HERE THERE BE MONSTERS

INTERVIEWS AND ESSAYS ON CLASSIC (AND NOT SO CLASSIC) HORROR CINEMA

By
Bryan Senn

HERE THERE BE MONSTERS:
INTERVIEWS AND ESSAYS ON CLASSIC (AND NOT SO CLASSIC) HORROR CINEMA
By Bryan Senn
Copyright © 2021 Bryan Senn
No part of this book may be reproduced in any form or by any means, electronic, mechanical, digital, photocopying, or recording, except for inclusion of a review, without permission in writing from the publisher or Author.
No copyright is claimed for the photos within this book. They are used for the purposes of publicity only.

Published in the USA by:
BearManor Media
1317 Edgewater Dr #110
Orlando, FL 32804
www.bearmanormedia.com

Perfect ISBN 978-1-62933-824-8
Case ISBN 978-1-62933-825-5

BearManor Media, Orlando, Florida
Printed in the United States of America
Book design by Robbie Adkins, www.adkinsconsult.com

Cover art created from this
Dracula's Daughter *Poster*

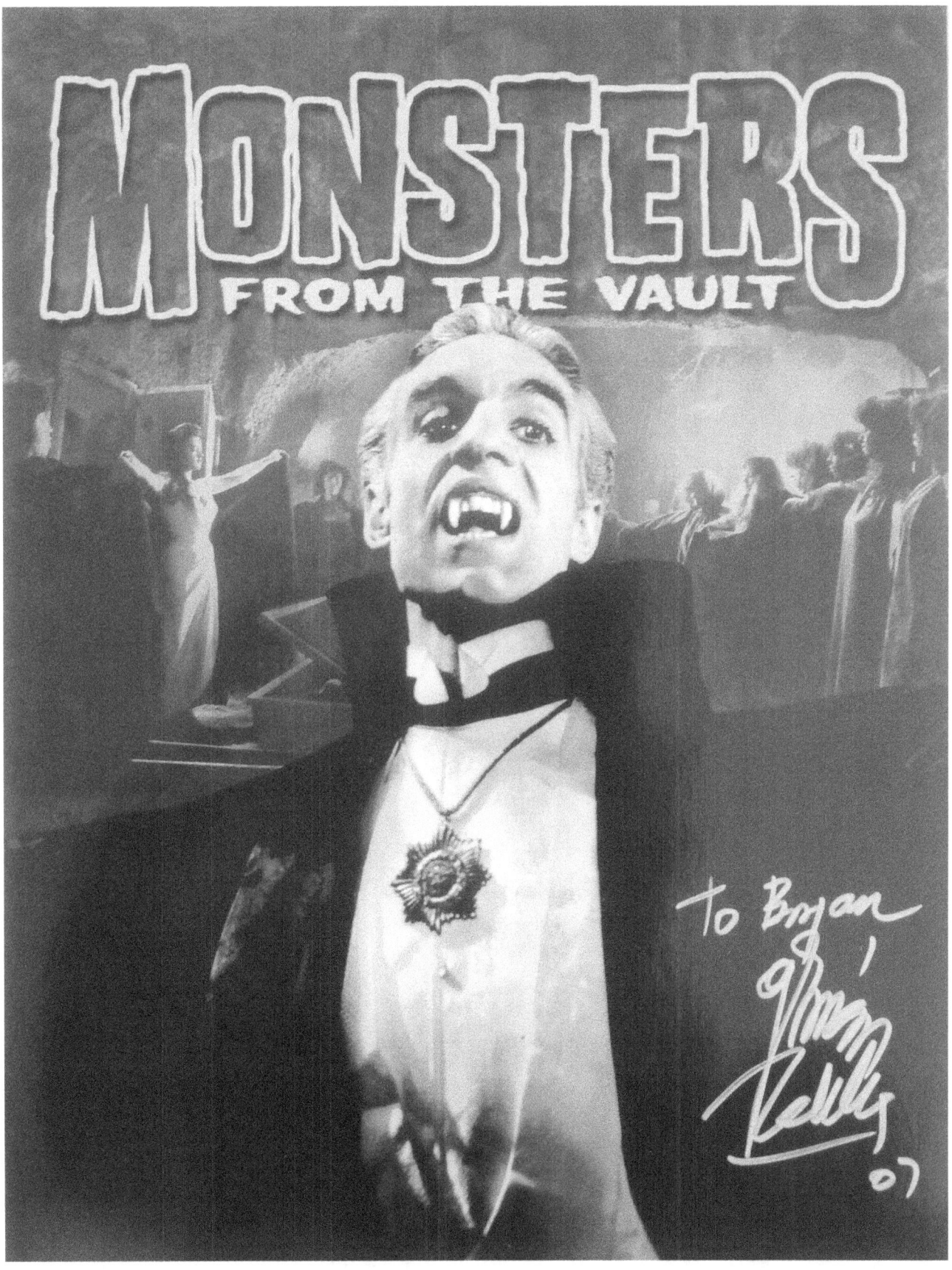

Cover artwork of Germán Robles as El Vampiro *(Monsters from the Vault magazine, issue 24).*

*For Sharon Senn, whose love of literature
inspired my own.*

*And for Lynn Naron, who good-naturedly
dragged me into all this way back when,
and inadvertently opened up a whole new (writing) world for me.*

ACKNOWLEDGMENTS

The interviews, essays, and reviews collected here would not have been possible without the magazine publishers and editors who provided an outlet for these cinematic musings. So a tip of the hat to the following dedicated genre print promoters: Buddy Barnett and Michael Copner (*Cult Movies*), Marty Bauman (*The Astounding B Monster*), Ted Bohus (*SPFX Special Effects Magazine*), Jim Clatterbaugh (*Monsters from the Vault*), the late Don Dohler (*Science Fiction Invasions*), Dennis Druktenis (*Scary Monsters*), Bruce Holecheck (*Cinema Arcana*), the late Don Leifert (*Movie Club*), Rod Lott (*Flick Attack*), Denis Meikle (*The Fantastic Fifties*), Don May (Synapse Films), David Miller (*Shivers*), Ted Okuda, Michael Stein, and James J.J. Wilson (*Filmfax* and *Ultra Filmfax*), Stephen D. Smith (*Monsterscene*), Gary Svehla (*Midnight Marquee*), Susan Svehla (*Mad About Movies*), Dan Taylor (*Exploitation Retrospect* and *The Hungover Gourmet*), and Jon R. Warren (*Collecting Hollywood*)

Of course, there would have been no content at all without the filmmakers themselves, and I'm particularly grateful to those who agreed to put up with my prompting and probing back in the day as I interviewed them for various publications. Sadly, so many of them are no longer with us. There's Veronica Carlson, the late Rosalie Crutchley, Audrey Dalton, the late Robert Day, the late Alex Gordon, the late Richard Gordon, the late Joseph Green, the late Robert Horton, Ricardo Islas, the late Tim Kelly, the late Janet Leigh, the late William Marshall, Caroline Munro, the late Robert Quarry, the late Germán Robles, Stu Segall, the late Barbara Shelley, Sam Sherman, the late Curt Siodmak, the late Gloria Stuart, the late Don Sullivan, Jack Taylor, the late Del Tenney, Robert Tinnell, and the late Robert Wise.

TABLE OF CONTENTS

Introduction IX

Interviews 1
Rosalie Crutchley Experiences *The Haunting* 1
  (and Other Bumps in the Night)
Alex Gordon on *Voodoo Woman* (and Sundries) 4
Richard Gordon on *Curse of the Voodoo* and 7
  Naked Evil
Lasers and Monsters and Mini-skirts, Oh My! ... 11
  Robert Horton Remembers *The Green Slime*
Ricardo Islas Howls at the Moon with *Plenilunio* .. 14
Robert Quarry Faces Off Against *The Zombies* 15
  of Sugar Hill
El Vampiro Speaks! An Interview with 18
  Mexican Horror Star Germán Robles
Stu Segall Orchestrates a *Drive-In Massacre* 23
Hammer Heroine Barbara Shelley 25
Zombies and Crustaceans and Gila Monsters, ... 26
  Oh My! An Interview with Don Sullivan
Jack Taylor Remembers Paul Naschy and 37
  Dr. Jekyll and the Wolfman
Del Tenney's Science and Ceremony: *I Eat* 39
  Your Skin
Robert Tinnell Makes You *Believe* 43
Robert Wise Sets *The Haunting* in Motion 45

Overviews 50
An Angel for Satan: The Gothic Eurohorrors 50
  of Barbara Steele
Drums of Terror: Sixty-Five Years of 58
  Voodoo Movies
Economy of Budget, Economy of Scale: 69
  The Golden Age of Made-for-TV Terrors
Guest List: Bryan Senn's Top 7 Unsung 72
  Were-Gems
One More Time! Were These Films Really 77
  Necessary?
Overrated or Underrated? Performances 80
Things That Came: Significant Horror 82
  Movie Trends (1963–2003)
Universal vs. Hammer: Cinematic Grudge 84
  Match of the Century
Werewolf Anthologies... or How to Have a 89
  Howlingly Good Time in Twenty-Five Minutes or Less

The Classics: 1930s and '40s 91
The Beast with Five Fingers (1946) 91
The Black Cat (1934) 92
Bride of Frankenstein (1935): A 75th Anniversary ... 94
  Appreciation
Elsa "The Bride" Lanchester: A Candid Look 97
  at the Fairest Monster of Them All!
Captive Wild Woman (1943) 99
From Villain to Hero: Lugosi and Chandu – 101
  Chandu the Magician (1932), *The Return of Chandu*
  (1934), and *Chandu on the Magic Island* (1935)
Dead Men Walk (1943) 103
The Devil-Doll (1936) 105
Dr. Cyclops (1940) 109
Sexy Beast: *Dr. Jekyll and Mr. Hyde* (1931) 110
Warner's Terror Twins: *Doctor X* (1932) and 114
  Mystery of the Wax Museum (1933)
Dracula (1931 Spanish Language Version) 125
Redux: *A Game of Death!* (1945) 127
House of Horrors (1946) 132
Voodoo Poetry: Val Lewton's *I Walked with* 134
  a Zombie (1943)
The Invisible Man (1933) 138
The Golden Age of Horror: *Island of Lost* 140
  Souls (1933) and *Mad Love* (1935)
King of the Zombies (1941) 150
Bela's Dark Triad: Three Overlooked Films 151
  from Lugosi's Golden Era – *Murder by Television*
  (1935), *The Mystery of the Mary Celeste* (1935), and
  The Dark Eyes of London (1939)
Lugosi: Hollywood's Dracula (Documentary) 158
The Mad Monster (1942) 160
Mad Science Meets Grand Gothic: *The* 162
  Man Who Changed His Mind (1936)
The Mummy (1932) 167
The Mummy's Curse (1944) 169
The Golden Age of Horror Cinema: *Murders* ... 171
  in the Zoo (1933)
The Return of the Vampire (1944) 178
Tod Slaughter's Terrifying Trio: *Sweeney* 180
  Todd, the Demon Barber of Fleet Street (1936), *The*
  Crimes of Stephen Hawke (1936), and *The Face at the*
  Window (1939)

Universal's Return to Glory, Double Feature–.... 183
    Style: *Son of Dracula* and *The Mad Ghoul* (1943)
Tower of London (1939) 189
The Vampire's Ghost (1945): Vampires and 191
    Voodoo on the Dark Continent
Voodoo Man (1944) 194
Retrospect, the Classics in Review: 196
    The Walking Dead (1936)

The Fantastic Fifties 202
Back from the Dead (1957) 202
The Colossus of New York (1958) 203
Fiends Who Walked the West: *Curse of the* 205
    Undead (1959)
French Frights: *Eyes Without a Face* (1959) 207
Of Fiends and Men: *Fiend Without a Face* 210
    (1958) and *First Man Into Space* (1959)
Frankenstein 1970 (1958) 215
Frankenstein's Daughter (1958) 216
Boris Back-to-Back: *Grip of the Strangler* and 218
    Corridors of Blood (1958)
House on Haunted Hill (1959) 223
Of 'Hypnomagic' and 'Hypnovista'...Keeping ... 227
    a *Hypnotic Eye* on the *Black Museum* (1959)
Twin Bill Terrorama! *Invasion of the Saucer Men* ... 231
    and *I Was a Teenage Werewolf* (1957)
Drive-In Demons: *It! The Terror from Beyond* 236
    Space and *Curse of the Faceless Man* (1958)
Big Beasts, Small Budgets: *The Killer Shrews* 240
    and *The Giant Gila Monster* (1959)
Robot Wars! *Kronos* (1957) 245
The Monolith Monsters (1957) 247
The Monster That Challenged the World (1957).... 249
Roger Corman's *Not of This Earth* (1956) 251
The Pharaoh's Curse (1957) 253
Changing Times: *The Son of Dr. Jekyll* (1951)..... 254
    and *Daughter of Dr. Jekyll* (1957)
Battle of the Bugs: *Tarantula* (1955) vs. *The* 258
    Deadly Mantis (1957)
Voodoo Woman (1957) 262
War of the Colossal Beast (1958) 263

The Sensational Sixties (and Beyond) 265
Assignment Terror (1969) 265
"Roaring Guns Against Raging Monsters!" 268
    The Dubious Thrills of *Billy the Kid Versus Dracula*
    and *Jesse James Meets Frankenstein's Daughter* (1966)
The Most Dangerous Game Meets the 1960s: 270
    Bloodlust! (1961) and *Confessions of a Psycho Cat* (1968)
The Brain That Wouldn't Die (1962) 282
Clown Hunt (2012) 284
Curse of the Swamp Creature (1966) 285

Curse of the Voodoo (1965): African Sorcery in 286
    Regent's Park
Science vs. the Supernatural: *Dr. Jekyll and* 290
    the Werewolf (1972)
Frankenstein and Me (1996) 294
The Giant Spider Invasion (1975) 296
One Big Bad Mama! *Gorgo* (1961) 298
The Haunting (1963) 299
Lost and Found: William Shatner's *Incubus* (1965) .. 300
The Last House on Dead End Street (1977) 302
Macumba Love (1960) 303
Naked Evil (1966) 306
The Navy vs. the Night Monsters (1966) 308
The Plague of the Zombies (1966): A Rare 310
    Hammer Original
Scream Blacula Scream (1973): A Vampire 315
    Sequel Deserving Resurrection
Seizure (1974) 318
Sugar Hill (1974) and Her Zombie Hitmen! 319
They Came from the Swamp: The Films of 324
    William Grefé (Documentary)
They Live (1988) 326
Tormented (1960) 327
Tower of London (1962) 329

Mexican Monster Movies 332
Mexican Monsters Invade America! Fans 332
    Rejoice!
Of Lobos and Hombres: Mexican Werewolf 342
    Cinema, 1958–1976
The Aztec Mummy Collection (1957/58) 358
Blue Demon vs. el Poder Satanico (1964) 362
The Curse of the Doll People (1961) 363
Doctor of Doom (1962) / *The Wrestling Women vs.* ... 364
    the Aztec Mummy (1965)
Infraterrestre (2001) 366
Santo Contra Hombres Infernales (1958) 367
A Santo Cinema Smack-Down! 368
Santo Cinema Smack-Down: Round 2! 371
Santo Cinema Smack-Down: Round 3! 375

Brief Bites 378
The Amazing Colossal Man (1957) 378
American Gothic (1988) 379
Assignment Outer Space (1961) 380
The Astounding She Monster (1957) 380
A 1950s Double Bill: *The Beast of Hollow* 381
    Mountain (1956) and *The Neanderthal Man* (1953)
Beyond the Time Barrier (1960) 383
The Bride and the Beast (1958) 383
Cannibal Holocaust (1980), or How I learned 384
    to Stop Worrying and Love the Long Pig

- *Captive Women* (1952) 385
- *Castle of the Creeping Flesh* (1968) 386
- *The Children* (1980)........................386
- *Children Shouldn't Play with Dead Things* (1973)....386
- *Colossus: The Forbin Project* (1969)..............388
- *Comin' Round the Mountain* (1951) 388
- *Corman's World: Exploits of a Hollywood Rebel* ....388 (Documentary)
- *The Crater Lake Monster* (1977) 389
- *Curucu, Beast of the Amazon* (1956)............390
- *The Diabolical Dr. Z* (1966)..................391
- *Doomsday Machine* (1967) 392
- *Dracula's Daughter* (1936).....................392
- *The Earth Dies Screaming* (1965)..............394
- *Earth vs. the Flying Saucers* (1956) 394
- *The Eye Creatures* (1965).....................396
- *Five* (1951)................................396
- *The Flying Serpent* (1946) 397
- *Frogs* (1972)...............................398
- *Halloween Home Haunts* (2013) 398
- *The Lair of the White Worm* (1988) 399
- *The Legend of the Seven Golden Vampires* (1974) 400
- *The Living Corpse* (1967) 401
- *The Mighty Gorga* (1969) 402
- *Missile to the Moon* (1959) 403
- *Monster in the Closet* (1987) 403
- *The Most Dangerous Man Alive* (1961) 404
- *Night of the Lepus* (1972) 404
- *Onibaba* (1964)..............................405
- *The Phantom Planet* (1961) 406
- *Return of the Killer Tomatoes* (1988) 407
- *Scared Stiff* (1988)...........................408
- *She Demons* (1958) 408
- *Slugs* (1988) 409
- *Sorority Babes in the Slimeball Bowl-o-Rama* 410 (1988)
- *12 to the Moon* (1960).......................410
- *The Unknown Terror* (1957)..................412
- *Voodoo Dawn* (1990)........................414
- *Voodoo Dolls* (1990).........................414
- *Westworld* (1973) 415
- *The Wild Women of Wongo* (1959) 416
- *The Woman Eater* (1959).....................416
- *Women of the Prehistoric Planet* (1966) 417
- *The Yesterday Machine* (1965) 418
- *Zombie Holocaust* (1980)....................419

Film Book Reviews........................420
- *The American International Pictures Video Guide*.....420
- *Crab Monsters, Teenage Cavemen, and Candy* .....421 *Stripe Nurses—Roger Corman: King of the B Movie*
- *Creature Features: Nature Turned Nasty in* ....422 *the Movies*
- *Film Alchemy: The Independent Cinema of* ....422 *Ted V. Mikels*
- *The Hammer Vampire*........................423
- *The Hideous Sun Demon: The Original Screenplay* ..424
- *The Horror Hits of Richard Gordon*..............425
- *House of Dan Curtis: The Television Mysteries* .....425 *of the* Dark Shadows *Auteur*
- *Keep Watching the Skies! American Science* ....426 *Fiction Movies of the Fifties, the 21st Century Edition*
- *Mexploitation Cinema: A Critical History* ....427 *of Mexican Vampire, Wrestler, Ape-Man and Similar Films, 1957-1977*
- *Mind Warp! The* Fantastic *True Story of Roger* ....428 *Corman's New World Pictures*
- *Muchas Gracias Senor Lobo: Paul Naschy* ....429 *Memorabilia*
- *No Traveler Returns: The Lost Years of* ....430 *Bela Lugosi*
- *Perverse Titillation: The Exploitation Cinema* .....431 *of Italy, Spain and France, 1960-1980*
- *Regional Horror Films, 1958–1990:* ....432 *A State-by-State Guide with Interviews*
- *Showmen, Sell It Hot! Movies as Merchandise* .....433 *in Golden Era Hollywood*
- *The Television Horrors of Dan Curtis:* Dark ....433 Shadows, The Night Stalker, *and Other Productions, 1966–2006*
- *Urban Terrors: New British Horror Cinema,* 434 *1997–2008*
- *The Weird World of Eerie Publications*............435
- *The Worst of Eerie Publications*..................436

This Time It's Personal......................438
- Dr. Clatterbaugh, or How I Learned to ....438 Stop Worrying and Love *Monsters from the Vault*
- Fanex Memories.........................439
- Halloween 365 Days a Year: *The American* ....441 *Scream*
- Jackie Chan: Super*chef?*.......................443
- Nightmare Theater...and a Pair of Binoculars.....444
- The Price Is Right: A Vincentennial ....445 Celebration
- Richard Gordon Tribute 447
- *The Thing* (1951)...........................448

INTRODUCTION

I began writing about movies during the heyday of the VCR era: the mid–1980s. Initially, it was just for my own amusement, putting my after-viewing thoughts down on an index card along with a numerical rating. But timing is everything, and mine was impeccable (i.e. lucky), as this also proved to be the heyday (or at least second coming) of the genre magazine. After getting my first book published in 1992 (*Fantastic Cinema Subject Guide*, McFarland and Co., Inc.), I began submitting articles to various genre-centric publications. Amazingly, more often than not, these were accepted—starting in 1993 with the long-running *Midnight Marquee* magazine. I soon branched out to other publications, some of which actually *paid* me! Though I was never going to buy that coveted Jaguar E-Type with my magazine earnings, it was good to receive at least some token monetary validation for all my hard work (and countless viewing hours). (Note: I did make enough cash from one rather lengthy article to replace a dying refrigerator with a brand new one—which I promptly dubbed the "Franken-fridge" due to the bankrolling essay's subject matter. But this windfall proved an exception rather than the rule, as most submissions garnered far more modest sums, or simply a word of editorial thanks or a free plug for an upcoming book as payment.) In any case, filthy lucre wasn't the point—it was to get my thoughts and phrases out there to that select few who might care (i.e. horror film fans).

And for the last thirty or so years I've been doing just that—submitting interviews, articles and reviews to a myriad of publications, happy in the knowledge that they were being read by fellow fans who might appreciate the Gothic aesthetics of a Universal graveyard, or the enjoyable bombast of a Bela Lugosi Poverty Row performance, or the entertaining craziness of a masked wrestler battling a monster. The thing about magazines, however, is that, unlike books, they are transitory and fall squarely into that impermanent category of literary ephemera. In other words, they're printed, they're read, and they're most often discarded (or forgotten), letting their contents drift away like vampire dust in the morning sun (cue James Bernard's *Horror of Dracula* theme). In fact, the vast majority of the genre periodicals referenced herein are, sadly, no longer in business.

So during the worldwide pandemic of 2020, when isolation became the norm, I had the idea to gather this material together (at least all that I could still find) and put it into a book, thereby preserving all those thoughts and words (of others—in the case of the various interviews—as well as my own) in a central and more accessible form. (The lightbulb wasn't wholly my own, however; credit for flipping the switch should go to my friend and fellow writer Holger Haase, who did a similar thing with *his* writings, though in eBook form.) But lest one think that I've simply succumbed to the Seventh Deadly Sin (sloth) and am merely trying to "double-dip" (literally speaking), many of the pieces you'll find within these pages *are* new (or at least new to print). Others have been considerably expanded from their original form, as I've gleaned new information, the results of which I've integrated into the essay in question. In the case of interviews conducted with actors and filmmakers for various magazine articles and book projects, many were truncated due to the magazine's space limitations, and now see the light of day in their full form for the first time.

A note on organization: for most of the chapters—"The Classics: 1930s and '40s," "The Fantastic Fifties," "The Sensational Sixties and Beyond," "Mexican Monster Movies," and "Brief Bites" (which consists of short essays/reviews of less than 750 words)—I've arranged the articles and write-ups alphabetically, based on the film covered rather than the article's title. The "Interviews" entries are arranged alphabetically by the subject's last name. The "Overviews" essays (which focus on subgenres, subsets and trends rather than individual films) and the "This Time It's Personal" articles (which spotlight more… quirky musings), on the other hand, are organized by essay title.

So, this book represents three decades of writings and ramblings on genre cinema. Some of these articles I've dusted off and polished up (adding bits here and there to create more bang for the buck, so to speak), while others I've just tossed out there as is, like a chipped table lamp at a garage sale. And that's basically what this book *is*: a literary yard sale offering a collection of old (and new) bits and bobs—everything from big heavy furniture to light shiny cutlery—that served their initial purpose and now need to find a second home in some other hands (yours, gentle reader). I'm hoping you'll find this walk down magazine memory lane as illuminating, entertaining, and amusing as it has been for me. If not, well, to paraphrase Edward Van Sloan's opening curtain speech from *Frankenstein* (1931):

> Mr. Bryan Senn feels it would be a little unkind to present this book without just a word of friendly warning. We are about to unfold the story of Horror Cinema, a genre of terror, which sought to create shocks in its own way without reckoning upon the viewer. It is one of the strangest tales ever told. It deals with the two great mysteries of genre cinema—monsters and madness. I hope it will thrill you. It may shock you. It might even *horrify* you. So, if any of you feel that you do not care to subject your nerves to such a strain, now's your chance to… well, I've warned you…

Bryan Senn
Philipsburg, Montana
November 2020

CHAPTER 1
INTERVIEWS

Beginning on stage in 1938 (at the tender age of seventeen), and in films from 1947, Rosalie Crutchley became one of England's busiest character actresses, playing a variety of roles ranging from Sigmund Freud's mother in *Freud* (1962) to the primitive fur-wearing shaman shaking her bone beads at the *Creatures the World Forgot* (1971). Her nearly one hundred film credits include John Gilling's comedic political sci-fi/horror/fantasy *The Gamma People* (1956), Hammer's unusual (and mummyless) *Blood from the Mummy's Tomb* (1971), Amicus' eerie *And Now the Screaming Starts* (1973), and the visually impressive *The Keep* (1983). Undoubtedly her best genre feature, however, is Robert Wise's chilling masterpiece of understated terror, *The Haunting* (1963). In it, the actress made a lasting impression as Hill House's morose housekeeper, Mrs. Dudley. Her unsettling soliloquy in which she intones "there won't be anyone around if you need help ... in the night ... in the dark" is one of the most memorable in the genre.

I interviewed the still-working actress by phone on November 4, 1995, ostensibly for a book chapter I was writing on *The Haunting*, but really to learn more about this fascinating actress with the ability to make such a big impression in such a small amount of screen time. In real life, this formidable on-screen personality turned out to be a kind and charming English Rose.

ROSALIE CRUTCHLEY EXPERIENCES *THE HAUNTING* (AND OTHER BUMPS IN THE NIGHT)

BRYAN SENN: *Are you still active in film and theater or are you retired now?*

ROSALIE CRUTCHLEY: No, no, I still do various bits and bobs. I had a small bit in *Four Weddings and a Funeral*, which many of us did. Then I do an awful lot of television really, and some of it gets over to America and some of it doesn't. But I don't really do theater anymore now. I haven't done that for a long time because I find that too heavy going.

SENN: *You started in theater though, back when you were only seventeen.*

CRUTCHLEY: That's absolutely correct. I think we all did then. But now, of course, young people don't have the chance to do that. The repertories have gone and everything else, and they just have to either go straight into series television or they just do one occasional television show and then there's a long pause before something else comes up. It's not a good long career for young people anymore. It's all sort of bits and pieces.

SENN: *Regarding* The Haunting, *how were you cast in the role of the housekeeper?*

CRUTCHLEY: I don't know really, it just cropped up, I think. Robert Wise must have seen me in something and thought 'we'll have her, she'll be alright.' I did a lot of films at that particular time in the fifties and sixties, and I think he just saw the right face for it and that was it.

Rosalie Crutchley's creepy housekeeper sets the uneasy tone that will swell into a full symphony of terror in The Haunting (1963).

SENN: *Did you read the Shirley Jackson novel* The Haunting of Hill House *before you did the part?*

CRUTCHLEY: I didn't actually, odd enough. I didn't. It has become a cult now I think, hasn't it rather?

SENN: *It's more than that, it's considered a bonafide classic.*

CRUTCHLEY: Well, Robert Wise was a very brilliant director. It was the first psychological thriller, wasn't it?

SENN: *Did you go to Ettington Park where they filmed the exteriors or did you stay strictly in London for the interior shoot.*

CRUTCHLEY: No, I just did where the house was. I think it was just outside London, wasn't it? [near Stratford-on-Avon]. It was a strange house which looked very threatening from the outside but it wasn't actually at all. But it was brilliantly shot, you see, so that it looked very very threatening.

SENN: *That particular house was reported to be haunted.*

CRUTCHLEY: So they said, yes.

SENN: *I don't suppose you experienced any ghostly goings-on?*

CRUTCHLEY: Absolutely not. The only ghostly goings-on was our acting [laughs].

SENN: *Russ Tamblyn reported that he did experience something rather chilling. He went out to the little graveyard behind the house where he felt a "presence," but he was too afraid to turn around and see what it was.*

CRUTCHLEY: Oh really? Perhaps it was the camera [laughs].

SENN: *Was there much talk of ghosts and that sort of thing among cast and crew?*

CRUTCHLEY: No, I don't think so. We all just more or less got on with it, you know, Claire Bloom and Richard Johnson, who I've recently done something with, something called *Anglo Saxon Attitudes* by Angus Wilson, I don't think we'd seen each other since *The Haunting*. That was only about two years ago. And I think Julie Harris, she's still working. And, of course, Claire Bloom is; she and I were in something together the other day, a Joanna Trollup film. It's very funny because we all crop up again and we all remember this from years ago—when we were young.

SENN: *So it was a memorable experience shooting the film?*

CRUTCHLEY: I think it was, yes. I think we all knew it was very good and very interesting and not at all like the usual film of the time.

SENN: *How long did you work on* The Haunting*?*

CRUTCHLEY: That I can't remember. It was over several weeks, I think. Everything took much longer then. You know, everything is so quick now. As you know it has to be, because of finances I suppose. It's a pity because one was able to take much more time over things and there was more rehearsal. Now there isn't. You just rush into the studio and do it as quickly as you can and they get it over as quickly as they can and that's it.

SENN: *So did you do quite a lot of rehearsing with director Robert Wise then?*

CRUTCHLEY: Oh yes, yes we did. I think he's a very nice man, lovely man. I remember him very well.

SENN: *Your rather off-kilter dialogue delivery and chilling smile really set the film's tone. Did Wise coach you much on how to play your role.*

CRUTCHLEY: No, I don't think so. At the time I was always playing rather mysterious young women, spies and things like that. And I've always played an enormous amount of non–English parts, although I'm essentially English. I think he just thought mine was the right face for it. And it was such a good script. As you know, we're all ninety percent as good as our script, most of us. And that *was* a good script.

Something amusing happened recently when my grandson, who has just finished his degree in physics at the University, was over in France with a friend. They bought the video of *The Haunting*, and it showed his grandmother from thirty years ago [laughs] which surprised him, I think. It's all over Europe I gather; it's extraordinary.

SENN: *How was the rest of the cast?*

CRUTCHLEY: We were all fairly experienced theater actors, you see, although Claire Bloom had done more films than most of us. Most of us had done an awful lot of theater. That was how films were cast in those days. They saw you in the theater or they saw you in another film. It wasn't the sort of casting sessions which they have now—and never through agents, though one has an agent. It was always the director himself who spotted people and asked people to do it. It's a different method altogether now, which I'm sure you wouldn't remember because that's years before your time.

SENN: *What's your opinion of the finished film?*

CRUTCHLEY: I don't remember when I originally saw it, that was years—*donkey's* years—ago. I don't remember what I thought when I saw it. I mean we obviously knew it was very good. But I *did* see it three or four years ago and I remember thinking it was *extremely* good—and so does, I say, the young generation like you.

I remember working with Robert Wise as an excellent experience. He was such a very good director. And I seem to remember he was terribly kind and friendly. I think we all felt it was rather like working in a theater company; we were all working together, you know what I mean? You didn't just turn up and do your bit and disappear. I mean we all kind of worked together. We probably had several general rehearsals together. But as I say, it was all much more in those days, not nearly so hectic because money didn't come into it to the same extent. And if somebody like Robert Wise wanted to make a good film he was given the time to do it—and the cast that he wanted too, of course.

SENN: *Did* The Haunting *have any noticeable impact on your subsequent career?*

CRUTCHLEY: I'm amazed that people remember it, how many old people remember it and young people that have seen it recently. No, I think in those days one was just sort of going on from picture to picture. There were a *lot* of British films being made at that particular time. Now, of course, they aren't being made to the same extent.

SENN: *You appeared in a number of other horror and fantasy films. In 1956, you did a picture called* The Gamma People.

CRUTCHLEY: That I remember nothing about.

SENN: *It was directed by John Gilling.*

CRUTCHLEY: Yes, I remember him. I think that may be the one I did up in Austria where I had to have hysterics and rush about or something, but I can't really remember. [Playing the wife of a murdered scientist, Ms. Crutchley did indeed "have hysterics and rush about"—to convincing effect.]

SENN: *This one I bet you* do *remember—*Creatures the World Forgot.

CRUTCHLEY: [Laughs] Oh, do I not! We did that in what is called Namibia, which is in southern Africa. But it was then called Southwest Africa, and then when it attained its freedom it became Namibia. It was *incredibly* uncomfortable. We were all *miles* away from anywhere—in a tent. We were all put up in different tents. But it was quite an extraordinary experience actually. It was a very silly film, one of those nonsenses, you know [laughs].

SENN: *You had quite a substantial role in it.*

CRUTCHLEY: I don't know *what* I was meant to be. I was sort of head of some clan.

SENN: *I think you were supposed to be some sort of Shaman.*

CRUTCHLEY: Oh, something like that. I remember I had to have awful things like beans put up my nose in order to extend my nostrils. The whole thing was highly uncomfortably and very unpleasant. It was absolute nonsense. I remember being told it was going to be a documentary but it really turned out to be a Hammer horror.

SENN: *In fact, you did another "Hammer horror,"* Blood from the Mummy's Tomb *[1971].*

CRUTCHLEY: Oh yes, I did a lot of those at that particular time. That was very much of that particular period. I remember I was killed by a cat, I think.

SENN: *Yes, supposedly a statue come to life.*

CRUTCHLEY: Those things suddenly turn up [on television], but it's usually much too late for me. They usually turn up on the television about midnight, and as I haven't got a video I don't see them.

SENN: *How was it working at Hammer. Did you get that "family feeling" so often talked about?*

CRUTCHLEY: Yes, we all did. We all thought it a bit of a joke, you know, but we all did what we could. There was a very nice man named Michael Carreras who ran it. A lot of those things go into the blue because I was bringing up my children at the same time at that particular stage. I remember thinking much more, 'Oh dear, I hope the children are alright.' But I did my best, a double life you know—quite difficult.

SENN: *Oh yes, in fact I'm experiencing that myself. I have a five-month-old son.*

CRUTCHLEY: Well, there you are; it's not easy is it? But I do feel it's very important to put the children first—because if you haven't, you find out after they've grown up that they think, 'oh, well, they never bothered about us.' So from an old lady—a granny now—giving you advice: don't ever put your career before your children, although you must get on with your career as well.

SENN: *You did a second ghost picture—*And Now the Screaming Starts *[1973]. Do you recall that one?*

CRUTCHLEY: No.

SENN: *It was directed by Roy Ward Baker. You play the housekeeper (again), and this time you are actually killed* by *the ghost.*

CRUTCHLEY: Vaguely.

SENN: *Peter Cushing was in it, but I don't think you had any scenes with him.*

CRUTCHLEY: No, I don't think I did. I knew him, but I didn't have scenes with him in that.

SENN: *Ian Ogilvy played the hero.*

CRUTCHLEY: Oh yes, I think that was with a young Stephanie Beacham. I *just* remember it; it just comes because I remember I had to kind of fall down the stairs with a tray. But it wasn't me, it was a splendid stunt girl, a very nice girl whose name, of course, I can't remember. These come back to me in time, but I really have to think *very* hard to remember them.

SENN: *Well, you did so many.*

CRUTCHLEY: As I say, we *did* in those times you see. There was a *lot* of British films being made, all the time. When I look back it was extraordinary, because now people have *long* pauses, you know, young people between jobs. Whereas I think we didn't [have long stretches between projects] once we got going. People saw you in one thing and put you in another.

SENN: *In 1982 you did a TV version of* The Hunchback of Notre Dame.

CRUTCHLEY: That was with Anthony Hopkins, I think. He had a kind of fall-down makeup I remember. But I don't remember a great deal about it.

SENN: *You did a picture called* The Keep *[1983]*.

CRUTCHLEY: Oh yes, though I never understood what that was about. I simply didn't understand it at all. I never knew what it was about or what I was . . . Ian McKellen and myself sat in a station yard pretending we were in Poland, I think, on a couple of suitcases for four or five days. And that's all I remember about it.

SENN: *Were your scenes shot in England?*

CRUTCHLEY: Yes. It was meant to be somewhere else.

SENN: *Romania.*

CRUTCHLEY: Yes, something like that, I think. And I never understood what it was about at all.

SENN: *So did you see the picture after it came out?*

CRUTCHLEY: No, I didn't [laughs]. There are a whole lot of things, and some of them I remember and some of them I simply don't. But anyway, it was very nice to talk to you and I don't think I've been much help to you.

SENN: *Oh no, you have, very much. I greatly appreciate it.*

CRUTCHLEY: Anyway, I'm very pleased that young people are still interested in *The Haunting*, because it's worth it when a film *is* good. It's worth remembering these things.

While writing my book *Drums of Terror: Voodoo in the Cinema*, I reached out to producer Alex Gordon by phone in August 1995 and enjoyed a very informative interview with this knowledgeable filmmaker and delightful man.

ALEX GORDON ON *VOODOO WOMAN* (AND SUNDRIES)

When initially asked what he thought of his film *Voodoo Woman* (1957), producer Alex Gordon unhesitatingly replied, "It was a nice little group of professionals—cast *and* crew. They didn't look down on it because it was a 6-day picture made for $80,000. They took pride in their work and worked as hard as if they were on a bigger picture."

The project, originally titled *Black Voodoo*, was dumped in Gordon's lap. "I only got the script a couple of weeks before shooting started so we had to work very very hard and very fast," recalled Gordon. "The Milner brothers, who made *Phantom from 10,000 Leagues*, were going to make it. And then something happened between their setup and American International. So Sam Arkoff and James Nicholson took it over and virtually handed it to me to produce with about two weeks' notice."

Gordon's first choice for the mad scientist role was Peter Lorre. "Unfortunately, we had a very bad experience with his situation on *The She Creature*, which I also produced at AIP. Although the Jaffe Agency had committed him to the picture [*The She Creature*], when he saw the script he refused to do it. Frankly, I don't really blame him. But there was a big ta-do about it. *Voodoo Woman* was supposed to be an additional project for him. So, of course, he never saw it and never got to the point of serious discussion about it, but I was thinking about him."

Gordon next tried to tap the talent of veteran villain George Zucco, perennial mad scientist and horror villain of the previous decade (who hadn't done a film in over four years). Sadly, Gordon found the actor in poor health. "His agent told me that unfortunately by that time Zucco was quite elderly [the actor was 71] and had problems remembering lines. In fact, he was on the senile side; but that he would like to bring him in anyway and have me meet him at the agent's office because it would sort of give Zucco a boost to think that he was still wanted. So I went over to the agent's office and I met Zucco who was with his wife, and they were

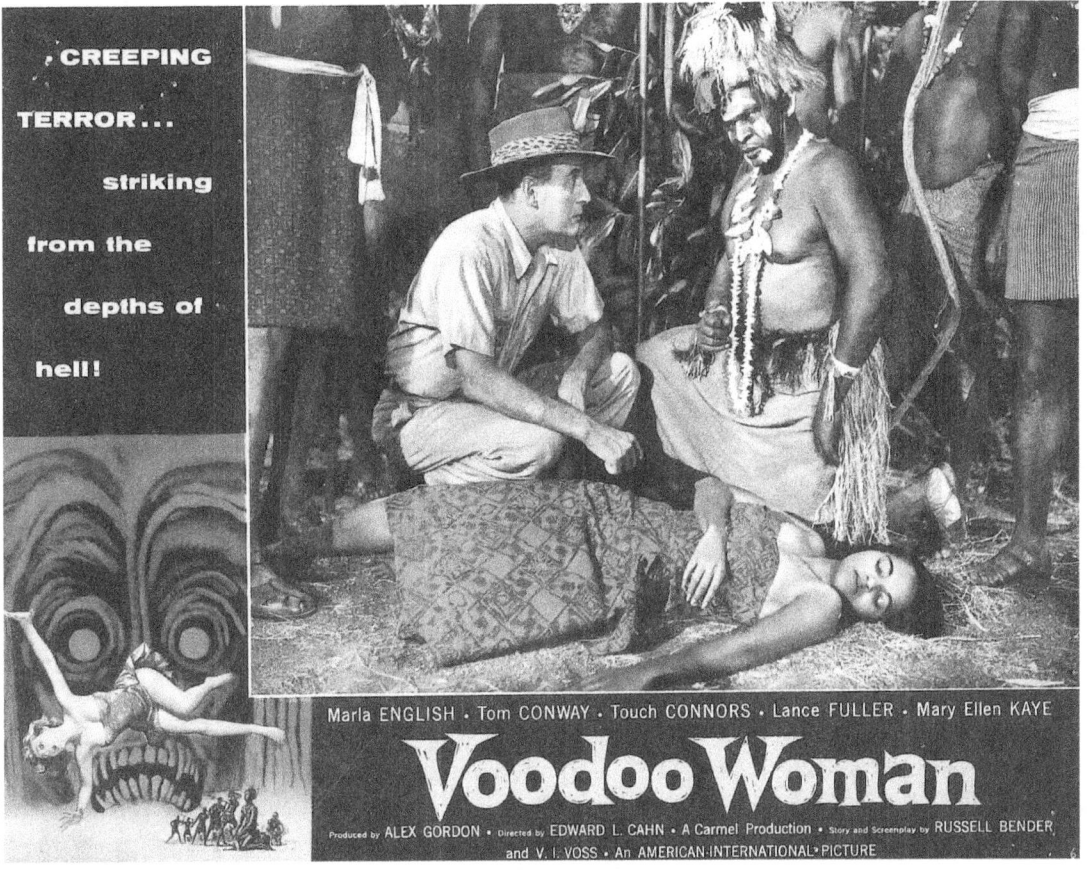

Producer Alex Gordon brought the Voodoo Woman *to life (and the screen) in 1957 (though in the film it's actor Tom Conway, pictured here, who does the honors).*

very very nice people. And, of course, I started off talking about all his old pictures, and he was thrilled that somebody would remember him and would remember all that work, especially the non-cheap horror pictures, the bigger things. And he said that much as he appreciated our offering him this picture, he didn't really want to do this kind of picture anymore. What he would like to do is go back to England and do some of the classics, like a picture based on a Dickens story, and not do any more of the low-budget horror type of things. So it was a nice conversation and everybody left happy; except, of course, I regretted that I was unable to get him. But I realized that he wouldn't have been able to do it even if he had decided that he would consider it."

The producer contemplated a few others, including John Carradine. "But Carradine had thrown a fit when we offered *him The She Creature*, because he had just done *The Ten Commandments* with DeMille and he was now back to his big picture and Shakespearean stage appearance mode and refused to do any more low-budget horror films. Of course, later he did, but at that time he didn't want to do any more."

With time running out, Gordon turned to one of his favorite actors to work with, Tom Conway. "We had a commitment with Tom Conway. He had really rescued us twice. Once by coming into *The She Creature*—we had a lot of problems there, not only with Peter Lorre but also Edward Arnold, who was supposed to co-star with him in that and died a couple of days before the picture was due to start. The point is, Tom Conway and AIP sort of owed each other, so I thought even though this was *reaching* a little bit to get Tom Conway to do the mad scientist there."

But reach Gordon did, and Conway came aboard. "He's just a terrific person," beamed the producer. "It was a real pleasure to work with him. He had a great sense of humor and we were always kidding around about his brother, George Sanders, and his escapades with ZsaZsa Gabor and all this kind of stuff, how Tom had to pull him out of various scrapes and things. But he was a very serious actor."

Though it has been intimated that Conway (paid $2500 for a week's work) had difficulty with his lines, Alex Gordon remembers no such problems. While Conway *had* become ill while making AIP's *Runaway Daughters* (with a cerebral hemorrhage), necessitating his replacement on that picture, Gordon reported that "he had no trouble on *Voodoo Woman* whatsoever; he was in very good shape.

"Frank Lackteen was originally set to play the role [Chaka, the witch doctor] that Martin Wilkins played. Frank became ill (he was quite elderly), and I had to have him replaced very suddenly. And his agent brought in this Martin Wilkins. I was very reluctant when I saw his credits—Shakespearean roles and stage stuff, and he had massive credits. To offer him a role like that, I thought it would be very demeaning to him. Although at that time we were not yet that race conscious, of course, as we were later—showing the blacks like that. Anyway, I guess he needed the money or whatever; he wanted to do it, and he appreciated my attitude. I said if you want to do it, of course we'd be delighted to have you, but I don't want you to think we're trying to insult you by offering you a role like this when you have these kinds of credits, you know. So, anyway, he worked out very nicely and that was fine."

The film's hero, Mike Connors (at the time Touch Connors) was "a very nice guy, really a pleasure to work with," praised Gordon. "He hadn't yet done *Tightrope* and *Mannix*, so he was still struggling, so he was agreeable to being in that."

Of the Voodoo Woman herself, Gordon remembered that "Marla English had a multiple deal with us and was a delight to work with. She really wanted to make westerns, so she wanted to do things like *Flesh and the Spur*, which I also produced there. But she agreed to do this and she was quite content with it."

Fourth-billed Lance Fuller, however, "was always a bit of a problem. He was a very nice guy personally, although a bit strange. But he wanted to really be a good actor, almost like a method actor type of thing. He would think up more gimmicks—he always wanted to have some kind of little bit of business to do, and he would dream up all kinds of things. It was difficult to keep him on the straight and narrow and have him just remember his lines. He maybe felt a little uncomfortable just standing there delivering the lines and wanted to *do* things. He was always fiddling around with stuff, wanted to pick things up and put them down, and that sort of thing. ... He took up a lot of time discussing the motivation of his role (laughs).

"Paul Dubov was a *very* good actor," continued Gordon, going down the *Voodoo Woman* cast list. "He started with us [AIP] in *The Day the World Ended* and he was virtually in every picture that I made and a lot of Roger Corman's as well at AIP. He was very reliable and never held us up or anything—a very useful actor." Dubov was also a writer. With his wife he wrote the 1968 Doris Day film *With Six You Get Eggroll*, inspired by their own domestic situation—they had six children between them.

Black actor Otis Green played the typical servant role—but one with the particularly demeaning moniker of "Bobo." So perhaps it's unsurprising that, according to Gordon, "he was really making quite a lot of noise trying to get better working conditions for blacks and getting going with decent black roles and things. He later became assistant to some well-known producer at one of the major studios.

"I pretty much had carte blanche on my casting on my own pictures," concluded Gordon. "That was something that I had battled Arkoff and Nicholson on for years and always pushed my way through using old-timers and people who were recognizable from other pictures. Whereas, as you know, Roger Corman was very clever in using newcomers that he could get very cheaply; and that's how he got people like Jack Nicholson started. Mainly I think because they would work for scale. Whereas, of course, my people I wouldn't offer them scale—I offered them reasonable salaries commensurate with what they were getting elsewhere."

Gordon became a bit defensive when the conversation turned to director Edward L. Cahn. "I resent the fact that people, so-called self-styled critics, that know nothing about him denigrate and write nasty things about him in these publications. They don't realize that the pictures he had to do at the end of his career, these small things were under tremendous budget restrictions and he always brought them in on time and budget. He was very loyal to the producer."

Cahn's career stretched all the way back to the beginning of the sound era, when he became an editor at Universal. "His first big thing came along when he re-edited *All Quiet on the Western Front*," Gordon pointed out. After a few test screenings, studio brass decided that they needed to replace comedienne Zazu Pitts with Beryl Mercer. "But the opening of the picture had been set for New York, and Eddie Cahn had to reedit the picture, take out Zasu Pitts and insert the Beryl Mercer scenes on a *train* going from Los Angeles to New York. So he was editing on this train, and he got it done in time so Universal gave him a chance. And he directed a highly acclaimed picture called *Law and Order* with Walter Huston and Harry Carey. But he wanted to be a producer as well as a director, and he wanted the independence rather than just working under the studio system. And I think that's what hurt his career, because he went to England to make pictures.

"The reason James Nicholson brought him in there [on *Voodoo Woman*]," continued Gordon, "was because he knew he could bring in pictures on time and on budget. But I hit it off with him tremendously. We really just loved talking about the old days and all that. And we respected each other for our mutual knowledge, he

Producer Richard Gordon (brother of Alex) put the Curse of the Voodoo *on viewers back in 1965. L-R: executive producer Kenneth Rive, director Lindsay Shonteff, actress Lisa Daniely, executive producer Richard Gordon, and actor Dennis Price.*

his career deteriorated because he had a drinking problem. [On *Curse of the Voodoo*] there was always a problem keeping an eye on him and shooting when he was at his best rather than late in the day. He wasn't drinking to the point where he'd show up drunk on the set, but he liked to drink at lunchtime and he…wouldn't be at his best, let's put it that way. But that didn't necessarily cause any delays or significant problems. It was just a matter of being aware of the fact. He really had a *cameo* role; he's not in the major bulk of the picture. It was an easy situation to handle. Later, at the time I had him in *Tower of Evil* [1972] and *Horror Hospital* [1973], he was *only* taking cameo roles because he couldn't sustain a full-length role in a feature film any longer."

To play the voodoo-practicing natives, Gordon inadvertently added a dose of authenticity. "They were professional actors; they were actually mostly West Indians, Jamaicans, from the West Indies, Barbados."

Gordon was equally pleased with Tony O'Grady's screenplay. "He brought it in and it was pretty good the way it was. There were some dialogue rewrites and so on, done by a man named Lee Vance who was also a script-writer in England, but more or less it was like the script that was brought in to us." Gordon, who paid about 1000 pounds for the screenplay, now feels that "We should have expanded the script and put more voodoo into it, but it didn't seem necessary at the time.

"I thought the voodoo scenes probably worked better than anything else in the picture. And I wished we'd devoted more time to the whole idea of the voodoo and less to some of the other things. Because the picture is sort of slow and it has a number of dead spots where you're really waiting for something more interesting to happen. I wished we'd had more voodoo-type footage. If it hadn't gone over budget to begin with, we might have decided to shoot some addition stuff. As it was, the finances were already rather strained."

In the end, opined Gordon, "it was the weather that really botched up things and also sort of depressed everybody because there's nothing worse when you're shooting a film than when you suddenly find yourself in a situation where for one reason or another you have to stand around doing nothing. It wasn't the easiest shoot I've ever been on."

Curse lived up to its name at the box office. "Over a period of time it was financially successful because of television and video but not really on its initial release," explained Gordon. "Yes, it did alright because it was such a low-budget film, but it didn't lend itself to being exploited separately—like *Devil Doll*, which we released as a single feature in the United States and it did extremely well."

RICHARD GORDON ON *NAKED EVIL* (1966)

"The point at which *Naked Evil* came about," explained Richard Gordon, "I had been representing Steven Pallos (who was a very very well-known producer in England and used to be a partner of Alexander Korda) in the United States for many years on the sale of his pictures here through Gordon Films. And we had talked about doing something together in production, and he sent me this play by John Manchip White which had been done on the BBC called *The Obi*, which I read and liked and thought would make a very good genre movie. And he suggested we do it together, and I said fine. And he had a director, Stanley Goulder, who had just done a film for him called *Silent Playground*, which was a very exceptional no-budget movie about a child molester, which was extremely well done and received a lot of critical attention in England also. And he suggested that Stanley would direct the picture, and it seemed a perfectly valid suggestion to me and we became co-producers on it." (Gordon labeled writer-director Stanley Goulder "a very pleasant and talented guy, a guy who knew exactly what he wanted.")

"*Naked Evil* was made as a quota picture," continued Gordon, "to fulfill a certain requirement by Columbia to fill a certain slot because they needed to have a certain amount of British product in distribution and the theaters needed to play a certain amount of British product. It wasn't intended to be anything more than that. That's all that happened to it in England. If it had been the genre picture that I'd *hoped* it would be, it might have gone on a double bill with another English X-rated movie [the British "X" certificate signified horror rather than porn] as a horror bill, it might have done a lot more. But it really didn't lend itself to that.

"When the subject came up just before shooting started of doing it in color, because everything was switching to color at that particular moment, Columbia wouldn't go along with the idea. Even if Steven and I had put up the extra money, Columbia didn't want it because their distribution expenses would have been much higher because they would have had to make color prints instead of black and white prints. In those days that involved a substantial difference in costs. And for the slot for which they had figured *Naked Evil*, they didn't think it was warranted.

"The budget was approximately 60,000 pounds, which at that time was close to $150,000. The exteriors were shot in and around London. The house that served as the school was one of those country houses that you could rent. The studio was a studio called Bushee in Hartfordshire on the outskirts of London. The shooting schedule was four weeks." And the film *did* come in on-schedule and on-budget, according to Gordon.

It also carried a wonderfully exploitative title. "Steve Pallos came up with the title. *The Obi* didn't seem like a title that would be practical to use and we were looking for something that would give it a little bit of *flair*, and Steve came up with *Naked Evil*. I thought it was a very good title.

Due to the low budget, Gordon was forced to utilize a cast of largely unknowns. "Anthony Ainley came from television and I don't think ever had a real movie career. Suzane Neve also. Basil Dignam was the only actor in it who had a strong theatrical movie background. Dignam, who plays the head of the institute, the one who was murdered, was an extremely well-known stage and screen actor in England. He made literally dozens if not hundreds of movies. You'll find him repeatedly playing Scotland Yard inspectors, school heads, Members of Parliament, those kinds of roles. He is a very, very familiar face in British films." Dignam not only appeared in prestige pictures like *Lawrence of Arabia* (1962), but in genre fare like *The Quatermass Xperiment* (1955), *Corridors of Blood* (1958) and *Gorgo* (1961).

"I didn't have much to do with the actual filming of it," admitted Gordon, who served in an executive producer capacity, "because this was at the same time as I was working on *Island of Terror* and *The Projected Man*. It all came on top of each other. You know I suddenly found myself feeling like a studio executive [laughs], juggling a number of pictures around. Steve was in charge of the production—we were actually joint executive producers—and Jerry Fernback was involved with me financially, with whom I was doing *Island of Terror* and *The Projected Man*. Then, of course, it was understood that I would take care of distribution outside the Columbia territory."

"It didn't quite work," admitted Gordon in his frank assessment of *Naked Evil*. "I'd thought it would be a real horror picture, and that there would be much more use made of the voodoo stuff and less of the gangsterism and all that. It's not what I would really call a genre picture in its present form. It's sort of neither fish nor fowl. You can see what it might have been if there'd been more emphasis on that [creepy] aspect of the story rather than on the kid's romance with the girl and being chased by the gangsters and the gang warfare and all that.

"I think the budget was too low, it was hampered by the deal with Columbia Pictures (in the Eastern Hemisphere they wanted something in black and white at a certain price that could be used as a second feature with one of their pictures). It just didn't come out the way we hoped it would. That's why we had a problem with it in the States and I eventually made the deal with Sam [Sherman]—for purely financial considerations."

"First we tried to release it as *Naked Evil* through a man that Alex [Gordon, Richard's Stateside brother] knew and was working with in California; his name was Robert Saxton. He, unfortunately, was not able to do much with it. It had *some* play as *Naked Evil*, but he didn't do anything much with it, and then he had to fold his company because he didn't have enough product to keep it going. So we took the picture back, and then I made the deal with Sam Sherman at Independent International [several years later]." Said deal resulted in Sherman filming some new scenes (in color and with a down-on-his-heels Lawrence Tierney as a psychiatrist[!] in a framing story), tinting the black-and-white footage, and releasing the film as the nonsensically-titled *Exorcism at Midnight* (to take advantage of the, you guessed it, post-*Exorcist* craze).

Actually, it wasn't Sherman and I.I. that did most of the tinting, but the original U.S. distributor. "Saxton and [my brother] Alex," recalled Gordon, "arranged the original tinting of the picture. In fact, Saxton's release publicity said it was in 'Evil Color' [laughs], which I thought was a nice gimmick. It promised a lot but didn't guarantee anything. Then Sam redid some of the color tinting to match up also with what else he was shooting and putting in there when he acquired the picture." It didn't help.

> The following article/interview was penned for *Filmfax* magazine (issue 92, August/September 2002). At the bottom I've included a few additional comments made by Horton that were not included in the article itself.

LASERS AND MONSTER AND MINI-SKIRTS, OH MY! ROBERT HORTON REMEMBERS *THE GREEN SLIME*

"The film has everything. It has all the cliches that you could possibly put into a film—including running out of ammunition and throwing the gun at the monster! Give me a break." –star Robert Horton

"The Green Slime are coming!" –bumper sticker promo

What kid growing up in the 1960s could resist such a title? And what adult going to the video store nowadays could resist *sniggering* at such a title? For all those "camp" followers out there, however, *The Green Slime* has become something of a mainstay, thanks to its encased-in-amber sixties sensibilities. In the words of the film's star, Robert Horton, "It's so bad it became a cult film." Well, actually it's not *that* bad.

The Green Slime half-sheet poster.

The first half of the movie is basically *Armageddon* (though not nearly as laugh-out-loud funny as that overblown and overpriced unintentional laugh-fest): Orbiting space station Gamma III must dispatch a crew to land on an asteroid, drill holes into its surface, and plant bombs that will blow it to smithereens before it collides with the Earth and destroys the human race. Horton plays Jack Rankin, the trouble-shooting specialist dispatched to the station to head the asteroid mission. Richard Jaeckel is Vince Elliot, the well-meaning but weak space station commander and former best friend of Rankin—until he stole Rankin's girl, the beautiful space station medico (former *Thunderball* Bond girl Luciano Paluzzi). Although the mission is successful, one astronaut inadvertently brings back to the station a mysterious green substance that grows into one-eyed walking slime monsters who feed on electricity and electrocute their victims. It's up to Rankin and Elliot to set aside their differences and find a way to defeat the ever-growing and seemingly unstoppable monsters.

According to *The Hollywood Reporter*, Robert Taylor(!) was originally scheduled to star in this first ever Japanese-U.S. co-production. But when cameras rolled in late 1967, it was a *different* Robert (Horton—of TV's *Wagon Train*, *Alfred Hitchcock Presents* [eight episodes, more than any other lead actor], and *As the World Turns* fame) in the heroic hotseat. Horton does fine in his square-jawed, underwritten role of a hard-line military man-of-action who must pull rank on his friend to get the job done. ("It's alright," opined Horton of his own performance. "There are two or three scenes that seem to work alright, that are isolated; but the overall impact of the film I would think is just nonexistent.") And Richard Jaeckel (*The Dirty Dozen*, *Grizzly*, *Starman*) does equally well in the part of the nice-guy-but-no-leader space station commander. (According to Horton, Jaeckel's casting was somewhat true-to-life, at least the "nice guy" part: "Oh, he was a very nice guy; I'd known him a long time. He was a very nice fella.") The film's main bit of human interest comes from the friction between these two characters and their different approaches to the responsibility of leadership. "The basic plot is very much the same as *Marooned* and *Alien*, et cetera," observed Horton, "but not very well done. As a matter of fact, the man who wrote it, when we were talking about the script and whether I was going to do it or not, we had this discussion and I said I didn't think that the script was really very good, and he was telling me that the script was about the agony of command. I said, 'Is that so? Well, if that's what you think it's about, ok, but that's not what *I* think it's about.'" This "agony of command" angle is indeed one of the few worthwhile things to be found in *The Green Slime* (apart from the space-age go-go boots and silver mini-skirts, of course). When Elliot's reasonable—but ultimately wrong—decisions cost several of his men their lives, Jaeckel's confusion-tinged remorse does indeed encapsulate "the agony of command."

But that's about as deep as this space age shoot 'em up gets. The rest is clean, shiny, plastic-looking model rockets docking at the equally phony-looking revolving space station; "dramatic" love triangle interaction between the three leads; and battles with the tentacled terrors (not to mention one "party" sequence in which the space station crew lives it up via a bout of go-go dancing!).

(Really) big laser guns and *Star Trek* sensibilities (shoot first and ask questions later) are the order of the day. And the monsters, with their squat green bodies, giant solitary red eye, and impossibly long (and ungainly) tentacles, are unique, if nothing else. "I have a photograph of me feeding one of the monsters a *cookie*, because that's what I thought of the monsters," laughed Horton. "I thought they were ridiculous." Even so, thanks to some frantic staging by director Kinji Fukasaku (as well as some heroically straight-faced playing by the principals), these Little Green Globs From Gamma III do generate a few moments of suspense, with Our Heroes desperately weaving and dodging the waving appendages whose touch means instant (and gruesome) death by electrocution.

Arguably the most amazing thing about this film is the fact that the movie's title song ("Is it just something in your head? / Will you believe it when you're dead? / GreeeeenSliiiiime!") came out as a 45 single. Apparently, there was plenty of singing going on *behind* the scenes as well… "When you go to work for a company in Japan, you sing a song at the beginning of the day—like 'The Star-Spangled Banner' or 'God Bless America'—that's got to do with that particular company," explained Horton. "The Japanese, as you know, are extraordinarily dedicated. Once they work for a company, they almost never leave it, almost never—it's a job for life. And they have this little pep talk, this little pep song, like a fight song before a football game…. Every morning on the set, before they shot a single foot, the crew and the actors—who obviously were not about to sing the lyrics—they'd sort of sit there while the song was sung [by the Toei Company crew]." (No, the Toei Company "fight song" was *not* the theme from *The Green Slime*).

Filming took place at a studio just outside Tokyo over a three-month period at the close of 1967 (MGM didn't release the picture until 1969). The entire crew was Japanese (excepting the first assistant director, who was in the Army and was instrumental in acquiring the Caucasian extras—soldiers stationed in Japan—who made up the space station crew), and the entire cast was Caucasian.

Horton has nothing but praise for the crew. "They were very easy to work with, and very hard-working…. [The Director] didn't speak a word of English, but we had absolutely no trouble [communicating] at all. I think at one time he asked me—because Japanese people tend to run with a little gait, they never walk anywhere, they run, they run in very small steps, but they run—at one of the critical points of the film if the hero,

Star Robert Horton (left) deals with co-stars Richard Jaeckel and Luciana Paluzzi before tackling The Green Slime *(1968).*

which is supposedly me, would run or stride. And I said he would stride, because you're not going far enough to make running that important a facet of the movie. Other than that question, we had absolutely no problems. I thought it was quite remarkable. I knew what the script was about and I knew what the demands of the moment were, and he moved the camera and we had absolutely no problem. Neither did Dick Jaeckel or Miss Paluzzi."

Despite his poor opinion of the finished film ("There are some individual scenes that work fine, but put it all together and you don't have an awful lot," is the kindest he can be), Horton has no regrets about starring in *The Green Slime*. "They paid me very well and I had three months in Japan, which we enjoyed very much. We had wonderful accommodations at the Okura Hotel. My friend Lee Marvin came over to ballyhoo *The Dirty Dozen* while we were there; he and I have been friends for a long time. We had a good time while we were there."

The picture was actually shot as *Battle Beyond the Stars*, but MGM—yes, *that* MGM—decided to retitle it for exploitation purposes. (Ironically, Roger Corman's New World Pictures later employed the *Battle Beyond the Stars* title for a much *more* exploitative sci-fi entry in 1980.) "One day, nine or ten or twelve months after we finished the film," recalled Horton, "I was living in New York at the time, my wife walked in with a *Variety* and said, 'I think they've changed the name of your picture, it's now called 'The Green *Slimmie*.'" I said, 'That's "The Green *Slime*." She said, 'I don't think I ever saw the word *slime* written down.'"

Well, *that* soon changed, since MGM's PR boys went all out in their promotional ploys. "And then all over Manhattan," continued Horton, "on the curbs all up and down Manhattan, were printed '*The Green Slime, The Green Slime, The Green Slime*'! And I remember we went down to see it on 34th Street, and about three minutes before I knew the film was going to be over with, I said, 'Let's get out of here; I have no desire to have anybody see me' [laughs]. The picture was dreadful."

Dreadful…but in a *good* way. With its comic-book iconoclastic cyclopean monsters, plasticine rockets, bright color schemes, "mod" wardrobes (and go-go dancing!), and fabulously campy theme song, *The Green Slime* remains an entertaining bit of late-sixties kitsch. It's a pulp sci-fi cover come to life.

ADDITIONAL COMMENTS

Horton worked with famous filmmaker Alfred Hitchcock on his television show on numerous occasions. Of the notorious Master of Suspense, Horton opined, "He was alright. I was very pleased that he asked for me to do the show, but I never knew why.... He was very pleasant; he was very nice. He had a dreadful reputation, but he certainly was very nice to me."

In assessing the no-budget Uruguayan(!) horror movie *Plenilunio* for my book *The Werewolf Filmography*, I wrote: "One of the great pleasures of watching foreign films is seeing a different set of sensibilities shape and mold familiar themes. Filmmakers from other cultures often bring an unusual (and frequently fascinating) perspective to their storytelling, not only in purely technical terms but in tone and approach. For American viewers raised on predictable Hollywood fare, with its expected rhythms, characters, and tropes, this can add the spice of novelty, and, more importantly, unpredictability—an 'anything-can-happen-at-any-time' quality. In *Plenilunio*, Uruguayan director/screenwriter Roberto Islas stars himself alongside a group of tween and teen children. Obviously not professional actors, this rag-tag bunch overcomes their awkwardness to react and interact like real children would in such a bizarre and frightening situation. Consequently, they seem far more real than the typical pint-sized Hollywood action hero tykes. Likewise, Islas himself eschews the clichéd he-man role to portray a man whose fear is palpable but who does what he can with his limited skills to try and save the children whom circumstance has thrust into his care. This adds some much-needed verisimilitude to the climax in which an average adult and group of everyday kids must try to save themselves from a horrible (and horribly unconvincing) situation.

"This early, micro-budgeted, shot-on-video effort offers a faint glimmer of the promise that brought Ricardo Islas to America in the late 1990s for a PBS producing career in Chicago, and subsequent directorial turns on genre fare like *Headcrusher* (1999), *Night Fangs* (2005), and *Zombie Farm* (2009). Though still low-budget (under the $1 million mark), these later productions are miles away from the peso-pinching backyard effort that is *Plenilunio* (which translates as 'Full Moon')."

I conducted this interview with Ricardo Islas in January 2015.

RICARDO ISLAS HOWLS AT THE MOON WITH *PLENILUNIO* (1993)

BRYAN SENN: *The IMDB has* Plenilunio *as a 1993 production. Is that correct?*

RICARDO ISLAS: Yes, it was shot between the end of 1992 and the beginning of '93.

SENN: *And what kind of distribution did it get, in both Uruguay and abroad; any U.S. distribution? (I found a VHS copy with subtitles at a local video store here in Seattle but was unable to ascertain whether it was a "legit" release or not.)*

ISLAS: In Uruguay it had major distribution via HALVEN, which was (maybe still is) a mainstream distribution company. At the time, it was VHS only. It was also shown in some selected theaters, festivals, and it made it to cable as well. In the U.S. it did have a "legit" release via Sub Rosa Studios (I think they're still around). So the VHS copy you saw was probably from that badge. It never made it to DVD though. It's on YouTube now.

SENN: *Did you create the werewolf yourself? And what was it made of? Also, you never showed it too clearly—any reason for that?*

ISLAS: Yes, I'm guilty as charged.[laughter] It was made out of sponge with a wire frame. The hair was similar to cotton; don't know the name in English, but it's stuff they use to stuff jackets when they're not using feather. Teeth and claws were hand made out of clay, and the eyes were stuffed animal glass eyes.

Plenilunio (1994)—the first (and last, to date) Uruguayan werewolf movie.

The reasons not to show it were mainly two: because I don't like to show monsters a lot, even when well made. And… because this one wasn't precisely a successfully crafted creature…

SENN: *Where'd you get all those kids to be in your movie? And the gentleman who played the wolf-in-human form, was he a professional actor? (I thought his voice was effectively menacing.)*

ISLAS: The kids were (still are) a group of friends that used to get together in real life with me at the old TV station where I was working in actuality when we shot the movie. There's a lot of truth to that group of kids and the older "brother" type that I was, simply because in real life I had been their teacher in either English as a second language (which I taught for a living for years in Uruguay) or in art (I used to teach comics). So the group was real, and that's probably why the interaction works pretty smoothly. I even recorded them talking about werewolves and then wrote my dialogues trying to be faithful to the way they talked.

I agree Martin Cabrera, who played the werewolf in its human shape, was very effective. He came up with the whisper, and it was very well used. My mistake (one of them) was not to trust him enough to have him play a conventional wolf man with make up as opposed to creating a gigantic puppet. Yet, to many, it's the crazy creature what makes the movie "memorable." Oh well, I could say it was planned, but I wouldn't be honest. It just happened.

SENN: *How long did it take to shoot? Was it all done at once or piece-meal over time?*

ISLAS: I can't exactly remember, but I believe it took about 30 days, and even when we didn't shoot every single day, it was pretty much shot continuously. We took no more than a couple of months from front to end.

SENN: *You wrote some pretty hard-hitting dialogue for the climax (such as "Desperation will finish off your stupid friendships; you will become animals; that's what we were and will be"). Any comments on the philosophy of this?*

ISLAS: Thank you for seeing this; I believe it's the first time it's been brought up in over twenty years. There is thought behind it, yes. Now, it's been a long time, and reality evolves. At the time, I did believe that a group of friends with a positive attitude might attract an evil counterpart. It was half way between the belief in metaphysical forces and influences from Stephen King. I was in my early twenties. I've been around now, and I can't say that I have the same beliefs today. However, back then and now also, I believed/believe that in desperate moments is when you can see the true nature of people.

And when the werewolf has them all trapped in the house, some will chicken out and others will brave up. I was trying to make sort of a primitive statement about human nature overshadowing animal instincts. But I guess the crazy wolf overshadowed them all, hahaha.

SENN: *And finally, any particular anecdotes or intriguing things you recall about the production?*

ISLAS: It was a very technical shoot, like any monster movie is. When you add a budget of less than 500 dollars, the technicalities become way more challenging. The wolf was falling apart towards the end of the movie, and it was beyond repair. To man it, it took three people, one for the head and one for each claw. I remember very long nights to get a few shots. We went through a big setback when the TV station where we started shooting the movie moved its operation to a different place. The whole plot about Roberto getting hired to work in a new cable station was made up as a solution to having lost our main location. It was quite a challenge, but we enjoyed every damn minute of it.

In 1974, actor Robert Quarry starred in AIP's blaxploitation horror film *Sugar Hill* (aka *The Zombies of Sugar Hill*). Two decades later I conducted this in-person interview with the charmingly acerbic Mr. Quarry in the Towson Sheraton bar, Baltimore, in July 1995. Some of the material ended up in my book *Drums of Terror: Voodoo in the Cinema*. But the talkative and refreshingly forthright AIP star had *much* more to say (as you'll read here).

ROBERT QUARRY FACES OFF AGAINST *THE ZOMBIES OF SUGAR HILL*

BRYAN SENN: *What attracted you to the project?*

ROBERT QUARRY: Nothing. Absolutely nothing. I was forced to do the movie, I had a pay or play contract. They were going to make an all-black movie, but that meant that they were going to have to pay me or play me, and Sam [Arkoff] wasn't going to pay me and not play me. So thrilled was Elliot Schick and Paul Mazursky who were doing this all-black exploitation horror film suddenly end up with me playing the head of the black mafia. It made about as much sense as me playing Bernadette of Lourdes. So I was just suddenly flown off to Houston to do this movie. I hadn't even read the script. When I got there I read it, and I thought what the hell am I doing playing *this* part? I mean this was a black man's role. And they had a black actor kind of tentatively set for it, but Sam said no, we'll use Quarry. And I ended up doing the movie. And then as it turned out, it was a very happy work relationship with Paul and Elliot Schick, because I was doing good work except that it was just all wrong for the movie. So I thought if anybody believes that I could be the head of the mafia for New Orleans and Houston, they're not very astute people.

SENN: *Well, you did have a couple of white henchmen, though. Were they added later too?*

QUARRY: No, I didn't have any white henchmen. I had a white girlfriend. All my henchmen were black. They were all black.

SENN: *What about Marki Bey [who played the eponymous Sugar Hill], how was she?*

QUARRY: Oh, she was darling. I don't think she ever made another movie. Because Marki had just come from, she was in the Pearl Baily black *Hello Dolly*, playing Irene, the second lead. And she was as pretty as could be and she was as nice as could be. We shot for about a week, and when the dailies started coming in, Sam didn't think she looked black enough so we had an afro wig made for her and darkened her makeup. So half of the time she had sort of light red hair with a very pale skin which they covered over. But she had kind of freckles, so they just covered *those* over and had her with this kind of red hair. Well, I'm not sure, but Sam Arkoff with his usual class probably said, 'she don't look like a nigger to me.' Mr. Class. So they insisted they put her in an afro wig. She was beautiful. But she'd never go out. And I finally got her to go out to dinner with me one night. And she said, 'well, I don't want problems.' And you know there was still – you can say what you want about civil liberties in the south—and they still are like that. We walked into a restaurant, a very fashionable and sheik restaurant. And we walked in at six o'clock, because Marki wanted to eat early and go to bed. So we went in there and there wasn't a person in the room and they said, 'do you have a reservation.' And she was now in her light skin and red hair. Only in the South would anybody have known that she was 'a black,' and Afro-American. And the guy says, 'do you have a reservation.' I said 'we'd just like to have dinner and it's early. And people don't usually come in and have dinner until 7:30 or 8:00 and I promise you we'll be out of here by then.' And I could see her shrinking back—because she knew what it was. So I said, 'Excuse me a minute Marki, I want to talk to this man.' And I went and I said, 'Listen, what is this *shit* that you're giving me? Is it because the young lady with

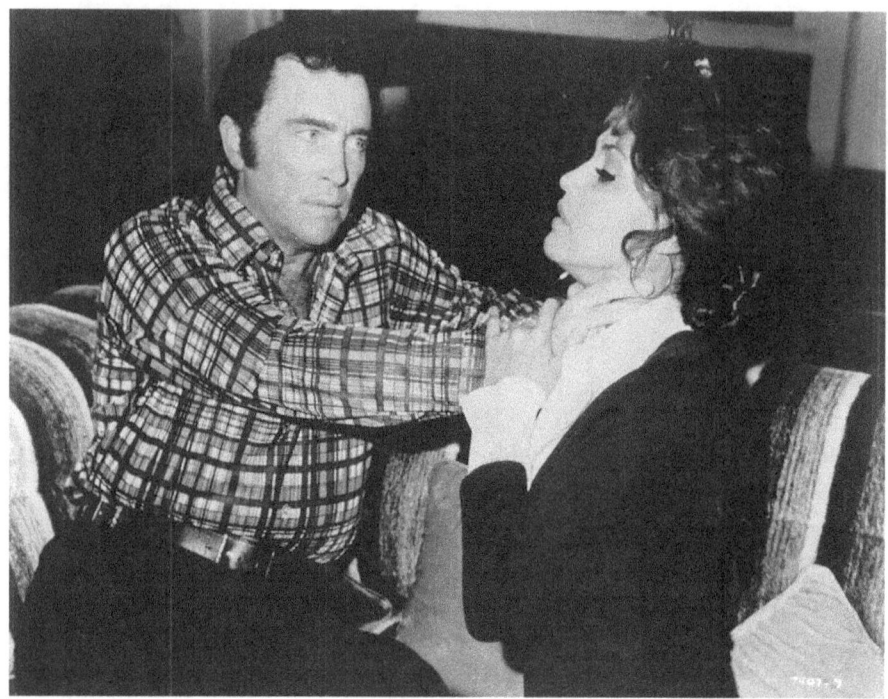

Villain Robert Quarry uses his powers of persuasion in The Zombies of Sugar Hill *(1974).*

me is black?' And he said, 'Oh no, no no.' And I said, 'I'll tell you what's up. I know a *lot* of people. Because the press in Houston, I'd known them when I had been working there for a year – well, before that I had been at the Alley Theater in Houston for a year on a Ford Foundation grant. And I said, 'you start fuckin' around with me with this shit and I promise you I'm calling every newspaper man and newspaper woman I know in this town and telling them what you've done.' 'Oh, we've got a table for you.' Well now by that time the evening was ruined for poor Marki. She never went out again, she stayed in the Holiday Inn and ate breakfast lunch and dinner there. It was just awful.

But I was there making an all-black movie. And I had a lot of friends, very rich, very influential friends that I had made when I was there in 1960, ten years before. They took me around and oh they were wonderful. And they had 'Alley Theater actor returns to star in movie'—and it was called 'All Black Cast.' Well I think they were so afraid I was going to bring a *nigger* to lunch. I mean that was their attitude. Nobody called me, nobody asked me, nobody said, 'how are you.' They just *ignored* my being there. Since I was there under those circumstances. And it was just shabby. But poor Marki—I mean to watch this beautiful, sweet, darling girl just cringe. Because as I said she sensed it before I did. I wasn't quick enough to catch what was going on. And I suddenly realized from her reaction what this maître d was pulling on me. He wasn't going to seat us because, you know, black and white do not *go together* in Houston Texas, even in 1972 or whatever the hell it was. I mean civil liberties were in and they no longer had segregated toilets and segregated theater seats or segregated anything, but they had their own *way* of segregating themselves. And this was a very social, a very kind of tony restaurant which I had taken her to because I wanted her to have a good dinner and I knew the restaurant—I'd been there for years. So I just said 'I'll call every newspaper in town and I'll tell them what you're up to, you rat-fuckin''—I mean I just was screaming—quietly. So, 'Oh, well no, we'll seat you, we'll do this.'

SENN: *How long did you have to stay there?*
QUARRY: I guess we were there four weeks.
SENN: *Do you know what the budget was?*
QUARRY: Well, it couldn't have been enormous. It wasn't that good. Well, it was a budget movie. They kind of started off with a kind of nice idea with the voodoo stuff and her vengeance on me who had her black lover killed. So, you know, it had some kind of stuff in it that was kind of scary. They did kind of good makeups on the voodoo people, the zombies. But all of those people were local people they picked up there, they didn't use actors. So, of course, the black actors there hated me because I was calling them "nigger." I mean that was what the script did. Well it's alright for a black to call a black nigger, but they were seeing a *white* guy doing this. And they didn't know from acting. They thought that was what I was like, that it was *my* doing. So we had a very nice actor named Charlie Robinson, who was at the Alley Theater, who later was in [TV series] *Night Court* and then he went into that other thing [*Love and War*] when that wonderful black actor died and he took over as the bartender. So Charlie, I got him my agent. And at that time they were trying to hire a lot of black actors because of the Affirmative Action thing and the Guild was raising hell about not employing black actors when they could have used somebody white. So Charlie got going on that, but he was the one who had to straighten 'em all out. So he went to all these extras around—I mean, I thought they were going to *kill* me, they started *at* me—after I'd been screaming, you know, 'back you black bastards, you

fuckin' coons' or whatever the wonderful dialogue was, which as I said was perfectly all right to say if you were black, but not for Mr. White Chops over here to be doing it. And he explained to them that it was just acting and that that was the part, and what it was all about. So we settled down and it was all right. But it was, you know, it was a fast shoot.

SENN: *How did director Paul Maslansky compare to [*Count Yorga, Vampire *director] Bob Kelljan, for instance? Who did you enjoy working for more?*

QUARRY: Actually, I enjoyed working for Paul. Bob was an absolute amateur. Bob had never directed zippo, until we did the two Count Yorga movies. And then they fired the director from *Blacula* and brought Kelljan in to finish up the movie. He wasn't the original director of *Blacula*.

SENN: *The guy who played Baron Samedi in* Sugar Hill...

QUARRY: Don Pedro Collins, one of the most pretentious bastards. He had a better dressing room than I did. That was in his contract, that he had to have a van or the whole thing. And he would sit outside and sort of, you know… and he would go over and play tennis somewhere. He was so full of affected shit. I *don't* think he ever worked another day after that movie. He had worked up until that time. He had done something, I don't remember what. But it had kind of made him—he thought it made him a star. So he behaved like he was the star of the movie. I mean, in *his* mind he was the star of the movie. So it was always "Makeup! Costume! Wardrobe!" You know, he was so full of that shit.

The whole thing to me was a fiasco. Because I didn't want to do the movie and I was forced to do it—and they didn't want me. They finally came around and said gee, you're doing a good job. Well, of course there weren't that many actors in it. So at least I was the only pro in the whole bunch that really knew movies. Don [Pedro] thought he was a *big movie star*—never made one movie, *never* done a film before. And we were watching it not long ago, Fred [Olen Ray] got a print of it somewhere, and, I don't know, there were a couple of people that were over there that night. And he said Jesus, you're good in this movie. And I looked at him and I thought, well so I was. But it worked out and I played the scenes well and I was nasty, you know. I ran fast, screamed, and died. So I was kind of amazed, I wasn't that embarrassed by it. I mean, I was only embarrassed by *Madhouse*, not that I gave a bad performance in *Madhouse*. I mean that to me was really a *rotten* movie. We had a rotten script, there was no way out of it.

SENN: *Was* Sugar Hill *the first contract film you did for AIP?*

QUARRY: No, the second one, [*Count*] *Yorga* was the first. Between the first and second, I had done *The Deathmaster* because a friend of mine had put up the money. So we did this movie, and while I was in England making Dr. Fib-bees [*Dr. Phibes Rises Again*], my co-producer hired some alcoholic to write the script so it was a mess. I mean I just came up with the idea of why don't we just have like a Charlie Manson vampire—with all those kids and whatever it was, you know, take 'em over and turn 'em into vampires.

SENN: *There was a scene in* Sugar Hill *where you receive on your doorstep a cannister and you open it up—*

QUARRY: That's the print that Fred [Olen Ray] had—and you never saw the heart. There was a heart that was ripped out and it was pulsating, bleeding, and steaming.

SENN: *So you actually saw it then, there* was *a heart in there?*

QUARRY: Yeah, they had a beef heart, yeah. The funniest thing was I had my little dog, I had my little poodle, and so she was in the scene with me. During rehearsal, they opened the thing and she just kind of sat there. When they went for the take, I opened the lid and she went 'aaah' and jumped off the couch and ran [laughs]. She got a big hand, you know, everybody thought that was terrific she'd done that. She was a little ham. But that's all out of the movie now, at least the print Fred has. Because they obviously took it out, I don't know why. You can show John Wayne running a pitchfork through a dog.

SENN: *Was that your real dog?*

QUARRY: That was my dog.

SENN: *What was the dog's name?*

QUARRY: Virginia Woof. I had just done *Virginia Wolfe*, so when I got her I called her Virginia Woof.

SENN: *Did she get paid?*

QUARRY: They sent out for a steak for her—from the take. I mean, I had a terrible time keeping a straight face through the take. Because she just played the shit out of that thing. And everybody applauded and carried on about Virginia because everybody adored her – the craziest dog that ever lived. So somebody sent out and got her a steak for lunch. So she was queen for the day there with that thing going on. But I remember when they cut that out, because as I said when I saw it, I turned to Fred and said, well Jesus, wait a minute. He said, 'well, what's in the thing there?' and I said 'a human heart.' It was a cow's heart or something that they'd cut out and put it. But it was all wired to sort of like pulsating in the bowl. So *that* went. But it was like the cat-eating scene in *Count Yorga, Vampire* when the girl eats the cat. They cut that out. They cut out about twenty minutes of that movie, which was a short movie.

SENN: *Before release?*

QUARRY: No, when they sold it to CBS. CBS made these horrendous cuts in the movie. And they cut like twenty minutes out of it—I mean to the point where the critic in the *TV Guide*, who loved *Count Yorga* and had given it three stars, she said 'We're taking a star away.' CBS absolutely hacked the movie to pieces. So they put it back together again for Elvira—and they got the star back again, so it had three checks instead of two. But the critics said, 'I'm taking a star away, they just hacked this film to pieces.' They wouldn't show the girl, you know they had a little pussy cat and they kind of sedated it. And then they put lasagna on her tummy, to look like the guts. It's just a flash. But they cut that out, so nobody knew what in the hell she was doing in there, because nobody ever saw that kitten. And the next night they ran a John Wayne movie, I think it was *McClintock* or something and he took a pitch fork and ran it through a dog, speared the dog. *That* they left in because it was John Wayne.

SENN: *Do you remember the actor Richard Lawson? He played the cop in* Sugar Hill, *the detective.*

QUARRY: No, I don't remember him.

SENN: *He was also in the* Blacula *sequel as well.*

QUARRY: I can't place him.

SENN: *At the close of* Sugar Hill *in the quicksand, it looks like when you go down, like your mouth's open. You must have got a mouthful.*

QUARRY: Oh, I did. Of course, I got a mouthful of that *crap*. Jesus, but I couldn't get it out of my ears, I couldn't get it out of my hair. God, I was hours trying to wash that shit out. That stuff was very unpleasant.

SENN: *What was it?*

QUARRY: I don't know, it's some kind of stuff that they make—it's a mixture. They've got some name for it—they use it for quicksand in movies. And it's full of kind of like, little tiny pieces of stuff. But it was gritty and kind of flaky stuff. It wasn't like sand. But it was, Jesus, I got it in my ears, I got it in my nose, I thought I was never going to get rid of it.

SENN: *Your pad there in the film, was that an actual house or was that a set? It was kind of a "mod pad."*

QUARRY: No, they used somebody's house. We used about three or four different houses there, the old haunted house, you know, that kind of thing.

It took three of us to bring about this interview with arguably the most well-known (non-wrestling) actor in Mexican horror cinema. Circumstances at the time dictated that I was unable to attend the in-person meeting with Senor Robles (star of such genre fare as *The Vampire*, *The Vampire's Coffin*, *The Brainiac*, *The Living Head* and the *Nostradamus* quartet), and so editor Jim Clatterbaugh served as the conduit for my questions. This (cover) piece was published in *Monsters from the Vault* magazine, issue 24, in the Winter of 2008, with this explanatory introduction: "The following interview is the joint effort of Bryan Senn (supplied the questions), Richard Sheffield (Germán Robles' good friend who helped coordinate the interview and provided his translation skills on various questions and answers during the interview), Jim Clatterbaugh (conducted the interview), and Marian Owens Clatterbaugh (transcribed the interview). The interview took place in June 2007 at Ron Adams' Monster Bash Convention, held annually near Pittsburgh, Pennsylvania. …..*MFTV* #24 marks only the second time Robles has been featured on the cover of a monster magazine in the United States, the other being *Famous Monsters of Filmland* #124 (published in 1976)…"

EL VAMPIRO SPEAKS! AN INTERVIEW WITH MEXICAN HORROR STAR GERMÁN ROBLES

MONSTERS FROM THE VAULT: *You were born in Spain, Germán, so what brought you to Mexico?*

GERMÁN ROBLES: During the civil war in Spain, there were two factions—the Fascist faction, which was General Franco, and the Republican faction. My father was a Republican and relocated to Mexico. My mother was put in jail for two and one-half years, and in 1945 my father had put together sufficient money to send to Spain to get her released from prison. She was released in 1945, and in 1946 my mother and I joined my father in Mexico.

MFTV: *How did you go about breaking into the movies?*

ROBLES: It was just a casual happening. I was working in a theater; Abel Salazar, the producer, saw me acting onstage and said, "That guy is my vampire!" He offered me a part in his film. I said, "Of course, right away, absolutely!" [laughter] And in 1957, the movie was made, and it was premiered the 22nd of June in 1957. Four days ago, no, two days ago—was its 50th anniversary!

Germán Robles became a Mexican horror icon when he starred as El Vampiro *(The Vampire) in 1957.*

MFTV: *The first day of this years' Monster Bash! Was your Spanish accent a hindrance or a help in securing roles in Mexico?*

ROBLES: It was a help, and, well, the producers said to me that I can't change the Spanish mode [of speaking], I can fake [the pronunciation of words] like azul [meaning "blue" and pronounced "athúl" in Spain], and in Mexico, it is [pronounced] "asúl"—with an s [sound]. The producers asked me, can you change your language color? I said, "Of course I will." And I changed my speaking style. My voice had to have a cadence [for the role].

MFTV: *Was* El Vampiro *[1957; The Vampire] your first film?*

ROBLES: Yes, it was my first—my debut.

MFTV: *And what a great debut!* El Vampiro's *producer (and co-star), Abel Salazar, has stated that he wanted to make "*Dracula *in a Mexican hacienda." Had you seen Lugosi in* Dracula *[1931], or even Carlos Villarias in the 1931 Spanish-language version of* Dracula, *before making* El Vampiro?

ROBLES: No. Never. Because *Dracula* is a Bram Stoker novel, si? I didn't want to be Dracula. I wanted to film a vampire history, a vampire tale—in this case, *The Vampire*. How did it look [the film]? First, there was the Mexican hacienda, the Sycamores. And the place was Sierra Negra—the black mountains. And the movie had a nice look –with the presence of the fog, the light, the design. The producer said I had the look of El Greco [the Spanish artist].

MFTV: *Did you ever see Lugosi's* Dracula *or the Spanish version of* Dracula?

ROBLES: Much later, I saw the Lugosi picture—I was curious about how it looked compared to *El Vampiro*. Also, I saw the Klaus Kinski *Nosferatu*—my favorite vampire.

MFTV: *What was your approach to creating the character of El Vampiro, and did you receive much input from director Fernando Méndez?*

ROBLES: Yes, thanks to the director, Fernando Méndez. He asked me if this was my first picture. I said, "yes, indeed." He said, "I want the figure of the vampire not to be a monster—I don't want a monster. I want a lover who looks at the girl from the top down and thinks about taking her to bed, si?" Violation—that's the principle thing about the vampire. The vampire takes the forbidden things, like a girl, a kid, or something like that. The attacks of the vampire usually take place in private…in the bedroom…in the bed. The vampire comes in the window and attacks her—very sexual, sensual, and possessive. See what I mean?

MFTV: *You were the first on-screen vampire to ever*

sport fangs. Lugosi never showed his teeth, and the Christopher Lee Dracula *came along after* El Vampiro. *Any problems with the lengthy teeth?*

ROBLES: Yes. Because it was very hard to [have] a nice pronunciation of the words. [laughter] So, sometimes on the screen, the camera angle would allow me to remove the fangs to say my lines; later, I put them back in. I brought the original fangs with me to the Monster Bash and had planned to wear them to my talk, but one was broken. I glued it back together but I couldn't get it to stay in.

MFTV: *During the scenes with dialogue, did your fangs ever fall out accidentally?*

ROBLES: No, no, no, of course not.

MFTV: *Speaking of Christopher Lee, it has been said that Lee actually patterned his vampire after yours. Do you know Mr. Lee, and what do you think of his performance as Dracula?*

ROBLES: No, unfortunately, no [does not know Mr. Lee]. However, a friend of mine met Lee in London at a BBC broadcast. My friend went over to Christopher Lee and said, "Hello, I am from Mexico." Mr. Lee said to him, "Oh, from Mexico! Do you know Germán Robles?" My friend said, "Yes, of course, he's a friend of mine." So, Christopher Lee said to my friend, "When you see Germán, tell him that thanks to his performance in *El Vampiro*, I copied (or something like that) his kind of lover-figure of the vampire." I appreciate the point of view of Mr. Christopher Lee because his picture [*Horror of Dracula*] was made in 1958, and *El Vampiro* in 1957.

Mexican lobby card for the sequel The Vampire's Coffin *(1958).*

MFTV: *Did you like Christopher Lee's* Horror of Dracula?

ROBLES: Yes, but not Coppola's *Bram Stoker's Dracula*. Now, I like Christopher Lee's Dracula because of his very powerful, very dominating, presence.

MFTV: El Vampiro *is one of the most beautifully shot and atmospheric Mexican horror movies. What are your memories of director Fernando Méndez and cinematographer Rosalío Solano?*

ROBLES: *El Vampiro* is iconic. Mexican cinema was not considered in very high esteem on an international level until *El Vampiro* was released—it was a landmark film. It put Mexican cinema on the map. [Regarding his memories of Méndez]: Good. He treated me very well, and he asked me, "Germán, this is your first picture?" I said, "Yes, sir." He said, "Now, I give you two advantages—two: First, the movie is 'eyes.' If you think well inside you, that reflects in your eyes. You must be sincere with your acting." I said, "Thank you very much." Then, he said, "Secondly, I want a vampire—a monster, not! I want a vampire that's very suave, very elegant." And the results turned out well, with my vampire. [Regarding his memories of Solano]: We became very, very close friends. He gave me advice: don't look there, don't look down, don't look very high, look and sense the light and the shadow. He told me the right way to look photographic. A good guy—very good guy.

MFTV: *Is Solano still alive? If so, do you ever see him?*

ROBLES: Si, si. He is 91. A month ago in Mexico, they held the equivalent of the Oscars, and they gave him a lifetime achievement award. But Fernando Méndez—no. He died many, many years ago.

MFTV: *Your next film was a sequel to* El Vampiro *called* El Ataúd del Vampiro *[1958;* The Vampire's Coffin*]. Did you have any compunction about playing the same character yet again?*

ROBLES: Yes, but I wanted to make my mark. I didn't want to be typecast in just the horror genre, which happened to Boris Karloff, Vincent Price, Lon Chaney, Bela Lugosi. I made 98 pictures, and in the first and second, I was a vampire. The others—no. In the others, king, bandit, scientist, cowboy, swordsman, many things, many personalities.

MFTV: *How do you think the sequel compares to the original?*

ROBLES: It's not as good as *El Vampiro*. It's very hard to try and make a successful second part. They tried to just capitalize quick on the success of *El Vampiro*. It was successful, but *El Vampiro* was much more successful.

MFTV: *I found the more modern hospital and apartment settings to be far less visually engaging than the dilapidated hacienda/castle milieu seen in the original. It also simply looks cheaper. Do you know if the budget was lower than on the original?*

ROBLES: The problem was Abel Salazar—he was a shylock, a Scrooge! [laughter] He wanted to do everything with less—or as much with less. He played poor.

MFTV: *Because the first film was so successful, did they give him more money the second time around?*

ROBLES: Yes, but he was cheap! Salazar became a millionaire because his films were so successful. *El Vampiro* has been dubbed in 52 languages, even more than *Gone with the Wind*. And subtitled in 14 languages.

MFTV: *Speaking of dubbing, have you ever seen the K. Gordon Murray English-dubbed version of* El Vampiro?

ROBLES: Yes, it's splendid. Because the voice is very similar to my own—very deep. It was a very good choice. However, it was very funny hearing it dubbed in Japanese—very strange. [laughter]

MFTV: *Were you well-paid for* El Vampiro *and its sequel? Did you at least get a raise for the second one?*

ROBLES: No, I was unknown—it was nothing, nothing. They paid me 7500 pesos—at exchange rate of 12.50 pesos pers dollar [$600 U.S. dollars], and 13,000 pesos [$1040 U.S. dollars] at the same exchange rate when I made the sequel.

MFTV: *You played the character of El Vampiro for a third time in the horror/comedy* El Castillo de los Monstruos *[1958;* Castle of the Monsters*]. How was the shift from straight horror to comedy?*

ROBLES: [Director Julian Soler] asked me, "You are filming right now *Coffin*. Would it be possible for you to come over and do a cameo part for me? With the same costume?" Salazar didn't even know about it. Méndez gave me permission.

MFTV: *After three films as El Vampiro, you played another vampire in four more movies:* La Maldicion de Nostradamus *[The Curse of Nostradamus]*, Nostradamus y el Destructor de Monstruos *[The Monster Demolisher]*, Nostradamus, el Genio de las Tinieblas *[Genie of Darkness]*, La Sangre de Nostradamus *[The Blood of Nostradamus] [all 1960]. These were adapted from a serial. Were the individual* Nostradamus *episodes ever shown in Mexican theaters in serial form (or on television as such), or were they released simply as feature films?*

ROBLES: They misrepresented themselves to me: They told me they were filming 30-minutes episodes—like fill-in shorts for theaters. When I finished the filming of these episodes, they put three episodes together to make one full-length picture. It ended up as being four full-length motion pictures. It is really uncomfortable to even think about this—it was a very unpleasant situation, because they actually cheated me. Very unpleasant situation. So, I erase from my mind the memory of these films. I have always tried to treat everybody at a nice, professional level. And it hurts, that they would take advantage of me—make fun of me, literally. Because I always try to do things right.

MFTV: *What did you do to differentiate Nostradamus from El Vampiro and make him a wholly different character?*

ROBLES: For Nostradamus, it was the first time I used a beard. And Greco still stayed with me [fresh in my mind]. So, it wasn't difficult to make that change, because I had just finished doing his Vampiro, and the figure of Vampiro was right at my fingertips.

MFTV: *How long did it take to shoot all of the episodes?*

ROBLES: I don't remember. I don't know—I'm sorry.

MFTV: *Two of the* Nostradamus *features costarred an American actor named Jack Taylor, using the name Grek Martin (he played the character of Igor), who went on to a long and prolific career in European films. Any memories of him?*

ROBLES: No, I don't know him. I have no idea who he is.

MFTV: *That's OK—it's probably because that was such a bad experience—the whole* Nostradamus *thing! And I have to ask, Why the name "Nostradamus"? I mean, it's not like your character makes any* predictions. *[laughter]*

ROBLES: The writers [Alfred Ruanova and Charles Taboada] picked Nostradamus. Why Nostradamus? Because the name Nostradamus is very phonetic—very emphatic, as opposed to a name like George—not so scary. [laughter]

MFTV: *El Barón del Terror [The Brainiac] holds a special place in the hearts of Mexican horror film lovers. What do you recall of working on this film?*

ROBLES: It's junk. [laughter] It's a classic—a

guilty pleasure. For me, it was a sad memory—but I had a small part.

MFTV: *And how about working with your frequent costar, Abel Salazar?*

ROBLES: Very funny guy. Cheap! A Scrooge—a shylock. [laughter] But, still very fun to work with.

MFTV: *Was that Salazar himself wearing the [Brainiac monster] mask, or did a stuntman step in for those scenes?*

ROBLES: It was him—yes, yes! Except for the very long [in duration] shots, because of the heat, sweating, and so forth.

MFTV: *Do you recall any problems with the production or run-ins with Salazar while he was wearing his producer hat?*

ROBLES: No, no. All I really remember is that Salazar mentioned to me that he preferred doing characterizations of the hero without having to use makeup or masks. All the heavy makeup and more complicated characterizations he left to the real actors.

MFTV: *How long did the feature movies in which he starred (for example,* Vampire's Coffin*) take to film?*

ROBLES: Four weeks, if there were very complicated scenes.

MFTV: *What was the mood on the set as you filmed this decidedly bizarre tale [*The Brainiac*]? Was it deadly serious or was it more lighthearted? Any practical joking going on?*

ROBLES: The best part of the film was the beginning. In the role I played, the first part of the picture was great, but the rest, when the monster appeared—not good! The beginning of the picture was good—about the religion, Inquisition. [Regarding the mood on the set]: Serious, very serious! But when the director said "cut," everybody laughed! But they didn't approach the film as a joke—they were very serious about it, treated it with respect.

MFTV: *La Cabeza Viviente [*The Living Head*; 1959] was another of your early horror film roles, though you played a good guy this time. Did you enjoy being a villain or did you like the hero role more?*

ROBLES: Villain, of course! People remember you more for being a villain than hero—everyone knows Dracula—Bela Lugosi….Jack Palance, great! Even though he did other roles, people always think of him as playing the bad guy

MFTV: *You worked with director Chano Urueta several times [*El Barón del Terror, La Cabeza Viviente*] on some of the best-loved films of the genre. What are your memories of him as a director?*

ROBLES: If Emilio Fernández, known as "El Indio," hadn't been around, Chano Urueta would be considered the greatest Mexican director of all time. This is what happened with Maria Félix and another actress, Elsa Aguirre. Aguirre was as beautiful as Maria Félix—and a much more superior actress than Maria Félix. But Félix was number one. Elsa Aguirre was never able to get to that first place. Same with Emilio Fernández and Chano Urueta. See what I mean? A good guy could never get to the top. In the case of Cahno Urueta, he was sensitive, would ask, "Can you do this for me, Germán?" "Yes." "OK, give me…blah blah blah blah…, but in this case, don't look up, don't look down, and you finish your talk." Very sensitive. But Emilio Fernández, he was always at the top. Poor Chano Urueta.

MFTV: *Most of your early roles were in horror films. Were you worried about being typecast at that time? And do you think they helped or hindered your subsequent career?*

ROBLES: Didn't help. I have done 98 films. So I have a battle—a conflict—of trying to get my public to forget *El Vampiro* and *Vampire's Coffin* so I could move on to other roles.

MFTV: *Do you have an affinity for horror movies (do you enjoy watching horror films yourself)?*

ROBLES: Yes, very very much! Very fun!

MFTV: *Do you ever catch your own films on television or on video? If so, what do you think of them?*

ROBLES: Yes, on both [television and video] it brings back many memories of things I did, and from time to time a tear slips out.

MFTV: *Do you have a personal favorite of all the horror pictures you've made?*

ROBLES: *The Vampire* and *The Vampire's Coffin*, of course! [laughter] But there are lots of horror films I like, *The Howling* [1981], *The Black Room* [1935] with Karloff I like very much, Klaus Kinski in *Nosferatu the Vampire* [1979].

MFTV: *Who are your favorite actors?*

ROBLES: From the past, Cary Grant, James Stewart, William Powell, Robert Taylor, Marlon Brando. From today, Al Pacino, Donald Sutherland. Jack Nicholson, of course! Paul Newman, Richard Gere, Harrison Ford I like very much, Sean Connery. They are actors of the old school, like studio actors, or the Global Theater in London. Al Pacino in Shakespeare's *Mercante di Venezia* [*The Merchant of Venice*; 2004].

MFTV: *In* Neutron contra los Asesinos del Karate *[1965] you acted opposite such lucha libre stars as Wolf Ruvinskis and Fernando Oses, and later Mil Mascaras and Superzan in* Los Vampiros del Coyoacan*[1974]. How was it working with these legends of Mexican wrestling?*

ROBLES: I took much care—they were "monsters" with biceps! [laughter]

MFTV: *Are you a lucha libre fan yourself?*

ROBLES: No, I think that lucha libre is a lark. They're good actors…unique…in the ring.

MFTV: *In* El Pistolero Fantasma *[1970;* The Phantom Gunslinger*] you play perhaps the ultimate villain—the Devil. Any thoughts about filling such diabolical shoes?*

ROBLES: Yes, because I was a devil who came to the Earth to fight the "saint," this guy played by Troy Donahue. Good guy, nice guy. I loved the characterization—I loved the part because I was a gunslinger. Good picture.

MFTV: *In your career you've moved back and forth between television and films (and theater), even at a time [the 1960s and 1970s] when such boundary-crossing was frowned upon—at least in Hollywood. Did you ever encounter any stigma about being a "TV actor," or was there even such a prejudice in Mexican pop culture at the time?*

ROBLES: No. It was that way in Hollywood, but it wasn't true in Mexico. There are three types of media that exist in Mexico: theater, television, and film. Those people who work in film do not work in theater, and those who work in theater do not work in television. But I have fans from all the categories—it's very curious. [Regarding any stigma about being a TV actor]: No, no problem whatsoever. I am primarily a stage actor. As a stage actor, I can do films, television, dubbing, and radio. But my base is theater.

MFTV: *Though you've done far more work outside of the horror genre than within it, you'll forever be known (in the U.S., at least) as a "horror actor" in general, and as El Vampiro in particular. Any resentment over that fact?*

ROBLES: No, never, of course not.

MFTV: *The last credit I could find for you was a television series in 2000. Have you retired? If so, how does El Vampiro fill his time these days?*

ROBLES: [Retired?] Of course not! [laughter] I have my own school, I'm a teacher. My wife Anna-Maria wrote a play that I'm going to work in about Leonardo da Vinci. It has to do with the last four or five days of da Vinci's life. Now, I'm making another soap opera for television called *Passions*. I had to change my arrival plans for Monster Bash because I was filming until three o'clock in the morning on Friday. The character I play is from the 18th century, owner of a large estate who has slaves. I marry one of the slaves. She has been stolen and sold into slavery—was from a very good family. It will be a very exciting show, and it will start in September this year.

In 2013, for my book *The Most Dangerous Cinema: People Hunting People on Film*, I interviewed Stu Segall about his 1972 movie *The Suckers* (a soft-core take on the classic "Most Dangerous Game" story). Though he carved out his modest industry niche by making sex films (first soft-, then hard-core), Segall made the occasional "legit" movie too, including the proto-slasher film *Drive-In Massacre* (1976). Forthright and forthcoming, the following are his comments on his sole foray into horror history.

STU SEGALL ORCHESTRATES A *DRIVE-IN MASSACRE*

"I used to be a private investigator," began Segall to explain how he found himself making movies. "And I ran into a guy through a mutual female friend who was a make-up artist in titty movies, the T&A business. He was fascinated by me being an investigator, and I was fascinated by what he did, so he said to me, 'Why don't you come on up to the set, and you'll help me on the movie.' So I said, 'Yeah sure, but I don't know what I'm doin'.' He says, 'Aw, come up.' So I hit it off with him, the guy's name was Ray Sebastian. And Ray Sebastian was a very well-known make-up artist in the early days of—we'll call it the T&A business. And we got to be very very good friends. So I worked for Ray as an assistant make-up artist on my first time on the set. My first job was to take make-up and put it on naked women. This was a movie that was made by—it might have been Russ Meyer, I don't remember the name of it. But they were all large-busted women. They were all 44D and above. So my job that day was to put body make-up on all these girls that were naked. And because of the way they used to light things in those days—they used a tremendous amount of light—these girls if they didn't have an overall tan, which most of them did not, needed body make-up. So I was making up tits and ass and crotches. You know you have them lined up on tables, and you just went down this line and put make-up on these girls. That was my first [movie] job that I got paid for. I was fascinated by being on the set, a lot of people doing a lot of things. There was an excitement about it—in a very small way—but it was exciting. So one thing led to another, and Ray says, 'Hey, I got another job. You want to take it—you'll have to unload this truck.' So I did a little grip work, I schlepped the lights. One thing led to another and I said I think I can do this. So I went out

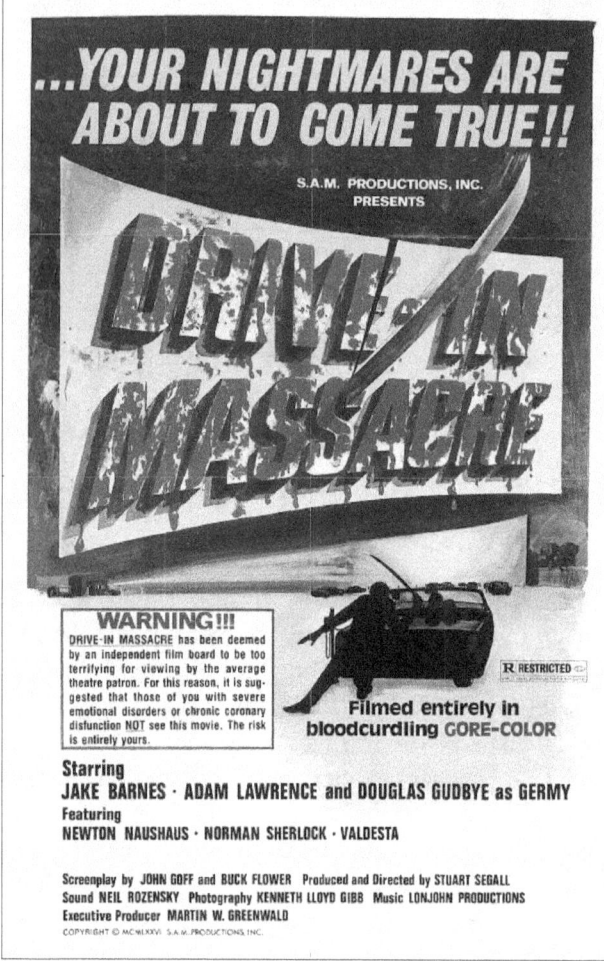

Drive-In Massacre *poster*.

and borrowed some money, and I put together my first movie [1969's *Harvey* and its sequel, *Harvey Swings*, 1970]. And I had no clue about anything. I had never directed anything, never produced anything. The editor I hired had never edited anything. And the distributor I wound up with never distributed anything. We were all a bunch of newcomers. But we were young, it was great. That's how I got out of the investigative business and into the movie business."

Segall usually employed a pseudonym. "I never put my name on any of the low-budget movies I made because they were T&A." After a few more early-seventies soft-core entries, like *Teen-Age Jail Bait* (1973), Segall eventually joined the early wave of hard-core porn that formed in the middle of the decade, directing and producing under a variety of aliases (with Godfrey Daniels being a favorite) such XXX fare as *The Spirit of Seventy Sex* (1976, with Annette Haven) and the "classic" *Insatiable* (1980), with Marilyn Chambers and John Holmes. Under his real name, Segall also produced and directed the slightly more "legit" early slasher pic *Drive-In Massacre* (1976).

"I made four movies at one time. *Drive-In Massacre* was actually shot in four days. Then there was another movie called *C.B. Hustlers*. And I had two other movies that we did R-rated versions of: *Saddle Tramps*, which was a western, and one more which I can't remember the title of. But we made four movies in 14 days, all at the same time. Same cast, and we changed the cast wardrobe and locations every day. You could never double-bill the movies because it *was* the same cast. It was a lot of fun. We did 20- and 22-hour days. You know, you're young, and when you're in your early twenties and doing stuff like this, it was a lot of fun.

"The drive-in location in which we shot was the Simi Valley Drive-In. We had one night to shoot the drive-in stuff, so we got there on whatever night they weren't open, it might have been like a Tuesday night or a Monday night, and we shot for from before the sun went down to just before the sun came up. All the R-rated movies I was making were for that circuit—the drive-ins.

"When I was growing up and started driving, you'd go to a drive-in movie. When you had a date and wanted to make out, that's where you went. Nobody had an apartment, we were all teenagers. So you always went to a drive-in. And I always thought, gosh wouldn't it be kind of strange if you reached out of a window to get your speaker, and some asshole would cut your head off."

Despite having made *Drive-In Massacre*, Segall is no fan of the genre. "I will not watch a horror movie," he declared. "I'm too freaked out to watch. I look at trailers now and I say, 'I'm not gonna see *that* one.' Like *Saw*, I would never go see that. That's way too spooky for me. I've never seen *The Exorcist*—I had to look through my fingers to watch. It scared the shit out of me. So I am not what you would call an aficionado of horror films. But I could certainly make an attempt to make one. It was really about making movies."

Drive-In Massacre turned out to be a one-off for Segall, and he quickly returned to his sexploitation roots. "The reason we didn't make more movies for drive-ins," he explained, "was that the financing wasn't there. So we went where the financing was [which was adult films]."

Abandoning porn (and directing altogether) in the mid-1980s, Segall (sans pseudonym) became a television producer/executive producer, overseeing series like *Hunter* (1984–87), *Renegade* (1992–97), and *Silk Stalkings* (1991–99, something of a return to his sexploitation roots), as well as a whole slew of low-budget made-for-TV movies like *Beastmaster: The Eye of Braxus* (1996), *I Married a Monster* (1998), and *Alien Fury: Countdown to Invasion* (2000). Since 1991 he has owned and operated a 70,000-square-foot studio facility, Stu Segall Productions, in San Diego. Among others, the popular cult TV series *Veronica Mars* was shot there. After 9/11, Segall transformed his production studio into a military training facility called Strategic Operations, Inc., and garnered contracts with the Navy, the Marines, and Special Forces. Explained Segall, "We use all the movie and TV effects in actual training. We brought that to military training. We've supported the training of about 700,000 soldiers, sailors, marines and coast guard. ...We've got an 'Afghan village' in the back that's now full of sailors and corpsmen, explosions going off. We've run 130,000 marines through this space before they went into combat in Iraq and Afghanistan. ...It's kind of similar to traditional movies in a way—battlefield special effects, movie special effects, make-up special effects. We do a tremendous amount of medical training. We'll take amputees and we'll put gore on them, put eviscerations and huge wounds on them so the corpsmen can train on something that looks very realistic."

Segall holds no illusions about his filmmaking career. "It was low-budget, down and dirty stuff," he said. "I never really wanted to be big or anything. I loved doing what I did because I was in control. On anything of any size or consequence, you've pretty much lost that control, and you're just another person doin' the job. ...I always like working for myself, and if I wanted to move on and move up—I might not have had the talent to do it, either; it's not just about what I wanted. It just didn't happen to me, and I'm fine with that. Some people aspire to that, but I just never had that aspiration.

"I was very proud of what I did. It got me to where I'm doing whatever I've done in my life. Producer of a thousand hours of television. Probably every studio in Hollywood, from Disney on down, we've made shows for—not as a director but as a production company."

I met actress Barbara Shelley at a Fanex convention in Baltimore in July 2001, and she graciously agreed to a quick conversation about her various horror credits. Though too brief for a comprehensive article, her illuminating comments are still worth recording. To wit:

HAMMER HEROINE BARBARA SHELLEY

CAT GIRL (1957)

"Big Chief Horrible Noise," [the leopard seen in the film], was his name, and we called him 'Chiefy.' I said [to the animal's trainer/handler, Frank], 'Is he tame?' He said, 'No, he's not vicious but he's not tame.' Chiefy used to come and rub his head against my hand, and in the end, he would lick it. It came to the point where he'd come into my dressing room. He was a lovely animal, I loved him."

VILLAGE OF THE DAMNED (1960)

On the film's concept: "A child who is evil is really more than frightening, it's deeply disturbing."

On said child, actor Martin Stephens: "[He was] a delightful young man."

On co-star George Sanders: "Great sense of humor. ...And George always played chess with Martin." Shelley likened Sanders to another famous actor she worked with—Christopher Lee. "Both won't sit down in a room until all the ladies are seated. These two gentlemen were wonderful to work with—such communication…"

On the film itself: "It was a very happy coming together of certain things that make a film. Very, very happy movie. I think it was a classic. I loved that movie."

THE SHADOW OF THE CAT (1961)

"The set was pretty tense—it wasn't completely pleasant on the set." Shelley put this tension down to director John Gilling's lack of humor. Nor was she happy with the final script. "[Screenwriter] George Baxt had written a completely different film. The cat never appeared in George's script—it was implied it was the evil in the family that caused all the trouble. But the director decided to film it all through the cat's eyes."

"[Co-star] Andre [Morell] was a man known to be very crusty. Didn't suffer fools gladly, expected people to be professional. But he was wonderful. ...Andre and I got on terribly well, and he was a very nice man."

THE GORGON (1964)

Shelley, who labeled *The Gorgon* "one of my favorites," wanted to play the Gorgon with real grass snakes woven into her hair and wig, but producer Anthony Nelson Keys felt it would hold up the production schedule and ordered another actress be made up as the Gorgon (with fake snakes). But after seeing the rough cut, Keys, who, according to Shelley, was a very stubborn man, approached her. "'Hrrmph,' he said. 'You were right.' And that's all he ever said."

Of her co-stars, she commented, "Peter [Cushing] I used to call 'the Propmaster.'" Patrick Troughton, who played a Prussian police officer, "used to greet me in the morning by clicking his heels and saying, 'Guten

Barbara Shelley ran afoul of Dracula, Prince of Darkness *in 1966. (lobby card)*

morgen Gorgan.' …I'd rather work with Chris [Lee] than anyone else."

DRACULA, PRINCE OF DARKNESS (1966)

"I thought a vampire is kind of the evil inside us that we all try and suppress…the repressed Victorian side."

RASPUTIN THE MAD MONK (1966)

As research for the story, Shelley "got some books from the library."

The actress was highly impressed by co-star Christopher Lee, particularly his intensity. "I was frightened to look at him in case he really would mesmerize me! I thought if I stared at him too hard he would have hypnotized me. …His actual acting in *Rasputin* is really of a quality that was never recognized in England."

QUATERMASS AND THE PIT (aka FIVE MILLION YEARS TO EARTH) (1967)

"We used to call it 'Quaterpiss and the Mat.'" [laughs]

"[Andrew Kier] was slightly ill-at-ease on the set because he thought [director] Roy [Ward Baker] didn't want him—but he did."

Full disclosure: the quirky, charming, never-fails-to-make-me-smile *The Giant Gila Monster* (1959) is one of my favorite creature features (in fact, it's the very first monster movie I showed my son). So I was thrilled when *Monsters from the Vault* editor Jim Clatterbaugh asked me to interview its star, Don Sullivan (who also headlined another favorite, *The Monster of Piedras Blancas*, as well as *Teenage Zombies*—which is *nobody's* favorite). Mr. Sullivan proved very warm and forthcoming, so much so that many of his comments had to be cut for length when the piece ran in issue 27 (Spring 2010). Here's the full, unabridged interview. Sadly, Don Sullivan passed away in 2018.

ZOMBIES AND CRUSTACEANS AND GILA MONSTERS, OH MY! AN INTERVIEW WITH DON SULLIVAN

In the mid–1950s a young man from Idaho went to California and fell into the acting business. While he never made an A-movie during his five-year stint in Tinseltown, Don Sullivan brought his boyish good looks and easy charm (not to mention his ukulele skills) to bear on such fondly-remembered creature features as *Teenage Zombies*, *The Monster of Piedras Blancas*, and *The Giant Gila Monster*. In 1960 he left one form of "glamour" for another to forge an illustrious career as a cosmetics chemist. Still active in the cosmetics industry today, Don talks about his all-too-brief Hollywood career, meeting Elvis, lobster-hunting with Lon Chaney, Jr., the dangers of ill-fitting swimsuits, and why you should never jump from a moving hot rod.

BRYAN SENN: *According to some sources [including the IMDb], you were born in Salt Lake City in 1938...*
DON SULLIVAN: That's incorrect. What happened is, I think some of the historians going back to the '50s saw me playing the part of a 17 or 18-year-old kid and assumed I was 17 or 18. I had already graduated from high school, spent four years in the Marine Corps, and four years in college before I got to California and into movies. I was born in 1929.
SENN: *You were raised in Idaho, right?*
SULLIVAN: That's correct, a little town named Shoshone, Idaho – a railroad stop with 300 people. So it was very, very small, and actually a fabulous place to grow up as a kid. There were pheasants and duck hunting, and you could be the star of every athletic sport [laughs] because at school there were so few kids.
SENN: *So how did a young man from a small town in Idaho end up in Hollywood making movies?*
SULLIVAN: When I first came to California I had no idea; I arrived here with 3 dollars in my pocket. I knew that Idaho was not a place, at that time, for the opportunity that I'd hoped for in my life. So I just packed up the car and came to California. Then the next morning I went up the Sunset Strip and found a gas station that could use an attendant, and I got an advance from the guy at the gas station. And I was in business until I could find a better area to go into or another profession. I wasn't thinking acting.

But I did hang out at that time at a place called Schwab's Drugstore on the Sunset Strip. A lot of actors frequented the place, and I ran into and got to know an actress named Judy Meredith [*The Night Walker*, *Queen of Blood*]. So we dated and were going steady, and I used to go down and pick her up at an acting class three times a week. I would sit in the back until she finished. And she said finally, "Don, why don't you join the class, it's fun." And I thought [hesitating], "Well..." And maybe waaay in the back of my mind I had a yearning to be an actor, I don't know. There are recesses we don't even reach into, you know? So I joined the class, and we put on a play strictly for family members, 30 or 40 people coming in to watch the play. And just as luck would have it, [producer/director/writer] Hugo Haas and his wife Bebe came in and liked my performance. He came backstage and said, "The next movie that I do, I want you to star in it as the young romantic lead." So I was thrilled. He brought a script about three months later. I looked it over and it was great, and I was happy. But it was with Cleo Moore, who was kind of the Marilyn Monroe of the day in Hollywood. So when he showed Cleo Moore a picture of me as the young romantic lead, she said, "Hugo, he's too young for me, I can't do it with him." So Hugo came back to me and said, "I'm sorry, Don, I've gotta change this." Cleo Moore was his 'belle cow,' the one who was securing the money for this thing. And he had to go along with her. So I thought, "Ok, fine, that's Hollywood," and paid no attention to it. But a year later Hugo was back with a second script. And I did the young romantic lead with Carol Morris, who was Miss Universe of the day, and I was on my way.
SENN: *And what was that first film?*
SULLIVAN: It was *Paradise Alley*.
SENN: *So basically you were refused the part because you were "too young," when, in fact, you were in your mid- to-late twenties at the time?*
SULLIVAN: That's correct, but I looked young. That youthful look was there—I was always a kid until I got to be about 45 or 50, and all of a sudden there was a transition and I became the old man. Then I had gray hair along both sides. Of course I've been pretty fortunate; I'm going on 80 this year, and I look pretty good for my age. I held together.
SENN: *You did a number of television shows, too. Did you go into TV right after you made that first film?*
SULLIVAN: I went into whatever I could get into. You had an agent, and they would send you out for both TV and films. But you find in Hollywood—I don't know what it's like today—but in those days it was not so much how good you were, it was who you knew. My fishing buddy Charlie Weintraub, an attorney, sold foreign film distribution. We used to go deep sea fishing down in San Diego. Well, he knew the casting director at MGM. So he's talking to the casting guy and says, "Hey, a friend of mine, Sullivan, is a good young actor." So I get *Not for Hire* with Ralph Meeker, I did a show there. In Schwab's Drugstore I met Eddie and Millie Dein, a director-writer team who did a lot of stuff with Warner Brothers in different areas. We got to be friends, and everything that Eddie would do, he'd find a part in it for me. I worked two times at Warner Brothers on *Hawaiian Eye*, and things like this. And he had an independent movie, one of the monster movies, that

I had a small part in.

SENN: *That Eddie Dein "monster movie" was, I take it,* Curse of the Undead *[1959]?*

SULLIVAN: Yeah, Eddie called me up and said, "I'm doin' a western-monster thing, and you get one day's work and one line." But it was Christmastime and I was grateful for that one day's work. It was a couple or three hundred dollars. In those days I didn't have the back-up here—there was no home here, no friends here, nothing for me to fall back on. I was trying to make a living. To survive in Hollywood is more than an accomplishment, it's a matter of survival. It still occurs to a great degree, I think. I was just down having breakfast with my daughter [Lucia Sullivan], who's an actress, and every one of the waiters and waitresses there are actors. It's a tough route.

SENN: *So your daughter is following in your footsteps?*

SULLIVAN: Yeah, she's doing really well. She's worked three times this last month. She did *The Mentalist*, she's in another TV show, and she did an independent movie. She's just getting smaller parts, but she's rapidly rising, so we'll see what happens. Most of all she's having a lot of fun, and I think that's the answer – to really *enjoy* it. Day by day in today's environment is pretty hectic.

Top billing…in a bottom feeder.

SENN: Teenage Zombies *came along in 1957.*

SULLIVAN: Made by Jerry Warren. It's interesting—I think we set a record for that movie. I don't know any other movie that was shot in 24 hours. The sound guy would say, "Jerry, you can't hear him." Jerry would say, "We'll dub it later." And the lighting technician would say, "There are a lot of shadows." And Jerry would say, "Well, that's atmosphere." And we'd do a master and that was it, then go to the next. And he would line you up on a wall and get reaction shots. He'd yell to the wall, "Fear!," "Love!," "Scared!," "Who's that?!" And you're supposed to give a reaction to that verbal command. He only had, I think, a budget of $10,000, and Jerry was probably taking half of that for himself. [Note: The budget was $15,000, according to Bri Murphy, *Teenage Zombies* co-star and wife of Jerry Warren.]

SENN: *I've read in interviews that Warren was something of a "screamer."*

SULLIVAN: No, I didn't find that to be the case. Not on that movie, he didn't scream at all.

SENN: *Did you get any money out of that gig?*

SULLIVAN: I think I was the only one that did. At the time I was a SAG member. So Jerry said to me that he could get in real trouble with the SAG office [because it was a non-union shoot]. Jerry said, "We're not paying any salaries for this." They were paying $100 or something like that. And I said, "I'm a member of SAG, and I don't work for less than SAG minimum. So you'll have to find somebody else." So he agreed to pay me SAG minimum. I think it was $250 or $300 at that time.

SENN: *You were top-billed in the movie; how'd you negotiate that?*

SULLIVAN: That was funny. Again Schwab's Drugstore plays a big part in my life for some strange reason. I'm in Schwab's having coffee one evening, and a friend of mine comes running up to me. He says, "Hey Don, you want to be in a movie? They're not paying any money, but it'd be fun to do. C'mon with me, Jerry's down the street." So Jerry and I talked for a few minutes. And Jerry says, "I want you to do the lead in this." But my buddy had already committed to play the lead for Jerry, so Jerry says [to my friend], "Do you mind if you play that second role?" And he said, "No, I don't mind." I felt kind of guilty having done this, but I didn't feel so guilty that I turned it down [laughs].

SENN: *There's a fight scene you have in there, and it looks like you're throwing some pretty good punches. Did you have any kind of fight choreography help, or did you just get in there and wing it?*

SULLIVAN: We just sort of winged it. Steve Conte, who was in that movie, was a very close friend of mine. Steve insisted that we have some time to work out the fight routines because he didn't want anybody to get hurt. Me, at that time, I was never concerned about getting hurt; I would have fallen off the top of a building if it was in the script [laughs]. I was the 'young immortal,' as a lot of young guys are.

SENN: *So Warren wasn't too concerned about it either; he was just going to let you go at it.*

SULLIVAN: Nah, Warren wasn't too concerned about the film, period. Quite frankly, he just wanted to get the thing on film and get it over with. He was not interested in making a good movie or anything that might resemble a good movie.

SENN: *To his credit, Warren came out and admitted, "On* Teenage Zombies *I just put together a picture that was long enough to play the lower half of my double bill." And that's all he was looking for.*

SULLIVAN: Yep, we'd request a little rehearsal time, or ask, "Could we shoot a scene a second time?" and it was "No, no, no."

SENN: *Did you ever do any promotion for, or attend a screening of,* Teenage Zombies?

SULLIVAN: No, not on that film I didn't. Actually, on the first film, *Paradise Alley*, with Hugo Haas, we had a premiere. I got ahold of Kookie Burns' girlfriend, Lisa Maynard, a beautiful blonde, and rented a T-bird convertible. And we drive up, and they had the stands at the movie theater, with all of these people screaming, and we get out of the car, and they're all screaming. And they're wondering, "Who is it?" They had no idea who I was or anything else [laughs]. Lisa and I go up, and they had George Jessel on the mike as the M.C. And he says, "This is the young romantic lead in the film—John Sullivan." And I said, "No, *Don* Sullivan." And then we talked for a few minutes. And we get done and George says, "Well, that's great, thank you." And as I walk off I hear him say, "And that was John Sullivan" [laughs].

After the premier was over I came outside. There was a very successful young actress at the time named Coleen Gray [*The Vampire*, *The Leech Woman*]. Coleen Gray all of a sudden is up in front of me. "Oh Don, can I have your autograph?" I looked at this beautiful girl and thought, "Wait a minute, there's something wrong here." And so I just played it very straight. Normally, at that time I would have said, "I'll give you the autograph if you give me your phone number," or something like that. But I didn't and just signed it. And I look over at Hugo Haas and Lance Fuller, and they're laughing

Jeanne Carmen and Don Sullivan pose with The Monster of Piedras Blancas *(1959).*

their heads off. They'd sent Coleen Gray up because they figured I'd react in some way, trying to get her number or whatever. It was a joke played on me, but I was pretty hip to it—at least I'd recognized it.

It was a fun premiere. Not many B actors have a premiere of their movie, so I enjoyed that.

SENN: *Speaking of B films, how were you cast in* Monster of Piedras Blancas?

SULLIVAN: That was through an agent [Red Herzog]. Jeanne Carmen, as I understand it—it may or may not be true—put up the money for that movie. I think she was engaged to somebody in Texas who was very wealthy, and in order to keep her happy or whatever, they said we'll back the movie; or maybe they were trying to make money, I don't know. But she picked me from a batch of pictures—that's how I got it. The agent called and said, "You got a movie."

SENN: *You two work pretty well together onscreen; what are your memories of her?*

SULLIVAN: Oh, I like Jeanne a lot; she was so terrific. As a matter of fact, I saw her down here at a celebrity autograph signing convention in the Valley. She and I were side-by-side, and I couldn't believe she looked so great. She was 70-some years old and looked incredible. And she was so mentally sharp. And wouldn't you know, about three months later I get word that she'd died. She had leukemia and didn't tell anybody about it. She was a sweetheart.

She played a lot of sex-bimbo types in a lot of things, and played that imagery up, because it was successful for her. But she wasn't that way at all; she was a very very sweet gal.

SENN: *Also in* Piedras Blancas *was one of my favorite old-time actors, Les Tremayne.*

SULLIVAN: He was one of my favorites, too. I *loved* Les Tremayne. You know, I have a warped sense of humor, and I say that *with* a sense of humor. But Les Tremayne was fun because he also had a good sense of humor. He knew what was good in life, bad in life, and what was worthwhile. He'd been doing B movies and really had probably far more talent—he'd done some A-movie work before—but even on a B movie he knew it was part of the industry, and he enjoyed the people, and knew that you're just lucky to be working as a creative artist. I loved Les Tremayne; he was a sweetheart.

SENN: *I thought you, Les Tremayne, and Forrest Lewis, who played the sheriff—you were the three heroes—had a nice, easy chemistry going that helped keep things more believable, relatively speaking.*

SULLIVAN: Forrest was a nice man; he did a lot of film work. It was fun, it was a good group. I have to tell you, though. You'll find in interviews that actors and actresses all are grateful to be working. They're of a nature that they seem to bond together—you know, it's a birds of a feather-type relationship. There are a few cases where on the set they get into fights and so forth—I guess that's more prevalent today. But at the time I was working, God, everybody was happy to be working, and they loved the people they worked with because they were of the same ilk.

SENN: *Sounds like it was pretty idyllic back then.*

SULLIVAN. It was. Everything was. Not to show my age, but it was an idyllic time in the United States and in California. Every positive thing you could want in life was here at that time. It's a different world today, and I think there are new positives that take the place of the old ones, but for me, I'm an old-fashioned type, coming from Idaho and all, and I enjoyed that period very much.

SENN: *Was it awkward filming that romantic sequence on the beach when you pulled that* From Here to Eternity *trick [kissing in the surf] with Jeanne Carmen?*

SULLIVAN: [Laughs] It was *terrible*. I'll try to keep this in the right frame while explaining it, so it doesn't offend anybody. Number one, I was embarrassed to begin with because, as you probably noticed in the scene, I was kind of a skinny young actor—I didn't have the bulging muscles of a *From Here to Eternity* Burt Lancaster. I was a thin kid; I wasn't eating so well, maybe. In any event, when I first read that I thought, "Oh God, I don't want to be photographed in a swimming suit." But you do what you have to do in movies and theater. So we get out there in Cayucus in Northern California, and the townspeople had come down to watch the shooting of the film. And there were probably 30 or 40 teenagers from high school there, mostly girls. Before we shot the scene, the director said, "Do you have a swimming suit?" And I said, "No, I thought wardrobe would bring a suit." He said, "Wait, in the trunk of my car I've got a suit." And he comes back with almost a bikini-type of a suit. And I put it on, and it was too small for me. It was *really* tight—bikini tight. So that's preying on my mind also. Now I come out of the water during the scene and have to sit down next to Jeanne and then go into the romantic clinch. Well, we're shooting, and I come out of the water and I sit down. Some of the "private parts" come out of the suit! They're exposed. And all the teenage girls are laughing and giggling and carrying on. And I'm mortified, absolutely mortified. Well, we get things straightened out. I go back out. I come out of this water and I sit down again. And the same thing happens again. This time they erupt in great laughter. They're pointing and carrying on. Now I get angry. So I go to the director and say, "Look, this will probably happen every time we shoot this; I can't help it. Can you shoot me from the waist up?" He says, "Good idea, son." Of course, I go out and come in, and the same thing happened. But we shot it from the waist up and got it done [laughs]. It was not a fun scene to do. Of course, Jeanne thought it was very *very* funny.

SENN: *In that scene you can plainly see a tattoo on your shoulder. Was that real?*

SULLIVAN: Yeah, it's a Marine Corps emblem. I was four years in the Marine Corps. Like most young guys, I felt I needed to get a tattoo.

SENN: *What did you think of the monster suit? It was designed by the producer, Jack Kevan, who also helped create the* Creature from the Black Lagoon *suit.*

SULLIVAN: The suit really was the star of the movie, because it was unique and a really scary thing. It would still be in vogue, that look and that suit. You could still use it for a monster movie in today's environment.

SENN: *It looked impressive, and they photographed it well. Did it look rubbery in person or did it look good?*

SULLIVAN: It looked scarier in person than it did on film, I swear. It was pretty frightening with the guy in it, a big guy, and it was pretty scary. If I'd have encountered it on a dark evening somewhere I would've gotten scared.

SENN: *The climax on top of the lighthouse looked a little daunting for the players; was that you way up there scrambling up the ladder on the top?*

SULLIVAN: Absolutely. As I said, I would have jumped off a building if they had told me to in those days. I had no concern about safety, just to make it as realistic as I could.

SENN: *Were there any mishaps during filming?*

SULLIVAN: No there wasn't, it went very smooth.

SENN: *I read that the budget was about $30,000. So I assume you were, again, making SAG minimum.*

SULLIVAN: That's all I ever made, was SAG minimum. The most successful movie that I made earned me SAG minimum. And that's still true today. Around Hollywood, my daughter is doing some of these TV shows and independent movies. She's up to a couple hundred more than minimum now. But you're either at that minimum level or you're a star and you're making the big dollars. There's not too much of an intermediate positioning in film. In fact, that was one of the reasons that in 1960 I left the acting industry. At that time, though it didn't turn out to be true, the thought process around Hollywood was that if you were doing B movies you were a B movie actor and would never be in any of the big films. And after six years of never getting a decent film and doing a number of B movies, I sort of felt that I didn't have anywhere to go, really.

SENN: *For* Piedras Blancas, *did you attend any kind of premiere?*

SULLIVAN: No, but it's interesting that, as I understand it, in Cayucus they celebrate every year—and have been celebrating for the last 50 years—the movie! They have a day where they have a big picnic and play the film and drink beer and have a good time. I think Jeanne had gone up there once or twice.

SENN: *Sounds like fun!*

SULLIVAN: It would be a lot of fun. You know, you get to be my age—I'm still working in the cosmetics industry, creating new products—but I enjoy this little renaissance of the film industry that I was part of in the '50s. It's fun. I've been to a number of science fiction and monster conventions; you know, the only reason you go is for a little bit of acknowledgment that you were part of that genre in the '50s, and it's fun.

You see, I'd gotten out of the acting industry and into hair care and skin care, creating products for Vidal Sassoon and other companies, and I didn't even realize that there was anybody that even knew or was interested in these B movies of the '50s. Only last year did I discover that there are a whole bunch of websites and different things on it.

SENN: *Have you watched* Piedras Blancas *lately, and what did you think of it then as compared to now?*

SULLIVAN: I have to tell you that I never watch any of those films. I don't have any particular *reason* for not watching them, but by the same token, I don't have any real reason to watch them again. I've seen them all. I probably was less impressed by them than some of the people who are fans of the monster movie genre. I will say this, and it's an interesting thing. Some of the films that I did, TV and different things, at the time I was so critical of them. I thought, my God, at the time there was James Dean and Marlon Brando and Paul Newman, and they were doing these A movies that were just incredible. It was maybe the most interesting time in Hollywood because of the talent that existed then. So my movies in comparison were so mediocre—compared to *East of Eden* with Jimmy Dean—that I just felt… kind of demoralized as an actor. And I didn't have anybody behind me to say, "Look, you have to go through these stages; it's a learning process and it may take 10 years or 15 years to mature into a real actor, to get everything out of your acting talent that's there. Stay with it." I didn't have anybody telling me that, and I just kind of lost heart when I didn't see the progression into the top A movies; but you're not going to get an A movie out of a B movie on $15,000.

SENN: *Let's go on to* The Giant Gila Monster, *which is a real favorite of mine and the first monster movie I ever showed my son. I find it to have a wholesome charm that is very appealing, not least because of your "role model" portrayal.*

SULLIVAN: It's interesting because I didn't realize it at the time, but when I compared the work that I was doing in the beginning to what I was doing at the end, which was *The Giant Gila Monster*, you could see a progression where I was getting better—more relaxed, more into character. There was quite a bit of improvement, and this was my favorite movie. [*Gila Monster* producer] Ken Curtis was probably one of the big influences on me at the time, because Ken came to me and said, "Look, anything you don't like, a line or a word, throw it out and put your own words in there; any direction you want to go, just feel free to do it." Boy is that a great attitude to have with an actor! It just relaxes you because that's saying, "Don't worry about mistakes." And without that concern I felt very relaxed on that movie. And some of that may have shown through.

SENN: *Was Ken Curtis a real hands-on producer, then; was he on-set a lot during shooting?*

SULLIVAN: No, no, no. These movies were made, this and *The Killer Shrews*, were made to play the lower half of movies at drive-ins. They had a budget of oh, I think $250,000—an adequate budget for an independent little monster thing. We came in at $185,000, so we were actually under budget because everything went well and smoothly and happily. But no, Ray Kellogg was the director, and he was directing because he was a special effects man at MGM, and had done a lot of special effects work and was very talented. [Note: Kellogg provided the photographic effects for such diverse films as *The Snows of Kilimanjaro*, *Niagra*, *The Robe*, and *Love Me Tender*.] So Ken made a deal with him: "Do the special effects and I'll let you direct this movie." And Kellogg was very nice and very easy to work with. But Ken actually wasn't around that much, quite frankly.

SENN: *Ken Curtis also starred in* The Killer Shrews, *as well as producing both films, so I assume he was pretty busy.*

SULLIVAN: You know, I've never seen *The Killer Shrews*, so I didn't know. I don't know [*Killer Shrews* lead actor] James Best either, although I admire him because I know 10 percent of anything that James Best ever made went to an orphanage. That's pretty admirable.

SENN: *Also putting in an appearance in* The Killer Shrews *was Gordon McLendon, who was the financial backer of both films. Did you have any interaction with him?*

SULLIVAN: I did meet him. I didn't have great conversations with him, but I did meet him, yes. A nice man. He had all these drive-in movie theaters, and he made these two movies as second billing for his theaters.

SENN: *How did you get the* Giant Gila Monster *gig?*

SULLIVAN: My agent got a call from a photo that was sent to Ken Curtis, so I had an audition with Ken. And I went over, and I always had a little ukulele, a banjo-ukulele. And Ken says, "Can you sing?" And I answered, "I write songs. I'm really not a singer, but I can carry a tune." He said, "Really? Jay Simms is the man doing the script for the moment. He's got three days to put this together, so we'll tag some music in this also." So it was pretty simple. He just got to know me; I didn't have to read or do any acting for him, or audition really, it was just a personal thing. We got along very well, maybe because we're both Irish. He said, "Fine, you've got it. But I do want the songs." So of course I said, "Sure, you can have the songs." I was just happy to get the movie.

But I remember when we finally got down to Dallas, Texas, getting ready to shoot the film, Ken comes to me and says, "Let me hear you sing this song." So I sang the song, and he said, "Well, you know, maybe just a little more..." and he took the ukulele and starts singing. I didn't realize he was a singing cowboy at Republic Studios—certainly on the John Wayne films

Actor (and ukulele aficionado) Don Sullivan sings "The Mushroom Song" in The Giant Gila Monster *(1959).*

he sang a lot—and he had this beautiful voice. And that intimidated me to have someone with a *real* voice [singing my song]. But I think if you're acting, sincerity will do a lot to cover up for a lack of talent [laughs]. When [in the movie] I sing the song to my little crippled sister, you don't pay any attention to the fact that I'm not a great singer. It's just sort of absorbed into the scene, because the scene works. You don't have to have a great voice to make a song work. I know that in Hollywood, because I wrote about 80 songs over that 5-year period, I met a lot of singers, and some of them were so great and so talented and went on to have *no* career. And others, who just had secondary-type voices, went on to be stars.

SENN: *You did three songs for* The Giant Gila Monster. *Had you already written these songs, or did you write them especially for the film?*

SULLIVAN: No, I'd already written those. I wrote the songs with somebody else in mind because I wasn't a singer. I can say that very honestly today. I'm like everybody else—in the shower you sound pretty good. And with an echo chamber in the studio I can sound pretty good. I wrote "I Ain't Made That Way" for Elvis. "Laugh Children Laugh," that one I wrote for me, that was mine. I was raised by a Christian Scientist grandmother. Not that Christian Science comes into it, but there's a love of family that came from her that I absorbed. I always liked to write songs that had a spiritual background and a family background. I wrote one song called "Little Match Girl," set in England; another one, "Ramie, the Daydreams of a Little Boy," I wrote for a series that was never made, but that was a real good song. So I had a lot of fun writing a lot of songs.

SENN: *And the third song for* Gila Monster *was "My Baby She Rocks."*

SULLIVAN: That again was written for Elvis. I was hoping somehow to accidentally bump into Elvis. Which I *did*, incidentally, and never ever thought to suggest the songs to him at the time. Which is pretty funny: I'd taken the time to write songs for Elvis, and when I finally met him I didn't even think about it [laughs]. Next to Schwab's was a restaurant called Googie's. And after 10:00 at night a lot of actors and actresses would hang out there and have cheeseburgers and so forth. So I'm in there one night. At that time my hair was long, and I had a black heavy sweater and a black sport jacket and black pants—really playing the actor bit. And a guy comes over to the table and says, "Elvis just heard that you did a couple of movies and was wondering if he could talk to you." And I look over, and Elvis is there with a couple of the guys that he ran around with. And I wasn't an Elvis fan, because I was a little older than Elvis, but I knew that he'd been on *The Ed Sullivan Show*. So I said sure. I go over to Elvis; he gets up, we shake hands and introduce ourselves. He said, "You know, it's awful noisy and busy in here. Can we go out to the parking lot; I want to ask some questions." So we went out there, and he wanted to know about directing and lights and hitting the marks and all those things. Of course, you know how you make a king: a king is only made if the people around him proclaim him the king. So when Elvis is acting like I'm the star, and I'm now feeling like a star, I'm saying, "Well now, the director does this..." and I'm giving him all this great advice—as if I really knew what I was talking about. But anyway, after about 20 minutes of this, we ended up getting philosophical, because he came from Memphis and I came from Idaho, and we're talking about "ain't life a funny thing" and this and that. We're looking up at the stars, saying, "I wonder what it's all about,"—you know, the thing that young guys do a lot. So we're out there about three-quarters of an hour. And he's one of the nicest young guys I've ever met. It's a nice part of my memory to have had that time with him.

SENN: *You received a special credit: "Special Songs by Don Sullivan" on* The Giant Gila Monster. *Did that net you any extra cash, or did you just throw the songs in?*

SULLIVAN: I just threw those songs in.

SENN: *The film's pressbook claims these songs were "scheduled for early release on the Rosco Record label." Did anything come of that?*

SULLIVAN: I've never heard that before. No, none of the songs in that movie were of the quality to be released. I think that was just PR. For example, I think "I Ain't Made That Way" was a *great* song—had it been made right. But what happened on it was when I sang the vocal to it, it was in conjunction with the music, which was on tape. And they blended the two at the time; therefore, if you wanted to raise the vocal, you automatically raised the music. There was no adjustment possible. So it wasn't done correctly. If you notice in the song, you can't hear the singing. So it wouldn't have been of the quality to release. And the other two songs, "My Baby She Rocks" didn't have any music, so that wouldn't have been released; and "Laugh Children Laugh" wasn't of a *nature* to be released. So no, they were never released.

SENN: *"My Baby She Rocks" is one I've always wanted to hear in its entirety; it's always frustrated me that we only get about 15 seconds of it—I want to hear the whole song [laughs]!*

SULLIVAN: [Laughs] Well, I think Elvis could have made it work, that's for sure.

SENN: *On* Gila Monster, *I assume you did your own stunts again.*

SULLIVAN: Yeah I did, but I learned a lesson on that—a little late, by about five years—that actors should *not* do their own stunt work. We're shooting the scene where I drive the hot rod with the nitroglycerin in it, I leap out and it runs into the gila monster and blows it up. Well, we're doing it, and Ken Curtis says, "Don, do you think you can dive out of the car? Put it in neutral and then dive out of the car, and the car will slow down on its own; you're not going that fast anyway." I go, "Sure, I can do anything. Absolutely. No problem." Well, I'm doing about 8 or 10 miles an hour in this little hot rod, and I open the door and dive out. I had no idea that at 10 miles an hour when you hit the ground how hard it is. Oh God [laughs], I laid there for about 5 minutes; I thought I'd broken about half the bones in my body. I told Ken, "If you want to retake that scene, you get a stunt man because I'm crippled [laughs]." Actors shouldn't do their own stunt work. And we didn't have any pads or anything. If it was an A movie you'd have a straw pit there that looked like the ground. And you'd have had knee pads and elbow pads, and then the stunt man would have done it rather than the actor. But on a B movie, I tell ya, it's pretty tough on the actors and actresses sometimes.

SENN: *You learned your lesson. I assume you were a little sore the next day.*

SULLIVAN: Yeah, I was in good shape, so I was fine the next day. I'm exaggerating when I say I was all busted up. I was bruised a little bit. But I healed rapidly in those days, so the next day I was fine.

SENN: *Speaking of the hot rods, where did they get all* *those cool cars, and did you enjoy driving yours around? It certainly looked like fun.*

SULLIVAN: It *was* fun. These were two national champion hot rods. McLendon got them from someplace, I don't know where. But they were so fast. The scenes where I had to start up and drive out of a driveway, it was very difficult because if you pushed down on the gas pedal, the wheels would spin out of control and throw gravel all over, so you had to do a steady fast tapping of the gas pedal, and it'd go "bupbupbupbup," to get out of there. But they were so fast. Which leads to an interesting story; the insanity of this one ought to scare everybody. When we're doing the scene when I'm driving down the road and the wind is whipping my face, they had mounted on the front of the hot rod a rack, the camera, the cameraman, and the director. They were all at the front of the hot rod, and I couldn't see *anything* in front of me. So the only visibility I had was glancing to the left at the edge of the road. I'm in that hot rod doing 75 miles per hour down the highway, *no* visibility, just glancing out the side. I'm assuming they had blocked off traffic three or four miles up the road; but it was a country road, so maybe there wasn't much traffic. But it was very very dangerous. There could have been a major accident there and killed three or four people. But nobody seemed very concerned. It didn't concern me, and it didn't concern the director or cameraman.

SENN: *The Giant Gila Monster was filmed near Dallas, Texas; did they take good care of you while "on location" for the shoot?*

SULLIVAN: Yeah, we stayed at the Adolphus Hotel, which was one of the nicer hotels in Dallas. I had an interesting experience there. The second day of the shoot I went down early to the hotel restaurant for breakfast. I've always been one—as you can tell, I'm relatively social—if I'm eating, I really enjoy it much more with company than if I'm eating alone. So I get my bacon and eggs and I start to sit down, and I look and there's a gentleman sitting at a table. So I went over and said, "You mind if I join you?" And he says, "No, no, sit down." So I sit down, and it's Edgar Bergen, the ventriloquist. Of course, I was very impressed because he was a nationally-known comedian through the *Edgar Bergen/Charlie McCarthy Show*. We're sitting there, we have a nice conversation and have our breakfast together. We finish about 6:30 and he says, "You know, I've got a young daughter and I'd like you to meet her." Well, I looked across the table, and he had a bulbous nose, and he was bald, and I thought, "Oh yeah, I really want to meet your daughter. Thank you but *no* thank you." [laughs] I didn't realize his daughter was Candice Bergen. He gave me her number but I never did call.

SENN: *I don't suppose you ever met the Gila Monster himself—or his handler?*

SULLIVAN: No, that was all done back in California. Ray Kellogg did all of that; I never saw it.

SENN: *How was Ray Kellogg as a director? [The shot-back-to-back* Giant Gila Monster *and* Killer Shrews *were his first full directing assignments.]*

SULLIVAN: Ray kind of left us alone; we worked out our own little routines. We didn't get much direction, but there wasn't much direction to give. It was pretty simple stuff.

SENN: *You had some pretty good chemistry with your leading lady, Lisa Simone, a former Miss France.*

SULLIVAN: Yeah, I felt kind of guilty in retrospect on that because, as I said before, you have to *make* a king—you can't play the king, it has to be made by other people. She couldn't play the sexy female in this thing unless I *made* her the sexy female in this thing. And I must say, I was just young enough to be impressed by the blonde girl over the brunette or the short girl over a tall girl. I had all the problems of youth. So I didn't find Lisa to be that attractive to me, even though she was Miss France. So I don't think I really treated her in the movie as well as I could have. I could have done some ad-libbed things and so forth. In retrospect I could do much better now than I did then—but everybody will say that. That's the first thing you do when you finish a movie, you sit down and say I wish I'd done this, I wish I'd done that. But I don't think I gave her a real fair shot in that movie. She was fine, she was good, she was a nice person, but *I* was a little weak in that area; I should have been a better actor.

SENN: *So she just wasn't your type?*

SULLIVAN: No, she wasn't. Now in *Teenage Zombies*, the little gal in there—that was my type. And I played it entirely differently, I played protective of her, as much as I could. Anyway, my type was always smaller, very gentle, and generally blonde—although I've been married a couple of times and both were brunettes. That's just the way life goes I guess.

SENN: *Publicity materials claim, "A handpicked crew of 27 experienced Hollywood technicians were flown in" for this movie. Did you run into "27 people" on set [laughs]?*

SULLIVAN: [Laughs] Well, I have to admit, if you're an actor doing a movie, you have no concept about a lot of things. Because you're involved with yourself—it's an "all about me" type of thing. I have no idea how many people were on the set, no idea.

SENN: *Did you do any publicity for* Gila Monster*?*

SULLIVAN: No, no publicity at all. There was no desire to make that movie available across the country other than through the drive-in movie theaters in second billing. Although it was interesting that 50 years later Coors Beer gave a free DVD of the movie with a 6-pack of Coors on a national basis. I think that had something to do with the number of people that have been exposed to the movie.

SENN: *Any thoughts on why it's remained so popular over the years—it's a beloved film.*

SULLIVAN: Oh yeah, I've spent the last part of the year trying to analyze why that movie [is so popular]. It's a great symbol, as far as I'm concerned. The number one thing is, it is a movie that anybody can watch with their children. There's no profanity, no sex, no drinking—it's a clean movie. That's number one—for children. Number two is, it probably has [religious appeal]. I didn't realize when I wrote "Laugh Children Laugh" that I wrote it as an Adam and Eve type of thing, a song about Adam and Eve. I wasn't thinking religiously, I just felt it was an interesting topic that would make a nice song. But I think that it probably has an appeal for Christians in that sense. So between the song and the nature of the movie being great for kids, I think that's a great deal of the popularity. [Screenwriter] Jay Simms tried to throw in everything from the kitchen into this movie. He had songs, he had hot rods, he had monsters [laughs]. He had a little of everything.

SENN: *As I said, it's the first monster movie I showed my son, and we both enjoy it very much.*

SULLIVAN: It's the only one of the films I did that I really enjoy. I should have qualified before—I do on occasion see that film and enjoy watching it. Because in a minor B movie way it was a tour de force. I wrote the songs, sang the songs, and starred in the movie—who could ask for more?

SENN: *I wanted to ask about one more film of yours—* The Rebel Set. *You play a very different character; you're not the clean-cut hero but a beatnik, goateed ladies-man type.*

SULLIVAN: Let me tell you how I got that movie. I'm walking down the street on Hollywood Boulevard on Saturday morning about 7:00 to get a cup of coffee. A car pulls up, a big black Cadillac. "Hey you! You're an actor." And I said [hesitantly], "Yeeeeah." "Come here!" And I said, "No, no, no." And he says, "I'm an agent; here's my card." And he says, "Look, Richard Long has a movie at Columbia, and he's unable to fulfill the movie because he broke up with his wife or his girlfriend, and he's so distraught he's not going to be able to do the movie. I told the producer I had another actor as good or better than him. Are you interested?" I said, "Of course." We drove down to Columbia Studios, I read for the producer and director. They said fine, we start shooting on Monday.

The only thing that was bad on the movie, that I didn't like, was—I was never a great memorizer of scripts. My daughter, I envy her because she could take five or six pages of dialogue and in a matter of an hour have it down pat. But it was never that easy for me, so to have a whole script to try to learn in one day was almost impossible for me. To really be able to do a *good* job with it. I felt that if I could have had that script for a week I could have done a much better job with the movie. But you do what you have to do.

SENN: *How was the director, Gene Fowler [*I Was a Teenage Werewolf, I Married a Monster from Outer Space*], to work with?*

SULLIVAN: He was very good. I was really unhappy because it was the only time in my career that I really went *up* on lines. Today I have no idea why I went up. We were shooting a scene where I had to talk about my mother. And I just blew it about six or seven times. And Gene finally said, "Aw, forget it, we'll work around it." And he went on, which I don't think he handled very well. He could have said, "Look, let's go in for five minutes, we'll run through the script and I'll talk to you, and then we'll come back and do it." But he didn't do that. A movie is so budget-oriented. Unless you get an A movie, and then they'll shoot the scene 27 times to get a good take. But B movies, they don't shoot a scene 6 or 7 times.

SENN: *So he basically just decided to drop the scene?*

SULLIVAN: Yeah, he dropped the scene out. And that didn't make me happy at all. But I wasn't unhappy with *him*, I was unhappy with *me* because I blew the lines.

SENN: *You worked with Lon Chaney Jr. at one time.*

SULLIVAN: I did. It was a movie—well, it turned out to be, unfortunately, a farce. I flew down to Florida to play the young lieutenant in a movie with Lon Chaney Jr. called *Chivato*, which I think is "traitor" or "coward" in Spanish. It was a movie about Castro, and Castro was the *hero* of the movie. And I was one of Castro's men, one of the heroes of the movie. So we get about half-way through shooting, and the politics of the United States change from pro-Castro to anti-Castro. Very abruptly. So now we've finished the movie, and the director says, "What am I gonna do? I've got a pro-Castro movie and an anti-Castro United States." So he tried to dub in words to make it just the opposite of how the movie was shot. For instance, when I came up to some little kids, I say, "Here, take this [bread] home to your family; it'll at least feed you for a day, and we'll try to get more tomorrow." But with the dubbing, I'm now going up to little kids saying, "Here is this bread; you keep that for me later, and if you eat one crumb I kill you!" Only I'm smiling and saying these ugly things. And the same with everybody else. It never worked and was never released, as I understand. [The film appears to have been released later as *Rebellion in Cuba*.]

But Lon Chaney, we had our moments with him. He liked to go out on the edge and everything. He'd tell me that Jack Dempsey said that Lon could have been the Heavyweight Champion of the World. Lon used to box with Jack Dempsey. I guess he was pretty good, because he was certainly strong enough. But he was drinking quite a bit. There was an electrical tower where we were shooting some of the scenes. It was up 50 or 60 feet in the air, and Lon would climb up about 35 feet and grab the rail and be hanging out over the cement by one hand, hollering at the director. And the director [Albert Gannaway] would say, "Lon, goddammit, come down from there!" Lon would say, "Yeah, I'm pretty macho!" He was too much. He and I had a lot of fun because from up on top of the tower you could look down at a pit where the water came in and went out the other side of this electrical thing. And in the water pool, at the bottom, were lobsters that got in there and couldn't get out. So we got a hold of a three-pronged metal spear, tied a cord to it, and we'd drop that spear and try to spear a lobster. Lon was fascinated with it because he thought he could do it. Well, we tried for a couple of days every time we were between takes and never got one lobster [laughs].

[Acting-wise], Lon would get into what he was doing, he was a deep-concentration type of a guy. He liked to succeed, and felt he was capable.

SENN: *Back to your songwriting—you wrote a lot of songs; have any of them been recorded or published.*

SULLIVAN: No. Well... not other than in *The Giant Gila Monster*, no. For me, songwriting was kind of a therapeutical thing, because in the acting industry I'd work for a week and then be off for three months. And I'm just a very active individual anyway, so I needed something to fill in the space. And at that time I was running around with Warren Oates and [Harry] Dean Stanton, and we would drink a little wine and sing our songs. They'd bring one they'd written; I'd bring one I'd written. We were just having fun. And I didn't have the contacts at all, because I'm a little kid from Idaho in big Hollywood. I didn't know anybody, had no musical connections at all. So I wrote the songs, but none of them were ever recorded.

I did write a complete script for a movie called *Sousaphone*, which is the story of a little girl who falls in love with a talking sousaphone. I wrote all the songs in there—it was a musical—and sent it to Disney. It came back unopened, with a note saying, "We do not open or solicit outside [submissions], we have our own inside writers." I sent it to Hanna-Barbera; it came back unopened [laughs]. So it was thrown into a trunk which five years later was lost, and that went down the drain with four songs. They were good songs; it was a beautiful little Disney movie. If I'd had any contacts at all, I'd have known there were other ways to get to Disney; but I didn't know about that then.

SENN: *You were hanging out with Warren Oates and Harry Stanton; that sounds like a pretty fun crowd!*

SULLIVAN: Well, it was a fun crowd; we used to enjoy it. The funny part about it is that in my own mind I would say, "I know why *I'm* in the acting industry; I don't know why *these* guys are—they're never going to go anywhere" [laughs]. Well, they both became stars—that's Hollywood.

SENN: *You alluded to this before, but back then you were a good-looking young man with an easy charm before the camera, but you left acting after only a few years. Why?*

SULLIVAN: In 1959 I did a pilot called *Tightrope*, with Touch Connors. They were gonna change a half-hour show into an hour show. [Producers Russell] Rouse and [Clarence] Green called me in and said, "We liked you in this pilot very much. We're going to write you in as the second lead in the hour TV series." So I was all thrilled about that, and spent the next two months getting scripts and auditioning and so forth. And then the sponsor got into a fight with the network over the time slot, and the whole thing fell apart. So I'd wasted three months. Now Rouse and Green called me in and said, "Look, we apologize about what happened, but we're doing a new television pilot. It's a young Abe Lincoln of the north woods up in Oregon [a modern-day attorney in Oregon], and we'd like you to star in the pilot." So I said, "Terrific," and we got scripts and all. But the money people said, "Alright, we'll put up the money, but we like another actor, we like Andrew Prine. We don't know Sullivan, but Andrew Prine has done a number of things." So they called me and said, "We're really sorry a second time, Don, but it's not gonna go."

So I was so disgusted I called up a friend of mine [Paula Kent], an actress who was married to a promoter that had quite a bit of funds available for different things. And I had lunch with her, and I said, "Look, I've got a bunch of songs, and I'm going to start a company producing songs. Would you like to get Miller—

Frank Miller was his name—involved?" Well, she said, "I've already started a company with Jheri Redding—a hair care company [Redken]—and it's doing extremely well." And she said, "You have a chemistry background." I said, "Yeah, from the University of Idaho." "Why don't you come and work for a while, make some money, and then you can go back into the acting." So, at the time I was getting pretty hungry because there was an actor's strike, and it went on for a year and a half, so I'd gone over a year and a half without working, from '59 to '60. So I said, "Alright, let's do that." So I went out and did some [trade] shows and stuff on the road for her, and then worked with Jheri Redding creating a couple of new products, and I became fascinated by it. Plus, there was the fact that I was also eating steaks and living well! And creating. You know, you don't have to be an actor to be creative. You can be a creative account, a creative salesman, a creative bricklayer, whatever. If you have the creative talent, it will come out in the work you do. So that creative desire can be fulfilled in a lot of areas. I never looked back. I went on and, over the years, was acknowledged as one of the top creative cosmetic chemists in the industry during the '60s, '70s, '80s, and '90s. I created products that sold literally hundreds of millions each year. For example, liquid silk, which is used in products all over the world, was my creation. I was the one that hydrolyzed liquid silk in the beginning and created the concept. So that was when I got out of the [acting] industry and had another career that in itself was maybe as good or better than I would have done in the film industry. You never take the same road over again.

SENN: *So you basically got fed up with being jerked around and out of work for so long.*

SULLIVAN: Well, I didn't feel jerked around, I just felt that the *nature* of the industry is one of uncertainty, and it just wasn't where I wanted to be. I wanted something where I had a little more control of my own life [laughs], rather than just floating around and hoping that somebody on Saturday morning would just pick me up off the streets to do a movie.

SENN: *So the movie fans' loss was the cosmetic industry's gain.*

SULLIVAN: [Laughs] I guess so, yeah. I had a lot of fun. I did over 5000 [cosmetic] shows around the world, taught university courses, wrote a book [*The Perfect Look*], and created dozens and dozens of new concept products. So I've had a tremendous amount of fun.

I'd certainly be dishonest if I said I didn't have some feelings that I wish I had stayed in the acting industry. But as I said, I just didn't know. I was a little on the insecure side in those days about talent, because I thought talent was something that just would automatically be there if you had it. But I didn't realize that… let's take an actor like Rock Hudson. In the beginning days they used to shoot him one line at a time because he was so bad. They'd shoot it a dozen times and then put the lines together and make a scene. Later on, because of the nature of working and so forth, he got to be a very good actor. And I didn't realize at the time that James Dean had been 10 years in the industry before he did any of the big movies.

SENN: *Anything you'd like to add in closing?*

SULLIVAN: Just thank you very much for the interest, I'm most appreciative.

In March 2015 I contacted American actor Jack Taylor, who forged a long career making films in Spain (and who, at the time, still lived outside Madrid), for his remembrances of the film *Dr. Jekyll and the Wolfman*. He also shed some illumination on that doyen of Spanish horror, Paul Naschy.

JACK TAYLOR REMEMBERS PAUL NASCHY AND *DR. JEKYLL AND THE WOLFMAN* (1972)

BRYAN SENN: *What attracted you to the* Dr. Jekyll y el Hombre Lobo *project, and how were you approached to star in it?*

JACK TAYLOR: I had worked with [director] León Klimovsky before and appreciated his way of doing things. He realized the limitations imposed at the time, budget, censorship, etc. and produced acceptable products. He was a very kind, educated gentleman… always courteous to his actors and crew. I continue to be friends with his widow Erika who was his script girl on most of his productions. I had also worked for [producer] Arturo Gonzalez, so when the project was offered, I accepted. The so-called "industry" was very limited at the time.

SENN: *What were the shooting conditions like? (Where was it shot? Did the production seem to have enough money?)*

TAYLOR: Shooting conditions were a bit primitive—no caravans for costume or makeup. However, this was done at an eighteenth-century complex near Madrid, and at least we had a roof. No worse than what actors had to put up with on more famous films such as *The African Queen*. Actors are made of resilient stuff. We do what is required, dressed in summer clothes in the freezing cold or sporting woolen capes in the heat of summer. There were no financial difficulties with Gonzalez.

SENN: *Any thoughts on the werewolf figure in general? From what do you think the appeal of this popular monster stems?*

TAYLOR: Everyone likes a fright as long as you can be sitting in your favorite chair or protected by the audience surrounding you in the theater. The werewolf is a victim of destiny, a sensitive creature who suffers just like Pearl White and a long line of male or female characters. Have you ever considered that perhaps Hamlet could have been one during his off moments? It would be difficult to be invited for dinner at some aristocratic event or Fourth of July picnic and suddenly realize that the moon is getting fuller and fuller.

SENN: *How was working with co-star Paul Naschy? He has the reputation of being somewhat egocentric; did that manifest itself on the set, and if so, how did you deal with it?*

TAYLOR: Working with Paul was very easy. He was a very private person, as am I; there were never any conflicts. He respected me, as I him. After many years of not working together he became more relaxed with me, possibly knowing that I respected his work. Thanks to Paul, the genre films began in earnest in Spain.

SENN: *What is your opinion of Naschy as a performer?*

TAYLOR: He did very few films that weren't genre related and probably felt that he deserved to be offered other things. In "WAX" there is a recording of his voice taken from a representation of a period piece "Dance of Death" where he does a superb job.

SENN: *From reading his autobiography, Naschy appears to have developed quite the persecution complex. He said, "Like Waldemar, I too have been left aside and misunderstood. I have spent all my life swimming against the current." Did you see any manifestation of that during filming?*

TAYLOR: Paul did feel unappreciated I know. Most of those genre films were never shown in Spain or at least not at the main theaters. They were considered B rated pictures...but the interesting fact is that they have survived and the supposedly A grade ones are mostly forgotten. Who is interested in child singers, a happy day at the convent when the one who strayed returns, or the nice looking guy/girl who goes buzzing around on an outdated motor bike wearing flared trousers and wowing the other sex? Much kissing wasn't allowed either, so a trip to some spooky spot was exhilarating. I do think Paul was burdened with complexes because he didn't feel that he was respected as an artist.

SENN: *This was Naschy's sixth werewolf film. Had you seen any of Naschy's earlier werewolf efforts?*

TAYLOR: I really don't remember if I had seen any of Paul's films before *Dr. Jekyll and the Wolfman*, but I did know him.

SENN: *How was León Klimovsky to work with as director? Did he give you much guidance or consult with you?*

TAYLOR: Klimovsky was great...none of the directors did much indicating. However, he did create a harmonious shoot. If you hit your mark and remembered your lines, that was pretty much enough. These films didn't require great amounts of "methoding." It was up to you to do your job...good or bad.

SENN: *In interviews, Naschy seemed less than impressed with Klimovsky, saying of his direction of* Dr. Jekyll and the Wolfman: *"The short-sightedness of León Klimovsky made for some careless moments." Do you concur?*

TAYLOR: I wasn't aware that Paul felt less than impressed with León. He did seem more content with Carlos Aured, now that I think back. He never expressed that to me at any time. [Note: Both Taylor and Naschy appeared in the Carlos Aured–directed *The Mummy's Revenge* in 1975.]

SENN: *Of course, Robert Louis Stevenson's* The Strange Case of Dr. Jekyll and Mr. Hyde *is a literary classic. Had you read it before playing Dr. Jekyll's grandson, and if so, what were your thoughts on it?*

TAYLOR: Yes, I had read the Stevenson book several times and was fascinated by it. I also remember seeing Bergman and Tracy in their [1941] production, and two earlier ones with March [1931] and Barrymore [1920]. As for me, it was a job; and as with every job I do/did the best I can/could. People tend to over-intellectualize films, which leads me to understand that once a picture is edited and put in a can, strange things take place, and those "things" become obvious when the images are projected onto the screen and the film takes on a life of its own.

SENN: *In an earlier interview you alluded to Mr. Hyde being your favorite monster. What is it that intrigues you about this character? And how did you feel about playing the grandson of Dr. Jekyll?*

TAYLOR: Playing his grandson was another role. I think we all have a bit of the two in our makeup. We've all seen perfectly normal people suddenly losing it. Divorce is an obvious example of "if I can't have you I want your house, car, money, children, your mother's rosary—just so I can fling it into the garbage, etc. and then I'll destroy you!"

SENN: *On a different tack, I personally quite enjoy the Mexican horror and masked wrestler films of the 1960s.*

As Dr. Jekyll, actor Jack Taylor tries to free Paul Naschy's Waldemar Daninsky from the curse of the werewolf but only gets a knife in the back for his troubles (as shown in the artwork on this Mexican lobby card).

You appeared in a trio of Nostradamus *movies as well as a pair of* Neutron *entries. Any particular reminiscences about those?*

TAYLOR: After a year in Hollywood where I was fortunate enough to get small jobs on *The Jack Benny Program*, and deliver ice to Claudette Colbert on hers, I decided that I had little to do there and wanted to go to Italy. But unable to afford that, Mexico was my second choice. There I was a different type, and because of this I was offered these strange roles. I fondly remember Federico Curiel [director of *Neutron el Enmascarado Negro*, *The Curse of Nostradamus*, *The Monster Demolisher*, *Genii of Darkness*, and *Neutron contra el Dr. Caronte*, all with Taylor], who was responsible for hiring me first and who continued to do so until I left to come to Spain with *Redhead*, the musical comedy. But that's another, and long, story.

Connecticut-based filmmaker Del Tenney is best known for directing the cult classic *Horror of Party Beach* (1964). But among his short, four-film filmography was a little-known voodoo opus crassly titled *I Eat Your Skin*, about which I interviewed Tenney back in 1997. The article/interview appeared in *Cult Movies* magazine, issue 28.

DEL TENNEY'S SCIENCE AND CEREMONY: *I EAT YOUR SKIN* (1964/71)

Shot in 1964 but not released until 1971, *I Eat Your Skin* is actually a better film than its horrendous title would suggest. (Thankfully, no skin—or any other body part—is ever eaten). Filmed in and around Miami and Key Biscayne, Florida, as the nondescript *Caribbean Adventure* (to disguise its horror status from local merchants/investors, according to second unit director

William Grefe), the film's title metamorphosed into *Zombie* and then *Voodoo Blood Bath* before ultimately becoming *I Eat Your Skin* upon its much-delayed release. (Grefe later made his own low-budget features, the most [in]famous being 1967's dreadful *Death Curse of Tartu*.)

"I always thought that voodoo was very interesting, an interesting kind of religious ceremonial, and the whole thing of killing the chicken or whatever they did, was an interesting theatrical event and was kind of 'fun'—if you want to call it that," related writer/director Del Tenney about why he chose to spice up his self-proclaimed "low-budget adventure film" with voodoo. "It had a certain sense of theatricality."

After producer/director/scripter Tenney's success with *Horror of Party Beach* and *Curse of the Living Corpse*, he was on a roll (these films, along with his *Psychomania* had made Tenney over a million-and-a-half dollars!). Unfortunately, with his new voodoo project, the momentum couldn't quite carry Tenney over that next distribution hill—for *Voodoo Blood Bath* remained unreleased for seven years. (Tenney had planned to make a ready-made double feature consisting of a Frankenstein/Dracula film [succinctly titled *Frankenstein Meets Dracula*] and the voodoo picture. When *Voodoo Blood Bath* generated no distribution interest, however, the 'Monsters Meet' project died on the celluloid vine.)

Even in 1964, shooting a low-budget horror film in black and white and expecting to find a decent (or *any*) distributor was an act of pure optimism. "What happened," Tenney recounted, "was that the bottom fell out of that kind of genre—grade-B black and white movies with no names—about that time. So I couldn't sell the package of *Frankenstein Meets Dracula* and *Voodoo Blood Bath*. I thought it was a good package but 20th Century-Fox said I don't think we're going to be able to take these pictures. So [*Voodoo Blood Bath*] was the last one I did." Tenney shelved his final feature and worked for the remainder of the sixties as a television producer before ultimately returning to the legitimate theater, his first love. ("I'm a stage director, you know, and have always been sort of a 'priest of the theater.' I've directed probably 150 to 200 plays and have been involved with certainly over 300 plays. All this [movie work] was done sort of tongue in cheek, for the commerciality of it.") Tenney also began a very lucrative real estate business, which he supervises to this day. He never made another feature. ("I am currently working on another film project," Tenney related in July of 1997. "I wrote an original treatment called *Infidelity Inn* which is kind of an Edgar Allan Poe turn-of-the-century murder

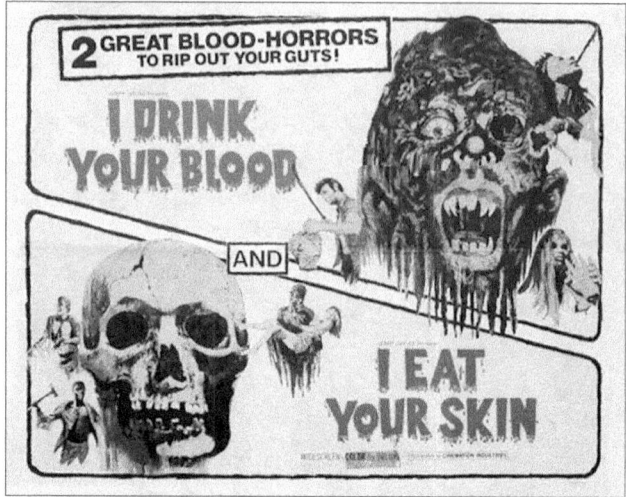

After sitting on the shelf for seven years, Del Tenney's Voodoo Blood Bath *was rechristened* I Eat Your Skin *and finally released in support of the rabid hippie opus* I Drink Your Blood *in 1971.*

mystery. So I'm still fooling around with it; it's still in my blood. I'd love nothing better than to work on motion pictures again." But that was not to be, and Tenney's proposed 'comeback' film was never made.)

Tenney's voodoo movie might still be moldering on the cinematic shelf today had it not been for producer Jerry Gross who, in 1971, needed a second feature for his rabid hippie opus *I Drink Your Blood*. Gross purchased *Voodoo Blood Bath* for about $40,000 dollars (only a third of its cost—"on *Voodoo Blood Bath* I took a bath," laughed Tenney) retitled it *I Eat Your Skin* and advertised the pair as "Two Great Blood Horrors To Rip Out Your Guts!" Compared to the mean-spirited *I Drink Your Blood*, Tenney's cheesy co-feature becomes downright enjoyable.

Writer/playboy Tom Harris (William Joyce) journeys with his agent (Dan Stapleton) to a small private island in the Caribbean (succinctly named "Voodoo Island") to research and write his next bestseller. Upon arriving, Tom is menaced by zombies, meets a scientist (Robert Stanton) combining snake venom and radiation to find a cure for cancer, and falls for the doctor's beautiful daughter, Jeanine (Heather Hewitt). The natives seem intent upon kidnapping Jeanine and sacrificing her to their voodoo gods, Jeanine being the only blonde virgin around for miles (though Tom's irresistible charm soon changes *that*). After more encounters with the oatmeal-faced zombies and escapes from the natives, Tom rescues Jeanine from under the sacrificial knife and makes his escape.

As their boat speeds away, the dying scientist (who'd taken a native knife in the back) makes his confession/

explanation: "Instead of getting closer to a cure for cancer, the bombarded snake venom was setting up a curious reaction in the body tissues, making the subject devoid of will – a human vegetable" (as well as turning their faces into oatmeal and their eyes into what looks like fried eggs). The local plantation overseer (Walter Coy), posing as the voodoo high priest Papa Negro, had been blackmailing the misguided scientist into "creating an army of these unfortunate people." The island blows up (the scientist had set the equipment in his lab to explode) and Tom returns with Jeanine to civilization.

Principal photography was completed in three weeks (a luxurious schedule for Tenney, whose three previous features had all been shot in two). This longer schedule, however, was not the director's idea. "That was simply the way it worked. Union-wise you had a certain schedule. I even had to have union *drivers*; it suddenly became a whole different ball park." Had it been a non-union picture (like his other films), Tenney would probably have completed it in his usual fortnight time-frame.

"We had a lot of trouble," Tenney recalled about filming *I-Eat-Your-Caribbean-Zombie-Blood-Bath*. "First of all we had a hurricane which caused about a week's delay. Secondly, it was the first film that I did union. When 20th Century-Fox picked up *Curse of the Living Corpse* and *Horror of Party Beach* and played them at the drive-ins, being union, they insisted that the next film I did was union. So instead of costing the usual forty or fifty thousand dollars which is what the others cost, this one cost me about a hundred and twenty thousand." Unused to union regulations and restrictions, Tenney tried to circumvent them whenever he could. "When I closed down the filming with actors, I did a lot of pick-up stuff. And I used my friends and my crew and whatever people I had that were not union people that I'd brought down—and myself and my brother and my wife (who's an actress) and so on."

Such nefarious (by union standards) activities turned around and bit him in the end. "They [the union] got wind of the fact that I was shooting off the cuff. And they did not like it at all. I threw a party at my house that we were renting on Key Biscayne for the whole cast and crew and everybody that was involved and catered it—quite a nice affair I thought. They set all the curtains on fire and ruined several sofas—they poured drinks on the sofas, the union guys—to get back at me. It cost me four or five thousand bucks in repairs and damages. So I'm not a very thankful person as far as the unions go [laughs]." Of course, Tenney went on to remark that he himself has belonged to several unions, including SAG, Equity, and AFTRA, and is not anti-union per se. "I just thought that those *particular* [union] people down there treated the situation badly. And the fact that I was funding the thing myself was never taken into consideration."

Other (non-union) difficulties arose as well. "Half the crew was going to the hospital with snake bites or malaria or whatever the hell was going on," remembered Tenney. "Everybody was getting sick because they weren't used to being out in the jungle like that."

A few tropical bugs were not the only physical menace around, however, and, though ignorant of it at the time, one cast member narrowly escaped disaster. "You remember the sequence where the heroine was swimming out in the bay?" asked Tenney. "Well, the day after we shot that movie, we were talking to the Coast Guard and the Coast Guard told us that that particular bay was infested with sharks! I was like, aaargh, I can't believe that I would put her in jeopardy like that!"

Despite the contrary weather, unions, viruses, and just-missed predators, Tenney still found *I Eat Your Skin* "an enjoyable picture to shoot. It was a fun movie to make. The cast was terrific. Everybody was very cooperative. For a low budget film, we had a lot of special kind of stuff with the boats and the airplane and all the special effects, the makeup and the snakes and all that stuff. It was very interesting and fun to do. I enjoyed working on the film."

Though not as enjoyable to *watch* as Tenney's wacky *Horror of Party Beach*, and not as slick as his *Psychomania* or *Curse of the Living Corpse*, *I Eat Your Skin* still maintains that combination of hard-edged violence (shocking decapitation; gruesome zombie faces) and raw energy (ceremonial sequences and chase scenes) which make Tenney's features as memorable as they are.

Technically, the film plays just slightly *below* the competency level. Most scenes had to be overdubbed, and the poor-quality sound and (mis)matching shows. ("I could never get good enough sound [on location]," commented Tenney, "we did a lot of looping.") Also, apart from the few ceremonial sequences (which admittedly make atmospheric use of sinister shadows and flickering firelight), the film is often poorly lit in that dull, flat style common to black and white pictures of the fifties and early sixties. The trashy model of the island blowing up (with bits of papier mâché flying into the air along with tiny gouts of flame) is about on a par with Ed Wood. The acting ranges from adequate (Walter Coy giving a fairly good Cameron Mitchell impersonation) to downright annoying (Betty Hyatt Linton's nasal interpretation of the agent's air-headed wife). Lon E. Norman's intrusive and often inappropriate jazz score (with trumpets blaring and drums pounding like a *Johnny Quest* episode) doesn't help.

Tenney's occasionally absurd script (combining the old mad-science-zombie and radiation chestnuts of the previous decade with large doses of cheese) does little to flesh out the characters, though he seemed to want to make his writer hero into a literary version of James Bond since he alternately jumps into action and jumps into the sack with equal aplomb. (In fact, Tenney told the locals that this was *exactly* what he was filming – a 007-style adventure film. "There was kind of a stigma about turning Caribbeans into zombies and so on," remarked the filmmaker, "and I thought they would be more receptive if they thought it was a James Bondish-type of thriller rather than a zombie film. As I look back on it, it was stupid because, you know, they didn't really care [laughs].") Fortunately, Tenney keeps the story moving at a fairly brisk pace via the various zombie encounters and native chase scenes.

"It has been a long time since any [monsters] have come along as terrifying as the humanoids in *I Eat Your Skin*," (over)stated the film's pressbook. "These weird humanoids are enough to make one jump out of his skin, which, incidentally, is exactly what this horror-chiller is all about." Though the PR boys definitely exaggerated their merit, the movie's zombies do provide a few genuine shudders, and so fulfill the first rule of zombie cinema – dead people should be scary. With their cataract-covered eyes, flaking, wrinkled skin, and tall, gaunt frames, these "humanoids" (as the pressbook labels them) wield machetes (one decapitates a local fisherman) and take bullets to the chest (the holes appearing in the dead flesh one by one) without missing a step. Never mind that they're really a product of science rather than sorcery (and consequently *should* be stopped by bullets since they're actually live people transformed into "human vegetables"). It still makes for some startling moments. ("I had to hire two or three union makeup people, which was very expensive," complained Tenney, "but they did a good job.")

Apart from the zombie encounters, the film's highlights are the convincing voodoo ceremonial scenes. This is a rarity in voodoo cinema, since so often filmmakers stage their dancing/sacrifice/ceremonials in such an ineffectual, lackluster, and trite manner that these supposedly sacred ceremonies become moments of voyeuristic derision. Fortunately, Tenney took care with his rituals, ensuring that the participants invest both enthusiasm and energy into their roles, their bodies writhing in ecstatic rhythms as shadowy lighting plays over their rapt forms. Consequently, one actually comes to believe in their beliefs—or at least in their earnestness—which carries the viewer beyond the sensationalism of the moment to feel some small measure of the *appeal* of Voudoun.

Tenney reported that he "read several books on voodoo," before writing the screenplay, but noted that at the time "there wasn't a lot actually, there's not a lot on it. So, basically, we sort of had to make it up as we went along as to the ceremonies and so on. Actually, most of it was just our imagination."

"We did have a kind of a [voodoo] expert as an advisor," continued Tenney. "And he told me basically that some of the story had a basis of truth in it—that snakes, of course, are always used in voodoo ceremonies, and chickens, and so on and so forth. Also, there *was* a cult of voodoo Caribbeans that did believe that snake venom was a *cure* actually for whatever particular thing they had down there at that point. So there was sort of a basis of truth in the storyline." Hmm. Perhaps a bit of wishful thinking?

Reviews were (and are) invariably harsh. *Castle of Frankenstein*'s Calvin T. Beck labeled it an "execrable zombie cheapie" in which "crusty-looking native monsters walk around amid endless tribal dancing and *Disembodied*-level dialogue. Even Mantan Moreland couldn't have saved this." *Fangoria*'s Dr. Cyclops called it "a feeble voodoo picture." Singling out the "horrible acting" and "terrible makeup," he concluded, "Certainly atrocious on every count, but not as laughably inane as *Horror of Party Beach*, Tenney's masterwork."

When asked what he thought of the finished film, Tenny laughingly admitted, "I didn't like it very much; I thought it was sort of silly." While definitely far from the best voodoo pictures of the sixties and seventies, *I Eat Your Skin* is not as bad as all that and still deserves a look for its effective zombies and involving voodoo sequences. Despite his sci-fi denouement, Del Tenney did Damballah proud.

> In 2000 I interviewed friend and filmmaker Robert Tinnell about his (then) new film *Believe*. I subsequently penned this piece for a ghost book that never (ahem) materialized. *Believe* is a wonderful, family-friendly specter spectacle and deserves to be seen (and read about). So without further ghostly ado…

ROBERT TINNELL MAKES YOU *BELIEVE*

"ALL THE QUIET ON EARTH CAN'T SILENCE THE DEAD." –ad line

Director Robert Tinnell makes "family films," and he makes them well. He has a way of exploring important issues, such as familial communication, trust and loss, by coalescing emotions into a series of subtly potent moments. Oh, and he also loves monster movies. A life-long fan of classic (and not so classic—*Believe* features two scenes inspired by the 1941 Bela Lugosi Monogrammer *The Invisible Ghost*!) horror cinema, Tinnell turned his earlier *Frankenstein and Me* (1997) into a touching homage to growing up with monster movies. So for those of us with children ourselves (or for the monster movie-loving child in all of us), Tinnell makes *our* kind of movies. And *Believe* (2000) is his even more polished attempt to put some fright (and insight) into family fare. "I wanted to make a film where Hardy Boys meet the Wuthering Heights, and I hope that's what I did," explained Tinnell (who also concocted the film's story line). Indeed he did, with a touch of Val Lewton thrown in for good measure.

Shot in a mere 20 days near Montreal, Canada, and in a small Canadian town near the New York border, on a relatively low budget, *Believe* centers on Ben Stiles (Ricky Mabe), the 14-year-old son of a diplomat, whose absentee parents have put him in a succession of boarding schools. Ben has a very unusual way to liven things up—he stages elaborate fright gags to scare his fellow pupils. After his latest stunt gets him expelled, he's sent to stay with his estranged grandfather (Jan Rubes), a reserved and imposing man who lives in a large, forbidding mansion. As the two try to establish some sort of relationship, Ben comes to realize that the estate is haunted by the ghost of a young woman—something his grandfather refuses to discuss. With the help of a recently orphaned girl named Katherine (Elisha Cuthbert), Ben attempts to unravel the mystery, leading to a

Believe *DVD cover.*

confrontation between his grandfather and Katherine's great uncle (Ben Gazzara) over tragic events that transpired long ago and have affected their lives ever since.

"I wasn't scared, but it *was* scary," announced my five-year-old son after viewing *Believe*. Well, there are two or three moments when his considerably older father *was* scared. One in particular induced a shiver when Ben's rather stolid tutor (Charles Powell) comes face to shuddery face with the apparition (whose hollow eyes and stark white face contrasts creepily with her blood-red gown). It's a moment of suspenseful buildup, with the wind rustling, curtains billowing and doors abruptly opening, that teases the character (and viewer) with a chilly unease before culminating in a startling shock.

Another moment of note comes when Ben, not yet sure of its spectral status, chases the ghost to the cemetery. With the camera behind the mysterious figure, Ben runs towards her, and she literally vanishes; at this, we see *through* her to the bewildered Ben, who stops so suddenly that he slips and falls—only to have his shocked sensibilities startled even further by a creepy carved face on a nearby sepulcher.

Tinnell fills his film with nice eerie touches; shots

of a shadow on a wall, leaves rustling in the wind, and shafts of illuminating moonlight (not to mention some evocative, prowling camerawork) generate an uneasy atmosphere. "I feel like this is the first time I've made a film that really visually does what I want it to do."

And what exactly (visuals aside) did he "want it to do"? "My goal in this one was really to find out if I can scare people," explained Tinnell. "I'm not a guy who runs away from that label; if you point and say 'he's a horror filmmaker,' I say great. So my goal was to prove I could do that."

But there's more to Tinnell's movie than just scaring young 'uns. "My other goal was to do something that would provide an entry level horror film for kids, with a positive message. And again, there's been a theme that's run through all four of my films pretty much: communication, the family. And I thought, what better way to demonstrate how just not talking to one another, the damage it does to families. And I really do believe in that."

Believe is a particularly well-acted movie, with top honors (along with top billing) going to Jan Rubes. "Jan Rubes, who you probably best remember as the grandfather in *Witness*, was an opera singer for years and years and years," reported Tinnell, "and he is just an absolutely wonderful person, a perfectionist, *very* hard on himself. Interestingly enough, the part was not originally envisioned as a foreigner, and Jan is Czech. And when they cast him, he said to me, 'Now look, do you have a problem, because I have this accent?' And I said, 'Not at all; I'm trying to do a Gothic here, and you're the mysterious foreigner.' I said no, I think it makes it even more interesting, that there's just yet another barrier between these people. I think he's just wonderful, and now I just couldn't envision anybody else playing the part. I think he delivers probably the best performance in all my films."

Believe is not altogether perfect, however. The characters of the two teen protagonists come off as a bit too reasonable and level-headed (for *their* age, anyway), while all the adults seem to be complete jerks and fly off the handle far too easily. "The character of Ben really doesn't grow," offers Tinnell, "it's not his job to grow. He's actually the same person in the film—he's just trying to get everybody *else* together."

Also, during the climactic confrontation with the ghost, she finally talks…and talks…and talks. So, while there's been a very effective and atmospheric buildup (as well as a priceless subplot that sees Ben employing his "spectral skills" to put a pair of bullies in their place), the climax is rather *anti*climactic. (This talky climax was in part a result of pressures applied by the project's distributors to deliver a longer, 96-minute movie.)

But, these few flaws aside, there's plenty to *Believe* in here. Arguably the film's best scene is the touching final denouement, in which the grandfather finally comes to terms with Ben and tells him how he feels. *Believe* is really a story of families and relationships and the importance of communication—with a gripping ghost yarn on which to hang these ten-gallon emotional hats. Tinnell is obviously quite invested in investing his movie with more than surface gloss.

"One of the things I did in the film was I staged a lot of things in doorways and windows," he revealed. "Because to me—I'm not trying to be Bergman or something—but I just thought it was a really neat way to demonstrate the barriers that everyone in this family has. Between he and the grandfather—the grandfather twice shuts him out of his personal space. They're always seeing each other from room to room, from window to window, from doorway to doorway, and—not to belabor anything—I think it's an interesting way to do things, to make film just a little more interesting. Maybe it doesn't make it any better or anything, but it is neat to inject that kind of symbolism. Did anybody notice it, I don't know; but the fact that that stuff's there makes it a better film."

Don't be put off by *Believe*'s so-called target audience. "It's primarily for kids from, say, eight to fourteen—primarily," admits Tinnell. "But I like to think that children of all ages, from eight to eighty, can enjoy this film. I think the best family films—this is not a children's film, obviously—I think the best *family* films are the ones in which the parents are sitting and watching with the kids, which is what they should be doing anyway, but don't. …I think that it works for all ages." Indeed it does.

Tinnell's heart (and, given the finished product, head) is in the right place. "I'm not going to condescend to the kids," emphasizes the director. "They deserve a good scare. Nowadays if they want to see any kind of contemporary horror, there's so much misogyny and just gratuitous bloodletting—and it's just not scary and there's no real supernaturalism. I just wanted to make a film that, if I was 12, I would have *loved*."

In the movie, Ben explains why he stages his terror tricks by observing, "People *like* to be scared." Yes they do, and here Tinnell has offered up his own fright frolic, with some important ideas and involving sentiments thrown in for good measure. Aimed at those monster movie lovers who've grown up and had kids of their own (as well as those who've never really grown up at all), *Believe* is a sometimes scary, often affecting and always entertaining movie for the whole family. And *that* is a rare commodity these days.

> Robert Wise began his long and illustrious career as an editor at RKO, where he cut such classics as *Citizen Kane* (1941) and *The Magnificent Ambersons* (1942). Wise graduated to director under the tutelage of producer Val Lewton with the subtle horror entries *The Curse of the Cat People* (1944) and *The Body Snatcher* (1945). While his subsequent career has been as varied as it has been successful, with pictures ranging from war films (*Run Silent, Run Deep* [1958], *The Sand Pebbles* [1966]) to westerns (*Blood on the Moon* [1948], *Tribute to a Bad Man* [1956]) to musicals (*West Side Story* [1961], *The Sound of Music* [1964]) and all points in between, Wise has periodically returned to the genre that launched his filmmaking career. His horror and science fiction credits include *A Game of Death* (1945*)*, *The Day the Earth Stood Still* (1951) *The Andromeda Strain* (1970), *Audrey Rose* (1977) and *Star Trek: The Motion Picture* (1979). In 1963 Wise returned to his roots yet again to produce and direct a "Lewtonesque" masterpiece of understated terror, *The Haunting*, arguably the greatest ghost film ever made. The erudite, energetic, and enthusiastic Oscar-winning director reminisced with me in November 1995 about making this landmark film.

ROBERT WISE SETS *THE HAUNTING* IN MOTION

BRYAN SENN: *How did* The Haunting *come about?*

ROBERT WISE: I actually got it started when I was in post-production on *West Side Story* at the old United Artist company, Goldwyn Studios. I'd read a copy of the book [*The Haunting of Hill House* by Shirley Jackson], found out it was available, and persuaded United Artists to buy it for me and finance a screenplay. And I got Nelson Gidding, who did *I Want to Live* for me, to write the screenplay. When we got it done, however, for some reason or another United Artists got a little cold on it and didn't want to proceed with it. So I talked to my agent about it. I had left a contract with MGM a few years before; I got out of the contract early but I had to promise to give them another film. My agent suggested that maybe this could be the film that would fulfill that commitment to MGM. So we took it over to them and they liked it very much – but they didn't want to put over a million dollars into it. And the best budget I could get out of MGM Culver City here was a million-four [$1,400,000]. I was about to go over to London for a command performance of *West Side Story*, and somebody said 'well, you know MGM has a studio outside of London, and maybe they could get you a better budget on the script over there than at Culver City.' So I took it along with me when I went to London and gave it to the people at the studio. They liked the idea and came back with a budget of a million-fifty [$1,050,000]. And so that's why we made it over there, as strictly what we call a runaway production – runaway because I could do it cheaper there.

However, I did keep the New England background of Shirley Jackson's original story because I thought that haunted houses were *fresher* there than the haunted houses around England and London, one on every corner, you know. So I managed to shoot it over there but keep it located in New England.

SENN: *You didn't have any problems transforming Olde England into New England, particularly with the few city scenes?*

WISE: No, the scenes in the city were nothing; it's just out on the road when [Eleanor] was driving to Hill House. I had to block off the road for a mile or more so I could have her driving on the right side and that kind of thing. It was very simple, wasn't hard at all.

SENN: *The four principal actors [Julie Harris, Richard Johnson, Claire Bloom, Russ Tamblyn]—were they the original choices you had in mind?*

WISE: Yes I think pretty much so. I can't guarantee right down the line, but I always had Julie Harris in mind. I thought she was just perfect for the lead. I don't know where or when Claire Bloom came into the casting picture; it must have happened before I went over there [to London]. Of course, Richard Johnson I met over there. He was on the stage in a very big hit play, and he seemed to be just right and available for me. And, of course, Russ Tamblyn came into it because he was under contract to MGM, and we needed this young man, the nephew of the lady who owned the house, so that just fell together there. Then, of course, there were all the supporting players. The few we had were all from over there.

SENN: *Russ Tamblyn said that he actually turned you down when you offered him the part initially.*

WISE: That could be, I don't remember.

SENN: *The pressbook for* The Haunting *claimed that you doubted you'd have actually done the film without a guarantee from Julie Harris in the role. Was that just publicity hype?*

WISE: I think probably so; I don't know that for sure. But I certainly was very keen on her from the very beginning to do it.

SENN: *So you don't remember considering any other actors for the principal roles?*

WISE: No.

SENN: *Were there any particular problems during shooting, any mishaps, or was it a smooth shoot?*

WISE: No, it was pretty much of a smooth shoot. I had a marvelous art director/production designer, Elliot Scott, who, along with Boris Levin, who did so many of my films here in Hollywood [*West Side Story*, for instance], was one of the best production designers I ever had. And he recommended Dave Bolton, who was a cinematographer, and did an outstanding job for me. I did it all over there [in England], post-production and everything. And I had a man who, I've forgotten his name right now [Humphrey Searle], did the score for me, whose first feature was, I believe, *The Haunting*. He had been very well known for composing and arranging for the ballet in London. I don't know who recommended him. So it all went along very well. [Note: Searle's first film score was actually the 1957 Hammer entry *The Abominable Snowman of the Himalayas*, though the composer went uncredited.]

Of course, I love the fact that I shot *The Haunting* in black and white. For that kind of film, the mood and quality of it, and the look of the thing, you could only get from black and white, I think.

And, of course, we were fortunate in finding the house we finally found, which was a house about ten miles outside of Stratford-on-Avon, an old manor house [called Ettington Park].

SENN: *Russ Tamblyn has said that he had a rather chilling experience there in the small cemetery behind the house—when he felt a presence behind him but was afraid to turn around to find out if indeed it was a ghost.*

WISE: [Laughs] He told me about that.

SENN: *Did you experience anything like that?*

WISE: No, not at all.

SENN: *Did you and the cast or crew talk much about the "ghostly" subject?*

WISE: We didn't talk about it too much. I'll never forget this house, though. I made it look a little bit more monstrous than it might have been because I shot all the exteriors with infra-red film, which brought out the kind of exaggerated striations of the rock. It was just the long shots of the house I'm talking about; you couldn't photograph *people* with that. The infra-red film turned the skies blacker and turned the clouds whiter. It added an eerie feeling to it. What I liked about the house too, and I was able to really use it that way to make a character out of it, was that it had that kind of tower there with those windows, you know. So I could cut to the windows and then down to Julie getting out of her car and going in, like the *house* was watching you. I tried to capitalize and use the house just as much as I could.

But anyway, I went out a day or two ahead with the crew only, the photographic crew, to shoot some of those long shots, the atmospheric shots. And I was shooting one morning the second day we were there, and I saw a big Princess limousine coming in at the gateway down the way and drawing up in front, and I knew that that was Julie and Claire coming to report on location. I went to greet them, opened the door of this limo, and they were on the other side of the limo clutching each other saying 'do we have to stay in there?' [laughs]. Because we stayed in the manor house, it was being run as a hotel. And there was supposed to be a ghost around there. Supposed to be a young lady a century or two before who was kept from her lover and all, another tragic love story, and she jumped out the tower window or something. I didn't experience her myself.

SENN: *How long was the shoot?*

WISE: Oh, I can't remember now. I think it was a decent time, probably nine or ten weeks, something of that nature.

SENN: *At the house itself you spent about a week, is that right?*

WISE: I would think not *over* that. I don't think over a week there because the major part of the film, as you know, was shot inside, and that was all back at the old MGM Boreham Wood studios outside of London.

SENN: *The interiors are fabulous.*

WISE: We got this marvelous production designer that did such a wonderful job for me.

SENN: *So that was not an actual house, the interiors, it was all on the studio soundstage.*

WISE: No, all the sets were at MGM Boreham Wood. They're gone now. The studios, oh I think not longer than five or six years after I was there, were torn down and put into something else.

SENN: *When the picture came out, did you do much promoting?*

WISE: I went around and did some promotion on it. I did a tour of six or eight cities I recall.

The Haunting *artwork*

SENN: *I've read that it was mildly successful.*

WISE: Mildly. I don't know that it ever broke even; I don't think so. It just didn't take off to the degree that it has attained over the years. It's become a real favorite of so many people. I can't tell you how many people have said to me, 'Mr. Wise, you made the scariest picture I've ever seen and you didn't show anything! How'd you do it?'

SENN: *Well, that goes back to your training with Val Lewton.*

WISE: Absolutely. It's kind of an homage to Val.

SENN: *A few years ago, at the Seattle International Film Festival, you were here, and you showed* The Haunting. *I was there, and we spoke briefly at that time. But boy, it just gave me chills.*

WISE: [Laughs] I have to be immodest and say I really like *The Haunting* because that's one of my best directorial jobs. I really think it worked well, really worked well.

SENN: *The cast themselves, were there any problems with them or did they just do a bang-up job?*

WISE: No, they worked pretty well. I told you Richard Johnson was in the stage show, so for the first, oh I guess maybe half the shooting, first few weeks of shooting, I had to juggle the schedule a little to accommodate him. Over there, even in those days, you only shot five days a week. But on Wednesday I had to finish with him by twelve or twelve-thirty, so he could go in and do his matinee.

SENN: *I read in the pressbook that he was still acting in a play during shooting, but I just thought that was more hype.*

WISE: No, no, that was true. I don't know that that lasted all the way through the shooting, but for a few weeks into the shoot I had to release him about noon on Wednesday so he could make his matinee.

SENN: *Well, it's a marvelously acted film.*

WISE: Isn't it though?

SENN: *Just wonderful. Did you work closely with the actors on their demeanor?*

WISE: Yeah, and, of course, with the writer on the screenplay. I thought Nelson Gidding did just a *fine* job on the screenplay. I loved the way he got the whole history of the house, the whole background, which was so important to us, before we got into our actual story. Because that opening, a kind of semi-montage, you know —the carriage turning over and the little girl at the funeral and then in the bed growing older—I thought that just worked wonderfully well.

I have a rather amusing story you might like. It has nothing to do with the actors or anything. The film was in black and white, of course. It was also in Panavision anamorphic—that's the wide screen. And at that time, the widest angle that they had was about a 35mm, and I was just wishing that I had something wider for some more extreme angles. So from London I called Bob Gottshalk, who was the head of Panavision and whom I knew very well. I said, 'Bob, don't you have anything wider than 35 that I could use in the film to get some special angles?' He said, 'Well, we're working on a 28mm but it's still got distortion in it.' I said [excited], 'Oh Jesus, that's just what I *want*! I want that distortion.' After much persuading on my part, he finally agreed to send it over to me. But I had to sign a document saying that I would not come back at him and complain about distortion in the lens. I used that for some of the shots down the long hallway, upstairs, the kind of spooky shots.

I'll tell you another interesting item. Do you recall the shot in the film where we're at the bottom of the library stairs, just a loose camera, and it climbs up the circular stairway, going all the way to the top?

SENN: *Yes, on the spiral staircase.*

WISE: I've been asked so many times how in the world did we get that shot. Well, we had that whole stairwell railing designed specially to take a little rig, a little dolly that would hold a hand-held camera. There was a wire underneath to guide it. So all we did was light the whole set the way we wanted it, started the camera at the top, turned it on, let it wind all the way down to the bottom, turned it off, and then when we printed the film, we just reversed it.

SENN: *That's pretty inventive.*

WISE: Trick of the trade.

SENN: *Well, you used quite a few tricks of the trade on that film.*

WISE: Yes we did. I thought that [circular] staircase was a particularly wonderful piece of construction. There was a man at the studio there called "Terry the Tinsmith"—I don't know his actual name. That was his department. He designed and constructed that whole thing, a marvelous piece of work.

I've also been asked many times about the door [a very frightening effect in which the parlor door seems to "breath"—bulging in and out]. As you recall, the door is kind of a carved door, and that was made out of laminated wood. And so it would *give* – at the back of the door. So across the back of the door was a big two-by-four and in back of the two-by-four was another one making a 'T.' And a prop man would be holding the board and I would say, 'Okay Steve, shove her,' and he'd shove the two by four and it would make the door bulge and buckle.

SENN: *Sometimes the simplest things work the best.*

WISE: Another amusing little thing – who was the old lady that played the owner of the house?

SENN: *Fay Compton.*

WISE: Fay Compton – I can never remember her name. I recall talking to her when we interviewed about doing the part. Of course, you know, I kept the New England background because haunted houses around England are a dime a dozen. And she said to me, 'You know, I had a house down in the West Country there, and you know I had to have it exorcized *twice*. It didn't take the first time' [laughs].

SENN: *So she was a believer then? How about yourself?*

WISE: Oh, I'm a believer in there being something out there beyond what we can feel and see and touch and smell. I've never had a real psychic experience myself, but I believe in the possibility of it.

CHAPTER 2
OVERVIEWS

Here you'll find a series of essays focused not on one or two films but on the Big Picture (well, cinematic subsets, subgenres and trends, anyway).

> Though I originally penned this essay for an aborted book project (tentatively titled *Eurohorror 101*), it ultimately found its way to editor Dan Taylor's eclectic *Exploitation Retrospect* magazine (issue 51) in 2012. (Note that at the time I wrote it, Steele's final Eurohorror, *An Angel for Satan*, had only recently appeared in an English-friendly version.)

AN ANGEL FOR SATAN: THE GOTHIC EUROHORRORS OF BARBARA STEELE

"I had such ambivalence at first about making these [horror] films," recalled English actress Barbara Steele at a 1992 showing of several of her pictures at San Francisco's Roxie Cinema. "There was a part of me that didn't embrace it, and a part of me that felt haunted and spooked by the fact I was doing so many horror films. I felt uneasy that maybe I shouldn't screw around with all these murderous forces all the time. Now I can look at it with humor and it's ok." It is indeed, as, thankfully, Steele overcame her unease to become the undisputed queen of Sixties cinematic horror, starring in eleven terror titles over the course of the decade. Nine of them were Italian productions or co-productions, and all but one of these (*The She Beast*, a "modern" British-Italian effort) offered a decidedly Gothic flavor. (The American *The Pit and the Pendulum* [1961] and the British *Curse of the Crimson Altar* [1968] complete Steele's Eleven.) The actress' angular, beautiful face, lustrous black hair, penetrating eyes, and enticing figure were a perfect fit for the Gothic horrors then proliferating on the Continent. But looks alone do not a queen make, and Steele often showed her broad-ranging talent by portraying everything from wide-eyed innocence to narrow-eyed demonic fury—sometimes even within the same film. This ability to embody both lightness and dark, to both attract and repel, to both entice and terrify, is what set her apart from the many other Euro-heroines of the day and made her such an in-demand actress with Eurohorror filmmakers. "Horror films are all about duality—and eroticism," she declared. "I *have* always had this duality within myself, as most of us do. But it's very odd, you see, because when you are an actress and you acquire any kind of cult following, it's really not you. You have inadvertently become some archetypal creature, having nothing to do with yourself, that people project some aspect of themselves onto." And in the nine Eurohorrors detailed below, Steele not only became archetypal, she became a veritable icon.

BLACK SUNDAY (1960)

"The Undead Demons of Hell Terrorize the World in an Orgy of Stark Horror!" –poster

As so often happens with cinematic series or groupings, the first of Barbara Steele's Eurohorrors turned out to be the best. "THE MOST FRIGHTENING MOTION PICTURE YOU HAVE EVER SEEN" trumpeted the Allen Theater marquee in Cleveland for *Black Sunday*'s "world premier" in 1960. While such hyperbole is not uncommon in the movie biz, truth in advertising *is*—but *Black Sunday* was one film that actually lived up to its ballyhoo. While it may no longer be the "most frightening" film for today's viewers, in 1960 there were few that could argue the point. Britain's Hammer Films were glorifying in the Gothic, but, though often colorful and engrossing, few of Hammer's Draculas or Frankensteins or Mummys could truly be termed terrifying (perhaps the closest the studio came to making a seriously scary film was *The Plague of the Zombies* in 1966). In America, Roger Corman's Price/Poe cycle was just beginning, but, again, though well-mounted and enthralling, these American Gothics weren't all that frightening either. (Steele herself co-starred in Corman's second Poe outing, *The Pit and the Pendulum* [1961], which became the actress' sole American effort of the decade.)

Enter 45-year-old Mario Bava, who for 20 years had toiled as a cameraman in the Italian film industry. After taking over the directorial reins on two different Galatea productions (*The Giant of Marathon* and *Caltiki the Immortal Monster*) when the directors walked out on the projects half-way through production, the Italian film company gave Bava the green light to choose anything he wished for his full directorial debut. Enamored of Russian literature, Bava chose Nikolai Gogol's ghost story *The Vij*. "The genius of the screenwriters—myself included," admitted Bava, "saw to it that almost nothing remained of Gogol's tale." (Of course, this didn't stop AIP from bandying about the literary heavyweight's name in its advertising.)

Originally titled *Mask of the Demon* (and called *Revenge of the Vampire* in England when it finally made it past the British censors *eight years* later), *Black Sunday* begins literally on Black Sunday, the day on which legend says the dead may walk the earth, as Princess Asa Vaida (Barbara Steele) and her satanic lover Javutich (Arturo Domenici) are condemned as witches and vampires in 17th century Moldavia. Before being executed in a particularly horrific fashion (the executioner hammers a metallic mask lined with spikes onto their faces!), Asa places a curse on the house of her accuser—her own brother. (The deadly mask was sculpted and cast in bronze by the director's father, Eugenio Bava.) Two centuries later, a pair of doctors (John Richardson and Andrea Checchi) traveling to a medical conference stumble upon the crypt holding Asa and inadvertently revive the witch, who vampirizes the elder doctor and resurrects her undead lover. The witch intends to possess the beautiful Princess Katia (Steele again), Asa's lookalike descendent. It is up to the young physician and a well-versed local priest to stop the evil vampiress/witch before she can change places with Katia and live another 100 years until the next Black Sunday.

Galatea urged Bava to shoot *Black Sunday* in Technicolor, but he refused. Bava's experienced cinematographer voice told his fledgling director's persona that the atmosphere he wanted to convey could only be captured in black and white. Said sentiments were echoed by the film's star. "I think that black and white movies are much more subjective," Barbara Steele opined to interviewer Christopher Dietrich. "They reach the unconscious on a much more profound level than films in color, especially in [the horror] genre. You put your own reading into black and white, whereas color is so literal that it's less intimate." (In the late 1960s, an American producer offered Bava the opportunity to remake *Black Sunday* in color. The maestro declined.)

Black Sunday certainly is intimate. Bava builds his nighttime atmosphere and imagery into a shadowland of doom and dread. Steele told film historian Mark Miller that because Bava "was a fabulous director of cinematography, he actually chose that script, I think, so that he could show all of his visual tricks." Bava's prowling camera and moody lighting conjure up shuddery images (such as a lantern suspended in total blackness or a face suddenly appearing out of the darkness) that both startle and chill. "[Bava] really geared it to play out all of his cinematographic visual fantasies," opined Steele, "and I think that the strongest point of the movie is its visual look." Indeed.

"YOUNG STARS MAKE AMERICAN FILM DEBUT IN 'BLACK SUNDAY'" read a headline in AIP's *Black Sunday* pressbook. It's an amusing claim

Barbara Steele became a horror icon with Black Sunday *(1960).*

considering the film is one-hundred percent *Italian*—AIP only picked it up for American distribution after the movie was completed. One of these "young stars" referenced was Barbara Steele. Though she'd been seen in a number of small-scale British movies, this was the actress' first starring role. It's an iconographic performance (at least visually—since her voice was unfortunately dubbed by another actress), one that would come to embody Steele's mix of beautiful innocence and smoldering sensuality. Such a persona codified the good and evil that could drive men to their nirvana or to their doom (sometimes simultaneously—as with *Black Sunday*'s Dr. Kruvajan, whom Asa orders to "embrace me; you will die, but I can bring you pleasures mortals cannot know").

"I was very young when I did *Black Sunday*," noted Steele in *Film Comment* magazine, "it was right at the beginning of my career, and so I was terrified on that set. Maybe some of that terror and intensity translated onto the screen." *Black Sunday* proved the beginning of an intense association for Steele with European horror. Though she'd prefer to be remembered for her work in art house fare like Fellini's *8½* and *Young Torliss*, it is her image as the ultimate Siren of the Scream that lingers.

Filming *Black Sunday* was no Sunday picnic. "We were all dying during the shooting of *Black Sunday*," recalled Steele to interviewer Christopher Dietrich. "It was freezing. We shot for three or four weeks in December. There was no heat, and it was one of those arctic Roman winters. Everyone had some terrible virus, and everyone was totally asphyxiated by all the dry ice! It's just as well that the film was dubbed later, because everyone was utterly nasal."

While perhaps lacking the obvious impact of today's modern gore-fests (though the mask-nailing and re-animation sequences still pack a visceral wallop), *Black Sunday* weaves its potent spell to draw the viewer into a shadowy world of palpable evil, making it one of the most atmospheric, eerie and frightening horror films of the 1960s. "The producers of *Black Sunday* recommend that it be seen only by those over 12 years of age!" warned the posters. Indeed, those of us who visited this world at an impressionable age were not soon to forget—as Barbara Steele herself learned: "I remember a nightmare experience when [my son] Jonathan was very young, about three, when we were living in New York. He was in a terrible state because his babysitter let him watch *Black Sunday* on television. There was that terrible scene, you know, where I got that awful mask lined with nails pounded on my face. This was really traumatic for Jonathan. Little children think television's real when they're three. I wanted to kill that babysitter." Babysitters—and viewers—beware.

THE HORRIBLE DR. HICHCOCK (1962)

"The candle of his lust burnt brightest in the shadow of the grave!" –ad line

After *Black Sunday*, this may be the most famous (and most notorious) of Barbara Steel's Italo-gothics. It's also one of the best.

Shot as *Raptus*, the story begins in 1885 London, where the brilliant, wealthy surgeon Dr. Hichcock (Robert Flemyng) displays one little quirk—he's a necrophile ("His secret was a coffin named DESIRE!" shouted the not-so-subtle ads). Hichcock's wife Margherita (Maria Teresa Vianello) willingly submits to her husband's funereal sex games by playing dead—helped along by the doc's experimental anesthetic. Their happy home life comes to an abrupt end when Hichcock accidentally kills Margherita with an overdose. The grief-stricken doctor abandons his ancestral manor house (and, apparently, his sick sexual proclivities), but returns twelve years later with a new (and unknowing) wife, Cynthia (Barbara Steele). Soon Cynthia is terrorized by the seeming specter of Margherita, and then by the now-unhinged doctor himself, who appears to have fallen under the spell of his adored, dead former wife and intends to make a corpse out of his current live one.

Cinematographer Raffaele Masciocchi's gorgeous Technicolor photography and lighting sets the uneasy tone. Deep graveyard blues in exterior scenes contrast starkly with the warm yellow interior light, while the occasional spot-specific red tint (pointedly appearing when the doctor's lust rises) creates a feeling of danger and heat, and the white of the phantom Margherita's gauzy gown fairly glows. Such illuminated imagery would do even Mario Bava proud. "The good thing about this picture, it's beautifully shot," observed star Robert Flemyng to interviewer Alan Upchurch. Indeed it is.

The entire film was lensed at the rented Villa Perucchetti in the district of Parioli in Rome. The villa's baroque architecture and archaic furnishings perfectly complement the picture's bizarre theme and gothic atmosphere. "You know, that villa was absolutely the only thing that was used," recalled Flemyng. "The kitchen of the house was all tile, so the various pantries and such-like had been turned into the mortuary. We shot everything in that villa."

"We were all influenced by the films of [Alfred]

Steele solidified her position as Europe's premier scream queen when she met The Horrible Dr. Hichcock *in 1962. (American lobby card)*

Hitchcock, who was the master of masters," admitted screenwriter Ernesto Gastaldi to *Video Watchdog*'s Tim Lucas. Gastaldi filled his screenplay with borrowings from several Hitchcock films, including a (possibly) poisoned glass of milk from *Suspicion*, and the new wife haunted by the memory of the dead wife from *Rebecca*—not to mention the doctor's sinister housekeeper, played by Harriet White Medin ("[Here] I was definitely thinking of *Rebecca*," Gastaldi stated). In a brilliant masterstroke of exploitability, Gastaldi gave his necrophile antagonist the same name as the Master of Suspense (though dropping the "t" in "Hitchcock" to ward off any potential lawsuit).

English actor Robert Flemyng paints a startling and commanding portrait of obsession, of a man battling his inner demons. His powerful presence infuses every frame of the perverse picture. The subtle struggle in Flemyng's face as the "respectable" doctor fights against his compulsion (after seeing a woman's corpse wheeled by at the hospital at which he works), or the intent gaze with which he fixes a female cadaver in the autopsy room, speak volumes. Such moments of strain and barely-held-in-check "passion" contrast starkly with his generally clipped, cold speech patterns and formal manner. "I just hammed away at it and hoped for the best," the actor recalled; and "the best" is exactly what he delivered.

Flemyng admitted that he took the part simply because he wanted to go to Rome. "I thought, 'What the hell, no one will ever see it.'" The allure of Rome also secured the services of Steele herself. Having come to the city to work on Fellini's *8 ½*, Steele told Upchurch: "I did [*Hichcock*] because I'd found a glorious little apartment with fabulous terraces and I was determined to stay there."

"That's the movie that [director] Riccardo Freda did on a bet, you know," continued Steele. "Freda said, 'I bet I can write and shoot a film in ten days,' and one of his friends bet him a race horse that he couldn't. And he shot it in ten days. He wanted this horse very badly, and we all felt obliged to help him. We were running at top speed through the entire movie." (Note: It was actually a 14-, rather than 10-day shoot.)

Steele does well enough in what, unfortunately, turns out to be a sorely underwritten role that asks little more of her than to look frightened and scream at the appropriate moment. Freda fails to exploit that sinister, dangerous quality in Steele that made her so alluring, leaving her to play a standard, put-upon heroine who faints at the drop of a hat (after the third fainting-from-terror episode, one begins to wonder…). Even so, Freda and Masciocchi's masterful visuals and moody build-up keep the menace thick in the heavy Gothic air.

A rather tangential sequel-of-sorts, *The Ghost*, followed a year later, again starring Steele (in a far meatier role) and directed by Freda. Though intriguing in its own right, it's not quite up to the delirious Gothic perversion that is *The Horrible Dr. Hichcock*.

THE GHOST (1963)

"Horror…sharp as a razor's edge!" –tagline

Made in 1963 in Italy, but not dubbed and released in the U.S. until 1965, *The Ghost*, an unofficial sequel to writer-director Riccardo Freda's earlier *The Horrible Dr. Hichcock*, has Dr. Charles Hichcock return as a cuckolded cripple who is killed by his wife (Barbara Steele) and her lover (the doctor's own physician). But the ghost of the vengeful Hichcock seemingly returns to torment the faithless couple…or does he?

Barbara Steele claims *The Ghost* was made on a bet (just like its "inspiration," *The Horrible Dr. Hichcock*). "Freda made a bet one day at lunch with a producer, Pietro Pupillo," reported the actress to *Fangoria* magazine. "He said he could write a script *and* shoot a movie in a week. He wrote it in a day; we had a day of pre-production, and he shot it in three days. One night I slept on the set, because I knew we would be shooting again in four hours."

Despite the obvious pressures such a rushed production put on its cast and crew (such as the actors having to literally learn their lines between scenes as the crew hurriedly set up for the next shot), Steele didn't see that as necessarily a bad thing: "I like working with a certain sense of urgency. It has its pluses because it creates an interesting energy, a kind of nerving sort of charge, a crisis energy on the set which I really think the film picks up on. I think that film on some subconscious level picks up this magnetism, this energy, when it's really happening. Somewhere I think it translates."

If so, then in *The Ghost* something was *lost* in translation, as it suffers from a decided *lack* of energy. Though opulently presented (with its wonderfully Gothic set dressings and old manor house setting), and possessing occasional moments of atmosphere and shock (such as a ghastly-lit face slowly emerging from the shadows; or an eerie visit to a twilight-lit, fog-enshrouded graveyard; or a vicious, well-edited straight-razor murder, complete with blood spattering the camera lens), the film's pacing matches the principals' turn-of-the-century garb—stately and demure.

The small cast does a superb job with some demanding roles, led by Steele, who does what she does best—seductive in one scene, terrified in the next, and totally mad at the end.

Filled with shots of billowy curtains, chess pieces that suddenly scatter from the board, drops of blood mysteriously appearing, disembodied ghostly laughter, and Charles' eerie voice issuing from the housekeeper medium's mouth, *The Ghost* offers up sporadic Gothic-flavored chills, but its measured tread and predictable ending (the poetic "twist" is anything *but* unexpected) make this *Ghost* a rather pale entry in the Italo-gothic sweepstakes of the 1960s.

CASTLE OF BLOOD (1964)

"The Living and the Dead Change Places in an Orgy of Terror!" –ad line

Journalist Alan Foster (Georges Riviére) meets Edgar Allan Poe and Lord Blackwood in a tavern. Blackwood owns a haunted castle and challenges the impetuous reporter to spend a night at the castle on All Souls Eve ("the Night of the Dead"). Despite Poe's warnings, Alan accepts and witnesses several ghosts reenact their murders. He also falls in love with Elizabeth Blackwood (Barbara Steele), a mysterious inhabitant of the castle. The spirits need the blood of the living so that they may rise yet again on the next All Souls Eve. With the specters clamoring for Alan's blood, Elizabeth, who's fallen in love with him, tries to help the young man escape.

One of Steele's weaker Continental horrors, *Castle of Blood* plays like a campfire ghost story that's outstayed its welcome. Though chilling at first, with Foster tentatively exploring the admittedly creepy castle (filled with sinister shadows, cobwebs and archaic furnishings), these I-mustn't-succumb-to-my-frightened-imaginings sequences stretch endlessly, quickly becoming tedious. And very soon after the flesh-and-blood "ghosts" show up, it becomes painfully obvious to everyone but the protagonist that these oddly behaving "people" are not what they seem to be. The one-note story is too thin to sustain a full feature, and padded scenes begin popping up more frequently than the apparitions.

Barbara Steele's dark beauty and odd mannerisms make her both alluring and dangerous, but she's undone by the banal dubbing and lack of real characterization (her "heroine" declares her love for the living stranger mere minutes after they meet!). "How I love you Alan—uselessly, absurdly," she avows. Absurdly indeed.

Filmed in 10 days using the three-camera technique common in television, *Castle of Blood* was "exhausting," recalled Steele. "It meant sometimes working eighteen hours a day!" The movie was advertised as being based on the Edgar Allan Poe story "Dance Macabre," but no such story exists. Obviously, the distributors felt they could gain a few extra box-office dollars by riding the coattails of AIP's Poe series. In the U.S. the Woolner Brothers released *Castle of Blood* on the top half of a double bill with *Hercules in the Haunted World*.

A few moments of *frisson* (such as when Foster rests his head on Elizabeth's breast and discovers that his lover has no heartbeat, or when a gruesome entombed corpse suddenly begins to breathe) and an ironic ending help make a visit to this *Castle* at least bearable, but the viewer, like the film's desperate protagonist, is ready to leave long before the show's over.

Director Margheriti remade this film in color as the rather more energetic yet still unnecessary *Web of the Spider* in 1970.

THE LONG HAIR OF DEATH (1965)

"A film that will chill your spine and keep you gripped in your seat!"–trailer

Set in the fifteenth century, *I lunghi capelli della morte* (The Long Hair of Death) tells the story of a woman wrongly accused of murder and burned at the stake as a witch, witnessed by her daughter (Barbara Steele). The daughter is murdered but seemingly returns from the dead to torment and finally engineer the death of the real killer, the son of a powerful nobleman.

Co-screenwriter Ernesto Gastaldi admitted that his film's ending (with the murderer trapped and helpless inside the wicker effigy of Death as the locals unknowingly set it alight to celebrate the passing of the plague) was inspired by the shock conclusion of a popular 1961 Roger Corman Poe film. "*The Pit and the Pendulum* had a big influence on Italian horror films," Gastaldi told interviewer Tim Lucas. "Everybody borrowed from it." Too bad Gastaldi and Co. didn't borrow *more* from that American horror classic, since *The Long Hair of Death* turned out to be a slow, ponderous, only intermittently entertaining Eurohorror.

In a 1994 interview with Peter Blumenstock, director Antonio Margheriti said, "*The Long Hair of Death* was done in three weeks, but I don't like that one too much. I don't like the story. The screenplay we had was very badly written and a lot of things were not really fixed in it. On the set, a lot of things turned out to be stupid or impossible, so we had to invent a lot and improvise every day. We shot only a few days in the studio, with the rest done on location at the *castello* in Anzio. There was hardly any time to think, to invent, or write something down properly, because we had to shoot, shoot, and shoot. Something is wrong with that film."

Indeed. Though Margheriti keeps his camera mobile, prowling about the marvelously dressed castle setting and cobweb-drenched catacombs, and even offers the occasional chill (such as when a lightning strike blows the lid off a stone tomb, exposing the skeleton within—which then, amidst the rain and mud, begins to take on flesh), he can't overcome the rambling, tedious script. The film spends far too much time on the antagonist's convoluted scheme to murder his unwanted wife, and the subsequent is-she-dead-or-isn't-she? shenanigans. The evil antagonist proves so unlikable that no suspense or real interest arises from the "haunting" proceedings. An unexpected sting in the ghost tale relieves some of the previous tedium (but only some), and Barbara Steele, who first entices, then terrifies, both extends and justifies her claim to the Queen of Eurohorror crown. But when it comes to entertainment value, *The Long Hair of Death* is really nothing more than a Continental buzz cut.

TERROR-CREATURES FROM THE GRAVE (1965)

"They Rise from Dank Coffins in the Dead of Night to Inflict and Evil Curse of Doom, Murdering Their Victims in an Orgy of Slaughter!" –ad line

In 1911 a lawyer (Walter Brandi) journeys to a remote villa (a former 16th century plague victim hospital) only to find that the man who sent for him has already been *dead* for a year. Soon mysterious deaths begin occurring around the village, and it comes to light that the dead man (who was well-versed in the occult) was murdered, and his spirit has summoned the plague victims from their graves to exact his vengeance.

While *Terror-Creatures from the Grave*'s American distributor tacked on the credit "Inspired by Edgar Allan Poe" in a desperate attempt to ride the coattails of the then-lucrative AIP Poe cycle (*Terror-Creatures*' story has *nothing* to do with Poe), the claim may not be that far wrong—at least in *spirit* if not actuality. Much like the putrid atmosphere brought by the plague itself, a macabre pall hangs over *Terror-Creatures*, with death (literalized by the restless plague victims) permeating every frame of the picture. The wonderfully Gothic castle setting, some eerie nighttime photography and hand-held camerawork (courtesy of cinematographer Carlo Di Palma, who went on to lens several Woody Allen movies, including *Hannah and Her Sisters* and *Bullets Over Broadway*), and somber/frightened acting by the principals (including Barbara Steele as the…er, steely widow) generate a creepy—and downright malevolent—atmosphere.

Taking a page from Val Lewton's book, director Ralph Zucker employs some subjective camerawork that keeps the ghosts/zombies of the ancient plague victims unseen (with only a shadowy outline visible, or a bubbly, deformed hand entering the frame), raising the film's *mysterioso* level and allowing the viewer's imagination to do the shuddery work. But this being a 1960s horror movie, it's not all shadows and suggestion; Zucker throws a few gruesome scenes into the spine-chilling mix as well—such as the shocking sight of a man's intestines oozing out a small hole in his belly after he impales himself on a sword.

Though the film's direction has been erroneously credited to Massimo (*Bloody Pit of Horror*) Pupillo (aka Max Hunter), *Terror-Creatures* (according to film historian Alan Upchurch *and* the movie's co-star, Walter Brandi) was actually helmed by a 25-year-old American named Ralph Zucker. It was his first—and last—directing job. Zucker worked in many other film capacities in Italy, however: as an actor in Pupillos's *Bloody Pit of Horror* (1965), as technical director on *Star Pilot* (1966), as producer of *King of Kong Island* (1968), and as scenarist and executive producer of *The Devil's Wedding Night* (1973), not to mention working on the English-dubbed export versions of other Italian movies and as a distributor of foreign films in Italy. Zucker died in Los Angeles in 1982 of a heart attack, age 42.

Given its novel and intriguing storyline, Lewtonesque sensibilities (spiced with a few shuddery shocks), effective acting, and its pervasive atmosphere of dread, *Terror-Creatures from the Grave* can be counted among the best of the Italo-gothics from the 1960s.

NIGHTMARE CASTLE (1966)

"So Weird, So Terrifying…Do You Dare See It?" –trailer

After *Black Sunday* (1960), and perhaps the American-made *The Pit and the Pendulum* (1961), the Gothic Italian period horror film *Nightmare Castle* may very well be Barbara Steele's best horror movie, as well as being the entry that best serves Steele the actress, allowing her far greater range than most (even *Black Sunday*).

Steele plays Muriel, the sexy but shrewish wife of sadistic scientist Stephen (Paul Miller), who likes to experiment with electricity. When Stephen finds his wife in the arms of her lover, he tortures them both to death (dripping burning acid on Muriel, and using a red-hot poker on her paramour). Learning that Muriel left all her wealth to her stepsister Jenny (Steele again), Stephen woos the naïve, high-strung girl. (Amazingly, these two "stepsisters" appear to be identical in every way except hair color!) Stephen plots to drive his new bride mad, and soon Jenny is wearing Muriel's clothes, playing Muriel's music, drinking Muriel's brandy, and behaving as if possessed by the dead woman's ghost. Is it delirium, or has the dead wife returned to seek retribution?

As the heartless Muriel, Steele is at her coldest *and* most alluring. With Muriel's death and Jenny's arrival, the actress transforms herself into a nervous and ultimately terrified victim—before turning terrifying herself at the end as she gleefully exacts Muriel's gruesome revenge. "I loved the duality of it," Steele told interviewer Brad Lineweaver. "First to play the victim and then use that energy to turn it into the revenge part, that's good. It's got power. It's good to have both, because we all need justification in our lives…. Duality makes drama, and not just in horror films."

Veteran Swiss character actor Paul Muller's (*Fangs of the Living Dead*, 1968; *Count Dracula*, 1970; *Lady Frankenstein*, 1971) cold, assured, arrogant portrayal of Stephen matches Steele's impressive playing scene-for-scene, making him a calculating villain you love to hate.

One of the film's few missteps comes in the form of some poor old-age make-up on the duplicitous housekeeper Solange (Helga Line), making her look like a cut-rate she-mummy. Fortunately, she soon transforms into the young and beautiful Ms. Line (explained with a simple offhand comment from Stephen about having "restored your youth"!). The film later takes an intriguing detour into *Awful Dr. Orloff/Eyes Without a Face* territory via a subplot in which Stephen uses a serum derived from the murdered Muriel's blood to scientifically sustain his new mistress' youth (youth in danger of fading again without the infusion of *more* blood).

Fortunately, the rest of the make-ups prove disturbingly effective, beginning with the bloody, scarred visage of Muriel's lover after Stephen smashes in his face with a metal poker. Following their torture (and electrocution), Stephen coolly and scientifically cuts the hearts from Muriel and her lover and drops them into a small tank in full gory view—the blood spreading slowly, almost gracefully, through the clear water. Stephen cremates their bodies and places the ashes in an ornate pot—which we next see the maid *watering*, as it now houses a potted plant! It's a cold, cruel and startlingly macabre moment, perfectly summing up the film as a whole.

Further chilling moments arise in this *Nightmare Castle*, such as Jenny watching in horror while the aforementioned plant mysteriously drips blood, or hears the frightening disembodied sound of twin heartbeats, or jumps when the wind blows open a door to the sound of diabolical laughter. And the climactic appearance of the ghosts remains one of the eeriest sequences in Sixties cinema. As Muriel slowly approaches the disbelieving Stephen, her raven tresses hang down, obscuring her beautiful face. Stephen abruptly pulls back the hair to reveal a horribly ruined countenance—the gruesome shock augmented by Muriel's demonic laughter. (And this over three decades before Japanese entries like *Ringu* made such an image a horror movie staple).

With its mix of gruesome shocks and shuddery Gothic atmosphere (augmented by the opulent—and authentic—castle setting, mobile camerawork, intriguing angles and evocative lighting), *Nightmare Castle* truly lives up to its name, standing as one of the best Italo-horrors of the decade.

THE SHE BEAST (1965)

"Deadlier than Dracula! *Wilder than the* Werewolf! *More frightening than Frankenstein!" –poster*

A newlywed couple (Ian Ogilvy and Barbara Steele) vacationing in Transylvania run their car off the road into a lake. Two hundred years earlier, a hideous witch named Vardella was drowned by the villagers in that same lake. When the wife emerges from the water, she is possessed by the spirit of the vengeful witch, causing her to take on the visage of an ugly old crone and embark on a murder spree.

Of the nine Continental-based Barbara Steele-starring horror films released in the 1960s, *The She Beast* ranks near the bottom. Though it offers a few arresting moments (such as the brutal, unflinching sequence in which the townsfolk tie the screaming witch to a seesaw-like contraption, drive a spike though her torso, and proceed to dunk her in the lake—a presage, perhaps, of things to come in director Michael Reeves' later *Witchfinder General*), this obviously cheap production (the protagonists even drive a VW bug!) ultimately becomes an uneasy blend of half-baked horror and *un*-baked slapstick.

Fortunately, the likable Ian Ogilvy (who starred in all three of Reeves' films before the director's untimely death at age 25) and the alluring Barbara Steele do much to ground the proceedings in believability. And former Roger Corman stock player turned Italy-based Jack-of-all-Cinema-Trades Mel Welles (who dubbed, acted in and even directed numerous Continentals), as the bloated, buffoonish communist innkeeper, actually makes some of the ham-fisted comedy work.

Charles B. Griffith (who served as second unit director on *She Beast*, and appears in the picture as well) told interviewer Dennis Fischer: "I wrote that in three days to get an airline ticket for my girlfriend. That was originally a comedy about communistic Transylvania with Barbara Steele, Mel Welles and Paul Maslansky, who played a cop and produced." (Maslansky also produced the superior *Castle of the Living Dead*, on which Reeves served as uncredited second unit director.)

"Paul couldn't make up his mind whether he wanted to do it as a comedy or not," recounted Mel Welles to film historian Tom Weaver. "It was a real farcical script, and by watering it down they kind of spoiled it. We made that entire picture in Italy and looped it there—in Italy you don't make direct-sound pictures because you can't keep an Italian crew quiet long enough [laughs]!"

Though occasionally the poke-fun-at-communists comedy works (the witch attacks and kills the corrupt innkeeper with a *hammer and sickle!*), most of it is so broad that it becomes both tiresome and incongruous, given the film's otherwise dark tone. Sample exchange:

First communist official: "Is he able to talk?"
Second official: "No, he's already dead."
First official: "Then he's obstructing justice."

Add to this scenes of the Keystone Kommunists taking pratfalls, and a speeded-up car chase involving a Model A and moped(!), and the slapstick antics fatally undermine the more horrific themes of vengeance and possession.

She Beast's reputation rests on the fact that it was 21-year-old wunderkind director Michael Reeves' first full feature—plus, of course, the fact that it starred Barbara

Steele at the height of her Eurohorror popularity. (Ms. Steele's fans must feel disappointment, however, at the actress' limited screen time here—which amounts to about 15 minutes, despite her star billing. The budget was so low that the filmmakers could only afford her for four days of shooting—at a fee of $5,000.)

Steele described Reeves (to interviewer Mark Miller) as "quite shy, very gentle, and obviously very intelligent. I think he could have been a terrific talent. He was so young and a little overwhelmed doing the picture, but he had quite a lot of control. He knew exactly what he wanted."

Uneven, yet still moderately intriguing, *The She Beast* proved to be more of a promise of things to come from first-timer Reeves than a wholly successful effort in and of itself.

UN ANGELO PER SATANA / AN ANGEL FOR SATAN (1966)

Barbara Steele's final Eurohorror, unfortunately, went unreleased outside of its native Italy. It's the Gothic period tale of a sculptor (Anthony Steffan) who arrives at a large estate to restore an ancient statue recovered from the nearby lake. The local villagers live in fear of the statue's 200-year-old "curse," placed upon it by a homely woman who'd murdered her own beautiful sister out of bitter jealousy. When the estate's rightful heir (Steele) returns home to claim her inheritance, the sculptor notes that she bears an uncanny likeness to the statue. Soon a rash of mysterious deaths has the villagers talking of witchcraft. Given its intriguing storyline (complete with a clever twist to the tale), beautiful cinematography and a particularly alluring—and dangerous—performance by Steele (whose provocative presence inspires lust, madness and murder), it's a pity that an English-language version didn't surface sooner (a subtitled DVD finally emerged in 2009).

"Film is a very strange, witchy substance," stated Steele at her San Francisco Roxie appearance. "I think it picks up things on a lot of subliminal levels, literally picks up the energies that are in effect between people when filming." Though her nine Eurohorrors vary wildly in quality, from the shuddery classic *Black Sunday* to the horror-humor hybrid misfire *The She Beast*, they each offer various "subliminal levels" and "energies" sure to please any fan of Gothic cinema. And it's no accident that they all starred the then-reigning queen

Steele's final Eurohorror makes of her An Angel for Satan *(1966).*

of Continental terrors, for she quickly became an iconic presence in world cinema—the two-sided coin personified, embodying both the light of innocence and the dark lure of evil. Perfectly suited for the peculiar blend of Gothic storytelling and European cinematic sensibilities found on the Continent in the 1960s, Barbara Steele truly was the ultimate *Angel for Satan*.

> As I was putting the finishing touches on my book *Drums of Terror: Voodoo in the Cinema* (Midnight Marquee Press, 1998), I contacted *Monsterscene* magazine editor Stephen D. Smith to see if he'd be interested in an overview article on the topic. He answered with a resounding "oui," and this was the result, printed in issue 11 (Winter 1998).

DRUMS OF TERROR: SIXTY-FIVE YEARS OF VOODOO MOVIES

"In many out of the way corners of the earth there may still be found remnants of races that believe implicitly in the religious formulas that have come down to them from the dim and distant past. Of all these strange beliefs, perhaps the most inexplicable and disturbing is that of the Haitians, known to white men as 'VOODOO.'" –opening narration for the 1935 film *Ouanga*

"This is a religion of major stature, rare poetic vision, and artistic expression." –experimental filmmaker turned Voudoun initiate Maya Deren

As demonstrated by the above *Ouanga* quote, moviemakers initially took a condescending (not to mention racist) attitude toward the practice of the religion known as Voudoun (or "voodoo" as it's called in common parlance). Sadly, this attitude hasn't changed much over the subsequent six decades, either in the average citizen or (with *very* few exceptions) in celluloid portrayals.

This system of "strange beliefs" which proved so "inexplicable and disturbing" to the common moviegoer has inspired dozens of filmmakers over the last sixty-five years to paint their voodoo visions on the silver screen. In the art of cinema, voodoo films possess their own unique flavor and attraction. Filled with bizarre rituals, tropical locales, frenzied sensual dancing, deadly hexes, powerful sorcerers, and the dreaded walking dead, voodoo movies appeal to the western audience's thrill of the exotic, the strange, the inexplicable.

Not unexpectedly, filmmakers have been more inclined to exploit rather than explore the topic. After all, with all due respect to those serious practitioners of Voudou and its variations, legitimate worship is *not* the stuff of celluloid dreams—or nightmares. As veteran screenwriter Tim Kelly (who penned the 1974 blaxploitation voodoo entry *The Zombies of Sugar Hill*) observed, "naturally with films, much of the historical accuracy is dropped and the sensational aspects sort of take over." Just as few people would buy a movie ticket in order to witness a full Catholic Mass (in Latin, of course), most viewers don't wish to see the drawn-out dancing and intricate rituals of legitimate Voudoun worship. No, moviegoers want to see spells, human sacrifices, and zombies. Consequently, that is just what filmmakers have provided.

As a result, most voodoo movies aren't too concerned with the spiritual aspect of their topic and tend to focus on more sensationalistic traits, portraying the religion as an evil practice centered on malevolent hexes and walking corpses. While it is true that Haiti is full of protective ouangas (charms) and that practitioners do sometimes seek out the aid of bokors (sorcerers), the main thrust of true Voudoun is to provide a venue by which the initiate develops a personal relationship with the loas (the spirits or gods) and so becomes part of the spiritual (as well as temporal) community. Much as the true Christian loathes those who pray for personal gain at the expense of others, however, so does the devout Voudounist disdain those who seek the loas' direct aid for ill. Consequently, judging Voudoun by its cinematic incarnations would be like evaluating Christianity by watching movies like *Brotherhood of Satan* (1971) or *The Devil's Rain* (1975).

In spite of what most moviemakers would have us believe, Voudoun is a legitimate religion born of a genuine spirituality. Though the dogmatic Christian may cringe at the thought, true Voudou is fairly close to Catholicism in its structure—but on a more personal, intimate, and vibrant level. (In fact, most Voudoun alters are adorned with lithographs of Catholic saints; and "Santería"—the Cuban form of Voudou—literally means "the worship of saints.") Like the Catholic, the Voudounist believes in the one true God (*Bon Dieu*) as the creator of all things. Voudoun's various loas (spirits or lesser deities) act (much as the saints do) as intermediaries between the believer and the Supreme Being. Whereas Catholics pray to the saints, however, the Voudounist goes that extra mile and welcomes the loa into their very bodies. Through ritual and dance, the Voudounist seeks possession by the loa. As the Haitian saying goes, the Catholic goes to church to speak about God while the Voudounist dances in the hounfour (a Voudoun place of worship) and becomes God.

In pop culture (and, consequently, film), apart from the drums and the ever-present voodoo doll (which, ironically, is more a product of western witchcraft than the African-based religion), voodoo's most recognizable icon would have to be the zombie. (Note: There are many more zombie films than voodoo movies. Though the screen's Walking Dead originated with voodoo [in 1932's *White Zombie*], subsequent filmmakers have often abandoned voodoo in favor of a scientific or Satanic explanation for their preambulating corpses.) The investigations of Harvard ethnobotonist Wade Davis (chronicled in his somewhat sensationalized book *The Serpent and the Rainbow* and further in his more scholarly tome *Passage of Darkness*) offer convincing evidence that zombies do indeed exist—though not as the revived corpses of Hollywood fantasy. Through an engulfing tide of cultural tradition and psychological belief, and aided by the physiological properties of neurotoxins and psychotropic drugs obtained from local flora and fauna, a victim's will and individual identity can be stripped from him. These unfortunate creatures are not decomposing cadavers, however, but a living person whose memory and personality has been sublimated and even partially erased.

But *why* create a zombie—an expensive, complicated, and dangerous feat for all involved? According to Davis (in *Passage of Darkness*), "zombification is a form of social sanction imposed by recognized corporate bodies—the poorly known and clandestine secret Bizango societies—as one means of maintaining order and control in local communities." In other words, it is a form of capital punishment—a living death—meted out by the community leaders. Unlike cinematic zom-

White Zombie ad.

bies, who are generally portrayed as the innocent victims of greedy sorcerers eager for slaves or as mindless instruments of revenge, the Haitian zombie is a convicted criminal serving out a sentence for his crimes against the community. Also, in contrast to the movies, these will-less creatures hovering between the natural and spirit worlds are not to be feared but rather to be pitied. For the Haitian Voudounist, the fear is not of being harmed by a zombie but of *becoming* one.

Apart from the deep South, voodoo didn't enter the general American consciousness until William B. Seabrook published *The Magic Island* in 1929, his intriguing, sensationalized account of Haitian voodoo. This popular book first inspired a Broadway play, then (indirectly) the highly successful Bela Lugosi vehicle *White Zombie* (1932). With *White Zombie* the idea (if not exactly the spirit) of voodoo took root in popular culture—and in cinema. One of the best known (and best) of all voodoo movies, this Golden Age horror classic created a malevolent milieu populated by the walking dead and lorded over by the iconographic presence of Bela Lugosi as zombie-master Murder Legendre. Under the guidance of the brothers Halperin (Victor and Edward, whose subsequent ineffectual efforts—including the abysmal *Revolt of the Zombies* [1936]—indicate that their initial success was more a matter of luck than of skill), *White Zombie* remains today one of the most atmospheric horror films ever made, a darkly gothic shadowplay of good against evil. Legendre's zombies (whom the voodoo-master refers to as his "angels of death") are both imposing and frightening, their cadaverous appearance the result of makeup maestro Jack Pierce's sinister shadings. It proved an auspicious and promising beginning for voodoo (and zombie) cinema—a promise that, sadly, has rarely been fulfilled in the subsequent six decades. (Note: This article will deal solely with those voodoo films in which the topic plays an integral role in the story; there are many other pictures that contain a negligible or tangential voodoo element. Also, a number of films—such as *Bride of the Gorilla* (1951) and *Burn, Witch, Burn* (1962)—have traditionally been thought of as voodoo movies but in fact contain little or no overt voodoo and rely upon some other source for their supernatural surprises.)

Within a year of *White Zombie*'s 1932 release, several other independent voodoo films went into production, with a trio of hoodoo horrors hitting the big screen in the first half of 1934. Unfortunately, the only real 'horror' inspired by this triad comes from struggling to stay awake through their torpid tellings. In rapid succession came *Drums o' Voodoo* (aka *Louisiana*; an all-black curiosity based on an unsuccessful Broadway play penned by black actor/playwright J. Augustus Smith), *Black Moon* ("the weirdest romance of our time"—according to the ads), and *Chloe: Love Is Calling You* (an overtly racist fear-of-miscegenation story using voodoo as a backdrop).

Of the three, *Drums o' Voodoo* can boast of being the most voodoo-friendly (shining a relatively benign light on its topic while touching on the sense of community integral to Voudoun spirituality)—as well as the most *un*cinematic and technically primitive, for it's little more than a filmed stageplay (with director Arthur Hoerl utilizing the failed play's cast and costumes to save money while anchoring his immobile camera on a solitary cramped soundstage).

It being a Paramount production (albeit a low-budget one), *Black Moon* remains the slickest of the trio and the best acted (thanks to good turns by Fay Wray and Jack Holt), but it still fails to generate any real thrills. Despite the involvement of diabolical voodoo and human sacrifice, nothing is made of the mystical (much less horrific) aspects of the West Indian religion. No zombies, no curses, no talk of vengeful spirits or voodoo gods, not even a single ceremonial snake rears its sacred head. The story might just as well have taken place in the wilds of India as a tale of civil upheaval or in darkest Africa as some Tarzan movie subplot. In making voodoo nothing more than the driving superstition of fanatical savages (while at the same time failing to generate any of the expected thrills or shudders attendant thereon) *Black Moon* did the subject (and its viewers) no favors.

Until recently a lost film (as was *Black Moon*, which only re-surfaced a couple of years ago), it would have been no *real* loss had *Chloe: Love Is Calling You* stayed that way, for there is absolutely nothing to recommend in this poorly-acted, slow-moving, nastily bigoted picture of bayou romance. With little action and no merit (its sole distinction being the most openly racist voodoo vision in cinema history), *Chloe* stands as one of the *worst* voodoo films of all time.

Obviously, the 1930s was *not* a good decade for screen voodoo, as the two remaining pictures to deal with the subject, *Ouanga* (1935) and *The Devil's Daughter* (1939), demonstrate. *Ouanga* was made by British Paramount (using an American cast and crew) as an English quota quickie. It didn't see release in the U.S. until 1941 under the altered (and slightly silly) title of *The Love Wanga*. A tale of inflamed love and voodoo vengeance on a Haitian plantation, *Ouanga* has little to offer but a few bits of local color (it was filmed on Haiti and Jamaica) and the screen debut of perennial gangster (and later TV mogul) Sheldon Leonard. (Leonard, by the way, does a rather poor job in his role of a love-sick overseer.) As for *The Devil's Daughter*, it was an even cheaper (and worse acted) all-black remake of *Ouanga*!

The 1940s showed a decided upswing in voodoo variants and provided the subgenre with the second of its genuine classics: *I Walked with a Zombie*. Before Val Lewton could create his famous "West Indian version of *Jane Eyre*," however, Monogram ushered in the decade with the first of its hoodoo horrors (two more were to follow): *King of the Zombies* (1941). More a vehicle for black comedian Mantan Moreland than anything else, this tale of a mad Nazi employing zombies and island voodoo to elicit military secrets from a captured American admiral proved mildly amusing despite its cheap look and puerile plotting.

Though also relatively cheap (with a budget of only about $150,000), there's nothing childish about the moody, graceful, adult-oriented *I Walked with a Zombie*. Not only is it the best voodoo film ever made, it is truly one of the most literate and poetic of all horror movies. Produced by the (justly) venerated Val Lewton, guiding hand of such 1940s classics as *Cat People* (1942), *The Body Snatcher* (1945), and *Bedlam* (1946) (and whom Boris Karloff once gratefully characterized as "the man who rescued me from the living dead and restored my soul"), *I Walked with a Zombie* was the first feature to take a truly adult approach to voodoo. None of that human sacrifice business or devilish sorcery mars its maturity. Instead, the picture shows the pervasiveness of this alternative religion in the lives of its island inhabitants. "[Voodoo] is part of everyday life here," states one character matter-of-factly, hinting at the normalcy of their voodoo worldview. The film also touches on the religion's cornerstone—possession. "They sing and dance and carry on," says the hero. "And then as I understand it one of the gods comes down and speaks through one of the people." (Amusingly, Lewton applied his wry sense of humor to the topic by inserting this declaration among the fine print of the opening credits: "The char-

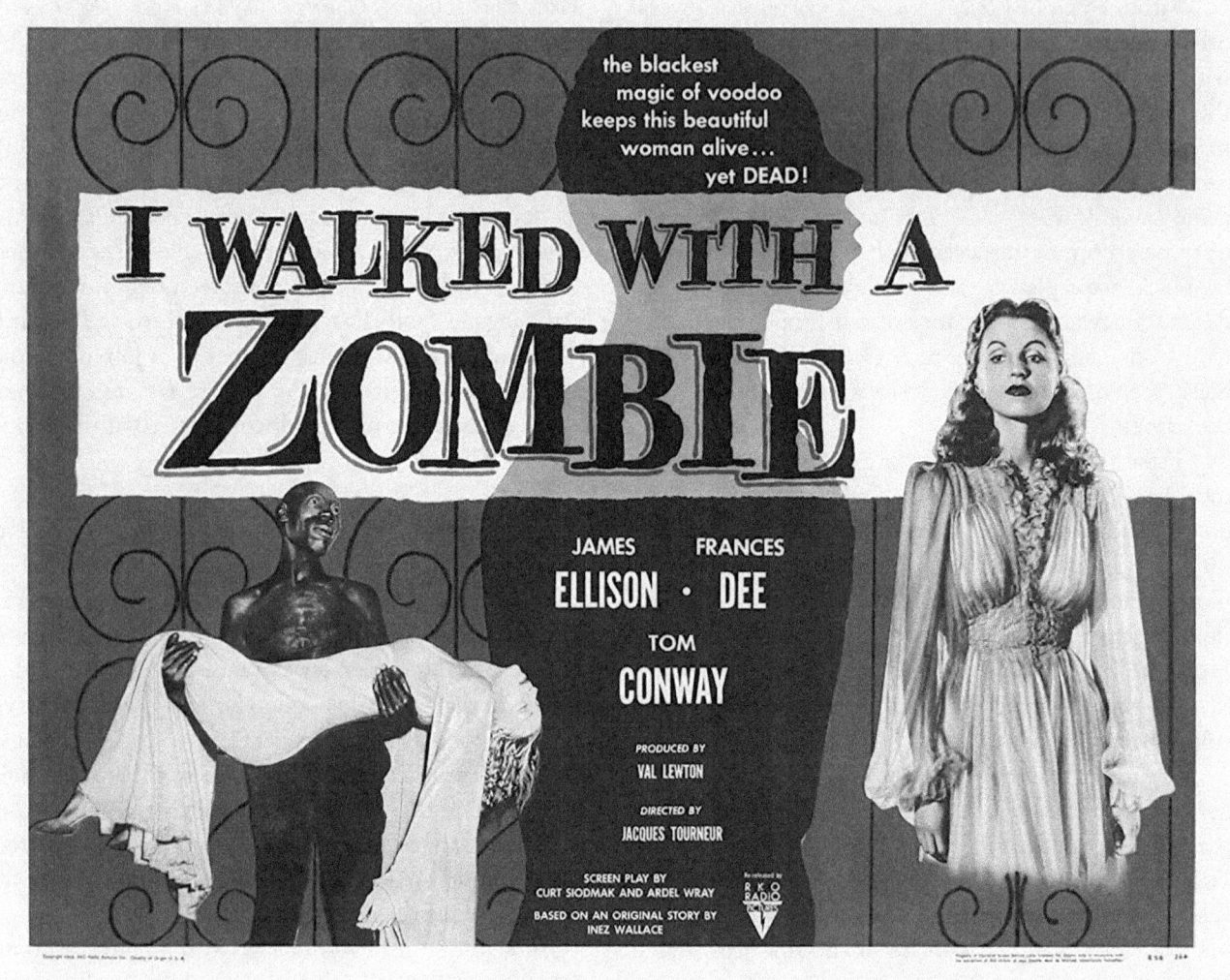

I Walked with a Zombie *lobby card.*

acters and events depicted in this photoplay are fictional. Any similarity to actual persons, living, dead, or *possessed*, is purely coincidental.")

After *I Walked with a Zombie* scored both with the critics and (more importantly) the public, the next three years saw five more variable voodoo films attempt to distract the war-weary masses. In rapid succession came the wacky-yet-entertaining (for all the wrong reasons) *Voodoo Man* (1944; Monogram's second voodoo venture); Universal's dull Inner Sanctum entry *Weird Woman* (1944; starring the laughably miscast Lon Chaney, Jr.); the surprisingly moody and intelligent poverty-row production of *The Vampire's Ghost* (1945); RKO's silly comedic follow-up to *I Walked with a Zombie* called *Zombies on Broadway* (1945); and a more serious-minded mix of sane science and mad voodoo in *The Face of Marble* (1946; Monogram's third voodoo outing).

Despite the (misguided) efforts of major studios like Universal and RKO, the standouts among this questionable quintet are (surprisingly) the two poverty-row entries *The Vampire's Ghost* (Republic) and *The Face of Marble* (Monogram). Via some imaginative staging, clever plotting, and down-to-earth acting (avoiding the over-the-top bombast indulged in by the principals of *Voodoo Man*, for instance), both pictures manage to rise above their bargain-basement roots to create something better than the sum of their worn parts. And while *The Face of Marble* displays the usual unimaginative take on voodoo as an evil conveyance of dastardly doom, *The Vampire's Ghost* manages to (no doubt unintentionally) raise a few issues concerning religious tolerance and cooperation (the vampire is destroyed, for instance, through the joint efforts of a Christian priest and the local voodooists).

So, of the eight voodoo productions of the 1940s, we have one undisputed classic, two more worthy low-budget additions, and several other mildly entertaining entries. Only one leg of this cinematic octopod really came up lame—the painfully unfunny *Zombies on*

Face of Marble *pressbook*.

Broadway. All in all, not a bad voodoo showing.

The next decade, however, can lay no such claim. With only half as many voodoo films released in the 1950s, none of them managed to be even half as good as the bulk of their predecessors. *Voodoo Tiger* (1952; a tepid Johnny Weissmuller/Jungle Jim drama), *Voodoo Island* (1957; one of Boris Karloff's worst films—with a performance to match), *Voodoo Woman* (1957; featuring a ludicrous monster in a ridiculous story), and *The Disembodied* (1957; the dullest of the four—and that's saying something) not only all failed to significantly explore their voodoo subject, they failed miserably to *exploit* it as well. Populated by silly 'natives' and embarrassed 'stars' (like Karloff in *Voodoo Island* and Tom Conway in *Voodoo Woman*), this sorry quartet remains as dull and lifeless as the zombies most of these features sorely lack. (Things appear even bleaker if one includes the execrable *Serpent Island*, 1954, which was so bad that it couldn't even manage a theatrical release and went straight to the undiscriminating wasteland of television.) If one were (hard) pressed to pick the best of these, it would have to be *Voodoo Woman*—simply in default of it possessing a "monster" (in the funny form of Paul Blaisdell's recycled *She Creature* suit topped by a dime-store skull mask and fright wig). With nary a creditable entry in sight, the 1950s proved to be voodoo's cinematic nadir.

Fortunately, the 1960s was a time of vast improvement in silver screen voodoo. After two false starts with the unblushingly bad Brazilian-lensed *Macumba Love* (1960) and the equally awful but homegrown (or, more aptly, home*groan*) *The Devil's Hand* (1961), the decade settled into a steady groove that saw five worthwhile voodoo releases. Along with the 'British Invasion' of pop music came the British Invasion of voodoo movies, for all five of these features came from England!

First up was *Curse of the Voodoo* (1965), an earnest-but-somewhat-stodgy tale of an African tribal curse afflicting big-game hunter Bryant Haliday. Originally titled *The Curse of Simba* in the U.K., in America the film met the ignoble fate of standing in support of the so-bad-it's-good *Frankenstein Meets the Space Monster* on a demeaning double bill. Though the weakest of the five British hoodoos, *Curse of the Voodoo*'s heartfelt and occasionally imaginative production makes it deserving of a better fate than it has thus-far received.

The next bit of voodoo to voyage across the Atlantic proved a groundbreaking production from Amicus, Hammer Films' main competitor in the English horror market. The first horror omnibus in over twenty years, *Dr. Terror's House of Horrors* (1965) began a long and successful string of anthology films that

Voodoo Island *lobby card*.

stretches forward to this day (as evinced by the recent *Tales from the Hood*, 1995). Though best remembered for its excellent "Disembodied Hand" segment starring Christopher Lee and its creepily effective wraparound involving Peter Cushing, *Dr. Terror's* also features a rather droll tale of "Voodoo" in which a jazz musician (singer/entertainer/comedian Roy Castle) incorporates "the sacred music of the great god Damballah" into his latest arrangement—much to his eventual regret. ("To my mind," stated director Freddie Francis about the segment's wry tone, "it was a *fun* thing, obviously not to be taken seriously.")

The following year, Hammer did their friendly rival Amicus one better by devoting a whole film to voodoo in the form of *The Plague of the Zombies* (1966). A visually exciting, occasionally frightening, and thoroughly entertaining horror yarn, *The Plague of the Zombies* stands near the top of voodoo's cinematic ladder and, if not on the top *Hammer* rung as well, then at least solidly positioned on its second step.

"The authentic and thoroughly researched sequences of voodoo practices shown in the film," proclaimed a Hammer publicity article, "are said to follow the actual rituals performed in Haiti." This was undoubtedly "said" *only* by the studio's PR writers, for the "voodoo practices shown in the film" are about as authentic as a mail-order voodoo doll. Delusions of authenticity aside, the ceremonial scenes are well handled by director John Gilling to infuse a sense of danger and excitement into the proceedings.

Regarding zombies, *Plague* features some of the most effective in the voodoo subgenre. Dressed in sackcloth shrouds, these walking corpses are quite frightening with their dead-gray pallor, flaking skin, wide-staring filmy eyes, and evil grins and smirks (admittedly a ridiculous trait for a creature supposedly lacking a will of its own—but a visually chilling one nonetheless). The dream sequence in which these cadavers rise up from their graves en masse is as relentless and frightening a scene as can be found in *any* Sixties horror, and one that probably inspired George Romero in filming his seminal *Night of the Living Dead* (1968) (and surely served as a blueprint for Bob Kelljan's effectively creepy opening for *The Return of Count Yorga*, 1971). Without a doubt, *The Plague of the Zombies* is the best voodoo film of the 1960s and arguably among the best of the entire subgenre as well.

Less than a year after English producer Richard Gordon's initial, disappointing foray into voodoo territory with *Curse of the Voodoo* (1965), Gordon took another shot at the subject and co-executive produced *Naked Evil* (1966). While *Curse of the Voodoo* is a difficult enough picture to see these days, *Naked Evil* is nearly impossible. This is a great pity, for the film is a unique, engrossing, and suspenseful addition to voodoo's cinematic subset. Shot in four weeks for about $150,000 as a "quota picture," the story has an English college beset by Obeah (the Jamaican form of voodoo) as some of the students become embroiled in a gang war between two rival crime lords, one of which employs an obi-man (sorcerer) to work his evil. Apart from its novel plotline, *Naked Evil* is one of the few films to effectively juxtapose Christianity and voodoo (though, naturally, it shows a bias towards the former) by pitting the power of the Christian faith (in the person of the rather obviously-named Father Goodman) against the power of voodoo sorcery (in the form of the obi-man Amazan).

Unfortunately, *Naked Evil* received the scantiest of U.S. releases when its American distributor went bankrupt. Consequently, in 1978, Gordon sold the rights to exploitationer Sam Sherman, who bookended the black and white film with about twenty (awful) minutes of color footage starring Lawrence Tierney (all shot in one day at a cost of about $5,000). Sherman then released the 'new' feature to television as *Exorcism at Midnight*. Even this bastardization (which Sherman readily admits was "just a way of getting another pressing out of the grapes") has disappeared from view.

While perhaps not as well-crafted as say *The Plague of the Zombies*, *Naked Evil* remains one of the more atmospheric and thought-provoking of its voodoo contemporaries. "I'd thought it would be a real horror picture," remarked a disappointed Richard Gordon, "and that there would be much more use made of the voodoo stuff and less of the gangsterism and all that. It's not what I would really call a genre picture in its present form. It's sort of neither fish nor fowl." Despite Gordon's regrets, *Naked Evil* is still a fairly tasty bird. It's a pity that at present it's not readily available, for (unlike so many of its more accessible brethren) it deserves to be seen.

The final voodoo film of the 1960s was a belated entry in AIP's Edgar Allan Poe series (starring Vincent Price, of course). "*The Oblong Box* is the fifth Edgar Allan Poe subject to be made by AIP in England," reported the film's pressbook (with the other four being *The Masque of the Red Death*, 1964; *The Tomb of Ligeia*, 1964; *War-Gods of the Deep*, 1965; and *The Conqueror Worm*, 1968). Like its two latter sister productions, *The Oblong Box* takes nothing from Poe but the name. Still, as AIP publicity takes such pains to point out, "It is typical of Edgar Allan Poe terror-territory, where the atmosphere is one of impending doom, where every awful happening is the harbinger of something worse." While not as good as its Anglo predecessors (the muddled misfire *War-Gods of the Deep* excepted), *The Oblong Box* manages to generate a substantial and melancholy atmosphere which does indeed conjure up the mood of America's greatest terror scribe.

Perhaps because it is *not* one of the 'Corman Poes' and sports a decidedly different texture as well, this period tale of a man disfigured and made mad by a voodoo curse who subsequently takes revenge on those he feels have wronged him has long been looked upon as a weak afterthought in the AIP/Price/Poe cycle. Conventional fan 'wisdom' has it that *The Oblong Box* is a dull, weak, disappointing entry in AIP's Poe series—when, in fact, nothing could be further from the truth. Thanks to excellent acting, a lively storyline, convincing period settings and costumes, and some involving direction from Gordon Hessler, it remains one of AIP's better non–Corman films from the 1960s.

Voodoo-wise, the opening ceremonial sequence and the few scenes with the "witchdoctor" (played with a calm menace by Danny Daniels) sitting before his bubbling cauldron create a terrifying voodoo ambiance that effectively permeates the rest of the picture.

The Oblong Box did well at the box office, earning AIP just over a million dollars in film rentals. Long thought of as the 'poor relation' to AIP's Poe family, *The Oblong Box* deserves respect from both Poe lovers and voodoo fans alike, closing the Sixties on a high voodoo note.

For voodoo cinema (just as for fashion and for music) the Seventies proved to be a wildly uneven time period. Moreso than in any other decade, screen voodoo fell into the crass hands of exploitationers everywhere (not only in the U.S. but in far-flung filmlands like Mexico, Spain, and Italy). In fact, the 1970s became voodoo's busiest decade, with ten full-fledged theatrical releases hitting the big screen. Too bad only a few of them are worth the celluloid they were filmed on.

First up were two hold-overs from the 1960s: *Isle of the Snake People* and *I Eat Your Skin*. Both these features sat on the shelf (for three and *seven* years, respectively) before finally hitting the big screen in 1971. Sadly, neither was worth the wait. The Mexican/American co-production of *Isle of the Snake People* cast Boris Karloff (in one of his final four film appearances) as a wealthy plantation owner by day and a black-clad voodoo priest by night. Cheap and garish, the picture's only redeeming facet is Karloff's game performance (but since the venerable veteran is onscreen for only about ten minutes, it comes as too little and too late).

Though definitely on the cheesy side, *I Eat Your Skin* is actually better than its exploitative title would indicate (thankfully no skin—or any other body part for that matter—is ever eaten). Made by low-budget Connecticut-based moviemaker Del (*Horror of Party Beach*) Tenney, the bizarre story has a mad scientist turning the voodoo-practicing island natives into oatmeal-faced zombies via radiation and snake venom(!). While no undiscovered classic, this voodoo obscurity is certainly more entertaining than the three Spanish hoodoo horrors that followed: *Vengeance of the Zombies* (1972; Paul Naschy's silly mix of voodoo, Hinduism, and the walking dead), *The Night of the Sorcerers* (1973; a gory but devastatingly dull tale of vampiric leopard-women(!) on the Dark Continent), and *Voodoo Black Exorcist* (1975; a lackluster combination of voodoo and mummies, and the worst of the lot).

Into the multi-national mix came the British *Vault of Horror* (1973), Amicus' less successful follow-up to their hit anthology *Tales from the Crypt* (1972). Considering the poor quality of most of this omnibus' sorry stories, it would have been better had Amicus simply closed the door of this *Vault* and walked away. The final tale ("Drawn and Quartered"), however, proved a clever and innovative voodoo variation on *The Picture of Dorian Gray* and the film's sole redeeming feature.

The House on Skull Mountain (1974) was an obscure, unimportant, bloodless (and actionless) tale of family voodoo in Georgia, while Lucio Fulci's Italian splatterfest *Zombie* (1979) proved just the opposite; its fiscal success both in the U.S. and abroad inspired an entire subgenre of European zombie gut-munchers. Mean-spirited, gruesome, and unpleasant, *Zombie* does deserve credit for utilizing voodoo as the source for its title creatures (*all* other flesh-eating-ghoul features have turned elsewhere, relying instead upon mad science, Satanism, and even Etruscan sorcery). *Zombie* also depicted the first (and only) zombie-vs.-shark sequence in cinema history, a truly amazing and exciting display.

Remarkably, the two best voodoo variants of the decade came from a rather unlikely source—the burgeoning blaxploitation arena. In 1972 the screen's first black vampire took the drive-ins by storm in the enormously successful *Blacula*, thanks in no small part to the imposing and cultured presence of Shakespearean actor William Marshall in the title role. Naturally, fiscal success led to a sequel, and American International talked their new star into reprising his role in their proposed *Blacula Is Beautiful* (a working title thankfully soon abandoned for the less ludicrous label of *Scream Blacula Scream*, 1973). When asked his opinion of the sequel, William Marshall complained that "It didn't add anything to the first one." His viewpoint, however, peeks strictly from behind Mamuwalde's cape, and in that sense he's right—*Scream Blacula Scream* added nothing to the character of "Blacula." What it did add, however, was a new twist (voodoo) on a tired old theme (vampirism).

Scream Blacula Scream possesses an effective and involving storyline—thanks to a liberal borrowing from a certain gothic soap opera, for it bears more than a passing resemblance to the popular 1970 feature film *House of Dark Shadows* (based on the cult hit daytime drama *Dark Shadows*). Both pictures center on an unhappy vampire seeking a cure from a sympathetic female (with *Scream* changing *Dark Shadows*' medical doctor into a voodoo priestess) while at the same time reluctantly wreaking undead havoc all around them. *Scream* even 'borrowed' *House*'s striking imagery of a troupe of uniformed policemen facing off against the lead vampire's minions. In substituting a voodoo for a scientific treatment and a black vampire for a white one, *Scream Blacula Scream* added even further interest to an already potent and pathos-laden (not to mention audience-tested) premise.

To its credit, *Scream Blacula Scream* is one of the few films to depict the *healing* power of voodoo. As Blacula himself states, "[Voodoo] can be used for good as well as evil." While not particularly profound, at least it's a more balanced portrayal of the concept.

When asked what he thought of the voodoo vs. vampirism theme in *Scream Blacula Scream*, Marshall replied "not much" and laughed. Fortunately, he still took his job seriously and, while letting a bemused humor come to the fore when appropriate, he thankfully played his character straight, becoming a truly ferocious figure when aroused while at the same time projecting a powerful pathos. Thanks in large part to leads William Marshall and Pam Grier (as well as some effective touches of humor), *Scream Blacula Scream* remains a fairly involving horror hybrid.

Voodoo's second Seventies success is 1974's black-oriented *Sugar Hill* ("It's a Face, Not a Place" rhymed the ads). Though saddled with more than its fair share of 1970s quaintness (jive talk, big hair, and powder blue pantsuits abound), *Sugar Hill* is a well-produced and often atmospheric tale of voodoo vengeance. The story has Diana "Sugar" Hill (Marki Bey, who "hated it, hated the whole thing," according to co-star Robert Quarry) call upon the voodoo deity Baron Samedi (Don Pedro Colley, whom Quarry remembers as "one of the most pretentious bastards") and his troupe of zombies to take revenge on the gangsters that killed her lover.

As a voodoo film, *Sugar Hill* possesses more integrity than most thanks to scripter Tim Kelly's genuine fascination with the Haitian religion. Though saddled with the vengeance motif so popular with AIP at the time, Kelly injected some authenticity-minded dialogue and convincing voodoo scenes into his supernatural story. Also convincing—and genuinely creepy—are the film's zombies. With their bulging, filmy eyes a milky white, their hair matted with leaves and spider webs, and their pasty gray skin highlighted so that one can almost *see* the bones beneath the dead flesh, they present a terrifying image of death revived. In one shuddery shot, two of them sit up simultaneously from their shallow graves, turn their heads slowly toward one another, and *smile*—a horrible, ghastly rictus grin. These are creatures of *evil*.

Sugar Hill's subject matter apparently spooked some of its participants. "Some of the people were quite uncomfortable with making the film, because they really were a little upset about the voodoo aspect," recalled Kelly. "I'm speaking of the local people they used in Houston [where the film was shot]" who felt "that maybe you shouldn't fool around with this stuff." Nervous bit players aside, no serious mishaps (voodoo-induced or otherwise) occurred during the four-week shoot.

Apart from these two moderately successful blaxploitation entries, voodoo cinema took a qualitative nosedive in the 1970s. Fortunately, relief was waiting just around the corner...

In the 1980s, voodoo finally came of age, breaking into the big-budget arena with a trio of thought-provoking and well-made major studio releases. *Angel Heart* (1987), *The Believers* (1987), and *The Serpent and the Rainbow* (1988) all proved worthy voodoo vehicles that took a stab at balancing the spiritual aspects of the religion with the sensationalistic traits typically flaunted by filmmakers.

At 18 million dollars, *Angel Heart* is the most expensive voodoo film to date. Amazingly (for money rarely guarantees quality and more often than not results in an *inverse* ratio—the more cash, the less innovation), it's also one of the best, thanks to a unique and involving story, evocative photography, superb acting (including Robert DeNiro's sardonically chilling turn as the Devil), and inspired direction. Under writer/director Alan Parker's artistic hand, *Angel Heart* took voodoo into the shadowy region of *film noir*, mixing the hard-

Angel Heart *poster*.

boiled detective genre with both voodoo and Satanism to create an exquisitely photographed film which often emphasizes both beauty and horror almost simultaneously. Unfortunately (for the voodoo fan), *Angel Heart* focuses primarily on Satanism (especially considering one of the pivotal characters is Lucifer himself) with voodoo utilized only for background and so adds little to Voudoun's cinematic canon. But it treats its topic better than most and shows that voodoo has its place among the very best (directors, actors, production designers, cinematographers) that the silver screen has to offer. To his credit, Parker also utilized actual Haitian ceremonial music for the film's one sacramental sequence, and choreographer Louis (*Fame*) Falco studied genuine Voudoun ceremonies before creating the scene's dance arrangements.

Shot at roughly the same time as *Angel Heart* (and released only three months later) was the only full-fledged voodoo film to date that deals with the Hispanic voodoo variation of Santería. While it's difficult to argue that *The Believers* is as good a *film* as the atmospheric, noirish *Angel Heart*, it definitely stands as a better *voodoo* movie, since *The Believers* places voodoo firmly in the fore rather than relegating it to simple background color like its sister production. The story revolves around a New York police psychologist (Martin Sheen) who runs afoul of a Brujeria (a twisted form of black magic) cult sacrificing children to attain their material goals.

The Believers is one of the few films in voodoo cinema to take a respectful (rather than exploitative) view of its subject. "[Santería] is a religion with much strength and dignity," opined screenwriter/associate producer Mark Frost, "a force for good that is often used for healing." Beginning with Frost's script, this respect for its topic traveled through the director down to the cast.

"We made a very strong point in the movie of separating this mad cult [Brujeria], which is sacrificing children," reflected star Martin Sheen, "from the practices of Santería, which is, in New York City, a very important part of the Hispanic community."

In his quest for authenticity, director John Schlesinger utilized a source from his own cast. Actress Carla Pinza (who plays Sheen's Santería-practicing housekeeper) is actually a real-life santera (Santería priestess). Revealing this fact only *after* she'd landed the role, she was immediately drafted as a technical advisor in addition to her acting duties. "Carla was also our go-between with the elders of the Santería church," recounted Frost. "They read the script and gave us their explicit approval. They even helped with suggestions. So we had their blessings in making the picture—which the more superstitious of us thought was a good idea."

Though occasionally uneven (with too much time spent on the sometimes-cloying character relationships), *The Believers* is one of the most intriguing and well-intentioned voodoo variations, presenting a fairly sympathetic picture of the religion while still remaining an entertaining (if flawed) horror film. Not an easy task, actually.

The Eighties saved the best (voodoo-wise, anyway) for last with the release of *The Serpent and the Rainbow* in 1988. Based on Harvard ethonobotonist Wade Davis' nonfiction book of the same name, the (fictionalized) cinema story has a young anthropologist (Bill Pullman) journey to Haiti (on the eve of the revolution) in search of the mysterious 'zombie powder' which can seemingly make a person appear dead while still alive. There he becomes embroiled in the local Voudoun religion as well as coming up against a political figure named Petraud (ZakesMokae), head of the dreaded Ton Ton Macute (Haitian secret police) *and* an evil voodoo sorcerer. ("The villain [Petraud]," explained director Wes Craven, "is the symbol for all the terrorism going on in the country.")

Employing the book's author as a guide and technical advisor, Craven shot for a month in Haiti in February 1987. Through Davis, Craven sought the blessing of a Voudoun priest (an American-educated houngan named Max Beauvoir), who performed rituals offering the protection of the loas for the production's cast and crew. "[Producer] David [Ladd] and I attended real voodoo ceremonies," declared Craven, "and talked with real voodoo priests. We told them we wanted to do a movie about voodoo and that we wanted to treat the subject fairly. And to prove how serious we were, we asked that we be given protection, through a voodoo ceremony, before filming actually started."

Despite such spiritual precautions, shooting in the poorest country in the Western Hemisphere proved a daunting task. With disease running rampant and sanitation nearly non-existent (food and water were often contaminated, and raw sewage ran in open ditches along the streets), Craven reported that "nearly three-fourths of the cast and crew had come down with something…just about everybody was suffering from nausea, vomiting, or dizziness." Craven also recalled how the production was "faced with riots because the estimated 2000 extras we were using kept asking for more money." As a consequence, location shooting was completed over the next eight weeks in the more stable environment of the neighboring Dominican Republic.

The film's authentic source material and locales provided opportunities for Craven to capture—more than any other fictional film before or since—the feel of Haiti and of Voudoun. Scenes of abject poverty appear with an alarming casualness, offering glimpses of the wooden shacks and rusted roofs, the rutted dirt streets, and the ragged clothing and bare feet of the local populace. Such dismal sights alternate with scenes of sublime beauty as a candlelit Voudou procession moves through the forested mountains or Voudoun acolytes bathe in the restorative waters of a sacred waterfall (a Voudoun "cathedral," as one character calls it). "There is great beauty and compassion in [Voudoun]," states one character, and Craven's camera bears this out. *The Serpent and the Rainbow* is perhaps the only film to effectively capture the almost desperate appeal of the Voudoun worldview felt by Haiti's impoverished millions.

For most of its running time, the film deals in a naturalistic and mature manner with such central Voudoun topics as possession by the loa ("In Haiti," explains a character, "our god is not just in his heaven, he's in our bodies, in our flesh"), the incorporation of Catholic iconography into Voudoun worship ("Haiti is eighty-five percent Catholic and one hundred and ten percent voodoo; for us, Erzuile and the Virgin Mary are the same"), and, of course, zombies.

Regarding zombies, *The Serpent and the Rainbow* comes the closest of all its cinematic brethren to an accurate depiction of the phenomenon (discounting, of course, the film's climactic mystical pyrotechnics as the expected visual poetic license). Not surprisingly, however, the movie both romanticizes and simplifies the motivation behind zombification. The 'recovered' zombie whom the protagonist contacts in the film, Christophe Durand (poignantly played by Conrad Roberts), is the big screen counterpart of the real-life Clairvus Narcisse, whose extraordinary case had drawn Wade Davis to Haiti in the first place. In reality, however, Clairvus was not "a grade school teacher [who] wasn't afraid to speak out for the people, for freedom" (as his character is described in the film), but a greedy, ambitious pariah at odds with his family and his community (even coming to blows with his own siblings). "Clairvus had been involved in innumerable disputes with his various brothers," reported Davis in his book. "Land [the most important economic factor in rural Haiti] was often an issue but there were others." Because of this, Clairvus was judged and condemned by a tribunal of the secret Bizango society, the unofficial authority among the rural Haitian peasantry. According to those Davis interviewed, the complaint was undoubtedly lodged (and the process paid for) by members of Clairvus' own embittered family. So while the reel story casts this former zombie as a martyr to an evil sorcerer's political ambitions, the *real* story shows him to be a hated outcast tried and condemned by his own community—his own *relations*—for his irresponsible and antisocial behavior.

While (artistic license aside) the authenticity-minded *The Serpent and the Rainbow* stands as voodoo cinema's veritable poster child, it's also a fine horror movie in its own right (in fact, one of the best of the decade). Wes Craven, maker of such seminal horrors as *The Hills Have Eyes* (1977), *A Nightmare on Elm Street* (1984), and, most recently, *Scream* (1996), knows his craft as well as he knows his genre. With *The Serpent and the Rainbow* he brings all his considerable talent to bear on the topic of voodoo, creating one of the most thoughtful, frightening, and entertaining entries in voodoo cinema.

The 1980s also saw a number of borderline hoodoo releases as well, including the underrated and craftily creepy *Dead and Buried* (1981; which features a small-town undertaker employing some ill-defined combination of science and voodoo to populate his little burg with normal-looking zombies), the comic-style and very entertaining anthology *Creepshow* (1982; whose wraparound involves an angry father, his vindictive child, and one mail-order voodoo doll), and the suspenseful and surprisingly effective *Child's Play* (1988; which employs a voodoo ceremony to transfer the soul of a serial killer into a two-and-half-foot plastic doll and so created one of the decade's most profitable and entertaining film franchises).

Of course, for every *Angel Heart* or *Serpent and the Rainbow*, there were two or three direct-to-video aberrations like *Zombie Island Massacre* (1984), *Zombie Nightmare* (1987; arguably Adam West's worst film—and that's quite a boast), and *Headhunter* (1989), none of which are worth the video tape they're recorded on.

The only other theatrically released voodoo film of the 1980s fell well short of its three hoodoo brethren. Though called *Scared Stiff* (1987), this muddled and dull low-budget bastard-child would have been more accurately named *Bored Stiff*. Still, three out of four ain't bad, and, though admittedly a bit sparse on the big screen, the 1980s stand as a triumphant decade for voodoo cinema.

Discounting such direct-to-video dreck as *Voodoo Dawn* (1990), *Voodoo Dolls* (1990), *Maniac Cop III* (1992), *Shrunken Heads* (1994), and *Voodoo* (1995), the current decade has seen only one theatrically-released voodoo film, 1995's *Tales from the Hood*. Though uneven (as are all anthologies), this black-oriented omnibus with a social conscience (Spike Lee served as the executive producer) put a supernatural spin on such heavy topics as police brutality, child abuse, racism, and black-on-black violence. Sadly, its voodoo episode ("KKK Comeuppance") is the weakest of the four segments, due mainly to the unconvincing playing of Corbin Bernsen as a racist Southern politician who encounters a legion of dolls inhabited by the souls of murdered slaves. Though disappointing on the voodoo front, *Tales from Hood* still remains one of the better horror anthologies extant.

Over the years, the Voudoun religion has seen a lot of bad press, largely because those who wrote of it were outsiders who feared what they often termed this "savage cult." This fear stemmed from the slavery within which the religion was born (or, more accurately, *re*born from its African roots). The white masters saw Voudoun as a powerful unifying force, one that could incite action and build hope in their oppressed slaves. (In fact, it helped do just that, for, after a thirteen-year struggle beginning in 1791, Haiti became the site of the only successful and lasting slave revolt in the history of the Western world.) As such, Voudou was something to be feared. For the most part, voodoo cinema has reflected and emphasized such sentiments. "The Relegation of 'voodoo' to the horror genre," conjectures Joseph Murphy in his book *Working the Spirit*, "reflects mass America's real horror of independent black power. If voodoo was powerful enough to free the slaves, might it not free their descendants?" Food for thought, anyway.

If, as some have asserted, movies mirror life, voodoo movies often seem to take the form of a *funhouse* mirror, reflecting a bizarre and distorted image of its subject. Just as with gazing at one's reflection in the carnival looking glass, however, seeing such an anomaly can be both entertaining and a little frightening. Many voodoo pictures also possess a shard of verisimilitude here and there, making a glance into their depths even more worthwhile. Keep in mind, however, as you follow a zombie through the cane fields or watch an unfortunate writhe in pain when some painted witch doctor stabs a pin into a doll, that most of these movies are no more accurate a reflection of the Voudoun religion than *Rosemary's Baby* (1968) is of Christianity.

While some hoodoo horrors are good, many are bad, and a few are downright ugly, most voodoo movies contain at least the promise (occasionally fulfilled, more often not) of a glimpse into an alternate worldview and spirituality that can be both fascinating and unsettling. Besides, without voodoo, where would George Romero be today?

> I originally penned this piece for a friend's proposed fanzine (to be titled *There Is No Yeti*)—hence its more informal tone. But when that failed to materialize, editor Jim Clatterbaugh kindly "aired" it in *Monsters from the Vault* magazine, issue 21 (March 2006).

ECONOMY OF BUDGET, ECONOMY OF SCALE: THE GOLDEN AGE OF MADE-FOR-TV TERRORS

Back in the late 1960s and early '70s, we pre-teens and adolescents enamored of all things ghoulish dwelt in a halcyon heyday of television horror. While local programs like *Nightmare Theater* ruled our late Friday Night airwaves with welcomed repetitive showings of cinematic "classics" like *Horrors of the Black Museum* (I lost count of how many Junior High slumber parties culminated in the near-ritualistic watching of this gruesome delicacy presented by Channel 7's "The Count"—the damned thing seemed to be running at least once a month!), a bevy of original, made-for-television primetime terrors further tickled our shiver-hungry spines.

At the forefront of this TV Gothicism stood Dan Curtis, originator of the classic (and campy) soap opera *Dark Shadows* (dubbed "*Mike* Shadows" by industry wags, due to the near-daily gaffs so clearly visible on this seat-of-your-pants production). Vampires, werewolves, ghosts, zombies, witches, warlocks, disembodied hands, Frankenstein's Monster, Jekyll and Hyde, Dorian Gray, The Turn of the Screw, Death Takes a Holiday—anything and everything in the horror vernacular was plundered by Curtis and Co. during the show's five-year run. But ol' Dan wasn't content to sit on his Dark Laurels. No, he needed to make movies. So, after a couple of *Dark Shadows* theatrical features (one good, one bad—and fans of the show [and movies] need not ask which is which), he settled in for a long run of what he knew best—TV terror. Though Curtis' output could be most charitably described as "uneven," he brought a wring-every-dollar sensibility to his airwave action, not to mention a literary-mindedness that saw him variously write, produce or direct (sometimes all three) TV movie versions of *Dr. Jekyll and Mr. Hyde* (1968), *Dracula* (1973), *Frankenstein* (1973), *The Picture of Dorian Gray* (1973) and *The Turn of the Screw* (1974). While none of these often impoverished (with some even shot using that shoddy, soap opera–style, never-looks-quite-real videotape) productions could be labeled "definitive" versions (all of them have far superior antecedents—and often descendants—in the cinematic world), they at least exposed a generation of boob tube babies to these classic stories (sort of a cinematic rendition of *Classics Illustrated*). And while some came off as rather dull costume dramas (*Picture* and *Turn*), others brought a bit of innovation in terms of casting and handling (*Jekyll*, *Dracula* and *Frankenstein*). Then there was the memorable and far-reaching (*X-Files* anyone?) *The Night Stalker* TV movie and subsequent series, though I've always felt the telefilm's success was due primarily to Richard Matheson's clever script and Darren McGavin's quirky characterization. (Forget the inferior follow-up, *The Night Strangler*, with its too-dull-to-be-believed plot and "monster," played by the too-dull-to-be-withstood Richard Anderson; though the "Underground Seattle" setting was an eerily clever conceit—too bad the *real* Underground Seattle is nothing like the expansive subterranean lair seen in the movie. There *is* an Underground Seattle tour you can take in that fair city; and while it's very interesting—and slightly creepy—you won't find the lofty, backlit atmosphere seen in the telefilm, just a few dusty storefronts and a rather amusing, still-standing early version of a flush toilet!)

Anyway, the now mostly forgotten literary variations (mere blips on the television horizon) and the still-potent *Night Stalker* were mere warm-ups for Curtis' Halloween valentine to TV terror lovers everywhere: *Trilogy of Terror*.

Your first kiss, the day JFK was assassinated, and the first time you saw that little Zuni Fetish doll may be the most memorable milestones in an American movie-lover's life. OK, perhaps that's a bit strong (drop out the first kiss part), but no other TV movie has seemingly had such a far-ranging effect on so many viewers as the final segment of the omnibus *Trilogy of Terror*. The stark ridiculousness of the whole thing (a 12-inch *doll* with a steak knife, for god's sake!) was transformed into something palpably real by Curtis' roving, floor-level camera, low angle shots and (un)steadycam proclivities, not to mention a truly terrified tour de force by Karen Black. And that final, shuddery shot of the squatting, toothsome Black with her butcher knife certainly peeled the psyches of more than a few of us couch potatoes. *Brrrrr*!

Another horror highlight from the land of TV terror came in the uniquely bizarre form of *Gargoyles* (1972). Though there's not much here acting-wise to differentiate it from its run-of-the-mill boob-tube contemporaries (Cornel Wilde has never been the most dynamic of leads—even in his younger days; and then-nobody Scott Glenn obviously took some heavy-duty acting lessons between here and *The Right Stuff*), and director Bill L. Norton relies a bit too heavily on the old slo-mo effect, *Gargoyles* remains intriguing for its highly original story line and Ross Wheat's effective monster costumes.

But for me, the absolute pinnacle of delicious airwave agony came in the form of *Don't Be Afraid of the Dark* (1973). This is the one—the single most terrifying TV movie ever made. Though I haven't seen it in nearly three decades, images of those little dried apple-faced demons who lived in the bricked-up bottomless pit behind the fireplace (or something) haunt me still. The film plays upon the fear of the dark (obviously), and brilliantly conjures up the terror of the unseen—while also *not* disappointing the viewer when it finally solidifies that fear and brings it into the light. It's one of the few movies that has its chill-inducing cake and eats it too.

Don't Be Afraid of the Dark—*unless these three terrors are after you.*

I have to confess, however, that I have little desire to revisit this television gem—for two reasons. First, since it was one of the few films (much less *TV* movies) that really, truly scared me, I want to savor that rarest of rare memories rather than clutter it up with my now-adult sensibilities and skepticism. And second, I'm almost positive it's not nearly as good as my on-the-cusp-of-adolescence memory has made it out to be. Never mind, that final shot of Kim Darby's body being dragged into the blackness, and the triumphant creatures' demonic whisperings—with Darby's voice now among them—is enough for me.

There's one more TV terror I'd like to ballyhoo, a little-seen and seemingly forgotten bit of boob-tube uniqueness (an oxymoron, perhaps?) not to be missed by fans of the particularly literate (and literal!) shudder: *An Evening of Edgar Allan Poe* (1970). Financed by AIP-TV, and produced, directed and co-adapted by Ken Johnson (who came from directing *Adam-12* episodes, and went on to direct/produce/write/etc. various *Incredible Hulk*, *V* and *Alien Nation* TV movies/miniseries/etc., not to mention a turn on *The Bionic Woman*—perhaps he leaves *that* one off his resume), this is a word-for-word recitation of four Poe stories. Dull, you say? Not a bit—at least not when the storyteller is the mellifluous master of menace himself, Vincent Price (even my five-year-old son was enthralled). Price, the only cast member, performs faithful recitations of four Poe stories: "The Tell-Tale Heart," "The Sphinx," "The Cask of Amontillado," and "The Pit and the Pendulum." Each recitation takes place on an appropriate and realistic set, ranging from 19th century drawing room

Television terror at its finest (and most literate): the 1970 Poe-stravaganza An Evening of Edgar Allan Poe.

to sumptuous dining hall to rat-infested dungeon. The marvelous sets are matched by equally striking costumes for Price. Price proves himself a storyteller supreme, going from drawing room civility to the passion of raging madness and all points in between. Poe's stories, macabre and fascinating, are brought to palpable life by the inflections of Price's resonant voice, the gestures of his hands, and the exquisite glint of madness in his eyes. The camerawork (including well-timed zooms, and changes in focus and perspectives that punctuate the frisson at hand) accents Price's movements and pointed tones, and the lighting effects and camera angles are used as effective exclamations. The full terror to be found in the dark genius of Edgar Allan Poe is made frighteningly accessible by the storytelling talent of Vincent Price. If Poe himself were alive, even he would give a shudder.

In pondering these brilliant moments in television horror history, it becomes apparent that the one thing all these small-screen gems have in common (and which so many big-screen extravaganzas lack these days, especially in today's blockbuster-mentality Hollywood) is a clever and original story. Lacking in cash and resources, the television filmmakers who created these fantastic frightfests made certain that their productions began with unique plots and characters upon which they could hang their small-screen shivers. It just points up the fact that nothing gets under your skin like a good story—and nothing leaves you as cold and empty as expensive, pretty images stretched over a bad one.

> Shortly before the publication of my book *The Werewolf Filmography*, blogger Rod Lott asked me to come up with a piece for his excellent *Flick Attack* website. Whether the fact he posted it on April 1, 2017, has any significance or not, well…

GUEST LIST: BRYAN SENN'S TOP 7 UNSUNG WERE-GEMS

When horror buffs turn their attention to werewolves (and who among us hasn't done *that* on occasion?), a number of tried-and-true titles invariably spring to mind: *The Wolf Man*, *I Was a Teenage Werewolf*, *Curse of the Werewolf*, *The Howling*, *An American Werewolf in London*, etc. But alongside these well-known classics lurk a pack-ful of impressive beasts prowling mostly unseen through the darkness of obscurity. So I thought it'd be (ahem) illuminating to shine a full moon light on a few lesser known and underappreciated specimens of lycancinema. Folkore dictates that the seventh son of a seventh son is destined to become a werewolf, so here are seven werewolf movies you didn't know you needed to see, but by God you do…

The Werewolf of Woodstock (1975; USA)
Premiering on January 4, 1975, on *ABC's Wide World of Entertainment*, this made-for-television attempt to cash in on the Woodstock phenomenon was executive produced by none other than Dick Clark. Which begs the question: Why is the film's music so *awful*? In any case, it's all here: cheesy rock riffs played on an abandoned Woodstock stage; a hippy chick heroine who keeps re-naming her dog according to the signs of the zodiac; a lycanthropy-causing lightning strike(!); *King Kong*/Beauty and the Beast thematics; goofy cops (including a laid-back detective sporting an ever-present Mike Nesmith beanie); a music-hating werewolf lured out of hiding by a loud rock band; and, best of all, a wolfman making his getaway in a dune buggy! Of course, what's *not* here are Emmy-winning performances, a cogent screenplay, or any semblance of objective quality. Still, given the right frame of mind (mood-enhancing substances recommended), *The Werewolf of Woodstock* can be a deliciously entertaining slice of made-for-1970s-TV cheese that, at a mere 66 minutes, never outstays its groovy welcome.

It's a shame that, after its initial airing, *The Werewolf of Woodstock* disappeared like some festival crowd after the reefer's run out, and has received no legitimate video release. For those dying to see flower power combat lycanthropy, or who just have to see a dune buggy–driving wolfman, it's well worth hunting down this *Werewolf* online or via bootleg DVD.

Night of the Howling Beast (1975; Spain)
This seventh entry in Spaniard Paul Naschy's thirteen-strong Waldemar the Werewolf series may not be the best (1981's *The Craving* wins that honor), but it may very well be the most entertaining of the bunch. It's certainly the most eventful and uncategorically the wildest, tossing Tibetan bandits, sexy cannibal she-demons, a beautiful sorceress, and the Abominable Snowman(!) into its lycan-mix. Leaving off his beloved Gothicism (which permeates nearly all his other were-flicks), writer-star Naschy penned a tale of anthropologist Waldemar Daninsky (Naschy) joining an expedition to search for the fabled Yeti in Tibet. Containing nearly as many outré elements as there are yak hairs on Lawrence Talbot, this *Night* offers the following:

Night of the Howling Beast *(1975): Paul Naschy's seventh—and craziest (wolfman vs. yeti, anyone?)—Waldemar the Werewolf entry. (Mexican lobby card)*

cannibalistic nympho-demons; Tartan bandidos; outdoor gunfights (in which a trio of brave Europeans take down more bad guys with their tiny revolvers than a score of bandits manage with full-on machine guns); a brutal despot who skins girls alive as "treatment" for his nasty boils; a beautiful witch whose sadism and lust for power leads her to offer her own body to Waldemar while intoning "You will obey me—as a man and as a beast!"; a prisoner revolt of half-naked nubiles (led by a captive *princess*, no less); half a dozen werewolf attacks; several naked women with the flesh from their backs peeled off in sheets (a sequence that earned the film a spot on the infamous "video nasties" list in England in the 1980s); and, of course, a cameo by the Abominable Snowman himself, culminating in an exciting monster-vs.-monster showdown between our heroic lycanthrope and the enraged yeti.

Naschy himself characterized this anomalous film as "a comic-strip brought to the screen; with the Wolf Man, Tartars, the Yeti, action, the ever-present curse of the werewolf, and the Tibetan flower which frees Waldemar from this curse. In short, a film that I find very amusing." And so will most lycan-fans, particularly those with a taste for offbeat Eurohorror.

Dog Soldiers (2002; UK)

"It's a monster movie full of outrageous blood and guts but given some truly unique twists," said *Dog Soldiers* star Sean Pertwee. "It begins like an Army documentary, develops into a scary chase movie and then becomes *Zulu* with werewolves…" A platoon of British soldiers on a training exercise in the Scottish Highlands fall prey to a pack of werewolves. The soldiers hole up in an isolated farmhouse and try to find a way to defend themselves against the seemingly unstoppable lupine marauders. It's a simple, straightforward action/horror scenario that springs to vivid life due to an electric pace, crisp writing, well-drawn characters, intense human conflict, brilliant acting, evocative direction (courtesy of Neil [*Descent*] Marshall making his feature debut), atmospheric photography, thrilling action set-pieces, a shocking (and judicious) use of gore and black humor, and absolutely *the* most terrifying lycanthropes ever to slash across the silver screen. (These werewolves mean business: at one point a beast literally rips the head off one soldier and *throws it* at another!)

What *Aliens* did for the hoary old otherworldly B.E.M.s (bug-eyed monsters), *Dog Soldiers* did for werewolves—transforming the generally solitary tortured-soul creature into a group of lightning-fast, cunning, vicious, and near unstoppable killing machines.

Though its opening weekend gross was the biggest for a horror film released in the U.K., *Dog Soldiers* failed to find an American theatrical distributor and ended up premiering (in an edited version) on the Sci-Fi channel. Which makes about as much sense as leaving The Slaughtered Lamb for a midnight stroll on the moors, since *Dog Soldiers* stands hairy head and shaggy shoulders above most other New Millennium werewolf efforts.

Audie & the Wolf (2008; USA)

It doesn't take a lot of money to make a great film. All it takes is a clever script, well-drawn characters, a unique tale to tell, a talented cast and crew that will work for next to (or exactly) nothing, and the superhuman determination to pull it all together. Yes, that's "all" it takes to make a low-budget winner. And one wonders why they come so few and far between...

But it *can* be done. Just look to the likes of George Romero (*Night of the Living Dead*), Tobe Hooper (*The Texas Chain Saw Massacre*) or John Sayles (*Return of the Secaucus Seven*). Writer-director Brian Scott O'Malley (a Roger Corman alumnus) may not have that pedigree, but lightning definitely struck on his *Audie and the Wolf*, a fresh, original, and clever low-budget horror romcom filled with engaging characters brought to likable life by excellent (if largely unknown) actors. The story of a "reverse werewolf" (as lead Derek Hughes put it) has a wolf transform into a man (dubbed "John" by the grocery delivery girl, Audie, who falls for him) during the three-day cycle of the full moon. As John struggles valiantly (and fails) to curb his appetite for fresh meat (with his partially-eaten victims becoming undead zombies kept locked in the basement!), Audie must find a way to tame the beast inside him.

Audie and the Wolf carries a professional gloss missing from most ultra-low-cost efforts. With a miniscule budget under $50,000, keeping locations to a minimum (mostly a large Hollywood home and its well-manicured grounds), the gore realistic, and the gags flowing (but flowing naturally from the story and characters, not grafted-on jokes flying willy-nilly) proved imperative. The witty dialogue at times softens the horror of the situation and at others intensifies it. For instance, Audie tells an occultist, "[John is] afraid to leave the house, he doesn't know anything, and he can't stop eating meat." At this, the woman quips, "Sounds like a typical American." At another point a shocked witness to one of John's killings exclaims, "You were going to eat her!" to which a crazed John shoots back, "If she didn't want to get eaten, she shouldn't have been made of *meat*!" Indeed.

Werewolf Fever (2009; Canada)

There's something very appealing about a hamburger. Simplicity itself—a bun, a well-grilled piece of meat and a few condiments—it's meant to be eaten quickly, enjoyed in the moment, and then forgotten. One could say the same about *Werewolf Fever*, a low-budget indy filmed on weekends at the real-life Kingburger Drive-In restaurant in Renfrew, Ontario, Canada. Simple, self-contained, and ultimately satisfying, *Werewolf Fever* is the cinematic equivalent of a tasty fast-food meal.

A simple tale of a werewolf laying seige to the local hamburger joint, picking off the employees (plus a few late visitors) one by one, *Werewolf Fever* was shot at the Kingburger during weekends in the summer of 2007 (it didn't see post-production completion until 2009, when it played the festival circuit before a 2011 DVD release).

Though *Werewolf Fever* starts slow, once the lycanthrope shows up fifteen minutes in, it's beasts, blood and burgers for the duration. Unlike so many micro-budgeted efforts, *Werewolf Fever* never outstays its welcome. Jack-of-all-cinema-trades Brian Singleton (director, writer, co-producer, cinematographer *and* editor) avoids that deadly trap into which so many amateur auteurs fall—seeing every shot as a masterpiece. Consequently, Singleton trimmed the footage fat to a lean, easily digested 66-minute running time.

Singleton manages to create a number of memorable moments, the most striking being when the beast attacks roller-skating waitress Sandy. After a swipe of his clawed hand sends her to the ground, she looks up to see her own leg, severed at the knee, rolling upright across the parking lot on its solitary skate until finally falling over. ("We rolled the skate across the parking lot more than 30 times to get the right take," laughed Singleton.) Later, as the survivors creep out to see what has happened to Sandy, they look up to spot the creature standing atop the drive-in gnawing on her severed limb—roller skate still attached—before lifting it above its head like a trophy, roaring in triumph, then tossing it down at their feet.

Horrific and humorous at the same time, these scenes encapsulate the outrageous enthusiasm of this hey-let's-put-on-a-werewolf-show production.

Game of Werewolves (2011; Spain)

Kurt Vonnegut once said of the concept of black humor that "The biggest laughs are based on the biggest disappointments and the biggest fears." And few fears are bigger—or more primal—than that of being dismembered and eaten. In this "Comedia Bestial" (Bestial Comedy), as *Game of Werewolves*' Spanish poster proclaims it, black comedy gallops through the film like a mighty were-steed as struggling writer Tomas (Gorka Otxoa) returns to his ancestral village only to be targeted as a sacrifice to a werewolf imprisoned in the town catacombs, a sacrifice necessary to prevent the activation of a "second curse" that could destroy the entire town.

The comedy arises naturally from the characters' reactions to the horrific absurdity of the situations, with the attacks coming fast and furious as vicious counterpoints to the dark humor of the situation. Far from a silly spoof, this *Game* is played straight, as are the truly terrifying monsters. Writer-director Juan Martinez Moreno wanted his werewolves to have substance, heft, and therefore eschewed CGI in favor of stuntmen in impressive-looking weresuits. These creatures, with their hullking hirsute bodies, sport striking red eyes set deep in a wolfish, fang-filled face.

Though taking the standard werewolf-stalking-the-village approach for the first half, the movie turns things upside down when the "second curse" kicks in and the *entire village* transforms en masse into vicious lycanthropes who then chase and attack the small group of humans. Such a clever switch not only ups the lycan-ante but the action (and horror) quotient as well, leading to an exciting werewolf car chase (with the old auto driven by Tomas' tough *grandmother*), some impressive stunt work as werewolves leap twenty feet through the air to pounce on their victims, and a desperate final stand in the old church that ends with a literal bang.

Game of Werewolves does for lycanthropes what *Shaun of the Dead* did for zombies... except *Shaun* was a big hit and received wide distribution in the U.S., whereas *Game* remains woefully—and unfairly—obscure to most American viewers. Don't let the nonsensical title fool you ("In America it's *Game of Werewolves* I guess because of *Game of Thrones*," posited Moreno); for those looking for a funny, scary, affecting, and highly entertaining werewolf outing, this *Game* is one well worth playing.

WolfCop (2014; Canada)

A werewolf policeman...who's an alcoholic...and who loves donuts? Yep, the low-budget ($1 million) Canadian horror-comedy *WolfCop* (shot in and around Regina and Moose Jaw, Saskatchewan) offers this and so much more when Lou Garou (Leo Fafard), the worst cop in the local Sheriff's department, falls victim to a Satanic ritual and emerges as... WolfCop, who sets about cleaning up the mean streets of Woodhaven, Canada.

WolfCop's appearance carefully walks that line between horror and comedy like a tightrope performer navigating above a circus audience, but with booze and donuts as his metaphorical balance pole. With dark skin, coarse hair, a black canine nose, red-rimmed lips and white protruding fangs, he appears fierce enough to be taken seriously yet, with his hulking bulk encased in a now-too-tight cop's uniform, incongruous enough to raise an amused eyebrow.

The juggling act extends to WolfCop's behavior as well. While reveling in his newfound power, which includes brutal and gruesome limb-ripping, head-decapitations, and an audacious face-skinning, WolfCop also retains at least some of Lou's humanity, communicating in brief, guttural utterances ("Lou, you're a wolf!" his friend exclaims, to which Were-Lou growlingly adds, "Cop!"); feasting on hooch and donuts (which, like Popeye and his spinach, seems to give him a boost) rather than human flesh; and acting like a cop (well, a cop in the Dirty-Harry-Meets-the-Wolfman mode anyway) by thwarting criminals not only with his claws but by using his gun as well. He even has sex while in werewolf form—resulting in the first consensual were-bestiality scene in lycancinema!

Sometimes scary, sometimes funny, sometimes shocking but always engaging, *WolfCop* breaks down the door and offers you the right to remain entertained.

The clever, suspenseful, frightening, funny, and criminally obscure Spanish horror-comedy Lobos de Arga transformed into Game of Werewolves for its English-language release.

> The year 1998 saw a raft of remakes float onto theater screens, inspiring editor Marty Bauman to solicit this essay for his groundbreaking internet magazine *The Astounding B Monster* (number 31).

ONE MORE TIME! WERE THESE FILMS REALLY NECESSARY?

The Cat and the Canary (1939)

John Willard's successful 1922 Broadway play *The Cat and the Canary* (starring Henry Hull—the *Werewolf of London* himself) had originally been filmed in 1927 by Paul Leni at Universal, and was first remade with sound in 1930 as *The Cat Creeps* (now a lost film). Universal considered yet another remake in 1938 but subsequently sold the rights to Paramount, who mounted this production. The two previous versions were both straight thrillers, whereas this 1939 rendition was tailored to the comedic talents of Bob Hope. While arguably one of the best mystery-horror films of the 1930s, *The Cat and the Canary* is also the premier mystery-*comedy* of the decade. With enough reaching hands, hidden passages and unusual plot twists to keep any Old Dark House fan happy, some genuine suspense, a hideous killer and Bob Hope one-liners make this stellar production a "streamlined, screamlined" winner (as the *New York Times* reviewer so colorfully put it). Bob Hope is likable, funny and even heroic, but he's at his best when making fun of his own fears—a sort of comedic whistling in the dark—something that audiences can identify with and admire. (When told by the sinister housekeeper that "There are spirits all around you," Hope nervously quips, "Well, could you put some in a glass, I need it badly.") Paulette Goddard makes a likable, strong-willed heroine, a pleasant and intelligent change from the standard window dressing screamer. And the supporting players all do well, headed by the urbane George Zucco and the mysterious Gale Sondergaard. Production values are high, and the climax, though brief, is unexpected and edge-of-the-seat material. One could do much worse than to sit in *this* catbird seat.

Scared Stiff (1953)

Though this slavish remake of *The Ghost Breakers* (1940) sports the same director and follows that previous film's script almost to the letter (with a half-dozen low-rent musical numbers thrown in for bad measure), it can't hold a candle to its comedy classic model. Retooled slightly for the talents of Dean Martin and Jerry Lewis (in the roles originally assayed by Bob Hope and Willie Best), the film sends the 'boys' to Cuba where they aid a lovely young girl (Lizabeth Scott) who's just inherited a haunted castle.

The script splits the wisecracks between the two stars (whose mean-spirited interplay quickly grows tiresome, with Martin constantly ordering Lewis to shut up or threatening to hit him). Sadly, Dean Martin is no Bob Hope, and the zingers fall flat coming from this sleepy-eyed crooner. And as for Jerry Lewis… well, Lewis' brand of heavy mugging and high-pitched howling can safely be called an acquired taste. Having no Gallic blood in my ancestry, I seem to lack those particular buds that would allow me to enjoy his facial calisthenics and harpy-like vocalizations. Lewis' only funny moments are those that arise from the clever script or those bits of comedy cribbed from Lou Costello (such as the "arm chair" routine seen in *Abbott and Costello Meet Frankenstein*)—which the short fat man does exceedingly better than the tall thin one. Lewis flatly stated (in *The Jerry Lewis Films*, by James L. Neibaur and Ted Okuda), "We didn't feel that *The Ghost Breakers* needed to be remade in the first place." They were right.

The Lost World (1960)

This tepid Saturday matinee filler doesn't deserve to share the same name with the 1925 Willis O'Brien silent classic. O'Brien filled his version with over 50 excitingly realistic stop-motion animated dinosaurs. In this weak remake, producer-director Irwin Allen decided a few dressed up lizards would do just fine. What's worse (in an unkind bit of irony), the talented, down-on-his-luck O'Brien worked on this production as an "effects technician" but was *not* allowed to work his stop-motion magic. This version sticks to the standard story of a small group of disparate individuals finding a lost prehistoric plateau where they encounter dinosaurs and primitive peoples before making their escape when it all blows up. The great Claude Rains stars as Professor Challenger, the leader of the expedition; Michael Rennie ("Klaatu" himself) plays a big-game hunter; Fernando Lamas is the experienced local helicopter pilot; and David ("Help meeeee!") Hedison acts as the standard hero. Unfortunately, Allen is not a good enough director to get the most out of this talented cast. Rains goes over the top with his eccentric and blustery portrayal; Rennie seems to be just walking through his role; Lamas isn't given much to do except glower; and Hedison is obviously trying too hard. The effects are anything *but* special, consisting of terrible matting and unconvincing miniatures. But Allen simply goes *too* far when he has Rains label a lizard with a frill a "brontosaurus" and a baby alligator with horns glued to its head a "tyrannosaurus rex"! Sad.

Tower of London (1962)

With a cast like Boris Karloff, Basil Rathbone, Ian Hunter and Vincent Price... wait a minute, that's the *other Tower of London*, the one released by Universal in 1939. *This* one stars the not-quite-so-illustrious personages of Michael Pate, Joan Freeman and Robert Brown. Oh yes, and Vincent Price graduates from his supporting role as the sniveling Duke of Clarence in the original to the lead part of the evil Richard himself in this remake. Here, director Roger Corman gives us a tale of murder and ghosts and conscience involving the fifteenth century monarch Richard III and his nefarious crimes to gain the English throne. As might be expected, Corman's revision comes nowhere close to the earlier film in production quality; but then the 1939 version was a relatively high-priced effort ($580,000) from a major studio whereas Corman's project was a low-budget (less than $200,000—twenty-five years later) independent entry. (Corman even borrowed some of the original's battle footage to flesh out his minimalist fight scenes.) The tones of the two films are miles apart as well, the earlier entry being an historical melodrama with horrific highlights, while the latter focused on the themes of madness, guilt and death—more in the vein of Edgar Allan Poe than medieval history (not surprising, since Corman was at this time right in the middle of his successful Poe series for AIP). Corman's version proved the more intimate of the two, with the weight of the film resting on the humped shoulders of Vincent Price playing a man who tortures and murders to achieve his ends yet suffers from his own conscience to the point of madness. The role of Richard is a fascinating one, with the script portraying him as a man who knows what is right and what is wrong, but chooses the path of evil anyway. "Is it what men do that darkens the sky, or do the skies blacken the souls of men?" asks this reflective villain. Unfortunately, *Tower of London* fails to live up to its potential. The script is structured so that the film will rise or fall with the performance of Vincent Price. He provides a larger-than-life portrayal, sprinkling his wild-eyed, open-mouthed, full-blooded delivery with moments of subtlety and emotion. It's an enjoyable performance without doubt, but an uneven one. Still, 1962's *Tower of London* remains an entertaining movie, filled with intrigue and shock and bizarre situations. More importantly, something worthwhile lurks beneath the garish surface. "He escaped the headsman's block, but he could not escape his own conscience." At least it's something to think about.

The Eye Creatures (1965)

Larry Buchanan, a Texas-based schlock filmmaker, was contracted in the 1960s by American International Pictures to produce and direct several features that the company could release directly to the seemingly bottomless pit of television. AIP gave him free reign to plagiarize their past properties, and *The Eye Creatures* is what happened when Larry decided to remake *Invasion of the Saucer Men* (1957). Despite the fact that entire scenes are copied word for word from *Invasion*, this version possesses none of the charm, humor or fun of the original. Instead, we get a 30-year-old John Ashley playing a teenager, a supporting cast of non-actors, static (non)direction, inconsistent day-for-night photography (black night sky alternating with shots of blue noonday sky *in the same scene*), and, worst of all, ridiculous, pitiful, ineffectual monsters. The original Saucer Men, with their huge bulbous heads, bug-eyes, and leathery, veined skin, are an icon of '50s monster movies. The Eye Creatures look like the Michelin Tire Man on acid doing a bad Frankenstein's Monster imitation. The scene in which they weakly try to get into a car with a crowbar is simply pitiful. And "pitiful" is the operative word for this entire tired mess. Watch *Invasion of the Saucer Men* again instead.

One Million Years B.C. (1966)

Despite its rather hackneyed story, *One Million Years B.C.* ranks as one of the best prehistoric/dinosaur films ever made (and certainly far superior to its 1940 model, the Hal Roach-produced *One Million B.C.*). While the drawing card may have been the stunning face and figure of Raquel Welch (whose generous pulchritude is the most prominent feature in the film's posters and ads), the real star of the show is stop-motion superstar Ray Harryhausen, whose meticulous animation work took nearly nine months to complete. Harryhausen's pre–*Jurassic Park* dinosaurs are so exciting and lifelike that something new can be seen with each successive viewing. He brings to vibrant life a lumbering brontosaurus, a startling realistic giant sea turtle, a lithe and deadly allosaurus, a thrilling and bloody battle to the death between a triceratops and ceratosaurus, and a swooping and diving pterodactyl who carries off the heroine as food for her hatchlings (though, fortuitously, it drops her in the surf in order to combat another pterodactyl in an exciting aerial dinofight). Costing about a dollar

This photo of Raquel Welch from One Million Years B.C. *(1966) makes it self-evident that, yes, this particular remake was* necessary...

for every year in its title, *One Million Years B.C.* grossed over $8,000,000 worldwide, making it Hammer Films' biggest commercial success. For both stop-motion and dinosaur fans, this is one remake not to be missed.

Zontar, the Thing from Venus (1966)

Aaaaargh!!! Larry Buchanan, that grade-Z filmmaker from Texas, strikes again with this uncredited remake of Roger Corman's 1956 "cult classic" *It Conquered the World* (no great cinematic treat itself, if truth be told). The cheap sets are of the "Motel 6" variety, the acting amateurish, and what new dialogue was written is contemptible. Add to this some unimaginative direction, inept camerawork, muddy lighting and a sad, dime-store monster, and the total comes to a big fat cinematic zero. John Agar is the only "name" in the cast (and the only real professional), but is given so little direction that his already flat acting style reaches new heights in banality. Agar (who starred in three of Buchanan's features) once observed, "Larry, God bless him, is a nice guy but he really was not a director." The viewer can only agree. A few bits of dialogue provoke a snort or two of derisive laughter ("I hate your living guts for what you've done to my husband and my world!"), but it's not enough to justify 80 minutes of tedium. When one character exclaims, "Zontar, you're slimy, horrible," she could just as well be describing the whole movie.

Godzilla (1998)

Despite what the cranky critics and annoyed armchair pundits said, this recent update is a thoroughly enjoyable monster romp for the '90s. Die-hard Godzilla fans complained that the Big Guy in this version didn't look anything like the original. Indeed, it's a huge relief not to have to watch yet another laughably awkward and slow-moving man-in-a-suit clomp about on tiny models. Who wants to see *that* again, when you can now watch a frighteningly realistic-looking and fast-moving giant menace brought to life via the magic of CGI? (Perhaps if the film had been named *Giant Monster Movie* rather than *Godzilla* it would have fared better.) Another frequent complaint falls on the shoulders of the *Jurassic Park* raptor-like "baby godzillas." While they may indeed conjure up images of those rapacious Spielberg dinos, the Madison Square Garden hatching/pursuit sequence is both well-shot and suspensefully-staged, and its inclusion brings the gigantic spectacle of the huge monster down to a more approachable scale. Given a good buildup, some extremely clever and exciting set-pieces (the "old fisherman" sequence and the helicopter pursuit through the canyons of Manhattan spring readily to mind), a gigantic monster that's both convincing and menacing, a horde of smaller creatures to generate a more personal menace, and a *Beast from 20,000 Fathoms*–style ending, what more could one ask? Well, more engaging *human* characters, perhaps—but this is a *monster* movie, after all (and Jean Reno's enigmatic Frenchman proved quite entertaining). Though this newest incarnation of Japan's worst nightmare may lack the brooding ambiance and topical-for-the-time subtext of the original, it remains one of the more entertaining recent remakes. And, thankfully, Raymond Burr is nowhere to be found.

Mighty Joe Young (1998)

As remakes go, this joins that all-too-rare breed of film that turns out better than its model. Scripters Lawrence Konner and Mark Rosenthal (*Star Trek IV*) and director Ron Underwood (*Tremors*) did an admirable job of transforming what was a charming yet juvenile children's film into a more mature yet still-charming update. By adding such subtexts as global ecology, hunting for profit, personal revenge (personified by a well-integrated *human* villain—something the original lacked) and the pain of childhood loss, the

1998 version surpasses the 1949 entry in terms of story and concept. It also stands (gorilla-sized) head and shoulders above the original in both acting (with Charlize Theron and Bill Paxton bringing a likable enthusiasm and determination to their lead roles) *and* special effects. While die-hard O'Brien/Harryhausen fans and stop-motion animation purists may take issue with the new, improved CGI version of Mr. Joseph Young, there's no denying its technical superiority over the admittedly well-done but uneven stop-motion effects from the original. Thankfully, those hands involved in the remake managed to instill in their 15-foot gorilla a charisma and personality that reflects and enhances O'Brien and Harryhausen's original creation. (And it does a fantasy fan's heart good to finally see Ray Harryhausen step *in front of* the camera for a brief and amusing cameo.) While 1949's *Mighty Joe Young* may please the nostalgic child in all of us, 1998's *Mighty Joe Young* satisfies both the Inner Child and the Demanding Adult in what turned out to be one of the most enjoyable adventure films of the decade.

Psycho (1998)

Once having seen it, who can forget Alfred Hitchcock's classic 1960 tale of Momma's-boy-gone-bad Norman Bates? Certainly not anyone who plunked down eight dollars to see the new colorized replica—er—remake. Oh, I'm sorry, there *were* new actors in it. But, apart from the addition of color, a few new Vince Vaughn mannerisms in place of Anthony Perkins twitches, and some loud retro wardrobe worn by Julianna Moore (playing Marion Crane's sister), there's nothing updated nor innovative here, since director Gus Van Zandt simply copied Hitchcock's film word for word and shot for shot. While this makes the new *Psycho* a good movie for those unfamiliar with the original, it makes it impossible for anyone else to really enjoy it, since the seasoned viewer spends the whole time comparing the two versions scene-for-scene. While this remake may serve Van Zandt's intent of bringing *Psycho* to those gen-Xers who think that black-and-white is simply a synonym for Geritol, it's a pointless and frustrating exercise for anyone who's seen the Hitchcock version. Not only did the Master of Suspense's original cause an avalanche of knock-offs (from such diverse sources as England's Hammer Films and America's own William Castle) and create a whole new cinematic subgenre (the "psycho-thriller"), it made an entire generation of moviegoers think twice before drawing that shower curtain. The new *Psycho* may very well make that same generation think twice before patronizing another remake.

> I was one of eight writers asked to participate in a 2003 *Midnight Marquee* magazine article (issue 67/68), edited by Anthony Ambrogio, which featured a decade-by-decade look at overrated/underrrated genre performances. So, for what it's worth, here are *my* highly opinionated selections.

OVERRATED OR UNDERRATED? PERFORMANCES

1930s:

Underrated: Bela Lugosi (as Anton Lorenzen) in *Phantom Ship* (1935; aka *The Mystery of the Mary Celeste*). One of the more infrequently seen Lugosi performances is also one of his best, as he deftly balances pathos with his more usual chilling delivery. The film isn't great, but Lugosi *is*.

Overrated: Boris Karloff (as Janos Rukh) in *The Invisible Ray* (1936). Ironically, Lugosi, who's famous for his bombast, provides the subtlety here, while Karloff, considered the more subtle and polished of the two, flails about wildly, sometimes overplaying to a near painful degree. It's as if Boris, tiring of his repeated bogeymen roles, decided to spice up his latest assignment by laying on the theatrical mannerisms gleaned from 20 years in stock theater.

1940s:

Underrated: John Carradine (as Professor Randolph) in *The Face of Marble* (1946). Carradine went from John Ford classics to Poverty Row dreck like this in just a few short years (forget 'Poor Bela,' what about 'Poor John'?). In his remarkably restrained performance here as a soft-spoken humanitarian, he downplays any opportunity the ridiculous script provides for melodramatic histrionics, opting instead for a more realistic portrayal of a misguided man driven by the best of motives.

Overrated: Hurd Hatfield (as Dorian Gray) in *The Picture of Dorian Gray* (1945). Though Hatfield is perfectly adequate as the beautiful, innocent Dorian in this classic '40s entry, his rather one-note performance has been consistently over-praised. Rarely changing expression, Hatfield walks through the role as if a blank slate—which works well at the beginning, but fails to wring any juice out of the later scenes after he's become a debauched sadist.

Even the 'King of Horror' occasionally proved fallible, as evidenced by Boris Karloff's (left) overwrought performance in The Invisible Ray *(1936). (lobby card)*

1950s:

Underrated: Any performance ever given by Whit Bissell. The ubiquitous authority figure of the 1950s and '60s, Bissell added weight and credence to whatever film he appeared in, be it via cameos (*Invasion of the Body Snatchers*, 1956) or starring roles (*I Was a Teenage Werewolf/Frankenstein*, both 1957). *Nobody* besides Bissell could have uttered "Speak, you've got a civil tongue in your head; I know you have because I sewed it back myself" and actually make the ludicrous line *work*.

Overrated: A tie: Gene Barry (as Clayton Forrester) and Ann Robinson (as Sylvia) in *War of the Worlds* (1953), who form the stiffest, most vapid and unappealing hero-heroine partnership of the decade. (Hell, even John Agar and Yvette Mimieux would have been preferable!) This film remains watchable solely for its amazing special effects and involving presentation by Byron Haskin (not to mention a classic H.G. Wells story).

1960s:

Underrated: Lon Chaney, Jr. (as Bruno) in *Spider Baby* (1964). Chaney plays Bruno as an open, honest, simple man who is placed in the unenviable position of trying to maintain a charade of normalcy in an insane situation. Much of this brilliantly quirky film's humor comes from Chaney's delicate balancing act (and he even sings the opening theme song!).

Overrated: Barbara Steele (as Katia/Asa) in *Black Sunday* (1960). Though an iconographic presence in this gothic gem (thanks to her striking angular face that somehow captures a good/evil duality—*and* to Mario Bava's impressive direction/photography), Steele's is not much of a traditional *performance* per se. She does far better *acting* in many other movies; here it's her *presence* that matters.

1970s:
Underrated: Robert Quarry (as Biderbeck) in *Dr. Phibes Rises Again* (1972). While Price provides more of the same from the first *Phibes* (but does it well, mind you), it's Quarry's prickly performance that adds the spark to this excellent (and underrated) sequel.

Overrated: Harrison Ford (as Han Solo) in *Star Wars* (1977). Though subtlety is not this cherished space oater's strong suit, Ford overacts and over-*re*acts to an almost embarrassing degree. Perhaps he misread the "Use the force, Luke" line as "Use the comical scowl/rakish grin, Harrison."

1980s:
Underrated: Terry O'Quinn (as Jerry Blake) in *The Stepfather* (1987). Nobody seems to have seen this intelligent and well-acted thriller-in-slasher's-clothing; if they had, O'Quinn's name would join the likes of Anthonys Perkins and Hopkins as providing the most fully fleshed and chilling psychopath portrayals in screen history.

Overrated: Jack Nicholson (as Jack Torrance) in *The Shining* (1980). Though his amusing-yet-chilling "Heeere's Johnny!" became a cinematic touchstone, the overrated Nicholson remains a weak spot in this underrated shiver-fest. From the first we see of him, with his evilly arching eyebrows and wild-eyed glare, we have no doubt that this man could just as easily have gone 'round the bend in a banal Motel Six setting as at the ghost-infested Overlook Hotel. Unlikable and scary to begin with, Nicholson makes for a disappointingly one-dimensional boogeyman.

1990s:
Underrated: Brendan Gleeson (as Sheriff Keough) in *Lake Placid* (1999). This overlooked winner about a 30-foot crocodile is chock full of (ahem) biting humor, offbeat characters, exciting action, and some *King Kong*-style sensibilities. The Irish Gleeson (with a dead-on American accent), as the put-upon, Twinkie-eating sheriff sensitive to sarcasm, remains believably likable while providing most of the comedy in this clever, suspenseful, funny and *fun* big-budget B-movie.

Overrated: Brad Pitt (as Louis) in *Interview with the Vampire* (1994). Not since Lawrence Talbot in *Frankenstein Meets the Wolf Man* has there been such a whiny 'cursed' protagonist. Which is fine, except that Pitt plays him like a constipated sourpuss (more fiber in his all-blood diet is obviously needed). Ironically, Tom Cruise as Lestat steals the show—after he was pegged to fail by just about everyone (Anne Rice included).

> *Midnight Marquee* magazine editor Gary Svehla asked a number of writers to come up with five "defining moments" in the evolution of horror cinema during the forty years in which the magazine had been publishing. The following is my humble contribution to that group article, which appeared in issue 69/70 in July 2003.

THINGS THAT CAME: SIGNIFICANT HORROR MOVIE TRENDS (1963-2003)

October 1, 1968: *Night of the Living Dead*, whose immense success and subsequent notoriety brought a whole new visceral take on terror (and spawned an entire subgenre of films), hits the screens. *NOTLD* showed fans and filmmakers alike that it was time for horror to get *nasty*.

December 26, 1973: The phenomenon that was *The Exorcist* brings big-studio respectability to the horror genre (and spawned its own little Satan-possessed subgenre), earning a head-spinning number of Academy Awards and nominations. From then on, 'horror' was no longer a dirty word, and big-budget bogeys became part of the Hollywood vernacular.

June 13, 1980: Though *Halloween* preceded it by two years, it took the poorly-made, poorly-acted (future-star-to-be Kevin Bacon shows none of the thespian talent here that would later propel him to the heights of Hollywood), ultra-successful *Friday the 13th* to open the floodgates and let the sea of slasher cinema spray out. Blame the countless "slice-and-dice," "stalk-and-slash," "slay-and-spray" teen-kill pics that every producer in the 1980s without an original idea in his or her head suddenly rushed into production on this mean-spirited, unpretentious popcorn-muncher. Whether you love it or loathe it, there is no denying the importance of this film in genre history. The sheer number of imitations and variations that followed, made solely to jump on the slasher bandwagon, ensures this (and its far superior predecessor, *Halloween*) a place in cinema history.

The Early 1980s: The VCR revolution takes root. When those initial top-loading, two-head, mono VCRs abruptly dropped their outrageous $1000-plus price tags down to the still outrageous but more affordable $400 region, and the $25 tapes themselves eased

Night of the Living Dead proved a game-changer for horror cinema in 1968. (lobby card)

into the $5 category, viewing habits changed forever, and genre aficionados received the priceless gift of accessibility. Affordable sell-through movies were still a few years off, but rental stores were multiplying like the oversized rabbits in *Night of the Lepus*; and now we could scour our *TV Guide* for upcoming broadcasts of our favorite horrors to tape. Suddenly, innumerable genre films—the classics, the dross, and the in-betweens—were readily available. It was an exciting time of taping, trading and building, allowing fans, researchers and writers access to things undreamt of in the pre–VCR philosophy. Fuzzy third-generation dupes, cut television prints, grainy film-chained 16mm copies—we didn't care, as we finally were able to see such elusive then-rarities as *Murders in the Zoo*, Karloff's *The Ghoul*, and even *Invasion of the Saucer Men*. I know I could never have written the books I have without the extensive film library I compiled during that oh-so-wondrous time. *Viva la Revolucione*!

June 11, 1993: The amazingly life-like dinosaurs of *Jurassic Park* make a thunder lizard–sized leap in special effects technology. For better or worse, the success of *Jurassic Park* brought computer generated imaging (CGI) to the forefront of horror/sci-fi (and mainstream) effects. After this, *anything* was possible, from the overdone wall-to-wall CGI silliness of *Attack of the Clones* to the more judicious (and more effective) CGI thrills of *Lake Placid*, *Reign of Fire* and *Eight Legged Freaks*. Technology had finally caught up with imagination. (And let's hope the latter sees as much use as the former).

> In 2000, *Monsters from the Vault* magazine (issue 11) allowed me to referee the ultimate Battle of the Horror Fan when I went ringside for Universal vs. Hammer. Who won? Read on…

UNIVERSAL VS. HAMMER: CINEMATIC GRUDGE MATCH OF THE CENTURY

Strange electrical machines crackle and spark menacingly, lightning pierces the sky overhead, peals of thunder reverberate off the massive dank stone walls of the hidden laboratory in which Colin Clive, his face a mask of insane zeal, shouts hysterically, "It's alive! It's alive! It's alive!" Soon after, a hulking figure backs out from the gloom. As it turns toward us the camera focuses in tighter and tighter to reveal the ghastly yet sadly sympathetic visage of Boris Karloff as—The Frankenstein Monster.

In an ornate hall of Castle Dracula, Peter Cushing races down a long table to leap upon the heavy red velvet curtains covering a window, ripping them down so that a shaft of life-affirming sunlight pierces the room. Then, using crossed candlesticks as a makeshift crucifix, he forces Christopher Lee's ferocious Count Dracula into the blazing sunlight. The undead fiend disintegrates into a gray, desiccated mass until all that's left of the King of the Vampires is a pile of dust—which then scatters on an unholy wind.

Separated by more than a quarter-century, these two memorable movie moments remain etched in the cinematic memories of horror film lovers everywhere, two time-capsules of shuddery excitement that represent the best of both worlds—the two very different worlds of Universal and Hammer.

In the early sound era of the late 1920s and early '30s, there was no "horror" genre per se. Movie fans had to wring their chills from tired stage melodramas and hoary Old House tales like *The Gorilla* and *The Bat Whispers* (both 1930). In 1931, however, a somewhat less-than-respected Hollywood studio named Universal (considered by the industry to be a decidedly *minor* "major") changed all that with their February 12 release of *Dracula*. At the time, however, Universal was none-too-sure of their new property and opted to promote their vampire picture along a romantic rather than horrific line, billing it as "The story of the strangest passion the world has ever known!"

Dracula's huge success at the box office quickly convinced the studio that "horror" was simply another word for "dollars," and Universal went all out in their promotion of shock and terror with their next offering of the macabre—*Frankenstein* (1931). The studio even went so far as to shoot a brief pre-credit prologue to the picture in which cast member Edward Van Sloan advises the audience that "I think it will thrill you; it may shock you; it might even *horrify* you. So if any of you feel that you do not care to subject your nerves to such a strain, now's your chance to—well, we've warned you!"

Curiously, the wholly unexpected success of *Dracula* made little immediate impact among the other studios. "U Has Horror Cycle All To Self," reported *Variety* on April 8, 1931. "With *Dracula* making money at the box office for Universal, other studios are looking for horror tales—but very squeamishly. Producers are not certain whether nightmare pictures have a box-office pull, or whether *Dracula* is just a freak. To date, no other studio has tried to follow in U's steps, one of the few occasions when a hit wasn't followed by a cycle of similar pictures." The monumental success, however, of Universal's follow-up venture, *Frankenstein*, proved that *Dracula* was no "freak" after all, and horror was here to stay. While only two other studios, Paramount and MGM, had a horror project in production at the time *Frankenstein* hit the screens in late November 1931 (*Dr. Jekyll and Mr. Hyde* and *Freaks*, respectively), by fall of 1932 five of the eight major studios had climbed aboard the horror bandwagon. With Universal as the flagship, the genre sailed into its Golden Age. The next eight years saw the creation of many of the greatest films of horror cinema: Paramount's *Dr. Jekyll and Mr. Hyde* (1931); Warner Bros.' *Doctor X* (1932), *Mystery of the Wax Museum* (1933) and *The Walking Dead* (1936); RKO's *The Most Dangerous Game* (1932) and *King Kong* (1933); MGM's *Freaks* (1932), *Mark of the Vampire* (1935) and *Mad Love* (1935); and Columbia's *The Black Room* (1935). But the undisputed champion of horror cinema, the Tinseltown Titan of Terror, was Universal.

Universal's reign as the Home of Horror lasted until 1948, when the studio finally gave up the monster ghost by introducing their stable of fiends to a flagging contract comedy team in what has proven to be one of the best horror-comedies of all time, *Abbott and Costello Meet Frankenstein*. After this, atmospheric horror gave way to the terrors of nuclear mutants and alien invaders, whose menace was presented in an almost documentary-like style.

Then, in 1957, a British film company named Hammer rescued the horror film from the cheesy clutches of assorted giant insects and B.E.M.s (Bug-Eyed Monsters) by pulling the stake from the heart of gothic horror. The commercial success of *The Curse of Frankenstein* (1957), *Horror of Dracula* (1958) and *The Mummy* (1959) breathed new life into the old monsters. Presented in living (and bloody) color for the first time, these hits insured a slew of sequels and spin-offs which transformed a small-scale outfit called Hammer Films into the new custodians of traditional horror, a job they held for nearly two decades.

But who is the superior of these two genre giants— the Germanic gothic of Universal or the colorful opulence of Hammer? Though both subsets of films have their place in this cinematic world, the advent of video has brought them into a close proximity that was never intended nor conceived of by their makers. Thus, comparisons, whether desired or not, are inevitable. Without a doubt, both studios brilliantly filled the horror niche appropriate to the cinematic climate of the time. Both were innovators who helped forge the horror genre and send it in new directions. While many horror aficionados take the safe, politically correct stand that contrasting the two studios is like comparing apples to oranges, most knowledgeable viewers ultimately declare a preference for one or the other when pressed.

While "apples and oranges" may be the common idiom of choice, a more accurate analogy for Universal vs. Hammer would be to compare German chocolate cake to Yorkshire pudding. Not only is the Germanic reference appropriate considering Universal's Teutonic influence (the studio was a haven for European filmmakers steeped in the German Expressionism of the 1920s), but Universal's films appear as dark, heavy, multi-layered confections. Hammer, on the other hand, took a more straightforward, meat and potatoes tact. In fact, just like Yorkshire pudding itself, so many of Hammer's films look weighty and delectable on the outside but sadly deflate into a formless mass when a fork breaks the crust to probe the interior.

In terms of sheer volume, the two studios produced roughly the same number of horror pictures (between fifty and sixty using a rather broad definition of "horror" that includes, for example, Universal's "Inner Sanctum" series and Hammer's many post–*Psycho* "thrillers"). While the quantity may be the same, however, *quality* is a very different matter.

Both studios, especially in their second decade of horror production, churned out their share of inferior product, usually tired continuations of their various monster series, tepid psycho-thrillers, or weak stabs at creating new horror franchises. Most Universal advocates admit that the studio's horror output went into decline in the early forties, while the Hammer junkie confesses that the late sixties saw the downward spiral of their favorite horror haven. Though both studios bucked the trend to produce some notable exceptions during their later years (Universal with such solidly entertaining programmers as *Son of Dracula* [1943] and *Abbott and Costello Meet Frankenstein* [1948], and Hammer with fairly innovative additions like *Twins of Evil* [1971] and *Vampire Circus* [1972]), it's more illustrative to look at the power hitters of their initial decades—when both companies were in their prime.

Facing facts, time and posterity have not been as kind to Hammer as that studio's advocates would have liked. When one looks at that (admittedly overused) category of "classic" horror films, Universal completely outstrips its later imitator. On a conservative tally, Universal includes in its top tier of recognized classics: *Dracula* (1931), *Frankenstein* (1931), *The Mummy* (1932), *The Old Dark House* (1932), *The Invisible Man* (1933), *The Black Cat* (1934), *Bride of Frankenstein* (1935), *Son of Frankenstein* (1939), *Tower of London* (1939), and *The Wolf Man* (1941). Okay, I can hear the Hammerphile's cry of "foul" at the inclusion of *Dracula* (which has taken more critical heat than any of the other Universal stalwarts) and *Tower of London* (a truly underrated horror-drama). So, dropping these two "questionable classics" from the Universal lineup still leaves eight heavy hitters at bat (the wood, not animal, variety). And this fails to recognize such solid second-tier gems as *Murders in the Rue Morgue* (1932), *The Raven* (1935), *Werewolf of London* (1935), *The Invisible Ray* (1936), and *Dracula's Daughter* (1936).

On the Hammer side, after the trio of *The Curse of Frankenstein* (1957), *Horror of Dracula* (1958), and *The Brides of Dracula* (1960), there are few that can even *reach* the "classic" pedestal, much less sit upon the throne. So in terms of classic horror, Universal out-strides Hammer by more than two-to-one. Even if one becomes generous with the "classic" classification and begins embracing the studios' second stringers (the Universal features listed above vs. Hammer's *The Revenge of Frankenstein*, 1958; *The Mummy*, 1959; *The Curse of the Werewolf*, 1960; *Kiss of the Vampire*, 1964; and *The Devil's Bride*, 1968), Hammer still can't close the gap, with Universal fielding a team of 15 to Hammer's 8. (Note: While one could argue that Hammer has a few *science fiction* classics held in reserve, such as *The Creeping Unknown* and—stretching a bit—*X the Unknown*, these came *before* the studio's horror period begun with *The Curse of Frankenstein* in 1957. Besides, if we step outside the horror and timeframe boundaries for Universal as well, that company later released its fair share of sci-fi classics, such as *It*

Came from Outer Space, Creature from the Black Lagoon, and *This Island Earth.*)

A comparison on a direct film by film basis also leaves Hammer in the backseat while Universal sits behind the wheel driving serenely down the cinematic highway of posterity. Beginning with *The Curse of Frankenstein*, Hammer produced six remakes which are more-or-less directly traceable to Universal originals: *Horror of Dracula*, *The Mummy*, *The Curse of the Werewolf* (Hammer's take on *The Wolf Man*), *The Phantom of the Opera* (we're speaking of Hammer's 1962 entry vs. Universal's 1943 version), and *The Old Dark House* (1966).

Most reasonable cinephiles (even avowed Hammerheads) admit without a squawk to Universal's *Frankenstein* (1931) and *The Mummy*'s (1932) superiority to Hammer's later counterparts. And absolutely no one has ever claimed Hammer's farcical abomination *The Old Dark House* to be anything but a putrid parody of James Whale's quirky, brilliant 1932 version of J. B. Priestley's novel *Benighted*. Of the three remaining matchups, only *Horror of Dracula* presents a case strong enough to sway an impartial jury in Hammer's favor. While Universal's Lugosi version opens with what may be the two finest, most atmospheric reels in horror history, its subsequent staginess, glacial pacing, and missed opportunities have caused it to age rather badly. (But then again, *Dracula* is the very *first* all-out sound horror film—and a damn fine effort for the first of its kind.) *Horror of Dracula*, on the other hand (without a doubt Hammer's best-loved production and an undisputed masterpiece), remains a vibrant, energetic, alluring take on Stoker's tale—arguably the best cinematic interpretation to date. So, to review the tally so far: It's Universal 3 and Hammer 1.

Of the two remaining matchups, Universal's *The Wolf Man* remains a far more watchable and satisfying film than Hammer's overlong, often tedious (and nearly monster-less) *The Curse of the Werewolf*. The two *Phantoms*, however, are much the same (though Universal's is the more opulent of the two), with little to choose between them. Call it a draw. The final tally by direct comparison? Universal 4, Hammer 1 – a resounding drubbing in any competition!

Acting-wise, both studios fostered a tandem of horror stars—Boris Karloff and Bela Lugosi at Universal, and Peter Cushing and Christopher Lee at Hammer. A consummate actor, Peter Cushing may be the only thespian to rival Karloff's superiority in the horror pantheon. Both actors possessed the uncanny knack of making the impossible believable and both could play sympathetic men in one picture, then ruthless monsters in the next. And with Lugosi and Lee, each studio nurtured a forceful, charismatic personality to complete the team. Further, both studios filled their productions with solid character actors in support of their terror titans, professionals like Lionel Atwill, Dwight Frye, and Ernest Thesiger for Universal; and Michael Gough, Andre Morell, and Michael Ripper for Hammer. It is *behind* the camera, however, that the gap between Universal and Hammer widens to an insurmountable gulf.

Looking at the two studios' bodies of work, one sees a definite pattern or style emerging. The Universal features are a study in dark mood and sinister atmosphere. House art directors like Charles D. Hall (*Dracula, Frankenstein, Murders in the Rue Morgue, The Old Dark House, The Invisible Man, The Black Cat, Bride of Frankenstein*), Albert S. D'Agostino (*Werewolf of London, The Raven, The Invisible Ray, Dracula's Daughter*), and Jack Otterson (*Son of Frankenstein, Tower of London, The Wolf Man*) create massive, almost overpowering sets which the studio's top-notch cinematographers, such as Karl Freund (*Dracula, Murders in the Rue Morgue, The Mummy* [as director]), Arthur Edeson (*Frankenstein, The Old Dark House, The Invisible Man*), and John J. Mescall (*The Black Cat, Bride of Frankenstein*), paint with pools of light and shadow to create an atmosphere rife with unearthly possibilities. The realm of horror was born in darkness (man's primal fear of the unseen and unknown lurking just beyond the flickering firelight), and terror films that exploit this fear with moody lighting and strategic shadows will invariably touch a nerve in their viewers. Universal's house talent was superb at doing just that.

The Universal horror films have survived as examples of some of the most stylistic in the genre. The 1930s carried with it an expressionistic style overtly Teutonic in origin. As Andrew Tudor observed in his cultural analysis of the horror film, *Monsters and Mad Scientists*, "the thirties horror-movie was the major beneficiary from the twenties influx of German technicians and from German stylistic influences in general." The Germanic style, with its emphasis on shadows, darkness and odd perspectives, lent itself brilliantly to the macabre themes of the burgeoning horror genre. As Tudor notes, "this 'German Style' proved highly effective in suggesting a world in which dimly seen and dimly understood forces constrained, controlled and attacked its unsuspecting inhabitants" (*and* unsuspecting audience).

Hammer, on the other hand, prided itself upon its opulent (though cramped) sets and Victorian-style bric-a-brac set decoration. Consequently, its contract cinematographers (Jack Asher, Arthur Grant, et al.) tended to turn up the Kleig lights to full power, often

shooting in a straightforward, pedestrian manner rather than carefully staging scenes for maximum visual impact. It's almost as though the filmmakers felt that the color and sets were enough to attract one's eye and carry the day, so presentation took a back seat to set decoration.

Pacing creates another major gulf between the two studios' styles. The average Universal feature is a taut 70 minutes, whereas the average Hammer film runs about 90 minutes. While Hammerphiles may argue that their studio gives you more for your ticket price, only seldom does that extra 20 minutes contain any bang for your buck. For the most part, Hammer pictures are too long—filled with talky expository scenes that add nothing to the film and only generate heavy eyelids for the viewers. *The Curse of the Werewolf*, long cited as one of Hammer's better offerings, is a prime example of a 70-minute plot stretched out to an overlong (and over*dull*) 91 minutes.

What Universal horror films have to offer today's viewer (above their nostalgia value) is a strong sense of atmosphere. Hammer also created its own special brand of ambiance, but primarily with hard, physical qualities such as authentic-looking period settings and costumes—whereas Universal's filmmakers (besides also utilizing some brilliant art direction) relied more on the artistic use of the camera and lighting to create shadowy subtexts in their sinister stories. One of the reasons those Hammer pictures set in modern times remain so unsatisfying (*Dracula A.D. 1972* being an obvious—and noxious—example) is because those pictures abandoned the qualities that truly made Hammer great: meticulous costuming and set design.

Universal generally came out ahead of Hammer in a toe-to-toe, film-to-film monster match-up, and their Wolf Man *proved to be no exception.*

sacrificing opportunities for intriguing shadowplay in order to (over)expose the detail of their drawing room settings.

Even more importantly, Hammer's trademark became its garish color. By the process' very nature, shooting on color film stock at that time required much more illumination than black and white photography, particularly if one desired the deep color saturation sought after by the Hammer teams. So while Hammer films nearly leapt from the screen in vibrant color, they sacrificed much in terms of mood.

Though the Hammer-makers took great pains with their vivid hues, they often failed in their presentation,

Further, much of Hammer's impact came from their prolific, bright-red stage blood and assorted body parts thrust upon the viewer for the very first time in startling, vivid hues. So many of Hammer's most memorable moments revolve around bloody stakings, gooey meltdowns, and other assorted visceral shocks. While these scenes of grue certainly grabbed the viewer's attention in the 1950s and '60s, they don't carry the same impact with today's jaded audiences. Over the years, those once-astounding and cheeky Hammer shots have been tamed by the ever-evolving (or is that ever-*revolting*?)

craft of the special effects artist. Universal, however, eschewed such cheap visceral shocks and instead focused on creating an almost palpable mood, weaving their macabre threads into a rich tapestry often startling in its bizarre beauty.

Sometimes it's what is *not* shown that makes the most impact, an axiom Hammer never took to heart. Producer-screenwriter Val Lewton, in his string of intelligent, subtle chillers from the 1940s, took this principle to its highest level in films like *Cat People* (1942), *The Leopard Man* (1943) and *Isle of the Dead* (1945). But even before Lewton, the Universal-makers took advantage of this "fear of the unseen" as well. Looking at the Universal and Hammer *Mummy* movies, for instance, provides an illustrative example of the two studio's differing approaches to screen terror.

In Universal's version, the sequence in which the mummy first comes to life is an unforgettable introduction to one of the screen's classic monsters. As young archeologist Ralph Norton (Bramwell Fletcher) silently mouths the words while he transcribes the Scroll of Thoth, the camera moves from him to the still form of the mummy in its upright sarcophagus, then back again to Norton. The next shot focuses on the mummy's desiccated head. After a moment of pregnant stillness, the eyes slowly open. The camera pans down the mummy's torso, and the arms, crossed on its chest, slowly slide down its body, breaking free of the rotted bandages which held them for 3700 years. The camera cuts to Norton, still engrossed in his translation, and then pans down to the scroll on the table. A hand enters the frame, a long, bony, withered hand which briefly touches the scroll, almost in a caress, before drawing it away. Norton looks up, gives a startled yell, and backs away. He begins to laugh, starting low but gaining in intensity until it becomes a horrible, uncontrollable laugh of madness. The camera pans to the floor and we see two trailing bandages drawn out the door as Norton's mad laughter continues—the only sound punctuating an otherwise silent soundtrack. This subtle scene, fraught with tension and terror, is truly one of the most memorable moments of horror ever filmed. Though we never see the Mummy walk, the bits and pieces revealed let our own imaginations create a more striking and terrifying scene than if we'd seen him stalk in full view from his sarcophagus.

In Hammer's take on this sequence, stalking (or, more precisely, *lurching*) in full view is exactly what the less-than-convincing Mummy does. Told in flashback (the initial discovery takes place completely off-screen, with only a piercing shriek to mark the moment), it begins with archeologist Stephen Banning (Felix Aylmer) removing the "Scroll of Life" from its wall niche. Suddenly, a secret wall panel opens to reveal the upright mummy slumped inside. The camera cuts back to Banning as he continues translating the scroll, then to another medium shot of the Mummy raising its head. After another cut to Banning, a medium-long shot of the Mummy reveals its arms moving. Banning continues to read from the scroll, and the camera cuts to a master shot of the archeologist in the foreground with the Mummy seen behind him in the background. Finally, the Bandaged One begins staggering forward (in long shot) and, after a close-up of Banning breaking off to turn and look at the revived corpse, we get a brief medium close-up of the Mummy standing stock still, gazing at the offending archeologist—who promptly utters his horrified yell. This ineffectual scene holds none of the power of Universal's version, since the Mummy staggers awkwardly forward (like a stiff automaton) in disappointing long shot—without an iota of mystery or menace.

In the end, one must realize that without Universal there would *be* no Hammer. Had Universal not taken a chance on *Dracula* in 1931, the horror genre as we know it may never have taken off like it has. Without Universal's library of cinematic horror classics to raid and reshape, Hammer would probably have died an early death in the 1950s after overstaying its welcome with a string of tepid adaptations of radio plays like its *P.C. 49* and *Dick Barton* dramas. Yes indeed, when one raises the issue of Universal vs. Hammer, it's time to bring the Hammer down.

AUTHOR'S NOTE: Having written *Golden Horrors: An Illustrated Critical Filmography of Terror Cinema, 1931-1939* (McFarland, 1996), it's little wonder I've taken the Universal side of this admittedly unnecessary-but-still-amusing argument; yet I must admit that I do also appreciate Hammer films as well. In fact, I talk up Hammer's *The Plague of the Zombies* rather highly in *Drums of Terror: Voodoo in the Cinema* (Midnight Marquee Press, 1998). So keep this in mind as you're getting out those poison pens and addressing those letter bombs (which, by the way, should be aimed at editor Jim Clatterbaugh for having the temerity to publish such rabble-rousing rubbish).

> I *believe* I penned this portmanteau piece for an on-line magazine, but at this point I can't be sure if it ever saw (virtual) print.

WEREWOLF ANTHOLOGIES... OR HOW TO HAVE A HOWLINGLY GOOD TIME IN TWENTY-FIVE MINTUES OR LESS

Alongside vampires and zombies, werewolves complete the Big Three of monster subgenres. So it's only natural that lycanthropes be well represented in the anthology arena. If you're looking for a little hirsute horror in your portmanteau, the following will (like a lycan with fleas) scratch that itch: the good, the bad, and the transformatively ugly...

Dr. Terror's House of Horrors (1965): The first of the renowned Amicus anthologies may not be the best (most cite 1972's *Tales from the Crypt* as their finest), but this one opens with an Old Dark House episode that spirals into lycan-territory for its twist ending. Nothing groundbreaking, but classy and well-acted.

Rider of the Skulls (1965): Mexican delirium as a masked rider battles monsters—including a werewolf—in a trio of tales. Bizarre and highly entertaining, it offers plenty for those enamored of south-of-the-border monster thrills, and anyone who enjoys a huge helping of the offbeat with their segmented terrors.

Dr. Terror's Gallery of Horrors (1967): John Carradine once cited *Billy the Kid vs. Dracula* as the worst movie he ever made. He must have forgotten about *Dr. Terror's Gallery of Horrors*. Not to be confused with the superior Amicus anthology (which undoubtedly the distributors of this pathetic collection intended), *Gallery* features five short stories of the supernatural, including one dull tale of vampirism with a werewolf kicker.

The Monster Club (1981): The cheesy wraparound (which even genre vets Vincent Price and John Carradine can't salvage) for this trio of below-average tales features a suit-and-bow-tie-wearing werewolf, complete with golden locks and a little dog nose that makes him look more like a mutant Pomeranian than a man-wolf. Played strictly for laughs, he gets none.

Tales of the Third Dimension (1984): This drive-in obscurity from North Carolina–based Southern fried movie mogul Earl Owensby offers yet another tale of vampires with a werewolf coda—but that's not the reason to watch. See it for the hilarious, disturbing, over-the-top granny-gone-bad Christmas episode that must be seen to be believed—and then make it a holiday viewing tradition.

Deadtime Stories (1986): This unevenly paced low-budget horror-comedy anthology from Connecticut raked in nearly $3 million on its U.S. theatrical release and was a big hit on video as well (largely due to its impressive video box graphics and the inclusion of the *Deadtime Stories* trailer on a number of compilation tapes—not to mention one of the *pun*niest movie titles of all time). The film's middle tale, "Little Red Runninghood" (she's a jogger), offers an amusing lycanthropic updating of the famous fairy tale that turns out to be the movie's best episode.

Waxwork (1988): "More fun than a barrel of mummies," claims the film's trailer. While this seriously overstates the case, this mired-in-the-'80s nostalgia-fest does indeed offer up the occasional homage-and-gore-soaked bit of "fun" for the diehard genre fan (most of it revolving around some comedic gore and re-creations of far better horror movie scenarios, such as Hammer's *The Mummy* and *Night of the Living Dead*). The first "waxwork" episode, though lasting only six minutes, offers a fairly decent *Howling*-esque werewolf, as well as gratuitous John Rhys-Davies.

Twisted Tales (1994): One of the three tales in this shot-on-video, micro-budget horror anthology focuses on a man trying to cope with being not only a werewolf but a vampire as well. Unfortunately, whatever novelty value such a premise might hold sinks beneath the weight of the amateurish acting and camcorder ineptitude on display.

Blood of the Werewolf (2001): This awful, awful, awful SOV production (that somehow secured a DVD release) remains the only all-werewolf omnibus to date, with all three tepid tales devoted to lycanthropes. Sadly, quantity does *not* ensure quality. Did I mention awful?

The Three Faces of Terror (2004): Italian monster-maker Sergio Stivaletti (*Demons, Cemetery Man*) steps up to the driver's seat to pilot this omnibus. Patterned

Trick 'r Treat *(2007) was a treat indeed for horror fans, not least because of its surprising werewolf segment.*

after *Dr. Terror's House of Horror*—but with a lot more blood—it serves as a showcase for Stivaletti's excellent special effects, including an impressive beast-man and remarkable werewolf transformation. Too bad the poor script, acting, and direction can't match its monsters.

CreepTales (2004): The fifth story (of six) in this no-budget, disjointed anthology offers little more than some blood spray and an immobile werewolf mask over the course of its brief seven-minute running time. And it is *not* seven minutes well spent.

Trick 'r Treat (2007): Saving the best for last, this criminally underrated anthology relays a scary, funny and often ironic group of interwoven Halloween-night tales, with one, starring *True Blood* heroine (and Academy Award winner) Anna Paquin, taking a surprising and shocking lycan-turn.

CHAPTER 3
THE CLASSICS: 1930s AND 1940s

> This review of *The Beast with Five Fingers* crept into *Filmfax* magazine, number 57, back in 1996.

THE BEAST WITH FIVE FINGERS (1946)

The Beast with Five Fingers is undoubtedly the finest Disembodied Hand movie ever made. While this rather grandiose statement may *sound* impressive (as long as you don't *bite* that tongue in your cheek), it loses much of its thunder when one considers the competition: a cheesy inanity called *The Crawling Hand* (1963), a well-staged but ultimately unconvincing (poor effects) 20-minute segment from *Dr. Terror's House of Horrors* (1965), a tangential subplot in the convoluted Hammer-wannabe *And Now the Screaming Starts* (1973), and the mean-spirited and miscast *The Hand* (1981).

Though the idea of a detached hand crawling about by itself is pretty absurd, the thought does possess a decidedly grisly and terrifying quality. Not many things are more horrible than dismemberment, but to have the missing member take on a malevolent life of its own to act out its independent intentions represents the ultimate loss of control. Too bad *The Beast with Five Fingers* weakens this nightmarish element with a murder-mystery denouement at the end—the old "*Mark of the Vampire* Syndrome" rearing its ugly head again. (Screenwriter Curt Siodmak and producer William Jacobs must shoulder most of the blame, since director Robert Florey was so dissatisfied with the script and shooting schedule that he took a three-month studio suspension before finally capitulating and directing the picture.)

Francis Ingram (Victor Francen), a once-famous pianist now paralyzed, dies soon after changing his will to make his live-in nurse (Andrea King) his sole beneficiary. When the new will is contested by Ingram's greedy relatives, terror unfolds as Ingram's one good hand is mysteriously severed and apparently creeps away to kill one member of the household and haunt another. The shocks that follow are only a mad deception though, since the killer turns out to be all too human (a *whole*

Peter Lorre encounters The Beast with Five Fingers *(1946).*

human), with the crawling hand being merely an hallucination created by the madman's guilt-ridden insanity.

As the demented killer, Peter Lorre gives such a chilling and believable performance that it saves *The Beast with Five Fingers*. Much like the actor did with his first starring role in Fritz Lang's *M* sixteen years earlier, Lorre's sensitive portrayal of the disturbed, obsessed murderer inspires both sympathy as well as fear, bringing an important resonance to what (as written) is a rather ridiculous and one-dimensional role.

Also effective is J. Carrol Naish as the congenial, cigar smoking Commissario of Police investigating the murder and strange goings on. The burden of comedy relief falls upon Naish's capable shoulders and he carries it well, finding a perfect balance between the Comedic Persona and the Authority Figure. At one point, Naish states in a serious tone, "Sometimes people tell me things—after it is too late," with just the right pointed look. Later, when Naish orders everyone to remain in the house yet the servants run out anyway, someone remarks, "They're more afraid of ghosts than the law," to which Naish candidly replies, "If I were not the Commissario I would be right along with them."

The remainder of the cast, however, proves less than adequate, headed by Robert Alda as the cynical, world-weary hero/love-interest. Alda plays it so flat and toneless, never speaking above a low monotone (in an attempt to convey a jaded suaveness, one supposes), that he becomes an insipid bore.

Curt Siodmak's (*Frankenstein Meets the Wolf Man, Bride of the Gorilla*) script (based on Willaim Fryer Harvey's creepy short story) is no better, with the first two reels coming off as a painfully dull melodrama filled with flowery lines like, "I have something to offer you—hope, courage, devotion, a new life." Then, when things finally get rolling with the dreaded hand seemingly out and about, the script makes little use of the opportunities for suspense and buildup. Right away, the authorities (in the person of the Commissario) are convinced of the hand's existence: "In my mind there is no doubt the hand is walking around," absurdly asserts the Commissario. And then there's the disappointing aforementioned 'it-was-all-in-your-mind' ending that concludes with a shoot-yourself-in-the-foot final scene in which the condescending Commissario turns directly to the camera and derisively snorts, "Can you imagine anybody believing a hand can walk around?" Suddenly, a hand begins to creep up his chest toward his throat ... before the camera pulls back to reveal that it's the man's own perambulating paw. With a sheepish grin and dismissive shrug, he goes out the front door and it is THE END (of credibility). This silly, unnecessary, *unfunny* final bit merely serves to trivialize the whole scenario.

As with every film from this strange little sub-genre, *The Beast with Five Fingers*' special effects prove uneven. At times they are startling, as in the long shots of the hand playing the piano, while at other times the malevolent member looks like a dime-store rubber joke prop pulled along by a string. (The hand in question, when not a rubber one, belonged to director Robert Florey, who 'lent a hand' by using his own digits for the live close-ups.)

Thanks to Florey's atmospheric staging, cinematographer Wesley Anderson's low-key lighting, and Lorre's sensitive, insightful playing, however, the picture possesses some effective, disturbing touches—such as the hand scuttling behind a row of books with the camera tracking its progress by the movement of the books themselves. And the scene leading up to the hand's first appearance is a masterful sequence of direction, lighting, and editing. Shots of a guitar's strings suddenly breaking, a book inexplicably falling off a table, the fire giving a startling sputter, intercut with views of an anxious Peter Lorre becoming more and more unnerved, create a chilling prelude to the small wooden box on the desk slowly opening seemingly by itself to reveal ... *brrrrr*! With Lorre or the hand present, Florey manages to elicit some solid chills, but the script ultimately defeats him as it contains too much tepid filler to sustain the macabre mood over the film's 88-minute running time. Though you gotta 'hand' it to Florey for trying, this *Beast* turned out to be no beauty.

The following assessment of the 1934 Karloff-Lugosi classic yowled from the pages of *Filmfax* magazine (no. 57) in 1996.

THE BLACK CAT (1934)

"We shall play a little game, Vitus, a game of death if you will." –Hjalmar Poelzig.

Though the film's credits claim that *The Black Cat* is "suggested by the immortal Edgar Allan Poe classic," screenwriter Peter Ruric (with story help from director Edgar Ulmer) created a scenario about as far from Poe's short story as one could get. Of the many adaptations of Poe's "The Black Cat," Ruric and Ulmer's vision is perhaps the least faithful to the storyline but the most faithful to the *spirit* of Poe. A spirit of melancholy, madness, and death permeates this film, just as these feelings are embedded in the brilliant, tortured works of the 19th century author.

The story follows a honeymooning couple, Joan and Peter Alison (Jacqueline Wells and David Manners), who, along with fellow traveler Dr. Vitus Werdegast (Bela Lugosi), seek shelter at the bizarre home of Hjalmar Poelzig (Boris Karloff). It turns out that Poelzig and Werdegast possess a long and hate-filled history. Poelzig's treacherous actions during WWI resulted in Werdegast's lengthy imprisonment. Werdegast has returned to seek his revenge, and find his wife and daughter whom his rival had stolen. Poelzig, now the leader of a satanic cult, intends to sacrifice Joan, but Werdegast, who has taken on the role of the couple's protector, intends to prevent this. With the innocent couple trapped in the middle, the two antagonists play out their baroque "game of death," which climaxes in a gruesome and explosive finale.

Nearly the whole of the film takes place within the walls of Poelzig's fascinating, ultra-modern house. This house is built upon the very foundations of the WWI Fort Marmorus, "the greatest graveyard in the world." From the start, a brooding, dark atmosphere permeates the story as the drama unfolds upon "the graves of ten thousand men." The intriguing art-deco sets were

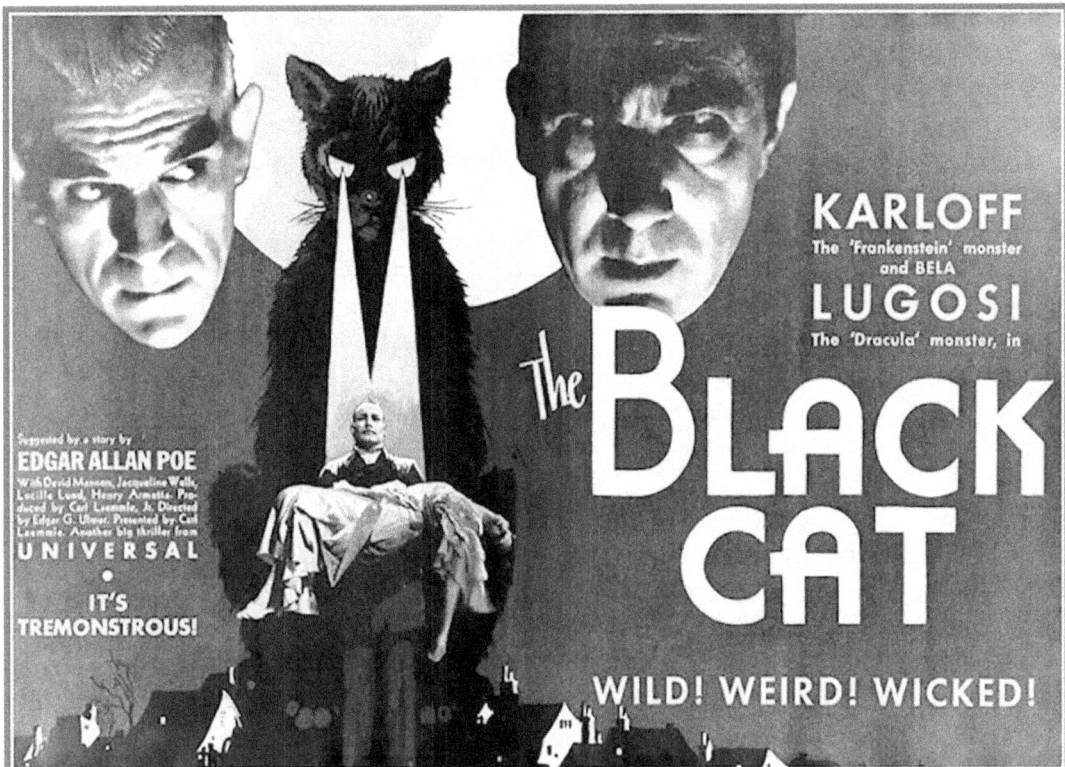

The first teaming of Boris Karloff and Bela Lugosi resulted in one of the greatest films from Horror's Golden Age.

designed by director Edgar Ulmer himself (who began his career as a set designer in Germany). Consisting of square panels, interior-lit walls, sliding doors, and stark white furniture, this setting rests atop the massive stone vaults and cold iron doors of the fort's cellars. Consequently, underneath the modernistic exterior is a tomb-like structure in which one can "still sense death in the air." This reflects the very essence of *The Black Cat*: of things lurking just below the surface, of death and decay—painted over but still there, exerting their brooding influence.

In *The Black Cat* both Karloff and Lugosi were at the peak of their acting prowess, and they gave two very different but very fine performances. As Poelzig, Karloff is the embodiment of all things evil and sinister. From his black flowing garments ("one of the things [Karloff] found most exciting in the film was the wardrobe," claimed Ulmer) to the sharp widow's peak on his forehead, malevolence nearly oozes from his person. Karloff's extraordinary use of body language comes into full play here. His movements are slow, measured, without waste, and very forceful. Karloff's delivery is equal to his movements as he imbues every line of dialogue with hidden meaning. Even a phrase as innocuous as "sleep well" takes on sinister connotations coming from Karloff's lips.

As Werdegast, Lugosi plays a man tortured in spirit, driven almost mad by circumstance, returning to seek justice or at least find retribution. With Karloff as the evil antagonist, Lugosi plays the 'good' protagonist. But the struggle between the two characters is not a struggle of good and evil, not black versus white, but more one of black versus gray, for Werdegast's motivations and actions are themselves twisted. (As originally written and shot, Werdegast intended to rape the heroine rather than set her free! This was omitted from the final release print, and new scenes filmed to maintain the continuity. Despite the change, the character is still far from benign, since Werdegast is motivated solely by vengeance and ultimately slips into the madness of his obsession.) This makes for a much more interesting conflict than a simple good versus evil scenario. Here Lugosi rises to the challenge and delivers one of the best performances of his career. One scene in particular should put to rest those critics who have claimed that Lugosi was strictly a one-dimensional actor. It comes when Poelzig takes Werdegast down to the underground vaults to show him the macabre sight of Werdegast's dead wife, her body preserved and suspended upright in a weird glass case. Subtle emotions play across Lugosi's face as he tearfully demands, "Why is she like this?" With a tremor in his voice, his eyes misting with sadness, and sorrow etched into the lines of his face, Lugosi's performance is genuinely moving. Such a tender, emotional portrayal is something far above a "one-shot Dracula."

Another striking aspect of *The Black Cat* is its wonderfully dark dialogue. The choice of words adds tremendously to the brooding, unearthly feel of the film. When Peter discovers the phone doesn't work, Poelzig turns to Werdegast and declares, "You hear that Vitus, the phone is dead. Even the *phone* is *dead*." The emphasis on darkness and death is underscored by the dialogue.

Throughout the picture, director Edgar Ulmer's brilliant visual flair prevails. For instance, the shot in which we first see Poelzig makes masterful use of light and shadow and movement. In silhouette, we see his upper body rise stiffly from a bed, like a corpse rising from a coffin. He reaches out to touch a lamp, but instead of the lamp coming on to illuminate the room, the entire wall behind him lights up. This only deepens the blackness of Poelzig's silhouette, emphasizing the mysterious, dark nature of the man. Of course, the contribution of cinematographer John J. Mescall (*Bride of Frankenstein*) cannot be overlooked. The fact that Ulmer never again achieved quite the level of artistic success he did with *The Black Cat* suggests that much of the merit of this picture is due to Mescall and the other technicians Ulmer utilized.

Recalling *The Black Cat* three decades later, Boris Karloff laughingly lamented: "The things we did to Poe when he wasn't around to defend himself!" These "things" ultimately proved quite lucrative; with the final cost a mere $95,745, *The Black Cat* made over $140,000 profit for Universal, making it the top grosser of the studio's 35 films released in 1934.

The Black Cat has held up very well over the years, losing very little of its power and mood. The imaginative sets; evocative lighting; two brilliant, contrasting performances from Karloff and Lugosi; and the timeless themes of love, hate, and death all combine to make *The Black Cat* a truly unique classic.

> Many consider *Bride of Frankenstein* to be one of the greatest horror films ever made. So when *Monsters from the Vault* editor Jim Clatterbaugh asked me to pen an article to celebrate the film's 75th anniversary, who was I to say no? This appeared in issue 28 (February 2011).

BRIDE OF FRANKENSTEIN: A 75th ANNIVERSARY APPRECIATION

Glass cylinders hum and glow, electricity jumps between metal rods, a bank of conductors spark violently, a circular generator shoots electricity around its perimeter, and rows of contacts emit small explosions and plumes of white smoke. Inside an ancient stone watchtower, the makeshift laboratory seems to come alive with sparks, light and smoke, while a steady thump, thump, thump—like the beat of a cosmic heart—pounds underneath the crackling and booming of the machinery and the violent storm raging outside. With this six-minute sequence (beginning when Henry Frankenstein and Dr. Pretorius remove the sheet covering the bandaged female body, and ending with Pretorius' feyly proud pronouncement upon revealing the creature in all her grotesque glory), director James Whale creates one of the most exciting sequences from the Golden Age of Horror by calling down the bolts from Heaven to bring life to the *Bride of Frankenstein*.

Universal planned *The Return of Frankenstein*, a sequel to their 1931 blockbuster, as early as the summer of 1933, with James Whale to direct and Boris Karloff (naturally) to star. Whale, however, resisted the idea, telling his friend R. C. Sherriff, "I squeezed the idea dry on the original picture, and never want to work on it again." Whale avoided the dreaded sequel assignment by helming *The Invisible Man* (scripted by Sherriff) instead. After further delays to the Frankenstein project due to Universal's fiscal difficulties (the studio saw red in 1933 to the tune of over one million dollars), Whale finally capitulated. The director then sat down with John Balderston to shape and refine playwright William Hurlburt's (*Lilies of the Field*) initial draft into the Swiftian screenplay that became *Bride of Frankenstein*.

Whale uses *Bride* as his personal showcase, bringing his considerable directorial prowess to bear on the bizarre story. (Whale even designed the Bride's distinctive beehive-gone-mad hairstyle.) A master of shadows and angles, Whale works with cinematographer John Mescall to create a brilliant collage of visual imagery and mood. Upon Pretorius' introduction, the gaunt doctor stalks into Henry's bedroom where the lighting casts a huge, foreboding shadow of the invader upon the wall. Whale then cuts to a medium close-up of the cadaverous Pretorius in which the shadows cast by the smoke rising from the room's huge fireplace ripple across the intruder and the wall behind, conjuring up a hellish, demonic connotation. Later in the same scene Pretorius proposes, "We must work together." At this, Henry leaps out of bed, protesting, "I'm through with it; I'll have no more to do with this *hellspawn*!" Agitated, Henry walks a few paces, wringing his hands. He stops abruptly, right in the spot where a shadow of the window's crosshatching forms a web-like pattern on

Boris Karloff as the Monster makes a pitiable suitor in Bride of Frankenstein *(1935).*

the wall behind him. With Pretorius hovering at his shoulder like a great black spider, Henry seems caught in Pretorius' web, held fast by his own curiosity while the demented doctor talks of his experiments.

As the prissy, disdainful, and thoroughly intriguing Dr. Pretorius, Ernest Thesiger steals every scene he's in—an amazing accomplishment considering he must frequently vie for attention with Karloff's Monster. Universal originally announced Claude Rains for the role, but when Rains began work on *The Mystery of Edwin Drood* instead, Whale, in an inspired bit of casting, recruited his old friend Thesiger for the part. "I've had a terrible lesson," whines Henry Frankenstein, to which Pretorius mocks, "That is *sad*, very *sad*." Thesiger's slight sneer and subtle emphasis on "sad," his tilt of the head and smug mouth all make it obvious how truly "sad" he feels. When Pretorius makes his macabre toast, "To a new world of gods and monsters," Thesiger's eyes widen slightly and his mouth momentarily twists into an off-kilter grin before he gives a dismissive half-laugh and returns to his precise speech and pinched expression, allowing us a glimpse of the subtle madness lurking beneath his cultured exterior. Alone in a crypt, he later toasts, "I give you the Monster," to a skull he's set up on a coffin. Thesiger's mirthless, unwholesome laughter at his grisly joke becomes truly disturbing, though it soon pales in perversity to the actor's smirking leer when the Monster joins him and requests, "Woman—friend—*wife*."

Fourth-billed in the original, Boris Karloff earned top billing in *Bride*. In fact, the actor was enjoying so much popularity and prestige at the time that Universal billed him by surname alone, simply as "KARLOFF" (an honor awarded to only a handful of actors over the years). In addition to better billing, *Bride* provided Karloff more range than he had in the original, allowing the full pathos of the Monster's pitiable existence to shine forth. The Monster has now outgrown his initial innocence in the first film and become "wise in his generation." Seeing his hideous reflection in a pool, Karloff's face hardens and anger flares in his eyes as he growls and strikes the water to erase the hated image. He now knows that it is his ghastly appearance that separates him from the world of men.

Though Karloff often complained of the decision to have the Monster speak, the few words he utters add much to the character, and the actor's insightful delivery makes the most of them. When confronting his creator for the first time, Karloff growls, "Frank-en-stein," his gutteral voice deep and hard, edged by the obvious hatred he feels in that single word. Just as he does with his brilliant pantomimic gestures and body language, Karloff uses his few brief lines to express a full range of emotion, from joy to anger, from heartfelt pain to fleeting pleasure.

With *Bride of Frankenstein*, Whale (alongside cinematographer John Mescall) raises the science of camera angles to a fine cinematic art. In preparation for the Great Experiment, Henry and Pretorius set everything in place. As they move their large gurneys of instruments and equipment, the tilted camera makes it look as though they're struggling to push the cart *uphill*. The next shot shows them shoving another cart directly toward the camera, but this time the angle makes it appear as if the gurney is coming *downhill*, so that if they let go the surgical instruments would come crashing into the camera—into the viewer. With a strategic use of angles, Whale adds an unsettling feel to this key anticipatory moment.

Whale angles his camera to draw parallels between Frankenstein and Pretorius as well. In a close-up of Henry working in the lab, the angle makes it appear as if he looks upwards to the right, while in the next shot the camera tilts in the opposite direction to show Pretorius looking upwards to the *left* in a mirror image that emphasizes the two characters' connection. With this visual link established, Whale then cleverly makes a distinction between the two very different personalities in the next shot. With both of them now together, Whale has Pretorius standing behind some equipment, his face seen through the opening of a gigantic gear wheel, while Henry stands in the open. The dark wheel shape forms a barrier between the two men to underscore the difference and distance between the idealistic Henry and the sinister Pretorius. With this point made, Whale again jumps back into their dichotomous relationship by returning to the tilted angles mirroring one another as the two scientists take up the discussion of their work—and Henry's scientific zeal (their bond) surges again.

While *Frankenstein* harbors subtle subtexts beneath its gothic surface, *Bride* simply *explodes* with thematic allusions involving individuality, sexuality, and religion.

Whale's insistence on including the Mary Shelley prologue and casting the same actress in the two roles of author and creature (i.e. creator and creation) is perhaps a specific reflection of the homosexual director's distrust of women, or, more generally, a revelation of the-monster-in-us-all. "James' feeling was that very pretty, sweet people, both men and women, had very wicked insides…evil thoughts," remembered Elsa Lanchester (in Greg Mank's *It's Alive!*). "…So James wanted the same actress for both parts to show that the Bride of Frankenstein did, after all, come out of the sweet Mary Shelley's soul." Though Mary is afraid of storms and can't stand the sight of blood, beneath the surface of "that bland and lovely brow" lies a soul that "conceived a Frankenstein." Mary, in fact, *is* the monster. Just as the sensitive, high-strung Henry Frankenstein possesses a doppelganger in the Monster, so the perceptive, elegant Mary Shelley possesses a secret double in the monstrous Bride.

No doubt Whale identified more with Dr. Pretorius than any of his other characters. As Thesiger plays him, Pretorius' prissy manner and obvious disdain for women reflect a decidedly alternative sexuality. "My business with you, Baron," he says to Henry and looks toward Elizabeth, "is private." Thesiger's hawkish nose turns up in the air while his mouth nearly puckers with distaste when contemplating the negligee-wearing female. Later, when Pretorius' miniature King escapes his jar and runs over to the tiny Queen, Pretorius remarks acidly that "even royal amours are a nuisance." Then, of course, there's a backhanded stab at conjugal bliss with Minnie the maid's tearful observation, "Oh what a *terrible* wedding night."

Through Pretorius, Whale not only pokes fun at conventional sexuality but at religion as well. While much of this irreverence stems from William Hurlbut and John Balderston's witty script, Whale expands upon it with his (occasionally overdone) visual references and particularly with his direction of Ernest Thesiger. "I also have created life—" boasts Pretorius before adding disdainfully "—as we say, 'in God's own image'" (a blasphemous remark which Pennsylvania's censor board demanded be excised). Later in the same scene, Pretorius toasts, "To a new world of gods and monsters," obviously placing himself in the first category. If considering himself something of a deity, Pretorius definitely leans more toward the devilish end of the spectrum than the holy. Upon revealing his Mephistophelian miniature creature to Henry, Pretorius observes, "There's a certain resemblance to me don't you think? Or do I flatter myself?" He follows this up with, "Sometimes I have wondered whether life wouldn't be much more *amusing* if we were *all* devils, and no nonsense about *angels* and being *good*." Pretorius urges Henry to "leave the charnel house and follow the lead of *nature*—" adding with a slight sneer, "—or of God if you like your *bible* stories."

Even Thesiger's dress (supervised by Whale) carries a perverse religious inference. When first seen, Pretorius wears a black cloak and hat with a white collar visible only as a thin band encircling the neck—looking very much like a priest's collar. Of course, when he doffs his coat, we see that this collar is simply a regular ascot-like garment, but the first impression is unmistakable. Later, when Pretorius takes Henry to his lodgings, Thesiger sports (for no discernible reason) a black yarmulke-like skull cap. (Apparently, Whale aimed his sharp lampoons at the entire Judeo-Christian spectrum.)

Beyond such backhanded satirizing, the script features one passage which rationally and intelligently answers the age-old caveat about men meddling in God's domain. When Henry goes on about finding the secret of life, Elizabeth admonishes, "Henry, don't say those things, don't *think* them. It's blasphemous and wicked. We are not *meant* to know those things." To this Henry answers, "It may be that I'm *intended* to know the secret of life. It may be part of the Divine Plan," giving an obvious and truly sensible response to such an irrational argument.

For *Bride*, Colin Clive's Henry Frankenstein has become a sniveling, self-pitying wretch who never shows any backbone. He exhibits little of the drive and sheer force of will which led him to create the Monster in the first place, and his helpless whining about not hearing from Elizabeth or not being able to work with the Monster around does little to engender sympathy. While on the surface this may seem a liability, it serves to increase the focus on the Monster and makes of Henry's creation a more sympathetic figure by contrast. Thus, our allegiance has shifted from Henry (with whom we sided in the first *Frankenstein*) to the Monster.

Given $37,500 to work with, art director Charles D. Hall created a series of detailed sets to match and surpass even those of *Frankenstein*. While his interiors fit the story perfectly, it is actually his *exteriors* for this studio-bound production which create the most impact on tone and mood. The first time the Monster enters the woods, he walks through a sunlit forest filled with lush underbrush, a placid stream, and contented sheep. Seeking only companionship, the Monster is attacked in this beautiful setting, once more rejected by humanity despite his efforts to save a young girl from drowning (obviously having learned a lesson from his fateful meeting with little Maria in the first film). When next we see the Monster, the bloodthirsty villagers are hot on his trail. The woods have changed, however, and the Monster flees through an almost surreal landscape of stark, limbless tree trunks, jutting rocks, and dark, denuded forest floor. The change in environment reflects the change in the Monster—from hopeful innocent to beleaguered prey.

Franz Waxman's music for *Bride* adds immeasurably to the picture's overall success by brilliantly evoking a scene's mood. When the villagers carry Henry's "corpse" home, a slow rhythmic dirge conjures up images of a funeral march. For the Monster's first appearance, ominous drums build as the creature's hand and arm move into view, coalescing into the harsh, five-note "Monster Theme" when the creature steps fully into the frame. Waxman's magnificent score brilliantly utilized leitmotifs to evoke the personalities and mood of key characters such as the Monster, Pretorius, and the Bride. So effective was the music that it became a keynote of Universal's stock library. The score later became the object of a lawsuit when Waxman sued Oscar Hammerstein for stealing his wonderful "Wedding Theme" for the song "Bali Ha'I" in *South Pacific*. Waxman was awarded a substantial settlement.

While *Bride* no longer has the power to frighten (one could argue that even in 1935 that was not its maker's intent, as Whale steered his sequel more towards the realm of the Gothic fairy tale than outright horror), it offers today's viewers moments of technical brilliance, exquisite excitement and rich thematic depth. Even outstripping its progenitor in some respects, *Bride of Frankenstein* stands tall as a timeless masterpiece from the Golden Age of Horror.

Filmfax magazine published this profile of the Bride herself in issue 58 (1996).

ELSA "THE BRIDE" LANCHESTER: A CANDID LOOK AT THE FAIREST MONSTER OF THEM ALL!

Few movie images are as memorable as the Bride of Frankenstein: a wild, grotesquely beautiful creature who ultimately rejects the Frankenstein monster, responding to his awkward affection with a piercing shriek. It's an image indelibly etched in the minds of horror movie fans everywhere, and it's a role that earned actress Elsa Lanchester celluloid immortality.

Born Elizabeth Sullivan in 1902 in Lewisham, England, Lanchester had studied dance as a child. At age 16, she acted in a children's group, and within a few years gained a reputation as an accomplished actress, appearing in several West End plays; her film career began in the late 1920s.

Lanchester married actor Charles Laughton in 1929; they would appear together in numerous films

(*The Private Life of Henry VIII*, *Rembrandt*, *The Big Clock*, *Witness for the Prosecution*) and stage productions. In 1934 she signed a contract with MGM and was seen in *David Copperfield* and *Naughty Marietta* (both released in 1935). For her third and final picture under this contract, MGM loaned her out to Universal for what would become, ironically, not only her best-known role, but one of the most celebrated film portrayals of all time: the *Bride of Frankenstein*.

Bride was the (first) sequel to *Frankenstein*, Universal's smash hit of 1931. Repeating their roles from the original were Boris Karloff (the Monster) and Colin Clive (Dr. Frankenstein); James Whale would again sit in the director's chair.

"Who will be the Bride of Frankenstein? Who will dare?" asked Universal's publicity department. Among the names bandied about were Arletta Duncan (one of Mae Clarke's bridesmaids in *Frankenstein*) and Brigitte Helm (of *Metropolis* fame). Publicity-generating prognostications aside, James Whale had his mind set on an elfin actress he had worked with during his early days on the London stage: Elsa Lanchester.

The following advertisement was placed in *The Hollywood Reporter*:

ELSA LANCHESTER
wishes to express her gratitude to that
charming director….JAMES WHALE
and to UNIVERSAL STUDIOS
for the courteous cooperation in one of
the most interesting and distinctive roles of
her theatrical experience. Playing the Monster's
Mate in *The Bride of Frankenstein* with Karloff
was a great pleasure….E.L.

"I have an odd face," Lanchester told Gregory William Mank in *It's Alive! The Classic Cinema Saga of Frankenstein*, "and James was absolutely dead set that my face was the face for the Bride of Frankenstein!" Not only did Whale envision Ms. Lanchester in the role of the monster's mate, but as Mary Shelley as well. "James Whale in his production of *The Bride of Frankenstein* did deliberately used me to play both 'Mary Shelley' and the monster's bride," wrote the actress in a letter to *Life* magazine (April 5, 1968), "because he wanted to tell that Mary Shelley indeed had something in common with the dreadful creature of her imagination." Despite the *Hollywood Reporter* ad, Lanchester received screen credit for playing Mary only, and gamely went along with a "?" in the opening and closing credits. (At least the double role yielded a double salary: $1,250 for each part.)

Elsa Lanchester in her iconic role as the Bride of Frankenstein.

In the film's prologue, Lord Byron (Gavin Gordon), Percy Bysse Shelley (Douglas Walton), and Mary Wollstonecraft Godwin (the scene occurs prior to her marriage to Shelley) lounge in an elegant drawing room. The conversation comes round to Mary's story *Frankenstein* and Byron briefly recalls moments from the first film. "I do think it a shame, Mary, to end your story so suddenly," remarks Shelley. To this Mary replies, "That wasn't the end at all. Would you like to hear what happened after that?" And so begins the "rest" of the tale.

James Whale's insistence on including the Mary Shelley prologue and casting the same actress in the two roles of author and creature (i.e., creator and creation) is perhaps a specific reflection of the homosexual director's distrust of women, or, more generally, a revelation of the monster-in-us-all. "James' feeling was that very pretty, sweet people, both men and women, had very wicked insides…evil thoughts," Lanchester told Gregory William Mank. "These thoughts could be of dragons, they could be of monsters, they could be of Frankenstein's laboratory. So James wanted the same actress for both parts to show that *The Bride of Frankenstein* did, after all, come out of sweet Mary Shelley's soul."

Although Mary is afraid of storms and cannot stand the sight of blood, beneath the surface of "that bland

and lovely brow" lies a soul that "conceived a Frankenstein." Mary, in fact, *is* the monster. Just as the sensitive, high-strung Henry Frankenstein possesses the doppelganger I the monsters, so the perceptive, elegant Mary Shelley possess a secret double I the monstrous Bride.

As the Bride, Lanchester was covered head to toe in bandages. Though publicity shots show her sipping tea in costume during breaks, it was just for the benefit of the still photographer. In her autobiography *Elsa Lanchester Herself*, the actress wrote, "I drank as little liquid as possible. It was too much of an ordeal to go to the bathroom—all those bandages, and having to be accompanied by my dresser."

Once the bandages are removed, the Bride is seen in all her glory, compete with that memorably frizzy, streaked hair. As for Jack Pierce, the legendary makeup artist who created the "look" of the Bride (as well as the definitive versions of the Frankenstein Monster, the Mummy, and the Wolf Man), Lanchester remembered, "[He] was elevated even further in his own heaven when a Bride was to be born. He had his own sanctum sanctorum, and as you entered (you did not walk in; you entered), he said good morning first. If I spoke first, he glared and slightly showed his upper teeth. He would be dressed in full hospital doctor's operating outfit. At five in the morning, this made me dislike him intensely."

Budgeted at $293,750 (just $2,000 more than *Frankenstein*'s final cost), *The Return of Frankenstein* (which was the picture's working title) began filming on January 2, 1935, on a 36-day shooting schedule. The director's meticulous methods, however, took the picture ten days over schedule and more than $100,000 over budget. (The final cost was $397,023.)

While *Bride of Frankenstein* possesses touches of undeniable brilliance, and moments of exquisite excitement and depth, it also sports several seriously marring liabilities which pull the audience away from the story, reminding the viewer that, indeed, this gothic fairy tale is simply a movie. As a directorial showcase, *Bride* outstrips its progenitor, but as a horror film it comes in a definite second.

For some, the fact that the monster has dialogue in the sequel is a detriment. "Many people like *The Bride of Frankenstein* better than the first one," observed the Monster himself, Boris Karloff (in *Movie Monsters* #3), a few years before his death, "but I don't know. I've always preferred the original film. In that picture the monster didn't speak, you remember. But when we made the sequel about the bride, they had me speaking all sorts of dialogue. Time and time again I argued that the monster shouldn't speak. If he spoke, he would seem too much more human, I thought. But the director won his argument." Indeed, he did, though it's not so much the monster's speech that detracts from the film but the overplayed parody (Una O'Connor's comic relief, the regrettable homunculi sequence).

For Elsa Lanchester, *Bride of Frankenstein* provided her with the role of a lifetime. Although she would go on to play many more film, stage, and television characters before her death in 1986, none of them had the same impact as "The Bride." In *Scream Queens* (by Calvin Beck), Lanchester stated, "Television runs the old picture every Halloween. …It's nice to be remembered for one part. I don't mind the trademark."

This *Captive Wild Woman* was released to *Filmfax* magazine (issue 61) in 1997.

CAPTIVE WILD WOMAN (1943)

In the mid–1940s, Universal's stable of monsters were tiring, unable to cross the finish line without help (resulting in the teaming and re-teaming of their classic monsters in features like *Frankenstein Meets the Wolf Man* and the two *House Of...* films). In this climate of quiet desperation, the studio sought a fresh thoroughbred which would inject new life into the horror race. They found it in a little franchise philly called 'Paula the Ape Woman.' Paula ambled through three features before she died of ennui. While the last two pictures, *Jungle Woman* (1944) and *Jungle Captive* (1945), proved to be tired, repetitive potboilers, the first, *Captive Wild Woman*, was something else indeed.

John Carradine plays Dr. Sigmund Walters, a respected scientist who, through some ambiguous use of "gland extracts," turns a man in an ape suit (Ray "Crash" Corrigan) into the beautiful Acquanetta. He dubs his new creation Paula Dupree and takes her back to visit the circus from which she was stolen. There she proves a 'natural,' since all the animals seem to fear her. Consequently, animal trainer Fred Mason (Milburn Stone), unaware that Paula is actually his missing ape, Cheela, incorporates her into his new and dangerous act—mixing lions and tigers in the same ring. The trouble is, "terrific emotion destroys the new tissue in [Paula's] gland growths," causing her to revert back to a half-simian form. And Fred's fiancée, Beth (Evelyn Ankers), inspires in Paula just such a "terrific emotion" in the form of violent jealousy. After the ape woman's abortive attack on Beth, Dr. Walters must perform another gland operation to restore Paula's human characteristics, and plans to use Dorothy, Beth's sister, as an unwilling donor. Beth arrives at Walters' private sanitorium just in time to release Paula (now in full ape form) from her cage so that she can attack and kill the evil doctor. Meanwhile, Fred is in big trouble at the circus, since a violent storm has sent the big cats into a violent frenzy right in the middle of his act. Paula/Cheela heads for the circus grounds and arrives just in time to save Fred from the attacking cats. An over-zealous guard shoots the helpful ape as she carries her beloved trainer from the ring. The ape dies and the (human) lovers are reunited.

Not the best of plots, nor the biggest of budgets (much of the time is filled with stock footage of famous lion-tamer Clyde Beatty), but this fun cheapie packs its brief 60-minute running time with plenty of vintage thrills. The film begins with an exciting sequence in which a tiger gets loose on the shipyard docks and is promptly cornered by Fred. From then on it never lets up, alternating thrilling lion and tiger taming footage of Beatty from *The Big Cage* (1933) with laboratory chills, presided over by the ever-villainous Mr. Carradine at his subdued best.

Carradine is excellent as the brilliant but amoral scientist, turning in an even-tempered, effective characterization that's a far cry from his many desultory poverty-row portrayals. Carradine looks downright dapper in his tailored suits and snap-brim hats, and shows a real sparkle in his eye and genuine enthusiasm for his work—to the exclusion of all else, including anything so trivial as morality. When Carradine asks of his protesting nurse, "Why should a single life be considered so important?" his earnest, quizzical expression and serious, questioning tone leave no doubt that he truly cannot fathom her concern.

As his reluctant but devoted nurse, Fay Helm (*The Wolf Man*, *Night Monster*, *Calling Dr. Death*) makes a heartfelt plea for Walters to stop his mad experiment. Her (perfectly reasonable) query, "And suppose your experiment *is* successful—what will you have?" makes *Captive Wild Woman* one of the few 'mad science' movies in which someone actually questions the *practicality* of the resident mad doctor's 'work.' Ms. Helm's sincere pleadings with the doctor are tinged with a desperate, affectionate sadness as she frantically tries to convince the brilliant but cold scientist to mend the error of his ways. Of course, she ends up involuntarily donating her "cerebrum" to the experiment for her troubles, but Helm's genuineness adds a bit more feeling to her role of assistant-turned-victim than can be found in most mad medico movies.

Acquanetta, "The Venezuelan Volcano," erupts as the Captive Wild Woman *(1943)*

Milburn Stone (later to achieve modest fame as "Doc" on TV's *Gunsmoke*) as Fred, and Evelyn Ankers as his fiancée, are solid audience identification figures, making their characters both approachable and likable. As the titular terror, the exotic Acquanetta (a model-turned-actress inexplicably dubbed the "Venezuelan Volcano"—though she was actually from an Arapaho reservation in Wyoming) looks striking as the gorilla-turned-woman who possesses a strange power over the circus animals ('animal magnetism'?). She's not asked to do much more than stand about with an intent look on her beautiful face (though at one point she does manage to effectively convey an ill-controlled rage). This is just as well since she subsequently proved herself (in films like *Dead Man's Eyes*, 1944) to be an actress of decidedly limited range.

Captive Wild Woman boasts some deft transformation scenes in which Jack P. Pierce performs his usual top-flight job of turning men (or, in this case, women) into monsters. Via filters to show Acquanetta's face suddenly darken (á la 1931's *Dr. Jekyll and Mr. Hyde*) and effective dissolves (á la *The Wolf Man*), Paula loses her humanity right before our very eyes.

An acknowledgment in the film's opening credits intimates that famed animal trainer Clyde Beatty "staged" the "thrilling animal sequences in this picture." All Beatty really did, however, was allow Universal to lift shots from his film *The Big Cage*. Still, the plentiful stock circus footage is exciting filler and generally well mixed with Stone's lion-tamer close-up scenes (though the occasional poor rear-screen process shot, or the fooling-absolutely-nobody technique of simply slowing and reversing the film to make a lion appear to *back* away from its handler, reminds one of the movie's bargain-basement origins).

Shaggy in ape form and sexy in human guise (thanks to the dark beauty of the "Venezuelan Volcano"), Paula made for an acceptable Jekyll/Hyde animal update. And, at least for her debut outing, this longshot came in a winner. Sure, *Captive Wild Woman* is horror hokum, but it's exciting, vintage 1940s hokum nonetheless.

> The following exploration of Bela Lugosi's three Chandu the Magician films appeared (out of thin air) in *Midnight Marquee* magazine (issue 57) in 1998.

FROM VILLAIN TO HERO: LUGOSI AND CHANDU

Chandu the Magician was born, innocently enough, in 1931 as a children's radio program. Noting the program's popularity, Fox purchased the screen rights to the character and cast their contract player and all-around leading man Edmund Lowe in the title role. Opposite Lowe, Fox chose Bela Lugosi (fresh from his success in *White Zombie*) as Chandu's nemesis, the power-hungry madman Roxor.

The story of *Chandu the Magician* (1932) revolves around Frank Chandler (Edmund Lowe), aka Chandu, a Westerner who has just attained the rank and power of 'Yogi' in Tibet. "The world needs thee," proclaims Chandu's aged mentor. "Go forth in thy youth and strength and conquer the evil that threatens mankind." This evil takes the form of Roxor, a megalomaniac scientist who has kidnapped Chandu's brother-in-law, Robert Regent (Henry B. Walthall). Robert has perfected a death ray and Roxor intends to pry the secret from his captive and use its destructive powers to rule the world.

What follows is 72 minutes of rescues, escapes, and confrontations in which Chandu utilizes his Yogi powers of hypnosis and illusion to perform all manner of daring-do. This gives *Chandu the Magician* the feel of a simplistic serial (like the later 1934 and '35 serial condensations *The Return of Chandu* and *Chandu on the Magic Island*)—with the added advantage, however, of a feature-film budget and the production staff to go with it.

Chandu the Magician's sets and photography are both excellent, not surprising considering that famed set designer William Cameron Menzies (who served as art director on such classics as *The Thief of Bagdad* [1924], *Gone With the Wind* [1939], and *Foreign Correspondent* [1940], and who later directed *Things to Come* [1936], *Invaders from Mars* [1953] and *The Maze* [1953]) co-directed, and celebrated cinematographer James Wong Howe (*The Thin Man* [1934], *Mark of the Vampire* [1935], *Hud* [1963], *Seconds* [1966]) served as director of photography. In smooth tracking shots, for instance, Howe's camera glides through the imposing temple sets (filled with huge columns, forbidding statues, and dark corners) like some silent desecrator, generating a feeling of uneasy wonder.

While the picture *looks* good, however, little can be said for the one-dimensional characters or the melodramatic acting. As Chandu, Edmund Lowe so underplays his role that he falls flat in his feeble attempt to bring his character to mystical life. Lowe once studied for the priesthood before becoming an actor, though perhaps not *well* for he fails to imbue Chandu with any semblance of spiritualism.

At the other end of the acting spectrum stands Bela Lugosi who goes overboard and makes his overripe Roxor *bigger* than life. Lugosi draws out his enthusiastic rule-the-world speeches with such relish that one simply can't take this madman seriously. Still, while no more convincing than Edmund Lowe, Lugosi becomes infinitely more *fun* to watch. In their review of the film, the *New York Daily News* made special mention of Bela Lugosi, calling him "the very devil of a villain," and maintaining that "the sight of him sends shivers up and down one's back." Roxor proved a perfect vehicle for Lugosi's particular brand of bombast.

Though the raw materials were present to make *Chandu the Magician* an all-out horror film in the vein of the same year's *The Mask of Fu Manchu* (world-hungry madman, threatened captives, death ray, exotic locale, etc.), *Chandu* focuses on romance and adventure rather than the darker elements of sexual deviance and torture. In so doing, *Chandu the Magician* becomes a hokey, mildly entertaining adventure fantasy pleasing to the eye but bland to the palate.

Fox originally intended to do a series of Chandu pictures, but the returns on this first one proved disappointing and so no further installments materialized. (This didn't stop Charles Pressley, however, from creating a *Chandu the Magician* waxworks exhibit—featuring Lugosi's Roxor—in his Hollywood Motion Picture Museum and Hall of Fame shortly after the film's release.)

Chandu soon rose from the box-office ashes, however, when independent producer Sol Lesser obtained the character rights and filmed *The Return of Chandu* in 1934 as a 12-chapter serial. Riding this celluloid phoenix was none other than Bela Lugosi—but in a very different role. This time Lugosi, the arch-villain in the

Bela Lugosi, as the villainous Roxor, menaces the heroine in Chandu the Magician *(1932). A scant two years later he was playing Chandu himself in* The Return of Chandu *and saving the heroine this time. (lobby cards)*

original picture, was cast as Chandu—the hero!

When Lesser proposed to produce a Chandu serial, he began searching for the ideal actor to fill the mystical/romantic shoes of this popular radio character (one with a bit more charisma than the tepid Edmund Lowe). "By a surprisingly easy process of elimination," stated Lesser in his film's publicity material, "I reached the conclusion that Bela Lugosi, the Hungarian star, was the ideal I sought. On his own native stage—at the National Theatre of Budapest—his greatest successes had been achieved in romantic roles, such as Cyrano de Bergerac, Romeo, Hamlet and Petruccio in *Taming of the Shrew*. Yet in America he had been 'typed' as a 'heavy.' as in *Dracula* for instance. His voice, I found, could assume the modulations of Chandu as heard in all those countless homes throughout America where a radio was installed, and of course, his skill as an actor could be depended upon to complete the realization of what Chandu looks, acts, and talks like."

Lugosi, fresh from a more-or-less benign characterization in Universal's *The Black Cat* (1934), welcomed the chance to play a more romantic (though still mysterious) character. "*The Black Cat*," boasted the actor in a *Return of Chandu* publicity piece, "was the picture that secured for me my present stellar part in which I am at last permitted to appear before American audiences in a distinctly romantic characterization." *The Return of Chandu* wrapped on August 4, 1934, after a hectic three-week shooting schedule. A *Hollywood Reporter* item (August 15, 1934) noted that Lugosi, now having finished *Chandu*, was checking in at Universal "for a top spot in *Daughter of Dracula*" (which ultimately evolved into *Dracula's Daughter—without* Lugosi).

An enterprising filmmaker, Lesser released *The Return of Chandu* in two forms, offering the standard 12-chapter serial to those theaters who played such fare, and also creating a seven-reel film condensed from the first five chapters for cinemas whose venue required features. (Lesser later hired editor Carl Himm to create a 'sequel' feature out of the remaining seven chapters as well, calling it *Chandu on the Magic Island*.)

The plot (of both features) has Frank Chandler (aka Chandu) using his mystic Yogi powers to foil the plans of a strange cat-worshipping sect located on "the lost island of Lemuria." The Lemurians need a sacrifice to restore their high priestess to life. Using their agents throughout the world, they attempt to kidnap and offer up the beautiful Princess Nadji of Egypt (Maria Alba), a friend (and, ultimately, love-interest) of Chandu. Thus the picture consists of numerous kidnapping attempts (some successful, some thwarted) and rescues of the fair Princess by Chandu and his tag-along nephew Bobby (Deane Benton).

Of the two features culled from the serial, *The Return of Chandu* is by far the superior entry. Lugosi's hypnotic talents (complete with his patented *Dracula* gestures) and forceful presence are fully exploited here. While it sports some vintage Lugosi histrionics, *Return*, however, also possesses those flaws one would expect from a cheap serial—crude, static photography, shallow characterizations, hollow sound, and an over-loud, often inappropriate, musical score—as well as the inevitable and sometimes laughable continuity lapses that result when someone shoehorns half a dozen serial episodes into a solitary feature.

For *Chandu on the Magic Island* (the second 'film'), such faults are multiplied, since this second pastiche offers little to either the serial or the Lugosi fan. Unfortunately (for the viewer), Chandu loses his mystical powers in this feature, and so Lugosi's hammy but entertaining hypnotic battle of wills with the evil villains is supplanted by endless stretches of Chandu ineffectually skulking about trying to get out of one mess after another. (And—unlike in *Return*—said situations lack the verve and thrill-a-minute excitement one expects from a quality serial.) As the now-powerless hero, Lugosi can only creep about trying to avoid capture, contact his spiritual mentor (the Yogi), or lament the loss of his preternatural powers (due to an "invisible barrier of black magic"). At one point, the villain traps Chandu in an underground maze and gloats, "You may walk the passages for years and find no way out." With the amount of footage devoted to Lugosi moving slowly through these tunnels, one fears this may indeed become a dreary reality. About the only thrill found in *Chandu on the Magic Island* is in seeing (in full daylight) the mammoth gate from *King Kong* (used to represent the temple of Lemuria) and the Dakang port set from *The Son of Kong* (utilized as the town of Suva), which producer Sol Lesser borrowed from RKO. Not surprisingly, Lugosi appears listless and less enthusiastic here than in *The Return of Chandu* (perhaps he grew tired of the lackluster role after making the first half-dozen episodes).

Lesser's serial/feature ploy failed to impress the critics (or moviegoers, for that matter) and the planned series of Chandu features and two-reel shorts the producer had proposed for Lugosi failed to materialize.

Even so, despite their obvious flaws, *The Return of Chandu* and (to a lesser extent) its sister feature *Chandu on the Magic Island* still remain intriguing to Lugosiphiles, if for no other reason than that for one brief moment in his Hollywood career, Bela Lugosi shouldered the burden of heroics rather than villainy.

> The following is a somewhat expanded version of a review that strolled through *Cult Movies* magazine (issue 13) in 1995.

DEAD MEN WALK (1943)

"REVENGE! Back from the grave to put a devil's curse on his own brother! ...*A Thrill-Shocker That Keeps You Tingling!*" –ad line

There are two main reasons to watch *Dead Men Walk*: George Zucco and George Zucco. He plays twin brothers, one a kind-hearted doctor and the other an evil student of the occult who returns from the grave as a vampire to seek revenge on his saintly twin. You see, the good brother had murdered the bad to rid the world of his "foul presence," and a malevolent bloodsucker is not one to forgive easily. Zucco plays his two polar-opposite roles well, giving even Karloff a run for his money

Two George Zuccos for the price of one in Dead Men Walk *(1943). (newspaper ad)*

in the kindly doctor role, while imbuing the thoroughly evil vampire with a cultured yet ruthless quality. "I do remember that George Zucco couldn't have been nicer," praised co-star Mary Carlisle to interviewer Don Leifert. She also recalled how working at PRC (the most impoverished of the Poverty Row studios), as opposed to working at a major studio, "was the difference between a Rolls Royce and a Ford. We'd shoot a picture at PRC in anywhere from ten days to two weeks." For *Dead Men Walk* it was even less—a mere *six* days.

Though a long way from his horror heyday with *Dracula* and *Frankenstein*, Dwight Frye also leaves a lasting impression in his final maniacal henchman role. Frye's plaintive cries for help as he lies trapped under a heavy dresser at the fiery climax are both pitiful and chilling in their delivery. By this point Frye had been reduced to working as a tool dye maker at night and prowling the casting offices by day seeking acting rolls. As his son, Dwight David Frye, recalled (in *Dwight Frye: His Life and Career*, by Gregory William Mank),

"From what I heard from my mother, my dad was obviously very worried about finances, frustrated, and maybe even a bit bitter about the fact that nobody would give him work except in films like *Dead Men Walk*." Frye died this same year, on November 7, 1943, of a coronary thrombosis. He was only 44 years old.

Dead Men Walk's nondescript plot follows the usual love interest between hero and doctor's daughter before closing with the standard climactic conflagration, which consumes both twins. For those willing to dig, Fred Myton's (*The Mad Monster*, *Nabonga*) generally uninspired screenplay does contain an intriguing underlying theme. If one looks at the twins as separate manifestations of the same entity—two sides of the same Jekyll-and-Hyde coin, as it were—then by having the good twin die in the process of destroying the bad, it demonstrates that one cannot upset the balance in human nature and remain intact. Pure good cannot function without the balance of the other, darker side. Or, without the symbolism, a more cynical viewer might see the dual-death as simply Myton having to bow to the omnipresent Production Code in not letting a crime (even the murder of an evil twin) go unpunished. All in all, *Dead Men Walk* remains a low-budget diversion enriched by Zucco's and Frye's performances but little else.

Though a generally forgotten film, *Dead Men Walk* inadvertently accrued a cinematic legacy by indirectly fostering the cinematic career of none other than *Jean Rollin*, France's erotic vampire champion of the 1970s (and maker of such *films fantastique* as *The Nude Vampire*, *Caged Virgins*, and *The Grapes of Death*). "Originally, [my first movie] was supposed to be the extension of an American horror film," recalled Rollin to interviewer Peter Blumenstock, "a PRC film called *Dead Men Walk*, starring George Zucco and Dwight Frye. Jean Lavie, a young distributor and a good friend of mine, told me he had bought this very film, and it was supposed to be shown in the Scarlett and Midi-Minuit theaters in Paris, two cinemas specializing in this type of cinema. But they couldn't show it because it was too short, scarcely an hour long. He proposed to me that I shoot about thirty minutes of film so they could add it and show the film without problems." So Rollin made *Le Viol du Vampire* (Rape of the Vampire). Rollin's financial backer, Sam Selsky, then suggested to Rollin "that if we could make half an hour of film for practically nothing, we could also make a feature-length film for practically nothing. ...Thus we had to add a second part to *Le Viol du Vampire*." Rollin's effort earned "quite some money" and launched the career of one of Europe's most iconoclassic horror filmmakers—all thanks to the brevity of *Dead Men Walk*...

> Herein represents my first foray into the *foreign* magazine market—namely, the British publication *Shivers*. While editor David Miller expressed his enthusiasm for (and amusement at) this piece, it proved to be the only one of mine they ever published (in issue 51, March 1998). It would be nearly two decades before I cracked a British magazine cover again.

THE DEVIL-DOLL (1936)

Though rarely considered among the first tier of Golden Age horror classics, *The Devil-Doll* remains an admittedly uneven though thoroughly entertaining mix of horror, science, and fantasy that boasts a bizarrely enthralling story, memorable performances (*two* by Lionel Barrymore alone!), and startling special effects. It's also the fourth and final time that the enigmatic Tod Browning (*Dracula, Freaks, Mark of the Vampire*) dipped his unsteady hand into the sound horror pool.

The Devil-Doll actually began as a voodoo property called *The Witch of Timbucktoo*. Before the project could proceed, however, the story was severely altered—reportedly to pacify the British censors (with *The Hollywood Reporter* complaining that "once again a foreign government has stepped in to censor a Hollywood script for political reasons.") Apparently, Her Majesty's government felt concern that the voodoo sequences would "stir up trouble" among its black subjects throughout the empire and requested that all black characters be dropped. MGM not only removed all the black characters, but erased all traces of voodoo as well, and basically started over with a new (scientific-oriented) storyline.

Said story follows the unjustly convicted Paul Lavond (Lionel Barrymore) as he escapes from Devil's Island with his friend, a scientist named Marcel (Henry B. Walthall). (Sadly, Walthal succumbed to a chronic illness two months before *The Devil-Doll*'s release.) Marcel, along with his companion Malita, has developed a method to shrink people down to one-sixth their normal size. The imperfect process, however, wipes out the subjects' memories and they become "creatures capable of responding only to the force of another will." When Marcel expires from a heart attack, Lavond sees this process as a way to wreak his vengeance against his three former banking partners who had framed him for *their* crimes. With Malita's help, Lavond returns to Paris disguised as an old woman toymaker named Madame Mandelip. Using his living dolls, he exacts his revenge. As Madame Mandelip, Lavond also steals a few bittersweet moments with his unknowing daughter, Lorraine, to whom he dare not reveal himself. In the poignant ending, Lavond, posing as a friend of her 'dead' father, takes his final leave of Lorraine. Realizing that his retribution has cost him dear, the implication is that he must quit this world to atone for his crimes—however justified they might have been.

The screenplay's credited co-writers proved an unusual trio, and one with more than passing interest to classic horror fans. Garrett Fort, for instance, was a horror veteran of the first rank, having scripted or co-scripted the screenplays for *Dracula* (1931), *Frankenstein* (1931), and (later) *Dracula's Daughter* (1936).

French novelist and screenwriter Guy Endore was no stranger to horror either, having co-authored two other Golden Age terror scripts—Browning's earlier *Mark of the Vampire* (1935) and Karl Freund's final film as director, *Mad Love* (1935). Endore also worked up a treatment for *The Raven* (1935), but his contribution was passed over. In 1961, Endore's novel *The WereWolf of Paris* (published in 1933) inspired Hammer's *The Curse of the Werewolf*.

The Devil-Doll's third screenwriter was Erich von Stroheim, the fallen "homme terrible" of Hollywood. Von Stroheim had been an actor/director of the first order in the 1920s (with lavish pictures like *Greed* [1924] and *The Wedding March* [1928]) but had been denied the chance to direct in the 1930s due to his legendary extravagance and volatile temperament. He returned to acting and screenwriting. Having acted in only a handful of films in the first half of the decade, von Stroheim jumped at the chance of a regular salary when MGM offered him a position as a staff writer. The formerly great director who had commanded budgets upwards of a million dollars ten years previously was offered the low-end salary scale of $150 per week—and took it.

Another intriguing figure lurking behind the scenes on *The Devil-Doll* was E. J. Mannix. A high-ranking Metro executive and member of Hollywood's 'Old Guard,' Mannix served as executive producer on *The Devil-Doll*, a position he also filled on both of Tod Browning's earlier MGM horrors, *Freaks* (1932) and *Mark of the Vampire* (1935). One suspects that Mannix, who was only infrequently assigned to supervise individual films, played the role of Metro watchdog on these pictures, sent to keep an eye on the alcoholic, semi-reliable Browning. While an important figure in Hollywood history, Mannix

The Devil-Doll *poster.*

has also become something of a bizarre footnote. In the book *Deadly Illusions: Jean Harlow and the Murder of Paul Bern*, author Samuel Marx claims to have confirmed the long-standing rumor that Mannix had murdered George "Superman" Reeves in 1959. Reeves' death was officially labeled suicide at the time, though the actor's mother (and many others since then) insisted it was murder. Apparently, Reeves was the third point of a romantic triangle involving Mannix and his wife. (Reeves, in fact, willed his estate to Mrs. Mannix.)

The Devil-Doll is a rather sentimental film which seems to be at odds with itself. On the one hand it wants to be a horrific special effects picture. On the other, it strains for sentimental tragedy. At times it comes perilously close to being maudlin. Fortunately, Lionel Barrymore is there to add substance to the sympathetic scenario. As the grievously wronged Paul Lavond, Barrymore's kindly, stoic, and likable portrayal lends an air of dignity (yes, even while in drag) and sincerity to the story. Lavond is a tragic figure, one who could easily become both insipid and ridiculous in his self-pity, female disguise, and fantastic scheme of vengeance. Barrymore's genuine and heartfelt performance anchors a picture which continually threatens to fly off in opposing directions.

Barrymore's fellow actors ably support him on all sides. As Lorraine, Maureen O'Sullivan balances both the bitterness and love felt by Lavond's daughter, creating a complex and realistic character. Frank Lawton (also in the same year's *The Invisible Ray*), while given the rather thankless role of Lorraine's love interest, makes the best of his brief (but well-written) scenes, infusing his portrayal with compassion and down-to-earth common sense. (This makes *The Devil-Doll* one of the few Golden Age horror pictures to feature a good performance by the juvenile male lead.) The ever-reliable Pedro de Cordoba (as the lead villain) slips from suave urbanity to concerned nervousness to near-hysterical anxiety (having received a note from Lavond warning him to confess his crimes or die at ten o'clock that evening) with an effective smoothness. His mounting tension and ultimate breakdown would make even Basil Rathbone envious; De Cordoba's increasing irritability and nervousness is steadier, less violent, more subtle, and ultimately more effective than Rathbone's similarly distraught Wolf von Frankenstein (in *Son of Frankenstein*), adding a sharp edge to the suspenseful scene.

The top honors, however, should go to Rafaela Ottiano. She takes her unsubtle, rather one-dimensional character of Malita and delivers a convincing portrayal of obsessive madness. With her eyes wide and wild, her eyebrows arched, her visage contorted with a mad zeal, she forces her words out with breathless excitement and insane conviction. Malita's physical appearance adds to the effect. Walking with a limp and leaning on a crutch, her unkempt dark, wiry hair sporting a shock of white (á la *Bride of Frankenstein*), the gleam in her eye and her animated face paint a convincing picture of mad enthusiasm. Malita reminds us that this picture is indeed a horror film, and Ms. Ottiano's zealous energy permeates every scene she plays. She is truly the decade's best (albeit only) female mad scientist.

The Devil-Doll is without question the best *acted* of Tod Browning's horror pictures. Browning has been characterized as giving little direction to his actors (perhaps stemming from his close association with Lon Chaney, who was a near-autonomous thespian entity), so possibly the major credit for the excellent acting in *Devil-Doll* should lie with the players themselves, professionals all. In any case, the supporting performances do much to ground the fantastical film in reality.

Aside from the actors, much of the film's effectiveness stems from the superb special effects, specifically the incredible realism of the oversized props and sets. When a miniaturized 'devil-doll' crawls out of a gigantic crib, climbs a three-story dresser, or pushes open a mammoth bedroom door, the colossal surroundings leave no doubt that she truly is only a foot tall. Stan Rogers and Edwin Willis' sets (with supervision from MGM Art Department head Cedric Gibbons) are intricately detailed and convincingly scaled. To Browning's and cinematographer Leonard Smith's joint credit, they are well-photographed and realistically lit as well, with oversized shadows adding depth and realism while high-angle camerawork adds to the illusion of diminutive size.

While the scenes involving the oversized sets are impeccable, other miniature effects, however, are not. Some matte shots appear particularly weak in places, falling far short of the standard set by *King Kong* three years earlier. The tiny creatures (dogs, horses, humans) moving about on table tops don't quite appear three dimensional, and the lighting never matches convincingly, with the over-bright living subject standing out conspicuously from the more naturally-lit background.

A few un-special effects are not the film's only foible, however. Though a unique production, *The Devil-Doll*'s uneasy combination of horror, science, and heartrending tragedy bleeds together into an odd hodgepodge of fantasy and drama. Early on, for instance, we see a gloomy old dark house situated in a swamp, complete with a dead tree silhouetted in front. This eerie shot dissolves to the candle-lit interior where a woman plays an ominous tune on an organ. Suddenly, this moody scene switches to a brightly-lit modern laboratory outfitted with gleaming bottles and a shining, sterile table. This change from a menacing atmosphere ripe with dread possibilities to one of bright, sunny science is jarring and ill-conceived.

The picture having passed the baton from horror to science, Marcel then gives a brief, grade-school lecture on the building blocks of matter—and even finds time to pithily explain away the demise of the dinosaur (a hotly contested issue even to this day) by implying that they all starved to death(!) because of their great size. The scientific focus quickly blurs into pure fantasy with the notion that Marcel's scientifically-shrunken beings can be controlled by hypnotic willpower—a "beam of thought." This mesmeric angle makes the diminutive creatures seem more alchemic homunculi than an achievement of modern science. The picture has now slid into the realm of fantasy.

Unfortunately, rather than focus on this (admittedly intriguing) fantasy aspect the story shifts gears yet again, driving toward something akin to Greek Tragedy. The fantasy becomes a mere tool used briefly in the scenario of injustice, revenge, and atonement which plays out in the remaining hour. For the rest of the film, horror rarely rears its ugly head, science is all-but-forgotten, and fantasy pops up only briefly as a mere implement of revenge. These elements are left sadly untapped and unexplored in the midst of the human drama.

Said drama *is* effective, however, thanks in large part to Barrymore and co.'s cogent playing—though even this proves uneven. While Barrymore does well with the sentimental aspects of the tale, he fails to round out his character with the very necessary dark elements of bitterness and hate Paul Lavond purportedly possesses. In discussing his burning hatred and thirst for vengeance, Barrymore's manner remains flat and devoid of the feelings he professes to have. "You see, when a man saves an ambition in a dirty dungeon for seventeen years," he says while casually putting his hands in his pockets and rocking back on his heels, "it becomes almost an insane obsession. With Marcel it was science. With me it was hate—hate and vengeance." Barrymore puts little emphasis on these last three emotional words, delivering them in an almost lackadaisical manner. Throughout this potentially charged and revealing soliloquy, Barrymore's attitude is one of almost casual detachment, as if he's explaining the workings of a combustion engine rather than the workings of a combustible state of mind. Barrymore is so easy-going that one just can't take his professed hatred seriously. This weakens the structure of the picture, which revolves around Lavond's justified thirst for retribution. If Barrymore doesn't seem to believe it, why should we? The actor is much more animated as Madame Mandelip and seems to enjoy playing the elderly female, showing much more spark as the "poor, toddling old woman" than as the supposedly hate-filled Paul Lavond. (Amusingly, in the film's pressbook, Barrymore complained of the hazards of playing a man disguised as an old woman, a part ballyhooed as "the strangest role of his screen career": "I never realized how difficult it was to change sex. The make-up alone was an ordeal. I was never meant for wigs and dresses! When my false hair wasn't slipping out of place, my feet were getting entangled in the hem of my skirt.")

Tod Browning's direction is straightforward but uninspired. Once again, he fails to make full use of the camera. It moves occasionally, but never to any great purpose (usually just following a character from one end of a room to the other). Most often the camera is static and Browning relies on different set-ups within a scene for variety. Rather than utilizing the camera for emphasis or interest, Browning counts on his editor to keep the scenes moving visually. Admittedly, Browning shoots enough varied footage to make this work adequately, but one comes to expect something more than "adequate" from a director of Browning's stature (a stature that is quickly being cut down to its proper size in the more recent reassessments of his work). Still, at least for *The Devil-Doll*, Browning did not make the downright *poor* decisions which nearly ruined *Dracula* (1931).

After *Dracula* (1931), *The Devil-Doll* became Tod Browning's most successful film of the decade (financially speaking), earning a modest $68,000 profit for his home studio, MGM. Though it *did* turn a profit, such an underwhelming box-office performance did little to revitalize Browning's fading career, and he made only one more film before withdrawing from the industry altogether to live out the last two decades of his life in hermit-like obscurity. Considering the erratic director's uneven output, the flawed-but-worthy *Devil-Doll* proved an appropriate genre swan song.

Filmfax magazine set their eye on Dr. Cyclops *via this review back in 1997 (issue 61).*

DR. CYCLOPS (1940)

In this first-ever full color horror film, Albert Dekker plays the mad Dr. Thorkel ("the world's greatest living authority on organic molecular structure"), who utilizes radiation from a secret uranium mine in the jungles of the Amazon to shrink living things down to one-sixth their normal size. Due to his poor eyesight (the myopic man can't even function without his thick, coke-bottle spectacles), he sends for a team of scientists to use as his eyes. After a cursory glance at some microscope slides, the trio identify the one element which has been holding Thorkel back in his work. No longer in need of them, the polite but arrogant Thorkel summarily dismisses his colleagues. Outraged, they discover the nature of his secret experiments, and are promptly shrunk down to a foot in height by the unscrupulous Thorkel for interfering. After Thorkel callously murders one of his new 'specimens,' the intrepid band of Tom Thumbs escape the doctor's compound only to face the perils of the jungle's now-gigantic flora and fauna. With Thorkel on the hunt for his diminutive prey, the surviving little people must find a way to kill the gigantic evil genius before he can destroy them first.

Dr. Cyclops starts out with great promise, beginning with an exceedingly effective opening sequence in which two men, Thorkel and his assistant, argue over the doctor's work. Bathed in a weird flickering green light (emanating from the radiation-directing machinery), Thorkel suddenly grabs his mutinous subordinate and forces his head down between two conductor-like devices. The unfortunate's face glows an even deeper shade of green and the victim's skull seems to shine through his very skin as he dies. It is a shocking and rather horrific opening, a moment that, sadly, the film will never come close to again.

Thereafter, producer/director Ernest B. Schoedsack concentrates more on the adventure/fantasy aspects of the tale than on the terrifying ones. Though disappointing for the horror fan, this should come as no surprise considering that the man twirling the director's baton co-created *King Kong* (1933), the greatest adventure film ever made. Consequently, *Dr. Cyclops'* tone is one of *wonder* as scene after scene focuses on the ingenuity shown by the protagonists in coping with their incredible situation. Schoedsack rarely touches on the truly terrifying emotional component which would arise from such a complete loss of control. Even the obligatory threatened-by-a-giant-cat sequence carries little menace, as it's shot in a straightforward, mundane manner that fails to exploit the horror of a fifteen-foot feline of furry fury. Seventeen years later Jack Arnold showed the cinema what a terror a gigantic housecat could *really* become in the far superior *The Incredible Shrinking Man* (1957).

Under Shoedsack's direction, cinematographer Henry Sharp turns the carbon arcs up full blast to bathe the sets in bright light. Though the colors are rich (and one of the reasons so much light was necessary), the absence of shadowy settings and dark recesses (even in the potentially shudder-inducing jungle) keep the picture from building any sort of malevolent atmosphere.

Schoedsack again undercuts the story's horrific possibilities by placing a heavy emphasis on *humor* rather than horror. The timid group scurry about the compound yard comically pointing in amazement at all manner of gigantic props, and flinch when an oversized chicken flutters as they walk past (accompanied by 'cute' music on the soundtrack in which piccolos trill up and down to match the 'amusing' actions).

Tom Kilpatrick's screenplay allows for little characterization, taking the protagonists strictly from the stock shelves. There's the pompous professor (sporting the 'funny' moniker, Dr. Bulfinch), the lazy engineer with a boyish (or, in this case, *boorish*) charm, the laconic hired man, the brainy but beautiful female scientist (who screams at the drop of a hat), and the ethnic comic relief in the form of an Hispanic simpleton.

The players are generally adequate (though Thomas Coley invests his hero/engineer part with about as much personality as the gigantic cactus the group ducks

Shrunk to six-inches tall by the nefarious Dr. Cyclops *(1940), the protagonists must face all manner of massive menaces.*

under). The one standout is Albert Dekker as Thorkel. Possessing a self-possessed soft-spokenness that flares into outright mania when provoked, Dekker brings a sense of humor to his amoral mad doctor. "You'll find the world far away—for legs as short as yours," he chides one of the scientists with just the hint of a chuckle in his voice and twinkle in his eye. "These mice are not for you," Thorkel tells his cat who's gazing at the pint-sized humans with a hungry look, before adding, "at least not yet." Dekker's almost whimsical attitude as he pokes gentle fun at his tiny, doomed captives becomes downright chilling.

One of the biggest assets (literally) found in *Dr. Cyclops* are the wonderfully realistic oversized sets and props. The cast runs around and through and over and into all manner of huge crates, buckets, tables, and even a gigantic cactus plant (under whose protecting thorns they seek refuge more than once). The gigantic books, scissors, eye glasses, shotgun, et al. are all so convincing that one quickly comes to believe that these people truly are only a foot tall.

Unfortunately, the illusion is occasionally spoiled by the less-than-perfect rear-projection shots, whose grainy appearance doesn't quite integrate with the more vibrant actors and scenery in the foreground. Special Effects artist Farcoit Alexander Edouart (1895–1980) provided these effects, which proved inferior to what had been done four years earlier in Tod Browning's *The Devil-Doll* (1936). The Academy of Motion Pictures Arts and Sciences didn't think so, however, and rewarded Edouart with an Oscar nomination for his work. He didn't win.

Also disappointing is the gigantic hand that grabs Dr. Bulfinch (or, more accurately, that waits while Bulfinch awkwardly backs into it). The huge, unwieldy extremity looks phony and moves too slowly, so that it appears out of sync with the gigantic rear-projected Albert Dekker.

All in all, *Dr. Cyclops* remains a fairly entertaining adventure movie, thanks to the lavish color, elaborate props, and engaging performance by Albert Dekker. Still, with a less adventure-oriented and more mood-minded filmmaker at the helm, it could have become so much more.

> I have no memory of why or for whom I penned this piece. Fortunately, most fans have no such difficulty remembering (and venerating) this best-ever adaptation of Stevenson's classic tale.

SEXY BEAST: *DR. JEKYLL AND MR. HYDE* (1931)

"It's the things that one *can't* do that always tempt me." –Fredric March as Dr. Jekyll

There's no denying how important sex is to the human animal. Apart from the obvious issue of species propagation, sex has been linked to the very formation of modern society itself. Most mammals copulate only during intermittent periods of ovulation, whereas humans indulge incessantly (albeit some more successfully than others). Sigmund Freud, among other scientists, postulated that it is this constant sexual drive that gave rise to the family structure (since animals that breed cyclically have no impetus to form a strong familial bond) and consequently to the very framework of the civilized world itself. So if we have sex to thank for our modern civilization, it's little wonder that art (including cinema) has found it such an intriguing topic.

With all their attendant anxieties, the themes of sex and death have become two of the principal topics explored (and/or exploited) by the horror/sci-fi genre. Both of these issues generate a great deal of apprehension (I'm sure even Valentino felt his fair share of performance anxiety, and I know of no one who hasn't had some qualms about his or her own inevitable demise); and fear is what this genre is (mostly) about. The horror film lets us explore these two powerful subjects within the safety of fantasy, and the best ones bring some insight and build (dare I say?) a bridge over these troubled waters.

Even in the 1930s sexuality was an important part of motion pictures (particularly in the pre–Production Code days prior to 1934), and the burgeoning horror genre provided viewers with a particularly intriguing avenue of exploration. The sound horror film was born awash in the themes of Eros and Thanatos. Much of *Dracula*'s (1931) appeal can be seen as outright sexual attraction. The mesmeric presence of Bela Lugosi as Count Dracula ("Ah, what letters women wrote me," declared the actor, "...letters of horrible hunger") provides the ultimate confidence figure to the uncertain males in the audience as he unfailingly conquers his swooning objects of desire. Alongside Dracula stand his three beautiful wives, who descend en masse on the hapless Renfield, intent on draining him of his life-giving fluids (perhaps the ultimate heterosexual male fantasy).

The genre's follow-up entry, the sci-fi-tinged *Frankenstein* (1931), with its doppelganger motif, can be seen (using an admittedly elastic imagination) as a homoerotic struggle between Dr. Henry Frankenstein (played by Colin Clive) and his creation. One can interpret the conflict caused by Frankenstein's creation of a man as the conflict arising from homosexual love and its subsequent rejection. In light of director James Whale's open homosexuality (and Clive's reported closeted bisexuality), this theme becomes particularly intriguing. The discord arises when Henry rejects his creature out of hand, feeling it ugly and brutal. Is this what happens when one disavows one's own sexual instincts? "There can be no wedding," announces Henry, "while this horrible creation of mine is still alive." Frankenstein cannot consummate 'normal' love while his homosexuality lives to assert itself.

But the third sound horror film offered by the fledgling genre proved to be the ultimate erotic thriller of its generation. Released on the last day of 1931, *Dr. Jekyll and Mr. Hyde* unleashed the literal 'Monster from the Id' upon an unsuspecting moviegoing public.

The story of Robert Louis Stevenson's *The Strange Case of Dr. Jekyll and Mr. Hyde* has become so ingrained in our popular consciousness that detailing it here would be a waste of space. Suffice it to say that, given only seven weeks and less than $500,000 (only slightly more money than *Dracula* and less than *half* the amount needed to make MGM's inferior 1941 Spencer Tracy version of *Dr. Jekyll and Mr. Hyde*), director Rouben Mamoulian took Stevenson's classic work on the duality of man and created a brilliant cinematic study of man's struggle to control his primitive instincts—with *lust* being foremost among them. In Mamoulian's own words (quoted in *Cinefantastique* magazine no. 3): "Mr. Hyde is the exact replica of the Neanderthal man, so he's our ancestor. We *were* that once. The struggle or dilemma is not between evil and good, it's between the sophisticated, spiritual self in man and his animal, primeval instincts." (Never mind that the filmmaker got humanity's family tree wrong here, as it's been shown that the Neanderthal took a wholly separate branch from homo sapien and so is *not* "our ancestor." Still, Mamoulian's sentiments remain salient.)

Mamoulian chose to extend the metaphor even further and explore the conflict of society vs. the individual (Dr. Jekyll as the representative of the repressed Victorian "proper" society, and Mr. Hyde as the personification of individual gratification). While Hyde does not live by society's rules (his actions are governed only by the cravings and whims of his own Id), Jekyll is restrained—and frustrated—by the dictates of societal mores. Mamoulian daringly explores this theme of repressed desires and pent-up sexuality, intimating that it is these unfulfilled longings that lead Jekyll to destruction, causing him to seek relief in the "evil" form of Mr. Hyde. And this release *is* evil, as Stevenson's story and Samuel Hoffenstein & Percy Heath's screenplay take great pains to point out. In the best tradition of the morality play, one of the major messages of *Dr. Jekyll and Mr. Hyde* is that just as repression can lead to dangerous risks, so can unbridled self-gratification lead to complete self-destruction.

The movie becomes a cautionary tale balancing the two extremes of repression and self-gratification, which, via the sci-fi device of splitting one personality into two, become personified in the same individual. And when Jekyll fails to strike a balance between the two, his total destruction ensues. So Mamoulian's (and Stevenson's) *Dr. Jekyll and Mr. Hyde* tells us that moderation in sexual matters, as in most things in life, is a consummation devoutly to be wished.

Such a message undoubtedly reflected, at least in part, the climate of the times. Nineteen-thirty-one saw the Great Depression nearing its peak, with the American economy on the brink of collapse and millions of men out of work (emasculated economically, so to speak). As a prelude to this calamity, the 1920s saw the American woman come into her own (at least partially), earning not only the vote, but some measure of sexual liberation as well (as witnessed by the rise of the "flapper" subculture). While one cannot ascribe a cause-and-effect relationship to these two developments, their proximity on the cultural timeline (not to mention basic human nature, which generally resists change) surely helped cast women's sexual liberation in a negative light, generating a backlash against the burgeoning sexuality of the American female and the lessening of male control (both in the workplace and in the bedroom). But, cleverly, Mamoulian demonstrates that in order to regain such control, the male (Jekyll) must literally become a sexually controlling monster (Hyde). Again, the film informs us that a balance, a happy medium, must be found.

On the technical side, Mamoulian paints his sexually-charged canvas with strokes both bold and subtle, utilizing a plethora of techniques and themes to create one of the most cinematically *alive* films ever shot (in any genre). Even something as simple as a dissolve becomes a fluid purveyor of thought and emotion. For instance, during a scene change in which Jekyll has just left Muriel (his chaste fiancée), the fading image of Muriel is superimposed for a few seconds onto the next scene of Jekyll walking with his friend Lanyon, demonstrating that her image is embedded deep within Jekyll's mind, and thoughts of her fill his head. Later, after Jekyll's first rather steamy encounter with chorus girl/prostitute Ivy, Mamoulian superimposes a shot of Ivy's swinging naked leg as the scene dissolves to Jekyll walking down the stairs. This second image serves a dual purpose. Not only does it expose what lingers beneath the surface of Jekyll's mind, it also distracts the viewer just as Jekyll himself is distracted, and so allies our thoughts and feelings with Jekyll's own. This serves to further cement the bond between the character and the viewer, which Mamoulian has taken such pains to forge with his various point-of-view shots at the film's opening.

Mamoulian even employs the split screen technique as a process of changing scenes and emphasizing conflict, allowing the audience to see one scene as it finishes while at the same time viewing the next as it begins. In one transition we see both Ivy and Muriel at the same time—before Ivy is finally wiped away as Jekyll meets with Muriel. This split image underscores Jekyll's inner conflict between the "good woman," Muriel (society's daughter and as such unattainable), and the "fallen woman" of the streets, Ivy, who is willing and able and oh-so-tempting. Thus we see simultaneously the two women in Jekyll's life—and the two very different sides of his "romantic interest." The duality of man (and his desires) is again emphasized.

One sequence in *Dr. Jekyll and Mr. Hyde* stands out as the most erotically charged scene in the film—indeed, of the entire decade—thanks to the alluring presence and seductive playing of Miriam Hopkins, and the astute and involving direction of Rouben Mamoulian. It occurs when sexy saloon singer Ivy Pierson (Hopkins) receives the mild medical attentions of Dr. Jekyll (Fredric March) after she's roughed up by some rogue. "Now you're the kind a woman would do something for!" she tells the good doctor as he gallantly tends to her bruised thigh. Her eyes flash wickedly and her lips curve enticingly. Undressing for bed after the good doctor prescribes rest, Ivy looks at Jekyll—and directly into the camera—and smiles, delicious and inviting. This point-of-view shot transforms the viewer from a detached voyeur into an involved participant in Ivy's game of coquettish seduction. We *become* the bemused (and aroused) Dr. Jekyll, to whom this beauty beckons so delectably. Reaching down slowly, Ivy pulls her petticoat up to expose her long, shapely legs. Gracefully, she removes her stockings and garters and playfully tosses them to Jekyll—to us—with a delightful laugh. Now naked in bed, Ivy reaches up impulsively and draws Jekyll to her. With a muffled, ecstatic "mmfff," she kisses him passionately. Throughout it all, the only flesh we actually see is her exposed back and a bit of leg, but oh does it fire the imagination! After all, eroticism begins in the mind, and the enticing glimpses and inviting glances provided by the sexy Ms. Hopkins gives one plenty of food for thought. She's not through with us yet, however. As Jekyll takes his leave ("I'll call that kiss my fee," he laughs), Ivy sits up in bed. Clutching the rumpled bedclothes to (barely) cover her nude body, she looks at Jekyll (at *us* again) and whispers seductively, "Come back soooon," while her naked leg swings saucily to and fro over the edge of the bed. Mamoulian then superimposes this shot of Ivy's swinging leg over the scene as Jekyll makes his exit—the lingering sexual image revealing that the seed of lust has been planted. For a full twenty-five seconds this arousing image of beautiful flesh is transposed over the sight of Lanyon (Jekyll's friend) chiding Jekyll about controlling his instincts. Controlling instincts be damned; we know what the good doctor is thinking about—and what *we* are pondering as well. The implied promise of erotic delights to come has set Jekyll's libido racing.

After this dose of highly-charged eroticism, Mamoulian goes on to explore the other side of the erotic coin through the unbridled character of Mr. Hyde, who ultimately turns a natural sexuality into hateful, bestial lust. One scene in particular embodies both the picture's horrific content and height of emotional/sexual power. In it, Hyde is at his most loathsome—a sadistic satyr who subtly plays on his victim's (Ivy's) mounting fears to build her emotional agony into a crescendo of terror. It begins as Hyde tells Ivy that he is going away. The sneering brute quickly dashes her ill-concealed hope, however, by asking, "You wouldn't have me go tonight, would you? Of course not; quite unworthy of our great love, hmm?" Clutching her, he forcefully presses his lips to her bosom. Reveling in the loathing and fear this inspires in her, he continues his verbal torture: "That's right, my little bird. The last evening is always the sweetest, you know." Trapped in his arms, struggling to control her dread of the sexual horrors to come, Ivy nearly collapses in panic. Enjoying her torment, Hyde continues his mocking taunts: "And what a farewell this one will be. What a farewell! I don't know

Dr. Jekyll and Mr. Hyde *(1931)—the premier 'erotic thriller' of its day, thanks in no small part to the alluring Miriam Hopkins as Ivy ("Come back soooon...").*

delight after his first release, or lifts his face to the rain in an exuberant display, March shows him to be the Id incarnate, determined to revel in every sensation. Later, when Hyde becomes a bit more "sophisticated" (i.e. sexual) in his pleasure-seeking, March adds to his brutal physical performance a dimension of subtle cruelty—namely, his sadistic dialogue delivery. In the scenes in which Hyde verbally taunts Ivy, March's sarcastic and double-edged emphasis (coupled with his sudden physical movements and quick shifts in demeanor) creates a terrifying picture of unpredictability. While he at first confines himself to the *verbal* torture of Ivy, it is a certainty that uncontrollable violence lurks just beneath the surface. March's brilliant mannerisms and mocking tones reveal the depths of mental as well as physical cruelty that this evil being is wont to inflict.

March is well supported by a cadre of fine actors. Miriam Hopkins matches March's Mr. Hyde with a flawless performance as the streetwise Ivy Pierson. At ease singing bawdy songs in a tavern or coquettishly lifting up her skirt to reveal her shapely legs, her unpolished charm and good humor make of her a very likable and sympathetic figure. Ivy's brazen sexuality is not a "dirty" thing, not a secret to be hidden away behind locked doors, but a breath of fresh air amongst the stuffy Victorian attitudes portrayed in the film.

While Rose Hobart (*Tower of London* [1939], *The Mad Ghoul* [1943], *Soul of a Monster* [1944]) is given the rather thankless role of Muriel, her earnest and intelligent performance manages to make her character real. Ms. Hobart admitted that playing the "good" half of Jekyll's romantic interest was not entirely satisfying. "I would have given anything to play the Miriam Hopkins part," she said. "That's why Ingrid Bergman chose it in the [1941] remake." Ironically, Hopkins initially wanted Hobart's role, and it took a persuasive Mamoulian to convince her otherwise. Ms. Hopkins later realized the allure of playing the "bad girl," admitting (in *Bad Girls of the Silver Screen*, by Lottie Da and Jan Al-

whether I shall be able to tear myself away from you at all. In fact, I shall only go as far as the door and the sight of your tears will bring me back. Does that please you, my dear?" March (utterly convincing in his role of tormentor) and Miriam Hopkins (the embodiment of barely-suppressed horror) create one of the most chillingly cruel scenes ever filmed.

Fredric March gives an Oscar-winning performance as Jekyll and Hyde (literally, since March won the 1932 Best Actor award, tying with Wallace Beery). As March plays him, Hyde is a beast, a brute in the form of a man (though Hyde's "form" is not altogether human, thanks to Wally Westmore's wonderfully simian make-up). March excels in the physical aspect of the role, his quick movements showing his impatience to wring every possible pleasure from his newfound freedom. As Hyde stretches with an almost animal exander), "I enjoyed playing that sort of woman. They have the courage of the damned. They know what they want and go right ahead."

Yes indeed, with the alluring "bad girl" Miriam Hopkins at his beck and call, that Mr. Hyde was one lucky monster. And within the horrific framework of *Dr. Jekyll and Mr. Hyde*, Rouben Mamoulian demonstrated how such "luck" comes with a steep price, and how both stifling repression and unbridled sexual excess are simply two sides of the same coin—the coin of extremism that ultimately buys disaster.

> Here's a long essay I put together back in the 1990s as a submission for one of the various genre magazines I was writing for at the time. For whatever reason (probably its length), it never saw print (though a considerably truncated version did appear in *Filmfax* magazine). Whether that was a bad or good thing, I'll leave up to you, as I'm including the full-length version here.

WARNERS' TERROR TWINS: *DOCTOR X* AND *MYSTERY OF THE WAX MUSEUM*

Doctor X (1932) and *Mystery of the Wax Museum* (1933) have much in common. Both were made by Warner Brothers (as that studio's first forays into sound horror), and both dealt with the horror of a hideous crazed killer. Both films shared much of the same production team and cast, including director Michael Curtiz, cinematographer Ray Rennahan, art director Anton Grot, editor George Amy, and actors Lionel Atwill, Fay Wray, and Arthur Edmund Carewe. The studio also allotted both productions the two-strip Technicolor treatment. Consequently, *Doctor X* and *Mystery of the Wax Museum* share a similar 'feel,' and, while differing slightly in quality, both remain genuine classics from the Golden Age of Horror.

DOCTOR X

"The human mind will only stand so much; we are all a little strange up here." –Otto, Dr. Xavier's butler [pointing to his temple]

Warner Brothers' first foray into sound horror, *Doctor X* traces its genesis to a 1928 play by Howard W. Comstock and Allen C. Miller called *Terror*. When first produced, however (in January of 1931), the play was retitled *Doctor X* to avoid confusion with the better-known Edgar Wallace property *The Terror*. Though *Doctor X* played on Broadway and received some good reviews, it closed after 80 performances. Warner Brothers purchased the film rights for $5,000 in January 1932 and assigned writer/actor George Rosener to pen the screenplay. Dissatisfied with Rosener's work, the studio set Earl Baldwin and Robert Tasker to rework it and consoled Rosener by awarding him the rather juicy part of Otto in the film.

Shooting commenced on March 19th, and director Michael Curtiz worked his cast and crew mercilessly in order to finish within the production's tight 24-day schedule. Fifteen-hour days quickly became the norm, and with the formation of the Screen Actors' Guild still two years away, the workers had little recourse for complaint. On one day (Saturday, April 2nd), the *Doctor X* company worked a grueling 24 hours straight as Curtiz completed an amazing 27 set-ups (which accounted for nearly eight minutes of screen time—one tenth of the finished picture!). Despite the company's herculean efforts, *Doctor X* wrapped two days *over* schedule.

"We are not here to preaching with pictures, to take political sides or bring a great message; we are here to entertain," opined Hungarian-born director Michael Curtiz in his trademark broken English. The talented director brought this philosophy of movie-making to bear fully on *Doctor X*, creating a fast-paced, visually exciting gem of spine-tingling entertainment. No deep issues of facing death, responsibility, or rebirth here, just a plethora of surface thrills and chills centering on morgues, mad scientists, cannibalism, and "moon-killers."

The story revolves around the search for a vicious murderer known as the "moon killer," who strikes only during a full moon. When Dr. Xavier (Lionel Atwill) and his staff at the Academy of Surgical Research come under suspicion, Xavier plans to conduct tests that will either clear the Academy or finger the guilty party. Retiring to his isolated mansion to conduct his experiment, Xavier reluctantly employs his own daughter Joan (Fay Wray) in a reenactment of the latest crime in order to flush out the killer. When things go awry and the (truly surprising) identity of the fiend is exposed (accompanied by a rather horrific revelation involving "synthetic flesh"), the film's nominal hero, Lee Taylor (Lee Tracy), a nosy reporter, must save the day.

Master filmmaker Michael Curtiz doesn't miss a trick in wringing every shudder from his lurid storyline. Even for simple introductions he plays up the bizarre, off-center qualities of his characters. Staff member

Ad for Doctor X.

Professor Wells is introduced sitting at a desk peering intently at a heart inside a glass jar while electricity crackles in the background. Professor Haines is first seen in silhouette, his profile (complete with satanic goatee) illumined by an eerie blue-green light flickering behind him so that the shadow creates a sinister, even diabolical impression. Dr. Rowitz, seen bending over a huge globe, looks up with a menacing slowness and forbidding expression as the door opens.

Curtiz makes good use of multiple camera angles—shooting from below, from above, at a slant (to create an impression of imbalance)—even within a single scene. Not only does this create a rich visual experience, but the varied viewpoints serve to instill a feeling of unease by keeping the viewer slightly off-kilter in his perspective.

Under Curtiz' skilled direction, Ray Rennahan's camera moves almost constantly, following the characters in a flowing rhythm that captures and enhances the mood of the moment. Warner's publicity department made much of the picture's deft camerawork (even going so far as to stick it with a painfully cute appellation). "The 'curious camera,'" states a *Doctor X* publicity piece, "is responsible for much of the feeling of suspense... Director Michael Curtiz has named it that because he puts the camera in the place of an interested and curious person, poking it into dark hallways and mysterious closets, investigating this and running down that and trying as best it can to solve the mystery."

Carefully placed objects in the foreground add a visual depth to the camera movement. "The smells," taunts Otto, holding up the soiled garments of the moon-killer's victim for the frightened maid to see, "don't they remind you of an embalming parlor, eh Mamie?" As he steps closer to her, Mamie retreats and the camera pans with them so that the glass tubes of some peculiar device pass between the camera and the actors, creating a distorted vision of the characters and adding to the weird, uneasy feel of the moment. For a full thirty seconds the camera makes its slow pan, staying with Otto as he taunts the increasingly hysterical maid all the way across the cavernous room.

Born Mihaly Kertesz in Hungary, Michael Curtiz started his career as an actor at the Royal Acadamy of Theater and Art in Budapest at the tender age of fourteen. He entered films in 1912 and soon after journeyed to Sweden where he became a director. (He supervised the great Greta Garbo in only his second assignment, *History's Great Women*.) After World War I, Curtiz made films in Austria, Germany, Italy, France, and England before Harry Warner brought him to America in 1926. Over the next three decades, Curtiz made close to one hundred features for Warner Brothers (*five* in 1932 alone). With *Doctor X*, Curtiz joined the studio's 'A' director list, subsequently helming many of Warner's most prestigious successes, including *Captain Blood* (1935), *Angels with Dirty Faces* (1938), and *Casablanca* (1942; for which Curtiz won an Academy Award).

Cinematographer Ray Rennahan was not an employee of Warners/First National but instead worked for the Technicolor Corporation, who supplied him to the studio for this specialized technique. (Rennahan also shot Warner's follow-up entry, *Mystery of the Wax Museum*, a scant six months later.) Rennahan was the premier 'color' cinematographer of his day, lensing the very *first* two-strip Technicolor feature (1921's *The Toll of the Sea*) and also the first *three-strip* Technicolor feature (1935's *Becky Sharp*). The cinematographer received nine Academy Award nominations over the course of his career, winning twice—for *Gone with the Wind* (1939) and *Blood and Sand* (1941). Like his contemporary, Karl Freund, Rennahan eventually turned to television, photographing over 500 features and series episodes from 1957 to his retirement in 1972.

Due to Curtiz's deft direction, Rennahan's eerie lighting, and George Amy's precise editing, the sequence of Doctor X's initial experiment (in which the various suspects are all hooked up to a bizarre piece of equipment that works as a sort of emotional lie detector) becomes a tension-filled, chilling reenactment of one of the killings. With the lights dimmed, Xavier narrates the weird scene taking place on the impromptu stage set before the three experimental 'subjects' hooked up to the baroque detection device. "She is passing through an alleyway," intones Xavier, "when suddenly, a terrible figure steals out—and starts creeping towards her." A shot of the black-robed Otto, arms raised menacingly, quickly gives way to a series of frantic, odd-angled closeups of each of the observers, briefly revealing their heightened tension. "As old Annie stoops to pick up a newspaper," continues Xavier's voice as the scene shifts again to the drama onstage, "the figure suddenly takes her throat in his powerful hands—" At this, Annie/Mamie lets out a shriek of terror. A quick cut to a hand throwing an electrical lever and the stage, the three spectators, the entire room, goes black—save for two glass globes glowing green on each side of the frame. As Mamie's continued shrieks are joined by alarmed shouts from the men, in rapid succession we see a closeup of hands struggling free from their equipment restraints, the tell-tale glass tubes, a shadowy pair of legs advancing, crutches crashing to the floor, and finally the blackness again—pierced only by the two glowing spheres. Suddenly, a shaft of light opens up between the two radiating orbs and Xavier steps into it to exclaim, "Look at that tube!" The camera then pans up the bizarre glass structure to reveal the liquid boiling up at the top. After three quick cuts to the suspects and their horrified reactions, the camera focuses on Xavier standing beside the glass tubes. "It's a success!" declares Xavier triumphantly. "The guilty man is—" A panicked scream of terror erupts before Xavier can name the culprit and we see Rowitz in closeup, his mouth open wide in horror as he emits a long, tortured shriek. Cutting back to Xavier, the undaunted doctor cries, "The guilty man is *Rowitz*!" Another shot of a hand closing a circuit switch and the lights come up to reveal Rowitz lying dead on the floor.

Editor George Amy employs twenty-five cuts in only fifty seconds to produce a sense of chaotic urgency and excitement. The near-hysterical shrieks and shouts uttered by the players ("Stop it!"; "I can't stand it!"; "The lights!"), along with the sounds of stumbling movements and falling objects, pierce the semi-darkness to augment the disordered intensity of the moment. Even during the few brief instances of ominous silence, the steady high-pitched hum of the machinery creates an impression of dire forces in motion.

"The primary purpose of set designing," stated art director Anton Grot in the *Doctor X* pressbook, "is to establish the mood of the story." Fresh from his Oscar nomination for *Svengali* the previous year, Grot (born Antocz Franciszek Groszewski in Poland) went on to explain the special needs of a horror picture: "When we design a set for mystery and melodrama we know that it must be of heavy construction with dark colorings and shadows. When we want to add menace to that, we put in a top-heavy effect over doors and windows, we build in low arches which give the feeling of overhanging danger. We design a set that imitates as closely as possible a bird of prey about to swoop down upon its victim, trying to incorporate in the whole thing a sense of impending calamity, of overwhelming danger." True to his word, Grot provides some marvelously eccentric sets and furnishings, creating a multi-textured canvas upon which Curtiz paints his cinematic portraits. Heavy stone pillars and recessed archways, high ceilings with oversized beams, massive carved wooden ballustrades topped with gargoyle-like figures, and dark heavy wooden furniture surround all manner of strange machinery. Rounded glass pyramids held in metallic prongs hover above the raised seats, while rods of metal spark dangerously and dials swing wildly. The futuristic equipment, all sharp angles and glass tubing makes a striking contrast to the massive pillars and archways of the gothic sets. The forbidding surroundings serve to cloak the 'scientific' experiments in a shroud of ominous mystery, inspiring thoughts more along the lines of medieval alchemy than of modern science.

Ray Renahan's varied lighting increases the sinister menace of the sets. Shadows create mysterious pools of blackness while bands of light and dark add an uneven, disturbing quality to the surroundings.

Lionel Atwill, making his horror debut with *Doctor X*, was arguably the screen's most effective mad doctor, a character type he excelled at throughout the 1930s and '40s. Atwill (earning $2,000 a week for his turn as Dr. Xavier) steals the show by creating a quirky, complex, and *suspicious* character out of what could easily have been a more transparently benign role. When the apprehensive maid asks Xavier what part she'll play in the upcoming reinactment, Atwill replies impatiently, "The scrubwoman of course," then adds, "the one who was *murdered* last night." Upon uttering "murdered," Atwill's lips curve upwards ever-so-slightly as if evincing a subliminal enjoyment in verbalizing the gruesome topic.

Atwill, a Broadway matinee idol before abandoning the legitimate theater for the 'bastard art' of films, put great stock in the motion picture industry. Returning to New York at the time of *Doctor X*'s release, the actor told *The New York Times*: "I am one of those few stage actors who really like the films, and admit it!" He went on to explain that "There are two different techniques. That is why some stage actors are not good in the pictures and why some movie stars fail on the stage. It is easier for the former to learn the other mode that the latter."

Fay Wray never looked lovelier than in *Doctor X*. Photographed in soft focus and gentle highlighting, her face nearly glows with an ethereal beauty. The character of Joan gives her a more complex and well-rounded role than most of her subsequent genre parts (including those in next year's *Mystery of the Wax Museum* and *King Kong*). As Joan Xavier, she ranges from righteous indignation to coquettish flirtation to genuine love and concern—not forgetting her famed screams of terror. Ms. Wray runs the gamut well and her natural innocence and charm make of Joan a genuinely likeable character.

Like Lionel Atwill, *Doctor X* was Fay Wray's first horror picture. Ms. Wray talked of her director, Michael Curtiz, in her autobiography *On the Other Hand*: "Michael Curtiz was a machine of a person—efficient, detatched, impersonal to the point of appearing cynical. He stood tall, militarily erect; his calculating, functional style made his set run smoothly, without humor. He had a steely intelligence and moviemaking know-how that made you feel there was a camera lens inside his cool blue eyes." The actress went on to relate several amusing anecdotes about Curtiz. "Looking through the finder one day at a group of extras," she recalled, "he called out to one, 'Move to your right… more… more… more… *now* you are out of the scene. *Go home!*' So wicked, it was almost funny."

On location for this picture's beach scene, remembered Ms. Wray, the director "paced back and forth in front of a crew and cast who were having the usual cold box lunch. He paced and muttered, 'Why should they eat? I don't eat! Why should we be wasting this time…?'"

Fay Wray commented on the film itself in *Starlog* (issue 194): "I saw *Doctor X* in Minneapolis just a couple of years ago. I thought it was paced a little too fast, and everyone talked too fast, that would be a criticism of it. But that didn't seem to bother the audience—they were pretty fascinated."

Doctor X was the first *color* horror film. The two-strip Technicolor process utilized for the picture, while appearing washed-out and unnatural compared to today's refined color process (or even the three-strip technique developed later in the decade), becomes an effective asset in *Doctor X*. Dominated by subdued greens and reds, the muted coloring adds an otherworldly feel perfectly suited to the bizarre storyline and macabre characters.

Sadly, *Doctor X* was seen in color in only a handful of select first-run theaters, the majority of prints struck being in standard black and white. In 1929 (when the color process was still in vogue) Warners had signed a hefty long-term contract with Technicolor (possibly in an attempt to corner the color market for their own product). Even though by 1932 the two-strip process had fallen out of favor with the public, Warners was still obliged to fulfill their contract (especially with a $25,000 *non-refundable* deposit already paid for each proposed feature staring them in the face).

Therefore, while Ray Rennahan filmed in color, another cinematographer, Richard Towers, manned a second camera unit to shoot simultaneously in black and white. The two outfits generally shot side by side, or, if the setup were more complex, Towers would shoot immediately after Rennahan. Though the lighting remained the same (with Towers utilzing filters and adjusted exposure to adapt to Rennahan's color-oriented illumination), the camera angles sometimes differ slightly in the two versions.

Shooting in color posed its own unique technical difficulties. "Color photography requires about twice as much light as does black and white work," related the *Doctor X* pressbook, "and twice as much light on the set means twice as much heat. The wax figures provided for the setting of the demonstration began to look discouraged after the first few minutes of work under the heat of the lights used. At the end of a half hour their faces were longer than Director Curtiz' arm. Their hands hung to the floor and their noses began to rest on their chins." Curtiz solved the problem by sending to the Warners' casting office for four live extras to replace the melting dummies. (Unlike Francis Drake's futile attempts to impersonate a wax statue in *Mad Love*, the four players in *Doctor X* did a marvelous job of holding still.)

While *Doctor X* provides more than its fair share of thrills and chills, the picture is not altogether perfect. Though thoroughly entertaining, *Doctor X*'s rather outlandish script contains a few suspiciously convenient lapses in logic. Where, for instance, did Xavier scare up four life-like wax statues of the moon-killer's victims on only 24-hours' notice? And how did Wells know about the secret lab—in Xavier's *private* home—and set up his own equipment so quickly? Luckily, Curtiz keeps things moving so briskly that one tends to overlook such contrivances in the excitement of the moment. Unfortunately, the picture's major liability remains painfully obvious, holding center stage throughout much of the film.

The only thing worse than arbitrarily inserting abrasive comedy relief into a horror movie is to saddle a main character with this burden. In *Doctor X*, the screwball reporter is the hero and as such receives a great deal of screen time. He is also the Comic Relief which means a thick layer of humor coats the picture. Admittedly, this can be very effective—but only if it is the right performer working with a witty script (Bob Hope in *The Cat and the Canary* or Glenda Farrell in *Mystery of the Wax Museum*, for example). Lee Tracy is *not* the right performer, and the series of lame insults and bland practical jokes (centering on a dime store hand buzzer) are far from witty. When Tracy is onscreen, the picture suffers, for the writers abandon their subtle, sardonic brand of humor for a more obvious (and awful) buffoonery. When Joan catches Tracy on the fire escape of the Institute and demands to know what he's doing there, Tracy lamely comes back with, "I'm a building inspector—I work nights so I won't get sunburned." When she brushes aside this 'witticism,' he tries, "I'm a somnambulist—I probably came up here to have my head examined." Tracy, rather than endearing himself to the audience with his 'zany' outlook and fun-loving attitude, becomes an annoying boor. Not only does this constant, prattling 'humor' detract from the mood and tension of the film, it also dispels audience sympathy by turning the hero (the audience identification figure) into an irksome clown. Consequently, at the climax, while we feel definite concern for Fay Wray's character when menaced by the real moon-killer, once Tracy shows up interest declines as we watch the murderer wrestle with an irritating hero for whom we have lost all empathy. Thus the climax becomes nothing so much as a common brawl since we no longer have any real emotional interest vested in the proceedings. At this point, while it is a foregone conclusion that Tracy will somehow come out on top, one's mind begins to conjure up alternative endings which feature Our Hero dying in a variety of nasty ways.

Lee Tracy became typecast early in his career as the ideal fast-talking reporter when he made the role of Hildy Johnson in Broadway's *The Front Page* his own. He played dozens of newspapermen in his subsequent film, theater, and television work. Born William Lee Tracy, he worked for a time on the railroad before turning to the stage in 1921. By 1924, he was making a name for himself on Broadway. Tracy entered films in 1929 but constantly returned to his first love, the theatre. Late in his film career, he received an Academy Award nomination for his role of Arthur Hockstader in Gore Vidal's *The Best Man* (1964), a part he'd made famous on the stage. Tracy died in 1968, leaving his $2,000,000 estate to his wife and upon her death to a number of charities, including the Motion Picture Relief Fund, the Salvation Army (because, said the actor, "they were the first ones on the job in both world wars"), and the Midnight Mission ("I couldn't leave that one out," said Tracy, who had been a heavy drinker in his day, "because there, but for the grace of God, go I"). Fay Wray reported that her co-star "was just like you see him on the screen—kind of casual, easy-going and very snappy."

Doctor X garnered generally favorable reviews. Mordaunt Hall of *The New York Times* (August 4, 1932), for instance, had nothing but praise for this "production that almost makes *Frankenstein* seem tame and friendly. That the audience which filled the theatre was duly impressed was obvious from the nervous giggles and the sudden explosions of relieved laughter." Mr. Hall observed that the film possesses "some remarkable laboratory settings," as well as an effective director in Michael Curtiz, "who always keeps his eyes open wide for chances for striking camera work, and here his penchant in that direction is assisted by the impressive settings, the more or less natural color effects, and also by the weird sounds emitted during Doctor Xavier's experiments." Incredibly, the reviewer also found merit in the film's "vein of adroitly conceived comedy relief," calling Lee Tracy's portrayal "splendid" and noting that "the timing of his comedy is very shrewdly accomplished."

Variety (August 9, 1932) was also impressed with the picture as a whole: "*Doctor X* combines the horripilating [sic] and the mysterious successfully enough on both counts, plus a good color job, to insure results that top recent house averages. …A lot of *Doctor X* is routine, including the love interest and the conventional murder mystery technique and background, but with material of three cycles involved, it does not become tedious."

This reviewer also noted the frequent bouts of laughter occasioned by *Doctor X*: "At the Strand on opening night, many people laughed when sinister hands appeared out of the dark, someone was suddenly dropped through a trap or a monstrous, weird face came into focus." Interestingly, however, this particular reviewer interpreted the audience laughter differently than the above-quoted Mr. Hall: "The laughs might indicate that hardened film-goers, including women, are getting used to seeing some of these things overdone. Nothing could be more unwelcome-looking than the makeup of Preston Foster, murder maniac, yet the Strand's audience accepted it humorously."

Preston Foster ("murder maniac") first entered the legitimate theater as an opera singer. After working as a bus driver, clerk, ad salesman, and professional wrestler(!), Foster finally won a spot with the Philadelphia Grand Opera. He quickly rose to operatic prominence and shifted over to Broadway where he was spotted by Mervyn LeRoy of Warner Bros., thus beginning his long career on the screen (over 100 films). *Doctor X* was one of Foster's first screen appearances. Foster never gave up his music and published a number of songs over the years, including "To Shillelagh O'Sullivan" (recorded by Bing Crosby) and "Let's Go, Padres" (the official song of the San Diego baseball team!). *Variety*'s obituary (July 22, 1970) reported that "His chief interests in Pacific Beach [where he retired in 1966], his wife said, were 'boats, music and baseball … in that order.'" One of Foster's final films was the low-budget but imaginative science fiction outing *The Time Travelers* (1964).

In promoting their film, Warner's publicity department stressed the 'aura of mystery' surrounding *Doctor X*—and the dollars that could be wrung by ballyhooing its surprise ending. "Climax in *Doctor X* Kept Secret from Cast," headlined one pressbook article, which related that "no visitor was allowed upon the stages or locations while this company worked and many members of the cast and crew were kept in the dark concerning the amazing denouement until the last moment when those scenes were made." In an "IMPORTANT NOTE" to theater managers, the pressbook advised, "Be sure to ask your patrons, via theatre front signs and the screen, not to reveal the exciting climax of *Doctor X* to their friends." Even further, the pressbook suggested that theaters have their patrons sign the following pledge upon leaving the cinema: "Because I realize that to reveal the climax of *Doctor X* might detract from the enjoyment others will get from the picture, I promise to keep the name of the murderer a secret."

Unconvinced of the viability of the fledgling "horror" genre, Warners further advised its exhibitors to soft-peddle the horror angle. "Sell its importance," counselled the *Doctor X* pressbook, "—its bigness—its novelty—its combination of mystery-thrills, love and comedy—its splendid technicolor effect. AVOID any suggestion of horror or shock. The picture contains more laughs and more romance than any mystery thriller ever made. It is important to get this over in your promotion." Catchlines like "The Most Mystifying Mystery in Years" and "It's the Miracle Film of 1932" were supplied to do just that.

While attempting to put a pleasant face on their rather gruesome horror property and avoid the dreaded "H-word" in their advertising, the Warners brass quickly came to realize that "horror" was simply another word for "dollars." After an enthusiastic *Doctor X* preview, Warner Brothers immediately began planning a follow-up thriller: *The Wax Works*.

MYSTERY OF THE WAX MUSEUM

"I am going to give you immortality; you will always be beautiful!" –Ivan Igor

Early in July of 1932, Warner Brothers loosed their legal eagles to track down and acquire the rights to an unpublished story entitled "The Wax Works," written by a reporter-turned-screenwriter named Charles Belden. (Belden's rather unremarkable screenwriting career climaxed with a series of Charlie Chan pictures for Fox in the mid-thirties, the best being *Charlie Chan at the Opera* with Boris Karloff. Married to actress Joan Marsh in 1938, Belden died in the Motion Picture Country Hospital in 1954 at the age of fifty.)

The studio paid Belden $1,000 for his story before they discovered to their fiscal chagrin that in February Belden had sold a play (obviously based upon his short story) entitled *The Wax Museum* to independent producer Charles Rogers. To further complicate matters, Rogers was threatened with a copyright infringement suit by Ralph Murphy, co-author of the Broadway play *Black Tower* (in which a mad sculptor creates statues by injecting victims with embalming fluid). Though this 'human statue' element was the only (tenuous) connection between the two stories, Rogers dropped his option on *The Wax Museum* to avoid legal entanglements—happily leaving the way clear for a more intrepid Warner Brothers. On the one hand, studio attorney Ralph E. Lewis advised Warners' head office that "there is a closer analogy between these two scripts than there was between *Wings* and *The Dawn Patrol*, and we only got clear on *The Dawn Patrol* by the skin of our teeth," while on the other hand citing Thorne Smith's novel *Night Life of the Gods* (later filmed by Universal) as safe evidence that the idea of turning people into statues was nothing original. Warners went ahead with their property and apparently encountered no further legal difficulty.

The studio handed *The Wax Works* (an initial working title which gave way to *Wax Museum* during shooting and finally transformed into *Mystery of the Wax Museum* a scant two weeks before its premier) to Hollywood newcomer Don Mullaly, a moderately successful playwright recently awarded a contract at the studio. *The Wax Works* was his first assignment. Mullaly turned in his initial treatment on July 27, and the studio immediately set one of their contract writers, Carl Erickson, to create an "optional outline" (adding a few ideas and refinements to Mullaly's scenario). Pleased with both contributors, the head office assigned them to continue work on the screenplay as a team. Four collaborative re-writes later and *Wax Museum* was ready to go before the cameras.

The classic storyline has master wax sculptor Ivan Igor (Lionel Atwill) betrayed by his business partner, resulting in the destruction of his life's work and the physical ruination of his face and hands (by fire). Over a decade later, Igor has re-opened his museum, ostensibly supervising the work of others but actually murdering people and stealing cadavers that he then encases

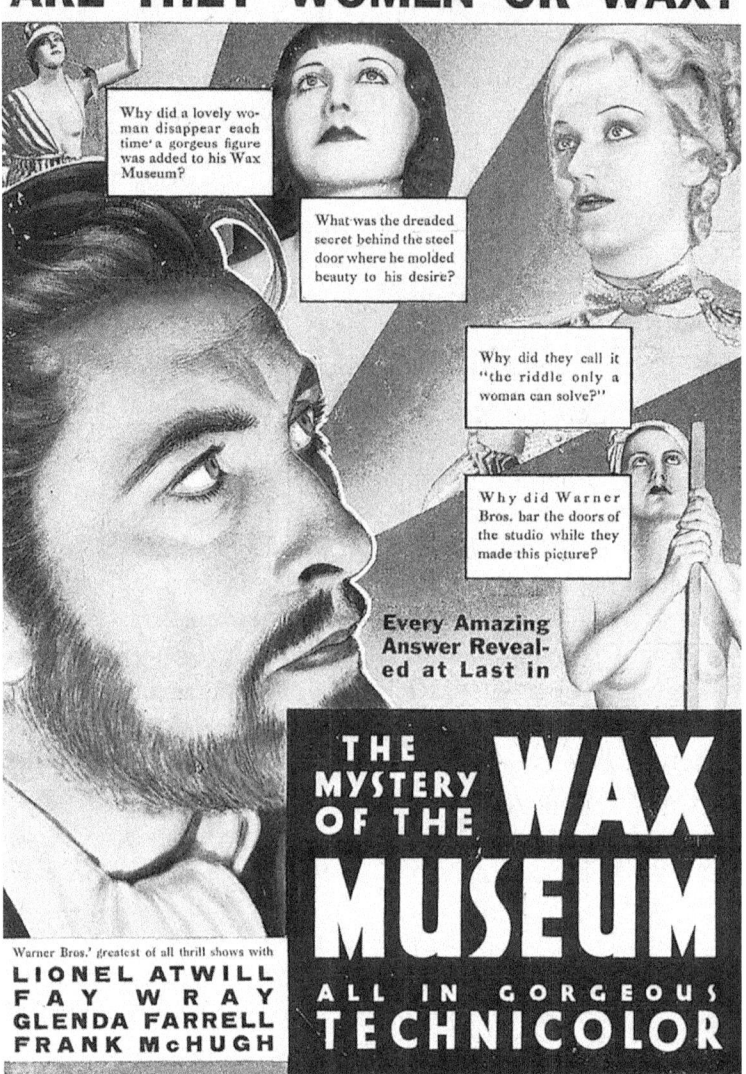

Ad for Mystery of the Wax Museum.

in wax to create his lovely "works of art." It's up to an intrepid, wise-cracking reporter (Glenda Farrell), her innocent roommate (Fay Wray), and her roommate's fiancé (Allen Vincent), who works for Igor, to discover the truth and stop the madman.

Warner Bros., wishing to repeat the earlier success of their gruesome shocker *Doctor X* (1932), again placed the horror reigns in the deft hands of Michael Curtiz for *Mystery of the Wax Museum*. Taking no chances, Warners also reassembled much of the original *Doctor X* cast and crew (including Lionel Atwill, Fay Wray, Arthur Edmund Carewe, art director Anton Grot, and editor George Amy) *and* allotted the production the same two-strip technicolor process. Given a better script in *Mystery* and a superior lead in Glenda Farrell (as opposed to a boorish Lee Tracy from *Doctor X*), Curtiz created a witty, exciting, frightening tale of the macabre which rose above even the high standards set by *Doctor X* (much as Universal's *Frankenstein* outshone *their* initial horror effort, *Dracula*).

Curtiz, a gifted, hard-working filmmaker (seven of his films were released by Warners this same year!), set down his views on filmmaking for the *Mystery of the Wax Museum* pressbook: "Odd, unusual camera angles should never be used for their own sake though the temptation to do so is often great, especially to the man who has an aptitude for thinking in them. The only reason for using an angle, in presenting a scene that would not seem the usual one to the onlooker, is to obtain a definite effect upon the spectator, which can be gained in no other way. You wish to arouse at that point a feeling of surprise, of terror, of repulsion, of admiration—and to emphasize it, the person or thing you are photographing must be presented from a special angle. Otherwise the natural, straightforward method of recording a scene in pictures is the one that holds the spectator's interest, keeps the story moving and preserves the flow and tempo of the action. It is very easy, in a story like *The Mystery of the Wax Museum* [sic], for instance, to overdo the use of bizarre, startling angles. That is why I used them throughout the picture sparingly, and always with a definite purpose in mind. Unless one is wary of the employment of them, their effect is very quickly blunted, and thereafter they become a nuisance instead of a help." In *Mystery*, Curtiz succeeded in utilizing these "odd, unusual camera angles" both judiciously and brilliantly.

Just as he did in *Doctor X*, Curtiz (with the help of Ray Rennahan's mobile cinematography) makes the camera an active participant rather than simply a passive recorder, creating mood, shocks, and thematic parallels with his use of varied set-ups and angles. At the picture's very beginning, before we've ever met the unscrupulous Joe Worth, Curtiz shows us Igor's partner lurking near the corner of a building. In medium closeup, an off-kilter camera angle generates an uncomfortable impression of this unsavory character. Near the climax, when Igor abruptly rises from his wheelchair to threaten the heroine, Curtiz reveals the astonishing action via a low-angle shot so that the madman appears to tower menacingly as he stands. When Charlotte strikes out at the fiend, shattering his wax mask into fragments to reveal the twisted death's head beneath, Curtiz shoots from behind the terrified girl's shoulder, placing the viewer almost literally in her shoes so it seems as if it is *our* fists which lash out again and again to expose the horrid ugliness underneath. Thus, the viewer experiences first-hand the shock of the moment.

In another sequence, the camera picks up a dark-clothed figure and follows the retreating back all the way across a litter-strewn street, the mobile camera keeping pace with the mysterious figure until it enters a building. Once inside, the camera again picks up the unknown individual and continues to track a few paces behind. As the shape walks into a room, the camera chases, moving ever closer until the figure sits down and finally turns to reveal the unexpected profile of Igor's duplicitous partner, Joe Worth. By turning the viewer (via the camera) into an unseen pursuer, Curtiz increases the impact of the final startling revelation.

When the police find the missing Judge Ramsey's watch on Igor's assistant, the drug-addled D'Arcy, they usher the cowering addict into an office, hold up the watch, and ask accusingly, "That yours?" The scene dissolves to a closeup of a liquid boiling away furiously. The camera quickly tracks back to reveal the huge vat of bubbling liquid wax in Igor's laboratory—an amusing visual representation that D'Arcy, in fact, truly is in 'hot water.'

Macabre touches abound. For an establishing shot of the morgue exterior, Curtiz places the camera at a high angle looking down on the ill-lit street and shadowy morgue entrance below. He then moves the camera slowly forward to take us in closer to the dread entryway only to stop short as two menacing shadows creep across the threshold, their owners left unseen to exacerbate the unease of the moment.

Shots of the wax statues melting in the fire add a genuinely gruesome touch, the eye sockets widening into corpse-like stares as the wax dissolves and runs, the melting wax sloughing off the face like layers of leprous skin, the head finally folding in upon itself and dropping sideways from the neck as if from a guillotine blade (with which Curtiz ends the scene as the fire burns through the execution exhibit rope, sending the blade slicing downward to sever the wax neck below with a shuddery 'thunk').

Curtiz went on to direct one other Golden Age horror classic, *The Walking Dead* (1936), as well as completing over a hundred other features for Warner Brothers. With three horrific triumphs to his credit (*Doctor X*, *Mystery*, and *The Walking Dead*) Michael Curtiz can truly be called a grand master of horror's Golden Age, second perhaps only to James Whale in his stylishly macabre accomplishments.

On *Mystery of the Wax Museum*, art director Anton Grot even surpasses his brilliant work in *Doctor X*, melding shadowy gothic with angular modernism to provide settings that underscore mood and create an eerie stage upon which the bizarre passion play can unfold. The morgue interior, for instance, is a quirky circular space in which the walls curve upward and inward to suggest the confining cap of a vaulted dome. The pillars set at regular intervals and arching toward the center create an aura of oppression, as if the massive supports were hovering just above us and could drop like the Sword of Damocles upon our unprotected heads at any moment. A cluster of heavy, conical lamps hang down like metallic vultures. Strange red and green-hued shadows lay along the recessed walls and among the shrouded gurneys. The oh-so-still occupants spread out along the circular room point toward the center to create a ghastly fence of (thankfully covered) cold flesh enclosing the viewer.

Igor's basement laboratory creates a very different impression, all angular modernism with suspended metal catwalk and curved staircase encircling and dominating the pit-like space below. Huge metal girders serving as pillars stand uneasily at weird angles, while banks of esoteric machinery, dials and switches along one wall testify to technological terrors. (Grot reused some of the laboratory equipment from *Doctor X* to dress his sets; the nozzle of Igor's wax dispensing machine, for instance, is a piece from Xavier's bizarre lie detector machine.) On the staircase above, huge metal bars for railings conjure up images of a stifling prison cell. The room's centerpiece, a gigantic cauldron filled with molten wax, its fumes and light casting a nightmarish hue throughout the chamber, creates a modernist's vision of Hell.

Don Mullaly and Carl Erickson's screenplay thankfully replaces the puerile 'humor' found in *Doctor X* with witty dialogue delivered with rapid-fire precision by Glenda Farrell. Farrell tosses off lines like, "I'm fired—I have to make news if I have to bite a dog," and "I've been in love so many times my heart's calloused," with a rat-a-tat delivery that brings her character to vivacious life. A lively bickering and comedic tension define her relationship with her hard-nosed editor (played by Warners perennial supporting actor Frank McHugh). When she gives him a raspberry over the phone, her boss quickly comes back with "a cow does that and gives milk besides" before hanging up.

Glenda Farrell's wisecracking reporter served as a blueprint for her later *Torchy Blane* series in which the actress played the nosy newshound in seven pictures. Farrell began in stock theater at the tender age of seven (playing Little Eva in *Uncle Tom's Cabin*) and made it to Broadway in 1928 (at age 24). After a bit part in 1929's *Lucky Boy*, she gained her first prominent screen role in Warner's *Little Caesar* (1931). Ms. Farrell "preferred stage and TV" to film work, according to *Variety*'s obituary (May 5, 1971), and she guest starred in a number of television series in the fifties and sixties inbetween stints on Broadway (including *Bonanza*, *Wagon Train*, *The Fugitive*, and *Dr. Kildare*). Her small screen work culminated in an Emmy for an appearance on *Ben Casey* in 1963.

Sadly, tragedy soon engulfed *Mystery of the Wax Museum*'s two screenwriters. Mullaly died of tuberculosis a mere six months after completing the final script for *Mystery*; Erickson committed suicide a scant two years later at the age of 27, reportedly despondent over his upcoming divorce.

While *Doctor X* was a fast-paced carnival ride of macabre thrills, *Mystery* adds that element so important in creating a lasting impression in a horror tale—pathos. Ivan Igor is an eccentric, likable, even kindly man. We smile as he lovingly talks of (and to) his beautiful wax creations—his "children"—and share his subsequent anguish as he helplessly watches them "die" in the consuming flames. We understand his bitterness at the slow, painful, imperfect recreation of his art (and life) through the hands of others, and can comprehend (if not entirely condone) his short temper and irate outbursts at those less deft than he. And finally, while we gasp in horror at his ghoulish activities, we can still find pity for this 'fiend,' so painfully wronged and only longing to recapture the beauty—the life—that was once his. His innate humanity has been twisted and blackened along with his mangled face and hands, yet it remains; and our shudders and cheers at the climactic demise of the fiend and rescue of the heroine are tempered with a pang of sympathy.

Lionel Atwill imbues Ivan Igor with a genuineness and passion that brings the character fully to life. Atwill is charming at the beginning as the humble sculptor proudly showing off his "children." The hint of an accent, his surprised delight and gratitude at the critic's praise, and his genuine affection demonstrated toward his work makes him a warm, affecting character. When the fire consumes his work—his life—Atwill displays real rage at the act and when all is lost, the helpless anguish on his face as he stands aghast, watching the flames engulf his "children," is truly heartrending.

A consummate actor, Atwill can inspire terror just as effectively as he elicits compassion. At the climax, when Igor rises from his wheelchair and grasps Charlotte with an impassioned "My Marie Antoinette!,"

Atwill's eyes go wide with a mad ardor and fix her with a searing stare so painfully intent it seems capable of burning a hole through mere mortal flesh. Little wonder that she screams under the crazed scrutiny of the agonizing glare.

Yet even at the height of his menace, Atwill still evokes a certain sympathy. Atwill's intense sincerity when he promises Charlotte "immortality" as a wax statue—as though offering his greatest gift—is pitifully touching. Then, after she cracks his mask to reveal the loathsome ugliness beneath, Atwill turns his head away and bows it slightly, averting his eyes to avoid the look of horror which would cut into his heart like a knife. When she recovers her shocked voice and finally screams, his head droops even lower in dejection at the reaction he inspires.

Igor's indominatable passion refuses to be extinguished and flares again under Atwill's fierce command. "There *was* a fiend," he answers heatedly when Charlotte affronts him with the hated appellation, "and this is what he did to me." Atwill suddenly whirls and stalks determinedly across the room toward an upright box resting against the wall, quickening his pace to violently rush the final few steps with one fist raised in anger to bitterly shout, "You! You did this!" at the heedless box. A stinging anguish shows through his madness and we pity him.

In the 1970s, after viewing the "rediscovered" *Mystery of the Wax Museum* at a midnight showing at Grauman's Chinese Theatre (for years *Mystery* was considered a "lost" film until located and released to television in 1975), Fay Wray commented on the merits of the picture: "I loved the color and Lionel Atwill's schmaltzy delivery and wisecracking Glenda Farrell."

"Schmaltzy" star Lionel Atwill reveled in his villainous roles, and worked hard to perfect his characterizations (sometimes *too* hard, as the actor revealed): "They fooled me in the *Wax Museum* thing, or rather, they let me fool myself. I'd been practicing before a mirror for weeks, learning how to keep my face as stiff as a board and just wiggle my jaws in talking, eyes set and staring—a grand effect. But then, in the finished picture, I looked so much like a stone image that they had to cut all those close-ups for fear of giving away that fact that my face was supposed to be a wax mask!"

Atwill, a complex man both in front of and behind the camera, enjoyed playing villainous roles—so long as they were not one-dimensional. While still a matinee idol on the Broadway stage, he began acting in early Silents. In a 1919 interview for *Motion Picture Classic*, Atwill commented on the future of moving pictures, and his views on screen villainy: "I honestly think pictures have possibilities, but not until some of these old-fashioned ideas are combed out of them. For instance, to the picture director, a character is either a hero, who is all good, or a villain, who is all bad. ...No one is wholly good or evil. ...I, for one, will never play in pictures again until I am assured that the director is broad-minded enough to present a villain who has lovable qualities, or a hero who has a few weaknesses." While not holding true to this vow on every occasion, his role of Ivan Igor in *Mystery of the Wax Museum* proved to be just such a complex and rewarding one.

Later, in 1933, after becoming an established screen star, Atwill further expounded upon his convictions as to the duality of man (and himself) in *Motion Picture* magazine: "See, one side of my face is gentle and kind, incapable of anything but love of my fellow man. The other side, the other profile, is cruel and predatory and evil, incapable of anything but the lusts and dark passions. It all depends on which side of my face is turned toward you—or the camera. It all depends on which side faces the moon at the ebb of the tide."

While Lionel Atwill received an even better part in Ivan Igor than he had as *Doctor X*, Fay Wray was sadly short-changed on *Mystery of the Wax Museum*. Her thankless roll as the vapid Charlotte gives her little to do and allows for even less range, making her a poor follow-up to the well-rounded Joan from *Doctor X*.

In her autobiography, Ms. Wray related how she experienced one of the hazards of working in a horror picture. "There is a scene in *The Mystery of the Wax Museum* [sic] when, in self-defense, I hit the face of Lionel Atwill. His face cracks and falls away, revealing horrible scarring underneath. This couldn't be rehearsed. Only two wax masks had been made. When the mask broke and I saw the repulsively scarred face, I absolutely froze instinctively, wanting not to touch that face again." The actress, having never seen the makeup before, was genuinely shocked (a testament to make-up man Perc Westmore's handiwork) and the scene had to be reshot using the second mask. She continues: "Curtiz, with his camera-eyes watching over my shoulder, wanted to see the whole revolting visage at the first strike. 'You should have kept on hitting!' So we did it again with the second mask. Now that I knew what to expect, I could do it technically."

Ms. Wray acted in *Mystery of the Wax Museum* and *King Kong* simultaneously. She remembers the making of *Kong* as "just doing little bits and pieces all the way through that whole year; when I was at Warner Bros. doing *The Mystery of the Wax Museum*, [*Kong* director

Merian C.] Cooper would wait for me, so I'd go over to RKO and work on a weekend. It was kind of a paradox; here it was the middle of the depression, and it seems in retrospect that for me, it was a period of an enormous amount of work."

"I don't know what he was, but he made Frankenstein look like a lily!" exclaims Florence when describing the ruined visage of Ivan Igor. (Florence fell into that age-old trap of referring to the Monster as 'Frankenstein,' when, in fact, Colin Clive [as Frankenstein] was considered quite attractive. Even a mere fifteen months after its cinematic birth, this unjust misidentification dogged the Monster's heavy footsteps.) Ms. Farrell's mis-appellative observation aside, Perc Westmore's disfiguring makeup for Igor's grotesquely burned countenance is both unique and shocking, the gnarled walnut-like skin appearing hard and twisted, almost like petrified wood—or wood warped and blackened by fire. The ghastly visage inevitably draws the eye in horrible fascination. Many took note of Westmore's work—not least of all the British censors, who labelled Atwill's horrific makeup "the most nauseating and by far the worst of its type." The offended Brits even demanded that the picture's establishing title of "LONDON 1921" be removed from their prints in an attempt to distance their country from the vile production. (The English public, however, held a different opinion from the outraged blue-nosed bureaucrats; after *Forty-Second Street*, *Mystery of the Wax Museum* was Warners' biggest overseas hit of 1933.)

While scripters Don Mullaly and Carl Erickson create several fascinating characters (Ivan, Florence, her editor, the drug-addicted Professor D'Arcy), they fail to bring to life the two juvenile leads (hero and heroine). Ralph comes across as a weak, dreary drone, little more than a whipping-boy for Ivan's bitter artistic disappointments. Charlotte is a silly, bloodless character, all-too-easily startled by the smallest of things. Fortunately, the snappy go-getter Florence provides the viewer with someone to focus on (and admire).

Another drawback to the film was the mixing of live actors posing as statues with actual wax dummies. The actors do well enough in holding still to convince the viewer of their authenticity and add credence to Ivan's waxing poetic (so to speak) about their realistic beauty. However, the real wax images look ridiculously phony in contrast, making one wonder if Ivan had one hellaciously bad sculpting day to produce such obviously inferior works. It would have been better had Curtiz utilized only actors throughout (as he did in *Doctor X*) to represent the statues.

If one listened to the bulk of reviewers, the film would be better titled *MISERY of the Wax Museum*. Thornton Delehanty of *The New York Evening Post* felt that the film "never achieves anything but a wax-like imitation of horror. The newspaper scenes are filled with painfully unfunny dialogue, so that even such good actors as Glenda Farrell and Frank McHugh are made to seem bad. The picture, incidentally, is photographed in Technicolor, which leaves it about where it would have been in black and white."

Variety's "Abel" (February 21, 1933) was a bit kinder, noting that the cast "struggle about as effectively as did Mike Curtiz, the director, with a loose and unconvincing story, to manage a fairly decent job along the *Frankenstein* and *Dracula* lines." Impressed by Perc Westmore's creation, he added, "Makeups are about the last word in gruesomeness." Less impressed by the wisecracking reporter angle, he commented, "Like most newspaper stuff, the flippant, cynical and hardboiled manifestations in the role essayed by Miss Farrell rarely convince."

The timorous Mordaunt Hall, reviewing for *The New York Times* (February 18, 1933), had his sensibilities shocked by the "ghastly details" of a film "going too far." Apparently, "glimpses of covered bodies in a morgue and the stealing of some of them by an insane modeler in wax" was simply too horrifying. Grateful for any relief from the horror, Mr. Hall continued: "As an antidote to the abhorrent scenes, there is some good comedy afforded by Glenda Farrell…and by Frank McHugh. …It is a relief to hear Miss Farrell wisecracking to Mr. McHugh, and she gives a vivacious and clever performance." The reviewer concludes by saying, "After witnessing this unhealthy film it is very agreeable to gaze upon a short subject dealing with the wonders of Yellowstone Park."

Like *Doctor X* (1932), its predecessor and model, *Mystery of the Wax Museum* was shot in the two-color Technicolor process. This red and green process, which was unable to reproduce the full range of the spectrum, originated in the mid-twenties (utilized for select insert sequences in Silents) but achieved its greatest popularity in the early talkies, specifically in musicals. As early as 1931 this process' popularity had waned with the public and *Mystery of the Wax Museum* became the final significant feature to be shot utilizing this technique. Nineteen-thirty-four brought the development of the more natural-looking three-color process and color films were once again a viable (and profitable) option.

Director Michael Curtiz, in the *Mystery of the Wax Museum* pressbook, extolled the virtues of color (and lighting) in building mood in a picture of this type: "Much more effective is the specialized type of lighting we used to establish and build up a mood that we wished to communicate with the spectator. This was particularly true of the sequences laid in the two wax works—the London one and the New York museum. In each, without being too obvious in our lighting, we tried to arouse in the spectators' minds a vague, intangible feeling of uneasiness, mystery, a sinister something lurking in the shadows, never shown but only suggested. The use of color is an asset in creating such moods in a story of this type. To be sure, stories of the fantastic, the horrible, the bizarre have been told with fullest success in black and white photography. But it has always been a question in my mind whether those very stories would not have been more gripping, more realistic, if they had been photographed in color such as we have employed with such unusual success in *The Mystery of the Wax Museum* and previously in *Doctor X*."

Color worked particularly well in the *Mystery of the Wax Museum* fire sequence. The predominant reddish color-scheme of the two-strip process adds a hellish quality to the conflagration, turning the blazing museum into a livid purgatory as shades of fiery red and orange dance and blend together.

The horror genre had to wait another seven years until *Dr. Cyclops* brought color terrors back to the big screen in 1940—long after horror had toppled from its 'Golden Age' aerie into the 'Silver Age' valley of B-movies. In *Doctor X* and *Mystery of the Wax Museum*, Warner Brothers gave us two of the most entertaining classics of the genre, unique not only for their historical value but for their enduring appeal to fans of the Fantastique.

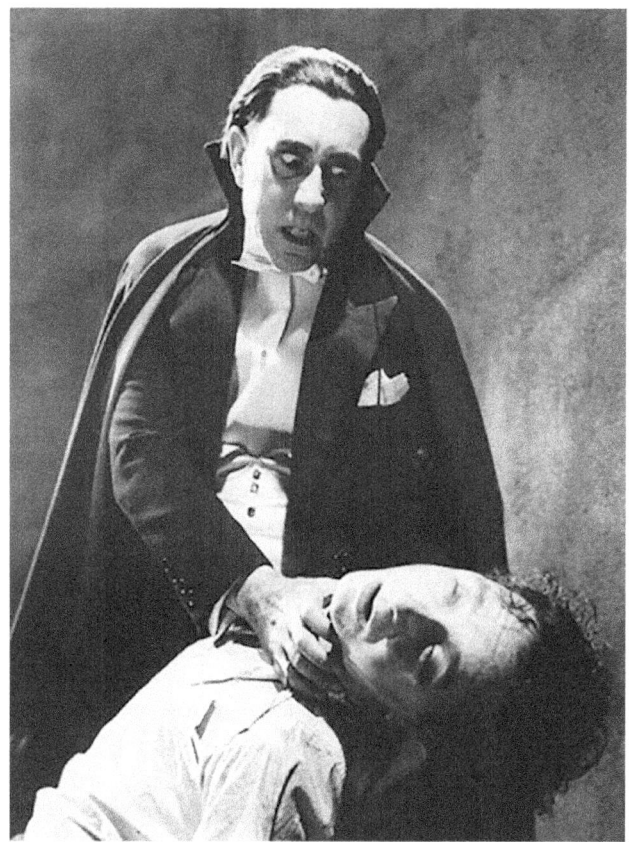

Universal's Spanish-language version of Dracula *(1931) proved superior to its classic English counterpart in almost every way—except where it counted most. Here Carlos Villarias' Dracula throttles Pablo Alvarez Rubio's Renfield.*

> This comparative essay about Universal's Spanish-language variation on their genre-forming groundbreaker *Dracula* appeared in *Filmfax* magazine, issue 57 (August/September 1996).

DRACULA (1931 Spanish Language Version)

In the burgeoning sound era, before the advent of practical dubbing, studios would occasionally produce alternate language versions (most often Spanish) of their more prestigious pictures to sell in the lucrative foreign markets. By utilizing the same sets and low-cost foreign actors, the studio could create a second picture for a fraction of the cost of the original. At the suggestion of producer Paul Kohner, Universal slated their upcoming "Terrific Vampire Thriller" (as the pressbook labeled it) for the foreign-language treatment. Shooting at night on the same sets after the American cast and crew had gone home, Kohner and director George Melford filmed this alternate version for a mere $66,000 (about one seventh the cost of the English language *Dracula*). Melford ("a wonderful man," according to female lead Lupita Tovar), whom the cast affectionately dubbed "Uncle George," directed through an interpreter to create a vision parallel yet *superior* to Tod Browning's version. Though lacking the (truly essential) iconographic presence of Bela Lugosi (thirty-eight-year-old Spanish stage actor Carlos Villarias makes a poor substitute), Melford's visual acumen outshines Browning's haphazard helming at nearly every turn.

Everyone has seen Tod Browning's *Dracula* (or at least everyone reading *this* magazine). The Spanish-language version follows Browning's almost exactly—with a few minor changes and some additional footage (which was ultimately discarded from the English-language print [or simply never shot]).

In the Spanish language version, Melford managed to avoid the directorial carelessness exhibited by his counterpart. For instance, in no fewer than four shots in Mina's bedroom Browning left in full view a tattered square of cardboard (utilized to shield a lamp while the set was being lit). Melford managed to shoot *his* identical scenes without including that pesky piece of trash.

Melford allowed a much freer visual mobility in the Spanish language version and, unlike Browning, took full advantage of Charles D. Hall's magnificent Castle Dracula and Carfax Abbey sets by letting cinematographer George Robinson's camera prowl about and explore these wondrous gothic settings. (Lupita Tovar remembered just how effective these sets were: "I was always an hour early because I wanted to be ready. And many a time I walk in there and I was all alone and it was really scary to see the sets and everything. If anybody will touch me, I think I would *scream*.")

Happily, Melford didn't share Tod Browning's odd affinity for misplaced mammals. Browning populated his cobwebbed cathedral with such bizarrely out-of-place fauna as cuddly possums and American armadillos (native Texans must have simply howled at this animal anomaly). While a solitary opossum did manage to creep onto Melford's shoot, he thankfully kept the lid down on the armadillo cages.

In scene after scene, Melford's staging proves far superior to Browning's, who seems simply to have chosen the path of least resistance. For instance, Browning 'cheats' his audience by first showing Dracula's coffin lid rise, then panning the camera away to a window while the noise of the lid slamming down is heard, before finally tracking back to reveal the vampire standing upright next to his coffin. Browning does this not once but *twice*, shooting the two scenes in an almost identical fashion! Granted, one wishes to avoid showing the sinister Count struggling to free his cape from beneath him as he swings a leg out of the box, but the director makes no effort to imbue his cheap avoidance trick with any sense of justification. At the very least, Browning could have shown the light fading behind the window to give some excuse for the camera (and audience) to look in that direction (as Lambert Hillyer later did in *Dracula's Daughter*). But no such reason is provided. This directorial laziness becomes almost unforgivable when compared to Melford's effective and atmospheric handling of this same scene in the Spanish version: The coffin lid opens of its own accord while an eerie cloud of white smoke issues forth, rising upwards to dissolve and reveal the imposing figure of Count Dracula.

Even in matters so simple as actor placement, Melford shows more savvy than Browning. When Dracula first encounters Dr. Seward and family at the symphony, for example, Browning allows Dracula to stand on a lower step as he meets Seward. This results in Dracula appearing a full head *shorter* than Seward and places the Count in the subservient position of having to look up at his soon-to-be-enemy. Why Browning would shoot the all-powerful Dracula in such a subordinate position is a question with no logical answer—except that the scene was carelessly staged. Melford avoids this mistake by having Dracula meet Seward just after the latter steps out of his opera box so that the two stand on level ground, allowing the half-a-head-taller Dracula to look down upon his shorter nemesis.

Melford utilized more varied shots than Browning, which makes the Spanish language version seem less stage-bound. For instance, for the scene in which Jonathan jumps about waving his arms at the bat hovering over Mina for what seems an interminable period of time, Melford shoots some additional close-ups to provide inserts that break the monotony of Browning's loooong single shot.

The Spanish version is much less circumspect than its English-speaking model about the inherent sexuality found in this vampire tale. Both Lupita Tovar as Eva (Mina) and Carmen Guerrero as Lucia (Lucy) are far more appealing in their provocative form-hugging gowns of black lace and plunging necklines than the vapid, virginally-garbed Helen Chandler and Frances Dade. The three rather prim, expressionless vampiresses in Browning's version (hair tightly braided, hands clasped demurely in front of their high-necked frocks) give way to Melford's trio of ferocious, sensuous creatures of the night, their hands raised like claws, hair loose and wild, faces livid in anticipation, creating a much more animalistic—and sensual—image. Even the slightly altered dialogue in the Spanish version plays up the subject's sexual aspects. Eva, after describing her 'dream' of the vampire's visitation, says, "The next morning I felt very weak, as if I had lost my virginity" (an overt simile the English version would never even *consider* using).

Pablo Alvarez Rubio's Renfield is every bit the maniacal madman as Dwight Frye's. Rubio's tortured laughter and plaintive pleadings, though more violent than Frye's, creates a more naturalistic dementia than his American counterpart's sometimes strained delivery. And Rubio's juxtaposition between unpredictably violent outbursts and cowering in fear (at the howl of wolves, for example) makes his Renfield seem more real than Frye's jittery madman. Rubio is further aided by the fact that, due to some extended scenes in the Spanish version, his Renfield receives more screen time and additional dialogue. Since, next to Dracula himself, Renfield is the story's most fascinating character, this makes the film's slow pacing and drawing room settings of the latter half more palatable in the Spanish version.

Browning's version supersedes Melfords in only one instance. Sadly, this is a vital one—the presence of Bela Lugosi. Though Carlos Villarias tries to emulate Lugosi's carefully choreographed movements, he cannot match the Hungarian's subtle expressions, sublime intensity, and powerful screen presence. Instead, Villarias must forge his character with gross mannerisms (such as baring his teeth, showing the whites of his eyes, grimacing grotesquely, and all manner of eyebrow calisthenics) that turns his Dracula into a melodramatic fiend which cannot match Lugosi's unholy bird of prey.

Also, not unexpectedly, the film's classic dialogue occasionally loses something in translation. Dracula's timeless phrase "There are far worse things awaiting man than death" turns into the rather awkward "Something worse than death lies in wait for the living." And Dracula's poetic observation "For one who has not lived even a single lifetime, you are a wise man, Van Helsing" becomes the almost comically banal "Considering that you have not lived an entire life yet, you know a lot, Professor."

A few dialogue demerits aside, and with one substantial exception in its pivotal casting, the once-obscure Spanish-language *Dracula* outshines its famous and classic cousin. Now, with the long-thought-lost Spanish version released on video, devotees of the Golden Age of Horror can see what *Dracula* truly *might* have been.

> While most genre fans have seen (or at least heard of) RKO's famous 1932 film version of *The Most Dangerous Game*, many have no idea the studio remade this classic in 1945, under the direction of future Oscar-winner Robert Wise. To help rectify this, I interviewed Wise for my book *The Most Dangerous Cinema: People Hunting People on Film*, and later submitted this modified essay to *Filmfax* magazine (issue 121) in 2009.

REDUX: A GAME OF DEATH!

"Let me tell you Rainsford, there is no game in the world that can compare with it for a moment." –Erich Kreiger

Robert Wise's all-but-forgotten remake of The Most Dangerous Game.

A Game of Death is the country cousin—or, more appropriately, given RKO's insistence on slavishly aping their own original, the slightly-less-attractive younger brother—of the studio's earlier hit *The Most Dangerous Game* (1932). Almost a carbon copy of the 1932 film, *A Game of Death*, just like a literal facsimile from the old mimeograph days, is a little bit fainter and features a few more smudges when compared to the original. But it also boasts one of the genre's—and cinema's in general—best directors, and even the occasional improvement here and there. Consequently, *A Game of Death* cries out for reappraisal, and this long-lost cousin deserves to take its rightful place on the Most Dangerous Family Tree.

Given his immense stature among both critics and moviegoers, director Robert Wise has given many, many interviews over the years. Rarely, however, has anyone ever asked about *A Game of Death*, which seems to be his own personal "forgotten film." And, truth be told, the director himself wishes it *were* forgotten. In a 1996 interview with this writer, Wise, when asked if he screened the original prior to shooting his remake, answered, "Yes," before adding, "unfortunately." The director continued: "I was not too keen about doing it but I was under stock contract at RKO. I don't like the idea of remakes and wasn't keen to do this, but yes, I had to look at the original picture because there were shots of these Great Danes going through the jungle or whatever in the hell it was, lots of shots of those. They wanted me to use those out of the original picture in order to save money and not have to re-shoot them. So I had to run the whole picture just to see those eight or ten or twelve shots of the Great Danes going through the forest or jungle just to see how I could use them. And what was bad about it for me was that every time—because it was a remake, there were similar scenes between the new one and the old one—and every time I'd get into a sequence not to do with the dogs but the story part of it, I kept getting flashes back to the original scene I'd seen. It was just terrible; it kept haunting me. Every time I got into it I couldn't get the original out of my mind, and that's no way to make a picture. I did it, but it was not a favorite experience." Favorite experience or no, *A Game of Death* can still be a *rewarding* experience for those viewers dedicated enough to seek it out. (To date, *A Game of Death* has received no legitimate video or DVD release, and only sporadic television airplay.)

Based (as was the 1932 film) on prolific novelist, playwright and screenwriter Richard Connell's 1924 O. Henry Memorial Award-winning short story "The Most Dangerous Game," *A Game of Death* has famous big game hunter and author Don Rainsford (John Loder) sailing back to New York when his yacht captain (Jason Robards Sr.) notices that some safety buoy lights don't match the reefs on his charts. They decide to turn back, but it's too late—the ship hits a reef and the cold seawater streaming through the breach in the hull quickly explodes the ship's boilers.

His companions are taken by sharks, but Rainsford makes it to the nearby island. There, Rainsford finds a castle, built by pirates but now owned and occupied by Erich Kreiger (Edgar Barrier), a man with an all-consuming passion for hunting, and who is more than pleased that his latest "guest" is a world-renowned hunter. At Kreiger's castle, Rainsford also meets Robert and Ellen Trowbridge (Russell Wade and Audrey Long), survivors of a previous shipwreck. While Bob overindulges in Kreiger's fine brandy, their host tantalizes Rainsford with his boast of having stocked his private island with "the most dangerous game." Mysteriously, he is unwilling to disclose the nature of said game (nor open up his locked "trophy room"). Meanwhile, Ellen surreptitiously relates her concern to Rainsford. "Don't trust him," she warns, "Don't believe anything he tells you…there's something evil going on in this place—we're all prisoners."

That night Ellen comes to Rainsford's room, worried because her brother Bob has disappeared. Hearing a scream from outside, they creep downstairs, only to find the trophy room unlocked. Inside they discover Kreiger's "trophys"—human heads mounted on the wall and bobbing in tanks. They also find Bob, who only pretended to be drunk to keep Kreiger off-guard, and who has been nosing around on his own. Rainsford slips out of the castle and sets traps in Kreiger's private jungle, intending to "beat him at his own game."

The next day Rainsford confronts Kreiger. "You hunt human beings," Rainsford states, before adding, "Kreiger, you're a genius—I congratulate you." Kreiger is surprised. "Really, Rainsford? I was afraid you might have some romantic notion about the value of human life." After gaining his confidence and accepting Kreiger's invitation to join him that night in hunting Ellen's brother, Rainsford reveals his plan to Ellen: "Don't worry, when I get Kreiger out in that jungle the hunt will be short and the victim won't be your brother."

Unfortunately, Kreiger discovers Rainsford's ruse and traps him in his room, guarded by Kreiger's "man-killing" monster of a dog. Kreiger then hunts Bob, using a bow (Kreiger's favored weapon after having become too proficient with a gun)—with the expected result. When Kreiger and his men return with his newest "trophy," Rainsford goads Kreiger into hunting *him* that same night, and Ellen insists on going with Rainsford.

After Kreiger spots Rainsford's previously-set deadfall trap, the madman trades his bow for a high-powered rifle. When Rainsford and Ellen seek cover in the island's foggy swamp, the hunter calls for his dogs to track them. Finally cornered on a seaside cliff, Rainsford is set upon by one of the dogs. As Rainsford struggles with the brute, Kreiger shoots, and man and dog tumble over the cliff to their doom.

With Ellen locked safely away back at the castle, Kreiger smugly plays his piano, reveling in his triumph. Suddenly, the castle's door opens and in walks Rainsford, disheveled but very much alive. "Rainsford, I congratulate you, you beat me," stammers the astonished Kreiger. "Not yet," growls Rainsford, "You hit the dog, not me. I took a chance and went over with him." Kreiger grabs for a Lugar in a drawer and the two men struggle. Kreiger's henchman joins the fray, but Rainsford overpowers him and continues grappling with Kreiger. They fall over the back of a couch, with Kreiger clutching the pistol. A shot rings out…but it is Rainsford who stands up from behind the sofa, Lugar in hand. As Rainsford and Ellen flee through the horrid trophy room to the hidden boat launch and speed away, the wounded Kreiger grabs his rifle and staggers to the window—only to topple onto the terrace below, into the slavering jaws of his own vicious hounds.

Anyone familiar with the 1932 *The Most Dangerous Game* will feel a strong sense of déjà vu reading the preceding synopsis. *A Game of Death* follows the same pattern as its predecessor, hewing closely to

Connell's classic storyline and deviating only in the details. Apart from the various name changes (Connell's exotic-sounding "Sanger" Rainsford becomes the more mundane—and approachable—"Don" [or "Bob" in the first film], while "General Zaroff" ["Count Zaroff" in the 1932 picture] transforms into the topically Teutonic "Erich Kreiger," no doubt to take advantage of the then-current anti-German sentiment), *A Game of Death* deviates from Connell's story along the same lines as its 1932 template: adding a female character (and her brother); telescoping the three-day hunt into one night; staging a more dramatic shipwreck rather than having Rainsford simply fall overboard; and keeping the hero's hands relatively clean at the end of the tale by avoiding Connell's deliberate-killing-of-the-antagonist closer.

As a result of such fidelity, *A Game of Death*, like its predecessor, retains much of the power of Connell's original story, with the various changes made either to 1) increase the drama (the added characters and tightened time frame), 2) play to the camera by making events more "cinematic" (adding the exciting shipwreck sequence), or 3) appease the censors (modifying the ending). Apart from the last, each of these alterations actually strengthens the story's power to help create yet another cinematic triumph—though one that, as we shall see, ultimately becomes redundant.

When it comes to visual symbolism, for instance, this *Game* is far less dangerous than its predecessor, no doubt due to the more stringent demands of the Production Code, updated in 1934. The satyr doorknocker of the 1932 version has given way to a generic gargoyle face here, while the woman held in the arms of the satyr in the huge tapestry prominently displayed in the madman's castle is no longer topless (as it was in the original film). *Game* makes a half-hearted attempt to put the sexual subtext over via a line of dialogue when Kreiger pronounces, "First the hunt, then the kill, then the woman. Only when you have experienced all that can you know complete ecstasy." But it seems only a token effort to recapture the significant subtext running through James Ashmore Creelman's more adult *Most Dangerous Game* screenplay.

Speaking of Creelman, had he not died by his own hand in 1941, that scribe could very well have brought a plagiarism suit against RKO, since so much of *A Game of Death* is simply Creelman's 1932 script with a few words and incidents changed by "new" screenwriter Norman Houston, a veteran scribbler of mostly B-oaters whose credits stretched back to the Silents. When Rainsford marvels that all his companions are now dead, labeling such a thing "incredible," Kreiger counters with, "Death is always incredible, always for others, never for ourselves." It's nearly a word-for-word steal from the original ("Such things are always incredible; death is for others, not for ourselves").

Unfortunately, few of those dialogue changes that Norman *did* make turned out to be improvements. A case in point:

Zaroff in *The Most Dangerous Game*: "One night as I lay in my tent with this, this head of mine, a terrible thought crept like a snake into my brain—hunting was beginning to bore me…When I lost my love of hunting, I lost my love of life—of love."

Kreiger in *A Game of Death*: "Then one night, lying in my tent, unable to sleep, my head throbbing, a terrible thought began pushing its way into my mind. The idea gave me actual, very real physical pain. Hunting had begun to bore me. It had ceased to be a sporting proposition."

Case in point number two:
Zaroff: "An hour with my trophies and [my guests] usually do their best to keep away from me."
Kreiger: "After seeing my trophy room, my guests invariably accept my invitation [to hunt]."

Not content with stealing much of the original's script, *A Game of Death* re-uses actual footage from *The Most Dangerous Game*, including all of the shipwreck sequence and various shots of the pursuing hounds. The original Zaroff, Leslie Banks, even stands in for Edgar Barrier's Kreiger at one point, when, in silhouette, he urges on his hounds. There's also one instance in which John Loder and Audrey Long magically transform into Joel McCrae and Fay Wray as they flee through the fog!

Sometimes, however, Norman makes the occasional improvement. The first is having the heroine's brother only feign inebriation. Not only is Russell Wade's character far less obnoxious than the original's Robert Armstrong, his alertness to danger and cleverness at pulling off the ruse makes his fate that much more chilling—particularly since we actually see him run for his life, something we don't in the original.

The concept of Rainsford having discovered Kreiger's secret and making plans to preemptively respond by building traps and working a deception (pretending to go along with the madman's obsession) adds a further layer of suspense to the already taut story. Quickly recovering from the initial horror of Kreiger's trophy room, Rainsford indeed lives up to "the most dangerous game" appellation by applying logic and cunning, formulating a plan to string Kreiger along and then kill him at the first opportunity. Of course, circumstances are against him and he's found out, but this little twist on the original offers moments of additional suspense and character revelation.

To his credit, Norman cleverly tapped into the WWII zeitgeist by transforming a Russian Count (or General in Creelman's story) into a German (his henchmen answer with "Javol" and deferentially refer to him as "Herr Kreiger"). Norman even makes Kreiger something of a Nazi spokesman, as he spouts such sentiments as, "The weaklings of this world were put here to give us pleasure, to die for us if need be."

Further reflecting the war-torn times, particularly the WWII America gung-ho/can-do attitude, in which Rosie the Riveter and war hero Audie Murphy were the role models of choice, *A Game of Death* makes a few further subtle alterations. Rainsford taunts Kreiger into hunting him immediately (rather than after resting) by accusing, "You stack the deck. No Kreiger, tonight or not at all…The trouble with you is you want all the odds. You wouldn't dare match your brain against my brain, your skill against mine." This puts the challenge into the mouth of the hero rather than (like in the 1932 version) the villain, casting *A Game of Death*'s Rainsford in a more pro-active light than the hero of the original, who simply *re*-acted. Additionally, Rainsford sets his traps well before he becomes the prey, showing a far-thinking preparedness not exhibited by the 1932 protagonist.

Like the original, *A Game of Death* touches on the morality of hunting for sport. At the film's beginning, Rainsford discusses this issue with his photographer friend Collings aboard the ship.

Rainsford: "To me it's the greatest sport in the world."

Collings: "Sport for the hunter, I imagine, not for the hunted. Take this jaguar, for instance [holds up photo of Rainsford about to shoot the big cat]. Look at the expression on that face. What do you suppose his feelings are?"

Rainsford: "Look Collings, there are two kinds of creatures in the world, the hunter and the hunted. I happen to be a hunter. Frankly, I'm not concerned with that fellow's feelings. As a matter of fact, he's probably enjoying himself just as much as I am. After all, he has a sporting chance of getting me."

Of course, such a nonchalant dismissal of the morality of hunting comes back to haunt this Great White Hunter when he himself becomes the prey. Though nothing explicit arises in the subsequent dialogue, the film suggests that Rainsford's outlook may indeed have changed over the course of his ordeal. Near the climax, after Rainsford has turned the tables on Kreiger, Rainsford pointedly asks, "Kreiger, you're the hunted now, and I'm the hunter; how does it feel?" Rainsford, in asking the very same question that Collings posed about the jaguar, appears now to side with the animals. It's a subtle shift that suggests that the issue is far more complex and worthy of consideration than Rainsford's earlier "two kinds of creatures" dismissal.

Art directors Albert D'Agostino (*The Invisible Ray*, *Dracula's Daughter*, various Val Lewton films) and Lucius Croxton, along with set decorators Darrell Silvera and Jame Altweis, create a studio jungle setting that, while not up to the impressive (and oppressive) vine-strewn, overgrown jungle hell of the original (itself constructed for the bigger-budgeted *King Kong*), proves perfectly serviceable. So too does the smaller-scaled but well-dressed castle interiors, with its massive wooden and iron door, stone flagstones, solid-looking walls festooned with animal heads, and heavy furniture.

Likewise, Kreiger's trophies are equally effective and a truly ghastly sight. In a particularly grisly moment, director Robert Wise offers us a horrified reaction shot, as Rainsford's eyes widen and Ellen sucks in her breath, then a close-up of their object of horror—a head suspended in a glass tank. The low-key lighting makes it seem to glow in all its hideousness, the warped features, sunken eye sockets and exposed teeth bared in decay seeming to push forward out of the surrounding darkness. It's a startling and gruesome tableau, and one that hammers home the horror of Connell's concept.

Given that 1932's *The Most Dangerous Game* boasted such thespian heavyweights as Joel McCrae, Fay Wray, Leslie Banks, and Robert Armstrong, the cast of lesser lights in *A Game of Death* come off remarkably well by comparison. At least partial credit should go to director Robert Wise, as confirmed by actor Russell Wade (who played Bob Trowbridge). "Bob Wise was helpful to me," explained Wade to Michael G. Fitzgerald (in *Filmfax* issue 52), "always giving me little tidbits. Bob deserves the great success he has attained."

Affecting a slight accent, precise speech patterns and an aristocratic bearing very much in the vein of Leslie Banks' original Count Zaroff, Edgar Barrier offers up an involving portrayal of Connell's archetypal hunter. When Kreiger asks Rainsford if he slept well, and receives the response "Like the dead," Barrier pauses ever so slightly before giving a slight knowing smile as he answers, "My guests always do." Barrier's subtle expression adds a whole other meaning—and a welcome touch of black humor—to the innocuous idiom. Later, Barrier's eyes shine with a mad excitement as Kreiger, his bloodlust aroused, calls for his dogs and urges his quarry to "Run, run, run, give them a good chase!"

New York-born stage and screen actor Edgar Barrier was a member of Orson Welles' prestigious Mercury Theatre group, and lent his voice to a number of Welles' radio productions before making a minor name for himself in Hollywood in various B pictures in the early 1940s, including several Jon Hall-Maria Montez fantasy costumers. Barrier played Banquo to Orson Welles' *Macbeth* in that director's 1948 film adaptation of the famous Shakespearean play. Among his more "interesting" credits are Universal's 1943 remake of *The Phantom of the Opera*, *The War of the Worlds* (1953; uncredited as a scientist), and *The Giant Claw* (1957; as another scientist, this time credited—though no doubt wishing he hadn't been). Beginning in the early 1950s Barrier made frequent appearances on television until his premature death in 1964 of a heart attack at age 57.

Though often painted with a "bland" brush by critics, John Loder puts forth an impression of level-headedness and dependability, so that one can easily posit him turning the tables on his blood-maddened host. Loder's calm, confident and authoritative (but not overbearing) demeanor, coupled with a natural likability and lack of arrogance, makes him an ideal choice for the story's hero. When Kreiger excitedly proclaims, upon learning the identity of his new guest, "Rainsford—not the famous author and hunter?!" Loder gives a self-deprecating laugh and answers, "I don't know about the 'famous' part," immediately endearing him to the viewer.

The son of a British general, John Loder served as a lieutenant at Gallipoli in World War One, where he was captured and became a prisoner of war. After appearing in a number of German silents, Loder came to Hollywood in the late 1920s, where he played in early talkies. Returning to his native England in 1931, he became a star of the British screen, even appearing opposite Boris Karloff in 1936's *The Man Who Changed His Mind* (aka *The Man Who Lived Again*). Loder went back to Hollywood during World War Two and appeared in a score of pictures over the next seven years (including the intriguing 1945 poverty-row witchcraft entry *The Woman Who Came Back*). Failing to attain the level of screen stardom he had achieved in Britain, Loder turned to Broadway and then finally returned to England, where he made several more pictures before retiring to his fifth wife's ranch in Argentina. Hedy Lamarr was among his previous wives.

As already mentioned, Russell Wade's doomed character in *A Game of Death* is far more engaging than Robert Armstrong's counterpart in the original film. In contrast to the blustery Armstrong's obnoxious drunk, Wade's quietly inebriated, even apologetic Trowbridge becomes a far more likable and identifiable character—particularly when we learn of his clever deception and masked alertness. Wade, never the most dynamic of actors, is well cast as the quiet, unassuming, gentle Trowbridge, making his plight and eventual demise that much more affecting.

Russell Wade is best remembered for a trio of Val Lewton horrors: *The Ghost Ship* (1943), *The Leopard Man* (1943), and *The Body Snatcher* (1945). After earning his first studio contract at age 18, Wade worked primarily in B films for the next decade before forging a new career in real estate in Palm Springs. "I still haven't seen the original [1932 *Most Dangerous Game*]," he said in the 1990s, "so I don't know if [*A Game of Death*] was a worthy remake. I would assume that our version was better than the earlier one, but then, some of that antique footage was put into our film and it looked it. You could easily see that the footage didn't match." (Wade's observation notwithstanding, said footage is integrated fairly well into *A Game of Death*.)

Not all the *Game of Death* principals measure up to their predecessors, however. While attractive enough in her own right, Audrey Long lacks that ethereal beauty and innate vulnerability possessed by *Most Dangerous Game* heroine Fay Wray. As the de facto heroine-in-peril, Long fails to recreate the desperation and sheer terror so convincingly put across by Wray in the 1932 film. And the people at RKO seemed to agree, since her screams in *A Game of Death* were dubbed from an old soundtrack recording of Ms. Wray!

Audrey Long had a relatively brief decade-long career in B movies, with her starring turn in *A Game of Death* being a highlight (though she did appear this same year in the Ray Milland classic *The Lost Weekend*—uncredited, as a cloak room attendant). In 1952 she became the fourth wife of novelist and screenwriter Leslie Charteris (creator of "The Saint") and retired from the screen. The union lasted until his death in 1993.

As Kreiger's stony-faced right-hand man Preshke, Gene Stutenroth makes a poor substitute for Noble Johnson's scowling, imposing and forbidding "Ivan." Sleepy-eyed Stutenroth comes off as a bland Raymond Burr-type heavy, too soft-spoken and polite to generate much menace. (Ironically, Johnson appears as Kreiger's secondary henchman, Carib, but makes little impression.) Stutenroth, renamed Gene Roth, found a home in low-budget Bs and on television, playing support in such fare as *She Demons* (1958) and *Attack of the Giant Leeches* (1959).

Though constrained by a nearly word-for-word and incident-for-incident script that offers too-few innovations, director Robert Wise, working with cinematographer J. Roy Hunt was still able to invest a few flourishes in this remake. The mobile camerawork of cinematographer J. Roy Hunt (whose career stretched all the way back to 1916, and whose credits include *I Walked with a Zombie* and 1949's *Mighty Joe Young*) keeps things visually active, even during the early dialogue scenes, while his low-key lighting enhances the ambiance and helps set the mood. When Rainsford and Ellen sneak into the trophy room at night, the lighting casts ominous shadows as they make their way through the castle's main room. Shadows from some ornate iron grillwork fall across them, subtly suggesting prison bars and reflecting the duo's trapped condition.

Though not the most prestigious of the Dangerous Game adaptations, and nowhere near the best-known or most popular, *A Game of Death* boasts the most prestigious *director* ever to tackle Connell's story—Robert Wise, who went on to helm such classics as *Curse of the Cat People* (1944), *The Body Snatcher* (1945), *The Day the Earth Stood Still* (1951), *I Want to Live!* (1958), *West Side Story* (1961), *The Haunting* (1963), *The Sound of Music* (1965), and *The Sand Pebbles* (1966). Consequently, *A Game of Death* holds the distinction of being the only adaptation of Connell's story to have been helmed by an Oscar-winning director (Wise won for *West Side Story* and *The Sound of Music*).

Though early in his career (*Game* was only his fourth picture), Wise's camera placement and choice of angles displays the superb craftsmanship and good cinematic judgment that would lead him to the Oscar podium two decades later. For instance, when Kreiger gives his self-revelatory "hunting was beginning to bore me" monologue, which segues into his hint-dropping about his having "found a new animal to hunt," Wise positions his camera and actors so that Rainsford and Ellen are seated in the foreground, their backs to us, while Kreiger stands in the background, looming larger than the two seated listeners. The placement, coupled with Kreiger's vaguely threatening dialogue and Edgar Barrier's mannered yet intense delivery, creates an ominous, brooding mood and offers a foretaste of the terrors to come.

When said terrors materialize in the form of the chase, the centerpiece of the film's second half, Wise utilizes some quick editing (a former editor himself, Wise cut such classics as 1939's *The Hunchback of Notre Dame*, *Citizen Kane* and *The Magnificent Ambersons*) and clever camerawork (with the camera alternately pursuing and running alongside the frantic, fleeing Ellen and Rainsford) to make the scene as exciting as it is disturbing. Though not quite capturing the raw energy and large-scale grandiosity of the original, it still remains a thrilling pursuit; and there would be no cause for complaint had not the brilliant original *Most Dangerous Game* sequence superseded it.

When Kreiger returns from another successful hunt, his servant places the body, wrapped in burlap, on a table in the trophy room. As Kreiger steps up to gloat over his latest kill, Wise's camera moves forward, *over* the body on the table, forcing the viewer to come into horrifically close proximity to the covered corpse, stopping only in close-up on Kreiger, whose distant gaze and trance-like expression, as he unconsciously strokes the scar on his forehead, hammers home the subtle madness of the man and the situation.

Near film's end, Kreiger sits triumphantly playing his piano. The shadow of the huge castle door slowly opening appears on the wall in front of him, followed by Rainsford's silhouette, which towers over the sitting—and startled—Kreiger. The tables have been turned and the balance of power shifted, and Wise's clever presentation and use of angles underscores this.

Though a worthy, well-acted and well-crafted thriller in its own right, even with its few token changes and even occasional improvement, *A Game of Death* remains too slavish a remake for its own good when juxtaposed with its 1932 predecessor. Back in 1945, however, with *The Most Dangerous Game* only a hazy 13-year-old memory for most moviegoers, the project was a viable one, reintroducing the classic tale to a new generation of cinemagoers. And had the 1932 *Most Dangerous Game* disappeared into the limbo of the lost film, this remake would enjoy pride of place among fans today.

Ultra Filmfax magazine opened the door to this *House of Horrors* in issue 67 (June/July 1998).

HOUSE OF HORRORS (1946)

Generally regarded as a rather distasteful late-hour entry in Universal's second horror cycle, *House of Horrors* is a better movie than it gets credit for. The slightly disagreeable smell that hangs like a pall over this *House* no doubt arises from the stigma attached to Universal's supposed exploitation of acromegalic actor Rondo

House of Horrors *insert poster*.

Hatton. While some may see Universal's (repeated) casting of the disfigured actor in the role of a grotesque murderer as a film studio crassly trading on the unfortunate results of a man's tragic disease, others may see a former bit-player and Hollywood wannabe making the best of a bad situation (and in the process attaining a much higher level of success than he ever had before). In any case, if one can look past the modern-era PC reactions, then *House of Horrors* becomes a quick-paced, atmospheric, well-acted, and entertaining chiller.

After a nasty art critic (Alan Napier) puts the kibosh on a potential sale, starving sculptor Marcel DeLange (Martin Kosleck) decides to end it all by throwing himself into the river. Before he can take the plunge, however, he sees a huge man (Rondo Hatton) struggling to drag himself out of the water. Marcel pulls the half-conscious form from the river and gleans the inspiration for his next masterpiece from the figure's misshapen head ("The perfect Neanderthal," he marvels). Marcel befriends the ugly giant and takes him home to use as a model. Upon learning that his newfound subject is the notorious Creeper, who kills by breaking his victims' spines, Marcel plants the suggestion that they would both be better off if certain art critics were silenced. Quick as a snap, the Creeper sets to work…

Though initially touted in the trades back in late 1944 as an A-level, big-budget production, when filming finally started in September 1945 (nearly a year after its first announcement) *Murder Mansion* (*House of Horror*'s shooting title) carried the typical B-level budget and rushed shooting schedule. Even so, all involved did their best to make this more than the average B-horror potboiler.

With much of the film taking place at night (especially during its first and final thirds), the fog-shrouded and shadow-filled streets give the picture a noirish feel. Add to this a hideous spine-breaker (in the form of Rondo Hatton as the Creeper) and an unhinged artist, and *House of Horrors* becomes a potent little programmer.

With careful staging and evocative photography (utilizing sinister shadows and silhouettes, for instance), director Jean Yarbrough (whose prolific but undistinguished output includes *The Devil Bat*, *King of the Zombies*, *She-Wolf of London*, *The Brute Man* [a poor prequel to *House of Horrors*], *The Creeper* [no relation], and the execrable *Hillbillys in a Haunted House*) rose above his usual workmanlike efforts to craft what is arguably his best picture. No doubt

Maury Gertsman's (*She-Wolf of London*) atmospheric lighting and precise low-angle photography helped tremendously.

House of Horrors benefits from a pair of likable leads in the attractive forms of Robert Lowery and Virginia Grey, who generate an amiable chemistry as they jovially kid one another and engage in witty repartee. Their fast-paced encounters keep things moving briskly and quickly establish their personable characterizations. The supporting players also prove effective, particularly the cultivated Alan Napier playing an acerbic art critic and Bill Goodwin as a clever, ever-smiling, flirtatious detective.

The "star" of the film (at least to horror fans), however, doesn't fare so well. Rondo Hatton, though "a very gentle, sweet man" (as remembered by *House of Horrors* co-star Virginia Christine), was not much of an actor. Partly due to his disease and partly due to a simple lack of thespian talent (as evidenced by his early failures to break into the profession before his affliction), Hatton could not deliver dialogue with anything even remotely resembling inflection. Nor could he effectively portray emotion with his oversized features. Consequently, his monotonous delivery and impassive countenance severely limit his performance. In other words, the less dialogue the better. Though his lines in *House of Horrors* come few and far between, they are not few nor far enough between, and he nearly spoils the show whenever he opens his mouth. His Creeper is simply a hulking, ugly killing machine—devoid of any pathos or identifiable humanity.

Fortunately, Martin Kosleck is there to step in, for his Marcel is the real "monster." Thanks to Kosleck's smoldering intensity and sensitive underplaying, Marcel inspires both sympathy *and* unease. Though he received only fourth billing and the lowest salary of all the principals ($1,334), Kosleck's meaty role and insightful playing make him the film's real star.

As Kosleck plays him, starving artist Marcel DeLange becomes a rather tragic figure. (Ironically, Kosleck was himself a recognized artist in real life, having garnered critical acclaim for his portraits and landscapes in both California and New York—with Albert Einstein as one of his biggest fans!) "Before you came into my life," Marcel tells the Creeper, "I felt put upon. I was haunted constantly by the feeling I was persecuted, helpless to fight back." Though obviously several slices short of a full loaf, the poor guy has indeed been "put upon" by the cranky critics around him (even one who professes to be his friend condescendingly calls him "little man"). Kosleck's twisted, weird intensity (complete with glint in his weasely eye) makes him seem like a coiled spring ready to snap (and snap he does—spines that is—at least vicariously through his newfound friend). Kosleck keeps the melodrama toned down to an effective level, however, relying on dialogue nuance and subtle expression rather than obvious shouting and gross facial tics. And he laces his lines with a hint of self-pity (some of it seemingly justified), so that this "crazy" (as one character calls him) arouses some small sympathy.

Due to Kosleck's sensitive playing, Marcel becomes a classic worm-turns character which later became so popular in the slasher films of the 1980s (though Kosleck shows much more sophistication and taste than the slice 'n' dice put-upons who came later). At film's end, Yarbrough dots the tragic exclamation point when Marcel's devoted cat comes sniffing and meowing around his master's lifeless body—a sad and touching sight.

With another actor as the muscle behind Kosleck's mania, *House of Horrors* could have become a B-movie classic. As it is, despite the wooden performance and inevitable stigma that comes with any Rondo Hatton appearance, *House of Horrors* still remains one of Universal's better (and more enjoyable) low-budget efforts from the 1940s.

I Walked with a Zombie…in *Scary Monsters* magazine (issue 27) in 1998 to explore one of the best (and certainly most poetic) horrors of the 1940s. Here's what I found…

VOODOO POETRY: VAL LEWTON'S *I WALKED WITH A ZOMBIE* (1943)

"I walked with a zombie [laughs]. It does seem an odd thing to say."
–Frances Dee as Betsy uttering the film's opening lines

Over the years *I Walked with a Zombie* has (rightly) garnered much attention for its restrained atmosphere and near poetic tone. (Along with *White Zombie*, this is probably the best known—and the best—of all voodoo films.) Much of the film's literate quality can be put down to one man: producer Val Lewton. More than any other Hollywood producer, Lewton proved a hands-on supervisor whose touch pervaded every aspect of his productions (he nearly always re-wrote scripts, for instance, usually without taking credit). Lewton's RKO 'horror unit' operated for three years (1942 to 1945) and generated nine low budget (about $150,000 apiece) terror films, many of them—such as *Cat People* (1942), *The Body Snatcher* (1945), and this feature—the very best of the decade. Boris Karloff (whose 1940s horror pictures consisted mainly of repetitious mad doctor roles or juvenile entries like *The Ape* and *House of Frankenstein*), starred in three of the producer's intelligent pictures and dubbed Lewton "the man who rescued me from the living dead and restored my soul."

Even before shooting began on the Lewton unit's first horror feature (*Cat People*), RKO executive Charles Koerner called Lewton into his office and gave him the title of his B-unit's second production: *I Walked with a Zombie* (to be based on a recent *American Weekly* article of the same name by Inez Wallace). To add insult to this titular injury, Koerner also told the dismayed producer that screenwriter Curt Siodmak would be penning the script. For the previous two years Siodmak had toiled away on the more conventional horrors churned out by Universal: *Black Friday* (1940), *The Invisible Man Returns* (1940), *The Invisible Woman* (1940), *The Wolf Man* (1941), *Invisible Agent* (1942), etc. Granted, *The Wolf Man* turned out to be one of the decade's classics, but Lewton must have balked at having a writer thrust upon him whose last assignment was the Universal monster rally *Frankenstein Meets the Wolf Man* (1943). "[Editor] Mark Robson remembers," wrote Joel E. Siegel in *Val Lewton: The Reality of Terror*, "that Lewton's face was white and his manner impossibly gloomy when he returned from that meeting with Koerner." The following day, however, Lewton showed up in an inexplicably exuberant mood and triumphantly told his staff that they would make "a West Indian version of *Jane Eyre*." (Before leaving his job as David O. Selznick's story editor for the RKO producer's post in early 1942, Lewton had helped prepare a film production of the Charlotte Brontë novel which was ultimately made by Orson Welles. Undoubtedly, Lewton had spent the night figuring out a way to make his ridiculously-titled zombie project respectable and seized upon the Brontë classic as a literary out.)

Blessed with the sensibilities of a sensitive artiste rather than the crass traits of the typical Hollywood mogul, Lewton told his unit: "They may think I'm going to do the usual chiller stuff which will make a quick profit, be laughed at, and be forgotten, but I'm going to make the kind of suspense movie I like." To this end, Lewton brought in a second writer, Ardel Wray, and even rewrote the script's final draft himself (uncredited). Though it's difficult to pinpoint who contributed what to the finished screenplay, Curt Siodmak told *Filmfax*'s Dennis Fischer that "[Lewton and Wray] made some changes. My idea was a little different. I started with the beautiful wife married to a plantation owner who every year went to Paris. He wants to keep her forever, so when he finds out that she wants to run away, he will not let her go. So he makes her into a zombie—then he can keep her, have her whenever he wants. But she has no reactions toward him. That's why she walks around. She was in a living death. But I don't know if he [Lewton] kept it this way. I never saw the picture afterwards." Obviously, Wray and Lewton heavily rewrote Siodmak's initial draft (which sounds very much like a reworking of *White Zombie*).

On October 26, 1942, cameras rolled on *I Walked with a Zombie* with Jacques Tourneur (who won the assignment on the strength of his excellent efforts on *Cat People*) twirling the director's baton. Like most facets of American life at the time, World War II also affected film production. Anticipating the necessity of cutting down on location trips because of the implementation of gas rationing, RKO eliminated five days of location shooting from the script. The changes necessitated the erection of three additional sets at the studio and added three days to the schedule. On November 19, a little over three weeks after principal photography began, the greatest voodoo film of all time was in the can.

Canadian nurse Betsy (Frances Dee) journeys to the West Indian island of St. Sebastian to care for the invalid wife of sugar planter Paul Holland (Tom Conway). Though Holland refers to his wife Jessica (Christine Gordon) as "a mental case," local legend has it that she's been turned into a zombie, a creature "with no will of her own." Soon Betsy learns the sordid story involving the Holland family—that Jessica fell in love with her husband's half-brother, Wesley Rand (James Ellison), and had planned to run away with him before succumbing to the fever that left her in this catatonic state. Betsy first hears of it when a melodious calypso singer (Sir Lancelot) captures the tale in musical verse:

"There was a family that lived on the isle,
Of St. Sebastian a long, long while.
The head of the family was a Holland man,
And the younger brother his name was Rand.

Ah woe, ah me, shame and sorrow for the family.

The Holland man he kept in a tower,
A wife as pretty as a big white flower.

She saw the brother and she stole his heart,
And that's how the badness and the trouble start.
The wife and the brother they want to go,
But the Holland man he tell them no.
The wife fall down and the evil came,
And it burned her mind in the fever flame.

Ah woe, ah me, shame and sorrow for the family"

When medical measures fail to alter Jessica's condition, Betsy determines to take her charge to the voodoo priest, but she must first brave the terrors of the night, including the guardian zombie Carrefour (Darby Jones)…

The visual poetry of I Walked with a Zombie *(1943).*

I Walked with a Zombie is without a doubt the most haunting and poetic of voodoo films (and perhaps of horror films in general as well). From the moody lighting, death-oriented dialogue, and low-key, serious playing of the principals, an almost palpable air of tragedy hangs over the picture.

A meticulousness and attention to detail helped add to the richness of the film's tapestry. "The sets were beautifully dressed," observed director Jacques Tourneur to Joel E. Siegel in *Cinefantastique* magazine. "Val was very fussy about furnishings and it paid off. You don't know why you like a thing in a film. Every time you see a film that you like, somebody stayed up at night, somebody didn't sleep, somebody worried, somebody was fussy, somebody made enemies. Good pictures don't just happen…Val and I were both craftsmen. We were proud of our work."

About their working relations and various contributions, Tourneur had this to say: "Val was the dreamer and I was the materialist. I always had both feet on the ground. We complemented each other. By himself, Val might go off the deep end and I, by myself, might lose a certain poetry." Fortunately, the chemistry proved just right on *I Walked with a Zombie* to keep it afloat in "the deep end" with a series of poetically graceful strokes.

Among these are the elegant use of Sir Lancelot's calypso ballads to move the story along (acting like a musical Greek Chorus), the beautifully staged and lyrically tragic ending, and, most memorably, the pivotal 'walk'—the picture's centerpiece.

Without a note of background music, the eerie sequence in which Betsy takes Jessica to the houmfort fills the ears with only those disturbing sounds heard by Betsy herself—the low howling of the wind, the eerie humming made by punctured ceremonial gourds, the mysterious rustling of the cane brake all around her, and the thundering silence when her light betrays the presence of the sentinel-like zombie, Carrefour.

For the eyes, the sequence becomes a veritable feast of menacing shadows and unseen presence as the two women (one fearfully alert and the other literally dead weight) pass. (Though accompanied by the zombified Jessica, Betsy is worse than alone on her nocturnal journey, her mute companion's unseeing, unknowing, and *unnatural* demeanor only intensifying Betsy's isolation and unease). It begins with an eerie shot of Carrefour standing motionless in black silhouette to set the menacing tone. Then, the smooth camera motion and alternating viewpoints (following alongside, behind, in front of, and even shooting from Betsy's point of view) draws the viewer into this nocturnal trial of subdued terror as Betsy comes upon such disturbing sights as a human skull in a circle of stones (which Jessica's gown brushes over as she walks past—perhaps signifying the zombie-woman's closeness to death), a sacrificial goat suspended from a tree, and the zombie himself—first revealed as a pair of naked feet in the tiny pool of Betsy's flashlight which then shoots frantically upwards to illuminate his unearthly, staring countenance towering above her (and us). Thanks to the clever, sensitive, and evocative staging of director Jacques Tourneur, the atmospheric lighting and fluid visuals provided by cinematographer J. Roy Hunt, and the determined-yet-uneasy playing of Francis Dee, this three-minute sequence becomes one of the most effective and poetically moody moments in all of voodoo cinema (or any other celluloid branch, for that matter).

The uniformly naturalistic, even subdued acting by the principals does much to weave a thread of believability into the film's dark cloak of the mystical and supernatural. (Even as late as two weeks before filming, Anna Lee [*The Man Who Changed His Mind*,

I Walked with a Zombie: *here Betsy (Frances Dee, center) does just that. (lobby card)*

1936; *Bedlam*, 1946] was set to play the role of Betsy, with Francis Dee stepping in only at the last minute. Though Ms. Lee showed herself time and again to be an extremely capable actress, Ms. Dee's intelligent and sensitive portrayal proved a great asset.) The characters speak and act in normal tones and everyday inflections, with no trace of theatricality or melodrama—a rarity in horror films of the 1940s. But then nothing in *I Walked with a Zombie* (including its brooding, otherworldly atmosphere, highly literate dialogue, adult attitude towards both its story and characters, and its elegant visuals) indicates *any* close kinship with the Universal monsterfests or Poverty Row horrors proliferating at the time. Director Jacques Tourneur strove for such unaffectedness in his actors. "In [*I Walked with a Zombie*], as in others," explained Tourneur in Charles Higham and Joel Greenberg's *The Celluloid Muse*, "I made the people talk very low, as I think this indicates sincerity… it makes for the effect I want. I'll have an actor replay a whole scene as though he's just talking to me in a normal voice, and it's effective."

Lewton obviously strove for a modicum of authenticity. "We all plunged into research on Haitian voodoo, every book on the subject Val could find," remembered co-scripter Ardel Wray in Siegel's *The Reality of Terror*. "He was an addictive researcher, drawing out of it the overall feel, mood and quality he wanted, as well as details for actual production. He got hold of a real calypso singer, Sir Lancelot he was called—a charming, literate, articulate man. He, in turn found some genuine voodoo musicians. I remember they had a 'papa drum' and a 'mama drum,' that the crew on the set were fascinated by them, and by one particular scene in which a doll 'walks' in a voodoo ritual. They managed a concealed track for the doll, and it was effective. I particularly remember that doll because Val sent me out to find and buy one 'cheap.' Everything had to be cheap because we really were on a shoestring."

Lewton even employed a "technical advisor" versed in the ways of authentic Voudoun. On October 29,

1942, *The Hollywood Reporter* announced that "LeRoy Antoine, who is one of the country's leading authorities on Haiti and Haitian folk music and voodoo, will be the technical advisor on *I Walked with a Zombie*. Antoine will also teach the Negro actors Haitian rhythms for use in voodoo ceremony."

With such research incorporated into its literate and intelligent script, some sincerity couldn't help but penetrate the film's voodoo veneer. In fact, *I Walked with a Zombie* was the first feature to take a truly adult approach to voodoo. None of the usual human sacrifice business or diabolical sorcery mars its maturity. Instead, the picture focuses on showing the pervasiveness of this alternative religion in the lives of St. Sebastian's inhabitants. "[Voodoo] is part of everyday life here," states one character matter-of-factly, hinting at the normalcy of their voodoo worldview. The film also touches on the religion's cornerstone—possession. As Paul describes voodoo early on: "They sing and dance and carry on. And then as I understand it one of the gods comes down and speaks through one of the people." (Amusingly, Lewton applied his wry sense of humor to the topic by inserting this declaration among the fine print of the opening credits: "The characters and events depicted in this photoplay are fictional. Any similarity to actual persons, living, dead, or *possessed*, is purely coincidental.")

Even the sensationalistic idea of zombies remains ambiguous and unexploited. The voodooists seem astonished when they realize Jessica is a true zombie, and Carrefour never attacks anyone; obviously, there is little real danger from these 'zombies'—despite the white outsiders' fear.

Director Jacque Tourneur considered *I Walked with a Zombie* "the best picture I've ever done. Very poetic." Indeed, not only is it among the greatest horror films of all time, it is, without a doubt, the most *elegant* voodoo picture to date. Despite a disparaging stumble here and there, it remains arguably the finest example of voodoo cinema ever set to celluloid.

> *Filmfax* magazine (issue 57) brought some visibility to my take on *The Invisible Man* in 1996.

THE INVISIBLE MAN (1933)

With four bonafide genre classics to his credit (*Frankenstein*, *The Old Dark House*, *The Invisible Man*, and *Bride of Frankenstein*), James Whale is undisputedly *the* most important director from the Golden Age of Horror. Though the quantity is quite impressive, it's the quality that sets Whale apart—and above—his contemporaries. Several other directors have provided us with multiple classics (Tod Browning with *Dracula* and *Freaks*; Michael Curtiz with *Doctor X*, *Mystery of the Wax Museum*, and *The Walking Dead*; Karl Freund with *The Mummy* and *Mad Love*; the Cooper/Schoedsack team with *The Most Dangerous Game* and *King Kong*), but no other of the decade's filmmakers possess such a prolific—and perfect—record as James Whale. His third, *The Invisible Man*, is yet another 'Whale of a Picture.' Of the director's four genre ventures, it may be the most balanced—it's more sophisticated than *Frankenstein*, less idiosyncratic than *The Old Dark House*, and avoids the heavy-handed symbolism and directorial grandstanding of *Bride of Frankenstein*. Deftly blending humor and horror, Whale places his stamp on every portion of *The Invisible Man* (from his trademark jump cut introduction of the title character—á la *Frankenstein*—to his mocking sense of humor) to facet yet another cinematic jewel.

The well-known story begins with struggling chemist Jack Griffin's (Claude Rains) frantic attempts to counteract a formula that has rendered him invisible. The serum, however, begins to affect his mind and, after being hounded by inquisitive townsfolk, he becomes a violent megalomaniac. Intending "to make the world *grovel* at my feet!" he embarks upon a reign of terror that only an invisible madman could accomplish. Despite the efforts of his loving fiancée and her scientist father, Griffin must finally be tracked down and killed by the police.

Whale, with the help of cinematographer Arthur Edeson, uses the camera like a brush to paint his story upon the celluloid canvas. Utilizing varied angles and perfectly-framed shots, Whale takes care not to repeat himself (even altering the camera angle or distance slightly when returning to a character or scene) in order to add a visual variation and keep the viewer slightly off-balance.

Whale builds upon R. C. Sherriff's script to infuse the film with a wicked sense of humor which sometimes bubbles up into near-hilarity. Once having seen it, who can forget the priceless moment when a seemingly disembodied pair of trousers comes skipping down a country lane jauntily singing "Here We Go Gathering Nuts in May"?

Sherriff's clever screenplay sports enough rich dialogue to make *The Invisible Man* one of the most quot-

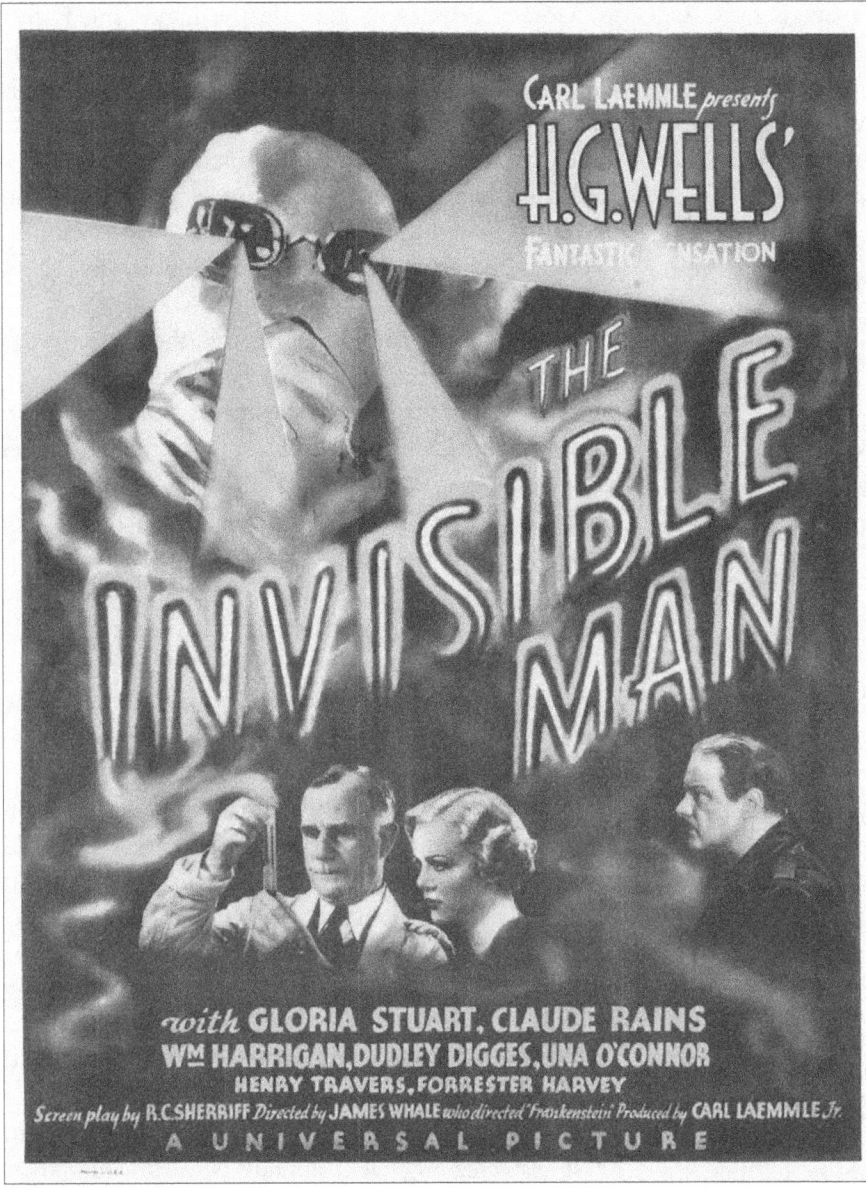

Another James Whale masterwork.

He ends it, however, with a brutal blow to the bobby's face with a wooden stool—killing the man. Griffin has now crossed the line; our worst fears have been realized and the madness seizes him fully as he embarks on his reign of terror. Even when Griffin becomes a truly frightening figure (wrecking trains and murdering with abandon), however, he never completely loses his humanity (still showing tenderness towards his fiancée, for instance). Ultimately, we still care about Griffin's condition and feel genuine sorrow at his plight and (sadly necessary) death.

Though originally announced as a vehicle for Boris Karloff (who dropped out of the project due to a contract dispute with Universal), it's difficult to imagine anyone but Claude Rains (making his screen debut) in the role of "The Invisible One." Through his intelligent, sympathetic voice and expressive body language, Rains creates a character who, though faceless, becomes more real (indeed, more *visible*) than many other star portrayals. The empathy Rains generates gives the film a powerful resonance so that when Griffin turns into a dangerous megalomaniac, the change inspires an anxious sympathy as well as fear. Co-star Gloria Stuart (playing Griffin's fiancée) recalled that Rains himself possessed a rather hearty ego, complaining that "he used to back me into the scenery." Despite this, she also felt that he was "a very nice person and a brilliant actor."

John P. Fulton's amazing special effects add the finishing touches that bring the scenario to realistic life. When we see a shirt running around the room on its own, arms waving in mockery at the dumbfounded spectators, or a cigarette and box of matches rise and light themselves (complete with a subsequent exhalation of smoke issuing out of thin air), we have no doubts that invisible hands really are manipulating these objects.

able films from Horror's Golden Age. Memorable lines like "Look, e's all eaten away!" and "Even the Moon's frightened of me!" and "How can I handcuff a bloomin' shirt?!" proliferate.

The characters are delightfully drawn, particularly Jack Griffin. Though his transformation from beleaguered scientist into maniacal killer comes fairly quickly, it is nonetheless believable. Frustrated to the point of distraction, he initially lets loose with a volley of malicious (and amusing) pranks—tipping over a grandfather clock, tossing glasses around the pub, throwing an old man's hat into a pond. Later, when Griffin disrupts the inquest at the tavern, he begins comically enough by throwing ink in the face of the doubting policeman.

Thanks to James Whale's perfect staging, R. C. Sherriff's grandiose dialogue, Claude Rains' brilliant inflection and physical acting, and John P. Fulton's flawless effects, *The Invisible Man* stands as one of the most thrilling and entertaining classics from the horror genre's greatest decade.

> This tandem piece was my very first published magazine article, and I have Gary Svehla, editor of the venerable *Midnight Marquee* magazine, to thank. This was adapted from my book *Golden Horrors: An Illustrated Critical Filmography of Terror Cinema, 1931–1939*, which I was writing at the time; and I was absolutely thrilled to see it in print in issue 45 (Summer 1993), quirky subheadings and all (which at least makes it easier for readers to skip those tedious synopses).

THE GOLDEN AGE OF HORROR: *ISLAND OF LOST SOULS* and *MAD LOVE*

ISLAND OF LOST SOULS (1933)

"What is the law? Not to run on all fours, are we not men?" –the 'Sayer of the Law.'

SYNOPSIS

Island of Lost Souls opens as Edward Parker is rescued at sea by the SS Covena after his own ship went down. Parker was headed for Apia where he was to marry his fiancée, Ruth. Onboard the Covena is Montgomery, a disgraced physician and current assistant to Dr. Moreau. Montgomery is overseeing the transportation of a load of exotic animals bound for Moreau's private island.

After Parker regains his strength, he confronts the drunken captain when the man cruelly attacks Montgomery's strange servant, M'ling. Later, when the cargo ship nears the island, Dr. Moreau meets the boat with his schooner and takes possession of the animals. Just as the large ship pulls away, the disgruntled captain spots Parker and throws him over the side onto Moreau's boat, despite both Parker's and Moreau's protestations. With no other options, Moreau and Montgomery take Parker to their island. Once there, Parker catches glimpses of the strange, misshapen inhabitants which populate the island. "Strange looking natives you have here," comments the innocent Parker, with his only answer a slight sardonic smile from Dr. Moreau.

Moreau decides he can use the handsome Parker to his advantage and introduces him to Lota, "the only woman on the island." Unknown to Parker, Lota is one of Moreau's 'manimals'—the human-like creatures which populate the island and which Moreau has created from animals. Lota is his most perfect creation and Moreau wishes to observe her reaction to this man. "Will she be attracted," the Doctor muses, "has she a woman's impulses?"

Later that night, Parker learns the horrors behind the mysterious "House of Pain" (the name given Moreau's laboratory by the pitiful beast-men who have endured countless sessions of painful vivisection as Moreau shapes and molds them under the knife). Disgusted, Parker attempts to flee with Lota. They are accosted by the manimals but saved by Moreau, who then tells Parker the whole story. "With plastic surgery, blood transfusions, gland extracts, with x-ray baths… with what I have discovered in my own work among the cellular organisms—*my* work, *my* discoveries, mine alone—with these I have wiped out hundreds of thousands of years of evolution."

With Parker set to leave the following day, Moreau has his own sailing sloop scuttled so Parker is forced to remain on the island. Meanwhile, Ruth learns that Parker was dropped off (literally) at Moreau's Island. The American Consulate arranges for Captain Donohue to take his ship to the island, with Ruth going along.

Back on the island, Lota is attracted to Parker and he momentarily succumbs to her 'animal charms.' But Lota's hands give away her true nature ("the stubborn beast flesh creeping back," laments Moreau) and Parker learns the truth of her origin (she was created from a panther). In a fury of indignation, he assaults Moreau. Despite this, Moreau still plans to keep Parker on the island and continue his 'experiment' with him and Lota. "He is already attracted," reasons Moreau, "time and monotony will do the rest."

When Captain Donohue and Ruth arrive on the island, Ruth is reunited with Parker. However, darkness has fallen and the three must spend the night at Moreau's compound. After the trio has retired, the manimal brute called Ouran attempts to break into the house to get at Ruth, apparently with the sanction of Moreau, who views it as another 'experiment' in attraction. Ruth's screams rouse Parker and Donohue, causing Ouran to run off into the jungle. Montgomery finally confronts Moreau: "I'd have stood for anything," he disgustedly tells Moreau. "I *have* stood for plenty. But not this!" Montgomery helps Captain Donohue

Island of Lost Souls' harrowing climax.

leave the compound, intending to bring back his crew in force. Moreau observes this and orders Ouran to kill the captain: "I want you to follow him and put your hands around his throat—" Ouran succeeds in his mission and takes the body back to the manimal village. This puts the beast-men in an uproar and they set fire to the village. The Law Sayer and leader of the manimals confronts Ouran with what he has done. "What is the law? Not to spill blood. Are we not men? *You* broke the law," he cries, pointing at Ouran. "Law no more" is Ouran's response. "*He* tell me spill blood." This is the beginning of the end of Moreau's god-like control over these creatures.

Moreau goes out to subdue them but the beast-men no longer fear his whip and "the Law." As the creatures advance, chasing Moreau back to the house, Montgomery, Ruth, Parker, and Lota sneak out the back and head for the boat. Ouran follows, but Lota, trailing behind, gives her own life to defend the three from the beast-man.

The manimals carry Moreau to the House of Pain where they pin him to the operating table. Clawed hands reach for knives and scalpels as a hideous wail of agony issues from the center of the slashing creatures gathered around the table. While Moreau meets his fate at the hands of his creations, the three protagonists row away from the now-burning island. "The fire will destroy all of Moreau's work."

MEMORABLE MOMENTS

One of the most frightening and brutal moments in this very frightening film comes when Moreau confronts the manimals at their village for the final time, only to find he can no longer control them. As the creatures steadily advance, the camera becomes Moreau and focuses on the lead beast-man advancing towards him (and the viewer). Moreau cracks his whip and it winds about the beast-man's neck--to no effect, and the creature continues his inexorable advance. Then another of the creatures has the whip wrap around *his* neck—again to no effect—as Moreau futilely continues trying to stop them. Finally, one more creature advancing towards the camera is struck by the whip, which this time winds about its *face*, but it keeps coming. The combination of the low lighting and surrounding darkness with the manimals' constant wailing and murmuring and the sight of the whip cracking futilely across their hate-filled countenances creates a frightening tableau, drawing the viewer in to feel Moreau's own panic and terror.

A second memorable sequence comes a few minutes later when the advancing beast-men have forced Moreau back to his house. In desperation, Moreau shouts at them: "Have you forgotten the House of Pain?!" This momentarily stops the manimals and, in an overhead shot, we see the creatures huddled and cowering in remembered fear. Suddenly, the Law Sayer stands up and cries, "You—you made us in the House of Pain!" and the camera tracks downward to close in on him. "You made us *things*!" he wails as the camera moves in tight on his bestial form. "Not men!" he shouts and takes a step towards the camera. "Not beasts!" he adds and takes another step closer. The camera abruptly cuts to the terrified Moreau, then back to the beast-man. "Part man, part beast..." continues the Law Sayer, moving still closer. "THIIIINGS!" he screams and the hideous hairy face fills the screen. Then in quick succession a half dozen creatures rush at the camera one at a time until they too fill the screen with their hideous bestial visages, echoing "Things!", "Part man!", "Part beast!", "Things!" The claustrophobic effect is both powerful and horrifying.

Even the power and ferocity of these scenes pale in comparison to the climactic demise of Dr. Moreau—the most chilling fate ever to befall a villain in the Golden Age of Horror. The sequence is truly horrific and once seen is not soon forgotten. While no overt bloodshed is seen (as would be the case in a modern film version), the sights and sounds and feel of the sequence are terrifying. Carrying Moreau into the laboratory, a dozen bestial hands hold him down while a dozen more shatter a glass cabinet to grab at knives and scalpels. Soon a hideous wail of agony emanates from the center of the bestial forms huddled around the operating table. As the camera pulls back and the scene dissolves into a shot of the laboratory entrance, the frantic screams from Moreau are almost too much to bear. This is undoubtedly the most horrific, certainly the most sickeningly exciting, and arguably the greatest climax in the Golden Age of Horror, comparable only to the shuddery ending of Tod Browning's *Freaks* (1932).

ASSETS

Any way you look at it, *Island of Lost Souls* is strong stuff, particularly for 1933. So strong was it, that for thirty-five years the film was banned outright in England (a country known for its sensitivity to animal rights and vivisection). H. G. Wells, on whose novel the film is based, heartily denounced the picture (and eagerly endorsed the British ban). With the subjects of vivisection, sadism, and implied bestiality running throughout the film to assault the sensibilities of puritanical censors and critics, it's not hard to fathom such outrage. But even beyond these ostensibly offensive elements, *Island of Lost Souls* was met with hostility because it simply worked too well as a horror film—it actually *horrified* people.

The frightening manimals, the claustrophobic jungle setting, the hideous experiments, the painful wails from the House of Pain, and Moreau himself—devoid of compassion, sadistic in his work; all these add up to an unrelenting 72 minutes guaranteed to disturb even the most jaded film viewer. The film is relentless. No comedy relief softens the harshness. The standard love-interest is minimal, with most of the focus instead on the relationship between the hero and the blossoming panther-woman. The implication of bestiality is clear, and the film doesn't hold back or apologize for its subject matter. Dr. Moreau even spells it out for the hero (and the audience): "Lota [the panther woman] is my most nearly perfect creation," beams Moreau. "I wanted to prove how completely she was a woman, whether she was capable of loving, mating, and having children. She was afraid of Montgomery and myself. Then *you* came. Well, she was very much attracted to you. You can see, of course, the possibilities that presented themselves."

Charles Laughton (in his sixth American film in a little more than a year) gives us the greatest mad doctor of them all. Moreau is *not* experimenting for the good of science, *nor* is he a wronged man using his genius for revenge. No, he knows what he is doing and he knows why. "Mr. Parker," he asks, more to himself than to his guest, "do you know what it means to feel like God?" (A line similar to this was cut from *Frankenstein* soon after its initial engagements. While Universal did not want its Dr. Frankenstein uttering such blasphemy, apparently Paramount had no such compunction about their Dr. Moreau.) Unlike Colin Clive's impassioned, high-strung Henry Frankenstein, Laughton's Moreau is a cool, calm creator, reveling in the monstrosities he lords over. As the Law Sayer intones the ritual phrase, "*His* is the hand that makes. *His* is the hand that heals. *His* is the House of Paiiiiiin," Moreau beams down at the beast-men like a god accepting homage. In another revealing scene, Moreau examines one of his monstrous creations strapped to an operating table. He casually turns the thing's head this way and that, examining his handiwork, while the pitiful beast-man screams in pain—a wail that starts low and grows steadily until it becomes an unbearable cry of agony—but the preoccupied doctor pays no attention. Laughton's Moreau can also be lascivious (in a somewhat detached manner, anyway). When he spies Lota saying goodnight to Parker in a rather tender fashion, he comments, "How that little scene spurs the scientific imagination onward." Laughton's low, intense delivery leaves little doubt that more than *scientific* imagination has been inflamed. Laughton's Moreau characterization is a brilliant study in control and composure—a sinister, perverse composure with an underlying power strong enough to hold his island in a grip of fear.

The bulk of the film takes place on Moreau's private jungle island and the setting creates a moody oppressiveness, a growing claustrophobic feeling of unease. On-location shooting at Catalina Island lends a great deal of authenticity to the production, and the realistic setting is lush and dark, with overripe foliage and decaying greenery closing in on all sides. Moreau's weird house, made of stone blocks and iron bars (almost prison-like), overgrown inside and out with the decay of the jungle creeping in, only adds to this trapped, closed-in feeling, and mirrors the moral decay of Moreau himself.

Island is filled with memorable performances. Aside from Laughton's Moreau, Lugosi turns in a weird, tortured portrayal as the Sayer of the Law. His pronounced accent, halting speech, and odd inflections add further texture to this unusual—and unnatural—character, perfectly complementing his bizarre hirsute appearance. Lugosi's innate authoritative presence, coupled with his anguished emoting as he recites his litany of "the Law" or wails at Moreau ("You made us *things*!"), make his character a brutally eloquent spokesman for the pitiable beast-men.

Newcomer Kathleen Burke creates an unforgettable character in Lota, the panther-woman. The combination of her odd, angular, yet very attractive face and her unaffected body language (as she languorously lounges against the hero, almost purring in satisfaction) creates a heady mixture of animal sensuality and primitive innocence.

Karl Struss' camerawork is impeccable. The Oscar-winning cinematographer makes good use of foreground placement, framing, and the mobile camera. Perhaps the film's most distinctive cinematic feature, however, is the relatively little-used subjective technique of keeping the camera steady and having the actors advance straight at the camera (and at the audience). Director Kenton and Struss used this procedure with the manimal monsters, accentuating the shock appeal of Wally Westmore's grotesque makeups. The resulting impact felt by viewers as the bestial creatures rush straight at them is one of a fierce claustrophobic head-on charge.

Director Erle C. Kenton handles the directing chores admirably, bringing each element together to form a powerful, frightening whole. While Kenton's work is effective, not a small portion of the picture's success stems from the cast and technical crew. Struss' camerawork, Hans Dreier's atmospheric jungle sets, Wally Westmore's gruesomely original makeup, Waldemar Young and Philip Wylie's no-holds-barred screenplay, and Laughton and Burke's excellent characterizations give the picture its power and impact. Kenton continued to work both within and outside of the horror genre, but his subsequent output (efficient but undistinguished) indicates that for *Island of Lost Souls* Kenton became something of an over-achiever.

LIABILITIES

Richard Arlen as the hero delivers a very ineffective performance which weakens this otherwise compelling production. Arlen alternates between obvious overdramatics (which don't gel with the very subtle performances of Laughton and Burke and the solid playing of the rest of the cast) and toneless acting. His supposedly 'revealing' expressions of disgust (particularly when he learns the truth about Lota) and anger are unconvincing on his wooden countenance. His voice generally does not carry the conviction of his words. When Arlen confronts the doctor, for instance, saying, "Moreau, you don't deserve to live," his words are fierce but his tone remains bland and unconvincing. It is unfortunate that this classic film suffers from the same 'ineffectual

Though largely overshadowed by the likes of Dracula, Frankenstein *and* The Mummy, Island of Lost Souls *stands as one of the greatest Golden Age horrors.*

lead' syndrome that mars *Dracula* (1931), *The Mummy* (1932), and to a lesser extent *The Black Cat* (1934).

Nevertheless, *Island of Lost Souls* stands up and dares to be counted among the handful of films that were unafraid to break ground and walk on American cinema taboos. It pulls no punches and makes no apologies. It is powerful, enthralling, and (much like its contemporary, *Freaks*) was ahead of its time.

REVIEWS

The New York Times' Mordaunt Hall (January 13, 1933) was reservedly impressed: "Although the attempt to horrify is not accomplished with any marked degree of subtlety, there is no denying that some of the scenes are ingeniously fashioned and are, therefore, interesting. The general effect of the film is enhanced greatly by Mr. Laughton's urbane impersonation. …Richard Arlen portrays Parker acceptably. Arthur Hohl does quite well as Moreau's agent, Montgomery."

Variety's Waly (January 17, 1933) noted the exploitability of what he termed "a freak picture": "Paramount will make money with this picture, and so will every exhibitor, including the first big runs, who pays some attention to its exploitation." He also noted that "with such actors as Charles Laughton, Richard Arlen and Bela Lugosi in the cast, *Souls* is provided with a mainstay assuring wider patronage than had their roles been filled at random. …While the action is not designed to appeal to other than the credulous, there are undoubtedly some horror sequences which are unrivaled. Those studies of a galaxy of Dr. Moreau's 50–50 man and beast creations, as an example, will pique any type of mentality. …Romance is essentially light, and, with a story of this kind it should be. …There are too many reminders of grammar school mystery in this. Laughton's Moreau, however, lends even these a dignity suggesting realism."

The reviewer was not so appreciative, however, of Ms. Burke: "The extra billing given Kathleen Burke as Lota, Panther Woman, is strictly for the marquee. Girl is too much like a girl to even suggest transformation from a beast. Her part is little more than a *White Cargo* bit."

PRODUCTION NOTES

Director Erle C. Kenton went on to direct other notable (but far less effective) genre films, including *Ghost of Frankenstein* (1942), *House of Frankenstein* (1945), and *House of Dracula* (1945). A workmanlike director who got his start directing two-reel comedies for Mack Sennett, Kenton never lived up to the promise shown on *Island of Lost Souls*. In 1950 he left films for the new (and profitable) field of television, directing many episodes of *Racket Squad* and *Public Defender*.

Cinematographer Karl Struss was one of the greatest in the business. His illustrious career spanned four decades and included films such as *Ben Hur* (1926), *Sunrise* (1927; for which he received an Academy Award), *Dr. Jekyll and Mr. Hyde* (1931), and *The Great Dictator* (1940). After leaving Paramount in the early 1940s, Struss worked primarily on independent 'B' films, including half-a-dozen science fiction entries: *Rocketship X-M* (1950), *Mesa of Lost Women* (1953), *She Devil* (1957), *Kronos* (1957), *The Fly* (1958), and *The Alligator People* (1959; his next-to-last film). Throughout the sixties, Struss turned exclusively to photographing television commercials. He retired in 1970. Struss was impressed with Erle C. Kenton, claiming the director "had a greater command of the English language than anyone I ever worked with" (*Hollywood Cameramen*).

According to William Brown in *Charles Laughton: A Pictorial Treasury of His Films*, Laughton modeled his mad Dr. Moreau after an oculist he visited (to correct a minor eye malady) shortly before production on the film began. The actor was fascinated by the man's appearance, particularly by his small, satanic-looking beard.

Laughton felt a bit overwhelmed by the various manimal monsters. He later recalled, "I remember each horror and monster had more hair than the one before. Hair was all over the place. I was dreaming of hair. I even thought I had hair in my food" (from *The Laughton Story*, by Kurt Singer). According to author Charles Higham in *Charles Laughton, An Intimate Biography*, the actor "was disgusted by the story. His love of animals welled up; he felt a deep-seated repulsion at what he felt to be a crude exploitation of the theme of vivisection." (Laughton was not alone in these feelings, judging by the public outcry against the picture which culminated in a complete ban from the British Isles.) "I was never able to enjoy a zoo again," complained the actor himself. "The very smell of caged animals reminded me of the picture, and made me sick."

Apparently, Laughton's troubles did not end there, for he took issue with the intrusive hands-on directorial style of Erle C. Kenton (who was characterized as "pompous and bullying" by Laughton biographer Simon Callow in *Charles Laughton: A Difficult Actor*). Higham noted that Kenton "insisted on acting out scenes dressed up in the evil doctor's white tropical suit and hat, and even offered to teach Charles how to handle a whip," though the actor was already quite proficient with the prop. Karl Struss concurred that Kenton "played every scene through for the actors, even for Laughton, who was superb as Dr. Moreau." The cinematographer failed to characterize the director as bullying, however—far from it. "I admired Kenton," admitted Struss.

A disgruntled actor was not the worst of the problems faced during filming. William Brown (in *Charles Laughton: A Pictorial Treasury of His Films*) tells of a serious accident that occurred when one of the manimal extras ran too close to the tiger's cage on the ship and received a vicious swipe of the animal's claws which nearly tore his arm from the socket.

Two of Moreau's manimals were played by *one* man—stuntman Joe Bonomo. For the first creature, Bonomo merely sported fangs and Fredric March's fright wig from *Dr. Jekyll and Mr. Hyde* (1931). The second manimal required a more complex make-up application, however; for as the 'Tigerman,' Bonomo's hirsute countenance resembles that of Oliver Reed in Hammer's *Curse of the Werewolf* (1961). "All of us who played beasts in that picture wore animal suits," remembered Bonomo in his autobiography, *The Strongman*, "constructed with the torso built down nearly to the knees, with a fifty-pound sack of sand in the crotch, making any effort to walk exceedingly clumsy and grotesque." Bonomo's screen career began when he won a 1921 "Modern Apollo" contest sponsored by the *New York Daily News*, which included a film contract. Bonomo's first assignment was doubling for none other than Lon Chaney in *The Light in the Dark* (1922).

Square-jawed screen hero Richard Arlen (born Richard Cornelius van Mattimore) worked variously as a sports writer, swimming coach, and Texas oil field laborer before journeying to Hollywood. Arlen (quite literally) broke into motion pictures while employed at the Paramount film laboratory. He fractured his leg while on the job and ended up in the studio hospital where he was spotted by a director who promised him a film part once he recovered. While the high point of Arlen's career, perhaps, came in 1927 with a starring role in *Wings* (the film which received the first Academy Award for Best Picture), Arlen continued acting for a full five decades. Specializing in actioners and westerns, Arlen also appeared in three further fantastique films (though the latter two are far from 'fantastic' in quality)—*The Lady and the Monster* (1944), *The Crawling Hand* (1963), and *The Human Duplicators* (1965).

According to Paramount's publicity department, Kathleen Burke was a Chicago dental assistant before winning a much publicized, nation-wide "Search for the 'Panther Woman'" contest to obtain this, her debut role. (The film's pressbook claimed that she was chosen over *60,000* other entrants!) As reported by the *Los Angeles Examiner* (September 30, 1932), "The contest was decided by a board of judges composed of Ernst Lubitsch, Cecil B. DeMille, Rouben Mamoulian, Norman Taurog, Stuart Walker and Erle C. Kenton. A $200-a-week contract with a five-week guarantee is the prize."

Paramount's director of recording, Loren L. Ryder, created the unnerving manimal sounds by combining recordings of animal noises and foreign languages played backwards, then alternately speeding them up and slowing them down to produce a suitably bizarre and otherworldly cacophony. Ryder's innovative use of sound earned him twelve Academy Award nominations and netted him five Oscars over the course of his career.

Working as assistant director on *Island of Lost Souls* was Charles T. Barton. Barton graduated to full director a year later and embarked upon a prolific career, directing over seventy features (predominantly for Columbia and Universal). Among them were eleven Abbott and Costello vehicles (including *Abbott and Costello Meet Frankenstein* [1948] and *Abbott and Costello Meet the Killer, Boris Karloff* [1949]).

Four remakes of H. G. Wells' story have appeared on the big screen: *Terror Is a Man*, an interesting, small-scale version filmed in 1959; *Twilight People*, a cheap 1972 Filipino co-production; *The Island of Dr. Moreau*, a much bigger (though even less effective) production released in 1977; and the 1996 Marlon Brando-starring misfire likewise titled *The Island of Dr. Moreau*.

MAD LOVE (1935)

"Each man kills the thing he loves." –Dr. Gogol

SYNOPSIS

Yvonne Orlac is an actress at "Le Theatre Des Horreurs," a Grand Guignol theater in Paris which specializes in torture plays. Her most ardent admirer is Dr. Gogol, a famous surgeon who has rented the theater's best box for every performance. The doctor makes advances to Yvonne, but his attention is unwanted because Yvonne is happily married to a brilliant young pianist, Stephen Orlac. Gogol, undaunted in his obsessive love, goes so far as to buy the wax statue of Yvonne which the theater had used for advertising in its lobby. A compassionate doctor and healer of children by day, at night the obsessed Gogol sets the wax statue up in his private study and plays the organ for it.

On the way back from a concert tour, Stephen Orlac is in a train wreck and the pianist's hands are crushed beyond saving. Desperate, Yvonne takes advantage of Gogol's attraction to her and has Stephen brought to the great surgeon, but even Gogol cannot save his hands. Suddenly, Gogol is hit by an inspiration. With a phone call the influential doctor has the body of an executed murderer brought to his house. The unfortunate was 'Rollo,' a knife-thrower in a circus, who was guillotined earlier that day. Gogol had attended the execution (it seems he never misses one). The brilliant doctor attempts an experimental operation and grafts the hands of Rollo onto the arms of Stephen Orlac. The operation is a success, except now Stephen seems unable to play the piano. Worse still, his hands have a newfound penchant for throwing knives (Gogol did not tell him that he now possesses the hands of a murderer).

In the face of mounting debt, Stephen goes to his estranged stepfather for help. When the old miser rebuffs his stepson, Stephen becomes angry and his new-

Mad Love: *a brilliant study in obsession and madness.*

ly-acquired hand picks up a knife and throws it at a wall. Though his stepfather is unhurt, Stephen is nearly unhinged by the event and rushes out in confusion and despair.

After being finally and utterly rejected by Yvonne, the now-mad Gogol plans to utterly destroy Stephen, who is already in a weakened mental state because of his inability to play and resulting money troubles. Gogol dresses in a bizarre neck-brace and a set of metallic hands to convince Stephen that he is Rollo, brought back to life with his head restored by Gogol, and the murderous hands that were once his are now on the arms of Stephen (this last part being true). He plants the suggestion that Stephen has killed his stepfather (a crime Gogol has committed and framed Stephen for).

Stephen is arrested for the murder of his stepfather and Yvonne, suspecting the truth, goes to Gogol's house in search of proof. She is forced to impersonate her own statue, however, when the madman returns home laughing his triumph. When she is discovered, Gogol thinks the statue has come to life: "My love has made you live!" Yvonne tries to escape but is trapped by the madman, and just as he is about to strangle her with her own hair, the police arrive with Stephen. Using his new talent, Stephen throws a knife to kill Gogol before he can strangle Yvonne. The two lovers are reunited.

MEMORABLE MOMENTS

In one of the movie's most literate and revealing sequences, Gogol plunges deeply and irrevocably into madness. After being spurned a final time by Yvonne, Gogol is forced to leave an operation when her words come back to torment his tortured mind: "Liar! Hypocrite! You disgust me!" In a mirror, his reflection speaks to him: "They are laughing at you in there, go back." Then suddenly, from another mirror, his second reflection answers: "Let them laugh. Nothing matters to you but one thing—Yvonne, Yvonne in your arms." As he approaches the second mirror, he approaches this other side of his psyche, and the reflection changes from that of the white-gowned doctor (a surgeon, healer, bringer of mercy) to that of the black-suited Gogol (obsessed madman). Through his deft direction, Karl Freund brilliantly visualizes the two sides of this man's nature, the inner struggle of the tormented Gogol.

The film's most macabre moment comes when Gogol dons a bizarre disguise to convince the confused Stephen that he has killed his step-father. Entering a seedy hotel room, Stephen faces a shadowy figure across a rough table. The room is illuminated by a single lamp, which serves to keep the stranger in near-darkness. The camera is placed behind the figure, so that all we see is a dark silhouette. When Stephen implores him to tell what he knows about Stephen's hands, the figure answers in a sinister, rasping whisper: "They throw knives, ha!" "How do you know that?" demands the shocked Stephen. The camera moves in on the table and the stranger brings up his hands—or what serve as his hands: a pair of bizarre metal gauntlets. "I have no hands," hisses the figure. "Yours—they were mine once." Suddenly stabbing a knife into the table, he exhorts Stephen to "use it—when they try to arrest you." "Who are you?" demands Stephen. "I am *Rollo*, the knife thrower," is his answer. "They cut off my head—"(the figure suddenly stands). "But that Gogol," he continues in his hideous, gravelly voice, "he put it back—here." For the first time we see the figure from the front as he opens his coat to reveal a medieval-looking neck brace, all stiff leather and gleaming metal, which obscures the whole of his lower jaw and neck. The evil-looking brace, combined with dark wraparound goggles and slouch hat, makes him a grotesque, terrifying figure.

The camera moves in on the weird, frightening countenance, and the upper lip moves upwards in an unpleasant sneer while a dry cackle, devoid of all mirth, issues from the mouth. It is a shuddery moment, subtly gruesome in its implications.

ASSETS

Cinematographer-turned-director Karl Freund (who had directed *The Mummy*, one of the greatest horror films of all time, three years earlier) again creates one of the best entries from Hollywood's Golden Age of Horror. With *Mad Love*, his only other horror picture as director, Freund shows us that his earlier success was not merely a fluke. While not as fluid as *The Mummy*, and lacking the iconographic presence of Boris Karloff, *Mad Love* is still a literate, powerful, darkly beautiful film deserving of the title 'classic.'

Freund uses the camera like a brush, painting shadows and light upon a celluloid canvass to create mood and meaning in every frame. Nothing in this picture is flat, there are always layers upon layers of dark and light. Gogol's house, for instance, is not simply a collection of rooms and stairways, but a series of oversized shadows, mysterious spaces, and pools of darkness in the vein of the German Expressionist cinema (not surprisingly, since Freund had worked as a cinematographer for such famed German directors as Fritz Lang in the 1920s).

Freund never settles for the ordinary or mundane. From the opening credits, when we see a fist rise up and smash through the glass on which the credits are printed (a startling harbinger of dire events to come) to the climactic moment when Gogol is about to strangle Yvonne with her own hair, the film reeks of the macabre. Freund continually uses striking visuals to enhance a scene or explore a character. Even an act as simple as answering the telephone is turned into a macabre visual treat. Instead of the camera viewing Gogol's housekeeper pick up and answer the phone, we are shown her shadow on the wall performing this task. And then the shadow delivers this little gem of dialogue: "The Professor isn't 'ere," she states and gives an unpleasant little laugh before adding, "If you want to know, 'e's visiting 'Madam Guillotine.' He never misses one o' those head-choppins."

When we first meet Dr. Gogol, he is sitting in a theater box, watching Yvonne (the object of his 'Mad Love') on stage. Gogol's face is bisected by a line of shadow from the box curtain. By placing the subject's face half in and half out of darkness, Freund creates a visual introduction to the duality of the man. On the one hand Gogol is a kind, compassionate doctor, ca-

Peter Lorre as Gogol and Frances Drake as Yvonne, the object of his Mad Love.

pable of affectionately comforting a sick child. On the other hand, he is a demented, obsessed madman with a sick passion for death and a woman he cannot have. Gogol is indeed a man half in and half out of 'the darkness.'

Mad Love was Peter Lorre's first American film, and he gives a bravura performance as the obsessed Dr. Gogol—a performance which won him accolades from the critics. Andre Sennwald of *The New York Times* wrote (August 5, 1935): "Mr. Lorre, with his gift for supplementing a remarkable appearance with his acute perception of the mechanics of insanity, cuts deeply into the darkness of the morbid brain. It is an affirmation of his talent that he always holds his audience to a strict and terrible belief in his madness." Lorre's great passion was psychology, and in fact he studied for a time under Sigmund Freud. "An actor," Lorre said, "to be good, must be a psychologist. He must outstrip the professional psychologists, who concern themselves only with a few phases of a subject's mind. An actor must be *a hundred percent psychologist*—for he takes his character apart and reconstructs all his emotions. Then he takes those emotions into himself, becomes that character, be the character mad or not. The actor must be the character, utterly" (*Famous Monsters Yearbook*, 1966). Lorre's deep knowledge of the mind stood him in good stead for his role in *Mad Love* and indeed over the course of his entire career.

Also well cast are Francis Drake as Yvonne (a last-minute replacement for Virginia Bruce) and Colin Clive as Stephen Orlac. The fresh, wholesome beauty of Francis Drake contrasts strikingly with Peter Lorre's Gogol, who, with his bulging eyes and fleshy lips and completely shaved head makes a decidedly *un*wholesome figure. A very talented actress, Drake makes good use of her large expressive eyes and subtle movements and gestures to create a tragic figure of innocence. Colin Clive is perfectly cast as the nervous, high-strung, highly suggestible pianist. His Stephen Orlac is a direct outgrowth of his classic role in *Frankenstein* (1931)—a tortured, brilliant man on the verge of nervous collapse. (By all accounts this characterization was not far from reality. "I remember that Clive was a very talented actor," recalled co-star Ian Wolfe to interviewer Roger Hurlburt in *Filmfax* no. 39, "but a noticeably high-strung and nervous one.")

Mad Love is a stylish, rich, dark fantasy which lets us look into the mind and soul of a madman. It is a *Dr. Jekyll and Mr. Hyde*, but less fantastic, with the evil being released not by a magic potion, but by the magic of a human mind lost in obsession and madness. With the talent evident in this and his earlier effort, one can only wish that Freund had stayed with directing (he went back to cinematography after this feature), and that while directing he had taken more forays into the realm of the macabre.

LIABILITIES

Mad Love is not a perfect film. Gogol's death is too abrupt. The now-completely mad Gogol gets a knife in the back and promptly dies without a word. When so many choice words had been issuing from his mouth throughout the rest of the picture, it is rather disappointing to have him end in silence.

And even after the happy ending, there are plenty of concerns left—Stephen still is unable to play the piano, and, of course, there's the problem of his new hands still "wanting to throw knives" (a rather dangerous hobby).

Finally, there is the wax statue. At times it is indeed a wax figure (in a not-so-good likeness of Ms. Drake), and at other times, particularly in close-ups, it is obviously Francis Drake herself trying to hold her breath and keep perfectly still. This substitution isn't convincing and detracts from the scenes' realism by calling attention to the deception (is it live or is it memor*wax*?).

REVIEWS

Variety's "Char" (August 7, 1935) called this production "ideal starring material for the foreign actor, Peter Lorre," before adding, "the results in screen potency are disappointing…" However, Char detailed no specific faults to back up his broad criticism, and, in fact, lavished nothing but praise on the film: "No complaint can be raised against the production, given the story by John W. Considine, Jr., producer, and the director Karl Freund. Although the script situations are wildly fantastic, yet essential in telling the story, every ounce of horror has been wrung from the *Hands of Orlac* property. …Settings are strikingly effective and the camera work far above average. …Lorre's fine performance does the rest…"

Andre Sennwald, of *The New York Times* (August 5, 1935), began by calling *Mad Love* "not much more than a super–Karloff melodrama, an interesting but pretty trivial adventure in Grand Guignol." He went on to commend newcomer Peter Lorre, however, and his ability to hold his audience "to a strict and terrible belief in his madness. He is one of the few actors in the world, for example, who can scream: 'I have conquered science; why can't I conquer love?'—and not seem just a trifle silly."

Mr. Sennwald was unimpressed by the picture's comedy relief, complaining about what he terms "one of those absurd movie newspaper men, whose behavior is so inappropriately foolish as to cast a pall of burlesque over several of the most striking excursions in terror. … Ted Healy, a highly amusing comedian, has gotten into the wrong picture."

"But *Mad Love* is frequently excellent when Mr. Lorre is being permitted to illuminate the dark and twisted recesses of Dr. Gogol's brain. …Even if it is not quite what we might have looked for in Mr. Lorre's first American picture, *Mad Love* is an entertaining essay in the macabre…"

PRODUCTION NOTES

Mad Love is based on the novel *Les Mains D'Orlac* (The Hands of Orlac) by French author Maurice Renard. Four versions of the novel have been filmed to date. While not the first, *Mad Love* is the best and definitive one. The initial adaptation of Renard's novel was a dull, static German film made in 1925 (as *The Hands of Orlac*), with silent screen star Conrad Veidt agonizing over his new appendages. *Hands of a Stranger* was a weak American remake from 1962, and the British *The Hands of Orlac* was a slight improvement in 1965.

The filmgoing public of 1935 expressed little love (mad or otherwise) for this macabre picture. Costing $257,000 to produce, *Mad Love* suffered a net loss at the box office of $39,000. Even MGM's own discarded stepchild *Freaks* (1932) did better domestic box office than *Mad Love* (which fared better abroad than at home—due, no doubt, to European star Peter Lorre's name value).

After previewing *Mad Love* in Hollywood, MGM cut nearly fifteen minutes of footage before its official release. Among the rejected scenes: Gogol encountering a blind man begging in front of the theater whom the doctor had cured ("Being blind is my trade!"); additional footage of the hair-raising stage tortures at the Theatre des Horreurs; an encounter between a street girl (intent upon robbery) and Stephen's miserly (and apparently lascivious) stepfather; and the picture's gruesome centerpiece—Gogol restoring the guillotined Rollo to a modicum of life in order to facilitate the transplant operation's success. "The room is fitted up with glass pipes," described the screenplay, "tubes, wires, coils, all the appliances of scientific experiment. Camera pans slowly around until it catches Gogol and Wong in center of room. In front of them, on table propped against wall, is body of Rollo. His head is fastened by means of straps and iron braces to trunk. A glass tube is in his neck. This is attached by long rubber tube to beaker which holds blood fluid, under which gas flame is burning." With the revamped Production Code hovering above the production like the Sword of Damocles (not to mention the easily-shocked sensibilities of Louis B. Mayer), it is no surprise that this graphic, blasphemous sequence fell before the editor's censorial scissors.

After viewing Lorre's bravura performance in *Mad Love*, legendary comedian and director Charlie Chaplin declared him "the greatest living actor." This was Lorre's American debut. Following *Mad Love*, Lorre did one other film in America (*Crime and Punishment*, 1935) before journeying to England for Alfred Hitchcock's *Secret Agent* (1936). There, Lorre was contacted by Adolf Hitler and invited to join the German film industry. Der Fuhrer professed to admire Lorre's portrayals of murderers. Lorre's written reply was short and to the point: "Thank you, but I think Germany has room for only one mass murderer of my ability and yours." According to Ted Sennett in *Masters of Menace*, Hitler apparently had a long memory, for during WWII the FBI reportedly captured eight Nazi assassins possessing a hit list of one hundred names. Peter Lorre was listed third.

Many great actors were rather vain, and Peter Lorre was no exception. According to Francis Drake, Lorre insisted on meeting his leading lady *before* his head was shaved so that she could see him with hair. Also, Lorre would occasionally upstage his co-star by intentionally ruining a scene ("He didn't want you to be too good!" laughed the actress), ad-libbing "Don't you know me? I'm your little Peter!" (from *Karloff and Lugosi: The Story of a Haunting Collaboration* by Gregory WilliamMank).

Born Frances Morgan Dean in New York City in 1913, Frances Drake had no aspirations to a career in acting—or a career in anything for that matter. The daughter of a wealthy mining magnate, she was educated (including finishing school) in Canada and England. It was only the loss of her family's fortune in the 1929 stock market crash that sent Frances looking for employment. She began as a ballroom dancer in fashionable London clubs and then graduated to the legitimate theatre. She only entered movies because "they paid even better than the stage" (*Whatever Became Of...* by Richard Lamparski). Ms. Dean received several offers from Hollywood (including one from Universal), and ultimately chose Paramount because "they offered the most money." The studio then changed her name to Drake (and publicized that their new 'find' was actually related to the famous pirate!). In 1939 she married Cecil Howard, son of the Earl of Suffolk and Berkshire. At her husband's behest, Ms. Drake retired from acting in 1942, continuing as long as she did only because her husband had not yet come into his inheritance. Of her career and early retirement, she said: "From beginning to end my career was because of money. Yet, I did miss it a bit for a while. I consoled myself that at least I'd not have to be anywhere near such coarse, crass people as [studio executives] Al Kauffman and Harry Cohn."

Mad Love was Karl Freund's last film as a director, a career that spanned only three years and eight films. Freund dismissed directing, claiming "anyone can make a good cake if he has the right ingredients. It all depends on story, cast, and circumstances." After *Mad Love*, Freund returned to cinematography, shooting such classics as *Pride and Prejudice* (1940) and *Key Largo* (1948). He also won an Academy Award for Cinematography for *The Good Earth* (1937) and, according to a studio memo, was considered by David O. Selznick for the job of photographing *Gone with the Wind*. In the 1950s, Freund accepted the job of Chief Cinematographer at Desilu Studios, where he developed the three-camera technique while working on *I Love Lucy*, a process which became the standard for television sitcoms. It is interesting to note that Freund both began and ended his directing career with horror films (*The Mummy* and *Mad Love*, respectively), and that out of his eight credits it is only these two that are remembered.

While Freund demonstrated intense visual acumen, he was not what one would call an "actor's director." According to Francis Drake, Freund was too concerned with the camera to give much direction to the actors, leaving them largely to their own devices. Fortunately, these actors were all thorough professionals who could perform effectively without detailed direction.

Co-cinematographer Gregg Toland went on to become one of the most respected and influential cinematographers in film. His innovative use of high-key photography and the deep-focus technique set industry standards. Toland won an Academy Award for his work on *Wuthering Heights* (1939), and shot such classics as *The Grapes of Wrath* (1940), *Citizen Kane* (1941; for which he won a second Oscar), and *The Best Years of Our Lives* (1946). On *Mad Love*, Toland was forced into the role of simple cameraman rather than creative cinematographer by dictatorial director Karl Freund. "And Gregg Toland was a marvelous cameraman!" remembered Frances Drake. "Such a dear little man, and he looked rather haunted when this wretched big fat man [Ms. Drake's unflattering term for her director] would say, 'Now, now, we'll do it *this* way!'"

> *Filmfax* magazine made me feel like a king by including this short essay in their June/July 1997 issue (no. 61).

KING OF THE ZOMBIES (1941)

Of the eight voodoo films produced during the 1940s, five came from poverty row. Though far from the best of this questionable quintet (that would be 1945's *The Vampire's Ghost*), *King of the Zombies* can at least lay claim to being the *first*. Since it was concocted in 1941, it's only natural that scripter Edmond Kelso make his voodoo tale's bad guy an obviously Axis antagonist. Refreshingly, Kelso eschews the soon-to-be-cliched 'madman-creating-a-zombie-army' angle (introduced in the 1936 non-voodoo horror *Revolt of the Zombies*) to utilize voodoo in a rather novel way. Here our notorious Nazi makes use of the local priestess' powers to try and elicit vital information from a captured American admiral—a voodoo version of the third degree! The evil warmonger also possesses a half-dozen or so zombies, but they don't really do much except provide frightening foils for comedian Mantan Moreland.

The story begins when our three patriotic protagonists, Bill (John Archer), Mac (Dick Purcell), and their valet, Jeff (Mantan Moreland), crash their plane into a small West Indian island while on their way to undertake some vague mission for the Navy. On the island they find Dr. Sangre (literally "Dr. Blood," played by Henry Victor), his entranced wife, his suspicious niece, and a kitchenful of zombies. Though the doctor welcomes his unexpected guests, his hospitality proves false, as Sangre tries to hypnotize/zombify both Jeff and Mac. Sangre has captured an American admiral and plans to use the voodoo ceremony of "transmigration" (utilizing his own niece in some kind of soul transference) to wring vital war information out of him. Fortunately, during the climactic ceremony, Bill breaks through Sangre's hold over the zombified Mac and induces his entranced friend to lead the other zombies in an attack against the evil doctor. Sangre falls into a fire pit, Mac and Jeff recover, the admiral is saved, and all is well with the war effort.

When initially announced, *King of the Zombies* was to star Bela Lugosi under no-budget western specialist Howard Bretherton's direction. As the production got closer to its start-time, however, both Lugosi and Bretherton dropped from the project. Monogram sought Peter Lorre as replacement, but finally settled on Henry Victor (and director Jean Yarbrough) by the time cameras rolled on March 31, 1941.

While Henry Victor (best remembered as the loutish Hercules in *Freaks*, 1932) does an adequate job as the Nazi-cum-zombie-master, he lacks the flamboyance necessary for this type of production—a trait which his two near-predecessors (Lugosi and Lorre) possessed in abundance. Relying on his imposing stature and straightforward manner, Victor brings little aplomb to a role that simply cried out for a touch of bombast.

Jean Yarbrough's undistinguished directorial career stretched from 1936 to 1967 (ending—not inappropriately—with the dreadful *Hillbillys in a Haunted House*). He performed his usual dull service on *King of the Zombies*, which falls somewhere between his best (relatively speaking) genre efforts (*The Devil Bat*, 1940; and *House of Horrors*, 1946) and his worst (*The Brute Man*, 1946; *She-Wolf of London*, 1946; and *The Creeper*, 1948). Whatever visual interest the lethargically-staged *King of the Zombies* holds comes from a few bits of atmospheric lighting (courtesy of Mack Stengler) and the fairly lush potted-plant jungle sets.

In the usual just-get-it-done poverty-row tradition, the effects in *King of the Zombies* are less than special. For instance, the wire holding up the model airplane is plainly visible as it crash-lands on the miniature tabletop jungle. Also, the zombies receive no special makeup treatment, and must make themselves menacing with blank stares, lurching gaits, and a few rips in their clothing. Fortunately, they're not asked to do much except put a few scares into Mantan Moreland's Jeff, who's seemingly frightened by his own shadow anyway.

King of the Zombies' *best attribute proved to be the pop-eyed comic stylings of Mantan Moreland, here trailing behind Henry Victor, Dick Purcell, and John Archer.*

The one true highlight of *King of the Zombies*, and the only real reason to watch, is Mantan Moreland. Unlike his fellow black actor/comedians such as Stepin Fetchit or Willie Best (aka Sleep 'n' Eat), Moreland could generally overcome the stereotypical attitudes of the day (encapsulated in his contemporaries' denigrating stage names) and bring a likeable and self-possessed quality to his unprepossessing comedy characters, becoming a sort of pop-eyed, black Bob Hope. In *King of the Zombies*, Moreland was at his best—and he steals the show. His natural delivery and impeccable timing as he throws out quips and asides left and right make the often suspect dialogue and self-deprecating lines seem downright funny. Moreland knows just when to go for the obvious and milk a line, such as when he hears the drums begin to beat like some bizarre jungle marching band and quips "That's my cue for me to start parading outta here" or, when informed after the plane crash that he's not dead after all, he answers, "I thought I was a little off-color to be a ghost." Moreland also knows when to throw away a crack for a more subtle amusement, like when he tosses out, "If it was in me, I would be pale now" or, after Dr. Sangre assures him that "You will be taken care of," Moreland shoots back, "That's what I'm afraid of."

If looked upon as a poverty-row comedy, *King of the Zombies* fills the bill nicely; but seen as a voodoo horror film, this *King* wears only a paper crown.

> With this article I hoped to shed a little light on three of Bela Lugosi's less well-known films. This "Dark Triad" saw the light of day back in 1995 in *Filmfax* magazine (issue 48).

BELA'S DARK TRIAD: THREE OVERLOOKED FILMS FROM LUGOSI'S GOLDEN ERA

The immortal Count *Dracula* (1931), inspiring both passion and terror in his victims; the insanely zealous evolutionist Doctor Mirakle committing *Murders in the Rue Morgue* (1932); the benign yet twisted Vitus Werdegast, deathly afraid of *The Black Cat* (1934); the Poe-obsessed Dr. Vollin (a "god with the taint of human emotions") holding forth *The Raven* (1935) as his talisman—these are Bela Lugosi's best remembered moments of triumph. Later, toppled from his Hollywood aerie through the shortsightedness of producers and his own lack of business acumen, the fallen star brought us (courtesy of Sam Katzman) the kindly Charles Kessler, tormented by an *Invisible Ghost* (1941); the insanely devoted Dr. Lorenz, driven to see that *The Corpse Vanishes* (1942); the schizophrenic Professor Brenner/Mr. Wagner presiding over the *Bowery at Midnight* (1942); and the hypnotic Dr. Marlowe, the *Voodoo Man* (1944) himself.

In the early 1930s, Universal was Lugosi's meat and potatoes studio, offering the actor consistently choice cuts upon which to chew. For the following decade, Monogram became his bread and butter provider (though more often than not the threadbare productions seemed more akin to bread and *water*). Seen in stark contrast, these two well-known and oft-discussed cinematic subsets represent the apex and the nadir (excepting, of course, his final, sad Ed Wood phase) of Lugosi's Hollywood career. Though the films from these studios varied wildly in quality, each and every entry offered the actor a legitimate starring role and allowed Lugosi full reign to stretch his histrionic abilities. As such they remain dear to Lugosiphiles, the gold and the iron pyrite alike.

But what of the many pictures that fall between the diamonds of Universal and the zirconium of Monogram? Outside of these two studios, Lugosi often fared poorly, with sizable starring roles coming surprisingly few and far between. For every substantial characterization allowed by a *White Zombie* (1932) or *Chandu the Magician* (1932), a plethora of short-changed parts fell to the slighted actor in the likes of *Night of Terror* (1933) or *The Gorilla* (1939). Yet, throughout the latter half of the decade, a handful of offbeat starring vehicles presented themselves, some good, some excruciatingly bad, but each featuring a full-blooded Lugosi standing proud and erect at the helm. Here follows a look at three Lugosi films generally given short shrift or ignored outright (even by 'Lugostorians'). The three vary wildly in quality, but each deserves a second glance for the opportunity they afforded the most charismatic horror star of the Golden Age.

"I'll be truthful and admit that the weekly paycheck is the most important thing to me. …It's a good business—so I can buy steamship tickets, give tips and invite the boys for a drink. If I wouldn't make such pictures—maybe trash—I couldn't do it." –Bela Lugosi in 1935

The year 1935 saw Lugosi in two little-seen and even less talked about pictures, one a success both artistically and financially, the other a dismal failure on both counts. The first (the failure), released in October, was a farfetched technological mystery called *Murder by Television* produced on the cheap by a short-lived independent outfit named Cameo. Though *Murder by Television* scrapes the very bottom of the movie barrel (and falls with a resounding thud into Lugosi's "trash" heap), it *did* offer the actor a dual role.

MURDER BY TELEVISION (1935)

"The mad monarch of the laboratory waves his mighty hands and death-dealing rays strike down his hapless victims," promised the ads—a promise left sadly unfulfilled in terms of execution (so to speak). Interesting only as a Lugosi novelty, *Murder by Television* is a dismal little mystery involving the emerging technology of television. Professor Howland creates a new process by which he can observe any place around the globe through his television device. Of course, every communication corporation in the world (as well as numerous foreign powers) are intensely interested. A group of people gather at Howland's home/laboratory to witness the first public demonstration of his miraculous device. In the middle of the transmission, the professor collapses while onscreen—dead—and a vital tube is stolen from the apparatus. The police chief (who was present at the demonstration) now sets about sorting out the various suspects, motives, and opportunities—without much success. Bela Lugosi plays an assistant to the inventor, and does his best to draw suspicion upon himself by skulking about and looking guilty. He is, of course, merely a red herring, for he's promptly murdered himself. Fortunately for the actor (and the audience), there's a *second* Lugosi on hand—the man's twin brother—who ultimately cracks the fantastical case and gets to explain it all with this bit of scientific hokum: "Dr. Scofield's equipment radiated waves to Professor Howland's laboratory. When these waves came in contact with those the professor's equipment was radiating, they created an interstellar frequency—which is—the death ray." Of course, the professor was *televised to death*! In there somewhere is another bit of science fiction involving a doctor who has perfected a machine that can differentiate a criminal brain from a normal one (too bad Henry Frankenstein didn't possess such a device).

Static photography; a leaden pace (complete with tepid time-filling song "I Had the Right Idea" and unending scenes of the Inspector questioning each and

Murder by Television ad.

a long pause in which he half-closes his eyes in anguish and hardens his jaw as if steeling himself against the painful reply, "My brother." While Lugosi's twins can hardly compare favorably to Karloff's powerhouse Anton/Gregor of the same year's *The Black Room*, for instance, the dual role at least provided a modicum of range for the actor.

The picture contains several bits of dialogue which, looking back in hindsight, possess an (unintentional) humorous irony. "It is my hope," states the sincere inventor of a new television process, "to be able to prove that television is the greatest step forward we have yet made in the preservation of humanity." He grandiosely goes on to claim that TV "will make of this Earth a paradise we have always envisioned but have never seen." Obviously, he hadn't envisioned TV sitcoms. Dreadfully dull and abysmal on all counts, *Murder by Television* is a nonsensical mixture of (bad) science fiction and drawing room mystery, with the only point of interest in the picture being Lugosi's (dual) presence and his few sinister expressions.

Generally ignored, even by trade publications, *Murder by Television* received perhaps its kindest review from *Monthly Film Bulletin*. With considerate understatement, the reviewer reported that "Generous use is made…of modern electrical apparatus, but the murderer's method is…beyond the realms of probability. The actors are stiff and appear to be ill at ease with their parts."

Filmed at the old Tiffany Studios on Sunset Boulevard, this production (which carried a shooting title of *The Houghland Murder Case*) was Bela Lugosi's fifth picture (of six) released in 1935—and definitely the worst of the lot. Poorly distributed (a single print sufficed for all of New York state), *Murder by Television* died a quick (and deserved) death at the box office. The picture's closing line (delivered by Lugosi) serves as an appropriate epithet: "As Ah-Ling would say, 'even though the eyes may see, the mind will not believe.'"

every person in the house); puerile, racist humor (black 'mammy' ["Oh, Lordy Lordy I knows I seen a ghost!"] and pidgin-spouting Chinese servant with "a penchant for quoting Confucius and *Charlie Chan*"); and acting stiff enough to break your teeth on make *Murder by Television* nearly murder to sit through. Fortunately, Bela Lugosi is on hand to generate at least *some* degree of interest.

For Lugosi's dual role, (doubtful) pressbook advances claimed that Bela created his own makeup for the film, utilizing 43 different shades of grease paint on his face to achieve the desired look for this black and white production. Multi-layered makeup aside, Lugosi does manage to bring a differential depth to his twin characters (no mean feat, for Joseph O'Donnell's script gives the actor very little with which to work). For the first half of the picture, Lugosi acts almost furtively, with an air of uncertain hesitancy rarely found among the actor's standard barnstorming performances. In the film's second half, Lugosi (now playing the murdered man's brother) creates a more commanding presence, one self-assured (all sardonic smiles and arching eyebrows) in contrast to his deceased brother's circumspect demeanor. Lugosi takes the rather dry, stale characters and wrings from them all the juice he can. In one sequence he flirts with the heroine, allowing an almost coquettish smile to play across his lips, while in another scene he expresses a tightly-controlled grief over the death of his long-lost brother. When asked "With you here and alive, who was it that was killed?," Lugosi gives

THE MYSTERY OF THE MARY CELESTE (1935)

Several rungs up the ladder of quality from *Murder by Boredom…* er, *Television* stands Lugosi's final production of 1935—Britain's *The Mystery of the Mary Celeste*. While in New York awaiting departure for England, Lugosi admitted that he was unacquainted with the script of his upcoming project (the actor rarely read even so much as a scenario before signing on the dotted line). Fortunately, *The Mystery of the Mary Celeste* proved a much more (sea)worthy vehicle than his previous outing. Released in the U.K. in November 1935, *Phantom*

Ship (its new moniker when the picture finally docked at American shores) was a very early production by Hammer Films (in fact only their second), the British company which single-handedly revived gothic horror in the 1950s and '60s. This generally forgotten thriller provided Lugosi with one of his most sympathetic roles, allowing the actor a rare opportunity to stretch his all-but-atrophied thespian compassion without ignoring altogether the Lugosi trademark menace.

"LUGOSI CHANGES IMAGE ABROAD" read the *Los Angeles Examiner* headline on September 20, 1935. "Bela Lugosi…is definite proof that a change of scene is often of great value. …In his English picture, *The Mystery of the Marie Celeste* [sic], Lugosi abandons bizarre makeup and terrifying roles. Instead, he appears as an old sea captain, a sympathetic, crusty old salt, and his performance, playing straight, is reported to surpass any of his efforts in the improbable horror films of recent release."

The Mystery of the Mary Celeste takes its inspiration from a true incident in 1872 in which a clipper ship (the Mary Celeste) was found adrift with no sign of the crew, remaining a real-life enigma to this day. The suppositional story revolves around Captain Briggs and his new bride sailing on the Mary Celeste along with various unsavory crew members, many holding grudges against the Captain or his brutal first mate, Mr. Bilson. Preeminent among them is a grizzled, one-armed sailor named Anton Lorenzen (played by Lugosi) who six years earlier had been shanghaied by Mr. Bilson on this same ship and as a result lost his arm to a shark. Soon crew members are murdered or disappear one by one until… well, that would be giving it away. Denison Clift's no-frills direction, and Geoffrey Faithfull and Eric Cross' competent camerawork, prove unspectacular but adequate. The acting is melodramatic (not unusual for a British thriller of this period) and the characterizations shallow—with the exception of top-billed Lugosi. This is one of the more infrequently seen Lugosi performances, and that is a pity because it's also one of his best. For the most part his is a sympathetic role, and Lugosi deftly handles the pathos while occasionally balancing it with his more expected chilling delivery. The actor has several standout scenes, foremost among them the one in which he kills a man while defending the Captain's wife. Lugosi reacts to this heroic deed with horrified remorse, and his tortured statement, "I've killed my fellow man," is subtly effective. In another scene he explains that he was once "full of the hope of living" but, because of the brutal treatment he received, is now only a shell of his former self. "Now look at me," Lugosi invites, "my hair white, my arm—gone. Look at me now, derelict—like that ship" [pointing to a painting]. (For the Lugosiphile, this telling self-revelation possesses a chilling and prophetic sadness in view of the drug-dependent actor's final desperate years.) Lugosi's delivery is perfectly timed, with pregnant pauses and pointed emphasis, and his demeanor effectively evinces anger coupled with self-pity, inspiring compassion in the viewer. These scenes and Lugosi's performance in general demonstrate that the actor was much more versatile than his critics and film assignments generally allowed.

As an interesting footnote, *The Mystery of the Mary Celeste* contains two lines of dialogue unusual for a production of 1935 (particularly one from the prim and proper British Isles). The first occurs when the Captain scares up a crew in a sleazy waterfront bar. The proprietor states, "And here's your cook," pointing to a small white man in a dirty bowler hat. "If you don't like the look of his face I'll get you a chink or a nigger." Though filmed over sixty years ago, such a blatantly racist comment was shocking even by 1935 film standards. The second 'scandalous' bit of dialogue comes when the Captain, after having some trouble with the crew, orders his Mate to "Find out what the *hell* is happening"—and this a full four years before Clark Gable shocked the industry with his "Frankly, my dear…" soliloquy.

The Mystery of the Mary Celeste generally fared well with the critics, as did Lugosi. *Variety* (December 4, 1935) called the film "very strong stuff for those who like tragic entertainment," while noting that "Outstanding role is played by Bela Lugosi." *Daily Film Renter* labeled it "pretty grim fare…with sudden deaths and disasters galore. …Bela Lugosi has a part after his own heart as the bleary-eyed, one-armed Lorenzen, who stalks the decks like a sinister portent."

Though no classic, and not really a "horror" film per se (yet containing isolated moments of terror), *The Mystery of the Mary Celeste* remains noteworthy for its realistic settings and ship (the *Mary B. Mitchell*, a rented schooner); the air of dread laced with horrific undertones hanging over the doomed vessel; and most of all for Lugosi's controlled, excellent performance.

THE DARK EYES OF LONDON (1939)

Lugosi was so well-received for his return to a (mostly) straight dramatic role in *The Mystery of the Mary Celeste* that British Independent Pictures offered him a two-picture contract at $12,500 per film. However, when the actor learned that his four prized dogs would have to be quarantined for six months before

The Mystery of the Mary Celeste *pressbook*.

they would be allowed to join him in England (due to that country's strict animal import laws), he turned down the offer and returned to Universal to ultimately work on *The Invisible Ray* (1936). One can only wonder at the turn his career might have taken had he not been such a dedicated dog lover.

Ever looking to escape his role of Dracula and break out of the horror mold, Lugosi was encouraged by his success in *The Mystery of the Mary Celeste* to make plans to start his own independent production company. The actor made no secret of his dissatisfaction in being passed over for non-horror parts, telling Eleanor Barnes of the *Illustrated Daily News* (September 1935): "Every time I get my thoughts centered on a role that I believe fits me, some other actor—always a great actor—gets there first. So what am I to do? I'll finance my own company and star in pictures that I want to play in." *Cagliostro* (a tale of an eighteenth-century Wizard) was to be the first production of his new company, but the project (and the company) never fully materialized (nor did his longed-for escape from horror roles). An amusing remark made by Robert Montgomery (related by actress Audrey Totter in Doug McClelland's *Forties Film Talk*) illustrates Lugosi's inescapable image: "One day while filming *The Saxon Charm* [1948] we were in the [Universal] commissary and Bela Lugosi was there, with a young boy [undoubtedly Bela, Jr.]. Bob Montgomery said, in a melodramatic voice, 'I see that Bela Lugosi is having a small boy for lunch!'"

Like *The Mystery of the Mary Celeste*, the final (and certainly topmost) point of Lugosi's forgotten triangle of films blazed forth from the sodden land of Merrie Olde England. Unlike *Mary Celeste*, however, this production brought the actor (at least part-way) back to the horror fold. In November of 1939, *Dark Eyes of London* hit the U.K. cinema circuit as the first English film to receive the British Censor's new "H" rating for "Horror" (which prohibited persons under sixteen years of age from seeing the film). The reactionary rating had been created in 1937, largely as a response to another Lugosi picture, 1935's *The Raven*. By far the best of the overlooked triad, *The Dark Eyes of London* hit American shores in March 1940 under the more sensational appellation of *The Human Monster*.

In London, "five insured persons have been found drowned in the last eight months," and Scotland Yard has nary a clue. An Insurance company run by a certain Dr. Orloff (Lugosi) seems to be involved somehow, and Inspector Holt (along with Diana, daughter of the most recent victim) investigates. Their probing leads them to the "Home for the Destitute Blind" run by the kindly

The Dark Eyes of London *pressbook*.

Mr. Dearborn (himself sightless). "Somewhere between Orloff's office and the Dearborn place is the answer," Holt tells Diana. When the girl, after taking a job at Dearborn's institute, discovers evidence that her father was murdered, Orloff sends Dearborn's deformed assistant, an ugly, hulking blind brute named Jake, out to silence the girl. Diana places a call to Holt from her flat just as Jake breaks in. Hearing her screams over the phone, Holt rushes to the house and scares Jake off before the deed can be done. Inspector Holt has now figured out Orloff's nefarious scheme of murder, forgery, and profit, and puts out a warrant for Orloff's arrest. Despite a tightening police net, the murderer somehow manages to elude this "nation-wide search." Shortly thereafter, Diana (who had gone back to work at Dearborn's on the off-chance of learning something more) discovers her father's cufflink in a cupboard in Dearborn's office. When queried, the blind Dearborn replies, "I don't recall ever seeing this before" and *looks down* at the object in her hand. "You're no more blind than I am!" declares Diana. "You're a fake, and you're shielding the man who killed my father." But Diana is wrong; Dearborn is not shielding the murderer, for he *is* the murderer. Dearborn removes his dark glasses and wig and drops his disguised voice to reveal—Dr. Orloff! Orloff ties Diana up and forces her to watch as he drowns Lou (a blind musician who had served as Orloff's covert messenger) in a tub of water to silence him, and then dumps his body out the window into the Thames. Orloff summons Jake and orders him to eliminate Diana and "this time make no mistake." Diana, desperately kicking and screaming as Jake is about to immerse her, frantically asks, "Where's Lou, Jake? He's gone, Jake. Orloff got rid of him, like he got rid of all the others." The ploy works, and Jake, who had genuinely loved the blind violinist, goes on a rampage. Orloff enters and Jake moves to attack him, but Orloff shoots his former henchman. "I will have to settle with you myself," he tells Diana. Before he has a chance to "settle" with her, however, the police arrive and Holt breaks into the institute. Orloff mixes a few chemicals and sets up a smokescreen downstairs. Bolting up the stairs to his laboratory "hospital," he locks the door and starts to climb to the roof. Jake is not quite dead, however, and he grabs Orloff's leg. Staggering to his feet, the mortally wounded giant struggles with Orloff and finally pushes him out the window—to be sucked into the mud flats of the river below.

For what is essentially a crime-drama decorated with horror trappings (it *is* a Lugosi vehicle after all, and so the producers felt it *must* be a horror picture), *The Dark Eyes of London* possesses some nicely macabre touches. The tone is set in the opening credits, which begin with a shot of London Bridge and the Thames. Suddenly, Lugosi's unmistakable eyes are superimposed over the image and zoom towards us out of the foggy background. Perhaps director Walter Summers had seen *White Zombie* (1932) and felt that if the actor's trademark stare was good enough for that film, it was good enough for *his* picture. In any event it makes for a promising introduction. Following this, the pledge of macabre thrills is extended further with the startling sight of a body floating face up near a pier. In a series of quick cuts we follow the bloated corpse as it drifts out into the open water and finally washes up along the shoreline in a crumpled heap. Yes indeed, Summers wastes no time in getting to the chills, and this whets our appetite for the gruesome doings to come. Unfortunately, because this film *is* structured like a crime-thriller, we must labor through long stretches of detective work before any other shivers are forthcoming.

Summers, with the invaluable aid of cinematographer Bryan Langley, makes sure things move briskly, even through the less-active stretches. The fluid camera movements and varied set-ups draw the viewer into even the more mundane expository scenes. The camera is never left stationary for long—it moves almost constantly, though not to the point of intrusion. This roving eye not only looks from side to side, following a character across a room, but it also moves forwards or backwards at the same time, tightening or opening up the frame as desired. This adds a depth to the visuals which a simple linear, left-to-right motion lacks. Nor is all this movement without purpose. Summers utilizes these techniques to introduce or include characters in a shot. Instead of simply cutting from one character to another as they talk, for instance, the camera will pull back to reveal the second speaker, or follow the movement of one as he approaches another until they both stand within the frame.

Summers even utilizes the camera to create shocks, as in the introduction to Jake (the "Human Monster" of the American title). When the doorbell to the institute rings, our vision rests on Dearborn, a mild-looking, white-haired, elderly gentleman sitting peacefully in an overstuffed chair. In a gentle, pleasant-sounding voice, he says, "Answer it, Jake." The camera suddenly moves up and away from Dearborn and over to a large figure standing beside the chair. Then, in one fluid motion, the camera quickly zooms in to a close-up of Jake's hideous countenance. Lit from below, his face is seen in high-contrast with the shadows emphasizing his ugliness. The suddenness of the motion from the harmless-looking Dearborn to the shadowy, ugly Jake transforms a simple introduction into a startling shock. Of course, nothing shocking happens—Jake just answers the door—but this brief, almost inconsequential moment becomes an ominous portent of horrors to come.

Lugosi is excellent in the dual role of Orloff/Dearborn. At ease as the quick-thinking Orloff, he speaks glibly and smoothly with Holt while periodically injecting that patented Lugosi treatment (malevolent stare, odd inflections) to remind the audience of what's in store. His facial expressions and pregnant pauses work wonders. "Find me poor Stuart's number in the phone book," he tells his secretary. "I want to *communicate* with his daughter." Lugosi's odd inflection on "communicate" and his drawn out "dauuughter" invests this simple statement with hidden, sinister meaning. Summers took full advantage of Lugosi's talent for menace: as the actor speaks, the camera moves in ever-so-slowly—almost subliminally—to augment Lugosi's delivery and imbue it with even more malevolent intensity. Later, when Orloff drowns poor Lou, Lugosi's cruel, satisfied smile speaks volumes about the sadistic nature of his character.

Since Bela Lugosi's distinctive voice and accent would have immediately given away his identity as the kindly Mr. Dearborn, his voice was dubbed by British actor O. B. Clarence. The lip-synching is quite good. Unfortunately, the effect is betrayed by a technical sound problem. Dearborn's voice has an isolated, hollow ring to it, as if coming from inside a drum (or studio sound room). Also, it is just a bit too loud compared to the other performers.

Critics felt *Dark Eyes of London* was strong stuff indeed. *Variety* (March 27, 1940) was impressed: "*The Human Monster*, patently a British-made picture, is not only reminiscent of *Frankenstein*, but contains numerous horror scenes no longer permitted under the Haysian code. Additional asset is the presence of Bela Lugosi in a more villainous characterization than he's been in for some time. Film won't disappoint for theatres going in for sheer grotesque chills. …Lugosi acts with more relish than in recent times on the screen." *The New York Times'* B. R. Crisler (March 25, 1940) seemed positively aghast: "Even connoisseurs of the horror film will doubtless be constrained to admit that nothing quite so consistently horrid as *The Human Monster*… has ever befallen this hapless city. Brooded over by the batlike spirit of Bela Lugosi, it comes like an evil visitation compared to which the hunchback of Notre Dame (first and second string); the two Doctors Jekyll and Messrs. Hyde, and both King Kong *pere* and *fils* are about as intimidating as Ferdinand the Bull." Stuffed-shirt critic Crisler quickly recovered his innate condescension, however, remarking that "all Mr. Lugosi has to do is to look at people and they either get hypnosis or cramps from laughing. Our personal reaction was more hysterical than horrified, but that's a matter of taste."

Bela Lugosi's trip to England to work on this production in April of 1939 brought him close to the machinations of Hitler and the war looming upon the horizon. Returning to New York, an impassioned Lugosi told a reporter for *Az Ember* (a New York publication for the Hungarian community): "Seeing all the horrors overseas, we have to stick to this country fanatically. Here we can live in human peace and love while over there countries disappear overnight. After what Adolf Hitler has recently done to the people of Czechoslovakia, I wonder if there is still an American of Hungarian descent who can nurture anything but hate for the Nazis. The lie about liberation has been revealed, and honest people point their fingers at Herr Hitler, the land robber and conqueror of nations."

The Dark Eyes of London was adapted from the book of the same name by prolific English crime novelist Edgar Wallace. Between 1905 and 1930, Wallace wrote 175 novels, 17 plays, and several hundred short stories. It generally took him about nine days to dictate a novel, but on one occasion he managed to complete a book over a single weekend! According to Margaret Lane's *Edgar Wallace: The Biography of a Phenomenon*, Wallace held no illusions as to the lasting literary merit of his works, yet he was determined that he would be remembered for his unusual storylines. His final project was to be the screenplay for *King Kong*. Unfortunately, he died of pneumonia before the production could really get under way. Wallace posthumously received co-story credit on the film.

The Dark Eyes of London was later re-issued on a double bill with another British horror/mystery, *Chamber of Horrors* (1941), which was also based on an Edgar Wallace story.

On the basis of Orloff and Ygor (in *Son of Frankenstein*), it is evident that Lugosi was in fine form during his first year back after a fifteen-month exile from the screen. This makes it all the more regrettable that *The Dark Eyes of London* was Lugosi's last truly worthy starring vehicle. With few exceptions (*Ghost of Frankenstein*, 1942; *Return of the Vampire*, 1944; and *Abbott and Costello Meet Frankenstein*, 1948), it was leads in poverty-row potboilers or red-herring bits in major films from here on out. *The Dark Eyes of London* makes a fitting close to the actor's most glorious decade and deservedly rides the pinnacle of Lugosi's Forgotten Triangle.

> Along with Boris Karloff, Bela Lugosi remains a key player from horror's Golden Age. I penned a DVD review of this excellent documentary for *Monsters from the Vault* magazine, issue 16, in 2003.

LUGOSI: HOLLYWOOD'S DRACULA (2000 DOCUMENTARY)

In an onscreen interview with this documentary's writer/director (included as an "extra" on the DVD), Gary Don Rhodes states that his intent was to capture that "elusive quality" that was Bela Lugosi. Via a judicious use of still images (many of them rare, including a well-edited sequential set of shots showing Jack Pierce making up Lugosi as Ygor), stock footage to illustrate the narrative (e.g. a WWI battle scene while discussing Lugosi's military service), interviews with friends, col-

DVD cover.

leagues and historians, and all-important clips from the films themselves (or trailer footage from the non-public domain Universals), Rhodes has indeed succeeded in bringing to light that "elusive" quality that has made Bela Lugosi a classic horror icon.

From the documentary's opening, in which "Swan Lake" (*Dracula*'s—and Lugosi's—unofficial anthem) plays, it's obvious that this work is an affectionate labor of love from Lugosi historian Rhodes and all those involved (including co-producer Richard Sheffield, who was one of a group of teens that befriended the down-and-out actor in the 1950s). But don't construe this obvious fondness as "fannishness," since there's nothing amateurish about *Lugosi: Hollywood's Dracula*. Slickly edited, well-photographed (with varied camera movement on the still photos to keep things visually interesting), and offering intriguing audio (including evocative music and occasional thunderclaps for punctuation!), not to mention a well-written, insightful script narrated by actor Robert Clarke, *Hollywood's Dracula* generally appears as professional as anything seen on A&E's *Biography*. (There are the occasional blips, however, such as the unfortunate inclusion of a goofy song called "Lon Chaney Will Get You If You Don't Watch Out," and a somewhat pretentious montage that features biology-film shots of blood flowing through veins and—inexplicably—1930s derelicts sleeping in doorways edited in with the Lugosi footage, but these are brief and minor missteps.)

The documentary is peppered with fabulous curios, such as snippets from a 1939 cartoon, "G-Man Jitters," in which an animated Lugosi (as Dracula), along with a cartoonish Frankenstein Monster, menaces a duck! Other gems include: 1941 home movie footage shot outside a soundstage; color(!) footage of Lugosi and Karloff on the set of *You'll Find Out*; a shot from the filming of *Abbott and Costello Meet Frankenstein* showing an unsuspecting Lugosi descending the castle stairs during a take as someone wearing a dark cloak apes his movements behind him—while everyone in the scene cuts up...except Lugosi; and footage of a very aged looking Lugosi (in Dracula attire and dark glasses) leading a man-in-an-ape-suit on a chain into the theater for the premier of *House of Wax*—a publicity stunt Lugosiphiles have read about for years, and now can finally *see* (despite his haggard appearance, Bela is all smiles and seemingly eating up the attention of the surrounding crowd).

Also impressive is the range of interviewees assembled: colleagues Audrey Totter, Loretta King, the late makeup man Harry Thomas, Howard W. Koch, David Durston (who calls Lugosi "the Lawrence Olivier of Hungary"), Louise Currie, Richard Gordon, Lucille Lund, Robert Wise, Helen Richman (who talks of Lugosi making a pass at her during a summer stock tour of *Arsenic and Old Lace*) and even Sammy Petrillo (co-star of *Bela Lugosi Meets a Brooklyn Gorilla*, and who becomes teary eyed when reminiscing about how "sweet and quiet a man" Lugosi was, and how Bela cried when he talked of his impending divorce from Lillian). Along with some erudite comments from historians such as Frank Dello Stritto, there's also interviews with Lugosi family and friends, including Bela Jr., Richard Sheffield, Robert Shower (who claims Lugosi "fought in eleven duels"), and the late Hope Lugosi, Bela's fifth and final wife (who merely states, in the only onscreen interview she ever granted, that Bela "was too old, that was all in the past," and talks rather callously and dismissively of finding her husband's dead body). The full interview with the last Mrs. Lugosi (included as an extra) is a real eye-opener, since it's more frightening than any of Bela's movies. She comes off as a callous and bitter old woman, commenting about their marriage, "He saw a *sucker*, and I was it...I don't care too much for Hungarians," and how Lugosi (she only referred to him as

"Lugosi") was full of hot air. "Poor Bela" indeed.

A boatload of extras rounds out the proceedings, including 12 scenes deleted from the documentary (obviously due to time constraints), with more onscreen interviews (including comments from Poverty Row director Joseph Lewis, who didn't make the official cut) and film clips.

Further extras include: The full 1932 "Intimate Interview" with Dorothy West that fans have seen before—but never in such pristine condition; a 1948 *Texaco Star Theater* TV show that pits Lugosi against Milton Berle; 1918 lost film fragments; and the aforementioned Hope Lugosi interview. *Brrrr.* (Also, a hidden "easter egg" consisting of Rhodes' quite funny half-hour mockumentary on his trials and tribulations in acquiring a chair once owned by Bela can be found by going to the last page of the "DVD Notes" section, highlighting the "Back" menu, pressing the "Up" arrow key on your remote and then hitting "Enter.")

But wait, there's more… Also included is a bonus CD of five never-before-available 1940s radio shows featuring Our Villain. Some are silly (a Fred Allen broadcast in which the comedian visits Lugosi's house), and some are serious (a radio interview in which Lugosi talks passionately about the underground resistance in Hungary and his native land's need for liberation). The best is a very funny "Command Performance" episode in which Lugosi plays (what else?) a mad scientist opposite Bob Hope as… Superman! (Paulette Goddard plays Lois Lane).

The impressive documentary ends, appropriately enough, with an audio recording of Lugosi giving his famous curtain speech at the close of the *Dracula* play: "…remember, there are such things, heh heh heh." Thanks to Gary Don Rhodes and Co., every Lugosi fan will indeed remember.

Cult Movies magazine originally published this review in issue number 16 (Fall 1995). Since then, however, I've expanded it for a subsequent project, and present the more comprehensive edition here.

THE MAD MONSTER (1942)

One minute a harmless country boy…the next moment a snarling, ferocious Wolf Man! –ad line

Taking note of *The Wolf Man*'s (ahem) howling success, low-budget specialists PRC (Producers

The Mad Monster *(Glenn Strange) claims another victim.*

Releasing Corporation) concocted their own werewolf variation—in the form of a hirsute Glenn Strange, the product of mad doctor George Zucco's nefarious experiments. Directing/producing brothers Sam and Sigmund Neufeld (Sam having anglicized his name to "Newfield" while sibling Sigmund elected to keep the family's Teutonic surname intact) had their *Mad Monster* prowling cinemas less than five months after *The Wolf Man*'s premier, making this the first film to jump on the werewolf bandwagon set rolling by the Universal classic. Unfortunately, the haste shows in its slapdash script and threadbare production values. Still, it offers one point of originality, as *The Mad Monster* marks the first appearance of a scientifically-created werewolf.

Discredited scientist Dr. Lorenzo Cameron (George Zucco) has sequestered himself and his sympathetic grown daughter Lenora (Anne Nagel) in a swampland mansion to continue his experiments on the mixing of animal and human blood. Utilizing his simpleton handyman Petro (Glenn Strange) as his human guinea pig (the insensitive Cameron even refers to him as such in just those words), Cameron employs a serum extracted from wolf's blood to transform the unwitting Petro into a wolfman. Why? "This country's at war," the mad doctor explains (to a group of scoffing colleagues conjured from his own fevered imagination). "Just picture an army of wolfmen—fearless, raging—every man a snarling animal." But there's more behind Cameron's scheme than just an altruistic wish to produce a supersoldier, and he employs his Mad Monster to murder his detractors one by one.

The film's werewolf makeup, by Harry Ross (*Dead Men Walk* [1943]), is simply not in the same class as Jack Pierce's *Wolf Man* creation. As Petro, Glenn Strange (Universal's fourth Frankenstein Monster) looks more silly than savage, with long sideburns, fluffy, combed-back hair, and heavy cheekbones and nose that make him appear more ape-like than wolfish (resembling Bela Lugosi in *The Ape Man* or, worse, a male version of Paula the Ape Woman from *Captive Wild Woman*). Strange becomes what may be the screen's most lethargic werewolf, acting quite un-wolf-like as he slowly walks about in an upright posture exhibiting none of the animal intensity that made Lon Chaney's Wolf Man so memorable. "He's no longer human," observes Cameron. "He's a wolf—snarling, ferocious, lusting for the kill." Strange's lackluster, hesitant playing, however, makes this "wolf" into a tame lapdog. Adding insult to injury, this poor man's Larry Talbot initially sports a pair of Farmer Brown overalls, then later a cheap sport coat and felt hat, giving him the appearance of an unkempt derelict with a bad overbite. Strange does better in his human guise, delivering his simple dialogue in a slow, almost sing-song manner, so that Petro becomes an almost Lennie-like gentle giant. Though lacking subtlety, Strange's poor dupe engenders sympathy for his plight and underscores the dastardliness of Zucco's mad medico.

Speaking of which, the cultured, ever-malignant (and seemingly omnipresent—at least at PRC) Zucco is, as usual, superb, bringing as much understated menace to his role as the alternately vapid and bombastic script would allow. When Petro, not knowing that Zucco nightly transforms him into a wolfman (thinking only that he suffers from sleepwalking), innocently asks the "good doctor" if he can cure him of his nocturnal wanderings, Zucco tells him no and that he may have to be locked up at night. When Strange laments, "It don't seem fair to lock a man up—like an animal," Zucco's sardonic smile at the irony of the statement is truly chilling. And Zucco makes the most of his You-Think-I'm-Mad speech as he rails at his imaginary denouncers conjured up out of his own twisted imagination.

Though obviously a product of Poverty Row, the film boasts some decent (if cramped) sets, including Cameron's lab (with its entrance secreted behind a bookcase, naturally), all stone walls, shelves of chemicals and bubbling beakers, and an atmospheric mist-shrouded swamp that cleverly obfuscates the lumbering man-monster. Likewise, director Sam Newfield occasionally leaves off his standard medium shots to insert something a little more evocative, such as when Lenora opens the secret lab door to reveal the wolfman advancing towards her—and the camera—as the low-key lighting (finally) makes him look menacing rather than risible.

The film wastes no time getting right down to business, busting out the Mad Monster a mere four minutes in with the first transformation, the metamorphosis captured efficiently if unimaginatively through a few simple dissolves. Of course, this marks the sole onscreen transformation (unless one counts the reverse shot of same a mere five minutes later when Cameron delivers the antidote to change Petro back to human form). After this, the metamorphosis occurs either off-screen or is completely obscured by that ridiculous felt hat. Unfortunately, after transforming, this Mad Monster does very little (in fact, the first time we see him he remains securely tied to a couch). When Cameron does send his wolfman out into the night, the man-monster typically wanders around the cramped swamp set a bit before scaring a bystander or creeping through a window. The few sparse murders remain coyly off-screen (with the final attack on Carmeron relayed through the old shadows-on-the-wall ploy). Surprisingly, the script has the beast's first victim turn out to be a six-year-old girl, murdered (off-screen, of course) in her own bedroom. Even more surprisingly, though, the supposedly grieving parents, interviewed later, seem strangely nonchalant and unaffected by their loss.

Other scripting headscratchers include the convoluted way Cameron sets up his scheme of vengeance (somehow talking his victim into delivering the final injection to Petro himself and so sealing his own doom) and the motivation behind his grown daughter Lenora's devotion to her obviously potty papa—despite the fact he constantly flies off the handle and keeps her a virtual prisoner, with little contact allowed with the outside world. Though of scientific origin, the werewolf itself appears to be supernaturally invulnerable, as one backwoods denizen fires both barrels of his shotgun at the beast at close range, with no effect. And the fiery finale is even more contrived than usual, with the expected conflagration started by a providential *bolt of lightning*.

Though not particularly clever, veteran low-budget scripter Fred Myton was nothing if not prolific, with more than 150 screenplay credits stretching all the way back to 1916. Up until the early 1950s he worked steadily, penning mostly low-end Westerns for Poverty Row outfits like Supreme, Republic, and, of course, PRC. He wrote one other horror film (also for PRC, and again starring Zucco and directed by Sam Newfield)—1943's *Dead Men Walk*.

Like Myrton, busy director Sam Newfield's career began in the Silents and lasted into the 1950s, over which time he helmed close to 300 films. According to his nephew, Sigmund Neufeld Jr., Sam suffered from a gambling addiction throughout his adult life that kept him near penniless most of the time, spurring on his prodigious output (Newfield directed 20 pictures in 1942 alone, typically earning $500 a film). Newfield made so many movies for PRC that he utilized two different pseudonyms (Sherman Scott and Peter Stewart) to disguise the fact that most of PRC's output was directed by one man. Upon Newfield's retirement, he was so destitute that his brother Sigmund (the head of PRC from 1940 to its merging with Eagle-Lion in 1948) purportedly paid off his gambling debts and set him up in an apartment in Hollywood.

Saved only by a few atmospheric moments and Zucco's entertainingly villainous performance, *The Mad Monster*, with its poor script and poorer wolfman, merely crouches in the shadows of 1940s horror.

> I believe this essay was intended as a book chapter or magazine article for a science-fiction-oriented project that never left the launching pad (though don't hold me to that, because the details have faded into that hazy realm of decades-old memories). In any case, I can't find any record of it being published in any magazine; so here is my take on an early (and woefully underrated) Karloff sci-fi/horror.

MAD SCIENCE MEETS GRAND GOTHIC: *THE MAN WHO CHANGED HIS MIND* (1936)

Regarding science fiction versus straight horror films, I have always felt that the best sci-fi movies incorporate significant horror elements. They explore the darkness of terror as much as the brilliance of science. For example, where would *Alien* (1979) be without its dim, organic interiors and dungeon-esque atmosphere (not to mention its terrifying monster), or *The Thing* (1951) without its claustrophobic setting filled with dark corridors and forbidding passageways? (Of course, there *are* exceptions—the antiseptic sci-fi of *2001: A Space Odyssey* being a prime example—but they are few and far between.) Even in the 1930s, when silver screen sci-fi was in its infancy, this trait became readily apparent. Who, for instance, will argue that 'straight' science fiction like *Just Imagine* (1930) or even the ponderous *Things to Come* (1936) are more enjoyable than, say, *Dr. Jekyll and Mr. Hyde* (1931) or *Island of Lost Souls* (1933)?

One of the better and (sadly) least appreciated examples of this early sci-fi/horror hybrid came to us courtesy of the British film industry. *The Man Who Changed His Mind* (retitled *The Man Who Lived Again* in America) is one of those little-seen English pictures that had heretofore remained unreleased on video and seemingly never made it to television or into revival houses. (Fortunately, Koch's recent DVD release has remedied this situation). Unlike most others in this category—such as 1933's *The Ghoul*, for instance (which itself has recently come to light via DVD), *The Man Who Changed His Mind* does not disappoint once the determined fan finally gets a look. Not only does it feature a full-blooded Karloff performance, but its intriguing blending of mad science and gothic atmosphere makes it a welcome addition to the then-nascent realm of cinematic science fiction.

The Man Who Changed His Mind came about more by default than by design. In late 1935, Gaumont-British contracted with Boris Karloff to come to England and make a horror picture. As noted by *The Hollywood Reporter* (January 13, 1936), however, the "Middlesex County Council restrictions of horror pics" (which would severely limit a horror film's audience by slapping it with an "adults-only" tag) changed the studio's mind about the project. Gaumont-British then entered into negotiations with Karloff about a cash settlement over the aborted $30,000 contract. Failing to reach an arrangement with the actor, the British studio decided to bring Karloff to London after all, to star in a different type of picture than the straight horror film intended. On March 5, 1936, *The Hollywood Reporter* revealed that Gaumont had chosen *The Man Who Changed His Mind*, "a story relying on the thrills of a scientific experiment," as their Karloff project in order "to avoid the prejudice of local licensing committees against horror pix." L. du Garde Peach, Sidney Gilliat, and John L. Balderston then wrote *The Man Who Changed His Mind* specifically as a vehicle for Boris Karloff, with a more scientific rather than horrific emphasis.

Karloff plays "mad brain specialist" Dr. Laurience, who perfects a machine that transfers minds between bodies, successfully switching the minds of two chimps. But when the wealthy, pompous Lord Haslewood (Frank Cellier) withdraws his patronage, Laurience places the mind of his elderly, crippled helper Clayton (Donald Calthrop) into Haslewood's body. Now mad, Laurience intends to transfer his own mind into the body of the fiancé of his beautiful assistant, Clare (Anna Lee).

The Man Who Changed His Mind begins scientifically enough in a modern, brightly-lit hospital as we witness Clare leaving to go to work for the reclusive Dr. Laurience in a rural village. When she disembarks from the train, however, the "scientific" orientation quickly

In America, the cleverly-titled The Man Who Changed His Mind *became the more prosaic* The Man Who Lived Again. *(American pressbook)*

to heighten the ominous atmosphere. Though its subject may be science, *The Man Who Changed His Mind* is still a *horror* film.

The Man Who Changed His Mind was Karloff's first British film since making *The Ghoul* three years earlier (also for Gaumont-British). A founding member of America's newly-formed Screen Actors Guild, Karloff was appalled at the actor's lot in non-union England. He refused to work on Saturdays as the studio wished, and, as reported by co-star Anna Lee (in Tom Weaver's *Science Fiction Stars and Horror Heroes*), "he lectured us all quite firmly on the fact that we must have a union."

Along with *The Invisible Ray*, released earlier in 1936, *The Man Who Changed His Mind* was Karloff's initial stab at a mad scientist role. Fortunately, the actor turns in a much more effective performance in this picture than he did in *The Invisible Ray*. (Karloff and mad science proved to be such a successful character match that a substantial portion of his subsequent career was spent among the tell-tale test tubes and Bunsen burners.)

While Dr. Laurience may not be Karloff's most subtle characterization, the actor convincingly portrays a man driven half-mad by his obsession. During his introductory scene, for instance, Laurience turns away from Clare to stare at his own reflection in the mirror. "The leading surgeon in Genoa," he observes, his tone low and bitter. "The greatest authority on the human brain—" Karloff pauses, and his voice suddenly quickens with anger as he finishes, "—until I told them something about their *own* brains!" He turns back and runs his hand through his hair in frustration. "Then they said I was *mad*." Karloff's eyes flash, and he looks up as if suddenly remembering Clare's presence. He stares at her a moment, then breaks into a smile. "Look at me," he says benignly. "Am I mad?" Before she can answer, Clayton (thankfully) interrupts. While he may not be mad exactly, Karloff's mannerisms and volatile mood

gives way to more traditional horror trappings. Rather than getting into a modern taxi at the station, Clare steps into a horse-drawn carriage—and then the fearful coachman refuses to take her to Laurience's creepy doorstep. It's as if she (and the viewer) steps out of the modern world of operating theaters and powerful locomotives into a dark tableau of forbidding mansions, nineteenth-century carriages, and superstitious coach drivers. The sudden switch from bright modernism to a shadowy gothic marks a striking contrast that serves change let us know that Laurience is not far from it.

In the movie's pressbook, Boris Karloff expounded upon the appeal of his terror films: "My roles generally provide the kind of thrills which transcend human emotion. The fear generated is synthetic, but the movie-goer vicariously endures the tortures of the terror-smitten fictional character. His mind wanders into the unlimited and unbounded world of imagination where anything can and does happen. And then the escape—the grateful realization that, like a bad dream, the thing isn't real."

Anna Lee had nothing but praise for her co-star, calling Karloff "the kindest, sweetest, nicest, quietest man I think I've ever worked with." The two passed the frequent bouts of inactivity on the set by reciting poetry. "He would start a poem, like, 'Between the dark and the daylight, when the night is beginning to lower,' and I'd go on, 'Comes a pause in the day's occupation, which is called the Children's Hour.' We went on for hours and hours doing this, seeing if we could stump each other!"

Ms. Lee did not have such a favorable opinion of her two *non-human* co-stars, however. "Right next door to me, practically sharing my dressing room, were the monkeys—the chimpanzees that you see in the film. And they smelled awful! I remember holding my nose whenever I had to go into my dressing room!" Sam and Gonette's (the chimps) odiferous nature was not their only undesirable trait. For the filming of Karloff's death scene, complete quiet was necessary on the set while the microphone sensitivity was increased to record the actor's whispered last words. As the cameras rolled, the sound man picked up a dull, thumping noise coming from somewhere in the building. It was soon discovered that the annoying noise was caused by the two chimps wildly jumping up and down in their cages. According to the film's pressbook, "the only way they could be effectively quieted was by getting Momo, the black boy who looks after them, to take them out of their cages, put on their dressing gowns, and lead them onto the set where, in the glare of the arc lamps, they remained happily silent, under the impression they were once more appearing before the camera."

Witty dialogue peppers the film's clever screenplay by L. du Garde Peach, Sidney Gilliat, and John L. Balderston. (Balderston contributed to more Golden Age horror classics than any other writer; his credits include *Dracula* [1931], *Frankenstein* [1931], *The Mummy* [1932], *Bride of Frankenstein* [1935], and *Mad Love* [1935]). In one scene, Lord Haslewood reluctantly sits in the chair offered by Laurience. "You must understand that once my mind is made up—" begins Haslewood, but Laurience finishes with "You will not change it." With a quick motion, Laurience shackles Haslewood to the chair. "Perhaps I can do it for you," Laurience offers in a bit of darkly ironic humor (since he intends to literally 'change' Haslewood's mind with that of another). When Clare asks, "Haven't you a housekeeper?" Laurience answers, "Only Clayton, and you've seen him," at which Clayton chimes in with "And she was not amused." Many of the choicest lines go to Clayton. "I wonder which revolts you most," wonders the wheelchair-bound cripple, addressing Clare, "my miserable body or my perverted mind." Later, shortly after breakfast, Haslewood offers his Institute's scientific services, but Laurience objects that "I must work in my own way." Looking around the dingy house and makeshift lab, Haslewood asks, "How can you work in this atmosphere?" to which Clayton snidely pipes up, "If you refer to the smell of bacon, it is no obstacle to scientific research."

Clayton is indeed the film's most eccentric—and intriguing—character. "Most of me is *dead*," he remarks acidly. "The rest of me is *damned*. Laurience manages to keep the residue alive. *Why* is his own affair." As the cynical, misanthropic paraplegic, Donald Calthrop delivers a performance arch enough even for Ernest Thesiger. "Having been a cripple for thirty years," he remarks, "I've a rather nasty nature." Calthrop's sour expressions, biting tones, and clipped speech leave no room for anything but bitterness (and an acerbic sense of humor). Later, while briefly playing Haslewood in Clayton's body, Calthrop barks out a chilling, ugly laugh before his character drops dead. The harsh, mirthless, *evil* sound raises the very hackles. Only later do we learn of the ironic joke (that, unknown to its new occupant, Haslewood's body is itself diseased).

The remainder of the cast admirably brings to life their well-formed characters. Not only is *The Man Who Changed His Mind* one of the decade's better written sci-fi/horror pictures, but it is also one of the better *acted* entries. Anna Lee makes an intelligent, headstrong heroine, while John Loder plays Dick (her fiancé) as a likable, good-humored young man. Best of all is Frank Cellier's dual portrayal of the arrogant, self-important Haslewood and the bemused Clayton-as-Haslewood, who possesses a whole new set of mannerisms—along with a sense of humor. "Oh what a pompous ass I am," he remarks cheerfully, amused at reading that Haslewood lists "hard work" as his hobby.

Frank Cellier made his stage debut in 1905 and quickly rose to prominence in the theater. Though he made nearly forty films from 1931 up until his death in

Dr. Laurience (Boris Karloff, left) plays mind games with Lord Haslewood (Frank Cellier, right) in this lobby card sporting the American release title for The Man Who Changed His Mind *(1936).*

1948, Cellier was best known for his theatrical work. *Variety*'s obituary (September 29, 1948) called him "the stage's most polished murderer." Making an unbilled appearance in *The Man Who Changed His Mind* was Frank Cellier's future son-in-law, Bruce Seton (*Sweeney Todd, the Demon Barber of Fleet Street* [1936]; *Love from a Stranger* [1937]). Seton later married Cellier's daughter, actress Antoinette Cellier.

Born Joan Boniface Winnifrith, Anna Lee took her stage name from such diverse sources as Leon Tolstoy and the American Civil War. "I was reading Tolstoy at the time and I thought Anna—from *Anna Karenina*—was very romantic, a lovely name. Then I was also reading American history, and I thought Robert E. Lee was a rather good chap, so I decided to take the name Lee." Ms. Lee's other genre outings include *Bedlam* (1946), *Jack the Giant Killer* (1962) and *Picture Mommy Dead* (1966). Still acting in the 1990s (she was a regular on TV's *General Hospital* for years), Anna Lee reassessed *The Man Who Changed His Mind*: "I saw the picture again recently…and I thought it was very well done, that it stood up remarkably well. I think it is one of Karloff's better pictures." Indeed.

Anna Lee was the real-life wife of *The Man Who Changed His Mind* director Robert Stevenson. They met in Egypt in 1934 while working on a picture and were married upon returning to England. "They were both on location for my film *The Camels Are Coming*," remembered producer Michael Balcon, "and Bob was struck down by some form of desert fever which made him delirious. Anna, like everyone else on the unit, felt very sorry for him and came into his tent one day to ask if she could do anything for him. Just then—according to Anna—Bob was so far gone in his delirium that he was trying to climb up the pole of his tent. '*In that one instant,*' Anna solemnly declares, '*I knew I loved Bob.*' She persisted in this story, even though I asked her if she thought that this explained the popularity of the Tarzan films!" (from *Michael Balcon's 25 Years in Films*, by M. Danischewsky [ed.]).

Producer Michael Balcon started in films in 1919 as a distributor. He produced his first picture in 1922 (*Woman to Woman*) on which he employed a young Alfred Hitchcock as screenwriter, art director, and assistant director. Balcon provided Hitchcock with his first opportunity to direct, and thereafter supervised Hitchcock's early masterworks. Balcon also produced the earlier Gaumont-British Karloff vehicle *The Ghoul* (1933). As recognition for his services to the British film industry, he received a knighthood in 1948. Sir Michael Balcon is the father of actress Jill Balcon and grandfather of Daniel Day-Lewis.

Donald Calthrop began on the stage at about the same time as Frank Cellier and also quickly rose to prominence in the theatrical community, acting alongside Sir Henry Irving and even running his own theater, in which he acted and produced. Unlike Cellier, however, Calthrop turned to films early, making his screen debut in 1916. Among his nearly seventy films are two borderline horror pictures, *The Clairvoyant* (1935) and *Love from a Stranger* (1937). He died in 1940 at the age of 52.

Under Robert Stevenson's deft direction on *The Man Who Changed His Mind*, cinematographer Jack Cox's camera draws the viewer into the story and creates a rich visual interest, utilizing forward as well as lateral movement to keep things from growing static. The camera frequently glides smoothly forward to bring the characters into close-up or punctuate an important moment, even following its subject upstairs while peering past posts and pillars to add depth. In addition, Stevenson and Cox take care in setting up their shots. Rather than taking the easy way out and filming two characters in conversation side-by-side in a flat manner, the filmmakers opt to create depth and visual interest by shooting past the shoulder or arm of one to the other to place the listener (and the viewer) in the foreground. (Despite having photographed such prestigious British productions as Alfred Hitchcock's *The Lady Vanishes* [1938], cinematographer Jack Cox was not above shooting the 1954 arrival of the *Devil Girl from Mars*—and her giant toaster-oven robot—in his later years.)

With calculated precision, Stevenson and Cox make an emotionally charged sequence the film's cinematic centerpiece. It comes when Haslewood confronts Laurience in his lab after the doctor's disastrous presentation to the Scientific Society. In a heated shouting match, Haslewood rails, "Now you're *finished* here, and your apparatus is mine to do exactly what I like with!" When Laurience shouts back, "You shan't touch it!" Haslewood sends a stand of beakers and test tubes crashing to the floor in defiance. At this, Laurience's hands fly to his head in shocked consternation. Suddenly, the room begins spinning. Images appear, superimposed over Laurience's confused countenance: Haslewood proclaiming over and over, "I paid for everything! I paid for everything!"; Clayton condemning, "Finest laboratory in the world, and you sold yourself for it"; the members of the smug Scientific Society laughing at him; Clare warning, "You can't do that! You can't do that!" The phantoms appear at odd angles to mirror Laurience's off-kilter state of mind, while Karloff's haunted eyes dart this way and that in a vain attempt to escape the hated memories. Finally, as bouts of ridiculing laughter chase through the soundtrack, Laurience's dazed visage dissolves into a blur. When the picture slowly comes back into focus, we see Laurience slumped in a chair, head bowed and totally drained, with a now-calm Haslewood standing over him, asking, "Dr. Laurience, do you feel better?" The montage of images and spinning surroundings superimposed over and around Laurience's face brilliantly reflects the man's disturbed, confused state as the jumble of hostile sights and sounds finally push him over the brink into madness.

Born in Buxton, England, in 1905, Robert Stevenson never even saw a motion picture until he was 22 years old, upon which he immediately decided upon a career in the industry. Beginning as a reader at Gaumont-British, he quickly rose from dialogue director to editor to production supervisor to screenwriter and finally to full director in 1932. According to *Variety*'s obituary (May 7, 1986), "his first major hit was *The Man Who Lived Again*." This hit was also Stevenson's first (and only) venture into the sci-fi/horror genre; in 1956 he turned exclusively to family entertainment with Walt Disney Studios, directing such Disney classics as *Old Yeller* (1957), *Darby O'Gill and the Little People* (1959; a picture possessing some pointedly horrific content); and *Mary Poppins* (1964; for which he was nominated for an Academy Award). His final film was *The Shaggy D.A.* in 1976. In 1977, *Variety* reported that Stevenson was the most commercially successful director of all time, having placed a record 17 films (all of them Disney productions) on the *Variety* all-time box office hits list, earning over $250,000,000 in worldwide rentals.

Alex Vetchinsky's sets add much to *The Man Who Changed His Mind*'s careful blend of scientific gothic. Laurience's dilapidated house, for instance, sports heavy pillars topped with bizarre crenellations reminiscent of the paws of some gigantic art-deco beast. Jack

Cox' careful lighting creates a maze of angular shadows and dark recesses, while bands of light and dark add an almost expressionistic feel to the sinister surroundings. This moody lighting extends to the characters themselves. During close-ups, for example, blocks of shadows seemingly surround the figures to create an ominous milieu perfectly suited to the strange story.

Despite all the care taken by the principal cast and crew, however, *The Man Who Changed His Mind* carries a few nagging liabilities. While the film features an intelligent storyline revolving around an intriguing premise, the authors fell into the easy trap of expediency at certain points. Having Laurence suddenly fall in love with Clare so that he now wants to inhabit the body of her fiancé seems too pat a plot device. Its artificial abruptness doesn't jibe with the rest of the cleverly constructed story.

Also, the picture glosses over a rather important continuity problem involving Laurence switching bodies with Dick. When Laurence places Dick inside the experimental chamber, the young man is securely strapped into the chair, helpless, and yelling "Let me out!" After setting the equipment to work automatically, Laurence goes to the other booth and simply sits in the chair. After the switch, however, Dick's body (now housing Laurence's mind) easily gets up and walks out of the booth while Laurence (with Dick's mind) must struggle to free himself from the chair's restraints. Apparently, the steel clasps transferred along with the minds?

Finally, three full-blown transference sequences (not even counting the original monkey-switching scene)—Clayton/Haslewood, Laurence/Dick, and the Laurence/Dick reversal—proves to be at least one too many. While the various shots of the laboratory equipment glowing, flashing, and sparking are impressive enough for the first experiment scene, they become a bit tiresome by the third go-round. It is a redundancy that adds nothing to the climax and only serves to eat up a little time before the sequence winds down to its foregone conclusion. More stringent editing would have gone a long way to stem the viewer's growing complacency regarding this all-important moment.

The Man Who Changed His Mind generally received good notices. *Variety*'s (September 22, 1936) unnamed London reviewer had nothing but praise for this "spine tickler," calling the production "painstaking and realistic and, indeed, the whole thing seems all too feasible." Of the cast: "Nothing very horrific in Karloff's performance, his manner at most times being almost gentle. John Loder and Anna Lee as the lovers make an agreeable couple. Frank Cellier as the magnate and Donald Calthrop as the cripple give splendid characterizations."

Two months later, however, when the picture made it to New York, *Variety*'s American reviewer ("Char" in the December 23, 1936 issue) felt just the opposite, stating the "plot construction of *Man Who Lived Again* offers nothing very original nor exciting, let alone anything that is very believable." Char singled out Frank Cellier, just as his British counterpart did ("a standout performance"), but claimed that Donald Calthrop "evoke[s] no more than passing notice."

Fortunately, Char seemed to be the odd man out. The *New York Daily Mirror* noted that, "settings are on the grand scale and the players perform as melodramatically as any California director could have demanded. Karloff... is a matchlessly amusing monster. It is entertaining to see him resume the role."

The Cinema (September 16, 1936) observed that "the film is content to score on its strong story values and wealth of melodramatic treatment. Certainly it is most effectively portrayed, with Karloff again a curious figure of appeal and repulsion, and again insisting on our acceptance that such things as this scientist dallies with may well be."

While *The Man Who Changed His Mind* may not exactly be a household title (even to the serious fan), it remains Britain's best sci-fi/horror contribution of the 1930s and surpasses many of that decade's Hollywood offerings as well.

Filmfax magazine unwrapped this essay on the Karloff classic in their August/September 1996 issue (no. 57).

THE MUMMY (1932)

"You will not remember what I show you now. And yet I shall awaken memories of love, and crime, and death." – Imhotep to his reincarnated love

Often when one thinks of "The Mummy" an image comes to mind of a bandaged monster sent out to do the evil bidding of a sinister high priest. The creature's face is wrinkled and blank as it inexorably limps toward an intended victim, its single good arm outstretched to strangle the life out of anyone who stands in its way. This is the mummy of Universal's four sequels made to the original 1932 Karloff vehicle: *The Mummy's Hand* (1940), *The Mummy's Tomb* (1942), *The Mummy's Ghost*,

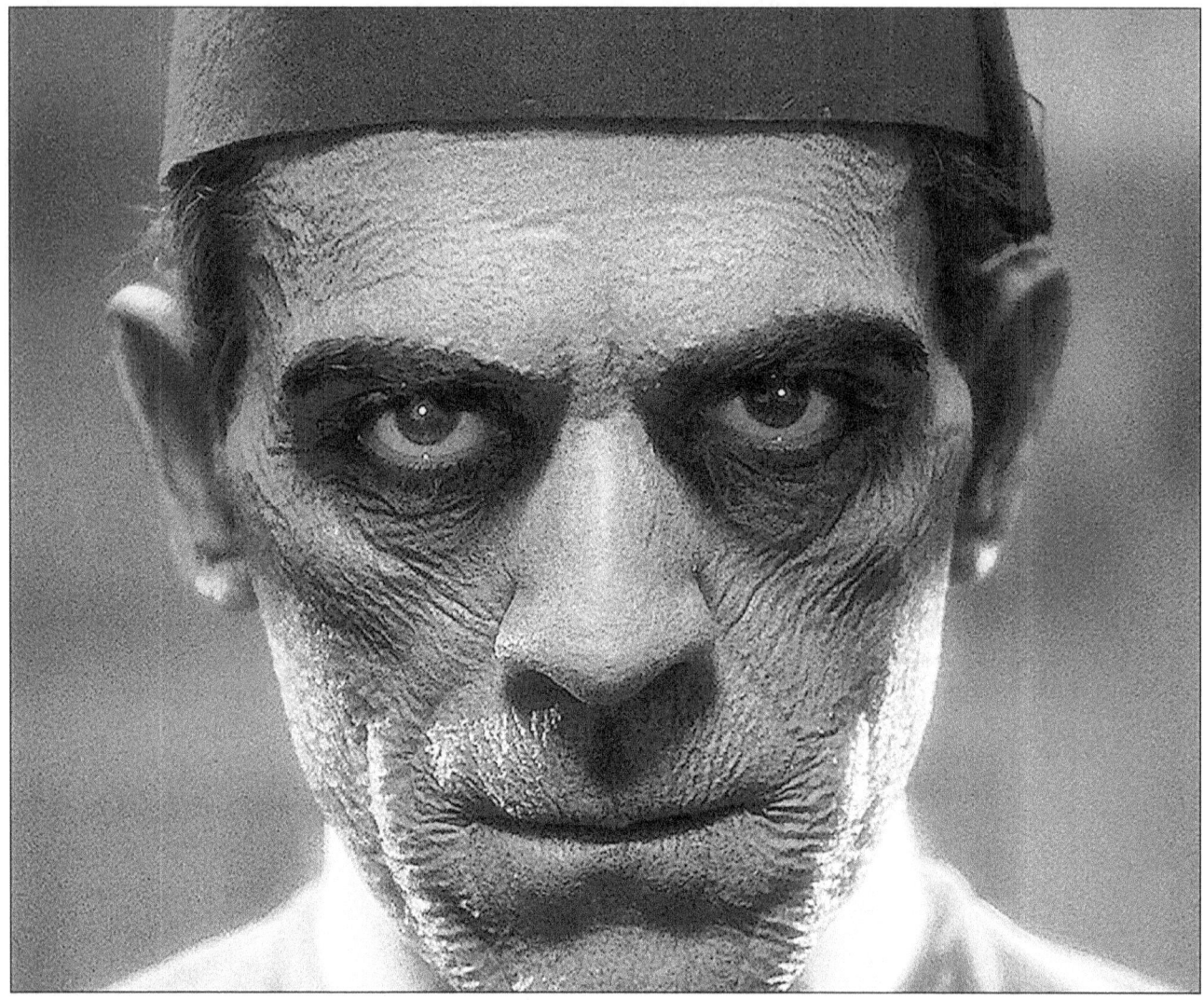

Boris Karloff is The Mummy *(1932).*

and *The Mummy's Curse* (both 1944). They are sequels in name only, for they create their own separate history (though not above borrowing much of the impressive flashback sequence from the original) and have little to do with the first picture. They also fail to come close to the quality and power of *The Mummy*, which is a subtle, intelligent masterpiece of horror presided over by Boris Karloff in the title role, giving one of the most memorable performances of his career. Karloff's mummy is not a shambling, inarticulate monster; he is an intelligent being of power, a master of the black arts. He does not kill through physical violence, but through the mere exertion of his indomitable will. Unlike those lumbering impostors that followed, he is more man than monster, a creature consumed by loneliness and love—monstrous, yes, but also distinctly human in his longings.

When a British archeological team discovers a secret tomb in the Egyptian desert, they find the mummy of Imhotep. They also find the ancient Scroll of Thoth, whose reading brings the mummy back to life, leaving a young archeologist raving. Eleven years later, a strange man informs archeologist Frank Whemple (son of the original expedition leader) where to dig to find the tomb of Princess Anck-es-en-Amon. The man calls himself Ardeth Bey, but he is, in fact, the living mummy Imhotep, who had been condemned to "a nameless death" when he attempted to use the scroll to revive his lover, Princess Anck-es-en-Amon, 3700 years before. Later, when Imhotep tries to raise the mummy of his lost love, his attempt fails for her soul has been reincarnated as Helen Grosvenor. Exercising his mystical powers, Imhotep wills Helen to come to him, intending to sacrifice her body in order to make her a living mummy like himself. When Imhotep raises his knife to strike, however, Helen/Anck-es-en-Amon intones some archaic rite to invoke the goddess Isis. In a blinding flash of light Imhotep crumbles to a pile of ancient bones and dust, and Helen returns to Frank (her new love).

The Mummy billed Boris Karloff as "Karloff the Uncanny," and his performance lives up to every adjective Universal's publicity department could dream up. With his imposing height, penetrating gaze, and slow, measured speech, Karloff creates a forceful and frightening figure. Aided by Jack Pierce's exquisite makeup, he truly does look 'uncanny'—his face a mass of tiny cracks and lines, eyes deep set, cheeks hollow and withered. (The talented makeup artist considered *The Mummy* to be his finest achievement; while Karloff, who had to suffer eight hours in Pierce's makeup chair, remembered it as "the most trying ordeal I have ever endured.") At the same time that Karloff projects an air of unholy menace and malignant power, he brings forth the pathos that made his Frankenstein Monster so memorable, investing his living mummy with enough humanity to lift him out of the category of 'monster' and into the realm of tragedy.

Karloff is ably supported by Edward Van Sloan as the occult expert, Professor Muller, who lends an air of calm authority to the part of Imhotep's chief antagonist. Likewise, Zita Johann, with her exotic beauty and wry charm, is ideal as the reincarnated princess torn between two worlds, bringing an inner strength and conviction to her role. (Perhaps Ms. Johann's sincerity is due in part to her personal beliefs. A self-proclaimed "mystic," she was a firm believer in reincarnation.) Screenwriter John Balderston suggested Katherine Hepburn for the demanding role, but the Broadway actress was unavailable at the time.

The Mummy was the directorial debut of Karl Freund, a cinematographer turned director (he'd photographed *Metropolis* [1926] and *Dracula* [1931], among others). With *The Mummy*, Freund, aided by his total control of the camera and its movements, creates a moody, tense, muted tale of obsessive love and understated horror. (The Rookie director even brought *The Mummy* in *under* schedule and *under* budget, despite an incredibly rushed beginning—he received the final script on a Saturday, cast the film on Sunday, and began shooting on Monday.) Freund worked with his cameraman, Charles Stumar, to combine fluid movement, a rich depth of field, and moody lighting into an atmosphere of supernatural antiquity. (Stumar was a talented cinematographer in his own right whose work enhanced both *Werewolf of London* and *The Raven* before his career was cut short by a fatal plane crash in 1935.)

The Mummy is one of those rare horror pictures of the Golden Age (or *any* age, really) that builds its foundation upon a firm bedrock of mysticism. An aura of the supernatural permeates this passion play as otherworldly forces ebb and flow across its surface. Only a few films, such as *Vampyr* (1932), have managed to immerse themselves so successfully in a supernatural dreamworld. Rather than providing the startling shocks and jolts of terror à la *Frankenstein*, *The Mummy* takes a subtle approach in weaving its cinematic tapestry of the strange and terrible. Touching on life, love, and death, *The Mummy* is poetic horror and truly one of the greatest, most original fantasy films of all time.

> A slightly shorter version of this essay appeared in *Filmfax* no. 77 in 2000.

THE MUMMY'S CURSE (1944)

"HANDS CREEPING LIKE COBRAS – EYES CRAWLING WITH MADNESS – THE MUMMY RUNS AMUCK!" –poster

For many monster movie fans, watching one of Universal's four "Kharis the Mummy" films (*The Mummy's Hand*, *The Mummy's Tomb*, *The Mummy's Ghost* and *The Mummy's Curse*) is like putting on a pair of comfortable old slippers—you always know how they'll feel and you're quite content with that. The final entry of the quartet offers yet another pleasant hour in which we're asked to do nothing more than sit back and visit once again with our predictable old bandaged friend. No thought involved, no emotional upheavals, no messages, issues, or subtext to deal with, just a nostalgic, seen-it-all-before-and-liked-it trip down mummery lane.

Thirty years after the events of *The Mummy's Ghost*, the U.S. government is draining the Louisiana swampland in which Kharis the mummy and his reincarnated love, Princess Ananka, had sunk to their supposed deaths. (Just *how* the New England marshes of the previous picture suddenly transformed into a Louisiana bayou is never explained, but then continuity between films was never one of Universal's strong suits.) Ilzor Zandaab (Peter Coe), current high priest of Arkam, and his servile assistant Ragheb (Martin Kosleck) have uncovered Kharis' body and revived the mummy. Soon, Ananka also rises from the mire, and the remainder of the film has Ilzor (repeatedly) sending out Kharis to retrieve the amnesiac princess.

Shot in a mere twelve days during the Summer of 1944, *The Mummy's Curse* remains one of Kharis' livelier outings. In fact, it features more mummy murders

Kharis (Lon Chaney Jr.) gets a touch-up from Ananka (Virginia Christine) in this gag shot from the set of The Mummy's Curse *(1944).*

and mayhem than any of the three other entries. At a rapid-fire 62 minutes, there's little time for characterization, but the local Louisianans in the form of Cajun Joe (Kurt Katch) and Tante Berthe (Ann Codee) are both colorful and compassionate. (The picture's one real shock comes when the mummy brutally strangles the beloved Berthe.)

While Virginia Christine is both likable and sympathetic (not to mention attractive) as the confused, amnesia-suffering Ananka (her tortured pleadings to "help me find myself" tug the heartstrings), the rest of the cast prove substandard. Dennis Moore is completely colorless as the deep-voiced but toneless hero, while Peter Coe presents the most passionless villain of the series. (His lowly assistant is much more interesting, but the ever-reliable Martin Kosleck receives too little screen time to bring the underdeveloped character to life.) And Chaney, who loathed these mummy movies (and by all accounts was hitting the bottle rather heavily during shooting), makes of Kharis nothing more than a slow-moving killing machine. He brings no nuances to the part, no doleful glances or tortured poses that would inspire pathos. (One *does* begin to feel sorry for Kharis after a while, however, simply because every time the poor old mummy tracks down his beloved princess, he has to strangle some third party—and the faithless reincarnate always slips away while he's taking care of business! It must be very frustrating.)

The Mummy's Curse contains arguably the most strikingly eerie scene in the whole Kharis series—the resurrection of Ananka. As a bulldozer pulls away from a just-leveled patch of swampland, a claw-like hand shockingly pokes up through the moist earth. Another hand and arm rise upward from the mire, and then a grotesquely twisted, mud-encrusted female form struggles to rise from its swampland tomb. Encased in a cracked, hardened shell of dried ooze, the fearsome figure staggers forward, seemingly gaining strength from the sunlight beating down. Virginia Christine (who later achieved fame as TV's Mrs. Olson in a 20-year-long string of Folgers Coffee commercials) does a remarkable job under what must have been horrendous circumstances. We see her stiffly rise, writhing and stretching upward like some unholy flower reaching for the life-giving sun, shedding the flaking, caked-on muck like decaying petals. It's a startling, uncanny sequence, made more so by Christine's painful pantomime and Jack Pierce's filthy, Golem-like makeup.

Said makeup took about five hours to apply and was no picnic for the young actress. "It was terrific," praised Ms. Christine about Pierce's work (to interviewer Don Leifert), "but the makeup hardened, you see, and we made a mistake in wardrobe. I wore a sleeveless dress and the same makeup was on my arms. Well, very human things happen, you know. I had to go to the john. Pierce's wife had to take me, and she treated me like a baby." An awkward toilette was only the beginning of the ordeal for the put-upon actress, for she next had to be buried alive! "It was just hell!" Christine recalled. "For a major star they would have had nice, clean dirt in a nice, clean studio. For me, they dug a hole in the ground on the backlot!… As I was lying there [buried], I began to think about what exactly was in all this earth, like how many worms." (Shooting this sequence attracted quite a few spectators to that backlot location, including Ingrid Bergman, who was at Universal filming exteriors for Alfred Hitchcock's *Spellbound*.) For all her troubles, the 27-year-old actress received a paltry $541.67—compared to the constantly complaining Chaney's hefty $8,000 fee.

Even without the cumbersome makeup, Virginia Christine experienced other trials and tribulations, including dealing with an intoxicated mummy. "[Lon] liked the bottle," confided the actress. "In the film we were supposed to climb up an old, ancient shrine located in back of Universal's lot, and the steps were very worn and crooked… Lon was weaving, and I thought, oh, boy. He was a big guy, a very sweet guy, but *big*. I kept thinking, if he falls on me, I've had it. Fortunately, the director, Les Goodwins, saw what was going on and got Lon out of there and put his double in the mummy suit."

Chaney's other co-star, Peter Coe (who became one of Lon's hunting *and* drinking buddies), recalled that Chaney was indeed imbibing heavily during production and, "as a matter of fact, he tried to get me to drink on the set of *The Mummy's Curse*. I told him: 'You're the f***ing mummy in this, all you've got to do is grunt. I've got to memorized three pages of dialogue for one scene!'"

While certainly no classic, *The Mummy's Curse* remains an enjoyable, unpretentious, fan-friendly horror entry that modestly delivers what it promises (and even goes for something extra in one instance). Lovers of Forties horror could do much worse than invoke *The Mummy's Curse*.

> In 1995, *Midnight Marquee* magazine graciously printed an excerpt from my then-in-progress book *Golden Horrors* for their issue number 48. I'm forever grateful to editor Gary Svehla for providing such exposure to my target audience.

THE GOLDEN AGE OF HORROR CINEMA: *MURDERS IN THE ZOO* (1933)

"If I had lacked the courage to kill for you, I couldn't expect you to go on loving me." –Eric Gorman

SYNOPSIS

[Note: Since, thanks to the miracle of DVD and streaming services, the film has now become readily available for viewing, I've considerably reduced the original synopsis in order to considerably reduce the tedium.]

Murders in the Zoo begins in the jungles of French Indo-China, where millionaire sportsman, and patron of the Municipal Zoo, Eric Gorman (Lionel Atwill) leaves a man to die—after *sewing his mouth shut*! Back home, the insanely jealous Gorman first disposes of his wife Evelyn's suspected paramour, Roger Hewitt (John Lodge), via deadly green mamba venom, and then kills his wife (Kathleen Burke) by dropping her into the zoo's alligator pit. When the zoo's young toxicologist, Jack Woodford (Randolph Scott), discovers evidence of Gorman's crimes, the villain attempts to silence him like the others. Forced to flee, Gorman releases the zoo's big cats as a diversion but ends up in the crushing coils of the zoo's huge python.

MEMORABLE MOMENT

Murders in the Zoo contains arguably the strongest opening from the Golden Age of Horror. In a small jungle clearing, an unidentified man lies on the ground, pinned by two native bearers. Another man (whom we later learn is Eric Gorman) bends over the captive's head, earnestly engaged in what at first glance appears to be *embroidery*. The bodies of the natives partially obscure the figure on the ground so we cannot be sure of what is really happening, though an occasional sharp grunt or sudden moan of pain issuing from the prostrate man (accompanied by a quick, spasmodic jerk of his legs) tells us that all is certainly not well. As Gorman works, sleeves rolled up, hands drawing back thread with a careful flourish again and again, he begins to speak. "A Mongolian Prince taught me this, Taylor—an *ingenious* device for the right occasion," Gorman states coldly. "You'll never lie to a friend again—and you'll never kiss another man's wife." Gorman finishes, wipes his hands on a handkerchief, and stands. He and the two natives walk off and now we can see the man stretched out on the ground, his hands tied behind his back. The man struggles painfully to his knees and then finally up to his feet, turning away from the camera to stumble off into the jungle. The scene shifts to Gorman mounting an elephant and moving away. Suddenly, the victim emerges from the brush and staggers toward the camera. In shocking close-up, we see his face for the first time and observe that his lips have been crudely *sewn shut*! His sweat-drenched countenance, the bloody lips closed unnaturally tight, and, most of all, the panicked, tormented look in the man's eyes shock the senses with the cruelty of this act. This harsh, horrific sequence, dwelling intently on barbarous torture so coldly and callously inflicted, could never have made it past the revamped Production Code a mere year later.

ASSETS

Fall of 1932 was a time of uncertainty for Hollywood horror. The mammoth successes of

The shocking opening from Murders in the Zoo *(1933).*

Dracula and *Frankenstein* (and to a lesser extent, *Dr. Jekyll and Mr. Hyde*) were a year old. The handful of Hollywood's follow-up pictures were a mixed bag of success and failure. While *Doctor X* was doing fair business and *White Zombie* cleaning up, Universal's *Murders in the Rue Morgue* was a box-office disappointment, and MGM's *Freaks* an outright bomb. Most studios (Universal excepted) were still on the graveyard fence as far as horror was concerned. One can easily envision the Paramount top brass sitting in the inner sanctum conference room debating what to do with their unwholesome little horror property, *Murders in the Zoo*. Their success with *Dr. Jekyll and Mr. Hyde* had encouraged them to mount a second horror film, *Island of Lost Souls*, then currently in production. "Still, it might be better," we can almost hear them say, "if we hedge our bets until we know if this horror-thing will last." Paramount had no such reservations about comedy, however, a tried and true box-office glamour gown. A solution: top-line one well-known and well-liked comedian in the form of Charlie Ruggles and place a director well-versed in comedy at the helm (Edward Sutherland). Paramount brass could now rest easy that their 'baby-scarer' would also be a 'laugh-riot.'

Though the emphasis on comedy in general (and the casting of Ruggles in particular) turned out to be a mistake, the choice of directors was a fortuitous one. While untried in the horror arena (the marginally mystical *Secrets of the French Police* being his only [small] step into The Dark Cinema), Sutherland brought a technical expertise and a sure knowledge of the medium to the production. Sutherland chose to eschew the standard gothic trappings and Germanic leanings of the genre and present his horrors in a straightforward, head-on manner befitting the picture's modern-day metropolis setting (a thinly-disguised New York). Midnight moonlight and graveyard atmosphere gives way to unflinching daylight and stark realism. In this way, *Murders in the Zoo* became one of the first films to take horror out of the nebulous land of mists and shadows and bring it into the everyday world of Joe Public. In *Murders in the Zoo*, horror was not the far-removed province of Eastern Europe or bizarre tropical islands or even the Nineteenth Century; the terror was right here and right now, pounding the pavement of our greatest city. This gives the picture an immediacy and realism (even to the more farfetched elements) which strikes a contemporary chord even today.

The opening credits herald *Murders in the Zoo* as something special. No standard static backdrops here as the camera tracks fluidly back along a jungle-like zoo path while the technical credits swipe across the screen. Then, each of the major players is introduced by shots of wild animals. A circus seal clapping its flippers dissolves into a shot of top-billed Charlie Ruggles clapping *his* flip– er, hands. A cuddly black bear dissolves into the equally cuddly Harry Beresford; a split screen image of a dove and owl precede Gail Patrick (placid heroine) and Randolph Scott (intelligent hero), while two panting cougars presage would-be lovers Kathleen Burke and John Lodge. Finally, a solitary tiger dissolves into the image of Lionel Atwill staring intently as he takes a drag on his cigarette and blows smoke through his predatory nostrils. Sutherland cleverly uses animals as visual metaphors to give the viewer a foretaste of the various characterizations and foster an immediate interest in the characters.

Through his technical expertise, Sutherland employs sequencing and motion to enhance the film's immediacy by bringing the viewer directly into the thick of things in the very first scene. The sequence opens with a shot of a contoured map of French Indo-China. The camera zooms closer and dissolves into a shot of a lush mountain range. Then, through a series of further dissolves (mountain range to valley to section of trees to specific foliage and finally into the clearing itself) coupled with the seemingly continual forward motion of the camera, Sutherland visually draws the audience into the picture and sets the viewer down in the steaming jungle right alongside his characters.

The director also knows when to keep the camera still for its greatest impact. After utilizing motion to bring the audience into his jungle setting, Sutherland then traps the viewer there by refusing to move the camera at a crucial moment. The moment comes when a man stumbles out of the brush to reveal that his mouth has been sadistically sewn shut. By keeping the grisly procedure a mystery during the awful operation and then having the victim stagger forward toward the stationary camera until his bloody, anguished countenance nearly fills the screen, Sutherland adds claustrophobic impact to the gruesome shock. We want to back away from the horrific sight—indeed, from the whole idea of this terrible deed—but the unmoving, unrelenting camera will not allow us to turn and flee, forcing us to see and learn what we do not wish to by crowding the screen with this hideous sight.

Sutherland utilizes transitional dissolves and horizontal wipes to create a smooth continuity between scenes. For instance, upon leaving the jungle setting, the camera focuses on a large round drum on which a native beats out a rhythmic sound. This dissolves into the similarly-shaped image of a life-saving ring mounted on the rail of an ocean liner. The visual unity provides a connection between the two diverse locales.

Ernest Haller's fluid camerawork enhances the picture's involving visuals. As Evelyn strolls along the ship deck in one scene, the camera tracks beside her past deck chairs, passengers, and doorways to add a visual expansiveness to the cramped set. Later, she relates the terrible fate of Taylor to Roger Hewitt. The camera focuses in medium close-up on the couple as Evelyn concludes that "there was no way of proving any—" She stops before verbalizing this last suspicion and stares past Hewitt's shoulder. When Hewitt turns his head, the camera tracks right to follow (and become) Hewitt's gaze, finally coming to rest on the figure of Eric Gorman, who momentarily stands there before advancing toward the couple. This type of personalized movement helps bond the viewer with the characters.

That Sutherland and Haller took great care with their visuals is evident from the marvelous composition and framing of scenes. When Roger Hewitt talks with Evelyn on the deck of the ocean liner, for instance, they stand at the rail, their bodies framing the shot on either side of the screen. "Please don't let [Gorman] see us together again," pleads Evelyn. In the background between the two figures is a window, the curtains half drawn. The nature and placement of this background detail adds further anxiety to the scene, suggesting that Gorman at any minute could easily spy them together. Evelyn glances over her shoulder (toward, and then past, the window) adding, "He'll be out any minute." The window becomes a metaphor for the couple's exposed position.

Philip Wylie and Seton I. Miller's intriguing screenplay works on a number of levels. From the opening 'sewing' sequence, one knows this film has bite. This bite is further barbed with a liberal dose of black humor. When Gorman tells his wife that her would-be lover had left, she asks what he said before departing. "He didn't say anything," is Gorman's sardonic reply. Later, when Evelyn accuses Gorman of killing Roger Hewitt at the zoo dinner, Gorman answers innocently, "Evelyn, you don't think I sat there all evening with an eight-foot mamba in my pocket, do you?" then quips, "Why, it would be an injustice to my tailor." Unfortunately, Wylie and Miller, whether by studio dictate or misplaced design, nearly bury these shining moments of subtle humor under a pile of lusterless sledgehammer 'comedy' bits involving Charlie Ruggles (see LIABILITIES section).

The plot clips along at a fast pace, with the cruel murders evenly spaced to generate ever higher peaks of intensity. The final climax, in which all the big cats are let loose, resulting in a ferocious feline free-for-all pitting lions against leopards and panthers against pumas, is exciting in its feral intensity (but something that filmmakers could only get away with in the pre-code days; it is too vicious to get past post-1933 censors). By releasing the caged animals, Gorman creates a veritable orgy of violence, paralleling the release (discovery) of his own previously secret savagery—only to have it turn and destroy him.

The screenplay pulls no punches in regards to sex, either. After Gorman cleverly murders another rival for his wife's affection, for instance, he focuses his amorous attention on his appalled spouse. Full of loathing, she exclaims disgustedly, "Now you want to make love to me!" Strong stuff for 1933. Undeterred, Gorman continues his ministrations, his hand slowly inching upwards as he holds her fast, crawling up her arm like a sensual snake. As his hand moves from arm to shoulder, Gorman brings it around to hover a moment over her breast, the hand *almost* touching, before moving sinuously up to grasp her shoulder. Then, overcome by his lust, he grabs her firmly and his right hand actually rests on her breast as his left arm crushes her unwilling form to him. This scene of blatant sexuality is a rarity, even *before* the enforcement of the Production Code, particularly considering the undercurrent of brutality which runs throughout the sequence. It makes for a powerful, disturbing moment.

Murders in the Zoo was produced during the worst of the Great Depression and Wylie and Miller's screenplay effectively reflects the mood of the time through its characters. Gorman, the picture's sadistic and despotic antagonist, is a millionaire. The two other wealthy characters, Evelyn and her would-be paramour Roger Hewitt, both display if not outright immorality, then a decided lack of propriety by scheming to run away together behind the husband's back. (While this may seem defensible given the circumstances, it still technically smacks of faithlessness.) All three of these moneyed characters meet gruesome fates, even the two more-or-less innocents (Evelyn is punished for allowing herself to have been seduced by Gorman's power and wealth, while Hewitt is destroyed for simply belonging to the same vile class as Gorman).

The hero, on the other hand, has no such bloated wealth. While a doctor, he still must worry about financing for his work and making enough money so that he can marry his sweetheart (new funding, he laughingly tells his fiancée Jerry, will "let you quit stalling about marrying me"). This protagonist occupies the same sinking financial boat as the bulk of middle America at the time.

Gorman becomes a metaphor for the wealthy elite, a symbol of responsibility for the financial ruin of the 'Average American.' In this light, the zoo, plagued with fiscal difficulties and teetering on collapse, is the American economy. The devious dealings (murders, in fact) of Gorman (the unscrupulous financier) cause the closing and ruin of the zoo (the economy). The scene in which a regretful Dr. Woodford must lay off a group of zoo workers brings the scenario powerfully home. "I know you boys have families," Woodford apologizes while handing out their final paychecks. "I *hate* to let you go but there's nothing else I can do." Gorman eventually pays the ultimate price for this disregard for others when a giant python slowly strangles the life out of him (much as the Depression slowly choked the financial life from millions of Americans). For audiences of the time, this could be (at least on a subconscious level) a most cathartic release. While often helpless in their fiscal reality, the Depression-era viewers could see the symbol of their financial misery receive his just deserts up on the silver screen—and watch an entertaining horror yarn at the same time.

Eric Gorman is a fascinating character. Civilized and generous on the outside, inside he is little better than a wild beast himself—worse, in fact, for he is infinitely more dangerous. Gorman identifies more with the animal he hunts than with fellow human beings. "I love them," he says of the beasts. "They're honest in their simplicity, their primitive emotions. They love, they hate, they *kill*." Atwill adds a pointed emphasis to this last word by drawing the corners of his mouth back in the briefest of grimaces. Gorman revels in the "primitive emotions" about which he speaks. Immediately after his first two murders, Gorman's passion spills over and he embraces Evelyn, his blood quickened by the kill. Sharing an obvious kinship with Count Zaroff of *The Most Dangerous Game* (1932), the jealous and sadistic Gorman draws a close link between sex and death.

While Gorman may espouse an admiration for the animals' "simplicity," this devious and complex man is anything *but* simplistic. His words are full of double meanings, and he invests his phrases with hidden messages. When Gorman comes to see Hewitt in his apartment and realizes that Evelyn had been (or still is) there, Gorman tells him, "You know, I was rather surprised to find that a man like you should take such an interest in something which is, shall we say, outside his province. I mean, on the boat you and I seemed to have a—mutual interest." Gorman's almost subliminal emphasis on key words further enhances the hidden meaning—and menace—of the dialogue. "I'm afraid I don't quite understand," replies Hewitt cagily, playing along with Gorman's game of civility. "I was referring to my animals," lies Gorman, who obviously means "my wife." Gorman hides behind his animals in his words just as he makes use of them in his murderous deeds.

The role of Eric Gorman was tailor-made for Lionel Atwill, one of the screen's best 'cultured' villains. Atwill relishes his part, imbuing lines like, "I can promise you a really *unusual* evening," with deliciously sinister undertones. After marking Roger Hewitt as a potential victim, Gorman states, "It'll be a great *pleasure* to show Mr. Hewitt through the zoo." Atwill takes the word "pleasure" and draws it out ever so slightly, giving it an unwholesome sound pregnant with dark, hidden menace.

Atwill utilizes gestures and expressions to further add depth and illumination to his character. When discussing his newly-delivered green mamba, Gorman relates how "it kills hundreds of natives every year—" with the trace of a smile forming at the corners of his mouth at this tragic thought before continuing, without pause, "—and no anti-toxin has ever been developed for it." While subtle, his expression conveys an image of sublimated sadism. The versatile Atwill can utilize broad expressions to great effect as well. As the crate containing the deadly mamba wheels away, the camera moves back onto the face of Gorman. Atwill then narrows and hardens his gaze, the half-lidded eyes conjuring up images of the serpent itself. Though a rather obvious ploy, Atwill's cold authority makes it an effective one. As emphasis, the picture then fades from Gorman's snake-eyed countenance to a close-up of the real snake as Woodford extracts venom from its fanged mouth. This juxtaposition drives home the slithery metaphor.

Kathleen Burke does well in the role of Gorman's wife, a woman bound to him by fear of this jealous and sadistic man. Her emotions spill forth when she finally rebels against his cruelty. "Oh, you're not human!" she cries, appalled and disgusted when he tries to kiss her after Hewitt's death. As he pulls her to him, she pushes away with a final, "Oh, I *hate* you!" Given the expression of loathing on Ms. Burke's face, the words become almost superfluous. Later, when she discovers the false snake head in her husband's study, she looks up with a cold hatred in her eyes. At her fateful confrontation with Gorman on the bridge, she finally overcomes her fear. Gathering strength, she excitedly, almost breathlessly, warns him, "You can't frighten me anymore. I'm going to tell them all—that you're a murderer, that you've no right to live!" The actress' shoulders shake with each word, her voice rising in pitch to near hysteria, her whole demeanor speaking of long-supressed hatred and horror boiling to the surface. (Unfortunately, while Kathleen Burke's effective performance is perfectly timed, the timing of her character wasn't quite so well thought out—much to the delight of the hungry gators.)

LIABILITIES

When Atwill is absent from the screen, the picture slows considerably. During these lulls, Sutherland focuses on unfunny bits of 'humor' with Charlie Ruggles, or simply inserts stock shots of zoo animals as time filler. One tedious sequence follows a messenger boy looking at the various zoo exhibits for a full two minutes!

Aside from Gorman (and to a lesser extent his wife, Evelyn) none of the other characters are fleshed out enough to generate much interest, nor do the players attempt to overcome this shortcoming. Professor Evans is alternately gullible (duped by the fast-talking inanities of Peter Yates' comical publicity man) and bumblingly ineffective (unable to act on the zoo's financial difficulties until Gorman arrives to take a hand). Harry Beresford simply walks through the part, investing just enough energy to keep it at the level of caricature. Hewitt and Dr. Woodford, though miles apart in their financial and social strata, could be interchangeable (the same can be said for actors John Lodge and Randolph Scott), both being rather stiff, brave, upstanding hero-types (the only difference being that one was bright enough to rely on brains—developing an anti-toxin—rather than dollars and so was able to save himself). As a heroine, Gail Patrick's Jerry simply hovers about the periphery, almost unnoticed, making little impact until her brief moment of heroism at the climax. Compared to Kathleen Burke, Ms. Patrick appears lifeless and lackluster.

The film's most serious flaw, however, takes the form of the painfully intrusive 'comic relief' of comedian Charlie Ruggles. He wastes many of the film's precious few 61 minutes variously cringing from caged lions, taking fright at his own reflection, or even soiling himself when he inadvertently traps the missing mamba with a pitchfork ("Is there a good laundry in this town?" he asks tremulously). His comical 'highlights' include cutting himself shaving every time a nearby lion roars or repeatedly tugging painfully on his ears while making an interminable dinner speech as an (unheeded) signal for the photographers to snap their pictures. Ruggles' dialogue consists of repeated inanities like "That's just a small idea of my ideas." Too bad this type of blatant, lowest-common-denominator humor was felt to

Murders in the Zoo *poster*.

be obligatory by Paramount at the time (Ruggles even received top billing). With more emphasis on the infrequent but effective *dark* humor rather than on the copious sledgehammer-style *light* humor, *Murders in the Zoo* could have joined the ranks of such hard-hitting classics as *Freaks* (1932), *Island of Lost Souls* (1933), and *Mad Love* (1935). Even so, it remains an effective, unique, and entertaining shocker from the Golden Age of Horror.

REVIEWS

Variety's 'Char' (April 4, 1933) noted that "this picture has what it takes to chill and entertain. A horror film compact in subject matter and action, it is also exceedingly well played and directed," though he adds, "…but the snakes in this one are apt to be more than some can stand." (Perhaps Char possessed a touch of ophidiophobia?) "Some of the animal scrapping in the big scene at the finish looks pretty legit," continues the reviewer. "Lions grapple with tigers and a general riot of jungle beasts is on. …Character [of Eric Gorman] is excellently played by Lionel Atwill." Of Comedy Relief stooge Charlie Ruggles, Char notes, "he's had better material and been funnier."

Andre Sennwald, reviewer for *The New York Times* (April 3, 1933), labeled *Murders in the Zoo* "a particularly gruesome specimen," and (incredibly) claimed to be "thankful for the generous footage given to Charles Ruggles as a timid and bibulous press agent for the zoo." Noting that "Lionel Atwill as the insanely jealous husband is almost too convincing for comfort, and Kathleen Burke as the wife suggests the domestic terrors of her life capably," Mr. Sennwald concludes that "judging by its ability to chill and terrify, this film is a successful melodrama."

PRODUCTION NOTES

According to the film's pressbook, "An entire zoo, complete in every detail, was constructed for the filming of the new thrill picture." While the "entire" claim can be put down to publicity department exaggeration, Paramount did construct several zoo sets on their lot specifically for this production, including the 'Alligator Pit' and 'Carnivora House.' Four professional animal trainers (headed by Chubby Guilfoyle) were employed to control the nineteen big cats released during "one of the most dangerous motion picture scenes ever filmed." "Three weeks of preparation" were necessary, claimed the pressbook, to allow the animals "to get accustomed to each other in neighboring cages." Noting that "sturdy fences were placed around the setting to give the crew space for cameras," Paramount's publicity writers dramatically described the hazardous scene: "Four animal trainers, who, according to the script, were to drive the beasts back into cages, entered the enclosure, and for an hour, while cameras ground, they sweated at the task. They had to work almost back to back to guard against attack from the rear. Three leopards and one puma found hiding places in dark corners, however, and would not return to their cages without a vicious struggle."

Paramount obtained most of the animals for their film from the nearby Selig Zoo. Transportation of the beasts required sixteen trucks (six for the alligators alone). The film's pressbook reported that "the caravan passed through Los Angeles at about 4 o'clock in the morning, so that danger of automobile collision and resultant possible escape of the animals was most remote." The pressbook also claimed that 50 alligators were employed, though this seems doubtful since only a fraction of that number are seen onscreen. In any case, once they arrived, the reptiles proved to be too torpid to 'act' due to the recent cool weather (alligators tend to sleep long and heavily through the winter months).

To rouse them, the crew had to warm the water in their tank at the steady rate of a quarter degree an hour. It took a week of gradual warming before the animals were once again wide awake and fully active.

Much of director Edward Sutherland's childhood was spent in vaudeville and on the 'legitimate' stage. In 1914, the nineteen-year-old Sutherland entered films as a stuntman, graduating to actor in a number of Keystone comedies and feature length Silents. He served as apprentice director to Charlie Chaplin on *A Woman of Paris* (1923) and became a full-fledged director shortly thereafter. Sutherland gravitated toward comedies, directing several W.C. Fields pictures (including 1933's *International House*, which featured a rare Bela Lugosi non-horror appearance); Laurel and Hardy's *The Flying Dueces* (1939); and Abbott and Costello's screen debut, *One Night in the Tropics* (1940). Though *Murders in the Zoo* was the director's only true horror picture (he was originally slated to direct *Dracula's Daughter* for Universal in 1935 but studio delays forced him off the project), he journeyed into the land of cinematic fantasy on two other occasions, exposing the mesmeric *Secrets of the French Police* (1932) and capturing the comical antics of *The Invisible Woman* (1942).

Renowned cinematographer Karl Struss, who photographed Sutherland's *Up Pops the Devil* (1931) and *Every Day's a Holiday* (1938), remembered (in *Five American Cinematographers*, by Scott Eyman) that "working with Eddie Sutherland was always a lot of fun." Struss also recalled that the director possessed a unique method of demonstrating his personal industry to the studio executives. "To show how efficient he was, he always watched everything sitting directly under the camera lens, and whenever he was satisfied, he would yell 'cut' and immediately jump up, blocking out everything, just to show the producers watching the rushes that he's right there on the job and alert."

Murders in the Zoo cinematographer Ernest Haller lensed 160 films over a career that spanned four decades, including such mainstream classics as *Dark Victory* (1939) and *Gone with the Wind* (1939; for which he won an Academy Award). Haller lent his considerable talents to two other horror productions (late in his career)—*Back from the Dead* (1957) and *What Ever Happened to Baby Jane?* (1962).

California native Charlie Ruggles began acting with a San Francisco stock company in 1905, eventually playing on Broadway. Entering films in 1915, Ruggles quickly rose to popularity as a likable, comedic 'averageman.' Apart from *Murders in the Zoo*, he also appeared in *Terror Aboard* (1933) and *The Invisible Woman* (1940). Ruggles was one of the first film stars to enter the fledgling medium of television, starring in *The Ruggles* in 1949 and several subsequent live TV shows. Charlie Ruggles' brother, director Wesley Ruggles, helmed *The Monkey's Paw* (1933).

Lionel Atwill's first snake-bite victim, lawyer-turned-actor John Lodge, retired from acting after serving in WWII and turned to politics, eventually becoming Governor of Connecticut in 1950. After serving his term as Governor, his political career took a diplomatic turn when he became U.S. Ambassador to Spain and then later Ambassador to Argentina. *Murders in the Zoo* was only his second film.

In a bit of ironic casting, Paramount awarded Kathleen Burke the role of Atwill's terrified wife who is ultimately eaten by animals (alligators). Earlier this same year she had played 'Lota' the panther-girl, who was *created from* an animal in *Island of Lost Souls*.

Born Margaret LaVelle Fitzpatrick, Gail Patrick studied law at the University of Alabama, intending to go into politics (with her sights set on the governorship of Alabama). Before completing her education, however, she entered and won a newspaper contest which sent her on a week's trip to Hollywood as Birmingham's "Panther Girl." (This contest was a publicity ploy orchestrated by Paramount to promote their upcoming production of *Island of Lost Souls* by searching the nation for the right young ingenue to play the mysterious Panther Woman in the film.) Though not chosen as their "Panther Girl" (as mentioned above, Kathleen Burke won the role), Paramount did offer Ms. Patrick a contract at $50 a week. "My dad never made more money than $175 a month in his life," the actress told Richard Lamparski in *Whatever Became Of...Fifth Series*. "I got them up to $75 a week and grabbed that contract." Among her over sixty screen credits is the Golden Age fantasy *Death Takes a Holiday* (1934). When she married prominent literary agent Cornwall Jackson in 1947, Gail Patrick retired from acting. In 1956, however, she returned to the entertainment industry as Executive Producer of the popular and long-running *Perry Mason* television series. Of her career in front of the camera, she stated, "I always felt self-conscious as an actress because I'm tall. I see that it came over as haughtiness. I just don't have an actress's soul. I think mine has a dollar sign on it."

The twenty-five foot, 360-pound python that puts the stranglehold on Lionel Atwill at film's end was named 'Oswald.' Fascinated by the creature, Atwill refused a stunt double (over the objections of director Edward Sutherland), and so the actor himself is seen

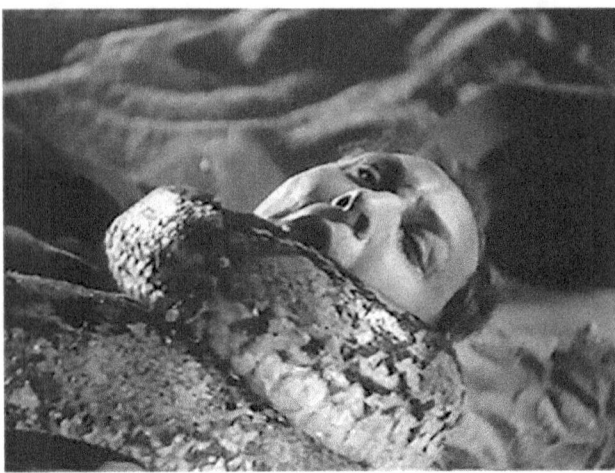

Eric Gorman (Lionel Atwill) meets his fate at the close of Murders in the Zoo *(1933).*

wrapped in the giant snake's smothering coils. Atwill was so taken with Oswald that he reportedly bought the reptile from its owner ("Snake" King, operator of a Texas snake ranch) and took him home after the film wrapped.

Lionel Atwill, with roles in *Mystery of the Wax Museum*, *The Vampire Bat*, and *Murders in the Zoo*, was fast becoming one of Hollywood's foremost screen villains. In 1933, *Motion Picture* magazine dubbed the actor "The MENTAL Lon Chaney," going on to say, "Here is a *handsome* man who makes women's hearts beat faster—*until he stops them*. Here is a charming and very polished gentleman who makes women's blood run warmer—*until he chills it*. This man murders with a smile, violates with a chilling laugh. …Here is a man with the most sardonic mouth I have ever seen, the coldest and most merciless eyes ever set in a man's skull."

Co-screenwriter Philip Wylie was well versed in the gruesome and macabre (not to mention animal stories), having previously co-scripted *Island of Lost Souls*.

When *Murders in the Zoo* opened in New York at the famed Paramount Theater, the picture shared the stage with a live comedic stage-show—headlined by a young vaudevillian named Bob Hope.

Filmfax magazine provided for The Return of the Vampire *in issue 61 (June/July 1997).*

THE RETURN OF THE VAMPIRE (1944)

Columbia, who for so long had been rather circumspect about producing horror films (relying on a series of scientifically-focused Boris Karloff 'mad doctor' movies as their ticket in the horror sweepstakes), finally broke down in 1944 to create a true gothic terror picture. From the opening frames (a 15-second pre-credit sequence showing a terrified woman backing away from a sinister cloaked figure; the silhouette menacingly raises its arms and she screams while a puff of smoke envelopes her and the film's title suddenly races out of the sinister cloud) we *know* that this is indeed a horror movie. If any doubts remain, the opening narration—"This is the case of Armand Tesla, vampire"—dispels them.

Originally titled *Vampires of London*, the story begins in 1918 with the staking of vampire Armand Tesla in London. One World War later and the Blitz uncovers the undead fiend's body. When two well-meaning locals remove the iron stake from Tesla's corpse (thinking it a piece of shrapnel), the vampire resumes his reign of terror and sets about revenging himself on those responsible for his earlier death and their descendants. In his plans he uses a poor thrall, Andreas (Matt Willis), who, under the vampire's spell, becomes a werewolf-like creature (but one that can still converse and think like a man).

Director Lew Landers (*The Raven*, 1935; *The Boogie Man Will Get You*, 1942; *The Mask of Diijon*, 1946) provides some subtly effective and frighteningly evocative staging for this macabre tale. For instance, when the vampire invades the bedroom of a little girl, the scene begins with mist swirling outside her French doors. The doors suddenly fly open of their own accord and wisps of fog stream into the room. The camera follows the invading mist and pans left across the floor where we see a moving shadow take the shape of a caped figure. As the shadow rises against the opposite wall and the silhouetted arms raise ominously, the little girl awakens and screams while a cloud of smoke suddenly envelopes her. Throughout the film Landers makes evocative use of shadows, the dark shapes letting the viewer's imagination work its wonder. (In fact, it's a full third of the way into the film before we ever see the vampire's actual form.)

After Universal passed up Bela Lugosi for the title role in *Son of Dracula*, opting instead for the jowly, flat-toned Oklahoman, Lon Chaney, Jr. (with disastrous results), the proud Hungarian jumped at the chance to play Drac– er, Armand Tesla in Columbia's *The Return of the Vampire* (for a Dracula by any other name beguiles just as sweetly). Lugosi appears to relish his role, bringing all the power of his hypnotic voice and stately presence to bear on this Dracula reprisal. Considering the quality of his other recent assignments (poverty row abominations like *The Ape Man* and *Ghosts on the Loose*, or, even worse, the downright embarrassing *Frankenstein Meets the Wolf*

Impressive theater ballyhoo marking The Return of the Vampire *(1944)*.

Man), Lugosi must have thought he'd died and gone to undead heaven. (To illustrate how low his fortunes had sunk, the actor received a paltry $3,500 total for starring in *The Return of the Vampire*).

Lugosi is ably supported by a well-chosen cast who go a long way toward bringing believability to this rather unlikely tale. Particularly effective are Matt Willis as the tortured Andreas, who alternates between convincing anguish when in human form and an evil glee while in his werewolf guise, and Miles Mander as the doubting Scotland Yard Inspector, who provides just the right mix of officiousness and sardonic humor (even venturing the occasional double-take).

On the technical end, *The Return of the Vampire* is top-drawer (looking much better than its slight $138,545.54 final cost should allow). Louis Diage provided some wonderfully detailed and moody graveyard sets up to even Universal's high standard. Makeup man Clay Campbell rendered some effective werewolf makeup (which he repeated twelve years later for *The Werewolf*) and special effects coordinator Aaron Nadley created convincing transformation scenes (with the image subtly distorting and the light changing so that the hair seemingly grows before our very eyes) which look smoother than those in many of the heralded Universal Wolf Man movies. And director Landers orchestrates some gritty bombing sequences, complete with convincing explosions and debris and neatly inserted bits of actual war footage that adds a nice touch of realism and veracity to the scene.

All is not perfect with this vampire's *Return*, however. While providing some masterful atmospheric lighting on the marvelous graveyard sets (not to mention employing an effectively eerie use of shadows), cinematographers John Stumar and L. W. O'Connell don't always photograph Lugosi to that actor's best advantage. In scenes which simply cry out for some moody low-key lighting, his face often appears overlit, so that the ravages of age (not to mention those of long-term drug use) becomes all-too-apparent on the sexagenarian actor's countenance. Also, the patented *Dracula*-like close-ups of Lugosi's hypnotic eyes carries no impact here due to the flat lighting awarded them. Ironically, though Charles Stumar had previously provided some potent pinpoint lighting effects for Boris Karloff's visage in *The Mummy* (1932), the usually reliable cinematographer let Lugosi down on *The Return of the Vampire*.

Since *The Return of the Vampire* really is a Dracula film in all but the name, I supposed it's unsurprising that it suffers from the same ills that plague that seminal classic – an overly talky and weak latter half. After a strong half-hour, *Return*'s story bogs down in characters running about discovering (or seeking to convince others of) what the audience already knows. While all is not lost (there's still plenty of atmosphere and an occasional chill or two), the film's latter half proves disappointing. Fortunately, *Return* avoids the anti-climactic climax Tod Browning laid on *Dracula* and instead provides the viewer with an exciting—and rather grisly—denouement (which includes a brief but effective vampire melt-down).

Columbia made only one other (half-hearted) stab at traditional horror, the weak *Cry of the Werewolf* (1944). With *The Return of the Vampire*, however, the studio not only provided a rare worthy vehicle for Bela Lugosi (the last time a major studio would grant him a starring role in a serious picture) but created an effective and entertaining (if flawed) gothic-style chiller. Though certainly not on the level of the Val Lewton pictures or of such prestige productions as *The Uninvited* and *The Picture of Dorian Gray*, *The Return of the Vampire* still remains one of the better horror films of the 1940s, and one certainly equal if not superior to most of Universal's rather tired offerings of the decade.

> Here's an essay that I wrote around the time I was working on my *Golden Horrors* book, with the intention of seeing it published in one of the then-numerous genre mags of the 1990s. Of course, magazine racks are paved with good intentions, and this one remained unseen…until now.

TOD SLAUGHTER'S TERRIFYING TRIO

Karloff and Lugosi, Rathbone and Lorre, even Clive and Frye—these are the names one most associates with the Golden Age of Horror. Though five of these six actors were born on foreign soil, they made their acting fortunes in Hollywood. Across the Pond, in Scary Old England, there was only one man who could match these horror icons' output. And his name, appropriately enough, was Tod Slaughter, who starred in a terror triptyche during the horror-heady heyday of the 1930s.

SWEENEY TODD, THE DEMON BARBER OF FLEET STREET (1936)

Tod Slaughter made a career out of villainous stage roles, the most famous being the murderous barber which he here plays onscreen. Slaughter was a stage actor of the old school, harking back to the great villains of Victorian melodrama. While he rarely made it to London's posh West End theaters, he became one of the most popular actors of the blue-collar East End stages and provincial playhouses. Newspaper accounts of the 1920s claimed that no actor in England had a bigger following than Tod Slaughter. According to *Who Was Who in Theater*, he appeared in over 500 different plays, sketches, and farces. His many stage plays include *Maria Marten, or, the Murder in the Red Barn*, *The Monkey's Paw*, *Jack the Ripper*, and *Dr. Jekyll and Mr. Hyde*. Slaughter's greatest success, however, came as the dastardly villain Sweeney Todd. The actor gave more than 4000 performances as *The Demon Barber of Fleet Street* over the course of his 50-year stage career. Though he achieved great success trodding the provincial boards, his mustache-twirling, hand-rubbing style of acting frequently failed to translate well to films, so that Slaughter, the self-proclaimed "Horror Man of Europe," could be better named the "Melodramatic Man of Europe." Even so, his following was large enough to support a string of villainous film appearances from 1935 to 1952. According to his own publicity (for 1939's *The Face at the Window*), Tod Slaughter "admits to at least two hundred murders on the screen and also confesses that he has never appeared in a picture in which, he too, like his victims, hasn't met violent death."

As the title character of *Sweeney Todd, the Demon Barber of Fleet Street*, Slaughter kills and robs sailors and gives their bodies to the nasty baker-woman next door as filling for her tasty meat pies. To accomplish this, Todd uses a special barber chair which, upon pulling a concealed lever, tips upside down to dump the unsuspecting patron through a trap door into the cellar below. Then Mr. Todd saunters downstairs to "polish off" his victim with his finely-honed razor. Todd's nefarious activities are finally discovered when he attempts to kill

Tod Slaughter, as Sweeney Todd, the Demon Barber of Fleet Street *(1936), gets to work.*

a young sea captain in order to reduce the competition for the sailor's sweetheart, who's caught Todd's eye. The young man escapes, the heroine is saved, and the villain comes to a sticky end.

Sweeney Todd looks much older than a film produced at the close of 1935, due primarily to its rather primitive production values. The straightforward direction and standard cinematography are unremarkable. The players' melodramatic acting also stems from an earlier time, though this fits in well with the style of the film's star. Slaughter's broad performance may lack subtlety, but his gleefully enthusiastic villainy is quite entertaining to watch.

In its native country, *Sweeney Todd* was treated fairly well by the critics. The *Monthly Film Bulletin* (March, 1936) noted that "Direction and much of the acting belong to the stage, and there are several inconsistencies in the development of the plot, but a certain amount of the necessarily gruesome atmosphere has been caught and the story itself is so good that the film has some success." *Kinematograph Weekly* (March 5, 1936) called the film a "colourful period thriller, smoothly adapted from the perennial provincial stage success. Approached mainly in a tongue-in-cheek manner, the old-time shocker mellows its hearty picture of diabolical villainy with plenty of robust comedy, thereby cultivating family as well as mass appeal." A butchering barber and cannibal cook the subject of "family" appeal?!

When the film finally made it to America three years later, however, the critics were not so generous. *Variety* (October 11, 1939) predicted that *Sweeney Todd* "will find the pickings none too certain in this country, although title may prove b.o.[box-office] in some cases. ...From the action and dialogue to the direction by George King the picture is stamped by mediocrity. ...Slaughter is a sinister enough type but the way he overacts creates new highs among Britishers. ...Technically, including photography, the film is away below standard."

The Slaughter film was not the first time Sweeney Todd sliced his way across the screen; two earlier cinematic adaptations came in 1926 and 1928, but it is Tod Slaughter's portrayal which makes this 1936 version the definitive (and remembered) one. In America, *The Demon Barber of Fleet Street* (the American distributor dropped the *Sweeney Todd* from the title) was released on a double bill with a straightforward mystery called *Return of the Frog*. Advertisements promoted it as "Europe's double-thrill horror show."

Stephen Sondheim adapted *Sweeney Todd: The Demon Barber of Fleet Street* into a musical in 1979. The New York show ran throughout the eighties and even enjoyed an acclaimed Broadway revival in 1990. It's hard to keep a good barber down.

THE CRIMES OF STEPHEN HAWKE (1936)

In his follow-up vehicle to *Sweeney Todd, the Demon Barber of Fleet Street*, Tod Slaughter eschews his razor for the "sinews of steel" in his bare hands. Kindly moneylender Stephen Hawke (Slaughter) leads a double life as the notorious "Spine-Breaker," a fiend who snaps his victims' spines in his crushing grip. Though a ruthless murderer/thief, Hawke exhibits a real love for his adopted daughter, and in the end even sacrifices his own life and liberty to prevent her unwanted marriage to a blackmailing police chief.

Tod Slaughter sets about committing The Crimes of Stephen Hawke *(1936).*

The character of Stephen Hawke allows Slaughter to step beyond his stock slimy villain characterization and portray a more multi-faceted figure. While the Spine-Breaker is a thoroughly loathsome killer (even snapping the spine of a young—though admittedly obnoxious—boy), Slaughter manages to inspire some pathos for the man via his unceasing love for his daughter and even (for a short time) place the viewer squarely on his side so that he might complete his murderous mission and eliminate the unscrupulous blackmailer. Director George King (who also helmed Slaughter's earlier *Sweeney Todd* and later *The Face at the Window*) makes the most of the realistic period settings. As with most Tod Slaughter films, however, the acting is flowery and melodramatic, and there are numerous slow points when Slaughter is absent from the screen. Still, *The Crimes of Stephen Hawke* possesses a few macabre thrills, such as the agonized screams of the fiend's victims as their life runs out through his vice-like fingers (accompanied by Slaughter's chilling chuckles), and one shuddery sequence in which a young man poses as his father's corpse come back to life in order to frighten Hawke into revealing himself. Also, in the best tradition of horrific henchmen, Hawke's ghoulish assistant is a one-eyed, one-legged (this infirmity belonging to actor Ben Soutten himself) hunchback. *Stephen Hawke* also allows Slaughter some priceless dialogue, rife with black humor. When the unsavory police chief approaches the reluctant Hawke about marrying his daughter, the following exchange occurs:

Chief (unaware he is addressing the 'Spine-Breaker'): "So, further discussion is in order, Sir?"

Hawke: "Naturally. Then, we can come to *grips* with the matter."

Chief: "Good. Then we can clinch the bargain, eh?"

Hawke: "'*Clinch*' is the word, Sir."

Of course, Hawke ultimately snaps the spine of this expectant suitor.

Don't be confused when the film opens on two tuxedoed radio performers named "Flotsam and Jetsam" singing a silly duet. This is the picture's novel 'hook'—the story is actually part of a radio broadcast related by Tod Slaughter, who appears as himself and elucidates with relish upon his earlier murderous screen deeds.

The Crimes of Stephen Hawke (known in America as *Strangler's Morgue*) is Slaughter's best film of the decade, and it received good reviews upon its initial release in England. *Kinematograph Weekly* (May 21, 1936) cited the picture's "gripping story, disarming treatment, great work by Tod Slaughter, good title, rousing comedy relief, and first-rate exploitation angles"; while the *Monthly Film Bulletin* (May, 1936) noted that "Tod Slaughter throws himself with zest into his part; the supporting cast is adequate, and the period settings are effective."

THE FACE AT THE WINDOW (1939)

In *The Face at the Window*, a British murder melodrama with horror overtones, Tod Slaughter plays a rich gentleman who is really the evil murderer known as "The Wolf" (shades of *Stephen Hawke*). This killer's nefarious crimes are always preceded by a horrible countenance staring in at the victim through a window (hence the title) just before the unfortunate receives a knife in the back. Add an innocent ingenue (Marjorie Taylor) and a young hero framed for The Wolf's crimes (John Warwick), and it's vintage melodramatics all around. The hero is courageous, the heroine bravely defiant, and the villain suave yet slimy. As expected, Slaughter plays his role to the hilt, and you're just waiting for him to tie the girl to the railroad tracks. The first two thirds of this already brief (65 minute) film

Tod Slaughter meets The Face at the Window *(1939).*

move rather too slowly and predictably as Slaughter makes advances to the heroine and goes about framing her lover; but the final 20 minutes hold the viewer's interest with glimpses of the horrible, drooling face in question and Slaughter's final surprise revelation as to his relationship with said face. There's a clever twist (borrowed—like its premise—from *The Crimes of Stephen Hawke*) in the way the hero forces the Wolf to reveal himself; and Slaughter's final ravings as we learn The Whole Truth are chilling in an over-the-top way. If you like British melodramas (along with ample arm-waving and prodigious posturing), this will adequately fit the bill; if, on the other hand, you're looking for some suspenseful horror, you'll have to look elsewhere.

Heroine Marjorie Taylor's short (four-year) screen career included three other Tod Slaughter vehicles: *The Crimes of Stephen Hawke* (of course), *It's Never Too Late to Mend* (1937), and *Ticket of Leave Man* (1937). "I have been dodging a fate worse than death for years," laughed Ms. Taylor in the *Face at the Window* pressbook. "Tod is always on my track trying to marry me, or trying to kill my screen-sweetheart but, fortunately, I have been saved in the nick of time in each instance."

Director George King was known in industry circles as England's "King of the Quickies." But his greatest claim to fame is his "discovery" of Laurence Olivier (at least according to the *Face* pressbook). King *did* direct Olivier at the beginning of his film career in 1930's *Too Many Crooks*, so perhaps it's sorta/kinda true?

F. Brooke Warren's turn-of-the-century stageplay *The Face at the Window* had been filmed twice before—first in 1920 starring C. Aubrey Smith and next in 1932 with Raymond Massey. But, like with *Sweeney Todd*, it took Tod Slaughter to bring it to full-blooded cinematic life.

> This terror-tandem essay ran in *Monsters from the Vault* magazine, issue 15 (2003).

UNIVERSAL'S RETURN TO GLORY, DOUBLE FEATURE-STYLE: *SON OF DRACULA* and *THE MAD GHOUL*

After the many big-budget horror productions of the 1930s (including the late-hour 1939 entries *Son of Frankenstein*, *Tower of London* and *The Hunchback of Notre Dame*), the forties saw the horror film shoved compactly and irretrievably into the "B" movie slot. With World War II came problems for the film industry, including shortages of film stock, set-building materials and leading men. Still, theaters remained busier than ever, since the real-life crisis brought with it a strong desire for escapist entertainment. Production difficulties, coupled with the voracious appetite of seemingly indiscriminate moviegoers, induced the studios to churn out low-level product simply to fill booking dates. Quantity began to rule over quality, and the double feature was born, with studios frequently offering two films for the price of one (and often spending less on both "B"s than the production cost of a single "A").

Universal was no different, as they began milking their stable of monsters for all they were worth, resulting in sequels, teamings and re-teamings, and ultimately encounters with a certain comedy duo. In 1943 Universal decided to return to their horror roots and resurrect the Count that started it all back in 1931. It proved a propitious returning, for in November 1943 Universal paired *Son of Dracula* with a macabre little thriller entitled *The Mad Ghoul* to create one of the studio's sharpest double-bills of the decade.

SON OF DRACULA

Son of Dracula proved to be the last of Universal's full-scale Dracula pictures (despite the title, no intimation that this is anyone other than the King of Vampires himself is ever given). Though the Count later appeared in the monster bashes *House of Frankenstein* (1944), *House of Dracula* (1945) and *Abbott and Costello Meet Frankenstein* (1948), he played a supporting role at best and generally received short shrift at the hands of Universal's other monsters (not to mention their most popular comedy team).

When Universal originally announced (in mid-1942) their intent to make a long-overdue second sequel to *Dracula*, horror expert George Waggner (*Man Made*

Lon Chaney Jr.'s Son of Dracula *throttles J. Edward Bromberg's Professor Lazlo in this noirish Universal horror.*

Monster, 1941; *The Wolf Man*, 1941; *The Ghost of Frankenstein*, 1942; *Frankenstein Meets the Wolf Man*, 1943) was slated to produce. Waggner, however, took on the supervisory chores for the studio's lavish *Phantom of the Opera* remake (starring Claude Rains) instead, and the job of producing *Son of Dracula* fell to former serial specialist Ford Beebe, fresh from an impressive producing/directing turn on *Night Monster* (1942). (Apart from working as a second unit director on 1939's *Tower of London*, Beebe supervised [and directed] one other horror picture—1944's *The Invisible Man's Revenge*.)

For *Son of Dracula*, Universal handed the scripting assignment to Curt Siodmak (*Black Friday*, 1940; *The Invisible Man Returns*, 1940; *The Wolf Man*, 1941; *Frankenstein Meets the Wolf Man*, 1943) and the director's baton to Siodmak's older brother, Robert. Though a successful director in Europe in the 1930s, *Son of Dracula* was Robert Siodmak's first film for Universal and something of a proving ground. It turned out to be a very *successful* proving ground. "He started on *Son of Dracula* and they gave him $150 a week," reported his brother Curt. "Two years later he was making $2,000 a day at Universal."

According to Curt Siodmak, he and his brother suffered from a severe case of sibling rivalry, so much so that Robert had Curt removed from *Son of Dracula*, ultimately replacing him with screenwriter Eric Taylor (*The Black Cat*, 1941; *The Ghost of Frankenstein*, 1942; *Phantom of the Opera*, 1943; *The Spider Woman Strikes Back*, 1946). "I finally got [my brother] a job," Curt recalled to interviewer Dennis Fischer, "and on the first day he starts working with another writer. I understand that, though, because who is going to have the authority? I wouldn't take anything from him, and he certainly wouldn't take anything from me. They had to have somebody else."

In late 1942 a new Universal horror star was on the rise. Boris Karloff had moved on to greener pastures and would work only sporadically for his old home studio. Bela Lugosi was looked upon by the Universal brass as something of a horror has-been whose age and fiscal desperation made him easy prey for producers wanting an inexpensive 'name' cameo for their horror properties. The new kid on the horror block, and the actor Universal's publicity department ballyhooed as "The Screen's Master Character Creator," was Lon Chaney Jr., son of Hollywood's first horror superstar. In rapid succession, Chaney Jr. scored in *The Wolf Man* (1941), *The Ghost of Frankenstein* (1942), *The Mummy's Tomb* (1942), and *Frankenstein Meets the Wolf Man* (1943).

Werewolf, Frankenstein's Monster, the Mummy... he'd played them all to booming box-office returns, and so it seemed only natural for Universal to cast their hot horror property as the King of the Undead himself. While the decision may have seemed reasonable at the time, in retrospect it proved a grave error (so to speak).

Though Universal snubbed the man who brought Dracula to (un)life on the talking screen, Lugosi was partially vindicated when Columbia cast him in the meaty role of Armand Tesla (Dracula in all but the name) in the same year's *The Return of the Vampire*. Even so, Lugosi reportedly never forgave Chaney for usurping his cape, and (according to director Reginald Le Borg) carried the grudge right onto the set of *The Black Sleep* thirteen years later, in which the elderly actor co-starred with the no-longer-young upstart.

On January 8, 1943, the cameras began rolling on *Son of Dracula*. A week into the shoot, however, near-disaster struck when the picture's leading man, Alan Curtis, was forced to bow out due to a knee injury he had received while starring in the talking screen's first fantasy anthology, *Flesh and Fantasy*. (Curtis' vignette was eventually expanded into a full feature entitled *Destiny*.) Though disastrous for Curtis (and expensive for Universal in terms of time and wasted footage), it ultimately proved a *happy* accident for the film itself, since Curtis' replacement, Robert Paige, provided what is perhaps the most effective, well-rounded horror hero portrayal of the decade.

Son of Dracula's unique story transplants Count Dracula (employing the rather obvious alias of Count Alucard) to small-town Southern America. Alucard (Chaney Jr.) is the invited guest of plantation heiress Catherine Caldwell (Louise Allbritton), whose "morbid" inclination drives her to seek eternal life through the Count. After becoming a vampire herself, Catherine plans to betray Alucard and then induce her true love, Frank (Robert Paige), to follow her into the world of the undead. But (to paraphrase poet Robert Burns) the best laid schemes of mice and vampires often go awry, and the undead meet their doom in a fiery finale.

Though generally thought of as the least of the Dracula trio (the other two, of course, being *Dracula* [1931] and *Dracula's Daughter* [1936]), *Son of Dracula* is a well-crafted chiller which ranks among Universal's best horror offerings of the 1940s. Director Robert Siodmak works with cinematographer George Robinson to carefully set the appropriate mood from the beginning. Alucard's introduction, for instance, starts with a shot of the black-tie party at Dark Oaks. While the elegant couples glide around the ornate ballroom, the camera tracks back from the gaiety and retreats through a curtained window into the darkness outside. Moving past shadowy shrubs, it swings left to reveal the pasty profile of Count Alucard, standing alone in the dark. The contrast of bright fellowship to shadowy solitude, coupled with some discordant notes on the soundtrack as the camera turns toward the undead Count, underscores the character's isolation from humanity while at the same time creating a startling moment of unease.

George Robinson's impressive illumination enhances the macabre mood. He fills the sets with planes of light and dark. Shadows of oversized banisters and spidery tendrils of darkness cast from the foliage outside a window splash across the interior sets, while isolated pools of light from lamps placed in the foreground add to the doom-laden atmosphere.

One of the first things to strike the viewer of *Son of Dracula* are the convincing—and unnerving—swampland sets. It took two art directors (John B. Goodman and Martin Obzina) and two set decorators (Russell A. Gausman and Edward R. Robinson) to create this studio-bound green hell. Spun with equal parts shadows and Spanish moss, the brackish water and tangled undergrowth form a perfect tapestry upon which to weave this weird tale of love and death.

On the special effects side, *Son of Dracula* sports some of Universal's more impressive visual trickery. Even the usually suspect rubber bat appears convincing, as the oversized flying rodent flaps smoothly (and steadily, for once) down a hallway, only to expand into an impenetrable shadow which then transforms into the caped figure of the Count himself—right before our eyes. (Another 'bat' scene required Fulton and co. to create a *live* bat. Actor Robert Paige told his cousin, James A. Healey, that Siodmak wanted to shoot a real bat crawling on the actor's neck during one scene. Understandably, Paige refused, so the effects people dyed a mouse brown and attached plastic wings to create the nocturnal marauder.) Even more impressive is the sequence in which Alucard's coffin rises from beneath the marshy water like an unholy u-boat, only to disgorge a stream of mist that forms itself into the shape of a man before solidifying into the figure of the undead fiend. Then, without so much as a whisper, Alucard's diabolical barge begins gliding forward, carrying the Count toward shore. It's quite unnerving as the immobile vampire flows forward (and we, along with the camera, retreat before him), with finger-like shadows from the surrounding trees playing across his face. Thanks to the visual wizardry of John P. Fulton, *Son of Dracula* boasts some of the most technically smooth and aesthetically well-staged special effects sequences from the Universal pantheon.

With one (critical) exception, *Son of Dracula* is a particularly well-acted entry in Universal's vampire cycle. Louise Allbritton is extremely effective as the "morbid" Catherine. Her penetrating-yet-faraway gaze, soft-but-impassioned speech, and almost blunted affect in the face of horrific circumstances complete the picture of a woman inexorably drawn to the dark mysteries beyond death.

Robert Paige, as Frank, contributes one of the most realistic—and *tragic*—hero portrayals in Universal history. Far from the bland pretty-boy of *Dracula*'s David Manners, Paige's awestruck horror at finding he's killed his fiancée, and his panicked flight through the swamp, make his character believably human. When he confesses his fears to Dr. Brewster, Paige's voice cracks with terror and anguish, his shaky hands rubbing his face in disbelief. "Harry, am I insane?!" he blurts out. "Could I have shot through Alucard and killed her without hitting him?" The words come in a frantic rush, with the urgency of the near-mad. Paige is totally convincing and completely sympathetic, giving the audience a solid handle upon which to hang the fateful and fantastic story.

Not all the principal players fare so well, however. At one point, Claire (Catherine's sister) observes that "There's something rather—*repulsive* about [Alucard]." While the comment may be a bit overstated, Lon Chaney Jr. cuts anything *but* a dashing figure. Chaney's fleshy face (complete with unsightly saddlebags under his eyes) and corpulent frame create a rather brutish-looking vampire that no amount of swank evening clothes can disguise. Though the actor tries his best to generate an old-world charm, Chaney's ineffectual efforts brand him as hopelessly *anti*-suave. When he asks the somewhat flowery question, "May I inquire as to what you are doing here?" his coarse inflections betray the refined dialogue, while his voice, in an effort to become soft and elegant, simply sounds flat and lifeless. Later, Alucard announces to his enemies that, "I am here because this is a young and virile race, not dry and decadent like ours." This evocative line of dialogue is rendered ridiculous by Chaney's flat Americana accent (which does little to conjure up the mysterious or exotic) and his comical mispronunciation of "decadent" as "dee-*kay*-dent." (Little wonder Universal replaced Chaney with the more sophisticated, Shakespearean-trained John Carradine for their subsequent Dracula portrayals.)

Apart from the liability of a miscast titular thespian, *Son of Dracula* also sports an occasional pat plot device that betrays its B-status. After Claire tells the family doctor that she suspects Catherine of seeing Alucard on the sly, the two nosy nellies invade the guest house where they find the Count's trunks—all empty. At this, the doctor suggests that they swear out an insanity complaint against Catherine, "to protect Kay from herself." If all it takes to get someone committed is a clandestine rendezvous with a man who travels light, one certainly wouldn't want to stop long in this little berg.

Despite these few foibles, the picture's otherwise strong script (which emphasized such an appealing element of tragedy), fascinating characters and darkly drawn atmosphere resulted in positive attention from both movie patrons and critics. *Variety* (October 28, 1943), for example, labeled *Son of Dracula* "a good entry of its type, and due for coinful box office reception from the thrill-inclined customers.... Direction by Robert Siodmak points up the scarey [sic] dramatics of the tale, while low key lighting by George Robinson assists materially in plotting the unfolding."

Son of Dracula proved to be a dark, moody, intelligent thriller that (sad to say for Chaney fans), given a better casting choice for the title character, could have attained something more than the slightly flawed, minor-classic status it enjoys today.

THE MAD GHOUL

Though conceived as nothing more than another B horror filler (and a mere supporting one at that—released on the bottom half of a double bill with *Son of Dracula*), *The Mad Ghoul* remains one of Universal's better 1940s horror entries. Thanks to a uniquely macabre storyline, some chillingly staged set-pieces, a dash of black humor, and exceptionally efficacious acting (headed by the terminally cultivated George Zucco at his restrained best), *The Mad Ghoul* rises above its second-string status to surpass many of the studio's more prominent efforts.

The highly unusual story has Dr. Alfred Morris (George Zucco) rediscovering a poison gas used centuries before by the Mayans. Said colorless and odorless toxin causes a "state of death in life" in its victims. In order to counteract this zombification, serum from a fresh human heart is needed to return the subject to normal (and stave off a 'true' death). Morris enlists star medical student Ted Allison (David Bruce) to assist him in his work. The doctor's goals are not altogether science-oriented, however, for he has set his venerable sights on Ted's fiancée, concert singer Isabel Lewis (Evelyn Ankers). When the guilt-racked Isabel confesses

George Zucco's Dr. Morris helps his Mad Ghoul (David Bruce) secure (semi) fresh hearts in this... er, ghoulish Universal horror.

to Morris (whom she views as a father figure) that she no longer loves Ted, Morris erroneously assumes that she's fallen for *him*! In order to get Ted out of the way, Morris secretly exposes his assistant to the gas, which transforms Ted into a mindless, cadaverous-looking zombie that will follow Morris' commands. He then takes his undead slave out to despoil a fresh grave and retrieve the restorative heart fluid. Now recovered, Ted thinks himself ill (unaware of what Morris has *really* done to him), and all seems clear for Morris' romantic plans. The doctor soon learns that the antidote's effects are merely temporary, however, and so orchestrates a rash of graverobbings and murders in order to procure the requisite human hearts and keep Ted around to do his bidding. On the romantic front, Morris also learns that the 'other man' is actually Isabel's pianist, Eric (Turhan Bey), rather than himself. With yet another rival to dispose of, Morris sends the once-again zombified Ted to kill Eric. But Ted (in his normal state) had previously discovered Morris' treachery, and had laid a trap for the doctor, exposing the scientist to the deadly vapor. Ted is shot down by police as he's about to attack Eric onstage, while Morris, the zombification process already taking effect, scrabbles desperately at a grave, only to succumb fully and die.

The Mad Ghoul, like its companion feature, is a particularly well-acted thriller. Both David Bruce as Ted, and Evelyn Ankers as Isabel, bring a likable naturalness to their pained characters. Bruce's boyish enthusiasm and naïveté (and subsequent tormented confusion at his inexplicable 'illness') wonderfully complements Ankers' guilt-racked, compassionate demeanor.

Top honors, however, go to George Zucco, who, along with Lionel Atwill, is perhaps the genre's most cultivated mad scientist/villain. "Zucco was one of the finest gentlemen I have ever worked with," commented co-star Turhan Bey to interviewer Tom Weaver, "and the last person in the world I would suspect to play horror parts. Except for his fantastic, menacing eyes and his voice, which he could manage so well, there was nothing horrible about him at all."

A master of subtle urbanity, Zucco presents a picture of calm control as the cultured, self-possessed Dr. Morris. When Ted, unaware that he's been exposed to the deadly drug, protests that he's fine, saying, "After all, I haven't gone through what [the experimental monkey] did," Zucco (who knows better) reacts with restrained subtlety to the tragic—and ironic—utterance. Instead of a broad facial twitch or obvious head bob, Zucco's eyes merely lower in reflective thought for an instant, the slight gesture suggesting both a steely control and perhaps a tinge of remorse.

When Morris learns that Isabel is throwing Ted over not for him but for Eric, Zucco reacts to this devastating blow with potent understatement. Only a slight increase in the intensity of his steady gaze and a brief flicker behind his eyes betray his emotion. So adept at portraying a man in near-total control of himself and his situation, Zucco makes his character seem that much more natural in his complete confidence.

Zucco also works wonders with the sometimes less-than-stellar dialogue. "I am a scientist," he tells Ted. "To me there is no evil, only true or false. You work with one, discard the other." Zucco's rapid, offhanded, yet conviction-laden delivery as he fiddles with his equipment makes the pretentious lines sound almost reasonable.

When an enthusiastic Ted answers Morris' offer to work as his assistant with "there isn't a fellow in the class who wouldn't give a *leg* to work with you in the lab," the doctor replies, "Well, that's rather more than the privilege is worth. You needn't give me a leg, just lend me a hand." Zucco's dry, cultured tone makes the line actually seem rather droll.

The film's comedy quotient remains both light and unobtrusive. As the clever and ebullient reporter Ken McClure (who sets a trap for the Mad Ghoul by posing as a corpse—to his eventual regret), Robert Armstrong becomes an amusing diversion, imbuing the comical cameo with the same enthusiasm he brought to *King Kong*'s Carl Denham.

Appropriately, much of the comedy arises from the macabre scenario. When McClure takes his place in a funeral home casket, the hovering mortician remonstrates, "Remember, for goodness sakes, whatever you do, don't mar this coffin!" Then, after Morris and Ted arrive, McClure abruptly sits up in the casket and brandishes a gun. Zucco, after a momentary start, deadpans, "The reports of your death seem to have been greatly exaggerated."

Though filmed on the cheap, the production *looks* good, thanks to some atmospheric art direction and careful composition. Scenes of appropriately misty graveyards generate the expected Universal-esque ambience, while James Hogan's occasionally inventive direction provides visual interest and the occasional chill. Hogan utilizes clever transitions (such as having the ghoul advance directly toward the camera to block it out and end the scene) and thoughtful staging to generate mood and *frisson*. At McClure's death, for instance, we see Ted surprise the unsuspecting reporter from behind. Then the camera focuses in tight on Morris's profile (with the zombified Ted to his left) while Morris chokes the life out of the man in the coffin—below screen. All we see of the deed itself is Zucco's straining face and arms as his hands work at their unseen task (now visualized in every viewer's mind). Ted's impassive, hideous face resisters no emotion at this heinous act. By allowing viewers to use their imaginations while focusing on the ghoul's blank visage, Hogan creates a moment that is coldly—dare I say *ghoul*ishly?—chilling.

"Hogan was very matter of fact," remembered Turhan Bey, "but an excellent craftsman. And a craftsman was what you had to be when you directed B pictures. You could be an artist at the same time, but mainly you had to be a craftsman, because you had X number of scenes to shoot every day and you had to keep on schedule."

Tragically, director James Hogan never saw his film released, for the 52-year-old moviemaker succumbed to a heart attack just one week before *The Mad Ghoul*'s national premier. Hogan began his directing career in 1920, helming over two-dozen silent films before successfully crossing over to the talkies. In the 1930s and early forties he carved out a niche for himself directing crime/mystery films, many of them in the Bulldog Drummond and Ellery Queen series.

Speaking of ghoulish, the striking 'ghoul' makeup is both subtly weird and hideously effective. Universal makeup ace Jack Pierce described how he was approached for the project: "All they told me was that they wanted [actor David] Bruce to look like a reasonably fresh cadaver. I said, 'How fresh?' They said a couple or three weeks buried. This was not much to go on but I did my best." Pierce's "best" was *more* than good enough. With dark shadings creating a sunken, hollow look; heavy-lidded, dead looking eyes; and wrinkled, parchment-like skin, Bruce indeed looks like a walking cadaver.

Such efficacy came with a price, however, at least for actor David Bruce. "They tinted me green and combed my hair over my eyes and for the later thing they put the false skin on, which was absolute murder," Bruce told *Famous Monsters* magazine. "I wore it for only three days and the third time I took it off my skin was bleeding because you had to peel the makeup off." (Apart from the borderline comedy-thrillers *The Smiling Ghost* and *One Body Too Many*, both 1941, this was David Bruce's only horror film.)

The Mad Ghoul's bizarre scenario, with its unsavory graveyard surgeries and warped love theme, grabs the viewer's attention and holds it—right up to the great climactic twist in which the 'mad doctor' is not merely destroyed by his 'monster' but actually *becomes* one himself. Such an ironic twist proves a clever (and welcome) innovation.

Unfortunately, like the Mad Ghoul himself, the film is far from blemish free. When Zucco or the zombified Ted are not onscreen, interest wanes, particularly during the overlong musical numbers in which Isabel does her songbird routine. (Universal originally had planned to allow Evelyn Ankers—who possessed a fine singing voice—to record the songs herself, but at the last moment opted instead to dub in the voice of professional singer Lillian Cornell.) Also, the climactic death of Ted remains both perfunctory and unsatisfying. Filmed mostly in medium-long shot, Hogan simply shows Ted walking across the stage toward Isabel and Eric before a policeman's bullets drop him. Such mundane presentation lacks both visual depth and suspense, and becomes an unworthy finale for the Mad Ghoul.

Its few faults aside, thanks to an innovative story, (usually) careful direction, grotesquely effective makeup and stellar playing (particularly from one of the genre's best-loved but least-appreciated grand old villains—George Zucco), *The Mad Ghoul* remains an entertaining and refreshingly original Universal horror from an often repetitive and sequel-plagued decade.

And with *The Mad Ghoul* cued up alongside the even better *Son of Dracula*, Universal had a near-unbeatable terror tandem to offer its horror-hungry audience. Though the razzamatazz theme music that heralded a Universal feature of the 1940s often disappointingly brought with it more razz than real razzamatazz, with the pairing of *Son of Dracula* and *The Mad Ghoul* the studio offered its wartime viewers a delightfully ghoulish glimpse back into the glory days of its 1930s chillers.

> Since I find the topic (and film) so fascinating, I've added a bit of historical background to this piece published by *Filmfax* magazine (issue 57) in 1996. Author's prerogative and all that...

TOWER OF LONDON (1939)

"DARK FASCINATING SECRETS LURK BEHIND THESE GRIM TOWERS!" –poster blurb

When Hollywood handles history it usually does so with kid gloves, whitewashing its subject in broad strokes of thrilling adventure and heroism. With a certain historical personage of the English monarchy, however, the exact opposite has been true. In 1483 Richard III became King of England amid the civil unrest and political upheaval of the Wars of the Roses. The last of the Plantagenet kings, Richard fell in battle less than three years later and the monarchy passed into the hands of the Tudors (of which Henry VIII is the best known).

If one recognizes the name of Richard III at all, it is probably as one of history's vilest villains, a humpbacked usurper who murdered members of his own family—including his two prepubescent nephews—to gain the crown. This is the Richard of William Shakespeare, who based his fictionalized play *Richard III* largely upon the highly biased and inaccurate tracts of Tudor chroniclers. Disregarding the fact that Richard was at the time of his reign a well-loved reformer (and also personally well-formed; i.e. no hump) who showed more mercy to his enemies than good sense would dictate, Shakespeare's popular play forever cast him in the public eye as an evil, scheming nephew-killer (despite a complete lack of evidence for same). Never one to fly in the face of popular opinion (not to mention established literature), it comes as no surprise that Hollywood took the same tact in its take on the tarnished tale.

Since it is a Universal film starring Basil Rathbone and Boris Karloff, and because it sports a plethora of tortures and murders, *Tower of London* has fallen seemingly by default into the horror realm. Much more than the average chiller, however, it's one of the best historical dramas of the age. Superb acting, grand spectacle, precise photography, a classic storyline and deft direction make *Tower of London* one of the most impressively-mounted productions from the Golden Age of Horror.

The story follows the clever and ruthless machinations of Richard (Basil Rathbone), brother of usurper King Edward IV, who claimed the English crown in 1471. With the aid of the Tower of London's chief torturer/executioner, Mord (Boris Karloff), Richard sets about murdering all those who stand in the way of his accession to the throne, including his own brother Clarence (Vincent Price) and his two young nephews. Winning his prize at last, Richard soon meets his fate at the hands of Henry Tudor at the battle of Bosworth field.

Almost immediately, the viewer is whisked inside Jack Otterson's magnificent castle sets, whose authenticity is only matched by their size and grandeur. Immense walls and towers rise seventy-five feet above the castle courtyard while the spacious-yet-forbidding interiors are made even more ominous by the huge stone fireplaces, mammoth pillars and massive wooden doors.

Boris Karloff (as Mord, the executioner) and Basil Rathbone (as Richard III) bring intensity and menace to the Tower of London *(1939).*

Otterson even built an authentic replica of the watery Traitor's Gate that leads to the river Thames, an imposing structure that opens and closes like the mouth of a great beast to devour the characters.

Robert N. Lee's (brother of director Rowland V. Lee) excellent screenplay is full of well-drawn, contrasting characterizations, the most notable being the strong King Edward (ebulliently played by Ian Hunter) and his cunning brother, Richard. Edward is a hearty, guileless, even good-humored man, whose misdeeds arise not from malice or forethought, but from the weight of leadership and the willingness to take the most expedient route. With an engaging impishness, he plays along with Richard's ploys, failing to see his sibling's darker motivations. Richard, however, schemes and plots to achieve his ends, drawing his brother in when necessary but never revealing to anyone but himself his true intent. One truly likes Edward, and wishes that he had a nobler advisor than Richard. Though Richard is definitely the villain of the piece (with Mord as a physical extension of his antagonism), he is not thoroughly evil. He exhibits a genuine affection for the woman he loves, and while we abhor his vile deeds, we also admire his cunning and even feel a pang of pity for this brilliant but misguided man.

Basil Rathbone was forced to decline a principal role in RKO's 1939 remake of *The Hunchback of Notre Dame* due to his Universal commitments. *Notre Dame*'s loss was the *Tower*'s gain, as he gives a vibrant performance to bring the character of Richard to full malevolent life. Rathbone's steely gaze and black eyes are like the stare of a snake. In an early execution scene, his gaze never wavers as the headsman's ax falls, though his eyes seem to glitter evilly and flicker with excitement, while a barely-detectable half-smirk deepens on his cold countenance.

Though for the most part a forbidding figure, Boris Karloff gives Mord a soul nonetheless. With gestures and hesitations at the murder of the young nephews, for instance, Karloff imbues his character with some small sympathy. When Mord picks up the sleeping Prince, the child's arm trustingly goes around the executioner's neck. At this, Karloff's face softens slightly and one can almost see the compassion struggling behind his eyes—before he again sets his face grimly and forcibly hardens his heart. For a brief moment, Karloff shows the man beneath the brute, adding a key dimension to his despicable character.

Little fault can be found with Rowland V. Lee's grand direction. Though creating a lavish spectacle filled with costumed extras, Lee does not neglect any attention to detail. As the herald mounts the execution platform, for example, the man casually reaches out to the body-sized wicker basket lying on the stage's corner to flip open the lid, readying the container for its imminent use. With a small but forbidding gesture, Lee adds a subtle shudder to the somber scene.

Tower of London sports more than its fair share of thrilling battle scenes, all wind and rain and clashing swords. Lee utilizes a montage of images—men swarming over the hill, knights battling hip-deep through a muddy stream—to create a sense of chaotic urgency, heightened by the driving rain and sounds of trumpets mixed with the clang of metal and the screams of dying men. (Lee had great difficulty in shooting these sequences. Three hundred extras were there ready for battle only to have their cardboard helmets and shields disintegrate under the onslaught of the rain machines. Lee finally overcame these obstacles by filming small bands of men fighting and transposing them against a background of battle scenes already shot to create the montage effect.)

Though often unfairly overlooked, *Tower of London* remains a grand historical epic boasting intense performances from two horror favorites, Basil Rathbone and Boris Karloff, and enough blood and thunder to please any genre fan.

> Back in 1998, *The Vampire's Ghost* haunted *Monsters from the Vault* magazine (issue 6). And here it is back again…

THE VAMPIRE'S GHOST (1945): VAMPIRES AND VOODOO ON THE DARK CONTINENT

1945's *The Vampire's Ghost* has long been dismissed as one of the lesser poverty-row horrors (and not even a Monogram or PRC product, but something from that no-budget *Western* studio, Republic!) which can't even boast a single Lugosi, Carradine, or Zucco. Yet despite its lack of genre stars or Monogram-style wackiness, *The Vampire's Ghost* is one of the best horrors to crawl out from Gower Gulch—a unique poverty-row sleeper possessing above-average intelligence (a rarity in its class) that remains both entertaining and potentially thought-provoking.

The West African plantation village of Bakunda is plagued by mysterious deaths in which the victims are drained of blood. The native voodoo drums speak of vampires, but the local whites, led by merchant Thomas Vance (Emmett Vogan), his daughter Julie (Peggy Stewart), her fiancé Roy (Charles Gordon), and missionary Father Gilchrist (Grant Withers), scoff at the notion. We soon learn, however, that the cultured saloon owner Webb Fallon (John Abbott) is the vampire. When Fallon sets his sights on Julie and flees into the jungle, the men pursue the monster and finally confront him at the taboo "Temple of Death."

Technically, *The Vampire's Ghost* is one of the better looking low-budget horrors of the 1940s. Director Lesley Selander, and co-cinematographers Bud Thackery and Robert Pittack, provide plenty of camera movement and effective set-pieces that raise the film above its poverty-row contemporaries.

The opening sequence, for instance, proves particularly strong. As John Abbott intones his melancholy narration, the scene dissolves from a primitive map of Africa to the darkened town of Bakunda. The camera moves through the village and, as Abbott concludes "I cannot rest…I cannot rest…I cannot rest," closes in on a dim doorway. A hand enters the frame to stealthily push open the portal. Inside, a beautiful native girl awakens, and as a shadow passes over her prone form, she screams. This carefully constructed and fluidly effective opening sets a wonderfully macabre and somber tone.

In another scene, Fallon stalks his victim. An unsavory ship captain (Roy Barcroft) walks home through

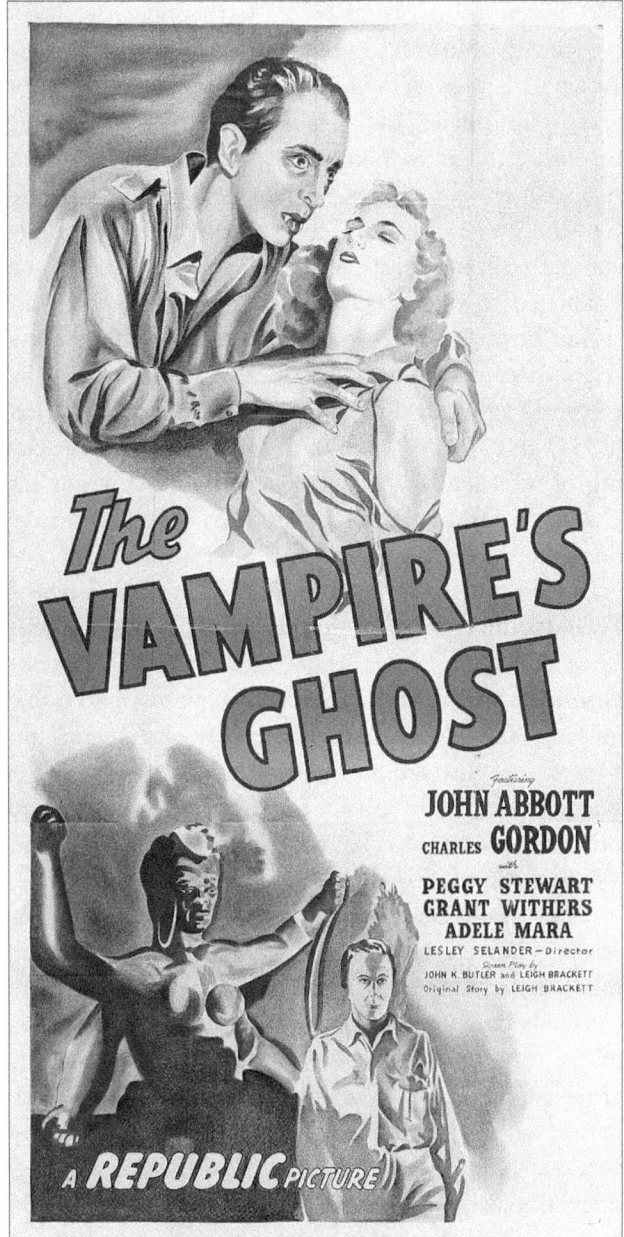

The Vampire's Ghost poster.

the darkened streets after cheating Fallon at cards. We see a pair of white trousered legs follow slowly. The man looks nervously behind him and quickens his pace while the pursuing legs continue following. Finally, the man is cornered against a locked gate. He turns and a man-shaped shadow rises up to fall across his body, growing larger while simultaneously the camera glides in closer. The terrified captain drops his raised knife and the shadow's hands move up toward the victim's throat. Throughout the sequence we never see the pursuer, even though we know who—and what—he is. The close shots of the pursuing legs, the menacing shadow, and the claustrophobic camera movement (effectively *pinning* the victim to the wall like a trapped insect) adds potent mystery and impact to the sequence.

Though it turned out he did a fine job, director Lesley Selander seemed an unlikely candidate to pilot a vampire movie, having made something of a name for himself as a low-budget *Western* specialist. Born in turn-of-the-century Los Angeles, Selander entered the film industry right out of high school as a lab technician. Becoming an assistant cameraman in 1920, he graduated to full cameraman two years later, and assistant director two years after that. After directing a series of comedy shorts, he went to MGM where he served as assistant director on films like *The Thin Man* (1934) and *Night at the Opera* (1935). With the backing of his friend Buck Jones, Selander finally got his chance to direct features in 1936. Over the next thirty-one years, he helmed over 150 films, most of them oaters (often starring Jones, Tim Holt, or William Boyd—Selander directed *twenty-five* "Hopalong Cassidy" features alone!). Selander also worked extensively in television. Between 1954 and 1958 he supervised 60 *Lassie* episodes and was also a regular fixture on *Laramie* and *Cannonball*. Though he rarely left the cinematic saddle, Selander did hitch up to the horror/sci-fi post on two other occasions—for *The Catman of Paris* (1946) and *Flight to Mars* (1951). He died in 1979 at age 79.

Not to argue too strongly against the notion that *The Vampire's Ghost* is really nothing more than a low-budget, mildly entertaining potboiler, but… the film *does* explore (no doubt purely by accident) significant issues of religious efficacy and conflict. In the film, the white colonialists are left to their largely impotent Christianity, while the natives possess their more accessible—and effective—voodoo. From the beginning, the "superstitious" natives know the cause of the mysterious plague of murders and quickly identify its source, whereas the whites haven't got a clue. Also, it is a voodoo-embroiled native that initially takes up arms against the vampire, and it is the voodoo drums that finally inform Father Gilchrist (Christianity's representative) of the truth and ultimately leads him to the unholy fiend. (There is one point where Christianity *does* become effective—when Roy, with the aid of Father Gilchrist, finally breaks free of Fallon's spell. This illuminates another intriguing tenent: A religion's power only works on the faithful of that religion. While the natives know what ails Roy, their voodoo magic cannot help him directly, for he is not of their faith. It finally takes Father Gilchrist and "the house of God" to overcome the evil spell placed upon Roy, demonstrating that each religion takes care of its own.)

The vampire himself laughs at the local religion—much to his eventual regret. When Fallon finds a voodoo doll pinned to his door with a knife, he shrugs the warning off with, "It's a lot of hocus-pocus; I don't let it bother *me*." Yet this dismissal of the sacred religion turns and bites him in the end, for it is the voodoo drums which lead his enemies to him and a native believer who sets the fire that destroys the vampire.

This religious dichotomy in a grade-B Hollywood screenplay inadvertently demonstrates one of the great differences between Christianity and the Voudoun faith: The Christian sees the supernatural as something distant and largely unaffecting (Heaven, angels, etc.) whereas the Voudounist sees the preternatural world of gods and spirits as a tangible force permeating their daily lives.

Though it's doubtful that Butler and Brackett intended to say any such thing, *The Vampire's Ghost* subliminally argues for tolerance and even cooperation between disparate religions. In the end, it's a combination of voodoo and Christianity that defeat the vampire: The crucifix stops the fiend from consummating his unholy bloodlust on the entranced heroine, while Roy (a Christian) takes up a native voodoo spear dipped in silver to incapacitate the vampire. And it's Simon Peter, a native voodoo drum-beater (though friendly to Father Gilchrist and the Christian faith), who sets the temple ablaze and finally kills the undead monster (for only fire can truly destroy the vampire). Okay, so *The Vampire's Ghost* may not be the ideal Unitarian treatise on religious tolerance, but it does offer some (inexpensive) food for thought to those hungry enough to look.

Despite *The Vampire's Ghost*'s backhanded support of the voodoo concept, on the surface it still took the expected condescending and stereotypical attitude toward the religion (characterizing the voodooists as "superstitious savages"). Regarding the age-old institution of vampirism, however, the picture proved much more liberal. Webb Fallon can move about in daylight (though he wears dark glasses to protect his eyes from the sun); he sleeps in a bed rather than a coffin (albeit with a small box of his native soil on the nightstand); he is *injured* by silver-tipped spears (rather than the traditional wooden stake) but *killed* only by fire; and he is healed by the restorative powers of moonlight. Like the more standard bloodsucker, however, Fallon *does* drain his victims of blood via two puncture marks in the neck; he shies away from crosses; he casts no reflection in mirrors; and his victims *do* turn into vampires themselves (though, disappointingly, this fact is revealed only through dialogue rather than visuals). Thanks to these rather innovative alterations, *The Vampire's Ghost* becomes an intriguing addition to the cinematic vampire canon (unless, that is, the viewer tolerates variation less well than Fallon tolerates the sun). NOTE: This whole notion of the 'right' rules of conduct and attributes of a vampire seems both artificial and absurd to this author. One of the most intriguing aspects of the horror genre is the presentation and exploration of The Unexpected. If these supernatural creatures always conform to what's expected of them from film to film, they become much less intriguing. And why *should* they be the same in movie after movie? As long as a vampire doesn't violate the reality built into its own particular film, clever variations can only add interest. I've never understood the vehemence of vampire-loving pedants in their insistence that *all* Creatures-of-the-Night conform to some arbitrarily concocted set of supernatural rules. And let us not forget that, thanks to Mr. Stoker himself, the most famous vampire of all could—and did—move about in broad daylight! (Please send all missives and complaints to the editor, care of the publisher, at the Vampire Variation League.)

Another frequent complaint by vampire purists is the casting of John Abbott as the bloodsucker. Though pop-eyed and slightly built (and lacking the *de rigeur* penguin suit and cape), Abbott's deep voice, cultured tones, forceful delivery, and confident physical movements make him an imposing figure nonetheless. Abbott's natural assuredness adds a much-needed efficacy to some of the suspect dialogue, bringing to life even potentially trite passages like, "Sometimes things drive a man, regardless of his will, things that may even tear his soul."

Abbott was no stranger to the role of vampire, having played *Dracula* himself in a London stage production. "In *The Vampire's Ghost*," recalled the actor to *Movie Club*'s Don Leifert, "I tried to make my character pass for a human being as near as I could and yet keep the undercurrent of the vampire's special propensities." He succeeded admirably.

"You're one of the nicest people I've ever met," the naïve Julie tells Fallon at one point. It's an amusingly ironic moment, but one possessing a grain of truth, for Abbott's vampire is one of the most sympathetic of the decade. Thanks to the actor's soulful eyes, deep baritone, and subtle, almost wistful expressions, an aura of sadness and tragedy hangs on Fallon like a shroud. When Fallon expounds upon the impending devastation of those around him, he states, "This has all happened before and it'll all happen again—until the end of time." Though Abbott speaks rapidly and matter-of-factly, his face and inflection betray a great sadness. "I enjoyed playing the role," enthused Abbott, and the discerning viewer enjoys *watching* him.

Born in 1905 to a London stockbroker, John Abbott was headed for a career in commercial art before the lure of the footlights swept him into the world of theater—ultimately landing him a position at the prestigious Old Vic (where he acted opposite the likes of Laurence Olivier and Alec Guinness). Abbott entered films in 1936, making half a dozen movies in England before coming to Hollywood in 1941 where he made over eighty more over the next five decades, including such prestige pictures as *Jane Eyre* (1944), *The Woman in White* (1948), *The Greatest Story Ever Told* (1965), and Disney's *The Jungle Book* (1967; as the voice of the Wolf Leader). For genre fans, Abbott's (all-too brief) presence livened up the otherwise dull Columbia effort *Cry of the Werewolf* (1944), and he added some much needed élan to Curtis Harrington's 1973 TV terror *The Cat Creature*. One of the actor's final film appearances before his death in 1996 (at age 90) was in the witty *Four Weddings and a Funeral* (1994).

The Vampire's Ghost is not, however, an undiscovered classic, for it admittedly carries its fair share of foibles. When things move indoors, for example, the expected poverty-row lethargy sets in, replete with statically-shot, talky dialogue scenes on cramped, underdressed sets. Adele Mara (under the guidance of "Dance Director" Jerry Jarrette) provides a truly awful and inappropriate gypsy-style (on the west coast of Africa?!) dance sequence that goes on for an embarrassingly long time. Apart from Abbott, the cast proves adequate but unremarkable—with the painful exception of Martin Wilkins as Simon Peter, who turns in an amazingly stilted and amateurish performance, even by low-budget standards. As the icing on the (fallen) cake, Grant Withers (playing Father Gilchrist) wearing a floor-length clerical smock in the middle of the African jungle topped by a *pith helmet* can't fail but induce derisive sniggers in the viewer.

The Rodney Dangerfield of vampire movies, *The Vampire's Ghost* simply "gets no respect." *Variety*'s Sten, for instance, was singularly unimpressed: "John Abbott, as the vampire, along with Charles Gordon, Grant Withers and Peggy Stewart, go through their paces in stilted fashion. Script, settings and camerawork just so-so."

The Hollywood Reporter complained that "There is little quality to the routine production, and Lesley Selander's direction reflects the confusion of the shabbily constructed screenplay." The reviewer did single out John Abbott, however, noting that "[Abbott's] own competence as an actor almost succeeds in making plausible the poorly-defined vampire story."

The Vampire's Ghost lacks even one champion among modern-day critics. Even the usually undiscriminating Michael Weldon called it "slow horror" in his *Psychotronic Encyclopedia of Film*. In *Poverty Row Horrors!*, Tom Weaver (the only film historian to date to give the film any kind of in-depth coverage) labeled it "bleak and silly," and concluded that "*The Vampire's Ghost*'s mix of vampire, voodoo and jungle film elements is offbeat enough to be almost appealing, but the film generates so few thrills and so little atmosphere that even at a scant 59 minutes, it nearly succeeds in wearing out its welcome." In *B Movies*, Don Miller complained of the film's "cheap production values, uninspired performances and a director (Lesley Selander) who obviously preferred the more outgoing pleasures of 'Red Ryder' Westerns, at which task he had been gainfully employed." Phil Hardy's *Encyclopedia of Horror Movies* called it "a real shoestring shocker which is quite unable to make anything out of a potentially intriguing story"—before going on to get several key plot points (including the climax) completely wrong. (Do 'critics' simply forget to *watch* these films before they write about them, or do they just fail to pay attention?)

To add insult to injury, just like *Voodoo Man* before it, *The Vampire's Ghost* was slapped with the restrictive "H" certificate (adults-only) by the BBFC when released in England.

Still, when one considers its Gower Gulch contemporaries (the amusing but puerile *King of the Zombies*, the entertaining but ridiculous *Voodoo Man*, and even the earnest but somewhat stodgy *The Face of Marble*), *The Vampire's Ghost* remains the best and most thought-provoking voodoo entry poverty-row had to offer.

Though I originally penned this assessment of the wacky Bela Lugosi favorite as a short, 600-word review for *Cult Movies* magazine (issue 16) in 1995, I subsequently expanded it for another project, and so present the updated version here.

VOODOO MAN (1944)

"Lugosi, the King of Horror, outdoes himself in Voodoo Man...*and with the help of two half-mad voodoo villains, Carradine and Zucco, you're assured a super thrill-chill show!"* –(over)enthusiastic radio spot

Monogram, that most prolific of Poverty Row studios in the 1940s, churned out numerous no-budget su-

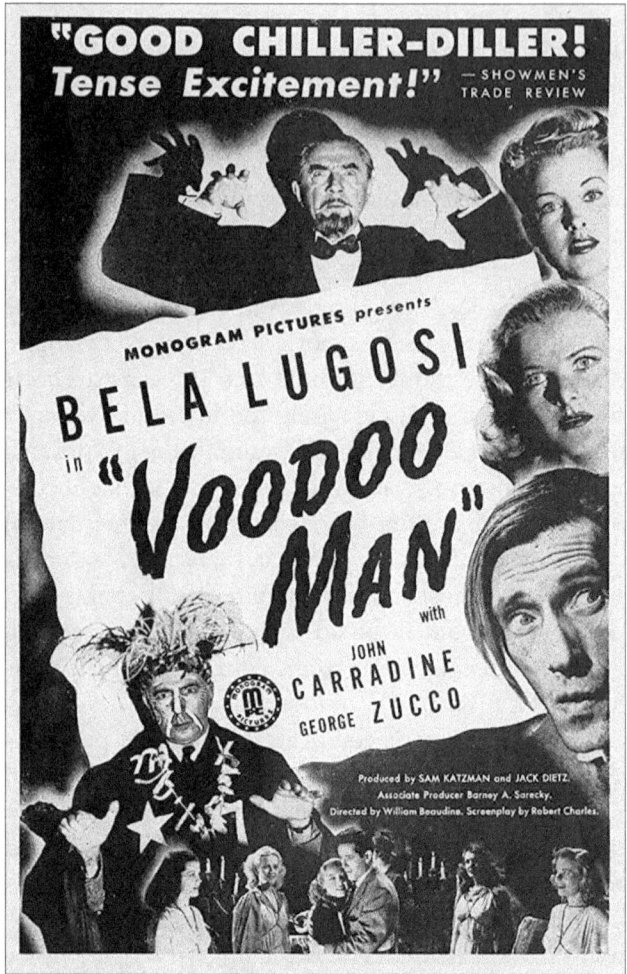

Voodoo Man *ad.*

pernatural potboilers to titillate the war-weary public. *Voodoo Man*, although no classic and not even a good film by "B" standards, is one of their better horror efforts.

In June of 1943 Monogram announced that their new production of *The Voodoo Man* would begin shooting in August. August came and went, and the studio next announced a start date in October (after Bela Lugosi had completed his current Hollywood stage engagement in *Arsenic and Old Lace*). William Nigh (*The Ape*, 1940; *Black Dragons*, 1942) was originally announced as the director, but he quickly gave way to Philip Rosen (*Spooks Run Wild*, 1941). A change of plans put Rosen on Monogram's *Return of the Ape Man*, which went into production first. When *Voodoo Man* finally began shooting on October 16, William "One Shot" Beaudine was twirling the director's baton. (Ironically, Beaudine had originally been slated to direct *Return of the Ape Man*[!]; Monogram's behind-the-scenes planning was seemingly just as muddled as their movie plots.)

Bela Lugosi plays Dr. Marlowe who, with the aid of gas station attendant Nicholas (George Zucco) and half-wit handyman Toby (John Carradine), kidnaps beautiful girls in an attempt to restore life to his zombie wife. To this end he hypnotizes the abducted girls while Toby beats out a rhythm on a tom-tom and Nicholas, decked out in astrologer's robe and feathered headdress, prays to the voodoo god "Ramboona." The process is apparently flawed, as the basement is full of zombie-girls. Into this mess step a Hollywood scenario writer (Tod Andrews) and his fiancée (Wanda McKay), who just happens to possess "the perfect affinity" for Marlowe's life-transferring ceremony.

Well-paced at the beginning (with the wild get-up and bizarre ceremony grabbing one's attention), the script soon bogs down in seemingly endless running about by the hero and sheriff. "What I remember about *Voodoo Man*," recalled Louise Currie (who played a zombie-girl) to interviewer Tom Weaver, "was walking around out in the woods with my eyes wide open, wandering around in a trance." Indeed, scene after repetitive scene of somnambulistic subjects shuffling about, combined with frequent sequences in which the non-zombified characters drive endlessly to and fro, almost bring the bizarre proceedings to a screeching halt.

With the story being so much hoke, the film's major asset becomes, of course, Bela Lugosi. Lugosi plays his role with a genuine relish that makes the film enjoyable to watch. *He* believes it, and consequently so do *we*. With Lugosi's commanding voice and powerful presence, one can almost give credence to Marlowe's much-touted hypnotic power.

In *Voodoo Man*, Lugosi gets to step beyond his usual 'evil incarnate' persona and slip in a bit of pathos—unusual in a Lugosi film. When someone asks, "Is your wife ill?," Marlowe replies, "She's dead." Lugosi's voice, while in full control, betrays just a hint of sadness. Later, when Marlowe's procedure momentarily revives his zombie wife, the doctor exclaims, "I have brought you back to me my darling; now we are together again." Lugosi's heartfelt delivery carries an almost tremulous joy. Even at the end, as Marlowe lay dying, his last line (referring to his dead wife)—"soon we'll be together"—is delivered with just the right amount of compassion to inspire a bit of pity for the old madman.

Lugosi even occasionally adds a touch of (unintentional) humor to his role. When the Sheriff asks Marlowe if he's seen anything suspicious around Laurel Road, Lugosi answers, "No, not that I remember. I'm quite off—the road." Lugosi's brief pause after "I'm quite off" adds a humorous connotation to the innocuous line. "Yeah, that's right," agrees the Sheriff—and so do we.

It's amazing how much effort Lugosi put into his role of the single-minded doctor, considering *Voodoo Man* was his *ninth* film for Monogram in three years. One would think that he'd have tired of the ridiculous plots and threadbare productions. Then again, at least he was the 'star' in these cheap features, whereas the major studios (when they cast him at all) generally offered him only cameos or supporting roles during the 1940s. *Voodoo Man* proved to be Lugosi's final film for Monogram (though not the last one to be released—*Return of the Ape Man* was shot before but released after *Voodoo Man*).

Sadly, Lugosi's horror veteran co-stars, Carradine and Zucco, don't fare nearly so well. Both these talented professionals are wasted in worthless roles (a fate these two actors suffered time and time again at the hands of cheap and unimaginative producers). Carradine, playing a mentally deficient henchman, must build his character with inanities like "You've got nice pretty hair." And Zucco, who could be such an elegant villain, mostly stays in the background muttering gibberish while wearing a silly feathered headdress. Carradine commented that Zucco was "a *very* good actor"—while probably secretly thanking his lucky stars that *he* didn't have to wear that preposterous chapeau. "I've done a lot of crap," admitted Carradine. "I only did 'em for the money. I had five boys to raise." His role in *Voodoo Man* certainly fits *that* description.

William "One Shot" Beaudine's direction is plagued with dull staging, a heavy reliance on the medium shot and an apparent aversion to interesting angles. It's no wonder that he could spare little creativity on *Voodoo Man*, for the busy Beaudine made a total of *twelve* features in 1944! Though he may not have been good, Beaudine was certainly prolific, directing over 175 features, 325 one- and two-reelers, and 350 episodes for various television series. At the time of his death in 1970 he was the oldest active member of the Screen Directors Guild.

What visual interest found in the film can be put down to cinematographer Marcel Le Picard's evocative lighting. He fills the cramped settings with sinister shadows and weirdly flickering light (from voodoo torches, one assumes) that add some welcome atmosphere to the cheap sets. Le Picard lensed a number of Lugosi movies, such as *Invisible Ghost* (1941), *Spooks Run Wild* (1941), *Return of the Ape Man* (1944), and *Scared to Death* (1947).

Voodoo Man's inappropriate music (by dentist-turned-composer Edward Kay), full of obvious cues and tinny strings (with an occasional harp arpeggio thrown into the mix), only cheapens the feel of this already threadbare production. Kay, who contributed(?) music to such horrors as *The Ape*, *The Ape Man*, *Return of the Ape Man* (theme, anyone?), *Revenge of the Zombies*, and *Ghosts on the Loose*, was an Academy Award nominee! He was nominated for his work on *King of the Zombies*. He did *not* win.

"Unlike most horror films," claimed the picture's pressbook, "*Voodoo Man* has no let-up of suspense, nor any comedy interludes to break the tension." Intentional or no, the film does offer up a few laughs (such as Carradine's howlingly funny observation upon finding one of the zombie girls missing: "She's not there—she must be somewhere else") to go along with its fine performance from that charismatic master of Poverty Row horror, Bela Lugosi. To balance this, however, *Voodoo Man* seems intent on *embarrassing* its two other genre stars, Carradine and Zucco. In the right frame of mind this horror cheapie can be a lot of fun. But take it seriously and one only laments the misuse of some of the genre's finest talents.

> This examination of one of Boris Karloff's better horror pictures appeared in *Collecting Hollywood* magazine, issue 5 (Spring 1994), and later became a chapter in my book *Golden Horrors*.

RETROSPECT, THE CLASSICS IN REVIEW: *THE WALKING DEAD* (1936)

"Can't you remember anything that happened—before you died?" –Dr. Beaumont.

SYNOPSIS

John Elman, a mild-mannered musician, has just been released from prison after serving 10 years for second degree murder. "It was my wife," he explains, "I struck a man, but I didn't mean to kill him." Elman has been dealt a rather harsh hand by the deck of fate and now only wishes to find a job and resume what is left of his life. Unfortunately for him, he's taken in by four powerful (and ostensibly "respectable") racketeers who frame him for the murder of an honest judge causing trouble for them.

Elman is convicted and sentenced to die. On the eve of the execution, two witnesses who can clear Elman, Jimmy and Nancy, finally overcome their fear of the racketeers and come forward—but it is too late and Elman is put to death in the electric chair.

Jimmy and Nancy both work for an eminent researcher named Dr. Beaumont. Beaumont, who'd been working on the restoration of life in animals, performs an experimental procedure on Elman's body and brings him back to life. Elman has changed, though, and is only the shell of the man he once was. He has very little memory and is almost an invalid. However, at certain times he gains some mysterious access to knowledge denied him in life—namely, the identities of his hidden enemies, those who had secretly framed him. "I'm positive Elman has some knowledge not given to him by Man," declares Dr. Beaumont.

One by one Elman confronts his enemies. Elman's very presence unnerves each of the racketeers, and their own guilt and terror leads them to their deaths. One man (the group's hitman) falls backwards in fright and shoots himself with his own gun; another flees into the path of an oncoming train; a third backs through an upper story window.

Finally, Elman retreats to a cemetery. "I belong here," he says quietly. The two remaining racketeers follow him there and shoot him, but receive their just reward when their fleeing car careens off the road and crashes into a power pole—sending them to their own impromptu electric chair.

As Elman lies dying (for the second—and final—time), Dr. Beaumont questions him: "John, look at me, try to remember, you must. ...Try John, try, that's why I brought you back from death. ...Tell me, what *is* death?" Suddenly, everything seems to become clear to Elman. "I think I can," he says. "After the shock I seemed to feel peace and– and–" and he dies, taking his mysterious knowledge with him as he rejoins his Maker. As Elman had said earlier, "The lord our God is a jealous God."

MEMORABLE MOMENT

The heart and soul of *The Walking Dead* is found in the first scene of retribution, when Elman confronts "Trigger" Smith, the racketeers' hired gun. Instructed to eliminate Elman, Trigger loads his weapon. The door to his room opens and he sees the figure of his intended victim. The scene quickly takes an unsettling turn when the camera views Elman from a slightly off-kilter low-angle. Although startled, Trigger quickly recovers himself: "Funny, here I been thinkin' of payin' you a visit and—you save me the trouble by walkin' in." Elman stands unmoving, his face a stone mask. With the camera peering up at his shadowy, cadaverous visage, Elman intones, "Why did you kill Judge Shaw?" His voice is flat and hollow, yet with a frightening certainty

As The Walking Dead *(1936), John Elman (Boris Karloff) goes about his mission of retribution*

and subtle force behind it. Trigger's facade crumbles. "Lay off that stuff!" he barks angrily. "That night, I thought you were my friend," Elman continues. Trigger panics and pulls his gun, shouting, "Put 'em up!" Elman slowly raises his hands. "You can't kill me again," he states, the flat monotone of that unearthly voice carrying a conviction that leaves no room for doubt. Arms upraised, Elman begins to advance. The dangling chain of the room's overhead lamp catches on his hand and the room is plunged into darkness. Moving steadily forward, the shadowy figure issues a statement: "You can't use that gun." Near hysteria, Trigger shouts, "Keep back, keep back!" Elman steps into a patch of light and stops. With a subtle, almost sorrowful, shake of his head, he says simply, "You can't escape what you've done." This stark statement of fact is the core of the picture—one must answer for one's actions. Trigger is now thoroughly terrified and, in trying to cheat fate, stumbles backwards and falls violently over a table. The gun fires accidentally and Trigger is dead. The killer has died by his own hand, his unthinking actions leading him on to his fatal destiny.

ASSETS

The Walking Dead is an often overlooked classic that frequently gets unfairly lumped in with Karloff's "Mad Doctor" and "Back-from-the-Dead" films (*The Man They Could Not Hang*, 1939; *Before I Hang*, 1940; etc.). These later horror films are basically low-budget potboilers, albeit with a touch more class than most of their contemporaries. It is a mistake, however, to dismiss *The Walking Dead* as simply another of Karloff's 'Mad Monster Movies.'

One point that sets *The Walking Dead* above its fellows is a very strong and literate script, which possesses a greater thematic depth than most. The confirmation of an afterlife, the revelation that the guilty *will* be punished, and the assurance that there is indeed a God watching over us, ready to take a hand, touch some very real and basic human needs. Screenwriters Adamson, Milne, Andrews, and Hayward utilize these needs in order to draw the viewer into their story. They deliver the goods in the end, for the film's message is one of reassurance, and as such is rather appealing and, ultimately, satisfying.

Also appealing is the character of John Elman. He is a likable but rather naive man who trusts people and the system but is betrayed by them. It's easy to empathize with Elman, because most of us have been taken advantage of at one time or another (though, it is hoped, not to the extent of Elman's case). The sympathy engendered by Elman's plight gives each viewer an emotional stake in the proceedings, and draws each viewer into the story. At the end, Elman (and, through him, the audience) receives assistance from, and finds solace in, a higher court than the American judicial system.

Elman is always a sympathetic figure. Even after he's brought back to life and sets out to bring retribution to the guilty, he is no monster; he's merely an innocent victim who, through some higher power, has become an instrument of justice. He never actually kills the guilty men; he merely confronts them with their guilt and lets their consciences press them on to their own deaths. This is an important distinction, one that separates him from—and sets him above—his enemies, for he could never intentionally kill as they did, even if in his case it might be justified. (Ewart Adamson and Joseph Field's original story for *The Walking Dead* [dated November 19, 1935] painted Elman in a drastically different light than the gentle being seen in the finished film. According to the original treatment, "Dopey" Elman is "a nervous wreck" due to drug and alcohol addictions. Even worse, after his resurrection, Elman "is a repulsive, vicious thing without the power of speech, which makes one recoil in horror." Thankfully, subsequent script revisions turned this vicious monster into a sensitive man.)

Warner Brothers signed Boris Karloff to a one-picture contract at a princely $3,750 per week. Out of the $217,000 spent on *The Walking Dead*, the actor's salary may very well have been the best $18,700 investment Warners made, for Karloff's performance here is among his best. His pleading at the trial, for instance, is heartbreaking: "You can't kill me for something I didn't do, I tell you—you can't, you can't!" Later, as he's about to be executed, we see his despair turn to bitterness. When the Warden offers him a last request, Karloff's sardonic reply is, "Take away my life and grant me a favor in return—now that's what I call a *bargain*." This momentary rancor is never directed at another person, however; it is simply a result of his unjust circumstance—and it doesn't last long. The actor's natural soft-spoken-ness and humanity shines through his performance, and no animosity or baseness is allowed to creep into the character. A kindness and innate belief in his fellow man shines through Karloff's eyes. Throughout the film Karloff inspires sympathy and the audience is behind him one-hundred percent.

After his miraculous revival from the dead, Elman presents a striking figure: cadaverous cheeks, half-veiled eyes, a streak of white in his hair, his left arm turned up tight at his side. His movements are slow and at first glance he puts forth an image of frailty. At the same time, however, his inexorable advancing gait and determined voice give an impression of strength and undeniable power. Karloff's body language is superb.

The character of Dr. Beaumont is quite fascinating. He is a good man, a kind man, who becomes obsessed with finding the elusive knowledge so far denied Mankind. "Dr. Beaumont has changed," complains Jimmy. "He's forgotten everything we started out to do. All he thinks of now is trying to find out what Elman experienced when he was dead, trying to put his soul under a microscope." Unlike the whiny and unimaginative Jimmy (some scientist!), we can certainly identify with this quest for knowledge, in wanting to *know* for sure, and only wish Dr. Beaumont would work faster in preparing those microscope slides.

Technically, the film is superior as well. The direction is purposeful and effective. There are varied viewpoints within a scene and good use is made of unusual angles and set-ups. In the memorable sequence in which Elman takes the long walk to the electric chair, the camera creates a moving tableau of sadness. In a slightly off-kilter angle we see the shadows of bars on the wall and a slowly rotating fan overhead. The camera moves in as Karloff swallows and raises his head upwards. In a low, soft voice he says, "He'll believe me."

Director Michael Curtiz utilized much of the skill and expertise for *The Walking Dead* that would later bring him such acclaim for classics such as *The Sea Wolf* (1941) and *Casablanca* (1942). Few directors are as adept at drawing their audiences into the action as the Hungarian-born Curtiz. One standout feature in *The Walking Dead* is the varied use of low-key lighting from the side, which effectively highlights the emotional changes in the characters. Curtiz would occasionally shift the lighting emphasis from the side to the front, thus emphasizing a new understanding on the part of a character or underscoring the fear in the faces of Elman's adversaries. An interesting example of these subtle but effective changes in lighting occurs at the climax, when Karloff describes his experience in the heavenly realm. Just as Elman utters his last words, the lighting shifts from the side to the front, illuminating his entire face. This subtle change, combined with a very soft focus, suggests an awareness of a supreme force at work and also conveys a sense that Elman himself has been absolved and can finally rest in peace and wholeness.

Along with Curtiz, much of the credit for the technical superiority of *The Walking Dead* must go to Hal Mohr, the film's ace cinematographer. This highly skilled craftsman, fresh from his Oscar-winning work a year earlier on *A Midsummer Night's Dream* (1935), plays an integral part in the dreamlike visual quality of *The Walking Dead*. Mohr's extensive use of lens focusing as a means of transition is smooth and fluid. In addition, his placement of objects and people in the foreground of the image creates three dimensional images which hold one's visual interest, perfectly complementing the story and actions unfolding onscreen. Mohr's varied use of unusual camera angles is equally outstanding. One fine example (of low angle positioning) occurs as Karloff takes that long walk towards his fated electrocution. The camera is set at such an angle that Karloff appears to be walking at an upward slant, symbolizing his impending ascent to the heavenly beyond. This sequence, which normally could be a very tense and suspenseful moment, is given a very different mood, one that is not at all frightening but more like the feeling of a sad but peaceful passing. Another effective use of camera perspective comes after Karloff is revived from the dead. Now that he has become the instrument of justice, he is photographed exclusively from below, as if he were a deity looking down in judgment. (To 'heighten' the effect even more, Karloff was made four inches taller. "According to prison authorities," reported the film's pressbook, "a man 'grows' an inch or two after taking the 'jolt' in the electric chair. It was necessary to increase Karloff's stature four inches to produce the effect.") Concurrently, the racketeers are usually viewed from a higher camera position so they appear smaller and not as powerful as Elman. All of these cinematic tools, combined with Karloff's ability to evoke sympathy and pathos, contribute to the dramatic impact of these scenes.

LIABILITIES

The Walking Dead did not escape the seemingly obligatory comedy relief. This time it comes in the form of an annoying character named "Betcha," who tries to wager on just about anything (including Elman's conviction). This coarse, unsuccessful comedy is so out of step with the serious, weighty tone of the film that it becomes a jarring intrusion rather than a smooth relief from tension.

Though the script is well-fashioned (the comedy relief notwithstanding), it has one troublesome area. The characters of Jimmy and Nancy (the intended audience identification figures) are too sketchily drawn. We don't really know *why* they didn't come forward until the eleventh hour (other than base cowardice), and their feelings are never fully explored. When they finally do present themselves (too late, of course), it happens in an abrupt way. There is no build-up revealing their change of heart (or acquisition of courage), no scenes of moral torment or conscience wrestling—just bam!, they're suddenly in Dr. Beaumont's office pleading with the doctor to help them stop the execution. In many films, this injudicious use of plot expediency would easily slide by, but *The Walking Dead*'s generally superior level of writing makes the lapse quite noticeable and rather disappointing.

REVIEWS

Variety's "Odec" (March 4, 1936) was unimpressed by this Warner Bros. foray into the realm of the macabre: "Those with a yen for shockers will get limited satisfaction from the story that has been wrapped around Boris Karloff's initial stalking piece under the Warner Bros. banner. The director and the supporting cast try hard to give some semblance of credibility to the trite and pseudo-scientific vaporings[sic] of the writers, but the best they can produce is something that moves swiftly enough but contains little of sustained interest. Karloff will have to be sold on past performances. *The Living Dead* [sic] lets him down badly on opportunities."

Newspaper ad.

Britain's *Kinematograph Weekly* (April 30, 1936) saw some merit in the production, however, calling it a "high voltage melodrama linking gangsterdom with the supernatural through the macabre histrionics of Boris Karloff," and stating that "this picture hands out holding entertainment for the masses, those who never tire at nibbling at the eerie. ...Boris Karloff gives a human and sympathetic performance in the fantastic role of Ellman [sic]; acting ability rather than grotesque make-up invests his portrayal with conviction."

The *New York Times*' Frank S. Nugent (March 2, 1936) noted that "there is no denying that he [Karloff] makes an impressive zombie. With a blaze of white streaking his hair, with sunken mournful eyes, hollow cheeks and a passion for Sindling's 'Rustles of Spring,' Karloff is something to haunt your sleep at nights. We didn't even dare laugh when he sat down to play the piano..." Of the production itself, the only thing the reviewer had to say was that "horror pictures are a staple commodity, and this one was taken from one of the better shelves."

PRODUCTION NOTES

The laboratory equipment featured in *The Walking Dead* was of a more authentic nature than the usual 'Mad Medico' apparatus seen in the films of the time. Several experimental devices in the picture were supposedly based on innovative medical inventions, including the "Lindbergh Heart" (a mechanical circulating system designed by famed flyer Charles A. Lindbergh and Dr. Alexis Carrel) and a motor-controlled, tilting operating table utilized by Dr. Robert E. Cornish in his experiments in the reanimation of dead dogs. According to the film's pressbook, "the studio built a working model [of the Lindberg Heart] from blue-prints sent from the Rockefeller Institute." The pressbook also claimed that "this is the first time either of these reanimating mechanisms have been shown on the screen." Warners' publicity department conveniently forgot about (or simply hadn't seen) Universal's *Life Returns*, released a year earlier, a banal boy-and-his-dog tale built around actual footage of an experiment conducted by Cornish on May 22, 1934, at the University of Southern California.

The sequence which employed these devices—Elman's resurrection scene—was not easy to shoot. According to the pressbook, it took twelve tries before everything went right: "The call for action was heard and the actor played his part. Something went wrong—a light flickered out, necessitating another take. Again and again Karloff rose from the dead only to be told that some important object in the scene was not recorded properly." After eight hours, Curtiz was finally satisfied. Karloff, however, was a bit the worse for wear. After see-sawing up and down for hours on end strapped to the tilting table, the actor could not bring himself to eat his dinner. Worse, he returned later that evening to play a scene "and had to eat, for the benefit of the cameras, six hotdogs smeared with mustard and drink six cups of coffee. He got them down, but they refused to stay."

"*Film Revives Controversy Over Capital Punishment*" read the headline in a *Walking Dead* publicity piece. "*Members of Cast of* The Walking Dead *Divided in Opinion*." According to the article, both Karloff and Barton MacLane were against the Death Penalty, but their enlightened viewpoint was not shared by the remainder of the cast. Henry O'Neill, Marguerite Churchill, Warren Hull, Edmund Gwenn, and Ricardo Cortez were all in favor (though Cortez limited it to men over 45, since "men over 45 haven't a chance to reform"). Director Michael Curtiz was "on the fence," believing "people should not be killed to pay a debt to society unless they have definitely committed a cold blooded, premeditated murder."

Beyond intellectual arguments over capital punishment, Warner Brothers ran into a bit of legal difficulty over *The Walking Dead*. According to *The Hollywood Reporter* (October 3, 1936), a writer by the name of Ferdinand Voteur charged that *The Walking Dead* plagiarized his story "Resurrection Morning." The studio answered that the film's four screenwriters concocted their screenplay from yet another script by Ewart Adamson and Joseph Fields. Nothing further seems to have come of Voteur's accusation.

Ricardo Cortez (born Jacob Krantz) entered films in the 1920s as a potential successor to Rudolph Valentino. In 1925 he appeared opposite Greta Garbo in her first American film, *The Torrent*. Cortez was top-billed in the production, making him the only performer who ever received better billing than the great Garbo in any of her American pictures. When sound came, Cortez successfully changed his 'Latin Lover' image to that of a suave heavy, becoming one of Hollywood's busiest villains (appearing in a total of forty-nine films in the 1930s). While continuing his acting career, he also directed, helming seven features between 1938 and 1940. Sensing that as a director he was fated to remain in the realm of the Bs, he once again concentrated fully on his thespian abilities. Cortez eventually retired from film work and became a stockbroker. His brother, Stanley Cortez, was a successful cinematographer (*The Black Cat*, 1941; *The Magnificent Ambersons*, 1942; *Flesh and Fantasy*, 1943; *Night of the Hunter*, 1951; etc.).

Trained at New York's Professional Children's School and Theatre Guild Drama School, Marguerite Churchill made her Broadway debut at 13. Six years later she made her first film, appearing opposite Paul Muni in *The Valiant* (1929). In 1933 she married cowboy star George O'Brien and retired from pictures. Ms. Churchill resumed her career only a few months prior to the start of *The Walking Dead* (and only a few months *after* the birth of their daughter). She also starred in *Dracula's Daughter* the same year. Marguerite Churchill's cinematic comeback was short-lived, however, for in 1937 she returned to Broadway, making only one more picture (1950's *Bunco Squad*) before retiring to Lisbon, Portugal.

Michael Curtiz directed nearly one hundred films for Warner Brothers, including two previous Golden Age horror classics, *Doctor X* (1932) and *Mystery of the Wax Museum* (1933). Curtiz, an established Warners

'A' director, commanded a hefty $17,660 fee for directing *The Walking Dead*—a salary nearly equal to that of his high-priced star! By all accounts, Curtiz was quite an outspoken character. Warners' publicity department was never slow to play this up: "When Michael Curtiz…saw Karloff for the first time in the ghastly yellow-and-green make-up he uses in portraying a man who's just got out of his grave, he said: 'Swell! Now I'll tell you of another job you can have. Go out and haunt the houses of those tenants of mine who are not paying their rent!'"

The Walking Dead was cinematographer Hal Mohr's only Golden Age horror film, though he photographed two in the 1940s: the lavish 1943 Claude Rains remake of *The Phantom of the Opera* (for which he won an Oscar) and the tepid *Phantom* follow-up, *The Climax* (1944). Mohr also shot such varied classics as *Destry Rides Again* (1939) with Jimmy Stewart, and *The Wild One* (1954) with Marlon Brando. The talented director of photography finished up his illustrious career shooting two low-budget sci-fi features: *Creation of the Humanoids* (1962) and *The Bamboo Saucer* (1968; his final film as cinematographer).

Various clips from *The Walking Dead* popped up in the 1964 Warner Bros. war comedy *Ensign Pulver* (1964), under the guise of "*Young Dr. Jekyll Meets Frankenstein*," a picture being shown on the deck to a crew of discontented sailors "hypnotized by despair."

It was not only the poverty-row outfits that came up with outlandish seat-selling slants for their pictures; even a studio as prestigious as Warner Bros. could generate some downright bizarre suggestions. "Think you can hold a screening at the morgue?" asked *The Walking Dead*'s pressbook. Or how about this angle: "Newspapers have been devoting considerable space to doctors who are conducting experiments on bringing dogs back to life after asphyxiation. If there's a local medico who ever conducted such an experiment or would be likely to try it, hop around to see him and see if he'll cooperate by working it—with proportionate tie-in for film." Imagine: Bring Rover to the Roxy on Friday to be gassed and restored to life at intermission!

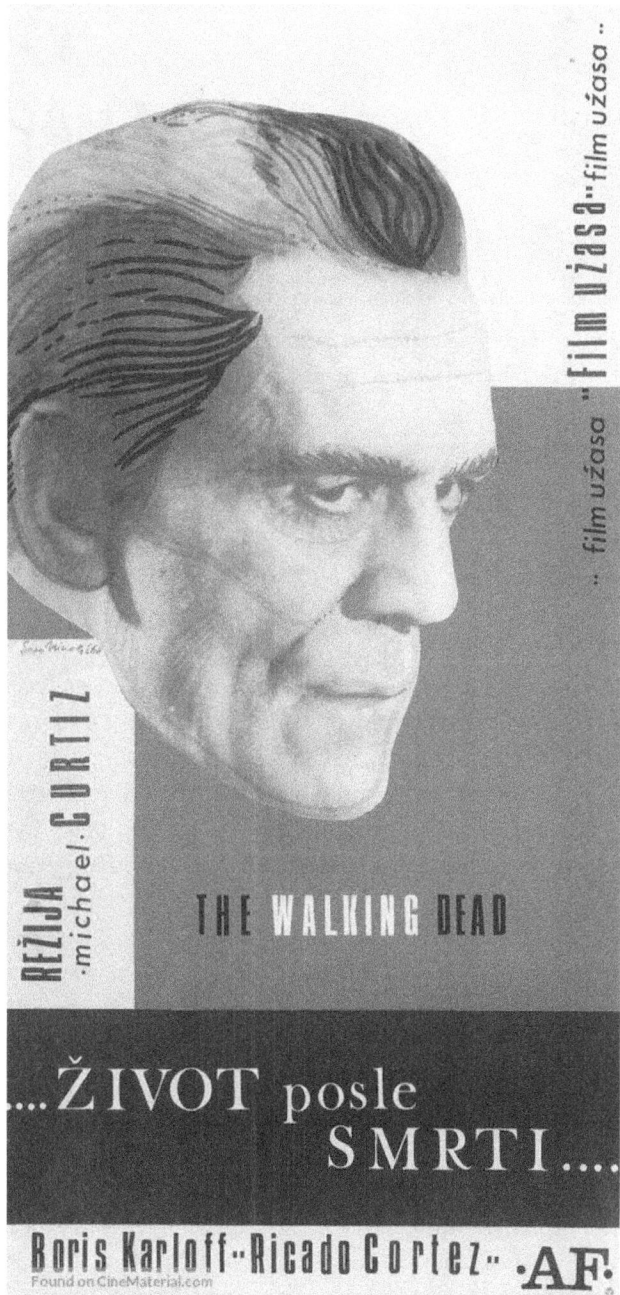

The Walking Dead *(1936) perambulated all over the world, as evidenced by this Swedish poster.*

CHAPTER 4
THE FANTASTIC FIFTIES

> Here's an expanded version of a review first published in *Cult Movies* magazine, issue 24 (December 1997).

BACK FROM THE DEAD (1957)

"Did She Come Back to LOVE or KILL? His First Wife in His Second Wife's Body!" –ad line

Though filmed in the 1950s, *Back from the Dead* feels like something from the previous decade—not in terms of its technical aspects, which are generally adequate (if unspectacular), but in its subject matter and approach. At a time when most genre fare focused on giant insects, alien invaders or teenaged monsters, *Back from the Dead* took a more intimate—and adult—turn (perhaps due to its literary roots, it being based on Catherine Turney's novel *The Other One*, which the author herself adapted for the screen). As one of a group of low-budget (about $125,000) features made by executive producer Robert Lippert, who contracted with 20th Century–Fox to provide cheap black-and-white 'Scope movies to support the studio's bigger pictures, *Back from the Dead* stars Arthur Franz as Dick Anthony, whose new wife Mandy (Peggie Castle) becomes possessed by the spirit of Dick's deceased first wife, Felicia, a practitioner of the black arts. Director Charles Marquis Warren (who also helmed this picture's co-feature) cleverly builds upon and exploits this intriguing concept by having Mandy startle Dick with things only Felicia would know, wearing a different (and shocking) style of wardrobe, and eventually setting out to commit murder to obtain what she wants (permanent possession of Mandy's body).

According to story editor Harry Spalding, director Warren was personally unimpressed with veteran novelist/scripter Turney (*Of Human Bondage* [1946], *No Man of Her Own* [1950]). "I remember…Warren and his sardonic sense of humor," recalled Spalding to interviewer Tom Weaver. "He was not a man who loved everybody, and he particularly didn't like lady writers with convertibles and huge dogs in the back seat—which is the way Catherine Turney arrived at Lucey's, a restaurant across from Paramount, where we met to discuss the script. This lady loved her dog and worried about it and brought it over with her. Halfway through this meeting, there was a problem involving a dog in the script [Mandy's dog, which suddenly bristles at his now-possessed owner]. I made some suggestions. [Producer Robert] Stabler made some suggestions—and Warren settled it: 'Why don't we just *kill* the dog?' Catherine *blanched*—but killed the dog anyway!"

Fifties genre stalwart Arthur Franz makes the most of his role as the beleaguered husband, going through the various stages of confusion, fear, and anger in a convincingly human manner. Though no bigger in scale than most of his other horror/sci-fi outings (*Abbott and Costello Meet the Invisible Man* [1951], *Flight to Mars* [1951], *Invaders from Mars* [1953], *The Flame Barrier* [1958], *The Atomic Submarine* [1959]), *Back from the Dead* offered the often frustrated Franz (he reportedly balked at the many one-dimensional supporting roles he found himself playing) a far grander challenge, acting-wise. He rose to the occasion to enact the more mature and well-rounded role with an assured turn as the horrified and desperate husband. For instance, when Felicia/Mandy, clad in a seductive nightgown, makes a play for him, Franz' look of confused attraction mixed with determined disgust speaks volumes.

After serving as an Air Force navigator during WWII (and spending time in a POW camp, from which he escaped), Arthur "Turo" Franz broke into film in 1948. Though he made periodic appearances on the Silver Screen for the next three decades (usually in secondary roles in bigger films or leads in smaller ones), television paid the bills, as he guested regularly on the small screen right from the medium's infancy, appearing on such early shows as *The Lone Ranger*, *Studio One* and *Kraft Television Theatre*. For the next quarter-century Franz became a familiar face (if not a household name) by riding the cathode ray into millions of homes in everything from *Gunsmoke*, *Bonanza*, and *Perry Mason* to *Voyage to the Bottom of the Sea*, *Mission Impossible* and

This publicity shot makes one happy indeed that Peggie Castle came Back from the Dead *in 1957.*

The Waltons. Franz died in 2006 at the age of 86 from emphysema and heart disease.

Alongside Franz, Peggie Castle (*Invasion USA* [1952], *Beginning of the End* [1957]) does equally well in her dual role, smoothly transforming from the sweet, likable wife to the conniving, self-centered and beguiling siren. The craggy coastline setting and brooding narration (the film opens with a woman's voice intoning, "Before I knew about this house and what went on inside those dark walls, I refused to believe that such things existed...") sets a melancholy tone and effectively creates a feeling of impending doom and inescapable disaster. Director Warren periodically closes a scene with a shot of the nearby pounding surf (into which Felicia had plunged to her death), utilizing the setting as a pointed symbol of unstoppable forces and malevolent intent.

Unfortunately, after its moody first-half buildup, *Back from the Dead* backs itself into a corner, thanks to its small-scale production and poorly-constructed script, which offers only a cheap Satanic ritual, some halfhearted black magic mumbo-jumbo and a decidedly anticlimactic climax in which Dick and his friend simply overpower the sinister Satanist (there's only one, apart from Felicia/Mandy), resulting in Mandy's abrupt recovery. Consequently, like February 29 (Arthur Franz's birthday), *Back from the Dead* remains an atypical but not-overly-noteworthy footnote on the (cinematic) calendar.

> This piece on the unique science fiction film *Colossus of New York* appeared in the short-lived *SPFX Special Effects Magazine* in 1999 (number eight of a ten-issue run).

THE COLOSSUS OF NEW YORK (1958)

"Towering above the Manhattan skyline, raining death and destruction!" –radio spot

Far from your typical 1950s sci-fi confection, *The Colossus of New York* is a serious, sober (and near-depressing) look at the dehumanizing effects of mechanization and alienation—taken to the absurd lengths that only B-movie Hollywood can go.

Ross Martin (of TV's *Wild, Wild West* fame) plays Dr. Jeremy Spensser, a modern-day scientific genius and loving family man whose work on world hunger has just earned him an "International Peace Prize." Tragically, Jeremy's future contributions to humanity are literally stopped dead in their tracks by a speeding Mac truck. Spensser's father (Otto Kruger, star of *Dracula's Daughter* [1936], *Jungle Captive* [1945] and *The Woman Who Came Back* [1945]), the world's preeminent brain surgeon, secretly removes his son's brain from his dying body and keeps it alive in a tank, then presses into service his *other* son, Henry (John Baragrey), an expert in mechanical automation. Henry constructs a giant metallic body for his sibling's brilliant brain, and Dad pops it in. Understandably, the now-mechanized Jeremy is less-than-pleased with these developments. As time progresses, Jeremy (or at least his brain) continues his important research in Dad's secret lab. No longer able to share human contact (physical or emotional), this mechanical Colossus develops extra sensory powers—including a hypnotic gaze and death rays that shoot from its eyes(!). Finally losing his last vestige of humanity altogether, the Colossus runs amuck at the United Nations building, striking down delegates and innocent bystanders right and left with his laser beam–gaze.

Thematically, *Colossus* indeed lives up to its name, for rather than focusing on some nebulous moral lesson disguised as a marauding menace (such as nuclear

The imposing Colossus of New York *(1958) stalks the city streets.*

testing spawning a giant insect, dinosaur or what-have-you) or exploiting an audience's xenophobia (via invading aliens), *The Colossus of New York* explores the more intimate and personally relevant horror of separation and alienation (though admittedly to the Nth degree). Such a personalized concept helped make *The Incredible Shrinking Man* (1957) one of the more profound pieces of celluloid science fiction from the 1950s.

While *Colossus* has its merits, it unfortunately falls well short of that earlier classic, and ends on a disastrously downbeat note rather than the enigmatic yet somehow uplifting tone of *The Incredible Shrinking Man*. Beginning with a senseless tragedy (the needless accidental death of a great man) and ending with still more pointless death, it seems an exceedingly grim way to learn that "the human mind, divorced from the sense of pain and mortality, would lose all decency and compassion" (as the film's pressbook phrased it).

Production-wise, the seams show through at times, such as when the same shot of the Colossus tramping across the bottom of the East River (a poor effect to begin with as the actor walks across a sound stage in slow motion while a cheesy superimposition produces a watery effect) is repeated twice. Poor rear-screen projection and periodically over-cranked photography of the Colossus (which creates a silent film–like, herky-jerky motion) go a long way toward dispelling the illusion of reality.

Fortunately, the Charles Gemora–designed Colossus looks impressive enough, with its bald dome, angular metallic features and huge frame (draped in a decidedly impractical yet visually impressive Romanesque cloak). 7-feet, 4-inch Ed Wolff played the Colossus, with Ross Martin's mechanized voice emanating from its mouth. Wolff began his cinematic career way back in 1925 when he played the leader of a mob that cornered Lon Chaney's Phantom of the Opera. Wolff also appeared in (among many other films) the 1936 *Flash Gordon* serial (inside a dragon costume) and 1959's *Return of the Fly* (wearing a giant fly head). The Colossus costume stood nine feet tall and weighed 160 pounds, and it took 40 minutes to get Wolff into the outfit. Between takes the beleaguered actor could only rest by reclining on the specially-built rack seen in the film. It's no wonder that "Ed Wolff was kind of moody" (as Martin related).

The then-relatively-unknown Ross Martin, who only made six films over the course of his career, joined the cast on the recommendation of screenwriter Thelma Schnee. Though onscreen for very little time, Martin's warm and enthusiastic portrayal added immeasurably to the poignancy of the scenario. And his mechanized voice in the initial Colossus scenes carries a pathos both heartbreaking and chilling. "The script said that [my character] was to be played as 'intellectually brilliant,'" remembered the actor shortly before his death in 1981 to *Filmfax*'s Al Taylor. "But that was not my major concern. Instead I played him as a warm and complete human being so his death would matter all the more." A consummate professional, Martin went a little too far in one scene. For the funeral sequence, Martin had to lie perfectly motionless in a satin-lined coffin. He held still so well and for so long that he fell asleep! "At one point during the filming, the members present were treated to the sound of a dead man snoring!"

Back in 1958, *The Colossus of New York* was released on a double bill with Jack Arnold's *The Space Children* (another unusually thoughtful sci-fi specimen). Paramount suggested as a publicity stunt that men six-foot-five or taller be given free admission! A grim and humorless film (seat-selling slants aside), *The Colossus of New York* may provide some food for thought, but one may need to approach this cinematic snack with a handful of anti-depressants at the ready.

> *The Fantastic Fifties* magazine took aim at this horror-western hybrid in their Summer 2020 issue (number 11).

FIENDS WHO WALKED THE WEST: *CURSE OF THE UNDEAD* (1959)

"HIS BODY IS AN EMPTY SHELL THAT HIDES A LUSTFUL FIEND!" –tagline

Curse of the Undead (like many things in life) began as a joke. "My wife and I were sitting around doing nothing," explained writer-director Edward Dein to interviewers Tom Weaver and Michael Brunas, "and one day she said let's do a little writing, just for practice. So I dove into the pool and came up with the craziest title in the world, *Eat Me Gently*, a Western horror story about a fag vampire running around the desert eating little boys. We wrote it as a screenplay; it must have taken about two weeks. We had a lot of fun with it. We had mimeographed copies made with red covers with thick letters which said '*Eat Me Gently*.' We decided to hand these copies around to our friends for laughs." One of those copies got into the hands of producer Joseph Gershenson, who told Dein, "I want to make this picture [but] I don't like your title. We are changing it to *Curse of the Undead*.' So, we had Michael Pate play it straight and this became a legitimate vampire picture." It also became a legitimate contender for Best Horror Western—an admittedly impoverished subset.

Black-clad gunfighter Drake Robey (Michael Pate) arrives in a small Western town beset by the usual ranchers' conflict. Local cattle baron Buffer (Bruce Gordon) wants the neighboring ranchland owned by kindly Doc Carter, resulting in his hired thugs smashing fences, diverting water, and stealing cattle. The tense situation goes from bad to worse when Robey, a vampire, arrives and begins draining the local girls of their blood. He also attacks and kills Doc Carter, driving the doctor's son Tim (Jimmy Murphy), thinking his rival responsible, to draw down on Buffer. With Tim now dead as well, the ranch goes to the doc's daughter, Delores (Kathleen Crowley), fiancée of local preacher Dan Young (Eric Fleming). But when Robey sets his lustful undead sights on Delores, Dan must uncover the truth about the gunslinger and find a way to stop the seemingly invincible vampire.

Dressing up a standard B-Western plot with Gothic trappings (including funeral coaches, shadowy nocturnal visitations, and an atmospheric graveyard set right out of a classic Universal horror) proved inspired. And the clever notion of a vampire making a "living" as a gunfighter (since bullets won't harm him, he need never worry about facing somebody faster) is worth the price of admission alone. In several quick-draw shootouts Robey proves slower than his opponent but still wins the showdown, leaving his antagonist dead. Such a transposition of the unearthly onto the mundane only enhances the scenario's otherworldly feel.

Director Dein, working with veteran cinematographer Ellis Carter (*The Incredible Shrinking Man*), creates a number of impressive sequences, foremost among them a suspenseful scene in which the preacher walks through the town on a full-moon night stalked by a shadow moving against the adobe walls. Thoroughly

Half-sheet poster for one of the better horror-western hybrids.

spooked by the sounds of pursuing footsteps, Dan dashes to the church, turning at the door to see Robey running at him—before stopping dead when caught in the shadow of a cross thrown from the crucifix atop the building, causing Robey to cringe and writhe in pain. Following a quick cut to a bewildered Dan, the dusty street is now empty. Robey has fled.

"Eddie [Dein] was an *amazing* character," remembered Australian actor Michael Pate (*The Strange Door*, *The Maze*, *Tower of London*) to Weaver. "He lived up in the hills just above Laurel Canyon with his wife Mildred, who was a real sweetheart (the *two* of them were), in an old castle with a moat and a drawbridge that you drove over to get inside the entrance courtyard. ...I got along tremendously well with Eddie, there was no bullshit about him, and we got through the filming of that picture pretty fast."

Writer-director Dein got his start as a screenwriter at Universal, penning such torpid thrillers as *Calling Dr. Death* (1943), *Jungle Woman* (1944) and *The Cat Creeps* (1946). On the up-side, he also wrote the unusually thoughtful *Soul of a Monster* (1944) and contributed to the Val Lewton horror *The Leopard Man* in 1943. Dein directed a handful of films beginning in 1952, but made his living in television, working on such shows as *Hawaiian Eye*, *The Wild Wild West* and *Black Sheep Squadron*. For Universal, he shot *Curse of the Undead* in December 1959, then immediately made (the lesser) *The Leech Woman* the following month (Universal sat on *The Leech Woman* for a year and a half before finally releasing it on a double-bill with *The Brides of Dracula*).

Dein and his wife Mildred's *Curse* script offers some deeper subtext than most simple Saturday afternoon horror movies (or Westerns, for that matter). When Robey warns the preacher to stop his inquiries, Dan answers, "If that's a threat it has no sting; I'm not afraid of dying." At his Robey retorts, "Most religious fanatics aren't—but how they struggle when that last moment arrives."

Rather than a simple soulless monster, Pate's vampire displays both a sensuality and ambivalence that suggests far more depth than just demonic evil. When Robey "attacks" his sleeping female victims, he kisses their lips and sensuously caresses their cheek with his mouth before moving to their necks to finally drain their blood. It's an erotically-charged, almost tender act that would do even Christopher Lee proud. At one point Robey explains about his profession as a hired killer: "Before I take a job I investigate thoroughly. You see, money's not enough. I must carry my client's anger in me. That's the way it helps me to justify my actions." It's an unexpectedly philosophical point coming from a bloodthirsty vampire (and hired assassin). And towards the end, after Dan has discovered Robey's horrific secret and denounces him as a monster, Robey angrily answers, "What I am is not my own choice! You should pity me and not judge me in my torment." Pate's angry yet tinged-with-sadness delivery hammers home the tragedy of the character as he concludes, "You think I wanted this?!" "I enjoyed [my role] very much," remembered Pate. "I thought the film went well, for what it was. It was stylized, it had good set design, very good lighting, it was photographed well."

Not everything makes this a *Curse* worth invoking, however. The obvious budget restraints hold things to a decidedly small scale, with characters simply *talking* about cattle thieving or having taken a beating. The action is confined to a few (admittedly well-dressed and authentic-looking) sets and one dusty main street exterior. The showdown climax sees Robey lying on the ground, dead, when suddenly his face and hands fade away and disappear (with a wavy special effect obfuscating the action) as his clothes deflate. "It was very cheap and we did it with dissolves," commented Dein on this disappointingly simple denouement. "Otherwise the special effects department would have to spend thousands of dollars."

And while generally well-acted, a thespian fly in the ointment comes in the form of the large and imposing, but stiff and humorless, Eric Fleming (who gained fame starring on TV's *Rawhide*) as Preacher Dan. As noted by co-star Pate, "Eric was a very well-meaning actor/person and worked very hard, but he was inclined to be a little dour." This certainly shows through in his portrayal, which sees him too often "preachifying," rather than simply speaking, for his character to be wholly realistic. (Tragically, Fleming drowned while filming a TV movie in Peru in 1966 when a canoe he was paddling on a river capsized. He was 41.)

Still, the film manages to sidestep its shortcomings and stand tall as a unique and atmospheric horror entry that made a fitting companion to Hammer's *The Mummy*. That's right, *The Mummy*(!), for in America, Universal released *Curse* on a double bill with that Hammer classic (advertising the duo as "TWICE THE SCREAMING TERROR ON ONE DOUBLE-THRILL SHOW!"). Though on the surface this seems an odd match (color British Gothic and black-and-white American Western), the two share surprisingly similar sensibilities, as well as the central premise of a supernatural horror plaguing a small town. *And* they're both simply good pictures.

In their pressbook, Universal urged theater exhibitors to emphasize the film's sagebrush sensibilities with a "WANTED POSTER" gimmick—"especially eye-catching if they appear in your cooperating merchants' windows. Combine Western flavor with mysterious horror—silhouetting face and figure of wanted character on board—with theatre and playdate." The ballyhoo boys went that extra (ludicrous) mile, however, when they noted that "Millions of people are still buying tranquillizer pills to calm their nerves and ease tension. Arrange window displays or/and counter cards in drug stores, tying in with these products. Use a tie-up card reading: 'Get a supply of these pills to calm your nerves before seeing the terrifying drama CURSE OF THE UNDEAD at the _____ Theatre!'"

Perhaps such a vampires-and-valium approach wasn't so ridiculous after all, since, as Dein observed, "*Curse of the Undead* got a lot of publicity and made quite a bit of money for the studio. For a small picture, it was excellent." Indeed it was.

> With their fifth issue (summer 2018), *The Fantastic Fifties* magazine allowed me to view—and present—this groundbreaking French classic with (ahem) new eyes.

FRENCH FRIGHTS: *EYES WITHOUT A FACE* (1959)

As frightening as anything you will ever see on a motion picture screen. –American trailer

Most critics consider 1959 the greatest single year in the history of French film. That year ushered in the *Nouvelle Vague*, and saw the release of recognized classics like Jean-Luc Godard's *Breathless*, Francois Truffaut's *The 400 Blows*, Alain Resnais' *Hiroshima, Mon Amour*, and Claude Chabrol's *Les Cousins*. Georges Franju's *Les Yeux sans Visage* (*Eyes Without a Face*) also belongs on the short list of France's 1959 masterworks—though it took years for film critics and historians to recognize it.

During its initial release, *Eyes Without a Face* (shot in eight weeks on a "not inexpensive medium-sized" budget) quickly grew notorious for its stomach-churning gore. According to Raymond Durgnat in his book *Franju*, when the film "was presented in the Film Festival at Edinburgh ... seven people fainted, and public and press were outraged. Franju didn't improve matters by saying that now he knew why Scotsmen wore skirts." Zing! Indeed, the film's British posters proclaimed that "BEAUTIFUL WOMEN WERE THE VICTIM OF HIS *FIENDISH FACIALS*!!!" reflecting a more, shall we say, innocent time. Unfortunate verbiage aside, it's no wonder ads played up the infamous face-removal footage, for this surely stands out as one of the most memorable and clinically gruesome scenes of the decade. London's *Daily Express* critic John Braine headlined his January 29, 1960, review "This One Is Revolting" and complained that "Someone had the idea of making a horror film even nastier than anything Hammer Films could do; and they succeeded." Only the second full-length feature by filmmaker Georges Franju, who'd made a handful of shorts and documentaries (including 1949's *Blood of the Beasts* about a Paris slaughterhouse—because "this is the realm of violence and poetry" as he explained to *Video Watchdog*'s Alain Schlockoff), with *Eyes* most critics felt Franju had returned to his slaughterhouse roots. But this enigmatic, thoughtful, and poetic tale of a father's obsession with restoring his daughter's ruined visage is so much more than a shuddery surgical sequence.

From the opening credits unspooling over shots of nighttime countryside whizzing by, the starkly-lit trees almost spectral against the inky blackness, as Maurice Jarre's jaunty, carnival-like theme plays incongruously on the soundtrack, you know this is not going to be the typical Eurohorror import. It begins as Louise (Alida Valli), assistant to the esteemed Dr. Genessier (Pierre Brasseur), dumps the body of a young woman into the Seine. When they find the body, police are aghast to discover the victim's face literally peeled from her head. Genessier, we soon learn, has undertaken a series of secret medical experiments to try to restore the ruined face of his daughter Christiane (Edith Scob), disfigured in a car crash. After Louise helps Genessier trap another victim, Edna (Juliette Mayniel), comes the film's most notorious scene: Genessier performing a grotesque "face lift" operation on Edna, using a scalpel and forceps to remove the skin from the still-living patient's face. Genessier labors with medical precision and without emotion. Franju documents every step of the procedure in sickening detail and icy clinical detachment, the matter-of-fact presentation serving to make the sequence that much more difficult to watch.

Franju recognized this scene's importance to the picture's tone. "The whole film hinges on that one scene, doesn't it?" he admitted to Schlockoff. "The operation, the mask, the decomposing mask." Franju realized, however, that he couldn't go *too* far with the gruesome realism of this tension-filled, squirm-inducing central sequence. "But we cut when the scalpel reaches the crayon lines around the eyes. Originally, the eyes came off with all the rest, but that shot, with the scalpel running around the eyes, was just... *terrifying*! ...I shot it but cut it out—except for the Japanese version."

Christiane, for most of the film, wears a mask Genessier has crafted in the likeness of her own, lost face. The expressionless mask lends her the unsettling appearance of an animated mannequin. Briefly, it seems that her father's treatment has succeeded, but Christiane's body soon rejects the skin graft from Edna's face, and the cycle must begin again. Franju presents the grotesque deterioration of Christiane's face in a series of ever-more-gruesome clinical photographs, accompanied by deadpan voiceover from Brasseur.

In the end, Christiane turns on her would-be benefactors, frees her father's next intended victim, and sets loose his experimental dogs and doves. In a shocking conclusion that recalls the classic *Island of Lost Souls* (1932), the dogs, snarling and barking, fatally maul Genessier. After an ironic shot of her father's prone form that reveals *his* face now mutilated beyond repair, Franju's camera follows Christiane as she wanders off, ghost-like, into the night while the freed doves flap and flutter around her.

When Franju first met with producer Jules Borkon about the project, "He asked me to make a true horror film," recalled Franju. "But he did not want any trouble with the censors—or his distributor! ...He didn't want dogs tortured with scalpels either, because the Brits love animals so much. He didn't want too much blood, because he was afraid the film could be rated this or that. And he did not want a mad doctor—the Germans had asked him to avoid that because it could evoke the 'medical experiments' conducted in concentration camps." The result: one disturbing dog surgery scene; one gory, blood-soaked face-removal sequence; and one coldly clinical mad medico at the story's center, as Franju chose to blithely ignore his producer's pleadings.

Franju also declined to make "a true horror film"—at least in the director's own eyes, since he didn't consider it a horror movie at all. "It's an anguish film," said Franju. "It's a quieter mood than horror, something more subjacent, more internal, more penetrating. It's horror in homeopathic doses."

Like Franju, 21-year-old female lead Edith Scob (in her first major role) didn't consider the picture horror either. "I feel it's a *fantastique* film," the actress told Frédéric Albert Lévy and Tim Lucas in *Video Watchdog* 107. "Horror films present another kind of violence. There is actually something poetic in *Eyes*, which makes it much richer."

Scob, spending nearly the whole of the film with her face behind an impassive mask, has the difficult task of acting only with her eyes and body language. "My face frightens me," Christiane says at one point, "my mask frightens me even more." Scob's large, luminous eyes behind her mask's eerie, unmoving blankness convey a haunted questioning, while she moves almost wraith-like in her floor-length tafetta robe. Her placid, otherworldly appearance is shattered only once over the course of the film—horrifically so—when we finally see her without her mask. Yet this vision of horror (with Georges Klein's gruesome makeup reminiscent of Lionel Atwill's twisted, burned visage from *Mystery of the Wax Museum*) comes only from a victim's point-of-view, awakening from an anesthetic sleep. Like the drugged girl's vision, Franju keeps the camera deliberately unfocused, the haziness of the image, combined with the low-key lighting as Christiane steps forward out of the shadows, providing just enough to allow the viewer's own imagination to fill in the grotesque details.

Making the film was often a lonely experience for Scob. "Wearing a mask all day long makes you a *thing*, with no expression," noted the actress. "You are put aside [like an object]. ...With my mask on most of the day, I was extremely isolated. ...There is only one sequence where I don't wear a mask. So I guess you could say I was isolated, just like my character was."

Still, it wasn't an unpleasant experience. "[Franju] had very precise images in his head," continued Scob, "and we had to get into his head. He always wanted to turn me into a sublime being, so I was constantly protected 'til the end of the shooting."

In a publicity article for the film's American pressbook, purportedly penned by Franju himself, the filmmaker stated, "I was very gratified that almost all of the film critics found my film...had *a touch of poetry*. It is my firm conviction that the modern 'horror film,' though fiction, must be plausible."

To attain such plausibility, Franju focused on realism. "I am a realist through the necessity of things," the director explained in Georges Sadoul's *Dictionary of Film Makers*. "An image on the screen has an immediate presence. It is perceived as if it were actual. Whatever one does, a film is always in the present tense. Past time is spontaneously made actual by the spectator. That is why what is artificial ages badly and quickly. Dream, poetry, the unknown must all emerge out of reality itself. The whole of cinema is documentary, even the most poetic. What pleases is what is terrible, gentle, and poetic."

The poetical Gallic horror Eyes Without a Face *(1959) suffered the indignities of a ridiculous title change and being paired with the ludicrous* The Manster *when it arrived in America. Here Christiane (Edith Scob) seeks respite from her nightmare existence with a canine friend.*

Completing Franju's determination to keep it real (so to speak) are the characterizations themselves. "Dr. Génessier would not be a Caligari, a Jekyll, a Mabuse, or any horror film doctor cliché," Franju told Schlock-off, "he would be a normal man. Because an abnormal man behaving abnormally is something fairly normal, while a normal man behaving abnormally is actually abnormal and far more disturbing. In the first case, our character belonged to the usual kind of *fantastique*; in the second, he'd belong to the Uncanny. And I'm only interested in the Uncanny—because I am afraid of it. And why? Because I *believe* in it!"

In the standard mad medico scenario, the doctor would be a self-absorbed, amoral megalomaniac prone to bombastic speechifying; and the reluctant patient a whitewashed wallflower cringing at every opportunity. But Genessier and Christiane are far more complex than that. He is not simply driven by the love of his daughter (and the guilt he feels over having caused the fateful crash), nor just by an obsessive hubris in his work (he talks more fearfully of "failure" in his experiments than of his daughter's plight), it's a convoluted combination of both. And Christiane, while seeking release from her prison of ugliness (even covetously caressing the face of an unconsious "donor"), at the same time voices her objection at being her father's "human guinea pig," as well as bitterly noting of her father: "He always has to dominate, even on the road; he was driving like a demon" (leading to the crash that ruined her life).

This conflicted, shades-of-gray internal complexity extends to the relationships with those around them as well. While Louise, trapped by her own overwhelming gratitude to the doctor for restoring *her* face, appears almost worshipful in her devotion, Genessier's treatment of her runs the gamut from a callous literal slap to the face (when Louise exhibits too much nervousness at their nefarious activities) to a gentle caress after she proudly shows him how her scars have all but disappeared. After it appears the latest face-grafting operation has been successful (during the brief period before Christiane's new face begins to decay), Genessier urges Christiane at dinner to "Smile..." before adding, "not too much," reminding her that her new face is not fully healed—and not her own. For these characters, the dark is never far behind the light.

Of course, along with the complex character development and general air of poetic horror comes a sometime languorous pace, with Christiane's former fiancé's suspicions and the involvement of the local police eating up time but accomplishing little. And Franju seemingly abandons his pledge to realism when Christiane finally rebels and stabs Louise in the throat with a scalpel (whose business end is a mere inch long). Despite the obvious non-life-threating nature of the wound (no artery was hit, given the tiny trickle of blood seeping from beneath the protruding blade), Louise expires almost immediately. Heart failure?

But these minor quibbles fade into insignificance against the emotional—and visual—power of the film's climax—one of the most unusual, poignant, and strangely beautiful in the entire horror genre, as Christiane achieves her symbolic freedom not through the clinically cold efforts of her father's restorative surgery but through the reclaiming of her own humanity—though at a violent cost filled with loss. (According to Scob, "at one point, [writers] Boileau and Narcejac considered having Brasseur or me fall into a vat of cement, but Franju preferred the ending to be more dreamlike.") What made it onscreen is indeed a remarkable end to a remarkable film.

"Franju never explained to me the meaning of these doves [at film's end]," said Scob of the enigmatic closing shot. "But, speaking for myself, it is Picasso's Peace Dove. ...It's the air, it's the sky, it's an open image of beauty."

Said Franju, "The lady with a dove. Is she crazy, or isn't she? She no longer belongs to our world. She sort of refuses misery and torture. She doesn't find refuge in the unreal, but in a reality that is no longer ours."

Critical disdain aside (fortunately, time has corrected the initial misperceptions, and *Eyes Without a Face* has taken its rightful place alongside the likes of *Diabolique* as a groundbreaking French classic), the worst insult the film suffered came when United Artists subsidiary Lopert Pictures finally released the film in America in 1962, incongruously retitling it *The Horror Chamber of Dr. Faustus* and pairing it on a double bill with the polar-opposite *The Manster* (a 1940s-style throwback about a two-headed monster). The poetry-in-horror that is *Eyes Without a Face*, like the ethereal Christiane herself, deserved better.

> Here's another essay I wrote (on a pair of favorites) that never saw the light of day. Sigh...

OF FIENDS AND MEN: *FIEND WITHOUT A FACE* (1958) AND *FIRST MAN INTO SPACE* (1959)

So what do a bunch of atomic-powered, thought-created ambulatory brains and a meteor-encrusted, blood-sucking astronaut-turned-monster have in common? Well, apart from them both being black-and-white horror/sci-fi features from the Fantastic Fifties, they were both British productions set in North America. Additionally, both feature science-spawned monsters marauding through the countryside to suck the life from anyone who crosses their path (the First Man desperately seeks human blood, while the Faceless Fiends devour the entire brain), with American leading man Marshall Thompson hot on their trails. What's more, both were shepherded onto the screen (and into horror lovers' hearts) by genre-loving executive producer Richard Gordon under his Producers Associates banner. Gordon, an American based in England, was responsible for putting together production packages for such well-respected genre features as the two Boris Karloff vehicles *The Haunted Strangler* and *Corridors of Blood* (both 1958), the underrated Peter Cushing starrer *Island of Terror* (1966), and a cadre of 'lesser' horrors that include *Devil Doll* (1964), *Curse of the Voodoo* (1965), *The Projected Man* (1966), *Naked Evil* (1966), *Tower of Evil* (1972), *Horror Hospital* (1973), and *Inseminoid* (1981).

"MAD SCIENCE SPAWNS EVIL FIENDS!" –*Fiend Without a Face* tagline

In their book *The Great Science Fiction Pictures II*, authors James Robert Parish and Michael R. Pitts called *Fiend Without a Face* 'one of the most underrated sci-fi fright films of the 1950s' which possessed 'some of the most frightening monsters ever to populate a genre outing.' *Fangoria* magazine (May 1985 issue) labeled it 'one of the classics of low-budget sci-fi/horror from the '50s' which offered 'a slam-bang, gory finale to be cherished by horror fans everywhere.' Obviously, these *Fiends* have felt the love. And rightly so, since *Fiend*

Fiend Without a Face poster.

Without a Face remains a 1950s creature feature that's not only clever and strikingly original, but unforgettable—at least in its last ten minutes. Unfortunately, it does take a bit to get there...

At the 'U.S. Air Force Interceptor Command Experimental Station' in Manitoba, Canada, Major Jeff Cummings (Marshall Thompson, giving his usual likable stalwart hero performance) oversees experiments using their atomic reactor(!) to boost radar range. But mysterious power drains hamper the work, while at the same time a series of gruesome killings—in which the victims' brains have been sucked out(!)—plague the small town nearby. Cummings' investigation leads to the eccentric and reclusive Professor Walgate (Kynaston Reeves) and his experiments in "the materialization of thought." Devising a machine to hijack some of the base's atomic power, Walgate has succeeded in creating "a being into which the thought, once released, could enter and preserve itself for all humanity. I envisaged something akin to the human brain, with life and mobility." Unfortunately, said beings turned out to be "mental vampires"—in the form of invisible disembodied brains that need both atomic power and human brains to survive(!!).

Fiend was born when literary agent (and lifelong sci-fi fan) Forrest J Ackerman brought his client Amelia Reynolds Long's short story "The Thought Monster" to AIP. (The story first appeared in the March 1930 issue of *Weird Tales*.) When AIP heads Sam Arkoff and Jim Nicholson demurred, frequent AIP producer Alex Gordon passed the project along to his brother Richard in England, who set up the production there.

In the original story, the (single) thought monster remains invisible throughout, but that simply wouldn't do in a horror flick, so Gordon and producer John Croydon met with and hired Baron Florenz von Nordhoff ('Flo' to his friends) to create the fiends (plural—as dozens lay siege to the protagonists by film's end). An Austrian artist and special effects technician (as well as genuine blue-blood), Nordhoff partnered with artist Karl-Ludwig Ruppel to engineer the impressive stop-motion animation effects. "Flo is a strange, likable man," recalled Croydon in *Fangoria* magazine, "a little crazy as his features and behavior suggested, with a penchant for eating vases of tulips when in his cups." Fortunately, Nordhoff remained stone-cold sober during the three weeks of "two frames per action motion-control" effects work ("it took approximately one full day to achieve one [fiend] death," noted Croydon).

Nordhoff and Ruppel shot the effects in Munich, with raspberry jam (made by Frau Nordhoff) standing in for the gore during the fiends' demise. "Liberally spread on carpet, furniture and walls," enthused Croydon, "in black-and-white photography [it was] an excellent substitute for blood." Indeed it was, particularly when augmented by the gruesome, repulsive, and oh-so-effective sound effects provided by technicians Peter Davies and Terence Poulton. For the film's first hour, in fact, it's primarily these audio outbursts (complete with a rhythmic, thumping heartbeat overlaid on what sounds like a cross between a strong wind and noisy slurpings) that represent the invisible creatures' presence. A few simple visual effects of parting bushes and moving straw, or the occasional spilled bucket of dirty water (through which a path is dragged by the invisible creatures via some convincing stop-motion animation) cements the illusion.

Croydon gives full credit to Nordhoff and Ruppel's work, "not only for the birth of the Fiend Without a Face but also their brilliance in the solution of its life and death that still manages to horrify, yet entertain, TV and cinema audiences, despite the censors" (in England cuts were made "to reduce the amount of blood," while Ireland banned the film outright).

Director Arthur Crabtree and cinematographer Lionel Banes don't neglect the more mundane matters, either. For instance, low-key lighting casts ominous shadows on the wall as the coroner delivers his autopsy findings, noting "The brain—it's gone...sucked out like an egg through those two holes." At this, Cummings pipes in with "Sounds like a mental vampire." Though far from subtle, the lighting (and dialogue) adds creepy atmosphere to a simple exposition scene.

Of course, much like the victims' inability to avoid the unseen fiends, the film can't quite escape the myriad time-filling episodes that frequently plague pictures of its ilk. Adding to the plentiful stock footage of radar dishes, flying jets, and dubbed-in pilot palaver is its mystery structure, as the plot follows Cummings' investigation into the inexplicable killings (as well as his low-key romantic pursuit of Barbara, the professor's plucky secretary). This culminates in an overlong interlude that sees Jeff locked inside the local mausoleum and nearly suffocating (the logic of which appears less likely than the creation of invisible thought monsters).

Fortunately, the characters—and actors—are more likable than most, while the periodic invisible stalking sequence keeps the viewer involved in the story until the gonzo final reel, when all *Fiend*ish hell breaks loose. These final dozen minutes become a horrific siege scenario—a full decade before *Night of the Living Dead* codified this horror movie trope. As the killer brains attack, the protagonists barricade themselves inside Walgate's house, boarding up windows and blocking doors with heavy furniture. There's even a cowardly character who goes to pieces under pressure (paging *Living Dead*'s Mr. Cooper…). Most importantly, however, here the fiends finally become visible (after the intelligent thought monsters attack the reactor room and boost the power output). They look like pulsing human brains with two antenna-like stalks, a series of leg-like tendrils, and an attached spinal cord that whips around like a tail (and which they use to inch-worm along or to spring through the air and wrap around the neck of a victim). These fiends rise up like a snake about to strike; and when shot, thick dark gore oozes and bubbles from their brain-bodies (complete with ghastly sound effects). The animation imbues them with personality via probing antennae, impatiently thrashing tail, or inquisitive sideways turn of the head… er, brain. There's even a wonderfully tension-filled bit in which a wounded fiend painfully drags itself towards a lit dynamite fuse in a desperate attempt to stop Cummings from blowing up the reactor. As the gruesome coup de grace, the loss of their atomic power sees the fiends melt into multi-hued puddles of goo.

Playing a rather more well-rounded heroine than that usually found in low-budget sci-fi of the time, Kim Parker (in her one major starring role) makes the most of her opportunities, convincingly running the gamut from tender sympathy to subtle flirtation to indignant anger. And, so important to a film of this type, she screams well. Ms. Parker (born Herta Padawer in Vienna, Austria, in 1933) made only nine films over a five-year period, two more of which were Fifties sci-fi—*Man Without a Body* and *Fire Maidens of Outer Space*—but neither of which could hold a candle to *Fiend*. The resilient actress-to-be survived Auschwitz as a child (her family was Jewish), then a bout of polio when a teenager. She entered the British fashion industry as a designer and model before (briefly) turning to acting. Married to Canadian actor Paul Carpenter (with whom she appeared in two films—*Action Stations* and *Fire Maidens*), she left show business in 1959.

Lest one think this is just a superficial (albeit brilliantly-titled) monster movie about disembodied killer brains, *Fiend* offers its fair share of topical subtext, with the fiends standing as physical manifestations of our fear of the atom (after all, they're powered—and created—by atomic energy). The film doesn't necessarily condemn nuclear power, however, just the misuse of it when employed by the wrong hands—in this instance, not some foreign power but those of a lone-wolf, misguided scientist who steals atomic energy from the protective, benevolent United States military. The film's conclusion implies that the reactor will be rebuilt with the cooperation of the local civilians for the benefit of all. And the message couldn't be clearer: nuclear power will help keep the Free World safe—but only if wielded by the all-wise and ever-responsible United States Government.

Such an attitude moves dangerously close to high camp when the military prove rather…cavalier in their approach to nuclear energy. During a radar test scene, the reactor attendant warns Major Cummings that "We've already exceeded the design limit. …If I take any more of those rods out, the reactor is liable to get out of control." At this Cummings answers, "Well, take some more out, we'll have to risk it—we've got to have more power." Resigned, the attendant complies, adding, "Well, it's your funeral," and, to himself, "Mine too, probably." So much for nuclear safeguards.

Fiend Without a Face was filmed back-to-back with its co-feature *The Haunted Strangler* on a combined budget of $300,000. *Fiend* flew solo in England, however, and the gruesome Little Picture That Could garnished some wonderful money-spinning publicity when it was denounced on the floor of the British Parliament.

"THE FIRST PICTURE THAT TAKES YOU INTO SPACE!" –First Man Into Space ad line

Despite its rather cold and clinical title, *First Man Into Space* is more moody horror film than sober science-oriented drama. And as a horror movie it works reasonably well, thanks to (reluctant) director Robert Day's (*The Haunted Strangler, Corridors of Blood, She*) atmospheric staging.

Hot-shot military test pilot Dan Prescott (Bill Edwards) disobeys orders and takes his experimental 'rocket-plane' too high (in a fairly convincing model effect—by effects artist Karl-Ludwig Ruppel, fresh from *Fiend Without a Face*—that proves far more convincing than the usual flaming toy seen in other productions of the time), leaving Earth's atmosphere to become the film's title character ("Who's gonna forget the first man into space?" he recklessly reasons). Dan encounters a cloud of "meteorite dust" that damages his ship and sends him spinning back to Earth. Oh, and his exposed head and space-suited body is now coated with a hideous "space crust." The man/monster now needs blood to survive and goes on a killing spree, while his mission commander—and brother—Charles Prescott (Marshall Thompson) tries to track him down. ("We first

First Man Into Space poster.

signed Marshall Thompson to appear in *Fiend Without a Face*," recalled Richard Gordon, "and he was so helpful and cooperative and such a nice guy that when it came to planning *First Man Into Space*, I decided to use him again.")

Though set in New Mexico, the movie was shot in England (where filming—at the time—was cheap). "We were so hamstrung with the budget," complained director Robert Day to this author. "We had just no money at all." (According to executive producer Richard Gordon, the British production cost about £100,000.) "And the script wasn't very good—*I* didn't think it was, anyway. Actually, we had hardly any script when we started shooting! [Producer] Chuck Vetter and I would meet after shooting, and prepare the next day's shooting—write the dialogue and everything!"

Indeed, the script—particularly "the dialogue and everything"—*is* suspect at times. "It's incredible to think of your brother as a blood-drinking monster," ponders Charles. Later he postulates, "If he can still drive a car, he still retains some intelligence—he's not all monster." Indeed.

Speaking of monsters, Day was less-than-enthusiastic about his movie's menace. "It was made of some plastic material," the director said of the monster suit, "and then touched up with makeup afterwards. It was okay. ...I hated the monster anyway, I thought it was dumb. My feeling at the time was, I thought that somebody could come back out of space with an aberrated mind, rather than the costume. I put that idea forward, but most of the people involved wanted the horror. Which I thought was almost a caricature. It's not one of my favorite movies." Fortunately for horror fans, Day was outvoted.

Playing the (not quite) First Monster from Space was no easy task for actor Bill Edwards (who wore the suit himself during the entire production). "It was basically a suit that Edwards was put into, with small holes in the mask for him to see out through," recounted Gordon to interviewer Tom Weaver. "One problem we did have was that he couldn't wear the outfit for very long because not enough air was getting through. It was extremely hot and uncomfortable, and would have given him breathing problems after a while, so he could only wear it for limited periods of time."

Despite his dislike of the 'horror' material, Day generated some very effective atmosphere, utilizing low-angle shots and moody lighting. Even the Mission Control–like sets are full of dark corners and shadows. Low-key lighting from below casts sinister shadows on characters as they hover over their instrument panels. There's also plenty of nighttime photography to compliment the spooky scenario.

Day also handled his hated 'monster' well. It's first-seen only as a menacing shadow on a wall (with heavy, strangled breathing on the sound track). Again, low-angle shots and darkened hallways generate a real sense of horror as the man/monster breaks into a blood bank. When Day finally exposes the creature to full view, it comes with a sudden (and brief) shot of the horrific face bursting forth from some bushes, making for a startling and memorable moment.

Cinematographer Geoffrey Faithfull's (*Phantom Ship, Village of the Damned, Corridors of Blood, Naked Evil*) camerawork compliments the film's atmospheric staging. There's some convincing shaky-cam photography to delineate turbulence (and up the believability quotient) in the rocket-plane, and a rotating POV camera simulates the ship spinning out of control. It's all very low-budget, but no less effective. Weird, low electronic blips and bleeps add to the film's ominous tone, and the rocket rising higher and higher—as the ground crew becomes more and more frantic—generates real suspense.

According to Gordon, *First Man Into Space* was originally filmed as a co-feature for the Boris Karloff vehicle *Corridors of Blood*, but due to a sudden public interest in the space program it was decided that the two should be released separately. *First Man* did quite well on its own, whereas *Corridors* was a dismal failure financially.

Oddly, MGM downplayed the film's horror angle in their advertising (there's no *hint* of a monster in any of the movie's posters, for instance). "MGM thought it would have more appeal to a general audience and that it could play much more widely than a horror picture might," explained Gordon, "so they decided to play up the science fiction rather than the horror or monster angles."

Even so, it's these very 'horror' and 'monster angles' that make *First Man Into Space* memorable—and watchable—today.

Cult Movies magazine resurrected *Frankenstein 1970* twenty-seven years too late—in 1997 (issue 24).

FRANKENSTEIN 1970 (1958)

"*Frankenstein 1970* was made because we had a three-picture deal with [Boris] Karloff," related producer Aubrey Schenck to interviewer Tom Weaver. "We had to pay him $30,000 whether we used him in a picture or not." While it may have *sounded* like a good idea at the time to update the tried-and-true Frankenstein legend with atomic reactors and the original monster himself, Boris Karloff (playing the doctor this time), *Frankenstein 1970* falls flat on its Franken-face.

Karloff plays a present day (or at least 1970, as the title would have us believe) Baron Frankenstein, a victim of torture at the hands of an unspecified (but obviously Nazi) regime, and the last of his line. He still inhabits the old family castle, but has built an ultra-modern laboratory in a secret room under the family crypt in which he plans to make a new, improved version of his infamous family's monster. For this he needs an atomic reactor (apparently the tried and true method of using plain old lightning was too archaic for him) and allows a TV crew to use his castle as the background for their show in exchange for the equipment he needs. When the atomic equipment finally arrives (from the ACME Reactor Company?), the Baron revives his monster. This, unfortunately, comes with great disappointment,

With Frankenstein 1970 (1958), *the Monster becomes the Maker (Boris Karloff as Baron Frankenstein).*

for instead of a terrifying graveyard ghoul, the monster is just a large man wrapped from head to toe in white bandages. And on that head rests a ridiculous box-like covering with eye holes cut out. Given this appearance, and the fact that the monster is blind (much of the plot revolves around the Baron sending the groping monster out to find a suitable set of eyes) makes the creature anything *but* menacing. ("That 'monster' of Karloff's," laughed Schenck, "that didn't scare you at all.")

The script gives Karloff (the only actor to work every day on the eight-day shoot) little to work with and saddles the veteran horror star with pointless clunkers like, "All radiation off; zero on Geiger modem dial." It's embarrassing, even for such a consummate professional as he, to wear silly goggles and apron and comment, "Ah Schuter, yours is not the brain I would have chosen, but at least you are obedient." In another scene, Karloff becomes the butt of an unintentional joke when he clumsily drops the jar containing the monster's intended eyeballs and comically slaps his hand on his thigh in an "oh shoot!" gesture. Occasionally some of the old power and menace shines through, however, such as when Karloff tells the story of the "inquisitive camp commandant" who was found with his tongue cut out ("a beautiful piece of surgery—beautiful"). Still, Karloff gives a painfully overripe performance, one of the worst of his career. "It was theatrical, it was overdone," agreed co-star Charlotte Austin. "I hate to say that, because he was such a gracious man. But when you're given this kind of dialogue, what can you do with it? I think he was just doing a job and wanting to go home." Director Howard Koch realized that Karloff was overdoing it, but was unwilling to rein him in. "I was in awe of him, and we just let him go," admitted Koch. "I was *afraid* to say to him it was too much!"

With one exception, the supporting characters (and actors) prove completely uninteresting. The only intriguing personality is Judy (Charlotte Austin), the TV director's feisty secretary and ex-wife. Unfortunately, she's the monster's first victim and so makes her tragic exit halfway through the film. This, by the way, is the source of another unintentionally humorous moment. When the Baron places her body in his oversized custom disposal unit and starts the machine, it sounds exactly like a toilet flushing! According to Koch, the original, more realistic "crunching" sound effects were removed at the behest of the censors. "When we showed that to the Code, they said, 'You can't have that sound effect in there, you've got to take it out! Christ, it's the most gruesome thing we ever heard in our lives!'" As it is now, it may very well be the *funniest*!

The quite predictable ending also disappoints. The monster, whose brain is that of a murdered servant, refuses to harm the heroine as ordered since she had previously been kind to the servant, and so turns on his master. As a result, the Baron kills both the monster and himself by releasing lethal radiation in the form of an unconvincing steam cloud. Quite an anti-climax: the Frankenstein Monster killed by radiation poisoning. It seems the atomic hysteria of the 1950s has reached back to claim even Mary Shelley's timeless creation.

Koch directs with a heavy-handed self-consciousness. Apparently, his idea of clever innovation is to use the sledgehammer approach to pound his ideas into the viewer's psyche. In one scene the blind monster (still seeking a pair of eyes) approaches his victim. Koch first shows the creature's empty eye sockets, then a shot of the victim's eyes, and finally a superimposition of the victim's eyes over the monster's empty eye holes. Subtle. And the impact of the ironic (if not wholly unexpected) twist of revealing that the Baron had created the monster "in his own image" is nullified by the off-handed shot used to present it. Koch himself admitted that "I don't feel I did such a great job on *Frankenstein 1970*," blaming it on the rushed eight-day shooting schedule and meager $105,000 budget. "I didn't have much time to really think."

Apart from an embarrassing, train-wreck-fascinating turn behind the test tubes by the original Monster himself, Boris Karloff, *Frankenstein 1970* offers little to the discerning horror fan. In their review of the film, the *Monthly Film Bulletin* summed it up best: "The whole inept effort is a slight on the horrific name of Frankenstein." Indeed.

> Strangely, this modest little essay was printed twice, in two different magazines (*Movie Club* issue 7 in the Summer of 1996, and then again in *Ultra-Filmfax* no. 68 two years later). Apparently, I didn't mind repeating myself...

FRANKENSTEIN'S DAUGHTER (1958)

Bride of Frankenstein, Son of Frankenstein... I suppose it was inevitable that somebody would eventually bring *Frankenstein's Daughter* to life (and to the screen). That somebody turned out to be a cheap outfit called Astor Pictures who, in 1958, took director Richard Cunha's $65,000 update on the Frankenstein legend and released it on a drive-in double bill with *Missile to the Moon*.

Dr. Morton (Felix Locher) works in his home laboratory trying to perfect a drug which will "wipe out all destructive cells and organisms that plague man." Morton's assistant, Oliver Frank (Donald Murphy), aka Oliver Frank*enstein* (grandson of the famous monstermaker), plans on using the serum in his own secret experiment, testing it out first on Morton's niece, Trudy (Sandra Knight), which results in her temporary transformation into a pasty-faced but harmless monster! In a secret room off Morton's lab, Oliver and his assistant Elsu (Oliver's faithful family retainer who poses as the gardener) have constructed a body. Procuring a head and brain from a reluctant date, Oliver brings his creation to life. After the expected (but decidedly small-scale) killing spree, the creature—and creator—ends up in the usual climactic conflagration while the now-recovered Trudy escapes into the arms of her heroic boyfriend.

Though there's much to scoff at in this gender-bending cheapie, Cunha and cinematographer Meredith Nicholson at least *try* to invest the proceedings with visual interest, utilizing depth of field, mirror images, and

Frankenstein's Daughter *half-sheet poster.*

even changing focus within a shot to bring a character into sharp relief at a dramatic moment. The suspicious gardener's introduction, for instance, begins with Trudy sitting on the couch reading a magazine when suddenly a sinister shadow passes over the world globe sitting on a table behind her. She looks up, alarmed, and the camera dollies back to reveal the unsavory old man hovering above her. The first glimpse of the monster is effective as well. The hulking form sits up in shadow and then advances slowly toward the camera. When it steps into a shaft of light, the low-angled shot adds an imposing quality to the shocking sight. Sadly, however, these carefully constructed set-ups are the exception rather than the rule, since Cunha and company could squeeze very little from their just-get-it-done six-day schedule for such time-consuming 'extras.'

Nicholson's shadowy lighting can't fully disguise the few cramped studio sets and banal exteriors (producer Marc Frederic's own home), and so the picture possesses a cheap, claustrophobic feel. And Cunha can do little with the awful Felix Locher as the elderly scientist, whose whining, oddly-accented delivery becomes so annoying that the viewer breathes a huge sigh of relief upon learning that Morton expired from a heart attack in the hospital and so will no longer be gracing us with his painful presence.

Then there's the outright non-acting of hero John Ashley, who, despite his preppie shirts and turned-up collar, never seems to look comfortable in front of the camera. His deadpan delivery and immobile countenance are so stiff you could light a match on them. When the two lovers see the monster for the first time, for instance, Sandra Knight gives a healthy scream and looks appropriately horrified while Ashley simply stares blankly, with no emotion crossing his impossibly bland face. "Maybe the key to my success with exploitation films is that I always liked those movies," the actor told interviewer Tom Weaver. "I just enjoyed doing them."

From Ashley's wooden demeanor in *Frankenstein's Daughter*, one could never tell.

Fortunately, as Trudy, Sandra Knight at least seems *alive* (and, in fact, comes off as quite likable), and Donald Murphy gives a hearty performance as the arrogant, brilliant Oliver. He imbues his scornful scientist with a superior air and a wealth of passion. Murphy's natural, sometimes intense, delivery even makes lines like "Tonight you'll be alive again, you little vixen," bearable. And he offers the insult "You nutty old man" with just the right level of bemused contempt to make the laughable line work.

Of course, the most important question to any hapless viewer caught by *Frankenstein's Daughter* is: Is it male or female? To borrow from *I Was a Teenage Frankenstein*, a sister (or is that brother?) production which advertised itself as "Body of a boy! Mind of a monster! Soul of an unearthly thing!," so could *Frankenstein's Daughter* characterize its creation as "Body of a boy! Head of a *girl*! Soul of a *gender-confused* thing!" Much ado has been made over why the creature looks male while the principals refer to it as "she." According to makeup man Harry Thomas, no one provided him with a script, and so he was unaware that his monster (played by Harry Wilson) was female. Though Thomas wanted to change the makeup when he learned the truth, Cunha couldn't spare the time on this six-day wonder, and so Thomas simply slapped some lipstick on Wilson's chops and sent his beefy "daughter" reeling in front of the camera. In any case, the face is so mutilated that it matters little whether it's a male or female countenance under all the stretched cotton, liquid plastic and spirit gum. As to the body, no one ever says anything to suggest that the *body* is female. In fact, Elsu is genuinely surprised when Oliver brings home a *female* head. So what we have is a male body with a female head and brain.

With tongue firmly in cheek, the monster's mix-and-match androgyny raises *Frankenstein's Daughter* to a level of deep social significance by inadvertently posing the question: Should a person's sex be determined by the brain or the body? If given half the chance, this poor creature might well have demanded that Oliver perform the ultimate sex-change operation and give it a female body to go with its feminine head, thus becoming the screen's first transsexual monster! The mind boggles.

Though Harry Thomas provides a fairly good road-accident makeup job on the monster's face, Thomas also capped his/her/its head with a pillbox-shaped, wrap-around white bandage reminiscent of the turban-style, high-fashion hats sometimes worn by middle-aged socialites of the previous decade. It makes for an amusing image. And an occasional guffaw is what the viewer must settle for with *Frankenstein's Daughter*, for nothing even remotely frightening ever happens during the whole ludicrous 85 minutes. After the monster's atmospheric introduction, the creature seems more comical than horrific, with its tremulous hands (the monster seems to suffer from some kind of palsy, for its appendages never stop shaking) held out perpendicular to its lumbering body, and its silly M.O. of slow karate chops to the victim's collar-bones. Despite game efforts from Sandra Knight and Donald Murphy, and a half-hearted stab at competence on the technical side, this *Daughter* must have been a deep disappointment to her parents.

> Since this article was written for the British publication *The Fantastic Fifties* (issue 10, Spring 2020), the Karloff film known to Americans as *The Haunted Strangler* is listed here under its U.K. release title *Grip of the Strangler*.

BORIS BACK-TO-BACK: *GRIP OF THE STRANGLER* AND *CORRIDORS OF BLOOD*

The 1950s were not particularly kind to horror legend Boris Karloff—at least cinematically speaking. The decade dominated by Big Bugs and Alien Invaders found little use for the Gothic-style terrors over which Karloff had reigned in the 1930s and '40s. Come the Eisenhower era, the "King of Horror" had to make do with a plethora of TV appearances (on various shows like *Suspense*, *Studio One*, *Playhouse 90*, and his series *Colonel March of Scotland Yard*) and second-rate Big Screen assignments like *The Strange Door* (1951), *The Black Castle* (1952), *Voodoo Island* (1957), and *Frankenstein 1970* (1958). The best of the battered bunch turned out to be a pair of 1958 British vehicles executive produced by Richard Gordon and directed by Robert Day: *Grip of the Strangler* (retitled *The Haunted Strangler* in America) and *Corridors of Blood* (aka *Doctor from Seven Dials*).

"THE BIG SCREAMS… ARE ON THE BIG SCREEN! AS KARLOFF CREATES A NEW MONSTER!" –*The Haunted Strangler* trailer

In 1880 London, novelist Jim Rankin (Boris Karloff) investigates the 20-year-old case of "the Haymar-

The Haunted Strangler *became* Grip of the Strangler *in the UK. (British quad poster)*

ket Strangler" (who half-strangled his female victims before finishing the job with a surgeon's knife). Convinced the man hanged for the crimes was innocent, and hoping to use the case to promote legal reforms, Rankin uncovers the shadowy figure of Dr. Tennet, who was involved in the case and then mysteriously disappeared right afterwards. Locating the killer's knife triggers something in Rankin, who transforms into the Strangler and takes up his old murderous ways! (Spoiler alerts need not apply, as the film makes this shocking revelation that Rankin is actually the amnesiac Tennet early on, with the remainder of the picture following Rankin's murderous activities after the periodic transformations, and his subsequent struggle to get the authorities to believe it.)

Though a relatively low-budget production (about $150,000, of which Karloff received $25,000), *Grip of the Strangler* looks like it cost far more, thanks to the convincing period dress and carriages, and some authentic-looking gas-lit interiors. Combine this with the moody black-and-white photography, and you really feel you're in Victorian London. (A minor gaffe: when Rankin searches the police archives we see a file box marked "Jack the Ripper"—but Saucy Jack didn't strike until 1888, eight years *after* the story's stated timeframe.)

For this three-week production, which, as director Robert Day told this writer, he "hardly had any money to spend," necessity truly became the mother of invention—with Karloff himself leading the economical charge when he affected the transformation from genteel novelist to insane killer with nary a brushstroke of makeup. The actor simply removed a dental plate, sucked in his lower cheek, squinted his eye, and grimaced. Amazingly, it worked, as Karloff's distinguished, kindly visage transformed itself into a grotesque, malevolent "graveyard ghoul whose claws were clenched with the wild, uncontrollable will to kill!" (as the film's trailer characterized him). "We talked about monsters, ghouls, and ghosts," wrote producer John Croydon in *Fangoria* magazine of their preproduction meeting on the transformation topic, "and were not getting very far when I noticed a twinkle in Karloff's eyes. 'Mind if I try my own [make-up]?' he asked. He turned his back and seemed to be remolding his features. When he swung back again, we were stunned. He had removed his false left upper and lower molars and drawn his mouth awkwardly sideways, sucked in his lower lip so that the upper teeth overlapped, his cheek drawn inwards. ...Our psychopathic monster had materialized before our very eyes, and that was how Karloff played the role. It was perfect." Indeed, though pushing 70, Karloff took the production on his stooped shoulders and crafted a dual-pronged performance that showcased the screen legend's talents both emotionally and physically (with the emphysema-plagued actor—destined to employ a cane and wheelchair—seen leaping down steps, struggling mightily against guards, ripping through a straightjacket, and running nimbly through dark woodlands).

"Boris realized in *The Haunted Strangler* he had a much better role than he'd been offered previously for quite a long time," remarked Day. "So he studied hard and was always the first one on the set. Word perfect—a *wonderful* guy." *Grip of the Strangler* provided Karloff with his finest role of the decade, and the veteran actor rose to the occasion to deliver his finest big-screen performance of the 1950s. Day remembered Karloff as "a wonderful man. It was just such an honor working with him. He was so kind and gentle, so much the reverse of the roles he played in the movies." As Rankin, Karloff's innate kindness shines through, expressing genuine affection for his wife and adopted daughter, and both compassion and determination to carry through his investigation no matter the cost to himself (the sensitive Rankin even faints at the sight of a prisoner being whipped at Newgate Prison). And as the Strangler, Karloff personifies madness and murderous intent, with his malevolent stare and quick movements. The film's American trailer, voiced by the ubiquitous Paul Frees, characterized his face as "a hideous mask of cruelty," and it's not far wrong. Though a handful of worthy big-screen roles were to come his way in the 1960s (via *The Raven*, *Black Sabbath*, *The Sorcerers*, and the fantastic *Targets*), *Grip of the Strangler* was to be Karloff's final "prime" picture, allowing him to showcase his power both emotionally and physically.

"Boris, when we shot the scene in the insane asylum," recalled Day, "he insisted on being in a proper straightjacket, and it worked very well I thought." Indeed, Karloff's desperate struggles against the attendants, coupled with his panicked protests and pleadings, paints a heartrending picture of a sensitive man driven to frenzy and near-madness by this dignity-stripping treatment. Karloff not only allows himself to be manhandled but engages in agitated pacing and futile pounding on his cell walls, as well as (in Strangler mode) setting fire to the straw in his cell and subduing a guard to effect a violent escape. Though he lived and worked for another decade, it's the last time the ailing actor would ever attempt such a physically demanding role.

"Boris didn't really like violence," noted Day, "and we avoided it when we could. ...We went for just suggesting the violence and not actually seeing it." And Day's "suggested violence" proved both economical and effective. For instance, for the shocking scene in which Rankin transforms into the Strangler and then kills his beloved wife, Day offers shots of Karloff plunging the knife downwards out-of-frame intercut with shots of the victim's arm laid on the carpet, her hand opening convulsively with each thrust of the blade. Such violence implied but not shown still creates a visceral shock without displaying the horrific deed.

Grip of the Strangler is by no means a perfect film, however. The script by Jan Read and producer Croydon (employing the pen name John C. Cooper) offers up rather too many time-filling can-can numbers at the dance hall the Strangler likes to frequent, and eats up further pointless minutes with a superfluous romantic subplot involving Rankin's daughter and his handsome research assistant. Both these characters prove completely colorless, with their love-fraught case not helped by the utterly bland playing of Diane Aubrey and Tim Turner. Still, thanks to Robert Day's sensitive direction and, most crucially, Boris Karloff's sympathetic performance of a tortured man transformed by the past, *Grip of the Strangler* becomes not just a period horror film but an involving tragedy—a real rarity in the sci-fi dominated 1950s.

"A N-E-R-V-O-R-A-M-A SHOCKER!" –Corridors of Blood trailer

With *Grip* in the can, executive producer Richard Gordon sought to continue his happy association with Boris Karloff. "We were looking for another subject for Karloff [after making *Grip of the Strangler*]," recounted Gordon to interviewer Tom Weaver, "and [producer] John Croyden came up with the original story idea for *Corridors of Blood*. A woman named Jean Scott Rogers wrote the screenplay. Her idea was to make a very serious picture about surgery in the days before anesthetics, which of course wouldn't have made a very commercial picture. So we tried to inject horror and melodramatic elements into it." Basically an historical drama with a few horror trappings (mainly the murderous Burke and

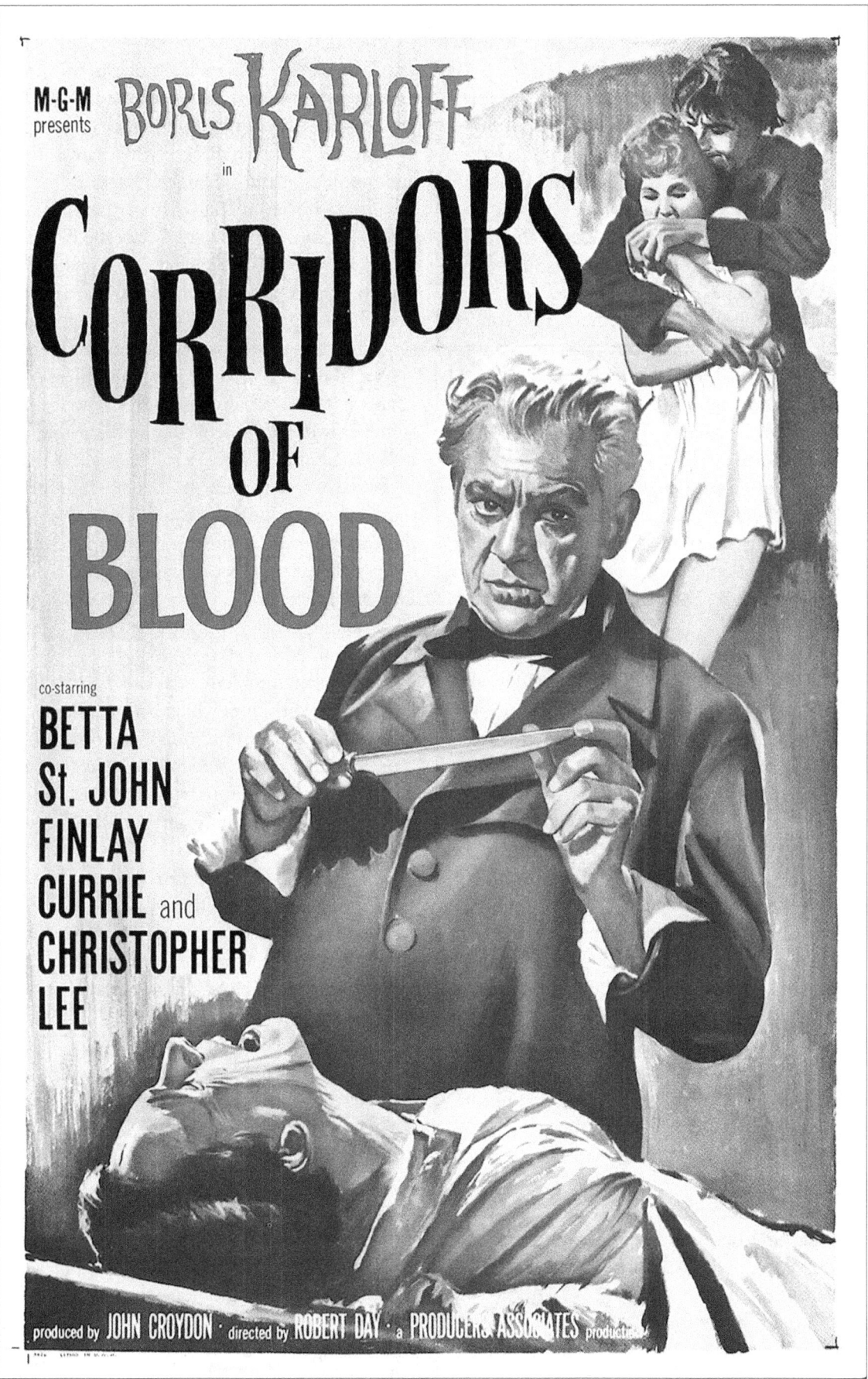

Corridors of Blood *poster*.

Hare/body snatching angle), *Corridors* offers a sumptuously-set, authentic-minded tale of a fascinating time in medicine's history.

In 1840 England, before the discovery of anesthesia, respected surgeon Mr. Bolton (Karloff) is working on a drug that can be used as an anesthetic. After an initial demonstration to prove that "pain and the knife are *not* inseparable" goes badly, Bolton is eventually dismissed from the hospital. In the course of his research, Bolton has become addicted to the drugs, and now finds his way to a seedy tavern where innkeeper "Black Ben" (Francis DeWolfe) and his partner, grave robber "Resurrection Joe" (Christopher Lee), use the doctor's addiction to blackmail him into signing phony death certificates for lodgers they have murdered in order to sell their bodies to anatomists.

"You'll take shock after shock after shock! Don't hold in your terror; shriek if you must!" warned the film's misleading trailer. Actually, there are few "shocks" (an antagonist taking a face full of acid; another falling to his death-by-impalement on iron posts) and even fewer moments of "terror" in this serious-minded historical melodrama.

Corridors is exceedingly well-acted, from FancisDeWolfe's ingratiating yet murderous Black Ben and Christopher Lee's cold-as-a-snake Resurrection Joe (obvious stand-ins for Burke and Hare), to Adrienne Corri's beguiling yet pitiless barmaid. In fact, it's Lee's chillingly calm delivery and convincing cockney accent—combined with a look of intensity-cum-madness in his eyes—that provides the movie with its little bit of "horror." ("Christopher [was] so good at that horror stuff," observed director Robert Day. "It was *his* interpretation, what he did [that added the horror].") The only thespian misstep is (surprisingly) Boris Karloff's overly melodramatic portrayal of the kindly Bolton trapped in horrible circumstances. His constantly furrowed brow, dramatic gestures, and plaintive tones contrast jarringly with the more naturalistic playing of the rest of the cast. (Even so, "the crew adored him to a man," recounted co-star Francis Matthews to interviewer Stephen Laws. "Boris was a disarming, cultured gentleman who was like a surrogate father to me. ...His running gag at the end of each day's work was to offer to sweep up the day's debris in the studio. So at the end of shooting party we presented him with a large broom signed by the entire cast and crew.")

With financial backing from MGM came that studio's substantial resources, allowing shooting at the plush MGM Studios in London, and the utilization of the MGM wardrobe and carpentry departments. As a result, *Corridors of Blood* features impressive (and authentic) costuming, and splendid sets far beyond what would be expected in a budget film of this nature. "We had nice sets on that show," recalled Day. "And that's where quite a bit of the money went."

Day (aided by Geoffrey Faithful's evocative lighting and mobile camerawork) nicely captures the back-alley squalor of the Seven Dials district. For instance, a seedy tavern-set scene opens with a close-up of the filthy legs and muddy feet of a sleeping street urchin—an attention to detail that brings the squalid settings vividly to life. "It's all spontaneous," said Day in reference to this sequence. "The way I work, I plan all my work the night before [the day's shoot]. ...But then there's always the spontaneity—like panning up from the feet of the boy to the crowded cafe. That's something that just comes in the moment." *Corridors* is filled with such moments.

Said Day, "I remember Richard Gordon saying, 'I think we need more blood, more bloodthirsty stuff' at the screening of my first edit of the movie. Richard didn't think it was bloody enough or horrific enough." Day *did*, however. "*Corridors of Blood* was part almost documentary and part horror movie. That was the blend I wanted."

"I think the problem with *Corridors of Blood* is that it's really a hybrid film which isn't one thing or the other," concluded Gordon. "It's not enough of a horror film like, let's say *The Haunted Strangler*, and yet it's too much of a horror film to be regarded as a picture dealing seriously with surgery and with the medical profession in that era."

Though filmed in England in 1958, *Corridors of Blood* went unreleased in the UK until October 1962 (where it was paired with *Nights of Rasputin*). It fared even worse in the United States, waiting until June of 1963 to see the cinematic light of day "because MGM didn't know quite what to do with it; they didn't have a picture to go with it," according to Gordon. Well, they finally found one—*Werewolf in a Girls' Dormitory*. Griped Gordon, "I think 'Nervo-Rama' was intended to suggest that the two pictures would put your nerves on edge. As far as I'm concerned, I think MGM had a *nerve* putting those two pictures together [*laughs*]! *Werewolf in a Girls' Dormitory* might have been all right on its own, but it was so inferior to *Corridors of Blood* that it upset the balance of the double bill." Indeed.

Sold as an out and out shocker to the horror crowd in 1963, *Corridors* was destined to disappoint. "The whole thing was a disaster," recounted Gordon. It was a fate undeserving of the well-crafted and engrossing *Corridors of Blood*.

In 1997 *Movie Club* magazine (issue 12) sent me to explore the hokey-but-highly-entertaining *House on Haunted Hill*.

HOUSE ON HAUNTED HILL (1959)

"I'm Vincent Price, and you're invited to my party in the House on Haunted Hill, where so far the ghosts have murdered only seven people. So won't you come and make it… eight?" –trailer

When one thinks of haunted house movies, the two that most readily spring to mind are likely to be *The Haunting* (1963) and *House on Haunted Hill* (1959)—for very different reasons. *The Haunting* because not only is it arguably the greatest ghost film ever made, but it's also one of the most frightening; *House on Haunted Hill* because it is perhaps the most unabashedly manipulative of all haunted house movies, pulling every trick in the spectral book (and adding several new ones) to try and raise a few goosebumps among its (obviously young) target audience.

House on Haunted Hill is one of those films that if seen as a child remains etched in the memory. (Cassandra Peterson—Elvira herself—credits *House on Haunted Hill* with starting her interest in film "when I was a little kid, probably seven or eight. …I'll never get over that movie as long as I live!") Though short on logic, it's long on fright gags, trotting out such archetypal scares as a hissing witch, blood dripping from ceilings, severed heads popping up in the most unlikely of places, a hanging woman, and as the *piece de resistance* of hoary horrors—a walking skeleton. With an unapologetic lack of subtlety, *House on Haunted Hill* appeals to that preadolescent in all of us that loves to be scared—but not *too* scared.

The film provides frights in the form of sudden shocks and obvious (phony) props that, once the initial jolt dies down, give us the opportunity to chuckle a bit and enjoy our shivery reactions. Unlike the truly great ghost films (such as *The Haunting* or *The Innocents* [1961]), there's never any danger at this *House* of having to face any *real* terrors (such as loneliness, sexuality, or even the basic fear of death itself). Perhaps that's the great appeal of *House on Haunted Hill*—it's like a backroad carnival Chamber of Horrors which offers up a series of 'safe' surface scares that provoke a jump and a giggle without popping the lid off one's own psychological Pandora's box. In any case, master showman William Castle provides an exciting ride for those willing to check their adult sensibilities at the gate and let their inner twelve-year-olds hop aboard this ghoulish exhibit.

The picture begins on a delightfully shuddery note, with a sudden shriek piercing the blackness of the screen, followed by ghostly groans, more screams, malevolent laughter, clanking chains, and heavy footsteps. Out of the darkness floats Elisha Cook Jr.'s disembodied head. "The ghosts are moving tonight, restless, hungry," he tells us in his soft, melancholy voice. "May I introduce myself? I'm Watson Pritchard. In just a minute I'll show you the only really haunted house in the world…"

Next comes the head of Vincent Price superimposed over the prison-like, Mayan-style structure of the Ennis-Brown house (the Frank Lloyd Wright-designed Hollywood dwelling which Castle chose to represent

Williams Castle's "amazing new wonder Emergo" gimmick was not the only treat in store for those who visited the *House on Haunted Hill* back in 1959. (newspaper ad)

the exterior of his House on Haunted Hill). "I'm Frederick Loren," he tells us, "and I've rented the House on Haunted Hill tonight so that my wife can give a party, a haunted house party. She's so amusing. There'll be food and drink and—ghosts, and perhaps even a few murders. You're all invited."

Price then introduces us to his five guests: Lance Schroeder (Richard Long), a test pilot; columnist Ruth Bridges (Julie Mitchum, Robert's sister); Watson Pritchard (current owner of the house after his brother was brutally murdered therein by his wife—"we never found the heads…"); psychiatrist David Trent (Alan Marshal); and Nora Manning (Carolyn Craig), a secretary who works for one of Frederick Loren's companies.

A multi-millionaire, Frederick has promised each of his five guests $10,000 if they will spend the night in the house along with himself and his wife, the beautiful Annabelle (Carol Ohmart), who hates her jealous husband and once even tried to poison him. At midnight they will all be locked inside, without any way out of the fortress-like house until released in the morning by the returning caretakers. All five are total strangers to Frederick and to each other. ("I had a reason for inviting each guest," he tells his questioning wife. "I wanted kind of a cross section, from psychiatrist to typist and from drunk to jet pilot. They share one thing—they all need money. Now let's see if they're brave enough to collect it.")

Soon things begin to happen. A chandelier falls; blood drips from the ceiling; Nora sees a hideous old crone in the cellar (which turns out to be the caretaker's blind wife); Lance receives a blow on the head by an unseen (un*dead*?) hand; and, most disturbingly, Annabelle is found swinging from the end of a rope—dead.

With everyone now armed (Frederick had provided each guest with a loaded pistol as "party favors"), suspicion focuses on Frederick. Meanwhile, the gruesome goings-on continue, seemingly centering on Nora. She finds a severed head in her suitcase, endures a terrifying visitation by Annabelle's apparition, and sees an old organ playing by itself. Near hysterical with fear, Nora shoots Frederick in the cellar when he approaches her.

We now learn that it's all been a plan to kill Frederick (or, more precisely, get him killed) concocted by Annabelle and her lover…Dr. Trent! "An hysterical girl accidentally shoots somebody?," Trent reassures Annabelle about the efficacy of their farfetched plot. "Who would suspect that we planned it that way—that we drove her to it?"

But things aren't quite what they seem, as Trent finds out when he tries to dispose of Frederick's body in the handy cellar acid vat, and as Annabelle learns when confronted with what seems to be Frederick's skeleton rising from the acid bath… "The crime you two planned was indeed perfect," a very much alive Frederick (he had loaded Nora's gun with blanks) tells the now-dead lovers (having by force and by fright sent the two lovers to their acidic doom) at the film's close. "Only the victim is alive and the murderers are not. It's a pity you didn't know when you started your game of *murder* that I was playing too."

"It's the SHIVER and SHAKE, QUIVER and QUAKE picture of the year," ballyhooed the film's theatrical trailer. With crashing chandeliers, self-playing organs, hairy clutching hands, dimming lights, and the proverbial 'dark and stormy night,' scripter Robb White and director William Castle trot out every Haunted House cliché imaginable—including the premise of a small group of people locked inside said house. "Having somebody trapped in a house, couldn't get out," laughed screenwriter Robb White to interviewer Tom Weaver, "that was just so basic that I'd written short stories about that for several years."

The movie's sense of fun (no matter what else you call it, *House on Haunted Hill is* a fun film) comes not only from the everything-but-the-kitchen-spook approach but also from White's amusing and often sardonic dialogue. When Frederick enters his wife's room, for instance, he announces, "Annabelle, your guests are here and fortunately still alive. Is your face on yet?" (an engagingly macabre bit of phrasing). When the downside-of-middle-age Ruth Bridges dismissively asks, "Who'd want to haunt me?," Frederick quips with mock gallantry, "I would say any self-respecting *male* ghost." The dialogue really comes alive, however, in the acerbic banter between Frederick and his scheming wife. "You remember the fun we had when you poisoned me?," asks Frederick, to which Annabelle laughingly shoots back, "Something you ate, the doctor said." Later Frederick leaves her with this final jab: "Don't sit up all night thinking of ways to get rid of me—it makes wrinkles."

Of course, without Vincent Price in the lead role, the picture wouldn't be half so enjoyable. Like no other 'horror' actor, Price had the ability to draw the viewer into the proceedings with a smooth and charming believability while simultaneously winking at the audience, reassuring us with a raised eyebrow or a subtle half-smile that it's-all-in-good-fun. "I thought *House on Haunted Hill* was a really very funny, kooky idea," related the actor to interviewer Bob Madison in 1979. "I must say I did enjoy that." It shows.

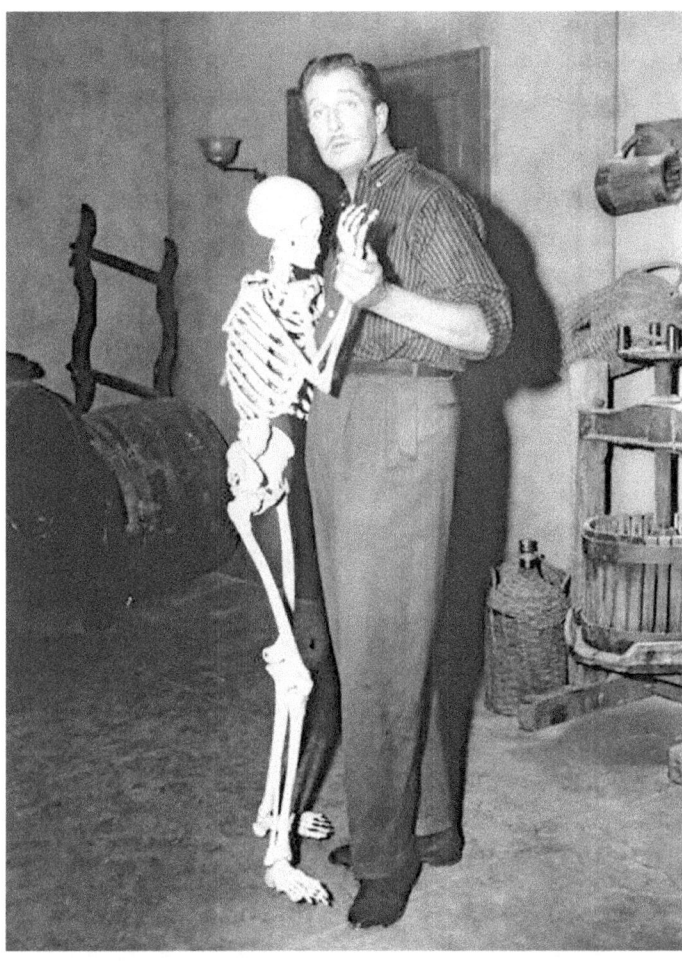

Vincent Price lightens the mood on the House on Haunted Hill *set.*

"The male lead had to be someone special—elegant, fey, with an offbeat personality," wrote William Castle in his autobiography *Step Right Up! I'm Gonna Scare the Pants Off America*. Castle found that "someone special" in Vincent Price. The producer/director related that he "lucked out on another rainy evening" when the filmmaker spotted Price sitting in a small coffee shop near the Samuel Goldwyn Studio. Castle introduced himself, made his pitch to the actor, and clinched the deal over a slice of pie. As reported by Castle, Price found the idea of dunking his conniving wife in the basement acid bath "charming."

The part of Frederick Loren proved an ideal venue for Price's particular brand of tongue-in-cheek charm. When the dour Pritchard remarks, "Seven [ghosts] now, maybe more before morning," Price arches his elegant eyebrows and glances at his companions before remarking in his soft, buttery voice, "That's cheerful."

In explaining the terms of the 'party' to his collected guests, Frederick begins, "If I should die—" and abruptly stops. Here Price glances pointedly at his wife, a faint smile on his lips and a chuckle in his throat, before continuing in a bemused voice, "—you will be paid by my estate." Later in the same scene, Loren hands Annabelle her "party favor" (a loaded pistol). She refuses to take it, however, saying, "I don't need it." In the silkiest of tones, Price cajoles, "Are you sure my dear? Who knows, you may want to use it on me before this night is over." At this Annabelle grasps the proffered weapon, whereupon Price gently pushes the barrel *away* from himself, almost—but not quite—suppressing a subtle smirk. Thanks to Price's bemused demeanor (and White's witty dialogue), the fact that his wife wants to kill him becomes more than simply a nasty plot point but a secret source of amusement.

"*House on Haunted Hill* was an enormous success," remembered Vincent Price to interviewer Gregory J. M. Catsos in the 1980s. "When William asked me to do it, my agent said, 'He won't pay you anything.' That's because William didn't have much money to work with. So I said, 'Well, let's take a percentage.' And I made a lot of money on it." Robb White (who was not only *House on Haunted Hill*'s screenwriter but Castle's business partner as well) remembered that the real reason Price was offered a percentage rather than flat salary was simply because Castle was too cheap to front the actor's relatively meager $12,000 asking price.

Price's costars perform admirably as well, particularly Carol Ohmart as the cold and conniving Annabelle Loren and Elisha Cook, Jr. (he of the perpetually-worried brow) as the credulous doom-sayer Watson Pritchard. Ms. Ohmart serves as a perfect foil for Price's self-possessed millionaire, exchanging quips with an icy coolness and calculated glance, while Mr. Cook serves as a verbal chorus for all the ghostly goings-on, periodically reminding us that "the ghosts are moving tonight, restless, hungry" or "[guns] are no good against the dead, only the living."

Even television pretty boy Richard Long (of *77 Sunset Strip*, *The Big Valley*, and *Nanny and the Professor* fame) fills the bill nicely as the handsome jet pilot(!)/hero who takes the beleaguered Nora under his protective wing. Long displays a naturalness in his acting (with his casual demeanor changing first to an amused concern and then to a determined steeliness as the hauntings unfold) that makes his character both likable and believable (in a decidedly *un*believable scenario). "I remember I objected to hiring the guy who played the hero, Richard Long," admitted White, "because he had a scar on his mouth which made him look like he was smiling all the time, even in the grimmest parts. But he turned out to be a good actor and I liked him very much."

While screenwriter Robb White conjures up some droll dialogue, he does less well with his general plotting, since *House on Haunted Hill*'s storyline is one of the most preposterously unlikely visions ever to haunt a house. One could have a field day pointing out all the plot holes, inconsistencies, and downright logistical impossibilities in this *House*. For instance, after contriving to get Nora to shoot and kill Frederick, Trent sets about secretly dumping his body into the acid vat. Wouldn't this completely negate all the convoluted conniving in which he and Annabelle had been engaged by destroying the evidence of Nora's crime and raising all sorts of further questions (such as who dumped the body)? Then, just as Trent goes to roll Frederick's apparently lifeless body into the acid, the lights suddenly go out and we hear a strangled cry and splash. *Who* turned out the lights (since only Trent and Frederick are present)—and *why*? (Obviously, Castle and Co. did – simply because it proved expedient to generate suspense by literally keeping things in the dark). And never mind the amazing amount of rigging each of the ghostly gags would have taken (particularly the physically impossible rope maneuvers), and how the two perpetrators seem to accomplish them almost instantaneously (such as when Annabelle appears outside Nora's window—even though there truly is no way out of the house—and mere seconds later appears back inside, trussed up in a hanging harness and swinging by the neck in the hallway). And let's not even dwell upon the climactic skeleton walk, with Frederick absurdly decked out in some Rube Goldberg version of a puppeteer's harness. (Incidentally, this fright gag—which Castle labeled "the most exciting scene in the picture"—is something of a disappointment as Mr. Bones awkwardly sidles, wobbles, and shuffles ["…off his mortal coil"?] forward, obviously pulled none-too-convincingly by wires. At this point, cinematographer Carl E. Guthrie, who has done so well with his low-key, mood-enhancing illumination, lets Castle (and the viewer) down by throwing too much light on the fleshless carcass, making it look like just what it is—a set of wired-together plastic bones.

All this rational carping is missing the point, however, for *House on Haunted Hill* is not a logic-driven movie. Whatever the script lacks in verisimilitude, Castle makes up for with macabre enthusiasm and good old-fashioned chills. Carolyn Craig and Carol Ohmart's piercing screams alone (some of the loudest ever put to celluloid) should cover up (or at least distract from) a plethora of plot holes. Obviously, Castle was more than willing to sacrifice plausibility for cheap thrills—and cheap thrills are what *House on Haunted Hill* is all about.

To this end, Castle employs some effective (if obvious) cinematic techniques, milking each spooky situation for all it is worth. When Frederick presents his guests with their "party favors" (seven miniature caskets, each containing a loaded gun), the camera, focused on the compact coffins, moves along with him as he opens the lids one by one. The angle of sight is such that we cannot see what's inside these intriguingly-shaped boxes until Frederick reaches the final two, prolonging the moment and building suspense.

Castle stages the film's first big shock—the abrupt appearance of the witch-like caretaker—with a simple effectiveness that underlines the jolt. The camera focuses in tight on Nora as she kneels down and searches a wall for a secret panel. When she stands up, so does the camera, abruptly revealing a hideous, hissing visage now hovering next to her.

In another scene, a terror-stricken Nora rushes into the living room calling for Lance. She stops and looks about her. The camera then pans across the lifeless room (in complete silence) to show how utterly alone she is. After what seems a one-hundred-and-eighty-degree motion, the camera (and our vision) encounters the room's dusty old organ—which suddenly begins to play of its own accord. A hoary device to be sure, but one given an added oomph by Castle's slow and careful buildup.

The film's true shuddery highlight (*not* the disappointing skeleton scene), however, comes when Nora sees the 'ghost' of the hanged Annabelle. In her room, the lights suddenly go out. By flashes of illumination from the lightning storm raging outside, we see a rope slither up through the bars covering the open window, slide along the floor, and wraps itself around Nora's ankles. Rooted to the spot in horror, Nora sees Annabelle floating outside the window, the noose end of the rope tied about her neck. Annabelle's apparition then recedes into the darkness and the rope uncoils itself from Nora's legs and follows. The immobilizing spell of terror broken, Nora rushes out of her room into the hall—and right into the hanging body of Annabelle. It's an eerily macabre sequence of sheer inventiveness which loses none of its impact after having been revealed as an elaborate hoax (despite the logistical impossibility of such a feat).

This brings up a potential complaint by viewers: that there really are no ghosts in this haunted house, since everything is (sort of) explained away as part of the convoluted murder plot(s). But even though all the ghostly manifestations prove to be of human rather than supernatural origin, one still feels that this house is indeed haunted (a feeling reinforced by the picture's beginning and end which feature the eerie, disembodied sounds of clanking, moaning, and shrieking). With admirable aid from cinematographer Guthrie, Castle creates an apparitional atmosphere so filled with spectral shenanigans that its residue remains long after the (lame) explanations fade. When Pritchard, staring into the acid vat, delivers the film's final words ("now there are nine; there'll be more—*many* more") one can scarce disbelieve it, particularly when the ghastly groans and spectral shrieks start up as he concludes, "They're coming for *me* now. And then they'll come for *you*!"

Shot in the dog days of Summer 1958 for about $150,000, *House on Haunted Hill* made over $4 million according to producer/director William Castle (who admittedly possessed a reputation for, shall we say, exaggeration). Whatever the real figure, there's no denying that the movie proved wildly successful at the box office, with lines of (mostly kids) queuing up around the block at those theaters rigged up with Castle's latest gimmick.

After the huge (and wholly unexpected) success of William Castle's first horror film, *Macabre* (1958), "Allied Artists wanted another picture immediately," (wrote the filmmaker in his autobiography), "and the exhibitors wanted another Castle gimmick…something original and more daring than the insurance policy." (As a promotional ploy for *Macabre*, Castle had insured every patron for $1,000 with Lloyds of London against death by fright. While this gimmick brought in the dollars by the bucketfulls, Castle was disappointed [reported Robb White] that he never got the chance to actually pay out on the policy [since nobody ever died while watching *Macabre*] and so reap even greater dividends from the attendant publicity.) This "more daring" gimmick for *House on Haunted Hill* turned out to be "Emergo." Castle enthusiastically described it in his autobiography: "We build a separate black box and install it next to the screen…. We build a plastic, twelve-foot skeleton [the actual ones were about half that size] and put it on a wire running over the audience's heads up to the projection booth. At the point where Vincent Price manipulates the skeleton on the screen, the projectionist pushes a button. The black box at the side opens, the skeleton lights up and moves on the wire, traveling electrically over the audience and up into the balcony."

It took some selling to convince the Allied Artists executives that it'd work, but soon theaters everywhere were equipped with these mysterious black boxes from which (as the *New York Times* so blithely put it) glow-in-the-dark skeletons "slid straight forward to the balcony, blankly eyed the first row of customers, and slid back."

But the best-laid plans of mice and hucksters… "We finally got it figured out so they worked all right," recalled Robb White, "and then the kids shot them down—they'd come in with everything short of bazookas, and kill our skeletons! They cost us more than the movie!" As critic Howard Thompson wryly observed about Emergo's flying skeletons: "Here was one performer who obviously couldn't wait to meet the public and instantly regretted it."

"I know I'm a darned good showman," boasted William Castle to interviewer John Brosnan, "no one could top my gimmicks." Indeed, but even without the questionable allure of a plastic skeleton gliding overhead, *House on Haunted Hill* remains a "darned good show." For a cinematic Halloween treat (that's chock full of tricks), one could hardly go wrong paying a visit to the *House on Haunted Hill*.

> Denis Meikle, astute editor of *The Fantastic Fifties* (issue 5, Summer 2018), declined to utilize my original title. Why? Well, I include it here in all its punny glory so you can answer that question yourself.

OF 'HYPNOMAGIC' AND 'HYPNOVISTA'… KEEPING A *HYPNOTIC EYE* ON *THE BLACK MUSEUM*

In the mid–1950s, the world (or at least a small corner of American pop culture) was entranced by the tale of Bridey Murphy—a phenomenon based on the dubious claims of Colorado housewife Virginia Tighe, who, under hypnosis, recalled a past life as a 19th century Irishwoman named Bridey Murphy. The resultant bestselling book, *The Quest for Bridey Murphy* by Morey Bernstein, bolstered by the 1956 feature film *The Search for Bridey Murphy*, inspired others to take up the hypno-flag, and for a short time hypnotism was all the rage—particularly at the cinematic hard tops and passion pits of the era. While hypnotism permeated such features as *The She-Creature* (1956) and *The Undead* (1957), two 1959 efforts went that extra hypno-mile and turned the technique into an audience-attracting gimmick: AIP's *Horrors of the Black Museum* and Allied Artists' *The Hypnotic Eye*.

"See the fantastic binocular murder!" –*Horrors of the Black Museum* ad line

And once you see it, you may never forget it...

The lurid *Horrors of the Black Museum*, about famous London crime writer Edmund Bancroft (a particularly bombastic Michael Gough) whose private basement crime museum rivals the famed "Black Museum" at Scotland Yard, and who employs a variety of bizarre weapons (including his own hypnotized and transformed assistant) to commit murders so that he can then write about them, is *not* a great film. Still, it remains embedded in one's psyche like, well, two needles to the eyes—due to that self-same "binocular murder." Arguably the most shocking and memorable movie opening of the decade, this "killer" scene remains a grabber that drops the jaw and flips the stomach. Few things disturb more than the idea of violent eye trauma, and here the filmmakers take it to the Nth degree, providing a metaphorical stab to the brain via the one suggested onscreen.

The movie offers a few other memorable moments as well, such as when a beautiful woman lays down to sleep only to look up into the face of a disfigured maniac operating a portable guillotine hovering above her headboard! (Needless to say, this was the *last* thing the unfortunate ever saw.) Then there's the scene in which an over-inquisitive doctor stands in the wrong place in Bancroft's "Black Museum" only to be skewered by a cartoon bolt of electricity, with his body subsequently disposed of in a gigantic open vat of flesh-eating acid.

"Every instrument of murder in *Black Museum* was from an actual murder and is in Scotland Yard's Black Museum," claimed producer/co-writer Herman Cohen to film historian Tom Weaver. "The murder with the binoculars happened in the thirties, in Kent, which is outside of London. A young stable boy who was very much in love with his master's daughter was fired for having sex with her in the stables. And she would have nothing to do with him after that. When the Royal Ascot meet started the following year, she received through the mail a pair of binoculars. She took them to the window, she focused them, and the needles penetrated through her eyes and killed her. The stable boy was found, was tried and was hung."

Fortunately, the film's shocking re-creation of this ingeniously horrible killing was staged more for suggestion than gore. As Cohen noted, "You really don't see anything happen in that scene. After the girl screams, 'My eyes! My eyes!' as the blood drips through her fingers, we then cut to a close-up of the binoculars on the carpet, with the needles extended. But you don't see it happen, you have to visualize it." Indeed, this then-tween author, watching it for the first time on television, visualized it with jarring impact...

Another striking aspect of these *Horrors* is star Michael Gough, who Cohen labeled "the cheaper version of Vincent Price," and whom he lauded as "a much better actor." As the calculating yet unhinged Bancroft, Gough alternates a velvety condescension with a strident near-hysteria to construct a volatile persona that, while not in the least believable, remains no less entertaining to watch—if for nothing else then to see what in the hell he's going to do next. Though vacillating between silky smoothness and noisy bombast, Gough's forceful delivery rarely disappoints. "You don't have time with a Herman Cohen production to actually explore anything, do you?" dryly noted the actor to interviewer Steven Eramo (perhaps recalling his ill-defined Bancroft character). "You're working against the clock a lot of the time. And they are very sort of weird and wonderful stories."

"Weird" indeed in the case of *Horrors of the Black Museum*; but as to "wonderful," well... one's mileage may vary—particularly given the picture's pacing problems (nothing much happens during the half-hour following the opening binocular incident) and a script littered with over-the-top misogynistic dialogue like "I tell you no woman can hold her tongue, they're all a vicious, unreliable breed." Yikes. (Even more damning, the film's three female characters—gold-digging mistress, blackmailing harpy shopkeeper, and vapid, bossy girlfriend—seem to bear out this nasty attitude.) Toss in a bank of *Star Trek*–level electrical equipment (all gauges, levers, and flashing lights) standing incongruously against one wall of his crypt-like "black museum," and a key plot point in which Bancroft employs some kind of wonder drug injection that temporarily transforms his assistant into a hypnotically-controlled, disfigured fiend ("The world thinks that Dr. Jekyll and Mr. Hyde were the figments of a great writer's imagination," Bancroft triumphantly announces, "but no, I have clearly demonstrated that it is a fact!"), and the atmosphere of pulpish morbidity becomes nearly overwhelming.

Ironically (given his *ex post facto* remarks about Michael Gough vs. Vincent Price), Herman Cohen initially sought *Price* for the Bancroft role. "But we couldn't afford Price at that time," explained the producer. "There were other people I was thinking about, too, like Orson Welles." Cohen finally decided to hire an English actor (to take advantage of the British "Eady Plan" and its attendant tax breaks), and so approached Gough. "We

Visitors to The Horrors of the Black Museum *were exposed to the wonders of "Hypnovista" in 1959...*

sat and we talked and I just flipped over him personally. He's a marvelous man, a wonderful person," enthused Cohen about his eventual star.

According to Cohen, those pesky killer binoculars bedeviled more than just impressionable viewers. "We opened up at a hundred theaters," recounted Cohen to *Scarlet Street*'s Jessie Lilley, "a big, big opening—and I flew in [to New York] with the binoculars. Ruth Pologe, the publicity gal I hired for *Black Museum*—she suggested I report that I lost the binoculars at the airport. Which I did. Which I reported to security. The police arrived, and we received the front page on two of the tabloids in New York—the *Post* and the *News*, I think." And despite an assistant D.A. calling Cohen "to try to prove that it was a publicity gimmick, which had cost the city a lot of money," the producer got away with the ploy scot-free. William Castle would have been proud.

Speaking of the "King of the Gimmicks," for *Horrors*' American release, AIP spliced onto the beginning of the film a 13-minute lecture on hypnotism by "internationally renowned psychologist" (according to AIP publicity, anyway) Dr. Emile Franchel who has "made bold ventures into the field of 'hypno-criminology'" (whatever *that* might be). "Jim Nicholson was looking for some gimmick," said Cohen, "because this was a big picture in Cinemascope and color. ...All kinds of gimmicks were working for Columbia, where Bill Castle was releasing his pictures, so Jim thought we should have a gimmick with *Horrors of the Black Museum*." Calling their gimmick "Hypnovista," AIP prominently played it up in their posters and advertising. As Franchel proclaims in the film's trailer, "Hypnovista—it is a psychological technique whereby you, seated in the auditorium, actually become part of the action you see on the screen."

Dubious hypno-gimmicks aside, *Horrors of the Black Museum*, which cost less than $400,000 to produce, returned $3 million to AIP by the close of 1959. So successful was it that, according to Cohen, it paved the way for AIP's long and profitable line of Poe pictures in the 1960s. Cohen told interviewer Stuart Galbraith IV that "*Horrors of the Black Museum* gave AIP its first picture in color and Cinemascope. That was their first big picture. Once they did that and released it, and it was a big, big hit, that's when they let Roger [Corman] do *The Pit and the Pendulum* and a couple of those pictures in color with Vincent Price." (Note: *House of Usher* was actually the first AIP Corman film in color and Scope; *Pit* followed later.)

In any case, and quite amazingly, *Horrors of the Black Museum* was inducted into the Museum of Modern Art(!) in the 1990s—at the request of filmmaker Martin Scorsese(!!). Apparently, those binoculars really left a mark...

"BEWARE OF THE EYE! Its hypnotic power turns human flesh into robots!" –The Hypnotic Eye poster

A beautiful woman rubs shampoo into her hair and, instead of approaching the kitchen sink, walks to the stove, lights the gas burner, and bends down to the flame. She raises up with her head and arms ablaze, and, suddenly realizing what she's done, screams in pain and fear. The scene goes black and the credits roll for *The Hypnotic Eye*, a rather grisly, ahead-of-its time gimmick-thriller.

The story concerns the Great Desmond (Jacques Bergerac), a successful stage hypnotist who uses a small hypnotic device resembling an eye to entrance young women onstage and plant post-hypnotic suggestions that induce them to later mutilate themselves in various ways. His motivation: his beloved assistant (Allison Hayes) is herself disfigured (but wears a very convincing mask), and wants to destroy the beauty of all those around her.

"Oh, that was such fun," recalled Merry Anders to interviewer Paul Woodbine. Anders plays a victim that washes her face with acid (and received top

...*While patrons of* The Hypnotic Eye *had to face the irresistible "Hypnomagic" the following year.*

femme billing, despite filling only a supporting role). "And it was such a weird picture." Weird indeed. Not only does the film contain the bizarre mutilation scenes (and some particularly gruesome makeup), it offers beatnik coffeehouse "cool, man, cool" poetry (delivered by real-life beatnik Eric "Big Daddy" Nord), the strikingly beautiful Allison Hayes, Fred "the Great Imposter" Demara as a doctor(!), and, of course, "HypnoMagic."

"HYPNOMAGIC: It makes YOU part of the show!" proclaimed the posters, while the movie's pressbook exhorted exhibitors to "sell HypnoMagic big and it will pay off big for you!" This "big sell" turned out to be a William Castle-style gimmick in which, just before the movie's climax, Bergerac, performing his stage show, asks that the house lights be turned on (which was the cue for the projectionist to raise the lights about 40 percent). At this point Bergerac speaks directly to the camera, merging the audience in the movie with the audience in the theater. Bergerac then demonstrates the "power of the mind" by squeezing the juice from a "bitter, bitter" lemon and informing the viewer how s/he can't help but salivate (which, amusingly, is true). Next comes a plethora of party tricks (one involving a balloon—handed out to each patron at the start of the show—supposedly becoming a lead weight in the viewer's lap) that, unlike the simple lemon bit, *don't* work and only serve to slow down the hitherto quick-paced proceedings. (Of course, the entertainment value of observing a theater full of people all rapidly raising and lowering their arms for one of these silly hypno-games would have been worth the price of admission alone!) "The potentialities of this new technique are tremendous," enthused producer Charles Bloch in the film's press materials. "HypnoMagic opens up whole new vistas to the director and is bound to work an organic change throughout the medium—something like when pictures first learned to talk." These "new vistas" were apparently limited ones, as nobody rushed to implement any "organic changes," and HypnoMagic became yet another obscure footnote in cinema showmanship history.

On the distaff side, poorly developed characters (there's little interaction—much less affection—between Desmond and his assistant, for whom he's supposedly doing it all) and too many on-stage sequences sometimes bring the story to an abrupt hypno-halt. Still, Allison Hayes' intense demeanor (and beauty), some shocking set-pieces, and an intriguing (though admittedly hokey) story line make *The Hypnotic Eye* worth a look.

At the film's close, a protagonist comes onstage and delivers this warning to Desmond's audience (and to the viewer): "Hypnosis, although an important and invaluable medical tool, can be extremely dangerous when improperly used by untrained or unscrupulous practitioners. Therefore, never allow yourself to be hypnotized by anyone who is not a medical doctor or who has not been recommended to you by your doctor—not even in a motion picture theater." Not just another amusing entertainment, *The Hypnotic Eye* serves as a public service announcement!

> Much like AIP did back in 1957, *Filmfax* magazine unleashed this twin-terror essay on their unsuspecting readership in 2002 (issue 93/94).

TWIN BILL TERRORAMA! *INVASION OF THE SAUCER MEN* & *I WAS A TEENAGE WEREWOLF*—A TANDEM TRIUMPH FOR TWO AIP DRIVE-IN FLICKS!

This was the 1957 AIP double-bill that opened the floodgates of teen-targeted terror that washed over the drive-ins in the late '50s. Beyond reaching their intended audience then frequenting the passion pits, both *I Was a Teenage Werewolf* and *Invasion of the Saucer Men* have managed to stand the test of time to become two of the most beloved genre entries of that all-important transitional decade.

The 1950s saw horror/fantasy cinema in flux, with traditional Gothic giving way to the more "modern"—and simplistic—terrors of science-gone-mad and alien invaders (reflecting the cultural fears of the time: namely, atomic annihilation and nonconformity/xenophobia), before the 1960s saw it move into a more self-conscious and sophisticated arena. Horror in the 1950s was (to borrow from the tacky world of advertising) "not your father's genre," as (like its intended viewers) horror went through its cinematic version of adolescence.

At the head of their class stood the big-screen cohorts *I Was a Teenage Werewolf* and *Invasion of the Saucer Men*. What set these two above their innumerable cinematic classmates (apart from clever scripting and superior presentation) are the way they addressed their issues through the eyes of the average teenager, validating the feelings and actions of this much-maligned and ostensibly powerless demographic. "If you're not part of the solution, you're part of the problem" is a favorite

With this combo, AIP provided one of the most entertaining horror/sci-fi double-bills of the decade. (pressbook)

saying of social activists everywhere, and in both *Teen Werewolf* and *Saucer Men* the adult establishment were definitely *not* part of the solution (with the disbelieving adults in *Saucer Men* hindering the scared-but-heroic teens at every turn, and Whit Bissell's "respected" doctor actually *causing* the problem in *Teen Werewolf*). Such resonance makes this modest yet wildly successful (both fiscally and posterity-wise) double feature worthy of a critical look.

So…turn up those tinny window speakers, douse the headlights and settle in to that rich Corinthian leather to revisit one of the best drive-in horror/sci-fi double-bills of the fabulous fifties…

"TEENAGE GUYS 'N' DOLLS…TERRIFIED, FOR DRIVING THIS BOY IS A SAVAGE LUST…TO KILL!" –I Was a Teenage Werewolf trailer

At the time of its release, *I Was a Teenage Werewolf* sparked a lot of controversy with its provocative advertising campaign. A Senate subcommittee even discussed the film, which (according to director Gene Fowler) cost $82,000 to make, was shot in six days, and earned over two million dollars before the year was out. Its tremendous cult appeal and success encouraged AIP (and others) to churn out dozens of other "teen" monster movies in the years to come, such as *I Was a Teenage Frankenstein*, *Blood of Dracula*, and *Teenage Caveman*.

But beyond its obvious exploitation value, *I Was a Teenage Werewolf*'s incisive script, inventive direction and excellent cast set it above its contemporaries and imitators. Without the werewolf angle, it would have been a tight and engrossing teen drama; with the lycanthropy, it became a superior sci-fi/horror entry; and with that *title*, it evolved into a cult classic.

The story centers on Tony (Michael Landon), an angry, sullen, but ultimately likable and well-intentioned high-schooler whose hair-trigger temper gets him into trouble with his school, his girl, and the law. When Tony unthinkingly beats up a friend, he realizes he needs help. The troubled teen goes to see psychiatrist Dr. Brandon (Whit Bissell), who, unfortunately for Tony, has been seeking the perfect human guinea pig for his secret experiment. And Tony indeed has "the proper disturbed emotional background" needed. "Through hypnosis [and a special serum]," the mad medico explains to his assistant, "I'm going to regress this boy back, back into the primitive past that lurks within him. I'm going to transform him and unleash the savage instincts that lie hidden within." The result? No, not a primitive Neanderthal but a werewolf! (Apparently, all those evolutionists and anthropologists got it wrong, and we're more lupine than primate.) Brandon's reasoning for such a bizarre achievement: "Mankind is on the verge of destroying itself; the only hope for the human race is to hurl it back into its primitive dawn, to start all over again." A bit reactionary, perhaps, but heartfelt. After killing several people as a werewolf, the confused Tony is identified as the monster and goes on the run, finally seeking out the doctor, leading to a final creation vs. creator confrontation.

Though low budget, *Teen Werewolf* shines in nearly every department, from the thoughtful scripting and well-drawn characters to the carefully staged technical aspects and spot-on acting. The werewolf slant is simply an added bonus (at least for those horror enthusiasts among us).

From the get-go, the film draws in the viewer, beginning with an exciting (and surprisingly violent and realistic) schoolyard fight enhanced by involving camerawork and editing, complete with split-second shots of battered faces and flying fists (flying even *into* the camera). Then Tony—the hero—picks up a shovel(!) to swing at his opponent's head, and even throws dirt in his eyes! None of the expected sedate fisticuffs or Queensbury Rules here; such employment of dirty tricks by Tony during his introduction makes him a much more intriguing character.

Though many "stars" who got their start in low-budget fare like this tend to try to sweep their early days as a take-anything-offered-actor under the rug, Michael Landon (who came to prominence via such television megahits as *Bonanza*, *Little House on the Prairie* and *Highway to Heaven*) regarded his debut effort with fondness, and always talked about it freely, even affectionately. And no wonder, considering the fine performance he delivered. Landon (who, according to producer Herman Cohen beat out Scott Marlowe and *Jack Nicholson* for the role) is fresh-faced and eager in his big-screen debut, full of energy and charm and possessing a winning smile—in contrast to his violent temper. The fledgling actor makes his character both real and intense. When Tony responds violently to an innocuous Halloween prank by viciously beating a friend and pushing his girlfriend to the floor, the look of pained confusion and self-loathing on his face when he realizes what he's done speaks volumes. It's a dramatic—and convincing—moment, one that drives Tony to do what he'd previously sworn never to: go see "head shrinker" Brandon.

Landon is just as effective in hirsute form. Running, snarling and leaping with a wild energy, he *becomes* the savage beast. In the attack in the gym, he lunges at the girl, heedless of the stack of folding chairs he crashes into in his frenzied bloodlust. It's an impressive physical performance that perfectly matches his intense emotional one. "[Michael] did all the stunts," recounted Cohen to interviewer Jessie Lilley, "he almost killed himself! In a way, it was kind of weird. When he had the makeup on, he told me, 'I really feel like a werewolf.' When he was chasing Dawn Richards in that gym to attack and kill her, we had to stop the camera and pull him off. He was really into it."

"You could ask [Michael] to do anything and he'd do it," remembered director Fowler to Tom Weaver. "I loved Michael—he was a very young kid at that time, maybe twenty years old, but he was good, a hard-working guy, always knew his lines."

As Dr. Brandon, reliable character actor Whit Bissell takes a rather ridiculous character and makes him utterly convincing. Far from the raving madmen found in the like-themed films of the 1940s, Bissell's "mad scientist" is cold and calculating yet no less committed, replacing bombast with a chilling single-mindedness. When Bissell rhetorically asks his dubious assistant, "What is one life, compared to such a triumph?" his tone of cold determinism both convinces and chills. Bissell's natural delivery and quiet intensity transforms this one-dimensional character into a 3-D villain, one who fully believes in what he's doing and whose demeanor communicates that belief to the viewer.

"Shooting *Teenage Werewolf* was more like shooting a television show," remembered Bissell to interviewer Pat Jankiewicz. "It had a very short schedule and Gene Fowler was a very fast director. You'd rehearse the lines, then shoot the scene. Michael Landon was a nice kid."

Former editor and first-time director Gene Fowler, along with veteran cinematographer Joseph LaShelle (*Laura*), does wonders with the paltry budget and inadequate schedule, taking the time and effort to build upon and enhance the solid script with fine technical touches. For instance, the camera tracks in slowly to focus on Tony as he recalls a violent memory under hypnosis. When Brandon suddenly and forcefully barks, "That'll be all; wake up!" the camera—just as suddenly—pulls back to take in the whole scene, the movement underscoring the dramatic shift *and* the power and control wielded by Brandon.

Then there's the now-classic scene of the attack on the high-school gymnast. As the leotard-clad young lady stretches and hangs upside down on the parallel bars, the school bell next to the watching Tony suddenly sounds, triggering a transformation. The girl then notices Tony, and we see—upside down—the snarling beast advancing towards us in a clever and disturbing victim's point-of-view shot.

Unfortunately, after the careful character build-up and the highlight of the gym sequence, the film begins to flag, and we must make do with a few poignant scenes involving Tony's confused and concerned father, some police procedural sequences, a rather listless dog attack on the werewolf (involving Fowler's own dog) and some tramping in the woods (complete with torch-wielding posse) until the final, admittedly exciting, confrontation when the monster turns on its maker. There's also a rather tepid (though obligatory, considering its target audience) teen party sequence, complete with silly song ("Eeny, Meeny, Miney, Mo") and goofy dancing. And scripter "Ralph Thornton" (a pseudonym employed by novelist Aben Kandel and—claims the man himself—producer Cohen) hauls out that hoary old chestnut (which was creaking with age even in the 1950s) for the film's closing line: "It's not for Man to interfere in the ways of God."

But overlook these few foibles, and *I Was a Teenage Werewolf* stands out as a shining example of artists and technicians taking an exploitable (and preposterous) premise and constructing an engrossing film suffused with themes and subtexts that (much like Fowler's other genre entry, *I Married a Monster from Outer Space*) belies its absurd title. And who can fail to love a movie that uses werewolfery as a metaphor for teen angst?!

"NATURALLY…LOVERS' LANE IS FULL OF FRANTIC LOVERS
UNNATURALLY…THE SKY'S FULL OF FLYING SAUCERS!"
–*Invasion of the Saucer Men* trailer

On July 26, 1952, several Air Force jets were dispatched to intercept UFOs spotted over the Nation's Capital (no, they didn't find them). "INTERCEPTORS CHASE FLYING SAUCERS OVER WASHINGTON D.C." read the headlines the day after the incident—even as the Air Force suggested the phenomenon was weather related. But blind credulity being a cheap commodity, the notion of flying saucers invading our Earth caught on—and stayed on (despite no hard physical evidence to support such an assumption—alien corpses in secret government labs notwithstanding). While most alien invasion movies of the 1950s remained deadly serious, one little B-picture took a decidedly different tack in its presentation of visitors from another world.

Based on the pulpish 1955 short story "The Cosmic

Frame" by Paul W. Fairman, *Invasion of the Saucer Men* opens at an Old Dark (farm)House as lightning flashes and thunder rumbles. "Spooky, huh?" begins the goofy-sounding narrator (Lyn Osborn). "I learned a long time ago you gotta start off your pitch with a bang." Osborn then leads us into the story as a pair of small-town teenagers (Steve Terrell and Gloria Castillo) accidentally run over a four-foot bulbous-headed alien with their car out at the local lovers' lane. When the two seek help from the authorities, the adults give their story no credence, particularly after the invader's companions have removed the alien body and left a human victim in its place—a drunken drifter (Frank Gorshin). (The creatures possess retractable needles in their fingers that inject a clear liquid into their victims—a liquid we later discover to be pure alcohol!) Meanwhile, a secret (and very small) Army detachment has found and accidentally blown up the aliens' saucer. The two teens—now held for manslaughter—elude police and, with the aid of Gorshin's skeptical partner (Osborne), discover the creatures' weakness (they disintegrate in bright light). Enlisting their lovers' lane cohorts, they surround the invaders with the teenagers' cars and "headlight" the aliens to death.

Unique among fifties sci-fi movies, *Invasion of the Saucer Men* possesses a charmingly tongue-in-cheek tone. While most of its contemporaries spend their time trying to convince us of their overblown earnestness as they throw all manner of giant bugs and mutant marauders at us, *Saucer Men* takes a "we're just here to have fun" attitude towards its preposterous premise. Such an approach makes its cramped sets, dark photography and all-too-frequent dull stretches much easier to forgive. (According to *Saucer Men*'s creature-creator, Paul Blaisdell, the film started out as just another straight AIP monster movie, but "It sort of collapsed into a comedy about three days into production." It seems rather unlikely, however, that writer Lou Rousoff ever intended his loopy script be taken seriously.)

Apart from its amusing attitude, one of the biggest things the movie has going for it are the quintessential Little Green Men that land in its little corner of Hicksburg (yes, that's the name of the film's small-town setting). Arguably frequent AIP monster-maker Paul Blaisdell's finest shoestring creations, these "cabbage-heads" (as their creator labeled them) have become the veritable poster children for BEMs (Bug-Eyed Monsters). (In fact, so popular has this iconographic image become that the movie poster for *Invasion of the Saucer Men*—featuring prominent full-color renderings of these BEMs—commands a four-figure price tag!) The real beauty of these bulbous-brained invaders is that they personify the pulp sci-fi ideal of Little Green Men From Mars so perfectly that they become the ultimate parody. (Ironically, Blaisdell painted said Saucer Men a reddish-brown color rather than green, though in the black and white film—which does indeed refer to them as "little green men"—one would never know. Also, these huge-headed extraterrestrials possessed even larger craniums as Blaisdell originally built them. Once the producers saw them, however, they instructed Blaisdell to make them smaller. Since they were made of unforgiving fiberglass, Blaisdell simply cut a wedge out of the back of the headpiece and pushed it together.)

Director Edward L. Cahn employs said saucer men (midgets in black jumpsuits sporting the ungainly cabbage heads and alien hands) to good effect, utilizing close-ups, quick cuts and herky-jerky motion to exploit the invaders' bizarre appearance and actions (including the dead alien's grotesque hand detaching itself from the corpse and scuttling about puncturing tires and menacing the heroine). "[Cahn] was a very underrated director," opined Blaisdell's assistant Bob Burns in *Monsterscene* magazine. "He was a get 'em done guy. One take unless everything went totally nuts… It's funny, he was an English guy with this real heavy English accent. He smoked a pipe all the time. The pipe was right in the middle of his mouth and when he talked you couldn't understand what he was saying half of the time."

Cahn stages a rather exciting mano-a-mano (or, more precisely, claw-to-horn) battle between an alien and the local farmer's cranky bull (resulting in a gruesome eye-gouging for the unlucky saucer man). "They shot the bullfight live with a Brahma bull," recalled Burns. "It didn't match the dummy head, but that's no matter, 'a cow's a cow' (studio logic, ha!)." For the gory goring, "we had the Styrofoam eyeballs which is all they were. [Blaisdell] drilled a hole and then put a piece of wax over the top and blended it in so you couldn't see it. I had an actual stuffed bull's head on a rod. We shot shots of it coming into the camera, and it was saved by quick editing…Then, when it gets gored in the eye, I could see where the waxed hole was. I just went and put a horn in there. Paul was behind with a grease gun full of chocolate syrup."

When an Army Colonel asks his Lieutenant if the local law bought their phony cover story about "crashed jets," his bemused underling (a former public relations man) reassures him with, "Colonel, sir, you're talking to the man that made the papers believe that 45-year-old B-girls were teenage maidens." It's a rather ironic line, for *Saucer Men*'s teenage protagonists look more like they're closer to 30 than 20 (a trait common to teen-targeted tales of the time). The movie throws this peculiarity into our faces more than most by continually harping on the idea that the protagonists need to find an "adult" who'll believe them—even though these "kids" should be paying off their mortgaged tract homes rather than hanging out at the malt shop!

But overaged teens are simply part of the charm of this fun little Fifties anomaly, which, when viewed in the right frame of mind, makes one long for a simpler, fairyland time of clean-cut teenagers, lovers' lane make-out sessions and inept Little Green Men From Mars.

I Was a Teenage Werewolf and *Invasion of the Saucer Men* offered to 1950s teenagers what *Cocoon* offered to 1980s geriatrics—validation. While *Teen Werewolf* explored (in a cleverly disguised—and hirsute—manner) the individual anguish and alienation that often comes with adolescence, *Saucer Men* explored (in a cleverly disguised—and tongue-in-cheek—manner) the group isolation and often unfair treatment experienced by teens. And the films did so in an intelligent, witty and entertaining fashion, making this a perfect double-bill time capsule for all those monster lovers with a special fondness for the simple innocence and blind naïveté of the 1950s.

Monsters from the Vault magazine showcased this 1958 double-bill in 2001 (issue 13).

DRIVE-IN DEMONS: *IT! THE TERROR FROM BEYOND SPACE* AND *CURSE OF THE FACELESS MAN* (1958)

"THE TWO MOST HELLISH HORROR HITS THAT EVER TURNED BLOOD TO ICE!!!" –United Artists pressbook

Though the UA pressbook may have put a bit too fine a point on it with their claim, there's no denying that the 1958 double feature release of *It! The Terror from Beyond Space* and *Curse of the Faceless Man* (both directed by the ubiquitous Edward L. Cahn and written by Jerome Bixby) was one of the more satisfying sci-fi/horror double-bills of the decade. This terror tandem is even more intriguing due to its mixing of the science fiction and horror subgenres (with the sci-fi oriented *It!* sharing the screen with the supernaturally charged *Faceless Man*). Granted, both are really monster-on-the-rampage *horror* movies (particularly given the claustrophobic, shadowy atmosphere Cahn infused into *It!*'s sci-fi setting), but the two make for a disparate yet still complementary pair.

"IT!...Reaches Through Space!...Scoops Up Men And Women!...Gorges on Blood!" –*It! The Terror from Beyond Space* poster

"$50,000 GUARANTEED! BY A WORLD RENOWNED INSURANCE COMPANY TO THE FIRST PERSON WHO CAN PROVE 'IT' IS NOT ON MARS NOW!" So promised the ads for what turned out to be one of the better sci-fi programmers of the 1950s (no… no one ever collected). While not on the level of such bigger-budgeted first-stringers as *The Day the Earth Stood Still, Invasion of the Body Snatchers* or *The Thing*, thanks to a solid (and much-copied) scenario, some evocative lighting and staging, and an almost noirish tone (complete with fatalistic narration), *It!* remains one of that decade's better benchwarmers.

It! took its inspiration from the best. "I had in my mind as a model," reported *It!*'s screenwriter Jerome Bixby to *Starlog*'s Pat Jankiewicz, "the Howard Hawks picture *The Thing*—the original, a fabulous suspense picture. I was thinking of an isolation situation and you've got these poor guys in the Arctic with this invincible critter who's picking 'em off one by one. What's a good way to adapt that? In a spaceship!" Bixby even went so far as to include overlapping, spontaneous-sounding dialogue *à la The Thing*. But "that kind of dialogue looks weird on paper (during shooting of *The Thing* it was extemporized in morning bull sessions), so nobody knew what the hell I was trying to do, and even if they had there wouldn't have been time to rehearse it on *It!*'s microscopic schedule."

Edited dialogue was the least of Bixby's problems, since *It!* could have easily become the screenplay that (literally) got away. "I was writing *It!* on the beach [in Venice, California]," recalled Bixby, "when a sudden squall came up out of the blue and most of the script went out surfing! I was splashing around and recovered maybe half of it." Fortunately, he was able to reconstruct the rest, and *It!* was ready for takeoff. (One final glitch involved the film's name; when the producers registered "*It! The Terror from Beyond Space*" with the MPAA Title Bureau, it drew protests from Universal-International who thought it too similar to their *It Came from Outer Space*—a film U-I were about to reissue. The matter seems to have been dropped, however, since nothing further came of the complaint.)

Double-feature poster.

Shot as *It! The Vampire from Beyond Space* (a title retained for its European release), the story (a blueprint for the later megahit *Alien*) is a great one for claustrophobic terror, as the titular bloodthirsty creature stows away on a rocketship leaving It's home planet of Mars. Soon, this Terror from Beyond Space begins picking off the crew one by one. The final siege, as the surviving crewmembers try to hold out in the very top compartment of the ship, with nowhere left to run, is thrilling. "Nothing to do but wait—" narrates hero Marshall Thompson as the tension mounts, "wait to see if the beast can reach us through the center hatch. We can go no higher. We are in the top level of the ship. This is where either we die—or it dies."

It! was the last creature feature to showcase an original monster suit from that prolific low-budget monster maker Paul Blaisdell, the man who created such '50s icons as the huge-headed "Saucer Men" from *Invasion of the Saucer Men* and the squat "Cucumber Monster" from *It Conquered the World*. "Ray 'Crash' Corrigan played the monster," recounted Blaisdell's assistant, Bob Burns, to *Filmfax*'s Ted Okuda, "but he wouldn't come to Topanga—where Paul lived—to get measured for the suit, so Paul had to sculpt the head over his own plaster bust. When Paul completed the outfit, the body of the creature was okay because Corrigan had sent over a pair of his long underwear, which Paul built the suit over. But when they put the head on Corrigan, his bulbous chin stuck out through the monster's mouth, so the make-up man painted his chin to look like a tongue. Everybody thinks the monster has a tongue, but it doesn't—it's just that Corrigan's chin kept snapping through the mouth because his head was so much bigger than Paul's." Blaisdell took six weeks to create the rather bulky suit for Corrigan to stomp around in, complete with plug-ugly face and three-fingered claws. Too bad those same claws frequently look awkward and useless, as do the floppy feet. The suit itself is baggy, and the bulky shoulder pads make It look like some weird alien linebacker.

Fortunately, director Edward L. Cahn (*Creature with the Atom Brain, The She-Creature, Voodoo Woman, Zombies of Mora Tau, Invasion of the Saucer Men, Invisible Invaders, The Four Skulls of Jonathan Drake*) builds suspense by keeping the creature predominantly off-camera for the film's first half. These proved to be the most effective of the monster scenes—as the beast rises up in silhouette or becomes a monstrous shadow moving across a wall—by playing upon the fear of the unseen, the unknown. Even with such obfuscating techniques, the film's author was unhappy with how much exposure the creature received. "I thought Eddie Cahn just shoved the monster down the audience's throat," complained Bixby. "Too much visibility." This was indeed the case for the film's final half-hour; yet, even in full view, the creature is large and ugly enough to make for a reasonably imposing menace, particularly when It dents a metal door or violently rips through a steel hatchway with its bare claws.

Apart from one overexposed monster, a few further glitches mar the perfect landing of this celluloid spacecraft. The rocket effects are primitive looking (complete with laughable smoke and sparkler effects); the two female astronauts play waitress to the male portion of the crew in true 1958 chauvinistic fashion; and the testosterone-charged crewmen seem to have no concerns about firing off guns, grenades and even a bazooka(!) inside a sealed rocket traveling through space. But the creature is menacing and the crew is likable (if admittedly clichéd), as are the players themselves. Thompson slips in a reaction shot of horrified surprise when he finds the pasty-faced body of a dead crewman. This momentary panic is something unusual for the typical '50s stalwart hero, who usually isn't allowed to let his terror show.

Shot in six days on just one (redressed) set, it's amazing that the film is as effective as it is. Cinematographer Kenneth Peach, Sr., provides some wonderfully evocative lighting, as well as plenty of camera movement. Atmospherically lit, the spaceship becomes a realm of shadows, dark corners and pools of blackness—admittedly impractical for a spacecraft but effective in creating a sinister and suspenseful tone. For moody monster mayhem 1950s-style, *It!*'s hard to beat.

"A Monster Loosed From The Bowels Of The Earth…On A Rampage For A Human Bride!"–Curse of the Faceless Man ad line

Southern Italy, August 24, 79 A.D.: Mount Vesuvius suddenly erupts, raining hot gas, ash and debris down upon the thriving Roman metropolis of Pompeii, killing inhabitants and encasing them in shells of molten muck. The terrified testament of a city destroyed was recorded in a letter by Pliny the Younger, who weathered the volcanic storm across the Bay of Naples at Misenum, 18 miles away. "Many raised their hands to the gods," he wrote, "and even more believed that there were no gods any longer and that this was one last unending night for the world…darkness and ashes came again, a great weight of them. We stood up and shook the ash off again and again, otherwise we would have been covered with it and crushed by the weight." After three days, the city of Pompeii was no more—buried under 30 feet of mineral ash. Reclaimed by nature and forgotten over the centuries, Pompeii was rediscovered in the 1700s by a farmer digging a well. Since then, many buildings and artifacts have been unearthed (and looted). The most striking of these "artifacts" are the victims themselves, their bodies having become molded forms of solidified ash—unmoving, faceless monuments to our frailty in the face of nature's fury.

Nearly two millennia after the devastation, *It! The Terror from Beyond Space* writer Jerome Bixby (*The Lost Missile*, *Fantastic Voyage* [story]) decided to strike back at nature and resurrect one of these petrified victims to enact the *Curse of the Faceless Man*. Okay, Bixby was actually just looking for a novel hook for a new horror flick, and so concocted a story of a Roman gladiator/slave hopelessly in love with an aristocratic girl in the city of Pompeii. A worshipper of the old Etruscan gods, Quintillus brings down the wrath of his deities upon the city that denied him his heart. Two Thousand years later a worker unearths the stone-encased body of Quintillus, which comes to life and goes after the reincarnation of his lost love (Elaine Edwards).

A cut-rate rehashing of the Boris Karloff classic *The Mummy* (1932), *Curse of the Faceless Man* is a fair-to-middlin' horror entry from the sci-fi-dominated fifties. Unfortunately, science fiction devotee Bixby felt the need to lessen the poignant mystery of his love-that-spans-the-ages concept with some lame, pseudo-scientific mumbo jumbo about "radioactivity in the ground, which has preserved the cells and provided energy" to the creature. And, of course, stuntman Bob Bryant in a bulky two-piece plaster suit is no "Karloff the Uncanny" in stunning Jack Pierce makeup.

Still, this "stone man" cuts a forbidding figure as it ever-so-slowly begins to move, then sits up and advances towards the camera/victim, the alien-ness of its hardened crust appearance highlighted by the shadows provided by cinematographer Kenneth Peach's moody lighting. While little more than a walking statue, this Vesuvian villain's doomed motivation and unique appearance combine to make it a monster both poignant and creepy.

Curse manages to give the impression that it actually takes place in Italy, an astounding feat considering that the entire seven-day shoot was completed in Southern California. The Griffith Park Observatory served as the "Museo Di Napoli," while the exotic-looking Portuguese Bend area near Palos Verdes and the beach at Malibu stood in for the "Cove of the Blind Fisherman."

California's Salton Sea became the Mediterranean when the monster literally dissolves at film's end (exactly *why* the "stone" creature disintegrates in salt water is never explained—another of Bixby's peculiar peccadilloes). "They had dry ice strapped to my legs so that the mist would rise up once I hit the water to seem as though I was dissolving," recalled stuntman Bob Bryant (who played the title terror) to interviewer Paul Parla.

The Faceless Man suit was created by Charles Gemora (who built—and played—the Martian in 1953's *The War of the Worlds*). "The costume they put me into," remembered Bryant (a former tackle for the California 49ers), "was simply a leotard which was in two sections… The head piece was just a simple stocking mold which they fitted over my head, and since the Faceless Man's eyes were supposed to be covered over with the lava crust, the only way I could see out of it was through two small camouflaged meshings which fit over each of the eye socket areas. The way the effect of my body being covered with lava crust was achieved was simply by sticking clumps of cotton to the leotard, and this took about two hours until they put this cotton all over me from head to toe and then layered me with a liquid coating of latex or glue of some sort."

Made for only about $100,000, *Curse* was indeed cursed with the expected low-budget problems. "The guy who set up all the break-away props like the doors I burst through and glass and so on was concerned if I would be able to actually burst though them, and he wondered if he had made the break-away doors a bit too thick," recounted Bryant. "Well, we didn't have the time or money to be going back and forth testing if they would work or not, so they told me to just give it all I had and kept their fingers crossed in that scene in the museum room when I smash through the doors. Well, I did give it all I had and not only did I go right through the doors with no problem, but almost went falling forward with the force I gave it." In the scene, it does indeed look like the Faceless Man is about to fall on his—er, face.

The *real* curse of *Faceless Man* is its pedestrian direction by veteran Edward L. Cahn, who offers few of the flourishes he displayed in *It! The Terror*, and uncomfortable performance by "hero" Richard Anderson (who plays a doctor called in to examine the stone man—*and* who just happens to be the fiancé of Quintillus' reincarnated love). Anderson (best known for his turn as Oscar Goldman on TV's *The Six Million Dollar Man*) remembers little about the film, despite it being his only starring movie. "That was another one I was doing just on my way to somewhere else, that trained me for television," was all he could (or cared to) recall to interviewer Tom Weaver. Understandable, really, since his dreary playing creates one of the dullest and least appealing heroes of the decade.

Though saddled with an unsteady script, occasional dull stretches and a leading man with a personality more petrified than Quintillus himself, *Curse of the Faceless Man* still manages to provide a rather unique—and modestly entertaining—variation on the time-honored mummy movie.

While *It! The Terror from Beyond Space* was an atmospheric and (mostly) effective progenitor of *Alien* (1979), and *Curse of the Faceless Man* was a rather stodgy but still (partially) effective variation on *The Mummy* (1932), they entertainingly combined to form two halves of one cinematic coin. A rampaging Martian monster and a love-struck crusty creature—both on the same bill. In 1958 it just didn't get any better than that.

> One can never have too many giant monsters, especially when the big beasts prove as engaging (and *unlikely*) as *The Killer Shrews* and *The Giant Gila Monster*. Thanks to *Fantastic Fifties* magazine (Special Edition no. 2) in 2019, I was able to spotlight a matched pair of my all-time favorites.

BIG BEASTS, SMALL BUDGETS: *THE KILLER SHREWS* AND *THE GIANT GILA MONSTER* (1959)

Gordon McLendon was a Texas millionaire who owned six radio stations and the ten-theater Tri-State Cinema chain. He also had ambitions to produce movies (perhaps inspired by other theater owners, like the AB-PT company, who decided to make their own movies to fill their cinema seats). So in 1959 the media tycoon formed McLendon Radio Pictures as a production/distribution company, banking on the synergy of radio advertising and theatrical exhibition to give him a leg up with the youth market. "If we can sell pictures," he stated confidently, "we can make pictures." His first pair of productions, however, also turned out to be his last, for while *The Killer Shrews* and *The Giant Gila Monster* (both produced by Ken Curtis and directed by Ray Kellogg) played successfully in Texas, they didn't fare so well across the country. McLendon eventually sold them to AIP, who subsequently peddled the TV

What's not to love?

rights to syndicator Screen Entertainment in 1963, where the duo spent many a late night and Saturday afternoon. It's a shame, really, as this one-off dualler remains a charmingly unique addition to the horror double feature subset.

> "This is station WKKK, and we urge you to report to your local authorities at once any sighting of a giant Killer Shrew!" –radio ad

Who would have thought that an animal such as the tiny shrew could become a movie monster menace? But then, the same people who brought us *The Killer Shrews* also made *The Giant Gila Monster* to complete a unique (and entertaining) double bill. The supposed giant mutant shrews are actually medium-sized coon dogs sporting stringy fur pelts, a long rat-like tail and fake fangs. None too convincing, especially with close-up inserts of an immobile puppet face added. But hey, this *is* low-budget filmmaking, and this engaging entry actually delivers some interesting situations and a few suspenseful moments—not to mention one of the most inventively bizarre climactic escapes ever filmed (in which three cast members duck-walk to safety under metal barrels with the hungry shrews snapping at their heels).

The story has a group of scientists conducting experiments on an isolated island in an attempt to find a solution to the world's growing population problem. The researchers consist of Dr. Craigis (Baruch Lumet), his zoologist daughter Ann (Ingrid Goude, Miss Universe 1957), and his two assistants, Dr. Baines (Gordon McClendon) and Jerry (Ken Curtis, a former singing cowboy who also produced the film and later achieved fame as "Festus" on TV's *Gunsmoke*). When boat captain Thorne Sherman (James Best) arrives with the week's supplies, things go horribly wrong as we learn that the scientists' experiments had inadvertently increased the size of their animal subjects a hundred-fold—and some have escaped. Now the island has been overrun with giant vicious mutated (and poisonous!) shrews. To make matters worse, a hurricane is coming and they can't leave the island. So the little group holes up in their house to wait out the storm and the night (when the hungry nocturnal monsters begin to prowl). Unfortunately, their house is made of adobe where, as Sherman points out, "anywhere that plaster's off that adobe is as soft as mush." And shrews are *digging* animals…

To first-time director Ray Kellogg's credit, the shrews initially appear quite menacing, since Kellogg (a prominent FX technician who provided the photographic effects for such diverse films as *Niagara*, *The Robe*, and *Love Me Tender*) keeps them in shadow as they make their first twilight attack (accompanied by frightening, discordant snarls and high-pitched, staccato chattering), only revealing their shaggy bodies and hideous deformed heads in quick edits via flashes of lightning. Later we see the mutated monsters close up—but only incompletely and in brief snippets seen through spaces in the house's fencing. With their grotesque muzzle, wicked fangs, and glaring eyes, they look both alien and alarming. Sadly, once we finally *do* see the killer shrews full on, the illusion dissipates and they look just like what they are—dogs wearing stringy throw-rugs and plastic teeth.

Even so, their rapid movements and aggressive actions keep things suspenseful. James Best recalled (to *Psychotronic*'s Steve Latshaw) that "They got all these coon dogs and fixed them with fangs and funny hair. I have a scene where they chase me all the way up the hill, through this wild woods with wind blowing and everything. They didn't know how to make the dogs chase me. And so, we got a raccoon…we put him in a crate and drug him up there and it left a scent. Now, wherever we drug the raccoon, that's where I would run. They hollered, 'Roll it!' and I took off running. Well, those dogs looked exactly like they were following me. And I looked back, and I wasn't sure they weren't. They had these fake fangs standing up. After awhile, I found myself running for real!"

Much of the film's, er, running time consists of the small cast trying to keep the vicious monsters from getting into the barricaded house, exploiting the claustrophobic horror of having to lock oneself into a confined area against a seemingly unstoppable menace. This fear of having nowhere to run helped make the 1968 classic *Night of the Living Dead* one of the most terrifying films ever made. Although it's quite a stretch to mention *The Killer Shrews* and *Night of the Living Dead* in the same breath, *Shrews* does possess a few moments which shadow that claustrophobic terror. In fact, it wouldn't be surprising if someone connected with *Night* (say scripter John Russo or director George Romero) had seen *The Killer Shrews*, especially since *Shrews* sports a scene suspiciously similar to one in the later zombie classic (Sherman is locked out by a cowardly companion, who then gets a licking once Sherman finally makes it back inside).

Though the sets are sparse, the active and enthralling human element holds one's interest. The three principals, consisting of boat captain hero, scientist's daughter and cowardly drunken research assistant, are all offbeat enough to lift them above the expected stock clichés. Though much of the film consists of talk (inevitable in low-budget productions), the likable and engaging characters keep things moving.

The Killer Shrews closes with what is undoubtedly one of the most unusual—and *inventive*—climaxes in 1950s horror/sci-fi. Though the protagonists employ a rather ridiculous-looking method of escape, it's actually both logical and ingenious. It's also quite exciting as they move slowly in their impromptu tanks with the shrews snapping around them and trying to force their way into the eye slits Sherman had cut from the metal drums. Director Kellogg and cinematographer Wilfred M. Cline stage and photograph the sequence to good effect. By frequently cutting to the three protagonists inside the drums and showing *their* view of the vicious fanged monsters thrusting their horrific snouts into the slits or under the barrels, they involve the viewer in the claustrophobic, near-panicky feel of the desperate moment.

James Best remembered that shooting this sequence was less than pleasant, since the scene concludes with the trio swimming to the safety of Sherman's boat. "Now, it was in December or January, in Texas," recalled Best, "and there was a thin layer of ice around the lake. They said, 'We'll have blankets and brandy for you when you get to the boat.' So we walked down under these stupid barrels until we get down to the water and then we dove under and swam to the boat. I have never been so cold in my life….But I wrapped a blanket around Ingrid and hugged her as tight as possible—and shot two or three brandies. After a while, I didn't care if it was cold or not."

Shot in Texas in six days back to back with its co-feature *The Giant Gila Monster* for a reported $123,000, *The Killer Shrews* stands up better than most of its similarly-budgeted contemporaries. (So tight was the production schedule, recalled Best, that "we actually would paint the sets and we would shoot the scene; you couldn't touch the set because you'd get paint on your hands.")

Director Ray Kellogg, a former special effects technician at 20th Century-Fox (where he worked on films like *The Day the Earth Stood Still* [1951], *Titanic* [1953] and *Prince Valiant* [1954]), made his baton-waving debut on *The Killer Shrews* and *The Giant Gila Monster*. Returning to Hollywood, Kellogg subsequently forged a new career as a second unit director on big budget films like *Cleopatra* (1963), *Batman* (1966), *The Green Berets* (1968) and *Tora! Tora! Tora!* (1970).

The Killer Shrews' financial backer, Gordon McLendon, plays the minor role of dedicated scientist Dr. Baines—so dedicated that when he suffers the poisonous bite of a killer shrew he quietly sits down to record his own death symptoms! An amiable Texas businessman, McLendon owned a string of theaters and radio stations (he *invented* Top 40 radio) and liked to dabble in motion pictures. About his role in *The Killer Shrews*, McLendon told reporter Dennis McDougal: "I had a minor, almost insignificant role in which I was on the screen maybe six or seven minutes. As I look back and view the picture now, I wasn't very good, but ,then again, I didn't much give a damn. I just thought it'd be a kick to do it."

If one can overlook the restrictions imposed by its tiny budget, *The Killer Shrews* remains good clean Fifties fun spiced with an occasional bonus thrill and chill. A five-decades-too-late sequel, *Return of the Killer Shrews* (co-written by and starring James Best) came out in 2012. Unfortunately, it wasn't a (mangy coon dog) patch on the original.

"ONLY HELL COULD BREED SUCH AN ENORMOUS BEAST…ONLY GOD COULD DESTROY IT!" –ad for *The Giant Gila Monster*

Or perhaps a young man's hot rod and some nitroglycerin…

In the backwoods Texas countryside, a Gila monster has grown to the size of a bus and graduates from taking cattle to eating the locals. Sheriff Jeff (Fred Graham) enlists the aid of young car mechanic/hot rod enthusiast/ukulele player Chase Winstead (Don Sullivan) and his car-crazy friends to help search for a missing teen couple. They find the wrecked car but no sign of the two young people. The oversized reptile derails and attacks a passenger train, then storms the barn dance hosted by Chase and his friends, leading to a fiery climactic confrontation between the hungry lizard and Chase's nitro-carrying ratrod.

Despite its puerile-sounding plotting, *The Giant Gila Monster* has it all (at least all that a 1950s drive-in horror flick might want): teenagers, rock 'n' roll, hot rods, and *monsters*. Add to that an authentic small-town setting, some creepily desolate countryside, a reassuring subtext of youth and authority combining in mutual respect to defeat a horrific threat to their insular world (much like in the better known and far-better-thought-of *The Blob*), a unique (if unlikely) menace, and likable characters acting in a reasonable fashion, and *The Giant Gila Monster* becomes a charming, wholesome, and refreshing addition to the Fantastic Fifties.

With the human villainy kept to a *Peyton Place*–level minimum, *The Giant Gila Monster* comes off as a feel-good monster movie. Like with *The Blob*, there really are no bad guys here. Even overbearing local bigwig Mr. Wheeler (who mistakenly feels Chase is a bad influence on his spoiled son and the rest of the local teens, and attempts to keep his exchange student ward Lisa apart from her true love, so that she and Chase have to sneak around behind his authoritative back) is more worried father than evil ogre. After all, it's *his* son (and the boy's girlfriend) that's gone missing, victims of the titular terror pre-credit attack, so it's almost understandable when he takes out his frustrations on those around him.

Then there's the eponymous horror itself. "What is the black menace that kills everything it sees and hears?" ominously asks the film's trailer. Well, it's a two-foot lizard made to look 25 times that size through some clever use of forced perspective, macro-camerawork, and miniature sets (including cars, train, and even a barn). While the effects (done by director Kellogg himself) were never in danger of winning any awards (never does the big beast appear in the same shot with any people), the effective photography, impressive model work, and well-spaced brevity (not to mention the lizard hisses and composer Jack Marshall's [creator of "The Munsters" theme] eerie Theremin-like theme music playing on the soundtrack) allows one to readily

Now that's *an ad!*

The Giant Gila Monster does his stuff.

suspend disbelief.

But it's the characters here that truly make the Gila show. From the folksy comedy relief of comedian Shug Fisher's Mr. Harris ("I ask what time it is and you tell me how to build a clock," remarks the exasperated sheriff when trying to get a straight answer from the inebriated curmudgeon) to the kindly, level-headed lawman capably, and naturalistically, played by stuntman/actor Fred Graham (back in 1938 Graham doubled Basil Rathbone in *The Adventures of Robin Hood* and frequently did stunt work for John Wayne), realistic—and likable—people populate this beleaguered stretch of backroad danger. And at the forefront are role-model Chase and his nice-girl Lisa. Note that the sweet ingénue whose status as a foreign exchange student reliant on Mr. Wheeler's sponsorship (the result of producer Curtis landing 1957's Miss France, Lisa Simone, for the role) furthers the plot not a whit but adds a nice touch of exoticism to the Nowheresville, Texas setting.

As the stand-up Chase (who works at the garage and drives the local tow truck to earn enough money to buy his crippled little sister Missy a set of leg braces *and* put food on his widowed mother's table), the likable Don Sullivan manages to make it seem reasonable that he also finds time to take a correspondence course in engineering, secretly date his best gal Lisa, good-naturedly keep the local hot-rodders in line, and write (and record) rock 'n' roll songs on the side. Oh, and he also works hand in hand with the friendly sheriff to comb the countryside for his missing friends, and sacrifices his finally-completed hot rod to stop the marauding beast at film's end. And one simply can't help but smile when Sullivan takes up his own tiny banjo-ukulele to sing the heartwarming "Laugh, Children Laugh (The Mushroom Song)," which Sullivan also wrote, to Chase's cute little page-boy-haircut sister.

Given all this, it's a testament to both scripter Jay Simms' well-drawn characterizations (not to mention periodic suspense scenes), and the wholesome, appealing Sullivan and co.'s heartfelt efforts, that it all doesn't collapse into The Giant Schmaltz Monster. But it doesn't, largely due to the sincere playing of the principals, the down-to-earth characters, and the fact that the Big Gila is always lurking nearby to keep things on the straight-and-monster-narrow.

Executive producer Gordon McLendon planned to tie the rock 'n' roll phenomenon to his picture by releasing and airing several songs written and performed by Don Sullivan in the movie. (The actor received a total of zero extra dollars above his SAG minimum salary for the three songs he contributed.) "Two featured songs from *The Giant Gila Monster* are available nationally through record distributors," announced the film's pressbook. "One, on the Rosco Record label, features star Don Sullivan singing his own hit 'I Ain't Made That Way.' Flip side, an instrumental, 'The Gila Monster Crawl.' Another, Cascade Record's 'The Gila Monster,' is a throbbing rock-and-roller on 'Top 40' lists throughout [the] country." Unfortunately, it proved to be wishful thinking on McLendon's part, as the songs never hit vinyl (and some not even a microphone—the latter two mentioned here were never recorded anywhere).

Though perhaps not as polished, maybe not as thematically rich, and certainly not as frightening as its lead-off co-feature *The Killer Shrews*, *The Giant Gila Monster* remains the more charmingly engaging of the duo. "The number one thing is," concluded Sullivan about *Gila Monster*'s appeal, "it is a movie that anybody can watch with their children. There's no profanity, no sex, no drinking—it's a clean movie. …Jay Simms, the author of this thing, tried to throw in everything from the kitchen into this movie. He had songs, he had hot rods, he had monsters [laughs]. He had a little of everything."

And on a personal note, it's no coincidence that *The Giant Gila Monster* is the very first creature-feature I showed to my young son. Everybody sing: "Laugh, children, laugh / The Lord said 'Laugh, children, laugh'…"

> Unlikely as it seems, the giant, energy-sucking robot dubbed *Kronos* heralded the start of "a beautiful friendship"—between me and the British publication *The Fantastic Fifties*, who included this essay in their fourth issue (Spring 2018), the first of many.

ROBOT WARS! *KRONOS* (1957)

"YOU'LL HAVE TO BE SHOCK-PROOF! TO WITHSTAND THE EMOTIONAL ASSAULT… OF SCIENCE FICTION'S BIGGEST THRILL SENSATION!" –trailer

Labelled "The Quickie King" by *Time* magazine in 1951, long-time cinema owner, distributor, and producer Robert L. Lippert oversaw the financing, distribution, and/or production of hundreds of low-budget features. An innovator, Lippert was the first to install popcorn machines in movie theaters (in 1939), and opened the first drive-in on the American West Coast in 1945. He also introduced the multiplex theater in 1965, starting the wave of the future for hardtop cinemas.

In the 1950s, Lippert, with his Regal Films, joined forces with 20th Century–Fox as an independent executive producer, resulting in a variety of horror/sci-fi features like *The Cabinet of Caligari* (1962), *Witchcraft* (1964), and this one-of-a-kind Fifties sci-fi effort about a gigantic robot threatening to suck the Earth dry of all its energies.

From the opening frames when lightning bolts dramatically crisscross the screen as kettle drums rumble on the soundtrack and out of the blackness races the title "KRONOS" in huge block letters—you know something BIG is coming. And that something turns out to be a towering alien robot that absorbs every form of energy it encounters. As the credits roll, the massive "KRONOS" remains onscreen, dwarfing each and every name listed like some sentient monolith.

A glowing spaceship flies through the star-studded night sky, observed by scientists Les Gaskell (Jeff Morrow) and Arnie Culver (George O'Hanlon, the voice of George Jetson in the beloved Hanna-Barbera cartoon series *The Jetsons*), who mistakenly label the alien object an asteroid. (This proves to be a rather amusing peccadillo running throughout the film's first third, as these brainy docs repeatedly talk about the strange-moving "asteroid" while gazing at its smooth oval contours and orbit-defying motion that's so obviously those of a flying saucer. No doubt, without seeing the optical effects added later, Morrow and co. could only go by what was indicated in the script and believed they were looking at a planetoid-like object.) The "asteroid" suddenly disgorges a ball of bright light that heads towards Earth, where it flies into the body of a local trucker driving in the desert, taking him over. Making his way to the nearby "Labcentral" government facility (a far-too-obvious sobriquet if ever there was one), the ball of light leaves the driver (dead) and enters the body of Labcentral director Dr. Eliot (John Emery). The possessed Eliot then apparently guides the spacecraft down to Earth

The world-destroying mechanical monster known as Kronos *(1957).*

(this telepathic control plot point remains rather hazy), where it lands in the Pacific off the coast of Mexico (via an impressive stock footage watery explosion, followed by some animated lightning and a massive tidal wave that washes over the camera to close the scene). Les, Arnie, and Les' love interest, lab photographer Vera (Barbara Lawrence), arrive in Mexico just in time to see a huge metal monstrosity rise out of the ocean and go on an energy-sucking rampage. Dramatically dubbed "Kronos" by an overawed Les, the building-sized behemoth destroys a Mexican power plant, fights off both the Mexican and American air force (all four planes' worth), and even absorbs an atomic blast. Can Les devise a way to stop the rampaging alien heading north to Los Angeles before it decimates the city—and Earth?

The film's trailer touted the colossal robot as "an awesome monster such as human eyes have never seen," and the PR boys were not far wrong. "Awesome" it certainly was, at least in terms of size; and never before had theater patrons seen such a cubist nightmare of a mechanical monster. Almost elegant in its minimalism, this "PLANET ROBBER" (as posters proclaimed it) rises hundreds of feet above the landscape (courtesy of some convincing matte work by effects experts Irving Block, Louis Dewitt, and Jack Rabin) as it "TRAMPLES THE EARTH." Block, who also served as associate producer, came up with the original story (and the name "Kronos," after a Titan from Greek mythology). He explained, "I wanted it to be anthropomorphic, to look like a robot, but at the same time I wanted it to look like a piece of machinery." And Block's effects team realized his concept to a tee. Awe-inspiring in its scope, yet with enough suggestion of the human form (with its two box-like upper and lower halves, domed crown, and piston-like legs) to make it vaguely—and menacingly—humanoid, Kronos stands not only as one of the (ahem) big screen's largest robots but as one of its most strikingly unique automatons as well.

Director Kurt Neumann fully exploits this (literal) model of ominous mechanized simplicity, sending it pounding across the landscape to seek out energy sources (and smash with its massive pistoning legs anything—or anyone—in its path) while shooting out superimposed lightning bolts that leave smoking ruins in its wake. Unfortunately, Block's team didn't do so well with the various miniatures, which explode into tiny gouts of flame whose obviousness deflates the grandiose balloon. Likewise, the spectacular robot meltdown at film's end—as molten cracks spider-web through its monolithic sides, its dome melts, and manic lightning coils around it like striking snakes—concludes with a final shot of the less-than-realistic steaming miniature wreckage that reinforces the uneven nature of the effects. Another issue is Kronos' movements, which are accomplished by obvious cell animation (courtesy of animator Gene Warren) that at times looks far too cartoonish to convince. Given the film's meager $160,000 budget (as detailed by effects man Jack Rabin), it's little wonder *Kronos'* ambitions far outstrip its cinematic execution.

Like Jack Arnold did in *It Came from Outer Space*, Neumann initially makes effective use of the high desert nighttime landscape and otherworldly plant life of Joshua Tree National Forest as the alien entity possesses the lone truck driver. Aiding Neumann was veteran cinematographer Karl Struss, a towering talent in Old Guard Hollywood (having lensed the original 1925 *Ben-Hur* and Chaplin's *The Great Dictator* in 1940, not to mention the 1931 horror classic *Dr. Jekyll and Mr. Hyde* and 1933's *Island of Lost Souls*) whose atmospheric lighting and roving camera build an eerie tableau. Unfortunately, Kurt Neumann is no Jack Arnold, and he quickly abandons the atmospherics for the more prosaic, stock-footage-heavy, documentary-like approach so common to the decade, focusing on the scientists in their lab and the various authorities mustering their resources. At least production designer Theobold Holsopple (*Rocketship X-M*, *The Fly*) fills the facility with impressive-looking banks of equipment, all knobs and dials and gauges and lights, not to mention a huge supercomputer dubbed "SUSIE" (for the amusingly nonsensical "Syncho Unifying Sinometric Integrating Equitensor").

This wasn't producer-director Kurt Neumann's first sci-fi rodeo, having ridden the *Rocketship X-M* in 1950, as well as wrangling *Kronos'* (inferior) double-bill co-feature, *She Devil*. Neumann's biggest success came in the form of the wildy popular *The Fly* less than a year later. Sadly, he had little chance to enjoy it, as he died a week before the blockbuster went into general release.

Kronos' likable cast keeps things grounded, adding the intimate immediacy so necessary for a story that focuses on a giant robot. The principals fly around the massive monster in their tiny helicopter (fortuitously, Les is a crack 'copter pilot as well as a brilliant scientist), even landing atop the stationary behemoth when it first appears in an up-close-and-personal encounter that concludes with the robot seemingly coming to life as the tiny humans scramble to escape. (The landing helicopter footage was filmed on nearby San Fernando Valley's Hansen Dam, with the dam portion later masked out and replaced by a close-up shot of the Kronos model in a simple but effective split-screen effect.)

The sometimes-unwieldy dialogue by frequent TV writer Lawrence Goldman (who also penned the low-budget efforts *The Viking Women and the Sea Serpent* and *War of the Satellites*) makes the actors, particularly top-billed Jeff Morrow, strive a bit harder for believability. For instance, Les finally comes up with a plan in which "a concentrated shower of omega particles, matter derived from energy, could cause change of polarity. The reversal process would trigger the conversion. Kronos' power to destroy could be turned upon himself." Right. It's a testament to Morrow's sincerity that this gobbledygook actually sounds plausible coming from the animated yet level-headed actor. "I did a little fast research beforehand," recalled Morrow, "so that when I wrote down on the blackboard the figures of the alphas and the betas and the gammas, I think I knew what I was talking about and I think I *sounded* as if I knew." And that goes a long way in a budget sci-fi feature.

The innovative *Kronos* even offers a proto–ecology movement sentiment when Eliot, having temporarily regained control of his mind, explains to Les that the alien's "planet has been depleted of energy. What has happened to them may well happen here—if we continue using our resources at the present rate." Though little more than a throwaway line, it's still a relatively novel notion to be found in a low-budget sci-fi film from the gas-guzzling, resource-destroying days of the Eisenhower era.

Another surprise, this one not so atypical, comes in the (stock footage) portrayal of the Mexican vs. the American authorities. The Mexican air force battles Kronos with what looks to be a quartet of (stock footage) WWII-era P51 Mustangs, while the U.S. Military later sends its (again, stock footage) state-of-the-art jet fighters against the monster. It's a subtle yet telling comment on American attitudes of the time towards our Southern Neighbor (one that seemingly hasn't changed all that much in sixty-plus years).

But lest one become lost in the lightning-pierced miasma of the oversized threat, *Kronos* offers more intimate horrors as well, particularly in a bizarre, strikingly creepy sequence that sees Eliot stagger about the Labcentral control room trying to fight off the alien possession. Collapsing from the effort, from out of his head seeps a mercury-like liquid, its tendrils stretching across the marble floor towards the vault's walls where it sparks and burns itself out. Though never fully explained, one can surmise this to be the energy alien's death throes (likewise for poor Eliot).

"*Kronos* was a very good little low-budget picture," concluded Jeff Morrow. And he should know, as he'd leant his solid talents to several other good little sci-fiers such as *This Island Earth* and *The Creature Walks Among Us*. (Of Course, Morrow was familiar with the distaff side as well, having followed up *Kronos* with the risible *The Giant Claw* and later *Octaman*.) "We made it in a couple weeks. The concept, I thought, was interesting, and it made good sense." Indeed, despite occasionally biting off more than it could chew, the scope and imagination of *Kronos* sets it apart as a unique and entertaining entry from the robot-mad 1950s.

With quotes from: *Keep Watching the Skies*, by Bill Warren, and *They Fought in the Creature Features*, by Tom Weaver.

This *Monolith Monster* essay thundered across the *Filmfax* editorial desk for issue 61 in 1997.

THE MONOLITH MONSTERS (1957)

"MAMMOTH SKYSCRAPERS OF STONE THUNDERING ACROSS THE EARTH!" screamed the ads for what turned out to be one of the most unusual sci-fi sleepers of the 1950s. Though the "skyscrapers of stone" tower to dizzying heights in the movie, the film itself has been unfairly dwarfed by its flashier contemporaries like *This Island Earth* (1955) and *Forbidden Planet* (1956). While certainly not up to the sheer spectacle of those well-known '50s science fiction stalwarts, *Monolith Monsters* in many ways proves itself just as worthy—if only for its novelty and adult approach (an attribute which *cannot* be applied to the two aforementioned "classics"). Thanks to excellent scripting, sincere acting, realistic effects and one of the most original menaces ever to cross the screen, *Monolith Monsters* remains a (sadly underrated) genre standout.

Based on a story by Jack Arnold, and competently directed by Arnold protégé John Sherwood, the film introduces a relatively inanimate yet quite frightening "monster" in the form of crystals from outer space. These seemingly harmless bits of rock are anything but—absorbing all the silicon out of humans, resulting in the victim's total body rigidity and death. Even more terrifying (and spectacular) is that fact that when the alien crystals come into contact with water, they grow to towering heights!

The straightforward, almost documentary style direction common to '50s science fiction films, the realistic dialogue and character behavior, and the sincerity of the principal players all combine to create an everyday

The Monolith Monsters *poster.*

tableau against which this ostensibly unstoppable and impersonal menace contrasts jarringly. The fact that the menace *is* impersonal (and not even *alive*) actually adds to the terror, making it more a force of nature (albeit an alien one) rather than a personal, intimate danger, thus exploiting our age-old fear of elements beyond our control.

The film is full of rich and believable dialogue, such as when one character, in figuring out how long before the destructive monoliths reach the city, grimly states, "The way I figure it we got seven or eight hours. Then St. Angelo is going to look more like a petrified forest than a town."

But the film's main asset is the monolith monsters themselves. Shots of the crystals growing to a height of ten stories before our very eyes and then crashing down—only to have the pieces grow up again in a never-ending cycle of destruction—are breathtaking. The unstoppable onslaught as the crashing stone towers crush farms, buildings and literally everything in their path is photographed so realistically that one has to strain to imagine that they are models. The lighting, so critical in miniature work, is very natural, and the towering crystals rise up in a believable manner and shape. The slow-motion photography, the excellent use of deafening sounds, and the attention to detail (such as having dust clouds rise up around the advancing juggernauts) completes the effects' believability.

The human element is handled well also, with a touching sub-plot about a small child slowly solidifying due to contact with the stones and the doctors' frantic efforts to find an antidote to the process. Grant Williams (best known for his sensitive portrayal as *The Incredible Shrinking Man*) is well cast as the geologist hero who first uncovers the menace. At the climax, after learning that salt stops the crystals' growth, he formulates a plan to destroy a nearby private dam which will wash through a salt plain and hopefully halt the monoliths' advance. However, the dam is privately owned and the authorities are waiting for a confirmation from the Governor to blow it. Williams, realizing that confirmation may come too late, takes the responsibility upon himself and blows the dam—then delivers the understatement of the film: "Well, let's hope the Governor makes the right decision." Williams plays the part with just the right amount of compassion and grim determination.

The remainder of the cast act quite naturally, a rare occurrence in low budget '50s films. Deserving of special praise is Les Tremayne, who plays the weary, good-natured editor of the only newspaper in this small burg where nothing ever happens. Tremayne, who was mostly wasted in stereotypical roles in low-budget films throughout the 1950s, brings a little extra to his character here, effectively mirroring the lost hope of unrealized dreams, giving us a glimmer of his talent which, unfortunately, went untapped on most occasions.

Of course, the film does have its faults. The script sports its share of standard '50s clunker lines such as, "You're absolutely right, it's ridiculous. But that's what someone said about the wheel when they first thought of it." And the ending still leaves a few fairly serious questions unanswered, such as just what are they going to do with the millions of tons of volatile crystals still trapped behind the impromptu salt lake? But this is splitting hairs. *The Monolith Monsters* possesses a wonderfully unique story, excellent effects, a high believability quotient, and, unlike many of its contemporaries, is exciting without being exploitative. These "mammoth skyscrapers" can thunder across my video screen any time.

Though perhaps a lesser known killer creature feature from the Fabulous Fifties, *The Monster That Challenged the World* proved to be one of the best. And here's why… (This essay appeared in *Fantastic Fifties* magazine, Special Edition no. 2, in 2019.)

THE MONSTER THAT CHALLENGED THE WORLD (1957)

"Crawling up from the depths…to terrify and torture!"
–tagline

What could be a more unlikely movie menace than an oversized sea slug? (Well, a killer shrew, actually—but that's another story.) Likely or not, thanks to an intelligent and mature script, offbeat casting, skillful acting, some realistic and gripping direction, and a very striking (and convincing) titular terror, *The Monster That Challenged the World* remains one of the unsung gems from sci-fi cinema's heyday.

Incongruously titled *The Jagged Edge* during pre-production (and changed to *The Kraken* mid-shoot before ultimately giving way to its final title), *The Monster That Challenged the World* concerns a group of giant mollusks (possibly revived by low-level radiation) released by an earthquake from the bottom of the Salton Sea (a salt lake situated in California's Mojave desert). When personnel from the nearby military base and local civilians begin disappearing, Navy Intelligence officer John Twillinger (Tim Holt, "a wonderful actor" and "lovely man; he was one of the nice ones," according to co-star Audrey Dalton) investigates. Discovering the nature of the menace (in a frightening face-to-pincers encounter), he spearheads a race against time to find and destroy the deadly giant caterpillar-like aquatic killers before they make their way through the nearby All-American Canal system and spread. It all culminates in a thrilling finale as the final monster menaces heroine Dalton and her young daughter at the naval base lab.

"There was an article in *Life* magazine," recalled screenwriter Pat Fielder to interviewer Tom Weaver about *Monster*'s genesis, "a true story about ancient shrimp eggs being discovered and reconstituted after millions of years buried in a salty pond. We transposed it all to the Salton Sea." (Fielder also cleverly put that very issue into the hands of one of the film's scientists to help illustrate the likely explanation for the monsters' reappearance.) Using an earlier (rejected) script by David Duncan as a springboard, first-time screenwriter Fielder did a substantial amount of research (including contacting the Pentagon to find out how the authorities would respond to such a threat) before tackling the project. She learned that the Navy would be responsible for dealing with the type of menace she proposed (it's reassuring to know that our Armed Forces have a contingency plan for battling giant sea slugs), and so the Twillinger character was changed from an Army officer to a Navy man.

The Monster That Challenged the World is one of the few horror/science fiction films from the 1950s written by a woman. This may or may not account for the veracity found in several powerful, adult-oriented scenes involving mothers and wives grieving over the loss of a loved one. In one sequence a local store owner, the sharp-tongued Mrs. Simms (Sarah Selby, veteran of the Val Lewton thrillers *The Seventh Victim* and *The Curse of the Cat People*, and perennial player in countless TV shows of the 1950s and '60s), confronts her daughter Jody (sensitively played by the lovely Barbara Darrow, whose swimsuited form in the clutches of the monster spearheaded the film's advertising) about her upcoming date with a "no good" sailor. When Jody fails to return from said date (the two go swimming and disappear beneath the waves in a suspenseful what-lurks-below sequence that would do Steven Spielberg proud), she summons the sheriff, and they find her daughter's scarf amongst some seaweed. At this, Mrs. Simms breaks down. "Jodi, Jodi! Oh baby, I could cut out my tongue for the things I said to you," she sobs, clutching the garment to her face and crying inconsolably in a truly heart wrenching scene. The movie's leading lady thought so too. "It hit me when I saw it," praised Audrey Dalton about the sequence. "She gave a wonderful performance." It's this unusual touch of scripting maturity and thespian genuineness that sets this *Monster* apart from—and above—its contemporaries. "All of these horror pictures have a grain of truth, and that's what makes them effective," opined Dalton, and *Monster* offers a whole beach-ful (giant sea slugs notwithstanding).

Upon viewing the film, the savvy sci-fi fan can't help but notice the plot parallels between *The Monster That Challenged the World* and the 1954 seminal giant creature classic *Them!* (with *Monster*'s canal system, for example, standing in for *Them!*'s L.A. sewers). "I had seen *Them!*," admitted Fielder, "and so had [producers] Arthur [Gardner] and Jules [Levy]. It was a fine picture, and I'm sure that it was the inspiration in some ways for *Monster*. I think it inspired a whole bunch of pictures of that era, but our independent research had allowed us to develop an awful lot of other material, too."

"The biggest and most ferocious monster ever built in Hollywood will be seen in *The Monster That Challenged the World*," boasted a United Artists publicity piece. While this may be something of an exaggeration, it's more truthful than most PR hyperbole. This monster (there was only one full-sized creature constructed) is indeed one of the most striking cinematic creatures created up to this time. With its bulbous eyes, glistening accordion body and deadly pincers, it whips its long neck around in an all-too-lifelike manner. To complete the illusion, a combination of a puma's growl and the cry of a bittern (a marsh bird) generated the creature's terrifying tones.

Heroine Audrey Dalton had to face down the beast at the exciting climax, in which she and her onscreen daughter Sandy (played by eight-year-old Mimi Gibson) were trapped in a closet as the monster begins to break through the door. Barely keeping her own terror in check, she says, "Sandy, I want you to close your eyes and put your head right here." Hugging the little girl tightly to her, she adds tearfully, "And Sandy, don't open them for awhile." The despairing resignation in her voice tugs the heart strings, while the relentless, noisy assault by the creature on the door generates a sense of near-panic. "It was this very large thing looming over you," Dalton recalled of the beast itself. "And I think the little girl was genuinely scared. She was young enough she was affected by it." This realistic reaction aided Dalton's own performance: "It brought out my motherly instincts."

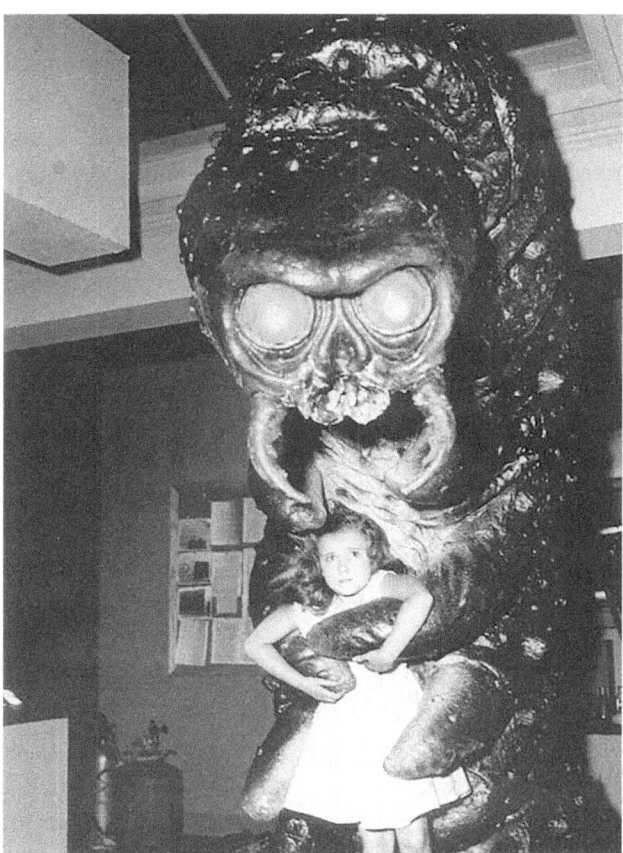

In this publicity still, little actress Mimi Gibson looks none-too-sure about posing with The Monster That Challenged the World *(1957).*

Veteran special effects artist Augie Lohman designed the $15,000 fiberglass "Kraken." (The UA publicity boys gleefully pointed out that sea monster-maker Lohman ironically suffered from severe seasickness.) It stood 11 feet high, contained three miles of mechanical wiring, and weighed in at 1,500 pounds. It took three to five people to operate. (After filming, the producers sold the monster to the Ocean Park Pier, where it served as a children's attraction for years.)

Director Arnold Laven (a "serious, intent, lovely man," according to Dalton) makes good use of Lohman's impressive creation, generating several potent shocks—such as when a sea slug abruptly enters the frame to grab an unsuspecting gate-keeper. Though it's a ludicrous notion (how could *anyone* fail to see or hear the approach of such a creature?!), the tense buildup and startling entrance of the marauding mollusk chokes whatever laughter may rise in one's throat—particularly when its mandibles engulfs the man's head, its glistening body undulating obscenely as the victim screams and struggles futilely. Laven also shoots several suspenseful swimming sequences that pre-date *Jaws* in their ability to generate fear of what is *not* seen lurking beneath the surface.

Rather than the expected stalwart John Agar or Ken Tobey types, *Monster* showcased some unusual casting choices. Former western star Tim Holt (*The Treasure of the Sierra Madre*), character actor Casey Adams ("My problem was that I was just so terrified of *water*," laughed Adams about his *Monster* experience), and comic actor Hans Conried (in a rare straight dramatic part) all add significantly to the film's sense of realism. It's not only their naturalistic acting but their playing against type that keeps things fresh and sidesteps the '50s sci-fi cliché trap. "We always looked to those actors who could bring something special to the part," commented director Laven to Weaver, "and who might be just a little different so there's a freshness to the films." (Tim Holt retired from acting shortly after this movie's release and managed a radio station in Oklahoma up until his death in 1973; whether his participation in this low-budget but delightfully entertaining sci-fier had anything to do with his career switch is purely a matter of conjecture.)

Since it was made for a modest $254,000 in 18 days (with an additional three days for background shooting), it's little wonder that this *Monster* sports a few blemishes among its barnacles. For instance, some not-fooling-anyone shot-through-a-fish-tank close-ups of the principals mar the otherwise effective underwater scenes. Then there are the gigantic egg sacs that look like oversized water balloons. And as the lead scientist, Hans Conried ludicrously shows a nature film (á la *Them!*, once again) on ordinary garden snails ("You'll note the remarkable similarities," he pronounces without a hint of irony when comparing them to the *not at all similar* creatures in question) to explain the workings of the gigantic sea mollusks.

But these are only minor ripples in this celluloid sea. While this *Monster* may not have exactly "challenged the world," it does indeed mount an effective challenge as one of the best creature features of the 1950s.

> I penned this assessment of one of director Roger Corman's best films for the premier issue of *Mad About Movies* magazine (July 2000).

ROGER CORMAN'S *NOT OF THIS EARTH* (1956)

"You are about to adventure into the dimension of the impossible," begins the film's opening written narration, which indeed seems to be *Not of This Earth*. "To

In Roger Corman's best sci-fier, Beverly Garland encounters a being (Paul Birch) that is Not of This Earth *(1956).*

enter this realm you must set your mind free from the earthly fetters that bind it! If the events you are about to witness are unbelievable, it is only because your imagination is chained! Sit back, relax and believe... so that you may cross the brink of time and space... into that land you sometimes visit in your dreams!" Whew! This seems an unlikely opening for a *science fiction* movie, but, apparently, we're not in Kansas anymore...

Arguably producer-director Roger Corman's best '50s sci-fi flick, *Not of This Earth* is an effective little thriller blending science fiction and vampirism in a quirky, believable manner (the above narration notwithstanding). Paul Birch plays a humanoid alien (using the alias of Mr. Johnson and dressing in a dark suit and wraparound sunglasses) sent to Earth to obtain blood and human specimens for his dying planet of Davanna. The Davannians have acquired a serious blood disease through constant exposure to radiation and require frequent transfusions in order to survive. Johnson periodically sends human specimens back to his world via a handy closet-like teleportation device (the first such gizmo seen in the movies).

Though low-budget (as all Corman's productions of this time were), the use of real Los Angeles streets, buildings and parks adds a touch of gritty realism to the few simple interior sets. "It was shot primarily on location," recounted Corman in Ed Naha's *The Films of Roger Corman*, "which went against standard Hollywood procedure. Back then, most movies were still being shot in studios. My theory, as I began studying some of my own films that were shot in studios, was that if I continued to shoot primarily in studios, my films would always look cheap. Budgets were so low and the sets we could afford were so small that we'd wind up giving the picture away as a low-budget film from the very first shot. You just knew it was going to be a little picture. If I filmed on natural locations, I wouldn't have such a low budget look."

Screenwriters Charles B. Griffith and Mark Hanna filled their tight script with good dialogue and believable characters who refreshingly speak like normal people (with the exception of Mr. Johnson—who is, after all, Not of This Earth). Beverly Garland, cast as the unwitting nurse hired by Johnson to attend to his blood transfusions, plays the part of tough, intelligent love-interest with a sense of humor and energy. Paul Birch, a mediocre actor at best, has his finest role as the emotionless, super-intelligent, thoroughly ruthless alien. His flat acting style is perfectly suited to the cold, precise character. And Dick Miller puts in a wonderful (albeit brief) comedic appearance as a cynical vacuum cleaner salesman insisting on giving a demonstration to the otherworldly bloodsucker.

Birch actually walked off the picture before it was completed. Fortunately, there was enough of his footage already in the can to complete the project by using a double for a few pick-up shots (such as when Johnson first enters a doctor's office, and when the alien gives a blood transfusion—mistakenly using *rabid dog blood*—to a fellow Davannian come to aid him). "Roger had Paul wearing contact lenses," explained creature creator Paul Blaisdell to interviewer Carl Del Vecchio. (Johnson sported a pair of milky white eyes that would fry a victim's brain whenever the alien removed his sunglasses.) "I'm not talking about the ones you slap on your cornea, I'm talking about the full-size ones which can become very painful after a few hours. And Roger just had Paul sitting around between takes all ready to go. A couple of hours passed and Birch felt like his eyes were burnt holes in a blanket. Then, he took the lenses out and his eyes hurt so bad he couldn't see straight." Birch became so angry that he and Corman nearly came to blows on the front lawn of the house where much of the picture was filmed, leading to the actor's hasty—and permanent—departure.

The film's creepy ending, though foreshadowing what was to become a genre cliché (the it's-finally-over-or-is-it? epilogue), remains chillingly effective. As the hero and heroine look upon the deceased Mr. Johnson's tombstone (inscribed "HERE LIES A MAN WHO WAS NOT OF THIS EARTH" [natch]), we see a figure approaching in the background—a figure wearing a dark suit and wraparound sunglasses...

Paired with Corman's *Attack of the Crab Monsters* for an offbeat and highly entertaining double bill, *Not of This Earth* was a resounding commercial success, earning a 400 percent profit its first week, according to scripter Griffith. Though not quite the unheralded classic some have made it out to be (but almost), *Not of This Earth* is a well-made, imaginative and entertaining sci-fi thriller.

> This review first appeared in *Cult Movies* magazine (issue 17) in 1996, now lost to the sands of time...I later expanded it into the more comprehensive essay included here.

THE PHARAOH'S CURSE (1957)

"A BLOOD-SUCKING MUMMY... A SEDUCTIVE CAT-GODDESS...*Unleashing 4000 Years of Horror Upon This Century!*" –poster

When is a mummy movie not a mummy movie? When it's the dusty *Pharaoh's Curse*. In 1902 Egypt, Captain Storm (Mark Dana) leads a trio of soldiers out to retrieve an Anglo-American archeological expedition, intending to head them off before they can despoil another tomb and cause more political upheaval. Going along is Sylvia Quentin (Diane Brewster), disaffected wife of the expedition's ambitious leader, Robert Quentin (George Neise). Along the way, a mysterious woman named Samira (Israeli actress Ziva Rodann going by the name of Ziva Shapir) walks out of the desert to show the band a shortcut to the Valley of the Kings, wanting to find her brother (local guide to the Quentin expedition) "before it is too late." But when they reach their destination, Quentin has already unearthed the mummy of a high priest—despite the dire warning carved into the sarcophagus: "Let ye who seek to disturb the eternal peace and sleep of the high priest beware—flesh of my flesh shall creep into thy body and the flesh of they spirit." At this, Samira's brother abruptly falls ill, aging decades in a day. Worse, he soon rises as a monster, stalking the secret passages of the tomb and emerging to suck the blood of the expedition members.

So what we have is possession by the spirit of a 3000 (or 4000) -year-old Egyptian priest (the archeologists—and script—seem at odds about the tomb's antiquity, with Robert labeling it "40 centuries old" while several others mention "3000 years"), with the possessed seemingly turning into a crumbling old man (literally, as at one point the Captain yanks the ersatz mummy's arm off!—the film's sole surprising moment).

What we also have is a dull, talky, barely feature-length (65 minute) film populated by cardboard characters, and a screenplay that offers little incident, a lackluster monster, and an action-less anti-climax that's as colorless as its sandy Death Valley shooting location.

Pharaoh's Curse was not only distributed, but financed by United Artists. "Our deal with UA," recalled producer Howard W. Koch to interviewer Tom Weaver, "was, as long as we could make our pictures for a price, we'd just give them the title, the lead in the cast, and go on. On *Pharaoh's Curse* I think all we did was give them the title, 'cause at that cost [about $90,000] they didn't care who was in it [*laughs*]!" Who "was in it" were a group of low-end television actors who do nothing to rise above the material. As Captain Storm, Mark Dana acts like a cut-rate Charlton Heston, all stiff posing and stentorian tones; while George Neise overacts up a storm as the driven Robert, stridently stomping and shouting. Ziva Rodann merely stands calmly and gazes off into space as the supposedly cryptic Samira, and Diane Brewster screams on occasion in her obligatory one-dimensional heroine role.

Known more for his speed than his artistry, director Lee Sholem marveled at how they filmed all their exteriors in one day: "We flew out of Burbank, early in the morning, and landed in the desert just as the sun was coming up. ...We started at one end of the canyon in

Ad for The Pharaoh's Curse.

Death Valley and worked all the way down to the other end. We moved with the sun. We shot all the desert exteriors, finished the day's work and came home. One day! That was really one for the books."

Of his director, executive producer Aubrey Schenck told Weaver, "Lee Sholem was the kind of director who, if you gave him a six-day schedule, he brought it in in *five*. In fact, Howard [Koch] gave him a nickname, 'Roll 'Em Sholem' [*laughs*]—Howard was the first to call him that, and then he was known all over the industry as that!" (Sholem did actually manage to shoot the entire film in a mere six days.)

The all-important tomb set (built at the ZIV studios in Santa Monica) consists of what looks like cheap cinderblock, papier-mâché "rock," and smooth plywood walls on which are painted large, simplistic figures, looking more like crude cartoons than Egyptian hieroglyphics. "You'd be amazed how little area we used in shooting those [tomb] scenes," recalled Sholem. "We did that by constantly redressing the sets. We'd put a piece or a prop in front of the camera, in the foreground, and we'd have a couple of run-bys. Then we'd move the pieces around, and you'd think it was a whole different area—but we'd only lit *one*!" Despite Sholem's enthusiasm, it shows.

The film's few "thrills" come in the form of the aged bloodsucker as he advances (slowly) on a cowering victim before the scene invariably cuts away to some *other* characters and we hear a distant scream. No visual attack, nor even gruesome aftermath, dares disturb the placid proceedings—which consist mostly of the principals arguing amongst themselves, or the hackneyed romantic triangle between Sylvia, Robert, and the intrepid Captain.

Though looking suitably withered, the mummy-man disappoints in his appearance as well. His thin white hair, drooping shoulders, shuffling gait, and half-lidded eyes (not to mention his suit of what looks like striped pajamas) projects more an aura of aged infirmity than supernatural menace. If his victims didn't simply stand rooted to the spot (presumably by fear), this doddering demon would go thirsty every time.

The film peters out at the end, with no real climax. The surviving principals simply find the "mummy" resting peacefully back in his tomb and realize their possessed guide was the reincarnation of the high priest (with his "sister" the embodiment of the "Cat-Goddess Babisti"). The sort-of human villain, Robert, doesn't even meet his deserved fate at the hands of the avenger—he's killed by a mundane minor cave-in.

Pharaoh's Curse is the kind of film in which the hero laboriously climbs through an opening in a chamber roof, the camera locked down on his every move, followed immediately by a scene of him climbing *back down* from said opening (with the camera again detailing every awkward movement)—only to *tell* his waiting comrades that he's found nothing but a dead end. Which pretty much sums up the picture as a whole.

> Though not the first piece I wrote for the excellent magazine *The Fantastic Fifties*, this double-dose of Dr. Jekyll was the first to *appear* in that publication (issue 3 in 2017).

CHANGING TIMES: *THE SON OF DR. JEKYLL* (1951) AND *DAUGHTER OF DR. JEKYLL* (1957)

Robert Louis Stevenson wrote his famous novella *Strange Case of Dr. Jekyll and Mr. Hyde* (the original title lacked the definite article) in about six weeks in the fall of 1885. (A probably apocryphal story told by the author's rather unreliable stepson Lloyd Osbourne claimed Stevenson scribbled it out in a mere three days after a dream—before chucking it all into the fire and then re-writing it at his wife's urging.) Since then the classic horror story of the duality of man has been translated, adapted, and filmed countless times, with two serious cinematic iterations emerging during the 1950s (a third—1953's *Abbott and Costello Meet Dr. Jekyll and Mr. Hyde*—offered more chuckles than chills).

Though separated by six years, these two filmic siblings display some remarkable similarities, no doubt bolstered by writer-producer Jack Pollexfen's involvement with both. Each revolves around progenies of the infamous Dr. Jekyll growing up without knowledge of their true heritage. Each features an ostensibly kindly guardian who, for the love of money, betrays his trust in the most heinous fashion. And both see the protagonist questioning his or her own sanity, believing they have indeed inadvertently followed in their father's fatal footsteps.

"*HERITAGE OF HORROR!* In his arms...in the night...in the middle of a kiss...*WILL HER MATE TURN INTO A* MONSTER*!*"–*The Son of Dr. Jekyll* ad line

First up in the Fantastic Fifties for the famous doc and his alter ego was *The Son of Dr. Jekyll*, a 1951 production that began as a *joke*. "Mort Braus and I," recalled producer/writer Jack Pollexfen, "were kidding one day about outlandish film titles, and we came up with *The Son of Dr. Jekyll*. We thought about it for a moment, thought it might sell, and knocked out a quick story. Columbia bought it at once." Though the two had nothing further to do with the production after Columbia took their initial treatment and ran with it (with Edward Huebsch crafting the shooting script), Pollexfen went on to pen and produce *Daughter of Dr. Jekyll* six years later.

Shot in a mere three weeks by journeyman director Seymour Friedman, and starring faded matinee idol Louis Hayward, *The Son of Dr. Jekyll* jumps right into the torrid tale with Mr. Hyde (original recipe) fleeing through the streets, pursued by a howling mob. Leaping over rooftops and onto the top of a moving Hansom cab in a thrilling display of monstrous agility, Hyde flees to Jekyll's home, desperate to obtain the transformative potion. He does so, but too late, as the pursuing mob sets fire to the house, forcing Hyde (now Jekyll again) to the roof, from which he falls to his death.

Though the fiend has murdered his own wife, Jekyll/Hyde leaves behind a healthy baby boy. Raised by Jekyll's friend Utterson (Lester Matthews), Edward (Hayward) only learns his true heritage upon his 30th birthday when he comes into his birthright inheritance. About to marry his fiancée Lynn (Jody Lawrance), he's understandably disturbed by the revelation. "You grew up hearing that name—'Hyde'—a fiend," he rancorously tells Lynn. "Your nurse frightens you with it. Then you find out your body and mind are the offspring of a *maniac* and you'll never be free of him." Finding his father's old notebook at the burned-out house, Edward decides to "Kill the legend" by taking up residence there, intent on showing the world that "there's no difference in being the son of Jekyll and the son of Jones." "Suppose I prove that my father actually discovered a new formula," he reasons, "that would clear him once and for all, wouldn't it?" Advised by his estate's trustee (and his father's former friend), psychologist Dr. Curt Lanyon (Alexander Knox), Edward sets about re-creating the infamous formula. Though he appears to succeed, a nefarious presence works behind the scenes to engender Edward's—and London's—belief that he has lost his sanity and committed monstrous murder, just like his father before him…

Edward Huebsch, who soon ended up blacklisted after running afoul of the House Un-American Activities Committee in the early 1950s, not only offers up some not-so-veiled commentary against the witch-hunting mentality running rampant during the anti–Commu-

Louis Hayward as The Son of Dr. Jekyll *(1951).*

nist "Red Scare" era ("Burning witches has always been a popular sport," comments Edward bitterly about his unwarranted persecution by his suspicious neighbors and the London press) but the occasional witty bon mot. When Edward promises a demonstration for the press of his father's formula (a demonstration sabotaged by the *true* villain), one skeptical reporter wonders if he's just pulling their leg. "If he is," answers a colleague, "believe me I'll take the 'Hyde' off Jekyll."

Unfortunately, this *Son* can't help but disappoint those viewers seeking a Hyde-filled follow-up, since, after the opening salvo, Stevenson's terrifying alter ego appears exactly *once*—and then only for a moment and without *doing* anything. Constrained by Braus' and Pollexfen's more mundane mystery plot, Huebsch must try to wring a modicum of suspense out of what turns out to be a rather ordinary wronged-man plot. Though he does what he can (including offering a circular conclusion dripping with poetic justice), there just isn't enough of a skeleton there to flesh out the sought-after Jekyll-and-Hyde horror.

Produced by one of Hollywood's major studios (though Columbia was admittedly a "minor" major), *The Son of Dr. Jekyll* at least *looks* good. The gas-lit parlors and shadowy nineteenth-century streets effectively evokes both the overstuffed interiors and sooty exteriors of Victorian England. The surface gloss extends to the film's sole transformation scene as well. It begins with a close-up of Edward's hand, which darkens and grows hairy as he flexes his fingers to reveal claw-like nails. Edward then falls to the floor, and his face darkens around the eyes and mouth and cheekbones to create a ghoulish cast. His hair lengthens and coarsens, and his mouth parts to reveal a set of scraggly teeth. Working with cinematographer Henry Freulich (*It Came from Beneath the Sea*, *The 27th Day*) and makeup artist Clay Campbell (*The 5000 Fingers of Dr. T*, *The Werewolf*), director Friedman creates a seamless visual transition through a convincing combination of filtered photography and stage magician trickery. Unfortunately, a few brief moments of visual flair can't overcome the script's overall mundanity, as Edward sets about figuring out what the viewer already knows (particularly after the game was given away half-way through, when we clearly see the guilty culprit sneaking into Edward's lab to switch some ingredients). Consequently, in the case of *The Son of Dr. Jekyll*, the apple rolled *very* far from the Jekyll/Hyde tree.

Luckily, another, rather more energetic, descendent loomed just over the big screen horizon…

"IS THERE A RAVAGING BEAST HIDDEN IN HER BODY?" –Daughter of Dr. Jekyll trailer

Note: Those unfamiliar with this low-budget entry may want to seek out and watch the film (if so inclined) before reading further, as detailing its dualistic qualities can't help but answer the above question and provide major spoilers. For those who already know the answer… read on.

Though 1957's *Daughter of Dr. Jekyll* offered even less Hyde than the *Son*, in the monster's stead stood… a *werewolf*! Called back home by her guardian Dr. Lomas (Arthur Shields) upon her twenty-first birthday, Janet Smith (Gloria Talbott) brings her fiancé George (John Agar) along. "You, my dear," reveals the kindly Lomas (who Janet formally refers to as "*Doctor*" throughout), "are an heiress to a sizable estate and fortune." He also reveals, somewhat reluctantly it seems, that she is not a 'Smith' after all but a *Jekyll*—the daughter of the infamous doctor-turned-monster. And "around here," Lomas explains, "they still believe that Dr. Jekyll, in the form of a werewolf, prowls thirsting for blood every time the full moon rises." This causes Janet to question whether she can marry George after all. Worse, she begins having nightmares in which she, in the form of an alluring, violent alter-ego, viciously attacks and murders people—waking up the next morning with blood on her nightdress! After several locals turn up with their throats torn out, Janet is on the verge of hysteria. George finally discovers, however, that the duplicitous Lomas has been inducing these dreams via hypnosis, and plans to make her kill herself so that *he* will retain control of the Jekyll fortune. And most terrifying, George learns that Lomas is the werewolf(!) who has been committing the murders.

Conflating the Jekyll/Hyde tale with lycanthropy (it's not Jekyll transforming into Hyde but man transforming into a werewolf) sets this *Daughter* apart from her brethren, marking out the story's duality in terms of the supernatural rather than the chemical. Further, one of only three werewolf titles from the 1950s (the other two being 1956's *The Werewolf* and 1957's *I Was a Teenage Werewolf*), *Daughter of Dr. Jekyll* distinguished itself as the only were-film of this science- (and science fiction-) minded decade to take a Gothic approach to its lycanthrope tale.

Made by bargain basement outfit Allied Artists (purveyors of such sci-fi efforts as *Target Earth*, *The Cyclops*, and *Attack of the 50 Foot Woman*, not to mention a slew of low-end oaters), the *Daughter* turned out to be a far more impoverished production than the *Son*. Set, like its more convincing sibling, in England at the end of the nineteenth century, careless anachronisms nearly destroy the illusion of time and place. Not only does the manor house possess incandescent lights, one can see 1950s cars whizzing by outside a lightly curtained window! And, remarkably, none of the principals sport even the hint of a British accent (Janet and George sound American, while Lomas affects an Irish lilt).

The film's trailer proclaims, "A vampire drawing sustenance from bestiality!" Apart from its rather unfortunate verbiage (due, one hopes, to simple ignorance regarding the term's connotations), such ad lines illustrate the picture's confusion regarding vampirism and lycanthropy—as well as the Jekyll and Hyde mythos. In speaking of his old friend and colleague Dr. Henry Jekyll, Lomas says that after Jekyll's death, "The villagers broke into his tomb and drove a stake through his heart—the only safeguard, according to ancient tales of witchcraft, that keeps a werewolf from rising out of the grave when the moon is full to hunt for human blood." Whether Dr. Jekyll was truly a werewolf or the locals merely mistook him for one due to his personality-altering experiments remains unclear.

It takes sixty minutes of this seventy-minute movie before we finally see Dr. Lomas transform into the werewolf—and it's not worth the wait. It begins with a close-up of his hand as it subtly grows hairier through some simple but clever changes in lighting (courtesy of "special photographic effects" men Jack Rabin and Louis DeWitt, who provided the effects for many a low-budget '50s entry, including *Cat-Women of the Moon, The Black Sleep, Pharaoh's Curse*, and *The Atomic Submarine*). Then Lomas' face darkens as *it* becomes hairier. Unfortunately, this is accomplished through some too-obvious face paint that becomes visible under special lighting (a technique that harkens all the way back to the 1931 version of *Dr. Jekyll and Mr. Hyde*, where it was utilized to far better effect). With his back to the camera, Lomas now turns around, fully transformed. Sparse hair on the sides of his face and temples, a pair of somewhat pointy fangs, slightly elongated ears, and a mad gleam in his eye are the only flimsy indications that man has become animal. And this were-Lomas, well-dressed in full suit and tweed coat, acts quite un-wolf-like. Rather than leaping and snarling and biting and clawing, he fights like an ordinary man, grappling with George and pushing him down a set of stairs before delivering a swift kick to the head to finally knock his opponent unconscious. The beast-man then rushes back up the stairs, exits the tomb, and *locks the door behind him*. Almost humorously, this werewolf then becomes a rather metaphorical "wolf" when he spies through a farmhouse window an attractive young woman dressing *and pauses to watch*—yes, he has now become a peeping wolf. A recovered George ultimately tells Janet that Lomas is "mad—worse than that, he changes into something; he isn't human." By this werewolf's actions (and even his appearance), however, one could barely tell. Perhaps Lomas takes on a lupine form of Mr. Hyde? If so, nothing in the film confirms this; he quaffs no potion, and the origin—the very nature—of his transformations remains unclear.

Though less elegant than the more sumptuous *Son*, this *Daughter* offers rather more food for thought. "Yearning for love," describes *Daughter of Dr. Jekyll*'s trailer, "and discovering on the eve of her marriage the monstrous inheritance that was her birthright of fear." If one were so inclined to look deeper into this 'B' potboiler, one might conclude that said fear has its roots in the dark recesses of sexuality. The female "monster" of Janet's nightmares, with her exotic beauty and low-cut, diaphanous nightgown, looks more sexy than monstrous (and far more alluring than the demurely dressed and rather plain-looking Janet). She's almost like a subconscious representation of Janet's repressed sexuality. Or perhaps it's a manifestation of her *fear* of sex, spawned by her impending marriage. Janet even tries to break off her engagement with George, ostensibly because she believes her bloodline to be tainted—though maybe it's something deeper... Of course, such a reading remains pure conjecture, as nothing else in the film explicitly points in this direction. (Director Edgar G. Ulmer shot the dream scenes—the most evocative sequences in the film—in some recently burned-out woodlands, using ultraviolet film, off-kilter angles, and a far sexier double for Gloria Talbott to generate a nightmarish atmosphere.)

"I did that picture strictly for the bread," admitted John Agar. "I didn't fluff it—I did the best I could with what I had to work with—but it wasn't my cup of tea, I just didn't believe it." Nor does the viewer. Agar, with his bland, corn-fed persona, never looks too comfortable in his Victorian Gothic surroundings (particularly when wearing a ridiculous striped leisure jacket that makes him look like he just stepped away from a barbershop quartet).

Gloria Talbott does better with her pivotal role of the confused, tortured Janet. "I'm mad," she concludes,

Gloria Talbott as the Daughter of Dr. Jekyll *(1957). (lobby card)*

exhorting George, "You've got to do something—lock me up or put me in a madhouse!" her tormented hysteria rising to become both unnerving and heartbreaking. "I had some good lines in the film," fondly recalled Talbott, "like, 'If you love me, you'll kill me'—I really felt it, and I can still make myself cry when I watch that scene." Of course, she also had some real clunkers to deliver. At one point she answers George's pleas to leave with "I can't make a decision—I'm not capable of it," painting her character as quite the shrinking violet.

Fortunately, at the helm of this muddled mess stood a man with both the ability and experience to make a silk purse out of a cinematic sow's ear. If anybody could save this *Daughter*, that person was director Edgar G. Ulmer. Ulmer helmed one of the greatest films of horror cinema's Golden Age—*The Black Cat* (1934), starring Boris Karloff and Bela Lugosi. During production of that dark, multi-layered classic, however, Ulmer fell in love with script girl Shirley Castle. Unfortunately, she was married to a Universal studio executive at the time, who had Ulmer blacklisted for stealing his wife. Consequently, Ulmer never made another studio picture and toiled for the next quarter-century in the land of low-budget independents. Even without major studio backing, however, Ulmer still produced a number of excellent pictures, including *Bluebeard* (1944), *Detour* (1945), and *The Man from Planet X* (1951). Of course he also directed the awful *Beyond the Time Barrier* and *The Amazing Transparent Man* (both 1960). In between these two polar-opposite subsets rests *Daughter of Dr. Jekyll*.

Ulmer employs plenty of fog to add atmosphere and a modicum of scope to the cramped settings and soundstage "exteriors" (much as he did with *The Man from Planet X* six years earlier). Working with cinematographer John F. Warren (*The Colossus of New York*, TV's *Thriller* and *Alfred Hitchcock Presents*), Ulmer fills the manor house (a real mansion in Los Angeles, near Hancock Park) with evocative shadows to match the baroque Victorian brick-a-brac. (Sadly, no amount of studio smoke can obfuscate the obvious table-top model used to represent the house and grounds in longshot.) Ulmer often moves his camera to good effect, slowly dollying in to punctuate a bit of dialogue, for instance. Of course, when said dialogue consists of awkward lines like "I still shudder when I recall that face, like some perverted mask of evil out of a legend of horror," all the fluid camerawork in the world can't save it. Fortunately, veteran player Arthur Shields (*How Green Was My Valley*, *National Velvet*, *She Wore a Yellow Ribbon*) delivers such dialogue with a naturalness that *almost* sells it.

According to *Daughter* writer-producer Jack Pollexfen, "Ulmer was an excellent director, at his best when he had his back up against the wall budget-wise." It's a rather disingenuous, self-serving statement by the tight-fisted Pollexfen, given that, post–*Black Cat*, Ulmer never had the chance to show what he *could* have done with a more generous budget.

"Edgar Ulmer—I liked him a lot," enthused Gloria Talbott. "He was [laughs] kind of insane, and I love people who are quirky and funny. He just was easy to work with—he was not a Douglas Sirk, who thinks he can get a performance out of somebody by scaring them to death. He was affable and fun—a pixie, sort of." Affable and fun—remarkable, given this put-upon pixie's tight schedule (about a week) and impoverished budget.

Though by no means a classic, this *Daughter* deserved better than becoming the bottom half of a double-bill with the Bert I. Gordon stinker *The Cyclops* (also starring Talbott).

While both these cinematic siblings exploit the Jekyll name, neither truly incorporates Stevenson's evocative duality theme (they don't even include the Hyde persona to any appreciable degree). Relying more on mystery and melodrama tropes than horror and Jekyll-and-Hyde thematics, both *The Son of Dr. Jekyll* and the *Daughter of Dr. Jekyll* must have been a disappointment to their old man (not to mention cinema patrons plunking down their hard-earned cash in the Fantastic Fifties).

With quotes from: *Interviews with B Science Fiction and Horror Movie Makers*, by Tom Weaver.

> I wrote this in conjunction with the late Lynn Naron back in 1999 for *Monsters from the Vault* magazine (issue 9). Lynn, whose unique humor shows through in his *Tarantula* assessment, was a consummate collector, film fan, and dear friend.

BATTLE OF THE BUGS: *TARANTULA* VS. *THE DEADLY MANTIS*

"CRAWLING TERROR 100 FEET HIGH!"

A gruesome-faced figure clad in striped pajamas staggers toward the viewer, collapses, and dies face down on the desert sand. So begins the first of many follow-ups to Warner Brothers' gi-Ant classic, *Them!* (1954). *Tarantula* (1955) returns director Jack Arnold

Tarantula *poster*.

to the lonely desert environs of his first science fiction success, 1953's *It Came from Outer Space* (penned by fantasist Ray Bradbury). Rather than working from a script based on a great writer's imagination, however, *Tarantula*'s tale sprang from the "No Food for Thought" episode of TV's *Science Fiction Theater*. Although R. M. Fresco and Martin Berkeley's weaker *Tarantula* script provides less silk from which to spin its web of suspense, Arnold takes every opportunity to exploit the desert locale's expanse and isolation to the fullest.

Leo G. Carroll plays Professor Deemer, research scientist extraordinaire, whose experiments with an artificial nutrient have created accelerated growth in usually harmless lab animals—a white rat, guinea pig, and the one *verrry* strange choice of a desert tarantula. It seems there's a slight problem with the nutrient's formula, however. Though it does cause the desired gigantism in the lab animals, its properties run amok in humans, deforming them with a case of fast-acting acromegaly *and* an unstable mind. Deemer's two associates, having grown impatient with slow lab testing, have injected themselves with the compound—and lived to regret it. The first dies just before the opening credits, and the other goes berserk, starting a lab fire and (for the expected plot twist) injecting the good doctor with a dose of the deadly nutrient before succumbing. In the ensuing conflagration the Volkswagen-sized tarantula makes its escape.

Meanwhile, grad-student-cum-lab-assistant Stephanie "Steve" Clayton (Mara Corday) arrives in Desert Rock with white gloves, pearls, and snazzy fashion ensemble to begin her tenure at Deemer's research facility. She and the town doctor, Matt Hastings (John Agar), strike up a budding romance. Matt has been investigating the death of Deemer's partner and in short order is out examining strange occurrences in the countryside. Cattle have been mysteriously killed, leaving behind only stripped bones and strange pools of white goop. (Here Matt displays his scientific acumen by first rubbing the substance on his fingers, then giving it a sniff, and finally—to the audience's surprise and *disgust*—performs a taste test!) Soon a corral of horses and its owner disappear, and a pair of sheep ranchers and their pickup are plucked from the road by the ever-growing spider.

Matt visits the big brain at the Arizona Agricultural Institute and learns that the giant pools of goop are venom from a spider. A very *big* spider. He alerts the sheriff and drives to Deemer's place, only to find it under siege by a now-mountain-sized tarantula. Matt grabs the fleeing Steve and, with the local law's help, tries to blow up the beast with dynamite. The TNT proves useless against the gigantic arachnid who pursues the protagonists back to town. As its multi-faceted sights fix on Desert Rock for dessert, the Air Force arrives and takes out the titular titan with a napalm strike (piloted by an unbilled U-I contract player named Clint Eastwood!).

At 80 minutes, *Tarantula* clips along at a rapid pace with only a few minor breaks to slow the action. Two of the most glaring are the obligatory science lesson (á la *Them!*) via a short Golden Science film sequence about tarantula life and an overlong scene in which Matt and Steve stop at an outcropping of rock to "enjoy the unique beauty" of the area. In reality, this "beauty" simply consists of a pile of pushed-up rocks that looks suspiciously similar to a spot the Lone Ranger and Tonto rode by on many occasions.

Leo G. Carroll gives this above-average entry its best performance, infusing his role of Professor Deemer with both pathos and intelligence. He gives the character as much (if not more) shading as the script will allow via his steady, understated playing. He inspires genuine sympathy, for instance, when the dying Deemer explains how he only wanted to prove the validity of his research in the short time he had left. Unfortunately, his death in long shot during the spider's house-redecorating rampage cheats the viewer out of any significant emotional involvement, lessening the impact of his demise. Carroll was a very capable thespian who is best remembered as Cosmo Topper from the *Topper* film/TV series and as Alexander Waverly, boss of Napoleon Solo and Ilya Kuryakin in *The Man from U.N.C.L.E.*

The rest of the cast turn in acceptable performances, with Nestor Pavia bringing his character enough believability (and adding just a hint of his *Creature from the Black Lagoon* Lucas characterization) to be convincing as a small-town police officer.

"Co-starring with a spider 60 feet high and 50 feet wide," stated John Agar in the *Tarantula* pressbook, "is an experience no man can easily forget. It adds to an actor's stature." Right. That said, Agar (whom the film's publicity claimed "was bitten by a tarantula as a child and spent a week in the hospital when the poison laid him low") and Mara Corday try their best as the romantic leads but, like most heroes and heroines in B-budget flicks, are hampered by a script that doesn't really allow them to develop as interesting characters. Their attempted romantic exchanges at various moments never really generate any chemistry. Still, Agar manages to pull off an occasional quip or meaningful glance. But Poor Mara Corday is saddled with one of the most bizarre "sexy moments" in a major studio production when she's ogled by a not only ravenous but apparently *lustful* giant arachnid! (The goofy spider head prop seen leering through the window produces shrieks all right—shrieks of *laughter*.)

The many victims of the huge tarantula are merely one-dimensional window dressing included solely as spider fodder. The viewer ends up feeling more apprehension at the imminent attack on the *horses* than on the cardboard-cutout humans.

Most actors who appear in '50s sci-fi films often feel some embarrassment over their involvement. Not so Mara Corday; when told her next assignment was to be *Tarantula*, her reaction was, "That's fine with me." And John Agar seems to have no regrets about his involvement in low-budget sci-fi programmers. He has made many appearances at film conventions throughout the U.S. over the past decade, and is always gracious about answering questions and signing autographs.

Of course, the most important feature of any Big Bug film is the special effects. Clifford Stine and his crew do an acceptable, albeit uneven, job considering tarantulas are not noted for their love of grease paint, hot lights, or rampaging on command. (Employing 60 of the multi-legged specimens for the title role, the production crew used compressed air to encourage the creatures to 'hit their marks.') Most of the matte work is adequate, with care being taken to include the star's shadow on roadways and hills. The night scenes, however, look as though Stine & co. simply employed an *empty* traveling matte that displays no detail inside the spider's outline. One of the most notable gaffs occurs when the spider chases after the hero's speeding car, and you can see the arachnid seemingly step into another dimension as part of its foreleg disappears into blank sky.

Universal-International took the full-bodied original Big Bug prototype, transformed many ants into a single spider, sifted the ingredients (including an expansive desert locale, a short Mr. Science-style nature film, and even a female lead with an easy-to-mistake-for-male name) and extracted most of the flavor from Warner Brothers' tale of giant ants in New Mexico to serve up their own brew of Big Bug horror. Though falling short of its model, *Tarantula*'s impressive marauding menace, solid thesping, and evocative desert setting still make this dish a tasty selection from the Giant Insect Buffet.

"THIS WAS THE DAY THAT ENGULFED THE WORLD IN TERROR!"

"In all the kingdom of the living there is no more deadly or voracious creature than the praying mantis." So states the resident scientist in *The Deadly Mantis* (1957), one of the more unusual variants in the Big Bug bombardment of the 1950s. Shot in two weeks in the dog days of Summer 1956, the film begins with a lengthy sequence of cold-war paranoia stock footage (courtesy of Air Force shorts such as *Guardians All*, *One Plane-One Bomb*, and *SFP308*) showing the military "racing against time to guard against sneak attack" by creating a radar defense network in the Arctic. This segues right into an impromptu lecture on the fact that "every action has an equal and opposite reaction," leading us to believe that nuclear testing in the South Pacific has melted a particularly large chunk of ice near the North Pole. The iceberg disgorges *The Deadly Mantis* to fly about attacking planes, ships, and Eskimo villages until being gassed in the Lincoln tunnel. In a nutshell: big bug appears, flies around, eats a few people, has the

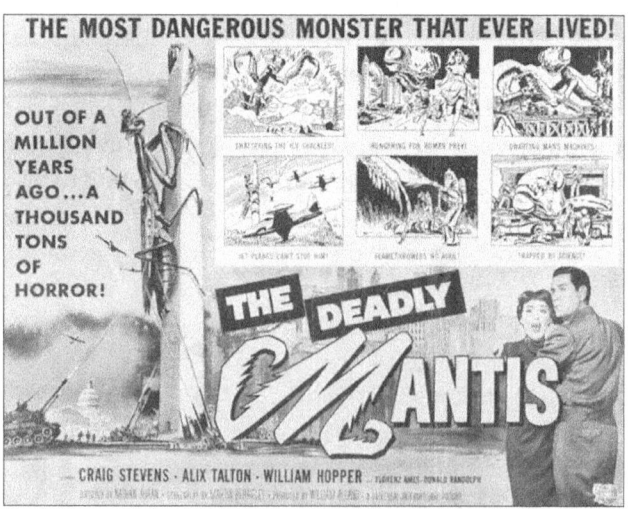

The Deadly Mantis *poster*.

entire United States Air Force and Civil Defense Corps out trying to find it, and finally lands in a major city to be cornered and killed. The End.

Sandwiched between the seemingly endless stock military footage and shots of the marionette-style model mantis rests the perfunctory human element, but it proves less memorable than usual in a Big Bug bonanza. The *homo sapien* characters consist of a young Army colonel (Craig Stevens, of TV's *Peter Gunn* fame, representing the might of the military), a youthful paleontologist (*Perry Mason*'s William Hopper covering the science angle), and a pretty woman photographer (Alix Talton as the coquettish love interest). Unfortunately, these bland human ciphers fail to generate any real interest, and the obvious potential for a love triangle remains unexplored. (When Universal-International originally announced *The Deadly Mantis* in mid–1956, *This Island Earth* lead Rex Reason and *Tarantula*'s Mara Corday were set to star. Reason, however, balked at his new assignment. "I knew that the monster would be the star," explained the deep-voiced actor to interviewer Tom Weaver, "and I felt that I was worth a little more than just to support a praying mantis.") The script contains absolutely no human conflict, so all the drama rests on the shoulders (thorax?) of one overgrown bug. Fortunately, said insect proves fairly impressive in appearance, with its long, spindly, barbed forelegs and its alien-looking head capped by giant, bulbous eyes.

Director Nathan Juran (*20 Million Miles to Earth* [1957], *The Seventh Voyage of Sinbad* [1957], *Attack of the Fifty Foot Woman* [1958], etc.), aided by cinematographer Ellis Carter, serves Mr. Mantis well by photographing it against some well-made models (cars, busses, buildings) using low-angle camerawork to emphasize its impossible size. ("The special effects in *Mantis* were fabulous," enthused producer William Alland to Tom Weaver. "Remember the scene in the tunnel, where the damn thing beats up all those cars [*laughs*]? That's the special effects department at their best. And they did it for peanuts, for *nothing*, you know.") Juran also shrouds much of the creature activity in shuddery shadow, staging the insect action at night or in an atmospheric fog. One particularly effective scene begins with a long shot of the Arctic base at night as light streams from a few of its tiny-looking windows. Suddenly, the silhouette of the giant mantis enters the frame and slowly moves towards the sleepy base. Cutting back and forth from the approaching mantis to the blissfully unaware human protagonists inside creates some genuine suspense. Of course, Juran takes said suspense to absurd lengths when, for seemingly several minutes, the oblivious heroine strolls back and forth in front of a large window through which the myopic mantis' bug eyes peer! In addition, the mantis moves much too slowly to convince us that it's all that "deadly," and it (embarrassingly) makes a rather annoying bellowing noise when it attacks—like an insect version of a stuck pig.

According to art director Alexander Golitzen, two different mantis models were created (Juran and company utilized a live insect for a few select shots as well). One model was designed for appearances on the ground and another for the "flight" scenes (which generally consisted of the model suspended on wires with its wings vibrating rapidly while rear-screen projected footage of clouds unspooled behind it). The 20-inch-long ground model was operated like a marionette, with the controller stick used to manipulate the head, mouth, torso, and legs as it crept across the miniature sets.

Martin (*Tarantula*) Berkeley's unimaginative script (based on a story by producer William Alland) does feature some occasionally amusing dialogue, such as when the paleontologist states, "I'm convinced that we're dealing with a mantis in whose geological world the smallest insects were as large as man. And that failing to find those insects for food it's—well, it's doing the best it can." And one can't help but chuckle at a newspaper headline that reads: "FEAR OF MANTIS MOUNTING."

The film possesses one particularly memorable scene, when the giant mantis descends on Washington D.C. and has the audacity to crawl up the Washington Monument. The mammoth mantis (this time a *real* praying mantis scaling a model) looks quite impressive as it moves straight up the huge obelisk, and we're treated to a frightening view from inside the monument through an observation window. Its huge abdomen passing across our field of vision, looking alien and monstrous as it moves up the side, is something no bug lover will soon forget. The mantis also does a nice bit of car tossing at the climactic confrontation in the tunnel, throwing the realistic-looking automobiles aside as if they were Matchbox toys.

Alas, the climax is a letdown. The mantis' final death throes, as the poison gas chokes the life out of its gargantuan body, are remarkably unexciting. It simply sinks to the ground and collapses, without any threatening thrashing or furious fanfare. Stay tuned for that one last "gotch," however, as the presumed dead mantis raises its claw one last time to menace the heroine (and 'bug' the audience).

As Big Bugs go, *The Deadly Mantis* is superior to

most (*Beginning of the End* and *The Monster from Green Hell*, for instance) but not quite up to the standards set by the sub-genre's queen bee, *Them!*, and her favored consort, *Tarantula*.

> *Voodoo Woman* stomped through *Cult Movies* magazine (issue 17) as a capsule review in 1996. Since then I've expanded upon her (as one does), and she's now "Bigger and Better[?] than Ever!"

VOODOO WOMAN (1957)

"A woman by day…a monster by night!" –poster

"Not since he starred in the *Cat People* and *I Walked with a Zombie* pictures," began a *Voodoo Woman* publicity piece, "has Tom [Conway] had a role like his current one." And I'm sure Mr. Conway thanked his *unlucky* stars that this was true, for *Voodoo Woman* may very well be his worst feature. Conway, brother of George Sanders, gained popularity in the long running *Falcon* detective series of the 1940s, and, while mostly eclipsed by his sibling's career, is a fine actor in his own right. Here, playing a mad doctor mixing voodoo with science, he's a long way from his notable appearances in those two aforementioned Val Lewton classics. The actor obviously badly needed the $2500 he was paid for the week's work. (Sadly, Conway would die alcoholic and penniless a decade later.)

Shot in six days for $80,000, according to producer Alex Gordon, the African-set story has Conway employing a local witchdoctor to aid in his scientific experiments to "create a new being—not man, not beast, but a combination of the best of each." His "new being" proves nearly indestructible, its armor-like hide withstanding an onslaught of bullets, fire and acid. Mike "Touch" Connors plays the jungle guide/hero and Marla English the ruthless treasure-hunter who, as a result of her own greed, is turned into the title monster—no less than the bulky rubber costume from *The She Creature* (1956) topped with a dime store skull-mask and fright wig.

Producer Gordon originally wanted Peter Lorre for the mad scientist role. But after Lorre balked at doing Gordon's earlier *The She-Creature* ("Frankly, I don't really blame him," commented the producer), he was no longer an option. Gordon next tried veteran villain George Zucco, but found the actor in poor health and unable to remember lines (he hadn't worked in over five years).

With time running out, Gordon turned to one of his favorites—Tom Conway. Conway's performance here is surprisingly poor (or perhaps *not* surprisingly, given the material), with the usually unflappable actor proving wildly unsteady. At times Conway seems unsure of just what he's supposed to be doing or saying, speaking his lines disjointedly and without conviction. At others he seemingly can't talk without constantly casting his eyes about (searching for cue cards?).

While Mike Connors, with his rugged good looks and straightforward delivery, makes an agreeable enough hero, Marla English turns her greedy villainess into a ridiculous caricature. Ms. English is easy on the eyes but hard on the ears, for she can't seem to say her lines without spitting and looking like she'd just love to bite the head off a chicken.

Despite *Voodoo Woman*'s minuscule budget and unreasonably short shooting schedule, director Edward L. Cahn took care to wring as much as he could out of the sorry scenario. The camera moves more often and with greater purpose than in most similar productions. And rather than exposing the silly-looking monster to full daylight (and disastrous scrutiny), Cahn limits its display to brief glimpses of a leg, arm, back, etc., or even as a menacing shadow. Unfortunately, one can't keep a determined Voodoo Woman in the dark forever, and when we finally do get a more substantial sight of the monster, we can only applaud Cahn's previous obfuscating techniques.

Apart from a ludicrous monster and some unconvincing acting, *Voodoo Woman* also suffers from an overabundance of the expected slapdash silliness that often accompanies low budget horror—including mismatched stock animal footage; angered Africans comically hopping from foot to foot in a visual parody of the old "restless natives" routine; and a native houseboy named…Bobo. (Bobo was played by Otis Green, whom Gordon characterized as "a young black actor who was…really making quite a lot of noise trying to get better working conditions for blacks and getting going with decent black roles and things." 'Bobo' was *not* a step in the right direction.)

After about an hour or so watching *Voodoo Woman*, it all begins to wear thin. "I realize that seeing it again leaves a lot to be desired," admitted Gordon. Yet it contains enough bizarre occurrences, occasionally effective ambiance and wacky monsters to make it a mildly entertaining 60 minutes. Too bad it actually runs 77 minutes.

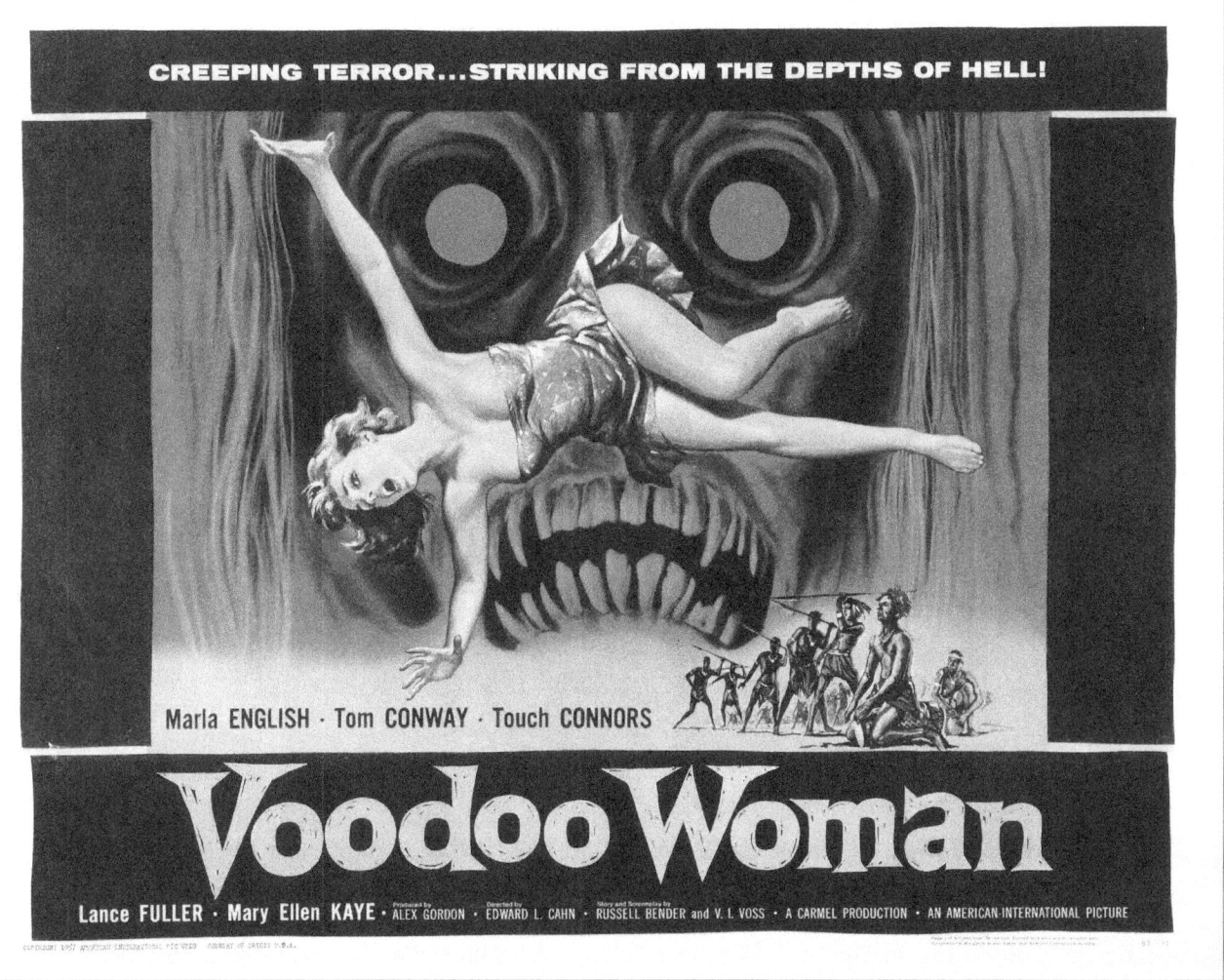

Voodoo Woman *poster*.

> When *Cult Movies* magazine printed my mini-review back in 1996 (issue 17), this *War* was more of a skirmish. I've since sent in reinforcements to swell the ranks…

WAR OF THE COLOSSAL BEAST (1958)

"What happens to our world if massive monstrous man-beasts—like this—invade us?" –an important question posed by *War of the Colossal Beast*'s trailer

While he scored with *Puppet People*, Mr. B.I.G. (Bert I. Gordon) dropped the (gigantic) ball with this follow-up to his *The Amazing Colossal Man* (1957). Prompted by AIP for a sequel, an unenthusiastic Gordon produced a listless rehash that did nothing to "heighten" his reputation.

The story, originally titled *The Revenge of the Colossal Man* (with AIP changing the moniker before release), picks up after Colonel Glenn Manning's (aka "the Colossal Man") fatal tumble off Boulder Dam, with the miraculously survived (though disfigured and amnesiac) giant now living on a mountain in Mexico(!) where he waylays local food trucks along the dusty highway. Manning's concerned sister Joyce (Sally Fraser) investigates, along with the U.S. Army's Major Baird (Roger Pace). They find the Colossal Beast, subdue him with a truckload of drugged bread, and transport him back to Los Angeles. There the unruly giant escapes, causes minor havoc at the L.A. airport (where he's been housed in an empty hangar), is recaptured, escapes again, and makes his way to Griffith Park (completely unseen, though he would have had to have passed though some of the most densely populated sections of L.A. to get there!). At the Griffith observatory the military lays siege while the Beast menaces a school bus full of children. Finally his sister gets through to him, and the Colossus, horrified at what he's become, commits gianticide.

In this sequel to The Amazing Colossal Man, *the "Colossal Beast" is less war-like than* hungry *(as he empties out a grocery truck).*

The screenplay by George Worthing Yates (from Gordon's story) is decidedly small-scale and filled with clunker lines that inspire chuckles rather than thrills. "I'm afraid the world doesn't think of a 60-foot man the way a sister does," observes one character in all seriousness. And when a scientist searching for Manning discovers a gigantic footprint and notes, "The foot that made that print is about ten times the size of a normal man; that'd make him about 60 feet tall," Joyce ludicrously chimes in excitedly, "Glenn was 60 feet tall!"—as if the Mexican countryside is littered with 60-foot giants. Yates fills his script with plenty of talk about the "Colossal Man," but the only action during the movie's first third comes in the form of a panicked Mexican truck driver frantically fleeing some *unseen* menace.

The special effects are typical Gordon (Bert, assisted by his wife Flora, did the opticals himself), with the now nearly-mindless giant (after taking that nasty spill at the close of *The Amazing Colossal Man*) seeming to change in size from one shot to the next. The titular titan also must be changing in density as well, since in some scenes he appears downright transparent. Even on those rare occasions when Gordon gets the proportions (and density) right, thick matte lines and obvious toy vehicles still erase all sense of reality. (The movie's few effective effects shots come courtesy of a six-minute flashback that features all the best footage from *The Amazing Colossal Man!*) On the plus side, the Jack H. Young Colossal Beast makeup is gruesome and well done. With half his battered face looking like a living skull, the monster's disfigured visage remains the most (only) memorable aspect of the film. (Young transformed Margaret Hamilton into the Wicked Witch of the West for *The Wizard of Oz* in 1939.) The climax, in which the Beast's sister inadvertently makes him feel guilty enough to commit suicide by grabbing high tension wires is anything *but* "electrifying" (even with the black-and-white film suddenly bursting into color for the final half-minute). After a few seconds of death throes, the 60-foot giant simply fades away—no smoke, no body, nothing (which definitely makes it easier on the cleanup crew). Also missing is the modicum of pathos found in the first film, the pity inspired by a man-turned-monster (generated by Glenn Langan's original poignant portrayal). Here the Beast (now played by Dean Parkin, whose only other acting credit was playing another mute giant in Gordon's earlier *The Cyclops*) can do nothing but growl inarticulately (sounding like a revving chainsaw).

Gordon himself thought so little of the film that he allotted it one solitary, nondescript sentence in his autobiography (though he obviously liked the grotesque makeup, since he put a rendering of the Colossal Beast on the book's cover): "My fourth film for AIP was *War of the Colossal Beast*, sequel to the extremely successful *Amazing Colossal Man*." That (not) said, *War of the Colossal Beast* should only be viewed (if at all) with a colossal sense of humor.

CHAPTER 5
THE SENSATIONAL SIXTIES (AND BEYOND)

> This was originally published as a mini-review in *Cult Movies* magazine, issue 10 (Spring 1994). I later expanded it to bring it up to speed for my book *The Werewolf Filmography*. Here's the Full (hairy) Monty version.

ASSIGNMENT TERROR (1969)

"The Ultimate in HORROR!" –ad line

Spain's Paul Naschy, who both scripted and acted in *Assignment Terror*, is the combined Christopher Lee and Peter Cushing of Continental cinema. In fact, to carry the Hammer analogy further, he's also the Terence Fisher (or at least Freddie Francis) of Eurohorror because, in addition to starring in over two dozen terror films (in which he plays everything from werewolves and mummies to hunchbacks and vampires), he also directed over a dozen of the features himself.

A professed lover of Gothic horror in general and the Universal classics in particular ("all the marvelous films made by Universal Studios in the 1930s are the main source of inspiration for all my work," he stated), Naschy almost single-handedly began a Gothic revival in Spanish cinema in the late 1960s and '70s with his scripting, acting in, and ultimately direction of the Waldemar Daninsky/Werewolf series. Though few Americans know his name or have seen his films, the dedicated Eurohorror aficionado and offbeat cineaste have been seeking out his movies for years. While the plots are sometimes trite, the production values often suspect, the acting usually bad, and the dubbing always atrocious, Naschy's films show an eccentric enthusiasm and appeal in a quirky, almost quaintly exploitative fashion that no American or British-produced horror film of the same era can duplicate.

What sets Naschy's movies apart from (and *above*) the often mean-spirited and cynically exploitative product of his contemporary countrymen is Naschy's respect and outright affection for the cinematic horror tradition. Though Naschy's budget-conscious and sometimes puerile journeys into Gothic fantasy are no better *cinematically* than most of the genre Eurotrash of the decade, their story lines possess an appealing dose of almost wistful nostalgia—spiced, of course, with the requisite dashes of sex and blood. "I wouldn't say that Paul Naschy was marvelous nor that he was very good," admitted the writer-actor-director himself, "but for any person who sits down to watch a film of mine on the big screen or on television, I believe it will communicate to him that what he is watching was made with love." And in the Spanish/West German/Italian co-production *Los Monstruos Del Terror* (which became *Assignment Terror* when released to U.S. television in 1972) Naschy wears this affection on his monstrous sleeve.

Alien Dr. Varnoff (Michael Rennie, a long way from Klaatu in *The Day the Earth Stood Still*) comes to Earth from the planet Ummo on a mission to destroy the human race by unleashing all the classic monsters upon humanity: Dracula, the Frankenstein Monster, the Werewolf, and the Mummy. (Naschy had also included the Golem in his original script, but the production had to pare down the monster roster for financial reasons.) To this end he inhabits a human body, sets up his lab in a castle, and goes about collecting his supernatural specimens.

"The idea occurred to me to make the definitive 'monsterthon,'" explained Naschy (who appears in the film as his signature character, Waldemar Daninski the Werewolf) about the movie's genesis, "including some extraterrestrials as well. The idea was that an alien agent would reunite all the monsters who had occasioned our most ancestral fears, and bring them to life in order to dominate mankind. The idea, that later was not in the film because we weren't able to finish it as we had wanted, was that he was going to create authentic clones of these monsters in order to help the extraterrestrials to dominate and colonize the Earth. It brought the most classic Gothicism to the modern-day theme of UFOs."

Working against such an outré plot, the film definitely appears of its time. The go-go dancers, miniskirts, sideburns, bright garish lights and generic psychedelic music nearly drowns it in the amber of the Love Generation. This "mod" feel contrasts jarringly

German lobby card for Paul Naschy's monster-fest, Assignment Terror *(1969).*

with the admittedly impressive authentic castle settings, cobwebbed torture chambers, creepy catacombs and general attempt to build a Gothic atmosphere around the classic monsters.

Makeup artist Rafael Ferrer wasn't quite up to the task of Naschy's ambitious monster-laden script. Waldemar the Werewolf (Naschy in his second lycanthropic outing—unless one counts the unfinished/unreleased *Nights of the Werewolf*) appears far less impressive here than in his previous incarnation in *Frankenstein's Bloody Terror* (1968). His wild-haired Lon Chaney Jr.–style makeup ends with coarse hair hanging off his head and cheeks, leaving the center of his face bare, with nary a nose-piece in sight. Consequently, despite an impressive set of sharpened teeth, he looks more ape-man than wolf-like. Worse, the "Living Mummy" (as he's referred to by several characters), from the way his head is bandaged, looks more like a skinny man with a splitting headache than a 3000-year-old undying monster. The Frankenstein Monster (referred to as the "Franksillian Monster" for no discernible reason) is a ridiculous ersatz copy of the Universal creation. The actor, in green face and half-closed eyes, looks more like a fatigued costume party-goer than a creature stitched together from dead bodies. "I had the bad luck," complained Naschy, "of having to count on the worst makeup man of my entire career, Rafael Ferrer, who defrauded us all."

Surprisingly, Naschy didn't give himself much dialogue, nor does the film develop much personality for Waldemar—apart from the tragic curse angle of his lycanthropy. He spends most of his few human scenes as the unwilling pawn of Varnoff (silently wielding a pickaxe and doing the heavy lifting while digging out the Living Mummy from his tomb). In fact, it's nearly 50 minutes into the picture before Waldemar utters his first line. But at least he gets the girl, as he asks the obviously adoring Ilona, "Why are you helping me?" and she answers, "I don't really know—perhaps because I'm a woman."

Assignment Terror adds a new wrinkle to the old silver bullet notion. After Varnoff and his helpers retrieve Waldemar's body from his family tomb, they operate to remove the bullet from his heart (cue the real-life open-heart surgery footage). Varnoff announces, "The Bullet in his heart only immobilized him, left him seemingly dead. His death is permanent only if the bullet is fired by a woman who loves him enough to die for him." A technicality, perhaps, but a romantic one. And a later dialogue exchange concisely coalesces the very nature of the beast, so to speak:

Ilona: "Is he [Waldemar] a man or a monster?"

Varnoff: "Both. The eternal dilemma of mankind—good and evil—the paradox."

According to Naschy, this *Assignment* did not go at all smoothly. "Filming took several months and was fraught with financial difficulties," he recalled. "Work on the film was halted numerous times for financial reasons, only to continue as the Italians and the Germans put in their part of the money." And then the original director quit. "After a few weeks [director Hugo] Fregonese walked off the job and was replaced by Tulio Demicheli, a good friend and wonderful director, who had to deal with all sorts of problems." Though Fregonese receives no on-screen credit, according to Naschy, "the bulk of the film was directed by Fregonese; percentage-wise, it was more or less 70 percent Fregonese and 30 percent Demichelli." Naschy also related how, during the shoot he became acquainted with an occult-obsessed German actress named Barbara Muller who turned out to be a Devil worshipper. She took him to a genuine Black Mass (involving animal sacrifices), which, wrote Naschy, was "something which has long haunted me and given me many sleepless nights."

Despite its rather rambling and disjointed feel (with numerous characters coming and going, and various plot threads unraveling into tangents that rarely weave back into the whole), and the disappointing appearance of its classic monsters, *Assignment Terror* still has plenty to offer the classic (and not-so-classic) horror and werewolf fan. First off, Naschy homages the movies he loves in the very names of his characters. The girl who ends up falling for Waldemar is named Ilona, sharing the same moniker as the female star (Ilona Massey) of Naschy's self-professed favorite horror film, *Frankenstein Meets the Wolf Man* (1943). And Varnoff's helpmate is called Maleva, a nod to the gypsy woman who guided and protected Larry Talbot's *Wolf Man* through his first two films. Most impressively, Naschy brings to malevolent life every little monster-lover's dream of pitting the classic creatures against one another—in this case treating viewers not only to a longer, more satisfying version of the battle royale between the Wolf Man and the Frankenstein Monster as seen (disappointingly briefly) in *Frankenstein Meets the Wolf Man*, but the novel sight of a Werewolf battling a Mummy—a first in monster history. "The film has a double climax," enthused Naschy, "the Wolfman (Waldemar Daninsky) engages in almost surreal combats with the Mummy and the Frankenstein Monster in two scenes which clearly pay homage to the classic *Frankenstein Meets the Wolf Man*." Naschy fills this nightmare-come-to-life with appropriate energy, as he snarls and leaps and slashes at his undead bandaged foe, who, despite occasionally tossing the Werewolf aside, appears to get the worst of it. Unfortunately, this ground-breaking encounter ends in something of a cheat when the Werewolf goes against his lupine nature and grabs a torch to set the Mummy ablaze. Every monster-loving *child* knows that no self-respecting savage werewolf would ever go *near* an open flame.

Assignment Terror turned out to be Michael Rennie's last genre outing. In his autobiography, Naschy wrote, "Very few people know that Robert Taylor, the great Robert Taylor, phoned me at home, much to my surprise. Somehow he'd read the script and was very keen to play the part of Odo Varnoff. ...I was full of enthusiasm and the next day I rushed to tell [producer Jaime] Prades the great news: Robert Taylor wanted to be in the picture. Prades, to my amazement, frowned and told me that Warners had insisted on the part being given to Michael Rennie. When Rennie turned up he was suffering from severe asthma and could only shoot very brief scenes at a time." The actor died the following year. Let's give one last "Klaatu barada nikto" before we bring the curtain down.

Though released (and re-released) successfully across Europe (and even Mexico and South America), *Assignment Terror* never saw the inside of an American movie theater. According to Sam Sherman (whose company Independent International unleashed *Frankenstein's Bloody Terror* on America), he intended to secure the U.S. distribution rights until he learned the film had already been sold to television.

With quotes from: "Interview: Paul Naschy," by José Luis González and Michael Secula, *Videooze* 6/7 (1994); *Memoirs of a Wolfman*, by Paul Naschy.

> I'm almost certain this piece saw print in one of the myriad monster magazines gracing the racks back in the 1990s or early 2000s. Unfortunately, my rather lax record-keeping won't let me *prove* it. In any case, here's my outlaw take on two remarkable (for all the wrong reasons) horror hybrids.

"ROARING GUNS AGAINST RAGING MONSTERS!" THE DUBIOUS THRILLS OF *BILLY THE KID VERSUS DRACULA* AND *JESSE JAMES MEETS FRANKENSTEIN'S DAUGHTER* (1966)

Horror Westerns are an odd breed. Their uneasy mix of gunfights, horseplay, gothic-style chills and monsters are often enough to leave a viewer shaking his or her head like a cowpoke trying to clear his rattled thoughts after a barroom brawl. Few films in this bizarre subset can be deemed successful (or even entertaining), with perhaps 1959's *Curse of the Undead* being the (relative) best of the lot. The strangest pair of ponies in this cinematic corral would have to be *Billy the Kid Versus Dracula* and its co-feature *Jesse James Meets Frankenstein's Daughter*—an outrageous double-bill that becomes almost train-wreck fascinating in its outlandish aplomb.

Billy and *Jesse* were first announced in May of 1961, with Joe Breen slated to direct the Dracula picture and Erle C. Kenton (*Island of Lost Souls*) earmarked for the Frankenstein. When finally filmed in 1966, the two were shot back-to-back (even *concurrently*, according to Howard W. Koch, Jr., who served as assistant to producer Carroll Case) under the direction of B-Western specialist William "One Shot" Beaudine. Shown together to unwary drive-in patrons across the country, the pair went down in history as the oddest western double feature (and horror double bill, for that matter) ever produced.

Billy the Kid Versus Dracula opens on a close-up of the highly made-up, pasty-faced John Carradine *yawning*—which proves a prophetic image for the tedious 70-odd minutes to come. Carradine plays Dracula—complete with top hat, cape, satanic goatee and (saddle)bags under his eyes—for the first time on the big screen in over 20 years; 1945's *House of Dracula* being his last cinematic go-round as the Count. (Oddly, the name "Dracula" never comes up in the film—though it does appear throughout Carl K. Hittleman's script.) The King of the Undead is now roaming the Old West, where he assumes the identity of a never-before-seen relative to infiltrate the household (or, more accurately, *ranch*hold) of Betty Bentley (Melinda Plowman). The randy old bloodsucker intends to make the beautiful Betty his undead bride. Standing in his way is the reformed William "Billy the Kid" Bonney (Chuck Courtney)—Betty's foreman *and* fiancé. (Courtney shot and killed himself in January 2000 at age 69, despondent after suffering a series of strokes.)

"I have worked in a dozen of the greatest, and I have worked in a dozen of the worst," pronounced John Carradine. "I only regret *Billy the Kid Versus Dracula*. Otherwise, I regret nothing." The Shakespearean-spouting actor often cited this as his poorest film. Taking into account some of the I'll-take-anything-with-a-paycheck actor's other movie appearances, it has plenty of (un)worthy competition. "I needed the money, to be honest," explained Carradine about why he accepted the assignment. "Actors have to live too, you know. It was a bad film. I don't even remember it. I was absolutely numb."

Said numbness may have come from a bottle, as the heavy-drinking Carradine would frequently drown his sorrows in the nearest cantina. In *The Dracula Book*, author Donald F. Glut recalled: "When I visited the set at Producers Studio in Hollywood…Carradine was doing a scene in which he was trying to seduce a pretty victim with his talk of a world of vampires. Carradine insisted that Count Dracula would be averse to using the term *vampire*, and substituted the word *un-dead*. When the shooting halted for lunch it was amusing to see Carradine, in full Dracula costume, relaxing in the bright sun and then crossing Melrose Avenue to enter a nearby bar."

Though he may have been "absolutely numb," Carradine's performance was anything *but* (though it is indeed numbing in its *badness*). While John Carradine produced some of the finest acting to grace the silver screen (one need only consider his sublime performances in features like *The Prisoner of Shark Island* and *The Grapes of Wrath*), he was capable of amazing excess when thrown into a take-the-money-and-run feature. Whenever Dracula notices something of interest, for example, Carradine's eyes comically widen into saucers. When confronted with the abhorred mirror, he gives a throaty "waaaaah" like some tantrum-throwing geriatric. Of course, director Beaudine and cinematographer Lothrop Worth were no help to the grand ac-*tor*. Every time Dracula uses his hypnotic powers, a colored spotlight turns his face a *bright red*, signifying the level of subtlety and sophistication employed by the filmmakers—and, no doubt, the level of embarrassment felt by Carradine.

The special effects are less than special, consisting of a bat gliding on a wire (in several silhouetted shots of the fake *fledermaus* flapping its wings it looks for all the world like the flying rodent is wearing its own miniature top hat!) and Dracula popping in and out of the scene à la a turn-of-the-century George Meliès short. At the climax, Billy empties his six-gun into the undead monster with no effect, but when the frustrated outlaw heaves the empty side iron at him, it lays the vampire low! So much for supernatural power (or dignity) in this David and Count Goliath encounter.

The picture also plays fast and loose with traditional cinematic vampire lore. Dracula walks around in broad daylight and sleeps in a bed rather than a coffin (oddly, in one scene we even get to watch him *make* the bed—the Count is nothing if not tidy, and director Beaudine is nothing if not *tedious*). The vampire drinks the blood of lambs and eats regular food (not even blood pudding), and a metal scalpel rather than a wooden stake sends him to his eternal rest at film's end. Said end is quizzical as well, for when Billy stakes Dracula, a bat flies unsteadily out of the cave to crash into some bushes while the vampire's body remains; perhaps it is the fiend's undead soul taking wing…or something?

"We did the Dracula thing with William Beaudine, who was a wonderful guy with a fine reputation," recounted cinematographer Worth to interviewer Jack Gourlay. "But he was so old by then, he'd have to rest between taking scenes." (At the time, the 74-year-old Beaudine was the oldest active member of the Screen Directors Guild.) "Beaudine said, 'You can't make the Academy Awards with these pictures—just take 'em and get the job done.'"

When John Carradine appeared on *Late Night with David Letterman* in the 1980s, the subject of this film came up:

David Letterman: "Do you remember some of the stranger films or the stranger parts that you played?"

John Carradine: "Well, I think the worst one was something called *Billy the Kid and Dracula*. *Billy the Kid Versus Dracula*—that makes it even worse!"

Letterman: "That was a true story though, right?"

Carradine: "No, no, I don't think so."

"True story" or no, the superior half of this terror tandem is *Jesse James Meets Frankenstein's Daughter* (faint praise, actually). In it the famous outlaw (John Lupton) and his muscle-bound (and muscle-headed) sidekick Hank (Cal Bolder) flee to Mexico after a stage holdup goes sour. There the pair stumble upon Maria Frankenstein (Narda Onyx), granddaughter of the infamous doctor, conducting her experiments in a Mexican mission (whose interiors, with their huge stone block walls, oversized nail-studded doors and ornate wall sconces, look more like a Transylvanian castle than a south-of-the-border monastery). Apparently, Maria and her weak-willed brother had been chased out of Vienna for her unorthodox experiments and have taken refuge in this little out-of-the-way corner of Mexico. Maria has been using the local peasants in an attempt to transplant the "artificial brains" her grandfather had created years before into new bodies. So far, the villagers have proven too weak physically to make her experiments a success, but Maria sees just what she needs in the buffed-up Hank. Maria's passion runs to more than her work, however, and she makes advances to the handsome Jesse. To her annoyance, the outlaw rebuffs her, having fallen in love with a local girl named Juanita (Estelita). Meanwhile, Marshall McVie (Jim Davis of TV's *Dallas* fame) tracks Jesse to the village but runs afoul of Hank who, thanks to Maria's successful experiment, has been transformed into a bald, shirtless automaton (and re-christened "Igor") under Maria's control. In the end, Igor turns on his female master and must finally be shot down by his former friend.

Just like its *compadre* did with vampire lore, *Jesse James Meets Frankenstein's Daughter* takes ludicrous liberties with its legends. Maria Frankenstein's experiments center on trying to successfully transplant the "artificial brains" her grandfather had created into new bodies—*not* in piecing together disparate body parts to create a new being. (Quite a comedown for a Frankenstein actually—rather than "playing God" and creating life, Maria's burning ambition is simply to insert a surplus organ she found lying around her grandfather's old lab into an already living body. I don't think grandpappy would have been impressed.)

As to Jesse James, this film turns the notorious thief and murderer into an Old West Robin Hood! At one point, the Marshall admits, "Well, folks say Jesse James steals from the rich and gives to the poor." Right. Then the ending has Jesse ride off willingly with the lawman to stand up and take what's coming to him, presumably reformed by the love of a woman. (Or perhaps battling man-made monsters in a Mexican monastery has made prison seem less unattractive?)

As expected, the film's grade-Z budget shows through frequently, such as in the unconvincingly flat, painted scenery viewed outside a set door or the disappointing lack of special makeup for the "monster" (excepting a thin scar encircling Hank's shaved head). To

Enough said.

veteran Western director Beaudine's credit, however, he takes his cast and crew outside to shoot on occasion, so that the gun battles and stagecoach scenes look relatively realistic (or at least up to the level of a 1960s Western TV series—which this film resembles more than a little for the first half-hour).

Ms. Frankenstein's "lab" also disappoints with its small-scale machinery and minimalist mad doctor equipment. Unable to afford even the most rudimentary pyrotechnics for the big "creation" sequence, Frankenstein's granddaughter must make do with placing a ridiculous piece of headgear on her monster (nothing more than a red and yellow motorcycle helmet with lightning-shaped neon rods attached) and waiting for the creature to sit up.

The picture's saving grace (apart from a wacky appeal inspired by the sheer audacity of it all) is the entertainingly energetic performance of Estonia-born actress Narda Onyx (whose career highlights consist of guest spots on TV's *One Step Beyond* and *The Man from U.N.C.L.E.*) as the female mad scientist. In the best Bela Lugosi/Monogram tradition, nothing will stop this maniacal medico from her warped, scientific goal. She bullies her brother mercilessly into helping with her "work" (it is Maria who obviously wears the pants in this Franken-family), employs (and kills) the locals in her experiments with a callous zeal, and even finds time to fall for the heroine—er—hero (as all the best madmen—and, apparently, mad*women*—do). When Ms. Onyx enthuses "I'm on the verge of a great experiment, and I know I will succeed this time!" her passionate delivery breathes some much-needed fire into the time-worn dialogue.

Jesse James Meets Frankenstein's Daughter proved to be William "One Shot" Beaudine's last feature. Beginning in 1915, Beaudine's directorial career spanned fifty years(!) and nearly every genre, including comedies (several Bowery Boys entries), detective films (various Philo Vance and Charlie Chan features), numerous horror movies (*The Ape Man* [1943], *Ghosts on the Loose* [1943], *Voodoo Man* [1944], *Face of Marble* [1946], *Bela Lugosi Meets a Brooklyn Gorilla* [1952]) and, of course, westerns. Though his baton held sway over myriad genres, all his pictures shared one thing in common—they were all low-budget "B" movies, often made for poverty-row studios. As usual, on *Jesse James Meets Frankenstein's Daughter*, old "One Shot's" direction is plagued with dull staging, a heavy reliance on the medium shot, and an apparent aversion to interesting angles. Though he may not have been good, Beaudine was certainly prolific, directing over 175 features, 325 one- and two-reelers, and 350 episodes for various television series before his death in 1970 at age 78.

While *Jesse James Meets Frankenstein's Daughter* may not be the ideal meeting of Wild West and Gothic Horror, its outrageous premise, absurd genre blending and Monogram-style mad scientist (female, no less) make it a moderately engaging cinematic curio. Partner it with the somewhat stodgier but no less offbeat *Billy the Kid Versus Dracula*, and this terrible twosome rides off into the sunset as the most unforgettable (for all the wrong reasons) double feature in cinema history.

> I assembled this spec article for *Video Watchdog* magazine, only to be told 'that dog don't hunt' (too long for a short piece and too short for a long one). Oh well, time to unleash the hounds…

THE MOST DANGEROUS GAME MEETS THE 1960S: *BLOODLUST!* (1961) AND *CONFESSIONS OF A PSYCHO CAT* (1968)

Hunting: the solid reassurance of the weapon in your hands, the thrill of spotting your prey, the adrenalin rush when you know you've hit your mark—it all culminates in a feeling of power, specifically of power over nature, staking your claim as *the* top predator in the food chain.

It's a primal impulse, and an archetypal one—the wielding of power over life and death. Carry that to the Nth degree—to, some might say, its logical conclusion—and you apply that power to fellow humans.

People hunting people for sport—it's an idea both shocking and fascinating. In 1924 prolific novelist, playwright and screenwriter Richard Connell published a short story that introduced this concept into the public zeitgeist, where it has remained embedded ever since, as evidenced by the many big-screen and small-screen adaptations, inspirations and rip-offs over the years. Since its publication, Connell's O. Henry Memorial Award-winning "The Most Dangerous Game" has been continuously anthologized and studied in classrooms throughout America. Raising questions about the nature of violence and cruelty, the needs of society vs. those of the individual, and, of course, the ethics of hunting purely for pleasure, the thrilling story spawned a new cinematic subgenre, beginning with RKO's 1932 production of *The Most Dangerous Game*, and followed the next decade by *A Game of Death* (1945), RKO's slavish remake of their own classic.

The next two "Dangerous Game" incarnations came in the 1960s, a decade that brought significant changes to the cinematic consciousness. One appears, on the surface, to be a throwback to the teen-targeted terrors of the 1950s (but with a taboo-breaking gruesomeness heretofore unseen), while another is a sleazy mishmash intended to titillate as much as shock. Both were low-budget quickies with a common theme that pushed genre boundaries, and they mark a fascinating juxtaposition of cinematic conceptions.

BLOODLUST! (1961)

"HE HUNTED HUMANS for the sheer sport of killing…and made his island paradise into a Hell on Earth!"
–poster

Here's your chance to see the father of *The Brady Bunch* hunted down like a wild animal (and who among us that grew up in the 1970s could resist such a satisfying concept?). Long before Robert Reed became a household name and face on television via "the story of a man named Brady," he was chased through a forest of potted plants by a crossbow-wielding madman thirsting for his blood.

This third "Most Dangerous Game" adaptation is the first truly low-rent version (though it wouldn't be the last). Budgeted at a mere $80,000, and starring a bunch of then-no-name actors, *Bloodlust!* turned out far better than its straitened circumstances should have allowed.

The story follows two young couples, Johnny and Betty, and Pete and Jeanne (Robert Reed, June Kenny, Gene Persson, Joan Lora), who charter a small boat for some fishing and skeet shooting. When their drunken captain, Tony (Troy Patterson), passes out, they decide to explore a nearby island. Walking through the jungle, Johnny falls into a pit trap—just as Mr. Balleau (Wilton Graff) and two servants arrive. Back at Balleau's house, their host explains, "I came here shortly after the war. I wanted to live in a world of my own—a world completely free from any kind of outside pressure." He also ominously adds, "I've developed a kind of passion for hunting." Though the four are uneasy, their host politely but forcefully insists that they stay the night

The foursome surreptitiously learns that Balleau's wife, Sandra (Lilyan Chauvin), and another man stranded on the island, Dean (Walter Brooke)—who pretends to be "a useless drunk"—are being held against their will. "He can never allow anyone to leave this place alive," Sandra laments. "And he's made sure no one ever will."

Meanwhile, Pete and Jeannie have found stairs leading to an underground tunnel and cave. There they find a room that appears to be some kind of butcher's workshop—except that there's a woman's corpse floating suspended in a glass tank set into the wall! When one of Balleau's henchmen enters, the two terrified teens hide, only to observe him removing a severed human foot and what looks like treated skin (including a human face mask!) from a vat of liquid. (And this nearly two years *before* H.G. Lewis decided to tread on taboo toes with his gore-laden *Blood Feast*.)

With the four youngsters now certain of the danger of their situation, Dean convinces them to cover for he and Sandra while the two make a run for a hidden cove and the boat that's moored there, promising to return with help. But Balleau is on to them, and he follows the pair into the jungle…

Two days pass and, with no word of Dean and Sandra, the quartet stumble across a secret door leading to a cave that serves as Balleau's "private trophy room." They find Balleau there, reclining in his throne-like chair, and the urbane madman proudly displays his trophies—human bodies posed in their death throes. Balleau explains, "I merely preserved my trophies as they were at the moment of my triumph"—just as he illuminates another alcove to reveal the preserved bodies of Dean and Sandra.

Back upstairs, the madman explains that he intends to hunt Johnny and Pete, leaving the two girls to supply

Bloodlust!: a Most Dangerous Teen Game.

him with "feminine company." Just then a henchman enters with a reluctant (and now sober) Tony. "I've paid you well to provide me with subjects in the past," an angry Balleau tells the cowering captain. "But since you've been so foolish as to allow these young people to find their way here without my knowledge, I think it only right that you should share their fate." Balleau further explains that Tony "was my source of supply for my subjects. In the past they were always convicts escaped from the penal islands."

Balleau plans to hunt the three men with a crossbow, armed with only three arrows. He gives Tony an unloaded gun and tells the trio that they'll find ammunition at the starting point of the hunt (a place "the natives call the 'Tree of Death'"). "When that gun is loaded, my life will also be subject to how the hunt goes," says the sporting Balleau. But when they find only one bullet at the designated tree, Tony takes the gun and abandons the two boys. Balleau tracks Tony, but the desperate man gets the drop on his pursuer, only to learn that the gun won't fire! "You've known me long enough to realize that I wouldn't give you a gun without first taking the precaution of removing the firing pin," deadpans the duplicitous Balleau—before sending an arrow through Tony's chest.

During the hunt the two girls escape from their room and make it to the sinister workroom, searching for weapons. One of Balleau's henchmen accosts the girls and tries to rape Betty, but she uses her judo skills (her father is an instructor) to flip her assailant into the standing acid vat!

The girls meet up with Johnny and Pete in the jungle, and elude Balleau (whose tracker, Jondor, has fallen into quicksand—with a displeased Balleau merely smiling as the man sinks) before doubling back to the house. When Balleau returns, the quartet hides in his trophy room. But Balleau, now armed with a pistol, finds them. As he contemplates how he'll "arrange" his soon-to-be-victims, Jondor staggers in—he has escaped the quicksand and leeches!

Balleau frantically fires his pistol at the steadily advancing Jondor, but the brute impales Balleau on the display stand meant for the teens before dying from his wounds. Contemplating their lucky escape, Johnny concludes, "I guess Balleau never thought he'd be the prize exhibit in his own museum."

Though snubbing Connell completely (giving no onscreen credit to the author's classic story), *Bloodlust!* remains more faithful than most to its source—which is just as much the 1932 RKO film *The Most Dangerous Game* as Connell's original tale. As *Bloodlust!*'s unit manager Bri Murphy (who later married *Bloodlust* writer-producer-director Ralph Brooke) related to interviewer Tom Weaver, "[*Bloodlust!*] was a remake of *The Most Dangerous Game*—Ralph figured that was one of the best horror pictures he'd ever seen, so why not do it again?" Why not indeed? To that end, Brooke adapted the story to his decreased budget, keeping the premise but changing the details. For instance, he dispensed with the rather costly use of trained dogs from the original, replacing them with a few extra actors (that could be had on the cheap), one even serving as the antagonist's lapdog, so to speak, who tracks the quarry through the jungle. Brooke also changed "Zaroff" to "Balleau" (dropping Connell's military leader status of "General" and RKO's aristocratic title of "Count") and transformed RKO's two main adult protagonists (or the solo protagonist of Connell's story) into a quartet of attractive young people, no doubt in a savvy effort to ride the coattails of the teen-targeted horror films then ruling the drive-ins (as led by AIP and their teenage monster movies like *I Was a Teenage Werewolf*, *I Was a Teenage Frankenstein*, and *Blood of Dracula*). In fact, it's rather surprising that *Bloodlust!* wasn't titled something like "I Was Teenaged Prey." Unfortunately, these teens apparently aren't resourceful enough to set any of the traditional jungle traps, so *that* thrilling portion of Connell's (and RKO's) story fell by the wayside.

Brooke did keep the tale's (and film's) private-tropical-island hunting ground setting, as well as the grotesque "trophy room" concept. He even expanded upon the latter by including some gruesome "trophy prep" imagery when the protagonists stumble across various body parts in Balleau's secret workroom.

Additionally, *Bloodlust!* offers a rather intriguing variation on the hunt, as Balleau, ever the sportsman, reduces his own odds by choosing to hunt his trio of victims with a crossbow and only *three* arrows—one for each. He also gives his quarry a gun and one bullet, though this turns out to be a ruse, as he's removed the weapon's firing pin (Balleau is not quite the "sportsman" he makes himself out to be).

Providing a somewhat different (and topical) take on the mad hunter's motivation, *Bloodlust!* posits that Balleau was *made* into a hunter of men by sanctioned killing—war. Upon displaying his "trophies" to the horrified teens, Balleau explains:

I hunted them. And shall I tell you why? I'd been a scholar all my life. I was curator of a large museum when the war began. I, who had never killed anything in my life, found myself assigned to duty as a sniper, a "sharpshooter," because of my steady hand and keen eyesight [chuckles]. It amuses me now that I found it distasteful—at first. Then as time went by I adjusted to my new activity, and what had been an unpleasant duty became a pleasure. Then it developed into a passion, and then into a *lust*—a lust for blood—a lust that has grown with the years, and one that I spend my entire life trying to satisfy.

It's a rather clever—and unsettling—extrapolation on the motivation of Connell's antagonist, made all the more chilling because it smacks more of logic than madness (particularly since there's no talk of an old head wound, as in Connell's story, or debilitating headaches, as in the RKO film, as a kind of motivational malady).

First-time director Ralph Brooke, aided by cinematographer Richard E. Cunha (a director in his own right, whose credits include *She Demons, Giant from the Unknown, Missile to the Moon*, and *Frankenstein's Daughter*—all from 1958!), seems remarkably self-assured in the visuals department, utilizing varied camera angles and evocative lighting to augment what little resources he has. For instance, the first shot of the goateed, rifle-bearing Balleau (appearing at the lip of the pit into which Johnny has fallen) is an up-angle perspective (accompanied by a dramatic chord sounding on the music track) that emphasizes the man's power and menace. The next scene fades in on a roaring lion's head, with the camera pulling pack to reveal it to be a stuffed and mounted trophy in Balleau's study, where Balleau serves as host to the quartet of "rescued" teens. The sudden juxtaposition of Balleau and the predatory beast furthers the unsettling feeling surrounding their mysterious "host."

Shortly thereafter, Balleau has a private word with Dean, warning, "I've worked out a very satisfactory design for living here. I think you realize that." The shot, focusing on Balleau, displays two lion heads mounted on the wall behind him, framing him on either side—three predators, with the deadliest of the trio firmly in the foreground. The camera then begins to slowly dolly forward as Balleau continues: "I hope you also realize that the presence of those four young people here changes nothing as far as we're concerned." As he concludes, "I've taken care of *everything*," the advancing camera is now tight enough to reveal the slight upturn of Balleau's lip and the faraway look in his eyes as he imagines that certain "everything." The subtle camerawork—and even subtler playing by Wilton Graff (augmented by his self-satisfied and calm-yet-menacing tone)—generates an ominous sense of unease that propels the story forward and *almost* overcomes the vapid characterizations and dull playing of the "four young people."

Unfortunately, triple-threat Ralph Brooke the Screenwriter fares worse than Ralph Brooke the Director. The four clean-cut "kids" (i.e., 20-something adults) are far too *Leave It to Beaver*-ish, with their bland politeness and gee-wiz demeanor, to take seriously. The banal dialogue they spout further scuttles their already-sinking credibility. For example, when told by Balleau of their impending doom, Johnny blandly retorts: "Listen, Mr. Balleau, fun's fun, but if you think we're going to be the day's pigeons in your shooting gallery, you're just a little far out."

Or how about this dreary exchange in which Pete relates his and Jean's horrific experience in discovering Balleau's gruesome "workshop":

Pete: "You'll never believe what we saw; I don't believe it myself."
Johnny: "We just heard about it [from Dean and Sandra]. I guess it's true then."
Pete: "If they told you about an unbelievable nightmare, it's true alright."
Johnny: "Well that settles it. We've got to try and get out of here tonight."

Adding dull insult to desultory injury is Brooke's (non)direction of his actors in this pivotal scene. Robert Reed's (as Johnny) reaction is nothing more than a furrowed brow and mild concern in his voice, while Gene Persson's (Pete) calm delivery is no more excited or shocked than had he been talking of his high school football team's recent loss to their cross-town rivals. While Brooke could get away with leaving his veteran actors to their own devices, the more inexperienced thespians—including Reed—obviously needed far more coaching than Brooke would, or could, give. Consequently, amateurish and passionless exchanges such as these tend to undermine the horror of the story. (To be fair to Brooke, time constraints may have been the *real* villain here, with eliciting nuanced performances rather far down on the day's to-do list.)

Director-producer-screenwriter Ralph Brooke, the younger brother of actor Walter Brooke, began as a bit player in the late 1940s/early 1950s before moving behind the camera (first working as art and second unit director for the infamous Jerry Warren on 1956's *Man Beast*) when he hooked up with low-budget director Richard Cunha as production manager on Cunha's four sci-fi/horror features (Brooke even co-wrote *Giant from the Unknown*). Brooke returned the favor by hiring Cunha as cinematographer on *Bloodlust!*

"Ralph was marvelous with the crews," reported Murphy, "he loved working with them; it was always light and fun and happy. We had one very complicated dolly shot through the jungle which took a lot of setting up. We rehearsed it several times and then we went to shoot it, and just at the end the sound man sneezed. Everybody gasped, 'Oh, my God!' expecting a big blow-up. But Ralph said, '*O-k-a-y*, somebody plug up the sound man and we'll do it again.' That got a big laugh, which was very nice, and that was typical of the way he directed." *Bloodlust!* was Brooke's first feature as director, and he helmed only two other short films before his untimely death in 1963 at age 43 from a heart attack.

Brooke's script offers up some choice inconsistencies to go along with the occasionally trite dialogue. "He had us alone in here with an unloaded gun," seethes Johnny after Balleau reveals his horrific plan—and the fact he's really unarmed. But the irony is that Johnny doesn't seem to realize that they *still* have him in the same room and Balleau is *still* unarmed. Plus, they outnumber him three to two (Johnny, Paul and Tony vs. Balleau and a solitary henchman). Why the two strong youths and sea captain don't grab and overpower Balleau and his toady instead of lamenting a lost opportunity that *is still there* becomes an obvious, and unaddressed, question—and smacks of rather disingenuous (or perhaps simply careless) scripting.

Fortunately, the subtly menacing playing of Wilton Graff as Balleau helps offset such banalities and gaffs, and injects some real style into the scenario. Graff receives the script's best lines—and delivers them with aplomb. During Balleau's explanatory soliloquy (quoted earlier), Graff begins by speaking calmly, levelly; but when he talks of his pleasure becoming a passion, Graff's voice quickens, becoming louder as he mentions his "lust for blood." Finally, his voice softens and slows again—almost in resignation—as he tells of trying to satisfy that lust, as if such a thing could never truly *be* satisfied. It's a well-modulated and subtly revelatory delivery on the character's own madness.

Later, when Balleau reveals his latest trophies— Sandra and Dean locked in a death embrace—in his underground lair, Betty screams. At this, Graff gives a wry smile and observes, "I see that my latest trophy has *really* impressed you. I'm glad, because I think it's the best thing I've done—" here Graff pauses ever so slightly, and the smile fades to a malevolent coldness as he pointedly adds, "—so far."

Born Wilton Calvert Ratcliffe, Wilton Graff got his start on the stage, appearing in over a dozen Broadway productions before moving to Hollywood in the early 1940s. There he appeared in supporting roles in scores of (mostly B) movies up until the early Fifties, usually playing judges, doctors, DAs and the like. Apart from *Bloodlust!* (his only starring role), Graff appeared in two other horror films, the Lon Chaney Jr.-starrer *Pillow of Death* (1945), and the Poverty Row entry *Valley of the Zombies* (1946). For the last decade of his career, until his death in 1964 (at age 65), Graff mostly worked in television, appearing on such shows as *The Virginian*, *The Alfred Hitchcock Hour* and *Dr. Kildare*.

While the other players make far less of an impression, at least two of them were competent (if unspectacular) professionals with some experience. Walter Brooke (playing the doomed Dean in *Bloodlust!*), brother to *Bloodlust!* director Ralph Brooke, for instance, made a handful of mostly uncredited appearances in the movies in the 1940s before turning to television as early as 1949 to make his living. For almost fifty years, until his death in 1986 at age 71, he appeared on the small screen, guesting on such series as *The Wild Wild West* and *Dragnet* in the 1960s, *M*A*S*H* and *Charlie's Angels* in the '70s, and *St. Elsewhere* and *The A-Team* in the 1980s. Among his sporadic film credits were supporting roles in *Conquest of Space* (1955) and 1967's *The Graduate* (Brooke once confided to his nephew that had he known his famous line about "plastics" would take off like it did, he would have invested in it himself!). Brooke's other genre credits include *The Andromeda Strain* (1971) and *The Return of Count Yorga* (1971).

Actress June Kenny was something of a drive-in stalwart in the late 1950s, having played female leads in such teen-targeted terrors as *Attack of the Puppet People*, *Earth vs. the Spider*, and Roger Corman's *The Sage of the Viking Women and their Voyage to the Waters of the Great Sea Serpent* (replacing Abby Dalton's sister, who injured herself in a fall from her horse during production), all in 1958. She left the industry in 1962 after a handful of TV appearances (including the "Waxworks" episode of Boris Karloff's *Thriller*).

Bloodlust! suffers from those seemingly unavoidable shortcomings arising from having more ambition than cash. Some of the most blatant evidence of the production's poverty lies in the faux cave, whose walls look like what they are—crumpled construction paper, and its *single* clichéd human skeleton and *two* accompanying rats (any more would have required a professional handler—far too expensive). The above-ground settings suffer just as badly. As the teen foursome creep around Balleau's house trying to figure out what's going on, the obvious redressing of the same sparse sets (including using the same two candelabras in room after room after room in a vain attempt to add some elegance to the meager set dressings) all but scream the word "cheapjack."

Though *Bloodlust*'s beach scenes were shot at Paradise Cove in Southern California, all the interiors *and* jungle sequences were filmed on a Hollywood soundstage, near the CFI Lab. "The jungle was all done on the stage," reported Bri Murphy, "every set-up, Ralph [Brooke] changed things around so it looked like a different part of the jungle. Ralph was production-managing that, too, so he had all the plants brought in from a plant supplier, but they didn't have any banana trees. Ralph got very upset—'How am I gonna do a jungle without banana trees?' Robert Reed said, 'Ralph, trust me, I'll fix it for you. Watch this take.' So they go to shoot the take and the kids are finding their way through the jungle, and Robert Reed says, 'Who ever saw a jungle without banana trees??' And the line stayed in!"

Robert Reed (born John Robert Rietz) is by far the best-remembered (*only* remembered) actor in *Bloodlust!* A drama major at Northwestern University, he journeyed abroad to further his studies at the Royal Academy of Dramatic Arts in London. Returning to the States, he joined an off-Broadway company called "The Shakespearewrights," playing leads in *Romeo and Juliet* and *A Midsummer Night's Dream*. Reed appeared in a number of television shows before landing the role that would make him famous, Mike Brady in *The Brady Bunch* (1969–1974), a role the method-trained, serious-minded actor reportedly hated. Post-*Brady* he appeared in dozens of television shows, TV movies and miniseries, earning three Emmy nominations along the way. Though he was HIV positive when he died in 1992, it was colon cancer that ended his life at age 59. Reed had a daughter from a brief 2-year marriage in the late 1950s, but it was Reed's *TV* offspring, Barry Williams (who played eldest son Greg Brady on the series), who helped make the arrangements for Reed's memorial service.

"[*Bloodlust!*] was Robert Reed's first picture," commented Bri Murphy, "and he was delightful. We called him 'the Boy Scout,' and the only problem we had with him was that his armpits sweated so much that it drove the wardrobe lady, Marge Corso, crazy—she was con-

See "Mr. Brady" (Robert Reed, far right) be hunted for sport in Bloodlust!

stantly changing sponges in his armpits. Unfortunately, she didn't realize that this was going to be a problem until after it was established that he was in a T-shirt, because it's hard to have sponges in your armpits and have them not show when you're wearing a T-shirt." In fact, there are several scenes in which Reed's sweat-stains show quite prominently, sponges or no sponges. "I was going to 'blackmail' Robert Reed with that picture," continued Murphy, "I had a 35mm print for a long time—but then he went and died, so I gave the print to Lilyan Chauvin, who was also in it [as Balleau's doomed wife, Sandra]. She teaches acting now, and still acts whenever she can."

Apart from unconvincing sets and missing banana trees, the lengthy early sequences in which Archie and Betty and Jughead and Veronica… er, Johnny and Betty and Pete and Jeanne, creep about the house trying to Find Out What's Going On engenders an unwelcome feeling of juvenilia. It gets to the point where one almost expects Deborah Wally or Erich Von Zipper to pop up on their way to some AIP beach party movie. (And the fact that Balleau's nondescript henchmen all sport striped shirts like some landlocked Disney pirate gang doesn't up the maturity level any.)

But just when you tire of the Hardy Boys/Nancy Drew-like shenanigans, Brooke and company toss out some genuine shocks. When two of the teens stumble across Balleau's underground workroom, they hide when one of his henchmen arrives. The servant promptly rolls up a window shade only to reveal a glass tank inset into the wall with a woman's body floating in it (nightgowned, of course). Brooke then treats us to the gruesomely macabre sight of the henchman retrieving human body parts from another tank—first a foot, then what looks like a batch of human skin, then a head (but with the skull removed, so that he promptly starts filling the skull-less skin with cloth packing material before carefully setting the gruesome relic on the table). The human taxidermy show concludes with the man dumping a load of offal into a second tank, the bubbling mist rising from it indicating its acidic nature. This is strong stuff for the time, and a rude awakening from the earlier '50s-style pleasantries. Combine such unexpected grue with some evocative camerawork and a well-played villain worthy of the title, and *Bloodlust!* frequently manages to escape from the many traps set by its budgetary and scripting deficits.

"I saw it again recently and I enjoyed it," recounted unit manager Bri Murphy thirty-five years after working on *Bloodlust!* "but maybe that was partly because of the sense of déjà vu. The paper caves—I wondered, how did we ever dare to try to get away with that?...[Nevertheless,] I think it was very good for what it was." Indeed, one could do much worse than this moderately entertaining Most Dangerous Game-on-a-shoestring outing.

CONFESSIONS OF A PSYCHO CAT (1968)

"What secrets are harbored deep within the sinister highways of the mind—what are the 'Confessions of a Psycho Cat'?!" –trailer

"ADULTS ONLY" warns the ads for *Confessions of a Psycho Cat*. Indeed, coming seven years after *Bloodlust!*, this New York–shot "roughie" (a more violent counterpart to the "nudie cuties" that proliferated in low-rent grindhouses during the 1960s) may very well be the sleaziest adaptation of Connell's tale to date—not to mention the cheapest.

"Dangerous Game" adaptations live or die by their antagonist, and *Confessions* at least offers a fresh twist: for the first time, the human hunter of Connell's story is a *woman*. "See the female cat as she really is!" dares the trailer, playing up this novel angle. This "female cat" is a wealthy, mentally unbalanced socialite denied a hunting trip to Africa with her brother (due to a recent nervous breakdown), and making up for it with her own special "safari."

After a brief prologue in which a woman sees her brother off at the airport, *Confessions of a Psycho Cat* opens at a cheap apartment where an in-progress swingers' party shows various people talking or having (simulated) sex. They're also waiting for their friend the dope dealer to arrive. "I'd like to do something stronger here than just pot," complains one dissatisfied party-goer, "—like real narcotics."

The scene abruptly switches to a man walking through the city streets suddenly attacked by a woman and her accomplice, who chase the victim into some nearby woods. The woman shoots a crossbow bolt at him, grazing his leg and dropping him into a river, whereby he makes his escape.

Suddenly the film cuts back to the grope-and-fondle gathering. The victim from the previous scene walks—or limps—in. It turns out he is the drug pusher everyone's been waiting for, but he has no "stuff." Instead, he offers a story. "It all started when I got this note to go to this apartment, this fancy apartment…"—and it's flashback time.

At said fancy apartment, three men—a washed-up actor named Charles Freeman, an ex-wrestling champ named Rocco (played by ex-boxing champ Jake LaMotta), and our storyteller Buddy—have been summoned by Virginia Marcus (Eileen Lord) for a little proposition: "I'll give either, any, or all of you 100,000 dollars—*if* you can stay alive in Manhattan for 24 hours." When asked, "What's the catch?" Virginia coolly responds, "Simple—I'm going to hunt you down, then I shall kill you." The men ask her why she picked them, and she answers, "You three men are all bona fide killers. Each of you has killed. Oh, I know you were *all* acquitted, you *all* went free. But each of you has killed." She then relates how each will receive a certified check, post-dated to the next day, which will signal that the hunt is on.

Back at the party, his listeners ask Buddy about the "killers." Cue three more flashbacks. First, Charles the actor, "shacking up with some guy's wife," is interrupted by her husband, who receives the sharp side of a straight-razor for his troubles. Second, the wrestler gets "carried away in the ring…*stomp!*" And Buddy himself (as related by one of his "friends" at the party) accidentally overdoses a young girl on heroine.

After scenes of more party "fun" (consisting of topless girls and hairy men trying to overcome either their natural ennui or nervousness), Buddy continues by relating the fates of the other two human targets. First, Virginia moves behind the scenes to secure a last-minute theatrical job for Charles, who, vain and desperate enough, accepts—despite having received the fateful check that morning. After Charles' performance that evening, Virginia traps him in the deserted theater and sends an arrow into his chest.

Next we see "the Champ" sitting in a cheap motel

Confessions of a Psycho Cat: *a Most Dangerous Sex Game.*

room with a young prostitute on the bed opposite him. Virginia keeps phoning him to taunt the once-proud pugilist into facing her. Finally he's had enough and tears out after his tormentor, who meets him at her apartment dressed as a matador(!). Virginia's manservant (named "Bi") sneaks up behind the raging wrestler and sticks two toreador spears into his back. Virginia then steps forward and twirls her matador's cape, dodging and weaving before finishing off the wounded man with a sword.

Back at the party, Buddy can no longer go without a fix. So, despite the protestations of his friends, he leaves the safety of the crowded apartment for the mean streets of Manhattan to score some dope. After he makes his score, he walks around a corner only to receive an arrow through the throat.

Meanwhile, Virginia's psychiatrist has become concerned about her increasingly erratic behavior, and has summoned her brother, Anderson, back from Africa. When Anderson and the doc arrive at Virginia's apartment, they discover the three bodies in her walk-in freezer. The picture ends with a close-up of Virginia shrieking in a straight-jacket.

As a cinematic adaptation of "The Most Dangerous Game," *Confessions of a Psycho Cat* takes little else from Connell's story than the central concept of hunting humans for pleasure (unless one considers the crowded island of Manhattan to be analogous to the deserted Caribbean isle of the original). Connell's characters are largely unrecognizable here. Instead of the world-traveling big-game hunter Sanger Rainsford, *Confessions* offers a trio of New York lowlifes: a womanizing over-the-hill actor, a barely-articulate ex-wrestler, and a cocky junkie. Zaroff's servant—the mute "gigantic creature" Ivan the Cossack—has transformed into a drink-making, average-sized houseboy whose ambiguous sexuality is reflected in his name: "Bi." Then, of course, the imperious and calculating Zaroff himself ("mine is an analytical mind, Mr. Rainsford") has morphed into a neurotic, ultimately psychotic, Manhattan socialite! And apart from a throwaway line at the beginning about her not being able to accompany her brother on his African safari (due to her recent "nervous breakdown"), and the fact that her "fancy" apartment is furnished like a taxidermy shop, nothing in the film addresses her obsession with hunting, nor why she's taken the "sport" to its ultimate amoral level. There's no revelatory monologue, no shocked reaction from the protagonist, and no human trophy room.

Even the hunts are only a pale reflection of Connell's gripping scenario. In fact, two of the three hunts are little more than simple murders, as Virginia lures her prey out of hiding and then strikes them down. The only real "hunt," in the purest sense of the word, comes at the very beginning, before we even know who's who or what's what, as Virginia and her toady chase a man through the woods. The prey initially escapes, only to be perfunctorily shot down at film's end when his need for a "fix" forces him to leave his sanctuary. There are no uncanny tracking abilities, no terror inspired by pursuing hounds, and no cleverly-laid traps. Gone is the sick and deadly concept of "outdoor chess…your brain against mine, your woodcraft against mine, your strength and stamina against mine." And gone is the pulse-pounding excitement of the terrifying hunt itself, the very core of Connell's engrossing story.

"EXCITING. EXOTIC.. EVIL…!" screams the film's poster in reference to its female antagonist. When it comes to Eileen Lord's performance, however, a more accurate tagline would be "REACTIONARY. RIDICULOUS.. RISIBLE…!" Lord is more petulant schoolgirl than clever master of the hunt, as evidenced by her sudden angry outbursts and gleeful cackling.

For instance, when Charles protests, "You must be joking," Virginia nearly screams, "I'm not joking!" Her over-shrill, over-the-top reaction, meant to suggest her unstable psyche, is about as subtle—and necessary—as a 10-pound sledge pounding in a one-inch nail. Even in more mundane conversation, Lord's voice sounds forced, her lips held taut, her eyebrows dancing in wild abandon.

When Virginia calls Rocco to taunt him into facing her, she mocks, "I challenge you, *Champ*. Come outside and fight." While she talks, Lord's free hand can't seem to stay still, as it tugs her hair and rubs her face like an agitated snake while she veritably spits out her mocking lines, her eyes and brows involved in some insane ocular calisthenics. At the end of the call she laughs maniacally, her mouth going impossibly wide. On the one hand, it's a shrill, painful, overplayed performance. On the other, however, it's never dull (unlike so many of the other amateur players in this half-baked movie), and makes up in sheer outrageous gusto what it lacks in verisimilitude.

With ad lines like "SHE WAS THE MISTRESS OF PLEASURE – AND THE SLAVE OF HER DESIRES!" and "HER BED WAS HER LAIR!" it's rather surprising that Virginia never engages in any of the erotic activity that comprises fully half the picture, remaining completely asexual and focused on the hunt. Of course, given that said undraped activity appears to have been added as an afterthought, it's little wonder

Lord took no part in the frisky festivities.

Speaking of which, though the picture offers up nudity in quantity, it definitely skimps on the quality. Very little of the lethargic, half-hearted couplings could be considered even mildly erotic, as the amateurish (and uncredited) participants look alternately uncomfortable and bored, with some being only marginally attractive at best. Consequently, despite all the casual nudity and unenthusiastic simulated sex, the film only comes (half) alive during the three stalking sequences, and when Lord indulges in her wild histrionics.

The only other performer of note is Jake "Raging Bull" LaMotta as Rocco. The ex-boxing champ looks lost. Granted, his punch-drunk performance occasionally suits the role, but he's unable to vary his delivery enough to make this "kill-hungry grunt-and-groaner" (as the trailer labels him) into anything more than a one-note caricature. Of course, the fractured script does little to aid this Raging Thespian, with perhaps the worst moments coming when Rocco alternately responds to Virginia's taunting on the phone and the (creepily underage-looking) topless prostitute's jibes from the bed (it's obvious said femme fatale is *not* in the same room with the ex-champ). LaMotta, bare-chested (and barely coherent) sits in a chair and "delivers" lines like "I'm not afraid of nothin'" and "Okay lady, now you get yours" with all the conviction of a, well, *Sleeping* Bull.

LaMotta, a former middleweight boxing champion known as "the Bronx Bull" and "the Raging Bull," is the only "name" attached to the production, either in front of or behind the camera. Beginning in 1941 at age 19, Lamotta enjoyed a highly successful boxing career over the next decade and a half, recording 83 wins (30 by knockout), 19 losses and 4 draws. Most famously, he was the first man to beat the great Sugar Ray Robinson. Most infamously, LaMotta later testified during an FBI investigation into the workings of organized crime that he'd thrown a 1947 fight with Billy Fox in order to curry favor from the Mafia and secure a World Title bout with French boxing champion Marcel Cerdan (which LaMotta won by technical knockout in 1949). Of the fixed fight with Fox, LaMotta wrote in his autobiography *Raging Bull, My Story*:

The first round, a couple of belts to his head, and I see a glassy look coming over his eyes. Jesus Christ, a couple of jabs and he's going to fall down? I began to panic a little. I was supposed to be throwing a fight to this guy, and it looked like I was going to end up hold-

The "Raging Bull" himself, Jake LaMotta, seeks the Confessions of a Psycho Cat.

ing him on his feet...By [the fourth round], if there was anybody in the Garden who didn't know what was happening, he must have been dead drunk.

After retiring from boxing, LaMotta bought a couple of bars and began a spotty career as an actor (winning mostly bit parts in 15 different films, the most famous being *The Hustler*, in which he played the bartender) and occasional stand-up comedian. He also wrote his tell-all biography detailing his often-violent life (at one point even confessing to rape!), upon which the Martin Scorsese-directed, Robert DeNiro-starring film *Raging Bull* (1980) was based.

Confessions of a Psycho Cat's very structure works against it. By opening on a dull "party" exchange and various sex scenes, then abruptly switching to a man fleeing through the woods before we've had any hint of introduction or explanation (it's as if a completely different movie had suddenly popped up), the viewer has no investment (nor any real interest) in what *should* be a thrilling, suspenseful centerpiece, making it all seem both disjointed and ridiculous. Rather than the multiple flashbacks, the story would have made far more impact had it run in a straight timeline, with the "hunts" escalating in action and intensity (the actor, the wrestler, and finally Buddy's frantic run) *after* the set-up had been established. Of course, this would have made it more difficult to shoehorn in the "titillation" scenes.

Besides the fact that *Confessions* was filmed on location in and around New York City, very little is known, or has been recorded, about the making of this obscure movie. Given the film's two different titles (the other being *3 Loves of a Psycho Cat*), and the different footage contained in each of the two respective trailers that exist, it appears that the movie was originally shot as a straight horror/suspense film but then morphed into a sex-laden "roughie" when the various nude/sex scenes were added later. The *3 Loves of a Psycho Cat* trailer contains none of the characters from the party sequences besides Buddy, and features plenty of footage not included in the *Confessions of a Psycho Cat* print (the only one available at present). In the *3 Loves* trailer, Jake LaMotta interacts *directly* with an underwear-wearing prostitute during his big phone scene, as opposed to his tangential verbal jousting with the obvious cut-ins of a topless prostitute (a different actress) seen in the *Confessions* print. The only character featured in both the hunt and party scenes is Buddy, and his variable appearance indicates some passage of time between the two sets of footage.

Besides its structural problems necessitated by its pastiche approach, *Confession*'s script offers some dialogue humdingers as well. Not surprisingly, most of them come from the movie's sexed-up portion. How about this exchange between two partygoers idly waiting for the "stuff" to arrive:

Man: You wanna ball?
Woman: Groovy.

Later, one of the somnambulant chippees responds to Buddy's shocking tale with a vapid, "That woman sounds real goofy." Indeed.

"All these people running around naked—look at them!" disdainfully sniffs one demure attendee (who nonetheless soon drops her top as well). This line becomes quite comical when the viewer realizes that none of the sex scenes feature more than three people in the same shot! Rather than a group gathering, this "party" is merely a disconnected series of two- and three-person vignettes.

But it's not just the tacked-on distaff portion of the script that contains head-scratching moments. During Buddy's flight through the woods, he ends up climbing a tree. The next shot shows him literally out on a limb, hanging above the river. Now *why* would he place himself in such an open and perilous position when running for his life? (So he could conveniently be shot in the leg with an arrow and drop into the water, that's why.) Later, in talking about Charles' demise, Buddy comments that it was "a spear right through the heart" when we clearly see said spear (an arrow, actually) sticking out of the victim's right *side*, nowhere *near* his heart. And how does Buddy know all this anyway, since he wasn't there?

In among its many fleapit flaws, *Confessions* does manage to pull off two effectively disturbing sequences. The first comes when Virginia tells her psychiatrist about a childhood trauma. With a distorted camera lens reflecting her fractured psyche, Virginia narrates an incident in which as a little girl she happily plays with her new puppy on the roof of a New York high-rise. "It was the cutest little thing," she says, before her voice abruptly changes, hardens: "I was glad when it died." Suddenly, a slightly older boy—her brother—rips the dog from her arms and shockingly hurls it over the roof edge! We watch as the (obviously *stuffed*) puppy spirals downward, even hitting the side of the building as it drops to its death. Here Virginia devolves into shrill shouting: "Killing is bad. I've never killed anything. I couldn't—I hate killing. I hate guns. Killing is bad!" Both shocking and disturbing, the sequence simultaneously answers and asks questions.

The second memorable moment is remarkable more for its jaw-dropping bizarreness than its shock effect. It begins as Rocco, lured out of hiding by Virginia's mocking phone calls, enters her darkened apartment and creeps through a set of patio doors, only to have Bi sneak up behind him and jab two toreador spears into the big man's back. The bleeding and enraged Rocco then staggers and lunges towards the cape-swirling Virginia, all decked out in a matador costume! The sequence's sense of disturbing surrealism is heightened by the fact that at the center of this bizarre human bullfight is Jake LaMotta, the former "Raging Bull" himself. The icing on this outré cake arrives when Virginia offers this epitaph: "He died like a brave bull."

While the huntress' lair exposes the production's poverty (all we see of Virginia's "fancy apartment" is an entryway and one cramped and cluttered room), it also reflects the chaotic mind frame of its owner. Nearly every inch of the two walls we see are covered with all manner of animal trophies—everything from a huge swordfish head to wolf pelts—while the floor is covered with animal-skin rugs, and every available surface displays stuffed ducks, weasels, badgers and god-knows-what. (Perhaps the picture's primary investor was a taxidermist?) Disappointingly, however, there's no human trophy room. Undoubtedly, such was beyond the film's meager budget.

Behind the camera, producer-director Herb Stanley, aided by cinematographer Paul Guffee, makes a few valiant attempts to create a mood, enhance a scene, or at least generate some visual interest—and even succeeds on occasion. During Buddy's panicked flight, the handheld camerawork, shooting from various angles, and moving both behind and in front of the frantic "prey," adds some much-needed motion and urgency. (Too bad we have so little investment in the moment, since at this point we've no idea what's going on.) Fast edits and some frenetic music (taken from library stock, but well-chosen nonetheless) further enhance the feeling of immediacy.

Later, as Virginia visits her psychiatrist, the camera shoots solely from Virginia's point of view as she enters the waiting room, talks with the nurse, picks up a magazine, and flips to an ad with a dog (triggering the pivotal soon-to-be-related memory of her doomed puppy), effectively forcing the viewer to identify—and sympathize—with the unbalanced Virginia. Stanley uses a wide-angle lens that slightly distorts what Virginia (and we) see to an almost fish-eye perspective, and occasionally goes in and out of focus (particularly when Virginia—and we—stare at the dog in the magazine), reflecting the instability of Virginia's state of mind.

Such occasional flashes of competence and creativity makes it doubly disappointing that Stanley's efforts are effectively undone by the static, poorly-filmed, tinny-sounding party and sex inserts; the jumbled and poorly-edited story structure; and the alternately toneless and wildly inappropriate playing of his non-actors. "See this shocking and bizarre motion picture," ordered the trailer. Well, they got it half-right, as it certainly lives up to the "bizarre" adjective in that claim. But apart from a few memorable moments, some unintentionally amusing dialogue, and the outrageously outré thespian shenanigans pulled by Eileen Lord as Virginia, the seedy *Confessions of a Psycho Cat* prove hardly worth hearing—or watching.

> This piece on the ultimate talking head movie was included as liner notes for the *Brain That Wouldn't Die* DVD put out by Synapse Films in August 2000.

THE BRAIN THAT WOULDN'T DIE (1962)

While not the first Disembodied Head movie, and not the best (1985's *Re-Animator* wins that title), *The Brain That Wouldn't Die* is undoubtedly the most offbeat and entertaining of its ilk. Filmed in thirteen days in 1959 (but not released until 1962 by American International Pictures), the New York lensed *Brain* remains a treasured guilty pleasure for many a horror/sci-fi aficionado.

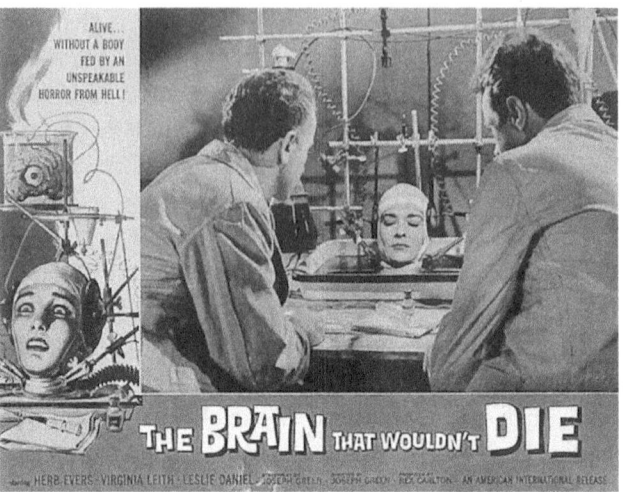

The decade's best head-on-a-table movie. Pictured: Leslie Daniel, Virginia Leith (as Jan...in the pan), and Herb Evers.

AIP's publicity department called the picture "an adventure into a terror-filled world of science gone mad where anything and everything can—and does—happen." For once, the PR crew was guilty of understatement. Arms ripped from sockets, flesh bitten from necks, decapitation, reanimation, misogynation... *The Brain That Wouldn't Die* is indeed a film in which anything can—and does—happen.

Inspired by producer Rex Carlton's suggested title of *I Was a Teenage Brain Surgeon* (this was right after Herman Cohen's "Teenage" monster films had come out), writer/director Joseph Green pounded out his outlandish script, now titled *The Head That Wouldn't Die*, in only three days. (AIP ultimately changed it to *The Brain That Wouldn't Die* before release).

The strange storyline has Dr. Bill Cortner (Herb Evers) keeping alive the decapitated head of his fiancée, Jan (Virginia Leith), after she 'dies' in an auto accident. Cortner then goes on a hunt for the perfect body, prowling sleazy nightclubs and "body beautiful" contests to find the prime pulchritude. Aiding him in his heady plan is his warped (both in mind and body) assistant, Kurt (Leslie Daniel), who's deathly afraid of 'the thing in the closet'—a horrible creature made from grafted tissues, the result of countless failed experiments. Jan is less than pleased with her current situation and merely wants to die. She develops a link with the unseen closet monster, and, at the propitious moment, exhorts him to break out of his cell. The mutant knocks over some chemicals which promptly burst into flame and then bites a chunk of flesh out of his creator's neck, tossing Bill's writhing body to the floor. As the flames rise higher, the creature scoops up Bill's intended body donor (a photographer's model) and carries her out while

Jan cackles hideously from inside the conflagration.

First-time director Joseph Green does wonders with a tight budget and little time. (In one interview Green put the cost at $62,000, though he later explained to this writer that the final budget was "about $125,000 to $150,000" with the $62,000 figure being "for certain preliminary work." Right.) The fatal car crash sequence, for instance, shows just how inventive a low-budget filmmaker can (and must) become. In close-up, Bill shouts in alarm and we see his foot frantically stamp on the brake before the camera runs directly into the guardrail and seemingly flips up into the air in a sudden, violent motion. Next we see Bill rolling over and over down a hill. He sits up and a pained look of horror crosses his face. The camera cuts to a close-up of the car's shattered side window, viewed from inside the automobile. Flames burn in the left foreground while a hand seemingly reaches upwards for help from the right. Bill staggers forward and reaches over the jagged glass toward the hand, but it collapses and falls out of the shot. Bill takes off his jacket and lowers it into the car out of camera range. When he draws it back again, there's *something* wrapped up inside.

Green shows some real ingenuity here, using camera angles and p.o.v. shots to give the feel of a fatal car crash without the expense (none of those overpriced stuntmen and pyrotechnicians with specialty vehicles here—just a junkyard car door, a hand-held camera, and some lighter fluid). Amazingly, it does the job by allowing our imagination (rather than money) to do the work. "It was all suggestion," recalled Green. "The picture was not a big-budget picture so I had to pick out ways to *suggest* a violent automobile crash and her head being severed from her body." Sometimes a suggestion is worth a thousand greenbacks.

Of course, the next sequence turns almost comically absurd as Bill dashes with his gruesome package through the landscaped woods (the manicured grounds of North Tarrytown's Detmer Estate) like an NFL running back. For a full minute and a half, the camera jogs alongside and in front like some macabre blocker intent on seeing his teammate carry the pigskin across the goal line. It is strange juxtapositions like these (inventive sequences alternating with moments of amusing preposterousness) which create much of the film's bizarre charm and make it so enjoyable.

The characters continually bicker and needle each other, setting up scene after scene of verbal friction that effectively distracts the viewer from the occasional spells of inactivity. Talk is cheap, and Green fills his low-budget picture with plenty of it. Fortunately, the frequently over-the-top conversations make for some fascinating moments of intense absurdity, with the disembodied head blathering away to the unseen monster in the closet ("I've *got* to see your hideousness; you've got to see *mine*... Nothing you can be is more terrible than I am—a head without a body—a head that should be in its grave") or the high-strung lab assistant petulantly sniping back at the insulting cranium ("I'm getting fed up with you and your *insidious talk*! He should have cut out your tongue while he was at it!").

The picture sports some downright priceless moments, such as when Bill, annoyed at Jan's vociferous objections, *tapes her mouth shut*! And the film boasts one of the most unintentionally amusing death scenes in the annals of cinema. After the closet creature pulls Kurt's arm from its socket(!), the maimed man staggers about for *two solid minutes*, running his mutilated shoulder into doors and walls so he can drag it along the surface and leave a gory snail-track of blood. (AIP originally cut this extended sequence, along with a few other gruesome tidbits, upon the film's initial release. Fortunately, the missing footage has been restored on video and can now be viewed in all its boffo gory glory.)

"Heading" up the cast was actress Virginia Leith. Publicity articles claimed that *The Brain That Wouldn't Die* was Virginia's "bid for renewed stardom." Sadly, the cerebral role didn't exactly take the actress to the head of her profession, for she only appeared in one more film, *First Love* (1977), and a few sporadic television shows. Much of *Brain*'s enjoyment factor, however, comes from her game performance as the bitter disembodied head.

Herb (later Jason) Evers, making his big-screen debut, does equally well, possessing a smooth manner and comfortable charm while mixing in quiet smirks and subtle leers to give his obsessed mad surgeon a human (if slightly sleazy) quality. (One wonders if starring in *Brain* had anything to do with Evers' subsequent name-change.)

Apart from these two players, most of the other *Brain* thespians emote as if they're performing nineteenth century grand guignol (which may not be so inappropriate after all, since they are, in fact, doing a cheesy form of *twentieth* century grand guignol!). As Kurt, Leslie Daniel (who worked primarily as a dubbing actor) reaches new heights in melodramatics, speaking his ludicrous lines with a near-violent fervor while sighing and gesturing with boundless theatricality. Daniel's painful sincerity and over-the-top mannerisms, while far from any sense of normalcy, are indeed *fun* to watch. (And since nothing in this picture is 'normal,' Daniel's hyperdrive performance works.)

The arm-removing "giant pinhead closet monster" (Green's appellation) was played by the exceedingly tall Eddie Carmel. A sometime Ringling Brothers and Barnum & Baily Circus giant, Carmel's publicity listed him at 500 pounds and nine feet tall! While these stats may have been 'heightened' just a bit, there's no denying the imposing impression he made as the hideous mutant behind the door. "He was a very fine young guy," remembered Green. "Every actor should be that easy to work with on the set. It was a shame he had this glandular problem." Sadly, this glandular problem, which made Carmel so suitable for his gigantic role in *Brain*, led to his early death in 1972 at the age of 36. (His director survived him by nearly three decades; Joseph Green succumbed to liver failure on September 1, 1999.)

While not particularly realistic looking, the creature's appearance certainly is *unusual*, with its oatmeal face, pointed bald head, off-kilter eye, and flaps of scarred, wattled flesh under its chin that make the poor wretch appear to sport some monstrous turkey-neck. "[Make-up man] George Fiala did a very good job," opined Green, "using a rubberized mask and regular makeup directly applied. I was very happy with the result."

Call it what you will, but *The Brain That Wouldn't Die* remains about as far from boredom as a film can get—despite the fact that it is indeed the ultimate "talking head" movie. For those viewers who maintain a sense of cinematic fun and love of the outlandish, *The Brain That Wouldn't Die* will forever remain *The* Movie *That Wouldn't Die*.

> Editor Dan Taylor enthused "Send in the clowns!" when asked if he'd like this piece for his magazine *Exploitation Retrospect* (issue 51) in 2012.

CLOWN HUNT (2012)

Yes, this is exactly what it sounds like—a satirical jab at the Most Dangerous Game theme (people hunting people for sport, first suggested by Richard Connell's famous 1924 short story "The Most Dangerous Game"), with circus clowns taking the brunt of the sardonic roundhouses (though the hunters themselves receive their fair share of derisive body blows). Shot in Texas in 2010 and released directly to video in 2012, the obviously low-budget *Clown Hunt* posits that clowns have become big game for Texas rednecks, who buy hunting licenses and join (semi)organized hunts to bag their limit of clowns out on the open range. In this particular chuckle-filled universe, clowns apparently live together in herds out in the wilds, performing random clown tricks as well as partaking in such odd activities as bouncing kittens off trampolines(!) and smashing baby chicks with their oversized shoes(!!). A group of rednecks run the gauntlet of "Save-the-Clown" protestors (whose activities are appropriately chronicled by KLWN-TV) to descend on local landowner B.J.'s (David Keith, the only "name" actor in the film—obviously there for one day and a quick paycheck) "Chuckle Ranch" and set up camp for the start of Clown season. "First week of the season is Happy clowns only," one hunter reminds the group. "Sad clown season doesn't start 'till the second week." As the band of hunters prepare for opening day, they drink, mud-wrassle (an hilarious homoerotic homage), and scout the local clown fauna. They also recall the legend of "Albino Willy," a famous clown who's "been seen all over the world, but nobody's been able to cap his ass." As the hunt begins, Albino Willy shows up and leads an impromptu clown revolt, so that the hunters soon become the prey.

Clown Hunt offers more gags and pratfalls than story and characters, the latter of which are pretty much ciphers, though one hunter (played by the film's writer/director/co-producer) appears more sensitive than the others (even offering the politically-correct observation that "they really don't like to be referred to as 'clowns' anymore; they would prefer to be called 'laugh-makers'"). In a clever riff on the notion of intolerance, he turns out to be a closeted clown himself (he retires to his tent each night to don clown makeup). When he finally "comes out" as a clown, the nonplussed expressions on the faces of his heretofore unsuspecting backwoods buddies speak volumes.

It being basically a one-joke movie, *Clown Hunt*'s entertainment value comes from the variations that branch off from said joke. Some are clever ("I was readin' *Big Shoes Big Guns* the other day..."; or the clowns dying in character, complete with comical feet in the air for their death throes), some are tasteless (such as Albino Willy placing a shovel under a hunter who's defecating into a hole, resulting in the drunken man's confusion when he finishes and finds nothing there), and some are tastelessly funny (when one clown becomes so frightened by the sound of a gun going off, he drops a load of jelly bean scat before running away). How much a viewer will enjoy this film stems from how one reacts to the various gags that come fast and furious

Clown Hunt—*it's just like it sounds.*

throughout the 70-minute running time.

Writer-director Barry Tubb foregoes any exploration into what kind of a society evolved (or *de*-volved) into hunting clowns, nor are there any explanations as to why clowns seem to behave like herd animals (given that they are indeed just *people* in make-up and oversized shoes, as demonstrated by the closeted clown hunter in the group). Consequently, Tubb sacrifices myriad opportunities for social or political satire, focusing instead on a stream of sight (and sound) gags (yes, there are fart jokes) that tend to become both puerile and repetitious over time. And Tubb obviously had difficulty coming up with a suitable ending for his Bozo opus. The climax begins well enough via an amusing, small-scale *Road Warrior* homage (as the few remaining hunters, driving an odd assortment of vehicles, try to run Albino Willy, riding an ATV decked out with a giant clown head[!], to ground), but deteriorates into the firing of a giant rocket-missile (complete with clown nose) and a nonsensical final shot of Willy's white wig floating in New York Harbor(?!). *Clown Hunt* might have done better as a concise comic short or even a faux trailer. As is, it comes dangerously close to wearing out its big-nosed welcome.

Director-producer-screenwriter-actor Barry Tubb forged a career appearing in supporting roles on television in the 1980s in such series as *Hill Street Blues* and the *Lonesome Dove* telefilms, and movies such as *Mask* (1985) and *Top Gun* (1986). Becoming disenchanted with Tinseltown, however, he worked on Broadway and then moved to France in the '90s, appearing there in a Wild West show (born and raised in Texas, Tubb was a champion bull rider at age 15). He eventually turned to the production side of filmmaking near the end of the decade, helming *Blood Trail* (1997) and *Grand Champion* (2002) before tackling the trials and tribulations of red noses and oversized shoes with *Clown Hunt*. Said Tubb, "I wanted to make my own movies because Hollywood just wasn't cutting it for me. The movies I was reading weren't as good as the stories I knew growing up."

While a tale of "clown hunting" may not qualify as a "good" story (and certainly wasn't something Tubb "knew growing up"), it at least makes for an intermittently amusing one that comes off as a unique pie in the face to Connell's concept.

> The following was my contribution to a compilation article aptly titled "Movies We Hate!!!" which appeared in *Midnight Marquee* no. 53 in 1997.

CURSE OF THE SWAMP CREATURE (1966)

"Never make a swamp picture," producer-director Larry Buchanan warned interviewer Greg Goodsell, "your film comes back and it's all...*strange*." Sadly, in the hands of the creator of *The Eye Creatures* (1965), *Mars Needs Women* (1966) and *Zontar, The Thing from Venus*, "strange" invariably translates into "boring."

In the mid–1960s, AIP contracted with Texas-based filmmaker Buchanan to produce a series of no-budget horror movies (most of them remakes of old AIP sci-fi properties) that could be sold directly to television. Along with the recycled scripts (from such '50s faves as *Invasion of the Saucer Men*, *Day the World Ended* and *It Conquered the World*), AIP sent Buchanan various fallen "stars" like Tommy Kirk, John Ashley, Yvonne "Batgirl" Craig and John Agar. It didn't help.

According to Buchanan, "[AIP heads Jim Nicholson and Sam Arkoff] said, 'Give us color in 80 minutes, and here's your check!' They never talked about aesthetics. Any time I would say, 'Look, I want to really do something right,' and we'd talk about $200,000 to $300,000…they didn't want to hear about it." But $20,000 to $30,000—*that* was another story…

Unlike other Buchanan opuses (like *Zontar* and *In the Year 2889*), *Curse of the Swamp Creature* was filmed from an original script (by failed Buchanan actor Tony Huston). Actually, that's not quite true; Huston stole the basic premise from AIP's *Voodoo Woman*, but made enough changes (none of which are improvements) in the setting and story to fob it off as "original." As a result, *Swamp Creature* lacks even the minimal interest that Buchanan's schlocky remakes possess. Shot in

A Curse *indeed.*

16mm on a budget of around $25,000, *Swamp Creature* may not be Buchanan's worst film (1968's *It's Alive* wins that [dis]honor), but it comes in a close second. And that's saying something, since Buchanan could easily be labeled the Ed Wood of the 1960s—correction, that should be the *Dead* Wood of the 1960s, since Buchanan's sorry movies are usually so listless that they prove unwatchable.

Curse's story has a mad doctor turning people into fish-creatures (he refers to his latest creation as "my beautiful indestructible fish-man") deep in the Texas swampland. Voodoo enters the picture when the "swamp dwellers" (poor black folk) come looking for their missing relatives at the doctor's compound. These 'natives' communicate via jungle drums(!), worship snakes (frequently talking of "snake magic") and hang the doctor in effigy. After a threadbare ceremony in which a woman performs what looks like a slow-motion watusi dance around a torch and plastic skull, the leader incites his followers to rise up against the evil doctor: "Our strong magic will destroy him. You must become the instrument of revenge. Go! Do what you will!" They "go" but they don't really "do" anything except mill about on the doc's front lawn. Rather than magic or restless natives destroying the doctor, it's his own zipper-suited, ping-pong-eyeballed "creation" that dumps him into his swimming pool full of (stock footage) alligators.

"We shot *Curse* at Caddo Lake, a huge swamp on the Texas-Louisiana border," wrote Buchanan in his (aptly-named) book *It Came from Hunger! Tales of a Cinema Schlockmeister*. "The small cast and crew were put up at the [also aptly-named] Fly 'n' Fish lodge, set among the green cypress trees. The nearest town was Uncertain, Texas. The Fly 'n' Fish [which served as a shooting location as well as lodging] would not take our black cast members, so we had to shuttle them from the swamp set to private black families in the little town of Uncertain."

"Larry, God bless him, is a nice guy but he really was not a director," recalled *Swamp Creature* star John Agar to interviewer Tom Weaver. "He did the best he could, but he didn't even know enough not to 'cross the line,' which is one of the simplest things there is in directing. In the beginning, he didn't understand *that*! The first picture I did for Larry was *Zontar, The Thing from Venus*; *Curse of the Swamp Creature* came next; then we did a war film called *Hell Raiders*. Of course, I never thought those things would ever see the light of day—that was the only reason I did 'em!"

Bare-bones sets, amateurish acting (an extremely sedentary Agar looks tired and really has nothing to do except sit around and smoke cigarettes), pacing that's more sluggish than the bayou current, deadening dialogue, dim lighting, tinny sound (much of it was shot silent with the sound and dialogue dubbed in later—people frequently say their lines without even moving their lips!) and muddy photography make this picture a firm contender in any Worst Movie contest. Viewers beware, for *Curse of the Swamp Creature* is actually the Curse of the Couch Potato.

> Here's another article (this one aimed at the British publication *Shivers*) that, for whatever reason lost to memory, went unpublished (despite my having interviewed producer Richard Gordon on the topic).

CURSE OF THE VOODOO (1965): AFRICAN SORCERY IN REGENT'S PARK

"Africa! Where primitive tribes still practice evil religions which weave a dark web of death around all who sin against their gods." –narrator

After tackling such terrifying topics as bodysnatching (*Corridors of Blood*), bloodsucking astronauts (*First Man Into Space*), *brain*sucking thought-monsters (*Fiend Without a Face*), and possessed ventriloquist dolls (*Devil Doll*), executive producer Richard Gordon felt the time was right to try his hand at voodoo. What resulted was an earnest but rather sluggish low-budget tale of African "black magic" (with London-area woodlands standing in for the Dark Continent).

In Africa, big-game hunter and safari guide Mike Stacey (Bryant Haliday) breaks taboo by following a wounded lion (the result of his client's inept shooting) into the dreaded Simbaza territory. "The Simbaza," relates colleague Major Lomas (Dennis Price), "are a tribe that worship lions. They also practice a very potent form of black magic." Accompanied only by his loyal native bearer Saidi (Dennis Alaba Peters), Stacey ultimately kills the wounded beast, but not before receiving a minor mauling in the process.

Later that day, a Simbaza witchdoctor (Danny Daniels) and several tribesmen walk into Stacey's camp and symbolically throw a spear into the ground at his feet. Then, on the way back from the safari, Saidi, under the influence of the Simbaza magic, tries to knife Stacey before being beaten off by Major Lomas.

When he gets back to his home in Johannesburg, Stacey finds that his wife Janet (Lisa Daniely) has left him (due to his inattention and heavy drinking), taking his young son and returning to her mother's estate in England. Stacey flies to London to attempt a reconciliation. When Janet stands him up for their meeting, Stacey picks up a woman in a bar (Valli Newby), who takes him back to her place. Once there, he passes out.

Back in Africa, the Simbaza have Saidi stretched out and tied to a pole. They perform some sort of ritual, paint his face with white powder, and stab a spear into his shoulder. At that very moment, Stacey awakens with a stabbing pain in *his* shoulder – the lion-inflicted wound has reopened. Walking through the park on the way back to his hotel, Stacey hears a lion growl and imagines something stalking him through the bushes.

When Janet finally does meet him later that day, Stacey suddenly hears jungle drums and sees a black man (in hat and trenchcoat) staring at him through the door. Pursuing the man, he boards a bus—but the man is not there. Stacey sits down to catch his breath, and when he glances around he sees the man sitting behind him, staring. Stacey turns away, looks again, and the man is gone.

That night Stacey fires off four pistol shots through his hotel room door when he sees the painted face of a Simbaza warrior there. When the police arrive, of course, there's no tribesman, and the inspector looks pointedly at the empty whisky bottle on Stacey's nightstand. The hauntings/hallucinations worsen, for the next day Stacey flees through the park, pursued by two spear-carrying tribesmen. He collapses and we next see him back in his hotel room with a doctor (Ronald Leigh Hunt) in attendance. His wife is also there, for she feels that in his weakened condition he needs her help. The doctor puts Stacey's hallucinations down to "delirium caused by that infected arm."

Three days of treatment and sedation fail to bring the infection and attendant delirium under control. "I've never seen a basically healthy man deteriorate so rapidly," declares the concerned doctor.

Janet goes to see an expert on African tribes and customs (Louis Mahoney), who tells her that the Simbaza penalty for killing a sacred lion would be "a curse, seeking out across continents, hounding and haunting a man no matter where he might hide—the gradual destruction of mind and body and spirit…. Some might call it the psychology of the guilt-ridden; others might call it praying a man to death." Stacey's only hope, he tells her, "is to return to the scene of his crime, seek out the man who cursed him, and slay him."

Janet relates this to her husband and, despite his weakness, he returns to Africa. When he gets to the Simbaza land, Stacey finds the witchdoctor and another tribesman beating Saidi. Stacey shoots the tribesman, but the witchdoctor runs off into the bush. The two men then play a deadly game of cat-and-mouse until Stacey has exhausted his ammunition. Now the hunter becomes the hunted, and Stacey makes a run for his jeep. The tables turn yet again when he reaches the vehicle; Stacey uses the jeep as a weapon and runs down the witchdoctor. "The curse is broken," concludes the narrator as Stacey limps out of the bush with Saidi, "broken as the gods demand—by *death*."

The picture's shooting schedule was four weeks, "but it went over [by one week]," recalled Richard Gordon, due to some bad weather. Largely becauseto these delays, the meager £35,000 budget escalated to £50,000 by the time it was completed. (Bryant Haliday recalled how crew members began bringing spirits to the location shoot in an effort to keep warm—at least on the inside. At one point, the now thoroughly "warm" actors playing the Simbaza got a little too lively, causing some concern when they "really started getting into the spirit, as it were, and waving their spears around.")

It's difficult to dislike *Curse of the Voodoo*, mostly because of its sheer earnestness. It is a deadly serious film with no touch of whimsy or camp about it (unlike so many voodoo pictures—either through intent or accident). The participants play their parts and treat their subject with a grim solemnity (whose somber tone is only enhanced by the gray skies and dark photography)—no doubt due, in part, to the lousy weather and uncomfortable conditions that prevailed during shooting.

Yet it's also nearly just as difficult to *like Curse of the Voodoo*, for its slow pace and cranky characters possess little appeal. Though he provides an intense yet effectively low-keyed performance, Bryant Haliday makes for a rather unlikable protagonist as the alcoholic, self-pitying Stacey. Humorless and continually scowling, Stacey's condescension and arrogant attitude inspires little sympathy in the viewer—a pathos vital in order to make the 'curse' scenario come to life for the audience. When Stacey treats Saidi (the only man possessing enough courage and loyalty to follow him into the taboo territory) with disdain and indifference, or when he sneers, "the Simbaza are just a backwards tribe that would come and carry your bags for two cents a day like all the rest," the viewer comes to think that perhaps this horrible curse is somewhat deserved.

Not only does the picture sport seemingly endless scenes of Stacey lying in bed suffering nightmares or of his dysfunctional attempts to reconcile with his wife, director Lindsay Shonteff includes numerous filler sequences that do nothing to advance the story or mood. One such is a long and dull nightclub scene (shot on a cheap and cramped set) in which a native woman (Beryl Cunningham) in bikini top and gold lame hotpants(!) does a silly gyrating dance to a drums and wah-wah trumpet tune, concluding with her lying on the floor and simply bobbing her head up and down for the 'big finish.' Ridiculous.

Even some of the (disappointingly few) 'action' sequences drag on far too long. For instance, the two tribesmen chase Stacey over the well-groomed expanses of Regents Park for what seems an interminable amount of time. (The image of two half-naked, face-painted, spear-wielding natives pursuing a man wearing a suit and raincoat across a vast well-manicured lawn looks more than slightly ludicrous.) Even worse, the looong sequence provides no payoff. Stacey simply collapses on the ground and the film cuts to show him lying in his bed with the doctor in attendance.

Brian Fahey's driving musical score, full of blaring horns and pounding drums, doesn't help matters. Such a 'rousing' score sounds very out of place here, since *Curse of the Voodoo* is definitely *not* an action-oriented film. The loud music comes on too often and frequently destroys the mood of a scene. Even during Stacey's Lewtonesque walk home through the park, trumpets blare and the music marches on. (According to Richard Gordon, this low-key, fear-of-the-unseen approach was purely intentional. "The idea was to do a kind of Val Lewton type of picture," related Gordon. "We had hoped that the sequence when he hears the lion roaring and it turns out to be from the zoo would play a little bit like the *Cat People* sequence and things like that." Hope springs eternal.)

Fortunately, the film is saved by its effective cast, whose solid, no-nonsense playing ground the events in reality and bring the various characters to life (if not to likability). Though playing a rather cold fish, Bryant Haliday brings an intense assuredness to the role of Stacey that adds efficacy and (some) poignancy to the plight of a man bedeviled by forces beyond his control.

Bryant Haliday originally had no designs on the entertainment industry, having first studied law and then for the priesthood (even winning several scholastic prizes in theology). After working as a teacher of Latin and Greek, he was bit by the acting bug and ultimately formed the prestigious Brattle Theater in Cambridge, Massachusetts, as well as co-founding Janus Films, which distributed many foreign films (such as the early work of Ingmar Bergman). While on a business trip in France, Haliday was asked by a French producer to star in a gangster film. This began a long association with French cinema and television (Haliday speaks fluent French), resulting in his permanent relocation to Paris. The actor made only four English-language films, all for producer Richard Gordon. Haliday died in the City of Light in 1996.

Dennis Price, as Stacey's friend and colleague Major Lomas, lends credence to the proceedings with his naturalness and sincerity. He tosses off lines like, "the Simbaza believe that the lion is a god and that anyone who kills one is instantly avenged," with such casual aplomb that the viewer has little doubt that he knows of what he speaks. Director Shonteff occasionally had to adjust the schedule to accommodate the alcoholic actor. "There was always a problem keeping an eye on him, and shooting when he was at his best rather than late in the day," recalled Gordon, who nonetheless stressed that Price's penchant for afternoon tippling never caused any major problems.

Often a suave leading man or an aristocratic villain in British films of the 1940s and '50s, Price's age and drinking relegated him to briefer and briefer roles (frequently in low-budget horror movies) in the 1960s and '70s. Among his many genre ventures are *Witchcraft* (1964), *The Earth Dies Screaming* (1964), *Venus in Furs* (1969) and *Vampyros Lesbos* (1970; two horror sex films from the notorious Jesus Franco), *The Horror of Frankenstein* (1970), *Twins of Evil* (1971), and *Theater*

Paired with Frankenstein Meets the Space Monster *in the U.S., the British* Curse of the Voodoo *proved to be the more... sober of the two.*

of Blood (1973). Price died in 1973 at the age of 58.

Though given the rather thankless role of Stacey's estranged wife, Lisa Daniely's sincerity adds substance to the poorly-drawn character. While the actress was subsequently quite active on British television and has remained so in the theater as well, her career never really flourished. As of this writing, she currently works in a bookshop in north London. Her most recent theatrical venture, a one-woman show called *Snakes About Her Cradle* presented in Edinburgh "was not a success" (in the words of the play's director, David McGillivray). Ms. Daniely has seemingly disavowed her film work, claiming not to remember anything about it. "Money" was her terse reply when asked what attracted her to *Curse of the Voodoo* and "Crap" her evaluation of it.

Visually, *Curse of the Voodoo* looks like all of its (meager) production dollars ended up on the screen, thanks in no small part to the clever use of some impressive stock footage. "We got some pretty good black and white stock footage to pump up the African scenes," remembered Richard Gordon. Indeed they did, and the well-integrated shots of African animals adds a bit of verisimilitude lacking in the closer jungle scenes (with English forests standing in for the African bush).

Though pacing was obviously not his strong suit, director Lindsay Shonteff, with the aid of cinematographer Gerald Gibbs (who lensed such early Hammer sci-fi entries as *X, the Unknown* and *Enemy from Space*, as well as Bryant Haliday's earlier feature, *Devil Doll*), does manage to create some effective scenes.

The sequence in which Stacey stalks the wounded lion, for instance, is a marvel of creative staging, camerawork, and editing. When the (stock footage) lion charges him, the film cuts to a shot of the camera rushing through the brush in a lion's-eye-view shot. Then, in quick cuts, Stacey raises his rifle, the camera seemingly leaps upon his chest, and we see a momentary extreme close-up of the beast's face. This ingenious sequence displays how inventive individuals can overcome a lack of money to create an exciting something out of nothing. (Too bad these occasionally effective moments are buried under a morass of drawn-out *in*effective ones.)

Originally announced as *The Lion Man* (the script's original title), the film became *Curse of Simba* in the U.K. and *Curse of the Voodoo* in the U.S., where it was double-billed with *Frankenstein Meets the Space Monster*. The American distributor, Allied Artists, decided that the original title of *Curse of Simba* wouldn't sell well as a horror picture and so changed the moniker to make no mistake about the voodoo element. (In England the picture was trimmed by 10 minutes in order to fit the UK distributor's need for a shorter supporting feature, making the retitled American version the definitive one.)

Too weak a picture to stand on its own or topline a double bill, *Curse of the Voodoo* made fortunes for no one. "Over a period of time it was financially successful because of television and video, but not really on its initial release," admitted Gordon. Still, though rather somber and leaning toward the dull side, *Curse of the Voodoo* stands as an offbeat, occasionally intriguing entry for the fan of voodoo cinema.

> The following essay was written for a proposed book on Jekyll and Hyde films. But, like with Henry Jekyll/Edward Hyde himself (themselves?), it turned out to be a doomed experiment.

SCIENCE VS. THE SUPERNATURAL: *DR. JEKYLL AND THE WEREWOLF* (1972)

When Robert Louis Stevenson's novella *The Strange Case of Dr. Jekyll and Mr. Hyde* was published in 1886, he probably never dreamed of the bizarre permutations his characters would undergo in the future. One of the oddest is this Paul Naschy European import.

Spain's Paul Naschy, who both scripted and acted in *Dr. Jekyll and the Werewolf*, is the combined Christopher Lee and Peter Cushing of Continental cinema. In fact, to carry the Hammer analogy further, he's also the Terence Fisher (or at least Freddie Francis) of Eurohorror because, in addition to starring in over two dozen terror films (in which he plays everything from werewolves and mummies to hunchbacks and vampires), he also directed over a dozen of the features himself.

A professed lover of Gothic horror in general and the Universal classics in particular ("all the marvelous films made by Universal Studios in the 1930s are the main source of inspiration for all my work," he stated[1]), Naschy almost single-handedly began a Gothic revival in Spanish cinema in the late 1960s and '70s with his scripting, acting in, and ultimately direction of the Waldemar Daninsky/Werewolf series. Though few Americans know his name or have seen his films, the dedicated Eurohorror aficionado and offbeat cineaste have been seeking out his movies for years. While the plots are sometimes trite, the production values often suspect, the acting usually bad, and the dubbing always atrocious, Naschy's films show an eccentric enthusiasm and appeal in a quirky, almost quaintly exploitative fashion that no American or British-produced horror film of the same era can duplicate.

What sets Naschy's movies apart from (and *above*) the often mean-spirited and cynically exploitative product of his contemporary countrymen is Naschy's respect and outright affection for the cinematic horror tradition. Though Naschy's budget-conscious and sometimes puerile journeys into Gothic fantasy are no better *cinematically* than most of the genre Eurotrash of the decade, their story lines possess an appealing dose of almost wistful nostalgia—spiced, of course, with the requisite dashes of sex and blood. "I wouldn't say that Paul Naschy was marvelous nor that he was very good," admitted the writer-actor-director himself, "but for any person who sits down to watch a film of mine on the big screen or on television, I believe it will communicate to him that what he is watching was made with love."[2] And in the creature-combining *Dr. Jekyll and the Werewolf*, Naschy wears this affection on his monstrous sleeve.

Dr. Jekyll and the Werewolf is the fifth outing for Naschy in his four-decade-spanning series featuring the tragic character of Waldemar Daninsky the Wolfman. Like many of them, here he not only starred but wrote the script as well (using the moniker Jacinto Molina, an abbreviated version of his real name: Jacinto Molina Alvarez). The convoluted story involves a descendent of Dr. Jekyll (Jack Taylor, a regular player in the films of the prolific Jess Franco) attempting to cure Waldemar Daninsky (Naschy) of his lycanthropy by using his grandfather's infamous "personality changing" serum—with the expected disastrous results (thanks to the evil machinations of Jekyll's jealous assistant, played with delicious bile by Mirta Miller). Now, instead of two personalities, the poor wretch has three to deal with: Waldemar, the Werewolf *and* Mr. Hyde.

A film of two halves, *Dr. Jekyll and the Werewolf* focuses on the latter during its initial stages, as we follow newlywed Justine (Shirley Corrigan), whose older husband Imre (Jose Marco) takes her on a honeymoon to his rustic childhood village in Transylvania, wanting to

Dr. Jekyll and the Werewolf *British poster.*

visit the graves of his parents (what a romantic). After the requisite ominous warnings from the local innkeeper ("Nearby that cemetery is the black castle; the man who lives there is a monster"), they run afoul of a trio of bandits at the dilapidated graveyard. The criminals murder Imre and attempt to rape Justine, but Waldemar intervenes, dispatching the ruffians and taking Justine to his castle to recuperate. There she discovers his horrible secret—he is cursed with lycanthropy—and, of course, falls in love with him. It's an all-too-familiar (and unlikely) scenario in the Naschy cannon, but director León Klimovsky infuses the proceedings with enough Gothic atmosphere (particularly when Justine, clad in black nightgown and with candelabra in hand, explores Waldemar's forbidding castle) to hold one's interest, as well as providing a simple but effective introduction for the werewolf. When the surviving bandit recruits two more cronies to rob the castle and kill Waldemar on a full moon night, the hunters become the prey. First revealing the monster's presence via a clawed, hairy hand, Klimovsky then cuts to a close-up of the wolfman's snarling face before the camera zooms in on its open, fang-filled mouth, making for a startling, dramatic intro.

Gothicism soon gives way to modernity when Justine takes Waldemar back to swinging London to see her good friend Henry Jekyll, hoping Henry can cure her newfound love. At this point the film settles down to some rather dull interplay between the various characters, as Justine tries to convince Jekyll to help ("A werewolf?" scoffs Jekyll, "It's all too fantastic," to which Justine reasonably retorts, "But how can *Henry Jekyll* be so skeptical?"), Jekyll acquiesces and performs various experiments in his makeshift attic lab, and Waldemar frets. Until Hyde finally breaks free towards film's end and engages in a bit of woman-whipping, prostitute strangling, and nightclub prowling, the only thing livening up the proceedings is an all-too-brief lycan-rampage when the amazingly unlucky Waldemar is trapped in a stuck elevator as the moon rises. "Why? Why must this happen?" whines Waldemar as he begins to writhe in pain. Three cutaways to the startled woman trapped in the lift with him reveal an increasingly hairy beast-man. Finally, the repairmen get the lift going. But when the door opens, Waldemar's bloody victim falls out, and the suit-wearing werewolf, crimson-tinged drool dripping from its mouth, rushes forward, scattering the onlookers.

With Stevenson's Jekyll and Hyde creation an almost spiritual cousin to the werewolf (both involve personality—and physical—transformation, and both reflect the two sides of man's nature), combining the two monsters seems a natural, even inevitable, pairing. (One might even see the lycanthrope as Nature's very own Jekyll and Hyde.) Such a juxtaposition presents the possibility of delving deeply into the duality of man, and even into the nature of evil itself—or the evil of Nature in all its amoral savagery. The werewolf personifies discord between the civilized and the bestial (moral man vs. savage animal), whereas Jekyll and Hyde represent a more sophisticated, more refined conflict (moral man vs. immoral evil). While the bloodlusting beast that is the werewolf may be amoral, Mr. Hyde is *immoral*, embracing evil for evil's sake. Yet both figures—the lycan and Hyde—seek personal gratification at the expense of all else. Hence, both fly in the face of society's codes; the difference being that the werewolf does so by nature (with ties to Nature with a capital 'N'), while Hyde does so by choice (representing the self-centered, hedonistic, impulsive side of humanity).

Beyond this dichotomy, *Dr. Jekyll and the Werewolf* highlights a struggle between the supernatural (Waldemar's werewolf) and science (Jekyll's chemical serum), or, on a less fantastical level, nature (the werewolf) vs. nurture (the artificially-molded Hyde). Intriguingly, while science initially triumphs over nature (with Jekyll effectively curing Waldemar of his lycanthropy by injecting him with his Hyde serum, watching as the apparently stronger Hyde persona overcomes the inner werewolf, then administering the antidote to vanquish Mr. Hyde and thereby leave Waldemar as himself), in the end, nature reasserts its dominance when Hyde runs out of Jekyll's serum and can no longer keep the Waldemar side in check. When the serum wears off, Hyde weakens, and Waldemar becomes himself once more—but almost immediately the full moon rises and Waldemar again transforms into the Wolfman. Nature has proven to be the strongest force after all—stronger than science, and stronger than societal constraints (personified by the "normal" Waldemar).

"[*Dr. Jekyll and the Werewolf*] established a kind of liberation from the bestial, unthinking level of the werewolf, only to unleash the consciously evil Mr. Hyde," enthused Naschy. "It's a pirouette within the world of these multiple personalities. I think it's an interesting film, above all for the re-creation so unique of Mr. Hyde."[3] Of course, the term "interesting" doesn't necessarily translate to "good."

As played by American ex-pat Jack Taylor, Dr. Henry Jekyll appears as a rather cold fish, never smiling and not suffering fools gladly. (One shudders at the thought of his bedside manner.) He agrees to help Justine only because of his unrequited love for her. Jekyll's arrogance extends from beyond the scientific (assuming that his serum will conquer the werewolf) to his own relationship with his mistress-cum-assistant. Jekyll pays for his hubris with a (literal) knife in the back, courtesy of his spurned lover ("Think of all I've done for you...have you forgotten all those patients who died like guinea pigs?"). Once again, a brilliant (if perhaps amoral) scientist is undone by love, twisted as it may be. And he's wrong on *both* counts, for in the end the werewolf re-asserts its dominance—science may temporarily halt the course of nature, but it cannot conquer it in the end.

Jack Taylor, born George Brown Randall in Oregon in 1931, took a circuitous route to the Euro-cinema scene. After a few small parts in '50s TV series (such as *The Jack Benny Show* and *Sheena, Queen of the Jungle*), Taylor, who "spoke a little Spanish," went to Mexico, where he made 13 films (including several in the vampiric *Nostradamus* series) before landing in Spain in 1961 with a stage show. There he stayed, making movies for the likes of Piquer Simon (*Where Time Began, Pieces*), Amando de Ossorio (*Night of the Sorcerers, Ghost Galleon, The Sea Serpent*), Jess Franco (*Succubus, Count Dracula*, and six more), and, of course, Klimovsky (*The Vampire's Night Orgy*).

Taylor brought to his role an admiring familiarity with the Jekyll & Hyde tale. "I had read Stevenson's book several times and was fascinated by it," recalled the actor. "I also remember seeing Bergman and Tracy in their production, and two earlier ones with March and Barrymore. As for me, it was a job, and as with every job I did the best I could. People tend to over intellectualize films which leads me to understand that once a picture is edited and put in a can, strange things take place and those 'things' become obvious when the images are projected onto the screen and the film takes on a life of its own."[4] Or *two* lives, in the case of *Dr. Jekyll and the Werewolf*.

While combining two classic monsters (the werewolf and Mr. Hyde) in one movie (and in one body) is a concept rife with possibilities, in the hands of director León Klimovsky it drifts dangerously close to dreariness—at least in the film's second half. It's almost as if the director lost interest after sending his wolfman to London and letting loose Hyde in the beastman's stead. The werewolf's few brief London appearances come with little vitality or suspenseful staging, the attacks listless and perfunctory (a quick grab, a bite, and off he goes). "This picture had the captivating novelty of a triple personality," opined Naschy. "It could have been quite good, but the short-sightedness of León Klimovsky made for some careless moments."[5] Such moments extend even to the disappointingly mundane climax, in which Justine waits, armed with silver bullets. When the werewolf arrives, she loses her nerve; it lunges for her, knocks the gun from her hand, and bites her throat. Dying, she manages to reach the pistol and, as the beast-man walks away, shoots him twice in the back (though no bullet holes nor blood splotches mar his pristine grey sweater). It's not much bang for one's lycanbuck.

Unlike in most of his previous (and subsequent) outings, Naschy makes for a disappointingly lackluster werewolf here. (Perhaps the struggle with Hyde sapped him of his wolfish ferocity?) He moves slowly, almost lethargically; and he walks in a very human-like manner that lacks the athletic, savage momentum of his usual portrayals.

The subpar werewolf makeup matches Naschy's subpar were-playing: coarse hair covering his entire face (disappointingly, no prosthetic nose piece differentiates it from a human proboscis), a mouthful of stained fangs, and small protruding wolf's ears. With drool dripping from his chin, he looks rather like a rabid victim of hypertrichosis (abnormal hair growth) and bad dentistry. He initially sports a black shirt and pants á la Naschy's beloved role model, Larry Talbot, though later he looks far nattier in sport coat and stylish sweater.

Both Klimovsky and Naschy do better with their *other* monster, however, as demonstrated by Hyde's

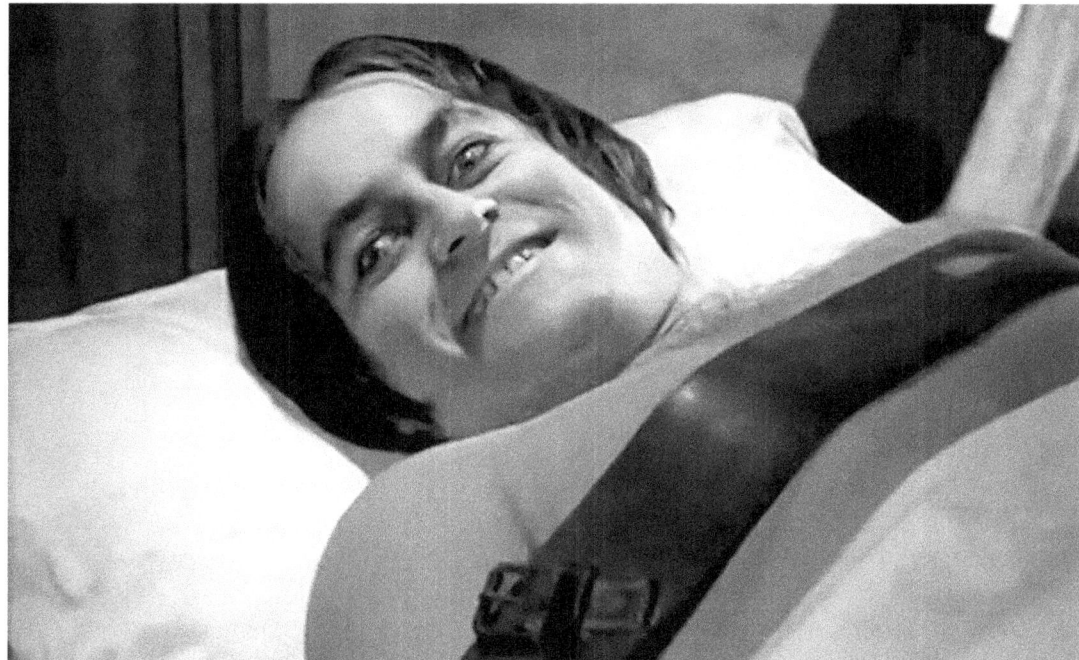

Paul Naschy (temporarily) shed the fur to become the depraved Mr. Hyde in Dr. Jekyll and the Werewolf *(1972).*

introduction. When Jekyll injects Waldemar, strapped to a gurney, with his grandfather's serum, a sweating Waldemar momentarily loses consciousness. Then his eyelids slowly open, his nostrils flare, and his eyes widen. Klimovsky shifts to a Hyde point-of-view shot, with the camera looking upwards into the concerned faces of Jekyll and Justine. A green filter clouding the image gradually clears as Hyde comes fully awake, with the picture finally taking on color to show Jekyll and Justine in stark relief, indicating Hyde has now entered our world. It's a clever visualization of evil (often represented by the color green) invading our realm. The Hyde makeup, though simple, is equally effective. A close-up of Waldemar/Hyde's face reveals a lank-haired fiend with yellowish eyes and pasty, veined skin. "Set me free!" Naschy's Hyde hisses, grinning evilly. "I must be free!"

Naschy infuses his version of Mr. Hyde with enough evil to choke a corpse, neatly strangling his latest female conquest just for the fun of it, and gaining real pleasure in flogging a half-naked bound beauty. But he becomes laughably old-fashioned walking around a mod 1971 London in a top hat and cloak. "The anachronism of [Hyde] going about modern-day Soho in his cape and top hat appealed to me," Naschy explained. "Had he been dressed as any normal city dweller, I don't think the character would have been as effective."[6] Effective? Well, the best laid plans of mice and werewolves…

This did result in a rather amusing incident during filming. "Dressed and made up as Mr. Hyde, filming in Soho, [London]," recalled Naschy, "these people in a sex shop started hurling insults at me. So I took my walking stick and went after them [laughs]. They were so scared they locked themselves inside the shop. They couldn't see the cameras that were hidden inside a car. …They just thought I was a nutcase."[7]

An apoplectically violent Mr. Hyde aside, "working with Paul was very easy," said Taylor. "He was a very private person as am I, there were never any conflicts. He respected me as I him." Still, "Paul did feel unappreciated, I know," continued Taylor. "Most of those genre films were never shown in Spain or at least not at the main theaters. They were considered B-rated pictures, but the interesting fact is that they have survived and the supposedly A-grade ones are mostly forgotten. …I do think Paul was burdened with complexes because he didn't feel that he was respected as an artist."[8]

Argentinean-born León Klimovsky (1906–1996) originally trained as a dentist before cinema's siren song enticed him to trade the dental drill for the director's baton. Relocating to Spain in the 1950s, he worked on comedies, dramas, war films and Westerns through the 1960s. In the 1970s his career took a turn toward the macabre when he was hired to direct Naschy's *The Werewolf vs. Vampire Woman* (1971) and *Dr. Jekyll and the Werewolf* in quick succession. He then went on to a string of Eurohorrors like *Vengeance of the Zombies* (1973; again with Naschy), *The Dracula Saga* (1973), *The Vampire's Night Orgy* (1974, starring Jack Taylor), *Devil's Possessed* (1974; with Naschy), *Strange Love of the Vampires* (1975), and *The People Who Own the Dark* (1976; Naschy again) before retiring in 1979.

According to Taylor, Klimovsky was "a very kind, educated gentleman" who "realized the limitations imposed at the time, budget, censorship, etc., and produced acceptable products. He was always courteous to his actors and crew." Taylor went on to note that "shooting conditions were a bit primitive ....no caravans for costume or makeup. However, this was done at an eighteenth-century complex near Madrid, and at least we had a roof."[9]

Two versions (select scenes, actually) of *Dr. Jekyll and the Werewolf* were shot—one for the homegrown Spanish market, and another for international distribution. The difference? In Spain at the time, under the repressive Franco regime, nudity in films was forbidden. So Spanish producers would shoot a clothed version for domestic consumption and then have the actresses drop their nighties for the export version. *Dr. Jekyll and the Werewolf* featured several scenes of this nature.

Of *Dr. Jekyll and the Werewolf*, Paul Naschy concluded, "I believe I made a strange contribution to the fantastic myths, mixing something so different yet at the same time so familiar as lycanthropy with the story of Jekyll and Hyde."[10] While it does indeed deliver two intriguing monster-characters, and possesses an obviously sincere effort on the part of its (triple) star, *Dr. Jekyll and the Werewolf* comes across as not only "strange" but uneven.

"I never thought of it as one of my better films," admitted Naschy.[11] Still, despite Klimovsky's occasionally dispirited direction and disappointing werewolf action, however, *Dr. Jekyll and the Werewolf* offers some effective Gothic atmosphere, the occasional moment of horrific artistry, and a boatload of novelty in linking the two (three?) classic horror figures together, making it worth a look not only for Naschy completists but for Jekyll & Hyde enthusiasts as well.

NOTES:
1 "Interview: Paul Naschy," by José Luis González and Michael Secula, *Videooze* 6/7 (Fall 1994).
2 Ibid.
3 Ibid.
4 Jack Taylor interview with the author, March 30, 2015.
5 "Interview: Paul Naschy," by José Luis González and Michael Secula, *Videooze* 6/7 (Fall 1994).
6 Ibid.
7 "Paul Naschy: Memoirs of a Wolfman," *Dr. Jekyll and the Werewolf* DVD.
8 Jack Taylor interview with the author, March 30, 2015.
9 Ibid.
10 "Horror with a Spanish Twist: Paul Naschy," by Dale Pierce, *Filmfax* 33.
11 "Interview: Paul Naschy," by José Luis González and Michael Secula, *Videooze* 6/7 (Fall 1994).

Monsterscene magazine fired up the electrodes to bring *Frankenstein and Me* to issue 9 (Fall 1996).

FRANKENSTEIN AND ME (1996)

"Only one person can bring the monster back to life…and he's twelve years old." –ad line

For those of us who grew up with cinematic monsters, *Frankenstein and Me* is not only a poignant trip down Memory Lane, but a validation of secret childhood wonder—feelings that monsters *do* exist and, if one believes strongly enough, anything *is* possible. The story, set in 1970, centers on a relatively poor but happy family living in a small community in the California desert (the film carried the shooting title of *Mojave Frankenstein*). The father, a likable, soft-spoken trucker (sensitively played by Burt Reynolds), is a dreamer, a man who loves to spend his time tinkering with impractical gadgets in the garage and indulging his two young sons in their love of monsters. The mother, however, disdains her husband and sons' penchant for imagination and cannot see past the more "practical" day-to-day drudgery of making ends meet. Tragedy soon strikes, however, for, in one of the film's most powerful moments, the father succumbs to a heart attack. It is a truly lump-in-the-throat scene, sensitively handled by director Robert Tinnell and his actors to evoke the awful pain and loneliness of this tragic moment.

After this, the story focuses on the two boys, particularly Earl (Jamieson Boulanger), who feels most keenly the loss of his father—his one validating adult. Temporarily leaving off his rich fantasy life (centering on monster movie scenarios), Earl visits a cheap traveling carnival that claims to have the "real" Frankenstein Monster—an imposing but lifeless figure. When the Monster falls off the back of a departing carnival truck, Earl gets it into his head to try and revive the creature. With help from his skeptical friends, he builds a primitive lightning rod apparatus (based on a design his father had doodled out for him before he died) in an old abandoned mining building. Everything comes to a head during the climactic storm, and the characters, in this milieu of trying to *create* life, learn something about life itself.

Tinnell's charming story wonderfully captures both the enthusiasm and loneliness often felt by monster lovers over the course of their childhood. It also deals thoughtfully with the pain of loss, making the boy's admittedly irrational actions a desperate tribute to his father, who always regretted that he didn't follow his dream. (Dad's dream was to make it big in Hollywood, but he lacked the conviction to stick it out. In one of the film's most heartwarming moments we see that as a present for their beloved father the two boys have built a makeshift HOLLYWOOD sign up on the rocks behind their house.) To screenwriters David Sherman, Richard Goudreau and Robert Tinnell's credit, *Frankenstein and Me* remains poignant without becoming cloying, and the script beautifully captures that sense of wonder so strong in childhood that makes such things as Frankenstein's Monster almost magically real.

Technically, Tinnell and his crew (filming exteriors on the very edge of the Mojave desert in Victorville, California, and shooting the interiors in Montreal, Canada) put their heart and soul into this production, creating beautiful, finely detailed sets (belying the film's relatively low two-million-dollar budget) which stand as loving homages to such films as *Frankenstein*, *The Wolf Man*, *The Brides of Dracula* and *Night of the Living Dead*. In these memorable settings, Earl plays out his rich, movie-influenced fantasy life. (Production designer Michael Marsolais transformed an old train warehouse into uncanny replicas of scenes from these seminal horror classics. Especially impressive is the windmill set from *Brides of Dracula*, which is so detailed that, as Tinnell laughingly related, Marsolais even placed fake pigeon droppings on the windowsills!)

The film sports some wonderfully evocative camerawork (courtesy of cinematographer Roxanne di Santo), utilizing shots both subtle and blatant to enhance a mood or punctuate a point. Fortunately, Tinnell sidesteps the dreaded "Young Directors Syndrome" (characterized by over-reliance on flashy film school technique) and swoops his camera only when appropriate. (Sadly, even "Old Directors" like Woody Allen and Martin Scorsese succumb occasionally, as evidenced by Allen's pointlessly circling camera in *Shadows and Fog* and Scorsese's wildly inappropriate aquatic ballet at the climax of *Cape Fear*.)

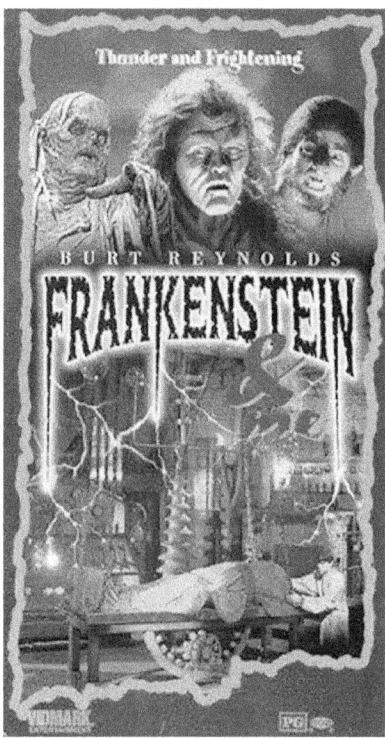

Robert Tinnell's charming homage to monster fans: Frankenstein and Me *(1996).*

Burt Reynolds sets aside his macho persona and sometimes broad, tongue-in-cheek acting style to deliver a subtle, touching performance (arguably his best since *Deliverance* and before *Boogie Nights*), bringing the sad scenario to painful life by emphasizing the quiet affection and deep bond between himself and his dreaming son. The child actors do an admirable job as well. The only fly in the acting ointment is Myriam Cyr (best known for starring in Ken Russell's *Gothic*) playing Earl's mother. Her reactions—moving from an almost bitter contempt for "dreamers" (which definitely includes all monster-lovers) to a tearful, wild-eyed, chest-swelling pride when she finally recognizes the wonder of that beautiful quality in her son—are a tad too sharp and jarring.

"It's what I've always wanted to do—," declares Burt Reynolds' character, "—paint my dreams across the silver screen." With *Frankenstein and Me*, writer/director Robert Tinnell has courageously put himself on the line to show his love and respect for the genre films of his youth and perhaps expose the roots of his own dream. In doing so, the dreamer has *lived* the dream. Bravo, Bob.

According to the film's publicity, "Robert Tinnell was able to share his enthusiasm for old movie monsters with [his child stars], who weren't necessarily familiar with Boris Karloff, Bela Lugosi and the other greats of that era." Though one should generally take such press releases with a grain of salt, the director himself related that his young thespians would eagerly gather in Tinnell's hotel room to watch the old classics. *Frankenstein and Me* wonderfully reflects this affectionate enthusiasm.

Leaving no homage unpaid, Fan-turned-filmmaker Tinnel even casts that guru of fandom, Forrest J Ackerman, in the cameo role of a priest (a rather amusing part for "Father Forry" who is a steadfast secular humanist!).

If you've missed *Frankenstein and Me*'s October debut on the Disney Channel (an ironic venue since, as Tinnell puts it, this is not so much a kid's movie but a fan's movie), I urge every monster-lover whose heart has remained true to his or her childhood dreams to run, not walk, to the local video store. You won't be disappointed.

> This was written for a 1998 one-shot magazine called *Science Fiction Invasions*, edited by Don Dohler.

THE GIANT SPIDER INVASION (1975)

It's only fitting that *The Giant Spider Invasion* was filmed in Wisconsin, because it is one of the biggest slices of cheese to ever land on a projection platter (and *Swiss* cheese at that, considering the size and number of its plot holes).

"Richard Huff originally had the idea," related Wisconsin-based director/co-producer Bill Rebane (who once gave up plans to run for Governor of Wisconsin in order to make a movie called *The Capture of Bigfoot*!) to *Fangoria*'s Keith Bearden, "and my friend Robert Easton came in to help him develop the script, and by the time shooting came around they were just at each other's throats and hadn't gotten anywhere. So we shot the film without a script, not knowing where it was going. We would get pages of dialogue, not knowing where they would lead to next. We had no idea how the film would end! It was crazy." 'Crazy' is the word, all right.

This Monogram-Movie-for-the-Seventies begins when a meteor lands in a rural Wisconsin community and somehow generates a miniature black hole that becomes "a doorway into a parallel universe." Said doorway disgorges baseball-sized geodes which contain not only diamonds (providing the film's greed-inspired subplot) but *spiders*—some of which grow to gigantic proportions. When things get out of hand (such as when the biggest spider stampedes a local softball game!), NASA scientist Steve Brodie and local astronomer Barbara Hale team up to "shower it with neutrons" using a "Cal-Tech Neutron Initiator" that causes the black hole to explode and the spider to melt down into a gooey mess.

Unfortunately, this all *sounds* like a lot more fun than it actually is. While peppered with an occasional dash of engaging wackiness (such as when a car drives into a giant spiderweb stretched across the road and a huge stuffed arachnid plonks itself down on the auto's roof), most of the overlong film consists of uninteresting filler scenes (endless and purposeless conversations, numerous one-sided phone calls with the perpetually-grinning Alan Hale Jr., stock fairground footage, etc.).

What makes it all bearable, though, is the fact that Rebane and company obviously didn't take it too seriously and so managed to inject a bit of humor into the puerile proceedings. For instance, the constantly-chuckling Alan Hale Jr. plays the sheriff like a "jolly red giant" (as one character labels him). Hale's first words (as a young reporter enters his office) are the amusingly Gilligan-esque greeting, "Hi little buddy!" while later he's seen intently reading a paperback called *Flying Saucers Want You.*"

Scripters Richard Huff and Robert Easton (who also provides the film with its most entertaining characterization by starring as the backwoods bozo who discovers the meteor) also generate a few chuckles with some amusing dialogue ("Sometimes the only way I know you're still alive is when I hear you flush the toilet," carps the farmer's bitchy wife).

By far the funniest scene, however, comes when the two fifty-something 'stars' (Steve Brodie and Barbara Hale) panic at the sudden appearance of a goofy-looking giant spider in the woods. Shots of the two falling and rolling over one another, arms and legs flailing as they slowly tumble down the hill's gentle slope like a couple of romping toddlers is a moment of sublime hilarity.

Ironically, the film's few sparse shudders come not from the cheap and unconvincing giant spider effects but from seeing the *normal*-sized (real) arachnids scuttling about (in drinking glasses, over countertops, on car seats, up pant legs). Conversely, the (unintentional) comedy quotient is provided by the oversized props standing in for the big bugs—everything from a laughable drawer-sized hand puppet to a dog-sized stuffed spider on strings (of the ridiculous *Missile to the Moon* variety) to the infamous car-sized 'Bug.'

"Bullets don't hurt [the giant spider]; the only thing I've got to stop it here with is a traffic light!" These laughable lines delivered by Alan Hale proved amusingly appropriate, for the biggest arachnid is nothing more than a stripped-down Volkswagen (a Bug, naturally) with oversized pipe cleaners stuck to the sides for legs.

This ultimate giant spider was actually an afterthought. "If you remember," explained Rebane, "the spiders came in all sizes, and originally the giant ones were not going to be that big. But [executive producer] Brandon Chase, who owns Group 1 Releasing, kept saying, 'It's in the title—I want a giant spider, I want one bigger than *Jaws*!'" To this end, local craftsman Bob Millay (who "loved beer a little too much," according to the director) came up with "the Volkswagen Bug monsters with the Plexiglas fronts." (Rebane also inserted a *Jaws*

Comic book–styled herald for the comical Giant Spider Invasion *(1975).*

reference to appease [or mock?] Chase by having one character ask, "Did you ever see that movie *Jaws*? Well, [the spider] makes that shark look like a goldfish.")

"Oh, they looked like hell," admitted Rebane about his giant spiders. "You'll notice that in the last shot I took some fire extinguisher foam and sprayed it all around so it looks like some secretion to cover up the car." Editor Barbara Pokras deserves some kind of 'Giant' award for her efforts on the silly spider scenes as well, for whenever possible she makes the cuts so quick that the illusion works... sometimes... well, not really, actually.

Budgeted at $320,000, Rebane claims *The Giant Spider Invasion* grossed over $15 million! If that is indeed the case, the film *should* have been called *The Giant Audience Swindle*.

> The following blu-ray review appeared in *Monsters from the Vault* magazine, issue 32 (Summer 2013).

ONE BIG BAD MOMMA! GORGO (1961)

Mother-love as the driving theme of a *Giant-Monster Movie*? That's the unusual premise for this entertaining monster-attacks-the-city entry from veteran dino-director Eugene Lourie (helmer of 1953's *The Beast from 20,000 Fathoms* and *The Giant Behemoth*, 1959). This time Lourie eschews the stop-motion animation of his previous dino-flicks (Ray Harryhausen's exemplary work in *Beast* and Willis O'Brien's for *Behemoth*) to offer up a man in a suit stomping on London town. Fortunately, said suited-up monster, combined with some outstanding miniatures and excellent integration of live-action panic scenes, puts the majority of Toho's efforts to shame (including their much-heralded original Godzilla series).

Gorgo's straight-ahead story has a pair of salvage divers (played by American ex-pat William Sylvester and Englishman Bill Travers) discover a 65-foot sea-based dinosaur recently freed by an earthquake off the coast of Ireland. Taking it to London in partnership with Dorkin's Circus, they exhibit the amazing beast at Battersea Park. But scientists inform them that this is not a full-grown specimen, and soon Momma comes calling, tracking her offspring to London, where, despite the best efforts of the Royal Navy and Army, she destroys most of the city's famous landmarks before freeing her progeny and calmly returning to the sea.

Often thought of as the least of Lourie's dino trilogy—primarily because it's a man-in-a-suit creature rather than a stop-motion creation—*Gorgo* actually surpasses its siblings in several respects. Yes, it lacks the more realistic mobility and unique personality of both the *Beast* and *Behemoth*, but it remains one of the best giant monster suits ever designed, far outclassing the rubbery Godzilla and its ilk. With its eyes, ears and tail moved by hydraulics to give it a more animated appearance, Gorgo features a sleeker body design, blood-red eyes, huge claws, dragon-like ears, and toothy mouth that cast it as something out of a nightmare (albeit a nightmare probably conceived by a pre-teen weaned on monster movies).

Gorgo's human element remains both straightforward and involving, with the two divers offering distinct personalities and perspectives on their "find" (and the moral issues that arrive with it). There's no forced love-interest subplot cluttering up the story (a dire distraction in *Beast*), and the human-sized drama (largely lacking in *Behemoth*) comes from the relationship the

Mother-love 200 feet tall in Gorgo *(1961).*

two protagonists develop with an orphaned Irish boy (understated yet touching, without being cloying), climaxing in a truly harrowing search for the lad through a dangerous, panic-stricken throng fleeing from the monster's rampage.

Excellent editing and clever camera angles make hundreds of extras look like thousands, and Lourie works wonders with his nighttime photography, complete with spotlights and red-limned clouds of billowing smoke, to make it appear that a 200-foot dinosaur really is stomping the scones out of Tower Bridge, Big Ben and Piccadilly Circus. Through the judicious use of military stock footage (for which the filmmakers even take the time and trouble to dub in appropriate dialogue), Lourie effectively portrays the transition from organized efficiency to organized chaos to general chaos to all-out mayhem. Some truly shocking scenes bring home the intimate horror resulting from such large-scale destruction, as we see people fall or leap from windows to their death, set on fire by the out-of-control conflagrations, and crushed by falling masonry.

Of course, just like the beast itself, *Gorgo* displays a few warts via some intermittent lags in pacing, some murky and unconvincing underwater scenes, and the occasional effect that appears not-so-special (including some obvious rear-screen work). But such blemishes are par for the course in a Giant Monster Movie from the 1960s, and *Gorgo* still towers fin-eared head and scaly shoulders above most of its contemporaries.

This blu-ray release marks a (Giant) Monster improvement over the old VCI DVD. While the amazing blu-ray clarity discloses noticeable grain in the film print (particularly in the nighttime and underwater scenes) and leaves some blue-screen matte lines painfully evident at times, the overall picture is much brighter and colors much richer than on the old DVD edition; plus, it's anamorphic. Also included on this new blu-ray edition is a Gorgo-sized cornucopia of extras: theatrical trailer; the complete *Gorgo, the Monster of the Sea!* Comic book; lobby card and poster gallery; toys and collectibles gallery; an excellent new 30-minutes documentary titled *Ninth Wonder of the World: The Making of Gorgo*; pressbook gallery; production notes; "Fumetto" comic; photo gallery; and a before-and-after restoration comparison. (Oh, and the giant claw that amusingly tears away the image when you switch from one feature to the next shows that the day of the clever menu graphic isn't over just yet.) All this, coupled with a presentation that finally does justice to this underrated monster flick, ought to leave any *Gorgo* fan with a grin as wide and toothy as Gorgo's himself.

> This essay (ahem) ghosted into *Movie Club* magazine's "Haunted House Thrillers" overview for issue 12 (Autumn 1997).

THE HAUNTING (1963)

"FEEL...Your Throat Grow Tight with Fear, Your Hands Twitch with Growing Terror" –ad line

If Haunted House Cinema held a heavyweight championship, the Muhammad Ali of the apparitional arena would be Robert Wise's chilling masterpiece of understated terror, *The Haunting*—a film that truly is "The Greatest."

The Haunting's story follows four psychic investigators (three of them non-professionals) who journey to the infamous Hill House, a house that was "born bad," in order to probe the depths of the supernatural forces said to walk there. Soon, horrible sounds and deafening poundings assail the quartet in the dark of night, while by day they experience sudden chills and "cold spots." During one of the audio assaults, the parlor door begins to bow inward—as if some monstrous force was pushing against it from the other side. (Wise achieved this frightening effect simply enough by having a burly prop man push on cue against the other side of the laminated wood with a two-by-four, causing it to bend inward and create a "breathing" effect.) As the hours pass, the hauntings seem to focus on Eleanor (a troubled woman sensitively played by Julie Harris) who becomes more and more ensnared by the dark forces inhabiting Hill House, ultimately leading to the film's tragic conclusion.

"It was such a good script," opined Rosalie Crutchley (who played Hill House's morose housekeeper). "As you know, we're all ninety percent as good as our script, most of us. And that *was* a good script." Robert Wise concurred: "I thought Nelson Gidding did just a *fine* job on the screenplay."

The film itself plays much better than a brief synopsis reads. Through realistic and complex characters, superb acting, creative direction, inventive cinematography and terrifying sound effects, the picture deftly sidesteps a gaping pit of haunted house clichés to take the viewer down a darkened path on which every shadow, every unexplained sound, every movement out the corner of one's eye conjures up frightful terrors of The Unknown.

On a deeper level, the film works as a carefully drawn character study, in which the disparate personalities

Claire Bloom and Julie Harris endure The Haunting *(1963).*

interact—and react—with both the turbulent forces within themselves and the terrifying forces surrounding them in Hill House.

Though a superbly acted picture, the movie's biggest "star" proved to be Hill House itself—a centuries-old English manor named Ettington Park. Now a very posh hotel, Ettington Park is itself purportedly haunted, with half a dozen different specters having been seen walking its halls over the years. When this author visited the site in the 1990s, he was shown the house's "haunted book." The mansion's library had been converted into a bar, and, according to the staff, every so often one particular book (*St. Ronan's Well* by Sir Walter Scott) is thrown to the floor by an unseen hand, always opened to the same page, which reads: "A merry place, 'tis said, in days of yore; but something ails it now—the place is cursed."

Wise used a special film stock in order to obtain the dark, moody and (pardon the expression) truly haunting image of the house itself. "I made it look a little bit more monstrous than it might have been," explained the director, "because I shot all the exteriors with infra-red film, which brought out the kind of exaggerated striations of the rock and turned the skies blacker and turned the clouds whiter. It added an eerie feeling to it.

"One of the things I liked about the house," continued Wise, "and I was able to really use it that way to make a character out of it, was that it had that tower there with those windows. So I could cut to the windows and then down to Julie [Harris] getting out of her car and going in, like the house was watching you. I tried to capitalize and use the house just as much as I could."

At one point a character states, "Ghosts are a visible thing." Not at Hill House. *The Haunting* is perhaps the only ghost film in which the specters are never seen. "I can't tell you," remarked Wise, "how many people have said to me, 'Mr. Wise, you made the scariest picture I've ever seen and you didn't show anything!'" Time after time Wise places his audience in literally hair-raising situations, not by exposing us to pasty-faced ghouls but by playing upon the terrors of our own individual imaginations. Through clever use of lighting, camera movement, sound and actor reactions, Wise terrifies with pure atmosphere, frightening us with what is *not* seen. "It's kind of an homage to Val Lewton," admitted the director, who cut his teeth under Lewton's tutelage.

"I have to be immodest and say I really like *The Haunting* because that's one of my best directorial jobs," declared the creator of such classics as *The Body Snatcher* (1945), *The Day the Earth Stood Still* (1951), *West Side Story* (1961) and *The Sound of Music* (1965). "I really think it worked well." Indeed it did—and still does.

For decades, the William Shatner starrer *Incubus* (the only film shot in Esperanto!) was thought lost. Found and restored (and subtitled) 30 years later, it finally reached an audience at the dawn of the new millennium. This assessment appeared in *Monsters from the Vault* magazine, issue 13 (Fall 2001).

LOST AND FOUND, WILLIAM SHATNER'S *INCUBUS* (1965)

"LOOK ON with Bewilderment as William Shatner Speaks in Tongues!" –(new) trailer

Bewilderment indeed, as (according the trailer again) *Incubus* is "the only film shot entirely in the artificial language of Esperanto." A failed experiment, Esperanto was designed to be a universal language that would unite the peoples of the world. Well, though a reported seven million individuals throughout the globe spoke this synthetic tongue in 1965, it never really caught on. And while director/screenwriter Leslie Stevens (creator of TV's *The Outer Limits*) was banking on these seven million rushing out to see the only movie made in "their" language, he forgot to take into account the fact that he could not get these scattered millions together for significant-sized theater screenings. As a result, *Incubus* failed to secure a distributor and, following a few film festival showings (Roman Polanski and Sharon Tate attended the movie's San Francisco premier), disappeared from the cinema scene to become a "lost" film. Thirty years later producer Anthony Taylor finally located a damaged print in Paris and restored it;

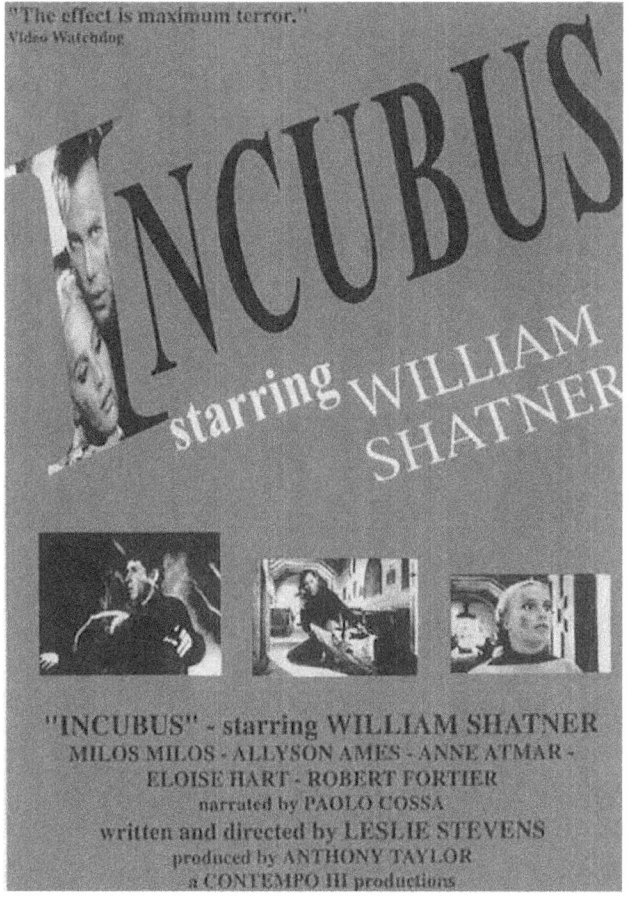

Incubus ad.

and *Incubus* was ready for the world again…but was the world ready for *Incubus*?

A beautiful succubus named Kia (Allyson Ames) tires of tempting already-lost souls to Hell and sets her demonic sights on corrupting a "good" man. Enter William Shatner as Marc, Kia's intended victim. When Kia becomes "tainted" by the love of this noble man, she vows revenge and summons up an incubus (Milos Milos) to corrupt and destroy Marc's sister. Marc must then battle the demon and his love for Kia for his very soul.

According to Shatner, Esperanto was spoken on-set at all times—as ordered by director Stevens, even though this meant nobody really understood anybody else (none of the actors actually knew Esperanto; they had the script's text in English on one side of the page and Esperanto on the other so they could recite it phonetically). Onscreen, this translated (no pun intended) into a dreamy, disconnected, almost otherworldly interplay between the actors. Since they really didn't know what they were saying to each other, their reactions are often oddly muted, almost surreal.

Even apart from the obvious novelty of Esperanto, *Incubus* remains a one-of-a-kind '60s film. One part *Outer Limits* (cinematographer Conrad Hall photographed that groundbreaking TV series—before winning two Academy Awards, for *Butch Cassidy and the Sundance Kid* and *American Beauty*), one part *Carnival of Souls* and two parts Ingmar Bergman, *Incubus* generates a timeless ambiance in its allegorical tale of good vs. evil. The internal struggles; the stark photography; the vaguely Scandinavian clothing (not to mention the overtly Scandinavian blonde succubae); and the use of Esperanto itself (with its faint Northern European flavor) all heighten the movie's Bergmanesque qualities. Whether this is a plus or a minus in a horror film—since *Incubus* also shares with Bergman a leisurely pace and overabundance of dull stretches (as the camera follows characters walking through the woods, reading, etc.)—remains a matter of taste.

In any case, Stevens and Co. managed to create a substantial something out of next to nothing, with its miniscule $100,000 budget and tight 10-day shoot. Particularly impressive (given its no-frills schedule) are some unique camera angles—shooting through water up at characters, tipping the camera upside down to follow a figure running past—and evocative lighting (including fog-shrouded back-lighting to generate some ominous atmosphere). And the incubus resurrection sequence, in which the (human-looking) demon literally rises from the earth in the dark of the night, is as frightening and eerie a scene as can be found in '60s cinema.

Incubus was William Shatner's last movie before *Star Trek*. Though a—little bit—of—Captain—Kirk creeps into his performance towards the end, he makes for a good-humored, likable protagonist. And Allyson Ames' ethereal beauty casts her as a convincing temptress (off-screen as well as on—she married, but later divorced, director Stevens).

Unfortunately, this atmospheric and surreal film becomes both prosaic and ridiculous at the end when the incubus transforms into an oversized *goat* (a baaaaad effect) to attack Kia as she tries to defect to "the God of Light" and aid the wounded Marc. Such a banal—and unconvincing—climax flies in the face of the movie's eerie, lyrical mood.

Though not exactly the self-described "lost cult classic" it claims to be ("lost" and "cult" apply, but "classic" definitely overstates), *Incubus* offers enough atmosphere, chills and just plain novelty to make it a lost movie worth finding.

In a bizarre life-imitates-art postscript, Milos Milos (Yugoslavian-born actor Milos Milosevicz), who plays the demonic incubus sent to seduce and destroy

Marc's sister, later mirrored this plot in real life when in 1966 he murdered his lover, Barbara Rooney (wife of Mickey), and then committed suicide. (In addition, actress Ann Atmar, who plays the sister ravaged by the incubus, also committed suicide shortly after the film wrapped.)

> In trying to recall for which publication I penned this DVD review in 2002, I've reached a Dead End (groan). But here it is anyway…

THE LAST HOUSE ON DEAD END STREET (1977)

Seventies horror is now back in vogue, as evidenced by such recent remakes of seminal seventies cinema landmarks as *The Texas Chain Saw Massacre* and *Dawn of the Dead* (not to mention the in-the-works redux projects *The Hills Have Eyes* and *Deathdream*), and the success of such '70s-*styled* horrors as *Cabin Fever*, *Wrong Turn* and *House of 1,000 Corpses*. The gritty, innovative, no-holds-barred low-budget terrors that proliferated in the 1970s have come full circle, undoubtedly due to the fact that a generation of filmmakers weaned on that decade's genre offerings have finally gained enough clout to get such projects made, and, perhaps more importantly, to the fact that those horror fans that 'came of age' in the '70s now have plenty of disposable income to splash about, and are willing to shell out the bucks to revisit their nostalgic favorites on DVD. So it's little wonder that Barrel Entertainment have dug deep—really, *really* deep—to unearth one of the most elusive American horror movies of the 1970s. It's a flick made notorious as much for its tantalizing absence (for years this 'lost' film has been seen only on murky bootlegs from countries like Venezuela) as for its content. Fortunately, thanks to the amazingly resourceful folks at Barrel, we can now see said content in all its gory…er, glory.

The Last House on Dead End Street, shot as *The Cuckoo Clocks of Hell* in 1973 and alternately released (ever-so-briefly) in 1977 as *The Fun House*, was the brainchild/labor-of-love/drug-induced fever dream of aspiring filmmaker Roger Watkins (aka Brian Lawrence, aka Norma F. Kaiser, aka Victor Janos, aka Steven Morrison, as the phony credits list the writer-producer-director-star), who scraped together $1,000, borrowed some camera equipment, talked friends and theater majors (and teachers!) at Oneonta State College into participating (including convincing several amateur actresses

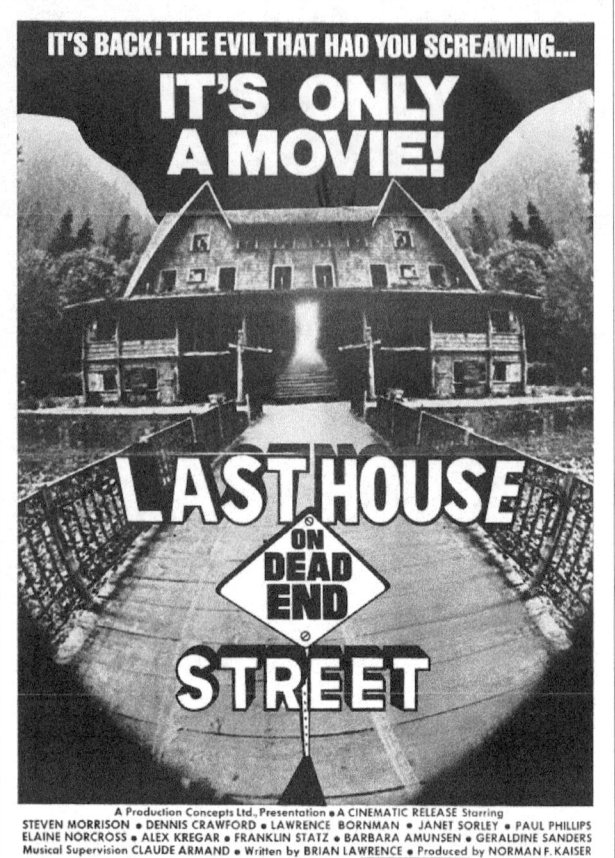

Last House on Dead End Street *poster*.

to drop their tops on cue), and engaged in several weeks of guerrilla filmmaking in Upstate New York. The result: a gritty, amateurish, exploitative, raw, nihilistic, unpleasant and ultimately fascinating movie about a low-rent porno filmmaker who gets out of jail and decides to "f**k the world" by producing a real snuff movie.

Despite its frequently mismatched dubbing (shot without sound, all dialogue was looped in later), poor lighting, slow pace in the opening reels, and swiss-cheese plot continuity, the film generates an intriguingly sleazy atmosphere that continues to build and build and *build* until it erupts into a crescendo of nihilistic violence in the final 30 minutes. The gore is not particularly impressive nor innovative (stage blood and cow's guts), but, unlike the H. G. Lewis oeuvre, *Dead End Street* offers the viewer no over-the-top, winking outrageousness to relieve the in-your-face intensity. *Dead End Street*'s centerpiece, a torture-dismemberment 'surgery' scene, is absolutely harrowing in its visceral power.

But the film is not all gore and grue. Watkins sprinkles in a number of bizarre images (such as a woman in blackface willingly bull-whipped at a party—by a hunchback[!], or a man forced to fellate a deer foot stuck into the pants of a topless girl[!!]). Such surreal sights, combined with the brutal acts perpetrated by the gang of snuff-makers (led by Watkins himself, whose intense eyes and high-pitched giggles make him a disturbingly believable psycho), generate an almost overwhelming miasma of voyeuristic unpleasantness (which seems appropriate for a film about filming—*extreme* filming). The final scene sums it all up. Shot primarily from the victim's point of view, the psychos look directly at the camera as they survey their 'handiwork.' It's the final grotesque joke: the victim is *us*, the voyeuristic viewers.

According to Watkins, the movie was completely improvised ("I made it up entirely as I went along," he confesses on the DVD's commentary track) by the drugged-out director (Watkins was "higher than a f**king kite on crystal methedrine" during filming). This seems apt, as *The Last House on Dead End Street* provides more of a disorienting, visceral viewing experience than a competent, cogent one.

Barrel entertainment must consider *Last House on Dead End Street* the *Citizen Kane* of '70s horror, for their double-disc DVD release features more extras than a Cecil B. DeMille epic. There are stills, outtakes, alternate title and closing sequences, a short-but-sweet trailer (with the "It's only a movie! Remember, it's only a movie!" rip-off tagline offset by a creepy and shocking image that's far scarier than anything in the film), a highly entertaining and informative commentary track (with Watkins and gore guru Chas Balun), a segment from a 1975 Joe Franklin show featuring Watkins and Professor Paul Jensen (the film's first victim), a (painful) 2001 music video tribute by Necrophagia that employs a few snippets from the film, and a 1973 60-minute radio interview with Watkins and co-star Ken Fisher. And that's just the *first* disc. Disc Two offers four of Watkins' short films (with commentary) and 70 minutes of behind-the-scenes recorded phone calls (an "audio diary") detailing the making of *Dead End Street*. Personally, I'm not really an 'extras' kind of guy (in fact, I rarely listen to even the seemingly now-de rigueur commentary tracks), but here I dove into this wealth of minutiae with gusto… and enjoyed every minute. Even if you don't like the film (and *Last House on Dead End Street* is not really a movie one 'likes'), these discs chart a fascinating course through the trials and tribulations of an enthusiastic and obviously bright (illicit substances notwithstanding) moviemaker.

> Here's another essay for which I have *no idea* why—or for whom—I wrote it, particularly given that it's on a genuine genre obscurity (maybe that is what drew me to it?). Though I'm unsure if it was ever published in this form, some of it did end up incorporated into my *Drums of Terror: Voodoo in the Cinema* book. Waste not, want not.

MACUMBA LOVE (1960)

"Blood-Lust *of the VOODOO QUEEN!*" –ad line

"Advance reports have it that we've a real 'sleeper' in our town over at the _____ Theatre," began a prepared UA publicity piece, "where the United Artists scary mystery drama, *Macumba Love*, is playing. In case you're not up on motion picture parlance, a 'Sleeper' is a film that unexpectedly turns out to be unusual." In *Macumba Love*'s case, the film proved a "Sleeper" only in the *literal* sense, for that's exactly what it induces in its viewers.

Macumba Love was filmed in Brazil, making it (along with *Curucu, Beast of the Amazon* [1956]) one of the few American-made horror films shot in South America. However, unless you're a fan of Brazilian beaches (upon which this picture spends an interminable amount of time) or June Wilkinson's talents (both of them), the film's glacial pacing and dull dramatics leave little to recommend to the discerning viewer.

On an island off the Brazilian coast, American "novelist, lecturer, and general debunker of mankind" J. Peter Weils (Walter Reed) runs afoul of the local voodoo cult headed by Mama Rataloy (Ruth de Souza). After finding two voodoo victims on his beach, Peter threatens to write an exposé of the cult—despite several sinister voodoo warnings. Mama Rataloy soon begins menacing those close to Peter: drugging his girlfriend Venus (Ziva Rodann), frightening his daughter Sara (June Wilkinson) by appearing as some kind of snake-woman, and kidnapping Sara's new husband Warren (William Wellman, Jr.) for sacrifice in a voodoo ceremony. The voodooists also capture Peter and force him to watch the ceremony. Fortunately, Sara arrives with the police, who scatter the voodooists in all directions. In the ensuing fracas, Mama Rataloy is killed (though *how* is unclear, since she simply falls to the ground, dead). As Peter looks on, the voodoo queen's face changes into that of a scaly creature before suddenly bursting into flame. Peter comforts Venus, and Warren and Sara are reunited.

While it's not unusual for a voodoo film to go light on the exploration of its sensationalistic subject, the typical hoodoo horror at least manages some level of entertaining *exploitation*. Not so *Macumba Love*, whose leaden pace and endless filler leave little room for excitement. The film opens on a promising note with a nighttime ceremony in which drums beat rapidly, participants chant, and dancers twirl about a bubbling cauldron. A corpulent mamaloi stabs a cloth doll with a pin and then drops it into the smoking pot. (When a huge cloud of smoke subsequently shoots up, the actress jumps back with a bewildered look on her face and looks questioningly into the camera, obviously startled and taken unawares. The fact that this gaff remained in the final print rather than being excised or re-shot amusingly exposes the film's level of [in]competency.) While initially impressive in its frenetic energy, the ceremonial sequence goes on far too long (seven full minutes!) and so ultimately inspires more boredom than interest. (Star Walter Reed told interviewer Tom Weaver that "there were real voodoo people in the movie! One guy came up to me and gave me this little figure that he'd carved out of soapstone, and somebody said, 'Oh, that's good luck.' I said, 'But it's *voodoo*!' And they said, 'Look, there's good voodoo and bad voodoo.' They *like* you!' I said, 'Good! I'm gonna have them keep *on* liking me!'"

Reed admitted that the film was "corny and also slow-paced. The first part of the picture, all that voodoo music and dancing–I thought they'd never get through with that! It went on and on and on! They got involved with the beauty of the dancing girls and things like that, they got carried away and forgot about the story sometimes. Actually, what they probably were really doing, if you really want to know, was purposely dragging it out, because you can't sell a picture that's too short."

In only two isolated instances does the film generate any excitement, and these are moments of pure visceral shock rather than of any thematic or artistic merit. The first comes as Peter and Venus frolic in the surf. When Peter playfully lifts Venus up and tosses her into the gently rolling waves, he ducks under the water for a moment and then comes up holding not the beautiful Venus as expected but the rigid corpse of a dead man, its eyes open and staring. Director Douglas Fowley hammers the shock home with an abrupt zoom into the face of the cadaver while Venus (now having surfaced herself) screams in horror. (Walter Reed recalled how "the guy that did that [played the corpse] didn't know how to do it, and finally the director, Fowley, took his shirt off and his pants off and jumped in the water and said, '*This* is the way to do it!'")

The second memorable moment comes when Mama Rataloy takes a hatpin and approaches a suffering captive tied to the back wall of her shack. "To disbelieve is to die," she tells him and abruptly jabs the long needle into his eye. The man screams and the screen then cuts to a literal victim's-eye-view as bright red blood suddenly gushes over the camera lens—as if we're seeing from behind the punctured orb itself. It's a gruesomely inventive (though arguably tasteless) bit of camerawork that remains one of the few memorable things in the picture.

Not surprisingly, the film's level of acting perfectly matches its technical (non)proficiencies. Though easy on the eyes, the two young leads, June Wilkinson as Sara and William Wellman, Jr. (son of famed director William A. Wellman, creator of such classics as *The Public Enemy* [1931], *A Star is Born* [1937], and *The Ox-Bow Incident* [1943]) as Warren, are excruciatingly bland. Even after finding himself staked out on the ground as a sacrifice, Wellman, Jr., never loses his blank expression. Ironically, the film's pressbook noted that "In *Macumba Love*, Wellman has his most challenging role to date, calling for a full display of dramatic emotion." The young actor must have simply forgotten to *answer* that call.

While one could never accuse June Wilkinson's 44-20-36 figure of being flat, the same cannot be said of her *acting*, for she perfectly complements the non-presence of her onscreen partner via her vapid demeanor and vacuous expressions. Wilkinson (known as "the most photographed nude in America" and, more amusingly, as simply "The Bosom" in the pages of *Playboy* magazine) enjoyed her moviemaking adventure in Brazil. "That was great fun," she told *Psychotronic*'s Ian Johnston. "I did have a wonderful time shooting that." Too bad the viewer can't say the same about *watching* it. (Reportedly, two versions of *Macumba Love* were shot. In the European version, Wilkinson went topless in some scenes whereas in the U.S. release—the only one currently available—she wears a one-piece bathing suit.)

Though veteran character actor Walter Reed may be the most experienced professional in the cast, his performance fails to reflect it. As Peter, he takes a smug, high-handed tone that makes him sound more like a conceited *caricature* than a concerned character. Reed doesn't speak his dialogue, he *announces* it. His harsh voice and strident manner rarely change, nor does his self-satisfied expression.

The film's one bright spot comes in the form of Israeli actress Ziva Rodann (whom the film's pressbook labels "the world's most glamorous army veteran—

June Wilkinson (dubbed "The Bosom" by Playboy *magazine) and friends run afoul of Brazilian voodoo in* Macumba Love *(1960).*

having served for a year in the Israeli army"). As Venus, not only is she sexier than the grossly pulchritudinous June Wilkinson, she out-acts her (and everyone else in the picture). In reviewing *Macumba Love*, *Variety*'s Holl (who had little good to say about the production) praised Ms. Rodann's "outstanding performance" and called her "an attractive and fiery performer who has a chance to make an important impact in future films." Sadly, such a chance never materialized, for, after half a dozen more unimportant and gimmicky pictures like *Giants of Thessaly* (1961) and *Three Nuts in Search of a Bolt* (1964; her last), she dropped from sight. Rodann's presence also enlivened one other exotic horror, *The Pharoah's Curse* (1957).

Macumba Love was the directorial debut of actor Douglas Fowley. As such, it proved a very inauspicious one, as Fowley fails in his pacing, staging (apart from the two aforementioned shocks), and direction of actors. It's little wonder that he was never entrusted with the director's baton again and, for the remainder of his career, worked only in front of rather than behind the camera.

Born Daniel Vincent Fowley in 1911, he began acting in films in the 1930s and subsequently played in over 200 pictures over the next five decades. While *Macumba Love* was his only job as a director, he had previously *acted* the part of one (to hilarious effect) in *Singin' in the Rain* (1952). Among his acting credits are the genre entries *One Body Too Many* (1944; with Bela Lugosi), *Mighty Joe Young* (1949), *Cat-Women of the Moon* (1953), *The Seven Faces of Dr. Lao* (1964), and *Homebodies* (1974).

According to Walter Reed, *Macumba Love* cleaned up at the box office. "Early on, they said I could have a salary or I could take five percent of the picture," the actor regretfully recalled. "I said, 'You must be out of your mind! I don't want five percent of this thing!' And it made $3,000,000 in this country–that wasn't including the foreign rights. I would have made a *lot* of money on that show."

Though successful financially, it failed aesthetically. *Macumba Love*'s final sequence epitomizes the picture's level of ineptitude. It begins when Mama Rataloy's face dissolves into an obviously papier-mâché mask with wrinkled skin and misshapen cardboard lips in one of the most amateurish makeup jobs ever seen in 35mm. Then, after an awkward (and very noticeable) jump cut, the fake head bursts into flame—just as the viewer bursts out laughing.

> The following (modified) essay served as liner notes for Image Entertainment's 2002 DVD release of *Naked Evil / Exorcism at Midnight*.

NAKED EVIL (1966)

Less than a year after producer Richard Gordon's initial, disappointing foray into voodoo territory with *Curse of the Voodoo*, Gordon took another chance on the subject and co-executive produced his second hoodoo horror. Though it proved no more successful financially than *Curse*, aesthetically speaking *Naked Evil* far surpasses its dull predecessor.

While *Curse of the Voodoo* is a difficult enough picture to see these days, *Naked Evil* is nearly impossible. (This author first saw it only when Gordon himself generously supplied a print.) This is a great pity, for the film is a unique, engrossing, and suspenseful addition to voodoo's cinematic subset.

The project began when Steven Pallos (a well-known producer in England and former business partner of Alexander Korda) brought the proposed production to Richard Gordon's attention. The film was designed as a low-budget (about £60,000, according to Gordon, which at that time was less than $150,000) British program filler.

Even though it was intended as an inexpensive second feature, Gordon and Pallos still wanted to make the most of their production. To this end they approached Columbia with the idea of filming it in color (since at that time color was becoming more and more crucial to film distribution). Columbia didn't bite, not wishing to pay the higher price of color prints.

The shooting schedule was four weeks, and (unlike Gordon's previous voodoo picture *Curse of the Voodoo*) *Naked Evil did* come in on-schedule and on-budget.

Based on a play called *The Obi* by John Manchip White, the production needed a new title, since the producers didn't feel that that rather non-threatening moniker lent itself well to exploitation. "We were looking for something that would give it a little bit of *flair*," remembered Gordon, and Pallos came up with *Naked Evil*. "I thought it was a very good title." Indeed it was, for as well as being mildly titillating, it captured the tone of the film very well—the idea of a raw, overpowering force of malignancy.

In the black section of an English town, a drug-dealing gangster uses Jamaican Obeah (a variation of voodoo) to decimate his competitor's ranks. To accomplish this, he sends his intended victims a dreaded obi (a bottle filled with graveyard dirt and "muck," topped with feathers). "With an obi, smash the bottle and you unleash the devil," explains one character. Three men have succumbed to the evil magic already ("a fall from a window of a locked room, a frightened man dashing in front of a bus, and yet another found in the canal"). Meanwhile, at a nearby university hostel for "colored students," its operator, Mr. Benson (Basil Dignam), receives a dreaded obi. It soon comes to light that the mysterious "obi-man" is the hostel's unsavory Jamaican caretaker, who's been selling his magic to the gangster (and applying it to Benson as well, since he knows the headmaster is about to fire him). Things soon go awry, culminating in death, possession, and exorcism.

The 1960s was one of the more successful decades for voodoo cinema, producing such diverse and effective entries as *Dr. Terror's House of Horrors*, *The Plague of the Zombies*, and *The Oblong Box*. *Naked Evil* fits into this company quite nicely and, while perhaps not as well-crafted as say *The Plague of the Zombies*, it remains one of the more atmospheric and thought-provoking of its contemporaries.

Naked Evil is one of the few films to effectively juxtapose Christianity and voodoo (though, naturally, it shows a bias towards the former) by pitting the power of the Christian faith (in the person of the rather obviously-named Father Goodman) against the power of voodoo sorcery (in the form of the obi-man Amazan). When Benson finds a ring of headless cockerels encircling the school, he calls in Father Goodman to perform an exorcism and "cleanse the grounds of whatever filthy spell was intended." The priest motions to the bloody talismans and comments, "You still believe in the power of these things, don't you," to which Benson replies, "I believe *your* magic is stronger." The padre also performs a benediction of sorts over the obi found in Benson's study and then concludes with a brisk, "Right, you can get rid of this now,"—confident that his Christian evocation has neutralized the power of the voodoo sorcery. At the film's end, it is Father Goodman's exorcism (with

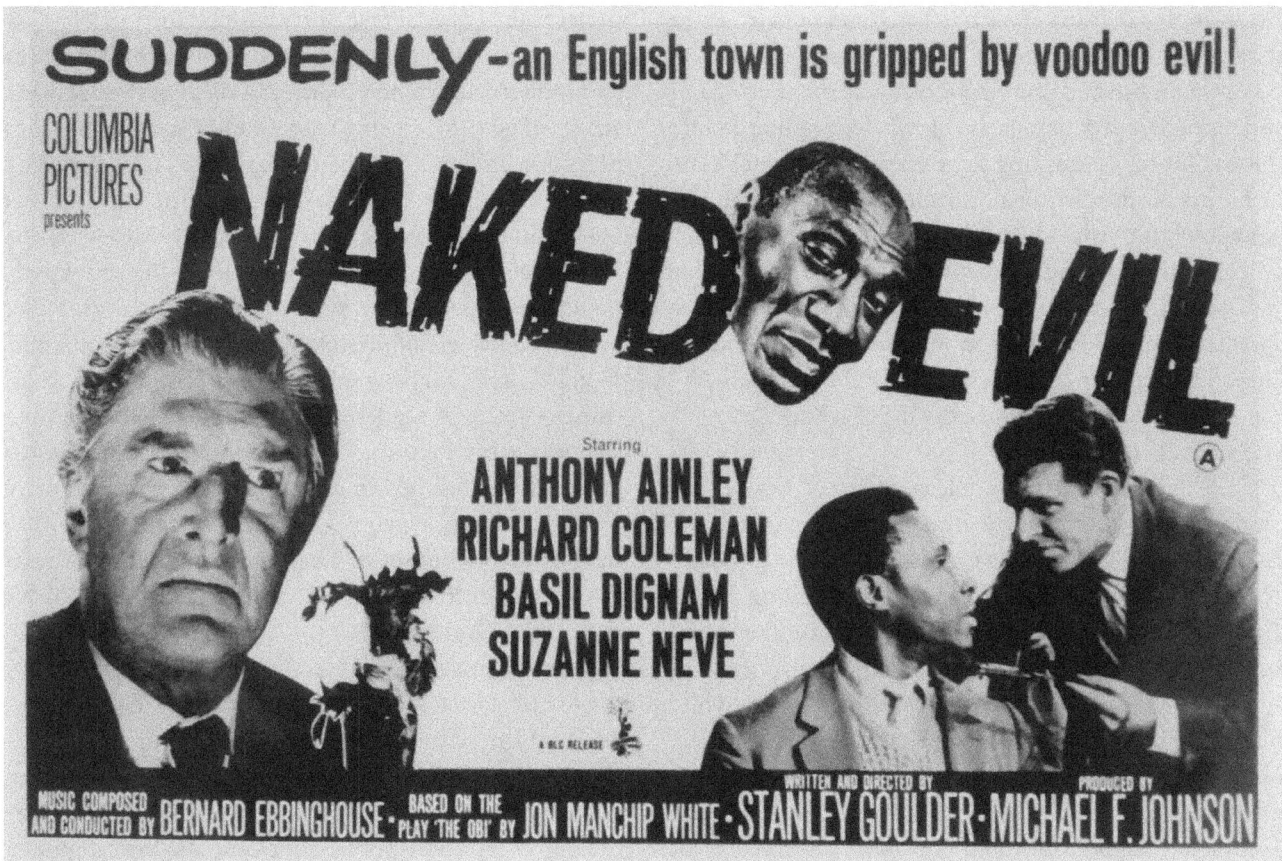

Ad for Naked Evil.

the priest thrusting a cross at a possessed man, who cringes from the sacred relic) that sends the voodoo demon packing.

These events lead to two possible lines of thought, each an intriguing interpretation. First, that voodoo magic relies primarily on the power of suggestion ("an obi only works on you if you're suggestible," states Benson at one point). Consequently, when a victim feels he's gained sanctuary from another source (the Christian church), he basically heals himself. The second possibility is that Christian magic is indeed inherently "stronger" than the evil voodoo sorcery. Either way, it makes for a fascinating conflict.

Though obviously low-budget and occasionally crude, *Naked Evil* often succeeds on a cinematic level. Director Stanley Goulder's clever staging, and cinematographer Geoffrey Faithfull's atmospheric lighting and camerawork, weave a palpable spell of evil around the sinister events.

Goulder ("a very pleasant and talented guy," recalled Gordon, "who knew exactly what he wanted") fills *Naked Evil* with eerie touches. When the protagonist drops the first obi bottle into the basement furnace, for instance, the cellar door suddenly slams shut and the dangling light begins swinging as if pushed by an unseen force. Even the credits sequence builds a macabre atmosphere when, as the credits roll, the camera silently prowls through a church graveyard at night, coming to rest at a graveside where we see a mysterious hand placing fistfuls of grave dirt into a shoebox.

Unfortunately, the picture's rather schizophrenic construction tends to weaken the film's overall impact and undermines Goulder and Faithful's careful staging. The more mundane gangster scenes and subplot (with the black wiseguys complaining about their 'business' troubles on cheap nightclub sets) seem dull and out-of-place next to the more fantastical Obeah angle. Even a frantic chase scene through the streets generates little excitement when transposed with the terrors of the obi. "It's not what I would really call a genre picture in its present form," griped Gordon. "It's sort of neither fish nor fowl." Despite Gordon's regrets, it's still a fairly tasty bird.

British films from this period are generally very well acted and *Naked Evil* is no exception. (There seems to be much less stigma attached to low-budget productions in general and horror pictures in particular in England. Consequently, competent British actors, even stars, are more likely to appear in them.) Worthy of note is Basil Dignam as Benson. His natural and authoritative delivery does much to lend conviction to the strange events. Dignam is quite believable as a man becoming more and more unnerved, his skepticism and stiff-upper-lipped demeanor slowly crumbling under the weight of a mounting fearfulness. A rational man, he knows his fear is ridiculous, but he cannot help it (labeling a shot of whisky "dutch courage" or ridiculing his unreasoning fear one moment yet asking Dick to stay "until I calm down" in the next). Dignam's familiar face and steady presence added to such pictures as *The Quatermass Xperiment* (1955; aka *The Creeping Unknown*), *Corridors of Blood* (1958), *Gorgo* (1961), and *Lawrence of Arabia* (1962).

In England, Columbia released *Naked Evil* as intended (as a supporting feature in black and white). In the United States, however, things didn't go quite according to plan. Gordon first tried releasing *Naked Evil* through Hampton International, but the company folded before it could offer more than spotty distribution. Worse, Hampton took the black-and-white film and *tinted* it, coloring scenes variously red, green, blue, and amber so that they could advertise it as being filmed in "Evil Color" ("which I thought was a nice gimmick," laughed Gordon, one that "promised a lot but didn't guarantee anything"). Nor did this unfortunate and unnecessary tinting *deliver* anything—except occasional confusion and eyestrain (not to mention washing out some of the picture detail by upping the contrast too high). *Naked Evil*'s trials and tribulations didn't end there. In the mid-seventies, Gordon made a deal with Sam Sherman and his Independent International company which allowed Sherman to put the film out on drive-in triple features along with other former Hampton International properties. "It had no value theatrically," said Sherman. "It was basically triple-billed just to load up a show at drive-ins."

In the late 1970s, Sherman was putting together a package of horror films to sell to television. "I was just looking to assemble what was available easily," related the enterprising producer/distributor. "I thought of *Naked Evil*." On December 1, 1978, Richard Gordon licensed Sherman the rights to distribute the film to television. Sherman couldn't sell the film as is, however, because "it was tinted senselessly. I'd have to be able to add some color footage to it. Basically, my idea was to create a framing story for the original film, and have the tinting be in some way explained—though I don't know if it explained it very well." To this end, Sherman wrote the 'new' script "in one evening," retitled it *Exorcism at Midnight*, and hired Steve Jacobson to shoot it all in a single day (on a budget of "about $5,000"). Using up

more than a few favors, Sherman obtained permission to shoot at a hospital on Roosevelt Island in New York and induced Lawrence Tierney (as well as several other actor friends) to act in this new mini-movie. Tierney plays Dr. Fuller, a psychiatrist who treats a disturbed young black man (portrayed by an actor who did *not* appear in *Naked Evil*) who supposedly witnessed the events seen in the original film. By using an experimental laser device that projects different colors, Fuller is able to bring out the man's memories (the original footage) and so (sort of) explain the various color tintings in these scenes. ("We found the color amber suggests restful scenes," clarifies Fuller. "Blue evokes scenes dimly recalled in memory, things that may have occurred at night, where red evokes scenes that may have tended to upset or frighten the patient. We use the various colors as we question him to draw out his thoughts." Right.)

Sherman used nearly the entire original picture for the flashback story. The few scenes the frugal Independent International decided to discard include an intimate (but G-rated) character-development sequence between Danny and his pregnant girlfriend and (surprisingly) an atmospheric shot of a shadowy figure—Amazan's spirit(?)—after the climax.

Here's another essay for which I have no explanation (much like the film itself), nor knowledge of whether it ever saw print. But, much like the acid-spewing Night Monsters themselves, it's presented here in all its gory glory and wobbly warts.

THE NAVY VS. THE NIGHT MONSTERS (1966)

"TERRIFYING ACID BLEEDING MONSTERS READY TO CREMATE THE HUMAN RACE!!" –
ad line

A long-time staple of late-night TV, *The Navy vs. the Night Monsters* is a cut-rate color monster movie that remains more entertaining than it should be. Though filled with jarring edits, dialogue that comes out of nowhere, and cheesy studio "jungle" sets (looking like rejects from a *Voyage to the Bottom of the Sea* episode), *Night Monsters* has gone on to become a fairly popular cult film.

Based on the novel *The Monster from Earth's End* by Murray Leinster (for whose rights director/screenwriter Michael Hoey paid $4,000), the story begins as

Who knew walking killer trees from Antarctica could be so cheesily entertaining?

a plane carrying a load of primitive carnivorous plants found in "the warm lakes area" of Antarctica(!) crash lands at the naval base on Gow Island in the South Seas. There they flourish and go on a rampage, picking up their roots and moving about to eat as many cast members as they can lay their tendrils on. Said members are led by put-upon base commander Lt. Charlie Brown (fallen leading man and former *Hawaiian Eye* TV star Anthony Eisley), nurse Nora Hall (blonde bombshell Mamie Van Doren), local lothario Ensign Chandler (former MGM musical star/heartthrob Bobby Van), comedy relief Petty Officer Twining (former child star Billy Gray [*The Day the Earth Stood Still*, TV's *Father Knows Best*]), recalcitrant scientist Dr. Beecham (prolific character actor Walter Sande), and petulant civilian meteorologist Spalding (Phillip Terry). After several people go missing or turn up dead, they realize what they're up against and battle the advancing tree monsters (who ooze acid rather than plant sap) with molotov cocktails. Things look grim, however, when the rapidly reproducing vegetation keeps on coming. Fortunately, they're able to get word to the mainland Admiralty, and the Navy sends in bombers to napalm the truculent trees out of existence.

The Navy vs. the Night Monsters is a strikingly visual film—not because of any efficacy on the part of first-time director Michael Hoey (whose straightforward staging could best be described as 'mundane'), but because of its amazingly garish color scheme. Vivid orange dirt, bright blue walls, intense red lighting, and cherry red oil drums predominate, turning this tropical island into a Mecca for Sixties-style sensibilities. To be fair, cinematographer Stanley Cortez (a long way from his heyday shooting films like *The Magnificent Ambersons*) does occasionally tone down the bright hues to create some effectively low-key lighting in some of the more suspenseful jungle scenes.

According to leading actor Anthony Eisley, the film was ruined by some severe tampering which took place after principal photography wrapped. "The [executive] producer [Jack Broder] re-cut that picture after it was made," Eisley told interviewer Tom Weaver, "and he totally destroyed any validity it might have had. Months after the picture was shut down, the producer put in this stupid stock footage of bombers blowing up the island at the end and shot these monotonous talking scenes of generals on the telephone that were not at all germane to the original story." Said "monotonous talking scenes" (which include boring banter between the plane's pilots and an unfunny sequence in which an inept sailor tries to inflate a weather balloon) were directed by Arthur C. Pierce (*Women of the Prehistoric Planet* [1966]).

"Broder had said to me, 'I need a 90-minute picture,' explained Hoey himself to Tom Weaver, "and I delivered him a 78-minute film. I didn't really believe that it had to be 90 minutes [for him] to sell it to television. So he had Arthur Pierce come in and shoot added scenes. Well, what Arthur did was not just shoot added scenes, but change the whole premise."

"That picture, as Michael Hoey wrote and directed it," opined Eisley, "would have been a very good little thriller." Even without Broder's tampering, such a claim seems rather dubious. First off, in a movie about killer plants, said vegetation needs to be effective. These terrifying trees look like some bizarre barrel-shaped automated car-wash mechanism with its long, flat 'tentacles' hanging limply at its sides. They're never really menacing—until a hapless victim *backs into them* (which happens at amazingly frequent intervals). "I wanted the [monster] trees to look like the other trees," complained Hoey, "so that there wouldn't be the feeling that they stood out like sore thumbs, which is what those stupid things did. Broder hired some guy who did them for $1.98. When they showed up on the set the first day, I refused to film them, I was so upset."

In addition, the picture possesses a disjointed feel—as if Hoey failed to shoot enough footage to cover himself. Characters often behave inexplicably—as if they've seen things *we* haven't, and we're forced to try and piece together what's going on through whatever meager clues the dialogue drops. Characters also seemingly pop in and out of locations without us having seen them arrive or go, adding to the general confusion. (While the inserted scenes exacerbate this confusion by negating some of the continuity, by no means did they *create* said confusion.)

Character-wise, the love-triangle between Brown, Nora, and Spalding (upon which Hoey spends an inordinate amount of time) never goes anywhere nor develops any real tension. Nora has no time for Spalding, though the poor guy professes several times that the only reason he stayed on this miserable island was to be near her. While Nora confesses her love to Brown, the laconic lieutenant can only tell her, "give me time baby." In the end, nothing is resolved, as the last we see of our tiresome threesome is them looking on at the (stock-footage) napalm strike—no resolution, no closure, just

an abrupt fizzle. And a fizzle is all one gets from this tacked-on climax. (The collected stock footage of this matches so poorly with what we've seen of the island that the cables simply snap on one's suspension of disbelief.)

Sprinkled in with the banalities, however, are a few truly effective moments—most of them centering on gruesome makeup (such as an acid burn victim courtesy of low-budget veteran Harry [*Frankenstein's Daughter*] Thomas) or gory activity (in one scene a sailor's arm is literally torn from its socket and we watch him stagger screaming through the jungle). And Hoey does manage a few moments of genuine suspense as various characters creep warily through the killer tree-infested jungle after dark.

And credit must be given for the innovative idea of having the monsters ooze acid rather than sap. Though admittedly little is made of this (apart from offering the excuse to show a couple of gross-out burn makeups) in *Night Monsters*, it did perhaps pave the way for a certain *Alien* possessing acid for blood (which concept *was* exploited effectively in this later sci-fi classic).

The film was shot (in 10 days for $178,000, according to Hoey) under the title *The Nightcrawlers* and released in the U.K. as *Monsters of the Night*. ("I remember the day when I was rehearsing and Jack Broder walked in and announced [that] the new title was going to be [*The Navy vs. the Night Monsters*]," recalled Hoey. "The entire cast was ready to walk out. They were furious that he would give it that title.") Whatever its moniker, it remains a risible yet oddly entertaining (in a snake-fascinating way) late-hour entry to the monster movie heyday of the 1950s and early '60s.

Midnight Marquee magazine (issue 54) unleashed this *Plague* in the Summer of 1997.

THE PLAGUE OF THE ZOMBIES (1966): A (RARE) HAMMER ORIGINAL

When someone mentions Hammer movies, one's thoughts naturally turn to monsters. In the annals of Hammer horror, the classic figures of Frankenstein and Dracula loom large. With seven entries each (not to mention a passel of vampire variations, including the Karnstein trilogy), these two figures have proved to be the monstrous cornerstones of Britain's Hammer Films. But these were not the only film franchises staked out by the studio. Hammer continued in its 'series' mentality with the Mummy theme (four features to its bandaged credit), a prehistoric subset (consisting of *One Million Years B.C.* [1966], *When Dinosaurs Ruled the Earth* [1970], and *Creatures the World Forgot* [1971]), the Quatermass triad, and innumerable post-*Psycho* "psychological thrillers" (such as *Taste of Fear* [1961], *Maniac* [1963], *Nightmare* [1964], ad infinitim, ad nauseum). Hammer was nothing if not repetitious.

Over the years, however, the studio occasionally left off beating their stable of (un)dead horses to venture outside the fiscal safety of its popular monster corral. Unique one-shot productions such as *The Abominable Snowman* (1957), *The Devil Rides Out* (1968), and *Countess Dracula* (1970; a "Dracula" in name only) are worthy efforts that have largely been overshadowed by the studio's various series, remakes, and clusterings. Among Hammer's originals are the two "Cornwall Classics" (as some devotees have overzealously labeled them), *The Reptile* and *The Plague of the Zombies*. The two were filmed back-to-back (*Plague* first and then, with only a week's break, *The Reptile*) utilizing many of the same sets and much of the same personnel (both in front of and behind the camera). Though similarly themed (exotic foreign deviltry invades a rural English village to spawn monsters that decimate the xenophobic locals), the two pictures are miles apart in efficacy. *The Reptile* is a slow-moving, predictable, sleep-inducing misfire while *The Plague of the Zombies* stands as a visually exciting, occasionally frightening, and thoroughly entertaining horror yarn.

In turn-of-the-century England, Medical professor Sir James Forbes (Andre Morell) journeys to a remote Cornish village to help his former pupil, Dr. Peter Thompson (Brook Williams), discover the cause of a mysterious rash of deaths plaguing the sleepy hamlet. When Peter's wife Alice (Jacqueline Pearce) dies of the malady, she rises from the dead (in a harrowing scene) as a zombie. Ultimately, the doctors discover that the local lord, Squire Hamilton (John Carson), is using voodoo to create a zombie labor force to work his tin mine. With Sir James' daughter Sylvia (Diane Clare) now imperiled, the doctors must do battle with Hamilton and his undead coterie.

One of the things that sets *Plague* apart from (and above) many a Hammer horror is the fact that things *happen* in this picture, and happen frequently. We have a sinister pre-credit sequence, then a scene in which the riding ruffians callously knock a funeral procession off a bridge to expose the shocking sight of the coffin spilled open in the ravine below. Next comes Alice's nighttime walk, and Sylvia's attack and abduction by the self-same riders. Then there's the horrific moment when a living corpse dumps Alice's dead body at Sylvia's feet.

Sadly (though perhaps not unexpectedly), at this point the film enters into a lengthy dull stretch (a seemingly inevitable occurrence in a Hammer production) in which the police question a suspect, Sir James questions the suspect, the two doctors talk and plan, Sir James pays a visit to the vicar's library, Hamilton visits Sylvia and through a complex subterfuge (lasting a full five minutes) acquires a few drops of her blood, and the principals attend Alice's funeral. These scenes add little to the film and simply allow the characters to discover what the viewer already knows—as well as eating up a significant portion (about thirty minutes) of the running time.

French poster for one of the better Hammer horrors of the 1960s.

Fortunately, while *The Plague of the Zombies* did not entirely escape The Plague of Hammer, the film picks up again with the graveyard sequence and from then on it maintains a shuddery and relatively fast pace to the end.

"Horror, as we at Hammer films know the word," pontificated producer Anthony Nelson Keys in *The Plague of the Zombies* pressbook, "has nothing to do with nastiness or cruelty or sadism for its own sake… We try to make horror films with a sense of taste and style, but whether we did or didn't, audiences still recognize that a horror film in period costumes is pure, honest-to-goodness fantasy."

Filming for a mere 28 days in late July/early August 1965, Keys and co. did indeed succeed in infusing *The Plague of the Zombies* with "a sense of taste and style." Director John Gilling, working with cinematographer Arthur Grant (whose steady hand and artful eye enhanced such Hammer productions as *The Abominable Snowman*, 1957; *The Curse of the Werewolf*, 1960; *The Phantom of the Opera*, 1962; *Frankenstein Created Woman*, 1967; *Dracula Has Risen from the Grave*, 1968; and *Frankenstein Must Be Destroyed*, 1969) stages and films scenes with an eye toward composition, movement, and atmosphere. When Alice comes upon the old tin mine during her fateful nocturnal walk, for instance, the camera shoots her through a huge disused gear-wheel, enclosing her image so that she looks small and trapped within the confines of the massive metal structure. The next moment she steps past the apparatus and moves closer to the camera. She stops, obviously seeing something, and her head turns aside just slightly as if she wants to look away (or scream) but cannot. Suddenly, the shadow of a hand rises up from the bottom of the frame. As the unseen figure advances towards her, the silhouette moves steadily up Alice's body before the shadow's bulk finally blots out her whole image with its ominous darkness. The staging and camera position, combined with the use of the sinister and intrusive shadow (further augmented by Jacqueline Pearce's uneasy demeanor) creates a moment ripe with dread—a dread that is realized fully a few minutes later.

In the next sequence, when a quartet of vicious riders converge on Sylvia in the woods, Gilling takes the time and effort to shift the camera back and forth from the attackers' perspective to the victim's, creating an involving—and harrowing—ambiance. First the camera is mounted high and appears unsteady, as if riding one of the horses that surrounds Sylvia. Then low-angled shots of the whirling and snorting beasts show us Sylvia's terrified viewpoint. Back and forth the perspective goes for several seconds until one of the toughs finally grabs Sylvia up and rides off. The camerawork and varied perspectives create an energetic immediacy and excitement that would have been completely lacking had we simply seen the ruffians chase her down and carry her off in the standard medium shot.

In the following sequence, the men have Sylvia inside the manor house. Here Gilling continues the motif from the previous scene (both thematically and visually) as she's roughly thrown from captor to captor and finally falls to the floor, hemmed in by the legs of the laughing men (just as she had been trapped by the charging horses). Low angle shots looking up at the forbidding enclosure of limbs as she desperately moves this way and that, seeking an opening, alternate between high angle shots that look down upon her from her attackers' vantage point.

Gilling stages the first appearance of a zombie (obviously a pivotal moment in something called *The Plague of the Zombies*) for maximum impact. It begins when Sylvia passes the same giant gear-wheel that Alice had come by earlier (with Sylvia's image momentarily framed behind it just as the doomed Alice had been). She rounds it and advances toward the camera (just like Alice) so that her worried face is backed by the dark sky and forbidding mine silhouetted behind. Then she suddenly whirls around and the scene cuts so that the camera is now above and looking down upon her now-shocked visage. The next shot has the camera start from behind her and swiftly zoom past, tilting upwards to reveal what she sees hovering on the rise above her— the horrible figure of the walking corpse holding Alice's lifeless body in its arms. A rapid zoom reveals the hideous grinning countenance in all its ghastly glory. Then, after a quick reaction shot of Alice cringing behind the gear-wheel, we see the creature gleefully dump its burden, which falls out of the frame seemingly at our very feet. Enhanced by careful positioning and camera movement, this scene, both shocking and terrifying, becomes one that, once seen, is not soon forgotten.

"The director that I got on with extremely well was John Gilling," recalled perennial Hammer favorite Michael Ripper (who plays a no-nonsense constable in *The Plague of the Zombies*) to interviewer Bruce G. Hallenbeck. "He was very good—and he thought a lot of me, I know that. He was very good as far as I was concerned, because I'm one of those actors who 'dies soon.' By that I mean, give me a few rehearsals and get to take three. After that I was dead, you know? If he saw me dying, he'd lean forward and say, 'Oh, Michael, when such and such a thing happens, say something like…'—which inspired me, you see, got me working again."

John Gilling entered the British film industry in 1933 as an assistant director. He turned his hand to writing in 1938, but didn't score a breakthrough until nearly a decade later with his screenplay for *Black Memory* (1947). After penning several more produced screenplays, he turned director on *Escape from Broadmoor* (1948), which he also scripted. Over the next two decades he directed nearly forty more features (many of which he wrote) as well as periodically working in English television (including the series *The Saint*, *Gideon*, and *Department S*). His first foray into the horror genre came in the pathetic form of *Old Mother Riley Meets the Vampire* (1952), which he directed but did not write. Fortunately, his opportunities soon improved, and he moved on to (somewhat) worthier projects like *The Gamma People* (1956), *Shadow of the Cat* (1961), *The Reptile* (1966), *Night Caller from Outer Space* (1966), and *The Mummy's Shroud* (1967). In 1959 he wrote and directed what proved to be the most effective and atmospheric Burke and Hare picture made to date, *Mania* (aka *The Flesh and the Fiends*). In 1970, Gilling relocated to Spain, but only made one more feature there, *La Cruz de Diablo* (*The Devil's Cross*; released in 1974) before retiring from films to devote himself to painting. Gilling died in 1984 in Madrid. After the underrated classic *Mania*, *The Plague of the Zombies* (which Gilling claimed he rewrote extensively as he shot) remains his best horror film. If one looks upon Gilling's directorial outings as a body of work, it doesn't really add up to much; but on at least two occasions (with *Mania* and *Plague*) he managed to construct that proverbial silk purse.

As with most Hammer productions, the acting in *The Plague of the Zombies* is first-rate. Andre Morell is simply a joy to watch, playing the elegant, no-nonsense Sir James with a twinkle in his eye and a droll half-smile on his lips. "I don't know why I put up with you at all," he offhandedly tells his daughter when she interrupts him, "I should have drowned you at birth." At this, Morell gives the hint of a soft smile at his feigned annoyance and gruff joke. When Hamilton angrily demands of Sir James, "Are you mad?!," Morell answers, "I almost wish I was, this business is so appalling," with just the right mix of throw-away glibness and introspective sincerity to make the rather unlikely line work.

Morell adds further depth to his character by making Sir James' assured, take-charge facade human enough to give way during the odd unguarded moment. Cleaning up after dinner, he tells Peter of his plans to illegally exhume a corpse. When the shocked Peter voices his objection, Sir James answers, "Why not? It's a full moon, couldn't be better. We'll start about midnight." Morell then promptly fumbles and drops the plate he'd been drying, his unsteady action and the slightly vexed look on his face belying his nonchalant words.

Born André Mesritz in London in 1909, Morell turned to amateur acting in 1930 and made his professional debut in 1934. Four years later he joined the illustrious Old Vic company and simultaneously started his screen career. After serving as a Major in the Royal Welsh Fusiliers during WWII, his stage and screen career flourished. Among Morell's seventy-plus film credits (which span forty years—right up until his death in 1978) are such prestige pictures as *Bridge on the River Kwai* (1957), *Ben Hur* (1959), *Julius Caesar* (1970), *QB VII* (1974), *Barry Lyndon* (1975), and *The Great Train Robbery* (1978). Morell's presence graced a number of genre pictures as well, including *1984* (1954), *The Hound of the Baskervilles* (1959; in which he created what some consider to be the screen's definitive Dr. Watson), *The Giant Behemoth* (1959), *Mysterious Island* (1961), *Shadow of the Cat* (1961), *She* (1965), *The Mummy's Shroud* (1967), and *The Vengeance of She* (1968). Of special note to Hammer fans is his marvelous turn in the little-seen crime thriller *Cash on Demand* (1962); in it, Morell plays a perfect foil to Peter Cushing, who gives one of the finest performances of his long career.

As *Plague of the Zombie*'s head villain, John Carson possesses the appropriately aristocratic bearing and cool charm of a James Mason (he even sounds like Mason), adding both weight and dignity to the rather ill-defined roll. (Sadly, the character of Squire Hamilton remains both one-dimensional and underdeveloped, and we're left simply to wonder at the motivations and root of his heinous actions.) Carson went on to appear in two other Hammer horrors, *Taste the Blood of Dracula* (1970) and *Captain Kronos, Vampire Hunter* (1973).

Of the female leads, Jacqueline Pearce (who essayed the title role in *The Reptile*) is the more effective of the two, for she is both attractive and affecting. In her introductory scene, her obvious relief at seeing her old school friend Sylvia seems subtly tempered by a guilty nervousness. She appears skittish and secretive, refusing to let Sir James look under her bandage (as if somehow knowing it's an unholy wound yet at the same time feeling protective of it). Pearce speaks rapidly, her eyes and head often downcast, though she frequently glances up as she talks in a furtive, almost pleading manner. The actress's demeanor immediately pulls the viewer in and arouses sympathy. "She was fine to work with," remembered Michael Ripper, "very good."

Diane Clare, though possessing a larger role, makes less of an impression. She appears rather stilted and never quite convinces, even in her potential showcase scenes of fear or anger. (No doubt the fact that Hammer dubbed her voice with that of another actress didn't help her cause any.) In any case, next to Pearce, the chubby-cheeked Clare looks girlish and passionless.

"The authentic and thoroughly researched sequences of voodoo practices shown in the film are said to follow the actual rituals performed in Haiti," proclaimed a studio publicity article. This was undoubtedly "said" *only* by the studio's PR writers, for the "voodoo practices shown in the film" are about as authentic as a mail-order voodoo doll. Delusions of authenticity aside, the ceremonial scenes are well handled by Gilling and his crew to infuse a sense of danger and excitement into the proceedings. While far from convincing (thanks to some outlandish 'heathen' headgear and bone necklaces sported by the trio of dark-skinned drummers, as well as the out-of-place white clerical-style robes and druidical masks worn by Hamilton and his cronies), these sequences possess an oppressive yet lively air due to the cave-like mine setting and the rapid, incessant drum rhythms. With the mine's overhanging rock ceiling and walls pressing in upon the scene, the drummers pound frantically in the foreground while (in contrast) the white-robed practitioners move slowly and deliberately about the paraphernalia-laden alter stone to pour

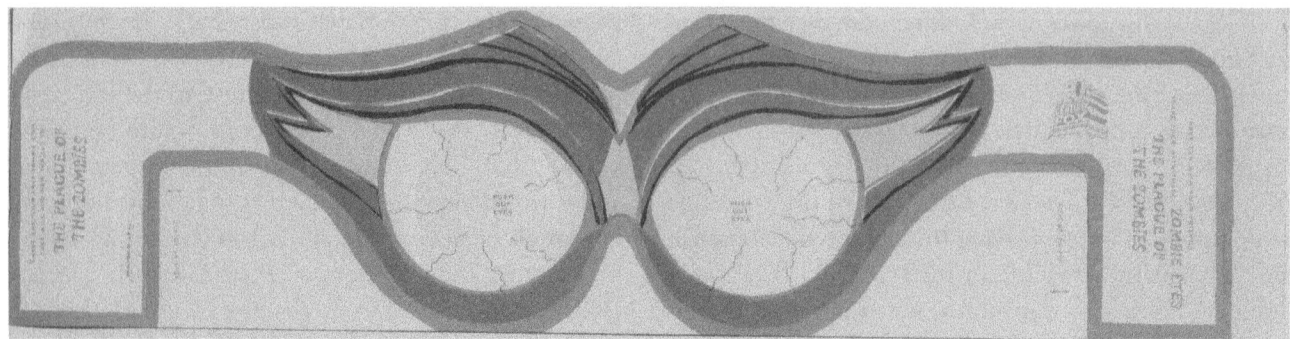

A set of "zombie eyes" promo giveaways—paper cutouts that read "THESE ARE YOUR FREE ZOMBIE EYES. THEY WILL ADD NEW THRILLS TO THE PLAGUE OF THE ZOMBIES.*"*

vials of blood over dolls in miniature coffins. It makes for an atmospheric and disturbing spectacle.

At one point, Sir James tells Peter that, "I spent the afternoon reading up on the subject [of zombies] in the vicar's library. And it's all there. It's all *clearly, scientifically* stated." Sir James must have found some amazing books, for until Wade Davis' 1985 book *The Serpent and the Rainbow*, there had been no clear, scientific investigation into the phenomenon of zombies, and the concept had been chronicled only as unsubstantiated stories, legends, and hearsay.

Regarding zombies, *Plague* features some of the most effective in the voodoo subgenre. Dressed in sackcloth shrouds, these walking dead are quite frightening with their dead-gray pallor, flaking skin, wide-staring filmy eyes, and evil grins and smirks (admittedly a ridiculous trait for a creature with no will of its own—but a visually chilling one nonetheless).

The film's horrific highlights center on these "undead" creatures (as Sir James labels them). The famed dream sequence, in which mottled hands thrust up through the newly dug graves as the zombies rise from their earthen tombs to close upon the frightened Peter (who stands motionless, seemingly rooted to the spot), may well be one of the most memorable (and chilling) scenes in the Hammer canon. The off-kilter camera angles, eerie flowing mist, gruesome makeup, and the inherent terror of death (symbolically represented by these perambulating corpses) make this shuddery sequence a justifiably revered one among horror enthusiasts in general and Hammerheads in particular. Macabre details, such as the rainwater lying on the raw, red earth looking like puddles of blood, combine with the horrific appearance and slow-but-inexorable movements of the hideous host to make the hackles stand on end. It's a brief, relentless, and frightening scene, and one that probably inspired George Romero in filming his *Night of the Living Dead* (and surely served as a blueprint for Bob Kelljan's effectively creepy opening for *The Return of Count Yorga*). (Note: This sequence is *not* tinted green as some uninformed writers have erroneously claimed, but features an effective use of *full* color—as exemplified by the blood-red puddles.)

Castle of Frankenstein's Russ Jones visited Hammer's Bray studios during the filming of *The Plague of the Zombies* and related how quickly and efficiently the production team worked. Lunching with Tony Keys, Jones wrote that, "across the room sat Andre Morell and the rest of the cast of *Plague of the Zombies*, deeply engrossed in discussing the afternoon shooting schedule. After our meal, Reg [Williams, who worked in the publicity department] was to take us to an interior set for a fight scene in which Andre Morell battled one of the zombie leaders. We walked to the set. Here an astonishing thing occurred. In the room were nothing but four walls and a bare floor. Within twenty minutes it was an English pub with a bar, bookcase, chairs, tables, carpets, pictures and various bric-a-brac. The cameras and crew came in, and the scene was put in the can after three takes."

Plague of the Zombies was placed on the bottom half of a double bill with *Dracula, Prince of Darkness* (which is rather unfair because *Plague* certainly moves faster and is arguably the more entertaining of the two). In the United States, the films were ballyhooed as "The Greatest All New Fright Show in Town!" and patrons were blessed with promotional giveaways: "Boys! Fight back… Bite back with Dracula Fangs! Girls! Defend Yourself with Zombie Eyes!" (cheap cardboard cutouts with small eyeholes).

Poor pairings and grotesque giveaways aside, *The Plague of the Zombies* stands near the top of voodoo's cinematic ladder and, indeed, if not on the top *Hammer* rung as well, then at least solidly positioned on its second step.

> While this essay never saw publication in this particular form (it was intended for the British mag *Shivers*), a modified version did make it into my book *Drums of Terror: Voodoo in the Cinema*. So there's that.

SCREAM BLACULA SCREAM (1973): A VAMPIRE SEQUEL DESERVING RESURRECTION

In 1972 the screen's first black vampire took the drive-ins by storm, thanks in no small part to the imposing and cultured presence of Shakespearean actor William Marshall playing the title role. Though cursed with a ridiculous name ("It was *not* going to sell with that title," Marshall laughingly recalled, adding, "I was quite wrong about that"), the actor brought a stately charisma to *Blacula* and added some much-needed respectability via his suggestions regarding the character. "The image that I suggested," Marshall told this author, "would be more meaningful to people—an African prince who had been nudged by his elders to go to Europe to do something about the *theft*, the continued thievery where African people were concerned."

Naturally, fiscal success led to a sequel, and American International talked their new star into reprising his role in their proposed *Blacula Is Beautiful* (a working title thankfully soon abandoned). "They believed it could do as well as the first one," recalled Marshall. This time, however, AIP proved less appreciative of the actor's input. "They were wary of me by then and didn't want to hear anything I had to say." As a consequence, the actor holds little love for *Scream Blacula Scream*.

When asked his opinion of the sequel, William Marshall complained that "It didn't add anything to the first one." His viewpoint, however, peeks strictly from behind Mamuwalde's cape, and in that sense he's right—*Scream Blacula Scream* added nothing to the character of "Blacula." What it did add, however, was a new twist (voodoo) on a tired old theme (vampirism).

A would-be voodoo priest raises Blacula from the dead in an effort to secure his sect's leadership. Mamuwalde (Blacula's real name) has other ideas, however, and makes his benefactor into a vampire slave while creating an undead coven of his own. When Blacula encounters Lisa (the voodoo congregation's legitimate priestess), however, he sees a way out of his nightmarish existence. The vampire reveals his true nature and pleads with a terrified Lisa to use her voodoo powers to "exorcise this demonic creature that inhabits my body." Though fearful, Lisa agrees. To this end, she takes clippings from his hair and prepares a voodoo doll in his likeness over which she performs a complex ritual. Lisa's boyfriend and the police interrupt the ceremony, however, resulting in a violent climactic battle between vampires and patrolmen—and the tragic demise of Blacula.

Scream Blacula Scream is one of the few films to depict the *healing* power of voodoo. As Mamuwalde himself tells Lisa, "Voodoo in the proper hands can unlock many mysteries. Yours is a power unlike mine. It can be used for good as well as evil." While not particularly profound, at least it's a more balanced portrayal of the much-maligned religion.

Unfortunately, little else is made of the voodoo angle in *Scream Blacula Scream*. After the very first scene, there's no exploration of (nor even a further appearance by) the voodoo group itself, so its dynamics and motivations remain mute. And after Lisa comments that "to us voodoo is simply a religion based on faith, a powerful, powerful faith," this premise disappears without a trace. In fact, the only time voodoo truly comes into play is at the picture's beginning (the resurrection ritual) and end (the abortive curative ceremony and subsequent lethal use of the voodoo doll). While the film carries a germ of voodoo extrapolation, the seed fails to sprout.

As entertaining blaxploitation/horror, however, the picture fulfills its promise to a much higher degree. Thanks in large part to leads William Marshall and Pam Grier (and, to a lesser extent, some effective touches of humor), *Scream Blacula Scream* remains a fairly involving horror hybrid.

With his imposing 6'5" frame, his deep baritone voice, and his charming and commanding presence, William Marshall takes total control whenever onscreen. Trained on the stage (with a number of Shakespearean successes to his credit—not to mention at one time serving as understudy to Boris Karloff's Captain Hook in *Peter Pan*!), Marshall's command of the English language and nuance of voice serves him well in the occasionally awkward role of Mamuwalde/Blacula. His powerful delivery makes even such potentially pretentious (and preposterous) lines like "I'm moved by powers no human is capable of comprehending" both sincere and affecting. Making something of nothing even in *this* instance, Marshall's pinpoint inflection and emphasis on the word "human" adds a subtle and poignant note of sadness.

At one point, Mamuwalde accepts an invitation to return the next day by answering, "Evening would be better for me; I'm rather a night person." Marshall's

Scream Blacula Scream *pressbook*.

slight accent on "night" adds to the secret humor of the statement. The actor's disarming charm then comes fully to the fore as, smiling, he continues, "I have the awful habit of sleeping away the daylight hours." Rather than going over the top with his eyes all a-twinkle and his tongue protruding visibly from his cheek, Marshall keeps his smile and twinkle subtle, thus displaying the *character's* wry humor rather than the *actor's* broad wink.

When asked what he thought of the voodoo-vs.-vampirism concept in *Scream Blacula Scream* Marshall replied "not much" and laughed. Fortunately, he still took his job seriously and, while letting a bemused humor come to the fore when appropriate, he thankfully played his character straight, becoming a truly ferocious figure when aroused while at the same time projecting a powerful pathos.

As Lisa, Pam Grier does an admirable job in what could have been a walk-through role (or a stock 'tough babe' part similar to those she so often played in her numerous action pictures). More than just being able to look good in pantsuits and throw a mean karate chop, Grier shows in *Scream Blacula Scream* that she indeed *can* act. When confronted by her friend rising from the dead and Blacula's subsequent frightening appearance, she effectively portrays a near-hysterical fear while still remaining lucid enough to demand an explanation through her terrified tears. Grier reveals a solid strength in Lisa while at the same time displaying a near-overwhelming (and natural) terror that makes her more human and more real.

Much of the fun of watching *Scream Blacula Scream* comes from its liberal doses of humor—some of it sly (such as Mamuwalde's occasionally droll dialogue) and some blatant. When a newly converted vampire starts to preen before a mirror only to realize that he can no longer see his own reflection, for instance, he lets out with "Hey look man, I don't mind bein' a vampire and all that shit but this really ain't hip. I mean a man has *got* to see his face." Crestfallen, he then keeps pestering a half-bemused, half-annoyed Mamuwalde with questions like, "Hey man, how do I look?" adding will all sincerity, "It's important." There's something about vampire vanity that tickles the funnybone.

Also amusing are the shots of Mamuwalde in bat form (in effectively animated silhouette) flapping down a modern traffic-filled avenue, past high-rise buildings, and through busy intersections—an anomalous sight that not only produces a chuckle but perhaps underscores the tragic gulf between the hapless vampire and the bustling world of humanity all around him. Fortunately, however, when the fangs come out and the action begins, all pretense of levity stops and vampires become a deadly serious subject.

Speaking of vampires, this film portrays them in a rather unusual light. Looking normal and thoroughly human when relaxed and sated, Blacula's undead followers take on a deathly pallor only when their bloodlust is aroused. Oddly, however, they also move in a slow, almost somnambulistic manner and so appear more like shuffling zombies than vicious vampires. It makes for an intriguing contrast and, because of their zombie-like gait and appearance, one that ties itself even more closely to voodoo. Alternatively, when Blacula swings into full vampiric action, coarse hair lines his cheeks and eyebrows to give him a ferocious animalistic image—and there's nothing slow or ponderous about *his* lethal movements.

The picture also possesses an effective and involving storyline – thanks to a liberal borrowing from a certain gothic soap opera, for *Scream Blacula Scream* bears more than a passing resemblance to the popular feature film *House of Dark Shadows* (based on the cult hit daytime drama *Dark Shadows*) released in 1970. Both pictures revolve around an unhappy vampire seeking a cure from a sympathetic female (with *Scream* changing *Dark Shadows'* medical doctor into a voodoo priestess) while at the same time reluctantly wreaking undead havoc all around them. *Scream* even 'borrowed' *House's* striking imagery of a troupe of uniformed policemen facing off against the lead vampire's minions. In substituting a voodoo for a scientific treatment and a black vampire for a white one, *Scream Blacula Scream* added even further interest to an already potent and pathos-laden (not to mention audience-tested) premise.

Technically, *Scream Blacula Scream* is competent—but no more. The same can be said for Bob Kelljan's earnest but uninspired direction. "I didn't feel the dramatic touch of a great director," deadpanned William Marshall. To Kelljan's credit, however, he at least *tries* different things, tossing in varied camera angles and techniques (extreme close-ups, high angle shots, unsteady cam, etc.). Unfortunately, they seem more arbitrary than impact-oriented and the rather obvious, unsubtle approaches often prove more distracting than enhancing.

A few things work quite well, however, such as the shock effect generated by first focusing on a character cautiously creeping about the vampire-infested mansion, then cutting to a close-up of Blacula, arms outstretched, as he zooms out of nowhere towards the camera (along with a jarring note on the soundtrack to complete the startle effect). Of course, this is simply a rehash of the same shock stunt Kelljan pulled in his two previous *Count Yorga* movies. Consequently, for those who've seen those earlier films, familiarity brings with it a liberal dose of contempt. (Kelljan also reuses from his *Yorga* pictures the [admittedly effective] ploy of having his human protagonist verbally spar with the vampire in a polite-but-guarded 'discussion' of vampirism.)

Another device Kelljan uses is to visually link two scenes with a similar image. As the bones burst into flame during Willis' resurrection ceremony, the film cuts to a shot of Lisa suddenly starting awake and glancing at the fire in her fireplace—as if some kind of mental contact had been made. Kelljan then zooms into the fire and when the camera zooms out again it's now focused back on Willis' supernatural flames—an obvious but nonetheless effective transition.

These are the exceptions, however, and most of the director's staging is of a more perfunctory manner. Blacula's resurrection, for instance, is a pivotal scene rife with excitement and possibilities which, under Kelljan's drab direction, ends up as an opportunity missed. When the supernatural fire dies down, Willis, angry and dejected, goes into the next room to get a drink. We then see the shadow of a man on the wall behind him, and the camera cuts to a close-up of black-clad legs and feet (and cloak) approaching the seated Willis. Willis then turns, and Blacula reaches down to bite him on the neck. The mundane staging generates little suspense, less excitement, and no terror.

Though cinematographer Isadore Mankofsky's lighting occasionally throws a token shadow, the film as a whole appears over-lit, fully displaying the pale, washed-out color so typical of the 1970s (particularly on TV—a place where director Kelljan soon sought career refuge).

Bob Kelljan (born Robert Kelljchian) began his career as an actor in New York. Coming to Hollywood in 1960, he appeared on television (including *The Twilight Zone* episode "The Jeopardy Room") and features (such as *The Glass Cage*, *Psycho-Out*, and *Hell's Angels on Wheels*). As a result of his association with actor Michael Macready, Kelljan turned director in 1969 with *Little Sister* (aka *Flesh of My Flesh*) which he also wrote. Kelljan next wrote and directed the highly successful *Count Yorga, Vampire* and its follow-up, *The Return of Count Yorga*. After a few more films (including *Scream Blacula Scream*, *Act of Vengeance* [aka *Rape Squad*], and *Black Oak Conspiracy*) he turned to television where he helmed the telefilms *Cry for Justice*, *The Plague*, *Angels on Ice*, and *Angels in Vegas*. He also directed in episodic television, working on series like *Fame*, *Beach Patrol*, and *Police Story*. Kelljan never completely abandoned his initial in-front-of-the-camera roots, however, for he continued to teach acting classes in Hollywood. He died in November 1981 at age 52 (from cancer), only six weeks after completing a *Hill Street Blues* episode.

Scream Blacula Scream remains an unusual, if flawed, entry in both the voodoo and vampire cinema subsets. Though it fails to carry its intriguing voodoo premise to its full conclusion, it still remains an entertaining film with a few shocks, a few doses of humor, and a few good performances to recommend it.

> I added to this *Cult Movies* magazine review (issue 24, December 1997) to, er, shake it up a bit.

SEIZURE (1974)

"You can never run from it; you can never hide from it: the breath-stopping panic of Seizure*!"* –trailer

This debut effort by then-twenty-six-year-old future Oscar-winning writer/director Oliver Stone (*Platoon*, *JFK*, *Natural Born Killers*) exhibits none of the power or fluidity of his later films. Having co-produced the low-budget sexploitationer *Sugar Cookies* in New York, the NYU film school graduate, along with his friend and co-producer Jeffrey Kapelman, raised $150,000 for his first feature by showing his student films to various Canadian investors. (*Seizure*'s final budget came in at $250,000, thanks to deferments and some additional investements.) Stone then shot his feature, written by himself and Spanish writer-producer-director Santos Alcocer (using the nom de plume Edward Mann), in Quebec in the fall of 1972, utilizing a mostly Canadian

Oliver Stone's debut. He got better. (half-sheet poster)

crew, and a mixture of Canadian and American actors.

The largely incoherent story centers on a writer (Jonathan Frid, of *Dark Shadows* fame) who invites a group of friends to his country home for the weekend and also inadvertently materializes three nightmare figures from his own imagination—an evil dwarf (Herve Villachaize, later of TV's *Fantasy Island*), a black executioner, and the "Queen of Evil" (played by Martine Beswick) who at one point is characterized as an incarnation of the goddess Kali(!).

The inexperienced Stone proved unable to fully meet the challenges of his impoverished budget, as the production looks shoddy, with poor sound and lighting. "I don't think they [Stone and Kapelman] had a firm grip on what it was like to run a production from a financial standpoint or a psychological standpoint," opined Tom Brumberger, *Seizure*'s makeup man, to interviewer Bob Martin. "They particularly didn't know how to handle the French-Canadian crew, who were very volatile." According to Brumberger, Stone was not easy to work with, as he "created a certain tension on the set—an atmopsphere I thought at first was an adverse environment to work in, and a good many others on the film felt that way." But when Brumberger finally saw the film a year and a half later, he "realized that it was that intensity that made it work." Too bad it didn't—work, that is.

Despite the inclusion of some talented actors (Frid, Beswick, and Mary Woronov in a throwaway role), the cast generally comes off as amateurish. The jump-cut editing (courtesy of Stone himself) and hand-held photography (tellingly, Canadian cinematographer Roger Racine's final film was the awful *Zombie Nightmare*) don't help matters, and the characterizations are either stereotypes or given little apparent motivation for their actions. A few bright points stand out from the murky proceedings, however, such as the scene in which Frid is forced to fight and kill a friend. The actor convincingly encapsulates his character's confusion and incredulousness at this nightmarish circumstance. And Stone handles the clichéd it-was-only-a-dream-or-was-it? ending well, with the revelation coming on an unusual and jarring note. But these few isolated scenes can't sustain the bulk of the film. The Queen of Evil herself sums it up best when she states, "You will do as you are told though nothing will make sense."

"I gave my blood to it, along with every last dime I could raise," stated Stone of his directorial debut. "I cut the film myself, with an assistant, while living in a $40-a-week hotel room. We eventually got chased out of Canada owing money, and I had to steal the answer print from the lab and run with it over the border to the U.S. in order to sell it." It hardly proved worth the effort, especially after Stone sold it to Cinerama Releasing, who fobbed it off as a stepchild second feature on a limited release double bill with the Amicus import *The Beast Must Die*. "It was totally ignored by the distributors," complained Stone. And by the public as well.

The director's experience with *Seizure* resulted in him becoming "totally disillusioned and spiritually depleted," so that he abandoned directing for the next decade. "I took a job with a godawful sports film company and kept writing, writing, writing," remembered the filmmaker. "I'd written fourteen original screenplays before *Midnight Express* was made [in 1978]." Stone finally stepped behind the camera again to direct *The Hand* in 1981, and never looked back.

Midnight Marquee introduced readers to the groovy *Sugar Hill* (and her Zombie Hitmen) in 1997 (issue 55). Ya dig?!

SUGAR HILL AND HER ZOMBIE HITMEN!

She found all the forces of evil,
Put them in a voodoo trance,
She used all her tools to put the fools away,
And evil never had a chance.
– "Supernatural Voodoo Woman" theme song

The 1970s were something of a cultural wasteland in America, full of bad fashion (polyester leisure suits and voluminous bellbottoms), bad hair (who can forget the gigantic afro phase?), and bad music (one word: Disco). Consequently, a 'modern' American movie from the '70s (particularly one that strove for a 'hip' contemporary look) is *instantly* recognizable for the cultural curiosity it is.

Though this author 'came of age' during the 1970s, he holds little nostalgic love for it, a personal prejudice perhaps, but one that seems justified when the decade's shortcomings are so bluntly exposed by films like *Sugar Hill* (1974). It's not a bad movie; in fact, it possesses a solid story, some moments of effective atmosphere, and decent production values. It's just hopelessly trapped in the thick amber of its time period. The dated dialogue and charmless 'jive' talk ("That's a very foxy lady"), the ridiculous she-bop Motown theme song ("Supernatural voodoo woman does her thing at night / Supernatural voodoo woman, do her wrong and you won't see the light"), and the wide lapels on powder blue pantsuits

Two of Sugar Hill's "Zombie Hit Men." (lobby card)

only serve to distract from the tale being told. Consequently, it's sometimes difficult to take seriously. Even so, for those with more tolerance for the sights and sounds of "K-Tel" and the like, *Sugar Hill* offers up a well-produced and often atmospheric tale of voodoo vengeance.

Marki Bey plays Diana "Sugar" Hill, whose lover is beaten to death by a gang of thugs headed by crime boss Morgan (Robert Quarry). Thirsting for vengeance, Sugar seeks the aid of Mama Maitresse (Zara Culley), a voodoo witch. The aged sorceress conjures up the voodoo god Baron Samedi (Don Pedro Colley), "keeper of the dead, king of the graveyards." Baron Samedi then raises up a band of zombies, the corpses of buried slaves, and instructs Sugar to "Put them to *evil* use." Via voodoo and her zombies, Sugar then sets about wreaking her revenge on the mobster and his men.

The genesis of *Sugar Hill* began in Haiti itself, for that's where screenwriter Tim Kelly acquired his interest and inspiration. Kelly, a prolific playwright (with over three hundred plays currently in print) who for a time made some extra cash penning blaxploitation pictures (and one other horror, *Cry of the Banshee*, which he remembers as "a painful experience"), had visited Haiti several times and "was absolutely fascinated by the island and wanted very much to do something in that genre" (as he related to this author). Feeling that "there was nothing [in films at that point] that was really hooked into the basic aspects of the voodoo religion," he wrote a script in 1972 called *Black Voodoo* "that was absolutely loaded with historical stuff that was completely accurate." Paul Maslansky, a producer who was looking to direct his first feature, took Kelly's script to AIP and received the green light—after a significant rewrite, of course, to make the concept fit the exploitable AIP mold. "At that time," recalled Kelly, "AIP was really intent on making *revenge* movies." So Kelly took *Black Voodoo* and (for the modest sum of $12,500) turned his historically accurate voodoo script into "the perfect wedding of the black exploitation film with something that was meant to be a little more serious."

Originally intended to be filmed in New Orleans (which makes more sense given its subject matter), the location was changed to Houston when AIP encountered "some sort of trouble with the teamsters," remembered Kelly. For the four-week shoot, director Paul Maslansky filmed in actual locations (real houses, hospital, office, mansion, etc.) rather than on a soundstage. As a result, the surroundings are realistic and more convincing than most, from the dusty deserted mansion to the eerie swampland.

Also convincing—and genuinely creepy—are the film's zombies. "They did good makeups on the voodoo people, the zombies," opined star Robert Quarry. With their bulging, filmy eyes a milky white, their hair matted with leaves and spider webs, and their pasty gray skin highlighted so that one can almost *see* the bones beneath the dead flesh, they present a terrifying image of death revived. In one shuddery shot, two of them sit up simultaneously from their shallow graves, turn their heads slowly toward one another, and *smile*—a horrible, ghastly rictus grin. These are creatures of *evil*.

Director Paul Maslansky (making his directorial debut *and* swan song—he never directed another picture though he continued as a highly successful producer) and cinematographer Robert Jessup take care with their supernatural charges, filming them to chilling advantage. In the resurrection scene, for instance, close-ups of gray hands poking up through the dead leaves of the mossy forest floor progress into atmospheric low-angled shots of the horrible corpses rising stiffly from the earth while the swirling mist turns the midday light into a hazy twilight punctuated by flashes of preternatural lightning.

As a voodoo film, *Sugar Hill* possesses more integrity than most—thanks to scripter Tim Kelly's genuine fascination with the Haitian religion. The story begins, for instance, with a voodoo ceremony in which authentically-dressed devotees dance and whirl, some clutching sacrificial chickens or sacred snakes. Suddenly, one of the participants starts screaming ecstatically, apparently possessed by a loa (voodoo god), and the others rush to gather around her writhing body.

While visually intriguing and well-staged, this authenticity-minded beginning also illustrates the film's '70s quaintness: instead of the expected rapid drumbeats, we hear the Motown rhythm of "Supernatural Voodoo Woman" playing on the soundtrack. Though this musical anomaly remains more than a little disconcerting, the sequence ends rather cleverly when the dancers suddenly collapse and we hear applause as the camera zooms in on a sign reading "Club Haiti." It was all just an outdoor nightclub act.

In amongst the 'hip' talk, screenwriter Kelly sprinkles some thought-provoking and credible dialogue. When Mama Maitresse admonishes Sugar, "Child, you have always been a *dis*believer; why do you now believe?" Sugar answers, "Because I want *revenge*!" making an interesting comment on the power of faith.

Later, in a ceremonial exchange, Mama Maitresse asks, "Where does the sun rise?" and Sugar answers, "In the east, Mama." The old woman continues, "Where does the sun *set*?" to which Sugar ritualistically responds, "In Guineé, Mama." Guineé was the term used by the Haitian slaves to designate their distant homeland in Africa and remains a symbolic Eden to the Voudounist.

The picture's subject matter apparently spooked some of its participants. "Some of the people were quite uncomfortable with making the film, because they really were a little upset about the voodoo aspect," recalled Kelly. "I'm speaking of the local people they used in Houston" who felt "that maybe you shouldn't fool around with this stuff." Nervous bit players aside, no serious mishaps (voodoo-induced or otherwise) occurred during the four-week shoot.

Sadly, *Sugar Hill* remains a decidedly flawed film. Beyond its appalling wardrobe and dated dialogue, the picture's main weakness lies in its acting. Apart from Robert Quarry, most of the major players are either amateurishly flat (the actors playing Morgan's henchmen) or too strained for credibility (Zara Culley as Mama Maitresse and top-billed Marki Bey).

According to AIP publicity, "Ms. Bey researched her part among various voodoo cults in and around the L.A. environs, thereby acquiring the proper authoritative menace to make her role as a voodoo high priestess believable." If so, it didn't work. Though pretty enough to look at, she brings little depth or distinction to her role. Bey was less-than-thrilled with her starring assignment, and this may have tempered her performance. In fact, co-star Robert Quarry remembered to this author that, "she hated it, hated the whole thing," even though Bey was the highest paid member of the cast (Quarry was second).

Quarry had nothing but nice things to say about Ms. Bey. "Oh, Marki, she was darling. I don't think she ever made another movie. [She made one more, *Hangup*, released later this same year.] Marki had just come from the Pearl Bailey all-black *Hello Dolly*, playing Irene, the second lead. And she was as pretty as could be and she was as nice as could be. We shot for about a week, and when the dailies started coming in,

[AIP president] Sam Arkoff didn't think she looked black enough so they had an afro wig made for her and darkened her makeup. So half of the time she had sort of light red hair with a very pale skin which they covered over. Well, I'm not sure, but Sam Arkoff with his usual class probably said, 'she don't look like a nigger to me.' Mr. Class. So they insisted they put her in an afro wig. She was beautiful."

Quarry, however, was not so enamored of his other co-star, Don Pedro Colley (playing Baron Samedi), calling him "one of the most pretentious bastards. He had a better dressing room than I did. That was in his contract, that he had to have a van and the whole thing. He was so full of affected shit. He behaved like he was the star of the movie. I mean, in *his* mind he was the star of the movie. So it was always 'Makeup! Costume! Wardrobe!' Don thought he was a *big movie star*."

Colley's performance certainly reflects this "star" attitude. Colley plays Baron Samedi in a broad, exuberant fashion—wide-eyed, big-voiced, and full of theatrical poses and dramatic gestures. Though a voodoo god incarnate is an admittedly unusual role which calls for an unusual portrayal, Colley makes him something of a caricature and so fails to convince. (This concept of a voodoo god appearing on earth strays far from the Voudoun canon, since the loas manifest themselves through *human beings*—via temporary possession—rather than owning corporeal forms themselves.) Colley's cause isn't helped by the echo chamber reverberation that his voice receives on the soundtrack—an obvious and distracting technical artifice.

As Morgan, Robert Quarry provides the only naturalistic and convincing performance in the film. His surface urbanity hides a brutal ruthlessness that periodically peeks out from under the mobster's thin facade via his subtle expressions and unsmiling eyes.

Initially, producer Elliot Schick and director Paul Maslansky felt that Quarry was *not* the right actor for the part of crime-syndicate head Mr. Morgan. In fact, they felt he was not even the right *color*. "I was forced to do the movie," recalled Quarry. "I had a pay or play contract. They were going to make an all-black movie, but that meant that they were going to have to pay me and not play me, and Sam [Arkoff] wasn't going to do that. Elliot Schick and Paul Maslansky, who were doing this all-black exploitation horror film, were not thrilled to suddenly end up with me playing the head of the Black Mafia. It made about as much sense as me playing Bernadette of Lourdes. So I was just suddenly flown off to Houston to do this movie. I hadn't even read the script. When I got there I read it, and I thought what the hell am I doing playing *this* part? I mean this was a black man's role. And they had a black actor set for it, but Sam said no, we'll use Quarry. And I ended up doing the movie. And then as it turned out, it was a very happy working relationship with Paul and Elliot, because I was doing good work—even though it was just all wrong for the movie."

Despite everyone's protestations (including Quarry's), Arkoff's money-conscious insistence paid dividends, for Quarry's fine performance is one of the film's prime assets. "I was kind of amazed [when I saw it recently]," concluded the actor, "I wasn't that embarrassed by it."

Quarry brought more than just *his* talent to the part, he brought his *dog's* too. For the scene in which Morgan and his girlfriend receive the heart in a jar, the poodle Morgan plays with on the couch is actually Quarry's own beloved dog, Virginia. ("I had just done the play *Who's Afraid of Virginia Wolfe*, so when I got her I called her 'Virginia Woof.'") Virginia was an instant success. "During rehearsal," remembered Quarry, "they opened the jar and she just kind of sat there. When they went for the take, I opened the lid and she went 'aaah' and jumped off the couch and ran [laughs]. She got a big hand, you know, everybody thought that was terrific she'd done that. She was a little ham." Virginia's "ham" paid off nicely for the canine thespian, for the director rewarded her sterling performance with a big steak at lunch that day.

Though he had small roles in a number of films, and scored some stage success in New York prestige productions like *Richard II*, *The Taming of the Shrew*, and *Who's Afraid of Virginia Wolfe*, Quarry didn't become a commodity until the low-budget drive-in horror *Count Yorga, Vampire* (1970) did unexpected blockbuster business. After the huge success of *Yorga*, AIP (who picked up the independent film for distribution) put Quarry under a five-year contract. The actor subsequently starred in two more vampire films, the inevitable *Return of Count Yorga* (1971) and *The Deathmaster* (1972), as well as *Dr. Phibes Rises Again*, *Sugar Hill* (1974), and *Madhouse* (1974). Quarry believes that AIP president Sam Arkoff saw him as a rival/successor to Vincent Price. This apparently caused some initial friction (which was soon smoothed over) between the two actors when they first worked together on *Dr. Phibes Rises Again*. In the late seventies, Quarry's acting career went on hiatus, due primarily to a serious car accident that kept him from seeking work for three years (as well as ending the life of his beloved poodle). The actor made a comeback of sorts when he began appearing in low-budget independents in the late

1980s such as *Cyclone* (1987), *Beverly Hills Vamp* (1989), and *Haunting Fear* (1990), usually directed by the prolific Fred Olen Ray (who affectionately refers to Quarry simply as "Uncle Bob").

Being one of the few whites in the predominantly black cast of *Sugar Hill* caused a few problems for Robert Quarry (both on and off the set), even in the civil rights-conscious year of 1971. Just how far attitudes had *not* come was brought home to him one evening when he took his co-star to dinner.

"Marki [Bey] would never go out," remembered Quarry. "And I finally got her to go out to dinner with me one night. And she said, 'well, I don't want problems.' We walked into a restaurant, a very fashionable restaurant. And we walked in at six o'clock, because Marki wanted to eat early and go to bed. So we went in there and there wasn't a person in the room and they said, 'Do you have a reservation?' And she was now in her light skin and red hair. Only in the South would anybody have known that she was 'a black,' an Afro-American. I said 'We'd just like to have dinner.' And I could see her shrinking back—because she knew what it was. He wasn't going to seat us because, you know, black and white do not *go together* in Houston, Texas, even in 1972 or whenever the hell it was. I mean civil liberties were in and they no longer had segregated toilets and segregated theater seats or segregated anything, but they had their own *way* of segregating themselves. So I said, 'Excuse me a minute Marki, I want to talk to this man.' And I went and I said, 'Listen, what is this *shit* that you're giving me? Is it because the young lady with me is black?' And he said, 'Oh no, no, no.' And I said, 'I'll tell you what's up. I know a *lot* of people. You start screwing around with me with this shit and I promise you I'm calling every newspaper man and newspaper woman I know in this town and telling them what you've done.' 'Oh, we've got a table for you.' Well now by that time the evening was ruined for poor Marki. She never went out again, she stayed in the Holiday Inn and ate breakfast lunch and dinner there. It was just awful."

Though Quarry had spent several years in Houston with a respected theater troupe, he suddenly found himself *persona non grata*. "I was there making an all-black movie. And I had a lot of friends, very rich, very influential friends that I had made when I was there in 1960 [with the Alley Theater], ten years before. And they read 'Alley Theater actor returns to star in movie'--and it was called an 'All-Black Cast.' Well I think they were so afraid I was going to bring a *nigger* to lunch. I mean that was their attitude. Nobody called me, nobody asked me, nobody said, 'how are you.' They just *ignored* my being there since I was there under those circumstances. And it was just shabby."

Quarry ran into some racially oriented difficulties *on* the set as well. "Many of those people [who played the zombies and such] were local people they picked up there in Houston; they didn't use actors. So, of course, the black actors there hated me because I was calling them 'nigger.' I mean that was what the script did. Well, it's all right for a black to call a black nigger, but they were seeing a *white* guy doing this. And they didn't know from acting. They thought that was what I was like, that it was *my* doing. So we had a very nice actor named Charlie Robinson [who played 'Fabulous,' Morgan's right-hand man], who was then at the Alley Theater and who later was in the TV series *Night Court* and *Love and War*. Charlie was the one who had to straighten 'em all out. So he went to all these extras—I mean, I thought they were going to *kill* me, they started *at* me—after I'd been screaming, 'back you black bastards, you fuckin' coons,' or whatever the wonderful dialogue was, which as I said was perfectly all right to say if you were black but not for Mr. White Chops over here to be doing it. And he explained to them that it was just acting and that that was the part and what it was all about. So we settled down and it was all right."

"*Sugar Hill* was not a title I wanted" complained screenwriter Tim Kelly. "Sugar Hill was at one time the wealthiest area of Harlem, sort of the Beverly Hills of Harlem, and I thought that that title was kind of vague. I wanted something up there that said what it was all about—like *Black Voodoo*." Why AIP, a company famous for coming up with an exploitable title first and the movie second, would choose such a nondescript and unilluminating name as *Sugar Hill* for their new horror feature remains a mystery. (Had AIP co-founder Jim Nicholson still been onboard, this film would have undoubtedly sported a much more effective—and exploitable—moniker, since Nicholson was renowned in the industry for his ability to create catchy film titles.) One possible explanation is that AIP was trying to follow in the lucrative footsteps of their previous vengeful-female blaxploitation feature, *Coffy* (1973). (If "Coffy" was good then "Sugar" must be better?)

Even so, the company seemed to recognize their marketing error, for their publicity refers to the film "proving to all and sundry that Sugar Hill is a curvaceous female creature—and not the geographical location the term so connotes..." At least when AIP sold the film to television, they changed the title to *The Zombies of Sugar Hill* (still no great shakes, but at least it gives the viewer a clue as to content).

AIP urged their exhibitors to promote *Sugar Hill* with such diverse tactics as a "Reptile Lobby Display" ("obtain several snakes and place on display in your outer lobby with information pertaining to the picture and/or voodoo ritual"), a "Candy Bally" ("print labels reading, 'I'm Sugar Hill, Try Me!' and affix to small plastic bags of any kind of candy"), and an "Ouanga or Voodoo Charm" giveaway consisting of "small plastic bones in a bag."

Plastic trinkets aside, the film itself didn't disappoint its intended audience (though modern viewers don't fare so well). Thanks to some well-staged and atmospheric sequences, Robert Quarry's convincingly ruthless portrayal, and the genuinely frightening zombies, *Sugar Hill* still remains a fairly entertaining blast-from-the-past curiosity.

> I reviewed this excellent two-disc DVD documentary set for *Monsters from the Vault* magazine, but it, like much of filmmaker William Grefé's oeuvre, has become lost to the ages. Let's fix that…

THEY CAME FROM THE SWAMP: THE FILMS OF WILLIAM GREFÉ (2016)

"SNAKES! SHARKS! SHATNER! OH, MY!"

So announces the colorful flyer for this colorful new documentary from Ballyhoo Home Entertainment about the unsung godfather of Florida-based drive-in filmmaking, William Grefé. In the 1960s and '70s Grefé supplied Southern drive-ins (and, in some cases, cinemas around the country) with crowd-pleasing exploitation fare like the swampland double bill *Sting of Death* (the first—and only—film about a jellyfish-man!) and *Death Curse of Tartu*, the *Willard*esque snake-fright flick *Stanley*, and the *Willard*-meets-*Jaws* variation *Mako: The Jaws of Death*.

Before watching this documentary, I'd only seen a handful of Grefé's films. And while I'd enjoyed them to varying degrees (particularly the cheesy entertainment of the jellyfish-man delivering the *Sting of Death*, and the creepy-crawly ooginess of *Stanley*), I never thought of Grefé as being some kind of maverick auteur. Hell, I hardly ever thought of Grefé *at all*. But after getting to know the man and his swampy oeuvre through this thoroughly engaging overview of his career, I was eager to seek out a few more of his films.

Unpretentious, soft-spoken, self-effacing, patient, and basically a heck of a nice guy (according to those who worked with him), Grefé admittedly isn't the most dynamic of speakers. Fortunately, the stories he tells (such as one involving the disastrous meeting of a valuable 1000-year-old Chinese vase and a clumsy film crew) keeps interest high. And Daniel Griffith, *They Came from the Swamp*'s director/producer/photographer/editor, livens up Grefé's on-camera presence by interspersing pertinent comments and stories from a plethora of interviewees. Thankfully, apart from a few bon mots by film historian Chris Poggiali, and some general comments from later indy filmmakers Frank Henenlotter and Fred Olen Ray, the documentary keeps to actual Grefé personnel—from actors and contemporaries (like fellow exploitation pioneers David Friedman and H. G. Lewis), to cameramen, sound men and even Grefé's long-time script girl—making this a fascinatingly up-close-and-personal bio-doc.

Organized as a career overview, *They Came from the Swamp* charts Grefé's moviemaking year by year, beginning with 1963's *The Checkered Flag*, and going through *I Eat Your Skin* (which Grefé worked on as second unit director), *Racing Fever*, *Sting of Death*, *Death Curse of Tartu* (shot in just *seven days* in the Everglades), *The Devil's Sisters* (shot in 10), *The Wild Rebels*, *The Hooked Generation*, *The Naked Zoo* (starring Rita Hayworth), *Live and Let Die* (more second unit work, complete with gators), *Stanley*, *The Godmothers*, *Impulse* (starring William Shatner), *Mako: The Jaws of Death* (with Richard Jaeckel), *Whiskey Mountain* (his final film as director), and 1985's *Cease Fire* (as producer).

Through interviews and clips, augmented by some truly fascinating behind-the-scenes footage (someone seemingly *always* brought along an 8mm camera to his shoots), we learn such intriguing tidbits like how Christopher George, *not* Burt Reynolds, was the first choice to play the lead role in *Deliverance*; and how just before shooting was scheduled to start, Grefé simply transformed his script about stock-car racers into one about bikers when Roger Corman's *The Wild Angels* became a huge indy hit. (The result: *The Wild Rebels*.)

Augmenting the excellent documentary is a cornucopia of bonus features: The usual still gallery (with an *un*usually excellent assortment of behind-the-scenes photos), a trailer collection (covering most of Grefé's oeuvre), a tantalizing docu-short on Crown International (who aspired to be the "new AIP") that just begs to be expanded to feature length, a 10-minute "*Mako: Jaws of Death*" promo piece, and two Bacardi Rum industrial films directed by Grefé, including a seventeen-

DVD cover.

minute pirate-themed promo short called *Bacardi: The Mixable One* that stars... William Shatner! But the most gratifying extra of all is the complete, rare 1977 Grefé feature film *Whiskey Mountain*, starring Christopher George (the first time it's ever been issued on DVD). Yes, one of this two-disc set's many extras is a full feature film! Being a Christopher George fan (who can forget the backwoods exploitation classic *Grizzly?*) made me appreciate the icing on this *Whiskey* cake even more, as this heretofore obscure effort (shot in the same area as *Deliverance*) proved to be an entertaining—and sometimes hard-hitting—hicksploitation winner. Talk about bang for your buck...

Smoothly edited to keep things lively and interest high, and featuring some wonderful clips and behind-the-scenes footage, this exhaustive (but by no means exhausting—I could easily have continued on for twice its length) capsule of a fringe filmmaker remains both edifying (at least for those interested in vintage exploitation moviemaking) and entertaining. And like the best filmmaker documentaries, *They Came from the Swamp* makes one want to view more of this intrepid moviemaker's work.

> I breathed a little extra life into this essay (i.e. expanded it), which first saw print in *Cult Movies* magazine, issue 16 (Fall 1995).

THEY LIVE (1988)

"I have come here to chew bubblegum and kick ass, and I'm all out of bubblegum." –John Nada

"Imagine that the Reagan Revolution is run by aliens from outer space," suggested director/screenwriter John Carpenter (to interviewer Dennis Fischer) in describing his new twist on the aliens-among-us theme pioneered by films like 1956's *Invasion of the Body Snatchers* and 1957's *Enemy from Space* (both favorites of Carpenter's). "It's a kind of modern, '80s *Invasion of the Body Snatchers*, but slightly different in that you don't lose your humanity when you get taken over—or at least, you don't become physically different—all you're doing is selling out your values. There's no change, you just get rich. Everybody wants to get rich, right?"

From the opening in which the off-center title "THEY LIVE" becomes a bit of graffiti on a ghetto wall, it's obvious that Carpenter is going to give us a sci-fi/horror film with a little bit extra. In the first half-hour of *They Live* Carpenter treats us to a masterful bit of mood building as he introduces John Nada (Roddy Piper), an honest, hard-working regular Joe down on his luck who's come to the big city looking for work. Focusing on a modern-day shanty town location, Carpenter effectively establishes the down-and-out climate of Reaganomics woes that existed side-by side with the bright shiny skyscrapers of prosperity just over the hill. Nada ultimately discovers that our whole economic and political system is run by aliens who keep the human populace unawares and complacent (save for a select few—the "power elite") through the use of a sophisticated system of subliminal control. The ugly aliens, skull-like in appearance, seem normal to humans due to the use of a perception-altering beam transmitted through TV. Nada stumbles onto a small resistance movement and acquires specially made sunglasses that enable him to see the aliens and his environment for what they really are. The sight of a normal cityscape transformed into a sterile-looking forest of messages like "OBEY," "CONFORM," "MARRY AND REPOPULATE," and "WATCH TV" plastered everywhere is unnerving. Billboards, business signs, magazines, and product labels all contain these subliminal messages designed to keep the human race apathetic and productive for the alien entrepreneurs running the show. Even the dollar bill carries a message in bold black letters: "THIS IS YOUR GOD." These scenes cleverly touch on the social and political paranoia inherent in many Americans—the distrust of government and authority, and the loathing of being duped or manipulated—while at the same time making a caustic statement about the power of greed. "Basically, the aliens are Republicans," remarked Carpenter, revealing his particular view of politics in the eighties.

Carpenter pushes some emotional buttons in the viewer by showing how Everyman (in the persona of Piper) can buck the system, in this case an evil alien manipulation. Of course, such nonconformist defiance is not without cost, and Carpenter wisely avoids shooting the ending through rose-colored lenses. The denouement is not downbeat, however, but neither is it neatly wrapped up in a bright tidy package.

The middle portion of the film, in which Nada tries to convince first TV station employee Holly (Meg Foster) and later fellow construction worker Frank (Keith David) of the nefarious conspiracy, drags somewhat. The sequence in which Nada has to fight his doubting co-worker in order to convince him to put on the revealing sunglasses, for instance, goes on far too long (seven-and-a-half minutes!). The seemingly endless bout of fisticuffs quickly becomes both ridiculous and

The alien-run Reaganomics world of They Live *(1988).*

tiresome, making one wish Nada would just hurry up and beat the guy senseless so he can place the glasses on his face. (According to Piper, Carpenter "wanted the longest fight scene in cinema history" and had his star watch John Wayne in *The Quiet Man* for inspiration.) The sequence is obviously a showcase for Piper's big-time-wrestling talents, since Piper was known as "Rowdy Roddy Piper" on the professional wrestling circuit when not acting in films.

Piper, not the most subtle of performers (see him in *Hell Comes to Frogtown* for some painfully broad histrionics), is here kept in check (fistfights aside) and on the whole does well. Some of the dialogue, however, proves beyond him. While Eastwood or Bronson can pull off lines like "Life's a bitch, and she's in heat," they sound forced coming from Piper. But these are fairly minor gripes. Carpenter throws in a few genre in-jokes to lighten the load, such as showing *The Monolith Monsters* on TV and making the alien walkie-talkies the same ectoplasmic detection devices seen in *Ghostbusters*. Carpenter again contributes an effective musical score (which he did for his first megahit, *Halloween*), which greatly adds to the feel of the film. And the movie's final 30 minutes, when Nada and Frank start shooting aliens and searching for the secret signal transmitter, offers great, non-stop action. As a political paranoia thriller *and* a shoot 'em up sci-fi actioner, *They Live* satisfies on both counts.

> *Filmfax* magazine *Tormented* its readers with this overview in 1997 (issue 61).

TORMENTED (1960)

"Flesh he couldn't feel…lips he couldn't touch…but a vengeance that haunted him to death!" promised the poster for this offbeat entry in the Bert I. Gordon cannon. Gordon (Mr. B.I.G. himself) took time off from filling the screen with huge humans (*The Amazing Colossal Man*, 1957; *The Cyclops*, 1957; *War of the Colossal Beast*, 1958), enormous arachnids (*Earth Vs. the Spider*, 1958), and gigantic grasshoppers (*Beginning of the End*, 1957) to make this small-scale but effective ghost story. No big bugs or mammoth anthropoids here, just Richard Carlson and one (normal-sized) vengeful ghost.

From the opening noirish narration in which (over moody shots of the island setting and its rocky beaches at twilight) Richard Carlson intones, "I once loved this island, this is where I found peace and quiet … but when the night wind rises and the fingers of fog steal in, they say you can hear voices—they say it's the dead growing restless and calling to the living," you know that this is not going to be the typical Bert I. Grotesque.

Carlson plays jazz pianist Tom Stuart, who's about to marry a wealthy young socialite, Meg (Lugene Sand-

Tom Stewart (Richard Carlson) is Tormented *by the ghost of his spurned lover in one of the few Bert I. Gordon movies that lacks a giant anything. (Mexican lobby card)*

ers). Tom's former mistress, Vi (Juli Reding), comes to his beach front cottage and threatens to expose their less than acceptable affair if he doesn't come back to her. Fate intervenes and Vi falls to her death from atop a lighthouse. However, Tom *could* have saved her, and Vi's vengeful spirit ("Nobody will have you but me") periodically pops up to prey on his guilty conscience.

The character of Tom Stuart is quite likable, and for the most part you're on his side as he's forced to contend with the likes of ghostly footprints, disembodied hands, a talking head, and bodies that turn to seaweed in his grasp. The ever-dependable Richard Carlson does a fine job playing an essentially good man who is pushed to the limit—and cracks. Carlson's genial manner quickly gives way to tortured preoccupation as his effective portrayal fully lives up to the picture's title. When pushed even further (by a ghost no less), he knowingly embraces the very crime he has been trying to deny (murder). "None of it could be helped—" Carlson forlornly states near the end of the film, before sadly adding "—except by me," realizing too late that he and he alone must be responsible for his own actions. Throughout the movie, the viewer sympathizes with Carlson and so becomes more involved with this story than with the typical Bert I. Gordon slice of cheese. And though the story here is an old one, it still carries impact—*and* a message: You can't escape your own conscience (even if it needs a little prodding from beyond the grave).

Frequent low-budget sci-fi scripter George Worthington Yates (*Earth vs. the Spider*, 1958; *Frankenstein 1970*, 1958; *War of the Colossal Beast*, 1958; many others) delivers what may be his strongest screenplay, creating a taut, effective script complete with believable dialogue and tragic situations, such as placing Tom in the painful position of having to kill Sandy, his fiancée's pre-teen sister whom he genuinely loves, because she accidentally saw him commit a murder. (Sandy is played by Gordon's own daughter, Susan, who does a good job in a potentially annoying role.) It's a situation distressing not only for Tom, but for the audience as well. Thanks to Carlson's empathetic portrayal and Yates' engaging screenplay, *Tormented* becomes Bert I. Gordon's most involving—and effective—film.

Gordon himself does much to make *Tormented* a potent little thriller. He employs some subtly creepy touches to indicate the presence of the sinister specter. When Tom embraces Meg in the lighthouse, for instance, a cold shadow suddenly envelopes the couple and Meg wonderingly smells a woman's perfume. Later, when Tom defies the ghostly Vi, a sudden gust of wind ruffles the lighthouse cobwebs to show the spirit's displeasure.

At the wedding scene, the church doors suddenly blow open of their own accord. As the camera moves down the church aisle, the flowers placed along the pews abruptly wilt when the camera glides past. Likewise, a gust of supernatural wind turns the pages of the minister's book from the marriage ceremony to the "Burial of the Dead" passage. Gordon also utilizes some off-kilter camera angles for his actor/reaction shots that enhance the creepy feel of the scene.

Of course, Bert being Bert, he couldn't stay subtle long, and soon superimpositions are running rampant across the screen. Gordon flirts with the ludicrous when he (for some inexplicable reason) has Vi's (superimposed) disembodied head taunting Tom from atop an end table. Though Carlson's sincerity nearly saves the rather laughable scene, it's completely spoiled when he picks up what is obviously a cheap mannequin head topped by a blonde wig. Fortunately, Yates' script follows this with a wonderfully tense scene in which Tom wraps the harpy's head in a cloth (while all the while it chants "Tom Stewart killed me" over and over) and rushes out of the house only to drop the bundle on the stairs. The gruesome package bounces down the steps to stop at the feet of a sea tramp intent on blackmailing Tom. When the panicked Tom wrestles the bundle away from the intruder, the incriminating cloth bursts open only to reveal a wadded-up bunch of flowers the landlady had brought by earlier.

As usual in a B.I.G. production like this, Gordon and his wife, Flora, did the "Special Visual Effects" themselves. Since this is a ghost film, however, Gordon's semi-transparent process work looks just fine for the ethereal phantom (unlike for his other films which feature more corporeal menaces; in fact, in Gordon's *The Amazing Colossal Man* the titular titan often looks more like *The Amazing* Transparent *Man*).

Apart from a few (un)special effects like the mannequin head, the film also suffers occasionally from some weak performances, such as Lugene Sanders as Meg, who comes across more like an immature spoiled child than a desirable young woman. From her tiresome and rather shrewish demeanor, we can only believe that Tom is marrying Meg primarily for her money.

The story's setting (a small island community) adds to the ominous tone of the film. The lonely derelict lighthouse, the windy boardwalk, and the crashing waves, all effectively photographed by Ernest Laszlo in melancholy hues of gray, create a brooding atmosphere in which to tell the story. (Of course, no doubt the picture was shot in black and white for budgetary rather than aesthetic reasons.)

Sadly, Bert soon returned to his first love (gigantism) with towering turkeys like *Village of the Giants* (1965), *Food of the Gods* (1976), and *Empire of the Ants* (1977). Though no classic, *Tormented* remains Bert I. Gordon's most intelligent film; and, while not his "biggest," it is definitely his best.

Cult Movies magazine graciously allowed me to visit the famous *Tower* for issue 16 (Fall 1995).

TOWER OF LONDON (1962)

"DON'T COME ALONE: YOU'LL NEED SOMEONE TO HANG ONTO WHEN YOU COME FACE TO FACE WITH THE BLOOD-CHILLING TERROR IN THE TOWER!" –poster blurb

Things in Hollywood had definitely changed in the near-quarter century since the original 1939 version of *Tower of London*—including big-screen terror. By the late 1950s and early '60s, the classic Teutonic-style horror spearheaded by Universal had largely given way to invading aliens and mutant bugs. Golden Horror icon Bela Lugosi was dead, while the two aging horror stars of the original *Tower of London*, Boris Karloff and Basil Rathbone, found themselves appearing in puerile productions like *The Black Sleep* (1956), *Frankenstein 1970* (1958) and *The Magic Sword* (1962)—when they could get movie work at all.

One *Tower of London* alumnus, however, found himself a hot horror property since his watershed year of 1958—which saw Vincent Price starring in both *The Fly* and *House on Haunted Hill*. In rapid succession, Price confirmed his "Master of Menace" title with appearances in films like *Return of the Fly* (1959) and *The Tingler* (1959), and the Edgar Allan Poe entries *House*

The everything-but-the-torture-chamber-sink artwork for Roger Corman's 1962 historical horror Tower of London.

of Usher* (1960), *The Pit and the Pendulum* (1961) and *Tales of Terror* (1962). Indicative of his rise to terror prominence was Price's advancement from supporting player (Clarence) in the 1939 version to lead villain (Richard) when Roger Corman took his low-budget stab at historical horror by remaking Universal's *Tower of London*.

First announced in February 1962 as *A Dream of Kings*, the film began shooting in mid-March. "The Tower of London, a monument to the corruption of the soul..." begins the narrator (omnipresent 1950s and '60s voice-over artist Paul Frees) at the film's opening. What follows is a 15th-century tale of murder and ghosts and conscience, in which Richard III (Vincent Price) kills his brother, his political rivals, his nephews and (accidentally) even his loving wife. The ghosts of his victims appear to Richard (or at least are conjured up out of his own guilt-riddled mind) to bedevil his existence and ultimately lead him to his death at the battle of Bosworth Field.

As might be expected, Corman's version comes nowhere close to the 1939 film in production quality; but then the earlier entry was a relatively high-priced effort ($580,000) from a major studio, whereas Corman's project was a low-budget (less than $200,000—twenty-five years later) independent effort. (Corman even borrowed some of the original's battle footage to flesh out his minimalist fight scenes.) The tones of the two films are miles apart as well, the earlier variation being an historical melodrama with horrific trappings while the latter focused on the themes of madness, guilt and death—more in the vein of Edgar Allan Poe than medieval history (undoubtedly intentional, considering the personnel involved).

Corman's proved the more intimate of the two, with the weight of the film resting on the humped shoulders of Vincent Price. The role of Richard is a fascinating one, for he is a man who knows what is right and what is wrong but who chooses the path of evil anyway. "Is it what men do that darkens the sky, or do the skies blacken the souls of men?" asks this reflective villain. This makes Richard a much more intriguing figure, one who is not totally evil but who embraces it nonetheless and therefore orchestrates his own destruction (it's almost a trial run for Price's portrayal in the later *Masque of the Red Death*). Richard has a conscience, and out of it he creates his own guilt-ridden hell by conjuring up the ghosts of his victims to torment him. As a morality play, the message could not be clearer—no one, no matter how corrupt, can truly escape their own conscience. And in the end, despite the somber, often brutal trappings, the film delivers an upbeat message—that people, despite their savagery and cruelty, are basically good, and this goodness will triumph in the end, whether it be by love...or by self-punishment meted out by one's own mind.

Praiseworthy missives aside, this *Tower* is built on shaky ground. The script is structured so that the film will rise or fall with the performance of Price (who is the focus of nearly every scene). Though at times Price sublimely points the production heavenwards, it never quite takes wing—due to that actor's uneven playing. Price (who began his career on the stage) sometimes acts as if he were back treading the boards, playing to the balcony's back row. He indulges in overblown arm-waving, lip trembling and histrionics that lessen the impact that a more subtle performance could have generated. The blame in part should rest with Corman, never noted as an actor's director, who failed to properly rein in the actor. ("He was very creative," commented Price of his director [to interviewer Lawrence French], "but more concerned with the story and effects than the actors.") Price provides a larger-than-life portrayal, sprinkling his wild-eyed, open-mouthed, full-blooded delivery with moments of subtlety and emotion. It's an enjoyable performance without doubt, but an uneven one.

1962's *Tower of London* is still an entertaining movie, filled with intrigue and shock and bizarre situations. More importantly, something worthwhile lurks beneath the garish surface. "He escaped the headsman's block, but he could not escape his own conscience." At least it's something to think about.

CHAPTER 6
MEXICAN MONSTER MOVIES

Ever since I caught my first glimpse of a Mexican horror movie on *Commander USA's Groovy Movies* in the mid–1980s, I've had a soft spot in my heart (head?) for this particular south-of-the-border brand of wackiness—in which living mummies stalk forth from their Aztec tombs, "crying women" fly into the night looking like desiccated corpses, 400-year-old sorcerers return to earth (via a passing comet!) to become brain-sucking monsters, and vampires don masks to wrestle Our Heroes in the ring (and then transform into werewolves when *un*-masked!).

The early 2000s saw a (sort of) legitimization of these gothic-styled Tijuana Terrors when American companies like BCI, CasaNegra, and Rise Above Entertainment began releasing them to DVD in English-friendly formats. Jim Clatterbaugh, *Monsters from the Vault* magazine's dedicated publisher/editor, shared my love of spicy cinema and commissioned me to review a number of Mexican classics (and not-so's), Aztec Mummy movies, and Santo imports. So grab a ringside seat for a flurry of Mexi-monster movie action…

> Much to Mexican Monster Movie lovers' delight, the first decade of the current century saw a flurry of south-of-the-border "classics" finally make their way north in DVD form. I was privileged to chronical this welcome cinematic emigration in *Monsters from the Vault* magazine (this piece seeing print in issue 24, Winter 2008).

MEXICAN MONSTERS INVADE AMERICA! FANS REJOICE!

Mexican horror movies of the 1950s and '60s are something of a throwback to the Universal Gothics of the 1930s and '40s in that they seemed determined to recapture the dark, brooding atmosphere of those earlier classics. But far from being mere rehashes, this subset of horror cinema possesses its own unique charm, due not only to the Latin legends and sensibilities it explores, but to its amazing graveyard ambiance coupled with the more gruesome shocks that the less restrictive time period allowed.

We primarily have two men to thank for bringing us a bevy of Mexi-monsters: actor-producer Abel Salazar, whose Cinematografica A.B.S.A. company more or less *created* the Gothic-styled Mexican horror movie in the late 1950s and early '60s, and theater owner-cum-producer K. Gordon Murray, who purchased the American rights to Salazar's movies (and numerous others), dubbed them into English, and exhibited them in a series of Saturday matinees before (and sometimes *after*) sending them off to television (via AIP-TV).

For years, fans could only obtain their south-of-the-border horror fix via dupey-looking, badly-dubbed television prints sourced from soft, cut-to-ribbons 16mm reels. But thanks to the fine folks at CasaNegra, this sorry state of affairs has changed, heralded by their inaugural dual release of *The Curse of the Crying Woman* and *The Witch's Mirror*, and continued with their subsequent issues of *The Brainiac*, *The Black Pit of Dr. M*, the double-feature disc *The Vampire/The Vampire's Coffin*, and the long-sought-after *The Man and the Monster* and *The Living Coffin*. Each of these films have received loving treatment in both the visual (gorgeous prints) and audio (restored Spanish-language dialogue, accompanied by excellent subtitles) departments.

THE MEXI-MONSTER CRYING GAME

For their debut offering, CasaNegra chose one of the best entries in the Mexican horror sweepstakes—director Rafael Baledon's *The Curse of the Crying Woman* (which premiered theatrically in the U.S. in 1969 as a co-feature with the delirious *The Brainiac*). Shot during the last two weeks of November 1961, *Curse*'s story centers on "La Llorona" (the Crying Woman), a prominent figure in Mexican folklore. In the film, a sinister woman summons her estranged niece, along with the niece's oblivious husband, to her isolated mansion, revealing that she is a descendent and follower of "the Wailing Witch." With the aid of her ugly, murderous, Ygor-like servant (complete with stiff neck, limping gait and a reference to being saved from the gallows), the evil aunt intends to use her young niece in a plan to resurrect the legendary witch and thus cement her own diabolical powers and immortality.

Given its creepy soundstage forest and (Spanish-style) castle (complete with cobwebbed, rat-infested interiors that'd make any Universal art director proud), and low-key lighting and evocative photography (courtesy of cinematographer Joseph Oritiz Ramos), *Curse* looks the part of a genuine Gothic horror. It also contains a number of arresting images. When exercising her evil powers, for instance, actress Rita Macedo wears appliances over her eyes that transforms them into large, shiny, black orbs—a simple but disturbing effect. In the film's most startling scene, the witch flies, bat-like, directly at the camera, only to abruptly change from a hideous corpse-like crone into the slightly less repulsive visage of Macedo with her oversized, blackened eyes.

Producer Abel Salazar cast himself as the hero (the husband); and to play his new bride (the niece), he chose Venezuelan-born actress Rosa (Rosita) Arenas—which wasn't much of a stretch, since the two were married in real life. Arenas also played the heroine in *The Witch's Mirror*, *Face of the Screaming Werewolf* and a trio of Aztec Mummy movies. Keeping it all in the family, villainess Rita Macedo's real-life daughter, Julissa del Llano (who went on to become a popular movie actress herself), has a small role as the young girl in the pre-credits sequence who's crushed under a coach wheel (a brutally shocking scene).

For years, fans of Mexican horror have had to make do with K. Gordon Murray's scratchy, faded television prints that sported awkward dubbing and stilted dialogue. CasaNegra's DVD of *The Curse of the Crying Woman* has caused Mexi-horror devotees everywhere to burst into a spontaneous Mexican Hat Dance (or maybe that was just me). The absolutely flawless film print makes every cobweb and rat hair on the impressive Gothic sets crystal clear (of course, it also makes the use of much younger stunt doubles in the climactic fight scene painfully obvious). And it is an absolute revelation to hear the original Spanish dialogue while reading the accompanying subtitles. Gone are the dubbing's impossibly banal tones and convoluted English, replaced by the original actors' voices and mellifluous speech. (For those nostalgic for the robotic tonalities we've all associated with this film lo these many years, CasaNegra thoughtfully included Murray's English-dubbed track as well.) As the icing on this Mexi-cake, CasaNegra offers a poster and still gallery; a booklet on "The Legend of La Llorona" by *Entertainment Weekly*'s Peter Landau; a "Loteria" game card; an informative text essay on filmmaker Rafael Baledon by Mexican film expert David Wilt; and a commentary audio track by Michael Luizza. Unfortunately, this last proves disappointingly sporadic—though appreciative—with only the occasional tidbit of information found amongst the obvious comments on the action, cinematography and direction. Nevertheless, this DVD release of *The Curse of the Crying Woman* affords us a pristine presentation of the apex of Mexican horror cinema; and, as such, there'll be no *Crying* over this *Woman*—unless they're tears of joy.

THROUGH THE LATINO LOOKING GLASS

Along with *The Curse of the Crying Woman*, CasaNegra's inaugural offering was yet another top-flight Mexican horror film, the intriguingly bizarre *The Witch's Mirror* (filmed in 1960 and released in the U.S. in 1968), an everything-but-the-graveyard-sink amalgam that horror film lovers can't help but appreciate for its amazing ambiance and sheer audacity.

After a famous surgeon poisons his wife, his housekeeper (a witch—who even turns into a black cat at one point!) vows revenge, since the murdered woman was her goddaughter. Later, the doctor remarries, but the housekeeper uses her witch's mirror to summon the ghost of the first wife, who torments and finally disfigures the new bride. The doctor commits murder to obtain "raw materials" that will restore his new wife's beauty, but the vengeful spirit intervenes, and the doctor meets his just fate.

The Witch's Mirror seems somewhat (ahem) reflective of a Barbara Steele Italian horror movie—but, admittedly, without Steele's arresting presence or Bava's/Margheriti's/Freda's artistic touches. Even so, there's much in this *Mirror* to admire. What makes this one stand out is its creepy Gothic atmosphere (the doc lives in a candle-lit castle and frequents a particularly eerie graveyard) and syntheses of various tried-and-true horror tropes. Apart from the witchcraft angle (including an appearance by Satan himself—as played by a shadow puppet) and the menace of a vengeful ghost, the movie offers elements of *Eyes Without a Face* (the doctor stealing cadavers and murdering women to obtain skin grafts), *Rebecca* (the new wife tormented by the memory—and ghost—of the old), and, amazingly, *Mad Love*! This crops up in a subplot involving the wife's horribly burned hands. To correct this, the mad medico transplants—in a shockingly gruesome scene for the time—a murdered girl's hands onto the arms of his wife. The ghost, however, intervenes and replaces the fresh hands with her own ghostly members. The new wife, now with the hands of the old wife, finds that her new limbs have a life of their own... Wow. And you have to admire a movie that casts a Satan-worshipping witch as the Good Guy!

Like with their *Curse of the Crying Woman* release, CasaNegra has managed to find near-pristine film elements, making it look like the picture was printed yesterday rather than nearly half a century ago. They also restored the original Spanish dialogue track (along with excellent subtitles), while still including the option of the more familiar K. Gordon Murray-produced dubbing track (for those who might wax nostalgic for toneless speech and awkward dialogue). Extras include a CasaNegra Loteria game card; a text essay on moviemaker Chano Urueta; cast and crew biographies; and a highly enjoyable audio commentary by IVTV founder Frank Coleman, who is nearly as informative as he is enthusiastic about what he's seeing on-screen, offering up interesting tidbits on the principal actors and filmmakers, including director Urueta, producer Abel Salazar, and even importer K. Gordon Murray.

CasaNegra deserves the grateful thanks (and accompanying dollars) of every horror movie fan for offering us the opportunity to see *The Witch's Mirror* in all its reflective glory.

OF BRAINS AND BOWLS

Here comes the Poster Boy for Mexican horror—like you've never seen him before! If there's one title in the Mexi-monster canon that brings a smile to the face of Latino-horror lovers everywhere, it's *The Brainiac*. Shot in two weeks in February of 1961, *The Brainiac* is something special. The story begins with Baron Vitalius (Abel Salazar, who also produced the film), a "sorcerer and heretic," being burned at the stake during the Inquisition. Engulfed in superimposed flames, Vitalius looks up and sees a comet moving across the heavens (a ludicrously unrealistic painting) and utters this curse to his executioners: "I shall return to your world in 300 years when that [comet] completes its cycle and is once again in these latitudes....I will kill each and every one of your descendants and I shall expunge your foul lineage from this earth." And he means it. Suddenly it's 1961 and the comet is spotted. Cut to a soundstage landscape, upon which drops a huge papier-mâché rock (conjuring up images of the oft-used "10-Ton-Weight" gag from a Monty Python skit). The comet fragment dissolves to reveal...the Brainiac!

Possessing an oversized, puffy head that inflates and deflates for horrific emphasis; a long, pointed nose; an even longer 12-inch forked tongue; and lobster pincers for hands, this is one of the most farcically fun monsters ever to suck brains. And that is just what he does with that unwieldy proboscis of his, sucking his victims' gray matter out through their necks. Moreover, he can change into human guise to hypnotize and lure his victims into range. Clever Brainiac that he is, he also keeps a bowlful of brains in a locked cabinet, which he can daintily spoon out whenever in the mood for a between-meal snack.

The cast's deadly seriousness only increases the unintentional hilarity, especially Salazar as the brain-sucking Baron. (Among the Baron's victims are Germán Robles, *The Vampire* himself, and Ariadne Welter, sister of *The Devil's Hand* star Linda Christian.) "[The on-set mood was] serious, very serious!" recalled Robles. "But when the director said, 'cut,' everybody laughed! But they didn't approach the film as a joke—they were very serious about it, treated it with respect."

If the film's boffo plot doesn't grab you, how about an endless array of painted paper backdrops? *The Brainiac* features absolutely *no* outdoor shots; it is completely studio-bound. Location shooting consists of having cast members stand in front of various blown-up photographic backdrops of an observatory, bridge, night sky, cityscape, etc. (Even Roger Corman, on his two-and-a-half-day wonder *The Little Shop of Horrors*, went outside to shoot once in a while!)

Further dubious assets include some wonderful "bad" dubbing-track dialogue ("I wish they'd find some way to control the subject of Man's studies—a maniac with a lot of knowledge is a threat!"), laughable effects, name problems (with characters alternately calling him *Baron* Vitalius and *Count* Vitalius) and a pair of inspectors who inexplicably show up with flame throwers to wrap it all up.

And most importantly, when the title terror is on-screen, it's no-holds-barred guffaws for bad cinema lovers everywhere—sort of a *Plan Nine from South-of-the-Border*. In the right frame of mind, even those not enamored of "golden turkeys" can enjoy this one-of-a-kind imported oddity—particularly now, since CasaNegra has done another bang-up job by offering *The Brainiac* in pristine condition in its original form (in Spanish with English subs). Of course, this may be one film you'll want to watch *twice*—once in its original Spanish, and again with the English dubbing option thoughtfully included by CasaNegra, so as not to miss the myriad aural howlers sprinkled throughout Murray and Co.'s delirious dub-job. Extras include a lively, appreciative commentary by Kirb Pheeler, creator of the Brainiac Interactive Presskit (also featured on the disc); biographies of the principals; a text essay; a poster and still gallery; and a U.S. radio spot.

Boffo drive-in herald for the boffo (but hugely entertaining) combo The Brainiac and The Curse of the Crying Woman.

THE PIT AND THE MEXI-MONSTER

One of the few Mexican horrors that crossed the border *without* the help of K. Gordon Murray (it was released Stateside by United Producers Releasing Organization, who generally handled nudie-cutie fare), *The Black Pit of Dr. M* has gone unseen for nearly four decades. Thanks to CasaNegra, *Misterios de Ultratumba* (*Dr. M*'s original-language title), one of the best Mexi-horrors of the 1960s, is now back in circulation (in its Spanish-language/English-subtitled form anyway, as the English dubbing track has remained lost).

"Take equal parts of an insane violinist, a doctor experimenting in black magic, and a crazed Gypsy woman, and shake well in an insane asylum, and the result has to be one of the most hair-raising suspense stories ever filmed." While the hyperbolic "hair-raising" adjective employed by this American pressbook article may not be the most accurate descriptor, insert "unusual," "eerie," or just plain "weird" and you'd be right on the money. The film opens with sanatorium head Dr. Masali (Rafael Bertrand) reminding his dying colleague, Dr. Aldama (Antonio Raxel), of the pact they'd made a year earlier: "The one who dies first must find the way so that the other one could go and come back from the other world without dying." Masali uses a medium to contact Aldama's spirit, who warns Masali of "the horrible price to pay." Masali remains adamant, however, and Aldama's ghost sets in motion a chain of events that ends in a tangled web of death, resurrection, madness and horrific irony.

The film's striking set design and art direction (all misty courtyards, Gothic-styled stone archways, and heavy ornate furniture), aided by some evocative camerawork and shadowy lighting, establishes an uncanny atmosphere so thick you'd need a headsman's axe to cut through it. During an opening burial sequence, for instance, the backlighting of the surrounding woods combines with the blazing foreground torchlight at the gravesite to give the proceedings a decidedly hellish cast—as if caught between two worlds. Director Fernando Méndez (who also helmed *The Vampire* and *The Vampire's Coffin*) and cinematographer Victor Herrera (*The Vampire's Coffin*, *Castle of the Monsters*) takes us further into this macabre milieu via a disquieting ground-level camera shot of the pallbearers lowering the coffin into the grave, before cutting to a close-in overhead shot of the casket disappearing into the dark hole—emphasizing the isolation, fear and (ironically, as it turns out) finality of death. Later, shadowy movements and subtle changes in lighting herald the appearance of the supernatural, so that even when Aldama's ghost is visually absent from the screen, its preternatural presence remains. Additionally, the gruesome acid-burn makeup on the doctor's assistant (horribly scarred while trying to subdue a violent patient)—reminiscent of Lionel Atwill's twisted, ruined visage from *Mystery of the Wax Museum* (1933)—hammers home the horror on a more visceral level. All these technical elements artistically combine to brilliantly establish the film's macabre mood and enhance the complex, eventful and otherworldly story unfolding.

Unfortunately, this *Pit* is not completely devoid of, er…pitfalls. The ingénue and nominal leading man (Mapita Cortes and Gaston Santos) make for a vapid and uninteresting pair, while the "lovers' destiny" angle seems mawkish and out-of-place. Likewise, the sudden shot from cupid's arrow into Dr. M's bosom appears so abruptly that it screams Lazy Plot Device. And the finale devolves into a rather standard mad villain moment that appears disappointingly mundane after the previous 70 minutes of macabre originality. But even with these few minor missteps, a viewer would do well to gaze into this *Pit*, as it offers a startlingly unique and creepily atmospheric look into the strange and wonderful world of Mexican horror cinema.

Apart from the gorgeous print of the "original uncut version" of the film, CasaNegra's DVD offers plenty of extras, including a photo essay on Mexi-monster movie imports; an audio commentary by Frank Coleman; biographies of the principals; a *Black Pit of Dr. M* progressive rock video (by Coleman's band); a poster and still gallery; the original Mexican theatrical trailer; a CasaNegra Loteria game card; and, most impressively, the original 1961 English-language continuity script (allowing a glimpse into the original English-dubbed version).

DRACULA ON A HACIENDA

This is the one that started it all. In 1957, Mexican actor-producer Abel Salazar (who, sadly, died of Alzheimer's in 1995) formed a new film company named A.B.S.A. (the first two initials of his name, with the "S A" being the Spanish equivalent of "Inc."), with the intention of putting a Latino twist on the Universal style of horror movies produced in the 1930s and '40s. "There was a period during which…the important [Hollywood film] companies were weak," explained Salazar to *Filmfax*'s David Wilt, "but there was a company that was very small in comparison with the others, Universal. I asked myself why Universal had the profits they had; it was because of the monster films and Deanna Durbin. They were what sustained Uni-

Pressbook for The Black Pit of Dr. M, *one of the few Mexi-horrors that made it north of the border* without *the help of K. Gordon Murray.*

versal. Therefore, I decided to make a horror film, and I chose *El Vampiro* [*The Vampire*]. I basically made Dracula set on a Mexican hacienda." The film's success led to a string of eight Salazar-produced horrors filmed over the next four years, several of which starred Salazar himself: *The Vampire*'s sequel, *The Vampire's Coffin* (also 1957); *The Man and the Monster* (1958); *The Curse of the Crying Woman* (1962); *The Living Head* (1963); and the (in)famous *The Brainiac* (1961; in which Salazar abandoned his usual role of hero to play the title monster). Salazar's producer-only genre credits include *World of the Vampires* and *The Witch's Mirror* (both 1960). All eight of Salazar's horror films were released Stateside in the mid-to-late 1960s by K.Gordon Murray's Trans-International Films.

The Vampire opens as a large box of earth from Hungary arrives at the small Mexican town of Sierra Negra. Also arriving in Sierra Negra is the heroine, Martha (Ariadna Welter), there to visit her sick aunt, co-owner (with her brother and sister) of "the Sycamores" hacienda. Ten years previously, a mysterious Count Duval (German Robles) moved nearby, and now no one will come near the Sycamores. Duval is actually Count Lavud, a vampire, who intends to wrest the Sycamores from its rightful owners and resurrect his vampiric brother. Standing in his way is Martha and her newfound paramour, Henry (Abel Salazar), a young psychiatrist secretly summoned to the Sycamores to assess the mental condition of the ailing aunt.

"They really tried to capture the style, the mood of the old-fashioned horror movies," explained leading lady Ariadne Welter to interviewer Paul Parla. "They kept talking about Bela Lugosi; he was the model for the part of the vampire."

In *The Vampire*, director Fernando Méndez aided by cinematographer Rosalio Solano, captures the "old-fashioned horror movie mood" beautifully. Through its well-framed photography (a funeral procession filmed at a distance through an archway creates a forlorn tableau) and moody lighting (Lavud suddenly appears by stepping out of a misty shaft of moonlight), not to mention some of the most impressive cobwebs seen outside of a classic Universal, *The Vampire* simply drips Gothic ambiance. Evocative (and *frisson*-inducing) images abound, such as pinpoint lighting making the Vampire's staring eyes appear to glow in the blackness (an effect borrowed from—and improving upon—Universal's *Dracula*), or one low-angle shot in which the wind swirls the mist behind a statuesque, black-clad vampiress, a cruel smile on her lips and an unhealthy gleam in her wide eyes.

All the players acquit themselves admirably, from the easy-mannered, likable Salazar as the skeptical hero, to Welter as the confused and vulnerable heroine who finds inner strength when needed, to Carmen Montejo as the vampirized aunt, full of dark intensity, to the crazed "good" aunt whose hollow-eyed anxiety reveals both terror and determination. Then there's Germán Robles as Count Lavud. His penetrating gaze, haughty manner, and fierce and swift attacks offer up the best of both worlds—the worlds of Universal's Bela Lugosi and Hammer's Christopher Lee. Ironically, *The Vampire* was made a year *before* Lee donned the cape for the first time in *Horror of Dracula*. (Robles claims that Lee told a mutual friend that Lee patterned *his* Count after Robles' portrayal! This seems unlikely, however, since Lee would have had little opportunity to see *The Vampire* prior to his work on *Horror of Dracula*, particularly since *El Vampiro* wasn't even seen in its English-language version until six years later.) Though Robles doesn't quite measure up to the imposing presence of either, combining the look and intensity of Lugosi (even wearing a near-identical penguin suit) with the ferocity of Lee serves *The Vampire* well.

Ironically, Robles was not the first choice as the Vampire. Salazar originally hired well-known Mexican character actor Carolos Lopez Moctezuma to play Lavud, but (as quoted by David Wilt in *Filmfax* magazine) decided "something wasn't right. The story was ready, we were ready to start, yet I was asking myself, what is it? Then I looked at American cinema again, and you know what is successful? The unknown actor! Lopez Moctezuma invariably had to be Lopez Moctezuma *before* he was 'the Vampire.' I talked to him and said, 'I'll pay off your contract because I made a mistake; I have to find an unknown actor.' Someone told me to go to a [certain] theater. I went [there, spotted Robles] and said, 'He is the Vampire!'"

By his own account, the Spanish-born Robles thoroughly enjoyed this, his first starring role. ("We had a tremendous amount of fun doing these films," agreed co-star Welter, referring to both *The Vampire* and its sequel, *The Vampire's Coffin*.) But the tight three-week shoot sometimes proved wearying. "There was a scene where I had to climb back into my coffin and close the lid over me," Robles told Parla. "So, I did the scene, but I wasn't aware of the fact that this was the last shot of the day. So, there I am, lying in this coffin, and I'm very tired. [Director] Fernando Méndez calls it a 'wrap,' and everyone left the set to go to dinner. At the restaurant, everyone asked Fernando, 'Where's Germán?' It suddenly dawned on him, and he ran back to the studio.

When he opened the coffin, there I was, in a deep sleep!"

Of course, this cinematic Gothic castle has its share of cracks. The often banal-sounding dubbing on the American release version does the cast no favors (thankfully, we no longer have to put up with this, as CasaNegra has restored the original Spanish language track and provided excellent subtitles). Also, some of the special effects prove either obvious and simple (the vampires abruptly appear and disappear in a crude stop-the-camera-I-wanna-get-off effect), or downright simple-minded (the ungainly and unconvincing flying rubber bats would be right at home in a Monogram movie from two decades earlier). But the engrossing story, adept playing, and wonderfully atmospheric ambiance set *The Vampire* astride the pinnacle of south-of-the-border horror cinema.

Released in Mexico in 1957, *El Vampiro* premiered theatrically in the U.S. on March 2, 1968, in Jacksonville, Florida, as a co-feature for *The Curse of the Doll People*. This came nearly four years *after The Vampire* first aired on television in 1964! (K. Gordon Murray—a pioneer in cinematic recycling...)

As with all of CasaNegra's Mexi-monster releases to date, *The Vampire* looks amazing, like it just stepped out of its coffin (or film can) for the first time. Extras include an audio commentary by Bob Cotter, author of *The Mexican Masked Wrestler & Monster Filmography*; a photo essay on Mexican horror cinema, 1953-1965, by expert David Wilt; cast bios; a poster and still gallery; a U.S. radio spot; and a *Boston Globe* obituary of Abel Salazar. But best of all is the inclusion of the film's sequel, *The Vampire's Coffin*, on a second disc(!), with the two-disc set labeled "The Vampire Collection."

THE VAMPIRE'S COFFIN, OR, YOU CAN'T KEEP A GOOD VAMPIRO DOWN

While the Mexican horror classic *El Vampiro* (*The Vampire*) was still drawing patrons to Mexico City theaters in 1957, producer Abel Salazar rounded up that film's principal cast and crew and began shooting a sequel.

A direct continuation of the original, *The Vampire's Coffin* opens at the big city hospital where young psychiatrist Dr. Henry Hetherford (Abel Salazar), the hero from *The Vampire*, works, and where Martha (Ariadna Welter), *The Vampire*'s heroine, recuperates from her terrifying ordeal. A curious colleague of Henry's tracks down Count Lavud's coffin and brings the staked corpse back to the hospital for study. Naturally, the doctor's greedy, grave-robbing assistant, Manson (Yeyre Beirute), inadvertently removes the stake from Lavud's heart, bringing the vampire back to life. Lavud then sets out to "avenge myself on those who buried my slumbering soul in the awful depths of death and stole my power that night" (i.e. kill Henry and make Martha his undead bride).

"The sequel was set in the city," observed co-star Ariadne Welter to interviewer Paul Parla, "which did not work as well as the original, which was set in the country." Indeed, the film's first half-hour unspools upon the unconvincingly cut-rate hospital sets (consisting of a few big, white, near-empty rooms), depriving the sequel of the original's lush atmospherics. Fortunately, the Vampire eventually chooses a much more appropriate (and better decorated) lair—the local wax museum, setting up shop amidst the guillotine, the Virgin of Nuremberg, and various creepy figures. The long, dark corridors and stone cellar, not to mention the eerie displays themselves, suits the subject far better than the stark hospital rooms and over-lit hallways.

The likable Salazar, who, despite starring in half-a-dozen horror movies, felt most at home in light comedies, does his usual comic, charming-yet-cowardly hero routine (kind of a Mexican Bob Hope, but without the zingers), while Ariadne Welter makes for a fetching damsel-in-distress. And Germán Robles continues his imposing turn as Lavud, combining the look of Lugosi with the lunge of Lee. Unfortunately, the mundane surroundings of the film's first half make of his Gothic-style Count a fish-out-of-water (or at least a vampire-out-of-crypt).

Director Fernando Méndez, aided by Victor Herrera's moody cinematography, frequently offsets the meandering script and banal setting with eerie lighting and shuddery shadows. One well-staged vampire attack has a woman pursued down a deserted street by the Vampire's shadow, which becomes the silhouette of a bat, before she abruptly turns to find herself suddenly facing the snarling fiend and his inch-long fangs. Too bad said scene is then juxtaposed with a cheesy Guys 'n' Dolls–style dance routine, as Martha, a professional dancer, rehearses at a theater. Fortunately, the climax offers a vigorous, exciting battle with the Vampire (and his slave) at the wax museum, marred only by some unconvincing bat-on-a-string action (but ending in a novel demise for the undead monster). Though falling short of the rich atmosphere and tight pacing of the original, *The Vampire's Coffin* still offers a passably creepy place for horror lovers to lay their heads.

The Anglicized version of *The Vampire's Coffin* premiered in the U.S. (in Cincinnati, Ohio) on a double bill with *The Robot vs. the Aztec Mummy* on November 17, 1965. Ironically, this sequel to *The Vampire* hit

In this sequel to The Vampire, *Germán Robles (as Count Lavud) once again occupies* The Vampire's Coffin. *(American lobby card)*

American theaters over two years *before* the original.

As expected, CasaNegra found an amazingly vibrant print of *The Vampire's Coffin*, and they offer both the original Spanish (with optional English subs) and English-dubbed audio tracks. Extras include a DVD-ROM version of a 1976 French photo-novel of the film(!); a poster and still gallery; and a U.S. radio promotion spot.

JEKYLL AND HYDE MEET THE DEVIL IN TIJUANA

The Man and the Monster, the third offering from producer/actor Abel Salazar's A.B.S.A. film company (after *The Vampire* and *The Vampire's Coffin*), is something of a south-of-the-border Faust-Meets-Jekyll-and-Hyde-by-Way-of-the-Phantom-of-the-Opera.

Mediocre pianist Samuel (Enrique Rambal) sells his soul to the Devil (and murders his beautiful and talented rival, Alejandra, to seal the deal) in order to become the world's greatest ivory tickler—the only hitch being that whenever he plays he transforms into a Hyde-like monster! Horrified by his monstrous alter-ego, Samuel intends to free himself from this curse by training a talented protégé, Laura (Martha Roth), to become the greatest pianist in the world ("I'll replace what I destroyed at last!" he proclaims). But the Maestro's evil piano-playing Mr. Hyde becomes jealous of Laura's phenomenal ability and attempts to kill her. Fortunately, the music promoter/hero (Abel Salazar), who has fallen for Laura, discovers the devilish doings, leading to the demise of both man and monster.

Apart from its tragic, tortured-soul story line, *The Man and the Monster* offers some fine production values and visuals, including fairly elaborate sets (creepy, cobwebbed hacienda contrasting with art deco-style, spacious apartments), evocative lighting (deep blacks and long shadows creating pools of light and dark), and fluid photography (the camera smoothly following the heroine, for instance, through the eerie hacienda as she frantically flees in terror from the homicidal monster). Directed by Raphael Baledon (*The Curse of the Crying Woman*) and photographed by Raoul Martinez Solares (*The Bloody Vampire, Invasion of the Vampires*, various Santo outings), *The Man and the Monster* remains one of the more visually impressive horrors to cross our Southern border.

Unfortunately, "visually impressive" doesn't readily spring to mind when one sees the Monster itself. With his bulbous nose, oversized buck teeth (that seem to be constantly on the verge of falling out), mutton-chop whiskers and wild fright wig, he looks like a cross between W.C. Fields and the Wolf Man. But at least, like Mr. Hyde, he's devoted to murder and mayhem (even killing a child—something *not* seen in Hollywood horrors of the time); and the believable cast handles it all with deadly seriousness (including hero Abel Salazar, who often portrayed a likable *comic* character but here plays it straight).

Unlike with the ludicrous makeup, director Baledon handles the pivotal deal-with-the-Devil sequence with both subtlety and panache (no horned, pitchfork-sporting Satan here; just a fervent wish and a clap of thunder on a bizarre, eerily-lit backstage set to signify the unholy bargain being struck). And, upping the macabre quotient, the slightly unhinged Samuel keeps the corpse of his murdered rival (and implied unrequited love object) in a closet of his music studio—and regularly *talks* to it.

To the tortured Samuel, playing the piano is like a drug—he must have his "fix" periodically. Though he tries to resist (and so hold his evil Id at bay), his hands shake and he pleads like an addict, ultimately succumbing to temptation. This addiction aspect imbues the proceedings with a weightier subtext than that found in the average Mexican monster movie.

If one can overlook the over-the-top makeup, the (not unexpected) unwieldy dubbing (though I recommend sidestepping this issue by watching the subtitled, more natural-sounding Spanish-language version), and (ironically) some inappropriate, bombastic music cues, *The Man and Monster* becomes a unique and satisfying foray into Mexican horror.

CasaNegra's crisp and clean print for *The Man and the Monster* lives up to their usual high standards, and though they eschewed the commentary track route, they offer up a photo gallery of poster art for two decades of Mexi-fright flicks, cast bios, a poster and still gallery, and a radio spot from its American theatrical release.

WAILING WOMEN, VALIANT VAQUEROS AND SMART STEEDS: THE LIVING COFFIN

As another of the Mexi-horrors imported and dubbed by K. Gordon Murray in the mid–1960s, *The Living Coffin* stands out for two reasons (unfortunately, neither has anything to do with quality): It's one of the few south-of-the-border horrors shot in color; and it's a horror–*Western*. A melding of two popular genres in Mexico, the *ranchero* (the Latino version of the B-Western) and Gothic-styled horror, *The Living Coffin* combines the native legend of La Llorona (the Crying Woman or Wailing Witch) with serial-Western sensibilities to create a hybrid that's one part Edgar Allan Poe (spotlighting the theme of burial alive), one part Tom Mix (featuring a super-intelligent horse that senses danger, rescues his master from quicksand, and even takes out the villain at the climax!) and one part Scooby-Doo (complete with not one, but *two* unmasking-the-phantom moments). In place of the "meddling kids" we have famous bullfighter-turned-actor (well, sort of) Gaston Santos and his perpetually sleepy comic-relief sidekick Pedro d'Aguillon (whose grating comments and annoying antics are frequently accompanied by "funny" noises on the soundtrack), who journey to a beleaguered hacienda plagued by mysterious deaths and the apparent ghost of "the Crying Woman" (whose pasty, cracked-and-peeling cadaverous countenance, coupled with cinematographer Victor Herrera's low-key lighting, generates most of the film's memorable moments). Decidedly human villains searching for a hidden gold mine in the nearby "Skeleton Swamp" are behind all the spectral shenanigans, and it's up to Santos to uncover the truth—after the requisite (substandard) fistfights and gunplay. Santos' horse even gets in on the act, pulling a string connected to a stationary firearm contraption to make the bad guys think there's a whole posse firing at them rather than just one lawman!

Director Fernando Méndez (*The Vampire*, *The Vampire's Coffin*, *The Black Pit of Dr. M*) builds an appropriately atmospheric mood, utilizing Herrera's layered lighting to turn the hacienda into a warren of torch-lit corridors and shadow-filled rooms (including an in-house mausoleum whose stone sarcophagi and iron-barred gate would be right at home in a Corman Poe entry). Unfortunately, the mood is shattered at regular intervals by the various riding, shooting and brawling scenes involving the brave-and-bland hero (not to mention his comical sidekick's continual search for a place to sleep, leading to innumerable scenes of him pulling chairs together to make a bed or climbing hay bales to lie down). And then there's the seriously unsatisfying "Scooby-Doo" ending that leaves the viewer feeling more cheated than enlightened—particularly since the cheesy masks removed from the faux phantoms bear only a passing resemblance to the previously highlighted spectral make-ups. Ruh-roh!

As an unofficial companion piece to the deadly dull *The Swamp of the Lost Monsters* (another color Mexican horror–Western starring Santos and d'Aguillon that featured an explain-it-all-away ending)—which has yet to find its way onto DVD—the intermittently creepy *Living Coffin* far surpasses its compatriot. But when compared to most "straight" Mexican horrors of the 1960s (including *all* the other films reviewed here), *The Living Coffin* seems disappointingly lifeless.

That said, for the Mexi-monster movie completist (or those enamored of the horror-Western hybrid), one can only applaud CasaNegra for their efforts, particularly since the disc features a sharp, colorful print with both English-dubbed and Spanish-language (with subtitles) audio. Perhaps not inappropriately, just as *The Living Coffin* offers the fewest horror thrills of all the CasaNegra releases, the disc offers the fewest extras: a brief poster-and-still gallery, short bios and an on-screen text article on Mexican horror-Westerns.

VIVA LA CASANEGRA!

Given the pristine presentations of all of these films (some of the finest and most entertaining horror movies made by our neighbors to the south), and with even more Mexi-monster releases by CasaNegra looming on the horizon, now (to paraphrase Dickens) is "the best of times" for Latino-horror fans everywhere, and for all those appreciative of the offbeat in their Uncanny. So invite your amigos, break out the popcorn (or chips and salsa), pop open the Corona, and settle back with this fabulous fistful of Mexi-horror. Oh, and don't forget to shout "Viva la CasaNegra!" as the credits unspool.

> This survey of Mexican werewolf movies was slated for the final issue of *Monsters from the Vault* magazine, but (like with Larry Talbot on the night of the full moon) things change. It might still see print; but until then, here's all the growlin', howlin', and wrasslin' full-moon fun.

OF LOBOS AND HOMBRES: MEXICAN WEREWOLF CINEMA, 1958-1976

The setting: a Mexico City wrestling arena filled with screaming spectators. The players: two mask-wearing wrestlers—one in silver and one in black. The action: as the crowd cheers, the two masked *luchadores* (wrestlers) grapple and toss each other about in a brutal athletic display of physical strength and endurance. Suddenly the silver-masked *technico* (hero) gains the upper hand and unmasks the black-cowled *rudo* (villain). But staring up at him is not the sweat-stained face of a defeated opponent but the snarling hirsute visage of a *werewolf!* Abruptly, the creature frees itself from the astonished hero's grip and transforms into a *bat* to make its escape!!

Welcome to the wild and wacky world of Mexican werewolves, a unique subset of south-of-the-border cinema which has, unfortunately, made only sporadic inroads north to the American market (though this sorry situation has improved of late, with a number of these films finally finding a home on subtitled DVDs or fan-subbed websites). Though not the first appearance of a wolfman in a Mexi-monster movie, this outrageous scene from 1962's *Samson vs. the Vampire Women* was undoubtedly the first glimpse for many American viewers into Mexican werewolf cinema.

Like most countries, Mexico has its own version of the werewolf figure. Based on ancient Aztec legends, the "nahual" was an evil warlock who could shape-shift into a dark coyote to drink the blood of its victims. Since the invading Spaniards didn't bring much in the way of werewolf lore when they colonized Mexico in the mid-1500s, the indigenous myths remained largely intact and unaffected by outside influence. The same *cannot* be said of Mexican horror cinema, however. Movie Mexi-wolves tended (like the rest of Mexican horror films from the 1950s onward) to follow the lead set by Hollywood, so that shapeshifting warlocks gave way to the more traditional tortured-soul "Larry Talbot" variety of wolfmen. Not content with merely aping their North American cousins, however, Mexican filmmakers put their own distinctive stamp on their lycanthropes, creating some unique and highly entertaining werewolf entries.

Ever since 1941's *The Wolf Man*, the werewolf has been a heavy hitter in the Monster ballpark, making increasingly frequent appearances throughout the years to become nearly as ubiquitous as the vampire. When Mexican moviemakers took notice of classic horror's renewed popularity in the 1950s (aided by the genre's inroads into television via the famous Shock Theater broadcasts), they decided it was time to put their own Latino spin on these horror classics. Pioneered by actor-producer Abel Salazar with 1957's *El Vampiro* (characterized by Salazer himself as "*Dracula* on a hacienda"), there emerged a subset of Mexican horror films that emulated the gothic atmospherics of Universal's classics while injecting a uniquely *Mexicano* sense into their shuddery stories. Though no producer ever tackled Universal's *The Wolf Man* directly, many a moviemaker utilized e*l hombre lobo* in one form or another. As such, our southern brethren offered up a baker's dozen (plus one) of cinematic lycan-treats during its horror heyday of the 1950s through the 1970s for us *gringos* to savor.

THE MEXI-WOLF AWAKENS

The first Mexican movie werewolf arrived in 1958 via the horror-comedy *El Castillo de los Monstruos* (Castle of the Monsters), which, sadly, failed to find its way north in dubbed or subtitled form. In the film, Clavillazo (comedian Antonio Espino) must rescue his lady love from a mad scientist named Dr. Sputnik who creates monsters in his castle lair. Said creatures consist of a Frankenstein Monster (who serves as the butler), a sportcoat-wearing ape-man kept behind bars, a poor man's Creature from the Black Lagoon, a living mummy, a vampire, and a wolfman. The latter sports a dark suit (Mexican monsters are nothing if not nattily dressed), hairy hands with long fingernails, and rather sparse makeup consisting of a mouth full of scraggly

The Mexican Lon Chaney–starrer La Casa del Terror *transformed into the near-unwatchable* Face of the Screaming Werewolf *after hack Jerry Warren got his hairy paws on it. (Mexican lobby card)*

teeth, large ears, slicked-back hair ending in a widow's peak, and unkempt beard and whiskers. Completely under the hypnotic control of Dr. Sputnik (who uses a whistle to summon his creatures), the werewolf doesn't even appear until an hour into the film, and then does little more than grab the misbehaving heroine and carry her to the lab before meeting his fate at the hands of the caged ape-monster, who chokes the life out of this *hombre lobo*.

Shadows, fog, a dank castle (complete with alligator pit and secret laboratory), and a bevy of classic creatures all bode well for some monstrous south-of-the-border entertainment. Unfortunately, the picture primarily focuses on the goofy antics of the comedic hero, with the creatures largely relegated to the film's final third, and then utilized mainly to chase Clavillazo around the *castillo*. On the plus side, director Julian Solar (*Santo vs. Blue Demon in Atlantis* [1970]) managed to secure the services of Mexico's premier vampire, Germán Robles (*El Vampiro* himself), for a bloodsucking cameo. "[Solar] asked me," recounted Robles, "'You are filming right now *Vampire's Coffin* [the sequel to the classic *El Vampiro*]. Would it be possible for you to come over and do a cameo part for me? With the same costume?' [*Coffin* producer Abel] Salazar didn't even know about it."[1] Solar also managed to insert some genuinely amusing demises for two of his monsters, having the gill-man devolve into a flopping fish when hit with a mysterious chemical and the Frankenstein Monster dissolve into a pile of bolts and clock parts upon being electrocuted.

A TERROR-CADE IN THRILLS! A NIGHTMARE IN CHILLS! –*Face of the Screaming Werewolf* trailer

Next in the lycan-line was 1959's *La Casa del Terror* (The House of Terror), though it didn't see play in America until five years later in a decidedly bastardized form when fringe filmmaker Jerry Warren (*Man Beast*, *Teenage Zombies*) acquired the rights to this Mexican horror comedy starring the popular Latin comedian Tin Tan (*and* featuring Lon Chaney Jr. as a werewolf!). Warren excised nearly all of Tin Tan's scenes (thus eliminating the original movie's *star*) and inserted footage from the 1957 *La Momia Azteca* (which Warren had already cannibalized to create the atrocious *Attack of the Mayan Mummy* in 1963). But Warren didn't stop there; *Face of the Screaming Werewolf* is really a combination of *four* different film snippets. In addition to the *Momia Azteca* and *Casa del Terror* footage, Warren recycled some of his own scenes shot with American actors for *Attack of the Mayan Mummy*, and included a few scraps of *new* footage lensed specifically to bridge some of the expository gaps in *Face*.

As might be expected from such a patchwork pastiche, *Face of the Screaming Werewolf* makes little sense and provides even less entertainment, offering only a few nostalgic moments of Lon Chaney in his trademark Wolf Man makeup (though a bit shaggier here than in his halcyon days at Universal) for those diehard fans desperate enough to sit through this painful 60 minutes (which feels like *twice* that length).

The story has a young woman, the reincarnation of an Aztec maiden, lead a scientific expedition to an ancient pyramid on the Yucatan peninsula where they find two bodies—an ancient mummy and a modern man in some sort of mummified condition ("placed in the pyramid only recently after an exchange of body fluid with the mummy in an effort to achieve an apparent state of death," as one character unhelpfully explains). The Aztec mummy comes to life, but the expedition subdues the creature and brings it—and the still-dead 'modern' mummy—back to the city for study (all, disappointingly, off-screen). A rival scientist steals the modern mummy and restores it to life, only to find that the man (Lon Chaney Jr.) is actually a werewolf! Meanwhile, the living mummy escapes, abducts the reincarnated girl, and is promptly killed when hit by a car (again, off-screen).

The two storylines have nothing to do with one another, and a paucity of dialogue (synching the dubbing was obviously too big a strain on Warren's grade-Z budget) ensures that the viewer often has no idea who is doing what to whom. Many of the scenes appear to be thrown in at random just to pad the running time (and the few new shots of Warren regulars—like Chuck Niles and Steve Conte—answering the telephone or delivering radio broadcasts eat up further time without adding anything appreciable to the confusing proceedings).

The first 20 minutes of *Face of the Screaming Werewolf* (a full third of the picture) consists of *La Momia Azteca* footage lifted from Warren's earlier *Attack of the Mayan Mummy* (1963). It didn't improve with age, for the looong ceremonial flashback sequence quickly grows tiresome, and the mummy only pops up in the last minute.

In an interview with Tom Weaver, Jerry Warren referred to his doctoring of Mexican imports as "a natural, easy way to make movies without an exceptional amount of work."[2] Well, with *Face of the Screaming Werewolf*, Warren put in even less work than usual—and it shows.

The *Casa del Terror* footage provides *Face*'s few highlights, including seeing Chaney Jr. in his black-shirt-and-trouser Lawrence Talbot get-up once more (he even leaps over a lab table at one point with a bit of the old Wolf Man ferocity); atmospherically-lit and unsettling insert shots of creepy wax figures (the villain's secret lab is at a wax museum—though this isn't made clear in *Face*, resulting in more confusion); and the boffo lab set itself, with a giant pressure cooker/tanning bed contraption (used to try and revive the mummy), various banks of electrical equipment, bubbling beakers, and a giant spinning apparatus of undetermined origin.

Working 12 to 14 hours each day, Lon Chaney Jr. completed all of his scenes for *Casa del Terror* in just two days. Director Gilberto Martinez Solares shot with three cameras to capture Chaney from various angles, as Chaney rapidly switched from normal makeup to mummy makeup to werewolf makeup. "He was a drunk," said Solares of his American star. "That was the first thing to say about him. All day long, every day. He had a small doctor's case that was supposed to contain make-up. But hidden in the middle, he had a tequila bottle—with a straw sticking out. Whenever he'd need a makeup change, he'd go for that straw. Also, Chaney didn't speak any Spanish, so his voice had to be dubbed in later. But the producer forced me to use him because of his status as a horror star."[3] Solares' preferred genre was comedy, and his favorite comedian was Tin Tan, with whom Solares made an amazing 40 films and who Solares considered "a genius." Solares made one further foray into werewolf territory with the deliriously entertaining *Santo and Blue Demon vs. the Monsters* (1970).

The nonsensical (but not in a good—nor entertaining—way) *Face of the Screaming Werewolf* is chock full of people we don't know doing things for reasons we don't know involving other characters we don't know. Why watch *Face*? I honestly don't know.

MANUEL AND JOSE MEET FRANKENSTEIN ...AND THE WOLFMAN

Universal's *Abbott and Costello Meet Frankenstein* (1948) is one of the most beloved horror-comedies of all time. And rightly so. The Mexican *Frankenstein* [sic], *el Vampiro y Compania* (1962) is one of the most overtly plagiaristic horror-comedies of all time, as it's a nearly scene-for-scene steal from that comedy duo's classic. But while the south-of-the-border filmmakers lifted the plot, characters, and even a number of gags from the earlier picture, they failed to replicate the truly funny Abbott and Costello dynamics (here substituting Manuel "Loco" Valdes and Jose Jasso, who display little chemistry and even less comedic artistry) as well as the original's genuinely frightening tone. Rather than treating its trio of monsters respectfully and utilizing their imposing personas to generate an atmosphere of suspense, as in the Abbott and Costello film, the Mexican remake casts its monsters as mere buffoons that serve only as the brunt of a few silly (and unfunny) jokes.

Though slavishly aping the Universal film's plot of two bumbling baggage handlers running afoul of a female mad scientist, Dracula, the Frankenstein Monster, and the Wolf Man (with the latter on the side of the "boys"—when not in hirsute form, that is), *Frankestein, el Vampiro y Compania* occasionally departs from its chosen model. For instance, the female mad scientist revives both the Monster and the vampire (with the newly-restored bloodsucker then taking hypnotic control of her), rather than Dracula himself having been behind the nefarious plan all along (as in the original). Replacing the A&C film's brain-transplant concept is the notion of a mind-transference, which is actually successful (if temporary), with the Monster hopping around goofily and acting "loco," while Costello stand-in Valdez stumbles about with arms outstretched, trashing the laboratory and menacing the principals. And for some reason, "el Vampiro" is never called Dracula (while, oddly, the Frankenstein Monster drops the "n" to become "Frankestein").

But for lycanthropic purposes, the most interesting change comes at film's end, when el Hombre Lobo battles el Vampiro (just as the Wolf Man fought Dracula in the original). Rather than an exciting chase/battle through the castle, ending in the Wolf Man lunging for Dracula in bat form and taking them both over the cliff to their deaths, the two Mexi-versions simply grapple in a dim basement room, with the werewolf finally choking the bloodsucker into submission before grabbing a handy stake to shove into his chest. The Wolf Man then clutches at his neck and succumbs to wounds apparently inflicted (unseen) by the vampire, while the room goes up in flames (consuming all three monsters) as Our Heroes make their getaway. Such a perfunctory finish for its werewolf, coupled with the curious choice to have the savage manbeast perform such a calculated, premeditated action (the staking), makes for a decidedly unsatisfactory conclusion for the film's lycanthrope.

Each of the three classic creatures prove subpar in every way, particularly the Frankestein Monster, whose frog-like features make him look cartoonish. The werewolf's wooly hair and beard, rubbery face, piggish nose, oversized Clark Gable ears, and set of inch-long vampire fangs stands as one of the worst werewolf makeups this side of an Andy Milligan movie. And most disappointingly, this ridiculous-looking Chaney-lite variation displays none of the original's savagery (no tearing the stuffing out of a chair here, for instance). Likewise, in keeping with the cramped sets and cheesy "exteriors" (which are no more convincing than the monsters' silly visages), the Mexican film offers no on-screen metamorphoses. Instead, the actor simply clutches his head, the film cuts away to another character, and then, viola, there stands the werewolf—who generally does very little. Sad.

Frankestein, el Vampiro y Compania has yet to receive an English-language release, which may be no great loss in the end. Two other horrors directed by *Frankestein* helmer Benito Alazraki this same year *did* see some screen time north of the border, however—the desultory *Spiritism* and the inferior Santo vehicle *Invasion of the Zombies*—completing a trifecta of Mexican horror cinema disappointment.

"GOD BLESS SANTO... er, SAMSON"

Finally, after three successive comedies, Mexico got serious about werewolves... sort of. 1962's *Samson vs. the Vampire Women* (*El Santo contra las Mujeres Vampiros*), the best of the three Santo movies dubbed into English and released on the Saturday matinee circuit and then to television (*Invasion of the Zombies* and *Samson in the Wax Museum* being the other two), stars that most famous of all Mexican masked wrestler heroes, El Santo (changed to "Samson" in the English dubbing), as the main opposition to a coven of vampire women (led by Lorena Velasquez). The bloodsuckers have awakened after 200 years to seek a new Queen of the Vampires (an innocent girl chosen at birth and destined to take her place among the undead upon her twenty-first birthday). Diana (Maria Duval), daughter of Professor Roloff (Augusto Benedico), is the chosen unfortunate, and it's up to Roloff's friend Samson (with a little help from the police) to take time out of his ringside activities and foil the bloodsuckers' plans.

Actress Lorena Velasquez (who also starred with the masked wrestler in *Invasion of the Zombies*, and who played a wrestler herself in several pictures, including *The Wrestling Women vs. the Aztec Mummy*) appeared on Britain's *Incredibly Strange Film Show* in 1989. About El Santo, she said: "He represented justice. He was the Mexican Schwarzenegger. And he was a very nice man, very kind man, very good actor—well, *not* very good, but he represented justice and this was very important for the people." Indeed, one doesn't watch a Santo movie to see classical thesping, but to watch an icon of Truth, Justice and the Mexican Way take out bad guys and monsters.

This film presents a rather unique take on vampirism. When the female vampires drink blood, they transform from grotesque hags into diaphanous-gowned, leggy beauties who pray to Satan, even conjuring up the "Lord of Darkness" himself (in silhouette, anyway)—aligning vampirism with Satanism. And this evil cult is definitely a Matriarchy (with hints of lesbianism, as they seem to prefer biting women), adding a bit of subtext to the tale by pitting Samson, the ultimate defender of Patriarchal society, against this aberration of matriarchal "deviants."

But lest one become lost in subtextual musings on women's liberation and alternate sexuality, the movie periodically reminds the viewer of what it's *really* all about, as Samson tackles a vampire opponent in the ring (a male minion who's secretly taken a wrestler's place). After the vampire-wrestler fails to kill Samson ("He's using karate!" Our Hero exclaims), Samson unmasks him—revealing the hirsute face of a *werewolf*, who then proceeds to escape by transforming into a bat! Though odd in the extreme, this scene is nothing if not novel. (Unfortunately, that's all we see of this unique were-vamp.)

And novel may be the operative word for *Samson vs. the Vampire Women*, which provides enough cobwebbed lairs, low-key lighting, and hideous dried crones transforming into beautiful vampire women to keep any Mexi-movie enthusiast satisfied. As the Professor so earnestly exclaims at picture's end: "God bless Samson!"

SAMSON, THE UNCONQUERABLE, UNEARTHS WEIRD BEINGS IN THE TYRANT'S DUNGEON OF HORROR... –ad line for *Samson in the Wax Museum*

It's *Mystery of the Wax Museum* gone south, south of the border, that is—as well as south of believability, since the film's hero is that purveyor of Truth, Justice and the Mexican Way, the silver-masked, crime-fighting professional wrestler Santo (dubbed "Samson" in the English version). In 1963's *Samson in the Wax Museum* (*Santo en el Museo de Cera*) Santo/Samson investigates a series of disappearances revolving around a sinister wax museum run by Dr. Karol (Claudio Brook). *Samson in the Wax Museum* sports a rather intriguing mystery motif in its first half, in which the police, Samson and the viewer receive evidence both for *and* against Dr. Karol's guilt. Along with the eerie atmosphere in Karol's cavern-like "museum" housing his weird, monstrous figures—many of which, including a wolfman, come to life to attack Our Hero—this initial ambivalence keeps the viewer off balance and interested. Of course, after 45 minutes the picture spoils it all by revealing the identity of the villain who transforms people into disfigured "monsters" with his flesh-eroding and trance-inducing serum.

Disappointingly, the faux monsters look like cut-rate *Island of Lost Souls* rejects (brawny man with unconvincing pig-snout, scraggly-faced wolfman, etc.), and they do very little until the climax, when, after turning on their creator, they briefly menace Samson before the Silver Masked Man dumps a vat of boiling wax over them. And the film makes up for its wrestling-free first third by tossing in a number of ringside scenes towards the middle and end, spoiling the picture's rhythm (though presumably giving the Santo enthusiasts what they really want). But for said Santo fans (and we know who we are), one could do worse than spend 90 minutes in this *Wax Museum*.

WEREWOLVES VS. A BLUE DEMON

The only sport in Mexico more popular than lucha libre ("free wrestling") is soccer, and from the 1950s through the 1970s the only luchadore (wrestler) more popular than Blue Demon was El Santo. Both wrestlers wore masks (Santo's was silver; Blue's was, well, blue), which they never removed in public, creating an almost mythic persona that transcended the wrestling ring to invade popular culture in the form of everything from toys to comic books to movies, making them into faux-superheroes. Santo began a highly successful series of films in the late 1950s in which the masked wrestler-cum-crime fighter battled all manner of baddies, from mafiosa to monsters. In 1964 producer Enrique Vergara (maker of many a Santo film) decided to showcase the 42-year-old Blue Demon in his own feature, perhaps as competition for, and a challenge to,

El Santo, whose growing popularity caused him to seek higher fees for his film appearances. Blue Demon subsequently starred in 25 features over the next 23 years. Nine of them co-starred Santo, though the two were far from friends in real life (much like Lugosi in terms of his relationship to Karloff, Blue seemed to resent his rival, who nearly always took the lead when they met, both in the ring and on the screen).

The rather redundantly titled *Blue Demon: El Demon Azul* (Blue Demon: The Blue Demon) stands as the first full-on werewolf movie produced in Mexico in which the lycanthrope plays more than a peripheral role. It opens with a couple necking in the woods, only to have their amorous activities rudely interrupted by a rampaging werewolf. Said lycanthrope, nothing if not unique in appearance (sporting big, rounded, fluffy ears to go with its big, rounded, fluffy face), grabs up the man in a deadly bear (wolf?) hug and then tosses his broken body down a hill before chasing the woman through the foggy forest (with the smoke pots obviously doing serious overtime) and squeezing her to death as well. Apparently, this type of lycanthrope has no need for claws or fangs. In fact, this werewolf sports a normal set of human choppers, the filmmakers curiously eschewing the *de rigeur* set of oversized canines altogether.

Here, masked Mexican wrestler Blue Demon, in his first starring role, plays... masked Mexican wrestler Blue Demon, who, through his learned professor friend, runs afoul of a young scientist attempting to create a "super hombre" via a serum derived from wolves. Unfortunately, those he injects have the nasty habit of transforming into werewolves when the moon rises. This includes one luchadore whom the scientist sends into a bout against the champion Blue Demon as a test of his subject's superhumanness. After the second round, however, the rattled wrassler transforms, causing Blue to execute a few more moves before tossing the hirsute were-wrestler out of the ring (after which the wolfman runs from the arena, his figurative tail between his legs).

The wrestler turned neophyte actor Blue Demon recounted how he was embarrassingly ignorant of filmmaking techniques when thrust into his first starring role: "In my first film I didn't realize that the scenes were shot out of sequence. The first scene I filmed was actually the last scene of the film. There was a character who, in the script, I had been close friends with. We had worked together in defeating the werewolf. But I had never met this man before and didn't realize that our characters were already friends. When filming began, I treated him as a stranger and ignored him. Everyone on the set thought this was very funny."[4]

Blue Demon: El Demonio Azul has never seen release outside of Spanish-speaking territories, which is a shame, as its atmospherically-shot, fog-drenched woodland settings; creepy castle (complete with copious cobwebs, gruesome skeletons, and hidden laboratory); and handful of fuzzy wolfman encounters (not to mention two vigorous Blue Demon wrestling matches) all add up to a fairly fast-paced, engaging luchadore-vs.-the-monsters outing.

THE SHE-WOLF HOWLS

The Mexi-trend of serious lycan-centric cinema continues with 1965's *La Loba* ("The She-Wolf"). The film begins with a shuddery bang as the lid of a sarcophagus in a lonely graveyard slides open to reveal a pair of clawed, hairy hands. Then, by the light of the full moon, out crawls a hairy figure. Creeping among the shadowy trees, the creature comes upon a man beside his campfire and acrobatically leaps, snarling and biting, upon the screaming victim. The beast-creature soon claims two more—a man and a woman—pouncing upon them to savage the woman to death, leaving the man bleeding but alive. Finally, the monster returns to its tomb, emerging from a connecting secret passage into a bedroom, where it lays down and transforms into a beautiful, naked woman!

Said woman is Clarisa (Kitty de Hoyos), grown daughter of Professor Fernandez (Jose Elias Moreno), cursed to transform into a she-wolf during the full moon. When a suitor arrives to ask for her hand, he is attacked and bitten by the wolf woman. The Professor works to save his life; unfortunately, the man has contracted the curse as well. Meanwhile, the earlier survivor has been hunting the creature that killed his wife, utilizing a werewolf-tracking dog. It all comes to a death-filled end during the next full moon when the two werewolves escape their confines to decimate the household before meeting their fates.

The first film in cinema history to feature an on-camera female werewolf transformation (and daringly—if coyly—flirt with the notion of nudity), *La Loba* stands on its two lycan-legs as a superior specimen not only of vintage Mexican horror but of classic werewolf cinema as well. It is atmospheric (the fog-shrouded graveyard, shadow-filled woodlands, and imposing hacienda all create an oppressive, near-gothic atmosphere), fast-paced (these werewolves attack frequently and viciously), and beautifully filmed (courtesy of talented cinematographer Raul Martinez Solares, under the concise direction of Rafael Baledon).

Baledon fills his film with impressive shots of the

she-beast moving rapidly through the forest. This werewolf doesn't simply lope through the woodlands, it leaps and bounds off logs, at times even catapulting through the air in impressive acrobatic displays. The mobile camera follows the characters and heightens suspense, even producing the occasional shock—such as when a man lies prone on an operating table before abruptly sitting up to reveal his snarling werewolf visage staring straight into the camera in a startling and unnerving display. And the frequent up-angle shots and shadowy lighting accentuate the story's dark sense of impending doom.

Baledon handles the pivotal transformation scenes with equal aplomb. Locked in her room when the changes begin, Clarisa sports hairy clawed hands and fangs in her shapely mouth. Then (taking a page from the original *Wolf Man*), the camera focuses on her feet as we see them darken and (via some effective time-lapse photography) grow hairy, with sharpened, misshapen claws in place of toenails. (Unfortunately, in a momentary misstep, Baledon reveals her still-bare legs, making it look like she's wearing a pair of unruly fur slippers). After a shot of the full moon, Baledon recovers by focusing on her head and bare shoulders as she lay gasping on the carpet, fur growing on her bare back. Her still-beautiful face is now framed by long hair and large wolf's ears. As the kicker, this all comes via the point of view of a small, terrified child peeking out unobserved from under the bed where she'd hidden, adding a sense of mortal danger to the weird transformation.

La Loba's behind-the-scenes personnel proved to be a who's who of Mexican horror cinema. Costa Rican–born screenwriter Ramon Obon concocted many of the classics of Mexi-horror, including *The Vampire* (1957) and its sequel *The Vampire's Coffin* (1958), *The Black Pit of Dr. M* (1959), and *The World of the Vampires* (1961). Tragically, Obon died in 1965 at the young age of 47. Near-ubiquitous cinematographer Solares (with nearly 300 credits to his name) had filmed a werewolf before in 1959's *Casa del Terror* (which became the bastardized *Face of the Screaming Werewolf* five years later), and shone light on multiple wolfmen in the entertaining *Santo and Blue Demon vs. the Monsters* (1970). Solares also shot (figuratively speaking) a were-*ape* in *Night of the Bloody Apes* (1968). Director Rafael Baledon was responsible for one of the best Mexican horrors of the time, the excellent *Curse of the Crying Woman* (1963).

As the doomed *La Loba*, sexy Kitty de Hoyos remains one of the most stunning she-wolves in cinema. Her perfect face, with its large eyes, dark lashes, aquiline nose and sensuous mouth, remains largely unaffected by the subtle makeup, making her a vicious yet still fetching wolf-woman. The long blonde wolf hair covering much of her body does just enough to suggest a gorgeous figure, barely concealing her nakedness. Curiously, this female lycanthrope sports a small tail as well (unlike her pants-wearing male counterpart).

The male werewolf is not nearly so attractive, looking like an escapee from Dr. Moreau's island, with his fright-wig hair, scraggly overgrown beard, mouthful of oversized teeth and fangs, and fur-covered torso, arms and feet.

Both these lycanthropes attack with animal ferocity, clawing, slashing and biting, all while emitting menacing growls and vicious snarls. Grappling with bloody, clawed hands, they rend and tear at their victims, leaving shockingly (for the time) bloody corpses, which the camera often reveals in close-up (even focusing on a gaping wound at one point). This was strong stuff for the 1960s, much less the generally conservative 1960s *Mexico*.

Bullets have no apparent effect on these supernatural creatures, but a silver knife is another matter—as is a well-trained attack dog. For the exciting climax, Baledon cuts back and forth between *la loba* and *el hombre lobo* violently attacking several human foes, culminating in the wolf man engaging in a fight to the death with the werewolf-hunting hound. The film closes with an almost romantic sense of tragedy, as the dying she-wolf (wounded by the silver knife) crawls to the body of her stricken wolf man mate. Lying together, the two return (via simple dissolves) to their human forms, finally finding peace in death. Even the victorious dog gets in on the tragedy act when it goes to lie forlornly next to the body of his fallen master, slain by the wolf man.

Besides the beautiful presence of Kitty de Hoyos, *La Loba* sports the authoritative yet haunted playing of Jose Elias Moreno as the doomed girl's anguished father. Having assayed the title role in the outlandish 1959 Mexican psychotronic oddity *Santa Claus* (in which Kris Kringle matches wits with a horned devil named "Pitch"!), Moreno went on to scientifically create his own were-creature as the scientist who inadvertently transforms his own son into a were-ape during the *Night of the Bloody Apes* (1968).

Sadly, *La Loba* has yet to howl outside of Spanish-speaking territories, though Columbia did allow a limited release in 1966 to a few select Spanish-language theaters in the U.S.

FROM THE SUBLIME TO THE RIDICULOUS

A werewolf *Western*? Check. A *Mexican* lycanthrope? *Si*. The *oddest* wolfman transformation in celluloid history? *Absolutamente*. The outré 1965 south-of-the-border monster mash *Rider of the Skulls* (*El Charro de las Calaveras*) offers all this and so much more.

Back in the Old (Mexican) West, a werewolf (David Silva, who played an inspector in the engagingly bizarre 1962 offering *The Brainiac*) terrorizes a village. Into the hamlet gallops the Rider of the Skulls (voiced by Dagoberto Rodriguez but represented in the physical action by rough-and-tumble former wrestler Fernando Oses), a mask-wearing, gun-toting, horseback-riding hero (kind of a sombrero-sporting Lone Ranger) dressed all in black and sworn "to fight evil in all its forms." Why does he wear a mask? "My identity doesn't matter," he says. "I represent justice; justice doesn't have a face." But the rampaging lycanthrope terrorizing the town does, and a rather unusual one at that. Long hair, mammoth eyebrows, protruding fangs, huge pointy wolf-ears, and veined wrinkly skin (as well as hairy arms and hands ending in sharp, 2-inch fingernail-claws) provide this wolf man's decidedly demonic look (well, as demonic-looking as a crude rubber and papier mâché mask can be). With the Rider on his trail, the werewolf claims two victims, terrifies his own stepson, and reveals himself to be the owner of the very hacienda at which the Rider is staying. Ultimately, the Rider tracks the beast to a rock quarry, where the wolf man finally tumbles over the edge. The now orphaned boy (his mother killed by the werewolf), along with a bumbling hired hand (the comic relief), follow the Rider to his next two adventures, first facing down a vampire in another town, and finally vanquishing a headless horseman.

Director/screenwriter Alfredo Salazar (brother of actor/producer/director Abel [*The Brainiac*] Salazar) shot *Rider of the Skulls* as three separate "mini" films, thus explaining the repetitive structure of the three monster-du-jour segments. Though this might indicate it was meant as separate episodes for television, that's not necessarily so, as union regulations in Mexico at that time often limited studios to filming shorts.

Spills and chills galore, as the Rider of the Skulls *takes on everything from headless horsemen to wobbly werewolves. (Mexican lobby card)*

Producers got around this by combining their half-hour episodes at a later date to create full-length feature films. A number of features were created this way, including the quartet of *Nostradamus* vampire movies starring Germán Robles.

Prolific screenwriter Alfredo Salazar, after twenty years of scribbling such delirious Mexi-horror "classics" as *The Aztec Mummy* trilogy, *The Man and the Monster*, *The World of the Vampires*, and numerous Santo outings (such as *Santo and Blue Demon vs. Dracula and the Wolfman*), takes the directorial reins for the first time with *Rider of the Skulls* (and even puts in a Hitchcock-like cameo as a victim of the vampire in the second tale). And while Salazar adds few flourishes to this obviously impoverished production (spending a lot of time filming medium-shots out of doors on dusty roads and fields, and in rundown buildings), he at least keeps things moving at a *rapido* pace, allowing little time to question the sheer absurdity of it all. For instance, in a nonsensically bizarre—but decidedly novel—twist on the classic werewolf transformation scene, the man stares at the moon outside his window, curses his fate, and then collapses to the floor where (via two simple dissolves) his body becomes first a skeleton(!) and then the (fully clothed) wolfman. Salazar seemed very pleased with this wacky take on lycanthropic metamorphosis, for he repeats it not one, not two, but *three* more times (all within the space of 20 minutes).

Things don't become any less *loco* as the tale gallops along. At one point the local witch aids the Rider by resurrecting a dead victim of the werewolf. The gruesome cadaver sits up in his coffin to regale the Rider about the werewolf's origin (unhelpfully admitting that "nobody knows where it came from") and reveal the beast's human identity. Later, the Rider catches sight of and chases the wolf man across an open field, relentlessly firing at the beast (he's either a terrible shot or the bullets have no effect, since he's only 20 feet behind the monster). Suddenly—and inexplicably—the Rider falls into a concealed pit. Instantly aware of this, the werewolf turns back and starts hurling oversized rocks down upon the trapped Rider! This all appears in the film's first third, with subsequent wackiness arriving in the form of a cape-wearing vampire with a dried-apple monkey face; a talking head in a box; and a headless horseman who, after reattaching his wayward cranium, rails against God Himself when a bolt of lightning takes out his two skeletal henchmen. *Ay Caramba*!

Of course, such outré inventiveness is often abetted (though not aided) by mere incompetence. For instance, the monsters' masks appear no less phony for their uniqueness. The third segment's papier mâché head in a box, whose mouth moves like a hand-puppet when it talks, takes the cheesiness to a whole new level. Despite the monsters prowling at night and characters often commenting on the "late hour," the action obviously takes place midday, with only the weakest of not-fooling-anyone day-for-night filters employed. At one point, while chasing the wolfman away yet again, the Rider states, "The werewolf won't show up for the next 15 days—not until the next full moon." Apparently, math is not his strong suit, as the full moon comes only once a month, not twice (blue moons excepted).

Additionally, due to its tripartite nature, *Rider of the Skulls* becomes rather repetitious in structure: initial monster attack; arrival of Our Hero; several inconclusive fisticuff-filled confrontations between Rider and monster; culminating in a final decisive battle resulting in the fiend's demise.

Continuity between segments (much like the werewolf itself) seems to fall by the wayside as well. For example, the boy's name inexplicably changes from "Perico" in the werewolf episode to "Juanito" in the vampire story (though the comical sidekick remains "Cleofas"). And the skull emblems on the Rider's costume metamorphose from a simplistic skull-and-crossbones image on the sleeves in the first segment to more artistically-rendered skull-only patches that migrate to the chest in the second segment. When the heroine of the vampire story asks Juanito if he's ever seen the Rider's face, Juanito answers, "No, I don't think anyone has ever seen it"—despite the fact that at the close of the werewolf episode mere minutes before, the rider unveiled his face to the boy and Cleofas (who even commented on how handsome the hero looks).

Even traditional werewolf lore can't escape Salazar's screenwriting peccadilloes. After the wolfman transforms back to his human form, he laments, "I've killed her" (referring to his latest victim), obviously remembering exactly what he did as the beast; most screen werewolves have no recollection of their actions in bestial guise. And while guns and knives seemingly have little effect, a simple fall down a thirty-foot embankment is enough to send this man-beast to his everlasting rest.

Though it's not all delirious *durazno y crema* (peaches and cream), *Rider of the Skulls* still offers dollops aplenty for those enamored of south-of-the-border monster thrills, and anyone who enjoys a huge helping of the offbeat with their horror.

"FROM THE MANSION OF HORROR ESCAPES THE BLOODTHIRSTY CREATURES YOU MOST HATE AND FEAR..."

Nineteen-seventy's *Santo and Blue Demon vs. the Monsters* (*Santo y Blue Demon contra los Monstruous*) rings in the new decade by introducing, like *Abbott and Costello Meet Frankenstein*, our two heroes and each of the featured monsters during the credits sequence. Except *Santo and Blue Demon vs. the Monsters* is not a comedy—well, not intentionally anyway.

The Mummy, the Cyclops, "Franquestain," the Wolf Man, the Vampire, and the Vampire Woman all receive their 15-seconds-of-fame introductory billing. But that's forgetting a diabolical bald hunchbacked dwarf named Waldo; a cadre of green-faced zombie henchmen; a big-domed alien-like creature with exposed brain (who merely stands around as background decoration); and the evil, cackling mad scientist who creates/revives all these monsters in his laboratory cave located beneath an abandoned castle!

Said scientist (himself revived from death by Waldo at the film's beginning) captures masked wrestler and all-around good guy Blue Demon, uses a "duplicating" machine to create an evil double, then sends the doppelganger, along with the scientist's mind-controlled monsters, out to attack the locals and kidnap the scientist's hated brother (who scoffed at his sibling's evil experiments) and niece. Of course, masked wrestling hero El Santo, the Man in the Silver Mask (friend of Blue Demon, boyfriend of the niece, and heroic defender of all), has something to say about this, and numerous set-to's with various monsters (including one ringside wrestling bout in which the Vampire disguises himself as a masked opponent named—get this—"The Vampire") ends in a free-for-all between Santo and the good Blue Demon on the one side, and the evil Blue Demon and all the monsters on the other.

Things move at a *rapido* pace (with monster attacks coming at frequent intervals), allowing little time for the frequent filler found in many a Santo and/or Blue Demon feature (one exception being a nightclub sequence in which the principals watch a silly Gene Kelly–style number that's obviously lifted from a completely different—and much older—movie). Plenty of day-for-night photography adds to the kitsch quotient (and contrasts comically with the occasional real nighttime shot).

The monsters prove more (unintentionally) amusing than terrifying. Santo himself admitted, "In the film there are some monsters that didn't look quite right."[5] For instance, the Vampire (nobody uses the 'D' word, but it's pretty obvious on what famous Count he is patterned) exhibits not only the expected evening dress, top hat and cape, but also a set of oversized fangs and gigantic pointed ears. The elfin bloodsucker does impressively launch himself into the air in bat pose, however.

The Mummy sports clean bandages and a five-day growth of beard; and the poor, inept sap never accomplishes anything more than serving as Santo's 3000-year-old punching bag. "The mummy was a poor skinny man, an actor," dismissed Santo.[6] The Frankenstein Monster is a tall gentleman in an obvious—and crude—mask (with a goatee), but he does a nice job of crushing one victim's head under his asphalt-spreader's boot in the movie's one moderately gruesome scene. Best of all is the Cyclops (recycled from the 1959 sci-fier *La Nave de los Monstruos*)—an unwieldy rubber-suited steroid-monster with one glowing eye, an oversized guppy-mouth, and big fuzzy ears.

The Wolf Man (played by Vicente Lara) seriously disappoints, with his bushy gray beard, lanky hair, oversized ears, sparse nose piece, and inch-long fangs. Sporting a dark suit, and walking about and opening doors like any normal person, he looks more like an old man in dire need of orthodontia than a bloodthirsty werewolf. He does receive more than his fair share of screen time, however, and takes pride of place when he becomes the first of the various creatures to see action—attacking and killing a farmer and his wife (for no apparent reason), leaving their young son horrified at their bloody corpses. Yet after this initial savage display, for the rest of the picture he behaves decidedly un-wolf-like, mostly standing around with the other monsters patiently awaiting orders or entering one fracas after another at the behest of the Blue Demon doppelganger. At one point he does try to bite Santo's throat, but for the most part he makes do with throwing punches and executing wrestling moves. At the climactic battle in the underground lab, this *hombre lobo* even grabs the torch waved at him by the good Blue Demon and tosses it aside—then picks it up *himself* to use as a weapon. A werewolf wielding *fire*? But *Santo and Blue Demon vs. the Monsters* remains unconcerned with such trivialities as lunar cycles, silver bullets or werewolf motivation, so that this lycanthrope becomes more of a supernatural henchman than a tortured soul or brutal blending of man and beast. No transformations, no human guise, no agonizing over his curse... this wolfman merely takes orders and throws punches. Such a no-nonsense, nuance-free approach does lycan-cinema no favors, but it fits in perfectly with the movie's central theme—the

It's a south-of-the-border monsterfest: Santo and Blue Demon vs. the Monsters. *(Mexican poster)*

battle between good and evil for Truth, Justice and the Mexican way.

Starring the two most popular luchadors (masked wrestlers) in the history of Mexican wrestling (and Mexican wrestling cinema), *Santo and Blue Demon vs. the Monsters* was the first true pairing of these two titans. (Santo made a brief appearance in the Blue Demon–starrer *Blue Demon vs. the Satanic Power* in 1966, but only in a cameo role.) Though they played "best friends" in *Vs. the Monsters*, they were anything *but* in real life, with Blue Demon being particularly resentful of Santo's number-one status in the ring and on the screen (Blue frequently being relegated to sidekick for Santo's hero). "We did have a fierce rivalry because we were both very popular," commented Blue Demon, "but I feel I was the superior wrestler. ... Outside the ring, our rivalry wasn't as strong. We weren't enemies, but we weren't exactly friends either." When asked which wrestlers he considered good actors, Blue Demon pointedly replied, "I don't like to be disrespectful, so I'd rather not answer that question."[7] While Blue Demon (real name Alejandro Munoz Moreno) made 28 films over the course of his career, El Santo (real name Rudolfo Guzman Huerta) starred in nearly twice as many. Whatever Blue's opinion of his rival's acting, Santo was nothing if not popular on the silver screen, and he and Blue Demon went on to make seven more movies together, including the werewolf-filled *Santo and Blue Demon vs. Dracula and the Wolf Man* (1973). (Note: Though *Vs. the Monsters*' closing credits lists Alejandro Cruz as playing Blue Demon, this isn't entirely accurate. Better known as the masked wrestler Black Shadow, Cruz, a friend and partner of the real Blue Demon, sometimes doubled for Moreno on the screen, including playing the "evil" Blue here.)

"*Santo y Blue Demon contra los Monstruos* is not bad," concluded Santo, the Silver Masked Man himself, "only some of the monsters don't look very scary."[8] No, but they *are* quite entertaining. Finally subtitled in English and released on DVD in America in the early 2000s, and chock full of cheesy fun, *Santo and Blue Demon vs. the Monsters* is not to be missed by those enamored of south-of-the-border psychotronica.

THE AMAZING PROFESSOR ZOVEK

Nineteen-seventy-three provided a bumper crop of Mexican werewolves, with no less than four productions showcasing our hirsute fiends to one degree or another. The first, *Blue Demon y Zovek en la Invasion de los Muertos* (Blue Demon and Zovek in the Invasion of the Dead), teams masked wrestler Blue Demon with "Professor Zovek," a Mexican escape artist who possesses psychic abilities (he studied in Tibet, he explains), in a *Night of the Living Dead* (or, more aptly, *Invisible Invaders*) zombie scenario.

A fireball lands in the Mexican countryside, disgorging a large black sphere which apparently sends out emanations that raise the dead. Caught in the middle of this nightmare scenario are a local scientist, his daughter, and escape artist/psychic/all-round hero Zovek (whom they called in to investigate some strange rock paintings that seem to foretell of a cosmic calamity). After numerous altercations and escapes from the walking dead, Zovek manages to destroy the black sphere and deactivate the reanimated corpses. But could this happen again elsewhere, wonders a worried Zovek...

"Professor Zovek" (Francisco Javier Chapa del Bosque), an illusionist and escape artist dubbed "the Mexican Houdini," signed on to do a series of films, this being his second (the first was *El Increible Profesor Zovek*). But before shooting on his sophomore effort concluded, Zovek died in a fall from a helicopter while performing a promotional stunt for the Suarez Brothers Circus. After Zovek's untimely death on March 10, 1972, the filmmakers hired Blue Demon to appear in a handful of scenes and so bring their production up to feature length. Blue never directly interacts with Zovek (though he supposedly communicates with him via telephone). And while Zovek battles literally scores of the walking dead, Blue faces a mere half-dozen, with one of them (played by Gerardo Zepeda) inexplicably looking like a werewolf. A burly fellow in a tight yellow t-shirt with an overabundant goatee, bushy sideburns, and protruding fangs, he attacks Blue Demon by swinging his muscular arms like a, well, trained wrestler. After Blue Demon delivers a few hits with no apparent effect, the masked hero simply runs off, while the werewolf-zombie is never seen again (though presumably he, too, becomes "deactivated" along with all the rest of the walking dead when Zovek destroys the mysterious orb).

Little happens in the film for the first thirty minutes apart from a whole lot of palaver and a five-minute Zovek nightclub act in which a straight-jacketed and chained Zovek escapes from a flaming sarcophagus. Finally, the dead rise in a creepy, atmospheric sequence set during a nighttime rainstorm. Eerily affecting, the pasty-faced ghouls climb from their coffins and tombs, and stride forth, backlit by atmospheric lighting. They battle Zovek in a smoky cavern, who then makes his escape by jumping into an underground river that nearly takes him over a waterfall. Fortunately, frequent fast and furious encounters with the undead keep the pace and the (low-budget) action level high.

Professor Zovek makes for an impressively active hero, sporting a chest-baring jumpsuit and headband emblazoned with his trademark "Z" as he runs, swims, and fights his way through the various zombies. And though Blue Demon has little to do in his few, largely superfluous scenes, it's always a lift seeing Mexico's number two masked wrestling superhero on the screen. Unfortunately, *Blue Demon y Zoveken la Invasion de los Muertos* never received an English-language release; the late Professor deserved better.

OVERSIZED CHILDREN AND UNDERUTILIZED WEREWOLVES

The next two werewolf entries from 1973 were a pair of comedies. In *Chabelo y Pepito Contra los Monstruos* (Chabelo and Pepito vs. the Monsters), a Mexican children's film that never received an English-language release, a pair of mismatched cousins, Chabelo and Pepito, go on an outing with their scout troupe, only to break away from the pack when Pepito's pesky older sister joins them (she's dating the scout leader). Encountering an escaped (man-in-a-suit) gorilla, the two scamps flee to a nearby cave, where they find a living mummy, a second-rate Creature from the Black Lagoon (who battles—and bloodily kills—the gorilla), a Frankenstein Monster (in a crude mask), a blue-faced Dracula, and *El Hombre Lobo* (the Wolf Man). After much running about in the cave and the "haunted" hacienda above it, they discover the monsters are robots created by a supervillain mining some new powerful element in the vicinity.

Aimed squarely at the kiddie crowd, *Chabelo y Pepito Contra los Monstruos* offers the odd—and more than a little creepy—sight of 38-year-old Javier "Chabelo" Lopez playing an oversized kid with a high-pitched voice and a "glandular condition" that causes him to eat almost constantly (cue the numerous hunger gags—including Chabelo chasing after a now-terrified Dracula when informed by Pepito that vampires make good sandwiches!). Childish in every way, the film delivers very little else and particularly short-changes its lycanthropic element. Onscreen for less than a minute, this Wolf Man howls in a couple of shots before being abruptly pushed into a snake pit by a gaggle of boy scouts. *El Hombre Lobo*, decked out in natty slacks and turtleneck (it *was* the Seventies), boasts effective Lon Chaney makeup, complete with full facial hair, canine nose and prominent fanged underbite, making him the most impressive-looking monster of the admittedly tatty bunch. Too bad the script gave this token werewolf so little screen time and nothing to do.

MORE COMEDY

Gaspar "Capulina" Henaine was a portly Mexican comedian who specialized in playing lovable imbeciles, generally alongside his partner Antonio "Viruta" Campos. This low-rent south-of-the-border Abbott and Costelloesque team split up in 1967, and Capulina went on to even greater success on his own, while his former partner (who initiated the split) fell into obscurity. With his intellectually-challenged antics aimed at the pre-teen set, Capulina met vampires (*Capulina Contra los Vampiros*, 1970), mummies (*Capulina Contra las Momias*, 1972) *plus* Frankenstein's Monster and the Wolf Man in *Capulina Contra los Monstruos* (Capulina vs. the Monsters, 1973). Though highly successful in Mexico, Capulina remained strictly a Latino phenomenon, and his films failed to break into the English-language market.

In *Capulina Contra los Monstruos*, newstand vendor Capulina is kidnapped by a mad scientist in order to employ the energy from the timid man's own overweening fear to restore life to the quartet of dormant monsters the scientist keeps in his secret lab. This done, the monsters frighten a few citizens in town, engage Capulina in a pillow fight, and end up back at the lab where they comically face off against Capulina and his quartet of kid friends (who vanquish the creatures with happy thoughts of ice cream!).

With its suitably savage and hirsute appearance (a cross between JoJo the Dog-faced Boy and Paul Naschy's Waldemar Daninsky), the Wolf Man comes off best of the four creatures, as the poor makeup jobs on the Vampire, the Frankenstein Monster, and the Mummy look more silly than scary. This werewolf sports a long furry tail, however, which the contentious Mummy bites at one point. He also incongruously wears a herringbone coat and cape *á la* Sherlock Holmes, and converses quite civilly with his four monstrous *companeros*.

Capulina inadvertently summed up this juvenile film best when he commented, "This [movie] has one of my favorite scenes: when I eat some onions and conquer the monsters with my breath."[9]

SANTO AND BLUE TOGETHER AGAIN

Saving the best for last (which in this context might be damning with faint praise), the final lycan-entry from '73 provides a happy (for their fans, anyway) re-

Those two shining pillars of Truth, Justice and the Mexican Way team up yet again to battle the forces of evil in Santo and Blue Demon vs. Dracula and the Wolf Man. *(Mexican poster)*

union for El Santo and Blue Demon. Though not as monster-heavy as the espectacular *Santo and Blue Demon vs. the Monsters* (1970), *Santo and Blue Demon vs. Dracula and the Wolf Man* (*Santo y Blue Demon vs. Dracula y el Hombre Lobo*) is no slouch in the Mexican monster rally department either. On the plus side, the film features Dracula (Aldo Monti, his '70s haircut and sideburns contrasting amusingly with his classic penguin suit); the Wolf Man "Rufus" (Agustin Martinez Solares Jr.), who serves the Vampire Lord in the bloodsucker's plan to rule the world by turning all humans into either vampires or wolfmen; and a kindly professor turned creepy zombie menacing his own granddaughter. Co-starring with the heroic "El Enmascarado del Plata" El Santo (playing himself) is his pal and near-equal in the crime-fighting superhero wrestler business, the blue-masked Blue Demon (also as himself). In the minus column, however, sits a meandering, mundane subplot in which the revived Dracula seeks vengeance on the descendants of those who initially staked him hundreds of years ago, while the Wolf Man—in human form—woos one of said female descendants in an ill-conceived and illogical vengeance scheme.

Then there's the overabundance of flatly staged wrestling action (three full bouts). Disappointingly for those Santo and Blue Demon fans who enjoy watching their heroes' energetic acrobatics in the ring, the locked-down camera and obvious studio staging (plain blue background, no visible audience) robs the movie's many wrasslin' moments of their sense of immediacy and excitement. In fact, it looks as if the brawny contests take place in some disconnected other dimension, with the piped-in sounds from the unseen crowd only underlining the feel of isolation. This is a real shame, because a well-shot Santo and/or Blue Demon bout (versus "The White Angel" and "Renato the Hippie," respectively) with a frenzied audience can get the blood pumping by showcasing the duo's agile abilities and their immense popularity with the crowds.

South-of-the-border werewolves apparently play by a very different set of rules. For instance, Rufus is revived from the dead just like his master, Dracula, by blood dripping onto his skeletal remains in his sarcophagus. Unlike Dracula's onscreen revival, however, the Wolf Man's resurrection occurs off-screen (no doubt to save on yet another round of special effects), after which the restored Rufus sits up in his Wolf Man guise (wearing what looks like a freshly-ironed yellow silk pirate shirt). He then calmly walks over to Dracula to declare, "I'm ready, Master." Obviously, this werewolf retains his full human faculties while in hirsute form, displaying not the savagery of the beast but the calculated coldness of a human villain. Appearance-wise, this Wolf Man sports a rather primitive Lon Chaney get-up: coarse hair covering every inch of his head and face save for his (brown colored) nose, and a pair of tiny fangs protruding from between his lips. Rufus' lycanthropy appears to extend only to his head and hands, thought, as his neck and partially bare chest remain free from any unsightly wolf hair.

Rufus' half-dozen wolfmen underlings (who come into play during the film's climax) vary in appearance and completeness of their makeup. Some have a full face of hair like Rufus, while others just a simple fright wig and bushy beard. One boasts little more than heavy eyebrows and a scraggly goatee. The two heroes battle the lycanthropes with punches and wrestling throws—and the wolfmen respond in kind, acting more like hairy henchmen than animalistic monsters. The film completely foregoes all the tortured, conflicted possibilities inherent in the man-into-beast concept and opts instead to utilize its werewolves as mere punching bags and wrestling fodder for the eponymous masked heroes.

After the brief resurrection scene, Rufus, "chief of the terrifying breed of the beast men" (as an old tome describes him), never again becomes a wolfman—at least until the very end when he battles with Blue Demon. (One sequence does offer an *implied* transformation, however, when Rufus escorts a woman on a nighttime stroll: over the shot of the full moon we hear a few grunts and growls, and then the girl's scream, but the metamorphosis, attack and assumed bloody result remain unseen.) At the climax, when tussling with Rufus in his human guise, Blue lands a punch that sends Rufus reeling to the ground. After a brief cutaway, Rufus rises as the Wolf Man, only to be dispatched shortly thereafter when Santo simultaneously kicks him and Dracula into the waiting pit of spikes. Furthering the lycan-disappointment, we never see just *how* Rufus transforms that cave full of captives into wolfmen (nor, for that that matter, do we see Dracula working on his assembly line producing vampire minions).

Apparently, any pointy object will do when dispatching these werewolves, with silver being superfluous. During the climactic free-for-all, as Santo and Blue Demon battle the wolfmen horde in their cave lair, Santo hurls a spear into one wolfman—who promptly falls to the ground and vanishes in a puff of white smoke, leaving the spear standing upright in the soil! And, of course, Rufus himself expires when the Silver Masked Man tosses him into the pit of spikes (*sans* smoke).

As well as the taint of lycanthropy (at least in *this* film), Wolf Man actor Agustin Martinez Solares Jr. had movies in his blood, being the son of cinematographer Agustin Martinez Solares (*100 Cries of Terror*), and nephew of both cinematographer Raul Martinez Solares (*Night of the Bloody Apes, Santo and Blue Demon vs. the Monsters*) and director Gilberto Martinez Solares (*Face of the Screaming Werewolf, Santo and Blue Demon vs. the Monsters*).

Even with its various pacing peccadilloes and lycanthropic lapses, *Santo and Blue Demon vs. Dracula and the Wolf Man* contains enough monstrous or outré elements to keep ennui from creeping into this cinematic ring, including a bloody resurrection scene right out of *Dracula Prince of Darkness* (bleeding out a victim suspended over Dracula's and the Wolf Man's bones) and a Dracula demise sequence borrowed from *The Return of Dracula* (did someone say "pit full of spikes"?). The movie also offers bright comic-book lighting (chock full of primary colors) contrasted with wonderfully shadowy Gothic illumination (particularly in some misty woodland settings). Then there's the lycan-heavy climax in which the two heroes face off against not only Drac and Wolfy, but a whole pack of savage werewolves. Never before was so much yak hair seen in one place at one time.

"The movies I make are not art," admitted Santo himself, "they are made to entertain. People go to see them to have fun." And those who come to see *Santo and Blue Demon vs. Dracula and the Wolf Man* with that in mind will not be disappointed.[10]

A FITTING FINALE

Classico Mexican horror cinema closed out its werewolf ways with a film that reflected the changing cinematic times by taking a grittier, more mature look at its hairy subject. *Santo vs. the She-Wolves* (*Santo vs. las Lobas*, 1976) also marks the fifth and final time the Mexican masked wrestling superhero/crimefighter El Santo tangled with werewolves. Here the Man in the Silver Mask faces off against an entire tribe of lycanthropes, led by a rejuvenating werewolf queen and her king.

Cesar Harker (Rodolfo de Anda) contacts masked wrestler and all-round-hero El Santo for help. Harker, who comes from a long line of werewolf hunters, has discovered that a local gathering of lycanthropes plan to create a new queen and thereby rule the world of men. After Santo is attacked by wolves (German shepherds), he journeys to Harker's village, where the werewolves lay siege. Harker tells Santo, "You must help us end the curse of the werewolves. ...We must succeed before the accession of the Red Moon." (Of course, nobody ever explains just what a *red* moon might be.) But Santo has been bitten, and "anyone who's bitten by one becomes a werewolf on the first Red Moon." After Cesar falls prey to the werewolf queen, Santo joins Eric, Cesar's twin brother, and the likable "Gipsy," Harker's bald-headed, bare-chested, leather-vested he-man servant (deftly enacted by Santo's real-life friend and manager Carlos Suarez), to battle the she-wolves and their male counterparts, led by Licar, King of the Werewolves, and save not only Santo himself but all of humanity.

Santo vs. the She-Wolves was shot towards the end of the *lucha libre* cinema cycle, when masked wrestler movies, popular for two decades, had lost much of their appeal (time marches on—even in wrestler-loving Mexico). Consequently, budgets for these productions shrank, and those few *luchadore* movies (never lavish to begin with) that *were* being made in the mid-to-late 1970s could charitably be called impoverished. *Santo vs. the She-Wolves* overcame this by taking a rather gritty turn, emphasizing bleak, seventies-style horror more than the candy-colored, kid-friendly tone of previous Santo films (even from only a few years before, like in *Santo and Blue Demon vs. Dracula and the Wolf Man*). Via hand-held photography, echoing sound effects, dim lighting (with silhouettes of hulking beast-men at twilight rising up into frame), an emphasis on real settings rather than artificial sets, and an absence of distracting, out-of-place time-filler like sappy nightclub musical numbers and/or dance routines (almost a staple of the *lucha libre* subgenre), *Santo vs. the She-Wolves* makes itself over into a fairly effective low-budget horror entry—with the added attraction of everyone's favorite Silver Masked Man at its center.

Directors Jaime Jimenez Pons and Ruben Galindo take every opportunity to underline this new emphasis on horror. At one point the werewolf queen tilts back her head and laughs—a sinister, hollow sound that echoes into the next scene, drawing the eeriness forward. When the wolves attack Santo, the point-of-view photography alternates between the backpedaling masked man desperately kicking at the canines, and close-ups of the slavering jaws snapping and lunging at the camera—at us. It's a cheap but involving horror trope that conveys the immediacy—and danger—of the situation.

At Harker's village, an outdoor dinner party turns into a chaotic, bloody brawl when the lycanthropes attack. The hand-held photography and rough, abrupt editing emphasize the chaos and highlight the bloody victims, as people flee in terror, leaving Santo and Gipsy to brutally battle the beast-men (and women). Perhaps the most effectively disturbing sequence comes when Gipsy and the heroine (who, of course, has fallen for Santo—"I love you," she tells him, to which the stalwart hero dismissively replies, "We'll discuss that later; right now we need to save those children's lives!") attempt to drive a station wagon full of village children to safety. As they drive through what appears to be an abandoned quarry, a gang of savage werewolves hurls rocks and flaming bundles of hay at the car before viciously assaulting the vehicle. The evil creatures paw at the windows and rock the car back and forth trying to get in, generating an almost *Night of the Living Dead* feel.

This darker, grittier tone continues even into the portrayal of the beloved central character, cracking the heretofore invincible El Santo's bulletproof persona—to the point he high-tails it up into the arena rafters to escape a pair of snarling wolves and screams for help until two guards arrive on the scene. Unlike in most Santo outings, Our Hero looks and acts genuinely frightened at times. And the final mano-a-lobo battle between Santo and Licar, though ending with Santo tossing the werewolf king over a cliff, remains surprisingly melancholy. Santo's victory is met by a thoughtful Santo simply staring after his victim while the lonely sound of the wind plays over an otherwise silent soundtrack. No triumphant music swells, no grateful bystander utters, "God bless Santo"; the curtain closes on this image of a solitary, introspective Silver Masked Man contemplating the horror and tragedy of the situation.

At first glance, the she-wolves look like big-haired, bearded ladies, though a closer look reveals slight variation, with some resembling cute Pekingese pups and others appearing more like fanged Lhasa Apsos. The queen herself sports a hairy face, long eyelashes, wavy locks of long werewolf hair, a mouth full of large (plastic-looking) fangs, and long (but still pretty) fingernails. Werewolfism apparently ends at the neck, though, for she boasts smooth skin wherever her fur bikini fails to cover.

Beyond these minor differences, there are two distinct types of werewolves—the human hybrid wolf-women (or wolfmen) and full-on wolves (played by German shepherds), who attack and bite Santo, opening the potential of Santo himself becoming a werewolf. In any case, all the werewolves retain their human faculties and have no ties to the moon. They are able to take on their lycanthropic guise whenever it suits them (one hirsute wolfwoman even peeks over a wall to spy on Santo in broad daylight). At one point, the local sympathetic doctor reveals that he, too, is afflicted with the curse of lycanthropy. But he somehow remains on the side of Good, staying friendly towards Santo even while in reluctant werewolf mode—which consists of a bushy beard, hairy hands and moderately long fingernails.

Of course, along with the various she-wolves, this tribe of lycanthropes features a number of male werewolves as well, including "Licar, King of the Lycanthropes," who arrives at their village sealed in a box sent from Transylvania. (Mexican actor Jorge Russek, who played Lican, appeared in a number of Hollywood productions, including *The Wild Bunch*.) "I've come to join you to eliminate the last of the Harkers," he tells his followers after they kill the train station attendant and liberate His Hairiness from the crate. Consequently, *Santo vs. the She-Wolves* marks the first portrayal of a werewolf *community*, years before the concept coalesced in the classic American entry *The Howling* (1981).

The film's one transformation scene consists of a simple dissolve when Licar, after being knocked unconscious by Santo at the attack on the party, reverts back to his human form upon regaining consciousness. Amazingly, not only does *he* transform, but the torn purple shirt he sported as a snarling werewolf magically becomes a neat, white dinner jacket, complete with bow tie!

One particular innovation found among these *Lobas* is making their symbolic scourge the protagonist himself. Santo is able to defeat numerous werewolves rampaging through the dinner party by using only his fists and wrestling moves, leaving many of the monsters unconscious or dead (whereas Harker and the rest require silver bullets to dispatch the lycanthropes). Unlike the others, Santo needs no silver bullets, as he himself, due to his legendary status as "The Man in the Silver Mask," is lethal to lycanthropes. As Cesar tells Santo, "The *Book of Licars* says that only a silver symbol can eliminate them [the werewolves]. Your mask is silver." So Santo, the Man in the Silver Mask, stands as the living bane of lycanthropy.

Loaded with grim situations and surprising deaths (nearly all the principal characters, including the She-Wolf queen herself, and the initial hero and heroine, perish within the first thirty minutes, allowing a whole new cast of characters to appear—including the murdered Cesar's twin brother—taking their place in the second half), *Santo vs. the She-Wolves* remains a rather bleak, rough-hewn, fascinatingly strange addition not only to Santo cinema but to big-screen lycanthropy.

Though two more werewolf-themed horrors popped up in Mexico—one in the Eighties, *Cazador de Demonios* (Demon Hunter; 1983), and one in the Nineties, *Colmillos, el Hombre Lobo* (Colmillos, the Wolf Man, 1993)—for all intents and purposes, south-of-the-border lycanthropy was done and dusted by the mid–1970s. But from 1958 to 1976, Mexican filmmakers created a cadre of unique lycanthrocentric movies that rarely failed to engage or entertain. Whether presenting brief monster cameos or wall-to-wall werewolves; whether childish comedies or gritty horror entries; whether filled with artistic touches or gonzo wackiness; whether good, bad, or downright ugly, Mexican filmmakers consistently offered unique and entertaining takes on one of horrordom's classic monsters, earning a big *gracias* from werewolf fans everywhere.

NOTES:
1 "El Vampiro Speaks!" by Bryan Senn, Richard Sheffield and Jim Clatterbaugh, *Monsters from the Vault* 24.
2 *Interviews with B Science Fiction Stars and Horror Heroes*, by Tom Weaver.
3 "Director Gilberto Martinez Solares," by Brian Moran, *Santo Street* 18.
4 "Meet the True Blue Demon," by Brian Moran, *Santo Street* 7.
5 "On Monsters and Imposters: Santo's Final Say," by Ruben Sano, *Santo Street* 13.
6 Ibid.
7 "Meet the True Blue Demon," by Brian Moran, *Santo Street* 7.
8 "On Monsters and Imposters: Santo's Final Say," by Ruben Sano, *Santo Street* 13.
9 "Investigating 'Investigador' Capulina," by Brian Moran, *Santo Street* 14.
10 "On Monsters and Imposters: Santo's Final Say," by Ruben Sano, *Santo Street* 13.

> In 2006, BCI put out an English language–friendly DVD collection of the three seminal Mexican mummy movies collectively known as *The Aztec Mummy* series. (Finally!) Here's my assessment of this classic(?) trio, penned (I thought) for *Monsters from the Vault* magazine (but I'll be damned if I can find which issue).

THE AZTEC MUMMY COLLECTION

In 1957, within the space of two months, Mexican filmmaker Rafael Portillo shot a series of three related horror movies, all scripted by Guillermo Calderon: *La Momia Azteca* (The Aztec Mummy), *La Maldicion de la Azteca Momia* (The Curse of the Aztec Mummy) and

The one that started it all: The Aztec Mummy. *(Mexican lobby card)*

La Momia Azteca vs. el Robot Humano (The Robot vs. the Aztec Mummy). Enter Jerry Warren in the 1960s, that tireless transformer of horror imports into senseless time-killers. Taking *La Momia Azteca* and adding footage of Warren "regulars"—such as Chuck (*Teenage Zombies*) Niles, George (*Invasion of the Animal People*) Mitchell and Bruno (*Creature of the Walking Dead*) VeSota—sitting around talking, drinking coffee and answering the telephone, Warren unleashed *Attack of the Mayan Mummy* on an unsuspecting American public. About half of the 70-minute feature consisted of new material shot by Warren, which means that half the picture consisted of lengthy exposition that explains very little, and dull, pointless soliloquies that add nothing. For these interminable interludes, Warren locked down his camera (it literally *never* moves) on threadbare sets (or in a real living room) and had his actors recite reams of "gobbledegook" (as Warren himself labeled his dialogue). Sample speech: "As the memory of Ann Taylor had functioned to the degree of pointing to the areas unknown to her present generation, the discovery of that which had filled the minds of everyone had become a reality." (Translation: "Hey, we found it!") Designed to do nothing more than eat up running time, these tangential conversations cover everything from regressive hypnosis to ulcer flare-ups! Inexplicably, Warren excised much of the original film's best footage, including about *four minutes* of mummy action! The unique and grotesque mummy is the film's major draw, but in Warren's version it appears in a mere two sequences. Even worse, Warren dispatches his titular terror off-screen (by having it *hit by a car!*), revealing its fate to the viewer only via a newspaper headline.

Fortunately, thanks to BCI-Eclipse's DVD box set release, English-speaking Mexi-monster movie fans now have the chance to see this iconic (well, marginally noteworthy, anyway) monster—and film—in its original form, and can now judge the feature (and its two sequels) based on its own merits (or lack of same) rather than try to *imagine* what it might have been before Warren sank his talentless talons into it.

The story of the original *Aztec Mummy*—with a reincarnation nod to Universal's Mummy films—has a female subject, under a radical form of regressive hypnosis, recall her past life as an Aztec princess. She subsequently leads a group of scientists to a secret chamber inside an Aztec pyramid, the site of her death after the discovery of her forbidden romance with the warrior Popoca. There the mummy of Popoca, cursed for his transgression to guard the secret of the Aztec treasure for eternity, comes to life and seeks to reclaim the sacred objects taken from its tomb. Meanwhile, a nefarious criminal mastermind/scientist known as "the Bat" sets his sights on acquiring the sacred breastplate and bracelet that reveal the location of the Aztec riches.

While it's a relief to finally see the full film rather than merely half of it (as we do with the nonsensical Warren travesty), *The Aztec Mummy* is no undiscovered Mexi-classic. The first hour focuses on various (often dull) human-centric activities: the scientists pontificating on their theories, the protracted hypnosis procedure, lengthy flashbacks to the Aztec ceremonies, the search for the hidden tomb, and the Bat skulking about and formulating his plans. Consequently, the film's raison d'être—the Aztec Mummy itself—receives very little screen time. Fortunately, director Portillo makes the most of the few minutes awarded his monster, beginning with an eerie introduction: from the darkness of the tomb we hear mysterious shuffling sounds coming closer and closer, the uncanny sound emanating from

The one that turned out to be the Curse of the Viewer: The Curse of the Aztec Mummy. *(Mexican lobby card)*

the blackness generating an ever-growing sense of unease, before the creature finally steps from the shadows to reveal its hideous visage. No clichéd bandaged Hollywood horror, Popoca is a dried and withered—but nonetheless imposing—figure of leathery skin and rotting garments. Of course, the immobile mask renders the monster largely expressionless, but his angry growls and menacing movements get the point across. Though requiring some modicum of patience, the Aztec Mummy (at least for the dedicated Mexi-monster fan) is worth the wait—just.

After the straightforward horror of the *The Aztec Mummy*, its first sequel, *The Curse of the Aztec Mummy*, veers sharply into serial territory, with some (poor) lucha libre–styled masked wrestler heroics tossed into the mix. An evil mastermind, a deadly snake pit, small-time hoods, fistfights, an Aztec treasure, a mask-wearing crime-fighter and an ancient Aztec mummy come to life—all in the space of 65 minutes—should be enough to make for a lively entry. Guess again.

Looking like nothing more than a low-grade serial, complete with cliff-hanging escapes and endless rounds of fisticuffs, *The Curse of the Aztec Mummy* occupies its brief running time with the exploits of the hammy master criminal dubbed "the Bat" (who was more of an ancillary character/subplot in the first film) and his gang of suit-and-fedora-clad thugs trying to find the Aztec treasure guarded by the living mummy Popoca. Popoca wears an ancient breastplate and bracelet that are the keys to locating the treasure. The Bat tries to get to the mummy through a scientist's fiancée, the reincarnation of Popoca's lost love. Opposing the criminals is the professor from the first film, aided by a mask-and-cape-wearing crime-fighting hero who calls himself "the Angel."

About the only enjoyment that can be gleaned from this tedious trial (which, in time-honored Universal Mummy fashion, trots out the flashback footage from the original *Aztec Mummy* to pad its threadbare plot) comes from a surprisingly brutal fight sequence in which one of the protagonists has his head repeatedly pounded into the floor(!) and the rather imposing appearance of the desiccated mummy itself. Unfortunately, said mummy appears only near the very end, in two brief scenes. Consequently, *The Curse of the Aztec Mummy*, the weakest of the three entries, becomes The Curse of Mexican Monster Movie Viewer.

But never fear, *The Robot vs. the Aztec Mummy*, the third in the Aztec Mummy trilogy (a fourth, *The Wrestling Women vs. the Aztec Mummy*, was made seven years later, but is only tangentially related to the earlier trio), stands as a significant improvement over both its lackluster progenitors (if only by dint of stealing the earlier films' few intriguing scenes while adding its own little touch of boffo sci-fi and mechanical-man outrageousness).

That evil criminal scientist "the Bat" is back and once again searching for the breastplate and bracelet guarded by the living mummy Popoca. The Bat constructs an atomic-powered "human robot" (a metal man with a human brain) in a convoluted plot to destroy the Aztec Mummy and obtain the treasure (which will finance his intentions to build an army of robots to conquer the world). It's up to the professor and his wife (the reincarnation of Popoca's lost love)—and Popoca himself—to once more thwart the madman's evil plan.

Over a third of *The Robot vs. the Aztec Mummy* consists of flashback scenes from the previous entries—

The one that finished it all (with a flourish): The Robot vs. the Aztec Mummy. *(Mexican poster)*

which is fine for the neophyte, but quickly turns tedious for those who've seen the other Aztec Mummy movies. For the veteran viewer, apart from the mummy flashback moments (always worth a re-visit), the picture only comes to life (or a risible semblance thereof) when the "robot" does the same—in the final ten minutes.

Unfortunately (or fortunately, depending upon one's "camp" sensibilities), said robot belongs to the goofy painted-cardboard-box-and-bucket variety. Laughably, the suit-wearer's face is fully visible behind the monster's faceplate—even though the mechanical monster supposedly houses merely a human *brain*. The climactic battle between the robot and the Aztec Mummy has the two titular titans taking turns awkwardly pushing each other back against a wall, before the Mummy finally tires of the game and dismantles his silly opponent. Though lacking the gravitas of the first (but, thankfully, avoiding much of the sheer boredom of the second), this final outing in the Aztec Mummy trilogy shapes up as an intermittently entertaining mix of Gothic horror and mad science, with some risible, salsa-flavored camp craziness seasoning the cinematic soufflé.

Housed on three separate discs, each in their own slim-case, BCI's prints of the three films are far from perfect (much like the movies themselves), with the subtitled *The Aztec Mummy* looking soft and dark, particularly—and most disappointingly—during the mummy sequences. The flipper discs for *Curse* and *Robot* offer the Spanish language versions (with optional subtitles) on one side, and the K. Gordon Murray English-dubbed import versions on the other. (*Aztec* was only released Stateside by Warren as the bastardized *Attack of the Mayan Mummy*; consequently, only its original Spanish language version is included in this set.) The sequels appear both sharper and brighter than the *Aztec Mummy* print—with the annoying exception of the mummy scenes. Aaargh! For some inexplicable reason, the mummy sequences look noticeably darker. (And, disconcertingly, the sequels' subtitles refer to the mummy as "she"!) Fortunately, the dubbed AIP-TV prints on the flipside suffer no such lack of light (or gender-confusion) during its key scenes.

The set's only extras are a brief photo gallery on the *Aztec Mummy* disc featuring a few stills and lobby cards, and a short, indifferently-written booklet that's only occasionally informative. Still, given the reasonable price for the three films, no self-respecting Mexican monster movie fan can afford to pass up this set, and the opportunity to enjoy the series for what it is—Mexi-warts and all.

> I'm fairly certain that I wrote this review to go along with the many others I submitted to *Monsters from the Vault* magazine back in the aughts (when niche companies like CasaNegra and Ground-Zero were putting smiles on fans' faces by importing all manner of Mexi-horror for American DVD consumption). Even so, this one apparently never saw print (perhaps due to it being a Spanish-only disc). Anyway, it's worth including here—if for nothing else than to give Blue Demon a fairer shake than he usually received while playing second fiddle to El Santo.

BLUE DEMON VS. EL PODER SATANICO (1964)

So often playing second fiddle to El Santo, Blue Demon finally earned his own film series in the mid–1960s—though not without frequent guest support from his rival, like in Blue Demon vs. el Poder Satanico *(1964).*

Stepping out from the shadow of El Santo's cape, masked wrestler Blue Demon finally got his own Mexican film series in the mid–1960s. Starting with the eponymous *Blue Demon* (also 1964), Santo's biggest rival in the ring became his biggest rival on the big screen as well. But just as in the world of lucha libra (Mexican wrestling), Blue Demon came off second best to El Santo in lucha cine, with *Blue Demon Contra el Poder Satanico* (Blue Demon vs. the Satanic Power) hammering this point home. Inferior in almost every way to the contemporary films of El Santo, *Poder Satanico* suffers from poor pacing, a scarcity of action, and an anti-climactic climax. Adding insult to injury, producer Luis Enrique Vergara even inserted a *Santo* wrestling match (which turns out to be more acrobatic and brutally exciting than any of Blue Demon's *three* featured bouts—poor Blue, upstaged by his rival even in his own film!). Vergara was also producing Santo's movies at this time (*Attack of the Witches*, *The Diabolical Axe*, etc.), and no doubt felt that a Santo cameo would help jumpstart his new luchadore film series. (In Santo's only other scene in *Poder Satanico*, the Silver Masked Man shows up before a bout to congratulate and encourage Blue, effectively putting the Santo seal of approval on the Blue Demon movies—a shrewd move on Vergara's part.)

El Santo and Blue Demon were the Karloff and Lugosi of Mexican horror (had Karloff and Lugosi worn masks and tights to fight bad guys and monsters, that is). Like Karloff, Santo made better solo films and generally dominated their joint efforts, while Blue Demon's *Poder Satanico* is the equivalent of a Lugosi B-movie for Monogram.

Poder Satanico (whose plot revolves around an evil villain who uses, well, satanic powers to hypnotize women, bed them and then consign them to the flames of his oversized oven) moves far too slowly for a lucha libra monster flick. The villain has no minions for Blue to battle, so the only action occurs *inside* the ring. Between several tepid nightclub sequences (including one featuring a chubby-cheeked chanteuse with mushroom-shaped hair!) and repetitive scenes of the villain hypnotizing his women, Blue Demon does little except sit around conducting research with old books and talking on the telephone.

Poder Satanico offers a bit of atmosphere via the foggy cave entrance to the monster's lair and the cobwebbed old mansion above it, but the climax pounds the last nail in the coffin as it sloooowly winds down to… nothing at all. Blue and a trio of cops wander around the mansion searching for the fiend, only to find that the villain, having lost his poder satanico, has reverted to a moldering corpse. There's no transformation, no confrontation, and no excitement.

Ground-Zero Entertainment's DVD is just as disappointing as the film itself. Apart from the fact that there are no subtitles (making it difficult to follow for those of us whose Spanish is limited to "dos cervesas, por favor"), the picture quality is on the level of a VHS tape (there's even some telltale tracking jumps at the bottom of the frame), and the muddy audio sports a near-constant crackling/buzzing sound. The fact that the DVD case names the film *Blue Demon* "contra"*el Poder Satanico*, whereas the film print itself reads *Blue Demon* "vs." *el Poder Satanico*, speaks volumes as to the level of care taken with this mishandled release.

> Below is a somewhat expanded review I wrote for *Cult Movies* magazine (issue 21) in 1997—*before* the Mexi-horror renaissance of the following decade (when fans could finally replace their poorly-dubbed dupes with pristine, subtitled DVDs).

THE CURSE OF THE DOLL PEOPLE (1961)

"GHOULS! SEE *IF YOUR BOY FIENDS CAN TAKE IT!"* –ad line

Like the loopy south-of-the-border bad movie "classic" *The Brainiac*, *The Curse of the Doll People* is one of a clutch of Mexican monster movies that carnival owner-cum-theater builder K. Gordon Murray acquired from Mexico City's Churubusco-Azteca Studios, selling them to American International Television (the TV distribution arm of AIP) as well as sending them out as theatrical double-features (sometimes years *after* they appeared on the tube!). AIP dumped these dubbed disasters onto the unsuspecting American air waves where they've resided ever since (and still pop up occasionally on Saturday afternoons).

Midgets in business suits set about fulfilling the Curse of the Doll People *(1961).*

One of the more unique entries in the package (though far from the best), this killer doll oddity follows the machinations of a voodoo sorcerer who (accompanied by his prune-faced, wide-brimmed hat-wearing zombie) sends out his life-like dolls to take vengeance upon those who stole an idol from his Haitian temple. The sorcerer creates his demonic dummies in his victims' images and traps their souls inside, then sends the "medium-sized dolls" (as one character describes them—though, in truth, they are actually about three feet tall) out to do his evil bidding. As a result, midgets dressed in half-pint business suits and doll masks (resembling homely middle-aged men—one even sports a gray goatee!) creep about with long nasty needles. A woman doctor (an expert on the occult) and her fiancé (another doctor—who seems to have trouble telling if a victim is alive or dead!), along with some *very* stupid policemen, try to stop them.

Talky and slow, and lacking the large doses of 1930s and '40s-style atmosphere (crumbling castles, dank crypts, fog-shrouded graveyards) featured in the best Mexican horror movies of the period, the main enjoyment gleaned from *The Curse of the Doll People* comes from the (unintentional) laughs it generates. For instance, when the voodooist calls the soul of his latest victim to enter the body of a doll he's constructed, said spirit flitting about the darkened chamber looks for all the world like a flying handkerchief! Other chuckles come when the heroine explores the sorcerer's lair and the zombie opens its sarcophagus lid while her back is turned—only to quickly close it again when she wheels about to see what was behind her (Abbott and Costello would have been proud). But best of all, the villain hypnotizes the heroine by using a large disco-style revolving glitter ball! Shake your boogey—er—booty.

The script was written by Abel (Anglicized as "Alfred" for the dubbed version) Salazar, a familiar name (and face) to those enamored of Mexican monster movies. An actor (who initially specialized in light comedy) in Mexico since 1941, Salazar soon turned his hand to producing and even formed his own company in 1957. He sometimes scripted, and often acted in, his own features (including taking the title role in *The Brainiac*) as well as those made by others (such as this one, produced by Pedro A. Calderon and Guillermo Calderon, which was combined into "William Calderon Stell" for American viewers).

As with most K. Gordon Murray jobs, the dubbing is generally toneless but the dialogue is often quite funny. "Your young fiancé," remarks the sorcerer to the heroine, "who denies the existence of all he is unable to measure or place under a microscope, is assuredly a drooling idiot!" Zing.

As far as the acting goes, however, the cast would be better suited to a film entitled *The Curse of the DULL People*. The picture is padded with scene after scene of people standing around talking, sitting around talking, even *laying* around talking. The dolls themselves manage to contribute one or two shuddery moments as they creep ever so slowly toward their intended victim, their face expressionless, needle in hand, sinister malice in every move… But don't get your hopes up; this is still your typical south-of-the-border celluloid junk—good for a few laughs, one or two shudders and some atrocious dubbing. But hey, at least nobody *wrestles* in this one.

Murray released *The Curse of theDoll People* theatrically in 1968 on a double bill with the far superior *The Vampire* (Mexico's take on *Dracula*), advertising the duo as "A psychedelic trip into the 5th dimension!" Well, it *was* the sixties, after all…

> This welcome DVD saw an all-too-brief release in 2003 before some murky rights issues caused Image Entertainment to pull it. Thus, my review, intended for *Monsters from the Vault* magazine, never saw print. Let's rectify that…

DOCTOR OF DOOM (1962) / THE WRESTLING WOMEN VS. THE AZTEC MUMMY (1965)

This presentation of a pair of wacky Mexican-Wrestling-Women-Meet-the-Monster movies from producer William Calderon Stell comes courtesy of our

*Sure, hombres like El Santo and Blue Demon can battle monsters—but so can wrasslin' chicas, as evidenced by this dynamic duo. (*Doctor of Doom *Mexican poster)*

fine-tooth-combing friends at Something Weird Video and Image Entertainment. While both flicks have been around since their U.S. kiddie matinee debuts in the mid–1960s by theater owner/entrepreneur K. Gordon Murray (including abominable altered versions of both films later put out by Rhino Video in the 1980s), they've never looked this good. Though far from pristine (with the picture rather soft and the blacks sometimes muted), this double-feature DVD offers what is probably the cleanest prints available these days.

The first of the two, *Doctor of Doom*, centers on a mad doctor (Roberto Canedo) who hides his identity beneath Ku Klux Klan-style hood and robes(!), and is obsessed with transplanting brains. To this end he sends out Gomar (Gerardo Zepeda), a man with the brain of a gorilla who wears a bullet-proof metal suit(!!), to kidnap women for his experiments. When the doctor chooses as his next 'donor' the sister of a professional female wrestler named Gloria Venus (Lorena Velazquez), Gloria and her partner in the ring, the Golden Ruby (Elizabeth Campbell), join up with a pair of police detectives (Armando Silvestre, Chucho Salinas) to stop the madman and his pet gorilla-man.

Whew! *Doctor of Doom* comes off more like a boffo episode of the old *Superman* TV show than a real movie. The mad doctor behaves like a deranged comic-book crime-lord, operating out of a secret lair (complete with a "room of death"—a chamber with moving, spiked walls), and sending out his gang of thugs to do his bidding (and augment Gomar's activities). The two policeman "heroes" even wear radio wristwatches straight out of *Dick Tracy*. (In a charming role reversal, the wrestling heroines must rescue these "heroes" from said room of death.) Throw in a handful of ringside scenes (which feature obvious—and chunky—*real* female wrestler doubles stepping in for Our Battling Beauties), some serial-like fisticuffs, bargain basement sets, ludicrously dubbed dialogue, and a secret identity mystery that's no mystery at all (there's only *one possible suspect*!), and *Doctor of Doom* becomes a naively charming guilty favorite among Mexican Wrestling Horror Movie aficionados.

Director Rene Cardona (unofficially) remade this feature in 1968 as the nudity-and-gore-filled exploitationer *La Horriplante Bestia Humana* (*Night of the Bloody Apes* in the U.S.). Ironically, Armando Silvestre, who stars as the heroic detective Mike Henderson in *Doctor of Doom*, took on the transplant-happy mad doctor role in *Bloody Apes*.

*The Wrestling Women's follow-up feature pitted Our Heroines against another Mexican legend of the screen—the Aztec Mummy. (*The Wrestling Women vs. the Aztec Mummy *Mexican poster)*

The Wrestling Women vs. the Aztec Mummy pits the wrasslin' heroines from *Doctor of Doom* against the dreaded Aztec Mummy, last seen in *The Robot vs. the Aztec Mummy* (made seven years earlier). The combining of the two series resulted in an odd amalgam of crooks and monsters, with plenty of catfights along the way.

This entry features a Fu Manchu-wannabe called "the Black Dragon," who (along with his two evil judo-champion sisters) seeks the fabled treasure guarded by the Aztec Mummy. Our two professional wrestler babes, Loretta (changed from Gloria in the earlier film; though still played by Lorena Velazquez) and the Golden Ruby (Elizabeth Campbell), along with their policemen boyfriends, oppose the Dragon and get to the mummy's tomb first, only to realize that the sacred breastplate which holds the secret of the treasure should remain where it belongs—under the watchful eye of the Aztec Mummy.

Much of *The Wrestling Women vs. the Aztec Mummy* moves about as slowly as, well, an Aztec mummy. In fact, it's a full hour before said monster first puts in an appearance—and then only briefly, since, upon seeing the creature rise from its tomb, the protagonists promptly run away! Fortunately, they take the sacred breastplate with them, so the Mummy follows them to the city (by transforming into a bat), where he manhandles (mummy-handles?) the Black Dragon's thugs and menaces the imperiled heroine until the coming dawn chases him back to his tomb.

The mummy's unique and unsettling appearance proves almost worth the wait, with his skull-like, parchment-skinned visage topped with wispy, matted hair, and his bony chest and leathery arms conjuring up images of the grave. And director Rene Cardona makes the most of this unique monster, offering shots of the mummy's desiccated legs and feet advancing through the darkened pyramid, shuffling inexorably through the shadows, its hideous countenance emerging from the blackness in a startling shock.

Intriguingly, this final entry in the Aztec Mummy series made several significant changes to the titular terror. He is now a sorcerer, "cursed for daring to love a sacrificial virgin," who can transform himself into a (rubber) bat or a (real) tarantula (he possessed no such powers in the previous three films); and, like a vampire, he must return to his tomb to sleep during the day.

In order to finally reach the delirious delights of the anticipated mummy mayhem, however, the viewer must wade through scene after scene of tedious talk—complete with risible dialogue ("The plan that Dr. Tracy worked out was for each of us to work alone so that we could defend ourselves." Right—*that* is clever…). Unfunny comic relief and lackluster encounters between the fist-throwing, body-blocking wrasslin' women and the Dragon's business-suited henchmen further weigh down the torpid proceedings. Two well-shot wrestling bouts—featuring varied angles, quick editing and even some hand-held photography—add a bit of excitement, but when the de rigueur staged wrestling matches prove to be a *highlight*, you know that the film is in trouble. (The gorgeous Lorena Velasquez was no wrestler, and was doubled in these sequences by a professional—which failed to please her. Interviewed for Britain's *Incredibly Strange Film Show* in 1989, she complained, "I had a double, and my double was a fat woman so I hate her [laughs]. I was just there in the close-ups.")

For the patient viewer, the picture finally kicks into gear for the last 20 minutes (after the Mummy rises), marking a vast improvement over the previous tedious hour; but in the end one can't help but wish that *The Wrestling Women vs. the Aztec Mummy* featured less Wrestling Women and more Mummy.

As usual, Something Weird offers a veritable cornucopia of fun extras, including a bevy of Mexi-movie trailers and TV spots, and a cascade of exploitation art. Also included is an episode from the odd "Ghoul-a-Go-Go" cable-access video program (a sort of Gothic, kids-oriented "Shindig"), which proves amateurish and embarrassingly silly. But it's really the battling beauties and Mexi-monsters that lovers of outré cinema want to see here; and in that, they won't be disappointed with this deliciously demented double-bill.

> Here's another DVD review that, for some reason (lack of interest?), failed to see print. Like with the movie itself, the Son of Santo deserved better…

INFRATERRESTRE (2001)

Infraterrestre (Infraterrestrial) features the return of that masked Mexican wrestling hero/icon El Santo!!! Hold on, before all you Santo-heads start body-slamming for joy, let the record show that this film stars the *Son* of Santo (though no one in the picture makes this distinction)—which seems reasonable, given that the *real* Santo died in 1984. But, more disappointing, *Infraterrestre* looks like an impoverished 1980s-style (not so) special effects trip into low-budget juvenilia—*without* the naïve charm that permeates the original Santo oeuvre.

The (hazy) plot has green, spiny-faced, hooded aliens, who landed on Earth eons ago and took up residence in the bowels of the Earth, finally come to the surface to try and infiltrate and conquer mankind. To this end they begin kidnapping people (*why* is never satisfactorily explained), and the Headquarters of National Security call upon their top agent, Santo (and his silly flying car!), to investigate. Oh, and one of El Santo's professional wrestler opponents, the Blue Panther, turns out to be an evil drone in service of the aliens

The Son of Santo follows in his father's footsteps… sort of.

(leading to several lackluster wrasslin' encounters).

Unbelievably, this all *sounds* far more entertaining than it is. Looking like it was made 20 years earlier (thanks to the cheesy video game-level graphics and bad synth score), *Infraterrestre* tries for a dark, urbane tone, which completely negates the Santo fun factor. Its gritty cheapness (most of the 'action' takes place in parking garages, dimly-lit Spartan offices and claustrophobic plywood tunnel sets) makes the picture feel downright unpleasant (which is something no previous Santo movie, no matter how poor, can be accused of). The Son of Santo's inflectionless voice proves anything *but* commanding, and the poorly-staged, half-speed wrestling encounters with Blue Panther (and the various commando-like alien henchmen) do little to enliven the glacially-paced plot. Sadly, *Infraterrestre* only proves (even to rabid Santophiles) that indeed you can never go home again.

Santo fans, you have been warned.

On the upside, the (1:66 letterboxed) print, in Spanish with English subtitles, looks great—for those few souls patient (and masochistic) enough to sit through it. And this "platinum edition" from Rise Above Entertainment features plenty of extras, including deleted scenes (mostly talk), outtakes, an interview with the director, the film's (pathetic) 'premier,' and even a videotaped bout between the Son of Santo and the new Blue Demon—in a gymnasium! Unfortunately, non–Spanish speakers will learn little from these bonuses, as they lack subtitles. But then again, who really cares.

> The following is a Santo film review that slipped through the ring ropes and went unpublished. Though far from that Mexican superstar's best, it still deserves its place ringside.

SANTO CONTRA HOMBRES INFERNALES (1958)

In 1958 the mega-popular Mexican wrestler El Santo finally tossed his mask into the cinematic ring via two low-budget movies shot back to back in Cuba: *Santo contra el Cerebrodel Mal* and *Santo contra Hombres Infernales* (Santo vs. the Infernal Men). Fortunately, Santo's subsequent films improved greatly.

Hombres Infernales tells the story of an undercover police agent infiltrating a drug smuggling ring at a seaside resort town. Santo shows up sporadically to aid the agent and ultimately rescue him when things go wrong.

Burdened with dull filler, static photography, and a sluggish plot, *Hombres Infernales* makes for a poor crime-thriller. And it makes for an even poorer Santo movie. The Silver Masked Man only appears onscreen in five scenes, for about the same number of minutes. And, amazingly, there's *no wrestling* (not even a wrestling *move*), with the two brief scuffles involving Mexico's greatest wrestler offering nothing more than mundane fisticuffs.

The movie begins with stock footage of an airliner flying, landing and taxiing; then segues into footage of cars driving, stopping and parking. It's ten minutes before the viewer even knows the identities of the characters inside the various vehicles. Santo finally surfaces (literally—as he rises out of the ocean to sneak up on a pair of dockside smugglers) 19 minutes into the picture. He engages in a brief fight with the two ruffians, then dives into the sea when one pulls a gun, and disappears. It's another 15 minutes before Santo shows his face—er, mask again. In the meantime, viewers must make do with a lengthy nightclub conversation between the Latino Tony Curtis lookalike protagonist and his girlfriend; a mariachi number on the patio; the Cute Couple frolicking on the beach; yet another musical number (this time with the chica serenading her beau—accompanied by the aforementioned mariachi band!); and an out-of-nowhere barroom-style brawl in the sand.

When the Masked Man (strangely, Santo is never referred to by his famous nom de ring) finally reappears, it's only to palaver for a moment with the protagonist. Another 10 minutes elapse before Santo shows up again—simply to read a note left by the gang-infiltrating agent. A lengthy sequence in which the smugglers make a watery pickup, and yet another nightclub sequence (featuring dancers and a cadre of castanets) eat up the running time before the agent's inevitable exposure prompts one more brief appearance by El Santo, who helps out in the brawn department and saves his partner's Mexi-bacon.

Ground-Zero Entertainment's (delete the "Ground," and the moniker accurately sums up the film itself) bare-bones DVD (with a few screen grabs as the only extras) is Spanish-language only, with no subtitles, making the many looong dialogue scenes that much more tedious for the average gringo. The barely adequate picture quality includes some tell-tale tracking lines at the bottom of the frame, exposing its videotape roots. Still, Santo completists will want *Santo contra Hombres Infernales* on their shelves for its historical position in the lucha libra firmament. However, very few will take it down off that shelf a second time.

Santo Contra Hombres Infernales *poster*.

> There's nothing quite like a Santo movie. And in the early 2000s, Rise Above Entertainment finally provided us gringos a bevy of English-friendly versions of that ol' masked magic. This piece appeared in *Monsters from the Vault* magazine, issue 17 (Fall 2003).

A SANTO CINEMA SMACK-DOWN! *SANTO IN THE TREASURE OF DRACULA* (1969); *SANTO IN THE VENGEANCE OF THE MUMMY* (1971); *SANTO VS. FRANKENSTEIN'S DAUGHTER* (1971); *SANTO & BLUE DEMON VS. DRACULA & THE WOLF MAN* (1973); AND *SANTO & BLUE DEMON VS. DR. FRANKENSTEIN* (1974)

Rise Above Entertainment has a Silver Masked Man in their corner—Santo, the most famous of all Mexican wrestling superhero crime-fighters! An institution south of the border, Santo has appeared in over fifty films from the 1950s through the '70s, but only a few have traveled north to English-speaking climes (with El Santo transformed into 'Samson' during the dubious dubbing process). Rise Above is determined to rectify this situation, and here offers five Santo-meets-the-monster movies on DVD, presented in English (subtitled) for the very first time.

First up (in chronological order) is *Santo in the Treasure of Dracula* (1969), which proves to be a splendid introduction to the uninitiated, as it's basically Stoker's *Dracula* tale with a Santo subplot (plus, we only see El Enmascarado de Plata wrestle once, which, some might say, is a silver-masked blessing). Released in atmospheric black and white (rather than the garish color of the other four entries covered here), the story has masked professional wrestler and amateur scientist Santo invent a time machine that transports a subject back to his or her past life. Santo tests it on his girlfriend (since women are "four times as resistant as men" [?]), who turns out to have been a Mina Harker substitute in her previous incarnation. Santo and his cohorts watch the unfolding supernatural drama on a monitor, with Our Hero pulling his beloved out of the past at just the right moment. But back in the present, a villainous gang of criminals discovers the whereabouts of Dracula's staked corpse and revives the Count, intent on stealing Drac's hidden treasure after the bloodsucker gets the meddlesome Santo out of the way.

The involving *Dracula* scenario (which apes both the cut-finger episode and the classic mirror sequence—though this time using a full-sized looking glass rather than the less dramatic cigarette case from the 1931 Lugosi version) unfolds amidst eerie lighting and foggy graveyard settings, while Aldo Monti as Dracula wears the aristocratic Lugosi get-up but snarls like Christopher Lee. The film offers less Santo screen time than most entries, but a little Santo often goes a long way, and it comes off as a perfect balance of eerie Mexican horror and the straight-arrow absurdity that is the Santo milieu.

Santo in the Treasure of Dracula *(1969)* came in two versions: the domestic iteration, and an 'El Sexo' edit for the international market in which the women—primarily Dracula's vampire brides—go topless.

The best of the quintet covered here, the atmospheric and highly entertaining *Santo in the Treasure of Dracula* wins a superior three-and-a-half out of four falls in the Santo Cinema Smack-down.

Next comes *Santo in the Vengeance of the Mummy* (1971), which turns out to be the worst of the bunch. It begins with a typical wrestling bout (as so many Santo features do), but this one is exceedingly well-shot, offering varied angles and involving point-of-view photography. Too bad the rest of the picture is so pedestrian in its staging and pacing.

The simple story has masked wrestler and all-around-do-gooder Santo accompanying his professor friend on a scientific expedition to discover the tomb of Nonoc. The mummified Nonoc rises from said tomb to decimate the interlopers one by one. Unfortunately, a plethora of pointless filler involving characters tramping through the jungle quickly brings the proceedings to a screeching halt (even the obligatory Mummy flashback sequence consists of little more than an overlong jungle chase scene). It's halfway into the picture before the Mummy even shows its withered head.

Bad comedy relief (centering on a bumbling, goofy academian and a terminally cheerful cook); banal staging (the Mummy's resurrection scene consists of him simply ambling out of the woods); a disappointing monster (whose dried apple face and penchant for shooting a bow and arrow make it more risible than frightening); over-bright lighting on unconvincing studio sets; and an insultingly stupid Scooby-Doo ending earn the dull, dull, dull *Santo in the Vengeance of the Mummy* a pitiful one out of four falls.

Fortunately, the same year's *Santo vs. Frankenstein's Daughter* cleanses the Santo palette with a wild and wooly monster-filled wrestling romp. The story opens, appropriately enough, upon a grave-robbing scene. Apparently, Frankenstein's daughter, Freda Frankenstein, is a chip off the old Frankenblock and has stitched together a new creature (dubbed Ursus, it looks like a

One of the best El Santo features: Santo vs. Frankenstein's Daughter *(1971).*

cross between the Karloff Monster and a barrel-chested wrestler). She's also concocted an "instant mummification serum" that has kept her and her fearful gang of henchmen alive and young long past their allotted three-score-and-ten. But the serum's effectiveness is rapidly failing, and she needs something special to prolong her unnatural life. That something is the "TR factor" (which "renews organic tissue") found in the blood of the heroic wrestler and national hero Santo. "I need the blood of the man in the silver mask!" she cries.

The fab lab set (filled with weird lights, sparklers, neon tubes and an explosive "red switch" right out of 1934's *The Black Cat*), garish color schemes (from the blue graveyard fog to the henchmen's fire engine red t-shirts to the heroine's orange hair), and cheesily horrific cave setting (offering mummified corpses, bats on strings, and a variety of stunt rats) all add to the wacky charm.

The film is so full of bizarre intrigue (including a subplot in which Dr. F. transfuses the blood of an ape into a human being to create a gorilla-man—which Santo then battles, naturally) that there's time for only one Santo wrestling bout (excitingly filmed and staged, with his bad-guy opponent even using illegal brass knuckles!) rather than the two or three matches usually thrown in as filler.

Lively, fast-paced, and chock full of outré elements and wacky scenarios (including the demented doc hypnotizing the heroine and ordering her to "gouge Santo's eyes out"…prompting one queasy henchman to turn away, proclaiming, "Bloody eyes always gives me goose bumps"!), *Santo vs. Frankenstein's Daughter* wins a solid three out of four falls in the Santo Cinema arena.

Santo & Blue Demon vs. Dracula & the Wolf Man (1973) ups the ante in the monster rally department, though it falls short of the cheesy delight that is *Santo vs. Frankenstein's Daughter*. On the plus side, the film offers Dracula (his '70s haircut and sideburns contrasting amusingly with his classical penguin suit), the Wolf Man (named "Rufus," who serves the Vampire Lord in the bloodsucker's plan to rule the world by turning all humans into either vampires or wolf men!), and Santo's pal and near-equal in the crime-fighting superhero wrestler club, the blue-masked Blue Demon. In the minus column, however, sits a meandering, mundane subplot (in which the revived Drac seeks vengeance on the descendants of those who initially staked him hundreds of years ago, while the Wolf Man—in human form—woos one of said female descendants in an ill-conceived and illogical vengeance scheme) and an overabundance of flatly staged wrestling action (three full bouts!).

Disappointingly for those Santo fans who enjoy watching their hero's energetic acrobatics in the ring, the locked-down camera and obvious studio staging (i.e. no audience) robs the movie's many wrasslin' moments of their sense of immediacy and excitement. In fact, it looks as if the contests take place in some disconnected other dimension, with the piped-in sounds from the unseen crowd only underlining the feel of isolation. This is a real shame, because a well-shot Santo bout with a frenzied audience can truly get the blood pumping, due both to Santo's agile abilities and his immense popularity with the crowds.

Still, there are enough monstrous elements to keep ennui from creeping into this cinematic ring, including a Dracula resurrection scene right out of *Dracula Prince of Darkness* (bleeding out a victim suspended over Dracula's bones) and a Dracula demise sequence borrowed from *The Return of Dracula* (did someone say 'pit full of spikes'?). The movie also offers bright comic-book lighting (chock full of primary colors) contrasted with wonderfully shadowy gothic illumination (particularly in some misty woodland settings). Then there's the climax in which the two heroes face off against not only Drac and Wolfy, but a whole pack of savage wolf men! Never has so much yak hair been seen in one place at one time!

Santo & Blue Demon vs. Dracula & the Wolf Man earns a respectable two-and-a-half out of four falls.

Sadly, the last of the five features is, like *Vengeance of the Mummy*, another dire disappointment. 1974's *Santo & Blue Demon vs. Dr. Frankenstein* has Irwin Frankenstein(!), grandson of the famous monster-maker, engaging in brain-switching experiments. The "evil genius" and "hateful criminal" (as the press labels this author of numerous kidnappings committed to procure his experimental subjects) seeks a new brain to restore life to his frozen wife. Oh, and he also intends to use his procedure to "control the leaders of humanity and rule the world." To this end he needs *Santo's* brain, for some reason. Though he hasn't quite gotten the cerebral concept correct (with twelve failed attempts to his credit), Frankenstein *has* conquered the aging process (he's 113 years old!) by developing a method of renewing "the beta factor in the blood."

Basically a retread of *Santo vs. Frankenstein's Daughter*, but without the fast-paced, anything-goes excitement of the earlier entry, *Santo & Blue Demon vs. Dr. Frankenstein* reduces the good doctor to a garden-variety criminal mastermind, and offers only one disappointingly normal-looking "monster" (named Golem) whom the doc controls with an implanted radio device. Four bouts of repetitive fisticuffs with Frankenstein's henchmen (offering the same old moves every time) and two full tag-team wrestling matches shot in the same stationary, disconnected manner seen in *Santo & Blue Demon vs. Dracula and the Wolf Man* deliver a double scissor-kick to the film's pacing. And numerous talky stretches (Frankenstein explaining his experiments; a police inspector palavering with his subordinates; even Santo and Blue Demon chatting over dinner) put a further headlock on the movie's entertainment value. Admittedly, the lighting is colorful; and Frankenstein's high-tech lab, with its stainless steel walls, sliding glass doors and banks of electrical equipment, at least offers an impressive setting. But it had all been done far better before, so this tired redux wins a paltry one-and-a-half out of four falls.

All five DVDs feature enlightening liner notes by Mexican movie scholar David Wilt; but the scanty 'extras,' consisting of a short collection of clips labeled "The Best of El Santo" and two pseudo-trailers, are identical on each disc (the exception being individual—but brief—still galleries). While the five Santo films reviewed here vary wildly in quality, Rise Above Entertainment deserves some kind of Championship Title for bringing those fans enamored of south-of-the-border pscyhotronica such a masked and monstrous mound of off-the-wall entertainment.

> Back in 2003, those Santo flicks just kept on coming. And I kept on reviewing, as shown in this *Monsters from the Vault* essay (issue 18, Summer 2004).

SANTO CINEMA SMACK-DOWN: ROUND 2! *THE WITCHES ATTACK* (1965); *THE DIABOLICAL AXE* (1965); *SANTO VS. THE RIDERS OF TERROR* (1970); *SANTO AND MATEQUILLA NAPOLES IN THE VENGEANCE OF THE CRYING WOMAN* (1974)

Here's another batch of Santo cinema from Rise Above Entertainment. Like those reviewed last issue, this quartet varies in quality, but each and every one offers something to both the Mexican Wrestler enthusiast and Mexican Monster Movie maven.

First up is, unfortunately, the worst up. After making five films for producer Alberto Lopez, masked Mexican wrestler-turned-movie star El Santo jumped ship and signed on with producer Luis Enrique Vergara (who later produced Boris Karloff's final four features). Santo made five pictures for Vergara (before moving on yet again due to a contract dispute), beginning with a guest shot in *Blue Demon Contra el Poder Satanico* (Blue Demon vs. the Satanic Power). Santo's first starring Vergara vehicles were the shot-back-to-back *The Witches Attack* and *The Diabolical Axe*. While El Santo did well for himself with the change (more than doubling his salary), this switch didn't do his films any favors, for the Vergara Santos generally appear slapdash and cheap, with the more luxurious sets and professionalism of his previous surroundings at Churubusco studios replaced with grimy location shooting and cut-rate technique.

The Witches Attack begins with a long pre-credit sequence (a rarity in Santo cinema) in which a beautiful girl, Ofelia, narrates her experience of being held captive by a Satanic cult in an old mansion, with Santo coming to the rescue—only to be captured himself. Resurrecting their Queen witch, the Satanists intend to sacrifice both Ofelia and Santo to their Unholy Lord, but, breaking his chains, the Silver Masked Man *does* finally rescue the girl—only to have her wake up: It was all a dream! But soon reality begins aping the dream events, as the all-too-real cult of witches tries to ensnare Ofelia and Santo in their hellish plans.

First off, *The Witches Attack* just feels shoddy. Confused, Ed Woodian day-for-night photography (my eight-year-old son, viewing the movie with me, asked why it was daylight on one side of the stone wall, then nighttime when Santo hops over to the other side), inappropriate stock music (climactic cues coming where there's no climax), and ridiculous effects (a 'menacing' rubber spider on a string is so laugh-out-loud ludicrous that you can see its little plastic cartoon eyes; while Satan himself is some guy in a bad papier-mâché horned mask wearing a cape and baggy pants) has this one scraping the bottom of the Santo barrel. (The movie even steals a shot—of Patricia Jessel being burned at the stake—from the 1960 American film *Horror Hotel*.)

But what really sinks this Santo ship is the film's tiresome repetitiveness. Santo makes *multiple* trips to the deserted mansion (and we watch him climb the same stone wall to gain entry each time!) in which little or nothing happens. Numerous boring battles between Santo and the witches' husky henchmen continue the monotony. Santo is captured and chained to the same sacrificial table on *three* different occasions; and he breaks free of the chains in an identical manner every time! (One would think the witches would finally wise up and secure some better-quality manacles.)

Granted, *The Witches Attack* offers a gaggle of beautiful girls in short Romanesque skirts (not to mention a seductive witch named Medusa in a spangled bikini putting the moves on El Santo), and some particularly exciting and acrobatic ringside action in front of a raucous, energized crowd. But it's not enough to gloss over the shabby production values and stultifying repetitiveness of it all; so that *The Witches Attack* wins a meager one out of four falls in the Santo Cinema Arena.

Fortunately, the next entry in the Vergara/Santo series significantly raises the bar. Shot back-to-back with *The Witches Attack* in December of 1964, *The Diabolical Axe* begins, shockingly, with the funeral of El Santo! But this turns out to be 1603 and the burial of the first in a long line of Santos. After the reverent monks tending to the burial have left Santo's gravesite, a black-masked executioner magically appears and swears to follow El Santo across time to exact his vengeance.

Cut to the 20th century, and the modern-day Santo wrestles at the Coliseum. The good news: It's an actual wrestling bout in an actual arena with an actual crowd (rather than the lackluster and unconvincing studio-staged matches that proliferated in later Santo entries). The bad news: Santo and his burly opponent seem to be operating at half speed. Fortunately, after a few minutes of dull grappling, the executioner from 1603 magically pops into the ring and starts swinging his axe at Santo's head! This leads to an exciting exchange involving Santo's trademark acrobatics as the two fly at each other across the ring. After Santo beats the stuffing out of the murderous interloper, the phantom executioner vanishes… but not for long, as he continues to turn up periodically to try and behead El Santo!

Our Hero seeks advice from a professor friend, and we learn that Santo's costume, made of "an indestructible material," has been passed down from father to son for generations. And his silver mask is magical, protecting against evil spells and reenergizing the wearer. The professor, whose home houses some bizarre lab equipment (spinning metal rectangles, flashing lights, an electric chair-like contraption), uses a device to electronically send Santo's spirit back into the past to investigate the mystery of the Black Mask (as they label the sinister executioner). Back in the seventeenth century, we learn that the original (soon-to-be) Santo was the swashbuckling lover of Lady Isobel. But an evil rival for her hand, who worships the demon Ariman (some kind of hairy man-bat statue), was transformed by satanic powers into the Black Mask and given a magical executioner's axe. Isobel's lover, after an

Santo's origin story! Mexican lobby card for The Diabolical Axe *(1965).*

inconclusive swordfight with the villain, seeks the help of an old hermit/sorcerer to defeat the Black Mask and find the kidnapped Isobel. "I'll give you the strength and power that will make you a superior man," intones the magician. "You'll never use weapons to fight your enemies; they would destroy your strength and eclipse your heart's kindness. You'll fight against the forces of evil for generations to come. You are now Santo, the Man in the Silver Mask." And, suddenly, we have the Santo origin story!

Back in the present, during a second wrestling bout, the Black Mask uses his diabolical powers to possess Santo's opponent, leading to some exciting, brutal, no-holds-barred ringside action. B.M. also murders Santo's current girlfriend (just as he did Lady Isobel in the past). El Santo must find a way to defeat the Black Mask and free his lost love's tortured soul (who appears to Santo as a helpful ghost).

In addition to the initial desultory wrestling match, a few additional chinks appear in this cinematic suit of armor. The wacky action slows to a crawl at times, as we follow Santo wandering through an Old Mansion (while first taking what seems like forever to get over the wall), with the camera following his every tedious step. And some awkward editing tries to… er, mask the generally cheap (or simple lack of) effects.

But with some fast-paced action (the final confrontation between Santo and the Black Mask, watched over by the eyeless skeleton of Santo's lost love, is both savage and exciting), some creepy cobwebbed crypt settings, the occasional macabre flourish (the villain's appearance is always preceded by the shadow of his headsman's axe), its bizarre plot and mystical motifs, and a decidedly dark tone (Santo loses not one but *two* girlfriends to the murderous Black Mask—one in the past and one in the present!), *The Diabolical Axe* stands as one of the most unusual—and intriguing—Santo entries, winning a solid three out of four falls in the Santo Cinema Smack-Down.

Santo contra los Jinetes del Terror (*Santo vs. the Riders of Terror*) takes a turn to the west—the Old West, that

Two Mexican legends finally meet—El Santo and La Llorona—in Santo and Matequilla Napoles in the Vengeance of the Crying Woman *(1974).*

painted with a monstrous brush, take on a more sympathetic hue over the course of the story—which even includes a romantic subplot involving the lead leper!), and some bloody Peckinpaugh-esque gunshot moments (with abundant blood squibs). And, despite its Old West setting, there's still the wrestling—courtesy of a temporary ring set up in the middle of the street by a traveling huckster and his man-mountain wrestler. Santo wrassles the brute at the behest of three nuns(!), who need the prize-money for their orphanage. (Unfortunately, this bout proves a pretty poor display, with the two combatants throwing obviously pulled punches, and Santo's trademark acrobatics conspicuous solely by their absence.)

Technically, the picture rates slightly above average for a Santo movie, with the expected phony-looking studio cave sets and over-bright lighting (not to mention pedestrian direction and locked-down camerawork) offset somewhat by an outdoorsy feel and authentic-looking western town.

Though the film lacks the expected mad doctor and bizarro monsters of most Santo entries (the handful of lepers aside), the sight of El Santo in his silver mask and tights (and silver boots!) riding a horse into an Old West town to talk with cowboys and townsfolk is surreal enough to engender that wonderfully childish and otherworldly feel found only in Santo cinema.

Santo vs. the Riders of Terror lands two out of four bullet hits in the Santo six-gun showdown. "Hi-ho Santo, Awaaaay!"

Santo and Matequilla Napoles in the Vengeance of the Crying Woman, another unique and intriguing Santo effort, teams the Man in the Silver Mask with famous Cuban-born boxer Jose "Matequilla" Napoles (the welterweight champion of the world at the time), and pits the duo against one of Mexico's legendary figures of horror: La Llorona (the Crying Woman). La Llorona is the tragic ghost of a woman who murdered her own children to spite her faithless lover (the kids' father), and now wanders the earth keening for her lost little ones. In this Santo outing, La Llorona also wears a

is, placing Santo in 19th century Santa Fe! The story has a small group of disaffected lepers escaping a leprosarium near Santa Fe, sending the townsfolk into a panic when the lepers break into a few farmhouses for food. A local band of thieves discover their hiding place and dupe the lepers into helping with their nefarious robberies. Things quickly get out of hand, and the sheriff sends for El Santo, who "defends justice wherever he's needed." Think of it: Santo as a wrestling Mexican version of the Lone Ranger (he even rides into town on a white horse)! Though he lacks the silver bullets (Santo doesn't even carry a gun), his silver mask and wrestling tights prove more than up to the task.

Apart from its obvious novelty (Santo in a *western*!?), *Santo vs. the Riders of Terror* features some disturbingly gruesome makeup on the lepers (who, though initially medallion that holds the secret to a vast treasure, which, centuries ago, she stole from her lover and hid before killing her children and herself. The "vengeance" of the title focuses on the descendants of her lover, who married another woman and began a new family. Professor Lira, one of the descendants, fears for the life of his grandson and so summons Santo and Matequilla to help him find the medallion (buried with La Llorona's corpse) and turn the treasure over to the Institute of Child Welfare, since (in a naïvely charming plot point) "the moment that fortune is used to save children's lives, the horrible vengeance of La Llorona will end." But also on the trail of the treasure is a gang of crooks…

The homegrown horror of La Llorona is well represented here, with the vengeful spirit portrayed as a mummified cadaver (aided by a beautiful, black-garbed female agent of the Devil) that comes to life after Santo removes the medallion from her desiccated corpse. With her withered face and one bad eye (making her look a bit like a female version of Lon Chaney Jr.'s Kharis from Universal's 1940s mummy series), fright wig hair, tattered grave clothes and omnipresent mist that swirls around her and announces her supernatural presence, she cuts a strikingly ghoulish figure. And her otherworldly, echoing wailing ("My sons!…") is the shuddery icing on the creepy cake.

But it's not only La Llorona who looks 'striking'; at one point, Matequilla sports the most amazing *hot pink* pantsuit (with puffy sleeves, no less) seen this side of a disco museum! (These clothes prove even scarier than La Llorona herself.)

On the action front, Santo has two (televised) fair-to-middlin' wrestling matches, while Matequilla gets his chance in the (boxing) ring as well. But, disappointingly, these are all studio-shot rather than actual arena bouts, and so lack the excitement generated by an energized crowd. In addition, the story's rather perfunctory resolution, though admittedly original, lacks any real thrills, chills or suspense.

Also disappointingly, Santo and Matequilla never encounter La Llorona themselves; in fact, they never even *see* her and must rely on the hearsay of others (apparently it just wouldn't do to have Our Heroes battle a *female*—even one who's a murderous, mummy-like walking corpse). As a consequence, all the fisticuff action comes during repeated encounters with the gangsters. Fortunately, Matequilla, though not a professional actor, proves an energetic and likable sidekick, with his semi-comic persona adding some levity to the proceedings (he complains incessantly about not having seen the ghost himself).

But the novel (and effective) monster, the addition of the likable Matequilla, the story's unusual premise, and a groovy James Bondian musical score (all drums, guitar riffs and jazzy horns) earns *Santo and MatequillaNapoles in the Vengeance of the Crying Woman* two-and-a-half out of four falls in the Santo-ring.

All four DVDs feature illuminating liner notes by Mexican movie scholar David Wilt. The scanty 'extras,' however—consisting of a short collection of clips labeled "The Best of El Santo" and a few pseudo-trailers—are identical on each disc (the exception being individual, but brief, still galleries). Though the variable Santo films can be good, bad and even ugly, each is worth a look for its entertaining glimpse into south-of-the-border psychotronica. Let's hope Rise Above Entertainment continues mining this rich vein of Santo gold.

> They say that all good things must end. Sadly, Santo Cinema proved to be no exception. The last gasp of the DVD company Rise Above Entertainment saw the release of two final Santo features. Though I intended this piece, like Rounds 1 and 2, for *Monsters from the Vault* magazine, for some reason they threw in the Santo towel before Round 3, leaving this tag-team essay standing outside the ring.

SANTO CINEMA SMACK-DOWN: ROUND 3! *SANTO VS. THE MARTIAN INVASION* (1966) and *SANTO IN THE BORDER OF TERROR* (1969)

Look out Santo fans, here comes a tag-team tandem that pits the defender of Truth, Justice and the Mexican Way against such diverse menaces as invading Martians and organ-stealing exploiters of illegal immigrants!

Santo vs. the Martian Invasion has the Silver Masked Man standing between the Earth and a horde (well, about ten anyway) of invading aliens. Eschewing the 'little green men' model, these Martians are blonde, muscle-bound hombres (and beauteous chiquitas) sporting silver tights and cape, a squarish skull-cap, and an "astral eye" stuck to their foreheads (a flashing eyeball-like device that serves as their own personal disintegrator ray—causing victims to just fade away in the cheapest of optical effects). Concerned about Earth's atomic capabilities, these Adonis-like aliens land in Mexico to demand total disarmament and insist the

When aliens look like this, an invasion might not be such a bad thing... Santo vs. the Martian Invasion *(1966).*

world "foster Earthly brotherhood" or face annihilation by the Martians' superior weaponry. ("We chose Mexico because it is a country dedicated to pacifism," they explain.) But *The Day the Earth Stood Still*'s Klaatu they ain't, as they demonstrate their power by killing thousands and kidnapping (via teleportation devices) select humans for study back on their home planet. The Martians turn their astral eyes toward Santo (as he represents the perfect physical specimen), and it's up to the Silver Masked Man to locate the invaders' ship, foil their plans and free the captives.

"A picture that breaks new technical ground with constant action and excitement!" proclaims the film's trailer (included on the disc as one of many extras). While the "new technical ground" is a hopeful overstatement at best (unless one counts Ed Wood–style effects and simple dissolves utilized by Georges Méliès himself over a century ago as "new"), *Santo vs. the Martian Invasion* indeed offers plenty of (campy) "action" and (cheesy) "excitement." Among the highlights: space-age tonalities "borrowed" from the *Forbidden Planet* soundtrack; the Martian spaceship (looking like two silver bowls glued together) landing in an obvious table-top forest; the flying saucer's sparse interior sporting a huge lever whose only purpose appears to be to blow up the ship if pulled (*Bride of Frankenstein* must be a particular favorite on Mars); the aliens interrupting a television broadcast and insisting, "We are not just actors performing in a scary movie"; a Martian materializing at an outdoor sports complex to disintegrate a crowd of people—including a group of children(!) Santo is coaching in wrestling techniques; a Martian taking the place of Santo's masked wrestling opponent in the ring (à la the classic vampire/werewolf in *Santo vs. the Vampire Women*); a camp-a-holic's dream of four Martian babes disguising themselves as a "ballet troupe" and proceeding to perform a hoochy-koochy dance number to a swingin' sixties instrumental beat; plenty of Santo-vs.-Martian grunting, sweating and fighting; and, of course, the Big Message closing narration: "The human race has been saved—for the moment. Will we learn our lesson? Or will we insist on carrying on crazy nuclear experiments until we disappear from the face of the Earth?"

Fast-paced, fun and utterly charming, *Santo vs. the Martian Invasion* wins a solid three out of four falls in the Santo Cinema arena.

The film's slightly letterboxed source print (in Spanish with removable English subtitles) looks (like the buxom Martian women themselves) gorgeous. A ringful of extras keeps the rabid viewer off the ropes. Apart from the movie's fun (and subtitled) trailer ("You have to see it to believe it!") and three additional (non-genre) previews, there's a lengthy onscreen interview with the Son of Santo (masked like his father, of course), a "commentary by Prof. Juan Carlos Vargas" (actually an informative 7-minute verbal overview, with photos), illustrated biographies of (lead Martian) Wolf Ruvinskis and El Santo (the latter with an excellent poster/lobby card gallery as background), and a useful Santo filmography. And for us mono-linguistic gringos, all these extras come with subtitles.

For those who like a little social consciousness served up with their cheese, Rise Above Entertainment offers *Santo in the Border of Terror*. Instead of Dracula, the Wolf Man or even invading Martians, here Santo wrestles with the issue of illegal immigrants!

A pair of Mexican workers in need of money (one for his ailing mother, the other for an operation to restore the sight of his fiancée's kid sister) sneak across the border to work at the big Texas farm of Mr. Richards. But things are not quite what they seem (one tip-off being the gaggle of machine-gun toting uniformed guards that patrol this barbed-wire enclosed compound!), as the farm's resident physician, the evil Dr. Sombra, runs an organ-stealing ring, killing the illegals and selling their vitals for profit. Oh, and the mad medico uses the proceeds to fund his crazy experiments (something to do with brain transplantation, though this remains maddeningly vague), which have resulted in two buff, zombie-like slaves to do his nefarious bidding. Into the mix comes El Santo and his bald, cowardly sidekick-manager Carlitos to bust up the doc's… er, operation and rescue their exploited countrymen.

Such a wacky scenario *should* have been a winner. Unfortunately, director Rafael Perez Grovas had neither the resources nor the talent to do it justice. Flat lighting, threadbare sets, hollow sound, and an overriding air of cheapness undermine the production from the get-go. Add in *four* time-killing musical numbers (two from the torch-singer heroine, and two from a rotund protagonist who bursts into song at the drop of a sombrero), and much walking to and fro along the same warehouse-like corridor, and the whole thing withers like an opponent under one of Santo's patented horse-locks.

"Take him to the dungeon!" orders the doctor at one point, upon which his henchmen escort their captive to what looks like a half-finished storeroom! So much for atmosphere. And later the doc imprisons the unconscious Santo in the ominous-sounding "Black Room"—which turns out to be a big empty chamber with *white* walls! Sheesh.

Missed opportunities fly by faster than scissor kicks. We never actually see any of the mad surgeon's handiwork (one victim has his eyes removed [off-screen], and not one but *two* different people lift the obfuscating sheet to view the mutilation—but the camera coyly keeps its distance). There's not even a single visit to the sinister surgeon's lab; he does all his mad raving from behind an office desk! Grovas throws us a bone by displaying the pair of purloined peepers in a jar, but apart from the doc's two muscle-bound (and normal-looking) mute slaves, nothing else out-of-the-ordinary steps forward.

On the plus side, the film offers two rather gritty, acrobatic and realistic (well, as realistic as these things get anyway) tag-team bouts in which Santo doles out (and takes) quite a bit of punishment (even tossing an opponent out of the ring into the first row). And there's a bit of amusingly goofy comedy relief involving Carlitos and a ticking bomb (to put up with the bumbling Carlitos, Santo must have had the patience of, well, a *santo*). But when a Santo movie's highlights are the time-filling *wrestling matches*, you know it's not going to win too many takedowns. In good conscience, *Santo in the Border of Terror* can only be recommended for Santo completists (and we know who we are), earning only one out of four falls in the Santo Cinema Smack-Down.

Rise Above's full-screen source print (in Spanish with optional English subtitles) looks a little the worse for wear (particularly towards the film's beginning), with some occasional blemishes and graininess, falling (like the feature itself) below the generally high standard set by most of their other Santo releases. Still, it's probably the best we'll ever see of this decidedly minor entry in the Santo oeuvre. The sparse extras are the same as those featured on all Rise Above's other Santo discs.

CHAPTER 7
BRIEF BITES

Back in the 1990s, a little genre publication called *Cult Movies* liked to print fistfuls of mini-reviews (alongside their longer, more in-depth articles) to inspire their readers to seek out, well, more cult movies. I contributed dozens of these easily-digested capsules. *Filmfax* magazine was another publication that sometimes ran a series of short essays to cover more genre ground, and I managed to weasel my way into *that* writers' den too. So, along with a few additional (less-than-750-word) contributions, here they are.

> Here's an updated version of a review I wrote for *Cult Movies* magazine, issue 16 (Fall 1995).

THE AMAZING COLOSSAL MAN (1957)

"I see myself as being a total filmmaker," proclaimed producer-director-screenwriter Bert I. Gordon to *Starlog*'s Ed Naha. "I can make any kind of film I have a feeling for. If I'm fascinated by a subject, I just go into it." Obviously, Bert was indeed "fascinated" by the idea of gigantism, having made *King Dinosaur* (giant lizards), *The Cyclops* (giant human) and *Beginning of the End* (giant grasshoppers) by 1957. He then went on to make *Earth vs. the Spider* (giant arachnid), *Village of the Giants* (giant teenagers), *Food of the Gods* (giant mosquitoes, rats and chickens!) and *Empire of the Ants* (giant ants). Of all these big-themed pictures, *The Amazing Colossal Man* is Bert's best (which, honestly, is not exactly "giant" praise).

"NEVER SINCE KING KONG SUCH A MIGHTY MOTION PICTURE!" trumpeted a *Kinematograph Weekly* ad for *The Amazing Colossal Man*. If one interprets "MIGHTY" as "FAIR-TO-MIDDLIN'," then the laudatory line isn't half wrong. Sure, the effects are laughable at times; sure, the script is occasionally banal; but while it's no classic (and certainly nowhere near *Kong*), *The Amazing Colossal Man* contains enough interest to keep the average '50s science fiction fan entertained.

Glenn (misspelled "Glen" in the credits) Langan plays Lt. Col. Glen Manning, who is caught in a plutonium bomb blast. He miraculously survives, regenerates new skin, and gradually grows to a height of 60 feet! As the scientists scramble to find a cure for his gigantism, the military try to quarantine the increasingly restless giant, and his fiancée (Cathy Downs) worries over her behemoth beau's deteriorating mental state. When he can stand it no longer, Manning breaks out of his confinement, takes a shot in the ankle with a gigantic syringe full of tranquilizer (and then hurls the oversized hypo through the body of his tormentor!), lumbers around Las Vegas, and faces down army bazookas at Boulder Dam.

Langan is the film's main asset, giving the excellent performance needed to pull off such a "big" role without looking too silly. His balance between depression, self-ridicule and, finally, uncontrolled fury makes this gargantuan a real, human character; and he nearly overcomes the handicap of a bald head and silly diaper that make him appear more like a 60-foot *baby* than a monstrous mountain of manhood.

Gordon, who (along with his wife Flora) did the special effects, denuded Langan's dome (and flooded the actor with light to blot out any shadows) to save on costs by cutting out half of the "travelling matte" process. (A proper travelling matte consists of a "positive" and "negative" matte; the negative blacks out the area so that when the positive image is laid over it, it won't appear transparent.) Gordon dispensed with the negative matte, and as a consequence of this penny-pinching technique, the Amazing Colossal Man often appears more like the Amazing *Translucent* Man. Similarly, Gordon short-changed his audience with the "money shots" of Manning rampaging through Las Vegas: The filmmaker simply superimposed the colossus onto *slides* of deserted Vegas streets and had a handful of screaming extras stand in the foreground. Fortunately, the film's most intriguing sequences (Manning bitterly raving in his circus tent) are enhanced by some realistic miniature props constructed by frequent AIP monster-maker Paul Blaisdell. And where else can one see a hypodermic syringe that measures *four feet long*?

The Amazing Colossal Man made an amazing colossal amount of money, grossing over $848,000 in its first

Mr. B.I.G.'s (Bert I. Gordon's) best-known film: The Amazing Colossal Man *(1957). (Mexican lobby card)*

six months of release. After such a gigantic take, Gordon, urged on by AIP, made a (much poorer) sequel in 1958 called *War of the Colossal Beast*, sans Langan.

Shabby sequels aside, with *The Amazing Colossal Man*, Mr. B.I.G. made his indelible mark on '50s sci-fi.

Cult Movies magazine (issue 15) offered up this inconsequential slice of *American Gothic* in 1995.

AMERICAN GOTHIC (1988)

An intriguing premise, ripe with possibilities, is mishandled in this poorly scripted, poorly acted, dark entry of the slasher/crazed family variety. Academy award winner Rod Steiger is the husband of Yvonne DeCarlo ("Lillian Munster" herself) and the puritanical head of a reclusive, looney family living alone on an island in the Pacific Northwest. Along comes half a dozen unlikable yuppies (including the main protagonist who is recovering from an emotional breakdown due to the death of her baby in a bathtub), and it's time for a little splatter fun and games. Rather than concentrating on the potentially interesting characters and warped dynamics of the sick, homicidal family, screenwriters Burt Wetanson and Michael Vines, and director John Hough, decide to make just another stalk-and-slash movie. Ma, Pa, Teddy, Woody, and Fanny, as the dark travesty of the American God-fearing family, are all fascinating characters, but they're left largely unexplored. The yuppie protagonists are all so shallow and unlikable that no empathy is generated, and therefore no real suspense or interest arises. Steiger and DeCarlo play their characters rather broadly, which is fine at first but soon grows tiresome as you long for a more subtle approach to bring things down to earth again. A few gruesome murders, an occasional disturbing sequence involving the family members, and a lot of running around in the woods is about all *American Gothic* has to offer.

> This mini-review appeared in *Cult Movies* issue 10 (Spring 1994).

ASSIGNMENT OUTER SPACE (1961)

This early Italian sci-fi entry seems to be one of the more serious attempts to portray space travel in a realistic way. Unfortunately, the budget, script, and special effects aren't up to this lofty goal. The events take place entirely in space or on space stations. By employing some interesting camera angles and photography, director Antonio Margheriti (under his anglicized "Anthony Dawson" pseudonym) and cinematographer Marcello Masciocchi do well in creating a tight, claustrophobic feeling. This closed-in, no-room-to-breathe atmosphere makes for a sharp and jarring contrast to the vast emptiness of space. More often than not, however, the effect is ruined by obvious-looking models and shoddy effects. Though the film is in color (fairly rare in a low-budget feature of this time), it is not used to best advantage. Instead of the bright, stunning visual atmosphere often found in other Italian SF (Mario Bava's *Planet of the Vampires* being a superb example), this film opts for silvers and grays as the predominant color scheme, making it much less interesting visually. The rather convoluted plot concerns a reporter risking his life to stop a runaway ship about to destroy the Earth. The dubbed dialogue is stilted and reaches absurd heights in melodrama. Lines such as "The world of human feelings has been much less explored than the whole universe" leads one to believe (or at least *hope*) that something was lost in translation. But at least the astronauts in this movie have to contend realistically with the lack of gravity in space (refreshing, since most other SF films cavalierly gloss over this serious bit of astrophysics).

> *Cult Movies* magazine published this mini-review in issue 16 (Fall 1995).

THE ASTOUNDING SHE MONSTER (1957)

"I remember that the director, Ron Ashcroft, planned to make that feature in a week's time and I think we ended up making it in five days. [It was actually *four*.] *That* was the astounding part of that picture!" related star Robert Clarke to interviewer Tom Weaver. Despite its title, there's nothing much "Astounding" in this ultra-cheap sci-fi entry.

Astounding poster for the decidedly less-than Astounding She Monster *(1957).*

A meteor/spaceship lands in the San Gabriel mountains and disgorges (off-screen) a beautiful female alien whose touch means death (by radium poisoning). Because of this she shimmers and glows (in a none-too-convincing cheap camera trick). Meanwhile, two hoods and their moll have kidnapped a socialite and they all end up at geologist Dick Cutler's (Robert Clarke) mountain cabin, where they're chased endlessly into, out of, and around the cabin by the "She Monster."

The Astounding She Monster (re-titled *The Mysterious Invader* when released in England) starts out nicely with a good introduction as we seemingly travel through space at incredible speed. Once we become earthbound, though (after about 20 seconds), it slows terribly. An annoyingly smug narrator with a gratingly cynical tone starts in with pretentious lines like, "There is our stage, our characters, unrelated, as apart from one another as the stars from the Earth."

Next we're treated to seemingly endless stretches in which just about every one of "our characters" wanders through the forest. To add dull insult to tedious injury,

Ashcroft has the various players meander through the same exact woods, using the same exact camera set-ups. Throughout the film, Ashcroft's direction remains flat, as he rarely moves the camera and fails to utilize even moderately interesting angles or setups.

The acting is poor, even from "star" Robert Clarke. Never the most expressive of actors, Clarke here falls below even his usual standard. Plenty of unconvincing day-for-night photography and lots of filler to pad out the already barely adequate running time of 62 minutes complete the sorry picture, as the no-budget theory of filmmaking shows through everywhere (especially when one notices that there is only one indoor set).

The She-Monster herself, played by the buxom Shirley Kilpatrick, doesn't do much except walk pensively around and deliver the touch of death to a few mismatched stock-footage forest animals. Strangely, we never see her turn around when she leaves; she always awkwardly backs away from the camera. Clarke tells the story "behind" this: "The gal playing the She-Monster, Shirley Kilpatrick—a well-endowed, buxom, beautiful girl, as I recall—had to wear a silvery, metallic-looking suit so that she would appear to be a monstrous yet appealing type of alien. It fit very tightly, and the first time she moved, the doggone thing split, right up the back. She was so generously endowed that they couldn't do anything but put safety pins to hold it together in the back. So you'll notice that the She-Monster always backs away from the camera—you never see her retreat from the scene other than she backs away—and the reason she was backing away was because, otherwise, she'd be showing her backside!"

The Astounding She Monster cost only $18,000 to make, and producer-director Ronnie Ashcroft (whose day job was owner of an editing service) sold the movie to American International Pictures for $60,000. It turned out to be a bargain, for AIP (according to Clarke) "did a tremendous business" with it. That is indeed *Astounding* (and unlikely).

This blu-ray review appeared in *Monsters from the Vault* magazine, no. 33 (Fall 2014).

A 1950S DOUBLE BILL: *THE BEAST OF HOLLOW MOUNTAIN* (1956) / *THE NEANDERTHAL MAN* (1953)

Though horror westerns are a relatively rare breed, most genre fans could name a fistful when pressed, everything from *Curse of the Undead* to *Billy the Kid vs. Dracula* to the more recent *Cowboys vs. Aliens*. But ask them to name a *dinosaur* western, and the average fan might stutter and stumble before finally remembering *The Valley of Gwangi* and... oh, that other one—you know—where the dinosaur only pops up at the very end. Well, that "other one" is *The Beast of Hollow Mountain*, a 1956 color and cinemascope tale of cowboys encountering a dinosaur down Mexico way. Locked firmly in *Gwangi*'s shadow (and justifiably so), this *Beast* is a relatively pedestrian and clichéd good vs. bad ranchers story, with a chaste love triangle thrown into the dusty mix, until the hour mark when a big T-rex shows up to chow down on a few of the principals. Once seen, the dinosaur (realized by a combination of replacement and stop-motion animation—and a pathetically phony-looking set of rubber legs worn by a stuntman) roars and snarls and impressively picks up a steer in its massive jaws to carry off. There follows an exciting fifteen minutes in which the Beast menaces a little boy and the heroine, tears the roof off a house, rips up the main antagonist, and chases and corners the hero in the local swamp. Though not always convincing (the tyrannosaur holds his little arms like he's about to begin a concerto, and waggles his looong tongue like a cretaceous Gene Simmons), the effects show both flair and an attention to detail, including some expressive snarling.

Though made only three years prior to *Beast of Hollow Mountain*, this set's second feature, *The Neanderthal Man*, seems like it should be thir*teen* years older, since it looks more a product of the 1940s than the '50s. The low-rent Jekyll and Hyde story has a put-upon scientist holed up in a backwoods community to prove his de-volution theories (or something). He utilizes a secret serum to turn a housecat into a saber-toothed tiger, and himself into the eponymous caveman—with the expected tragic results. As the (rightly) ridiculed scientist, Robert Shayne (misspelled "Shane" in the credits) overacts up a storm, all wide eyes, wild facial expressions, and strident dialogue delivery. He treats all those around him, including his own daughter and his adoring fiancée, with anger and contempt, thus robbing whatever meager pathos the scenario might have provided. E. A. Dupont's uninspired direction rarely deviates from the medium shot, and the flat lighting and largely immobile camerawork completes the picture of general dullness. Full of awkward dialogue delivered in stilted fashion ("You're nothing but a vacuum of ego"; "All of us are capable of doing when [sic] we give free play to the baseness which is a part of everyone"), the film wastes most of its time on characters speculating

That is some tongue: The Beast of Hollow Mountain *(1956).*

upon or trying to find out what we already know. The rubbery monkey-man mask, complete with curly wig and expressionless, painted eyes, coupled with shots of a live tiger (with no visible saber teeth) intercut with an obvious (and poorly) stuffed tiger head with huge tusks glued onto it, ratchets up the risibility factor to 10.

Out on blu-ray for the first time, *Beast* is a real beauty. Apart from a few scratch lines during the opening credits, the clear and vibrantly colorful print is nearly flawless. Also presented in near-pristine condition is its co-feature; though, truth be told, such clarity does it no favors by revealing the *Neanderthal Man*'s awful rubber mask and painted-on eyes in all its ridiculousness. The disc offers no extras, but that's fine; just consider *The Neanderthal Man* as a feature-length extra to the only real reason to purchase this set—the final 15 minutes of *The Beast of Hollow Mountain*.

> This modest little review broke the Magazine Barrier when it appeared in *Cult Movies*, issue 24 (December 1997).

larly the space flight sequences and the cartoonish paintings used to represent the futuristic city. Wooden characters (with lifeless thesping to match) and a general slowness of plot detract further from the lackluster proceedings. Too much time is wasted on Allison simply wandering around trying to figure out what is going on. *Beyond the Time Barrier*, however, is not completely beyond merit. The underground city interiors, created from an intriguing triangle motif, are fascinating. Triangular openings, inverted three-sided panels, and pyramid shapes abound in a bizarre amalgam that grabs the eye and holds it. Cinematographer Meredith M. Nicholson's varied lighting casts pools of light and shadow over the intriguing shapes to add a rich visual contrast. Still, though the sets themselves are unique, it's too bad that something more interesting wasn't *done* on them.

> Unfortunately, I have no idea where this review appeared (thank you, shoddy record-keeping system). But here it is anyway, in all its, er, beastliness.

BEYOND THE TIME BARRIER (1960)

"Fantastic sights to stagger the imagination!" –ad line

Director Edgar G. Ulmer has developed something of a cult following, based largely on a triumphant triad of films: *The Black Cat* (1934), *Bluebeard* (1944), and *Detour* (1945). His revered reputation has absolutely *nothing* to do with *Beyond the Time Barrier*. Filmed on the site of the 1959 Texas State Fairgrounds, and made back to back with *The Amazing Transparent Man* (another disappointing failure), *Beyond the Time Barrier* is Ulmer's low, low, low budget entry in the time travel sweepstakes.

While testing a new supersonic airplane, Major William Allison (Robert Clarke) somehow breaks the time barrier and lands in the year 2024. He finds a world decimated by the "cosmic nuclear plague of 1971." The surviving humans have gone underground and are now at war with the surface-dwelling mutants. Several subplots involving the leader's plans to mate Allison (a rare healthy male) with his daughter and the machinations of various revolutionary factions unfold before Allison escapes and flies his plane back to the world of 1960, there to warn mankind of the certain doom awaiting them if they hold to their present course of destruction.

The film suffers from poor special effects, particu-

THE BRIDE AND THE BEAST (1958)

A big game hunter (Lance Fuller) marries a girl (Charlotte Austin) who turns out to have been a gorilla in a past life. He then makes the mistake of taking her on safari in Africa for their honeymoon. The jungle urges prove too much and she summons an ape who, despite valiant protestations from her human husband, carries her off into the jungle to complete the 'honeymoon.' (Actually, the wife's final choice of mates doesn't seem so unreasonable when one considers that

Apes and Angora in The Bride and the Beast *(1958).*

she and her new hubby spent their wedding night in *separate* twin beds!) Sound absurd—and just a little bit kinky? It is.

Shot as *Queen of the Gorilla*, this no-budget exploitationer was scripted by none other than the notorious Edward D. Wood Jr., best known as the maker of such so-bad-they're-funny *anti*-classics as *Glen or Glenda?* and *Plan Nine from Outer Space*. This explains the script's rather perverse subject matter—as well as a certain bizarre non-sequitur involving angora (Wood reportedly loved to dress in women's clothing and had a particular penchant for angora sweaters). "Angora...beautiful things, soft like kittens' fur, it felt so *good* on me," coos the species-confused heroine for no discernible reason.

"When I read the script," remarked star Charlotte Austin to interviewer Tom Weaver, "I got physically sick to my stomach. I thought, 'Oh, my God, *who* wrote this thing? The dialogue was terrible, the whole premise, the whole idea—awful!"

Apart from the nonsensical (and occasionally amusing) 'Woodisms' such as "Basically, we're all animals, so her reversion just can't be ignored" (huh?), or this little howler: "That she had been a gorilla in a past life seems rather positive" (indeed?!!), *The Bride and the Beast* contains little of interest. In fact, a more accurate title would be *The Bride and the Boredom*. Most of the running time is eaten up by mismatched stock animal footage ("It was every stock shot that was ever shot in Hollywood, spliced together," observed Austin) and desultory scenes of the actors standing around talking or ineffectually shooting at something (characters make *six* different attempts to plug the same tiger—and miss *every time*).

The 'titillation' scenes of a nightgown-clad Charlotte Austin (the Bride) enjoying the animal embraces of a cheap-gorilla-suit-wearing Steve Calvert (the Beast) are just plain silly. Austin herself seems game enough in her acting but has little to do except stand around looking (appropriately) confused or allowing herself to be carried about by a hairy ape. As for Lance Fuller (playing her great white "Bwana" husband), he appears to have graduated from the John Agar school of acting (or perhaps flunked out would be more precise, since he proves less expressive than even the direst Agar performance).

The amusingly sleazy slant at the film's opening quickly levels out into a plain of boredom, so that even the story's bizarre premise falls flat. "Most of the time in that movie was spent biting our lips to keep from laughing," remembered Austin, who seemed to have enjoyed the experience. Too bad the viewer can't make the same claim. In all good conscience, *The Bride and the Beast* can be recommended only to stock jungle footage fans or that 'special' cinephile—the Ed Wood completist.

Here's a write-up I did for an online forum back in the day, this time on an infamous and controversial piece of Italian exploitation (and the granddaddy of the 'found footage' subgenre). *Cannibal Holocaust* (1980) features real animal violence and fake human torture in a tale of unscrupulous documentary filmmakers inciting a primitive jungle tribe to violence and cannibalism in order to satisfy their thrill-hungry camera lenses.

CANNIBAL HOLOCAUST, OR HOW I LEARNED TO STOP WORRYING AND LOVE THE LONG PIG

THE PRODUCTION:

The acting is crap (the four 'filmmakers' so overact and re-act that they become a quartet of goons), and the characters are cartoonish and poorly drawn (apart from the Professor, who's the only one that comes off as more than just two-dimensional), so that their motivations/actions seem forced. (For instance, I'd love to have learned *why* the girlfriend stayed with such a trio of abusive louts—all she ever seems to do is angrily shout at them; and even the sex scene is almost akin to rape, with the girl seeming to get little out of it. But there's nary a whiff of backstory, nor emotional revelation or motivation.) So there's little emotional connection when the quartet meet their demise.

On the other hand, everything else about the movie, from the script's clever structure to the camerawork to the inappropriate-but-oddly-affecting music, packs a wallop. The hyper-realistic photography (shot like a documentary, with much of the violence seen from a distance, with a shaky picture and/or obscuring trees) makes it seem all the more real and sets *Cannibal Holocaust* apart from other cannibal movies, which are primarily gross-out effects fests (some more effect-*ive* than others). Consequently, the human violence becomes that much more disturbing and powerful in *Cannibal Holocaust*—not because we care about the characters, white *or* native, but because director Ruggero Deodato has made it all seem so *real*.

THE ANIMAL VIOLENCE:

Though definitely disturbing (and morally questionable), the three instances of onscreen animal death didn't really seem that out-of-place or particularly shocking to me, as it does indeed seem intrinsic to the plot. Both the muskrat and turtle, for example, are killed for food, and done so quickly and efficiently. (Cue that Captain and Tennille song: "Muskrat Suzy, Muskrat Sam, get their throats slit out in Cannibal Land / As they wriggle, the cannibal starts to giggle…") The pig, of course, is another story, but it's a quick demise as well. This real-life (as opposed to *reel*-life) animal violence further heightens the sense of reality, so that the film's hyper-realism becomes that much more affecting when it comes to the (faked) human violence. Though admittedly distasteful, the animal snuff is the icing on the reality cake, so to speak. Whatever its dubious moral ground, the animal violence in *Cannibal Holocaust* definitely enhances the film's power. The animal aspect of *Cannibal Holocaust* is like a jungle field-trip to a slaughterhouse, where you finally see where our food *really* comes from. This hammers home the everyday necessity—and acceptance—of death in this environment (rather than the sanitized, plastic-wrapped Safeway methods we're all used to in 'civilization'), which feeds into one of the movie's major themes.

THE MESSAGE:

Cannibal Holocaust is unquestionably a powerful, affecting, thought-provoking, and shocking film; and I've been pondering what the point/message is. (And the damned thing got me thinking enough to make me want to believe there *is* a point—besides exploitation.) Of course, there's the obvious anti-media/voyeurism angle. But I'm thinking there's something more under the surface—perhaps a treatise on the nature of brutality itself. On the one hand, the anthropologist studying the found film footage concludes that it's the filmmakers (modern man) who are the *real* savages (since they terrorize and supposedly provoke the cannibals into horrific acts just to gratify their camera), while he paints the primitives with the old 'noble savage' brush. But the primitives were doing nasty things to each other already (the 'punishment' for adultery, the shockingly horrific late-hour 'abortion'). So perhaps it's the circumstances/environment itself that transforms men into brutal savages, since the only 'good' guys in the movie seem to be the Professor and—finally, after watching the film and being sickened by it—the TV people (the 'civilized' city-dwellers). Civilization arose to keep such savagery in check, and when the veneer is stripped away, the inherent brutality in man re-emerges.

It also may be Deodato's self-loathing ode to the crass business of filmmaking. The four filmmakers will do *anything* to get their footage—and they don't give a damn about how authentic, or even how 'good' their film is; they just want something that'll sell and make them famous and a ton o' cash. So perhaps *Cannibal Holocaust* is the ultimate subtle, subversive inversion of exploitation filmmaking. Ironically, one of the most powerful exploitation movies ever made is one big subversive treaty damning exploitation movies *That* is clever!

Cult Movies magazine (issue 21) released these *Captive Women* in 1997.

CAPTIVE WOMEN (1952)

"Man was born in brotherhood and in brotherhood must live if he is not to die in chaos."

Made by the same producer/screenwriter team (Aubrey Wisberg and Jack Pollexfen) that brought us the superior low-budget sci-fi film *The Man from Planet X* a year earlier, and featuring much of the same cast (Robert Clarke, Margaret Field, and William Schallert), *Captive Women* can't hold a candle to that earlier effort. *Captive Women* suffers from a weak storyline, inadequate acting, and, most severely, from the lack of Edgar G. Ulmer, who directed the atmospheric *Man from Planet X*.

New York in the 29th century is a ruined post-atomic mess populated by three warring tribes—the Upriver People (the bad guys), the Norms (indifferent, but still our heros because they look normal), and the Mutates (the good guys despite their scarred appearance from radiation poisoning). The Mutates periodically raid the Norms for normal women with which to breed in an attempt to eradicate the radiation sickness from their own gene pool. They do this only of necessity and are generally a peaceful people, given to talking about loving thy neighbor, rebuilding civilization, and so on. The Upriver people, on the other hand, are bent only on conquest, and send their army to conquer the Norms (their force consists of only six warriors, budgetary restrictions turning the "army" into a mini-platoon). What follows is an hour of dull intrigue, vapid love-interest, and stagey personal combat sequences; while Stuart Gilmore's lifeless direction robs the story of what little energy it might muster. On the plus side, there are some noble ideas of brotherhood and equality laid out along the way, but these noteworthy sentiments are lost among all the bickering and pointless running about. A few good shots of the scarred landscape, with the dark photography setting a somber mood, help to ease the boredom, but in the end, *Captive Woman* is best shown only to a Captive Audience.

> This mini-review crept into *Cult Movies* magazine (issue 10) in 1994.

CASTLE OF THE CREEPING FLESH (1968)

"A HAUNTED GOTHIC TALE OF MADNESS, LUST AND BLOOD" –ad line

Since it was made by the same man (Adrian Hoven, using the alias Percy G. Parker) who brought us the unpleasant and mean-spirited *Mark of the Devil* (1970) and *Mark of the Devil 2* (1972), one should not be surprised that *Castle of the Creeping Flesh* is as nasty as it is. The story concerns a small group of hedonistic partygoers, headed by a brutal Baron (Michael Lemoine), who stumble into the castle of the reclusive Count von Saxon (Howard Vernon—*The Awful Dr. Orlof* himself). The Count is trying to revive his dead daughter through some kind of mad medical operation and chooses one of the visiting girls as an unwilling donor. "Life and death—*they* are alike; but there is also love," justifies Von Saxon in a bit of off-kilter, homespun philosophy. "Love creates life; love has a right to kill. But he who kills for revenge will be cursed." Good to know.

With an overly talky script (not helped by atrociously dubbed dialogue) populated by unlikable characters, this piece of celluloid Eurotrash's only real asset is an overpowering sense of decadence that gives the proceedings a sleazy sort of attractiveness. (Tellingly, this West German production's alternate titles are *Castle of Bloody Lust* and *Castle of Unholy Desires*.) The photography and sets are lushly Gothic, and there are some truly erotic sequences involving actress Janine Reynaud, a sensuous beauty often found in the films of Jess Franco. There are also endless unpleasant close-ups of real-life open-heart surgery as the Count (a surgeon) tries to revive his dead daughter using "borrowed" organs; an unconvincing man-in-a-bear-suit inflicting ridiculous face slaps on a cast member with its, er, faux paws; several gratuitous rape scenes; and a gratingly bad piano-bar jazz score. Though not for everyone, *Castle of the Creeping Flesh* possesses a repellant albeit fascinating air that makes it (almost) watchable.

> Like *The Children* themselves, this piece was quite short (but not too short for *Cult Movies* magazine, issue 21, Spring 1997).

THE CHILDREN (1980)

Night of the Living Dead meets *Mr. Rogers* as a nuclear leak turns children into murderous zombies with black fingernails. The killer kids burn the flesh of their victims with their touch. The only way to stop them is to cut off their hands! On the plus side, this wacky movie sports an occasionally effective and suspenseful scene as the zombie children close in on their horrified parents. Also, the story raises some admittedly ludicrous but still rather frightening issues, such as how could you destroy your own child—even if it is a *horrible undead thing*?!! On the minus side, the effects are expectedly shoddy, highlighted (or, more aptly, "lowlighted") by silly hamburger faces and rubbery hand-less arms. Bad acting, characters you don't really like, and a sheriff who takes abuse from just about everyone make this a rather disappointing, albeit novel, horror outing.

> These *Children* played in *Cult Movies* magazine, issue 15 (Summer 1995).

CHILDREN SHOULDN'T PLAY WITH DEAD THINGS (1973)

Children Shouldn't Play with Dead Things is really two films in one—or, more precisely, one film with two different tempos. The first half is black comedy (which sometimes works and sometimes doesn't). A theater group, headed by Alan Ormsby (who also cowrote the screenplay as well as creating the effective makeup!), visits a graveyard located on a remote island. *Why* they visit this creepy place in the middle of the night is anybody's guess, except that the megalomaniac director (Ormsby) wants to play wizard with a satanic tome he's uncovered. He intends to cast a spell to raise the dead (or at least have a few laughs in the meantime).

This initial episode, consisting of a lot of bad wisecracks (usually revolving around a corpse these jokers have dug up and nicknamed "Orville") and a few good ones comes to a close when the spell is finally cast. Excellent camerawork and some (uncharacteristically) intense acting at this point make this bizarre scene a riveting set piece and an excellent jumping off point

Good advice.

for the film's no-holds-barred second half. For you see, the spell really works and the dead actually do rise in an incredible scene inspired by George Romero's *Night of the Living Dead* (and inspiration *for* Michael Jackson's *Thriller*). At this point the movie becomes as gripping and as terrifying as Romero's classic.

Unfortunately, *Children* is marred by the generally substandard acting (Ormsby should definitely remain *behind* the camera) of the cast (made up of many of director Bob Clark's college friends). Also, the hit and miss comedy of the sometimes slow-moving first half is only partially effective. But stay tuned, for the second half is well worth the wait. Alan Ormsby went on to direct the disturbing 1974 film *Deranged* (loosely based on the ghoulish crimes of Ed Gein) and wrote *Cat People* (1982). Director Clark's *Deathdream* (1972) is even better than *Children*; both are low-budget classics of the drought-ridden seventies. *Children Shouldn't Play with Dead Things* (what a great title!) was shot in 14 days on a miniscule budget of $70,000—an impressive achievement.

> This brief byte (ouch) appeared in *Cult Movies* magazine, issue 21 (Spring 1997).

COLOSSUS: THE FORBIN PROJECT (1969)

A taut, gripping translation from the book to the screen (a rarity in Hollywood), *Colossus: The Forbin Project* proves itself a top-notch sci-fi thriller. Two ultra-sophisticated, sentient defense computers (the American supercomputer dubbed "Colossus" and its Soviet counterpart named "Guardian") link up to hold the world in the palm of their circuits. They do this by holding out the threat of nuclear devastation in an effort to exhort from mankind an unwanted utopia ruled by the computers. The story centers on Charles Forbin (Eric Braeden), the principal builder of Colossus, and his attempts to outwit and disconnect his technological Frankenstein Monster. Unfairly overshadowed by its brother compu-thriller *2001: A Space Odyssey* (1968), *Colossus: The Forbin Project* is an entertaining, well-acted technological nightmare whose intelligent screenplay presents a gripping portrayal of the threat of nuclear devastation and the near-worse solution of computer domination and resultant loss of freedom. Bill Gates beware.

> *Movie Club* magazine published this brief bit of backwoods blarney in 1997 (issue 11) as part of their "Universal Comedy" overview.

COMIN' ROUND THE MOUNTAIN (1951)

In this low-end Abbott and Costello vehicle, the boys journey to the hillbilly country of Old Kentucky when Wilburt (Costello) learns he's a long-lost cousin of the McCoy clan, and that there's treasure buried somewhere thereabouts just waiting for him to claim. Of course, his bumbling soon re-ignites the old McCoy-Winfield feud (apparently the 'Hatfields' were out of town that decade).

Somewhere amongst the lowbrow shenanigans (which include waaaay too many silly songs from warbler Dorothy Shay), the duo visits an old backwoods witch called Aunt Hattie (Margaret Hamilton doing her Wicked Witch of the West shtick from *The Wizard of Oz*) to buy a love potion. Hamilton chants comical nonsense that sounds something like "Ardule la gummeegitchee gazoo" and molds an effigy of Costello when Abbott refuses to pay up front, sticking pins into the doll's derriere until the little fat man can take it no longer. Then, when the witch is not looking, Costello makes an effigy of *her*, and the two engage in a comical voodoo doll duel. The scene concludes when Costello notices the old witch's broom (complete with windscreen and windshield wipers!), touches a spot on the handle, and accidentally flies out the door to crash into the trees outside. (So much for voodoo—thrown over for the more traditional witchcraft for one final sight gag.)

The film's level of humor is reflected in this dialogue exchange:

Abbott: "She's making voodoo."
Costello: "She's making voo do what?"
Abbott: "Voodoo!"
Costello: "I do what?"

> This blu-ray review was intended for *Monsters from the Vault* magazine but somehow never made it into orbit.

CORMAN'S WORLD: EXPLOITS OF A HOLLYWOOD REBEL

Roger Corman has been called many things over the course of his nearly six-decades-long career, from "schlockmeister" to "genius" and everything in between. Though opinions of Corman's films, both those he directed personally and those he oversaw from afar via his various production and distribution companies (like New World, Concorde, and New Horizons), vary widely, the high esteem held by those who knew and worked for Roger Corman remains near-universal. Though his eye rarely strayed from the bottom line, and "parsimonious" may be one of the kinder adjectives frequently applied to his approach to filmmaking, Corman was always up-front and honest with his underlings, a straight-shooter in the crooked maze of Hollywood who gave countless Tinseltown luminaries their start in the biz.

In *Corman's World: Exploits of a Hollywood Rebel*, documentarian Alex Stapleton gathers a cast of Corman characters that looks like a Who's Who of Hollywood elite to talk about their early years learning the ropes via the informal "Corman School of Filmmaking." Movie makers like Peter Bogdanovich, Martin Scorsese, and Ron Howard, and actors such as Jack Nicholson, Bruce Dern and Robert DeNiro, all offer their two cents on the man, the myth and the legend that is Roger Corman. Via clips and comments from these and a score of other Corman cronies (from Peter Fonda and David Carradine to Jonathan Haze and Dick Miller, from Joe Dante and Jonathan Demme to Roger's wife Julie and brother Gene), and illuminating bon mots from the man himself, this fast-moving, well-edited documentary paints a fascinating picture of Roger and his career. The film covers all the Corman bases, including his humble beginnings as an independent in Hollywood (making movies like *Monster from the Ocean Floor*) to his linking up with AIP to create some of the most beloved films in the horror genre (including his classic Poe pictures), his establishing of the biker flick (with *The Wild Angels*), his political views and the volatile cultural climate of the times (including breaking ground with the drug film *The Trip*), his New World period, his cinematic love affair with the Philippines (where filming—and stuntmen—were cheap), his distribution of art films (Bergman, Fellini), his response to the industry sea change wrought by *Jaws* and *Star Wars*, his New Horizons phase, and the direct-to-DVD and SyFy Channel shift.

A well-integrated selection of film clips, photos, and some fascinating vintage interview snippets visually illuminate and augment the words of the various interviewees. Included are some priceless behind-the-scenes footage from the original *Piranha*, and some relatively recent shots of Roger in action down in Mexico as he supervised (and cameoed in) *Dinoshark*. A real highlight comes when Jack Nicholson breaks down in tears when speaking of Roger and how he not only jump-started but single-handedly sustained his career. It's a touching moment nearly worth the price of admission alone.

Extras consist of a slam-bang trailer worthy of the Corman factory itself, a handful of "extended interviews" with the likes of Eli Roth, Scorsese, Howard and Jim Wynorski, and a series of "Special Messages to Roger" in which the interviewees are instructed to talk to the camera as if it were Roger himself. These latter bits not only offer some amusing—and touching—denouements, but demonstrate how Roger Corman remains a vital part of the industry even now, as several folks make impromptu pitches and press Roger for work!

Though die-hard genre fans may find few groundbreaking revelations here, the erudite and affectionate outpouring, and the intelligent words of Roger Corman himself, offer an excellent overview of the contributions of an industry giant and true original. And, like nearly all Corman classics (and even the later classicks), it's fast-paced and never dull. Remember, it's *Corman's World*—we just watch it.

> These few words published in *Cult Movies* magazine (issue 15, Summer 1995) are probably more than this terrible turkey deserved.

THE CRATER LAKE MONSTER (1977)

"Hell, if things were different they'd be easier." This absurd observation from a cast member of *The Crater Lake Monster* sets the tone for this awful Loch Ness Monster variation. The only recommendation for viewing *The Crater Lake Monster* is the surprisingly good stop-motion animation of the title character created by animator Dave Allen (*Equinox*, 1971; *Flesh Gordon*, 1972; the *Puppetmaster* series). A meteor crashes into Oregon's Crater Lake and heats up the water just enough to hatch a dormant dinosaur egg lying on the bottom. So out comes a hungry plesiosaurus who commences to chow down on the locals, which is no great loss since by and large they all act like imbecilic yokels anyway. The script is bad, the acting worse, and the finale, when the hero sheriff takes on the house-sized thunder lizard with a snowplow, is ludicrous. Funds must have been running short, since so does this un-

A few scant scenes with this fella are the only *reasons to watch* The Crater Lake Monster *(1977).*

exciting climactic battle. The Sheriff obviously knew just *where* to find a plesiosaur's weak spot, because he merely runs into the towering monster's midriff with the front of the snowplow and miraculously kills the beast. Stop-motion fans will get a kick out of the proceedings, but everybody else will just kick themselves for sitting through it.

> I sent this one down the river to *Movie Club* magazine (issue 11, Fall 1997) for their "Universal Horror/Sci-Fi" overview.

CURUCU, BEAST OF THE AMAZON (1956)

"LIKE NOTHING YOUR EYES HAVE EVER SEEN BEFORE!" –poster

Though more of a (tedious) jungle adventure than horror film, *Curucu, Beast of the Amazon* still manages to deliver an occasional shock and one (rag-tag) monster. Granted, the title creature is revealed half-way through the film to be nothing more than a man wearing a cartoonish costume of feathers, tusks and bone, but at least the man/monster commits a few startling and gruesome murders before his (literal) unmasking.

Filmed on location over an 11-week period in Brazil (for the amazingly low sum of $155,000), *Curucu* understandably possesses an air of realism absent in most Hollywood jungle epics of this time and budget. *Curucu* also sports some absolutely breathtaking photography of spectacular jungle waterfalls. The realism, however, quickly cracks under the weight of mismatched stock footage and poor matting techniques periodically inserted into the film. (Watch for a downright laughable scene in which the actors face down a herd of stampeding wild buffalo.)

John Bromfield (fresh from *Revenge of the Creature*) plays the square-jawed hero named Rock, turning in a performance obviously inspired by his character's name. ("John Bromfield, God love him," confided co-star Beverly Garland to interviewer Tom Weaver, "was certainly not an actor—a good-looking, wonderful person, but I really don't think he was much of an actor.") Perennial Fifties fave Garland (who for five weeks in the Brazilian jungle was the only female among the 40-plus cast and crew) does better as Andrea, the strong-willed woman who nevertheless goes weak in the knees and screams whenever in the jungle (obviously "no place for a woman").

Writer-director Curt Siodmak (from whose typewriter sprang *The Wolf Man* for Universal fifteen years earlier) fills his tepid screenplay with scene after dull scene of dialogue—in an office, in a boardroom, in a nightclub, on a boat… ("I had no money at the time, so I wrote *Curucu*," confessed Siodmak about his motivation.) In between, there's plenty of travelogue footage as our intrepid protagonists traipse through the jungle searching for the legendary monster that's been murdering and frightening off the native plantation workers. (Ms. Garland's character, a doctor, goes along to procure a sample of the drug used by the deep-jungle headhunters to shrink tissue in the hopes it will aid in her cancer research.)

Most of the film's running time consists of the cast hacking their way through the underbrush or the hero saving the heroine from various mundane menaces—spider (which he shoots with a rifle in a moment of ludicrous overkill), leopard (obviously stuffed), snake, and headhunters. To be fair, the snake attack scene generates some small excitement, and Beverly Garland does some effective (and probably *real*) emoting. ("I was talking to Curt [Siodmak] one day twenty-five years later," related the actress, "and he said, 'You know, it's amazing you're still here…that snake in *Curucu* was very dangerous.'") And the picture possesses one final kick at the end—the very last shot—which embodies a touch of poetic justice that would feel at home in the pages of the notorious E.C. horror comics.

The most pointed criticism that can be leveled at the film (and, perversely, the picture's most *amusing* element) is the incredibly patronizing outlook it takes towards women (even for the 1950s). Hilariously sexist lines pepper the picture. Just before he meets Andrea (a prominent medical researcher), Rock reveals his "M.C.P." nature with this offhanded comment: "I know how it is—can't get a man so she chooses a career." Later, when Rock states, "You're not afraid of anything are you?" Andrea seemingly justifies his Neanderthal notions by answering, "Of course I'm afraid of some things—I'm a woman."

Beverly Garland has related how most of the cast and crew were sick with various jungle illnesses during filming. ("I never recovered, physically," stated Siodmak.) Viewing the finished product, one can readily believe it.

An even shorter version of this essay appeared in *Cult Movies* magazine (issue 13) in 1995.

THE DIABOLICAL DR. Z (1966)

"NOTHING EVER STRIPPED YOUR NERVES SCREAMINGLY RAW LIKE... THE DIABOLICAL DR. Z*"* –poster

This Spanish/French co-production from the diabolical director Jess Franco (using the pseudonym "Henri Baum") may be that prolific Spanish filmmaker's finest film. Best known to English-speaking audiences for his 1970 version of *Count Dracula*, starring Christopher Lee, Klaus Kinski and Herbert Lom, Franco has been turning out the European equivalent of drive-in fare since 1959 (reportedly over 150 features to date!).

The Diabolical Dr. Z centers on Dr. Zimmer (Antonio Jiminez Escribano), who has developed a strange machine that blends acupuncture and hypnosis to transform people into obedient slaves. Dr. Z explains his reasoning like this: "Thanks to me, all the killers, all the abnormal, all the sadists, all the maniacs could be transmuted into wise and good persons." Unfortunately, the poor physician never has a chance to prove his theory, for he dies of a coronary induced by his ridicule at a scientific convention. Consequently, his rather cold daughter (Mabel Karr) decides to avenge his death by destroying the three prominent scientists whom she feels were responsible. The instrument of her vengeance is a gorgeous exotic dancer with two-inch fingernails that goes by the stage name of "Miss Death" (played by the strikingly beautiful Estella Blain). Miss Zimmer

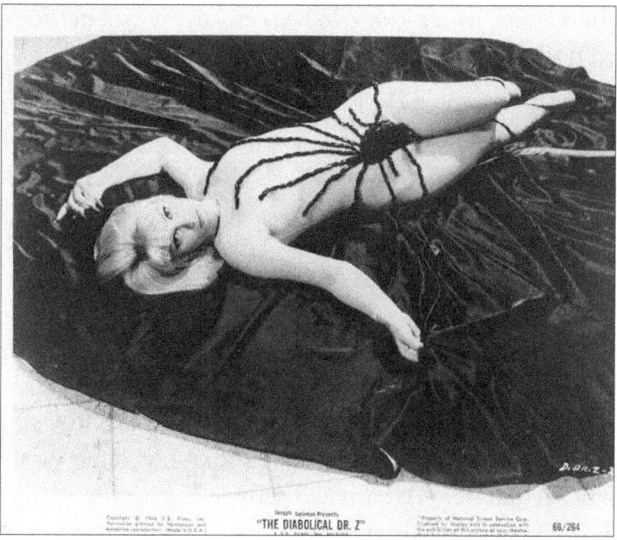

The stunning Estella Blain, as "Miss Death," becomes an instrument of vengeance for The Diabolical Dr. Z *(1966).*

kidnaps Miss Death, subjects her to the mind-control machine, treats her remarkable fingernails with the "poison" curare, and sends her out to exact vengeance.

Running throughout this unique film is an undercurrent of Sadean sensuality, largely due to the presence of Estella Blain (who, sadly, committed suicide in 1981) and Franco's voyeuristic approach. Blain's bizarrely erotic "dance of death" in the nightclub sequence is worth the price of admission alone. After being turned into an unwilling killer, she still manages to inspire flashes of sympathy, however, making the audience actually care about what happens to her—a rare occurrence in subsequent Franco films.

Franco peppers his odd-yet-clever scenario with striking set-pieces, including a suspenseful chase through village back-alleys; a sudden and vicious murder-by-auto; some wince-inducing facial self-surgery; the surreal mind-control machine, with its spider-like mechanical "arms" and oversized acupuncture needles, at work; a brutally realistic fight sequence; and, of course, Miss Death's unforgettable nightclub performance (involving her writhing about on a huge, stylized spider web). Aided by cinematographer Alejandro Ulloa's atmospheric lighting and gorgeous black-and-white photography (transforming stately manor homes and village streets into ominous dens of shadow and darkness), Franco here updated 1960s Continental horror with a striking eroticism and deliciously bizarre ambiance. (And watch for the filmmaker himself in an amusing cameo role as a sleep-deprived police inspector.) *The Diabolical Dr. Z* is a remarkably polished achievement for an off-kilter filmmaker who, in a few short years, would come to be seen largely as a perverted hack (when seen at all).

> *Cult Movies* magazine was doomed to print this little ditty in issue 16 (Fall 1995).

DOOMSDAY MACHINE (1967)

In the future of 1975 a mixed spacecrew is sent on a mission to explore Venus. Just after the ship takes off, the Chinese set off their "Doomsday Device" and the Earth is totally destroyed (looking like a big paper ball set aflame). After making their *Escape from Planet Earth* (the film's alternate title), the crewmembers first spend time agonizing over the loss of the human race, then (deciding they must make a brave new world on Venus) start alternately bickering and acting heroic. When they finally reach Venus, several crewmembers agree to sacrifice themselves so that the others can land safely. But miracle of miracles, they find another derelict spaceship (an old Russian ship which just happens to be floating by), and it appears as if everybody is going to make it and start up an Earth 2 on Venus. But wait, suddenly a "collective intelligence" pops up, refuses to allow the two ships to land, and abruptly wipes out these last survivors of the human race, sending the unwelcome astronauts on an "even greater journey."

This ultra-cheap, ludicrous mishmash of a film is filled with long, boring scenes of people sitting around, walking around, and just plain *hanging* around. The special effects are uniformly shoddy, with most of the rocketship shots borrowed from the 1956 film *Warning from Space*. Co-director Lee Sholem explained (to interviewer Tom Weaver) just what the hell was going on: "They called me in to see if I could make anything out of it. Everything was just a hodgepodge—I don't know why they let the director carry on as long as they did. They had nowhere to go, they didn't know what to do. They knew they had nothing, the cutter was proving that—they couldn't even cut what they had! It was a monstrous job—it was a patch-job more than anything." It *is* fun, however, to see Grant Williams, *The Incredible Shrinking Man* himself, play a weasely, cowardly, lecherous skunk; while Mike Farrell (pre–*M*A*S*H*) and Casey Kasem appear in bit parts. And the shapely Mala Powers, who'd been menaced by *The Unknown Terror* in 1957, is always a welcome sight. It took five years before somebody got up the nerve to release the *Dullsday*... er, *Doomsday Machine*.

> This was written as part of a "Dangerous Dames" compilation article presented in issue 57 (Summer 1998) of *Midnight Marquee* magazine.

DRACULA'S DAUGHTER (1936)

"She was beautiful when she died—a hundred years ago." So spoke Professor Von Helsing (Edward Van Sloan) at the close of *Dracula's Daughter* (1936), a film that arguably features the most fascinating female villain from horror cinema's Golden Age.

This titular vampire is a monster of a very different stripe. Not only is she a rare feminine bloodsucker in a (at the time) male dominated arena, but she's a *sympathetic* one as well. Gloria Holden's Countess Marya Zaleska is much more than a bloodsucking demon; she is a tortured soul, a pitiable victim (of her own despised heritage), as much as vicious victimizer. This sympathetic characterization adds a fascinating 'monster-as-victim' subtext (a theme which makes the Frankenstein films so intriguing) to what could otherwise have become just another straightforward vampire yarn.

Though her very nature has made her cold and aloof, Zaleska's haughtiness carries a decidedly hollow ring. While her face may remain passive, her voice can readily quicken with excitement to betray the hope and longing lurking beneath the cold countenance. Though a tortured soul, this reluctant vampire hasn't completely lost her sense of humor, for she displays a sharp wit that emphasizes her humanity. When psychiatrist/hero Jeffrey Garth makes a skeptical comment at a party, for instance, Zaleska cleverly disarms him with, "Possibly there are more things in heaven and Earth than are dreamed of in your—psychiatry, Mr. Garth."

Gloria Holden brings this tormented spirit to life with her restrained-yet-earnest performance, revealing the living being beneath the undead exterior. Holden truly uses her eyes to mirror her character's soul. She keeps her gaze almost unfocused at times, as if her inner self were concentrating elsewhere, attempting to escape from her own nightmarish existence. At other moments her staring eyes dart about, almost desperately, as if searching for the escape she craves. When she talks of living "a normal life" in which she'll "think normal things," the faraway look in her eyes and half-smile on her lips speak of the hopeful expectations stretched out before her. After her moral defeat during the piano scene (in which she once again succumbs to the bloodlust), her servant, Sandor, holds up Zaleska's black

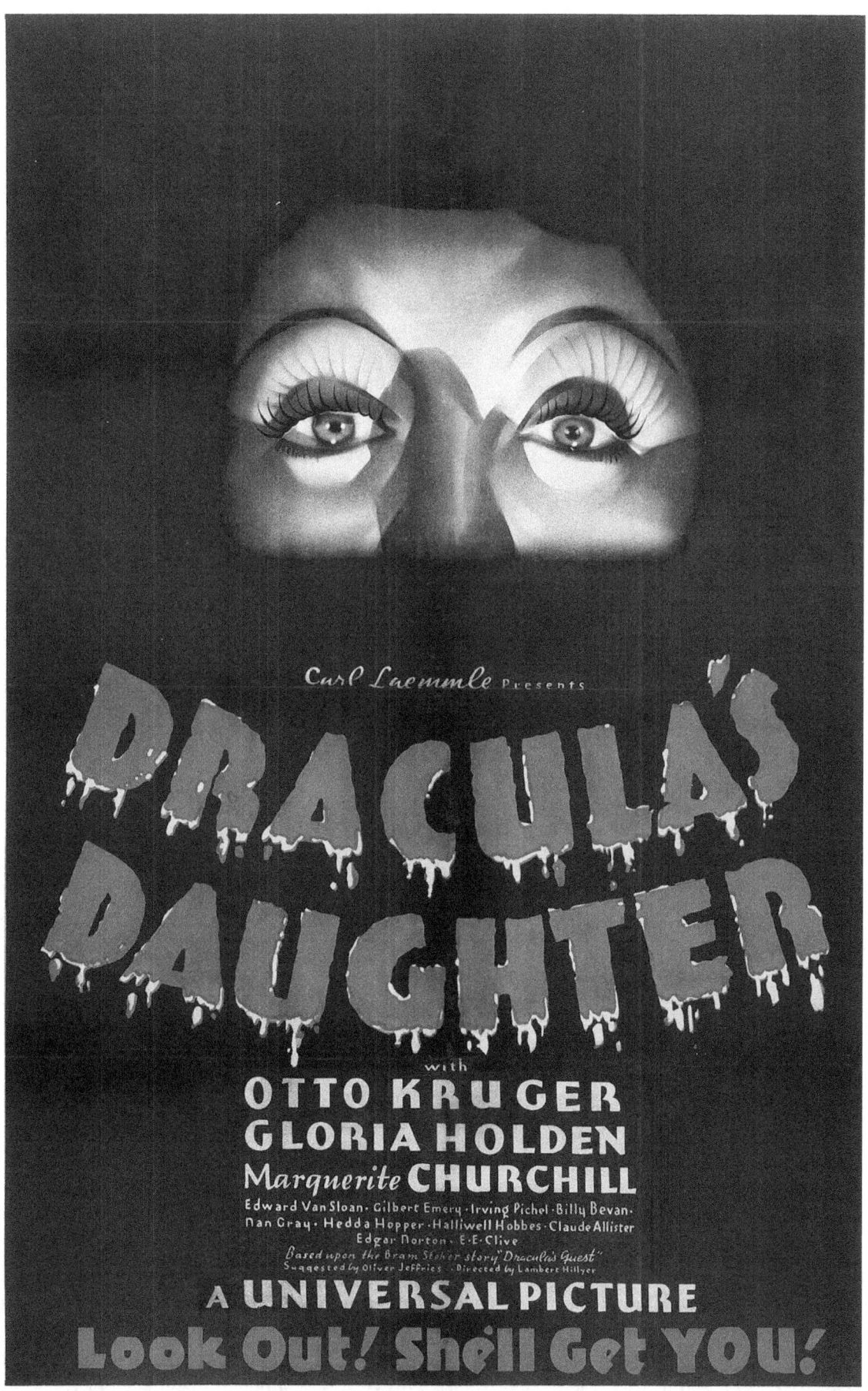

Look out indeed.

cloak and ring (the symbols of her nocturnal cravings) so she can venture out to claim another victim. Holden hesitates, gazing at the despised garment in ambivalent fascination. Unable to resist the lure, she finally turns and allows Sandor to drape the damning cloak on her shoulders. Holden's face remains outwardly impassive, but her eyes and downward turn of expression betray a poignant sadness at her defeat.

Such appealing torment, coupled with the irresistible lure of vampirism (symbolizing power over both sex and death), makes this diabolical daughter one of the most intriguing female villains of the Silver Scream.

> This is from *Cult Movies* magazine, issue 24 (December 1997).

THE EARTH DIES SCREAMING (1965)

"'THE EARTH DIES SCREAMING'… AND A NEW TERROR REIGNS!" –trailer

Great title, lousy movie.

Some unknown force has wiped out nearly the entire human population. Robots with silver heads and dressed in spacesuits roam a small English village where a handful of people who escaped the "gas attack" (including real-life husband and wife Willard Parker and Virginia Field) are trying to figure out what is going on. What's worse, robots are reviving the dead as white-eyed, mindless zombies. With elements like these (not to mention a real grabber for a name), *The Earth Dies Screaming* should be a sure-fire hit. But, sadly, you can't judge a film by its title. The production is obviously of very small scale. With only seven cast members, no special effects to speak of (we're never shown where the robots originate, for instance), and only two robots (looking like cut-rate escapees from an early *Dr. Who* episode), it's difficult to create a believable scenario through which our intrepid band can fight for their lives against insurmountable odds.

Terence Fisher, Hammer Studio's best resident director (who helmed such classics as *The Curse of Frankenstein* and *Horror of Dracula*) never takes advantage of the possibilities inherent in the story. We don't see any eerie shots of deserted towns, or kettles boiling over unattended, or any other trappings of a world suddenly devoid of people. Everything is filmed in a straightforward, almost casual manner.

Likewise, the horror and menace to be found when faced with walking corpses is never fully exploited. They move so slowly, and there are so few of them, that they fail to pose any real threat (particularly since they easily "die" a second time; no need to "shoot 'em in the head"—anywhere will do). It's almost as if their inclusion was an afterthought—"Right, some zombies would make for a jolly good show." The climax contains no surprises and little excitement. The two heroes formulate a plan to destroy the transmitter through which the robots and zombies are directed. They locate the transmitter and blow it up. That's it—straight to the point without any undue drama or suspense.

In the end, *The Earth Dies* not with a scream but a whimper.

> *Cult Movies* magazine (issue 15) published an even shorter form of this review in the summer of 1995.

EARTH VS. THE FLYING SAUCERS (1956)

"The ultimate (pre–*Independence Day*) "flying saucer" movie, *Earth vs. the Flying Saucers* is a marvel of special effects and a tribute to the genius of effects wizard Ray Harryhausen. SEE flying saucers destroy a battleship. SEE flying saucers over the capitals of the world—gliding past the Eiffel Tower, the London Parliament and the Capitol Building. SEE an out-of-control saucer smash into the Washington Monument, sending it crashing to the ground. SEE the dome of our capitol building crushed beneath a faltering saucer. These are just a few of the highlights provided by Harryhausen as he sends his stop motion-animated spaceships out to wreak havoc.

When Operation Skyhook (a satellite-launching project) keeps losing contact with its rockets, Dr. Marvin (Hugh Marlowe) is nonplussed. Things become crystal clear when a huge flying saucer lands at the rocket base, disgorging several robot-like creatures (whose metallic exoskeletons serve as the spindly aliens' outer shells). Soon, an invasion fleet is crisscrossing the skies and the aliens issue an order to capitulate within 60 days or face total destruction.

"The challenge on *Earth vs. the Flying Saucers*," recalled Harryhausen, "was to see if you could make a mechanical-looking object that would interest the public for an hour and a half—to keep the thing interesting and feel that there was an intelligence operating these saucers." Harryhausen rose to the challenge admirably; his creations, although inanimate objects, seem almost

Hugh Marlowe comforts Joan Taylor when it's the Earth vs. the Flying Saucers *(1956). (Mexican lobby card)*

alive as they flit about the sky, darting this way and that with incredible speed or gliding gracefully yet malevolently over our cityscapes. (Enhancing these scenes are the saucers' evocative sound effects, the result of recordings made at the Playa Del Ray Sewage Disposal Plant[!], where the film's rocket base scenes were shot.) Tim Burton later paid loving homage to Harryhausen's saucers in the quirky and highly entertaining *Mars Attacks!* (1996).

Harryhausen flawlessly integrates his unstoppable saucers into some excellent stock footage of exploding buildings, ships, and planes. When watching, there is no question that those fighter jets were just shot down by a destructive spaceship from another world. Aside from the convincing saucers themselves, the film also sports an excellent cast, headed by Hugh Marlowe as Dr. Marvin, the young brave scientist impatient with beaurocracy and unafraid to buck authority when necessary. This is a bit unusual in a film of this time—a time when the army was always right and authority was rarely questioned.

Earth vs. the Flying Saucers has its flaws, however, not the least of which is a simplistic and often contrived plot. (Producer Charles Schneer was dissatisfied with George Worthington Yates' original script and hired blacklisted writer Bernard Gordon to extensively rewrite it, using a pseudonym. Gordon received $1500 for his troubles.) Dr. Marvin whips up a totally new super-weapon with which to combat the invaders far too easily. The aliens stupidly (and too-conveniently) decide to send *all* of their saucers to Washington D.C. to attack, even knowing about our "super-weapon" and making no provision against it. The dialogue gets *awfully* technical at times: "You can take it from me, when a rocket blasts off it should circle the Earth for a long time." And the film as a whole often reflects the hostile paranoia permeating the 1950s: when the saucer first appears, it is *our* side that fires first, unprovoked, and no one questions this callous and ignorant act. A determined army Major puts it in perspective when he utters the film's funniest line: "When an armed and threatening power lands uninvited in our capital, we don't meet them with tea and cookies." Indeed.

But we're not here to pick apart the movie's Cold War attitude, we're here to see flying saucers destroy our nation's capital (an appealingly anarchic concept later stolen by the ultra-successful *Independence Day*). We're here to see humanity triumph and repel the alien invaders. And we do, in a spectacular way that is unsurpassed in the cinema of its day.

> *Cult Movies* magazine (issue 15) printed a scaled-down version of this essay in nineteen-ninety-*FIVE*.

FIVE (1951)

"One—*One girl…the last left on Earth!* Two—*two hours of the most spellbinding entertainment ever filmed!* Three—*A story of three elemental passions…love, hate, fear!* Four—*Four men…alone with the knowledge that in all the world there is only one woman!* Five!" –ad line

Five was the brainchild of former radio "genius" Arch Oboler (creator of *Lights Out*). Shooting on his Santa Monica Mountain ranch, the writer-producer-director utilized his own (Frank Lloyd Wright–designed) guest house as the primary set, housed the underpaid crew of four U.S.C. film students in his own home (which he mortgaged to raise the film's $75,000 budget), paid his five no-name actors (most of them recruited from radio) minimum scale, and filmed a script that focused on emotional reactions and personal interactions rather than costly special effects. And, surprisingly, it worked.

The idea for *Five* arose way back in 1938, when Oboler wrote a radio show for Bette Davis called "The Word." He then expanded the story, which told of a couple alone on Earth, into a feature film script (adding the nuclear element) while on an African Safari in 1948.

An atomic blast fills the screen, and we read that this is "a story about the day after tomorrow" as clouds and smoke obscure a montage of famous landmarks—Big Ben, the Kremlin, the New York skyline. Five survivors—a nice guy (William Phipps), an arrogant bastard (James Anderson), a black man (Charles Lampkin), an old man (Earl Lee), and a woman (Susan Douglas)—come together at an isolated mountain cabin. There they must deal with racism, radioactive poisoning, and jealousy over perhaps the last woman on earth. (Apparently, this particular last-woman-on-earth possessed a decidedly disagreeable disposition, as Phipps called

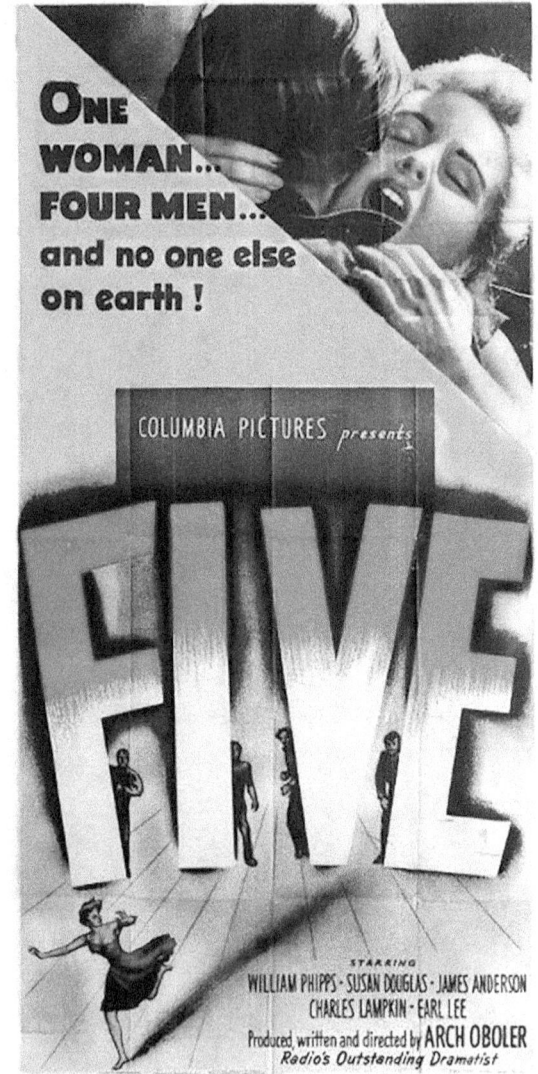

Poster for Five.

Susan Douglas "one of the biggest pain-in-the-asses I ever worked with!…. She bellyached and bellyached. She was just a thoroughly unlikable person.")

Five proved to be a contentious shoot all the way around. Oboler's dictatorial style failed to endear him to his cast and crew. "[Oboler] had clashes and run-ins with everybody," recounted William Phipps to interviewer Tom Weaver, and even came to blows with one crewmember, drawing blood.

Whatever his personal shortcomings, Oboler's careful direction adds some evocative touches. At the movie's beginning, a disheveled Douglas wanders along a country road. Finding a car, she opens the door only to see a skeletal hand protruding from the driver's sleeve. Rather than scream or cringe, she just looks blankly at the horrific sight and staggers onward—telling volumes of the horrors and despair she's already seen and experienced.

Later, in a deserted town, as she shouts almost hysterically, "Somebody, please—I'm alive!" we see newspaper headlines that tell the story: "WORLD ANNIHILATION FEARED BY SCIENTIST" and "SAVANT WARNS AGAINST NEW BOMB USE." It begins to rain and the cheap newsprint ink begins to run, washing away the words just as the "new bomb" washed away civilization.

Though heavy on dramatics (which, admittedly, serves the serious story well) and occasionally bordering on pretentious, Oboler's screenplay and dialogue frequently hit home. "I'm going hunting," one character says, dispiritedly. "I go every day. There's nothing to hunt, but I go anyway." The dialogue perfectly captures the man's despairing resignation.

The very first End-of-the-World-by-Nuclear-Holocaust movie, *Five* is a stark, personal look at "survival" after the bomb. Shot only five years after the bombing of Hiroshima and Nagasaki, *Five* points out the horror of nuclear devastation, not through shots of twisted wreckage and mangled bodies (the low budget couldn't support such expensive effects), but through the more personal terror of individual loneliness and isolation. It remains a thought-provoking, serious look at what-we-must-never-let-happen.

According to Sid Pink, who eventually picked up and distributed the film, *Five* (ahem) bombed on its initial release. Then Pink put together a program that would televise the film's "gala premier" in Hollywood (becoming the first-ever film to do so). With the aid of the fledgling small-screen medium (and an appearance at the premier by actress Bette Davis), *Five* became a huge success.

Cult Movies magazine let fly with this review in issue 15 (Summer 1995).

THE FLYING SERPENT (1946)

"Relic of an Ancient Terror Born a Billion Years Ago!" – poster

PRC stands for Producers Releasing Corporation, but just as easily could denote "Poverty Row Cinema." That second meaning is all too evident in *The Flying Serpent*. The story concerns an archeology professor (George Zucco) who has found the fabled treasure of Montezuma and, along with it, the prehistoric bird-monster the ancient Aztec's called Quetzalcoatl. Zucco sends this creature (described as half bird and half reptile) out to kill whomever gets too close to the treasure—or whomever annoys him. He simply places one of the monster's feathers on the victim and the Flying Serpent swoops down to rip out his or her throat. At least it is *supposed* to swoop down; what it actually does is glide sloooowly down (on visible wires) to be grabbed and held by the victim, who thrashes about trying to make it *appear* that Quetzalcoatl is indeed tearing at his or her jugular.

The smallish (four-foot-long) creature is so unconvincing, with its leathery wings and raggedy-looking stuffed body, that it's difficult to take seriously as a character meets his "death" at the beak of this ferocious fiend. And the not-fooling-anyone model of the monster's mountain temple (complete with approaching toy car) fails to add any further credibility.

Silly props and subpar model work are not the picture's main fault, however—that (dis)honor belongs to John Thomas Neville's unforgivably stupid story line. Though looking overly familiar (the plot borrows heavily from PRC's earlier—and better—1940 film *The Devil Bat*, also scripted by Neville), it starts out fine, with Zucco sending his feathered monster out to silence those meddlers interfering with his work. But soon the plot silliness sets in as the host of a radio mystery show (Ralph Lewis) bursts upon the scene and sets about solving the crimes while on the air during his radio program—with the complete blessing and cooperation of the local law! A centuries-old flying Aztec serpent-god is one thing, but a back-country sheriff allowing an interloping radio show host to head a multiple murder investigation is quite another. Credulity can only stretch so far... Even worse, the numerous scenes involving the radio host hero prove duller than an ancient Aztec axe as he slowly and tediously discovers what the audience already knows.

The Flying Serpent possesses one (considerable) asset among its many deficits, however: talented character actor and frequent screen villain George Zucco. Though given very little to work with, he manages to bring a cultured menace to his thankless role of monster-keeper, which lifts his performance above the banality and indifference of the other players. When Zucco came to Hollywood in 1936, the British-born former stage star was typically cast in varying shades of villainy, playing cultured cads in everything from prestige pictures like *The Hunchback of Notre Dame* (1939) and *New Moon* (1940) to enjoyable "lighter" fare such as *The Adventures of Sherlock Holmes* (1939, creating an unforgettable—and arguably definitive—Moriarty) and Bob Hope's

The two stars of The Flying Serpent *(1946): a natty George Zucco and a ratty puppet.*

My Favorite Blonde (1942). But more important to lovers of the macabre, he lent some much-needed dignity and a certain urbane élan to such low-budget horrors as *The Mummy's Hand* (1940), *The Mad Monster* (1942, also for PRC), *Dead Men Walk* (1943, PRC again), *The Mad Ghoul* (1943), and many others. Zucco once labeled himself "Hollywood's unhappiest actor, because I am always being cast as a blood-letting, law-breaking, evil old man." Still, as the actor's widow, Stella Zucco, noted (to interviewer Gregory Mank), "No matter what he was doing, George was a real professional; I honestly don't think he could go on and give a bad performance."

With George Zucco in the catbird seat, *The Flying Serpent* is worth a look. And the title creature *is* fun to watch as it glides about on its visible wires carrying out Montezuma's Revenge.

> *Frogs* hopped into *Cult Movies* magazine (issue 24) in 1997.

FROGS (1972)

Snakes, spiders, lizards, and various other creepy-crawlies star opposite Ray Milland and in this effective low-budget nature-strikes-back movie. Self-described "ugly rich" patriarch Milland and family represent the callous, polluting human race which nature, led by the seemingly intelligent and omnipresent frogs, has decided to take care of once and for all (in its own slithering, slimy manner). Inventive camerawork and effective editing, combined with the natural fear of reptiles and insects, turn the various creature attacks into everyone's worst nightmare. The script does at times go too far, however, such as when one victim is stalked by a ma-

Ribbit.

levolent *turtle*! And apart from Milland as the cantankerous manipulator, most of the characters are merely caricatures—and dated ones at that (hip black chick, playboy photographer, etc.). But if you want to cheer on a bit of ecological revenge or simply desire a few skin-crawling shudders, then *Frogs* is the animal for you. Be sure to stay tuned through the credits for one final fit of froggy fun.

> I reviewed this blu-ray (on a subject near and dear to my heart) for *Monsters from the Vault* magazine but am unsure if it ever saw the light of day (or moonlight of night).

HALLOWEEN HOME HAUNTS (2013)

Since you're reading this magazine, chances are you have a soft spot in your heart (or perhaps head) for that holiday phenomenon known as Halloween. And beyond the handing out of tiny treats to tiny tots in tiny costumes, you may even go that extra Hallow-mile and set up a few Styrofoam gravestones and plastic pumpkins on your front porch. Or you might toss around a handful of plastic body parts and paste a scary-looking cardboard skeleton to your door. Or, like me, you may build your own monstrous figures, set up the fog machine and eerie green and red floodlights, and transform your yard into a zombie-infested graveyard. If so, you may just want to take a look at this new documentary on "home haunts," which showcases a plethora of like-minded (or like-obsessed) folks who yearly transform their yards, garages, and even interiors of their homes into something out of a nightmare—all for the pleasure of scaring the bejeezus out of small children (and unwary adults) once a year.

Halloween Home Haunts interviews a select few of these individuals in the Sacramento, California, area, from the fill-your-yard-with-store-bought-props types to those who festoon their abode with beautiful homemade tombs and imaginative figures (one giant PVC-legged spider with a pumpkin-headed skeletal rider looks absolutely amazing!) to those who set up a full-on amateur haunted house in their garage (complete with live actors) to those who turned pro and orchestrate full-on professional haunted attractions, like "Heartstoppers."

Shot in a rather pedestrian point-and-shoot style, the film's format becomes somewhat repetitious, as the filmmakers interview a home haunter during the daytime as they set up, with the subject explaining their various exhibits. Then the camera takes a tour of the finished product, showing how it all looks at game time. And finally, they interview a few of the spooked and happy patrons after experiencing the haunt's shuddery thrills on the Big Night.

Unfortunately, the filmmakers take a politely distant approach to their subject, with the onscreen interviewer prompting the home haunter to explain the nuts and bolts of their operations, but failing to get to the real meat of the matter—*why* they do this and how it affects their lives. A timid turn in this direction elicits little more than "for the looks on their faces"-type responses, and we're left wondering what really motivates these obsessive and talented people. Consequently, we never learn much about these highly creative folks or what makes them tick, so there's little real excitement or involvement. While *Halloween Home Haunts* does a nice job of covering its surface subject—the "haunts" themselves—it fails to dig under the surface of the rubber props and dry-ice fog to the reality (and humanity) underneath.

If you're looking for ideas for your own home haunts (tips on the art of laying a thick fog layer, for instance, or how Spanish moss will bestow that aged, natural look upon your fake tombstones), *Halloween Home Haunts* fills the bill. If, however, you're searching for insight into why these people go all-out in time and expense on Halloween, you'll have to look elsewhere (to the far superior and more in-depth documentary *The American Scream*, for instance).

Extras include a trio of "teaser trailers" and one "official trailer"; a brief bit on "Hauntcast"—a podcast aimed at the home haunting community (covering everything from prop building to "haunt theory" to haunt reviews); a pointless segment on a man who built his own Disney-like "Tiki Room," complete with animatronic parrot; and an "Alternate Opening" which proves far more atmospheric and nostalgically-pleasing that the more mundane beginning the filmmakers went with.

> Here's a review I wrote for… well… for the life of me I can't recall (and it's not listed on my admittedly spotty writing 'resume'). So I have no idea where, or even *if*, it was published. I do recall that this quirky, disturbing, and entertaining flick made quite an impression on me (and I still return to it periodically). So, for what it's worth, here's my take on…

THE LAIR OF THE WHITE WORM (1988)

Ken Russell, who's been labeled the "enfant terrible" of British cinema, loves to shock his audience (his *The Devils* is one of the most sacrilegious films ever put to celluloid—at least according to the Catholic Film Board who both condemned and banned it). *The Lair of the White Worm*, Russell's offbeat entry into vampire territory, certainly bears this out.

The story, adapted (very loosely) from Bram Stoker's novel of the same name, takes place in Northern England, where there lives a huge worm-like creature of legend who is worshipped as a god and kept alive by a cult of vampire/snake-people headed by the exotic, sensuous (and pre–*L.A. Law*) Amanda Donohoe. Donohoe periodically makes human sacrifices to feed her 'god,' and eventually her slitted eye falls on the tale's two innocent heroines (Catherine Oxenberg and Sammi Davis).

Triple-threat producer/director/screenwriter Russell fills his film with unsettling (and some might venture

A vampiric Amanda Donohoe protects The Lair of the White Worm *(1988).*

'blasphemous') hallucinatory imagery, such as a crucified Jesus Christ with the giant snake/worm of the title wrapped around him, gnawing on his arm; or Roman soldiers raping nuns; or nuns impaled on wooden stakes; etc. While Russell puts forth some genuinely startling visions, he goes overboard with his religious and sexual symbolism, acquiring a heavy hand which pounds his symbolic ideas home with a sledgehammer. (One dream sequence has the hero watching a 'titillating' catfight between Donohoe and Davis while the felt-tip pen he holds in his lap gradually points upwards until it stands straight up in an 'erect' position!—a bit of symbolism that's simply laugh-out-loud ludicrous in its blatancy.)

The picture's effects are superb, especially when considering the extremely low budget (by today's standards) of 1.3 million dollars. The title monster appears both grotesque and hideous, and Russell cleverly keeps it off-screen until the climax in order to generate maximum anticipation and impact upon its ultimate appearance while at the same time allowing the film to focus on the more intriguing Donahoe and her vampiric acolytes. Said viper-vampires' make-ups are unique and effective (particularly the wickedly long, curving, snake-like fangs).

Like in most British productions, the film's cast does an excellent job (including a young Hugh Grant—before *Four Weddings and a Funeral* and an indiscreet run-in with a prostitute catapulted him into the international limelight). The actors work hard to make Russell's quirky characters both believable and likable (a rarity in a Russell film), adding interest and drawing the viewer into the bizarre proceedings.

The film generates an occasional unintentional chuckle, however, such as when Donohue writhes to the strains of snake-charmer music in an absurdly awkward fashion. Also, the intriguing nature of the vampiric snake people remains sadly unexplored. Where did they come from? How did they become what they are (apart from creating new acolytes via their poisonous bite)? Are they supernatural or *supra*-natural? And what exactly is their relationship with the title worm (who, though horrifyingly ugly, possesses no more sense of 'evil' than a landlocked Loch Ness Monster)?

With a more subtle approach and a more thorough exploration of the subject matter, *The Lair of the White Worm* could have become a cult classic in the vein of *The Wicker Man* (1972), which explores much of the same concepts of conflicting religions and repressed sexuality but in a more sophisticated and effective manner. As is, *The Lair of the White Worm* still remains a unique vision, sometimes shocking, often enthralling, always eccentric, but only partly effective.

> This appeared in the "Rotting in the Crypt: Vampire Mini-Reviews" section of *Midnight Marquee* magazine, issue 49 (Summer 1995).

THE LEGEND OF THE SEVEN GOLDEN VAMPIRES (1974)

"HAMMER HORROR! DRAGON THRILLS! The First Kung-Fu Horror Spectacular!" announced the proud posters for Hammer Films' final entry in their Dracula series. Made in conjunction with the Hong Kong–based film company Shaw Brothers (known for their martial arts adventure movies), the world's first kung-fu/vampire film is an audaciously action-packed but flawed attempt to meld Hammer's gothic to Shaw's chop-socky.

In China, Professor Van Helsing (Peter Cushing in his fifth and final outing as the unflappable arch-foe of Count Dracula) and his son (Robin Stewart) join forces with a family of native martial arts experts to rid their ancestral village of the dreaded Seven Golden Vampires—who are lorded over by Dracula himself. The film fairly explodes with exciting fight sequences in which the protagonists battle both humans *and* the undead (with the brothers thrusting fists through rotted zombie chests to extract their dusty hearts, impaling them with knives and swords, or dispatching them with battle axes). When our protagonists meet human opponents, Les Bowie's crimson stage blood flies nearly as fast and furious as the fists.

Director Roy Ward Baker generates some effective atmosphere by lingering on the nightmarish resurrection sequences (skeletal hands clawing up out of the earth) and slow-motion marching of the vampires' undead zombie slaves (their victims). And the cinematography team of Roy Ford and John Wilcox provides some effective nighttime photography—particularly for the climactic battle sequence in which the leaping, sword-wielding nosferatu are backlit by columns of fire. Peter Cushing is particularly strong as Van Helsing, keeping his now-familiar role as the chief opponent of the undead fresh and lively with his sincerity and steady performance. And rarely since the original *Horror of Dracula* (1958) has Van Helsing been so active—with the 60-year-old Cushing wielding a flaming torch and battling hand-to-hand his fiendish nemesis with as much vigor as in his first encounter 25 years earlier.

Where this *Legend* fails though, is in its uneven pacing and underdeveloped characters. Going from the slow-paced nightmarish undead sequences to frantically furious kung-fu fighting fails to meld properly, generating a disjointed feel, as if viewing two distinct movies or perhaps a series of unrelated set-pieces. As far as characterization goes, aside from Van Helsing, the remaining characters are merely ciphers—the brothers given so little distinction (apart from choice of weapons) as to be almost interchangeable. Oddly enough, one still likes them—if for nothing else then for their courage and sheer audacity at fearlessly meeting the undead with nothing but bare knuckles and knives. Scripter (and co-producer) Don Houghton handles the expected love-interest (kept to a minimum here so as not to interfere with the action) in a fresh and *un*expected manner by having the two young occidentals of the party (Robin Stewart and Julie Ege) fall not for each other as convention would dictate, but for Asians (the lead brother and the one sister of the fighting family), brazenly crossing the racial boundaries of romance. The powerful presence of Christopher Lee is missed, but John Forbes-Robertson fills out Dracula's cape adequately, and the role is small enough so as not to become a major issue.

One big disappointment, however, is in the effects department. The rubber bats are obvious, and the decomposition sequences of the vampires laughable. The defeated vampires simply *deflate*—looking a bit like Mr. Potatohead with the wind knocked out of him. Hammer had done better effects work in *all* of their previous Dracula entries, and to finish the series with such weak effects is a shame. Though no classic, and basically a failed experiment—but an entertaining one—*The Legend of the Seven Golden Vampires* deserved better than its sad fate of having to sit on the shelf for *six years* before receiving a shamefully spotty released in the U.S.

> Back when I'd never even *heard* of a Pakistani horror movie, this juicy little gem from 1967 came out of nowhere, released on DVD in 2003 by the Mondo Macabro label. Wow. Just… wow. I wrote this, I believe, for some on-line film forum I belonged to back in the day. (And, by the way, my *current* tally of Pakistani horror movies viewed stands at… one.)

THE LIVING CORPSE (1967)

From the opening credit proclaiming this Pakistani vampire flick has been "adopted" [sic] from the Bram Stoker tale, you know this puppy will be straying far from the beaten path. *The Living Corpse* proved to be unlike *any* vampire movie I'd ever seen—not through want of trying, however. It uses Hammer's *Horror of Dracula* as a blueprint; several scenes, including the Chris Lee entrance and the *vampiress interruptus* sequence (in which the Count brutally saves Harker from a lady bloodsucker), are outright steals (though *The Living Corpse* adds a disturbing touch to the latter sequence by having the male vamp toss a baby to the delighted vampiress and telling her to "feast on this" as she scampers happily away—an incident taken from Stoker's book but rarely seen onscreen). The film also borrows dialogue ("children of the night") and atmosphere (giant spider web anyone?) from the Lugosi *Dracula*.

Beyond such steals and embellishments, *The Living Corpse* offers plenty of uniquely bizarro touches to make it stand out. For instance, I laughed out loud when the hefty, size-16 female vamp attempts to seduce the film's Harker-like character by spontaneously erupting into an 'erotic' dance—a strange bit of '60s 'performance art' that looks like a cross between the Hula and the Swim! Then there's several traditional Indian-style musical numbers (one in which the heroine sings to herself about love in her garden; another in which a group of girls picnicking sing about the beautiful weather!).

Dance the night away with The Living Corpse *(1967)*.

During a nightclub musical interlude, the patrons even *join in* at one point. These are things one doesn't necessarily associate with an atmospheric vampire movie…

Btw, the main vampire *became* a vampire because of his fooling around with the "elixir of life." You see, he was a famous scientist(!) trying to find a cure for death, and… well, let's just say he found it. Now *that* is novel. (Of course, John Beal in 1957's *The Vampire* was a science-spawned bloodsucker, but *he* didn't acquire the penguin suit and cape, nor the mesmeric powers that *this* guy did.) Mind-boggling.

In all, I found *The Living Corpse* highly entertaining, and would recommend it to anyone whose taste in horror runs to the offbeat.

It took some Mighty Effort for *Cult Movies* magazine to include *The Mighty Gorga* in issue 16 (Fall 1995). No, it was *not* worth it…

THE MIGHTY GORGA (1969)

"The Greatest Horror Monster Alive!" –(grossly duplicitous) tagline

There's nothing "Mighty" about *The Mighty Gorga*, except perhaps that it's *Mighty Bad*. Clumsy camerawork, dull direction, a silly screenplay ("Mighty Gorga, I know that your thirst for the blood of young virgins is great, but leave our village in peace," entreats the local witchdoctor while exercising his powers of persuasion with a 50-foot ape) and amateurish acting are the highlights of this no-budget grade-Z *King Kong* wannabe.

The worst part of this production (using the term loosely here) are the insulting effects, which should be the primary *raison d'être* of this shoddy piece of celluloid. Gorga is a 50-foot gorilla who lives on a plateau in deepest Africa—or so the script tells us, since in actuality Gorga is director David L. Hewitt wearing a homemade gorilla suit, complete with immobile face and plastic eyes; and we can't really tell if he's 50 feet tall or not, since there are no miniatures to be seen, and the big ape is shown only with the sky or treetops as background. (This was because Hewitt, low on funds, decided to build only the top half of the suit!).

The story follows Anthony Eisley as the owner of a down-and-out circus come to Africa to capture the mighty monkey. He meets a female animal trapper (Megan Timothy) and they set off with nothing more than a couple of backpacks and one small land rover to retrieve this hostile 50-foot monstrosity from a Lost World–like plateau in the heart of an uncharted jungle. Thrown in there somewhere are those low-budget stalwarts, Scott Brady and Kent Taylor, to try and add at least a modicum of professionalism to the proceedings (unfortunately, they're onscreen for so short a time they add virtually nothing). The protagonists run afoul of a lost tribe, find the ridiculous-looking Gorga and an equally ludicrous Tyrannosaur, stumble upon a cache of King Solomon's treasure, and rush past a stock footage Jim Danforth–animated dragon from AIP's *Goliath and the Dragon*. After a few awful rear-screen projections; a battle between the Absurd—er—Mighty Gorga and the worst plastic-looking dinosaur ever to cross the silver screen (actually a hand puppet!); some high school-level dramatics from the overweight witch doctor (Bruce Kimball, who also—aptly—plays a clown in the opening scenes set at the circus); and the expected volcanic eruption (which we're only *told* about, since it happens off-screen), this mess finally comes to a close.

Special effects man turned director Hewitt was also responsible for the equally inept *Wizard of Mars* (1964), *Dr. Terror's Gallery of Horrors* (1966—not to be confused with the far superior *Dr. Terror's House of Horrors*) and *Journey to the Center of Time* (1967), making Hewitt a strong candidate for the title "The Ed Wood of the 1960s."

"I can't believe this thing's real," exclaims the heroine as *The Mighty Gorga* spools out before our disbelieving eyes—and neither can the viewer. The more you watch, the more you're convinced that this is actually an expanded 8mm high school project. *The Mighty Gorga* offers no budget, no sense and no thrills. The one or two unintentional laughs are only respite from the rest of the painfully bad experience.

I shot this Missile *at* Cult Movies *magazine (issue 17) in 1996.*

MISSILE TO THE MOON (1959)

"See the science-fiction thrill of the year, a sensational look into the future that is as close as tomorrow's headlines!"—trailer

Heaven forbid!

Director Richard Cunha (*She Demons, Giant from the Unknown*) made this inept remake of the already bad *Cat-Women of the Moon* (itself released by Astor Pictures back in 1953) as a second feature for his *Frankenstein's Daughter*. Cunha claimed (to interviewer Tom Weaver) that it was Astor's idea to remake their earlier sci-fier: "They thought, well, shucks, it'd be a good idea to redo the movie, they could get a little bit of sex in and have some pretty girls wandering through the scenes." Pretty girls notwithstanding, in retrospect it was *not* such a "good idea."

The witless story concerns your average scientist who builds a private rocketship near his house and blasts off with a couple of stowaway street punks and a bland hero/heroine duo (anticipating the first launching of a privately owned rocket by 23 years). Once the motley group reaches the Moon they encounter the typical lost-race-of-love-starved-women, a large gangly spider puppet (rented from the Universal prop department—"we paid practically nothing for it," recalled Cunha, "and they were kind enough to let us use it"), and a group of foam rubber rock men. These hilariously awkward monsters (looking like Gumby on steroids) are the film's highlight. Cunha later talked about the poor souls who had to play the Rock Men: "We had one scene where we had to plaster them to the sides of giant rocks, for them to break out. And, you know [laughs], it took a while for the plaster to dry with them in there! They'd be yelling, 'Get us out of here, get us out of here!' So, yes, that was very very difficult for them, but they were all good guys. We laughed over a beer about it later."

Cheap is the operative word here, with cardboard sets, silly costumes, and bottom-of-the-barrel effects. Dumb is the operative word for the script. At one point the protagonists take great pains to point out that fire can't burn on the Moon's surface because there is no oxygen. Yet later in the story, one of the cast mistakenly steps into the "lethal" sun's rays and spontaneously goes up in flames! And why did "Mr. Science" take along an ordinary gun, useless in an airless atmosphere since it can't be fired without a spark? The often trite and ridiculous dialogue doesn't help (e.g., "I am Lido, high ruler of our humble domain; I am told you are intruders from an unknown origin").

While *Cat-Women of the Moon* used the "Hollywood Covergirls" for its Moon Maidens, *Missile* employed several international beauty contest winners. Cunha recalled, "None of them were actresses as such, they were all beauty queens who couldn't hit marks and couldn't say lines—it was quite frustrating." No doubt, considering Cunha only had six days and less than $80,000 to work with.

Some unintentional laughs help ease the pain, but after a while it all gets too much and this misfired *Missile* just lies there…like a plastered Rock Man.

Cult Movies *magazine let this Monster* out *of the Closet for issue 17 (Winter 1996).*

MONSTER IN THE CLOSET (1987)

This rather engaging monster/comedy from Troma Inc. (the makers of *The Toxic Avenger*) is a wonderful find for monster and sci-fi movie lovers. Chock full of references (some subtle and some blatant) to such genre classics as *Psycho, The Thing, Close Encounters of the Third Kind,* and *Alien,* it walks the fine line between homage and parody, usually stepping off on the homage side.

Set in a small town, the story follows a sensitive, put-upon reporter named Mr. Clark (played by Christopher Reeves look-alike Donald Grant, complete with Clark Kent glasses) sent to investigate a series of "closet murders." The killer turns out to be a large, ugly, indestructible being from outer space who for some inexplicable reason likes to hang out in closets. The menacing man-in-the-suit monster (with 7-foot-2-inch Kevin Peter Hall inside) sports impressive claws, a humped back, and a retractable miniature head that shoots out of its mouth and grabs its victims like a, well, *Alien*. The acting is suitably broad, and the cast is filled with semi-name thespians such as Claud Akins (a tobacco-chewing sheriff), *Laugh-In*'s own Henry Gibson (a dotty old scientist attempting to create his own close encounter by communicating with the monster via a toy xylophone), and Stella Stevens (in an expected yet nonetheless effective *Psycho* shower scene take-off). Venerable genre vet John Carradine even puts in a brief

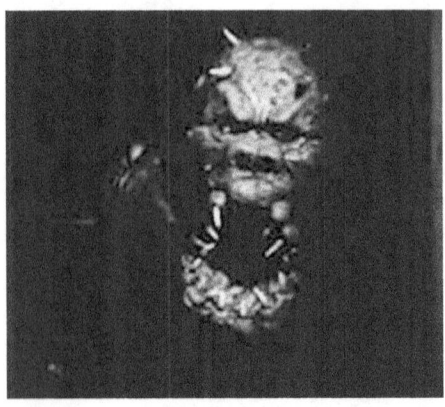

Yep, there's definitely a Monster in the Closet (1987).

appearance as a blind man with a less than cooperative seeing-eye dog. The script leaves too many unanswered questions and plot holes (such as where did the alien come from?; *why* did it come?; how did it get here?; and why *closets*?) for it to be solid science fiction, but taken simply as a fun, homage-filled monster-comedy it works well. The film occasionally takes a genre cliché and adds a comedic twist, such as having the monster pass over the heroine and lovingly carry off the swooning *hero* instead. And you can't help but like a movie whose last line is: "Oh no, it wasn't the closet—it was beauty killed the beast!"

> *The Most Dangerous Man Alive* attacked the pages of *Cult Movies* magazine for issue 17 (Winter 1996).

THE MOST DANGEROUS MAN ALIVE (1961)

"IN THE HEART OF AN ATOMIC TESTING AREA IT TAKES ONLY 10 SECONDS TO TURN A HUMAN INTO THE… MOST DANGEROUS MAN ALIVE" –poster blurb

The Most Dangerous Man Alive is a gritty blend of the sci-fi, horror and gangster genres. A framed gangster (Ron Randall) escapes from prison and wanders into the test site of a new type of cobalt bomb. The bomb detonates but he's not killed. Instead, he becomes a "man of steel"—his flesh absorbs metal. Randall uses his newfound talent to revenge himself on the gang that sent him up the river. To the mobsters' dismay, bullets won't stop him, electricity won't stop him, apparently nothing will stop him. Randall finally meets his match, however, when a battalion of police and national guardsmen runs him to earth and then fries him with a flame-thrower.

The tone of the picture is grim realism, with the principals playing their parts well. Beautiful Debra Paget, as the gangster's mistress, assays her role in a sensuous, daring manner (especially for 1961). Her seduction scene, in which she entices Randall to remove her shoe and stocking, is charged with a subtle erotic energy. Even though Randall plays a no-good gangster, he manages to arouse sympathy in the audience and put them on his side. One feels pity for him as the changes going on in his body begin to affect his mind ("I'm not human anymore… all I can feel now is hate!").

The script becomes rather simplistic and vague in its explanations (referring to a mysterious "Element X" contained in the cobalt and showing us some shabby "mutated" lab animals as explanation), but the plot does possess some effective twists, such as extending some hope to Randall in the form of scientific help only to dash that hope when the bad guys interfere at the wrong moment. The climax proves to be a major disappointment, however, with terrible flame effects poorly superimposed over shots of Randall shouting hysterically about ruling the world. And the obvious stock footage of flamethrower troops completely erases the film's sense of realism. Here the low budget becomes painfully apparent.

Still, *The Most Dangerous Man Alive* remains one of the more unusual sci-fi/horror entries from the early '60s and deserves better than its current status as one of *The Most Unseen Films Today*.

> *Night of the Lepus* is a personal favorite of mine (what's not to love about giant killer bunnies?!). After I'd written this review, I had the pleasure of meeting Janet Leigh. So naturally I asked this thoroughly charming lady about this particular film. She graciously responded to my questions with good humor; and said responses are now incorporated into my original review (from issue 16 of *Cult Movies* magazine in 1995).

NIGHT OF THE LEPUS (1972)

"What devil creatures grow in weight and size every day, hidden behind the eyes of horror?!" –trailer

It's hard to imagine a Hollywood producer sitting around thinking, "What kind of monster can we put in our next picture? What about giant killer bunny rabbits?" How can those cuddly little pink-nosed fluffballs come "from behind the shroud of night to become a scuttling, shambling horde of creatures destroying all in their path" (as the poster so vividly puts it)? By injecting one with some kind of untested serum and allowing

"There is a herd of killer rabbits heading this way!" during the Night of the Lepus *(1972).*

it to escape and breed with those in the wild, resulting in thousands of hungry bunnies as big as Saint Bernards—that's how!

As a consequence, Stuart Whitman, DeForest Kelley (*Star Trek*'s "Bones"), Rory Calhoun, and a white-haired Janet Leigh (who proves more successful in fending off a herd of giant killer rabbits in this film than a single *Psycho* back in 1960), along with an entire Arizona town have to think of some way to stop these wascally wabbits. The bunnies themselves are photographed in slow motion with macro lenses on miniature sets to create the (ahem) hare-raising effect of giant killer rabbits. Couple this with close-ups of big-toothed bunnies with blood-smeared faces and the sound of galloping horses on the soundtrack as they hop down a country road in an unstoppable mass of furry fury, and you've got one hell of an Elmer Fudd nightmare on your hands.

The screenplay by Don Holliday and Gene Kearney was adapted from a Russell Braddon novel, *The Year of the Angry Rabbit*. "I read the script, and I have to tell you that it read very well," remembers Janet Leigh. "*Night of the Lepus* was made at the time of science fiction pictures like *Willard* and *Ben* and *Frogs*, and I must repeat that the script read very well. No one twisted my arm and said I had to do it. What no one realized was that, no matter what you do, a bunny rabbit is a bunny rabbit! A rat, *that* can be menacing—so can a frog. Spiders or scorpions or alligators—they could all work in that situation, and they have. But—a *bunny rabbit*? How can you make a bunny rabbit menacing, what can you do? It just didn't work."

Metro-Goldwyn-Mayer (yes, believe it or not, *MGM*!) seemed to sense this when they pointedly left out any rabbit references in their ad campaign. The poster artwork, for instance, consisted merely of the protagonists menaced by oversized eyes and indistinct shapes, with the studio artists sagely deciding *not* to include images of killer bunnies.

In all fairness, Ted Voigtlander's photography and the Howard A. Anderson Company's visual effects are really quite good (as the marauding mammals march down a dimly-lit country road and trample over an authentic-looking miniature farmyard). And director William F. Claxton (who, having directed nearly a dozen Westerns over the previous two decades, was obviously at home among the sand and sagebrush of *Night of the Lepus*' southwestern milieu) makes good use of the forbidding desert environs (the film was shot in and around Tucson, Arizona). Incidentally, rabbits are herbivores and don't eat meat, and humans are definitely meat (couch potatoes included). The only real danger would be to the carrot industry; but giant rabbits attacking a Jolly Green Giant vegetable processing plant would not make for good drama, so the poetic license taken by the filmmakers can be excused.

Whitman, Leigh, and company all manage to keep straight faces (although we don't know how) and valiantly strive to keep things on a mature level. The production values are adequate but a bit reminiscent of a mid–1970s TV movie. Still, don't miss this one for offbeat fun and loud lepus laughter. And besides, where else can you hear a rabbit *roar*?

Cult Movies magazine (issue 10) printed this mini-review in 1994.

ONIBABA (1964)

A land rich with tales of demons and devils and ghosts, Japan's history is filled with wars, bloodshed and the honor of the Samurai. In Japanese cinema, history and the supernatural have often been combined to create complex morality plays. The anthology film *Kwaidan* (1964), for instance, remains one of the finest examples of a Japanese horror picture (forget the Godzilla movies and their imitators, they don't belong in the same genre with the serious Japanese horror films).

Onibaba is another excellent example of what Japanese cinema is capable of creating. It is the story of two women, a mother and daughter-in-law, during a time of war and chaos. The daughter's husband (the mother's son) has been taken off by Samurai to fight in the wars. The crops have died, and so the two women are driven to find stragglers from the battles, kill them for their armor, and sell the armor to buy food in order to survive. Their home and world exists in a seemingly endless forest of tall reeds along the shores of a lake. A man comes, a man who was taken at the same time as the son. He has escaped the battles and tells of how the son is now dead. This newcomer wants the daughter—and eventually the daughter wants him as well. The old woman, however, is afraid that the daughter will leave her to starve ("I cannot kill by myself," she moans). The mother pleads and pleads with her daughter-in-law, but the young woman continues to sneak out to meet her lover. A great Samurai warrior enters the reed-plain and becomes lost. His demeanor is regal and proud, but he wears a terrifying mask—a demon mask. The crafty old woman tricks and kills him. Now the old mother has a plan. Using the mask, she attempts to frighten the daughter into remaining in their hut at night and not go off to see her young man. But there is a twist—and the film winds its way to its inevitable cinematic justice.

Under director-producer-screenwriter Kanero Shindo, cinematographer Kiyomi Kuroda's stunning black and white photography makes the eerie sea of reeds a character unto itself. Continually shifting in the wind, the undulating foliage creates a feeling of forces moving just beneath the surface of consciousness. The film possesses a quiet stillness, yet beneath its calm exterior lies the sleeping specter of sudden motion, ready to awaken and burst upwards with a stunning ferocity. *Onibaba* is truly a work of cinematic poetry.

The *Phantom Planet* lobby card.

Cult Movies magazine unmasked *The Phantom Planet* for issue 17 (Winter 1996).

THE PHANTOM PLANET (1961)

In the near future, the rocketship Pegasus-4 takes off from Lunar Base-1 to investigate the recent disappearance of two of its spacecraft, attributed to a mysterious planetoid that has been zooming about the sector. Dean Fredericks, the pilot of Pegasus-4, crash lands on the elusive asteroid, is exposed to its atmosphere (never mind that something the size of an asteroid has no atmosphere to speak of, since its mass is too small) and inexplicably shrinks to only six inches tall. The people of the asteroid, called Rheton, look just like humans but also stand a mere six inches in height. The populace makes Fredericks one of their own (Francis X. Bushman, as the leader, even offers him his daughter in marriage). The Rhetons possess a machine capable of controlling gravity, and they seem content to flit about the galaxy minding their own business and trying to avoid other people. Too bad that the evil Solanites (a race of ugly, dog-faced humanoids) want the gravity device for themselves and periodically attack Rheton. This gives the viewer the chance to witness an epic space battle between what looks like a large piece of coral floating through space (the planetoid Rheton) and a flock of

Even the Return of the Killer Tomatoes *can't be as nefarious as such blatant product placement…*

flaming charcoal briquettes (the Solanite ships).

The script ignores the potentially intriguing *Gulliver's Travels* idea of tiny people, and the alien culture of Rheton remains largely unexplored (all we're shown is that they live in primitive caves, wear American-style haircuts and makeup, and duel to the death over their women). The thrills are minimal and the pacing slow (not helped by overlong scenes involving the complicated four-sided love story between the astronaut, the leader's daughter, a young Rheton and a sympathetic mute girl).

Seven-foot-tall Richard Kiel (later to achieve fame as "Jaws" in the James Bond film series) plays the slow-moving Solarite prisoner (with huge dog-like head, motley fur, cartoon eyes and pointy shoulders) who escapes and has to be pushed onto a "disintegration plate" by the hero. Though impressive in size, this creature's appearance is just too goofy to be taken seriously, and Kiel moves so slowly and clumsily in the cumbersome monster suit (almost tripping as he steps down from a small boulder) that he's not much of a menace.

"What will the future reveal, if this story is only the beginning…only the beginning…the beginning," echoes the closing narration as the words "THE BEGINNING" rush at us on the screen. Luckily, the filmmakers didn't attempt to answer this question with any further installments.

> *Cult Movies* magazine marked the *Return of the Killer Tomatoes* via this bemused review in issue 17 (Winter 1996).

RETURN OF THE KILLER TOMATOES (1988)

"Tomatoes are evil! A good tomato is a squashed tomato!"
—adamant protagonist

This is a superior follow up to the decidedly unfunny 1978 spoof *Attack of the Killer Tomatoes*—superior in both production values and laugh quantity but still *far* from a great parody. Those killer tomatoes are back, this time in human form headed by John Astin as Professor Gangrene, who takes the tiny vegetables and turns them into Rambo lookalikes set to conquer the world. He also makes a beautiful girl in the form of actress Karen Mistal to "fulfill my needs" (and *what* a tomato!). This good-looking vegetable provides the love interest for Our Hero, played by Anthony Starke (a poor man's Michael J. Fox). Together they foil the plans of the sinister Gangrene and his evil legumes.

The humor is mostly of the sledgehammer variety, silly and self-conscious. One can still find the occasional guffaw, however, and one particular running gag dealing with 'product placement' (that increasingly common practice among today's filmmakers of placing manufacturer's products on prime display within the movie in return for various fringe benefits) stands out. Here director John DeBello makes great sport of this crass commercialism as boxes of Kellogg's Cornflakes slowly creep into the shot, or the principal characters make blatant plugs for Crest toothpaste and Moosehead beer. Nothing is sacred. When the mad doctor Gangrene turns around at one point, we see a huge Pepsi logo on the back of his lab coat!

No one takes themselves seriously here, least of all the filmmakers, who even spoof themselves. Opening theme song (to the tune of the original "Attack of the Killer Tomatoes Theme"): "Retuuuurn of the killer tomatoes. Retuuuurn of the killer tomatoes. The theme song has remained the same, the plot itself has hardly changed..." And a film that starts out by showing a movie entitled *Big Breasted Girls Go to the Beach and Take Their Tops Off* before someone whispers, "Hey, aren't we supposed to be showing something called *Return of the Killer Tomatoes*?" can't be all bad. Nothing great here, but a few dumb laughs make it a harmlessly diverting 90 minutes.

Cult Movies magazine subscribers were far from *Scared Stiff* by issue 17 (Winter 1996), particularly after reading *this* mini-review.

SCARED STIFF (1987)

The title of this tired film is a misnomer, since it inspires more yawns than scares. The well-worn plot centers on a somewhat less than typical family of the eighties—a yuppie psychiatrist, a female rock star on the comeback trail, and her seven-year-old son—who move into an old house once owned by a notorious slave-trader named Masterson. Apparently, a curse was placed on the slaver by his mistreated slaves which gradually turned him into a hideous monster. We learn this via diary entries and visions experienced by the rock star/mom, who, incidentally, was recently a mental patient, so of course no one believes her. The curse worsened Masterson's disposition as well as his looks, for he ended up killing his wife and young son, aged (you guessed it) seven. So, of course, the yuppie psychiatrist gets a funny gleam in his eye and starts chasing everyone around the house.

It's all been done before (*The Amityville Horror*, *The Shining*) to better effect, and the only innovative aspects present—the use of the voodoo curse and the occasional physical transformations—are handled poorly. The dialogue is alternately banal and clichéd, especially the pseudo-psychiatric lingo spouted by Andrew Stevens as the very unconvincing psychiatrist. Stevens' performance is just too plastic to inspire any empathy, so when the possession finally comes there's no pathos or even interest in his character (he's just the handiest body present for the malignant spirit). The remainder of the cast is flat, when they're acting at all. A couple of spots do manage to rise from the tedium, however. During the climactic hallucination/other dimension sequence, in which the heroine gets a surprise behind every door she opens, she's greeted by a mental patient with a perverse sense of humor who shows her he's "cured" by literally unzipping the top of his skull and exposing his brain for her inspection. And the final transformation makeup, in which Masterson's head becomes a living African death-mask, is unique. But these momentary flashes can't relieve the 70 previous sleep-inducing minutes. A more accurate title would have been *Bored Stiff*.

Cult Movies magazine unleashed the *She Demons* in issue 17 (Winter 1996).

SHE DEMONS (1958)

"A FRIGHTmare of Blood-Chilling HORROR… FLAMES INTO THE Most Fiendish ADVENTURE THE SCREEN HAS EVER SHOWN!" –trailer

This fifties flick seemingly has it all: evil Nazi mad scientist, ritualistic dances by bikini-clad natives, putty-faced monsters, a beautiful heroine and stalwart hero, and even some non-P.C. ethnic comic relief. All prime ingredients for a $65,000, 1958 exploitation film. Unfortunately, these elements just don't come together well under the unimaginative direction of Richard E. Cuhna (who followed this up with the even more absurd *Frankenstein's Daughter* the next year).

She Demons came about simply because Astor Pictures wanted a co-feature for Cunha's first film, *Giant from the Unknown*. "[Astor] gave us $80,000 for *She Demons*," recalled producer Arthur Jacobs to interviewer Tom Weaver, "I think we spent $65,000." It looks it.

A quartet of boaters stranded on the proverbial uncharted island (Tod Griffin, Irish McCalla, Victor Sen Yung, and Charles Opuni) run afoul of mad Nazi scientist/war criminal Karl "the Butcher" Osler (Rudolph

Anders), who, aided by a handful of loyal Storm Trooper guards, has been on the island for a dozen years conducting experiments on captive native women in an effort to restore the face of his disfigured wife. Unfortunately, the only consequence of this "research" has been the transformation of young girls into animalistic "She Demons," whom Osler keeps in bamboo cages. Oh, and along the way, Osler has developed a new power source by harnessing the heat from molten lava, resulting in a climax that has our protagonists running past stock footage of lava flows, explosions, and the ubiquitous *One Million B.C.* destruction scenes before emerging at Bronson Canyon to wage a gun battle with Nazi guards and escape to a waiting rowboat.

"I was trying to get even with the world at the time and just having a good time," recounted director/coscripter Richard Cuhna to Weaver about his approach to *She Demons*. "These were really tongue-in-cheek films, and we enjoyed doing them a great deal and had as much fun as possible."

Indeed, the script carries more humor than most fifties genre films, and some of it is even funny.

Osler: "My only wish is to please you."

Heroine: "If you want to please me, *drop dead*."

Unfortunately, Cuhna relies too heavily on the medium shot and people talking through the action (he obviously bought into the old axiom "talk is cheap"), taking away much of the visual interest that Nazi-created, bikini-wearing She Demons skulking around a deserted island (actually Southern California's Paradise Cove and Griffith Park) can offer.

The acting is poor, with former *Sheena, Queen of the Jungle* TV star McCalla's (who earned $1,500 for a week's work) alternately petulant and stilted delivery making her appear uncomfortable, and Griffin's square-jawed demeanor and toneless heroics making *him* appear simply dull. But at least Rudolph Anders as the Nazi doctor is fun to watch, as his urbane cordiality alternates with over-the-top slimy menace.

Everything in this production is cheap, but cheapest of all is the ludicrous She Demon makeup. Consisting of nothing more than silly putty and fangs, one marvels at the audacity of the filmmakers who try to put this kind of thing over on their audience. Rather than being off-putting, however, the utter unbelievability of their appearance so oversteps the bounds of badness that the She Demons actually acquire a bizarre charm.

With the right attitude, this cheapie can be a fairly fun filmic frolic; but be warned—you may occasionally *bite* that tongue in your cheek.

> This mini-review crawled into *Cult Movies* magazine, issue 16 (Fall 1995), no doubt leaving a big slime trail…

SLUGS (1988)

"Killer slugs, for Chrissakes!" exclaims the protagonist of *Slugs*. "What'll it be next, rampaging crickets?" There aren't too many creatures on God's green earth more repulsive to human beings than the common garden slug. Anyone who's ever been out enjoying a barefoot summer and has stepped on one never quite forgets the experience. So it would seem that these slimy garden pests would be prime material for a creepy crawly horror movie. In the hands of the right filmmaker, yes; but, unfortunately for slugophiles, director J. P. Simon was not the man to prime the slime.

Looking fairly slick (kind of like MTV meets *Mayberry R.F.D.*), the story takes place in a small town which used to double as a toxic waste dump. Our hero, the local health inspector, soon comes to learn that the recent rash of grisly deaths have been perpetrated by carnivorous mutant slugs. There's the obligatory city

Oogey, oogey, oogey… Slugs *(1988)!*

politics and back door dealings, but the whole thing is handled in such a clichéd manner it becomes just another hackneyed sub-plot.

Slugs does present a few good set-pieces, however, such as when the bedroom floor of two copulating teens becomes covered by the marauding mollusk menaces. While admittedly not in the best of taste, a naked nubile nymph slipping and sliding around on a thousand slugs while they tear at her flesh exploits our fear of the slimy to the Nth degree (not to mention creating a landmark first in cinematic history). Several other slug attacks are well-staged as well, but these bits of oozing originality can't mask the snail's pace of the rest of the film.

Simon is definitely not an actor's director, since the performances turned in by the principals are as unsubtle as those of the title characters. And the climax, while containing plenty of flash and fire, remains unexciting and predictable. Our grotesque garden friends will have to wait for someone else to pick up the slime trail before their cinematic prowess will truly be defined. Though *Slugs* may be the first (and *only*, to date) Rampaging Carnivorous Mutant Slug movie, let's hope there's a better one just waiting on the lawn of the future.

Cult Movies magazine visited the *Slimeball Bowl-o-Rama* in issue 17 (Winter 1996).

SORORITY BABES IN THE SLIMEBALL BOWL-O-RAMA (1988)

"Goddamn she-demons—I hate 'em."

What a title. With a moniker like that, we're not talking art film here. What we are talking is a fun little exploitationer that doesn't take itself—or anything else—too seriously. Granted, the dialogue is bad (with a lot of four-letter expletives thrown in to give the characters at least *something* to say), the effects mediocre to nonexistent, and the acting... well let's just say the acting is about what you'd expect from a no-budget monster flick by a bunch of people out to have a good time making a movie. Everybody obviously had fun doing this and it shows, with sheer exuberance making up for most of the deficits.

The story involves your typical(?) sorority initiation in which the pledges have to break into a bowling alley and steal a trophy as proof of the deed (it must have been a slow night on Greek Row). Of course, the bitchy sorority sisters have a suitable set of scare tactics lined up, but things don't quite go quite according to plan. You see, there's an evil imp *imp*risoned (ouch) inside said bowling trophy, and when he gets out there's hell to pay. He begins by granting a few wishes, but his true nature shows through and the boons soon go bad. Then the fun begins.

We're definitely talking "imp of the perverse" here, as the ugly little fellow spends his time turning people into demons while cracking wise and standing over dead bodies talkin' cool. The story avoids the usual clichés of high school pranks and false scares; and thankfully missing are the tired old 'killer's-eye-veiw-shots-which-turn-out-to-be-just-a-harmless-jokester-ha-ha.' The ending, refreshingly, is not the standard cliché of 'The-End-Or-Is-It?' Instead, as the nerd-turned-hero and his newfound tough-punk girlfriend ride away into the sunrise on her motorcycle, we hear the Imp, who's now trapped in a large tobacco tin, offer, "Hey, you in the front row, you want a wish? Heh heh heh."

The effects are low-low-low-budget, consisting of a few face makeups and one decapitated head, and the imp is static and doesn't move around much. But where else will you see a sorority-sister-turned-demon who looks like a *Bride of Frankenstein* clone imitating Elsa Lanchester's famous hiss?! And it's a lot of fun to see petite Linnea Quigley (who's all of 5'2") beat up just about everyone.

Cult Movies magazine took this trip with me (and the 12) in issue 17 (Winter 1996).

12 TO THE MOON (1960)

"LAND ON THE MOON WITH THE FIRST INTREPID ASTRONAUTS!" –ad line

Obviously landing on the moon was a much bigger deal back in 1960 than now, when the Space Program is focused on Mars and beyond. But at the dawning of the Age of Aquarius, landing on the moon "with the first intrepid astronauts" perhaps did indeed rate that exclamation point for the film's original audience.

An international expedition is sent to the moon to claim it for all mankind. The only problem is, the "moon-people" already there take issue with this action. Once on the moon, two crewmembers (a man and a woman who happen to be in love) disappear and the ship starts receiving written messages from the lunar

Sorority Babes in the Slimeball Bowl-o-Rama *poster*.

inhabitants such as "We are not enslaved by your earthly emotions" and "If we find love turns to evil, we will destroy them [the missing couple] and mankind." Then the plot *really* gets silly.

What starts out as a fairly intelligent and progressive space-travel film, complete with such important themes as international and interracial cooperation, quickly degenerates into a juvenile, simplistic space opera. Admittedly, space operas have their place, but *12 to the Moon* fails to deliver even a single aria, much less the whole operetta. Hardly "the most exciting space adventure ever" (as the trailer so grandiosely labels it), the film's pacing is slow, the cast uninteresting, and the characters' petty squabbles, which take up much of the movie's running time, are just embarrassing. Adding dull insult to desultory injury, we never see the moon-people. We never even learn anything about them except that they like cats (one message requests that the two experimental felines onboard the ship be left behind). By the time they offer up their final message that "We have learned that all your Earth emotions are not evil and warlike; someday when you come back you will be welcome," it's difficult to care. Screenwriter Dewitt Bodeen, best known for penning a trio of excellent Val Lewton pictures at RKO—*Cat People* (1942), *The Seventh Victim* (1943) and *The Curse of the Cat People* (1944)—here evinces none of the poetic depth he brought to those earlier features. (Perhaps it was Lewton himself—a producer with the soul of a writer, and who often rewrote his projects' screenplays without taking credit—who contributed the quality to those classics.)

Production-wise, *12 to the Moon*'s low budget shows through everywhere. One crewmember talks about his "invisible electro-magnetic ray screen which forms a protective shield over our faces." Translation: there is no glass in the helmets. Talk about *low* budget ($150,000 for an eight-day shoot, which, come to think of it, should have at least bought some better space suits). The effects are minimal and substandard, consisting mainly of the same shot of a rocket travelling through space used over and over again (and it's not even a good shot—the stars shine right through the transparent-looking ship). The set for the lunar surface itself, however, is an exception, and one of the film's few highlights. It looks eerie and effectively alien with its cracks, craters, weird shadows, and smoke seeping from mysterious holes.

Overall, if you find outlandish, outdated space-travel films appealing then you may want to hitch a ride with these *12 to the Moon*. If, on the other hand, you prefer your sci-fi of the intelligent, stimulating variety, watch George Pal's *Destination Moon* (made 10 years earlier) instead. One final indication of the quality level found here: *12 to the Moon* was directed by the same man who made *They Saved Hitler's Brain*.

With this mini-essay, printed in *Cult Movies* magazine (issue 16), I tried to share a little knowledge about *The Unknown Terror*.

THE UNKNOWN TERROR (1957)

"Five thousand feet beneath the earth they sealed the horror of The Unknown Terror.*" –radio spot*

Another minor, little seen feature of the "Forgotten Fifties" ilk, *The Unknown Terror* is aptly named, since the movie itself is about as unknown as the terror (though the film carried a shooting title of *Beyond Terror*, that commodity is conspicuous solely by its absence). While not as outrageous in its monsters as most of its better-known contemporaries, and lacking any significant fright factor, *The Unknown Terror* does manage to build a bit of atmosphere, particularly in the picture's first half.

The story centers on three characters involved in a love triangle, with plenty of implied past history—but one in which the people are both realistic and likable. The trio, Mala Powers (wife), John Howard (husband) and Paul Richards (friend), are searching for Powers' brother, who disappeared in the Caribbean while looking for the "Cave of the Dead"—a legendary site of human sacrifice. The movie generates a mounting feeling of dread as they encounter covertly hostile inhabitants, evil rumors and bad omens. They find the cave, but they also find an exceedingly *large* mad scientist (Gerald Milton), who looks more like a big-time wrestler than a mad medico (and emotes more like one as well). This thinking-man's Tor Johnson is experimenting with some kind of weird fungus that he grows down in the cave, turning locals into fungoid monsters in the process.

"'The Unknown Terror' is a human being who has thrived on quickly-multiplying fungus growths, which have almost completely covered his body," explained a Twentieth Century Fox publicity piece. "Nerves of steel are wanted to view this 'beautiful specimen, a product of science fiction.'" Hardly. The creatures themselves are never shown too clearly, which is just as well since they inspire more menace in spongy silhouette than in full bubbly view (upon which they look just like what

Mala Powers menaced by The Unknown Soapsuds… er, Terror *(1957).*

they are—actors with bits of dirty cotton stuck to their faces). Fortunately, the fungus monsters play a relatively small part and appear in only two "close encounters." Screenwriter Kenneth Higgins' (husband of 1930s film and serial actress Lucille Lund) story opts to focus more on the human characters and, at the end, on the fungus itself (ridiculously represented by flowing soapsuds) as it begins to ooze down the cave walls and grow at an alarming rate. ("We can't let it out. We've got to seal it in this cave, otherwise it'll destroy the world!" cries the agitated doctor.) Unfortunately, this causes the climax to fizzle, since the finale consists of the two surviving principals trying to escape the ever-growing fungus—and it's difficult to make a bunch of advancing soapsuds look menacing. "In viewing the movie," recalled star John Howard to interviewer Tom Weaver, "I thought that [the fungus] looked like soap bubbles coming down the cave walls. I didn't see how this could frighten anybody, but it sure frightened the hell out of my kids—they were scared to death!" (They obviously never did their own laundry.)

On the plus side, the cavern interiors are realistic and convincing, and we're also treated to two melodious musical numbers performed (and written) by the talented Sir Lancelot, billed as "the King of the Calypsos." (The smooth-voiced singer previously made memorable appearances, both musical and dramatic, in the Val Lewton classics *I Walked with a Zombie* [1943], *The Ghost Ship* [1943] and *The Curse of the Cat People* [1944]).

Female lead Mala Powers does an admirable job with her Unknown Role, particularly given that she was "acting for two" at the time. "*Unknown Terror* was when I was pregnant," stated the actress to Weaver, "and nobody knew that. So for me it was quite a feat to go through morning sickness every morning and not let everybody know about it."

While not a great film, *The Unknown Terror* doesn't really deserve its status as The Unknown Movie. Those who paid money back in 1957 to see *The Unknown Soapsuds…* er—*Terror* also journeyed *Back from the Dead* with Arthur Franz on a rather dreary (though squeaky clean) double-bill.

> *Cult Movies* magazine let us see the (*Voodoo*) *Dawn* in issue 21 (Spring 1997).

VOODOO DAWN (1990)

Though possessing a few beautiful settings (sun-filled meadow, green leafy forest), and touching (briefly) on the humanistic theme of the plight of the migrant farm worker, *Voodoo Dawn* falls into the same trap that snares many a low-budget, straight-to-video effort: poor characterization and leaden plotting.

John Russo (of *Night of the Living Dead* fame) and his three co-writers concocted a tale of big-city college kids caught up in a struggle between immigrant farm workers from Haiti and an evil voodoo priest named Makoute. For some inexplicable reason, this rogue sorcerer is stalking and killing his former countrymen in order to obtain body parts to assemble a patchwork zombie creation. Why this voodoo version of Dr. Frankenstein does all this is never explained (he already has a handful of *whole* zombie corpses to do his bidding), nor is much else in this poorly-scripted and deadly dull movie (has Russo penned *anything* good since 1968?).

Poor Tony Todd (who made such an impression in the 1990 *Night of the Living Dead* remake and the *Candyman* series) has no dialogue as the voodoo villain and little to do except creep about in the dark with a machete. The only intriguing moments in this waste-of-time arise when the friendly mamaloi effectively uses a voodoo doll to make Makoute twist and jerk this way and that—*and* the final shot of one of the zombies (who, lacking significant makeup, simply look like slow-walking field workers). Having been run through (sideways) with an iron bar, the perambulating corpse can't get through the door because the ends of the bar jutting out from either side of his body keep catching on the door frame, and the mindless automaton simply bumps again and again at the portal. Sadly, one late joke at a zombie's expense and a few pretty images do not an entertaining movie make, and viewers should simply roll over and go back to sleep rather than face this *Voodoo Dawn*.

> I got to (briefly) play with (*Voodoo*) *Dolls* in *Cult Movies* magazine, issue 22 (Summer 1997).

VOODOO DOLLS (1990)

This direct-to-video cheapie from Quebec begins well enough with an atmospheric black-and-white prologue filled with clever film-school technique (slo-mo, freeze-frame, quick cuts, etc.). Unfortunately, once the story proper gets underway, the film settles down into just another by-the-numbers bottom-of-the-barrel VCR filler, whose technical competency fails to reach even the level of a low-end Fred Olen Ray or David DeCoteau production.

The convoluted story revolves around the Hanley School for Girls, where a brutal slaying took place forty years ago (the black-and-white prologue). Apparently, several of the kitchen help practice "black magic or voodoo or something" (as one character vaguely explains) and intend to draw the New Girl into their cult of death.

Director Andre Pelletier fills this boring picture with pointless scenes that go absolutely nowhere until the story finally winds down (or *falls* down) to its forgone conclusion. The bargain-basement budget shows through everywhere, from the fact that we only see about five students at this prestigious "school" to some horribly bad non-acting. As the voodoo priest, Graham Chambers is the token black in the cast, but he's also the *toneless* black since he appears less animated than his voodoo dolls.

These dolls provide the one novel notion in this otherwise senseless scenario, for these little bits of straw and cloth possess a life of their own. At one point a whole gang of voodoo dolls attack and kill a lecherous handyman. Sadly, the effects are far from special as the hapless victim rolls around with the obviously inanimate dolls pinned to his shirt while he holds one to his neck and shakes it in a desperate attempt to make it seem alive. Pelletier finally shows some good judgment, since this turns out to be the *only* scene to spotlight these pathetic stuffed menaces (misleading title notwithstanding). For superior (and far less tedious) voodoo doll action, see *Tales from the Hood* or even the south-of-the-border deviation *The Doll People*.

> This appeared in a 1998 one-shot issue called *Science Fiction Invasions*, published by *Movie Club* magazine.

WESTWORLD (1973)

This fast-paced futuristic thriller was the directorial debut of author Michael Crichton (whose novels *The Andromeda Strain*, *The Terminal Man*, *Coma*, *Jurassic Park*, and, most recently, *Congo* and *The Lost World* have all been turned into films). Beyond directing, Crichton also penned *Westworld*'s clever screenplay.

The story takes place at Delos, the ultimate adult amusement park of the future, which is composed of Romanworld, Medievalworld, and Westworld. There the high-paying guests ($1000 a day—in 1973!) can live out their fantasies in the authentic settings of past eras. Androids who look, sound, and feel exactly like humans (except for their hands which "they haven't perfected yet") populate the three worlds. These robots interact with, and attend to, the human guests—whether it be engaging them in swordfights (which the robots are programmed to lose), challenging them to shootouts, or even yielding to their amorous advances (yes, the "sex model" robots can even copulate). Our heroes, Richard Benjamin and James Brolin, two fairly ordinary guys looking for some fun at the ultimate escapist resort, choose Westworld where they enjoy gunfights, brawls, saloon gals, and even a jailbreak in the setting of an 1880 Old West town. But then something goes terribly wrong and a robot "program virus" takes over which causes the androids to stop losing the battles and start killing the guests. The scene in which an incredulous James Brolin is shot down in the street by the black-garbed gunfighter (Yul Brynner, sporting the same outfit he wore as the leader of *The Magnificent Seven*) whom Brolin and Benjamin had already "killed" on two previous occasions is well staged and riveting in its execution (so to speak). The remainder of the film becomes a suspense-filled cat-and-mouse chase through the three worlds as the seemingly unstoppable robot gunfighter stalks Benjamin with a chilling single-mindedness.

Benjamin and Brolin both come off as quite likable, and the low-key byplay between them effectively involves the audience in their Old West fun so that the viewer rides right alongside them as they enjoy each new twist Westworld has to offer. Thus, when the robots finally turn on the humans, the terror hits home in a frighteningly personal manner.

Crichton's direction is thoughtful and intelligent yet at the same time taut and gripping, and he establishes an air of believability (of first and foremost importance in science fiction) by showing us the organized chaos behind the scenes in the various control rooms and robot repair shops.

A well-crafted thriller, *Westworld* engages both the viewer's intellect and emotions while exploring the potential horrors of over-mechanization, making it truly one of the best sci-fi films of the 1970s. A sequel entitled *Futureworld* came out three years later (in 1976), but, lacking Crichton's involvement, it proved merely a pale imitation which focused on a ludicrous take-over-the-world plot.

Though readily available on video, Westworld has (thankfully) also been released on laserdisc. MGM/UA has found a pristine print for this laser transfer, releasing the film in its original widescreen format. While, disappointingly, the disc contains no extras (there's not even a solitary trailer to be found), this is still the only way to truly see one of the cinema's seminal sci-fi films in all its robotic splendor.

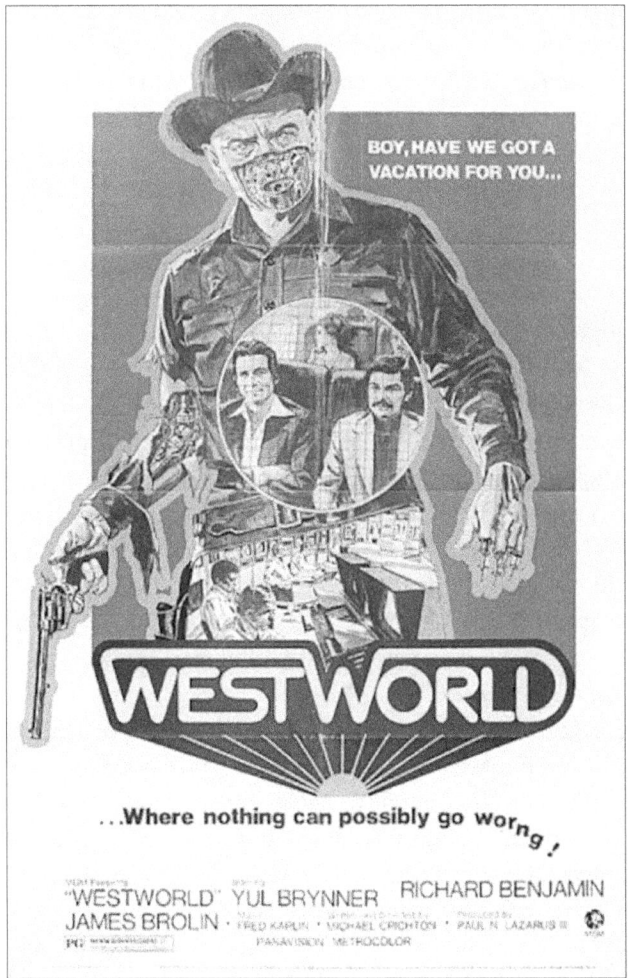

Westworld *poster*.

> Not all so-called "cult movies" are worth reviewing, even if half their cast are *Wild Women*. *Cult Movies* magazine helped me prove this in issue 17 (Winter 1996).

THE WILD WOMEN OF WONGO (1959)

"This one's mine, he's cute!" –one of the Wild Women of Wongo choosing a mate

This deservedly obscure oddity may be the worst (and certainly the dullest) scantily-clad-primitive-women movies ever made. On the island of Wongo there exists a tribe made up of beautiful women and ugly men. The land of Guhna is populated by handsome men and ugly women. Get everyone together, swap mates, and you have the general storyline for *The Wild Women of Wongo*. In the interim there's the occasional sacrifice to the "Dragon of Wongo" (an ordinary alligator), some spear throwing, and the most pitiful action sequences ever attempted outside a high school drama production. The big battle scenes consist of actors making ineffectual thrusts with their spears and trying desperately to look like they're actually doing something. Some even go so far as to employ the old hold-the-spear-under-the-arm trick when 'stabbed.' Sad. The only interesting thing about this bottom-of-the-barrel production is that it was shot in color. Why is anybody's guess. *The Wild Women of Wongo*'s intellectual level is best summed up in the film's final moments. The happily paired-off couples line up, and then turn and wink into the camera one by one. Aaaaaarg!

> The seed of this expanded review first grew in *Cult Movies* magazine, issue 24 (December 1997).

THE WOMAN EATER (1959)

"ONLY THE MOST BEAUTIFUL ITS VICTIMS!"
–poster

This English oddity about a bizarre carnivorous tree that eats nothing but buxom young girls (while a native bangs away on a tom tom and a mad scientist extracts from it a serum to restore life to the dead) is an admittedly silly but still rather engaging import.

The wealthy Dr. Moran (George Coulouris) discovers a monster plant in the Amazon jungle that is worshipped as a god by the primitive tribe caring for it. He brings the plant and its native caretaker, Tanga (Jimmy Vaughan), back to Merrie Olde England to keep in his basement dungeon so he can experiment with its life-restoring fluid. For those unorthodox laboratory procedures he periodically needs nubile young women to feed to the plant. At meal time, said shrub awkwardly enwraps the girls in tentacles and draws them towards its trunk (there to do god-only-knows-what, since we're not shown any further digestive developments—we just have to use our *limber* imagination). Heroine Sally Norton (Vera Day) is stranded in Moran's little village and, with the aid of local garage mechanic Jack Venner (Peter Wayn), gets a job at Moran Manor as a live-in housekeeper. The doctor soon sets his sights on Sally, and it's up to Jack and the local constabulary to rescue the girl from the doc's vegetable vagaries.

Though the production is definitely on the cheap, director Charles Saunders makes the most of both the English countryside (often going outside to shoot, which gives the picture a more expansive—and authentic—feel) and the huge old manor house that stood in for Moran's mansion. Art director Herbert Smith constructs a bang-up basement/dungeon lab set, its medieval-style stone staircase, pillars, dank walls and iron gates contrasting nicely with the tables of shining glass beakers and medical apparatus, generating an atmosphere of ominous menace. In the middle of this unhealthy milieu stands the Womaneater itself, a fairly impressive (if not wholly convincing) monstrosity sporting a huge trunk, moving tendrils and waving limbs draped in dank, mossy matter.

Saunders keeps the camera moving and selects his shots with care, even employing the occasional plant's-eye-view shot to enhance the horror (as well as provide an additional voyeuristic glimpse at the invariably luscious and semi-draped victim-to-be). Saunders, who directed his first film way back in 1930, also co-directed the (literal) talking head horror *The Man Without a Body* (again starring Coulouris) the previous year. He went on to make more explicit sexploitation pictures like *Nudist Paradise* (1959).

Admittedly, a large part of *The Woman Eater*'s appeal is its exploitation factor—featuring plenty of sparsely clothed beauties about to become plant food—but that old British aplomb rises above it all and lends an air of respectability to the tawdry tale.

Said aplomb comes in large measure from British character actor George Coulouris as the botanically obsessed Dr. Moran. Though cold, authoritative and forceful, Coulouris possesses an unhealthy gleam in his

The Woman Eater poster.

eye that reveals his character's mania. When a constable shows him the photograph of a missing girl and notes that she's "a looker," he answers "As a scientist I'm more interested in things with six legs rather than two; no doubt I'm in a minority" with a droll understatement that makes the line that much more amusing.

No great cinema here, but *The Woman Eater* offers something unusual enough to provide an entertaining 71 minutes. So *plant* yourself (ouch), sit back and enjoy this British guilty pleasure.

> As everyone knows, most planets are just plain inhospitable. Thanks, *Cult Movies* magazine, for showing us just that about the *Prehistoric Planet* (and its *Women of*) in issue 17 (Winter 1996).

WOMEN OF THE PREHISTORIC PLANET (1966)

"IT'S THE BATTLE OF THE SEXES AS SAVAGE PLANET WOMEN ATTACK FEMALE SPACE INVADERS" –ad line

Shot in 11 days and released by the same outfit (Realart) who brought us *Bela Lugosi Meets a Brooklyn Gorilla* (1952), this shoddy no-budget sci-fi clunker doesn't even deliver what its title promises. First of all, there is only one woman of note—and she's not even *from* the planet in question. Second, the "Prehistoric Planet" consists of nothing but a few tacky studio sets, some painfully obvious painted scenery and a single sub-standard table-top miniature. ("The sets were so cheap and phony looking," recalled female lead Irene Tsu to interviewer Tom Lisanti, "the cast was constantly worried that we would knock them down.") And worst of all, the closest this picture comes to any prehistoric menace is a six-foot photographically enlarged lizard and an ordinary boa constrictor.

The weak story follows a "Centarian" spaceship, captained by Wendell Corey and John Agar, searching for survivors from another ship that crashed on a primitive planet. The only survivor, however, is the now-grown son (Keith Larsen) of two of the original crew members, who immediately falls in love with "Leeta" (Irene Tsu), a girl from the rescue ship. After some pointless wandering around, the handy volcano erupts, the ship leaves, and the two lovers stay behind (presumably to "go forth and multiply"). As the ship speeds away, Corey states, "We'll enter it in the Galactic Registry... and call it 'Earth.'" (Orson Welles, who seems to have hosted every "ancient astronaut" film ever made, should have been narrator on this one.)

The movie is filled with ridiculous pseudo-scientific explanations (chief among them being the fact that since the spaceship travels so much faster than the planet's rotation, 18 years have passed on the planet in the one month it took the rescue ship to reach it—a bit of physics to set Einstein spinning in his grave). Tacky sets, an absence of interesting ideas, and "monsters" no more menacing that anything found in a grade-B Tarzan movie (there's even a chimp named "Teeka") make *Women of the Prehistoric Planet* hard to sit through. The mismatched stock footage of parrots and other "exotic" wildlife doesn't help either. The only redeeming factor is the color, which does manage to give what little there is to look at a sort of garish appeal.

Time to take the Wayback Machine—er, *Yesterday Machine* to the Fall of 1995 and *Cult Movies* magazine (issue 16).

THE YESTERDAY MACHINE (1965)

"Yesterday should be left alone because today we have enough problems trying to make sure there will be a tomorrow."

The Yesterday Machine is an obscure, all-but-forgotten little independent from the Lone Star state which, as it turns out, deserves its obscurity. Two college kids on their way to a football game encounter a pair of confederate soldiers in the woods. The boy is shot but escapes while the girl disappears. The police are baffled and it's up to a hard-bitten reporter (James Britton), paired up with the missing girl's sister (Ann Pellegrino), to crack this bizarre case. Eventually, they discover a time machine run by a crazed Nazi scientist whose ultimate goal is to use his miraculous device to raise up Hitler so that the Third Reich will rule the world "not for a thousand years but forever!" Of course, his plans are thwarted by our intrepid reporter, and the world is safe once more.

Such an outrageous plotline should be simply bursting with thrills—or at least a few laughs. Not so here. The talky script remains deadly dull; nothing even remotely resembling action ever takes place. Most of the

A VHS blast from the past—that should remain there.

time is spent following the characters walking through the woods, talking to the police, or listening to boffo, pseudo-scientific lectures. The old Nazi scientist takes up nearly *fifteen minutes* of screen time alternately raving about the Third Reich and offering up lengthy, ridiculous scientific explanations. The following is a *minute* portion of his never-ending time travel rantings: "If the velocity of ordinary light should be accelerated, then it will pass beyond the instant and no longer be moving in the direction of the future, but it will be moving in the direction of the past." Come again? And this goes on forever, making you feel like you're caught in some twisted Mr. Wizard time warp.

There are no special effects to speak of, unless one counts a few sparks shooting out of the cheap plastic tubing that makes up the time travel device. And nothing is made of the central theme of time travel. The closest we come to visiting another time is meeting a lone boy dressed in 18th century colonial garb riding a horse down a country road. For the most part we're stuck in modern offices or the cheesy lab set. The direction offers no help, with long talky scenes filmed in medium shot, little camera movement, and poor use of actors. Naturally, the acting is anything *but*. James Britton never raises so much as an eyebrow, much less do any genuine emoting, even when stumbling upon such wonders as a secret lab, teleportation device, and time machine. Ann Pellegrino does no better and turns out to be the most unattractive heroine of the decade. Tim Holt (a long way from *The Monster That Challenged the World*—and an even longer way from his turn in the classic *Treasure of* the Sierra Madres) is top billed and the only name actor in the cast, but puts in only a brief appearance. Billy Thurman, who has a small part as a police detective, became a regular in the movies of Texas schlockmeister Larry Buchanan (*Zontar the Thing from Venus*, *In the Year 2889*, *Mars Needs Women*, etc.). Round out the (in)action with a gratingly inappropriate modern jazz score, and *The Yesterday Machine* turns out to be a time-travel film that deserves to remain lost in the past.

> I penned this little mini-missive for one of the on-line forums I belonged to back at the turn of the century. (Wow, that makes me sound *old*…)

ZOMBIE HOLOCAUST (1980)

It's a New York–based cut of cannibal cinema. No, it's a New Guinea-set primitive flesheater flick. No, it's a bungle-in-the-jungle mad doctor movie. No, it's a zombie zinger! Well, I'm not really sure *what* it is, but it's a fact that *Zombie Holocaust* (aka *Doctor Butcher M.D.*) is unique in its blending of cannibals and walking corpses. Toss in some gratuitous surgery scenes, a statuesque painted beauty laid out naked in an ancient sacrificial stone (that somehow manages to match her measurements perfectly!), a mannequin fall that made me laugh out loud when it hit the concrete and *lost an arm* (with the subsequent scene of the bloodied actor showing the AWOL appendage re-attached!), and that always-welcome British actor whose name I can never recall [Ian McCulloch], and *ZH* sets the stage for an entertaining 90 minutes of Euro-wackiness.

In most ways, this Italian exploitationer fills the bill—*except* in the Zombie department. And a film called "*Zombie*" Holocaust had better deliver on its walking corpses. Though initially they appear creepily effective (as they slowly and inexorably advance towards their victims while ominous music and heavy breathing 'moodies up' the soundtrack), it soon becomes apparent that these ambulatory cadavers are no more imposing than the generic henchmen from an old *Batman* TV episode. (For all their effectiveness, they may just as well have been wearing Penguin muscle-shirts.) Of course, the boat-motor scene was a stunner. The facial makeups were unusual and, for the most part, superb; but it's a little disconcerting to see a decayed head atop a perfectly healthy body, with normal-looking arms and legs (I mean, come on, take the 10 minutes to do the limb makeup too, fercrissakes!).

CHAPTER 8
FILM BOOK REVIEWS

I not only love to write about genre films, I love to *read* about them as well. So why not combine the two and pen some book reviews? Fortunately, editor Jim Clatterbaugh at *Monsters from the Vault* magazine provided me a publishing outlet over the years, and the following book reviews (all printed between 2007 and 2014) are the result.

THE AMERICAN INTERNATIONAL PICTURES VIDEO GUIDE
by Gary A. Smith (2009; McFarland)

For genre film fans—whether lovers of horror, sci-fi, J.D., biker, blaxploitation, or even beach party flicks—the three words "American International Pictures" hold a special sort of magic. Over the course of two decades, the film production/distribution company founded by James Nicholson and Samuel Z. Arkoff in 1954 brought us everything from *I Was a Teenage Werewolf* and *The Abominable Dr. Phibes* to *Beach Blanket Bingo* and *Hell Up in Harlem*. AIP provided the outlet (and often the paychecks) for such talents as Francis Ford Coppola, Mario Bava, Martin Scorsese, and Jack Nicholson. For a decade, the names Roger Corman and American International Pictures were nearly synonymous; and the same could be said for Vincent Price, whose career was rejuvenated by AIP's Poe series. Consequently, books on this Little Indy That Could are *always* welcome.

The American International Pictures Video Guide, by Gary A. Smith, is "a comprehensive guide to AIP movies that are or have been available in home viewing formats such as DVD and VHS." In essence, it's a handy alphabetized recounting of every film "which had a theatrical release by American International Pictures or [was] purchased by AIP for television release," and which can be found on home video—some 210 features. Now, this is not the first tome to focus exclusively on AIP. Mark Thomas McGee's excellent history *Fast and Furious: The Story of American International Pictures* came out back in 1984 (with a revised edition, *Faster and Furiouser*, arriving in 1995). And the company has seen its fair share of ink in such books as *Beyond Ballyhoo*, again by McGee, and *Cheap Tricks and Class Acts*, by John Johnson (not to mention the autobiographies of Roger Corman and Sam Arkoff). One might say that the history of AIP has been well-chronicled. So what does this latest volume have to offer?

In the book's (brief) foreword by McGee himself, he writes, "[My] book [*Fast and Furious*] was a history of the company, and this one is a history of their product." Indeed, taken as a companion piece to McGee's volume, *The American International Pictures Video Guide* becomes a useful addition to anyone's AIP library. Unfortunately, this *Video Guide* doesn't fare so well standing on its own. First off, Smith provides only a cursory history of the company in his brief introduction—understandable, perhaps, given the wealth of information that can be found elsewhere, but a bit sketchy all the same. Second, the unfortunate decision to arrange the movies in alphabetical rather than chronological order compounds this dearth of historical content by denying the reader the ability to see the progression—and evolution—of AIP films over time. Granted, it's easier to look up a particular movie in this encyclopedic format; but I, for one, would gladly use the index on occasion in exchange for the opportunity to see the patterns and shifts in the company's output that a chronological listing would have provided. Most disappointing, however, is the brevity of the entries themselves. Covering 210 movies in 175 pages in "The Films" section (with a significant portion of that space taken up by movie credits and an admittedly excellent selection of photographs) leaves very little room for exposition and insight. And Smith fills the one or two paragraphs of text he allots each film with far more synopsis than analysis. For example, his only critical commentary on *The Dunwich Horror* is: "Lovecraft's classic story is given a lackluster presentation herein. Not much really happens and what does isn't all that exciting or interesting." Nor are these two meager sentences. Granted, the occasional factoid piques one's interest (in the same entry, for instance, he writes about the amusing ballyhoo over Sandra Dee's nude scene), and his straightforward, engaging style is eminently readable; but Smith offers disappointingly little substance. Where the book truly shines is in the appendices. The first, "American

International Television," offers entries on those films purchased by AIP for television release, including various Mexican horrors, Italian peplums and the Texas-based Larry Buchanan travesties (though Smith inexplicably lumps *all* of Buchanan's eight AIP titles under one [*Mars Needs Women*] entry!). Still, it's refreshing to finally read something about the brilliant Vincent Price TV vehicle *An Evening of Edgar Allan Poe*. Appendix 2 details "The Unfilmed AIP," which makes for a fascinating read of various what-might-have-beens and what-never-weres. Appendices 3 through 5 offer valuable listings of "Prepackaged Features" (the AIP double-bills), "Title Changes" (alternate titles for AIP flicks), and "Comic Book and Paperback Novel Tie-Ins."

Though somewhat disappointing when taken on its own, *The American International Pictures Video Guide* still serves as a sporadically useful adjunct to the prior chroniclings of that innovative, wonderful cinematic institution known as American International Pictures.

CRAB MONSTERS, TEENAGE CAVEMEN, AND CANDY STRIPE NURSES – ROGER CORMAN: KING OF THE B MOVIE
by Chris Nashawaty (2013, Abrams)

The Little Shop of Horrors, *House of Usher*, *The Wild Angels*, *The Big Doll House*, *Piranha*... if there was a new trend in independent cinema flooding the drive-ins of the '50s, '60s and '70s (and the video shelves of the '80s and '90s), it's even money that independent director/producer/studio head Roger Corman not only rode that wave but possibly even started it. Numerous articles, interviews, filmographies and biographies (including one by the man himself) have been published over the years detailing nearly every aspect of Corman's career as a B-movie mogul and innovator. So what could yet another book about this cinema patriarch have to say? How about page after page of tell-it-like-it-was stories from the people who were there—the colleagues, cohorts, and collaborators who have gone through "Corman University" to produce over 400 Corman-shepherded movies over the course of five decades (with some of said Corman grads even ending up at the Oscar podium). Such an approach forms a fascinating oral history, with short, well-written essays interspersed to bind it all together. Filled with striking images of posters, stills, frame grabs, and even candid shots (one amazing behind-the-scenes color photo from *Attack of the Crab Monsters* made this reviewer do a double-take), this coffee table book chronologically covers Corman's career as director and producer and company head as told by those who fell within the man's orbit. All Corman Creatures Great and Small provide illuminating reminiscences, from the likes of Dick Miller, Jonathan Haze, and Jack Hill, to Ron Howard, James Cameron and Jack Nicholson. In all, over 60 actors, friends and filmmakers (from Roger's producer brother Gene Corman to cameraman Haskell Wexler to megastar Robert DeNiro) share their memories and insights about working with, and for, the "King of the B Movies." And, of course, Corman's own thoughts and well-chosen words are sprinkled throughout. Through these informative, candid, funny and even occasionally poignant recollections, the picture of an intelligent, honest, and yes, economical filmmaker whose eye never strayed far from the bottom line takes shape and looms large—almost as large as Corman himself, who many credit with discovering and nurturing many of the greats of modern cinema. Joe Dante (*The Howling*, *Gremlins*) even goes so far as to say, "The stuff he made is probably what shaped the whole culture. If everybody that ever went through the Corman School was left behind, or just disappeared so there was nothing left but their clothes, this business [of movie-making] would not function. ... Everything leads back to Roger."

Though author Chris Nashawaty deserves high praise for interviewing, and compiling pertinent comments from, just about everyone who's anyone in the Corman Universe, it seems he takes implied credit for work he didn't do, as not all the quotes reflect original research. For instance, a passage on pages 76-77 quoting Jack Nicholson on *The Trip* is taken directly from Corman's own 1990 autobiography, with nary a citation in sight; while another Nicholson passage (on page 19) comes from the 2011 documentary *Corman's World*. And an amusing comment from Corman himself on *The Big Doll House* (page 107) is lifted from an onscreen interview in the excellent 2010 documentary on Filipino exploitation cinema *Machete Maidens Unleashed*.

But barring these occasional proprietary lapses, the oral history (and stunning visuals) that comprise *Crab Monsters, Teenage Cavemen, and Candy Stripe Nurses* stands as an engrossing and illuminating recap of the work of, and the man that is, Roger Corman—one of cinema's most important and influential figures.

CREATURE FEATURES: NATURE TURNED NASTY IN THE MOVIES
by William Schoell (2008; McFarland)

In his preface to *Creature Features: Nature Turned Nasty in the Movies*, author William Schoell perceptively observes that "Science fiction fans usually excoriate monster movies, because they don't understand that movies about resuscitated dinosaurs and gigantic, impossible insects are not science fiction, but *horror* (or dark fantasy if you want to get technical)." Indeed, monster movies (particularly *giant* monster movies) offer some of the most ridiculous and illogical menaces and situations seen on the cinema screen. Yet they also frequently capture the attention—and imagination—of movie-lovers both past and present. Hence this book, which, as delineated by its author, "concentrates on creatures....The monsters in this book are either behemoths...or normal-sized animals such as birds and bears that behave in strange ways." Schoell focuses on said monsters in seven largely self-explanatory chapters: "Here There Be Dragons" (covering dinosaurs, Godzilla, and various fantasy creatures); "Into the Ant Hole" (big bugs); "Humongous" (regular animals grown to gigantic proportions); "Nature Turned Nasty Part One—Birds, Bugs and Bats"; "Nature Turned Nasty Part Two—Fish Stories"; "Nature Turned Nasty Part Three—Day of the Animals"; and "The Indefinable: Blobs, Things, and Other Oddities."

Schoell thankfully keeps his synopses brief (generally to one paragraph), avoiding the pitfall of so many film books who use up far too much ink on dully recounting minute plot details. This leaves more room for his often astute observations and critiques. For instance, Schoell is refreshingly unafraid to point out that the (gigantic) Emperor has no clothes in his otherwise positive analysis of the original *Godzilla*. "It isn't just that the creature is only a man in a monster suit, but that the suit—especially the head—is so poorly designed.... With a dopey-looking face and a body like a flabby T-Rex, Godzilla is about as fearsome as a Muppet." And later, he (rightly) points out how the similar *Gorgo* suit is so much "better designed than Godzilla." Schoell's breezy enthusiasm often becomes infectious, though his unreasoning love for all things B.I.G. (Bert I. Gordon, that is) exposes the chinks in his critical armor, with one of the biggest holes being his labeling the awful *The Cyclops* "Gordon's best movie." Yikes.

And while his analyses are sometimes illuminating and amusing, it's rather disappointing—at least to the knowledgeable genre fan (for whom I'm assuming this book was written)—that Schoell offers so little production or behind-the-scenes information. (Quotes from participants, either primary or secondary, are as scarce as a convincing special effect in a Bert I. Gordon movie.) Rather tellingly, the entire bibliography consists of two websites and a mere nine magazine articles and books—with three of them being the author's own works! Schoell also fails to place these films into any significant context (apart from chronology), ignoring the fascinating societal shifts and sociological issues that brought about the big-bug and nature-strikes-back trends, missing out on a golden opportunity to put these subgenres into the "big picture" of their times and circumstances.

The author's criteria for inclusion is sometimes as curious and inexplicable as, well, gigantic creatures. Missing are such titles as the giant snake opus (and box-office hit) *Anaconda* and the ants-strike-back entry *Phase IV*, one of the most unusual and thought-provoking of all the nature-amok flicks. In his "Dragons" chapter, Schoell fails to include one of the best examples of this species, *Dragonheart* (though, to his credit, he awards long-overdue praise to the criminally underrated *Reign of Fire*). Other notable omissions come in the form of missing bats (*Chosen Survivors*), cats (*The Uncanny*), dinosaurs (*The Land Unknown*), fish (*Up from the Depths*), and rats (the obviously-titled *Rats: Night of Terror*).

All told, *Creature Features* is more of an introductory narrative sampling of giant creature and nature-amok films than an encyclopedic resource. In this respect, Schoell's approachable, engaging, and often witty prose fills the bill admirably. But due to its arbitrary selectivity and threadbare research, it fails to become the ultimate guide to these fascinating cinematic subsets that it could have been. Even so, reading this tome inspired this reviewer to revisit several of the creature features detailed within, which surely must be the highest praise a film book can earn.

FILM ALCHEMY: THE INDEPENDENT CINEMA OF TED V. MIKELS
by Christopher Wayne Curry (2008; McFarland)

Full disclosure: I am *not* a fan of the films of Ted V. Mikels. When the height of a moviemaker's oeuvre is the blinding ineptness of *Astro Zombies* and *The Corpse Grinders*, it becomes more than a little difficult to take said filmmaker seriously (or take him at *all*, given the awful dullness of both those movies). Still, I *am* a fan of the well-written bio-filmography. (In fact, one of my favorite filmic reads of the last decade was *The Ghastly Ones*, by Jimmy McDonough, a snake-fascinating look into the tawdry life and tawdrier works of Andy Milligan—a fringe filmmaker who makes Mikels seem like Orson Welles.) So I don't need to love the subject to love the book. And while I have little to no affection for the subject of *Film Alchemy*, I do at least *like* the book, which devotes a full chapter to each of Mikels' 13 theatrical releases and 6 direct-to-video flicks, as well as providing a moderately in-depth interview with the man himself.

"As has been made obvious by this point in the chronology of Ted V. Mikels' movie career," observes Curry in his *Astro Zombies* chapter, "the virtues and standards of Hollywood filmmaking cannot, and should not, be applied to him." Hmmm. Comments such as these suggest Curry wants us to give Mikels a free pass when viewing his "epics," but that's a tough sell. Good filmmaking is good filmmaking, whether it be in high-rent Hollywood or low-rent Brentwood; and there are plenty of moviemakers that have risen above their constraints to create fine films on a shoestring. As Curry constantly casts himself in the role of Mikels' apologist, however, the reader can't help but come to admire both his tireless efforts and amusing approach. For example, he follows up the above statement with: "Ted works entirely outside of the system, and almost every one of his movies flies directly in the face of Hollywood convention. Ed Grant of *Time* magazine seconded this on November 20, 2000, by stating that 'in an era when Hollywood entertainment is remarkably predictable, Mikels' work still comes as a cold slap in the face.' If Ted's first four films didn't succeed in delivering the 'cold slap in the face' that Grant spoke of, then *Astro Zombies* was going to make up for it with a one-two punch." Yep, but "cold slaps in the face" and "one-two punches" are not necessarily pleasurable—nor are the films of Ted V. Mikels, but I suppose your mileage may vary.

Though *Film Alchemy* is well written and researched, I can't help but wish Curry had done more in the biography department. I mean, the man worked as a magician, ventriloquist, accordion player, acrobat and body builder, and lived at one time in a huge, castle-like mansion with a harem of *eight* women that he labeled his "castle ladies"! Curry himself even writes in his Preface, "It is true that Mikels' actual life is sometimes far more interesting than the quirky tales that he manages to spin into movies. And, in part, it was Mikels' home life that attracted me to the oddball filmmaker." I, for one, would have loved to have read more about that life. Curry does offer an 18-page interview with Mikels at the end of the book (which boils down to about 12 pages of text without the photos) that addresses some of these "interesting" aspects of Mikels' life. It's definitely a highlight of the book; though, in truth, it left this reader asking more questions than the interview answered.

Of course, any fan of Mikels' movies will simply have to get this book; but Curry does a good job making *Film Alchemy* interesting enough even for Mikels' detractors (such as this reviewer). Filled with a wide variety of photos, both promotional and personal, and chock full of illustrative (and often amusing) quotes and anecdotes, *Film Alchemy* provides an intriguing glimpse into both the cinematic and personal world of an unusual man driven to make unusual movies.

THE HAMMER VAMPIRE
by Bruce G. Hallenbeck (2010; Hemlock Books)

Question: What *hasn't* been written about Hammer Films? Answer: Not much. Even more so than the classic Universals, more articles, interviews and books (both hefty and light, scholarly and fannish) have been penned about Hammer than any other cinematic subset in the horror genre. With such a wealth (some might even say overabundance) of information, interviews and critique, it seems only natural that some enterprising soul should break it down into smaller morsels to streamline this bonanza of cinematic attention. Said soul in this case is Hammer expert and frequent *Little Shoppe of Horrors* scribe Bruce G. Hallenbeck. (For those few who may be unawares, *Little Shoppe* is *the* preeminent Hammer-centric magazine.)

After a somewhat desultory 19-page prologue titled "The Vampire Film Before Hammer," in which Hallenbeck stodgily chronicles the subgenre from the silents up until 1958 (when the studio bared its first fangs), he hits his stride when he begins to write about his obvious first love—Hammer horror. In a highly readable, linear style he takes us from the Hammer vampire's Point A (1958's *Horror of Dracula*) to Point Z (1974's *Legend of the 7 Golden Vampires*), and all points in between, in an entertaining and sometimes illuminating fashion. Through chapters titled "The Terrifying Lover," "The Nature of the Beast," "The Vampire as Antichrist," "Sin, Sex and Sadism," "The Vampire in Society," and "Variations on the Theme," Hallenbeck chronicles the various undead twists and turns the British studio took with its bloodthirsty bunch. Sprinkling his text with well-chosen quotes and anecdotes, both secondary and primary (as Hallenbeck has interviewed many of the personnel involved in these productions over the years), he thankfully fleshes out the narrative of the Hammer vampire trajectory with cultural references to events of the time, raising the book above the expected "fan" level to that of cultural criticism. He explores, for instance, how the sexual revolution of the mid-to-late '60s resulted in the Hammer vampire transitioning from the classic male bloodsucker (Dracula) to focus more on the feminine nosferatu (e.g., the Karnstein incarnations). Utilizing evocative descriptors and turns of phrases ("where Lee's Dracula is forever leaping about, Pitt's Carmilla glides dreamily, wearing nothing but the allure of the grave beneath her diaphanous nightgown"), Hallenbeck offers history, critique and insight on all 16 of Hammer's much-beloved (well, for the most part anyway) vampire films.

Hallenbeck doesn't leave us hanging after the *7 Golden Vampires* drain their last victim, however, as he concludes with "The Vampire Film after Hammer," demonstrating how the Hammer influence continued to steer the direction(s) vampire cinema took post-Hammer (affecting everything from the Anne Rice novels to the *Twilight* films). Production-wise, the book, while attractive, is far from flawless (much like many of the Hammers themselves): though well illustrated with stills, behind-the-scenes shots and posters (including 8 pages in color), it disappoints by its lack of an index.

While not particularly surprising or innovative (again, like some of the films it covers) in its various conclusions, *The Hammer Vampire* offers an informative and solidly enjoyable ride through the graveyards of Hammer history, with a few sprightly side-trips into cultural territory to illuminate the road.

THE HIDEOUS SUN DEMON: THE ORIGINAL SCREENPLAY
edited by Tom Weaver (2011; BearManor Media)

Apparently, many genre fans have a soft spot in their movie-watching hearts (or is that *heads*?) for a little independent monster flick from 1959 called *The Hideous Sun Demon*. Produced and directed by B-movie actor Robert Clarke (a bit player in a couple of Val Lewton pics and star of the low-budget *Man from Planet X*), *Sun Demon* was a Jekyll-and-Hyde tale of a scientist accidentally contaminated by a new type of radiation that results in him transforming into a lizard-man when exposed to the rays of the sun. Hmm... sounds like a good excuse to become a night-owl, right? Given the amount of over-the-top whining, angst, and out-and-out hysterics exhibited by Mr. Clarke as the affected doc, however, I guess he didn't think so. Anyway, this little programmer, which Clarke shot over a series of weekends with mostly film students and family, came and went with little fanfare (losing Clarke a bundle of cash in the process). It's not a bad film as '50s monster movies go, but it's not a particularly good one either. So on the surface it's rather curious that genre historian/interviewer Tom Weaver should devote an entire book to such a minor production. Curious, that is, until one cracks the cover and delves into said tome, for this volume proves to be a fascinating chronicle of independent filmmaking from a bygone era.

Weaver had earlier collaborated with Clarke on that actor's autobiography, *Robert Clarke: To 'B' or Not to 'B,'* and pertinent excerpts from that book are featured here. Also included are an introduction from *Sun Demon* associate producer Robin C. Kirkman, who not only worked on the movie but co-financed it as well; a series of trivia and "Fun Facts" about the film (basically everything you might—or might not—want to know about the production and participants); an essay by Gary Rhodes detailing "The Sun Demon: Its Drive-In World Premier" (previously published in this very magazine); a piece "About Robert Clarke," by later associate Wade Williams; a reproduction of the complete "Showmanship Manual" (i.e. pressbook); and more fascinating behind-the-scenes photos than you can shake a sunlamp at. But the meat of the matter are copies of not one but *two* film scripts: "Sauros," by Phil Hiner, the first incarnation of the story that was to become *The Hideous Sun Demon*; and the final script, called "The Sun Demon" and credited to E.S. Seeley, Jr. Leaving no sun-drenched stone unturned, Weaver prefaces these two screenplays with a list of differences between the shooting script and the final film, illustrating how low-budget moviemakers so often have to improvise on the fly.

Consequently, even if you're not a Sun (Demon) worshiper, there's plenty here to ignite one's interest (in fact, reading all these various bits and bobs induced me to re-visit the movie, something I probably would not have otherwise done). With publisher BearManor touting this book as "No. 1" in "The Scripts from the Crypt Collection," one can only wonder (and eagerly anticipate) what genre flick(s) will become "No. 2" (and 3 and 4...). Personally, I'm hoping for one of *my* '50s favorites to receive the Royal Weaver treatment, such as *The Monster That Challenged the World*, *I Was a Teenage Werewolf*, or *I Married a Monster from Outer Space*. Of course, nothing would induced me to do a little happy dance more than to see a whole tome devoted to *The*

Giant Gila Monster (though I'm not holding my breath on *that* one). Are you listening, Tom…?

THE HORROR HITS OF RICHARD GORDON
by Tom Weaver (2011; BearManor Media)

In this "Book-Length Interview" (as this tome's subtitle labels it), interviewer and chronicler extraordinaire Tom Weaver turns his inquisitive spotlight on producer Richard Gordon to illuminate the ins and outs and whys and wherefores of every genre picture Gordon worked on, from favorites like *Fiend Without a Face*, *The Haunted Strangler* and *Island of Terror* to exploitation oddities like *Secrets of Sex*, *Tower of Evil* and *Inseminoid*. And boy does Gordon—and this book—shine. I've had the very great pleasure of meeting and interviewing Richard Gordon myself on several occasions and found him to be one of the most pleasant and knowledgeable filmmaking professionals I've ever pointed a tape recorder at. Couple this with the insightful, organized, and good-humored interviewing techniques of Tom Weaver, and *The Horror Hits of Richard Gordon* becomes a must-have volume for every fantastique fan's bookshelf.

Richard Gordon was a very hands-on producer, as he was involved with everything from setting up a production's financing to hiring a crew and casting actors, all the way through to securing distribution and overseeing promotional campaigns for the finished product. And, most importantly, he was frequently on-set during production, leading to a plethora of behind-the-scenes anecdotes and reminiscences. Gordon truly loves movies and moviemaking (he often populated his films with actors he'd seen onscreen as a child and young adult), and it shows in every erudite word of his myriad detailed recollections, from his wonderful stories of Karloff and Lugosi to his amusing encounter with some MGM brass.

While Gordon's film-by-film recollections are the meat of the book, Weaver, like any great chef, adds various garnishes to set off this tasty tome, be they transcripts of often amusing radio advertising spots, a synopsis of the original short story upon which *Fiend Without a Face* was based, a series of "fun facts" about each film, or the amazing selection of rare photos.

The book's size, shape and design brought a nostalgic smile to this reviewer's face, as, whether intentional or not, it brought back memories of the old "Films of…" series of books published by the late, lamented Citadel Press back in the 1970s and '80s. *Horror Hits* hits all the right nostalgic notes, not only in the cinematic symphony that comprises Gordon's filmography, but also in the research and presentation departments. Sadly, Mr. Gordon passed away in late 2011, the same year of this book's publication; thankfully, it was not before he saw this excellent overview of his career in print. And now those fans of his work (and who among us reading this magazine doesn't love such Gordon productions as *Fiend Without a Face* and *Island of Terror*?)—even those who may not immediately recognize the name of the often-unsung Richard Gordon—have a fitting compendium that indeed proves to be a Horror Hit.

HOUSE OF DAN CURTIS: THE TELEVISION MYSTERIES OF THE DARK SHADOWS AUTEUR
by Jeff Thompson (2010; McFarland)

This follow-up book to author Jeff Thompson's excellent *The Television Horrors of Dan Curtis* fills in the less fright-minded blanks in Dan Curtis' career left by the first tome's particular focus on the filmmaker's "television horrors." While some overlap from the previous volume is naturally expected (and occurs) when writing about the creator of such seminal video fare as *Dark Shadows*, *The Night Stalker* and *Trilogy of Terror*, I was initially dismayed to see that Chapter One of *House of Dan Curtis* was titled "The Career of Dan Curtis: An Overview"—the *same exact* title as the first chapter of *Television Horrors*. Terms like "redundant" and "filler" immediately sprang to mind. My trepidation only increased when I realized that this repeated "Overview" took up nearly *half* the book! Yikes. Well, I'm happy to report that I needn't have worried. A consummate researcher and engaging writer, Thompson offers enough additional information, quotes, and perspective (this "Overview" is more than twice as long as that in the prior book) to make it well worth reading, even for those already possessing Thompson's first volume.

Beyond this expanded monograph, the main value of *House of Dan Curtis* comes from the tome's second half, which focuses on what Thompson very elastically categorizes as Curtis' "mysteries" (basically everything not thoroughly detailed in *Television Horrors*, whether truly "mysterious" or not). These include chapters on *Dead of Night: A Darkness at Blaisedon* (Curtis' failed attempt "to recreate [the daytime serial] *Dark Shadows* at night"); Curtis' two tele-movies about *Melvin Purvis, G-Man*; the seven *Wide World Mystery* episodes—*Frankenstein*, *The Picture of Dorian Gray*, *Shadow of Fear*, *The Invasion of Carol Enders*, *The Turn of the Screw*, *Come Die with Me* and *Nightmare at 43 Hillcrest*; Curtis' heist-comedy *The Great Ice Rip-Off*; a chapter on "Three Unsold Pilots"; and another detailing his two-part miniseries on alien abduction, *Intruders*. The final (fascinating) chapter covers the "Productions That Never Were."

While many of these "mystery" productions may hold less interest for the average horror fan, Thompson's thorough coverage of their making (sprinkling in plenty of illuminating quotes from participants) and infectious enthusiasm made this reviewer want to find and watch many of these lesser lights in Curtis' oeuvre (even some I'd never even heard of before). For the casual fan, *House of Dan Curtis* may be a bit too far from the horror mark, but for those willing to cast their viewing (and reading) nets a bit further afield, it makes for an informative companion volume to *The Television Horrors of Dan Curtis*.

KEEP WATCHING THE SKIES! AMERICAN SCIENCE FICTION MOVIES OF THE FIFTIES, THE 21ST CENTURY EDITION
by Bill Warren (2010; McFarland)

Way back in the day (the late '80s/early '90s anyway), I ran across two film books (well, technically three) that not only took their less-than-respected topics seriously, but applied a heretofore unprecedented level of (approachable) scholarship to them. These two inspirational works set the bar for my own entry into film history and criticism; the high level of passion, thoroughness, wit and craft shown by these tomes was something I aspired to in my own writings. The two books, if you hadn't guessed by now, were *Universal Horrors* (1990), by Michael Brunas, John Brunas and Tom Weaver, and the two-volume set of *Keep Watching the Skies!* (1982 and 1986), by Bill Warren. So imagine my elation to learn that Warren had completed an updated "21st Century Edition" of his classic treatise, filling in the unavoidable gaps caused by the dearth of material of the day (remember, the original was written *before* the big video boom of the mid-80s).

Warren's goal was to cover every science fiction (or even sci-fi-*tinged*) film released in America during the period 1950 to 1962. And that is a *lot* of movies. In fact, it took two volumes for him to achieve this goal the first time around, because Warren refused to take the easy route and just do a quick encyclopedic-style compendium of bite-sized entries. Nope, Warren devoted pages and pages to each and every movie, creating the most thorough critical reading of a film genre written up to that time. And it was chock full of production info, cast and crew bios, and quotes from contemporaneous reviews to add weight and context to his critical assessments, all written in an approachable and entertaining style. Well, now Warren has updated this amazing body of work, adding numerous bits and pieces gleaned from the voluminous research published in the intervening quarter century (such as the many invaluable interviews conducted by the prodigious Tom Weaver, whom Warren always appropriately credits) to paint an even more complete picture of one of the most beloved genres of cinema. And, of course, he has filled in the various omissions and inadequately-covered films that were simply not available for viewing back in the '70s and early '80s, making this updating a now-truly complete work.

"Every entry, every single one, has been rewritten," states Warren in his preface, and it's a claim that appears justified. And fortunately, for this new edition Warren hasn't lost the personable, engaging tone; meticulous thoroughness; or, most importantly, clever insight that made the original recipe so tasty back in the '80s. For instance, he posits an excellent general hypothesis about the appeal of these films to today's modern viewer. "Most 1950s movies of whatever genre reflect [an] undercurrent of optimism; perhaps the SF movies do so more than others. ... Buoyant optimism is hard to find in American entertainment today...almost everything is suffused with jaded cynicism; irony has become the dominant tone." Modern viewers, most of whom were not even born when these movies hit theaters, "aren't nostalgic for the film," says Warren, "but perhaps they're nostalgic for the underlying sense of optimism, since they can't find anything like it in contemporary films, other than animated comedies." The always fascinating text is complemented and enhanced by an excellent selection of truly intriguing photographs (273 of them, including 24 *color* pages of movie posters). With the book's glossy paper stock and a dust jacket sporting what is arguably the coolest film book cover ever conceived (courtesy of artist extraordinaire Kerry Gammill), McFarland has produced what can only be termed a thing of beauty.

One questionable change to this updated edition, however, is the rearranging of the entries into alphabetical rather than the original's chronological order. It's an unfortunate choice that denies the new edition the collective historical perspective of the first. In his otherwise insightful "Preface for the 21st Century Edition," Warren merely notes the change and flippantly offers, "So here's another movie reference book that begins with several films titled *Abbott and Costello...*" with no real explanation. So with no historical/temporal perspective to be gained any longer by reading the entries in order, I found myself simply skipping around as the mood took me. Admittedly, this is certainly a legitimate way to read a collection of essays on various films, but it makes for a less holistic—and less satisfying—reading experience.

The only other criticism I can muster about this landmark (re)work is the length of many of the synopses. This is a HUGE book (it damn near puts your legs to sleep if held in your lap), and long, uber-detailed plot rehashes make up a large part of many of the entries. Granted, during its original publication, a number of these films were harder to find than convincing special effects in a Bert I. Gordon flick, so an in-depth recounting of a movie's plot was a useful and necessary tool for most readers who didn't have the film in question at their fingertips. But now, in the 21st century, nearly all of the movies covered can be easily acquired with the click of a mouse button. I, for one, don't need 1300 words detailing the activities on *Voodoo Island* (which, curiously, is a completely *new* entry—it wasn't even included in Warren's original volume). I understand that in writing a critical essay you pretty much have to do some plot rehashing (points of reference and all that), but I say keep 'em short and compact so that the savvy reader can skip forward a column or two to the good stuff. With his entry on *The Day the Earth Stood Still*, Warren demonstrated that he was capable of doing just that—by deftly outlining the well-known story in a compact 150 words. This makes it all the more unfortunate that he most often chooses the opposite tack (for instance, taking over *ten times* that many words to recap the equally-well-known *Forbidden Planet*!). The book (and reader) would have been better served had Warren, during his revisions, boiled many of these now-unnecessarily lengthy synopses down to a few paragraphs, thus reducing the page count, the mammoth price tag, and the strain on our leg muscles. Still, this really is a relatively minor quibble, as there's plenty of critical and informative meat below this tome's synoptic fat, and it's really only a minor inconvenience to trim away the extraneous bits.

With its c-note price tag, *Keep Watching the Skies! The 21st Century Edition* is a book even hard-core fans have to think twice about buying. But for those who truly appreciate insightful, balanced and well-researched criticism on a body of film with undeniable appeal, it truly is a no-brainer. In short, it's simply the best book on '50s sci-fi cinema ever written.

MEXPLOITATION CINEMA: A CRITICAL HISTORY OF MEXICAN VAMPIRE, WRESTLER, APE-MAN AND SIMILAR FILMS, 1957-1977
by Doyle Greene (2005; McFarland)

Ever since I caught my first glimpse of Mexican monster movies over two decades ago on *Commander USA's Groovy Movies* Saturday afternoon show, I've been fascinated by that peculiar and enthralling subset of horror cinema. With its popularity and accessibility growing by leaps and bounds of late (thanks to enterprising DVD distributors), it's gratifying to see the film literature and analysis spotlight turned towards these South-of-the-Border wonders.

"This project will focus on how mexploitation films, as products of a specific time and place, are entertaining, insightful, and yes, important cultural documents that address the conditions, contradictions, and visions of contemporary Mexican society, politics, and culture," writes author Doyle Greene in his introduction to *Mexploitation Cinema*. And via chapters and subheadings with such titles as "Camp, Cheese, and Counter-Cinema," "Santo as 'National Allegory,'" and "From Chica Modernas to Wrestling Women" he does just that—in a clear, concise, and frequently fascinating fashion.

So many movie books these days seem to lack a cohesive center, or fail to make any intellectual point, focusing instead on listings and loose criticism (often of the far-too-fannish variety). That's why it's so refreshing to find a book like *Mexploitation Cinema*, particularly since it covers a field that hasn't already been plowed to death.

In his analyses, Doyle explains and explores the fascinating historical and political backdrop that influenced these seemingly "simple" monster movies, and in so doing demonstrates how they may not be so "simple" after all. For instance, he makes a compelling case for the beloved monster-fighting masked wrestler El Santo being "a symbol of the values of Mexican culture embodied in an iconic, masculine, and modern superhero—the good patriarch, the countermacho political stereotype, the tecnico-as-technocrat who selflessly intercedes on behalf of the Mexican public."

Be advised, however, that *Mexploitation Cinema* is not an all-inclusive encyclopedia-type book, and Doyle doesn't mention every horror that came down the Mexi-pike. But he does cover a large number of the better-known entries (including such favorites as *Santo vs. the Vampire Women*, *Wrestling Women vs. the Aztec Mummy*, *The Brainiac* and *Night of the Bloody Apes*) and, more importantly, analyzes them in relation to Mexican cinema and culture of the time (as well as tossing out fun facts and production info for those triviots among us).

"Mexploitation cinema can be seen as a strange, challenging 'counter-cinema,'" writes Doyle, "both dependent upon and yet dialectically opposed to Hollywood conventions. Mexploitation can also be seen as a cinema that reflects 'national concerns'…[such as] mexicanidad, modernity, and gender politics." Though some monster movie fans might groan at such seemingly pretentious statements, the author makes strong cases for these academic assumptions—and does so in a readable and enjoyable manner (with the occasional welcome shot of humor launched over the literary bow). And lest you think that this is some stuffy tome by a turn-down-your-nose academian wishing only to condescend to and intellectually eviscerate his subject, Doyle shows time and again great affection for—and appreciation of—his topic. "Perhaps, as absurd as it may initially sound, it is possible to posit that *The Brainiac* or *Night of the Bloody Apes* might one day be mentioned in the same breath as *Bride of Frankenstein* or *Psycho*," he asserts. Right on, amigo!

Admittedly, all the discussion of "mexicanidad" and "countermachos" might put off the casual Mexi-monster fan, but for those who wish to look (and think) a bit deeper into what makes these wonderful and often maddening monster movies worthwhile, *Mexploitation Cinema* can be an eye-opening and thought-provoking read. (And don't let the ten-dollar Mexi-terms put you off; Doyle explains each and every esoteric expression he uses in a direct and accessible fashion, so that by book's end you'll be slinging around phrases like "chicamodernas" and "comedias rancheras" with the best of 'em.)

By delving in-depth into a number of mexploitation movies, and showing how these relate to the social and political climate of the time (climaxing with the horrific 1968 Tlatelolco Square massacre—Mexico's own Tienamen Square–like debacle), Doyle convincingly demonstrates that these movies are far more than simple slices of Latino cheese.

MIND WARP! THE FANTASTIC *TRUE STORY* OF ROGER CORMAN'S NEW WORLD PICTURES

by Christopher T. Koetting (2009, Hemlock Books)

In the 1930s and '40s it was Universal; in the 1950s and '60s it was AIP ; and in the 1970s and '80s it was New World Pictures. These are the studios that stood at the forefront of genre exploitation, with Universal parlaying their various monsters into numerous franchises and mash-ups, AIP spearheading the teen-targeted terror (and later the Gothic revival in American horror with their Edgar Allan Poe series), and Roger Corman's New World springing such exploitation gems on an unsuspecting public as *Death Race 2000*, *Forbidden World*, and *Humanoids from the Deep*. At the close of the '60s, Roger Corman had grown tired of seeing others (re: AIP) make mountains of money off *his* movies and so decided to go into the distribution business himself. So Corman opened the doors of New World Pictures in 1970, appropriately situated on Sunset Boulevard across the street from a burlesque house.

In *Mind Warp!* author Christopher T. Koetting details every film New World either produced or distributed, from their blaxploitation and horror movies to their bigger-budgeted "prestige" pictures (like *Capone*) and Corman's brief love affair with art house fare (like Bergman's *Cries and Whispers* and Fellini's *Amarcord*). Koetting discusses each film in terms not only of its place in the (ahem) New World order, but its relative merits as cinema. He also includes brief bios of the principals involved, weaving a fascinating picture of Corman's influence on future filmmakers (and the industry in general). It's a breath of fresh air to find a writer who can restrain himself to penning concise, one-paragraph (or less) synopses and then get on with the real business at hand—detailing the film's merits (and demerits) and production history. And it's an even fresher blast to find a writer that can do all this in an engaging, approachable, and entertaining style, complete with clever transitions (no easy task, given the breadth of his subject matter—even within each chapter) and smooth prose that weaves the various anecdotes into a cohesive story of a man and his studio.

Over the course of 275 well-illustrated pages, Koetting creates an admirable overall picture of a supremely successful film company—and the man behind it, warts and all. Given that it's impossible to separate the two, *Mind Warp* is as much about Roger Corman as it is about New World. But this is no fannish love letter to Mr. Corman. While Koetting gives all credit where credit is due the innovative filmmaker-turned-savvy businessman, he's unafraid to point out Corman's sometimes less-than-stellar proclivities. For instance, he fully covers Corman's frequent meddling with (even butchering of) films New World distributed, as well as his downright disingenuous attitude towards it. He quotes Corman saying, "We have occasionally made cuts in films, but we always make them in cooperation with the producer and the director. We never cut somebody else's film." Koetting's blunt response to this? "Mel Welles, Tamara Assayev, Curtis Hanson, Oscar Williams, Ernest R. von Theumer (director of *The Big Bust Out*) and now Cheng Cheh begged to differ. The list would only grow larger in the years ahead." And, refreshingly, Koetting details exactly *why* all these filmmakers "beg to differ."

At other times Koetting (rightly) defends Corman against his detractors. For example, he writes, "Over the years, [Paul] Bartel, [Chuck] Griffith, Joe Dante and others have maintained that what was now to become *Death Race 2000* was, in Dante's words to Gray, 'a real pop art masterpiece before Roger got to it.' Corman supposedly 'ruined' the film in post-production by cutting down the humor and increasing the graphic violence. But an examination of the shooting script by Griffith puts the lie to this. Nearly all of the humor in the script is present in the film—and most of the acts of violence in the film are present in the script as well. In fact, there is actually *more* humor in the film than there is in the script." It all makes for a very fair and balanced portrayal.

Koetting definitely did his homework while researching his subject, as he constantly inserts illuminating, pertinent quotes from the productions' main participants (as well as from the head man himself); snippets of contemporary reviews to illustrate a film's reception; and production facts and figures to show how each movie performed in regards to that all-important bottom line. The only disappointment comes from Koetting's lack of *original* research. Though he includes plenty of diverse quotes from secondary sources (and appropriately assigns credit), he apparently conducted no original interviews himself. So while he does a great job of collecting and collating in order to paint his New World Picture, it feels somewhat second-hand. And one other thing: If you go to all the trouble to create such an indispensable work, why oh why oh why wouldn't you index the thing and make it a truly *useful* one? Now, I know first-hand the tedium of indexing, but it makes a non-fiction book so much more user-friendly. It's a real disappointment that Koetting took the lazy route and short-changed his readers in this regard.

But even with these caveats, *Mind Warp!* still remains a well-written, engaging, and informative look at one of filmdom's true originals and the cinematic empire he built.

MUCHAS GRACIAS SENOR LOBO: PAUL NASCHY MEMORABILIA
by Thorsten Benzel (2012; Creepy Images)

If you've never heard of Paul Naschy, then this book will hold limited interest for you. (Of course, such a notion begs the question "Why *haven't* you?") But... if you've ever spent a slack-jawed 90 minutes watching *Assignment Terror* on your local TV affiliate at 1 a.m., or brought home a big clam-shell VHS box of *Frankenstein's Bloody Terror* to pop into your old top-loading VCR, or (more recently) inserted a shiny new disc into your DVD player only to sit mesmerized by the sheer strangeness of *Hunchback of the Morgue* or the melancholy madness of *Count Dracula's Great Love* or the wintry creepiness of *Horror Rises from the Tomb*, then *Muchas Gracias Senor Lobo* will be right up your Eurohorror alley.

Spain's Paul Naschy is the combined Christopher Lee and Peter Cushing of Continental cinema. In fact, to carry the Hammer analogy further, he's also the Terence Fisher (or at least Freddie Francis) of Eurohorror because, in addition to starring in over thirty terror films (in which he plays everything from werewolves and mummies to hunchbacks and vampires), he also directed over a dozen of the features himself.

A professed lover of Gothic horror in general and the Universal classics in particular, Naschy almost single-handedly began a Gothic revival in Spanish cinema in the late 1960s and '70s with his scripting, acting in, and ultimately direction of the Waldemar Daninsky/Werewolf series begun with 1968's *Mark of the Wolfman* (aka *Frankenstein's Bloody Terror*). While the plots are sometimes trite, the production values often suspect, the acting usually bad, and the dubbing always awful, Naschy's films evince an eccentric enthusiasm, and appeal in a quirky, almost quaintly exploitative fashion that no American or British-produced horror film of the same era can duplicate.

What sets Naschy's movies apart from (and *above*) the often mean-spirited and cynically exploitative product of his contemporary countrymen (such as Jess Franco) is Naschy's respect and outright affection for the cinematic horror tradition. Though Naschy's budget-conscious journeys into Gothic fantasy are no better cinematically than much of the genre Eurotrash of these decades, their story lines possess an appealing dose of almost wistful nostalgia—spiced, of course, with the requisite dashes of sex and blood.

In his introduction to this book, German author Thorsten Benzel, who has been collecting Naschy material for over 20 years, observes that "thanks to the DVD boom of the past decade, many of Paul Naschy's movies have again become available to a larger public. At the same time, though, the advertising materials that were once used to promote these films around the globe have vanished into oblivion." And it is Benzel's mission to rectify that. As he explains, "First and foremost, this book is meant to entertain the reader, but beyond that, I hope that it will also help to conserve a small part of that history of the European cinema for further generations."

Benzel writes, "While today's advertising campaigns are fairly identical worldwide, the world of movie promotion was much more colorful and exciting in the 1960s and '70s. Distributors in different countries created their own advertising materials and their own artwork, and often enough they would even change a movie's title to meet the expectations of their country's audience." With that in mind, Benzel takes us on a "journey through a lost world of movie advertising, the likes of which we'll not see again." Said journey begins in 1968 and travels through 1988 via nearly 400 oversized, glossy, full-color pages of image after astounding image (over 1200!) covering Naschy's thirty primary fantastique films (plus an additional dozen pages of material from many of the actor's other, lesser movie appearances). Posters, lobby cards, stills, ad mats, campaign manuals, sales brochures, and even magazine and book covers from multiple countries—not only the expected U.S., U.K., and Continental nations (like Austria, Belgium, Denmark, Finland, France, Germany, Italy, Spain, Sweden, Turkey, and Yugoslavia), but Argentina, Australia, Canada, Columbia, Mexico, Pakistan, and Thailand—veritably leap from the pages like a crazed Waldemar during the full moon. Each of the 30 chapters begins with an essay detailing the history of the film's distribution in various countries, followed by an amazing array of beautifully reproduced images. The text, first presented in German, then in English, is sparse but informative—at least on the advertising and distribution side. For instance, I learned that the Spanish poster for *La Marca del Hombre Lobo* (*Mark of the Wolfman*) that I've had up on my home office wall for years is actually a reissue from 1976 (the only difference from the original 1968 poster being the company logo in the upper left corner). The text offers very little production information, however, nor any real critical examination of the movies themselves. But that's not what this book is about, for *Muchas Gracias Senor Lobo* is a visual love-letter to the films of Paul Naschy, put together by, and aimed at, fans of the prolific Spanish filmmaker's work.

The book also includes such unique treats as a touching and humanizing introduction by Naschy's son Sergio, Naschy's own werewolf makeup sketches, "Facts" and "Trivia" sidebars regarding the films' release and promotion, and a handy memorabilia glossary of terms detailing poster production and sizes, country by country.

Paul Naschy died in 2009, but his cinematic legacy lives on. For producing this handsome and astoundingly detailed visual chronicle of the often convoluted and sometimes tortuous film career of Jacinto Molina Alvarez, ne Paul Naschy, one can only cry, "Muchas Gracias Senor Benzel!"

NO TRAVELER RETURNS: THE LOST YEARS OF BELA LUGOSI
by Gary D. Rhodes and Bill Kaffenberger
(2012; BearManor Media)

With the poignantly-named *No Traveler Returns*, Lugosi scholar extraordinaire Gary D. Rhodes teams up with Bill Kaffenberger to bring us a detailed treatise of just what exactly "Mr. Dracula" (as so much of his publicity labeled him) was up to in the lean postwar years of 1946 through 1951. Well, it turns out that said years were not quite so lean as has been believed, with Lugosi keeping busy (and solvent) via a variety of venues and media. Through newspaper accounts, personal and professional letters, reminiscences, and what must have been countless hours of painstaking detective work into the minutiae of local press and regional theaters, Rhodes and Kaffenberger take their readers on a fascinating journey that at times puts us right alongside Bela, his wife Lillian, and even their pre-teen son Bela Jr. (who contributes a brief but affecting afterword to the book) as they travel, sometimes hundreds of miles in a single day, in their Pontiac roadster from one summer stock or vaudeville venue to the next, giving the locals what they want—Lugosi as *Dracula* (or Jonathan Brewster in revivals of *Arsenic and Old Lace*). Then there were the occasional radio and television engagements, the personal appearances and "lectures," the various "spook show" appearances (including "The Bela Lugosi Horror and Magic Stage Show"), and, of course, the infrequent movie work in films such as *Scared to Death* (1946) and *Abbott and Costello Meet Frankenstein* (1948).

Through it all, the authors paint an intriguing portrait of a man whose name, face and voice were all over America at the time due to continual re-issues of his films in theaters and on television, yet who had to scramble to make a living traveling all over America when Hollywood turned its back on him. The trials and tribulations (and occasional triumphs) Lugosi experienced during this time are all chronicled here in this amazingly detailed account that's littered with first-hand reports and personal letters (many of them reproduced, along with a plethora of rare ads, promo materials, and photos, both official and candid). And through it all comes the image of a hard-working, caring, considerate actor who literally went that extra mile to support his family. Laudably, it's no whitewash job, however, as the authors aren't afraid to include a few unflattering reports as well, revealing the all-too-human side of this intriguing "traveler."

Like much of BearManor's output, *No Traveler Returns* could have done with some judicious copy editing to correct misspellings (there are *two* "L"s in "Edgar Allan Poe," for instance), the occasional ambiguous pronoun, and some repetitive verbiage in its rather unspectacular prose. But these are minor quibbles readily eased by the reasonable price tag of this clear, concise, and straightforward recounting of a fascinating time for a fascinating actor.

PERVERSE TITILLATION: THE EXPLOITATION CINEMA OF ITALY, SPAIN AND FRANCE, 1960-1980
by Danny Shipka (2011; McFarland)

The first words you read upon opening *Perverse Titillation: The Exploitation Cinema of Italy, Spain and France, 1960-1980* are these: "To all of those who have received grief for their entertainment choices and who see the study of weird and wacky films as important to understanding our popular culture." Now *that* is my kind of dedication. Who among us readers of this magazine can fail to relate? Author Danny Shipka means it, too, as evidenced from the get-go of this well-written chronicle of "Eurocult" cinema. For me personally, European exploitation films (what my enthusiastic film-loving buddies and I like to call "Eurotrash"—everything from Euro-gothics to giallos to Eurospy to krimis) have taken up a goodly portion of my viewing time over the past two decades, as I've explored one Euro-avenue after another. I find it to be a fascinating new-old cinematic roadway, and one that hasn't been mapped to death by genre scholars as yet. It's always good (and validating) to see the films you love receiving some positive attention; and when you're a lover of Eurotrash, it's downright fantastic.

I've often wondered just why I find Eurocult films so enthralling (nostalgic-tinged affinity, perhaps, as I lived in Europe for a time?), and Shipka offers at least some of the answers. As he goes about detailing the history and appeal of everything from cannibal and mondo flicks to nunsploitation and Paul Naschy movies, he offers such illuminating observations as: "European horror was different. I wasn't aware of the culture so I was always caught off guard when the plot would unfold. The different perspective put me at a disadvantage so I felt more vulnerable as a viewer, never knowing what to expect or how it would be portrayed on the screen." In other words, to American viewers raised on the tried-and-true tropes of Hollywood horror and slasher cinema, it seemed that Eurocult flicks were those in which anything could and did happen. They were unpredictable, unusual, odd—and, because of all that (and much more), exciting.

Shipka offers many perceptive observations. Regarding the transition from the cannibal flick to the "gut-munching zombie film" in Italian cinema, for instance, Shipka writes: "The zombie resonates on the idea that these 'others' bring with them disease that will effectively destroy all of society. Whether this disease be this [previously discussed] lack of religious conviction, commercialism, globalization, environmentalism, or products of war, the zombie film manifests the fear people have of a changing world. This fear can be eliminated by gleefully gunning down, video-game style, the hordes of zombies that populate the film. Without the burden of humanity that the cannibal subgenre was forced to deal with, the effective eradication of zombies is a simple, mindless pleasure audiences can take part in." With this short passage, Shipka captures the essence and appeal of the zombie subgenre in a clear, concise and insightful manner. I love this thoughtful, intelligent approach to a cinematic subset that has too often been dismissed as so much Eurojunk. While these films are indeed exploitative, they also offer plenty of, ahem, food for thought, and Shipka masticates with relish.

But what's really great about his book is that Shipka places these movies—and Eurofilm trends in general—in the cultural context of the times, bringing background and meaning to these cinematic subsets. It's a refreshingly intelligent approach to a type of cinema that, frankly, hasn't received the attention it deserves. In short, he details (in an approachable and winning style) how and why these fascinating films came to be.

The book is well laid-out. After an informative introduction, he divides the tome into three sections:

Italy, Spain and France. And each of these are broken down into myriad subsections. For Example, the Italy chapter includes (among others): "*I vampiri*: Italian Genre Beginnings"; "The '60s: A Return to Gothic"; "It's a Mondo World"; "The Color of Fear: The Italian Giallo"; "We Will Eat You: The Cannibal and Zombie Film"; and "Sexploitation: Italia Style." Though the chapters on Spain and France are not quite so extensive, they still offer numerous subsets, including in-depth sections on such iconic exploitation auteurs as Jess Franco, Paul Naschy and Jean Rollin. Following each individual section is a "Filmography" that offers specific capsule reviews of the movies mentioned in the section (plus some additional outliers). These allow Shipka's inner fan to really shine through, as he lets loose with a volley of humorous and tell-it-like-it-is assessments. As Shipka explains in his introduction, "When writing a book like this the question always arises: should the author take the scholarly approach, exploring themes and history outside the confines of what is actually on celluloid ('Boring,' says the casual Eurocult fan), or should he take the approach of a fan who loves these films and wants to share in spreading the fun ('You prove nothing,' says the academic). My thought is, let's do both!" Shipka does indeed do both—and exceedingly well.

Well illustrated with pertinent posters and ads for the films, the book's only fault is an overabundance of minor grammatical mistakes. Much like the movies it explores, the text is littered with numerous superficial flaws (e.g., "...most importantly, audiences interest in these films..."). More rigorous copy editing on the publisher's part could have easily corrected such minor annoyances; but this is a tiny quibble and shouldn't deter anyone with an interest in unusual cinema from purchasing such a unique and valuable tome. After reading the highly entertaining *Perverse Titillation*, I came away with a better and more cohesive view of Eurocult cinema. Like the best of the films it covers, *Perverse Titillation* proves both entertaining and enlightening. What more could a mondo-horror-zombie-cannibal-devil-loving film fanatic ask for?

REGIONAL HORROR FILMS, 1958-1990: A STATE-BY-STATE GUIDE WITH INTERVIEWS
by Brian Albright (2012; McFarland)

Question: What do *The Horror of Party Beach* (1965), *The Legend of Boggy Creek* (1972), and *The Evil Dead* (1981) all have in common? Answer: They're all "regional horror films"—i.e., non–Hollywood independent productions largely made with local cast and crew (in Connecticut, Arkansas and Tennessee, respectively). And with this unique, informative and entertaining book, author Brian Albright focuses exclusively on these sometimes amateurish, occasionally striking, but always colorful indies from around the country, including everything from the obscure (*Sting of Death*) to the groundbreaking (*Blood Feast*) to the notorious (*I Spit on Your Grave*). In his introduction, Albright writes, "Once you watch enough of these movies (and believe me, there were times when I thought to myself, 'I have watched enough of these movies...') you also start to recognized the distinct local flavor present in each one. There is a certain look and feel to the horror movies made in Texas or Florida that not only couldn't be duplicated in Hollywood, but that also couldn't be duplicated in Mississippi or Louisiana or Wisconsin." Indeed, any bleary-eyed viewer who's run across a late-night Larry Buchanan Texas terror or sat slack-jawed as North Carolina producer/actor Earl Owensby's *Wolfman* played across the TV screen can certainly relate. The thing is, though, *Regional Horror Films* is neither your typical masters-thesis scholarly tome (pontificating on the oedipal thematics of Kentucky killer flicks, for instance) nor a collection of critical reviews (which, the author points out, "are a dime a dozen" in this internet age). Instead, this is a book in two parts, the first being a fascinating collection of a baker's dozen in-depth interviews with regional filmmakers. Did you ever wonder how Florida filmmaker William Grefe came up with a flick about a *jellyfish man*? Ever ponder the political underpinnings of *Werewolf of Washington*? Or have you ever asked yourself, "How can I get an entire town to band together to make a monster movie like they did in Milpitas?" Well, it's all in here, in fascinating (and often amusing) detail.

The book's second section, "The Films," is a state-by-state listing of horror movies produced by locals around the country, everything from *Valley of Blood* in Alabama to *Wendigo* in Wyoming. It's astounding to see that nearly every state of the union is well represented in the indy horror arena (though, much to my dismay, my own state of Washington joins the likes of Idaho, Maine and North Dakota as homegrown horror slackers). Each entry consists of basic credits, a one or two-sentence synopsis, and some information/trivia about the film and/or filmmakers. "I've tried to take a 'just the facts' approach," writes Albright. While some may find this brevity and lack of critical analysis rather disappointing, a detailed account of each and every movie would have turned the volume into an astronomically-priced boat anchor. As is, Albright includes enough tasty tidbits and fun facts to keep the reader engaged (and chuckling), while piquing one's interest in tracking down some of these titles for him or herself. As Albright writes, "What I really wanted to create with this book was a primer; a guidebook to map out some otherwise poorly documented genre acreage. Each of you is going to pick and choose which twisted paths to follow, just as I have." And writing with good humor in an approachable, engaging, and even breezy style, he succeeds admirably. Now I'm off to track down a copy of the Louisiana-lensed *Nutriaman: Terror in the Swamp*…

SHOWMEN, SELL IT HOT! MOVIES AS MERCHANDISE IN GOLDEN ERA HOLLYWOOD
by John McElwee (2013; Paladin Communications)

An oversized, well-produced coffee-table book, *Showmen, Sell It Hot!* is about the sizzle rather than the steak, as it details the ins and outs and ups and downs of a bevy of screen classics and how they were sold to—and were received by—the moviegoing public of the time. Serving up a variety of choice cinematic cuts, author John McElwee begins in the Silent era with the salvaging/selling of Erich von Stroheim's eviscerated *Greed*, and ends with the 1967 "new cinema" phenom *Bonnie and Clyde*. McElwee focuses on the impact these films had on audiences at the time, and indeed upon pop culture of the day, via dollar figures, play dates, ballyhoo campaigns, and reactions from not only the critics but the all-important exhibitors themselves, with theater owners and managers giving thumbs up or down based upon the only truly objective way to evaluate a movie's success—the box office take. Along the way we masticate over how Fred Astaire was introduced to the public in *Flying Down to Rio*, how MGM turned Jean Harlow's premature death into a ghoulish money tree with *Saratoga*, how *Dracula* paired with *Frankenstein* to revive the horror genre, why *Stagecoach* wasn't the massive success one thinks of today, how RKO failed in their desperate bid to make the ahead-of-its-time *Citizen Kane* appealing to an indifferent public, and how exhibitors balked at Hitchcock's see-it-from-the-beginning mandate for *Psycho*—a successful publicity gambit that forever changed the way theaters operated and how patrons went to the movies. Further chapters detail the selling of such films as the Marx Bros.' *A Night at the Opera*, *The Wizard of Oz* (which didn't even make back its massive cost until subsequent reissues), *Sunset Boulevard*, *Ace in the Hole*, *On the Waterfront*, wartime propaganda pieces such as John Wayne's *Flying Tigers* and Humphrey Bogart's *Across the Pacific*, the hugely successful teaming of *The Public Enemy* and *Little Caesar*, and the James Dean phenomenon. A highlight is an excellent chapter on Val Lewton's output and his films' public reception. Another chapter recounts how the mighty 1933 blockbuster *Kong Kong* earned even more in its various re-releases than during its initial run. And horror fans will find additional interest in chapters on *Brides of Dracula* and *Whatever Happened to Baby Jane*.

McElwee employs a clipped, hyperbole-filled writing style in emulation of the trade mags and materials he so obviously pored over and loves (phrasing like "unusually sock for two oldies" abounds). Though overdramatic at times, his purple prose seems almost fitting given the book's subject matter, adding (much like the original ballyhoo itself) to the entertainment factor. And McElwee is unafraid to add the personal touch, recounting his days spent at his local North Carolina movie palace as a child, and his encounters with the exhibitors and operators throughout the South.

Page after page of eye-popping ads and heralds, and a plethora of amazing ballyhoo photos of theaters dressed to the nines in posters and lobby displays, makes one long for the days when exhibitors emphasized the "show" in showmanship. For those interested in exploring a lesser-known but supremely important side of the movie biz—namely, how great (and lesser) films were sold—*Showmen, Sell It Hot!* is (in the parlance of the day) a scorcher.

THE TELEVISION HORRORS OF DAN CURTIS: DARK SHADOWS, THE NIGHT STALKER, AND OTHER PRODUCTIONS, 1966-2006
by Jeff Thompson (2009; McFarland).

Most genre fans of my generation have them: memories of running home from school to catch the next installment of that oh-so-peculiarly-unique daytime soap opera *Dark Shadows*, on which all manner of ghosts, ghouls, vampires, werewolves and zombies cavorted in front of the teleprompters. Then there's the image of investigative reporter Carl Kolchak, his porkpie hat perched on his brash and inquisitive noggin' as he verbally spars with authorities (and his own apoplectic editor) or physically battles a vicious vampire in Vegas in *The Night Stalker* (*the* most successful made-for-TV movie to date). And who can forget that ferocious little Zuni fetish doll chasing Karen Black around her apartment with a steak knife, and her final evil toothy grin at the shuddery conclusion of *Trilogy of Terror*? Such seminal moments in television horror history can be put down to one man: producer-director-writer-creator Dan Curtis, who, in the 1960s and '70s, became the undisputed King of TV Horror. Curtis secured his crown with a plethora of television "events," including the (arguably superior) sequel *The Night Strangler*; critically-lauded TV adaptations of *The Strange Case of Dr. Jekyll and Mr. Hyde, Frankenstein, The Picture of Dorian Gray, Dracula* (with Jack Palance) and *The Turn of the Screw*; and the lesser-known (though not always lesser) television terrors *The Norliss Tapes, Scream of the Wolf, Dead of Night*, and *Curse of the Black Widow*. Finally, there's Curtis' big-screen outings: *House of Dark Shadows, Night of Dark Shadows*, and the truly terrifying (and underrated) *Burnt Offerings*. For over a decade Dan Curtis seemingly single-handedly made the airwaves both a frightening and literate place.

Now this genre luminary (who passed away in 2006) finally has a book to chronicle his considerable video and cinematic feats. Author Jeff Thompson has spun his doctoral dissertation on the works of Dan Curtis into an informative and surprisingly approachable tome. I say "surprisingly" because I've read my fair share of scholarly theses and know all about the pretensions, self-importance, and minutiae that academics can become so engrossed in that they lose sight of the forest for the trees. (I was involved in numerous research projects, presentations and papers during my academic career, and witnessed no end of petty jealousies, infighting, back-biting, and assorted silliness.) Consequently, dissertations can be some of *the* most excruciating things to read on the planet. Fortunately, Thompson has managed to avoid these many pitfalls to deliver a highly readable, insightful and enjoyable treatise on the life and career of an often-overlooked pillar of the horror film community. While the book (rightly) focuses on Curtis' terror productions (with self-explanatory chapters like "Curtis' Dream: Dark Shadows," "Curtis and the Classics," "The Kolchak Papers," and "A Trilogy of Trilogies of Terror"), Thompson also details the fascinating story of how Curtis brought WWII into millions of Americans' living rooms night after night with the mega-miniseries *The Winds of War* and *War and Remembrance* (a truly staggering feat that "was the equivalent of making 18 motion pictures back to back," as noted by co-producer Barbara Steele). Thompson even adds a personal touch with his final chapter, "Dan Curtis and the Emergence of Participatory Fan Culture," which details the rise of the *Dark Shadows* convention phenomenon and various fan activities surrounding this legendary soap opera (and in which Thompson himself has actively participated for nearly three decades).

However, like *Dark Shadows* itself (affectionately dubbed "Mike Shadows" by wags in reference to its frequent gaffs), this book is not without its flaws. Thompson's boundless admiration and enthusiasm appears to have put blinders on his critical faculties, as he hasn't a bad word for *any* Curtis production. And when an author brings out the old "so-bad-it's-good" sobriquet (as Thompson does for *Curse of the Black Widow*), you know he's watching this one through rose-colored lenses. While Thompson includes a plethora of illuminating quotes, anecdotes and observations from various Curtis cohorts (including such genre faves as John Karlen, Karen Black, and Barbara Steele), most of this is culled from previously-published interviews. But these minor quibbles are far over*Shadowed* (ouch) by his comprehensive approach, and Thompson manages to judiciously shape reams of research material into a cohesive whole that paints a vivid portrait of the man and his films. In short, no fan of the golden age of TV terror should be without this book.

URBAN TERRORS: NEW BRITISH HORROR CINEMA, 1997-2008
by M. J. Simpson (2012; Hemlock Books)

When one thinks of British horror cinema, thoughts immediately turn to the Hammer films made from the mid-1950s to early 1970s (as well as those produced by their tag-along cousins Amicus and Tigon). But after the famous studio closed shop in the mid-1970s, what then? Following Hammer's heyday, the British horror film went into something akin to cinematic hibernation. English author M. J. Simpson posits that British horror is back—and with a vengeance. Starting in the late 1990s, Merrie Olde England began producing horror movies at an increasingly rapid pace. As he notes in the book's introduction, "At the end of the 1990s, there were, on average, three British horror films released each year. A decade later, that number had increased tenfold." And these films offered a decidedly new slant—by replacing the crumbling Gothic castles of Hammer horrors with the urban (and suburban) sprawl of modern Gothicism. "The British Horror Revival grew over time to encompass many things," writes Simpson, "but its core titles, its most interesting and notable movies, have all explored life in contemporary Britain. Urban Gothic begat Suburban Gothic, Rural Gothic, Corporate Gothic and, of course, Hoodie Horror. In all of these, 21st century Britain was not just background but intrinsic to the story and the characters."

Employing a clear, intelligent and approachable writing style, Simpson details in *Urban Terrors: New British Horror Cinema, 1997–2008* the production, merits (or lack thereof) and cinematic place of 114 British horror films released over a 12-year period, from 1997 to 2008. Simpson places each film in the context of the British horror movie industry, includes quotes from the principals involved, and writes of its critical reception (and importance), citing reviews both in the mainstream press and genre-focused outlets (magazines and internet sites). Simpson also offers his own opinions on the films—and doesn't pull any punches when a flick's a stinker (even citing "Sturgeon's Law," which maintains that "ninety percent of everything is crap"). For every *Shaun of the Dead* or *28 Days Later*, for instance, there's a dozen lesser (or even *un*) known Brit films. And that's what makes this book so intriguing, informative and valuable—at least to a cinema Anglophile like myself (reading this book induced me to seek out a number of British obscurities, searching for that diamond in the Brit-rough).

A short-but-sweet Forward by horror fan turned actor Sean (*Dog Soldiers*, *Wilderness*) Pertwee (who cites Robert Wise's classic *The Haunting* as "a firm favourite") is just icing on this Brit-cake. And though a smallish-format book of less than 300 pages, *Urban Terrors* is illustrated with plenty of pertinent photos (including eight pages of color shots).

In his "Epilogue," Simpson notes that the British Horror Revival did not end in 2008. In fact, over 50 entries were released in 2010 alone. So why stop in 2008? Well, as Simpson writes, "extending the content of this book up to its delivery date [in 2012] would have more than doubled the number of films covered"; and "keeping track of all these pictures, let alone actually watching them, would be a full-time job." Hmmm. Difficult, perhaps, but not impossible (this reviewer covered more films than that—366 to be exact—in my book *A Year of Fear*). This rather arbitrary incompleteness, coupled with the fact that Simpson fails to include an index (a real no-no to this reviewer's way of thinking, for such an omission makes a film book much less useful than it could have been), makes one wish that Simpson had applied a bit more industry to go along with his obvious knowledge of, and enthusiasm for, the subject. Even so, *Urban Terrors* remains a valuable, even groundbreaking inaugural work on a little-covered subset of modern horror cinema.

THE WEIRD WORLD OF EERIE PUBLICATIONS
by Mike Howlett (2010; Feral House)

In the magazine publishing industry of the 1960s and '70s, the only thing hotter than *Playboy* and its imitators were horror rags. Local newsstands were flooded not only with monster movie periodicals like *Famous Monsters of Filmland* and *Castle of Frankenstein*, but horror comic magazines as well. Sure, the likes of Warren's *Creepy* and *Eerie* set the standard, but plenty of other publishers jumped on the horror-comic bandwagon to produce magazine-sized morsels of the macabre designed to separate teens and pre-teens from their hard-earned quarters. One such knock-off company was Eerie Publications (not to be confused with the Warren magazine named *Eerie*).

With impossibly lurid covers, filled with snarling monsters, gruesome gore (bloody decapitations and gooey entrails abound), and scantily-clad damsels in distress (and sometimes dismemberment), the cheaply-produced Eerie magazines were a hit. Their cover graphics and titles, like *Weird*, *Tales of Voodoo*, *Witches' Tales*, *Terror Tales*, and *Tales from the Tomb*, were cannily designed to appeal to one's inner sixth-grader. How could any horror-loving lad (or lass) resist a mummy staking a werewolf biting a sexy vampiress? Or one in which a living skeleton bloodily dispatches one vampire while a werewolf stakes another? Never mind that these traffic-stopping covers had absolutely nothing to do with the stories inside—primarily comprised of a series of (sometimes sub-par) pre-code horror comic reprints from the fifties. Fortunately, towards the end of the 1960s, the Eerie in-house editors and artists began beefing up a few panels with some blood splashes and gore (one artist was especially fond of adding gruesome "ripped cheeks" to victims, for instance). "The formula was simple," explains author Mike Howlett in *The Weird World of Eerie Publications*. "Pick a story from a pre-code horror comic and photocopy it. Get the copy to an artist with instructions to redraw the art, making it gorier and more horrific. Some artists ran with that concept and reinterpreted the art and panel layout, often improving the storytelling of the original. Others simply took the easy route and redrew the same thing, panel for panel."

In his forward, Howlett proclaims, "I enjoy [Eerie publications] for what they are: fun, cheap, gratuitous and entertaining. Some of my favorite films could be called the same thing: *Tombs of the Blind Dead* (1971), *The Gore-Gore Girls* (1972), *Werewolf vs. the Vampire*

Woman (1972), Hammer horrors, Santo flicks, and countless Italian zombie movies. I defy anyone to watch the finale of the Paul Naschy flick *Hunchback of the Morgue* (1973) and tell me that the battle between the hunchback and the primordial creature in an underground laboratory, with Rosanna Yanni laying prone in the foreground, doesn't look like an Eerie Pubs cover come to life." Ok, already I'm in Mr. Howlett's corner, as many of those cinematic trash-treats he cites are some of *my* favorite films as well. And anyone who draws on the name (and films) of Paul Naschy for an analogy is A-ok in my book.

Howlett, writing in an open and entertaining style, jumps in to explain just why this much-maligned subset of the horror comics/magazine boom is actually a worthy one (resulting in this beautifully-illustrated tome). "Look, I'm not an idiot," he candidly states. "I realize that [Eerie artist] Bill Alexander is no Frank Frazetta, and Oscar Fraga is no Berni Wrightson. Warren and Skywald magazines are timeless; their artwork is as valid today as it was in the '70s. Eerie Pubs, on the other hand, are now being appreciated (in 'mainstream' circles at least) as nostalgic and kitschy, a product of their time; a throwback to something that could never fly today. They were (and are) down and dirty, like 42nd Street in the '70s: dirty and dangerous."

The book begins with a concise history of horror comics, and how Eerie Publications came to be. Then comes the meat of the matter—the history of the company and its founder, Myron Fass, a man fond of brandishing a loaded pistol in his office and taking target practice down the hall(!). Howlett also details how Eerie and its parent company, Countrywide Publishers, did far more than simply flood the market with cheap horror comics; they produced crime magazines, girly mags (including an early *Playboy* knockoff called *Jaguar*), special-interest publications (with titles like *Dogs*, *Cycle*, and *Masters of Self-Defense*) and various one-shots (such as the bizarre *Nixon Cockeyed*, featuring "The Most Shocking Pictures of Pat Ever Published"[!]). It all makes for a highly engrossing—and amusing—recounting of what no doubt many of us Monster-Boomers hold near and dear to our nostalgia-loving hearts.

Reading this fascinating story of the company and its participants (particularly its trigger-happy head honcho) inspired me to seek out a number of these tawdry treasures to have a look-see for myself. And while I can't say all (or even many) of the stories inside were completely satisfying, each issue I read had at least *something* to tickle my horror-bone. And the covers... well, so many of them are worth the price of admission alone. Amazingly, this gorgeously-produced book shows you *all* of them in full color (one entire chapter is devoted to a "Cover Gallery").

About the only fly in this Eerie ointment is a largely pointless intro by comics artist Stephen R. Bissette consisting of an "ironic" diatribe against the shoddy subject; it simply doesn't work.

Rounding out the book are mini-biographies of all the principal players at Eerie (editors, artists, and even hangers-on like Myron's older brother Irving), a number of useful appendices, and even a brand new comic story by Eerie artist/writer extraordinaire Dick Ayers, commissioned especially for this book. Who in all the *Weird World* could possibly ask for more?

THE WORST OF EERIE PUBLICATIONS
by Mike Howlett (2014; IDW Publishing)

"Eerie Publications came into existence for one reason: to cash in on the popularity of Warren's *Creepy* magazine." So begins author Mike Howlett's detailed and enthusiastic introduction to *The Worst of Eerie Publications*. A companion volume to Howlett's earlier *The Weird World of Eerie Publications*, it adds little to that amazingly thorough and fully fascinating history in terms of information. But what it *does* bring to the Eerie table are 21 of the original (or, most often, *not-so-original*) stories lovingly reprinted (and gorgeously restored) for one's ravenous reading pleasure.

Beginning in 1965, Eerie Publications offered a line of cheaply-made horror comic magazines chock full of gory tales of infidelity and bloody revenge (often from beyond the grave). Most of *Weird*'s, *Tales of Voodoo*'s, *Horror Tales*', *Tales from the Tomb*'s, et al's stories were actually dressed-up reprints pilfered (without credit) from the less-well-known ranks of 1950s pre-Code horror comics. Eerie boss Myron Fass (a fascinating character [ouch] fond of wearing a loaded pistol in the office) would "supply photocopy pages from old comics and present them to the artist, with instructions to make them gorier and more prurient." And that they did, adding graphic renderings of bones poking through limbs, eyeballs flying from sockets, and flesh gruesomely ripped from cheeks (a trademark of Eerie stalwart Ezra Jackson). While the quality of both the art and the stories varies wildly, they all feature a macabre, over-the-top sensibility as a gruesome constant. The tales included here range from the absurd (sentient killer cacti in "Green Horror") to the outrageous (the gore-soaked acid trip of "Blood Bath"), with graphics to match.

"Today's fans have come to admire the audacity of the ideas," writes Howlett, "the ballsiness of the rip-offs and the sometimes sketchy art (both literally and figuratively), especially on the covers." If you are such a fan—or someone curious to delve into what Howlett labels "the porn of comic books"—then this handsomely-produced tome is for you.

CHAPTER 9
THIS TIME IT'S PERSONAL

Collected here are a handful of published pieces that reflect a more personal outlook on the genre we love. With them I do something a bit different and inject a little "me" into each essay. Whether that's for better or worse, I'll leave for you to decide...

> When *Monsters from the Vault* publisher Jim Clatterbaugh decided to finally hang up his editorial apron, he asked some of his regular contributors to write a few words about the magazine. Well, me being me, I wrote *more* than a few, and they can be found below. (Note: several years have now passed, and the "final issue" of *MFTV* has yet to see the light of day. Still waiting, Jim...)

DR. CLATTERBAUGH, OR HOW I LEARNED TO STOP WORRYING AND LOVE *MONSTERS FROM THE VAULT*

Yes, *Monsters from the Vault* IS 'the Bomb' (heh). Moving on from bad title puns... the mid-nineties was something of a heyday for genre publications, with fanzines and prozines like *Filmfax*, *Scarlet Street*, *Midnight Marquee*, *Movie Club* and *Monsterscene* going strong. So when Jim Clatterbaugh started up yet another classics-oriented genre mag, I was a bit doubtful about its longevity. Obviously (and not for the first—nor last—time), I was way off base. I failed to take into account not only Jim's enthusiasm, but his determination, dogged perseverance, commitment to quality, and powers of persuasion. Early on Jim asked if I'd like to contribute. My big hesitation at the time came from the fact that *Monsters from the Vault* didn't pay its contributors. "Outrageous!" you say. Well, I said the very same thing. At the time, after having a couple of books published, I grandiosely thought of myself as a "professional" writer. Yep, I wanted cold hard cash in exchange for the sweat of my brow (or fingertips). Magazines like *Filmfax*, *Shivers* and *Monsterscene* paid by the word (and I can be pretty verbose), so those were my first-choice submission spots. I'm not proud of this mercenary attitude, and have since amended my egotistical ways. I came to see the true purpose of researching and writing about these films and filmmakers: to share the cinema love and gently prod my fellow enthusiasts towards more worthy viewing experiences (those involving masked wrestlers or giant gila monsters, for instance). And I've been steadily doing just that via *Monster from the Vault* for the past two decades—and that I *am* proud of.

Anyway, back in circa 1995 I thought, "Well, Jim's a great guy who's been an integral part of Fanex from the get-go" (a convention institution that not only brought me opportunities to meet, interview and even befriend many of our beloved genre celebs, but forge deep friendships that last to this day), "so why not support his little undertaking?" Besides, if the likes of Greg Mank and Tom Weaver (who contributed from the very first issue) deem it worthy, who am *I* to say no? So, being the diehard Pacific Northwesterner that I am (a breed with

A flattering Monsters from the Vault *magazine cover.*

recycling in its genetic code), I dutifully dusted off a chapter I'd written for my *Golden Horrors* volume, made just enough modifications to assuage my conscience, and submitted it to Jim for his nascent mag. Now here is where the genius that is Jim Clatterbaugh shone through. When I received the issue, there on the cover read "Bryan Senn on *Tower of London*." Suddenly those paying rags were forgotten—*they* never put my name on the cover! Yep, it just goes to show that the ego is mightier than the pocketbook. From then on I was a staunch contributor (even going so far as to submit wholly *original* pieces). And by the time whatever tiny spec of genre cred my name possessed had faded like a 1962 Eastmancolor work print, I was ensnared by the magazine's beautiful layouts, incisive articles by fellow writers far more erudite than myself, and Jim's unwavering commitment, loyalty, and good-naturedness. Jim always made me feel like a valued member of a team, just like he did with all his loyal readers.

When it comes to genre mags, I've always privileged the word over the image (ironic, really, given that I write about movies), preferring the more adult articles of *Castle of Frankenstein*, for instance, to the photo-heavy, juvenile *Famous Monsters*. *Monsters from the Vault* did an amazing thing—it excelled at *both* (words and images) from the outset. It became a veritable beacon for the little corner of cinema scholarship that we call home, carving out a legacy that will live on via its inspiring melding of incisive writing, approachable style, and eye-catching graphics. I am truly saddened that there will be no more *MFTV*. I'll miss its insight, entertainment, and camaraderie. But I want to thank Jim from the bottom of my black heart for not only putting my name in lights—or at least on the cover (perhaps I'm a bit too focused on this?)—but for allowing me to be a part of such a wonderful endeavor. Like its very subject matter, *Monsters from the Vault* will never truly die so long as we hold it near and dear in our hearts and minds.

> Some years ago, *Midnight Marquee* magazine editor Gary Svehla asked me (and many others) to submit a few reminiscences about the various Fanex film conventions he and his wife Sue put on in Baltimore over the years. Though for some reason or another the article never saw print, here are my select ruminations.

FANEX MEMORIES

I began attending Fanex in 1991 (number 5) at the urging of my good friend Lynn Naron. Being from Seattle, this was no easy task, nor one to be taken lightly, given the time and expense involved. After all, I was going to fly 3500 miles to Baltimore and spend all this time and money on some silly movie convention! I was right then finishing up my first film book, so I justified it to my oh-so-patient and understanding wife (who even attended a few Fanexes over the years herself) by pointing out that it was tax deductible; and I told *myself* that it'd be a great way to make useful contacts (which was one of the truest things I'd ever said during an inner monologue). Well, after meeting Gary and Sue and many of the friendly Fanex staff and regulars, and having the time of my life for three days, I ended up flying 3500 miles *every year* to do it all again. I was hooked. And one of the memorable events that set that hook was breakfasting with John Agar. At this point I'd met very few celebrities, and I must confess that I was a bit awestruck. I began by introducing myself and stuttering something like, "I've been a fan of yours for years, Mr. Agar," at which point he stopped me, looked me in the eye, and insisted, "Call me John." As friendly and unassuming as could be. There passed an exceptionally pleasant hour of conversation covering everything from pancakes to his love of bowling to his film career. Though I no longer remember the details, I can vividly recall the ease and comfortableness this man inspired in myself and those lucky few present.

A few other memorable moments:

Seeing Christopher Lee kicked out (politely, of course) of the Hyatt Regency ballroom when the hotel staff finally insisted he wrap up his riveting talk—after two and a half hours! (Undoubtedly, he'd have gladly gone on—with the rapt audience's blessing—for *another* two and a half.)

Lunching with William Schallert at Baltimore's Inner Harbor, only to discover that we'd both recently read physicist Stephen Hawking's *A Brief History of Time*, then puzzling over how something could be both a particle *and* a wave during the salad course.

The honor of not only introducing one of America's greatest filmmakers, Oscar-winner Robert Wise, at the Fanex Awards Ceremony, but also of moderating one of his talks (the late Mr. Wise was by far the easiest interviewee I've ever encountered—posit a question and he'd be all over it like a highly articulate dog with a bone).

Now, I may not have the best recall in the world (one of the reasons I *always* use a tape recorder for interviews), and I often spent much of the time in a somewhat, shall we say, hazy state (due to a combination of lack of sleep

Would you discuss toilet training with this woman? Caroline Munro from The Golden Voyage of Sinbad *(1973).*

and the fact that Gary and Sue always picked hotels with great bars), but there remains many, many wonderful specific memories.

Scheduled Fanex events are great, no doubt about it. About the only thing that beats a spirited panel ("Hammer vs. Universal" anyone?), fascinating Q&A guest session, or entertaining Awards Ceremony (with its attendant, endearing snafus) is meeting up with friends—and guests—in the bar afterwards. One night in the hotel bar during Fanex 11 (1997) I found myself talking with the still-stunning Caroline Munro. And what was the topic of conversation with this gorgeous icon of glamour? Her modeling career? Her Hammer films? Her Bond appearance? Nope. We became animatedly involved in discussing… toilet training. At the time, my son was going through that dreaded stage, and she had experienced the same with *her* son a few years back. So there I was, swapping potty strategies with one of the most beautiful women ever to grace a Hammer horror. And she gave me some good tips, too.

I had the great pleasure of spending quite a bit of time with Veronica Carlson, leading to a lasting correspondence over the years. At Fanex 8 (1994) I had the good fortune to attend a screening of *Horror of Dracula* at Baltimore's historic Senator Theatre, accompanied by Ms. Carlson, who held my hand throughout the film. During the "owl" scare (Hammerheads will know whereof I speak), she jumped in her seat and bore down on my hand—*hard*. She laughed at her own reaction; then, being one of the most thoughtful people on the planet, she expressed concern for my crushed appendage. Truthfully, it *did* hurt—this statuesque beauty was no shrinking violet—but, naturally, I was too "macho" to admit such a thing. *That* kind of pain I'll welcome any day.

Veronica Carlson was one of the warmest people I've ever met. Invariably, she'd talk with—and charm—any and every person who approached her, which meant she was always one of the last to leave the bar. I don't think she ever made it back to her room before 2 a.m. In fact, she was sometimes a little *too* nice. One late, late night, after closing down the hotel bar, she was waylaid in the foyer by a, shall we say, rather intense fan who started shooting rapid-fire question after question at her. This gracious lady patiently listened and began answering said questions, though I could see a bit of strain (not to mention fatigue) creeping into her face. Standing next to her, my hands at my sides, I realized that Veronica had surreptitiously taken my hand and started squeezing it. After a few moments, the pressure in my hand began mounting. Finally, the (dim) light bulb turned on in my head, and I got the message through my drink-addled, sleep-deprived brain: too gracious and polite to walk away on her own, she was silently asking for help! (Yes, I finally interrupted Mr. Intensity to say how Ms. Carlson needed to be up early for the next day's activities and that it was time to go.) But what a class act she is, one who's genuinely interested in others and their feelings.

One of my *least* favorite guests was Michael J. Pollard. Half-way through his Q&A session, Mr. Pollard abruptly stopped his barely-coherent ramblings to announce, "I gotta take a piss." Upon which he got up and left the room, never to return. Later, in the bar, I observed him trying to drunkenly chat up the wife of a friend of mine by boasting about his deep knowledge of baseball and then promising her a movie role! Ugh.

Then there was Kevin McCarthy. "Kevin McCarthy?!" you ask, incredulously. Yep. Though a great actor and riveting raconteur, Mr. McCarthy earned another, less flattering, sobriquet from me during Fanex 12 (1998). Like many of the guest celebrities at this time, he'd brought a bunch of photos to sign and sell at his table during the autograph sessions. I happened to be standing nearby when a young boy of about 10 nervously approached him to buy an autographed photo. Well, Mr. McCarthy suddenly says to this star-struck fan, "You have to buy *two*." The young lad, obviously flummoxed, turned to his mother waiting behind him, who dutifully handed over another ten-spot. I was dumbfounded and disgusted at this petty and ungrateful behavior from someone whose work I so admired. Feet of clay indeed. From that moment on, in my eyes Kevin McCarthy became not "Dr. Miles Bennell" from *Invasion of the Body Snatchers*, but "Mr. Money-Grubber" from *Invasion of the* Money *Snatchers*.

Fortunately, bizarre and unpleasant incidents like these were the rare exceptions and not the rule. Over the years Fanex introduced me to many new friends, and opened many doors for me, enriching my life both personally and professionally. The Fanex experiences—the good, the bad, and even the ugly (mornings were often a little, well…rough)—are ones I'll always treasure.

> Halloween is my favorite time of year, so I put a bit of myself into this blu-ray review written for *Monsters from the Vault* magazine (issue 32, Summer 2013).

HALLOWEEN 365 DAYS A YEAR: *THE AMERICAN SCREAM*

For the last quarter century I've been hosting an annual Halloween party, and over the years have cobbled together, scrounged, bought, inherited, and built from scratch various props and scenes to enhance the Halloween ambiance—everything from full-sized figures of mummies, vampires, werewolves and zombies, to coffins, an electric chair, a full-on graveyard, and even a life-sized guillotine (constructed by a very talented friend). Yep, mine is definitely the "Halloween House" of the neighborhood.

So I can relate to this engrossing, insightful, and at-times-poignant documentary on "home haunters" (those who go the extra mile to make Halloween special)—at least to some small degree, as the three Fairhaven, Massachusetts, families showcased here make my what-I-feel-to-be-considerable efforts look like the work of a dabbling dilettante. First up is the well-spoken Victor, a computer engineer whose obsession-fueled perfectionism leads him (and his family) to spend much of the year planning and creating the ultimate amateur Halloween haunted house. Then there's the gruff-and-tumble Manny (and his wife and kids), who's much less a perfectionist than Victor but whose dumpster-diving sensibilities and inventive nature create some memorable scare-works. Finally comes the socially awkward father-and-adult-son team of Rick and Matt (whom Manny labels as "peculiar," though Manny himself may not exactly be the best judge of such things…); their efforts don't always come off, but their enthusiasm never flags.

Producer/director Michael Stephenson does an exemplary job of setting up the premise and letting the subject matter (and subjects themselves) play out. From the mood-setting music to the excellent camera work and editing, the film juxtaposes these men's obsessions with the more mundane daily rituals of life—Victor's pre-teen daughter helping out by fetching some plastic eyeballs for her dad, for example, followed by a shot of her pouring a bowl of breakfast cereal (Count Chocula, of course). As the days count down towards Halloween, things become more and more tense (at least for the stressed-out Victor and the bickering Rick and Matt). Interspersed with scenes of the haunters crafting their creations (some more successfully than others) and setting up their props are interviews with friends, family members, and even "professional haunters" that illuminate the reasoning behind such a time-consuming and demanding pastime. There's even a sequence showing Victor attending a "Haunt Convention" (who knew there even *were* such things?). Among the revelations, we learn that Victor's religious upbringing (he was raised as a Branch Davidian) precluded him from celebrating just about anything—not only Halloween but also Christmas(!) and even his own birthday(!!). Consequent, "it's his way of reclaiming all those celebrations he missed," observes Victor's wife, "jamming them all into one holiday." Victor himself wonders over his obsession, but offers some food for thought when he explains, "Halloween is a community thing, it's not just a family thing. Thanksgiving and Christmas are *family* holidays. Halloween brings the whole community together." And when the big day rolls around and we see the scores of people, young and old alike, screaming and squealing with delight at the Halloween scares and creations Victor and the others have devised, one can almost understand it. "They'll remember this," says Victor. "They may not remember me, but they'll remember what I've done." "My family were awesome, awesome, awesome this year," adds a teary Victor. "And I couldn't be happier." After taking this riveting journey with Victor and the rest, with its ups and downs, personal sacrifices and Halloween triumphs, any empathetic viewer with a modicum of Halloween spirit can't help but nod in agreement.

Extras consist of "Ghoulie Manor: Behind the

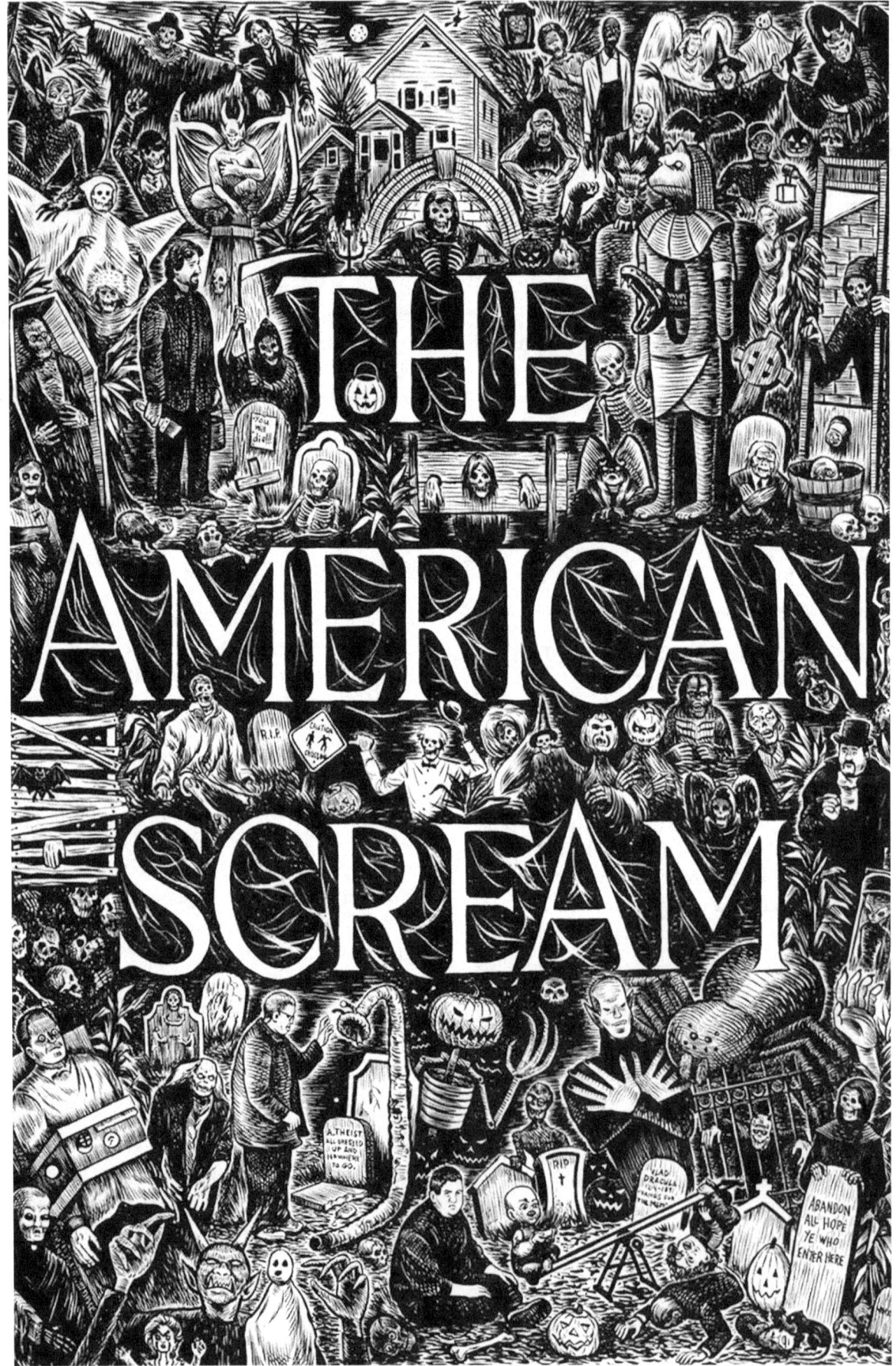

DVD cover.

Scenes," a brief follow-up piece on Victor's pro-haunt "Ghoulie Manor" (yes, Victor went "pro" a few months after the documentary was shot), a Ghoulie Manor TV spot, and a concise trailer for *The American Scream*. Don't let the disappointingly prosaic blu ray/DVD cover dissuade you, the excellent *The American Scream* is just the thing to get you in the Halloween mood.

> I penned this short piece—my one and only restaurant review—for my friend Dan Taylor's magazine *The Hungover Gourmet* (issue 10, May 2007). I include it here because... well... Jackie Chan!!

JACKIE CHAN: SUPER*CHEF*?

Who goes to the *mall* to eat while vacationing in Hawaii? Amazingly enough, I do—despite the fact that I'd sooner stuff red hot peppers into orifices I'd rather not think about than visit one of those soul-sucking monuments to consumerism. But this was different, since said shopping center houses the one and only food palace owned by my (and millions of others') favorite Asian action star – Jackie Chan. *Jackie's Kitchen* (open for about a year now), located in the Alamoana Shopping Center just West of Waikiki in Honolulu, is the first (and only, to date) of a proposed chain of restaurants around the globe. Its fairly extensive Asian-flavored (naturally) menu offers everything from smoked duck (a whole half-duck, with excellent seasoning and a tangy plum sauce) and noodles to steaks and local seafood dishes. But for me it wasn't the (surprisingly good) food that was the main draw—it was the All-Things-Jackie ambiance generated by the framed photos, movie posters and plasma TV screens (showing a Jackie Chan movie) that studded the walls. That's right, while you eat you can watch Chan-the-Man in action all around you (sans sound, but with helpful subtitles). The first night we ate there (yes, we returned to the scene of the *Crime [Story]* several days later) the film du jour was the newest *Police Story* movie (*San ging Chaat goo si*, or *New Police Story*), which wasn't even available in the West yet. The snippets I saw looked intense and brutal and well up to Chan's high action standards. The second go-round had us watching the *Around the World in 80 Days* remake (which, thanks to Jackie's acrobatic turn and comedic charm, isn't half-bad—silly gadgets, love story and all) in between courses.

Jackie Chan at the 2003 opening of Jackie's Kitchen in Honolulu.

The restaurant also sports an inviting flair bar, where the bartenders flip, spin and toss the glasses and bottles in an amazing display worthy of a scene in Jackie's next opus. As I whiled away some time at the bar waiting for the wife and kid to finish their shopping, one of the bartenders (from Liverpool, no less) told me that on opening day, when Chan himself was there to christen Jackie's Kitchen, the place was mobbed by thousands of fans. Fortunately, the screaming hordes were long gone, and, though the establishment was fairly busy, it only took a matter of minutes to get seated. For good food and fun, Asian action-style, Jackie's Kitchen earns a (*Project*) *A*.

Oh, and like all good (or not-so-good; re: Planet Hollywood) celebrity eateries, Jackie's Kitchen has its own (tastefully limited) line of merchandise, including various shirts, DVDs and magnets. And yes, I had to take home a couple of pilsner glasses (hey, for only two bucks more you get to keep the big glass after draining it of such amber ambrosia as the refreshing Hawaiian Longboard Lager, Oregon's well-balanced Drop Top Ale, and the classic British Newcastle Brown Ale).

> I wrote this in 2001 for a glossy, one-shot magazine focusing on the 1950s "Shock! Theater" TV package (which introduced many of the classic horrors to television in the 1950s). Called *Shock! Theater: An Illustrated History*, the mag was published and edited by *Monsters from the Vault*'s Jim Clatterbaugh. Along with reproducing the original promotional book, Jim solicited short essays from his usual writers, to be printed under the collective title "Shock! Theater Memories." For it, each scribbler would recount "how *Shock! Theater* (or the incarnation of it they watched) influenced their love of classic (and not so classic) horror/sci films." This is *my* particular account.

NIGHTMARE THEATER...AND A PAIR OF BINOCULARS

Growing up in the early 1970s in the middle-class Seattle suburb of Kent, Washington, offered a fairly whitebread-bland existence to a kid looking for something a bit more exciting than riding his bike around the neighborhood and playing penny-ante poker in his friends' basements. Smoking cigarettes, sneaking out in the middle of the night, and dabbling in drugs (fortunately, the low-grade, THC-challenged marijuana we were able to procure then was much less potent than that available today) were all typical wing-spreading activities of a burgeoning junior-high adolescent—and, thankfully, ones that didn't stick. Another escape from the mundane real world—and one that did indeed last (to this very day; hence this little reminiscence)—was a plunge into the *reel* world, the cinematic landscape of science-fiction, fantasy, and horror in particular. With the VCR revolution over a decade away, this young monster-lover had to rely on local programming for his escapist fare. Enter *Nightmare Theater* on the local CBS affiliate KIRO (Channel 7), which ran from 1968 to 1975 on Friday nights, and was hosted by "The Count" (one Joe Towey, whose day job was directing the daily kids' show *J. P. Patches*). Dressed in the de rigueur black cape and pancake makeup, sporting the expected (bad) Bela Lugosi accent, and armed with all manner of quips and puns, The Count introduced a (not so) new cinematic chiller every week.

While most of these late-night movie sessions with The Count have drifted off into the fog of a hazy memory, one in particular stands out as a defining moment in the shaping of my cinematic consciousness. It came during one of an endless stream of Friday night slumber parties. The usual group of us were engaging in the standard activities (cards, board games, listening to records) in my friend's basement when on the tube came The Count to introduce that night's feature: *Horrors of the Black Museum*. Now, we were prepared for the rather archaic terrors of a Universal Frankenstein movie or perhaps a Poverty Row mad scientist, or even a marauding Big Bug—all things our 12-year-old minds had seen and absorbed before. What we were *not* prepared for, however, was a pair of binoculars that shot needles into the eyes and brain of an unwary victim! We were stunned. The usual hooting and hollering ceased, and we sat there gaping while the blood gushed from between the woman's fingers as she screamed and covered her ruined eyes (actually, the blood just trickled, but to our shocked sensibilities at the time it seemed like a veritable geyser of hemoglobin). Of course, we were riveted to the screen for the rest of the admittedly mediocre movie. And though our now rather nervous pre-teen bravado soon returned, it had been A Moment.

That *scene*...

And now I have *Nightmare Theater* and *The Count* to thank every time I pick up a pair of binoculars and subconsciously twirl the focus knob before putting them to my eyes—just in case.

> To mark the 100th anniversary of Vincent Price's birth, *Monsters from the Vault* magazine asked a number of writers to pen an appreciation of the actor. This was my contribution, printed in issue 30 (Spring 2012).

THE PRICE IS RIGHT: A VINCENTENNIAL CELEBRATION

On those rare occasions when I'm laid low by the flu bug and stay home sick, without fail I turn to one of three films as a form of cinematic succor: *The Ghost Breakers* (1940), *Champagne for Caesar* (1950), or *His Kind of Woman* (1951). These are my "comfort movies," films that invariably make me forget, at least for a time, my ailment du jour. Of this spirit-lifting trio, two of them prominently feature Vincent Price. This is no coincidence. Vincent Price is one of those rare actors that not only *act* well but provide a real sense of themselves for each and every portrayal, so that the viewer takes away more than just a great performance, but the feeling that you've actually spent time with a real person. Consequently, the characters Vincent Price plays are not merely fictitious (or historical) figures, but seemingly real human beings. Even the broadly comical, egocentric, conniving soap magnate Burnbridge Waters from *Champagne for Caesar* enters the realm of realism through Price's humanizing performance—via the glance here, the aside there, the purring undercurrent in his voice, the twinkle in his eye. It's an amazing ability, an amazing gift. Boris Karloff had it; Peter Cushing had it; and Vincent Price had it in spades.

Karloff, Cushing and Price—this trio of horror stars, this triumvirate of terror, this troika of talent—to my mind, they stand head and shoulders above all the rest, not only due to their ability to imbue even the vilest of villains with an underlying reality, depth and even humanity, but because all three were, by all and sundry accounts, well-rounded, unassuming, thoughtful, professional, intelligent and erudite men. In the nearly quarter-century I've been writing about movies, I've met, spoken to, and corresponded with many different film people. Generally, I've found that I have more interest in, and affinity with, those who worked *behind* the camera (screenwriters, directors, cinematographers) than the actors who stood in front of it. Of course, as with every gross generalization, there are a host of exceptions. Charming and fascinating thespians like Janet Leigh, Robert Quarry, and Veronica Carlson immediately spring to mind. Yet I've also *missed* meeting a lot of film people, and topping my list of regrets are the three greats: Karloff, Cushing and Vincent Price.

So what makes Vincent Price so special? Like no other "horror" actor, Vincent Price had the ability to draw the viewer into the proceedings with a smooth and charming believability while simultaneously winking at the audience, reassuring us with a raised eyebrow or a subtle half-smile that it's-all-in-good-fun. A stellar showcase for this engaging quality is *House on Haunted Hill* (1959). The part of Frederick Loren in *House* proved an ideal venue for Price's particular brand of tongue-in-cheek charm. When one dour character remarks, "Seven [ghosts] now, maybe more before morning," Price arches his elegant eyebrows and glances at his companions before remarking in his soft, buttery voice, "That's cheerful."

In explaining the terms of his House on Haunted Hill "party" to his collected guests, Loren begins, "If I should die—" and abruptly stops. Here Price glances pointedly at his wife Annabelle (played by Carol Ohmart), a faint smile on his lips and a chuckle in his throat, before continuing in a bemused voice, "—you will be paid by my estate." Later in the same scene, Loren hands Annabelle her "party favor" (a loaded pistol). She refuses to take it, however, saying, "I don't need it." In the silkiest of tones, Price cajoles, "Are you sure my dear? Who knows, you may want to use it on me before this night is over." At this Annabelle grasps the proffered weapon, whereupon Price gently pushes the barrel *away* from himself, almost—but not quite—suppressing a small smirk. Thanks to Price's bemused demeanor, the fact that his wife wants to kill him becomes more than simply a nasty plot point but a secret source of amusement.

But being the consummate professional, Vincent Price was not all winking charm and knowing smiles, as he could play the very Devil-on-Earth when needed. Case in point: *Witchfinder General* (renamed *The Conqueror Worm* in America). The role of "Witchfinder General" Matthew Hopkins may be Vincent Price's finest performance in a terror film. It is certainly one of his most *unusual* portrayals in that he eschews the ingratiating charm and smooth flamboyance for which he had become so well known (and loved) to deliver a steely, subdued, and intensely menacing portrayal that becomes utterly convincing. While it may

As Matthew Hopkins, the Witchfinder General *(retitled* The Conqueror Worm *in America), Vincent Price delivers what may be his greatest performance in a genre film.*

not be every Price fan's *favorite* role, it is undoubtedly his most powerful.

"All screen villainy is fun," declared Price in the *Conqueror Worm* pressbook. "That is why I enjoy doing it so much. It gives me as big a kick as comedy, which I also love doing, besides being so much easier." About his character Hopkins, Price had this to say: "Despite his macabre and revolting occupation, this man Hopkins was not just a sadist. Else, I wouldn't have been interested in playing him. He was a human being—not a humane one, perhaps—but he had all the usual weaknesses, including a fondness for young women. I saw him as a man who, at first, really believed in the Christian justness of his cause, but who, when he found he could turn it to profit through the credulity of local magistrates in those lawless times, degenerated into an ogre whose lust for power and greed for money ran away with him. Having begun, he had to keep on, and finally his atrocities became more and more terrible. He became the complete hypocrite—cowardly as well as demonic."

From his very first scene, Price's skillful playing establishes his character's fascinating and diverse dichotomy. When his brutish assistant Stearne (Robert Russell) asks, "How much farther, Matthew?" Hopkins reacts forcefully with "You'll not call me 'Matthew.' I'm not one of your drinking cronies carousing and wenching in the taverns." Price's voice is hard, his flinty tones ringing with both authority and superiority. Obviously, Hopkins sees himself as one who stands above those around him.

Later, Hopkins comments on his assistant's enthusiasm: "You enjoy torture, don't you Stearne?" Price's hard voice carries a hint of disdain as he turns his face away from his compatriot to stare straight ahead. "And you?" asks Stearne, sneering, before insolently adding, "Sir." At this, Price's head jerks around, almost angrily, at the question. But instead of a reply, he simply turns back forward again, his face stony and unreadable. Perhaps Stearne has hit a nerve.

Price reveals further aspects of Hopkins' character when he and Stearne begin questioning an elderly priest accused of witchcraft. After Stearne slaps the old man, Price closes his eyes for a moment and turns his head slightly—as if momentarily repulsed by his assistant's debasing and violent action. Moments later, when the priest rejects their accusations, Price's head snaps back and he shouts with venom, "All you reject is the true God! Take him Stearne, look for the Devil's marks upon him." Then, tellingly, Price turns away and lets his assistant (rather than himself) get on with his cruel work. Hopkins obviously enjoys the power he wields and (on at least some superficial level) believes in his profession. Yet, unlike his coarse compatriot, he does not necessarily revel in the brutality that comes along with it. Price's subtle playing reveals the multifaceted character hiding beneath the cold mantle of "Witchfinder General."

One final cinematic example serves to illustrate not only the immense talent of Vincent Price the actor, but also the engaging qualities of Vincent Price the raconteur. This comes in a performance in which he is on-camera for literally the entire movie. In 1969, Price agreed to star in a made-for-television production financed by American International Pictures called *An Evening of Edgar Allan Poe*. Produced, directed and co-adapted by Ken Johnson (*Adam-12*, *Incredible Hulk*, *V*, etc.), this is a word-for-word recitation of four Poe stories by the mellifluous master of menace himself. Price, the only cast member, performs faithful recitations of "The Tell-Tale Heart," "The Sphynx," "The Cask of Amontillado" and "The Pit and the Pendulum." Each recital takes place on an appropriate and realistic set, ranging from 19th-century drawing room to sumptuous dining hall to rat-infested dungeon. The marvelous sets are matched by equally striking costumes for Price. Price proves himself a storyteller supreme, going from drawing room civility to the passion of raging madness and all points in between. Poe's stories, macabre and fascinating, are brought to palpable life by the inflections of Price's resonant voice, the gestures of his hands, and the exquisite glint of madness in his eyes. The camerawork (including well-timed zooms, changes in focus, and perspectives that punctuate the *frisson* at hand) accents Price's movements and pointed tones, and the lighting effects and camera angles are used as effective exclamations. Here the full terror to be found in the dark genius of Edgar Allan Poe is made frighteningly accessible by the storytelling talent of Vincent Price.

The actor labeled this little-seen and seemingly forgotten gem of small-screen uniqueness "probably the best thing I ever did in the way of Poe." And, even taking into account his magnificent work in such Poe classics as *House of Usher*, *The Pit and the Pendulum* and *The Masque of the Red Death*, he's right.

On a personal note, I have only ever written two fan letters in my life—one to Peter Cushing and one to Vincent Price. Both men graciously answered my letter with a brief note and a signed photo, even though I asked for nothing. Now that's class.

> When Richard Gordon—movie producer, film fan, and gentleman—passed away in 2011, my friend Bruce Holecheck, aware that I knew Dick, asked me to write a brief tribute for his website *Cinema Arcana*. This is what I had to say.

RICHARD GORDON TRIBUTE

I was truly saddened to learn of the passing of producer Richard Gordon, who brought to our movie screens such fan favorites as *Fiend Without a Face*, *The Haunted Strangler* and *Island of Terror*, as well as exploitation oddities like *Secrets of Sex*, *Tower of Evil* and *Inseminoid*. He also oversaw the importation of numerous Eurotrash entries, such as *The Playgirls and the Vampire*, *Tomb of Torture* and *Cave of the Living Dead*. Richard Gordon was a very hands-on producer, as he was involved with everything from setting up a production's financing to hiring a crew and casting actors, all the way through to securing distribution and overseeing promotional campaigns for the finished product. Dick was not only a gifted producer with countless stories of Boris Karloff, Bela Lugosi, and flying brains that

A young Dick Gordon meets the Vampire himself, Bela Lugosi, on the set of Old Mother Riley Meets the Vampire *(1952).*

melted into goo when shot, he was also one of the most cordial and knowledgeable film professionals I've ever met. Even more than that, he was a friend.

I first met Dick Gordon at a Fanex movie convention in Baltimore back in the early '90s, where our mutual love for classic (and not-so-classic) films from the 1930s and '40s forged an instant bond between us. He not only loved making movies, he loved movies period and had a truly encyclopedic knowledge of cinema. He was also one of the nicest men one could ever hope to meet, and he readily agreed to a lengthy interview I wanted to conduct with him for my then-book-in-progress, *Drums of Terror: Voodoo in the Cinema* (Dick had produced two voodoo films in the 1960s—*Curse of the Voodoo* and *Naked Evil*). Said interview led to many phone calls and much correspondence over the years, as well as several more meetings at various conventions (he loved to attend movie conventions, as he was as much a fan as frequent guest celebrity). Dick was always helpful and willing to go that extra mile for a fan and friend (he even loaned me some irreplaceable original artwork so I could reproduce it for one of my books). A man of old-school manners, with a wry sense of humor (though based in New York City, he originally grew up in England and possessed that country's famous dry wit in abundance), his conversation and letters were always amusing and engaging.

I still remember one time when Dick and I had a minor "disagreement" over the original British title of an old '30s film (it was a ridiculous thing—the issue being whether the title contained the name "Mary" or "Marie"), with each of us tossing various sources back and forth to support our respective positions (yep, it was a veritable movie geek-off)... until I finally came up with a copy of the film's British pressbook that confirmed *my* claim. Dick, being the gentleman he was, admitted his "defeat" with good grace, while I, being the immature gloater that *I* was, took great delight in telling all and sundry who were present the next time Dick and I met that I'd actually bested the walking cinema encyclopedia Richard Gordon in this one tiny thing. Yes, it was a victory to treasure—but not a tenth as much as I treasure the now-far-too-brief time I spent with one of filmdom's finest. Fandom has not only lost a prominent figure, it has lost a prominent member.

> I scribbled this personal reminiscence for a "Fifties' Sci-Fi Film Faves" compilation article that appeared in *Midnight Marquee* magazine (issue 51) back in 1996.

THE THING (1951)

When I was about eight or nine years old, my parents would periodically go over to their friends' house to play bridge. And sometimes they'd take along me and my younger brother (no doubt to save on babysitter wear-and-tear). After we'd tire of beating on each other or annoying our parents as they tried for that elusive grand slam, we'd go off to the den to watch the late movie. On one such evening, I remember my initial confusion when, at the beginning of that night's scheduled flick, a "Winchester" company logo (complete with crossed rifles and marching music) came up on the little 19-inch screen. "Oh no!" I thought, crushed. "It's a western." How could something with as cool a name as *The Thing* (as promised in the local *TV Guide*) be a regular old Cowboys-and-Indians movie? My disappointment quickly turned to delight, however, when that stupendous trademark title burned itself into the screen while its eerie sci-fi theme music boomed out of the TV speaker. Oh boy oh boy oh boy—it's a monster movie after all! Little did I know how my pre-teen sensibilities would be both shocked and enthralled by the next two hours of unrelenting suspense and excitement. Even an endless string of Cal Worthington (and his "dog Spot") commercials couldn't break the spell woven by Howard Hawks' *The Thing from Another World*.

The Thing title.

I don't recall what my little brother thought of it (he probably fell asleep anyway) since nothing could tear my rapt attention away from that small flickering box. My surroundings—stuck out there in a patch of dark, secluded forest (in a double-wide trailer on a wooded lot)—only enhanced the scenario's sense of isolation and danger. I was right there, slack-jawed, as Captain Pat and crew fried that "super-carrot" menace from outer space. Now, as a cinema-obsessed adult, I can appreciate the film's tight, overlapping (and downright witty) dialogue, exclaim at the superb characterizations and convincing acting, and marvel over the deft direction and atmospheric lighting. But at the time, my nine-year-old brain, eager for the weird and adventurous, only registered how *real* it all seemed as I was completely caught up in this "first invasion from another planet" (in the words of reporter Ned Scott).

And you know, whenever I revisit the North Pole with Scotty, Pat, and Professor Carrington—even with my now somewhat more mature thirty-three-year-old brain—it *still* seems real.

Index

Abbott and Costello Meet Dr. Jekyll and Mr. Hyde 254
Abbott and Costello Meet Frankenstein 77, 84, 85, 145, 158, 159, 183, 345
Abbott and Costello Meet the Killer, Boris Karloff 145
Abbott, John 193
The Abominable Snowman of the Himalayas 46, 311
Ackerman, Forrest J 212, 295
Acquanetta 100, **100**, 101
Action Stations 213
Adams, Casey 251
Adamson, Ewart 197
The Adventures of Robin Hood 244
Agar, John 79, 257, 260, 286, 439
Ainley, Anthony 10
Akins, Claud 403
Alazraki, Benito 345
Albright, Brian 432-3
Alcocer, Santos 318
Alda, Robert 91-2
Alexander, Ruth 7
Alien 162, 240, 403
All Quiet on the Western Front 6
Alland, William 261
Allbritton, Louise 186
Allen, Dave 389
Allen, Fred 160
Allen, Irwin 77
Allen, Woody 295
Allied Artists 8, 227, 256, 290
The Alligator People 144
Altweis, Jame 130
The Amazing Colossal Man 263, 264, 329, 378-9, **379**
The Amazing Transparent Man 258, 383
Ambrogio, Anthony 80
American Gothic 379
American International Pictures 4, 78, 212, 229, 231, 233, 282, 283, 285, 315, 323, 324, 363, 381, 389, 420
The American International Pictures Video Guide (book) 420
The American Scream 441-4, **443**

Ames, Allyson 301
Amicus 89
Amy, George 114, 116
And Now the Screaming Starts 3, 91
Anders, Merry 229-31
Anders, Rudolph 409
Anderson, Richard 70, 239-40
The Andromeda Strain 275
An Angel for Satan 58
Angel Heart 66-7, **67**
Anglo Saxon Attitudes 2
Ankers, Evelyn 100, 189
Antoine, LeRoy 138
Archer, John **151**
Arenas, Rosita (Rosa) 333
Arkoff, Sam 4, 15, 212, 285, 322, 420
Arlen, Richard 143, 144, 145
Armageddon 11
Armstrong, Robert 131, 188
Arnold, Edward 5
Arnold, Jack 109, 246, 247
Arsenic and Old Lace (stageplay) 194
Ashcroft, Ron 380, 381
Asher, Jack 86
Ashley, John 78, 217-8
Assignment Outer Space 380
Assignment Terror 265-7, **266**
Astor Pictures 216, 408
The Astounding B Monster internet magazine 77
The Astounding She Monster 380-1, **380**
The Astro Zombies 423
Atmar, Ann 302
Attack of the Crab Monsters 252, 421
Attack of the Giant Leeches 132
Attack of the Killer Tomatoes 407
Attack of the Mayan Mummy 344, 359, 361
Attack of the Witches 362
Atwill, Lionel 86, 114, 117, 122-3, 174, 175, 176, 177-8, **178**,
Aubrey, Diane 220
Audie & the Wolf 74
Austin, Charlotte 216, 384
The Awful Dr. Orlof 386

The Aztec Mummy 344, 350, 358, 359-60, **359**, 361
Back from the Dead 177, 202-3, **203**, 413
Bacon, Kevin 82
Baker, Roy Ward 26, 401
Balcon, Jill 166
Balcon, Michael 165-6
Balderston, John 94, 96, 162, 164, 169
Baldwin, Earl 114
Baledon, Rafael 333, 340, 347-8, 348
The Bamboo Saucer 201
Banes, Lionel 212
Banks, Leslie 129
Barrier, Edgar 129, 130-1, 132
Barry, Gene 81
Barrymore, Lionel 107, 108
Barton, Charles T. 145
The Bat Whispers 84
Batman (1966) 242
Battle Beyond the Stars 13
Bauman, Marty 77
Bava, Eugenio 51
Bava, Mario 51
Baxt, George 25
The Beast from 20,000 Fathoms 298
The Beast Must Die 319
The Beast of Hollow Mountain 381, **382**, 383
"The Beast with Five Fingers" (short story) 92
The Beast with Five Fingers (film) 91-2, **91**
Beatty, Clyde 100
Beaudine, William 194, 195, 268, 269, 270
Beauvoir, Max 68
Beck, Calvin T. 42
Beebe, Ford 184
Beery, Wallace 113
Beginning of the End 378
Bela Lugosi Meets a Brooklyn Gorilla 417
Belden, Charles 119-20
Believe 43-5
The Believers 66, 67

Ben Hur (1926) 144
Benighted (novel) 86
Benjamin, Richard 415
Benzel, Thorsten 429-30
Beresford, Harry 175
Bergen, Candice 34
Bergen, Edgar 34
Bergman, Ingrid 170
Berkeley, Martin 259, 261
Berle, Milton 160
Best, James 32, 241, 241-2
The Best Man 118
The Best Years of Our Lives 150
Bey, Marki 15-16, 66, 321, 323
Bey, Turhan 187, 188
Beyond Ballyhoo (book) 420
Beyond the Time Barrier 258, 383
The Big Cage 100
Billy the Kid vs. Dracula 89, 268-9, 270, **270**
Birch, Paul 252, **252**
Bissell, Whit 81, 234
Bixby, Jerome 236, 238, 239
The Black Cat (1934) 92-4, **93**, 102-3, 143, 151, 258
Black Friday 135
Black, Karen 70
Black Moon 61
The Black Pit of Dr. M 336, **337**, 348
The Black Room 153
The Black Sleep 185
Black Sunday (1960) 50-2, **51**, 56, 81
Black Tower (stageplay) 120
Blacula 65, 315
Blain, Estella 391, **391**
Blaisdell, Paul 235, 238, 252, 378
Bloch, Charles 231
Block, Irving 246
Blood Feast 271
Blood from the Mummy's Tomb 3
The Blood of Nostradamus 21
Blood of the Beasts 207
Blood of the Werewolf 89
Bloodlust! 271-7, **272, 276**
Bloody Pit of Horror 56
The Bloody Vampire 340
Bloom, Claire 2, 45, 46
Blue Demon 346-7, 347, 351, 353, 354, 354-5, 362, 370
Blue Demon: El Demon Azul 346-7
Blue Demon vs. El Poder Satanico 353, 362-3, **362**

Blue Demon vs. the Satanic Power (see *Blue Demon vs. El Poder Satanico*)
Blue Demon y Zoveken la Invasion de los Muertos 353-4
Bluebeard (1944) 258
Bodeen, Dewitt 412
Bogdanovich, Peter 389
Bolton, Dave 46
Bonomo, Joe 144-5
Boogie Nights 295
Borkon, Jules 208
The Bounty Killer 7
Bowery at Midnight 152
Bowie, Les 401
Boyd, William 192
Bradbury, Ray 259
The Brady Bunch (series) 271, 276
Brady, Scott 402
Bram Stoker's Dracula 20
Braine, John 207
The Brain That Wouldn't Die 282-4, **282**
The Brainiac 21-22, 332, 334, **335**, 338, 349
Braus, Mort 254-5
Breen, Joe 268
Bretherton, Howard 150
Brewster, Diane 253
The Bride and the Beast 383-4, **383**
Bride of Frankenstein 94-7, **95**, 97-9, **98**, 139, 164
Bride of the Gorilla 60
The Brides of Dracula 85, 206, 295, 433
A Brief History of Time (book) 439
Britton, James 418
Broder, Jack 309
Brodie, Steve 296
Brolin, James 415
Bromberg, J. Edward **184**
Bromfield, John 390
Brooke, Ralph 273, 274, 274-5, 276
Brooke, Walter 274, 275
Brown, William 144
Browning, Tod 105, 107, 108, 125, 126, 138
Bruce, David 187, **187**, 188
Brumberger, Tom 319
The Brute Man 133, 150
Bryant, Bob 239
Brynner, Yul 415
Buchanan, Larry 78, 79, 285, 286, 419

Burke, Kathleen 143, 144, 145, 175, 176, 177
Burn, Witch, Burn 60
Burns, Bob 235, 238
Burton, Tim 395
The Cabinet of Caligari (1962) 245
Cabrera, Martin 14
Cahn, Edward L. 6-7, 235, 236, 238, 239, 262
Calderon, Guillermo 364
Calderon, Pedro A. 364
Calling Dr. Death 206
Callow, Simon 144
Calthrop, Donald 164, 166
Caltiki the Immortal Monster 51
Calvert, Steve 384
The Camels Are Coming 165
Campbell, Clay 179, 256
Campos, Antonio (see Viruta)
Cannibal Holocaust 384-5
Cape Fear (1991) 295
Captain Kronos, Vampire Hunter 313
Captive Wild Woman 99-101, **100**
Captive Women 385-6
The Capture of Bigfoot 296
Capulina 354
Cardona, Rene 365, 366
Carew, Arthur Edmund 114
Carlisle, Mary 104
Carlson, Richard 328, **328**
Carlson, Veronica 440, 445
Carlton, Rex 282
Carmel, Eddie 284
Carmen, Jeanne 29, **29**, 30
Carpenter, John 326, 327
Carpenter, Paul 213
Carradine, David 389
Carradine, John 5, 80, 89, 100, 186, 195, 196, 268, 403-4
Carrel, Alexis 200
Carreras, Michael 3
Carroll, Leo G. 259
Carson, John 313
Carter, Ellis 261
La Casa del Terror (see *Face of the Screaming Werewolf*)
Case, Carroll 268
Cash on Demand 313
El Castillo de los Monstruos 342-3
Castle of Blood 54-5
Castle of Frankenstein magazine 439
Castle of the Creeping Flesh 386
Castle of the Living Dead 57

Castle of the Monsters 21, 336
Castle, Peggy 203, **203**
Castle, Roy 64
Castle, Shirley 258
Castle, William 224, 225, 226, 227
The Cat and the Canary (stageplay) 77
The Cat and the Canary (1927 film) 77
The Cat and the Canary (1939 film) 77
The Cat Creature 193
The Cat Creeps 77, 206
Cat Girl 25
Cat People (1942) 8, 135, 262
Cat People (1982) 388
Cat-Women of the Moon 305, 403
The Catman of Paris 192
C.B. Hustlers 24
Cellier, Antoinette 165
Cellier, Frank 164-5, **165**, 166
Cerdan, Marcel 280
Chabelo y Pepito Contra los Monstruos 354
Chamber of Horrors (1941) 158
Chambers, Graham 414
Champagne for Caesar 445
Chan, Jackie 443, **443**
Chandler, Helen 126
Chandu on the Magic Island 101, 103
Chandu the Magician (radio program) 101
Chandu the Magician (film) 101, **102**, 152
Chaney, Lon Jr. 35-6, 81, 170, **170**, 171, 178, 184-5, **184**, 186, **343**, 344
Chaney, Lon Sr. 107, 145
Chaplin, Charlie 149
Charlie Chan at the Opera 119
El Charro de las Calaveras (see *Rider of the Skulls*)
Charteris, Leslie 131
Chase, Brandon 296
Chauvin, Lilyan 276
Cheap Tricks and Class Acts (book) 420
The Children 386
Children Shouldn't Play with Dead Things 386-8, **387**
Child's Play 69
Chloe: Love Is Calling You 61
Christian, Linda 334
Christine, Virginia 134, 170, **170**, 171
Churchill, Marguerite 200

Cinema Arcana (website) 447
Citizen Kane 132, 150
The Clairvoyant 166
Clare, Diane 313
Clarence, O.B. 158
Clark, Bob 388
Clark, Dick 72
Clarke, Robert 159, 380, 381, 385, 424
Clatterbaugh, Jim 18, 26, 69, 94, 332, 420, 438-9, 444
Clatterbaugh, Marion Owens 18
Claxton, William F. 405
Cleopatra 242
Clift, Denison 154
The Climax 201
Clive, Colin 97, 98, 111, 148
Close Encounters of the Third Kind 403
Clown Hunt 284-5, **285**
Cocoon 236
Coe, Peter 170
Coffy 323
Cohen, Herman 228, 228-9, 233, 234
Cohn, Harry 149
Coleman, Frank 334, 336
Coley, Thomas 109
Collecting Hollywood magazine 196
Colley, Don Pedro 17, 66, 322
The Colossus of New York 203-5, **204**, 258
Colossus: The Forbin Project 388
Columbia Pictures 10, 10-11, 178, 255, 306, 348
Comin' Round the Mountain 388
Commander USA's Groovy Movies 332
Compton, Fay 49
Confessions of a Psycho Cat 277-82, **278, 280**
Connell, Richard 273, 279, 284
Connors, Mike 6, 262
The Conqueror Worm (see *Witchfinder General*)
Conried, Hans 251
Considine, John W. Jr. 148
Conte, Steve 29, 344
Conway, Tom 5, 63, 262
Cook, Elisha Jr. 225
Cooper, Merian C. 124, 138
Corday, Mara 260, 261
Corman, Gene 389
Corman, Julie 389

Corman, Roger 6, 78, 229, 252, 331, 388-9, 421, 428-9
Corman's World: Exploits of a Hollywood Rebel 388-9
Cornell, Lillian 189
Cornish, Robert E. 200
The Corpse Vanishes 152
Corri, Adrienne 222
Corridors of Blood 10, 215, 220-2, **221**, 308
Corrigan, Ray "Crash" 238
Corso, Marge 276
Cortes, Mapita 336
Cortez, Ricardo 200
Cortez, Stanley 200, 309
Costello, Lou 77
Cotter, Bob 339
Coulouris, George 416-7
Count Dracula 391
Count Yorga, Vampire 17, 18, 318, 322
Countess Dracula 311
Courtney, Chuck 268
Coy, Walter 41
Cox, Jack 166
Crab Monsters, Teenage Cavemen, and Candy Stripe Nurses – Roger Corman: King of the B Movie (book) 421
Crabtree, Arthur 212
Craig, Carolyn 226
The Crater Lake Monster 389-90, **390**
Craven, Wes 68
The Craving 72
The Crawling Hand 91, 145
Creation of the Humanoids 201
Creature Features: Nature Turned Nasty in the Movies (book) 422
Creature from the Black Lagoon 259
Creatures the World Forgot 3
Creelman, James Ashmore 129
The Creeper 133, 150
Creepshow 69
CreepTales 90
Crichton, Michael 415
Crime and Punishment 149
The Crimes of Stephen Hawke 182, **182**, 183
Crisler, B.R. 158
Cross, Eric 154
Croxton, Lucius 130
Croyden, John 212, 220
Cruise, Tom 82
Crutchley, Rosalie 1-4, 299

ry of the Banshee 320
ry of the Werewolf 180, 193
uhna, Richard 216-7, 274, 274-5, 403, 408, 409
ully, Zara 321
ult Movies magazine 39, 103, 160, 194, 202, 215, 262, 263, 265, 318, 326, 329, 363, 378, 379, 380, 383, 385, 386, 391, 392, 394, 396, 397, 398, 402, 403, 404, 405, 406, 407, 408, 409, 410, 414, 416, 417, 418
unningham, Beryl 288
uriel, Federico 39
urrie, Louise 159, 195
urry, Christopher Wayne 422-3
he Curse of Frankenstein 85, 86
he Curse of Nostradamus 21
he Curse of the Aztec Mummy 358, 360, **360**, 361
he Curse of the Cat People 250, 413
urse of the Crimson Altar 50
he Curse of the Crying Woman 332-2, **335**, 338, 348
he Curse of the Doll People 339, 363-4, **363**
urse of the Faceless Man 236, **237**, 238-40
urse of the Living Corpse 8, 40, 41
urse of the Swamp Creature 285-6, **286**
urse of the Undead 28, 205-7, **205**, 268
urse of the Voodoo 7-9, **9**, 63, 286-90, **289**, 306
e Curse of the Werewolf 86, 87, **87**, 105
urtis, Alan 185
urtis, Dan 70, 425-6, 433-4
urtis, Ken 31-2, 32, 240, 241,
urtiz, Michael 114, 115, 115-6, 117, 118, 118-9, 120, 121, 124, 124-5, 139, 198, 200, 200-1
urucu, Beast of the Amazon 303, 390-1
ushing, Peter 25, 64, 84, 86, 313, 401, 445
e Cyclops 264, 378, 422
r, Miriam 295
ade, Frances 126
'Agostino, Albert S. 86, 130
' Aguillon, Pedro 341
alton, Audrey 250, 251
ana, Mark 253
anforth, Jim 402
aniel, Leslie **282**, 283-4
aniels, Danny 65
aniely, Lisa 8, **9**, 289

Dante, Joe 389, 421
The Dark Eyes of London (book) 158
The Dark Eyes of London (1939 film) 154-8, **156**
Dark Shadows (series) 66, 70, 433-4
Darrow, Barbara 250
Daughter of Dr. Jekyll 254, 256-8, **257**
Davies, Peter 212
Davis, Bette 396, 397
Davis, Jim 269
Davis, Wade 59, 68
The Dawn Patrol 120
Day, Robert 213, 214, 219-20, 222
The Day the Earth Stood Still 242
The Day the World Ended 6, 7
Day-Lewis, Daniel 166
De Cordoba, Pedro 107
De Hoyos, Kitty 348
Dead and Buried 68-9
Dead Man's Eyes 100
Dead Men Walk 103-5, **104**, 160, 161
Deadly Illusions (book) 107
The Deadly Mantis 260-2, **260**
Deadtime Stories 89
Death Curse of Tartu 40, 324
Death Takes a Holiday 177
Deathdream 388
The Deathmaster 17
DeBello, John 408
DeCarlo, Yvonne 379
Dee Francis 136, 137, **137**
Dein, Edward 27-8, 205, 206, 207
Dein, Mildred 205, 206
Dekker, Albert 110
Del Bosque, Francisco Javier Chapa (see Zovek)
Del Llano, Julissa 333
Delehanty, Thornton 124
Deliverance 295, 324, 326
Demara, Fred "The Great Imposter" 231
Demicheli, Tulio 267
DeMille, Cecil B. 145
Demme, Jonathan 389
Dempsey, Jack 36
DeNiro, Robert 66, 389
Deodato, Ruggero 384, 385
Deranged 388
Deren, Maya 58
Dern, Bruce 389
Destination Moon 412
Destiny 185
Detour 258, 383
The Devil Bat 133, 150, 397

The Devil-Doll (1936) 105-8, **106**, 110
Devil Doll (1964) 7, 8, 9
Devil Girl from Mars 166
The Devil Rides Out 311
The Devils 399
The Devil's Daughter 61
The Devil's Hand 63, 334
Devil's Possessed 293
The Devil's Sisters 324
The Devil's Wedding Night 56
DeWitt, Louis 245, 257
DeWolfe, Francis 222
Di Palma, Carlo 56
The Diabolical Axe 362, 372-3, **373**
The Diabolical Dr. Z 391-2, **391**
Diage, Louis 179
Dignam, Basil 10, 307-8
Dinoshark 389
The Disembodied 63
Dr. Cyclops 109
Dr. Jekyll and Mr. Hyde (1931) 84, 110-14, **113**, 144, 172, 246, 257
Dr. Jekyll and Mr. Hyde (1941) 111
Dr. Jekyll and Mr. Hyde (1965) 70
Dr. Jekyll and the Werewolf 37-9, **39**, 290-4, **291**, **293**
Dr. Jekyll and the Wolfman (see *Dr. Jekyll and the Werewolf*)
Doctor of Doom 364-5, **364**
Dr. Phibes Rises Again 17, 82, 322
Dr. Terror's House of Horrors 63-4, 89, 91, 306
Dr. Terror's Gallery of Horrors 89, 402
Doctor X 114-9, **115**, 120, 121, 122, 123, 124, 125, 172
Dog Soldiers 73-4
Dohler, Don 296
Donohoe, Amanda 400, **400**
Don't Be Afraid of the Dark 70-1, **71**
Doomsday Machine 392
Douglas, Susan 396
Dracula (1931) 19, 84, 86, 102, 105, 108, 110-1, 125, 143, 151, 159, 164, 172, 186, 338
Dracula (1931 Spanish language version) 19, 125-7, **125**
Dracula (1973) 70
Dracula A.D. 1972 87
Dracula, Prince of Darkness 26, **26**, 314, 356
Dracula's Daughter 103, 105, 126, 177, 200, 203, 392-4, **393**
Drake, Francis 118, 147-8, **147**, 149, 150

Dreier, Hans 143
Drive-In Massacre 23-5, **24**
Drums o' Voodoo 61
Dubov, Paul 6
Duncan, Arletta 98
Duncan, David 250
The Dunwich Horror 420
Dupont, E.A. 381
Durgnat, Raymond 207
Durston, David 159
The Earth Dies Screaming 394
Earth vs. the Flying Saucers 394-6, **395**
Earth vs. the Spider 378
Easton, Robert 296
Eastwood, Clint 259
Edeson, Arthur 86, 138
Edouart, Farcoit Alexander 110
Eerie Publications 435-6, 436-7
Eisley, Anthony 309, 309-10, 310
Elvira 223
Empire of the Ants 329, 378
Endore, Guy 105
Enemy from Space 289, 326
English, Marla 6, 262
Ensign Pulver 201
Equinox 389
Erickson, Carl 120, 122, 124
Ettington Park 2, 46, 300
An Evening of Edgar Allan Poe 71-2, **71**, 421, 445
Evers, Herb/Jason **282**, 283
Exorcism at Midnight 11, 64, 308
The Exorcist 82
Exploitation Retrospect magazine 50, 284
The Eye Creatures 78
Eyes Without a Face 207-10, **209**, 333
The Face at the Window (stageplay) 183
The Face at the Window (1920 film) 183
The Face at the Window (1932 film) 183
The Face at the Window (1939 film) 180, 182, 182-3
The Face of Marble 62, **63**, 80, 194
Face of the Screaming Werewolf 333, 343-4, **343**, 348
Fahey, Brian 288
Faithfull, Geoffrey 154, 214, 222, 307
Falco, Louis 67

Monsters of Filmland magazine 439
Fanex convention 439-41
Fantastic Fifties magazine 205, 207, 218, 227, 240, 245, 249, 254
Fantasy Island (series) 318
Farrell, Glenda 120-1, 122, 123, 124
Farrell, Mike 392
Fast and Furious: The Story of American International Pictures (book) 420
Fernback, Jerry 10
Ferrer, Rafael 266
Fiala, George 284
Field, Joseph 197
Field, Margaret 385
Field, Virginia 394
Fielder, Pat 250
Fiend Without a Face 210-3, **211**
Film Alchemy: The Independent Cinema of Ted V. Mikels (book) 422-3
Filmfax magazine 12, 91, 92, 97, 99, 109, 114, 125, 127, 132, 138, 150, 151, 167, 169, 178, 189, 231, 327, 378, 438
Fire Maidens of Outer Space 213
First Love 283
First Man Into Space 210, 213-5, **214**
Fisher, Shug 244
Fisher, Terence 394
Five 396-7, **396**
Fleming, Eric 206
Flemyng, Robert 52, 53
Flesh and Fantasy 185
The Flesh and the Fiends (see *Mania*)
Flesh and the Spur 6
Flesh Gordon 389
Flick Attack website 72
Flight to Mars 192
Florey, Robert 91, 92
The Fly (1958) 144, 246
The Flying Serpent 397-8, **398**
Fonda, Peter 389
Food of the Gods 329, 378
Forbes-Robertson, John 401
Forbidden Planet 376
Ford, Harrison 82
Ford, Roy 401
Fort, Garrett 105
Foster, Preston 119
Four Weddings and a Funeral 1, 400
Fowler, Gene 35, 233, 234
Fowley, Douglas 304, 305
Fox, Billy 280

Franchel, Emile Dr. 229
Francis, Freddie 64
Franco, Jess 391-2
Franju, Georges 207, 207-8, 208, 209, 210
Frankenstein (1931) 84, 86, 97, 98, 105, 111, 139, 142, 164, 172
Frankenstein (1973) 70
Frankenstein and Me 43, 294-6, **295**
Frankenstein Meets the Space Monster 8, 63, **289**, 290
Frankenstein Meets the Wolf Man 135, 184, 267
Frankenstein 1970 215-6, **215**
Frankenstein's Daughter 216-8, **217**, 403, 408
Frankestein, el Vampiro y Compania 345
Franklin, Joe 303
Franz, Arthur 202
Freaks 84, 105, 142, 150, 172
Freda, Riccardo 53-4, 54
Frederic, Marc 217
Frees, Paul 331
Fregonese, Hugo 267
Fresco, R.M. 259
Freud, Sigmund 110, 147
Freulich, Henry 256
Freund, Karl 86, 139, 147, 148, 149, 169
Frid, Jonathan 319
Friday the 13th (1980) 82
Friedman, David 324
Friedman, Seymour 255, 256
Frogs 398, **398**
The Front Page (stageplay) 118
Frost, Mark 67
Frye, Dwight 86, 104, 126
Frye, Dwight David 104
Fuller, Lance 6, 29, 384
Fulton, John P. 139, 140, 185-6
Futureworld 415
"G-Man Jitters" (cartoon) 159
Gabor, Zsa Zsa 5
Galindo, Ruben 357
A Game of Death 127-32, **127**
Game of Werewolves 75, **76**
The Gamma People 3
Gannaway, Albert 36
Garbo, Greta 115
Gardner, Arthur 250
Gargoyles 70
Garland, Beverly 252, **252**, 390, 391

Gastaldi, Ernesto 52-3, 55
Gaumont-British Studios 162
Gausman, Russell A. 185
Gein, Ed 388
Gemora, Charles 204, 239
Genie of Darkness 21
George, Christopher 324, 326
Gershenson, Joseph 205
Gertsman, Maury 134
The Ghastly Ones (book) 423
The Ghost 54
The Ghost Breakers 77, 445
Ghost of Frankenstein 144, 158, 184
The Ghost Ship (1943) 413
The Ghoul (1933) 162, 166
The Giant Behemoth 298
The Giant Claw 131
Giant from the Unknown 274-5
The Giant Gila Monster 26, 31-5, **32**, 240, **240**, 242-4, **244**
The Giant of Marathon 51
The Giant Spider Invasion 296-8, **297**
Giants of Thessaly 305
Gibbons, Cedric 107
Gibbs, Gerald 289
Gibson, Henry 403
Gibson, Mimi 250, **251**
Gidding, Nelson 45, 48, 299
Gilliat, Sidney 162, 164
Gilling, John 25, 311, 312, 312-3
Gilmore, Stuart 385
Gleeson, Brendan 82
Glen or Glenda? 384
Glenn, Scott 70
Glut, Donald F. 268
Goddard, Paulette 77
Godzilla (1954) 422
Godzilla (1998) 79
The Golden Voyage of Sinbad **440**
Goldman, Lawrence 247
Goliath and the Dragon 402
Golitzen, Alexander 261
Gone with the Wind 149
Gonzalez, Arturo 37, 38
The Good Earth 149
Goodman, John B. 185
Goodwin, Bill 134
Goodwins, Les 171
Gordon, Alex 4-7, 11, 212, 262
Gordon, Bernard 395
Gordon, Bert I. 263, 264, 327, 329, 378, 379
Gordon, Flora 264, 329, 378

Gordon, Richard 7, 7-11, **9**, 64, 159, 210, 212, 214, 215, 220, 222, 286-7, 287, 288, 289, 290, 306, 307, 308, 425, 447-8, **447**
Gordon, Susan 328
Gorgo 10, 298-9, **298**, 308
The Gorgon 25
The Gorilla (1930) 84
The Gorilla (1939) 152
Gothic 295
Gottshalk, Bob 48
Goudreau, Richard 295
Gough, Michael 86, 228-9
Goulder, Stanley 10, 307
The Graduate 275
Graff, Wilton 275
Graham, Fred 244
Grant, Arthur 86, 311
Grant, Ed 423
Grant, Hugh 400
The Grapes of Wrath 150, 268
Gray, Billy 309
Gray, Coleen 29
The Great Dictator 144
The Green Berets 242
Green, Doyle 427-8
Green, Joseph 282, 283, 284
Green, Otis 6-7, 262
The Green Slime 11-3, **11**, **12**
Grefé, William 40, 324
Grey, Virginia 134
Grier, Pam 66, 315, 317
Griffin, Tod 409
Griffith, Charles B. 57, 252
Griffith, Daniel 324
Grip of the Strangler (see *The Haunted Strangler*)
Grot, Anton 114, 116, 121-2
Grovas, Rafael Perez 377
Guardians All 260
Guerrero, Carmen 126
Guffee, Paul 281-2
Gunsmoke 100
Guthrie, Carl E. 226, 227
Gwenn, Edmund 200
Haas, Hugo 27, 29
Hale, Alan Jr. 296
Hale, Barbara 296
Hall, Charles D. 86, 97, 126
Hall, Conrad 301
Hall, Kevin Peter 403
Hall, Mordaunt 118, 124, 143
Hallenbeck, Bruce G. 423-4

Haller, Ernest 173, 177
Halliday, Bryant 7, 8, 287, 288
Halloween (1978) 82, 327
Halloween Home Haunts 398-9
Halperin, Edward 60
Halperin, Victor 60
Hamilton, Margaret 264, 388
Hammer Films 84-8, 154, 310-1, 400, 423-4
The Hammer Vampire (book) 423-4
Hammerstein, Oscar 97
Hampton International 308
The Hand 91, 319
Hands of a Stranger 148
The Hands of Orlac (1925) 148
The Hands of Orlac (1965) 148
Hanna, Mark 252
Hardy, Phil 194
Harris, Julie 2, 45, 46
Harryhausen, Ray 78, 80, 394-5
Harvey (1969) 24
Harvey Swings 24
Haskin, Byron 81
Hatfield, Hurd 80
Hatton, Rondo 133, 134
The Haunted Strangler 213, 218-20, **219**, 222
The Haunting (1963) 1, 45-9, **47**, 223, 299-300, **300**, 435
The Haunting of Hill House (novel) 2, 45
Hays, Allison 231
Hayward, Louis, 255, **255**
Haze, Jonathan 389
Headhunter 69
Healey, James A. 185
Healy, Ted 148
Heath, Percy 111
Hedison, David 77
Hell Comes to Frogtown 327
Hell Raiders 286
Helm, Brigitte 98
Helm, Fay 100
Henaine, Gaspar (see Capulina)
Henenlotter, Frank 324
Hepburn, Katherine 169
Hercules in the Haunted World 55
Herrera, Victor 336, 339
Hessler, Gordon 65
Heubsch, Edward 255
Hewitt, David L. 402
The Hideous Sun Demon 424-5

The Hideous Sun Demon: The Original Screenplay (book) 424-5
Higgins, Kenneth 413
Higham, Charles 144
Hillbillys in a Haunted House 133, 150
Hillyer, Lambert 126
Himm, Carl 103
His Kind of Woman 445
History's Great Women 115
Hitchcock, Alfred 13, 52-3, 80, 166
Hitler, Adolph 149, 158
Hobart, Rose 113
Hoerl, Arthur 61
Hoey, Michael 308, 309, 310
Hoffenstein, Samuel 111
Hogan, James 188
Hohl, Arthur 143
Holden, Gloria 392-4
Holecheck, Bruce 447
Holliday, Don 405
Holsopple, Theobold 246
Holt, Jack 61
Holt, Tim 250, 251, 418
Homebodies 305
Hope, Bob 77, 160, 178
Hopkins, Miriam 112, **113**, 113-4,
Hopper, William 261
The Horrible Dr. Hichcock 52-4, **53**
The Horror Chamber of Dr. Faustus (see *Eyes Without a Face*)
The Horror Hits of Richard Gordon (book) 425
Horror Hospital 9
Horror Hotel 372
Horror of Dracula 20, 85, 86, 338, 400, 401, 440
Horror of Party Beach 8, 40, 41
Horrors of the Black Museum 69-70, 227-9, **229**, 444-5, **444**
Horton, Robert 11-13, **12**
Hough, John 379
Houghton, Don 401
The Hound of the Baskervilles (1959) 313
House of Dan Curtis: The Television Mysteries of the Dark Shadows Auteur (book) 425-6
House of Dark Shadows 66, 317
House of Dracula 144, 183
House of Frankenstein 144, 183
House of Horrors 132-4, **133**, 150
House of Usher 229, 329

House of Wax 159
House on Haunted Hill (1959) 223-7, **223**, **225**, 445
The House on Skull Mountain 65
Houston, Norman 129, 130
Hoven, Adrian 386
Howard, John 413
Howard, Ron 389
Howe, James Wong 101
Howlett, Mike 435-6, 436-7
The Howling 89, 358
Huerta, Rudolfo Guzman (see Santo)
Huff, Richard 296
Hughes, Derek 74
Hull, Henry 77
Hull, Warren 200
The Human Duplicators 145
The Human Monster (see *The Dark Eyes of London*)
The Hunchback of Notre Dame (1939) 132, 190
The Hunchback of Notre Dame (1982) 4
Hunchback of the Morgue 436
Hunt, J. Roy 132, 136
Hunter, Ian 190
Hurlburt, William 94, 96
The Hustler 280
Huston, Tony 285
The Hypnotic Eye 227, **230**
I Drink Your Blood 40, **40**
I Eat Your Skin 39-42, **40**, 65, 324
I Love Lucy (series) 149
I Married a Monster from Outer Space 234
I Walked with a Zombie 61, 61-2, **62**, 132, 134-8, **136**, **137**, 262, 413
I Want to Live 45
I Was a Teenage Werewolf 231-4, **232**, 236, 256
The Incredible Shrinking Man 109, 204, 249
Incredibly Strange Film Show 346
El Increible Profesor Zovek 353
Incubus 300-2, **301**
Independence Day 396
Independent International Pictures 11, 267, 308
Infraterrestre 366-7, **366**
Insatiable 24
Interview with the Vampire 82
Invasion of the Body Snatchers (1956) 326, 441

Invasion of the Saucer Men 78, 231-3, **232**, 234-6
Invasion of the Vampires 340
Invasion of the Zombies 345, 346
Invisible Agent 135
The Invisible Ghost 43, 152, 195
The Invisible Man (1933) 94, 138-40, **139**
The Invisible Man Returns 135
The Invisble Man's Revenge 184
The Invisible Ray 80, **81**, 107, 156, 163,
The Invisible Woman 135, 177
Iselin, Alan 8
The Island of Dr. Moreau (1977) 145
The Island of Dr. Moreau (1996) 145
Island of Lost Souls 140-5, **141**, **143**, 172, 177, 246
Island of Terror 10, 210
Islas, Ricardo 13-15
Isle of the Snake People 65
It Came from Outer Space 236-8, 246
It Conquered the World 79, 238
It! The Terror from Beyond Space 236-8, **237**, 239, 240
It's Alive (1968) 286
Jackie's Kitchen 443, **443**
Jackson, Cornwall 177
Jacobs, Arthur 408
Jacobs, William 91
Jacobson, Steve 308
Jaeckel, Richard 11, 12, 13
Jane Eyre (novel) 135
Janus Films 288
Jarrette, Jerry 193
Jasso, Jose 345
Jaws 296-8, 389
Jensen, Paul 303
Jesse James Meets Frankenstein's Daughter 268, 269-70, **270**
Jessel, George 29
Jessel, Patricia 372
Jessup, Robert 321
Johan, Zita 169
Johnson, Ken 71
Johnson, Noble 131
Johnson, Richard 2, 45, 48
Jones, Buck 192
Jones, Russ 314
Journey to the Center of Time 402
J.P. Patches (series) 444
Jungle Captive 99, 203
Jungle Woman 99, 206

Juran, Nathan 261
Jurassic Park 83
Just Imagine 162
Kaffenberger, Bill 430-1
Kandel, Aben 234
Kapelman, Jeffrey 318, 319
Karloff, Boris 61, 63, 65, 80, **81**, 84, 86, 93, **93**, 94, 95-6, **95**, 98, 99, 135, 139, 153, 162, 163-4, **165**, 167, 168, **168**, 169, 184, 190, **190**, **197**, 198, 198-9, 199, 200, 201, 215-6, **215**, 218, 219, 219-20, 220, 222, 315, 445
Kasem, Casey 392
Katzman, Sam 152
Kauffman, Al 149
Kay, Edward 195-6
Kearney, Gene 405
The Keep 4
Keep Watching the Skies! American Science Fiction Movies of the Fifties, the 21st Century Edition (book) 426-7
Keith, David 284
Kelley, DeForest 405
Kelljan, Bob 17, 314, 317-8
Kellogg, Ray 31-2, 34, 240, 241, 242
Kelly, Tim 59, 66, 320-1, 321, 323
Kenny, June 275
Kenton, Earl C. 143, 144, 145, 268
Kevan, Jack 30
Key Largo 149
Keys, Anthony Nelson 25, 311
Kiel, Richard 407
Kier, Andrew 26
The Killer Shrews 32, 240-2, **240**, 243
Kilpatrick, Shirley 381
Kilpatrick, Tom 109
Kimball, Bruce 402
King Dinosaur 378
King, George 181, 182, 183
King Kong (1933) 103, 109, 117, 123-4, 130, 158, 188
King, Loretta 159
King of Kong Island 56
King of the Zombies 61, 133, 150-1, **151**, 194, 196
Klimovsky, León 37, 38, 291, 292, 292-3, 293, 293-4
Knight, Sandra 217, 218
Koch, Howard W. 159, 216, 253, 254, 268
Koerner, Charles 135
Koetting, Christopher T. 428-9

Kohner, Paul 125
Konner, Lawrence 79
Kosleck, Martin 134, 170
Kronos 144, 245-7, **245**
Kruger, Otto 203
Kuroda, Kiyomi 406
Kwaidan 406
Lackteen, Frank 5-6
Ladd, Davd 68
The Lady and the Monster 145
The Lady Vanishes (1938) 166
The Lair of the White Worm (novel) 399
The Lair of the White Worm (film) 399-400, **400**
Lake Placid 82
Lamarr, Hedy 131
Lamas, Fernando 77
LaMotta, Jake 280, **280**
Lanchester, Elsa 96, 97-9, **98**
Landers, Lew 178, 179
Landon, Michael 233-4
Lang, Fritz 147
Langan, Glenn 264, 378
Langley, Bryan 157
LaShelle, Joseph 234
The Last House on Dead End Street 302-3, **302**
Laszlo, Ernest 329
Laughton, Charles 97-8, 142, 143, 144,
Laven, Arnold 251
Lavie, Jean 104
Law and Order 6
Lawton, Frank 107
Lawrence of Arabia 10
Le Borg, Reginald 185
Lee, Anna 136-7, 163, 164, 165, 167
Lee, Christopher 20, 25, 26, 64, 84, 86, 222, 338, 439
Lee Robert N. 190
Lee, Rowland V. 190
Lee, Spike 69
The Leech Woman 206
The Legend of the Seven Golden Vampires 400-1
Leigh, Janet 404, 405, 445
Leith, Virginia **282**, 283
Leonard, Sheldon 61
The Leopard Man 206
LeRoy, Mervyn 119
Lesser, Sol 101, 102, 103
Letterman, David 269

Levy, Jules 250
Lewis, Forrest 30
Lewis, H.G. 271, 324
Lewis, Jerry 77
Lewis, Joseph 160
Lewis, Ralph E. 120
Lewton, Val 7, 48, 61, 61-2, 88, 134-5, 135, 136, 137, 138, 412, 433
Life Returns 200
The Light and the Dark 145
Lights Out (radio show) 396
Lilli Marlene 8
Lindberg, Charles A. 200
Line, Helga 56
Linton, Betty Hyatt 41-2
Lippert, Robert L. 202, 245
Little Shoppe of Horrors magazine 423
Live and Let Die 324
The Living Coffin 341
The Living Corpse 401-2, **402**
The Living Head 22, 338
La Loba 347-8
Locher, Felix 217
Loder, John 129, 131, 164, 167, 175
Lodge, John 177
Lohman, Augie 251
Long, Audrey 129, 131
The Long Hair of Death 55
Long, Richard 225-6
Lopez, Javier "Chabelo" 354
Lord, Eileen 279, 282
Lorre, Peter 4, 91, **91**, 92, 147, **147**, 148, 150, 262
The Lost Weekend 131
The Lost World (1925) 77
The Lost World (1960) 77-8
Lott, Rob 72
Lourie, Eugene 298, 299
Love from a Stranger 166
Love Me Tender 241
Lowe, Edmund 101, 102
Lowery, Robert 134
Lubitsch, Ernst 145
Lugosi, Bela 60, 80, 86, 93, **93**, 94, 101, 101-2, **102**, 102-3, 110-11, 127, 142-3, 144, 150, 151-8, 158-60, 178-9, 179-80, 180, 184, 185, 194, 195, 196, 338, 430-1, **447**
Lugosi, Bela Jr. 159
Lugosi: Hollywood's Dracula 158-60, **159**
Lugosi, Hope 159-60
Luizza, Michael 333

Lund, Lucille 159, 413
M (1931) 91
Macabre 227
Macedo, Rita 333
MacLane, Barton 200
Macumba Love 63, 303-6, **305**
Mad About Movies magazine 251
The Mad Ghoul 183, 186-9, **187**
Mad Love (1935) 105, 118, 145-50, **146**, **147**, 164, 333
The Mad Monster 160-2, **160**
Madhouse 17
The Magic Island (book) 60
The Magnificent Ambersons 132, 309
Le Mains d'Orlac (novel) 148
Le Picard, Marcel 195
Mako: The Jaws of Death 324
Mamoulian, Rouben 111, 111-2, 145
The Man and the Monster 338, 340-1, 350
Man Beast 274
The Man from Planet X 258, 385
The Man Who Changed His Mind 131, 162-7, **163**, **165**
The Man Who Lived Again (see *The Man Who Changed His Mind*)
The Man Without a Body 213, 416
Mander, Miles 179
Mania 312
Mank, Gregory William 438
Mankovsky, Isadore 318
Manners, David 186
Mannix (series) 6
Mannix, E.J. 105-7
The Manster **209**, 210
Mara, Adele 193
March, Fredric 113
Margheriti, Antonio 55, 380
Mark of the Devil 386
Mark of the Devil 2 386
Mark of the Vampire 105
Marlowe, Hugh 395, **395**
Marlowe, Scott 233
Mars Attacks 395
Marshall, Jack 242-4
Marshall, Neil 73
Marshall, William 65-6, 315, 315-7
Marsolais, Michael 295
Martin, Dean 77
Martin, Ross 203, 204
Marvin, Lee 13
Marx, Samuel 107
Masciocchi, Marcello 380

Masciocchi, Raffaele 52, 54
Maslansky, Paul 17, 57, 320, 321, 322
Masque of the Red Death 331
Massey, Ilona 267
Massey, Raymond 183
Matheson, Richard 70
Matthews, Francis 222
Mayer, Louis B. 149
Maynard, Lisa 29
Mazursky, Paul 15
McCalla, Irish 409
McCarthy, Kevin 440-1
McCrae, Joel 129
McElwee, John 433
McGavin, Darren 70
McGee, Mark Thomas 420
McGillivray, David 289
McHugh, Frank 122, 124
McKellen, Ian 4
McLendon, Gordon 32, 240, 242, 244
Meikle, Denis 227
Melford, George 125, 126
Méndez, Fernando 19, 20, 336, 338, 339, 341
Menzies, William Cameron 101
Mercer, Beryl 6
Meredith, Judy 27
Mesa of Lost Women 144
Mescall, John J. 86, 94, 96
Metro Goldwyn Mayer (MGM) 45, 215, 405
Metropolis 98
Mexploitation Cinema: A Critical History of Mexican Vampire, Wrestler, Ape-Man and Similar Films, 1957–1977 (book) 427-8
"Michael Jackson's Thriller" (rock video) 388
Midnight Express 319
Midnight Marquee magazine 80, 82, 101, 140, 171, 285, 310, 319, 392, 400, 439, 448
A Midsummer Night's Dream (1935) 198
The Mighty Gorga 402
Mighty Joe Young (1949) 80, 132, 305
Mighty Joe Young (1998) 79-80
Mikels, Ted V. 422-3
Milland, Ray 398
Millay, Bob 296
Miller, David 105
Miller, Dick 252, 389
Miller, Don 194

Miller, Mirta 290
Miller, Seton I. 173, 174
Milligan, Andy 423
Milner Brothers 4
Milos, Milos 301-2
Mind Warp! The Fantastic True Story of Roger Corman's New World Pictures (book) 428-9
Missile to the Moon 216, 403
Mitchell, George 359
Moctezuma, Carolos Lopez 338
Mohr, Hal 198, 201
La Momia Azteca (see *The Aztec Mummy*)
The Monkey's Paw (1933) 177
Monogram Studios 194
The Monolith Monsters 247-9, **248**
The Monster Club 89
The Monster Demolisher 21
Monster from the Ocean Floor 389
Monster in the Closet 403-4, **404**
The Monster of Piedras Blancas 29-31, **29**
The Monster That Challenged the World 249-51, **251**
Monsters and Mad Scientists (book) 86
The Monsters from Earth's End (novel) 308
Monsters from the Vault magazine III, 18, 26, 69, 84, 94, 183, 236, 258, 298, 324, 332, 342, 364, 368, 371, 375, 388, 398, 420, 438-9, **438**, 445
Monsterscene magazine 58, 294, 438
Montejo, Carmen 338
Montgomery, Robert 156
Monti, Aldo 355, 368
Moore, Cleo 27
Moreland, Mantan 61, 151, **151**
Moreno, Alejandro Munoz (see Blue Demon)
Moreno, Juan Martinez 75
Moreno, Jose Elias 348
Morell, Andre 25, 86, 313, 314
Morris, Carol 27
Morrow, Jeff 247
"The Most Dangerous Game" (short story) 128, 273, 279, 284
The Most Dangerous Game (1932) 8, 127-8, 128-9, 131, 132, 174, 273
The Most Dangerous Man Alive 404
Movie Club magazine 216, 223, 388, 390

Muchas Gracias Senor Lobo: Paul Naschy Memorabilia (book) 429-30
Mullaly, Don 120, 122, 124
Muller, Barbara 267
Muller, Paul 56
The Mummy (1932) 86, 88, 143, 147, 164, 167-9, **168**, 180, 239, 240
The Mummy (1959) 85, 86, 88, 89, 206
The Mummy's Curse 168, 169-71, **170**
The Mummy's Ghost 167
The Mummy's Hand 167
The Mummy's Revenge 38
The Mummy's Tomb 167, 184
Munro, Caroline 440, **440**
Murder by Television 152-3, **153**
Murders in the Rue Morgue (1932) 151, 172
Murders in the Zoo 171-8, **172**, **176**, **178**
Murphy, Bri 28, 273, 275, 276, 277
Murphy, Bridey 227
Murphy, Donald 218
Murphy, Joseph 69
Murphy, Ralph 120
Murray, K. Gordon 332, 333, 334, 338, 341, 363, 364
The Mystery of the Mary Celeste 80, 153-4, **155**
Mystery of the Wax Museum 114, 116, 117, 119-25, **120**
Myton, Fred 104, 161
Nadley, Aaron 179
Naish, J. Carrol 91
Naked Evil 10-11, 64, 306-8, **307**
Napier, Alan 134
Napoles, Jose "Matequilla" 374
Narcisse, Clairvus 68
Naron, Lynn 258, 439
Naschy, Paul 38, 72, 73, **73**, 265, 266, 267, 290, 292, 292-3, **293**, 294, 429-30
Nashawaty, Chris 421
La Nave de los Monstruos 351
The Navy vs. the Night Monsters 308-10, **309**
The Neanderthal Man 381, 383
Neise, George 253
Neufeld, Sigmund 160, 162
Neufeld, Sigmund Jr. 161-2
Neumann, Kurt 246
Neve, Suzane 10
Neville, John Thomas 397
New World Pictures 13, 428-9

Newfield, Sam 160, 161, 161-2
Niagara 241
Nicholson, Jack 6, 82, 233, 389
Nicholson, James 4, 212, 229, 285, 323, 420
Nicholson, Meredith 216-7, 383
Nigh, William 194
Night at the Opera 192
Night Life of the Gods (novel) 120
Night Monster 184
Night of Terror 152
Night of the Bloody Apes 348, 365
Night of the Howling Beast 72-3, **73**
Night of the Lepus 404-5, **405**
Night of the Living Dead (1968) 64, 82, **83**, 89, 212-3, 241, 314, 388, 414
Night of the Living Dead (1990) 414
The Night of the Sorcerers 65
The Night Stalker 70
The Night Strangler 70
Nightmare Castle 56-7
Nightmare Theater (series) 69-70, 444-5
Nights of Rasputin 222
Niles, Chuck 344, 359
No Traveler Returns: The Lost Years of Bela Lugosi (book) 430-1
Nord, Eric "Big Daddy" 231
Nordhoff, Baron Florenz von 212
Norman, Lon E. 42
Norton, Bill L. 70
Nosferatu (1979) 19
Not of This Earth 251-3, **252**
Nudist Paradise 416
Nugent, Frank S. 199
Oates, Warren 36
The Obi (stageplay) 10, 306
The Oblong Box 64-5, 306
Oboler, Arch 396, 397
Obon, Ramon 348
Obzina, Martin 185
O'Brien, George 200
O'Brien, Willis 77, 80
O'Connell, L.W. 179-80
O'Connor, Una 99
O'Donnell, Joseph 153
Ogilvy, Ian 57
O'Grady, Tony 7, 9
Ohmart, Carol 225, 226
The Old Dark House (1932) 85, 86, 139
The Old Dark House (1966) 86

Old Mother Riley Meets the Vampire 312, **447**
Olivier, Laurence 183
O'Malley, Brian Scott 74
One Body Too Many 188, 305
One Million B.C. 78, 409
One Million Years B.C. 78-9, **79**
O'Neill, Henry 200
One Plane-One Bomb 260
Onibaba 405-6
Onyx, Narda 270
O'Quinn, Terry 82
Ormsby, Alan 386
Osbourne, Lloyd 254
O'Sullivan, Maureen 107
The Other One (novel) 202
Otterson, Jack 86, 189-90
Ottiano, Rafaela 107
Ouanga 58, 61
The Outer Limits (series) 300
Owensby, Earl 89
Paget, Debra 404
Paige, Robert 185, 186
Paiva, Nestor 259-60
Pallos, Steven 10, 306
Paluzzi, Luciano 11, 13
Paradise Alley 27, 29
Parish, James Robert 210
Parker, Alan 66, 67
Parker, Kim 213
Parker, Willard 394
Parkin, Dean 264
Passage of Darkness (book) 59
Pate, Michael 205, 206
Patrick, Gail 175, 177
Paxton, Bill 80
Peach, Kenneth 238, 239
Peach, L. du Garde 162, 164
Pearce, Jacqueline 312, 313
Pellegrino, Ann 418
Pelletier, Andre 414
The People Who Own the Dark 293
Perry Mason (series) 177
Pertwee, Sean 73, 435
Perverse Titillation: The Exploitation Cinema of Italy, Spain and France, 1960–1980 (book) 431-2
Peter Pan (stageplay) 315
Peterson, Cassandra (see Elvira)
Petrillo, Sammy 159
The Phantom from 10,000 Leagues 7
The Phantom Gunslinger 23

The Phantom of the Opera (1943) 86, 131, 184, 201
The Phantom of the Opera (1962) 86
The Phantom Planet 406-7, **406**
The Phantom Ship (see *The Mystery of the Mary Celeste*)
The Pharoah's Curse 253-4, **253**, 305
Pheeler, Kirb 334
Phipps, William 396
The Picture of Dorian Gray (1945) 80
The Picture of Dorian Gray (1973) 70
Pierce, Arthur C. 310
Pierce, Jack P. 60, 99, 100, 158, 169, 170, 188
Pillow of Death 275
Pink, Sid 397
Pinza, Carla 67
Piper, Roddy 327
Piranha (1978) 389
The Pit and the Pendulum (1961) 50, 55, 229, 330
Pitt, Brad 82
Pittack, Robert 191
Pitts, Michael R. 210
Pitts, Zasu 6
The Plague of the Zombies 50, 64, 306, 310-4, **311**, **314**
Plan Nine from Outer Space 384
Planet of the Vampires 380
Playboy magazine 304
Plenilunio 13-15, **14**
Pliny the Younger 238-9
Poe, Edgar Allan 71-2, 92, 94, 329-31, 447
Poggiali, Chris 324
Pokras, Barbara 298
Polanski, Roman 300
Pollard, Michael J. 440
Pollexfen, Jack 254-5, 258, 385
Pons, Jamie Jimenez 357
Portillo, Rafael 358-9
Poulton, Terence 212
Powers, Mala 392, 413, **413**
Presley, Elvis 33
Pressley, Charles 101
Price, Dennis 8-9, **9**, 288-9
Price, Vincent 64, 71-2, 78, 81, 89, 223, 224, 225, **225**, 228, 322, 329-31, 445-7, **446**
Pride and Prejudice 149
Prince Valiant 242
Prine, Andrew 36
The Prisoner of Shark Island 268

Producers Releasing Corporation (PRC) 397
The Projected Man 8, 10
Psycho (1960) 80, 403
Psycho (1998) 80
Psychomania 41
Pupillo, Massimo 56
Purcell, Dick **151**
Quarry, Robert 15-18, 66, 82, 321, 321-2, 322-3, 324, 445
Quatermass and the Pit 26
The Quatermass Xperiment 10, 308
The Quest for Bridey Murphy (book) 227
Quigley, Linnea 410
Rabin, Jack 246, 257
Racine, Roger 319
Raging Bull 280
Rains, Claude 77, 139, 140
Ramos, Joseph Ortiz 333
Randall, Ron 404
Rape of the Vampire 104
Rasputin the Mad Monk 26
Rathbone, Basil 190, **190**, 244
The Raven (1935) 105, 152, 156, 169
Ray, Fred Olen 17, 323, 324
Read, Jan 220
Realart Pictures 417
Re-Animator 282
Reason, Rex 261
Rebane, Bill 296, 298
Rebecca 53, 333
The Rebel Set 35
Rebellion in Cuba 36
Reed, Robert 271, 276, **276**,
Reed, Walter 304
Reeves, George 107
Reeves, Michael 57, 58
Regal Films 245
Regional Horror Films, 1958–1990: A State-by-State Guide with Interviews (book) 432-3
Rennahan, Ray 114, 115, 116, 117, 121
Rennie, Michael 77, 267
Reno, Jean 79
The Reptile 311
Republic Studios 191
Requiem for a Gunfighter 7
The Return of Chandu (serial) 101-3, **102**
The Return of Chandu (film) 101, 103

The Return of Count Yorga 64, 275, 314, 318, 322
The Return of Dracula 356
Return of the Ape Man 194, 195
Return of the Fly 204, 329
Return of the Frog 181
Return of the Killer Shrews 242
Return of the Killer Tomatoes 407-8, **407**
Return of the Vampire 158, 178-80, 185
Revolt of the Zombies 60
Reynaud, Janine 386
Reynolds, Amelia 212
Reynolds, Burt 294, 295, 324
Rhodes, Gary Don 158, 430-1
Rice, Anne 82
Richard III 189
Richard III (stageplay) 189
Richman, Helen 159
Rider of the Skulls 89, 349-50, **349**
Ripper, Michael 86, 312, 313
Rive, Kenneth 7, **9**
The Robe 241
Robinson, Ann 81
Robinson, Charlie 16, 323
Robinson, Edward R. 185
Robinson, George 126, 185, 186
Robinson, Sugar Ray 280
Robles, Germán III, 18-23, **19**, 334, 338-9, **339**, **340**, 343
The Robot vs. the Aztec Mummy 339, 359, 360-1, **361**, 365
Robson, Mark 135
Rocketship X-M 144, 246
Rodann, Ziva 253, 304-5
Rogers, Charles 120
Rogers, Jean Scott 220
Rogers, Stan 107
Rollin, Jean 104
Romero, George 314
Rooney, Barbara 302
Rooney, Mickey 302
Rosen, Philip 194
Rosener, George 114
Rosenthal, Mark 79
Ross, Harry 160-1
Roth, Eli 389
Rousoff, Lou 235
Rubes, Jan 44
Rubio, Pablo Alvarez **125**, 126
Ruggles, Charlie 172, 175, 175-6, 176, 177

Ruggles, Wesley 177
Runaway Daughters 5, 7
Ruppel, Karl-Ludwig 212
Ruric, Peter 92
Russek, Jorge 358
Russell, Ken 399-400
Russo, John 414
Ruvinski, Wolf 377
Ryder, Loren L. 145
Saddle Tramps 24
St. Ronan's Well (novel) 300
Salazar, Abel 18, 19, 21, 22, 332, 333, 334, 336-8, 338, 339, 340, 342, 343, 349, 364
Salazer, Alfredo 349, 350
Samson in the Wax Museum 345, 346
Samson vs. the Vampire Women 342, 345-6, 376
Sanders, George 5, 25, 262
Sanders, Lugene 329
Santa Claus (1959) 348
Santo 346, 347, 351, 353, 354-5, 356, 357, 358, 362, 367, 368, **369**, 370-1, **370**, 371-2, 373, 374, 375, 375, 376, **376**, 377, 427
Santo and Blue Demon vs. Dr. Frankenstein 371
Santo and Blue Demon vs. Dracula and the Wolfman 350, 353, 354-6, **355**, 370-1
Santo and Blue Demon vs. the Monsters 344, 348, 351-3, **352**
Santo and Matequilla Napoles in the Vengeance of the Crying Woman 374-5, **374**
Santo contra Hombres Infernales 367, **368**
Santo contra el Cerebrodel Mal 367
El Santo contra las Mujeres Vampiros (see *Samson vs. the Vampire Women*)
Santo en el Museo de Cera (see *Samson in the Wax Museum*)
Santo in the Border of Terror 377
Santo in the Treasure of Dracula 368-9, **369**
Santo in the Vengeance of the Mummy 369
Santo vs. Frankenstein's Daughter 369-70, **370**, 371
Santo vs. las Lobas (see *Santo vs. the She-Wolves*)
Santo vs. the Martian Invasion 375-7, **376**

Santo vs. the Riders of Terror 373-4
Santo vs. the She-Wolves 356-8
Santo vs. the Vampire Women (see *Samson vs. the Vampire Women*)
Santos, Gaston 336, 341
Saunders, Charles 416
The Saxon Charm 156
Saxton, Robert 11
Scared Stiff (1953) 77
Scared Stiff (1987) 69, 408
Scared to Death 195
Scary Monsters magazine 134
Schallert, William 385, 439
Schick, Elliot 15, 322
Schlessinger, John 67
Schenck, Aubrey 215, 254
Schneer, Charles 395
Schoedsack, Ernest B. 109, 138
Schoell, William 422
Science Fiction Invasions magazine 296, 415
Science Fiction Theater (series) 259
Scob, Edith 208, **209**, 210
Scorsese, Martin 229, 295, 389
Scott, Elliot 46
Scott, Randolph 175
Scream Blacula Scream 65-6, 315-8, **316**
Seabrook, William B. 60
The Search for Bridey Murphy 227
Searle, Humphrey 46
Sebastian, Ray 23
Secret Agent (1936) 149
Secrets of the French Police 172, 177
Segall, Stu 23-5
Seizure 318-9, **318**
Selander, Lesley 191, 192, 194
Selby, Sarah 250
Selznick, David O. 135
Sennwald, Andre 147, 148, 176
The Serpent and the Rainbow (book) 59, 68, 314
The Serpent and the Rainbow (film) 66, 67-8
Serpent Island 63
Seton, Bruce 165
The Seven Faces of Dr. Lao 305
The Seventh Victim 250
SFP308 260
The Shadow of the Cat 25
Shadows and Fog 295
Shakespeare, William 189
Sharp, Henry 109

Shatner, William 300, 301, 326
Shaun of the Dead 75
Shaw Brothers 400
Shay, Dorothy 388
The She Beast 50, 57-8
The She Creature 4, 7, 63, 227, 262
She Demons 132, 408-9
She Devil 144, 246
She-Wolf of London 133, 150
Sheen, Martin 67
Sheffield, Richard 18, 159
Shelley, Barbara 25-6, **26**,
Shelley, Mary 98
Sherman, David 295
Sherman, Sam 11, 64, 267, 308
Sherriff, R.C. 94, 138, 138-9, 140
Sherwood, John 247
Shields, Arthur 258
Shindo, Kanero 406
The Shining 82
Shipka, Danny 431-2
Shivers magazine 105, 315, 438
Shock! Theater: An Illustrated History magazine 444
Sholem, Lee 253-4, 392
Shonteff, Lindsay 7, **9**, 288, 289
Shower, Robert 159
Showmen, Sell It Hot! Movies as Merchandise in Golden Era Hollywood (book) 433
Siegel, Joel E. 135
Silent Playground 10
Silva, David 349
Silvera, Darrell 130
Silvestra, Armando 365
Simms, Jay 244
Simon, J.P. 409, 410
Simone, Lisa 34, 244
Simpson, M.J. 434-5
Singleton, Brian 74
Singin' in the Rain 305
Siodmak, Curt 91, 92, 135, 184, 390, 391
Siodmak, Robert 184, 185, 186
Sir Lancelot 136, 137, 413
Slaughter, Tod 180-3, **181, 182, 183**
Slugs 409-10, **409**
The Smiling Ghost 188
Smith, C. Aubrey 183
Smith, Gary A. 420
Smith, Herbert 416
Smith, Leonard 107
Smith, Stephen D. 58

Solano, Rosalio 20, 338
Solar, Julian 21, 343
Solares, Agustin Martinez 356
Solares, Agustin Martinez Jr. 356
Solares, Gilberto Martinez 344, 356
Solares, Raoul Martinez 340, 348, 356
The Son of Dr. Jekyll 254-6, **255**
Son of Dracula 85, 178, 183-6, **184**, 189
Son of Frankenstein 158
The Son of Kong 103
Son of Santo 366, **366**, 367, 377
Sondergaard, Gale 77
Sondheim, Stephen 181-2
Sorority Babes in the Slimeball Bowl-o-Rama 410, **411**
Soul of a Monster 206
South Pacific 97
Soutten, Ben 182
The Space Children 204
Spalding, Harry 202
Spellbound 170
SPFX Special Effects magazine 203
Spider Baby 81
The Spirit of Seventy Sex 24
Spiritism 345
Spooks Run Wild 195
Stabler, Robert 202
Stanley 324
Stanley, Herb 281-2, **282**
Stanton, Harry Dean 36
Stapleton, Alex 389
Star Pilot 56
Star Trek (series) 301
Star Wars 82, 389
Starke, Anthony 407
Steele, Barbara 50-8, **51**, **53**, **58**, 81
Steiger, Rod 379
Stengler, Mack 150
The Stepfather 82
Stephens, Martin 25
Stephenson, Michael 441
Stevens, Andrew 408
Stevens, Craig 261
Stevens, Leslie 300, 301
Stevens, Stella 403
Stevenson, Robert Louis 165, 166, 254
Stewart, Peggy 193
Stine, Clifford 260
Sting of Death 324
Stone, Milburn 100
Stone, Oliver 318-9, 319

The Strange Case of Dr. Jekyll and Mr. Hyde (novella) 38, 111, 254, 290, 292
Strange, Glenn 160-1, **160**
Strangler's Morgue (see *The Crimes of Stephen Hawke*)
Stritto, Frank Dello 159
Struss, Karl 143, 144, 177, 246
Stuart, Gloria 139
Stumar, Charles 169
Stumar, John 179
Stutenroth, Gene 131-2
Sugar Cookies 318
Sugar Hill (see *The Zombies of Sugar Hill*)
Sullivan, Don 26-37, **29**, **32**, 244
Sullivan, Lucia 28
Summers, Walter 157
Sunrise 144
Suspicion 53
Sutherland, Edward 172, 173, 177
Svehla, Gary 82, 140, 171, 439
Svehla, Sue 439
Svengali 116
The Swamp of the Lost Monsters 341
Sweeney Todd, the Demon Barber of Fleet Street (1936) 165, 180-2, **181**, 182
Talbott, Gloria 257-8, **257**, 258
Tales from the Crypt 65, 89
Tales from the Hood 69, 414
Tales of Terror 331
Tales of the Third Dimension 89
Tamblyn, Russ 2, 45, 46
Tarantula 258-60, **259**
Tasker, Robert 114
Taste the Blood of Dracula 313
Tate, Sharon 300
Taurog, Norman 145
Taylor, Anthony 300
Taylor, Dan 50, 284
Taylor, Eric 184
Taylor, Jack 37-9, **39**, 290, 292, 293, 293-4
Taylor, Joan **395**
Taylor, Kent 402
Taylor, Marjorie 183
Taylor, Robert 11, 267
Teen-Age Jail Bait 24
Teenage Zombies 28-9, **28**, 34
The Television Horrors of Dan Curtis (book) 425, 433-4
The Ten Commandments 5

Tenney, Del 39-42
Terror (stageplay) 114
Terror Aboard 177
Terror-Creatures from the Grave 55-6
Terror Is a Man 145
Thackery, Bud 191
Them! 250
Theron, Charlize 80
Thesiger, Ernest 86, 95
They Came from the Swamp: The Films of William Grefé 324-6, **325**
They Live 326-7, **327**
They Saved Hitler's Brain 412
The Thin Man 192
The Thing (1951) 162, 236, 403, 448-9, **448**
Things to Come 162
Thomas, Harry 159, 218, 310
Thompson, Howard 227
Thompson, Jeff 425-6, 433-4
Thompson, Marshall 210, 214
"The Thought Monster" (short story) 212
The Three Faces of Terror 89-90
3 Loves of a Psycho Cat 280-1
Three Nuts in Search of a Bolt 305
Thurman, Billy 419
Tierney, Lawrence 11, 64, 308
Tin Tan 344
The Tingler 329
Tinnell, Robert 43-5, 294, 295
Titanic (1953) 242
Todd, Tony 414
Toland, Gregg 150
Too Many Crooks 183
Tora! Tora! Tora! 242
Tormented 327-9, **328**
Totter, Audrey 156, 158
Tourneur, Jacques 136, 137, 138
Tovar, Lupita 125, 126
Tower of Evil 8, 9
Tower of London (1939) 78, 85, 184, 189-90, **190**, 331
Tower of London (1962) 78, 329-31, **330**
Towers, Richard 117
Towey, Joe 444
Tracey, Lee 118, 119, 121
Trans-International Films 338
The Treasure of the Sierra Madre 251
Tremayne, Les 30
Trick 'r Treat 90, **90**
Trilogy of Terror 70

The Trip 389
Troughton, Patrick 25-6,
Tsu, Irene 417
Tubb, Barry 285
Tudor, Andrew 86
The Turn of the Screw (1974) 70
Turner, Tim 220
Turney, Catherine 202
12 to the Moon 410-2
Twentieth Century–Fox 245
Twilight People 145
Twins of Evil 85
Twisted Tales 89
2001: A Space Odyssey 162
Ulmer, Edgar 92, 93, 94, 257, 258, 383
Ultra-Filmfax magazine 216
The Undead 7, 227
Underwood, Ron 79
United Artists 45, 236, 250, 253
United Producers Releasing Organization 336
Universal Horrors (book) 426
Universal Studios 84-8, 183, 189, 236-8, 260, 261
The Unknown Terror 412-3, **413**
Urban Terrors: New British Horror Cinema, 1997–2008 (book) 434-5
Urueta, Chano 22, 334
Valdes, Manuel 345
Valley of the Zombies 275
Vance, Lee 9
The Vampire (1957; Mexico) **III**, 18, 19, **19**, 20, 21, 22, 334, 336, 336-9, 348, 364
The Vampire (1957; USA) 402
Vampire Circus 85
The Vampire's Coffin 20, **20**, 22, 336, 338, 339-40, **340**, 348
The Vampire's Ghost 62, 150, 191-4, **191**
The Vampire's Night Orgy 292, 293
Vampyr 169
Van Sloan, Edward 169
Van Zandt, Gus 80
Vaughn, Vince 80
Vault of Horror 65
Velasquez, Lorena 346, 366
Vengeance of the Zombies 65. 293
Vergara, Luis Enrique 346-7, 362, 371-2
Vernon, Howard 386
Veronica Mars (series) 25
VeSota, Bruno 359

Vetchinsky, Alex 166
Vetter, Chuck 214
Victor, Henry 150, **151**
Video Watchdog magazine 270
"The Vij" (short story) 51
The Viking Women and the Sea Serpent 247
Villachaize, Herve 319
Village of the Damned (1960) 25
Village of the Giants 329, 378
Villarias, Carlos 125, **125**, 127
Vines, Michael 379
Viruta 354
Voightlander, Ted 405
Von Stroheim, Erich 105
Vonnegut, Kurt 75
Voodoo Black Exorcist 65
Voodoo Dawn 414
Voodoo Dolls 414
Voodoo Island 63, **63**
Voodoo Man 62, 152, 194, 194-6, **194**
Voodoo Tiger 63
Voodoo Woman 4-7, 63, 262, **263**
Voteur, Ferdinand 200
Wade, Russell 130, 131
Waggner, George 183-4
Walker, Stuart 145
The Walking Dead 121, 196-201, **197**, **199**, **201**
Wallace, Edgar 158
Wallace, Inez 135
Walt Disney Studios 166
Walthall, Henry B. 105
War of the Colossal Beast 262-4, **264**, 379
War of the Satellites 247
War of the Worlds (1953) 81, 131, 239
Warner Bros. 119, 120
Warning from Space 392
Warren, Bill 426-7
Warren, Charles Marquis 202, 203
Warren, Gene 246
Warren, Jerry 28, 29, 274, 343-4, 344, 359
Warren, John F. 258
Watkins, Roger 302, 303
Waxman, Franz 97
Waxwork 89
Wayne, John 244
Weaver, Tom 194, 424-5, 425, 438
Web of the Spider 55
Weintraub, Charlie 27
Weird Woman 62

The Weird World of Eerie Publications (book) 435-6
Welch, Raquel 78, **79**
Weldon, Michael 194
Welles, Mel 57
Welles, Orson 135
Wells, H.G. 142
Wellman, William A. 304
Wellman, William Jr. 304
Welter, Ariadne 334, 338, 339
The Werewolf 179, 256
Werewolf Fever 74-5
Werewolf in a Girl's Dormitory 222
Werewolf of London 169
The WereWolf of Paris (novel) 105
The Werewolf of Woodstock 72
The Werewolf vs. the Vampire Woman 193
West, Adam 69
West, Dorothy 160
West Side Story 45
Westmore, Perc 123, 124
Westmore, Wally 143
Westworld 415, **415**
Wetanson, Burt 379
Whale, James 94, 96, 97, 98, 111, 138, 140
What Ever Happened to Baby Jane? 177, 433
Wheat, Ross 70
Whiskey Mountain 324, 326
White, John Manchip 10
White, Robb 224, 225, 225-6, 227
White Zombie 59, **60**, 60, 61, 134, 135, 152, 157, 172
Whitman, Stuart 405
Who's Afraid of Virginia Wolfe (stageplay) 322
The Wicker Man (1972) 400
Wilcox, John 401
The Wild Angels 324, 389
The Wild Bunch 358
The Wild Rebels 324
The Wild Women of Wongo 416
Wilde, Cornel 70
Wilkins, Martin 6, 193
Wilkinson, June 303, 304, **305**
Williams, Barry 276
Williams, Grant 249, 392
Williams, Reg 314
Willis, Edwin 107
Willis, Matt 179
Wilson, Harry 218

Wilt, David 333, 339, 371, 375
Wings 120
Wisberg, Aubrey 385
Wise, Robert 1, 2, 45-9, 127-8, 130, 132, 159, 299, 439
Witchcraft 245
The Witches Attack 372
Witchfinder General 445-7, **446**
The Witch's Mirror 333, 333-4, 338
With Six You Get Eggroll 6
Withers, Grant 193
Wizard of Mars 402
The Wizard of Oz 264, 388
The Wolf Man (1941) 86, **87**, 135, 160, 184, 267
WolfCop 75
Wolfe, Ian 148
Wolff, Ed 204
The Woman Eater 416-7, **417**
Women of the Prehistoric Planet 310, 417-8
The Woman Who Came Back 131, 203

Wood, Edward D. 384
Working the Spirit (book) 69
The World of the Vampires 338, 348, 350
Woronov, Mary 319
The Worst of Eerie Publications (book) 436-7
Wray, Ardel 135, 137
Wray, Fay 61, 114, 117, 118, 123, 123-4, 129, 131
The Wrestling Women vs. the Aztec Mummy 346, 360, 365-6, **365**
Wright, Frank Lloyd 223, 396
Wuthering Heights 150
Wylie, Philip 143, 173, 174, 178
Wynorski, Jim 389
X, the Unknown 289
Yarbrough, Jean 133, 150
Yates, George Worthington 263-4, 328-9, 395
The Year of the Angry Rabbit (novel) 405

The Yesterday Machine 418-9, **418**
Les Yeux sans Visage (see *Eyes Without a Face*)
You'll Find Out 159
Young, Jack H. 264
Young, Waldemar 143
Zombie 65
Zombie Holocaust 419
Zombie Island Massacre 69
Zombie Nightmare 69, 319
The Zombies of Sugar Hill 15-18, **16**, 59, 66, 319-24, **320**
Zombies on Broadway 62
Zontar, the Thing from Venus 79, 286
Zovek 353
Zucco, George 4-5, 77, 103-4, **104**, 161, 186, 187-8, **187**, 189, 195, 196, 262, 397-8
Zucco, Stella 398
Zucker, Ralph 56

www.ingramcontent.com/pod-product-compliance
Lightning Source LLC
Chambersburg PA
CBHW081143230426
43664CB00018B/2780